# THE HANDBOOK OF
# FIXED INCOME
# SECURITIES

# THE HANDBOOK OF FIXED INCOME SECURITIES

*Third Edition*

*Frank J. Fabozzi, CFA*
*Editor*

*T. Dessa Fabozzi*
*Associate Editor*

*Irving M. Pollack*
*Associate Editor*

**1991**

**BUSINESS ONE IRWIN**
Homewood, Illinois 60430

Project editor: Jane Lightell
Production manager: Carma W. Fazio
Compositor: Publication Services
Typeface: 10/12 Times Roman
Printer: Arcata Graphics/Martinsburg

**Library of Congress Cataloging-in-Publication Data**

The Handbook of fixed income securities / edited by Frank J. Fabozzi with the assistance of T.
Dessa Fabozzi and Irving M. Pollack.—3rd ed.

    p.    cm.

    Includes index.

    ISBN 1-55623-308-6.—ISBN 1-55623-406-6 (pbk.)

    1. Bonds—handbooks, manuals, etc.   2. Preferred stocks—Handbooks, manuals, etc.   3.
Money market funds—Handbooks, manuals, etc.   4. Mutual funds—Handbooks, manuals, etc.

    I. Fabozzi, Frank J.   II. Fabozzi, T. Dessa III. Pollack, Irving M.

    HG4651.H265 1991

    332.63'2044—dc20                         90-3373

# FOREWORD TO THE THIRD EDITION

The confluence of heavy summer rains and an unplugged basement sump pump provided the incentive to sort through boxes of books and papers I had considered over the years too valuable to discard. One large, soggy container was filled with materials gathered during the initial stages of my career as a fixed income portfolio manager. Although some of the items were written in the early 1970's, this particular collection was dominated by pieces published between 1975 and 1982.

These were classics of their time. A few were merely photocopies, obtained from more seasoned professionals who handed them down to fledgling analysts and portfolio managers. Topics included the emerging mortgage securities and zero-coupon markets, term structure and valuation models, financial futures and options, dedication and immunization strategies, and, of course, discussions of the then–controversial risk parameter, duration. Represented were the efforts of Wall Street researchers, investment managers, academics and financial consultants.

I was proud of my motley library because, at the time, it provided the most current reflection of the state of our rapidly developing art. As I hired new analysts and portfolio managers, I was able to supplement their on-the-job training with copies of relevant publications which more often than not formed the nucleus of their own libraries. As the pace of development in our field accelerated, more and more documents were added to these libraries. The publications of the late 1970's and early 1980's were especially exciting because they reflected the breakthroughs in computer technology and financial research which propelled fixed income analysis from the empirical to the theoretical. While I rummaged through the assorted research papers, monographs, magazine articles and unpublished manuscripts, I was struck by how far we have come in so little time.

In the last few years, considerable editorial efforts have significantly reduced the need to maintain the sort of personal library that I had. The fixed income world is still evolving, although at a somewhat slower pace than in the past. The current edition of this *Handbook* successfully incorporates the recent developments in our field. No other book that I know of provides encyclopedic resource of relevant, useful and readable information. A expected, a number of the authors whose works I had collected are represented in the pages that follow. The range of subjects covered is extraordinarily broad and I would suggest that the investigation of any fixed income idea begin with this volume.

So, while I decided to save my musty collection for historical and sentimental reasons, I intend to keep my copy of the *Handbook* in an easily accessible and dry location.

**William L. Nemerever**
*Executive Vice President*
*Fidelity Management Trust Company*

# FOREWORD TO THE FIRST
# AND SECOND EDITIONS

Although buy-and-hold is a realistic option for investors who buy equities, it is an act of wanton imprudence for investors in debt securities. Ultimately, of course, a debt security reverts to cash, and thereafter earns nothing for its owner. Well before the maturity date, however, its entire pattern of market behavior changes with the passage of time. This means that active management of fixed income securities is an inescapable responsibility.

Lenders of money have two other factors to worry about. First, will the borrower meet all payments of interest and principal when due? Second, how much will those payments buy in terms of goods, services, and financial assets as the repayments come in?

From these three painfully obvious considerations—the impact of time, the credit-worthiness of the borrower, and the relation of predetermined dollar payments to a changing price level—stems an extraordinarily complex collection of tools, techniques, risk and return calculations, and forecasting models for the active manager to worry about. In a world in which the variety of issuers and issues seems to proliferate continuously, this is no job for people who are seeking soft berths.

It is, indeed, an area where constant study is essential. What happens in any given market, in any given moment, or in any given economic environment is relevant for all the other markets, moments, and environments. Our learning requirements give us no surcease.

This volume is essential for those who recognize the importance of meeting those requirements. It leaves no stone unturned, and has about the most skilled stone-turners one would want to put to this particular task. Whether we turn to it for a guide to action, for a grasp of the facts, or for an understanding of fundamental theory, the answers we seek are here.

**Peter L. Bernstein**
*President of Peter L. Bernstein Inc.,*
*and Consulting Editor of*
*The Journal of Portfolio Management*

# PREFACE

This book is designed to provide extensive coverage of not only the wide range of fixed income products but also investment management strategies. Each chapter is written by an authority on the subject. Many of these authorities have written books, monographs, and/or articles on their topic. Almost half of the 60 chapters in the *Handbook* are either authored or coauthored by a Chartered Financial Analyst.

The third edition of the *Handbook* is divided into nine parts. Part 1 provides investment information with which a money manager must be familiar in order to understand the risks and rewards associated with fixed income securities and portfolios. Coverage of horizon (or total) return, duration and convexity is included in this part.

Parts 2, 3 and 4 cover the myriad of fixed income products. In comparison to the second edition of the *Handbook*, there is greater coverage of the mortgage-backed securities derivative market (collateralized mortgage obligations and stripped mortgage-backed securities) and the high yield bond market. Coverage of guaranteed investment contracts (GICs) is also provided.

Part 5 provides coverage of options and futures products. There is expanded coverage of fixed income option pricing models, as well as methodologies for estimating volatility. Part 6 is devoted to the analysis of bonds with embedded options. The various approaches are explained and there is a chapter specifically covering the option-adjusted spread approach.

The more popular fixed income portfolio management strategies are covered in Part 7. In addition to structured portfolio strategies (that is, indexing, immunization and dedication) and active strategies, coverage includes the importance of selecting a performance bogey, performance evaluation, and asset allocation techniques with futures and options. There is expanded coverage on international fixed income investing.

Part 8 is devoted to customized interest rate agreements—interest rate swaps, caps, floors and compound options. These agreements are used by asset/liability managers to control the interest rate risk of a portfolio and/or enhance returns when market inefficiencies exist. Risk modeling and forecasting are covered in Part 9.

Money managers must justify their management fees to clients. Consequently, eventually all money managers must explain to their clients how much *value* they've added to portfolio performance above and beyond a passive management strategy. Similarly, as editors and associate editors of this book, we must justify to our current clients (those who have purchased the second edition of the *Handbook*) why they should pursue a book buying strategy and not simply continue using the second edition, thereby saving on the advisory fee (the cost of the third edition). That is, what value have we added to the book that is worth paying the fee?

The value can be seen from the information provided on pages xi and xii which summarizes the differences between the second and third editions. The third edition has 60 chapters compared to 58 in the second edition. Of the 60 chapters, 28 are new. For those topics that have been carried over, 13 have been substantially revised.

## ACKNOWLEDGEMENTS

We extend our deep personal appreciation to the contributing authors, the editorial advisory board, and the following individuals who provided us with various forms of assistance in this project:

Scott Amero (Blackstone Financial Management)
David Askin (Daiwa Securities Trust)
Rosario Benavides (Salomon Brothers)
Joseph Bencivenga (Salomon Brothers)
Jackson Breaks (McGlinn Capital Mangement)
David Canuel (Aetna Life and Casualty)
Rayner Cheung (Jefferies)
Daniel Coggin (Virginia Retirement System)
John Finnerty (McFarland Dewey & Co. and Fordham University)
Jack Clark Francis (Bernard Baruch College, CUNY)
Robert Gilligan (Bear Stearns)
Michael Granito (J. P. Morgan Investment Mangement)
Andrew Kalotay (Fordham University)
Tony Kao (General Motors)
Atsuo Konishi (Sumitomo Bank Capital Markets)
Martin Leibowitz (Salomon Brothers)
Matt Mancuso (Bear Stearns)
Nick Mencher (BARRA)
Llewellyn Miller (Sanford C. Bernstein & Co.)
Ed Murphy (Merchants Mutual Insurance Company)
Judith Otterman (Salomon Brothers)
Patrick Paridiso (Deutsche Bank Group)
Daralyn Peifer (General Mills)
Scott Pinkus (Goldman Sachs)

Scott Richard (Goldman Sachs)
Andrew Rudd (BARRA)
Ron Ryan (Ryan Labs)
Rob Smith (Bear Stearns)
Francis Trainer (Sanford C. Bernstein & Co.)
Sally Staley (Wisconsin State Investment Board)
Charles Webster (Lehman Brothers)
Leslie Webster (Chase Manhattan Bank)
Nate Weiss
N. R. Vijayaraghavan (Indosuez Carr Futures)

Frank J. Fabozzi
Editor

T. Dessa Fabozzi
Associate Editor

Irving M. Pollack
Associate Editor

## SUMMARY OF DIFFERENCES
## BETWEEN SECOND AND THIRD EDITIONS

*The second edition has 58 chapters and an appendix, divided into the following 8 parts:*

PART 1:  General Investment Information
PART 2:  Securities and Instruments
PART 3:  Credit Analysis
PART 4:  Fixed Income Portfolio Management
PART 5:  Options and Futures and Their Role in Fixed Income Portfolio Management
PART 6:  International Bond Investing
PART 7:  Interest-Rate Determinants and Interest-Rate Forecasting
PART 8:  Interest-Rate Swaps

*The third edition has 60 chapters divided into the following 9 parts:*

PART 1:  Background
PART 2:  Treasury, Agencies and Money Market Instruments
PART 3:  Senior Corporate Securities, Municipal Bonds and GICS
PART 4:  Mortgage-Backed and Asset-Backed Securities
PART 5:  Options and Futures
PART 6:  Analysis of Bonds with Embedded Options
PART 7:  Fixed Income Portfolio Management
PART 8:  Interest Rate Swaps, Caps, Floors and Compound Options
PART 9:  Modeling and Forecasting

*The following 28 chapters are new:*

3.  Risks Associated with Investing and Fixed Income Securities
7.  Price Volatility Characteristics of Fixed Income Securities
12.  Repurchase Agreements
18.  High Yield Bonds
20.  Investing in Chapter 11 and Other Distressed Companies
24.  Eurocapital Markets

*The following 13 chapters have been substantially revised:*

# CONTRIBUTING AUTHORS

**Larry Anderson**  Head of Fixed Income Research, London, Deutsche Bank

**Anand K. Bhattacharya, Ph.D.**  Vice President, Prudential-Bache Capital Funding

**Richard Bookstaber, Ph.D.**  Principal, Morgan Stanley & Co.

**John Breit, Ph.D.**  Director, Merrill Lynch Capital Markets

**Frank D. Campbell**  Portfolio Management Division, Securities Department, The Travelers Companies

**Steven J. Carlson**  Senior Vice President, Fixed Income Strategies, Lehman Brothers

**Andrew S. Carron**  Director, Fixed Income Research, The First Boston Corporation

**Paul B. Chau**  Senior Consultant, BARRA

**Peter E. Christensen**  Managing Director and Manager, Mortgage and Fixed Income Research Departments, PaineWebber, Inc.

**Theresa Conroy**  Applications Group, Gifford Fong Associates

**William J. Curtin**  Senior Vice President, Lehman Brothers

**Ravi E. Dattatreya, Ph.D.**  Senior Vice President, Sumitomo Bank Capital Markets, Inc.

**Chris P. Dialynas**  Managing Director, Pacific Investment Management Company

**John Drastal**  Vice President, Lehman Brothers

**Ernst-Ludwig Drayss**  First Vice President, Frankfurt, Deutsche Bank

**Lawrence J. Dyer**  Vice President, Morgan Stanley

**Frank J. Fabozzi, Ph.D., CFA, CPA**  Visiting Professor of Finance, Sloan School of Management, Massachusetts Institute of Technology

**T. Dessa Fabozzi, Ph.D.**  Vice President, Financial Strategies Group, Merrill Lynch Capital Markets

**Sylvan G. Feldstein, Ph.D.**  Vice President, Municipal Bond Research Department, Merrill Lynch Capital Markets

**Michael G. Ferri, Ph.D.**  Foundation Professor of Finance, George Mason University

**H. Gifford Fong**  President, Gifford Fong Associates

**Laurie S. Goodman, Ph.D.**  Vice President, Eastbridge Capital

**Kevin E. Grant, CFA**  Investment Director, Aetna Investment Management/Aetna Life and Casualty

**Adam M. Greshin, CFA**   Vice President, Scudder, Stevens and Clark

**Margaret Darasz Hadzima, CFA**   Principal, Scudder, Stevens and Clark

**Victor J. Haghani**   Interest Rate Arbitrage Group, Salomon Brothers Inc

**Lakhbir S. Hayre, D. Phil.**   Director, Financial Strategies Group, Prudential-Bache Capital Funding

**J. Michael Henderson, CFA**   Associate Director, Bear Stearns & Co., Inc.

**Jane Tripp Howe, CFA**   Senior Credit Analyst, Pacific Investment Management Company

**David P. Jacob**   Director of Fixed Income Research, J. P. Morgan Securities, Inc.

**Michael D. Joehnk, Ph.D., CFA**   Professor of Finance, Arizona State University

**Frank J. Jones, Ph.D.**   First Vice President and Associate Director of Research, Merrill Lynch Capital Markets

**Judith Jonson**   Senior Associate, Citicorp

**James V. Jordan, Ph.D.**   Associate Professor of Finance, Virginia Polytechnic Institute and State University

**Ronald N. Kahn, Ph.D.**   Manager, Special Projects, BARRA

**Robert W. Kopprasch, Ph.D., CFA**   Managing Director, Hyperion Capital Management Inc.

**Kenneth Lauterbach**   Vice President, Financial Strategies Group, Prudential-Bache Capital Funding

**Andrew Lawrence**   Vice President, Greenwich Capital Markets

**Anthony LoFaso, Ph.D.**   First Vice President and Manager, Portfolio Strategies Group, Fixed Income Research, PaineWebber, Inc.

**Nicholas C. Letica**   Assistant Vice President, BT Securities Corp.

**Robert D. Long, CFA**   Managing Director, The First Boston Corporation

**Linda Lowell**   Vice President, Mortgage Investment Strategies, Smith Barney

**John Macfarlane**   Managing Director, Salomon Brothers Inc and Treasurer, Salomon Inc

**Howard S. Marks, CFA**   Managing Director, Trust Company of the West

**Richard W. McEnally, Ph.D., CFA**   Meade Willis Professor of Investment Banking, University of North Carolina

**Sharmin Mossavar-Rahmani, CFA**   Senior Vice President, Fidelity Management Trust Company

**Daniel Nadler**   Lehman Brothers

**Brian K. Newton**   Senior Vice President, BARRA International

**David Z. Nirenberg, Esq.**   Associate, Cleary, Gottlieb, Steen and Hamilton

**Gregory J. Parseghian**   Managing Director, The First Boston Corporation

**Charles Pearson**   Director of Research, Gifford Fong Associates

**Mark Pitts, Ph.D.**   Senior Vice President, Lehman Brothers

**Chuck Ramsey**   Senior Managing Director, Bear Stearns & Co., Inc.

**John C. Ritchie, Jr., Ph.D.**   Professor of Finance, Temple University

**Oskar H. Rogg**   Vice President, Liability Management, The First Boston Corporation

**Michael R. Rosenberg, Ph.D.**   First Vice President and Manager, International Fixed Income Research, Merrill Lynch Capital Markets

**Daniel Ross**   Director, Dumas West and Co.

**Harry C. Sauvain, D. S. C.**   University Professor Emeritus of Finance, Indiana University

**Timothy D. Sears**   Vice President, Mortgage Research, Goldman Sachs & Co.

**Dexter Senft**   Managing Director, Fixed Income Research, The First Boston Corporation

**Klaus O. Shigley, FSA**   Vice President, The John Hancock Mutual Life Insurance Company

**Janet Showers, Ph.D.**   Director, Hedge Group, Salomon Brothers Inc

**Andrew Silver, Ph.D.**   Senior Analyst, Moody's Investors Service

**Tom Tong**   Vice President, Financial Strategies Group, Merrill Lynch Capital Markets

**Hung Q. Tran**   Director, Fixed Income Research, New York, Deutsche Bank

**Oldrich Vasicek, Ph.D.**   Senior Research Associate, Gifford Fong Associates

**Kenneth L. Walker**   President, T. Rowe Price Guaranteed Asset Advisors, Inc.

**Richard S. Wilson**   Managing Director, Research Products and Services, Fitch Investors Service, Inc.

**Kurt Winkelmann, Ph.D.**   Manager, Fixed Income, Vestek Systems, Inc.

**Benjamin Wolkowitz, Ph.D.**   Managing Director, Morgan Stanley & Co.

**W. David Woolford, CFA**   Managing Director, Prudential Insurance Company of America

**Yu Zhu, Ph.D.**   Vice President, Financial Strategies Group, Merrill Lynch Capital Markets

# CONTENTS

PART 4

*Method   Call-Adjusted Duration and Convexity*   Valuing the Embedded Call Option   *Features of a Call Option*   Portfolio and Asset/Liability Management Implications   *Indexing   Active Strategies: The Importance of the Benchmark   Immunization*

# PART 1

# BACKGROUND

# CHAPTER 1

## INTRODUCTION TO
## FIXED INCOME SECURITIES

*Frank J. Fabozzi, Ph.D., CFA, CPA*
*Visiting Professor of Finance*
*Sloan School of Management*
*Massachusetts Institute of Technology*
*and*
*Editor, The Journal of Portfolio Management*

*Michael D. Joehnk, Ph.D., CFA*
*Professor of Finance*
*Arizona State University*

Ever since interest rates began to climb in the late 1960s, the appeal of various types of fixed income securities has increased in a similar fashion. Today such securities as bonds, mortgage-backed securities, bonds with equity kickers, and preferred stock are found in an increasing number of investment portfolios and are being actively used to fulfill a variety of individual and institutional investor objectives.

Basically, two things have occurred to alter the investment appeal of fixed income securities: (1) Interest rates moved to levels that made such securities highly competitive with equities, and (2) at the same time, these market rates began to fluctuate widely, thereby providing investors with attractive capital appreciation opportunities from active portfolio management. Such behavior was, of course, predictable because the yields and price performance of good to high-grade fixed income securities are sensitive to changes in market interest rates.

This book is devoted exclusively to fixed income securities—to the different kinds of fixed income securities that are available to portfolio managers, to the various investment strategies that individual and institutional investors can employ to satisfy asset/liability objectives, and to the opportunities available in trading these instruments. Also, interest-rate control tools—options, futures, interest rate swaps, interest-rate agreements (caps, collars, and floors), compound (split-fee) options—will be discussed along with their use in asset/liability strategies.

The present chapter provides an introduction to and an overview of fixed income securities. The next chapter discusses the features of fixed income securities, and Chapter 3 provides an analysis of the risks associated with such securities.

## WHY INVEST IN FIXED INCOME SECURITIES?

Like any other type of investment vehicle, bonds and other forms of fixed income securities provide investors with two kinds of income: (1) They provide current income, and (2) they can often be used to generate varying amounts of capital gains. The current income, of course, is derived from the periodic receipt of interest and/or dividend payments. Capital gains, in contrast, are earned whenever market interest rates fall. A basic trading rule in the market for fixed income securities is that interest rates and security prices move in opposite directions.[1] When interest rates rise, prices fall; and when rates drop, prices move up. So it is possible to buy fixed income securities at one price and, if market interest-rate conditions are right, to sell them sometime later at a higher price. Of course, it is also possible to incur a capital loss should market rates move against the investor. Taken together, the current income and capital gains earned from bonds and other types of fixed income securities can lead to attractive and highly competitive investor yields.

In addition to their yields, fixed income securities are a versatile investment vehicle. They can be used conservatively by those who primarily (or exclusively) seek high current income to supplement other income sources. Or they can be used aggressively for trading purposes by those who actively seek capital gains. Fixed income securities have long been regarded as excellent vehicles for those seeking current income; it is only recently, with the advent of high and volatile interest rates, that they have also become recognized as excellent trading vehicles. This is so because investors have found that the number of profitable trading opportunities has increased substantially as wider and more frequent swings in interest rates have occurred. Finally, because of the generally high quality of many fixed income securities, they can also be used for the preservation and long-term accumulation of capital. Many investors regularly and over the long haul commit all or a major portion of their investment funds

---

[1] The reason for this relationship is explained in Chapter 6. Other reasons for the appreciation of a bond's price are given in the same chapter.

to fixed income securities because of this investment attribute. Some investors, in fact, may never use any other type of investment vehicle.

## Advantages of Ownership

One advantage of investing in fixed income securities is that highly competitive rates of return are available, even with nominal amounts of trading and minimal risk exposure. Another advantage is the occasional opportunity to realize substantial capital gains. Also attractive to some investors are the tax advantages that can be obtained with certain types of issues; municipal obligations and preferred stock for certain corporate buyers are perhaps the best known in this regard.[2]

## Disadvantages of Ownership

A major disadvantage to investing in fixed income securities is that the coupon rate or dividend rate (in the case of preferred stock) is fixed for the life of the issue and therefore cannot move up over time in response to inflation.[3] In fact, inflation is probably the biggest worry for fixed income investors. Not only does inflation erode the purchasing power of the principal portion of the investment, but it also has a strong influence on the behavior of interest rates. That is, inflation can lead to violent swings in interest rates, thereby producing violent swings in the market behavior of fixed income securities, which can cause substantial capital losses. Another disadvantage for some fixed income securities is the often inactive secondary market, which tends to reduce the opportunities for active portfolio management.

## WHAT ARE THE CHOICES?

Fixed income securities derive their name from the fact that their level of current income, as defined by the issue's coupon or dividend rate, is fixed for a stipulated period of time, usually the life of the issue. In essence, the security's claim on the income of the issuer is set at a fixed amount. A 12 percent coupon on a $1,000 bond means that the issuer has to pay the bondholder $120 per year for the use of the money—nothing more, nothing less. Likewise, a $5 dividend rate on a preferred stock means the same thing: that the issuer is required to pay "rent" of precisely $5 per year for each share of preferred stock outstanding.

Investors and portfolio managers can select from a number of different types of fixed income securities:

---

[2] See Chapters 21 and 16.

[3] There are exceptions, such as floating- and variable-rate instruments. See Chapter 14.

- Money market instruments
- Bonds
    - Treasury issues
    - Agency issues
    - Corporate bonds
    - Municipal bonds
- Mortgages and mortgage-backed securities
    - Mortgage pass-through securities
    - Collateralized mortgage obligations
    - Stripped mortgage-backed securities
- Asset-backed securities
- Preferred stock
- Convertible (exchangeable) issues
    - Convertible bonds
    - Convertible preferreds
- International bonds
    - Dollar-denominated bonds
    - Nondollar-denominated bonds

Each of the listed types will be reviewed in detail in later chapters, but just a glance at this list reveals that investors/portfolio managers can find fixed income securities with short-term maturities (money market instruments), or they can choose to go long term (with bonds, mortgage-backed securities, preferreds, and convertibles). We conclude this chapter with a review of these securities.

Briefly, money market instruments are low-risk, highly liquid, short-term, unsecured IOUs issued by banks, nonfinancial corporations, the U.S. Treasury, various agencies of the U.S. government, and state and local governments. The minimum denominations of these securities are relatively large (seldom less than $10,000), and trading lots can be substantial (usually $100,000–$250,000 or more). Major money market instruments include U.S. Treasury bills, federal funds, Eurodollars and domestic certificates of deposit, commercial paper, bankers acceptances, repurchase agreements, and notes and bills issued by federal agencies and municipal governments.

The size of the long-term debt market (bonds, mortgages, and pass-through securities) and its composition as of December 31, 1989 are summarized in Exhibit 1–1. Of the $7.9 trillion long-term debt market, the largest component is by far the mortgage market. Mortgage-backed securities (securities in which the underlying collateral is a pool of residential or commercial real estate mortgages) are the fastest growing sector of the long-term debt market. The second largest sector is the market for U.S. government securities (i.e., U.S. Treasury securities), whereas the smallest sector

**EXHIBIT 1–1**

**Composition of the U.S. Bond Market as of December 31, 1989 (dollars in billions; based on par value)**

| | | | | |
|---|---|---|---|---|
| U.S. Treasury Securities | | | $1,918 | (24.1%) |
| U.S. Agencies Securities (excluding agency pass-through securities) | | | 301 | ( 3.8%) |
| Corporate Bonds | | | 1,429 | (18.0%) |
| Domestic | 1,331 | (16.8%) | | |
| Yankee | 98 | ( 1.2%) | | |
| Municipal Securities | | | 802 | (10.1%) |
| Mortgages—Nonsecuritized (1-4 multifamily, farm commercial) | | | 2,564 | (32.3%) |
| Pass-throughs | | | 933 | (11.1%) |
| Total of All U.S. Bond Markets* | | | $7,947 | |

* Excludes asset-backed securities

Source: This exhibit was prepared from data supplied by Salomon Brothers Inc.

shown in Exhibit 1–1 is the U.S. government agency securities market.[4] The municipal sector is the "tax-exempt" segment, where state and local government bonds are traded.[5]

The major nongovernmental sector of the market is the corporate segment. The market for corporates is customarily subdivided into several segments, which include industrials (the most diverse of the groups), public utilities (the dominant group in terms of volume of new issues), rail and transportation bonds, and financial issues (bonds issued by banks and other financial institutions). The corporate bond market offers not only a full range of credit quality but also the widest range of issues. One particular sector of the corporate bond market that has drawn increased interest from institutional investors (and Congress) is the high-yield (or junk bond) market. This is the market for noninvestment grade bonds. In dollars, the high-yield market represents approximately 25 percent of the corporate bond market.

---

[4] As we will explain in Chapter 27, a majority of the securities backed by a pool of mortgages are guaranteed by a federally sponsored agency of the U.S. government. However, these securities are classified as part of the mortgage market rather than as U.S. government agency securities.

[5] Municipal issuers include states, counties, cities and other political subdivisions such as school districts and their authorities. These issues are considered tax-exempt because the interest they pay is free from federal income taxation and possibly from state and local taxation.

Although preferred stocks are actually a form of equity, they are considered fixed income securities because their level of current income is fixed (i.e., they carry a fixed dividend rate, which is paid quarterly). Most outstanding issues are utility issues, although there is a growing number of industrial preferreds. One attraction of preferreds as a form of fixed income security is that under the tax law a specified portion of preferred stock dividends received by corporations are tax-exempt (leading to yields on preferred stocks normally lower than those of comparable corporate bonds).[6]

Convertible or exchangeable securities, issued as bonds or preferreds, are convertible into shares of common stock. Convertible securities can be converted into the common stock of the issuer; exchangeable securities may be exchanged for the common stock of another corporation. Convertible and exchangeable securities have the same underlying attributes as any other fixed income security (bond or preferred), except that under certain conditions their price behavior is determined by movements in the underlying common stock.

International bonds are issued by foreign entities. From the perspective of the U.S. investor, international bonds can be divided into two categories: dollar-denominated (or U.S.-pay) bonds and nondollar-denominated (or foreign-pay) bonds. All the cash flows from dollar-denominated international bonds are in U.S. dollars. These bonds are further classified by the location of the primary trading market. When the primary trading market is outside the U.S., dollar-denominated international bonds are referred to as *Eurodollar bonds*; when the primary trading market is in the U.S., they are called *Yankee bonds*. Yankee bonds are issued by foreign-domiciled entities such as foreign governments, foreign corporations, and supernational agencies (such as the World Bank, the Asian Development Bank, and the InterAmerican Bank).

All cash flows from nondollar-denominated bonds are designated in a foreign currency or a basket of foreign currencies such as the European Currency Unit (ECU).[7] Nondollar-denominated bonds are typically traded outside the United States. Exhibit 1–2 shows the size of the non-U.S. government bond markets converted into U.S. dollars as of June 1, 1990. The Japanese government is by far the largest issuer of nondollar bonds, followed by West Germany and the United Kingdom. Because most corporations outside the U.S. rely heavily on bank borrowing, corporate bond issues make up only a small segment of the bond markets in foreign countries. Salomon Brothers, for example, estimates that nondollar-denominated bonds issued by foreign governments constitute about 81 percent of the nondollar-denominated bond market. There are Yankee bonds that are nondollar-denominated. Also, there are a handful of issues

---

[6] The percent exempted from federal income taxes has been reduced over time. This is discussed further in Chapter 4.

[7] The ECU is the official composite unit of the European Monetary System.

**EXHIBIT 1–2**

**Non-US World Government Bond Index** (as of June 1, 1990, in billions of U.S. dollars)

| Sector | Principal Amount | Market Value | Market Weight |
|--------|------------------|--------------|---------------|
| Japan | $472.1 | $460.4 | 37.34% |
| U.K. | 167.1 | 155.6 | 12.62 |
| W. Germany | 213.7 | 201.6 | 16.35 |
| France | 153.1 | 155.2 | 12.58 |
| Canada | 101.8 | 101.6 | 8.24 |
| Netherlands | 100.1 | 97.2 | 7.88 |
| Denmark | 33.3 | 34.0 | 2.76 |
| Australia | 21.8 | 21.1 | 1.71 |
| Switzerland | 7.1 | 6.6 | 0.53 |
| **Total** | **$1,270.1** | **$1,233.3** | **100.00%** |

Source: Salomon Brothers Inc.

that make coupon payments in a foreign currency and the principal payment in U.S. dollars. These are called *dual currency bonds*.

Asset-backed securities are securities collateralized by assets that are not mortgage loans. Although the two most common types of asset-backed securities are those backed by automobile loans, called CARs (Certificates for Automobile Receivables), and credit card loans, called CARDs (Certificates for Amortizing Revolving Debts), there are also securities backed by boat loans, recreational vehicle loans, computer leases, accounts receivable, and Small Business Administration loans. As of March 1989, $23.6 billion of asset-backed securities was outstanding. Of this, $10.3 billion (43.8%) was in CARS and $12 billion (50.8%) was in CARDS. Only $1.4 billion (5.4%) was backed by the other loans or receivables mentioned above.[8]

---

[8] These data were reported by Monica E. Barry of The First Boston Corporation at the Bond Management and Portfolio Management Strategies Conference in New York on June 9, 1989.

# CHAPTER 2

## FEATURES OF
## FIXED INCOME SECURITIES

*Frank J. Fabozzi, Ph.D., CFA, CPA*
*Visiting Professor of Finance*
*Sloan School of Management*
*Massachusetts Institute of Technology*
*and*
*Editor, The Journal of Portfolio Management*

*Michael G. Ferri, Ph.D.*
*Foundation Professor of Finance*
*George Mason University*

This chapter will explore some of the most important features of bonds, preferred stock, and mortgage-backed securities and provide the reader with a taxonomy of terms and concepts that will be of assistance in the reading of the specialized chapters to follow.

## BONDS

### Type of Issuer

One important characteristic of a bond is the nature of its issuer. Although foreign governments and firms raise capital in U.S. financial markets, the three largest issuers of debt are domestic corporations, municipal governments, and the federal government and its agencies. Each class of issuer, however, features additional and significant differences. Domestic corporations, for example, include regulated utilities as well as unregulated manufacturers. Further, each firm may sell different kinds of bonds: Some debt may be publicly placed, whereas other bonds may be sold directly to one or only a few buyers (referred to as a *private placement*); some debt is collateralized by specific assets of the company, whereas other debt may be unsecured. Municipal debt is also varied: "General obligation" bonds (GOs) are backed by the full faith, credit, and taxing power of the governmental unit issuing them; "revenue bonds," on the other hand, have a safety, or creditworthiness, that depends upon the vitality and success of the particular entity (such as toll roads, hospitals, or water systems) within the municipal government issuing the bond. Within the federal government, many departments and agencies have the authority to sell bonds. The U.S. Treasury has the most voracious appetite for debt, but the bond market often receives calls from such units as the Export-Import Bank, the Federal Home Loan Bank, and other agencies of the federal government.

It is important for the investor to realize that, by law or practice or both, these different borrowers have developed different ways of raising debt capital over the years. As a result, the distinctions among the various types of issuers correspond closely to differences among bonds in yield, denomination, safety of principal, maturity, tax status, and such important provisions as the call privilege and sinking fund. As we discuss the key features of fixed income securities, we will point out how the characteristics of the bonds vary with the obligor or issuing authority. A more extensive discussion is provided in the chapters in Part 2 of this book that explain the various instruments.

## Maturity

A key feature of any bond is its *term-to-maturity*, the number of years during which the borrower has promised to meet the conditions of the debt (which are contained in the bond's indenture). A bond's term-to-maturity is the date on which the debt will cease and the firm will redeem the issue by paying the face value, or principal. One indication of the importance of the maturity is that the code word or name for every bond contains its maturity (and coupon). Thus, the title of the Exxon bond due, or maturing, in 1998 is given as "Exxon 6.5s of '98." In practice, the words *maturity, term,* and *term-to-maturity* are used interchangeably to refer to the number of years remaining in the life of a bond. Technically, however, maturity denotes the date the bond will be redeemed, and either term or term-to-maturity denotes the number of years until that date.

A bond's maturity is crucial for several reasons. First, maturity indicates the expected life of the instrument, or the number of periods during which the holder of the bond can expect to receive the coupon payments and the number of years before the principal will be paid. Second, the yield on a bond depends substantially on its maturity. More specifically, at any given point in time, the yield offered on a long-term bond may be greater than, less than, or equal to the yield offered on a short-term bond. As will be explained in Chapter 8, how maturity affects the yield will depend on the *shape of the yield curve*. Third, the volatility of a bond's price is closely associated with maturity: Changes in the market level of rates will wrest much larger changes in price from bonds of long maturity than from otherwise similar debt of shorter life.[1] Finally, as explained in the next chapter, there are other risks associated with the maturity of a bond.

When considering a bond's maturity, the investor should be aware of any provisions that modify, or permit the issuer to modify, the maturity of a bond. Though corporate bonds (referred to as "corporates") are typically *term bonds* (issues that have a single maturity), they contain arrangements by which the issuing firm either can or must retire the debt early, in full or in part. Many corporates, for example, give the issuer a *call privilege*, which permits the issuing firm to redeem the bond before the scheduled maturity under certain conditions (these conditions are discussed below). Many municipal bonds have the same provision. Although the U.S. government no longer issues bonds that have a call privilege, there are outstanding issues with this provision. Many industrials and some utilities have *sinking-fund provisions*, which mandate that the firm must retire a goodly portion of the debt, in a prearranged schedule, during its life and before the stated maturity. Typically, municipal bonds are *serial bonds* or, in essence, bundles of bonds with differing maturities. (Some corporates are of this type, too.)

Usually, the maturity of a corporate bond is between 1 and 30 years. This is not to say that there are not outliers. Two recent examples are the $9\frac{7}{8}$ percent coupon Swedish Export Credit Corporation's bond issued in 1988 that matures in 2038 (the first 50-year publicly issued bond sold in the U.S. market for quite some time) and the Citicorp perpetual issue (i.e., no maturity date) sold overseas in 1986. Despite such issues, the average maturity of corporate bonds has been decreasing since the 1970s to suit the needs of investors. For example, in 1974 the average maturity of new issues of investment-grade corporate bonds was 19.93 years; by 1988, the average maturity declined to 11.05 years.[2] Government securities that make coupon payments have initial maturities of 2 to 30 years (though, technically, Treasury issues of 2 to 10 years are called "notes"). The number of outstanding government issues with maturities exceeding 10 years is relatively small. The "term component" of municipal debt—the longest lived part of the serial issue—tends to have a maturity between 15 and 20 years.

Though classifying bonds in terms of years of "short-term," "intermediate-term," and "long-term" is not universally accepted, the following classification

---

[1] Chapter 7 discusses this point in detail.

[2] This information was obtained from Table 3–5 of Chapter 3 of Richard W. Wilson and Frank J. Fabozzi, *The New Corporate Bond Market Corporate Bonds* (Chicago: Probus Publishing, 1990).

is typically used. Bonds with a maturity of between 1 to 5 years are generally considered short-term; bonds with a maturity between 5 and 12 years are viewed as intermediate-term. Long-term bonds are those with a maturity of greater than 12 years.

## Coupon and Principal

A bond's *coupon* is the periodic interest payment made to owners during the life of the bond. The coupon is always cited, along with maturity, in any quotation of a bond's price. Thus, one might hear about the "Alabama Power 7.875 due in 2002" or the "Sears 8 due in 2006" in discussions of current bond trading. In these examples, the coupon cited is in fact the *coupon rate*; that is, the rate of interest that, when multiplied by the *principal, par value* or *face value* of the bond, provides the dollar value of the coupon payment. Typically, but not universally, for bonds issued in the United States half of the coupon payment is made in semiannual installments. In contrast, for bonds issued in the European bond markets or the Eurobond market, the coupon payment is made once per year. Bonds may be *bearer bonds* or *registered bonds*. With bearer bonds, investors clip coupons and send them to the obligor for payment. In the case of registered issues, bond owners receive the payment automatically at the appropriate time.

There are a few corporate bonds (mostly railroad issues), called *income bonds*, that contain a provision permitting the firm to omit or delay the payment of interest if the firm's earnings are too low. They have been issued as part of bankruptcy reorganizations and to replace a preferred stock offering of the issuer.

*Zero coupon bonds* have been issued by corporations and municipalities since the early 1980s. Although the U.S. Treasury does not issue zero coupon debt, such securities have been created by government securities dealers. Merrill Lynch was the first to do this with its creation of Treasury Investment Growth Receipts (TIGRs) in August 1982. The most popular zero coupon Treasury securities today are those created by government dealer firms under the Treasury's Separate Trading of Registered Interest and Principal Securities (STRIPS) program. Just how these securities are created will be explained in Chapter 9. The investor in a zero coupon security receives interest by buying the security at a price below its principal, or maturity value, and holding it to the maturity date. The reason for the issuance of zero coupon securities is explained in Chapter 6.

In contrast to a coupon rate that is fixed for the entire life of the bond, there are *floating-rate bonds*. The coupon rate on such securities is periodically reset based on some predetermined benchmark. For example, the coupon rate may be reset every six months at a rate equal to some spread above the yield on a six-month Treasury security. The distinctions between a floating-rate bond and what is sometimes referred to as a *variable-rate bond* or *adjustable-rate bond* are the frequency at which the coupon rate is reset and the underlying interest-rate benchmark. A floating-rate bond resets more than once a year, and the interest-rate benchmark is a short-term interest rate. In contrast, a variable-rate bond does not reset more than once a year, and the interest-rate benchmark is a long-term interest rate. Institutional investors such as banks and thrifts have found floating-rate bonds indexed off an interest-rate benchmark attractive for asset/liability management.

Two last points about floating-rate securities. First, although the coupon rate on most floating-rate securities resets on the basis of some financial index, some issues have a benchmark for the coupon rate that is a nonfinancial index, such as the price of a commodity. Second, whereas the coupon on floating-rate bonds benchmarked off an interest-rate benchmark typically rises as the benchmark rises and falls as the benchmark falls, there are issues whose coupon interest rate moves in the opposite direction of interest-rate changes. Such issues, called *inverse floaters*, have been used by institutional investors as hedging vehicles.

In recent years, new structures in the high-yield (junk bond) sector of the corporate bond market have introduced variations in the way coupon payments are made. For example, in a leveraged buyout or recapitalization financed with high-yield bonds, the heavy interest payment burden the corporation must make places severe cash-flow constraints on the firm. To reduce this burden, firms involved in LBOs and recapitalizations have issued deferred-coupon structures that permit the issuer to avoid using cash to make interest payments for a period of three to seven years. There are three types of deferred-coupon structures: (1) deferred-interest bonds, (2) step-up bonds, and (3) payment-in-kind bonds.

Deferred-interest bonds represent the most common type of deferred-coupon structure. These bonds sell at a deep discount and pay no interest for an initial period, typically from three to seven years.[3]  Step-up bonds sell at a discount from par and do pay coupon interest. However, the coupon rate is low for an initial period and then increases ("steps up") to a higher coupon rate thereafter. Finally, payment-in-kind (PIK) bonds give the issuer an option to pay cash at a coupon payment date or give the bondholder a similar bond (i.e., a bond with the same coupon rate and a par value equal to the amount of the coupon payment that would have been paid). The period for which the issuer can make this choice varies from 5 to 10 years.[4]

---

[3] Because no interest is paid for the initial period, these bonds are sometimes referred to as zero coupon bonds.

[4] For a further discussion of PIK bonds, see Laurie S. Goodman and Alan H. Cohn, "Payment-in-Kind Debentures: An Innovation," *The Journal of Portfolio Management*, Winter, 1989, pp. 9–19.

Another high-yield bond structure allows the issuer to reset the coupon rate so that the bond will trade at a predetermined price.[5] The coupon rate may reset annually or reset only once over the life of the bond. Generally, the coupon rate will be the average of rates suggested by two investment banking firms. The new rate will then reflect the level of interest rates at the reset date and the credit spread the market wants on the issue at the reset date. This structure is called an *extendable reset bond*. Notice the difference between this bond structure and the floating-rate issue described earlier. With a floating-rate issue, the coupon rate resets based on a fixed spread to some benchmark; the spread is specified in the indenture; and the amount of the spread reflects market conditions at the time the issue is offered. In contrast, the coupon rate on an extendable reset bond is reset based on market conditions suggested by several investment banking firms at the time of the reset date. Moreover, the new coupon rate reflects the new level of interest rates and the new spread that investors seek.

One reason that debt financing is popular with corporations is that the interest payments are tax-deductible expenses. As a result, the true after-tax cost of debt to a profitable firm is usually much less than the stated coupon interest rate. The level of the coupon on any bond is typically close to the level of yields for issues of its class at the time the bond is first sold to the public. Some bonds are initially issued at a price substantially below par value (called original-issue, deep-discount bonds), and their coupon rate is deliberately set below the current market rate. However, firms usually try to set the coupon at a level that will make the market price close to par value. This goal can be accomplished by placing the coupon rate near the prevailing market rate.

To many investors, the coupon is simply the amount of interest they will receive each year. However, the coupon has another major impact on an investor's experience with a bond. The coupon's size influences the volatility of the bond's price: The larger the coupon, the less the price will change in response to a change in market interest rates. Thus, the coupon and the maturity have opposite effects on the price volatility of a bond. This will be illustrated in Chapter 7.

The principal, par value, or face value, of a bond is the amount to be repaid to the investor either at maturity or at those times when the bond is called or retired according to sinking-fund provisions. But the principal plays another role, too. It is the basis on which the coupon or periodic interest rests; the coupon is the product of the principal and the coupon rate. For most corporate issues, the face value is $1,000; many government bonds have larger principals starting with $10,000; and most municipal bonds come in denominations of $5,000.

---

[5] Most of the bonds have a coupon reset formula that requires the issuer to reset the coupon so that the bond will trade at a price of $101 per $100 of par value.

## Yields

Participants in the bond market use three calculations to describe the potential return from investing in a bond: current yield, yield-to-maturity, and, in the case of a bond that may be called, yield-to-call. The calculation and limitations of these yield measures are explained and illustrated in Chapter 6, but here is a nontechnical explanation of each.

The simplest calculation is the *current yield*, which is the ratio of the coupon to the current price. For example, a bond with a price of 91 (91% of par, or $910 for a corporate bond with a face value of $1,000) and a coupon of 9.5 (9.5% of par) has a current yield of 10.44 percent. The current yield is deficient because it neglects the principal to be paid at maturity. To account for this rather large cash flow, investors use the conceptually and computationally more complex measure of *yield-to-maturity*. The yield-to-maturity, often referred to simply as "yield," is the rate of interest an investor would have to earn if an investment equal to the price of the bond were capable of generating the semiannual coupon payments and the principal of the bond in exactly the time pattern promised by the issuer. For example, suppose a bond is selling at $961.60 and has a coupon of $80 per year for the next 20 years. The holder of such a bond would expect to receive $40 every six months for 20 years and $1,000 at the end of the 20th year. What rate of interest on an investment of $961.60 would be able to produce those cash flows and leave nothing after the payment of the $1,000? The answer is an annual compounded rate of 8.6 percent, which is the yield-to-maturity of this bond.

The yield-to-maturity is an application of the discounting technique known as internal rate of return (IRR). The IRR of any series of payments is the discount rate that makes the present value of the payments just equal to the price or cost of the asset that generates the cash flows. The yield and the price of any bond are inversely related: As the price of the bond rises, the yield falls, and vice versa. For example, had the price of the bond in the preceding example been $1,010.00, the yield would have been 8.05 percent; and if the price had been $847.80, the yield would have been 9.98 percent. Yield must rise if price falls because any given future cash flows can be generated with a lower investment *if* the annually compounded rate of interest increases. Similarly, yield would fall if price rises because it would take a smaller rate of interest to generate the set future cash flows if the initial investment were to increase.[6]

For callable bonds, a third measure of potential return is calculated: yield-to-call. This measure is calculated assuming that the bond will be held to the first call date and then called at that time. The IRR procedure is also used to calculate the yield-to-call.

---

[6] Further discussion of this principle may be found in Chapter 6.

## Price Quotes

The prices of most bonds are quoted as percentages of par value, or face value.[7]
To convert the price quote into a dollar figure, one simply multiplies the price
by the par value. The following table will illustrate the matter.

| Par Value | Price Quote | Price as a Percentage of Par | Price in Dollars |
|---|---|---|---|
| $    1,000 | 91 3/4 | 91.75% | $    917.50 |
| 5,000 | 102 1/2 | 102.5 | 5,125.00 |
| 10,000 | 87 1/4 | 87.25 | 8,725.00 |
| 25,000 | 100 7/8 | 100.875 | 25,218.75 |
| 100,000 | 71 9/32 | 71.28125 | 71,281.25 |

Treasury bonds and notes are quoted in thirty-seconds of a percentage point,
whereas corporate and municipal bonds are quoted in eighths of a percentage
point. Care must be taken in translating quotes into dollar prices because the
convention for Treasury bonds and notes is to quote, on dealer screens, the
number of 32nds after the decimal. Specifically, for a Treasury note and bond,
a quote of "91.24" means $91\frac{24}{32}$, or $91\frac{3}{4}$. A quote of "102.4" means $102\frac{4}{32}$, or
$102\frac{1}{8}$.

## Call and Refunding Provisions

If a bond's indenture contains a *call feature* or *call provision*, the issuing corporation or governmental entity retains the right to retire the debt, fully or partially,
before the scheduled maturity date. The chief benefit of such a feature is that
it permits the borrower, should market rates fall, to replace the bond issue with
a lower interest cost issue. The call feature has added value for corporations
and municipalities, which may in the future wish to escape the restrictions that
frequently characterize their bonds (about the disposition of assets or collateral).
The call feature provides an additional benefit to corporations, which might want
to use unexpectedly high levels of cash to retire outstanding bonds or might wish
to restructure their balance sheets.

The call provision is detrimental to investors, who run the risk of losing
a high-coupon bond when rates begin to decline. When the borrower calls the

---

[7] The exception to this rule is certain municipal issues, which are quoted on a yield basis. This
point will receive more attention in Chapter 21.

issue, the investor must find other outlets, which presumably would have lower yields than the bond just withdrawn through the call privilege. Another problem for the investor is that the prospect of a call limits the appreciation in a bond's price that could be expected when interest rates start to slip.

Because the call feature benefits the issuer and potentially places the investor at a disadvantage, callable bonds carry higher yields than bonds that cannot be retired before maturity. This difference in yields is likely to grow when investors believe that market rates are about to fall and that the borrower may be tempted to replace a high-coupon debt with a new, low-coupon bond. (Such a transaction is called *refunding*.) However, the higher yield alone is not sufficient compensation to the investor for granting the call privilege to the issuer. Thus, the price at which the bond may be called, termed the *call price*, is normally higher than the principal or face value of the issue. The difference between call price and principal is the *call premium*, whose value may be as much as one year's interest in the first few years of a bond's life and may decline systematically thereafter.

An important limitation on the borrower's right to call is the *period of call protection*, or *deferment period*, which is a specified number of years in the early life of the bond during which the issuer may not call the debt. Such protection is another concession to the investor and comes in two forms. Some bonds are *noncallable* (often abbreviated NC) for any reason during the deferment period; other bonds are *nonrefundable* (NF) for that time. The distinction lies in the fact that nonrefundable debt may be called if the funds used to retire the bond issue are obtained from internally generated funds, such as the cash flow from operations or the sale of property or equipment, or from nondebt funding such as the sale of common stock. Thus, while the terminology is unfortunately confusing, a nonrefundable issue may be refunded under the circumstances just described and, as a result, offers less call protection than a noncallable bond, which cannot be called for any reason except to satisfy sinking-fund requirements explained later.

Variations in call protection mirror the type of issuer of the bond. Long-term industrial corporate bonds generally have 10 years of refunding protection but are then immediately callable. Electric utilities most often have 5 years of refunding protection although, during times of high interest rates, issues with 10 years of refunding protection have been sold. Long-term debt of the former members of the Bell Telephone System have 5 years of call protection. Outstanding Treasury bonds that are callable can be called 5 years prior to maturity. Callable Treasury bonds are indicated on quote sheets by the citation of two different years. The first year indicates the first call date and the second the maturity date. It is important to note, however, that debt from federal sources is seldom called or refunded for purposes of saving interest payments; rather, government debt managers attempt to refund debt in a way that is consistent with stability in the capital markets.

A key question is when will the firm find it profitable to refund an issue. It is important for investors to understand the process by which a firm decides whether it ought to retire an old bond and issue a new one. A simple and brief example will illustrate that process and introduce the reader to the kinds of calculations an issuer will make when trying to predict whether a bond will be refunded.

Suppose a firm's outstanding debt consists of $30 million in a bond with a coupon of 10 percent, a maturity of 15 years, and a lapsed deferment period. The firm can now issue a bond with a similar maturity for an interest rate of 7.8 percent. Assume that the issuing expenses and legal fees amount to $200,000. The call price on the old bond is $1,050.

The firm must pay, adjusted for taxes, the sum of call premium and expenses. To simplify the calculations, assume a 30 percent tax rate. This sum is then $1,190,000 and the call premium is $1.5 million.[8] Such a transaction would save the firm a yearly sum of $462,000 in interest (which equals the interest of $3 million on the old bond less the $2.34 million on the new, adjusted for taxes) for the next 15 years.[9] The rate of return on a payment of $1,190,000 now in exchange for a yearly savings of $462,000 per year for 15 years is about 38 percent. This rate far exceeds the firm's after-tax cost of debt (now at 7.8% times .7, or 5.46%) and makes the refunding a positive economic transaction.[10]

## Sinking-Fund Provision

The *sinking-fund provision,* which is typical for publicly and privately issued industrial bonds and not uncommon among certain classes of utility debt, requires the obligor to retire a certain amount of the outstanding debt each year. Generally, the retirement occurs in one of two ways. The firm may purchase the amount of bonds to be retired in the open market if their price is below par, or the company may make payments to the trustee who is empowered to monitor the indenture and who will call a certain number of bonds chosen by lottery. In the latter case, the investor would receive the prearranged call price, which is usually par value. The schedule of retirements varies considerably from issue to issue. Some issuers, particularly in the private-placement market, retire most

---

[8] Both expenses are tax deductible for the firm. The total expense is the call premium of $1.5 million plus the issuing expenses and legal fees of $200,000. The after-tax cost is equal to the before-tax cost times (1 − tax rate). Hence, the after-tax cost is $1.7 million times (1 − .3), or $1,190,000.

[9] The new interest expense would be $30 million times .078. The after-tax cost of the interest saving is $660,000 times (1 − .3).

[10] Most analysts believe that the "hurdle rate" for refunding must be the after-tax cost of debt, which equals the product of the yield-to-maturity and (1 − marginal tax rate of the firm).

if not all of their debt before maturity. In the public market, some companies may retire as little as 20 to 30 percent of the outstanding par value before maturity. Further, the indenture of many issues includes a deferment period that permits the issuer to wait five years or more before beginning the process of sinking-fund retirements. Government debt is generally free of this provision.

There are three advantages of a sinking-fund provision from the investor's perspective. The sinking-fund requirement ensures an orderly retirement of the debt so that the final payment, at maturity, will not be too large. Second, the provision enhances the liquidity of some debt, especially for the smaller issues with thin secondary markets. Third, the prices of bonds with this requirement are presumably more stable because the issuer may become an active participant on the buy side when prices fall. For these reasons, the yields on bonds with sinking-fund provisions tend to be less than those on bonds without them, all else being the same.

Sometimes, however, the sinking fund can work to the disadvantage of an investor. Suppose that an investor is holding one of the early bonds to be called for a sinking fund. All of the time and effort put into analyzing the bond has now been wasted, and the investor will have to choose new instruments for purchase. Also, an investor holding a bond with a high coupon at the time rates begin to fall is still forced to relinquish the issue. For this reason, in times of high interest rates, one might find investors demanding higher yields from bonds with sinking funds than from other debt.

The sinking-fund provision may also harm the investor's position through the *doubling option*, a part of many corporate bond indentures. With this option, the corporation is free to retire twice (in some cases, more than twice) the amount of debt the sinking fund requires and to do it at the call price set for sinking-fund matters. Of course, the firm will exercise this doubling option only if the price of the bond exceeds the sinking-fund price (usually near par), and this happens when rates are relatively low. If, as is typically the case, the sinking-fund provision becomes operative before the lapse of the call-deferment period, the firm can retire much of its debt with the doubling option and can do so at a price far below that of the call price it would have to pay in the event of refunding. The impact of such activity on the investor's position is obvious: The firm can redeem at or near par many of the bonds that appear to be protected from call and that have a market value above the face value of the debt.

## Put Provisions

A putable bond grants the investor the right to sell the issue back to the issuer at par value on designated dates. The advantage to the investor is that if interest rates rise after the issue date, thereby reducing the value of the bond, the investor can force the issuer to redeem the bond at par. Some issues with put provisions may restrict the amount that the bondholder may put back to the issuer at any one put date. There are even some issues—we're not making this up—that allow an investor (more precisely, his or her heirs) to put the bond if the investor dies. An example of such an issue is The Cato Corporation $10\frac{1}{2}$s of '96. This is not very different from certain U.S. government bonds, popularly referred to as "flower bonds," that permit the heirs of an estate to use certain issues to pay estate taxes by turning in the issue. The amount that the Treasury credits the estate for taxes is equal to the par value of the bonds, regardless of their market value at the time. Thus, these U.S. government bonds can be viewed as putable bonds.

In recent years, put options have been included in corporate bonds to deter unfriendly takeovers. These put provisions are referred to as "poison puts."

## Convertible or Exchangeable Debt

A *convertible bond* is one that can be exchanged for specified amounts of common stock in the issuing firm. The conversion cannot be reversed, and the terms of the conversion are set by the company in the bond's indenture. The most important terms are *conversion ratio* and *conversion price*. The conversion ratio indicates the number of shares of common stock to which the holder of the convertible has a claim. For example, one convertible issue of Burlington Industries matures in 2008 and has a coupon rate of 8.75 percent; this bond has a conversion ratio of 20.619 shares for one bond. Equivalently, this means at the time of issuance the conversion price was $48.50 per share ($1,000 par value divided by the conversion ratio 20.619). The conversion price at issuance is also referred to as the *par conversion price*.

The conversion privilege may be permitted for all or only some portion of the bond's life. The conversion ratio may decline over time. It is always adjusted proportionately for stock splits and stock dividends. Convertible bonds are callable by the issuer. This permits the issuer to force conversion of the issue. There are some convertible issues that have call protection. This protection can be in one of two forms: Either the issuer is not allowed to redeem the issue prior to a specified date, or the issuer is not permitted to call the issue until the stock price has increased by a predetermined percentage price above the conversion price at issuance. For example, a convertible issue of National City Corporation could not be called prior to January 1, 1988, unless the common stock traded at a premium of 50 percent above its par conversion price.

An *exchangeable bond* is an issue that can be exchanged for the common stock of a corporation other than that of the issuer of the bond. For example, Dart & Kraft has an exchangeable bond issue that can be traded for the common stock of 3M. (Dart & Kraft obtained the 3M common stock in exchange for the sale of one of its subsidiaries.) Ford Motor Credit exchangeable bonds can be replaced with the common stock of its parent company, Ford Motor Company. There are a handful of issues that are exchangeable into more than one security.

General Cinema, for example, has an outstanding issue that is convertible into the common stock of R.J. Reynolds and Sea-Land Corporation.

Techniques for analyzing convertible and exchangeable bonds are described in Chapter 15.

## Warrants

A *warrant* is an option a firm issues that permits the owner to buy from the firm a certain number of shares of common stock at a specified price. It is not uncommon for publicly held corporations to issue warrants with new bonds.

A valuable aspect of a warrant is its rather long life: Most warrants are in effect for at least two years from issuance, and some are perpetual.[11] Another key feature of the warrant is the *exercise price*, the value for which the warrant holder can buy stock from the corporation. This price is normally set at about 15 percent above the market price of common stock at the time the bond is issued. Frequently, the exercise price will rise through time, according to the schedule in the bond's indenture. Another important characteristic of the warrant is its detachability. *Detachable warrants* are often actively traded on the American Stock Exchange. Other warrants can be exercised only by the bondholder, and these are called *nondetachable warrants*.

The chief benefit to the investor is the financial leverage the warrant provides. This is explained in Chapter 15.

## PREFERRED STOCK

Preferred stock is a form of equity or ownership in a publicly held corporation. As the term implies, the claims of the holders of preferred stock (or simply, *preferred*) are superior in some important ways to those of the owners of the other form of equity, common shares. The firm must pay dividends on preferreds before it is free to distribute earnings to holders of common stock. Also, in the event of liquidation, the owners of preferreds have a prior claim on any assets that may remain after the creditors have been satisfied. One difference between preferred and common stock is that holders of preferred are not normally permitted a voting power in the management of the firm.

The dividend on a preferred stock is, like the coupon on a bond, a fixed payment. A preferred with a dividend of 8 percent and a par value of $100 (which

---

[11] This long life contrasts sharply with the short life during which exchange-traded call options on common stock, similar to warrants, are exercisable.

is a typical value) would receive $8 per year. However, the dividend is unlike the coupon on a bond in that the firm is not legally bound to pay the dividend. The company may decide to omit or delay the dividend without suffering the legal consequences it would encounter if it omitted a coupon interest payment. Some dividends are cumulative, which means that the firm must eventually pay arrearages on any previously omitted dividend payments. Other dividends are noncumulative, and the firm may skip them without the liability of having to pay them later. A very small number of preferreds, called *participating*, entitle the investor to receive extra dividends whenever common dividends exceed the level of dividends on preferred issues.

Public utilities are the prime issuers of preferred stock. Their aim in using this hybrid security is to increase the equity portion of their balance sheet or to prepare the way for a later flotation of new debt. Industrial concerns use preferreds primarily in the special cases of a merger or acquisition. The type of preferred used then is *convertible preferred*, as discussed later. Industrial firms find preferred stock to be an unsuitable form of financing because the dividend payments are not tax deductible, as are interest payments on bonds. If the tax rate of a firm is 34 percent, then the true after-tax cost of debt capital is 66 percent lower than the rate on preferred equity. Utilities, by contrast, have an easier time passing costs along to customers and consequently are not reluctant to employ preferred stock in their capital structure.

The expected rate of return on preferred stock is easy to calculate. Because it is a form of equity and a perpetuity, preferred stock has no maturity or principal to be redeemed (with the exception of some cases to be analyzed later). Thus, the price of preferred is simply the discounted value of an unlimited series of fixed dividend payments. It can be shown that the return on preferred is approximately equal to the ratio of the dividend to the price. (This calculation resembles the current yield on bonds discussed above.) For example, if the Duke Power preferred with a dividend of $8.70 has a price of $61, then its yield is 14.26 percent.

As with bonds, the price and yield of preferred stock vary inversely: A rise in yield brings about a fall in price, and vice versa. Further, the yields on preferreds tend to correspond closely to and move in concert with the yields on other long-term fixed income securities. Any utility may have more than one preferred stock outstanding at any time, and the different instruments are designated by their dividend level. For example, Duke Power currently has at least four preferreds outstanding—one with a dividend of 8.7 percent, another with a dividend of 8.2 percent, a third with a dividend of 2.69 percent, and so on.

Preferreds have a number of characteristics analogous to those discussed in connection with corporate bonds. The first is the call provision. By such a provision the issuer has the right to redeem, under certain circumstances and at a price above par, the outstanding preferred stock. Normally the issuer will be motivated to call the stock when rates fall below the level in effect when the preferred stock was first issued. Again, as in the case of bonds, saved payments are the goal of early retirement. Also the issuer has usually granted the investor a deferment period during which the stock cannot be called. As in the case of bonds, the actual call provisions can vary considerably from stock to stock, company to company, and time to time.

Preferred stock also often contains a sinking-fund provision, which mandates that the issuer retire a given percentage of the issue at scheduled periods after issuance. Investors holding a stock with this provision tend to calculate its yield in a manner similar to the yield-to-maturity on bonds. Obviously, a preferred stock with a sinking fund bears a strong resemblance to a typical corporate bond: Both have fixed, periodic payments; both have maturities; and both have large par value payments at the time of maturity.

As mentioned above, some preferred stock is convertible into shares of common of the issuing company. This instrument has been popular in the arrangement of mergers and acquisitions. If an acquiring company offers convertible preferreds in exchange for common stock in the acquired firm, the owners of that stock have no immediate tax liability. By accepting the convertible preferred, the owners of the acquired firm can receive a steady stream of high dividends and decide when and to what extent they might want to convert into common shares of the acquiring firm.

Preferred stock also has been issued in the high-yield sector of the preferred stock market. About half of the nonconvertible preferred stock in this market sector has been payment-in-kind preferred stock. This structure shares the characteristics of payment-in-kind bonds discussed earlier.

One more interesting facet of preferred stock requires mention here. The dividends from preferred stock are not fully taxable if the owner of the stock is a corporation. As a result of this rule, corporations tend to be active buyers of the preferreds of other companies, particularly the utilities. This point will be treated in greater detail in Chapter 16.

## MORTGAGE-BACKED SECURITIES

A mortgage-backed security is an instrument whose cash flow depends on the cash flow from an underlying pool of mortgages. There are four types of mortgage-backed securities: (1) mortgage pass-through securities, (2) collateralized mortgage obligations, (3) mortgage-backed bonds, and (4) stripped mortgage-backed securities. Our purpose here is to provide an overview of these securities. A detailed discussion of the structure, analysis, and portfolio strategies of these securities is presented in Chapter 27 through 31.

## Mortgage Cash Flows

Since the cash flow for these securities depends on the cash flow from the underlying pool of mortgages, the first thing to define is a mortgage. A mortgage is a pledge of real estate to secure the loan originated for the purchase of that real property. The mortgage gives the lender (*mortgagee*) the right to foreclose on the loan and seize the property in order to ensure that the loan is paid off if the borrower (*mortgagor*) fails to make the contracted payments. The types of real estate properties that can be mortgaged are divided into two broad categories: residential and nonresidential (i.e., commercial and farm properties). The mortgage loan specifies the interest rate of the loan, the frequency of payment, and the number of years to maturity. Each monthly mortgage payment consists of the monthly interest, a scheduled amount in excess of the monthly interest that is applied to reduce the outstanding loan balance (this is called the *scheduled repayment of principal*), and any payments in excess of the mortgage payment. The latter payments are called *prepayments*.

In effect, the lender (mortgagee) has granted the homeowner the right to prepay (or "call") all or part of the mortgage balance at any time. Homeowners prepay their mortgages for one of several reasons. First, they prepay the entire mortgage when they sell their home. Homes are sold for many reasons, among them a change of employment that requires moving, and the purchase of a more expensive home. Second, if mortgage rates drop substantially after the mortgage loan was obtained, it may be beneficial for the homeowner to refinance the loan (even after paying all refinancing costs) at the lower interest rate. Third, if homeowners cannot meet their mortgage obligations, their property is repossessed and sold. The proceeds from the sale are used to pay off the mortgage loan. Finally, if the property is destroyed by fire or another insured catastrophe occurs, the insurance proceeds are used to pay off the mortgage.

## Mortgage Pass-Through Securities

A mortgage pass-through security (or simply, *pass-through*) is created when one or more holders of mortgages form a collection (pool) of mortgages and sell shares or participation certificates in the pool. A pool may consist of several thousand mortgages or only a few mortgages. The cash flow of a pass-through depends on the cash flow of the underlying mortgages, which, as just explained, consists of monthly mortgage payments representing interest, the scheduled repayment of principal, and any prepayments.

Payments are made to security holders each month. The amount and the timing of the cash flow from the pool of mortgages and the cash flow passed through to investors, however, are not identical. The monthly cash flow for a pass-through is less than the monthly cash flow of the underlying mortgages, by an amount equal to servicing and other fees. The other fees are those charged by the issuer or guarantor of the pass-through security for guaranteeing the issue (discussed later).[12]  Typically, the coupon rate on a pass-through security is 0.5 percent less than the mortgage or coupon rate on the underlying pool.

The timing of the cash flow is also different. The monthly mortgage payment is due from each mortgagor on the first day of each month. There is a delay in passing through the corresponding monthly cash flow to the security holders. The number of days that the payment is delayed varies by the type of pass-through.

There are three major types of pass-through securities guaranteed by the following organizations: Government National Mortgage Association ("Ginnie Mae"), Federal Home Loan Mortgage Corporation ("Freddie Mac"), and Federal National Mortgage Association ("Fannie Mae"). The last two are federally sponsored credit agencies. The Government National Mortgage Association is a wholly owned U.S. government corporation within the Department of Housing and Urban Development. The securities associated with these three entities are known as *agency pass-through securities*. About 98 percent of all pass-through securities are agency pass-through securities. There are also *conventional pass-through securities*, also called *private label pass-through securities*, issued by thrifts, commercial banks, and private conduits that are not backed by any agency.

Agency pass-through securities are not rated by commercial rating agencies such as Moody's and Standard & Poor's because they think it is inappropriate to do so. In contrast, conventional mortgage pass-through securities are rated. Although conventional mortgage pass-through securities are not guaranteed by the U.S. government or the other agencies, they are often supported by credit enhancements so that they can obtain a high credit rating.

Recall from our earlier discussion of the yield on bonds that given a cash flow and the price of the bond, the yield-to-maturity is just the internal rate of return. The difficulty with computing the yield on any mortgage-backed security is that the cash flow is unknown because of prepayments. The only way to calculate a yield is to make some assumption about the prepayment rate over the life of the underlying mortgage pool. Based on the prepayment rate assumption, the cash flow for a mortgage-backed security can be calculated. Given the estimated cash flow, a yield can be computed. A yield computed in this manner is called a *cash flow yield*. Cash flow yields are typically based on one of the following benchmarks for projecting the cash flow: constant prepayment rate or PSA standard prepayment model. These are discussed in Chapter 27.

---

[12] Actually, the servicer pays the guarantee fee to the issuer or guarantor.

## Collateralized Mortgage Obligations

With a pass-through security, there is considerable uncertainty about what its actual maturity will be. Consequently, market participants interested in purchasing a short-term security, say one to three years, find these securities unattractive; some long-term investors find these securities unattractive because a fast-pay pass-through security could substantially reduce its maturity. A collateralized mortgage obligation (CMO) reduces the uncertainty concerning the maturity of a mortgage-backed security and thereby provides a risk/return pattern not available with typical pass-through securities.

A CMO is a security backed by a pool of pass-through securities and/or mortgages. Because CMOs derive their cash flow from the underlying mortgage collateral, they are referred to as "derivative" securities. CMOs are structured so that there are several classes of bondholders with varying *stated* maturities. The principal payments from the underlying collateral are used to sequentially retire the bonds.

For example, in a plain vanilla CMO structure, there may be four classes of bonds, which we shall refer to as class A, class B, class C and class Z. (The classes are commonly referred to as *tranches*.) The first three classes, with class A representing the shortest maturity bond, receive periodic interest payments from the underlying collateral; class Z is an accrual bond that receives no periodic interest until the other three classes are retired. When principal payments, both scheduled and prepayments, are received, they are applied to retire the class-A bonds. After all the class-A bonds are retired, all principal payments received are applied to retire the class-B bonds. Once all the class-B bonds are retired, class-C bonds are paid off from all principal payments. Finally, after the first three classes of bonds are retired, the cash-flow payments from the remaining underlying collateral are used to satisfy the obligations on the Z-bonds (original principal plus accrued interest).

The cash flow for each class of a CMO can be derived only by assuming some prepayment rate for the underlying mortgage collateral. The prepayment benchmark used by mortgage-backed securities dealers to quote CMO yields is the PSA standard prepayment model.

There are other CMO structures. These include CMOs with a floating-rate class, an inverse floating-rate class, a planned amortization class (PAC), and a targeted amortization class (TAC). The last two bond classes provide, under all but extreme prepayment rates, a more stable cash flow. These are described in Chapter 29.

## Mortgage-Backed Bonds

The pass-through security is the most common structure used for the issuance of a security collateralized by a mortgage pool. Another structure is the mortgage-backed bond. This bond is a general obligation of the issuer, which may be a thrift or other entity that originates mortgages. While a pass-through security issued by a thrift does not appear as a liability on its balance sheet, a mortgage-backed bond does.

Payments of interest and principal are made like other corporate bonds: Interest payments are made every six months, and principal is paid at the maturity date. The difference between a corporate bond and a mortgage-backed bond lies in the structure. The mortgage-backed bond is structured so as to reduce the risk of default by the issuer. Consequently, most mortgage-backed bonds are given a high credit rating by the commercial rating companies.

A special type of mortgage-backed bond is a *pay-through bond* (also called a *cash-flow bond*). The pay-through bond does not have a fixed maturity as does a mortgage-backed bond. The maturity and principal payment of a pay-through bond will depend on the actual payments on the underlying mortgage collateral.

### Stripped Mortgage-Backed Securities

Stripped mortgage-backed securities, introduced by Fannie Mae in 1986, are another example of derivative mortgage securities. A pass-through security divides the cash flow from the underlying pool of mortgages on a pro rata basis to the security holders. A stripped mortgage-backed security is created by altering the distribution of principal and interest from a pro rata distribution to an unequal distribution. By doing so, at least one of the securities created will have a price/yield relationship that is different from the price/yield relationship of the underlying mortgage pool. As will be explained in Chapter 30, if properly used, stripped mortgage-backed securities provide means by which investors can hedge the risks associated with the ownership of pass-through securities and mortgages.

The first generation of stripped mortgage-backed securities were "partially stripped" mortgage-backed securities. We can illustrate this by looking at the stripped mortgage-backed securities issued by Fannie Mae in mid-1986.[13] The class-B stripped mortgage-backed securities were backed by a pool of 9 percent mortgage pools. The mortgage payments from the underlying mortgage pool are distributed to class B-1 and class B-2 in the following way. Both classes receive an equal amount of the principal. However, the interest payments are divided so that class B-1 receives one-third and class B-2 receives two-thirds. Since the coupon rate for the underlying mortgage pool is 9 percent, class B-1 receives 3 percent interest and one-half the principal, making it a 6 percent coupon security. The class B-2 will receive two-thirds of the 9 percent coupon

---

[13] For a further discussion, see Richard Roll, "Stripped Mortgage-Backed Securities," Chapter 18 in Frank J. Fabozzi (ed.) *The Handbook of Mortgage-Backed Securities*. (Chicago: Probus Publishing 1988).

from the underlying pool or 6 percent and one-half the principal, producing a 12 percent coupon security.

In early 1987, stripped mortgage-backed securities began to be issued in which all of the interest is allocated to one class (called the *interest-only*, or *IO*, class) and all of the principal to the other class (called the *principal-only*, or *PO*, class).

## SUMMARY

This chapter has provided an introduction to some of the fundamental attributes of bonds, preferred stock, and mortgage-backed securities. The chapter has explored, in a preliminary way, the key features of these fixed income securities. It is our hope that this chapter will supply the reader with a general knowledge of the instruments and provide a conceptual and terminological background for the chapters that will investigate in more detail each of the features discussed and the associated risks.

# CHAPTER 3

## RISKS ASSOCIATED WITH INVESTING IN FIXED INCOME SECURITIES

*Ravi E. Dattatreya, Ph.D.*
*Senior Vice President*
*Sumitomo Bank Capital Markets, Inc.*

*Frank J. Fabozzi, Ph.D., CFA, CPA*
*Visiting Professor of Finance*
*Sloan School of Management*
*Massachusetts Institute of Technology*
*and*
*Editor, The Journal of Portfolio Management*

*T. Dessa Fabozzi, Ph.D.*
*Vice President*
*Merrill Lynch Capital Markets*

The return obtained from a fixed income security from the day it is purchased to the day it is sold can be divided into two conceptual parts: (1) the market value of the security when it is eventually sold and (2) the cash flows received from the security over the time period that it is held, plus any additional income from reinvestment of the cash flow. Several environmental factors impact one or both of these two parts of return. We can define the risk in any security as a measure of the impact of these market factors on the return characteristics of the security.

The different types of risk that an investor in fixed income securities is exposed to are as follows:

- Market, or interest-rate, risk
- Reinvestment risk
- Timing, or call, risk
- Credit, or default, risk
- Yield-curve, or maturity, risk
- Inflation, or purchasing power, risk
- Marketability, or liquidity, risk
- Exchange rate, or currency, risk
- Volatility risk
- Political or legal risk
- Event risk
- Sector risk

Each risk is described in this chapter. They will become more clear as the securities are described in more detail in other chapters of this book.

## MARKET OR INTEREST-RATE RISK

The price of a typical fixed income security moves in the opposite direction of the change in interest rates: As interest rates rise (fall), the price of a fixed income security will fall (rise).[1] This property is illustrated in Chapter 6. For an investor who plans to hold a fixed income security to maturity, the change in its price prior to maturity is not of concern; however, for an investor who may have to sell the fixed income security prior to the maturity date, an increase in interest rates will mean the realization of a capital loss. This risk is referred to as *market risk*, or *interest-rate risk* which is by far the major risk faced by an investor in the fixed income market.

It is customary to represent the market by the yield levels on Treasury securities. Most other yields are compared to the Treasury levels and are quoted as spreads off appropriate Treasury yields. To the extent that the yields of all fixed income securities are interrelated, their prices respond to changes in Treasury rates. As discussed in Chapter 7, the actual magnitude of the price response for any security depends on various characteristics of the security such as coupon, maturity, and the options embedded in the security (e.g., call and put provisions).

---

[1] There are certain fixed income instruments whose price changes in the same direction as interest rates. Examples are put options and interest-only strips in mortgage-backed securities.

## REINVESTMENT RISK

As explained in the next chapter, the cash flows received from a security are usually (or, are assumed to be) reinvested. The additional income from such reinvestment, sometimes called "interest-on-interest," depends on the prevailing interest rate levels at the time of reinvestment as well as on the reinvestment strategy. The variability in the returns from reinvestment from a given strategy due to changes in market rates is called *reinvestment risk*. The risk here is that the interest rate at which interim cash flows can be reinvested will fall. Reinvestment risk is greater for longer holding periods. It is also greater for securities with large, early cash flows such as high-coupon bonds. This risk is analyzed in more detail in Chapter 6.

It should be noted that interest-rate risk and reinvestment risk oppose each other. For example, interest-rate risk is the risk that interest rates will rise, thereby reducing the price of a fixed income security. In contrast, reinvestment risk is the risk that interest rates will fall. A strategy based on these two offsetting risks is called "immunization" and is the topic of Chapter 42.

## TIMING OR CALL RISK

As explained in the previous chapter, many bonds contain a provision that allows the issuer to retire, or "call," all or part of the issue before the maturity date. The issuer usually retains this right to have the flexibility to refinance the bond in the future if market interest rates decline below the coupon rate.

From the investor's perspective, there are three disadvantages of the call provision. First, the cash flow pattern of a callable bond is not known with certainty. Second, because the issuer will call the bonds when interest rates have dropped, the investor is exposed to reinvestment rate risk. That is, the investor will have to reinvest the proceeds received when the bond is called at relatively lower interest rates. Finally, the capital appreciation potential of a bond will be reduced because the price of a callable bond may not rise much above the price at which the issuer may call the bond.

Many long Treasury and agency bonds, most corporate and municipal bonds, and almost all mortgage-backed securities have embedded in them the option on the part of the borrower to call, or terminate, the bond prior to the stated maturity date. Even though the investor is usually compensated for taking the risk of call by means of a lower price or a higher yield, it is not easy to determine if this compensation is sufficient. In any case, the returns from a bond with call risk can be dramatically different from those obtained from a noncallable bond. The magnitude of this risk depends upon the various parameters of the call as well as on market conditions. Timing risk is so pervasive in fixed income portfolio management that many market participants consider it next only to interest-rate risk in importance. A framework for analyzing callable bonds and mortgage-backed securities is presented in Chapters 36 and 37.

In the case of mortgage-backed securities, the cash flow depends on prepayments of principal made by the homeowners in the pool of mortgages that serves as collateral for the security. The timing risk in this case is called *prepayment risk*. It includes call risk—the risk that homeowners will prepay all or part of their mortgage when mortgage interest rates decline. If interest rates rise, however, investors would benefit from prepayments. The risk that prepayments will slow down when mortgage interest rates rise is called *extension risk*. Thus, timing risk in the case of mortgage-backed securities is called prepayment risk, which includes call risk and extension risk.

## CREDIT RISK OR DEFAULT RISK

*Credit*, or *default, risk* refers to the risk that the issuer of a fixed income security may default (i.e., the issuer will be unable to make timely principal and interest payments on the security). Credit risk is gauged by quality ratings assigned by commercial rating companies, such as Moody's Investor Service, Standard & Poor's Corporation, Duff & Phelps, McCarthy, Crisanti & Maffei, and Fitch Investors Service, as well as credit research staffs of investment banking firms and institutional investor concerns.

Because of this risk, most bonds are sold at a lower price than, or at a yield spread to, comparable U. S. Treasury securities, which are considered free of credit risk. However, except for the lowest credit securities (known as "high-yield," or "junk bonds"), the investor is normally concerned more with the changes in the perceived credit risk and/or the cost associated with a given level of credit risk, than with the actual event of default. This is so because even though the actual default of an issuing corporation may be highly unlikely, the impact of a change in perceived credit risk or the spread demanded by the market for any given level of risk can have an immediate impact on the value of a security.

## YIELD-CURVE OR MATURITY RISK

In many situations, a bond of a given maturity is used as an alternative to another bond of a different maturity. An adjustment is made (see the discussion on duration in Chapter 7) to account for the differential interest-rate risks in the two bonds. However, this adjustment makes an assumption about how the interest rates (i.e., yields) at different maturities will move.[2] To the extent that the yield movements deviate from this assumption, there is *yield-curve*, or *maturity, risk*.

In general, yield-curve risk is more important in hedging situations rather than in pure investment decisions. For example, if a trader is hedging a position [3] or if a pension fund or an insurance company is acquiring assets so as to enable it to meet a given liability, then yield-curve risk should be carefully examined. However, if a pension fund has decided to invest in the intermediate-term sector, then the fine distinctions in maturity are less important.

Another situation where yield-curve risk should be considered is in the analysis of bond swap transactions where the potential incremental returns are dependent entirely on the parallel shift (or other equally arbitrary) assumption for the yield curve.

## INFLATION OR PURCHASING POWER RISK

*Inflation*, or *purchasing power, risk* arises because of the variation in the value of cash flows from a security due to inflation, as measured in terms of purchasing power. For example, if an investor purchases a five-year bond in which he or she can realize a coupon rate of 7 percent, but the rate of inflation is 8 percent, then the purchasing power of the cash flow has declined. For all but adjustable- or floating-rate bonds, an investor is exposed to inflation risk because the interest rate the issuer promises to make is fixed for the life of the security. To the extent that interest rates reflect the expected inflation rate, floating-rate bonds have a lower level of inflation risk.

## MARKETABILITY OR LIQUIDITY RISK

*Marketability*, or *liquidity, risk* involves the ease with which an issue can be sold at or near its true value. The primary measure of marketability/liquidity is the size of the spread between the bid price and the offer price quoted by a dealer. The greater the dealer spread, the greater the marketability/liquidity risk. For an investor who plans to hold the bond until the maturity date, marketability/liquidity risk is less important.

---

[2] Usually a parallel shift assumption is made. That is, we assume that the yields at different maturities move by equal amounts.

[3] For a discussion of a technique for hedging yield-curve risk, see Ravi E. Dattatreya, "A Practical Approach to Asset/Liability Management," in Frank J. Fabozzi and Atsuo Konishi (eds.) *Asset/Liability Management for Depository Institutions* (Chicago: Probus Publishing, forthcoming).

## EXCHANGE RATE OR
## CURRENCY RISK

A nondollar-denominated bond (i.e., a bond whose payments occur in a foreign currency) has unknown U.S. dollar cash flows. The dollar cash flows are dependent on the foreign-exchange rate at the time the payments are received. For example, suppose an investor purchases a bond whose payments are in Japanese yen. If the yen depreciates relative to the U.S. dollar, then fewer dollars will be received. The risk of this occurring is referred to as *exchange rate*, or *currency, risk*. Of course, should the yen appreciate relative to the U.S. dollar, the investor will benefit by receiving more dollars.

In addition to the change in the exchange rate, an investor is exposed to the interest-rate, or market, risk in the local market. For example, if a U.S. investor purchases West German government bonds denominated in deutsche marks, the proceeds received from the sale of that bond prior to maturity will depend on the level of interest rates in the West German bond market, in addition to the exchange rate.

## VOLATILITY RISK

As will be explained in Chapter 36, the price of a bond with an embedded option depends on the level of interest rates and factors that influence the value of the embedded option. One of the factors is the expected volatility of interest rates. Specifically, the value of an option rises when expected interest-rate volatility increases. In the case of a callable bond or mortgage-backed security, since the investor has granted an option to the borrower, the price of the security falls because the investor has given away a more valuable option. The risks that a change in volatility will adversely affect the price of a security is called *volatility risk*.

## POLITICAL OR LEGAL RISK

Sometimes the government can declare withholding or other additional taxes on a bond or declare a tax-exempt bond taxable. In addition, a regulatory authority can conclude that a given security is unsuitable for investment entities that it regulates. These actions can adversely impact the value of the security. Similarly, it is also possible that a legal or regulatory action impacts the value of a security positively. The possibility of any political or legal actions adversely affecting the value of a security is known as *political* or *legal risk*.

To illustrate political or legal risk, consider investors who purchase tax-exempt municipal securities. They are exposed to two types of political risk that can be more appropriately called *tax risk*. The first type of tax risk is that the federal income tax rate will be reduced. The higher the marginal tax rate, the greater the value of the tax-exempt nature of a municipal security. As the marginal tax rates decline, the price of a tax-exempt municipal security will decline. For example, in 1986, there were tax proposals to reduce marginal tax rates. As a result, tax-exempt municipal bonds began trading at lower prices. The second type of tax risk is that a municipal bond issued as tax-exempt will eventually be declared taxable by the Internal Revenue Service. This may occur because many municipal (revenue) bonds have elaborate security structures that could be subject to future adverse congressional actions and IRS interpretations. As a result of the loss of the tax exemption, the municipal bond will decline in value in order to provide a yield comparable to similar taxable bonds. For example, in June of 1980, the Battery Park City Authority sold $97.315 million in construction loan notes. At the time of issuance, the legal counsel thought that the interest on the note would be exempt from federal income taxation. In November of 1980, however, the IRS held that interest on these notes was not exempt, resulting in a lower price for the notes. The issue was not resolved until September 1981 when the Authority and the IRS signed a formal agreement resolving the matter so as to make the interest on the notes tax-exempt.

## EVENT RISK

Occasionally the ability of an issuer to make interest and principal payments is seriously and unexpectedly changed by (1) a natural or industrial accident or (2) a takeover or corporate restructuring. These risks are referred to generically as *event risk*. The cancellation of plans to build a nuclear power plant illustrates the first type of event in relation to the utility industry.

An example of the second type of event risk is the takeover in 1988 of RJR Nabisco for $25 billion via a financing technique known as a *leveraged buyout* (LBO). In such a transaction, the new company incurred a substantial amount of debt to finance the acquisition of the firm.[4] Because

---

[4] For a discussion of event risk associated with takeovers, see N.R. Vijayarghavan and Randy Snook, "Takeover Event Risk and Corporate Bond Portfolio Management," in Frank J. Fabozzi (ed.) *Advances and Innovations in Bond and Mortgage Markets* (Chicago: Probus Publishing, 1989).

the corporation was required to service a substantially larger amount of debt, its quality rating was reduced to noninvestment grade quality. To see the change in yield spread demanded by investors because of this new capital structure, refer to Exhibit 3–1. The yield spread to a benchmark Treasury from the LBO announcement increased from about 100 basis points to 350 basis points.

There are also spillover effects of event risk on other firms. For example, if there is a nuclear accident, this will affect all utilities producing nuclear power. With respect to takeovers, consider once again the LBO of RJR Nabisco. Any LBO of $24 billion was considered highly improbable prior to the RJR Nabisco LBO. The RJR transaction showed that size was not an obstacle. Consequently, other large firms that investors previously thought were unlikely candidates for an LBO were considered possible. To gauge the spillover effect caused by the LBO announcement, see Exhibit 3–2, which shows how event risk fears caused yield spreads to widen for three large firms.

**EXHIBIT 3–1**
**RJR Nabisco—The Impact of the Initial LBO Bid Announcement on Yield Spreads**

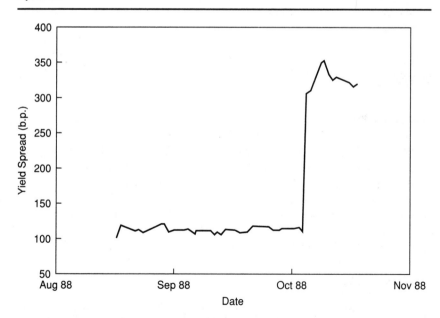

Source: N.R. Vijayarghavan and Randy Snook, "Takeover Event Risk and Corporate Bond Portfolio Management," in Frank J. Fabozzi (ed.) *Advances and Innovations in Bond and Mortgage Markets* (Chicago: Probus Publishing, 1989), p. 55.

**EXHIBIT 3–2**

**Anheuser Busch, Sara Lee & Union Pacific—Event Risk Fears and Widening Yield Spreads**

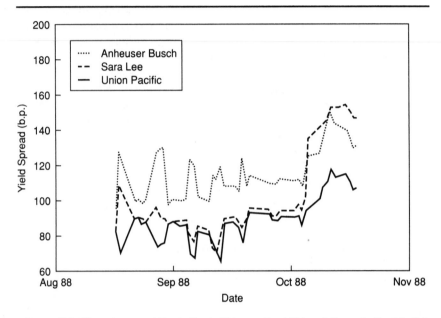

Source: N.R. Vijayarghavan and Randy Snook, "Takeover Event Risk and Corporate Bond Portfolio Management," in Frank J. Fabozzi (ed.) *Advances and Innovations in Bond and Mortgage Markets* (Chicago: Probus Publishing, 1989), p. 56.

## SECTOR RISK

Bonds in different sectors of the market respond differently to environmental changes because of a combination of some or all of the above risks, as well as others. Examples include discount versus premium coupon bonds, industrial versus utility bonds, corporate versus mortgage-backed bonds. The possibility of adverse differential movement of specific sectors of the market is called *sector risk*.

## OTHER RISKS

The various risks of investing in the fixed income markets reviewed in this chapter do not represent the entire range of risks. In the marketplace, it is customary to combine almost all risks other than market risk (interest-rate risk) and refer to it as *basis risk*.

## SUMMARY

In this chapter we have described 12 risks associated with investing in fixed income securities. Not all securities or investment strategies expose the investor to all of the risks we have discussed. As the instruments and portfolio management strategies are described in more detail throughout this book, these risks will be explained further.

# CHAPTER 4

## FEDERAL INCOME TAX TREATMENT OF FIXED INCOME SECURITIES

*Frank J. Fabozzi, Ph.D., CFA, CPA*
*Visiting Professor of Finance*
*Sloan School of Management*
*Massachusetts Institute of Technology*
*and*
*Editor, The Journal of Portfolio Management*

*David Z. Nirenberg, Esq.*
*Associate*
*Cleary, Gottlieb, Steen & Hamilton*

A knowledge of the federal income tax rules governing securities transactions is essential in understanding how fixed income securities are priced and why certain institutions and individuals participate in particular sectors of the market.

For example, consider bonds that are exempt from federal income taxes. These bonds will sell at a lower yield relative to taxable bonds because of the tax-exempt feature. Some institutions, such as pension funds, do not pay taxes and are not interested in tax-exempt bonds. However, individuals, who are subject to federal income taxes, will alter how they participate in the market for taxable and tax-exempt bonds depending on their expected marginal tax rates.

Both the prevailing tax law and the anticipated changes in the tax law have an impact on fixed income security prices. For example, when there is a likelihood that tax rates may be reduced for individuals, the price of tax-exempt bonds may fall (and the yield rise) because the tax-exempt feature has less value to individuals. As another example, the threat that the Internal Revenue Service may challenge the tax-exempt status of a particular municipal (tax-exempt) bond because of some perceived violation by the issuer will drive down the price of that bond so as to increase its yield.

This chapter explains the federal income tax treatment of fixed income security transactions.[1]   It is impossible to cover all of the nuances in the tax code that affect fixed income security prices and the tax provisions specifically applicable to certain institutions, some of which (such as banks, insurance companies, dealers in securities, and foreign investors) are subject to special rules. Some of these areas are covered in other chapters of this book. Since the tax law changes, it is important for investors to investigate how those changes will impact their current portfolio and investment philosophy.

## SOME DEFINITIONS

### Gross Income, Adjusted Gross Income, Taxable Income, and Alternative Minimum Taxable Income

Investors often use the term *income* in a very casual way. The Internal Revenue Code (IRC), however, provides a more precise definition of income. The IRC distinguishes between gross income, adjusted gross income, taxable income, and alternative minimum taxable income. *Gross income* is all income that is subject to income tax. For example, interest income and dividends are subject to taxation. However, there is a statutory exemption for interest from certain types of debt obligations, as explained later in this chapter. For such obligations, interest income is not included in gross income. Gross income for an individual and a corporation is determined in the same manner.

*Adjusted gross income*, for individuals, is gross income minus certain business and other deductions. For example, an important deduction from gross income to arrive at adjusted gross income is the deduction for certain contributions to individual retirement accounts (IRAs) and certain qualifying retirement plans.

*Taxable income* is the amount on which the tax liability is determined. It is found by subtracting the personal exemption allowance and other permissible de-

---

[1] This chapter does not discuss the taxation of mortgage-backed securities. For a discussion of those securities, see James M. Peaslee and David Z. Nirenberg, *Federal Income Taxation of Mortgage-Backed Securities* (Chicago: Probus Publishing 1989). This chapter also does not discuss so-called "applicable high yield discount obligations" which, under special rules enacted as part of the Revenue Reconciliation Act of 1989, are treated in part as stock and in part as debt.

ductions (other than those deductible in arriving at adjusted gross income)[2] from adjusted gross income. The concept of adjusted gross income does not apply to corporations; for a corporation, all permissible deductions are treated as business deductions. Therefore, adjusted gross income is meaningless for a corporation.

*Alternative minimum taxable income (AMTI)* is a taxpayer's taxable income with certain adjustments for specified tax preferences designed to cause AMTI to approximate economic income. For both individuals and corporations, a taxpayer's tax liability is the greater of (1) the tax computed at regular tax rates on taxable income and (2) the tax computed at a lower rate on AMTI. This parallel tax system, the alternative minimum tax, is designed to prevent taxpayers from avoiding significant tax liability as a result of taking advantage of exclusions from gross income, deductions, and tax credits otherwise allowed under the IRC.

## Tax Basis of a Capital Asset, Capital Gain, and Capital Loss

The IRC provides for a special tax treatment on the sale or exchange of a capital asset. The instruments described in this book—debt obligations and preferred stock—as well as shares of investment companies specializing in fixed income securities would qualify as capital assets in the hands of a qualified owner. In order to understand the tax treatment of a capital asset, the tax *basis* of a capital asset must first be defined. In most instances, the *original basis* of a capital asset is the taxpayer's total cost on the date of acquisition.[3] The *adjusted basis* of a capital asset is its original basis increased by capital additions and decreased by capital recoveries.

The proceeds received from the sale or exchange of a capital asset are compared to the adjusted basis to determine if the transaction produced a capital gain or capital loss. If the proceeds exceed the adjusted basis, the taxpayer realizes a *capital gain*; on the other hand, a *capital loss* is realized when the adjusted basis exceeds the proceeds received by the taxpayer.

---

[2] For individuals certain "miscellaneous itemized deductions" may only be deducted to the extent that they exceed, in the aggregate, 2 percent of an individual's adjusted gross income. One of the most important of these deductions is the deduction of expenses incurred in the production of income, including fees for investment advisors and accountants.

[3] When securities are purchased in a package, it is necessary to unbundle the package in order to determine the basis for each security. The general rule for determining the basis of each security is to allocate the cost of the package based upon the total fair market value of the unit immediately after the acquisition. For example, suppose that a unit package containing one bond and one share of preferred stock is purchased for $950. Immediately after the acquisition, the bond sells for $900 and the preferred stock for $85. The total value of the unit is therefore $985. The original basis of the bond is then 91.4 percent ($900 divided by $985) of the acquisition cost, or $868.30 (.914 times $950). The original basis of the preferred stock is $81.70 (.086 times $950).

## Classification of Taxpayers: Dealers, Traders, Investors

For tax purposes, taxpayers are classified as either dealers, traders, or investors. The classification is important because it determines whether capital gain or loss provisions are applicable and the treatment of transaction costs.[4]

Traders and investors are entitled to realize capital gains and losses. Dealers, on the other hand, are not. In the case of dealers, the securities held are considered inventory, and any gains or losses treated as ordinary gains or losses rather than capital gains or losses.[5] A dealer in securities is a merchant of securities who is regularly engaged in the acquisition of securities and subsequent resale to customers with a view to the gains and profits that may be derived as a result of such transactions. A dealer may be an individual, partnership, or corporation.

A trader is a person who buys and sells for his or her own account rather than the account of a customer, and the frequency of such transacting is such that the person may be said to be engaged in such activities as a trade or business. Investors, like traders, transact for their own accounts. However, transactions are occasional and much fewer than required in a trade or business.

Regardless of the classification of the taxpayer, expenses incurred to acquire a security are treated as part of the acquisition cost. Selling expenses, however, are handled differently for traders and investors as compared with dealers. Traders and investors must deduct the selling expenses from the sale price when determining whether a capital gain or loss is realized. For dealers, selling expenses are deducted as a business expense.

## INTEREST INCOME

Interest received by a taxpayer is included in gross income, unless a specific statutory exemption indicates otherwise. Therefore, if a taxpayer purchases $10,000 in par value of a corporate bond that has a coupon rate of 12 percent, the taxpayer expects to receive $1,200 per year. In the case of cash method taxpayers, such as most individuals, if that amount is actually paid by the issuer in the tax year, it is included in gross income. In the case of accrual method taxpayers, the interest income is included in income as it accrues without regard to when an actual cash payment is made.

---

[4] The classification is also important because it determines whether "wash sale" provisions are applicable. (A wash sale is defined in footnote 24.)

[5] There is an exception. If a dealer (1) clearly designates that certain securities are being held for investment purposes when the securities are acquired and (2) does not hold the securities primarily for sale to customers in the ordinary course of business after the designation, then gains or losses on the designated securities qualify for capital gain and loss treatment.

Interest received on debt issued by any state or political subdivision thereof,[6] the District of Columbia, and any possession of the United States is not included in gross income. For all taxpayers, interest that is otherwise tax-exempt on certain so-called private activity bonds (state and local bonds, the proceeds of which are used indirectly for private or commercial purposes) issued after August 7, 1986, nonetheless is included in alternative minimum taxable income. For corporations, 75 percent (50 percent for years prior to 1990) of the interest on any tax-exempt bond is included in AMTI indirectly through a special adjustment to AMTI for corporations.[7]

The statutory exemption of the interest received from debtors who are state and local governments (both referred to as "municipalities" in this chapter) is supposedly based upon the reciprocal immunity doctrine of the United States Constitution. This doctrine holds that states cannot interfere in the operations of the federal government, and the latter cannot interfere in the operations of the former. By taxing interest income on municipal obligations, it is argued that the ability of the state to finance its operations would be impaired.

Likewise, interest paid on debt issued by the U.S. government is exempt from income taxation by state and local governments but not from federal income taxes. Interest income by U.S. territories, and the District of Columbia, is also exempt from all state and local income taxes. Most states exempt the interest income derived from their own debt obligations, agencies, and political subdivisions from state and local income taxes. States may exempt the interest income from obligations of other states and political subdivisions.

As explained in Chapter 6, a portion of the income realized from holding a fixed income security may be in the form of capital appreciation rather than interest income. The tax treatment of the income component that represents capital appreciation differs depending on when the bond was issued. Prior to The Deficit Reduction Act of 1984, any capital appreciation that did not represent original-issue discount (to be discussed later) was generally treated as a capital gain.[8] As explained later in this chapter, the IRC provides for different tax treatment for certain capital gains and losses on the one hand and ordinary income and losses on the other. For bonds issued after July 18, 1984, part of the capital appreciation will be treated as ordinary income. Although under current law capital gains are taxed at the same rates as ordinary income, historically

---

[6] Because of financing practices by some state and local governments that Congress viewed as abusive, Congress imposed certain limitations on the issuance of tax-exempt obligations. The limitations involved industrial development bonds and arbitrage bonds.

[7] Under this adjustment, 75 percent of the difference between a corporation's "adjusted current earnings," essentially a proxy for economic income (or for years prior to 1990, one-half of the book income), and that corporation's AMTI (computed prior to the adjustment) is included in AMTI.

[8] Special rules, however, applied to original-issue discount obligations issued by individuals.

capital gains have been preferably treated for tax purposes and legislation is proposed from time to time to restore the preferential treatment of certain capital gains. In any event, even under the current law, taxpayers get less favorable treatment for capital losses than ordinary losses. Thus, the tax treatment of income from holding a debt instrument may have a major impact on the after-tax return realized by an investor. Because of the potential importance of distinguishing between income in the form of a capital gain (or loss) and interest income, the investor must be familiar with certain rules set forth in the IRC. These rules are summarized later in this chapter.

Unlike debt instruments, whose interest payments are taxable, the capital gain portion of a tax-exempt bond is *unattractive* for an investor who seeks tax-free income because, although the coupon interest received is exempt from federal income taxation, the capital gain portion is subject to taxation. This point should be kept in mind when considering the acquisition of a tax-exempt obligation.[9]

## Accrued Interest

Usually, bond interest is paid semiannually. The interest earned by the seller from holding the bond until the disposal date is called *accrued interest*. For example, if a corporate bond whose issuer promises to pay $60 on June 1 and December 1 for a specified number of years is sold on October 1, the seller is usually entitled to accrued interest of $40 ($60 times 4/6) for the four months that the seller held the bond.

Let us look at the tax position of the seller and the buyer, assuming that our hypothetical bond is selling for $900 in the market and that the seller's adjusted basis for this bond is $870. The buyer must pay the seller $940, $900 for the market price plus $40 of accrued interest. The seller must treat the accrued interest of $40 as interest income. The $900 is compared to the seller's adjusted basis of $870 to determine whether the seller has realized a capital gain or capital loss. Obviously, the seller has realized capital appreciation of $30. When the buyer receives the December 1 interest payment of $60, only $20 is included in gross income as interest income. The basis of the bond for the buyer is $900, not $940.

Not all transactions involving bonds require the payment of accrued interest by the buyer. This occurs when the issuer of the bond is in default of principal or interest, or if the issuer of the bond is contingent on sufficient earnings of

---

[9] As explained in Chapter 21, there is a formula suggested for determining the equivalent taxable yield for a tax-exempt obligation. This formula is only an approximation because it assumes that all of the income is tax free.

the issuer.[10] Such bonds are said to be quoted *flat*. The acquisition price entitles the buyer to receive the principal and unpaid interest for both past scheduled payments due and accrued interest. Generally, for bonds quoted flat, all payments made by the issuer to the buyer are first considered as payments to satisfy defaulted payments or unpaid contingent interest payments and accrued interest before acquisition. Such payments are treated as a return of capital. As such, the proceeds reduce the cost basis of the bond. On the other hand, accrued interest after the acquisition date is considered interest income when received.

For example, suppose the issuer of a corporate bond is in default of two scheduled interest payments of $60 each. The interest payments are scheduled on April 1 and October 1. The bond is sold for $500 on August 1. Assume that on October 1 of the acquisition year the issuer pays the bondholder $120. The buyer would treat the payment as a return of capital of $120, since it represents the two defaulted interest payments. Hence, the adjusted basis of the bond is $380 ($500 minus $120) and is not considered interest income. Suppose that two weeks later the issuer pays an additional $60 to the bondholder. This payment must then be apportioned between accrued interest before the acquisition date of August 1 and accrued interest after the acquisition date. The latter is $20, since the bond was held by the buyer for two months. Thus, $40 of the $60 payment reduces the adjusted basis of $380 prior to the second payment to $340 and is not treated as interest income. The $20 of accrued interest since the acquisition date is treated as interest income. If a bond is sold flat or is redeemed by the obligor for less than the par amount plus accrued interest, the amount realized is apportioned between principal and interest in a manner that reduces somewhat the amount of interest income realized and increases the amount treated as return of capital (or, if the amount returned exceeds the holder's tax basis, in a manner that increases the holder's capital gain).

## Bond Purchased at a Discount

A bond purchased at a price less than its redemption value at maturity is said to be bought at a *discount*. The tax treatment of the discount depends upon whether the discount represents *original-issue discount* or *market discount*.

*Original-issue Discount Bonds.* When bonds are issued, they may be sold at a price that is less than their redemption value at maturity. The difference between the redemption value and the purchase price is the original-issue discount. Each year a portion of the original-issue discount must be amortized (accrued)

---

[10] A bond whose interest is contingent upon sufficient earnings by the issuer is called an *income bond*.

and included in gross income. There is a corresponding increase in the adjusted basis of the bond.

For obligations issued on or after July 2, 1982,[11] the amount of the original-issue discount amortized is based on the constant-yield method (also called the effective or scientific method) and included in gross income based on the number of days in the tax year that that bond is held. With this method for determining the amount of the original-issue discount to be included in gross income, the interest for the year is first determined by multiplying the *adjusted issue price* (essentially, the adjusted basis the bond would have in the hands of the first holder of the bond) by the yield-to-maturity at issuance.[12] From this interest, the coupon interest is subtracted. The difference is the amount of the original-issue discount amortized for the year. The same amount is then added to the adjusted basis.

To illustrate the tax rules for original-issue discount bonds, consider a bond with a 4 percent coupon rate (interest paid semiannually), maturing in five years, that was issued for $7,683 and has a redemption value of $10,000. The yield-to-maturity for this hypothetical bond is 10 percent. The original-issue discount is $2,317 ($10,000 − $7,683). Suppose that the bond was purchased by an investor on the day it was issued, January 1, 1989. The constant-yield method is used to determine the amortization and the adjusted basis.[13] The procedure is as follows. Each six months, the investor of this hypothetical bond is assumed to realize for tax purposes interest income (including accrued original-issue discount) equal to 5 percent of the adjusted issue price. The 5 percent represents one-half of the 10 percent yield-to-maturity. The original issue price is the purchase price of $7,683. In the first six months the bond is held, the investor realizes for tax purposes interest equal to 5 percent of $7,683, or $384. The coupon payment for the first six-month period that the bond is held is $200. Therefore, $184 ($384 − $200) is assumed to be realized (although not received) by the investor. Thus, the amount of the original-issue from holding this bond for six months is $200 in coupon interest plus the $184 of the original-issue discount amortized. The

---

[11] For obligations issued prior to July 2, 1982, the original-issue discount must be amortized on a straight-line basis each month and included in gross income based on the number of months the bond is held in that tax year.

[12] In the case of bond callable at the option of the issuer (or puttable at the option of the holder) the option is ignored in determining yield unless it would result in a lower yield/cost to the issuer (or, in the case of a put option, a higher yield to the initial holder).

[13] If the obligation had been issued prior to July 2, 1982, the investor is required to amortize the original-issue discount of $2,317 on a straight-line monthly basis. Since there are 60 months to maturity, the prorated monthly interest on a straight-line basis is $38.62 ($2,317/60). Since the hypothetical bond is assumed to be purchased on January 1, the annual interest that must be reported from the amortization of the original-issue discount *each year* is $464 ($38.62 × 12). The total interest reported each year from holding this bond is $464 plus the coupon interest of $400 ($10,000 × .04).

adjusted issue price for the bond at the end of the first six months will equal the original-issue price of $7,683 plus the amount of the original-issue discount amortized, $184. Thus, the adjusted issue price is $7,867. The bondholder's adjusted basis in the bond (used in calculating gain or loss from sale) will also be increased by the amount of accrued original issue discount. This way, the increase in the value of the bond (as it approaches maturity) that is included in income as accrued original-issue discount is not taxed again as capital gain.

Let's carry this out for one more six-month period. If the bond is held for another six months, the amount of interest that the investor is expected to realize for tax purposes is 5 percent of the adjusted issue price. Since the adjusted issue price at the beginning of the second six-month period is $7,867, the interest is $393. The coupon interest for the second six months is $200. Therefore, the amount of the original-issue discount amortized for the second six-month period is $193 ($393 − $200). The $393 reported for holding the bond for the second six months is $200 in coupon interest and $193 in amortization of the original-issue discount. The adjusted issue price at the end of the second six-month period is $8,060—the previous adjusted issue price of $7,867 plus $193. If this bond, which was assumed to be purchased on January 1, 1989, is sold on December 31, 1989, interest income would be $777, consisting of $400 of coupon interest and $377 of the original-issue discount amortized. If this bond is sold on December 31, 1989, for $8,200 there would be a capital gain of $140, the difference between the sale proceeds of $8,200 and the adjusted basis of $8,060.[14]

Exhibit 4–1 shows the amount of the original-issue discount that must be reported as gross income for each six-month period that the bond is held and the adjusted issue price at the end of the period. Notice that amortization is lower in the earlier years, generally increasing over the life of the bond on a compounding basis.

Holders of original-issue discount tax-exempt bonds need to amortize the original-issue discount using the constant-yield method as well. However, the amount of the original-issue discount amortized is not included as part of gross income (but may be included in alternative minimum taxable income) because all interest is exempt from federal income taxes. As with taxable bonds, the amount of original-issue discount accrued on a tax-exempt bond is added to its adjusted basis.

The original-issue discount rules do not apply in two cases. The first is

---

[14] Because it is assumed that the investor purchased the bond at the original issuance, the bond-holder's, adjusted basis equals the bond's adjusted issue price. Had the bondholder purchased the bond in the secondary market, the bondholder's adjusted basis might have been greater or less than the bond's adjusted issue price.

**EXHIBIT 4–1**
**Amortization Schedule for an Original-Issue Discount Bond**
**Issued After July 2, 1982**

Characteristics of hypothetical bond:
| | | |
|---|---|---|
| Coupon | = | 4% |
| Interest payments | = | semiannual |
| Issue price | = | $7,683 |
| Redemption value | = | $10,000 |
| Years to maturity | = | 5 |
| Yield-to-maturity | = | 10% |
| Original-issue discount | = | $2,317 |
| Basis at time of purchase | = | $7,683 |

Amortization based on constant-yield method

| | | For the Period | | |
|---|---|---|---|---|
| Period Held (Years) | Adjusted Issue Price* | Gross Income Reported† | Coupon Interest | Original-issue Discount Amortized‡ |
| 0.5 | $ 7,867 | $384 | $200 | $184 |
| 1.0 | 8,060 | 393 | 200 | 193 |
| 1.5 | 8,263 | 403 | 200 | 203 |
| 2.0 | 8,476 | 413 | 200 | 213 |
| 2.5 | 8,700 | 424 | 200 | 224 |
| 3.0 | 8,935 | 435 | 200 | 235 |
| 3.5 | 9,182 | 447 | 200 | 247 |
| 4.0 | 9,441 | 459 | 200 | 259 |
| 4.5 | 9,713 | 472 | 200 | 272 |
| 5.0 | 10,000 | 486 | 200 | 286 |

* Adjusted issue price at the end of the period. The adjusted issue price is found by adding the original-issue discount amortized for the period to the previous period's adjusted issue price.

†The gross income reported is equal to the coupon interest for the period plus the original-issue discount amortized for the period.

‡By the constant-yield method, it is found as follows: (Adjusted issue price at the end of the previous period ×0.5) − $200.

the case of Series EE and E U.S. government savings bonds. The holders of these bonds may elect to have the original-issue discount on these bonds taxed when the bonds are redeemed rather than having the accrued interest taxed annually. The second exception is for noninterest-bearing obligations such as Treasury bills and many other taxable short-term obligations with no more than one year to maturity. When these obligations are held by investors who report for tax purposes on a cash rather than an accrual basis, the discount is not recognized until redeemed or sold. However, there are restrictions on the deductibility of interest to carry such obligations, as explained later in this chapter.

There are three more points the investor should be familiar with when dealing with original-issue discount bonds. First, original-issue discount is treated as zero if the discount is less than one-fourth of 1 percent of the redemption value at maturity multiplied by the number of complete years to maturity. For example, suppose a bond maturing in 20 years is initially sold for $990 for each $1,000 of redemption value at maturity. The discount is $10. The redemption value multiplied by the number of years to maturity is $20,000. The original-issue discount is .0005 of $20,000. Since it is less than one-fourth of 1 percent (.0025), the original-issue discount is treated as zero; that is, the investor does not have to amortize the discount and report it as gross income. Second, if an original-issue discount bond is sold before maturity, subsequent holders must continue to amortize the original-issue discount. However, if a subsequent holder purchases such a bond at a lower yield than the original holder (that is at a price in excess of the adjusted issue price) then the amount of original-issue discount included in income is appropriately reduced. The third point to keep in mind is that an investor may have to pay taxes on interest included in gross income but not received in cash. *Consequently, original-issue discount obligations are less attractive for portfolios of investors subject to taxation than for those of investors that are not (including IRAs).*

**Bond Purchased At a Market Discount With No Original-issue Discount.** When a bond is purchased at a market discount and there is no original-issue discount, the tax treatment depends on when the bond was issued.

For *taxable* bonds issued after July 18, 1984, any capital appreciation must be separated into a portion that is attributable to interest income (as represented by the amortization of the market discount with which it is purchased) and a portion that is attributable to capital gain. The portion representing interest income is taxed as ordinary income when the bond is sold. This is called *accrued market discount.* Unlike original-issue discount, the amount of the market discount that represents interest income is not taxed until the bond is sold or, if the principal on the bond is payable in installments prior to maturity, on each such an installment payment. Accrued market discount can be determined using either the straight-line method or the constant-yield method. It is important to remember that the amount of accrued market discount that is included in the income as interest is limited to the amount of capital appreciation on the bonds.

For taxable bonds issued on or prior to July 18, 1984 and for tax-exempt bonds when ever issued, any capital appreciation is treated as capital gain. Exhibit 4–2 shows the tax consequences for five assumed selling prices for a hypothetical bond. The results are shown for bonds issued before and after July 18, 1984. The results are also shown for the constant-yield and straight-line methods.

Two implications result from Exhibit 4–2. First, from a tax perspective, taxable bonds issued before July 18, 1984 and selling at a discount will be more

**EXHIBIT 4–2**

## Tax Treatment of Market Discount Bond for Five Assumed Selling Prices

Characteristics of hypothetical bond:

| | | |
|---|---|---|
| Coupon | = | 4% |
| Interest payments | = | semiannual |
| Bond price | = | $7,683 |
| Redemption value | = | $10,000 |
| Years to maturity | = | 5 |
| Yield-to-maturity | = | 10% |
| Market discount | = | $2,317 |
| Basis at time of purchase | = | $7,683 |
| Bond sold after 2.5 years | | |

*Bond issued before July 18, 1984*

| Sale Price | Accrued Market Discount | Capital Gain (Loss) |
|---|---|---|
| $9,500 | $    0 | $1,817 |
| 9,000 | 0 | 1,317 |
| 8,700 | 0 | 1,017 |
| 7,683 | 0 | 0 |
| 7,000 | 0 | (683) |

*Bond issued after July 18, 1984, with amortization based on constant-yield method*

| Sale Price | Accrued Market Discount | Capital Gain (Loss) |
|---|---|---|
| $9,500 | $1,017 | $  800 |
| 9,000 | 1,017 | 300 |
| 8,700 | 1,017 | 0 |
| 7,683 | 0* | 0 |
| 7,000 | 0* | (683) |

*Bond issued after July 18, 1984, with amortization based on straight-line method*

| Sale Price | Accrued Market Discount | Capital Gain (Loss) |
|---|---|---|
| $9,500 | $1,161 | $  656 |
| 9,000 | 1,161 | 156 |
| 8,700 | 1,017* | 0 |
| 7,683 | 0* | 0 |
| 7,000 | 0* | (683) |

* Actual accrued market discount is $1,017 ($1,161 for amortization based on the straight-line method), but the amount required to be included in income is limited to the excess of the sales price over the purchase price.

attractive than bonds issued after that date and selling at a discount. This will be reflected in the market price of those bonds. Consequently, investors that are in low marginal tax rates will find that they may be overpaying for bonds issued before July 18, 1984. The second implication is that it is not in the best interest of the investor to select the straight-line method to compute the accrued market discount because that method will cause the capital gain portion of any gain on sales to be lower (and the interest portion higher) than if the constant-yield method is elected.

Because of the difference in the tax treatment of original-issue discount bonds and market-discount bonds, the investor should check, prior to purchase, the type of bond and when it was issued.

## Bond Purchased at a Premium

When a bond is purchased at a price greater than its redemption value at maturity, the bond is said to be purchased at a *premium*.[15] For a taxable bond issued after September 27, 1985 and purchased by a nondealer taxpayer, the taxpayer may elect to amortize the premium over the remaining life of the security under a compound interest method similar to the method of accruing original-issue discount. Premium on a bond issued prior to September 28, 1985 may, however, be amortized on a straight-line basis. An election to amortize bond premium applies to all bonds held when the election is made and to all bonds acquired thereafter. In the case of a convertible bond selling at a premium, the amount attributable to the conversion feature may not be amortized. The amount amortized reduces the amount of the interest income that will be taxed. In turn, the basis is reduced by the amount of the amortization. For a tax-exempt bond, the premium *must* be amortized. Although the amount amortized is not a tax-deductible expense because the interest is exempt from taxation, the amortization reduces the original basis.

For example, suppose that on January 1, 1989 a calendar-year taxpayer purchased taxable bonds for $10,500. The bonds have a remaining life of five years, pay interest annually each January 1, and have a $10,000 redemption value at maturity. The coupon rate is 10 percent. The premium is $500 and the bonds have a yield-to-maturity of 8.72 percent. The taxpayer can amortize this premium over the five-year remaining life. If so, the amount amortized would be $84.01 for the first year (the difference between (i) the coupon of $1,000 and (ii) the product of the holder's basis, $10,500, and the yield, .0872).

---

[15] A bond will sell at a premium so that the effective interest rate of the bond is adjusted to reflect the prevailing interest rate on securities of comparable risk and remaining maturity. For further discussion, see Chapter 6.

The bondholder's basis would be reduced by the amortized premium. In the second year, $91.34 of the premium would be amortized ($1,000 − [($10,500 − 84.01) × .0872]). Each year the amortized premium would be sufficient to include, in income, interest (net of the amortized premium) at a rate equal to the bond's yield-to-maturity, and to amortize exactly 100 percent of the premium by maturity. Exhibit 4–3 sets out the amortization schedule of this hypothetical bond. If the bond is held until retired by the issuer at maturity, the adjusted basis would be $10,000, and consequently there would be no capital gain or loss realized. If the taxpayer does not elect to amortize the premium, the original basis is not changed. Consequently, at maturity the taxpayer would realize a capital loss of $500.

If our hypothetical bond was a tax-exempt bond, the premium would have to be amortized. The coupon interest of $1,000 would be tax-exempt, and the amortized premium each year would not be a tax-deductible expense. The basis would, however, be adjusted each year.

So far in our illustration we have used the original basis and the remaining number of years to maturity to determine the amount to be amortized. In the case of a callable taxable bond acquired after January 1, 1957, the taxpayer must elect to compute the amortization based upon the earlier call date if it results in a lesser amount of amortizable bond premium attributable to the period before the call date. Suppose that in the previous example the bond was callable on January 1, 1993 (four years after acquisition) for $10,300. The first election the investor must make is whether or not to amortize the premium. If the investor makes the election, then the investor must elect to base the amount of the amortization on the call price and date rather than on the redemption value at maturity, if the deduction is less. If the amount amortized is based on the redemption value at maturity, then the amortizable bond premium for 1989 is $84.01 (see Exhibit 4–3). If the call date and call price are used, the amortizable bond premium

**EXHIBIT 4–3**
**Amortization of Bond Premium on Bond Issued After September 27, 1989**

| January 1 | Basis | Yield | Income | Coupon | Amortized Premium |
|---|---|---|---|---|---|
| 1989 | $10,500.00 | .087237 | $915.99 | $1,000 | $ 84.01 |
| 1990 | 10,415.99 | .087237 | 908.66 | 1,000 | 91.34 |
| 1991 | 10,324.65 | .087237 | 900.70 | 1,000 | 99.30 |
| 1992 | 10,225.35 | .087237 | 892.03 | 1,000 | 107.97 |
| 1993 | 10,117.38 | .087237 | 882.61 | 1,000 | 117.38 |
| 1994 | 0.00 | | | | |

would be $43.66 (the coupon of $1,000 minus the product of the basis, $10,500, and the yield, 9.1080%). Thus, the net amount of interest required to be included in income in 1989 would be $956.34 ($1,000 − 43.66).

Should a bond to which an election to amortize bond premium applies be called before its maturity date, any unamortized portion of the premium is treated as an ordinary loss in the year the bond is called. For example, if our hypothetical 5-year bond was callable on January 1, 1991 at par, and if the bond was actually called on that date, an investor who had elected to amortize the premium would be entitled to an additional offset to interest income of $324.65 (the bondholder's then current basis of $10,324.65, or $10,500 minus amortized premium for the first two years of $84.01 and $91.34, respectively, minus the $10,000 received on the redemption). If premium is amortized to a call date but the bond is not then called, the remaining premium is amortized to the next call date (or maturity) as if the bond were newly acquired on the call date at a price equal to the holder's then current basis in the bond.

As noted earlier, no portion of the premium attributable to the conversion feature of a convertible bond may be amortized. For example, suppose a 15-year convertible bond with a 9.5 percent coupon rate is selling for $1,400. The investor must determine what portion of the premium is due to the conversion value. Suppose that the investor determines that nonconvertible bonds with the same quality rating and years remaining to maturity are selling to yield 8.1 percent, a 15-year bond priced to yield 8.1 percent would sell for $1,120.30 per $1,000 of redemption value at maturity.[16] Consequently, the premium that the investor may elect to amortize is based upon $1,120.30, *not* $1,400.

## DIVIDENDS

Preferred stock and investment companies specializing in fixed income securities pay dividends rather than interest. The general rules applicable to these investment vehicles are discussed in this section.

Corporations make cash distributions to shareholders. Not all cash distributions, however, are taxed. A *dividend* is defined as a payment made by a corporation out of its earnings and profits in the year of distribution or earnings and profits accumulated in all years prior to the date of distribution. Dividend income is taxed as ordinary income. Any portion of a distribution that does not represent a dividend or a redemption of stock is treated as a return of capital.

---

[16] See Chapter 6 for the pricing of bonds

No tax is paid on that portion: instead, the basis of the stock is reduced by that amount.[17]

Corporate recipients of dividend payments must include the entire amount in gross income. However, there is a special deduction that a corporation can take against dividend payments.[18] A corporate taxpayer is entitled to a deduction equal to (1) 70 percent of a dividend received from a domestic corporation,[19] (2) 80 percent of a dividend received from a domestic corporation in which the recipient corporation owns at least 20 percent of the stock, and (3) 100 percent of the dividend received from a corporation that is a member of a controlled group with the recipient corporation. For this reason, the treasurer of a corporation contemplating a fixed income investment would prefer a high-quality preferred stock issue to a high-quality, long-term debt instrument.

Dividends are also paid by regulated investment companies such as a mutual fund.[20] Investment companies sell their own securities to the public and reinvest the proceeds in a large number of securities. The shareholder of an investment company participates in the return generated from holdings and transactions involving these securities. The return earned by the investment company can therefore be in the form of interest, dividends, or capital gains. However, the dividend from an investment company to its shareholders is designated by the investment company, in a written notice to its shareholders not later than 60 days after the close of the taxable year, as either ordinary dividends or capital gain dividends. Ordinary dividends of a mutual fund are generally taxable as ordinary income. In the case of a corporate shareholder, however, a dividend received deduction may be available in respect of ordinary dividends paid out of dividends received by the mutual fund.[21] Further, any portion of the dividend that represents tax-exempt income realized by the investment company is under certain conditions tax-exempt to the shareholder.[22] The amount classified as a capital gain is considered a long-term capital gain.

Not all of the long-term capital gain realized by the investment company is actually paid in cash to the shareholders. In that case, the investment company

---

[17] If the distribution that is not a dividend exceeds the adjusted basis, the excess is treated as a capital gain.

[18] Section 243(a) and (c) of the IRC.

[19] There is a limitation based upon the taxable income of the corporation.

[20] Section 852(a) of the IRC sets forth specific requirements for a regulated investment company to be granted special tax treatment.

[21] Section 854(b) of the IRC specifies under what conditions a mutual fund dividend may be considered a dividend for purposes of the corporate dividend received deduction.

[22] Section 852(b)(5) of the IRC specifies under what conditions the tax-exempt portion of interest income may be tax free to the shareholder.

will pay the income tax on that portion retained. The shareholder, however, is deemed to have paid the tax on the undistributed capital gain, which can be refunded or credited to the shareholder. Moreover, the shareholder increases the basis of the share of the investment company by an amount equal to the excess of the long-term capital gains over the capital gains tax included in the shareholder's total long-term capital gains.[23]

## CAPITAL GAIN AND LOSS TREATMENT

Once a capital gain or capital loss is determined for a capital asset, there are special rules for determining the impact on adjusted gross income. As noted above, under current law, capital gains are taxed at the same rates as ordinary income. Thus, the importance of the capital/ordinary distinction is diminished. However, because capital losses are less favorably treated than ordinary losses and because proposals to amend the tax law to reinstate the preferential treatment of capital gains are raised on a regular basis and are likely to succeed at some point in the future, a basic understanding of the treatment of capital gains and losses is important. The tax treatment for individuals and nondealer corporations is explained in this section.

### Capital Gain and Loss Treatment for Individuals

To determine the impact of transactions involving capital assets on adjusted gross income, it is first necessary to ascertain whether the sale or exchange has resulted in a capital gain or loss that is long-term or short-term. The classification depends on the length of time the capital asset is held by the taxpayer. The general rule is that if a capital asset is held for one year or less, the gain or loss is a short-term capital gain or loss.[24] A long-term capital gain or loss results when the capital asset is held for one day more than one year, or longer.

---

[23] Section 852(b)(3)(D) of the IRC.

[24] An exception to this general rule applies to wash sales. A wash sale occurs when "substantially identical securities" are acquired within 30 days before or after a sale of securities *at a loss*. In such cases, the loss is not recognized as a capital loss. Instead, the loss is added to the basis of the securities that caused the loss. The holding period for the new securities in connection with a wash sale then includes the period for which the original securities were held. The rule is applicable neither to an individual who is a trader nor to a dealer.

Second, all short-term capital gains and losses are combined to produce either a *net short-term capital gain* or a *net short-term capital loss*. The same procedure is followed for long-term capital gains and losses. Either a *net long-term capital gain* or a *net long-term capital loss* will result.

Third, an overall *net capital gain* or *net capital loss* is determined by combining the amounts in the previous step. If the result is a net capital gain, the entire amount is added to gross income.

If there is a net capital loss, it is deductible from gross income but only to the extent of $3,000 (but $1,500 for married taxpayers filing separate returns). Unused capital losses can be carried over indefinitely until they are all utilized in subsequent tax years.

## Capital Gain and Loss Treatment for Corporations

The procedure for determining a net capital gain or loss for corporations is the same as that for individuals. The tax treatment of any net capital gain or loss differs from that of individuals in the following two ways.

First, the excess of net long-term capital gains over net short-term capital losses is subject to an alternative tax computation that limits the tax to 34 percent of the gain in any taxable year in which the corporation is subject to tax at a higher rate. The tax attributable to the excess of net long-term capital gains over net short-term capital losses is the lesser of (1) the tax liability on the taxable income when the excess is included in taxable income (i.e., regular tax computation) and (2) the tax liability on taxable income that is reduced by the excess, plus a 34 percent tax on the excess. The latter tax computation is the alternative tax computation. Because the regular tax rate is 34 percent, however, this rule is not meaningful under current law. Further, under current law, net capital gains are not otherwise preferentially treated.

Second, no deduction is allowed for a net capital loss. However, net capital losses can be carried back to the three preceding taxable years and carried forward five taxable years to offset any net capital gains in those years.[25] Although there are exceptions, the general rule is that any unused net capital loss after the fifth subsequent year can never be used by a corporate taxpayer. Net capital losses are not carried over in character. Instead, they are carried over as a short-term capital loss.

---

[25] There is a limitation on the amount that can be carried back. The amount cannot cause or increase a net operating loss in the taxable year to which it is carried back. Net capital losses are applied to the earliest year as a carry-back or carry-over.

## DEDUCTIBILITY OF INTEREST EXPENSE
## INCURRED TO ACQUIRE OR CARRY SECURITIES

Some investment strategies involve the borrowing of funds to purchase or carry securities. Although interest expense on borrowed funds to purchase or carry investment securities is tax-deductible, the investor should be aware of the following three rules relating to the deductibility of interest expense to acquire or carry securities.[26]

First, there are limits on the amount of current interest paid or accrued on debt to purchase or carry a market discount bond. Such interest expense may be deducted to the extent of any interest (including original-issue discount) earned on the bond. Any interest expense that remains can be deducted in the current year only to the extent that it exceeds the amortized portion of the market discount. The amount of interest expense that is disallowed can be deducted either (1) if the bondholder elects, in future years if net interest income on the bond exceeds the interest expense to purchase or carry the bond, or (2) when the bond is sold.

To illustrate this limitation, suppose that interest expense incurred to carry a market discount bond is $500 for the current year, the coupon interest from that bond is $200, and the amortized portion of the market discount is $140. The investor is entitled to deduct $200 (the amount of the coupon interest). In addition, since the remaining interest expense of $300 ($500 − $200) exceeds the amortized portion of the market discount of $140 by $160, an additional $160 may be deducted. Thus, the total interest expense that may be deducted in the current year is $260. The $140 can be deducted in future years, if it does not exceed the limit, or when the bond is sold.

There is an exception to the above rule. An investor can elect to have the amortized portion of the market discount taxed each year. In that case, the entire interest expense to purchase or carry the bond is tax-deductible in the current year. For example, if an investor elects to include the $140 of amortized market discount as gross income in the current year, he or she may deduct the $140 as current interest expense.

Second, the IRC specifies that interest paid or accrued on "indebtedness incurred or continued to purchase or carry obligations, the interest on which is wholly exempt from taxes," is not tax-deductible. It does not make any difference if any tax-exempt interest is actually received by the taxpayer in the taxable year. In other words, interest expense is not deductible on funds borrowed to purchase or carry tax-exempt securities. The nondeductibility of interest expenses also applies to debt incurred or continued in order to purchase

---

[26] In addition, Section 469 of the IRC sets out certain limitations on the deductibility of losses from the investment in any "passive activity."

or carry shares of a regulated investment company (e.g., mutual fund), that distributes exempt interest dividends.

To understand why interest related to debt incurred to purchase or carry tax-exempt obligations is disallowed as a deduction, consider the following example. Suppose a taxpayer in the 28 percent marginal tax bracket borrows $100,000 at an annual interest cost of 12 percent, or $12,000. The proceeds are then used to acquire $100,000 of municipal bonds at par with a coupon rate of 10 percent, or $10,000 interest per year. If the $12,000 interest expense were allowed as a tax-deductible expense, the after-tax cost of the interest expense would be $8,640. Since the interest received from holding the municipal bonds is $10,000, the taxpayer would benefit by $1,460 after taxes.

Finally, investment interest deductions may not exceed investment income (plus $1,000 in 1990).

# CHAPTER 5

---

# A REVIEW OF
# THE TIME VALUE OF MONEY*

*Frank J. Fabozzi, Ph.D., CFA*
*Visiting Professor of Finance*
*Sloan School of Management*
*Massachusetts Institute of Technology*
*and*
*Editor, The Journal of Portfolio Management*

The notion that money has a time value is one of the basic concepts in the analysis of any financial instrument. Money has a time value because of the opportunities for investing money at some interest rate. In this chapter we review the three fundamental concepts involved in understanding the time value of money: future value, present value, and yield. These concepts are applied in the next chapter, where we discuss bond pricing and yield measures.

## FUTURE VALUE

Suppose an investor places $1,000 in a bank account and the bank agrees to pay interest of 7 percent a year. At the end of one year, the account will contain $1,070, or $1,000 of the original principal plus $70 of interest. Suppose that the investor decides to let the $1,070 remain in the bank account for another year and that the bank agrees to continue paying interest of 7 percent a year.

---

* The material in this chapter is drawn from Chapters 2–4 in Frank J. Fabozzi, *Fixed Income Mathematics* (Chicago: Probus Publishing, 1988).

The amount in the bank account at the end of the second year will equal $1,144.90, determined as follows:

| | |
|---|---|
| Principal at beginning of year 2 | $1,070.00 |
| Interest for year 2 ($1,070 × .07) | 74.90 |
| Total in bank account | $1,144.90 |

In terms of our original $1,000 investment, the $1,144.90 represents the following:

| | |
|---|---|
| Original investment at beginning of year 1 | $1,000.00 |
| Interest for year 1($1,000 × .07) | 70.00 |
| Interest for year 2 based on original investment | 70.00 |
| Interest for year 2 earned on interest for year 1 ($70 × .07) | 4.90 |
| Total | $1,144.90 |

The additional interest of $4.90 in year 2 above the $70 interest earned on the original principal of $1,000 is the interest on the interest earned in year 1.

After eight years, $1,000 will grow to $1,718.19 if allowed to accumulate tax-free at an annual interest rate of 7 percent. We refer to the amount at the end of eight years as the *future value*.

Notice that the total interest at the end of eight years is $718.19. The total interest represents $560 of interest earned on the original principal ($70 × 8) plus $158.19 ($718.19 − $560) earned by the reinvestment of the interest.

## Computing the Future Value of an Investment

To compute the amount to which $1,000 will grow by the end of eight years if interest is earned at an annual interest rate of 7 percent, the following formula is used:

$$\$1,000(1.07)^8 = 1,718.19$$

To generalize the formula, suppose $1,000 is invested for $N$ periods at an annual interest rate of $i$ (expressed as a decimal). Then, the future value $N$ periods from now can be expressed as follows:

$$\$1,000(1 + i)^N$$

For example, if $1,000 is invested for four years at an annual interest rate of 10 percent ($i = .10$),then it will grow to $1,464.10:

$$\$1,000(1.10)^4$$
$$= \$1,000(1.4641)$$
$$= \$1,464.10$$

The expression $(1 + i)^N$ is the amount to which $1 will grow at the end of $N$ years if an annual interest rate of $i$ is earned. This expression is called the *future value of $1*. By multiplying the future value of $1 by the original principal, the future value of the original principal can be determined.

For example, we just demonstrated that the future value of $1,000 invested for four years at an annual interest rate of 10 percent would be $1,464.10. The future value of $1 is $1.4641. Therefore, if instead of $1,000, $50,000 is invested, the future value would be

$$\$50,000(1.4641) = \$73,205.00$$

We can generalize the formula for the future value as follows:

$$FV = P(1 + i)^N$$

where

$$FV = \text{future value (\$)}$$
$$P = \text{original principal (\$)}$$
$$i = \text{interest rate (in decimal form)}$$
$$N = \text{number of years}$$

Most calculators have an option that computes this value. Alternatively, there are tables available that provide the value of $(1 + i)^N$. Exhibit 5–1 is an abridged future value table that provides the value of $(1 + i)^N$. Notice that at the intersection of the 10 percent column and four period row, the value is 1.4641. This is the same value computed for $(1.10)^4$ in the above illustration.

The following three illustrations show how to apply the future value formula.

*Illustration 1.* A pension fund manager invests $10 million in a financial instrument that promises to pay 8.7 percent per year for five years. The future value of the $10 million investments is $15,175,665, as shown below:

$$P = \$10,000,000$$
$$i = .087$$
$$N = 5$$

$$FV = \$10,000,000(1.087)^5$$
$$= \$10,000,000(1.5175665)$$
$$= \$15,175,665$$

# EXHIBIT 5-1
## Future Value of $1 at the end of N Periods

| Period | 1% | 2% | 3% | 4% | 5% | 6% | 7% | 8% | 9% | 10% | 11% | 12% | 13% | 14% | 15% |
|---|---|---|---|---|---|---|---|---|---|---|---|---|---|---|---|
| | | | | | | | | | Interest Rate | | | | | | |
| 1 | 1.0100 | 1.0200 | 1.0300 | 1.0400 | 1.0500 | 1.0600 | 1.0700 | 1.0800 | 1.0900 | 1.100 | 1.1100 | 1.1200 | 1.1300 | 1.1400 | 1.1500 |
| 2 | 1.0201 | 1.0404 | 1.0609 | 1.0816 | 1.1025 | 1.1236 | 1.1449 | 1.1664 | 1.1881 | 1.2100 | 1.2321 | 1.2544 | 1.2769 | 1.2996 | 1.3225 |
| 3 | 1.0303 | 1.0612 | 1.0927 | 1.1249 | 1.1576 | 1.1910 | 1.2250 | 1.2597 | 1.2950 | 1.3310 | 1.3676 | 1.4049 | 1.4429 | 1.4815 | 1.5209 |
| 4 | 1.0406 | 1.0824 | 1.1255 | 1.1699 | 1.2155 | 1.2625 | 1.3108 | 1.3605 | 1.4116 | 1.4641 | 1.5181 | 1.5735 | 1.6305 | 1.6890 | 1.7490 |
| 5 | 1.0510 | 1.1041 | 1.1593 | 1.2167 | 1.2763 | 1.3382 | 1.4026 | 1.4693 | 1.5386 | 1.6105 | 1.6851 | 1.7623 | 1.8424 | 1.9254 | 2.0114 |
| 6 | 1.0615 | 1.1262 | 1.1941 | 1.2653 | 1.3401 | 1.4185 | 1.5007 | 1.5869 | 1.6771 | 1.7716 | 1.8704 | 1.9738 | 2.0820 | 2.1950 | 2.3131 |
| 7 | 1.0721 | 1.1487 | 1.2299 | 1.3159 | 1.4071 | 1.5036 | 1.6058 | 1.7138 | 1.8280 | 1.9487 | 2.0762 | 2.2107 | 2.3526 | 2.5023 | 2.6600 |
| 8 | 1.0829 | 1.1717 | 1.2668 | 1.3686 | 1.4775 | 1.5938 | 1.7182 | 1.8509 | 1.9926 | 2.1436 | 2.3045 | 2.4760 | 2.6584 | 2.8526 | 3.0590 |
| 9 | 1.0937 | 1.1951 | 1.3048 | 1.4233 | 1.5513 | 1.6895 | 1.8385 | 1.9990 | 2.1719 | 2.3579 | 2.5580 | 2.7731 | 3.0040 | 3.2519 | 3.5179 |
| 10 | 1.1046 | 1.2190 | 1.3439 | 1.4802 | 1.6289 | 1.7908 | 1.9672 | 2.1589 | 2.3674 | 2.5937 | 2.8394 | 3.1058 | 3.3946 | 3.7072 | 4.0456 |
| 11 | 1.1157 | 1.2434 | 1.3842 | 1.5395 | 1.7103 | 1.8983 | 2.1049 | 2.3316 | 2.5804 | 2.8531 | 3.1518 | 3.4785 | 3.8359 | 4.2262 | 4.6524 |
| 12 | 1.1268 | 1.2682 | 1.4258 | 1.6010 | 1.7595 | 2.0122 | 2.2522 | 2.5182 | 2.8127 | 3.1384 | 3.4984 | 3.8960 | 4.3345 | 4.8179 | 5.3502 |
| 13 | 1.1381 | 1.2936 | 1.4685 | 1.6651 | 1.8856 | 2.1329 | 2.4098 | 2.7196 | 3.0658 | 3.4523 | 3.8833 | 4.3635 | 4.8980 | 5.4924 | 6.1528 |
| 14 | 1.1495 | 1.3195 | 1.5126 | 1.7317 | 1.9799 | 2.2609 | 2.5785 | 2.9372 | 3.3417 | 3.7975 | 4.3104 | 4.8871 | 5.5347 | 6.2613 | 7.0757 |
| 15 | 1.1610 | 1.3459 | 1.5580 | 1.8009 | 2.0789 | 2.3966 | 2.7590 | 3.1722 | 3.6425 | 4.1772 | 4.7846 | 5.4736 | 6.2543 | 7.1379 | 8.1371 |
| 16 | 1.1726 | 1.3728 | 1.6047 | 1.8730 | 2.1829 | 2.5404 | 2.9522 | 3.4259 | 3.9703 | 4.5950 | 5.3109 | 6.1304 | 7.0673 | 8.1372 | 9.3576 |
| 17 | 1.1843 | 1.4002 | 1.6528 | 1.9479 | 2.2920 | 2.6928 | 3.1588 | 3.7000 | 4.3276 | 5.0545 | 5.8951 | 6.8660 | 7.9861 | 9.2765 | 10.761 |
| 18 | 1.1961 | 1.4282 | 1.7024 | 2.0258 | 2.4066 | 2.8543 | 3.3799 | 3.9960 | 4.7171 | 5.5599 | 6.5435 | 7.6900 | 9.0243 | 10.575 | 12.375 |
| 19 | 1.2081 | 1.4568 | 1.7535 | 2.1068 | 2.5270 | 3.0256 | 3.6165 | 4.3157 | 5.1417 | 6.1159 | 7.2633 | 8.6128 | 10.197 | 12.055 | 14.231 |
| 20 | 1.2202 | 1.4859 | 1.8061 | 2.1911 | 2.6533 | 3.2071 | 3.8697 | 4.6610 | 5.6044 | 6.7275 | 8.0623 | 9.6463 | 11.523 | 13.743 | 16.366 |
| 21 | 1.2324 | 1.5157 | 1.8603 | 2.2788 | 2.7860 | 3.3966 | 4.1406 | 5.0388 | 6.1088 | 7.4002 | 8.9491 | 10.803 | 13.021 | 15.667 | 18.821 |
| 22 | 1.2447 | 1.5460 | 1.9161 | 2.3699 | 2.9253 | 3.6035 | 4.4304 | 5.4365 | 6.6586 | 8.1403 | 9.9335 | 12.100 | 14.714 | 17.861 | 21.644 |
| 23 | 1.2572 | 1.5769 | 1.9736 | 2.4647 | 3.0715 | 3.8197 | 4.7405 | 5.8715 | 7.2579 | 8.9543 | 11.026 | 13.552 | 16.627 | 20.361 | 24.891 |
| 24 | 1.2697 | 1.6084 | 2.0328 | 2.5633 | 3.2251 | 4.0489 | 5.0724 | 6.3412 | 7.9111 | 9.8497 | 12.239 | 15.178 | 18.788 | 23.212 | 28.625 |
| 25 | 1.2824 | 1.6406 | 2.0938 | 2.6658 | 3.3864 | 4.2919 | 5.4274 | 6.8485 | 8.6231 | 10.834 | 13.585 | 17.000 | 21.230 | 26.461 | 32.918 |
| 26 | 1.2953 | 1.6734 | 2.1566 | 2.7725 | 3.5557 | 4.5494 | 5.8074 | 7.3964 | 9.3992 | 11.918 | 15.080 | 19.040 | 23.990 | 30.166 | 37.856 |
| 27 | 1.3082 | 1.7069 | 2.2213 | 2.8834 | 3.7335 | 4.8223 | 6.2139 | 7.9881 | 10.245 | 13.110 | 16.739 | 21.324 | 27.109 | 34.389 | 43.535 |
| 28 | 1.3213 | 1.7410 | 2.2879 | 2.9987 | 3.9201 | 5.1117 | 6.6488 | 8.6271 | 11.167 | 14.421 | 18.580 | 23.883 | 30.633 | 39.204 | 50.065 |
| 29 | 1.3345 | 1.7758 | 2.3566 | 3.1187 | 4.1161 | 5.4184 | 7.1143 | 9.3173 | 12.172 | 15.863 | 20.624 | 26.749 | 34.616 | 44.693 | 57.575 |
| 30 | 1.3478 | 1.8114 | 2.4273 | 3.2434 | 4.3219 | 5.7435 | 7.6123 | 10.062 | 13.267 | 17.449 | 22.892 | 29.959 | 39.116 | 50.950 | 66.211 |

*Illustration 2.* Suppose that a life insurance company has guaranteed a payment of $14 million to a pension fund four years from now. If the life insurance company receives a premium of $11 million and can invest the entire premium for four years at an annual interest rate of 6.5 percent, will it have sufficient funds from this investment to meet the $1 million obligation?

The future value of the $11 million investment at the end of four years is $14,151,130, as shown below:

$$P = \$11,000,000$$
$$i = .065$$
$$N = 4$$

$$FV = \$11,000,000(1.065)^4$$
$$= \$11,000,000(1.2864664)$$
$$= \$14,151,130$$

Since the future value is expected to be $14,151,130, the life insurance company will have sufficient funds from this investment to satisfy the $14 million obligation to the pension fund.

*Illustration 3.* The portfolio manager of a tax-exempt fund is considering investing $400,000 in an instrument that pays an annual interest rate of 5.7 percent for four years. At the end of four years, the portfolio manager plans to reinvest the proceeds for three more years and expects that, for the three-year period, an annual interest rate of 7.2 percent can be earned. The future value of this investment is $615,098.

Future value of the $400,000 investment for four years at 5.7 percent is as follows:

$$P = \$400,000$$
$$i = .057$$
$$N = 4$$

$$FV = \$400,000(1.057)^4$$
$$= \$400,000(1.248245)$$
$$= \$499,298$$

Future value of $499,298 reinvested for three years at 7.2 percent is computed below:

$$i = 0.72$$
$$N = 3$$

$$FV = \$499,298(1.072)^3$$

$$= \$499,298(1.231925)$$
$$= \$615,098$$

### Fractional Periods

In our illustrations, we have computed the future value for whole years. The future value formula, however, is the same if an investment is made for part of a year. Most pocket calculators can accommodate fractional exponents.

For example, suppose that $100,000 is invested for seven years and three months. Since three months is 0.25 of one year, $N$ in the future value formula is 7.25. Assuming an annual interest rate of 5 percent, the future value of $100,000 invested for seven years and three months is $142,437, as shown below:

$$P = \$100,000$$
$$i = .05$$
$$N = 7.25$$
$$FV = \$100,000(1.05)^{7.25}$$
$$= \$100,000(1.424369)$$
$$= \$142,437$$

## Compounding More than One Time Per Year

An investment may pay interest more than one time per year. For example, interest may be paid semiannually, quarterly, monthly, weekly, or daily. Our future value formula can handle interest payments that are made more than once per year. This is done by adjusting the annual interest rate and the exponent. The annual interest rate is adjusted by dividing the number of times that interest is paid per year. The exponent, which represents the number of years, is adjusted by multiplying the number of years by the number of times interest is paid per year.

Mathematically, we can express the future value when interest is paid $m$ times per year as follows:

$$FV = P(1 + i)^n$$

where

$$i = \text{annual interest rate divided by } m$$
$$n = \text{number of interest payments } (= N \times m)$$

*Illustration 4.* Suppose that a portfolio manager invests $1 million in an investment that promises to pay an annual interest rate of 6.4 percent for six years. Interest on this investment is paid semiannually. The future value is $1,459,340, as shown below:

$$P = \$1,000,000$$
$$m = 2$$
$$i = .032 \ (= .064/2)$$
$$N = 6$$
$$n = 12 \ (6 \times 2)$$
$$FV = \$1,000,000(1.032)^{12}$$
$$= \$1,000,000(1.459340)$$
$$= \$1,459,340$$

If interest is paid only once per year, this future value would be $1,450,941 instead of $1,459,340. The higher future value when interest is paid semiannually reflects the more frequent opportunity for reinvesting the interest paid.

## Future Value of an Ordinary Annuity

Suppose that an investor expects to receive $10,000 a year from some investment for each of the next five years starting one year from now. Each time the investor receives the $10,000 he plans to invest it. Let's assume that the the investor can earn an annual interest rate of 6 percent each time $10,000 is invested. How much money will the investor have at the end of five years?

Our future value formula makes it simple to determine to what amount how much each $10,000 investment will grow. This calculation is illustrated graphically in Exhibit 5–2. The total future value of $56,371.30 shown in Exhibit 5–2 is composed of the five payments of $10,000, or $50,000, plus $6,371.30 of interest earned by investing the $10,000 annual payments.

When the same amount of money is received (or paid) periodically, it is referred to as an *annuity*. When the first receipt occurs one period from now, it is referred to as an ordinary annuity.

The following formula can be used to calculate the future value of an ordinary annuity:

$$FV = A \left[ \frac{(1 + i)^N - 1}{i} \right]$$

where

$$A = \text{amount of the annuity (\$)}$$
$$i = \text{annual interest rate (in decimal)}$$

The term in the square brackets is the *future value of an ordinary annuity of $1 per year*. Multiplying the future value of an ordinary annuity of $1 by the amount of the annuity produces the future value of an ordinary annuity of any amount.

**EXHIBIT 5–2**
**Future Value of an Ordinary Annuity of $10,000 per year for 5 years**

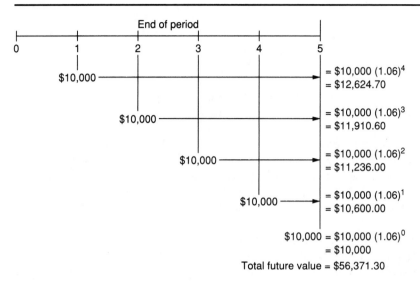

For example, in the previous example, in which $10,000 is invested each year for the next five years, starting one year from now, we have

$$A = \$10,000$$
$$i = .06$$
$$N = 5$$

therefore,

$$FV = \$10,000 \left[ \frac{(1.06)^5 - 1}{.06} \right]$$

$$= \$10,000 \left[ \frac{1.3382256 - 1}{.06} \right]$$

$$= \$10,000(5.63710)$$

$$= \$56,371$$

This value agrees with our earlier calculation.

Tables are available that provide the future value of an ordinary annuity of $1 per period. Exhibit 5–3 is an abridged version. The value from the table should then be multiplied by the annuity payment to obtain the future value of the annuity. For example, from Exhibit 5–3 the future value of an ordinary

**EXHIBIT 5–3**

**Future Value of an Ordinary Annuity of $1 per Period for N Periods**

| Number of Periods | 1% | 2% | 3% | 4% | 5% | 6% | 7% | 8% | 9% | 10% | 11% | 12% | 13% | 14% | 15% |
|---|---|---|---|---|---|---|---|---|---|---|---|---|---|---|---|
| | | | | | | | | | Interest Rate | | | | | | |
| 1 | 1.0000 | 1.0000 | 1.0000 | 1.0000 | 1.0000 | 1.0000 | 1.0000 | 1.0000 | 1.0000 | 1.0000 | 1.0000 | 1.0000 | 1.0000 | 1.0000 | 1.0000 |
| 2 | 2.0100 | 2.0200 | 2.0300 | 2.0400 | 2.0500 | 2.0600 | 2.0700 | 2.0800 | 2.0900 | 2.1000 | 2.1100 | 2.1200 | 2.1300 | 2.1400 | 2.1500 |
| 3 | 3.0301 | 3.0604 | 3.0909 | 3.1216 | 3.1525 | 3.1836 | 3.2149 | 3.2464 | 3.2781 | 3.3100 | 3.3421 | 3.3744 | 3.4069 | 3.4396 | 3.4725 |
| 4 | 4.0604 | 4.1216 | 4.1836 | 4.2465 | 4.3101 | 4.3746 | 4.4399 | 4.5061 | 4.5731 | 4.6410 | 4.7097 | 4.7793 | 4.8498 | 4.9211 | 4.9934 |
| 5 | 5.1010 | 5.2040 | 5.3091 | 5.4163 | 5.5256 | 5.6371 | 5.7507 | 5.8666 | 5.9847 | 6.1051 | 6.2278 | 6.3528 | 6.4803 | 6.6101 | 6.7424 |
| 6 | 6.1520 | 6.3081 | 6.4684 | 6.6330 | 6.8019 | 6.9753 | 7.1533 | 7.3359 | 7.5233 | 7.7156 | 7.9129 | 8.1152 | 8.3227 | 8.5355 | 8.7537 |
| 7 | 7.2135 | 7.4343 | 7.6625 | 7.8983 | 8.1420 | 8.3938 | 8.6540 | 8.9228 | 9.2004 | 9.4872 | 9.7833 | 10.089 | 10.405 | 10.730 | 11.066 |
| 8 | 8.2857 | 8.5830 | 8.8923 | 9.2142 | 9.5491 | 9.8975 | 10.259 | 10.636 | 11.028 | 11.435 | 11.859 | 12.299 | 12.757 | 13.232 | 13.726 |
| 9 | 9.3685 | 9.7546 | 10.159 | 10.582 | 11.026 | 11.491 | 11.978 | 12.487 | 13.021 | 13.579 | 14.164 | 14.775 | 15.416 | 16.085 | 16.785 |
| 10 | 10.462 | 10.949 | 11.463 | 12.006 | 12.577 | 13.180 | 13.816 | 14.486 | 15.192 | 15.937 | 16.722 | 17.548 | 18.420 | 19.337 | 20.603 |
| 11 | 11.566 | 12.168 | 12.807 | 13.486 | 14.206 | 14.971 | 15.783 | 16.645 | 17.560 | 18.531 | 19.561 | 20.654 | 21.814 | 23.044 | 24.649 |
| 12 | 12.682 | 13.412 | 14.192 | 15.025 | 15.917 | 16.869 | 17.888 | 18.977 | 20.140 | 21.384 | 22.713 | 24.133 | 25.650 | 27.270 | 29.001 |
| 13 | 13.809 | 14.680 | 15.617 | 16.626 | 17.713 | 18.882 | 20.140 | 21.495 | 22.953 | 24.522 | 26.212 | 28.029 | 29.985 | 32.088 | 34.351 |
| 14 | 14.947 | 15.973 | 17.086 | 18.291 | 19.598 | 21.015 | 22.550 | 24.214 | 26.019 | 27.975 | 30.095 | 32.392 | 34.883 | 37.581 | 40.504 |
| 15 | 16.096 | 17.293 | 18.598 | 20.023 | 21.578 | 23.276 | 25.129 | 27.152 | 29.360 | 31.772 | 34.405 | 37.729 | 40.418 | 43.842 | 47.580 |
| 16 | 17.257 | 18.639 | 20.156 | 21.824 | 23.657 | 25.672 | 27.888 | 30.324 | 33.003 | 35.949 | 39.190 | 42.753 | 46.672 | 50.980 | 55.717 |
| 17 | 18.430 | 20.012 | 21.761 | 23.697 | 25.840 | 28.212 | 30.840 | 33.750 | 36.973 | 40.544 | 44.501 | 48.883 | 53.739 | 59.117 | 65.075 |
| 18 | 19.614 | 21.412 | 23.414 | 25.645 | 28.132 | 30.905 | 33.999 | 37.450 | 41.301 | 45.599 | 50.396 | 55.749 | 61.725 | 68.394 | 75.836 |
| 19 | 20.810 | 22.840 | 25.116 | 27.671 | 30.539 | 33.760 | 37.379 | 41.446 | 46.018 | 51.159 | 56.940 | 63.439 | 70.749 | 78.969 | 88.211 |
| 20 | 22.019 | 24.297 | 26.870 | 29.778 | 33.066 | 36.785 | 40.995 | 45.762 | 51.160 | 57.275 | 64.203 | 72.052 | 80.947 | 91.024 | 102.44 |
| 21 | 23.239 | 25.783 | 28.676 | 31.969 | 35.719 | 39.992 | 44.865 | 50.422 | 56.764 | 64.002 | 72.265 | 81.698 | 92.470 | 104.76 | 118.81 |
| 22 | 24.471 | 27.299 | 30.536 | 34.248 | 38.505 | 43.392 | 49.005 | 55.456 | 62.873 | 71.402 | 81.214 | 92.502 | 105.49 | 120.43 | 137.63 |
| 23 | 25.716 | 28.845 | 32.452 | 36.617 | 41.430 | 46.995 | 53.436 | 60.893 | 69.531 | 79.543 | 91.148 | 104.60 | 120.20 | 138.29 | 159.27 |
| 24 | 26.973 | 30.421 | 34.426 | 39.082 | 44.502 | 50.815 | 58.176 | 66.764 | 76.789 | 88.497 | 102.17 | 118.15 | 136.83 | 158.65 | 184.16 |
| 25 | 28.243 | 32.030 | 36.459 | 41.645 | 47.727 | 54.864 | 63.249 | 73.105 | 84.700 | 98.347 | 114.41 | 133.33 | 155.62 | 181.87 | 212.79 |
| 26 | 29.525 | 33.670 | 38.553 | 44.311 | 51.113 | 59.156 | 68.676 | 79.954 | 93.323 | 109.18 | 128.00 | 150.33 | 176.85 | 208.33 | 245.71 |
| 27 | 30.820 | 35.344 | 40.709 | 47.084 | 54.669 | 63.705 | 74.483 | 87.350 | 102.72 | 121.09 | 143.08 | 169.37 | 200.84 | 238.49 | 283.56 |
| 28 | 32.129 | 37.051 | 42.930 | 49.967 | 58.402 | 68.528 | 80.697 | 95.338 | 112.96 | 134.20 | 159.82 | 190.69 | 227.95 | 272.88 | 327.10 |
| 29 | 33.450 | 38.792 | 45.218 | 52.966 | 62.332 | 73.639 | 87.346 | 103.96 | 124.13 | 148.63 | 178.40 | 214.58 | 258.58 | 312.09 | 377.16 |
| 30 | 34.784 | 40.568 | 47.575 | 56.084 | 66.438 | 79.058 | 94.460 | 113.28 | 136.30 | 164.49 | 199.02 | 241.33 | 293.20 | 356.78 | 434.74 |

annuity of $1 per period for 5 periods assuming a 6 percent interest rate per period is 5.6371. Hence the future value of an ordinary annuity of $10,000 is $10,000 times 5.6371, or $56,371.


## PRESENT VALUE

We illustrated how to compute the future value of an investment. Now we will illustrate how to work the process in reverse; that is, given the future value of an investment, we will illustrate how to determine the amount of money that must be invested today in order to realize that future value. The amount of money that must be invested today is called the *present value*.

### Present Value of an Amount to be Received in the Future

What we are interested in is how to determine the amount of money that must be invested today, earning an interest rate of $i$ for $N$ years, in order to produce a specific future value. This can be done by solving the future value formula given earlier for $P$, the original principal:

$$P = FV\left[\frac{1}{(1 + i)^N}\right]$$

Instead of using $P$ in the above formula, we shall denote the present value as PV. Therefore, the present value formula can be rewritten as

$$PV = FV\left[\frac{1}{(1 + i)^N}\right]$$

The term in the square brackets is equal to the present value of $1; that is, it indicates how much must be set aside today, earning an interest rate of $i$, in order to have $1 $N$ years from now. Present value tables are available. Exhibit 5–4 shows the present value of $1, which is found by dividing one by $(1 + i)^N$. The columns show the interest rate. The rows show the number of periods. The present value of $1 obtained from Exhibit 5–4 is then multiplied by the future value to determine the present value. For example, the present value of $1,000 seven years from now assuming 12 percent interest compounded annually is

$$
\begin{aligned}
PV &= \$1,000 \text{ (PV of \$1 from Exhibit 5–4)} \\
&= \$1,000(.4523) \\
&= \$452.30
\end{aligned}
$$

# EXHIBIT 5–4
## Present Value of $1

| | | | | | | | | | Interest (Discount) Rate | | | | | | | | | |
|---|---|---|---|---|---|---|---|---|---|---|---|---|---|---|---|---|---|---|
| Period | 1% | 2% | 3% | 4% | 5% | 6% | 7% | 8% | 9% | 10% | 11% | 12% | 13% | 14% | 15% | 16% | 18% | 20% |
| 1 | .9901 | .9804 | .9709 | .9615 | .9524 | .9434 | .9346 | .9259 | .9174 | .9091 | .9009 | .8929 | .8850 | .8772 | .8696 | .8621 | .8475 | .8333 |
| 2 | .9803 | .9612 | .9426 | .9246 | .9070 | .8900 | .8734 | .8573 | .8417 | .8264 | .8116 | .7972 | .7831 | .7695 | .7561 | .7432 | .7182 | .6944 |
| 3 | .9706 | .9423 | .9151 | .8890 | .8638 | .8396 | .8163 | .7938 | .7722 | .7513 | .7312 | .7118 | .6931 | .6750 | .6575 | .6407 | .6086 | .5787 |
| 4 | .9610 | .9238 | .8885 | .8548 | .8227 | .7921 | .7629 | .7350 | .7084 | .6830 | .6587 | .6355 | .6133 | .5921 | .5718 | .5523 | .5158 | .4823 |
| 5 | .9515 | .9057 | .8626 | .8219 | .7835 | .7473 | .7130 | .6806 | .6499 | .6209 | .5935 | .5674 | .5428 | .5194 | .4972 | .4761 | .4371 | .4019 |
| 6 | .9420 | .8880 | .8375 | .7903 | .7462 | .7050 | .6663 | .6302 | .5963 | .5645 | .5346 | .5066 | .4803 | .4556 | .4323 | .4104 | .3704 | .3349 |
| 7 | .9327 | .8706 | .8131 | .7599 | .7107 | .6651 | .6227 | .5835 | .5470 | .5132 | .4817 | .4523 | .4251 | .3996 | .3759 | .3538 | .3139 | .2791 |
| 8 | .9235 | .8535 | .7894 | .7307 | .6768 | .6274 | .5820 | .5403 | .5019 | .4665 | .4339 | .4039 | .3762 | .3506 | .3269 | .3050 | .2660 | .2326 |
| 9 | .9143 | .8368 | .7664 | .7026 | .6446 | .5919 | .5439 | .5002 | .4604 | .4241 | .3909 | .3606 | .3329 | .3075 | .2843 | .2630 | .2255 | .1938 |
| 10 | .9053 | .8203 | .7441 | .6756 | .6139 | .5584 | .5083 | .4632 | .4224 | .3855 | .3522 | .3220 | .2946 | .2697 | .2472 | .2267 | .1911 | .1615 |
| 11 | .8963 | .8043 | .7224 | .6496 | .5847 | .5268 | .4751 | .4289 | .3875 | .3505 | .3173 | .2875 | .2607 | .2366 | .2149 | .1954 | .1619 | .1346 |
| 12 | .8874 | .7885 | .7014 | .6246 | .5568 | .4970 | .4440 | .3971 | .3555 | .3186 | .2858 | .2567 | .2307 | .2076 | .1869 | .1685 | .1372 | .1122 |
| 13 | .8787 | .7730 | .6810 | .6006 | .5303 | .4688 | .4150 | .3677 | .3262 | .2897 | .2575 | .2292 | .2042 | .1821 | .1625 | .1452 | .1163 | .0935 |
| 14 | .8700 | .7579 | .6611 | .5775 | .5051 | .4423 | .3878 | .3405 | .2992 | .2633 | .2320 | .2046 | .1807 | .1597 | .1413 | .1252 | .0985 | .0779 |
| 15 | .8613 | .7430 | .6419 | .5553 | .4810 | .4173 | .3624 | .3152 | .2745 | .2394 | .2090 | .1827 | .1599 | .1401 | .1229 | .1079 | .0835 | .0649 |
| 16 | .8528 | .7284 | .6232 | .5339 | .4581 | .3936 | .3387 | .2919 | .2519 | .2176 | .1883 | .1631 | .1415 | .1229 | .1069 | .0930 | .0708 | .0541 |
| 17 | .8444 | .7142 | .6050 | .5434 | .4363 | .3714 | .3166 | .2703 | .2311 | .1978 | .1696 | .1456 | .1252 | .1078 | .0929 | .0802 | .0600 | .0451 |
| 18 | .8360 | .7002 | .5874 | .4936 | .4155 | .3503 | .2959 | .2502 | .2120 | .1799 | .1528 | .1300 | .1108 | .0946 | .0808 | .0691 | .0508 | .0376 |
| 19 | .8277 | .6864 | .5703 | .4746 | .3957 | .3305 | .2765 | .2317 | .1945 | .1635 | .1377 | .1161 | .0981 | .0829 | .0703 | .0596 | .0431 | .0313 |
| 20 | .8195 | .6730 | .5537 | .4564 | .3769 | .3118 | .2584 | .2145 | .1784 | .1486 | .1240 | .1037 | .0868 | .0728 | .0611 | .0514 | .0365 | .0261 |
| 21 | .8114 | .6598 | .5375 | .4388 | .3589 | .2942 | .2415 | .1987 | .1637 | .1351 | .1117 | .0926 | .0768 | .0638 | .0531 | .0443 | .0309 | .0217 |
| 22 | .8034 | .6468 | .5219 | .4220 | .3418 | .2775 | .2257 | .1839 | .1502 | .1228 | .1007 | .0826 | .0680 | .0560 | .0462 | .0382 | .0262 | .0181 |
| 23 | .7954 | .6342 | .5067 | .4057 | .3256 | .2618 | .2109 | .1703 | .1378 | .1117 | .0907 | .0738 | .0601 | .0491 | .0402 | .0329 | .0222 | .0151 |
| 24 | .7876 | .6217 | .4919 | .3901 | .3101 | .2470 | .1971 | .1577 | .1264 | .1015 | .0817 | .0659 | .0532 | .0431 | .0349 | .0284 | .0188 | .0126 |
| 25 | .7798 | .6095 | .4776 | .3751 | .2953 | .2330 | .1842 | .1460 | .1160 | .0923 | .0736 | .0588 | .0471 | .0378 | .0304 | .0245 | .0160 | .0105 |
| 26 | .7720 | .5976 | .4637 | .3607 | .2812 | .2198 | .1722 | .1352 | .1064 | .0839 | .0663 | .0525 | .0417 | .0331 | .0264 | .0211 | .0135 | .0087 |
| 27 | .7644 | .5859 | .4502 | .3468 | .2678 | .2074 | .1609 | .1252 | .0976 | .0763 | .0597 | .0469 | .0369 | .0291 | .0230 | .0182 | .0115 | .0073 |
| 28 | .7568 | .5744 | .4371 | .3335 | .2551 | .1956 | .1504 | .1159 | .0895 | .0693 | .0538 | .0419 | .0326 | .0255 | .0200 | .0157 | .0097 | .0061 |
| 29 | .7493 | .5631 | .4243 | .3207 | .2429 | .1846 | .1406 | .1073 | .0822 | .0630 | .0485 | .0374 | .0289 | .0224 | .0174 | .0135 | .0082 | .0051 |
| 30 | .7419 | .5521 | .4120 | .3083 | .2314 | .1741 | .1314 | .0994 | .0754 | .0573 | .0437 | .0334 | .0256 | .0196 | .0151 | .0116 | .0070 | .0042 |

The process of computing the present value is also referred to as *discounting*. Therefore, the present value is sometimes referred to as the *discounted value*, and the interest rate is referred to as the *discount rate*.

There are two facts you should note about present value. Look again at Exhibit 5–4. Select any interest rate and look down the column. Notice that the present value decreases. That is, the greater the number of periods over which interest could be earned, the less must be set aside today for a given dollar amount to be received in the future. Next select any period and look across the row. As you look across, the interest rate increases and the present value decreases. The reason is the higher the interest rate that can be earned on any amount invested today, the less must be set aside to obtain a specified future value.

The following two illustrations demonstrate how to compute the present value.

*Illustration 5.* A pension fund manager knows that he must satisfy a liability of $9 million six years from now. Assuming that an annual interest rate of 7.5 percent can be earned on any sum invested today, the pension fund manager must invest $5,831,654 today in order to have $9 million six years from now, as shown below:

$$FV = \$9,000,000$$
$$i = .075$$
$$N = 6$$

$$PV = \$9,000,000 \left[ \frac{1}{(1.075)^6} \right]$$

$$= \$9,000,000 \left[ \frac{1}{1.543302} \right]$$

$$= \$9,000,000(.647961)$$
$$= \$5,831,654$$

*Illustration 6.* Suppose a money manager has the opportunity to purchase a financial instrument that promises to pay $800,000 four years from now. The price of the financial instrument is $572,000. Should the money manager invest in this financial instrument if she wants a 7.8 percent annual interest rate?

To answer this, the money manager must determine the present value of the $800,000 to be received four years from now. The present value is $592,400, as shown below:

$$FV = \$800,000$$
$$i = .078$$
$$N = 4$$

$$PV = \$800,000 \left[ \frac{1}{(1.078)^4} \right]$$

$$= \$800,000 \left[ \frac{1}{1.350439} \right]$$

$$= \$800,000(.740500)$$

$$= \$592,400$$

Since the price of the financial instrument is only $572,000, the money manager will realize more than a 7.8 percent annual interest rate if the financial instrument is purchased and the issuer pays $800,000 four years from now.

### Fractional Periods

If a future value is to be received or paid over a fractional part of a year, the number of years is adjusted accordingly. For example, if $1,000 is to be received nine years and three months from now and the interest rate is 7 percent, the present value is determined as follows:

$$FV = \$1,000$$
$$i = .07$$
$$N = 9.25 \text{ years (3 months is .25 years)}$$

$$PV = \$1,000 \left[ \frac{1}{(1.07)^{9.25}} \right]$$

$$= \$1,000 \left[ \frac{1}{1.86982} \right]$$

$$= \$1,000(.53481)$$

$$= \$534.81$$

## Present Value of a Series of Future Values

In most applications in investment management and asset/liability management, a financial instrument will offer a series of future values. To determine the present value of a series of future values, the present value of each future value must first be computed. Then the present values are added together to obtain the present value of the series of future values. This procedure is demonstrated in the following illustration.

*Illustration 7.* An investor is considering the purchase of a financial instrument that promises to make the following payments:

| Years from now | Promised Payment by Issuer |
|:---:|:---:|
| 1 | $  100 |
| 2 | 100 |
| 3 | 100 |
| 4 | 100 |
| 5 | 1,100 |

This financial instrument is selling for $1,243.83. Assume that the investor wants a 6.25 percent annual interest rate on this investment. Should the investor purchase this investment?

To answer this question, the investor first must compute the present value of the future amounts that are expected to be received, as follows:

| Years from now | Future Value of Payment | Present Value of $1 at 6.25% | Present Value of Payment |
|:---:|:---:|:---:|:---:|
| 1 | $  100 | 0.9412 | $ 94.12 |
| 2 | 100 | 0.8858 | 88.58 |
| 3 | 100 | 0.8337 | 83.37 |
| 4 | 100 | 0.7847 | 78.47 |
| 5 | 1,100 | 0.7385 | 812.35 |
| | | Total present value = | $1,156.89 |

Since the present value of the series of future values promised by the issuer of this financial instrument is less than the price of $1,243.83, the investor would earn an annual interest rate of less than 6.25 percent. Thus, this financial instrument is unattractive.

## Present Value of an Ordinary Annuity

One way to compute the present value of an ordinary annuity is to compute the present value of each future value and then total the present values. There is a formula that can be employed to compute—in one step—the present value of an ordinary annuity:

$$PV = A \left[ \frac{1 - \frac{1}{(1+i)^N}}{i} \right]$$

where

$$A = \text{amount of the annuity (\$)}$$

The term in the brackets is the *present value of an ordinary annuity of \$1 for N years*. Exhibit 5–5 provides the present value of an ordinary annuity of \$1 for N periods for selected interest rates. The present value of an ordinary annuity is computed by multiplying the value from Exhibit 5–5 by the annuity payment. The following illustration shows how to apply the formula.

   *Illustration 8.*   An investor has the opportunity to purchase a financial instrument that promises to pay \$500 a year for the next 20 years, beginning one year from now. The financial instrument is being offered for a price of \$5,300. The investor seeks an annual interest rate of 5.5 percent on this investment. Should the investor purchase this financial instrument?
   Since the first payment is to be received one year from now, the financial instrument is offering a 20-year annuity of \$500 per year. The present value of this ordinary annuity is calculated as follows:

$$A = \$500$$
$$i = .055$$
$$N = 20$$

$$PV = \$500 \left[ \frac{1 - \frac{1}{(1.055)^{20}}}{.055} \right]$$

$$= \$500 \left[ \frac{1 - \frac{1}{2.917757}}{.055} \right]$$

$$= \$500 \left[ \frac{1 - .342729}{.055} \right]$$

$$= \$500(11.950382)$$
$$= \$5,975.19$$

Since the present value of an ordinary annuity of \$500 per year when discounted at 5.5 percent exceeds the price of the financial instrument (\$5,300), this financial instrument offers an annual interest rate in excess of 5.5 percent. Therefore, it is an attractive investment for this investor.

# EXHIBIT 5–5
## Present Value of an Ordinary Annuity of $1 per Period for N Periods

|  | Interest (Discount) Rate | | | | | | | | | | | | | | |
|---|---|---|---|---|---|---|---|---|---|---|---|---|---|---|---|
| Number of periods | 1% | 2% | 3% | 4% | 5% | 6% | 7% | 8% | 9% | 10% | 11% | 12% | 13% | 14% | 15% |
| 1 | 0.9901 | 0.9804 | 0.9709 | 0.9615 | 0.9524 | 0.9434 | 0.9346 | 0.9259 | 0.9174 | 0.9091 | 0.9009 | 0.8929 | 0.8850 | 0.8772 | 0.8696 |
| 2 | 1.9704 | 1.9416 | 1.9135 | 1.8861 | 1.8594 | 1.8334 | 1.8080 | 1.7833 | 1.7591 | 1.7355 | 1.7125 | 1.6901 | 1.6681 | 1.6467 | 1.6257 |
| 3 | 2.9410 | 2.8839 | 2.8286 | 2.7751 | 2.7232 | 2.6730 | 2.6243 | 2.5771 | 2.5313 | 2.4869 | 2.4437 | 2.4018 | 2.3612 | 2.3216 | 2.2832 |
| 4 | 3.9020 | 3.8077 | 3.7171 | 3.6299 | 3.5460 | 3.4651 | 3.3872 | 3.3121 | 3.2397 | 3.1699 | 3.1024 | 3.0373 | 2.9745 | 2.9137 | 2.8550 |
| 5 | 4.8534 | 4.7135 | 4.5797 | 4.4518 | 4.3295 | 4.2124 | 4.1002 | 3.9927 | 3.8897 | 3.7908 | 3.6959 | 3.6048 | 3.5172 | 3.4331 | 3.3522 |
| 6 | 5.7955 | 5.6014 | 5.4172 | 5.2421 | 5.0757 | 4.9173 | 4.7665 | 4.6229 | 4.4859 | 4.3553 | 4.2305 | 4.1114 | 3.9976 | 3.8887 | 3.7845 |
| 7 | 6.7282 | 6.4720 | 6.2303 | 6.0021 | 5.7864 | 5.5824 | 5.3893 | 5.2064 | 5.0330 | 4.8684 | 4.7122 | 4.5638 | 4.4226 | 4.2883 | 4.1604 |
| 8 | 7.6517 | 7.3255 | 7.0197 | 6.7327 | 6.4632 | 6.2098 | 5.9713 | 5.7466 | 5.5348 | 5.3349 | 5.1461 | 4.9676 | 4.7988 | 4.6389 | 4.4873 |
| 9 | 8.5660 | 8.1622 | 7.7861 | 7.4353 | 7.1078 | 6.8017 | 6.5152 | 6.2469 | 5.9952 | 5.7590 | 5.5371 | 5.3282 | 5.1317 | 4.9464 | 4.7716 |
| 10 | 9.4713 | 8.9826 | 8.5302 | 8.1109 | 7.7217 | 7.3601 | 7.0236 | 6.7101 | 6.4177 | 6.1446 | 5.8892 | 5.6502 | 5.4263 | 5.2161 | 5.0188 |
| 11 | 10.3676 | 9.7876 | 9.2526 | 8.7605 | 8.3064 | 7.8869 | 7.4987 | 7.1390 | 6.8052 | 6.4951 | 6.2065 | 5.9377 | 5.6870 | 5.4527 | 5.2337 |
| 12 | 11.2551 | 10.5753 | 9.9540 | 9.3851 | 8.8633 | 8.3838 | 7.9427 | 7.5361 | 7.1607 | 6.8137 | 6.4924 | 6.1944 | 5.9177 | 5.6603 | 5.4206 |
| 13 | 12.1337 | 11.3484 | 10.6350 | 9.9856 | 9.3936 | 8.8527 | 8.3577 | 7.9038 | 7.4869 | 7.1034 | 6.7499 | 6.4235 | 6.1218 | 5.8424 | 5.5831 |
| 14 | 13.0037 | 12.1062 | 11.2961 | 10.5631 | 9.8986 | 9.2950 | 8.7455 | 8.2442 | 7.7862 | 7.3667 | 6.9819 | 6.6282 | 6.3025 | 6.0021 | 5.7245 |
| 15 | 13.8651 | 12.8493 | 11.9379 | 11.1184 | 10.3797 | 9.7122 | 9.1079 | 8.5595 | 8.0607 | 7.6061 | 7.1909 | 6.8109 | 6.4624 | 6.1422 | 5.8474 |
| 16 | 14.7179 | 13.5777 | 12.5611 | 11.6523 | 10.8378 | 10.1059 | 9.4466 | 8.8514 | 8.3126 | 7.8237 | 7.3792 | 6.9740 | 6.6039 | 6.2651 | 5.9542 |
| 17 | 15.5623 | 14.2919 | 13.1661 | 12.1657 | 11.2741 | 10.4773 | 9.7623 | 9.1216 | 8.5436 | 8.0216 | 7.5488 | 7.1196 | 6.7291 | 6.2739 | 6.0472 |
| 18 | 16.3983 | 14.9920 | 13.7535 | 12.6593 | 11.6896 | 10.8276 | 10.0591 | 9.3719 | 8.7556 | 8.2014 | 7.7016 | 7.2497 | 6.8399 | 6.4674 | 6.1280 |
| 19 | 17.2260 | 15.6785 | 14.3238 | 13.1339 | 12.0853 | 11.1581 | 10.3356 | 9.6036 | 8.9501 | 8.3649 | 7.8393 | 7.3658 | 6.9380 | 6.5504 | 6.1982 |
| 20 | 18.0456 | 16.3514 | 14.8775 | 13.5903 | 12.4622 | 11.4699 | 10.5940 | 9.8181 | 9.1285 | 8.5136 | 7.9633 | 7.4694 | 7.0248 | 6.6231 | 6.2593 |
| 21 | 18.8570 | 17.0122 | 15.4150 | 14.0292 | 12.8212 | 11.7641 | 10.8355 | 10.0168 | 9.2922 | 8.6487 | 8.0751 | 7.5620 | 7.1016 | 6.6870 | 6.3125 |
| 22 | 19.6604 | 17.6580 | 15.9369 | 14.4511 | 13.1630 | 12.0416 | 11.0612 | 10.2007 | 9.4424 | 8.7715 | 8.1757 | 7.6446 | 7.1695 | 6.7429 | 6.3587 |
| 23 | 20.4558 | 18.2922 | 16.4436 | 14.8568 | 13.4886 | 12.3034 | 11.2722 | 10.3711 | 9.5802 | 8.8832 | 8.2664 | 7.7184 | 7.2297 | 6.7921 | 6.3988 |
| 24 | 21.2434 | 18.9139 | 16.9355 | 15.2470 | 13.7986 | 12.5504 | 11.4693 | 10.5288 | 9.7066 | 8.9847 | 8.3481 | 7.7843 | 7.2829 | 6.8351 | 6.4338 |
| 25 | 22.0232 | 19.5235 | 17.4131 | 15.6221 | 14.0939 | 12.7834 | 11.6536 | 10.6748 | 9.8226 | 9.0770 | 8.4218 | 7.8431 | 7.3300 | 6.8729 | 6.4642 |
| 26 | 22.7952 | 20.1210 | 17.8768 | 15.9828 | 14.3752 | 13.0032 | 11.8258 | 10.8100 | 9.9290 | 9.1609 | 8.4881 | 7.8957 | 7.3717 | 6.9061 | 6.4906 |
| 27 | 23.5596 | 20.7069 | 18.3270 | 16.3296 | 14.6430 | 13.2105 | 11.9867 | 10.9352 | 10.0266 | 9.2372 | 8.5478 | 7.9426 | 7.4086 | 6.9352 | 6.5135 |
| 28 | 24.3164 | 21.2813 | 18.7641 | 16.6631 | 14.8981 | 13.4062 | 12.1371 | 11.0511 | 10.1161 | 9.3066 | 8.6016 | 7.9844 | 7.4412 | 6.9607 | 6.5335 |
| 29 | 25.0658 | 21.8444 | 19.1885 | 16.9837 | 15.1411 | 13.5907 | 12.2777 | 11.1584 | 10.1983 | 9.3696 | 8.6501 | 8.0218 | 7.4701 | 6.9830 | 6.5509 |
| 30 | 25.8077 | 22.3965 | 19.6004 | 17.2920 | 15.3725 | 13.7648 | 12.4090 | 11.2578 | 10.2737 | 9.4269 | 8.6938 | 8.0552 | 7.4957 | 7.0027 | 6.5660 |

## YIELD (INTERNAL RATE OF RETURN)

The yield on any investment is computed by determining the interest rate that will make the present value of the cash flow from the investment equal to the price of the investment. Mathematically, the yield on any investment, $y$, is the interest rate that will make the following relationship hold:

$$p = \frac{C_1}{(1+y)^1} + \frac{C_2}{(1+y)^2} + \frac{C_3}{(1+y)^3} + \cdots + \frac{C_N}{(1+y)^N}$$

where

$$C_t = \text{cash flow in year } t$$
$$p = \text{price}$$
$$N = \text{number of years}$$

The individual terms that are being summed on the right-hand side of the above relationship are the present values of the cash flow. The yield calculated from the above relationship is also called the *internal rate of return*.

Solving for the yield ($y$) requires a trial-and-error procedure. The objective is to find the interest rate that will make the present value of the cash flows equal to the price. The following two illustrations demonstrate how it is carried out.

*Illustration 9.* A financial instrument offers the following annual payments:

| Years from now | Promised Annual Payments (Cash Flow to Investor) |
|---|---|
| 1 | $ 2,000 |
| 2 | 2,000 |
| 3 | 2,500 |
| 4 | 4,000 |

Suppose that the price of this financial instrument is $7,704. What is the yield, or internal rate of return, offered by this financial instrument?

To compute the yield, we must try different interest rates until we find one that makes the present value of the cash flows equal to $7,704 (the price of the financial instrument). Trying an annual interest rate of 10 percent gives the following present value:

| Years from now | Promised Annual Payments (Cash Flow to Investor) | Present Value of Cash Flow at 10% |
|---|---|---|
| 1 | $ 2,000 | $ 1,818 |
| 2 | 2,000 | 1,652 |
| 3 | 2,500 | 1,878 |
| 4 | 4,000 | 2,732 |
| | Total present value = | $ 8,080 |

Since the present value computed using a 10 percent interest rate exceeds the price of $7,704, a higher interest rate must be tried. If a 14 percent interest rate is assumed, the present value is $7,348, as shown below:

| Years from now | Promised Annual Payments (Cash Flow to Investor) | Present Value of Cash Flow at 14% |
|---|---|---|
| 1 | $ 2,000 | $ 1,754 |
| 2 | 2,000 | 1,538 |
| 3 | 2,500 | 1,688 |
| 4 | 4,000 | 2,368 |
| | Total present value = | $ 7,348 |

At 14 percent, the present value of the cash flows exceeds the price of the financial instrument. Therefore, a lower interest rate must be tried. Use of a 12 percent interest rate follows:

| Years from now | Promised Annual Payments (Cash Flow to Investor) | Present Value of Cash Flow at 12% |
|---|---|---|
| 1 | $ 2,000 | $ 1,786 |
| 2 | 2,000 | 1,594 |
| 3 | 2,500 | 1,780 |
| 4 | 4,000 | 2,544 |
| | Total present value = | $ 7,704 |

The present value of the cash flow is equal to the price of the financial instrument when a 12 percent interest rate is used. Therefore, the yield is 12 percent.

Although the formula for the yield is based on annual cash flows, the formula can be generalized to any number of periodic payments in a year. The generalized formula for determining the yield is

$$p = \frac{C_1}{(1 + y)^1} + \frac{C_2}{(1 + y)^2} + \frac{C_3}{(1 + y)^3} + \cdots + \frac{C_n}{(1 + y)^n}$$

where

$$C_t = \text{cash flow in period } t$$
$$n = \text{number of periods}$$

Keep in mind that the yield computed is now the yield for the period. That is, if the cash flows are semiannual, the yield is a semiannual yield. If the cash flows are monthly, the yield is a monthly yield. The annual interest rate is computed by multiplying the yield for the period by the appropriate factor (the frequency of payments per year). We reconsider this procedure for annualizing yields later.

*Illustration 10.* An investor is considering the purchase of a financial instrument that promises the following *semiannual* cash flows:

10 payments of $50 every six months
$1,000 10 six-month periods (five years) from now

Suppose that the price of this financial instrument is $1,243.88. What yield is this financial instrument offering?

The yield can be computed by a trial-and-error procedure, as summarized in the table below:

| Annual Interest Rate | Semi- Annual Interest Rate | Present Value of 10 Six-Month Payments of $50* | Present Value of $1,000 10 Six-Month Periods from now† | Total Present Value |
|---|---|---|---|---|
| 6.000% | 3.000% | $ 426.51 | $ 744.09 | $ 1,160.60 |
| 5.500 | 2.750 | 432.00 | 762.40 | 1,194.40 |
| 5.000 | 2.500 | 437.60 | 781.20 | 1,218.80 |
| 4.500 | 2.225 | 443.31 | 800.51 | 1,243.83 |

* $50 × present value of an ordinary annuity of $1 for 10 periods.
† $1,000 × present value of $1 10 periods from now.

As can be seen from the calculation, when a semiannual interest rate of 2.250 percent is used to find the present value of the cash flows, the present value is equal to the price of $1,243.83. Hence, 2.250 percent is the six-month yield. Doubling this yield gives the annual interest rate of 4.5 percent.

## Yield Calculation When There Is Only One Cash Flow

There is a special case when it is not necessary to go through the time-consuming trial-and-error procedure to determine the yield. This is the case where there is only one cash flow provided by the investment. The formula to determine the yield is

$$y = (\text{Future value per dollar invested})^{1/n} - 1$$

where

$n$ = number of periods until the cash flow will be received

$$\frac{\text{Future value}}{\text{per dollar invested}} = \frac{\text{Cash flow from investment}}{\text{Amount invested (or price)}}$$

*Illustration 11.* An investment offers a payment 20 years from now of $84,957. The price of the investment is $20,000. The yield for this investment is 7.50 percent, as shown below:

$$\frac{\text{Future value}}{\text{per dollar invested}} = \frac{\$84,957}{\$20,000} = 4.24785$$

$$y = (4.24785)^{1/20} - 1$$
$$= 1.07499 - 1$$
$$= .074999, \text{ or } 7.5\%$$

## Annualizing Yields

We can annualize interest rates by simply multiplying by the frequency of payments per year. The resulting rate is called the *annual interest rate*. For example, if we computed a semiannual yield, we can annualize it by multiplying by 2. Alternatively, if we had an annual interest rate and wanted to use a semiannual interest rate, we can divide by 2.

This procedure for computing the annual interest rate, given a periodic (weekly, monthly, quarterly, semiannual, etc.) interest rate is not correct. To see why, suppose that $100 is invested for one year at an annual interest rate of 8 percent. At the end of one year, the interest is $8. Suppose, instead, that $100 is invested for one year at an annual interest rate of 8 percent, but interest is paid semiannually at 4 percent (one-half the annual interest rate). The future value at the end of one year is $108.16. Interest is therefore $8.16 on a $100 investment. The interest rate, or yield, on the $100 investment is therefore 8.16 percent ($8.16/$100). The 8.16 percent is called the *effective annual yield*.

To obtain the effective annual yield associated with a periodic interest rate, the following formula can be used:

$$\text{Effective annual yield} = (1 + \text{Periodic interest rate})^m - 1$$

where

$$m = \text{frequency of payments per year}$$

For instance, in the previous example, the periodic yield is 4 percent and the frequency of payments is twice per year. Therefore,

$$
\begin{aligned}
\text{Effective annual yield} &= (1.04)^2 - 1 \\
&= 1.0816 - 1 \\
&= .0816, \text{ or } 8.16\%
\end{aligned}
$$

If interest is paid quarterly, then the periodic interest rate is 2 percent (8%/4), and the effective annual yield is 8.24 percent, as shown below:

$$
\begin{aligned}
\text{Effective annual yield} &= (1.02)^4 - 1 \\
&= 1.0824 - 1 \\
&= .0824, \text{ or } 8.24\%
\end{aligned}
$$

We can also determine the periodic interest rate that will produce a given annual interest rate. For example, suppose we wanted to know what quarterly interest rate would produce an effective annual yield of 12 percent. The following formula can be used:

$$\text{Periodic interest rate} = (1 + \text{Effective annual yield})^{1/m} - 1$$

Applying this formula to determine the quarterly interest rate to produce an effective annual yield of 12 percent, we find that

$$
\begin{aligned}
\text{Periodic interest rate} &= (1.12)^{1/4} - 1 \\
&= 1.0287 - 1 \\
&= .0287, \text{ or } 2.87\%.
\end{aligned}
$$

## SUMMARY

In this chapter several basic mathematical concepts are presented—future value, present value, and yield (or internal rate of return). In the next chapter we will see how these concepts can be applied to price fixed income securities and calculate various yield measures.

# CHAPTER 6 p.81-108

## BOND PRICING AND RETURN MEASURES*

*Frank J. Fabozzi, Ph.D., CFA, CPA*
*Visiting Professor of Finance*
*Sloan School of Management*
*Massachusetts Institute of Technology*
*and*
*Editor, The Journal of Portfolio Management*

In this chapter, the pricing of fixed income securities and the various measures of computing return (or yield) from holding a fixed income security will be explained and illustrated. The chapter is organized as follows. In the first section, we extend the present value analysis reviewed in the previous chapter to explain how a bond's price is determined. Then we turn to yield measures, first focusing on conventional yield measures for a fixed-rate coupon bond (yield-to-maturity and yield-to-call in the case of a callable bond) and a floating-rate coupon bond. After highlighting the deficiencies of the conventional yield measures, a better measure of return—horizon return—is then presented. Applications of horizon return are then given.

## BOND PRICING

The price of any financial instrument is equal to the present value of the expected cash flow. The interest rate or discount rate used to compute the present value

---

*Portions of this chapter are adapted from Chapters 5–8 in Frank J. Fabozzi, *Fixed Income Mathematics* (Chicago: Probus Publishing, 1988).

depends on the yield offered on comparable securities in the market. In this chapter we shall explain how to compute the price of a noncallable bond. The pricing of callable bonds is explained in Chapter 36.

## Determining the Cash Flows

The first step in determining the price of a bond is to determine its cash flows. The cash flows of a noncallable bond consist of (1) periodic coupon interest payments to the maturity date and (2) the par (or maturity) value at maturity. While the periodic coupon payments can be made over any time period during the year (weekly, monthly, quarterly, semiannually, or annually), most bonds issued in the United States pay coupon interest semiannually. In our illustrations, we shall assume that the coupon interest is paid semiannually. Also, to simplify the analysis, we shall assume that the next coupon payment for the bond will be made exactly six months from now. Later in this section, we explain how to price a bond when the next coupon payment is less than six months from now.

In practice, determining the cash flow of a bond is not simple, even if we ignore the possibility of default. The only case where the cash flow is known with certainty is for fixed-rate coupon, noncallable/nonputable bonds. For callable bonds, the cash flow depends on when the issuer elects to call the issue. In the case of a putable bond, it depends on when the bondholder elects to put the issue. In either case, the date that the option will be exercised is not known. Thus, the cash flow is uncertain. For mortgage-backed securities, the cash flow will depend on prepayments. The amount and timing of future prepayments are not known and therefore the cash flow is uncertain. When the coupon rate is floating rather than fixed, the cash flow will depend on the future interest rate on the benchmark index. The techniques discussed in Chapter 36 and 37 have been developed to cope with the uncertainty of cash flows. In this chapter the basic elements of bond pricing, where the cash flow is assumed to be known, are presented.

The cash flows for a noncallable bond consist of an annuity (that is, the fixed coupon interest paid every six months) and the par or maturity value. For example, a 20-year bond with a 9 percent (4.5 percent per six months) coupon rate and a par or maturity value of $1,000 has the following cash flows:

$$\text{Semiannual coupon interest} = \$1,000 \times .045$$
$$= \$45$$
$$\text{Maturity value} = \$1,000$$

Therefore, there are 40 semiannual cash flows of $45, and a $1,000 cash flow 40 six-month periods from now.

Notice the treatment of the par value. It is *not* treated as if it will be received 20 years from now. Instead, it is treated on a consistent basis with the coupon payments, which are semiannual.

## Determining the Required Yield

The interest rate or discount rate that an investor wants from investing in a bond is called the *required yield*. The required yield is determined by investigating the yields offered on comparable bonds in the market. By comparable, we mean noncallable bonds of the same credit quality and the same maturity.[1]

The required yield is typically specified as an annual interest rate. When the cash flows are semiannual, the convention is to use one-half the annual interest rate as the periodic interest rate with which to discount the cash flows. As explained at the end of the previous chapter, a periodic interest rate that is one-half the annual yield will produce an effective annual yield that is greater than the annual interest rate.

Although one yield is used to calculate the present value of all cash flows, there are theoretical arguments for using a different yield to discount the cash flow for each period. Essentially the theoretical argument is that each cash flow can be viewed as a zero coupon bond, and therefore the cash flow of a bond can be viewed as a package of zero coupon bonds. The appropriate yield for each cash flow would then be based on the theoretical rate on a zero coupon bond with a maturity equal to the time that the cash flow will be received. For purposes of this chapter, however, we shall use only one yield to discount all cash flows. In Chapters 9 and 37, this issue is reexamined.

## Determining the Price

Given the cash flows of a bond and the required yield, we have all the necessary data to price the bond. The price of a bond is equal to the present value of the cash flows, and it can be determined by adding (1) the present value of the semiannual coupon payments and (2) the present value of the par or maturity value.

Since the semiannual coupon payments are equivalent to an ordinary annuity, the present value of the coupon payments and maturity value can be calculated from the following formula:[2]

$$c \left[ \frac{1 - \left[ \frac{1}{(1+i)^n} \right]}{i} \right] + \frac{M}{(1 + i)^n}$$

---

[1] In Chapter 7, we introduce a measure of interest rate risk known as "duration." Instead of talking in terms of a bond with the same maturity as being comparable, we can recast the analysis in terms of the same duration.

[2] The formula is the same as the formula for the present value of an ordinary annuity for $n$ periods given in the previous chapter. Instead of using $A$ to represent the annuity, we have used $c$, the semiannual coupon payment.

where

> $c$ = semiannual coupon payment (\$)
> $n$ = number of periods (number of years times 2)
> $i$ = periodic interest rate (required yield divided by 2) (in decimal)
> $M$ = maturity value

**Illustration 1.** Compute the price of a 9 percent coupon bond with 20 years to maturity and a par value of \$1,000 if the required yield is 12 percent.

The cash flows for this bond are as follows: (1) 40 semiannual coupon payments of \$45 and (2) \$1,000 40 six-month periods from now. The semiannual or periodic interest rate is 6 percent.

The present value of the 40 semiannual coupon payments of \$45 discounted at 6 percent is \$677.08, as shown below:

$$c = \$45$$
$$n = 40$$
$$i = .06$$

$$\$45 \left[ \frac{1 - \left[ \frac{1}{(1.06)^{40}} \right]}{.06} \right]$$

$$= \$45 \left[ \frac{1 - \left[ \frac{1}{10.28572} \right]}{.06} \right]$$

$$= \$45 \left[ \frac{1 - .097222}{.06} \right]$$

$$= \$45(15.04630)$$
$$= \$677.08$$

The present value of the par or maturity value 40 *six-month periods* from now discounted at 6 percent is \$97.22, as shown below:

$$M = \$1,000$$
$$n = 40$$
$$i = .06$$

$$\$1,000 \left[ \frac{1}{(1.06)^{40}} \right]$$

$$= \$1,000 \left[ \frac{1}{10.28572} \right]$$

$$= \$1,000(.097222)$$
$$= \$97.22$$

The price of the bond is then equal to the sum of the two present values:

| | |
|---|---:|
| Present value of coupon payments | $ 677.08 |
| Present value of par (maturity) value | 97.22 |
| Price | $ 774.30 |

*Illustration 2.* Compute the price of the bond in Illustration 1, assuming that the required yield is 7 percent.

The cash flows are unchanged, but the periodic interest rate is now 3.5 percent (7%/2).

The present value of the 40 semiannual coupon payments of $45 discounted at 3.5 percent is $960.98, as shown below:

$$c = \$45$$
$$n = 40$$
$$i = .035$$

$$\$45 \left[ \frac{1 - \left[ \frac{1}{(1.035)^{40}} \right]}{.035} \right]$$

$$= \$45 \left[ \frac{1 - \left[ \frac{1}{3.95926} \right]}{.035} \right]$$

$$= \$45 \left[ \frac{1 - .252572}{.035} \right]$$

$$= \$45(21.35509)$$
$$= \$960.98$$

The present value of the par or maturity value of $1,000 *40 six-month periods from now* discounted at 3.5 percent is $252.57, as shown below:

$$M = \$1,000$$
$$n = 40$$
$$i = .035$$

$$\$1,000 \left[ \frac{1}{(1.035)^{40}} \right]$$

$$= \$1,000 \left[ \frac{1}{3.95926} \right]$$
$$= \$1,000(.252572)$$
$$= \$252.57$$

The price of the bond is then equal to the sum of the two present values:

| | |
|---|---|
| Present value of coupon payments | $ 960.98 |
| Present value of par (maturity) value | 252.57 |
| Price | $1,213.55 |

## Relationship Between Required Yield and Price at a Given Point in Time

The price of an option-free bond changes in the direction opposite to the change in the required yield. The reason is that the price of the bond is the present value of the cash flows. As the required yield increases, the present value of the cash flows decreases; hence, the price decreases. The opposite is true when the required yield decreases: The present value of the cash flows increases and, therefore, the price of the bond increases.

We can see this by comparing the price of the 20-year, 9 percent coupon bond that we priced in Illustrations 1 and 2. When the required yield is 12 percent, the price of the bond is $774.30. If, instead, the required yield is 7 percent, the price of the bond is $1,213.55. Exhibit 6–1 shows the price of the bond for required yields from 5 percent to 14 percent for the 20-year, 9 percent coupon bond.

**EXHIBIT 6–1**
**Price/Yield Relationship for a 20-Year,**
**9% Coupon Bond**

| Required Yield | Price of Bond |
|---|---|
| 5% | $1,502.05 |
| 6 | 1,346.72 |
| 7 | 1,213.55 |
| 8 | 1,098.96 |
| 9 | 1,000.00 |
| 10 | 914.21 |
| 11 | 839.54 |
| 12 | 774.30 |
| 13 | 717.09 |
| 14 | 666.71 |

If we graphed the price/yield relationship for any noncallable bond, we would find that it has the "bowed" shape shown in Exhibit 6–2. This shape is referred to as *convex*. The convexity of the price/yield relationship has important implications for the investment properties of a bond. We've devoted Chapter 7 to examine this relationship more closely.

## The Relationship Between Coupon Rate, Required Yield, and Price

For a bond issue at a given point in time, the coupon rate and the term-to-maturity for the issue are fixed. Consequently, as yields in the marketplace change, the only variable that an investor can change to compensate for the new yield required in the market is the price of the bond. As we saw in the previous section, as the required yield increases (decreases), the price of the bond decreases (increases).

Generally, when a bond is issued, the coupon rate is set at approximately the prevailing yield in the market.[3] The price of the bond will then be approximately equal to its par value. For example, in Exhibit 6–1, we see that when the required yield is equal to the coupon rate, the price of the bond is its par value ($1,000). Consequently, we have the following properties:

**EXHIBIT 6–2**
**Price/Yield Relationship**

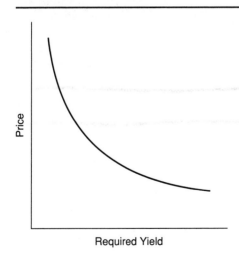

---

[3] The exception is an original-issue deep-discount bond such as a zero coupon bond.

*When the coupon rate equals the required yield, then the price equals the par value.*

*When the price equals the par value, then the coupon rate equals the required yield.*

When yields in the marketplace rise above the coupon rate at *a given point in time*, the price of the bond has to adjust so that the investor can realize some additional interest. This adjustment is accomplished by having the bond's price fall below the par value. The difference between the par value and the price is a capital gain and represents a form of interest to the investor to compensate for the coupon rate being lower than the required yield. When a bond sells below its par value, it is said to be selling at a *discount*. We can see this in Exhibit 6–1. When the required yield is greater than the coupon rate of 9 percent, the price of the bond is always less than the par value ($1,000). Consequently, we have the following properties:

*When the coupon rate is less than the required yield, then the price is less than the par value.*

*When the price is less than the par value, then the coupon rate is less than the required yield.*

Finally, when the required yield in the market is below the coupon rate, the price of the bond must sell above its par value. This occurs because investors who would have the opportunity to purchase the bond at par would be getting a coupon rate in excess of what the market would require. As a result, investors would bid up the price of the bond because its yield is attractive. It will be bid up to a price that offers the required yield in the market. A bond whose price is above its par value is said to be selling at a *premium*. Exhibit 6–1 shows that for a required yield less than the coupon rate of 9 percent, the price of the bond is greater than its par value. Consequently, we have the following properties:

*When the coupon rate is greater than the required yield, then the price is greater than the par value.*

*When the price is greater than the par value, then the coupon rate is greater than the required yield.*

## Time Path of a Bond

If the required yield is unchanged between the time the bond is purchased and the maturity date, what will happen to the price of the bond? For a bond selling at par value, the coupon rate is equal to the required yield. As the bond moves closer to maturity, the bond will continue to sell at par value. Thus, for a bond selling at par, its price will remain at par as the bond moves toward the maturity date.

The price of a bond will *not* remain constant for a bond selling at a premium or a discount. For all discount bonds the following is true: As the bond moves toward maturity, its price will increase if *the required yield* does not change. This can be seen in Exhibit 6–3 which shows the price of the 20-year, 9 percent coupon bond as it moves toward maturity, assuming that the required yield remains at 12 percent. For a bond selling at a premium, the price of the bond declines as it moves toward maturity. This can also be seen in Exhibit 6–3, which shows the time path of the 20-year, 9 percent coupon bond selling to yield 7 percent.

## Reasons for the Change in the Price of a Bond

The price of a bond will change because of one or more of the following reasons:

1. A change in the level of interest rate rates in the economy. For example, if interest rates in the economy increase (fall) because of Fed policy, the price of a bond will decrease (increase).
2. A change in the price of the bond selling at a price other than par as it moves toward maturity without any change in the required yield. As we demonstrated, over time a discount bond rises in value if yields do not change; a premium bond's price declines over time if yields do not change.
3. A change in the required yield due to changes in the spread between corporates and Treasuries. If the Treasury rate does not change but the

**EXHIBIT 6–3**
**Time Paths of 20-Year, 9% Coupon Discount and Premium Bonds**

| Years Remaining to Maturity | Price of Discount/Bond* | Price of Premium Bond† |
|:---:|:---:|:---:|
| 20 | $ 774.30 | $ 1,213.55 |
| 18 | 780.68 | 1,202.90 |
| 16 | 788.74 | 1,190.69 |
| 14 | 798.91 | 1,176.67 |
| 12 | 811.75 | 1,160.59 |
| 10 | 827.95 | 1,142.13 |
| 8 | 848.42 | 1,120.95 |
| 6 | 874.24 | 1,096.63 |
| 4 | 906.85 | 1,068.74 |
| 2 | 948.02 | 1,036.73 |
| 1 | 972.50 | 1,019.00 |
| 0 | 1,000.00 | 1,000.00 |

* Selling to yield 12%.
† Selling to yield 7%.

spread to Treasuries for all corporate bonds changes (narrows or widens), corporate bond prices will change.
4. A change in the perceived credit quality of the issuer. Assuming that interest rates in the economy and yield spreads between corporates and Treasuries do not change, the price of a corporate bond will increase (decrease) if its perceived credit quality has improved (deteriorated).
5. For bonds with embedded option (e.g., callable bonds, putable bonds, and convertible bonds), the price of the bond will change as the factors that affect the value of the embedded options change.

## Pricing a Zero Coupon Bond

So far, we have determined the price of coupon-bearing bonds. Some bonds do not make any periodic coupon payments. Instead, the investor realizes interest by the difference between the maturity value and the purchase price.

The pricing of a zero coupon bond is no different from the pricing of a coupon bond: Its price is the present value of the expected cash flows. In the case of a zero coupon bond, the only cash flow is the maturity value. Therefore, the price of a zero coupon bond is simply the present value of the maturity value. The number of periods used to discount the maturity value is double the number of years to maturity. This treatment is consistent with the manner in which the maturity value of a coupon bond is handled.

*Illustration 3.*  The price of a zero coupon bond that matures in 10 years and has a maturity value of $1,000 if the required yield is 8.6 percent, is equal to the present value of $1,000 20 periods from now discounted at 4.3 percent. That is,

$$\$1,000 \left[ \frac{1}{(1.043)^{20}} \right] = \$430.83$$

## Determining the Price When the Settlement Date Falls between Coupon Periods

In our illustrations, we assumed that the next coupon payment is six months away. This means that settlement occurs on the day after a coupon date. Typically, an investor will purchase a bond between coupon dates so that the next coupon payment is less than six months away. To compute the price, we have to answer the following three questions:

1. How many days are there until the next coupon payment?
2. How should we determine the present value of cash flows received over fractional periods?

3. How much must the buyer compensate the seller for the coupon interest earned by the seller for the fraction of the period that the bond was held?

The first question is the "day-count" question. The second is the "compounding" question. The last question asks how accrued interest is determined. Below we address these questions.

### Day Count

Market conventions for each type of bond dictate the answer to the first question: the number of days until the next coupon payment.

For Treasury coupon securities, a nonleap year is assumed to have 365 days. The number of days between settlement and the next coupon payment is therefore the actual number of days between the two dates. The day count convention for a coupon-bearing Treasury security is said to be "actual/actual," which means "the actual number of days in a month/actual number of days in the coupon period." For example, consider a Treasury bond whose last coupon payment was on March 1; the next coupon would be six months later on September 1. Suppose this bond is purchased with a settlement date of July 17. The actual number of days between July 17 (the settlement date) and September 1 (the date of the next coupon payment) is 46 days (the actual number of days in the coupon period is 184), as shown below:

| | |
|---|---|
| July 17 to July 31 | 14 days |
| August | 31 days |
| September 1 | 1 day |
| | 46 days |

In contrast to the "actual/actual" day count convention for coupon-bearing Treasury securities, for corporate and municipal bonds and agency securities, the day count convention is "30/360." That is, each month is assumed to have 30 days and each year 360 days. For example, suppose that the security in our previous example is not a coupon-bearing Treasury security but instead either a coupon-bearing corporate bond, municipal bond, or agency security. The number of days between July 17 and September 1 is shown below:

| | |
|---|---|
| Remainder of July | 13 days |
| August | 30 days |
| September 1 | 1 day |
| | 44 days |

### Compounding

Once the number of days between the settlement date and the next coupon date is determined, the present value formula must be modified to take into account that the cash flows will not be received six months (one full period) from now. The "Street" convention is to compute the price as follows:

1. Determine the number of days in the coupon period.
2. Compute the following ratio:

$$w = \frac{\text{Number of days between settlement and next coupon payment}}{\text{Number of days in the coupon period}}$$

For a corporate bond, municipal bond, and agency security, the number of days in the coupon period will be 180, since a year is assumed to have 360 days. For a coupon-bearing Treasury security, the number of days is the actual number of days. The number of days in the coupon period is called the *basis*.

3. Determine the first cash flow which is $w$ times the semiannual coupon payment.
4. For a bond with $n$ coupon payments remaining to maturity, the price is

$$p = \frac{w \times c}{(1 + i)^w} + \frac{c}{(1 + i)^{1+w}} + \frac{c}{(1 + i)^{2+w}} + \cdots + \frac{c}{(1 + i)^{n-1+w}} + \frac{M}{(1 + i)^{n-1+w}}$$

where

$p$ = price ($)
$c$ = semiannual coupon payment ($)
$M$ = maturity value
$n$ = number of coupons payments remaining
$i$ = periodic interest rate (required yield divided by 2) (in decimal)

The period (exponent) in the formula for determining the present value can be expressed generally as $t - 1 + w$. For example, for the first cash flow, the period is $1 - 1 + w$, or simply $w$. For the second cash flow, it is $2 - 1 + w$, or simply $1 + w$. If the bond has 20 coupon payments remaining, the last period is $20 - 1 + w$, or simply $19 + w$.

**Illustration 4.** Suppose that a corporate bond with a coupon rate of 10 percent maturing March 1, 1997, is purchased with a settlement date of July 17, 1991. What would the price of this bond be if it is priced to yield 6.5 percent?

The next coupon payment will be made on September 1, 1991. Since the bond is a corporate bond, based on a 30/360 day count convention, there are 44 days between the settlement date and the next coupon date. The number of days in the coupon period is 180 days. Therefore,

$$w = \frac{44}{180} = .24444$$

The number of coupon payments remaining, $n$, is 12. The semiannual interest rate is 3.25 percent (6.5%/2). The first coupon payment per $100 of par value will be

$$.24444 \times \$5 = \$1.222$$

The calculation based on the formula for the price is given in Exhibit 6–4. The price of this corporate bond would be $116.2797 per $100 par value.

The *total payment* (also called the *invoice price* or *proceeds*) that the buyer must remit to the seller is the price plus accrued interest.

### Accrued Interest and the Total Payment

The buyer must compensate the seller for the portion of the next coupon interest payment the seller has earned but will not receive from the issuer because the issuer will send the next coupon payment to the buyer. This amount is called *accrued interest* and depends on the number of days from the last coupon payment to the settlement date.[4] The accrued interest is computed as follows:

$$AI = c \left[ \frac{\text{Number of days from last coupon payment to settlement date}}{\text{Number of days in coupon period}} \right]$$

**EXHIBIT 6–4**
**Price Calculation When a Bond is Purchased Between Coupon Payments**

| Period | Cash Flow per $100 of Par | Present Value of $1 at 3.25% | Present Value of Cash Flow |
|---|---|---|---|
| 0.24444 | $1.222 | $0.992212 | $1.212704 |
| 1.24444 | 5.000 | 0.960980 | 4.804902 |
| 2.24444 | 5.000 | 0.930731 | 4.653658 |
| 3.24444 | 5.000 | 0.901435 | 4.507175 |
| 4.24444 | 5.000 | 0.873060 | 4.365303 |
| 5.24444 | 5.000 | 0.845579 | 4.227896 |
| 6.24444 | 5.000 | 0.818963 | 4.094815 |
| 7.24444 | 5.000 | 0.793184 | 3.965922 |
| 8.24444 | 5.000 | 0.768217 | 3.841087 |
| 9.24444 | 5.000 | 0.744036 | 3.720181 |
| 10.24444 | 5.000 | 0.720616 | 3.603081 |
| 11.24444 | 105.000 | 0.697933 | 73.283000 |
|  |  | Total | $116.27970 |

[4] Accrued interest is not computed for all bonds. No accrued interest is computed for bonds in default or income bonds. A bond that trades without accrued interest is said to be traded "flat."

where

$$AI = \text{accrued interest (\$)}$$
$$c = \text{semiannual coupon payment (\$)}$$

*Illustration 5.* Let's continue with the hypothetical corporate bond in Illustration 4. Since the number of days between settlement (July 17, 1991) and the next coupon payment (September 1, 1991) is 44 days and the number of days in the coupon period is 180, the number of days from the last coupon payment date (March 1, 1991) to the settlement date is 136 (180 − 44). The accrued interest per $100 of par value is

$$AI = \$5 \ \frac{136}{180} = \$3.777778$$

The total payment per $100 of par value the buyer would remit to the seller would be the price of $116.28 (the rounded price) plus accrued interest of $3.777778, or $120.067.

## CONVENTIONAL YIELD MEASURES

In the previous section, we explained how to compute the price of a bond given the required yield. In this section, we'll show how various yield measures for a bond are calculated given its price. First let's look at the sources of potential return from holding a bond.

An investor who purchases a bond can expect to receive a *dollar* return from one or more of the following sources:

- the coupon interest payments made by the issuer
- any capital gain (or capital loss—negative dollar return) when the bond matures, is called, or is sold
- income from reinvestment of the coupon interest payments

This last source of dollar return is referred to as *interest-on-interest.*

Three yield measures are commonly cited by market participants to measure the potential return from investing in a bond—current yield, yield-to-maturity and yield-to-call. These yield measures are expressed as a *percent* return rather than a dollar return. However, any yield measure should consider each of the three potential sources of return cited above. Below we discuss these three yield measures and assess whether they consider the three sources of potential return.

### Current Yield

The current yield relates the *annual* coupon interest to the market price. The formula for the current yield is

$$\text{Current yield} = \frac{\text{Annual dollar coupon interest}}{\text{Price}}$$

*Illustration 6.* The current yield for an 18-year, 6 percent coupon bond selling for $700.89 is 8.56 percent, as shown below:

$$\text{Annual dollar coupon interest} = \$1,000 \times .06$$
$$= \$60$$

$$\text{Current yield} = \frac{\$60}{\$700.89} = .0856, \text{ or } 8.56\%$$

The current yield considers only the coupon interest and no other source of return that will affect an investor's yield. For example, in Illustration 6, no consideration is given to the capital gain that the investor will realize when the bond matures. No recognition is given to a capital loss that the investor will realize when a bond selling at a premium matures. In addition, interest-on-interest from reinvesting coupon payments is ignored.

## Yield-to-Maturity

In the previous chapter, we explained how to compute the yield or internal rate of return on any investment. The yield is the interest rate that will make the present value of the cash flows equal to the price (or initial investment). The yield-to-maturity is computed in the same way as the yield; the cash flows are those that the investor would realize by holding the bond to maturity. For a semiannual-pay bond, doubling the interest rate or discount rate gives the yield-to-maturity.

Recall from the previous chapter that the calculation of a yield involves a trial-and-error procedure. While there is a *yield book* that contains tables that provide the yield-to-maturity given the price, coupon and remaining time to maturity, practitioners usually use calculators or software that produces this number. The following illustration shows how to compute the yield-to-maturity for a bond.

*Illustration 7.* In Illustration 6, we computed the current yield for an 18-year, 6 percent coupon bond selling for $700.89. The maturity, or par value, for this bond is $1,000. The yield-to-maturity for this bond is 9.5 percent, as shown in Exhibit 6–5. Cash flows for the bond are

1. 36 coupon payments of $30 every six months and
2. $1,000 36 six-month periods from now

Different interest rates must be tried until one is found that makes the present value of the cash flows equal to the price of $700.89. Since the coupon rate on the bond is 6 percent and the bond is selling at a discount, the yield must be

**EXHIBIT 6–5**

**Computation of Yield-to-Maturity for an 18-Year, 6% Coupon Bond Selling at $700.89**

Objective: Find—by trial and error—the semiannual interest rate that will make the present value of the following cash flows equal to $700.89:

36 coupon payments of $30 every six months
$1,000 36 six-month periods from now

| Annual Interest Rate | Semi-annual Rate | Present Value of 36 Payments of $30* | Present Value of $1,030 10 Periods from now† | Present Value of Cash Flows |
|---|---|---|---|---|
| 6.50% | 3.25% | $ 631.20 | $ 316.20 | $ 947.40 |
| 7.00 | 3.50 | 608.71 | 289.83 | 898.54 |
| 7.50 | 3.75 | 587.42 | 265.72 | 853.14 |
| 8.00 | 4.00 | 567.25 | 243.67 | 810.92 |
| 8.50 | 4.25 | 548.12 | 223.49 | 771.61 |
| 9.00 | 4.50 | 529.98 | 205.03 | 735.01 |
| 9.50 | 4.75 | 512.76 | 188.13 | 700.89 |

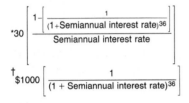

$$*30 \left[ \frac{1 - \frac{1}{(1+\text{Semiannual interest rate})^{36}}}{\text{Semiannual interest rate}} \right]$$

$$†\$1000 \left[ \frac{1}{(1 + \text{Semiannual interest rate})^{36}} \right]$$

greater than 6 percent. Exhibit 6–5 shows the present value of the cash flows of the bond for semiannual interest rates from 3.25 percent to 4.75 percent (corresponding to annual interest rates from 6.5 percent to 9.50 percent, respectively). As can be seen, when a 4.75 percent interest rate is used, the present value of the cash flows is $700.89. Therefore, the yield-to-maturity is 9.50 percent (4.75% × 2).

The yield-to-maturity considers the coupon income and any capital gain or loss that the investor will realize by *holding the bond to maturity*. The yield-to-maturity also considers the timing of the cash flows. It does consider interest-on-interest: *however, it assumes that the coupon payments can be reinvested at an interest rate equal to the yield-to-maturity.* So, if the yield-to-maturity for a bond is 9.5 percent, to earn that yield, the coupon payments must be reinvested at an interest rate equal to 9.5 percent. The following example clearly demonstrates this.

Suppose that an investor has $700.98 and places the funds in a certificate of deposit that pays 4.75 percent every six months for 18 years or 9.5 percent per year on a bond equivalent basis. At the end of 18 years, the $700.98 investment will grow to $3,726. Instead, suppose that an investor buys the following bond: a 6 percent, 18-year bond selling for $700.98. This is the same as the price of our bond in Illustration 7. The yield-to-maturity for this bond is 9.5 percent. The investor would expect that at the end of 18 years, the total from the investment will be $3,726.

Let's look at what the investor will receive. There will be 36 semiannual interest payments of $30, which will total $1,080. When the bond matures, the investor will receive $1,000. Thus, the total that the investor will receive is $2,080 if he or she held the bond to maturity. But this is less than the $3,726 necessary to produce a yield of 9.5 percent (4.75 percent semiannually) by $1,646 ($3,726 minus $2,080). How is this deficiency supposed to be made up? If the investor reinvests the coupon payments at a semiannual interest rate of 4.75 percent (or a 9.5 percent annual rate on a bond equivalent basis), it is a simple exercise to demonstrate that the interest earned on the coupon payments will be $1,646. Consequently, of the $3,726 total dollar return necessary to produce a yield of 9.5 percent, about 44 percent ($1,646 divided by $3,726) must be generated by reinvesting the coupon payments.

Clearly, the investor will only realize the yield-to-maturity stated at the time of purchase if (1) the coupon payments can be reinvested at the yield-to-maturity and (2) if the bond is held to maturity. With respect to the first assumption, the risk that an investor faces is that future reinvestment rates will be less than the yield-to-maturity at the time the bond is purchased. This risk is referred to as *reinvestment risk*. If the bond is not held to maturity, the price of the bond may have to be sold for less than its purchase price, resulting in a return that is less than the yield-to-maturity. The risk that a bond will have to be sold at a loss because interest rates rise is referred to as *interest rate risk* or *price risk*.

### *Reinvestment Risk*

There are two characteristics of a bond that determine the degree of reinvestment risk. First, for a given yield-to-maturity and a given coupon rate, the longer the maturity, the more the bond's total dollar return is dependent on the interest-on-interest to realize the yield to maturity at the time of purchase. That is, the greater the reinvestment risk. The implication is that the yield to maturity measure for long-term coupon bonds tells little about the potential yield that an investor may realize if the bond is held to maturity. In high interest rate environments, the interest-on-interest component for long-term bonds may be as high as 70 percent of the bond's potential total dollar return.

The second characteristic that determines the degree of reinvestment risk is the coupon rate. For a given maturity and a given yield-to-maturity, the higher the coupon rate, the more dependent the bond's total dollar return will be on the reinvestment of the coupon payments in order to produce the yield-to-maturity at the time of purchase. This means that holding maturity and yield-to-maturity constant, premium bonds will be more dependent on interest-on-interest than bonds selling at par. In contrast, discount bonds will be less dependent on interest-on-interest than bonds selling at par. For zero coupon bonds, none of the bond's total dollar return is dependent on interest-on-interest. So, a zero coupon bond has no reinvestment risk if held to maturity.

## Interest Rate Risk

As we explained in the previous section, a bond's price moves in the direction opposite to the change in interest rates. As interest rates rise (fall), the price of a bond will fall (rise). For an investor who plans to hold a bond to maturity, the change in the bond's price prior to maturity is of no concern; however, for an investor who may have to sell the bond prior to the maturity date, an increase in interest rates subsequent to the time the bond was purchased will mean the realization of a capital loss. Not all bonds have the same degree of interest-rate risk. In the next chapter, the characteristics of a bond that determine its interest-rate risk will be demonstrated.

Given the assumptions underlying yield-to-maturity, we can now illustrate the key point that yield-to-maturity has limited value in assessing the relative value of bonds. Suppose that an investor who has a five year investment horizon is considering the following four option-free bonds:

| Bond | Coupon Rate | Maturity | Yield-to-Maturity |
|------|-------------|----------|-------------------|
| W | 5% | 3 years | 9.0% |
| X | 6% | 20 years | 8.6% |
| Y | 11% | 15 years | 9.2% |
| Z | 8% | 5 years | 8.0% |

Assuming that all four bonds are of the same credit quality, which one is the most attractive to this investor? An investor who selects Bond Y because it offers the highest yield to maturity is failing to recognize that the bond must be sold after five years, and the selling price of the bond will depend on the yield required in the market for 10-year, 11 percent coupon bonds at that time. Hence, there could be a capital gain or capital loss that will make the return higher or lower than the yield to maturity promised now. Moreover, the higher coupon rate on Bond Y relative to the other three bonds means that more of this bond's return will be dependent on the reinvestment of coupon interest payments.

Bond W offers the second highest yield-to-maturity. On the surface, it seems to be particularly attractive because it eliminates the problem faced by purchasing Bond Y of realizing a possible capital loss when the bond must be sold prior to the maturity date. In addition, the reinvestment risk seems to be less than for the other three bonds because the coupon rate is the lowest.

However, the investor would not be eliminating the reinvestment risk since after three years he must reinvest the proceeds received at maturity for two more years. This return that the investor will realize will depend on interest rates three years from now when the investor must rollover the proceeds received from the maturing bond.

Which is the best bond? The yield-to-maturity doesn't seem to help us identify the best bond. The answer depends on the expectations of the investor. Specifically, it depends on the interest rate at which the coupon interest payments can be reinvested until the end of the investor's investment horizon. Also, for bonds with a maturity longer than the investment horizon, it depends on the investor's expectations about interest rates at the end of the investment horizon. Consequently, any of these bonds can be the best investment vehicle based on some reinvestment rate and some future interest rate at the end of the investment horizon. In the next section, we shall present an alternative return measure for assessing bonds.

### Yield-to-Maturity for a Zero Coupon Bond

In the previous chapter, we explained that when there is only one cash flow, it is much easier to compute the yield on an investment. A zero coupon bond is characterized by a single cash flow resulting from an investment. Consequently, the following formula, presented in the previous chapter, can be applied to compute the yield-to-maturity for a zero coupon bond:

$$y = (\text{Future value per dollar invested})^{1/n} - 1$$

where

$$y = \text{one-half the yield-to-maturity}$$

$$\text{Future value per dollar invested} = \frac{\text{Maturity value}}{\text{Price}}$$

Once again, doubling $y$ gives the yield-to-maturity. *Remember that the number of periods used in the formula is double the number of years.*

**Illustration 8.** The yield-to-maturity for a zero coupon bond selling for \$274.78 with a maturity value of \$1,000, maturing in 15 years, is 8.8 percent, as computed below:

$$n = 30(15 \times 2)$$

$$\text{Future value per dollar invested} = \frac{\$1,000.00}{\$274.78}$$

$$\begin{aligned} y &= (3.639275)^{1/30} - 1 \\ &= (3.639275)^{.033333} - 1 \\ &= 1.044 - 1 \\ &= .044, \text{ or } 4.4\% \end{aligned}$$

Doubling 4.4 percent gives the yield-to-maturity of 8.8 percent.

*Relationship Between Coupon Rate, Current Yield, and Yield-to-Maturity*
The following relationship should be recognized between the coupon rate, current yield, and yield-to-maturity:

| Bond Selling at: | | Relationship | | |
| --- | --- | --- | --- | --- |
| Par | Coupon rate $=$ | Current yield | $=$ | Yield-to-maturity |
| Discount | Coupon rate $<$ | Current yield | $<$ | Yield-to-maturity |
| Premium | Coupon rate $>$ | Current yield | $>$ | Yield-to-maturity |

*Problem with the Annualizing Procedure*
As we pointed out at the end of the previous chapter, multiplying a semiannual interest rate by 2 will give an underestimate of the effective annual yield. The proper way to annualize the semiannual yield is by applying the following formula:

$$\text{Effective annual yield} = (1 + \text{Periodic interest rate})^k - 1$$

where

$$k = \text{number of payments per year}$$

For a semiannual-pay bond, the formula can be modified as follows:

$$\text{Effective annual yield} = (1 + \text{Semiannual interest rate})^2 - 1$$

or

$$\text{Effective annual yield} = (1 + y)^2 - 1$$

For example, in Illustration 7, the semiannual interest rate is 4.75 percent, and the effective annual yield is 9.73 percent, as shown below:

$$\text{Effective annual yield} = (1.0475)^2 - 1$$
$$= 1.0973 - 1$$
$$= .0973, \text{ or } 9.73\%$$

Although the proper way for annualizing a semiannual interest rate is given in the formula above, the convention adopted in the bond market is to double the semiannual interest rate. The yield-to-maturity computed in this manner—doubling the semiannual yield—is called a *bond equivalent yield*. In fact, this convention is carried over to yield calculations for other types of fixed income securities.

## Yield-to-Call

For a callable bond, investors also compute another yield (or internal rate of return) measure, the *yield-to-call*. The cash flows for computing the yield-to-call are those that would result if the issue were called on its first call date. The yield-to-call is the interest rate that will make the present value of the cash flows if the bond is held to the first call date equal to the price of the bond (or total payment).

***Illustration 9.*** In Illustrations 6 and 7, we computed the current yield and yield-to-maturity for an 18-year, 6 percent coupon bond selling for $700.89. Suppose that this bond is callable in five years at $1,030. The cash flows for this bond if it is called in five years are

1. 10 coupon payments of $30 every six months and
2. $1,030 in 10 six-month periods from now.

The interest rate that we seek is the one that will make the present values of the cash flows equal to $700.89. From Exhibit 6–6, it can be seen that when the interest rate is 7.6 percent, the present value of the cash flows is $700.11, which is close enough to $700.89 for our purposes. Therefore, the yield-to-call on a bond equivalent basis is 15.2 percent (double the periodic interest rate of 7.6 percent).

**EXHIBIT 6–6**
**Computation of Yield-to-Call for an 18-Year, 6% Coupon Bond, Callable in 5 Years at $1,030, Selling at $700.89**

Objective: Find—by trial and error—the semiannual interest rate that will make the present value of the following cash flows equal to $700.89:

   10 coupon payments of $30 every six months
   $1,030 10 six-month periods from now

| Annual Interest Rate | Semi-annual Rate | Present Value of 36 Payments of $30* | Present Value of $1,030 36 Per-iods from now† | Present Value of Cash Flows |
|---|---|---|---|---|
| 11.20% | 5.60% | $225.05 | $597.31 | $822.36 |
| 11.70 | 5.85 | 222.38 | 585.35 | 805.73 |
| 12.20 | 6.10 | 219.76 | 569.75 | 789.51 |
| 12.70 | 6.35 | 217.19 | 556.50 | 773.69 |
| 13.20 | 6.60 | 214.66 | 543.58 | 758.24 |
| 13.70 | 6.85 | 212.18 | 531.00 | 743.18 |
| 14.20 | 7.10 | 209.74 | 518.73 | 728.47 |
| 14.70 | 7.35 | 207.34 | 506.78 | 714.12 |
| 15.20 | 7.60 | 204.99 | 495.12 | 700.11 |

$$*30 \left[ \frac{1 - \left[ \frac{1}{(1 + \text{Semiannual interest rate})^{10}} \right]}{\text{Semiannual interest rate}} \right]$$

$$†\$1,030 \left[ \frac{1}{(1 + \text{Semiannual interest rate})^{10}} \right]$$

According to the conventional approach, conservative investors will compute the yield-to-call and yield-to-maturity for a callable bond selling at a premium, selecting the lower of the two as a measure of potential return. It is the smaller of the two yield measures that investors would use to evaluate the relative value of bonds. Some investors calculate not just the yield to the first call date, but the yield to all possible call dates. Since most bonds can be called at any time after the first call date, the approach has been to compute the yield to every coupon anniversary date following the first call date. Then, all calculated yields to call and the yield-to-maturity are compared. The lowest of these yields is called the *yield-to-worst*. The conventional approach would have us believe that this yield should be used in relative value analysis.

Let's take a closer look at the yield-to-call as a measure of the potential return of a callable bond. The yield-to-call does consider all three sources of potential return from owning a bond. However, as in the case of the yield-to-maturity, it assumes that all cash flows can be reinvested at the computed yield—in this case, the yield-to-call—until the assumed call date. As we noted earlier in this chapter, this assumption may be inappropriate. Moreover, the yield-to-call assumes that (1) the investor will hold the bond to the assumed call date and (2) the issuer will call the bond on that date.

The assumptions underlying the yield-to-call are often unrealistic. They do not take into account how an investor will reinvest the proceeds if the issue is called. For example, consider two bonds, M and N. Suppose that the yield-to-maturity for bond M, a five-year noncallable bond, is 10 percent, while for bond N the yield-to-call, assuming that the bond will be called in three years, is 10.5 percent. Which bond is better for an investor with a five-year investment horizon? It's not possible to tell for the yields cited. If the investor intends to hold the bond for five years and the issuer calls the bond after three years, the total dollars that will be available at the end of five years will depend on the interest rate that can be earned from reinvesting funds from the call date to the end of the investment horizon.

More will be said about the analysis of callable bonds in Chapters 7, 36, and 37.

## Yield (Internal Rate of Return) for a Portfolio

The yield for a portfolio of bonds is not simply the average or weighted average of the yield-to-maturity of the individual bond issues. It is computed by determining the cash flows for the portfolio and the interest rate that will make the present value of cash flows equal to the market value of the portfolio.[5]

---

[5] In the next chapter, the concept of duration will be discussed. A good approximation to the yield for a portfolio can be obtained by using duration to weight the yield-to-maturity of the individual bonds in the portfolio.

***Illustration 10.***   Consider the following three-bond portfolio:[6]

| Bond | Coupon Rate | Maturity | Par Value | Price Value | Yield-to-Maturity |
|------|-------------|----------|-----------|-------------|-------------------|
| A | 7.0% | 5 years | $10,000,000 | $ 9,209,000 | 9.0% |
| B | 10.5 | 7 years | 20,000,000 | 20,000,000 | 10.5 |
| C | 6.0 | 3 years | 30,000,000 | 28,050,000 | 8.5 |

The portfolio's total market value is $57,259,000. The cash flow for each bond in the portfolio and for the whole portfolio is given below:

| Period Cash Flow Recieved | Bond A | Bond B | Bond C | Portfolio |
|---------------------------|--------|--------|--------|-----------|
| 1 | $   350,000 | $ 1,050,000 | $   900,000 | $ 2,300,000 |
| 2 | 350,000 | 1,050,000 | 900,000 | 2,300,000 |
| 3 | 350,000 | 1,050,000 | 900,000 | 2,300,000 |
| 4 | 350,000 | 1,050,000 | 900,000 | 2,300,000 |
| 5 | 350,000 | 1,050,000 | 900,000 | 2,300,000 |
| 6 | 350,000 | 1,050,000 | 30,900,000 | 32,300,000 |
| 7 | 350,000 | 1,050,000 | — | 1,400,000 |
| 8 | 350,000 | 1,050,000 | — | 1,400,000 |
| 9 | 350,000 | 1,050,000 | — | 1,400,000 |
| 10 | 10,350,000 | 1,050,000 | — | 11,400,000 |
| 11 | — | 1,050,000 | — | 1,050,000 |
| 12 | — | 1,050,000 | — | 1,050,000 |
| 13 | — | 1,050,000 | — | 1,050,000 |
| 14 | — | 21,050,000 | — | 21,050,000 |

To determine the yield (internal rate of return) for this three-bond portfolio, the interest rate that makes the present value of the cash flows shown in the last column of the table above equal to $57,259,000 (the total market value of the portfolio) must be found. If an interest rate of 4.77 percent is used, the present value of the cash flows will equal $57,259,000. Doubling 4.77 percent gives 9.54 percent, which is the yield on the portfolio on a bond equivalent basis.

---

[6] To simplify the illustration, it is assumed that the coupon payment date is the same for each bond.

## Yield Measure for Floating-Rate Securities

The coupon rate for a floating-rate security changes periodically based on some predetermined index (such as LIBOR or a Treasury Security).[7] Since the value for the benchmark in the future is not known, it is not possible to determine the cash flows. This means that a yield-to-maturity cannot be calculated.

A conventional measure used to estimate the potential return for a floating-rate security is the security's *effective margin*. This measure estimates the average spread or margin over the underlying index that the investor can expect to earn over the life of the security. The procedure for calculating the effective margin is as follows:

1. Determine the cash flows assuming that the index rate does not change over the life of the security.
2. Select a margin (spread).
3. Discount the cash flows found in (1) by the current index rate plus the margin selected in (2).
4. Compare the present value of the cash flows as calculated in (3) to the price. If the present value is equal to the security's price, the effective margin is the margin assumed in (2). If the present value is not equal to the security's price, go back to (2) and try a different margin.

For a security selling at par, the effective margin is simply the spread over the index.

*Illustration 11.*    To illustrate the calculation, suppose that a 6-year floating-rate security selling for 99.3098 pays a rate based on some interest rate index plus 80 basis points. The coupon rate is reset every six months. Assume that the current interest rate for the index is 10 percent. Exhibit 6–7 shows the calculation of the effective margin for this security. The second column shows the current interest rate for the index. The third column sets forth the cash flows for the security. The cash flow for the first 11 periods is equal to one-half the current interest rate index (5 percent) plus the semiannual spread of 40 basis points multiplied by 100. In the twelfth six-month period, the cash flow is 5.4 plus the maturity value of 100. The top row of the last five columns shows the assumed margin. The rows below the assumed margin show the present value of each cash flow. The last row gives the total present value of the cash flows. For the five assumed yield spreads, the present value is equal to the price of the floating-rate security (99.3098) when the assumed margin is 96 basis points. Therefore, the effective margin on a semiannual basis is 48 basis points and 96 basis points on an annual basis. (Notice that the effective margin is 80 basis

---

[7] Floating-rate securities are discussed in Chapter 14.

**EXHIBIT 6–7**
**Calculation of the Effective Margin for a Floating-Rate Security**

Floating-rate security:  Maturity = 6 years
Coupon rate = index + 80 basis points
Reset every six months

Present Value of Cash Flow:

Assumed Annual Yield Spread (in b.p.)

| Period | Index | Cash Flow* | 80 | 84 | 88 | 96 | 100 |
|--------|-------|-----------|-----|-----|-----|-----|-----|
| 1 | 10% | 5.4 | 5.1233 | 5.1224 | 5.1214 | 5.1195 | 5.1185 |
| 2 | 10 | 5.4 | 4.8609 | 4.8590 | 4.8572 | 4.8535 | 4.8516 |
| 3 | 10 | 5.4 | 4.6118 | 4.6092 | 4.6066 | 4.6013 | 4.5987 |
| 4 | 10 | 5.4 | 4.3755 | 4.3722 | 4.3689 | 4.3623 | 4.3590 |
| 5 | 10 | 5.4 | 4.1514 | 4.1474 | 4.1435 | 4.1356 | 4.1317 |
| 6 | 10 | 5.4 | 3.9387 | 3.9342 | 3.9297 | 3.9208 | 3.9163 |
| 7 | 10 | 5.4 | 3.7369 | 3.7319 | 3.7270 | 3.7171 | 3.7122 |
| 8 | 10 | 5.4 | 3.5454 | 3.5401 | 3.5347 | 3.5240 | 3.5186 |
| 9 | 10 | 5.4 | 3.3638 | 3.3580 | 3.3523 | 3.3409 | 3.3352 |
| 10 | 10 | 5.4 | 3.1914 | 3.1854 | 3.1794 | 3.1673 | 3.1613 |
| 11 | 10 | 5.4 | 3.0279 | 3.0216 | 3.0153 | 3.0028 | 2.9965 |
| 12 | 10 | 105.4 | 56.0729 | 55.9454 | 55.8182 | 55.5647 | 55.4385 |
| Present value | | | 100.0000 | 99.8269 | 99.6541 | 99.3098 | 99.1381 |

\* For periods 1–11:  Cash flow = 100 (Index+Assumed Margin) (0.5)
For period 12:  Cash flow = 100 (Index+Assumed Margin) (0.5) + 100

points, the same as the spread over the index, when the security is selling at par.)

There are two drawbacks of the effective margin as a measure of the potential return from investing in a floating-rate security. First, this measure assumes that the index will not change over the life of the security. Second, if the floating-rate security has a cap or floor, this is not taken into consideration. Techniques described in Chapter 37 can allow interest rate volatility to be considered and can handle caps or floors.

## HORIZON RETURN ANALYSIS

If conventional yield measures such as the yield-to-maturity and yield-to-call offer little insight into the relative value of bonds, what measure of return can be used? The proper measure is one that considers all three sources of potential dollar return over the investor's investment horizon. This requires that an investor first project the total future dollars over an investment horizon. The return is then the interest rate that will make the bond's price (total price) grow to the projected total future dollars at the end of the investment horizon. The yield computed in this way is referred to as the *horizon return*. The horizon return is also referred to as the *total return* and *realized compound yield*. In this section, we explain this measure and demonstrate how it can be applied in relative value analysis.

## Calculating the Horizon Return

The horizon return requires that the investor specify

- An investment horizon
- A reinvestment rate
- A selling price for the bond at the end of the investment horizon (which depends on the assumed yield at which the bond will sell at the end of the investment horizon)

More formally, the steps for computing a horizon return over some investment horizon are as follows.

**Step 1:** Compute the total coupon payments plus the interest-on-interest based on an assumed reinvestment rate. The reinvestment rate is one-half the annual interest rate that the investor believes can be earned on the reinvestment of coupon interest payments.

The total coupon payments plus interest on interest can be calculated using the formula for the future value of an annuity (given in the previous chapter) as shown:

$$\text{Coupon plus interest-on-interest} =$$
$$\text{Semiannual coupon} \left[ \frac{(1 + r)^h - 1}{r} \right]$$

where

$h =$ length of the investment horizon (in semiannual periods)
$r =$ assumed semiannual reinvestment rate

**Step 2:** Determine the projected sale price at the end of the investment horizon. The projected sale price will depend on the projected yield on comparable bonds at the end of the investment horizon.

**Step 3:** Add the values computed in steps 1 and 2. The sum is the *total future dollars* that will be received from the investment given the assumed reinvestment rate and projected required yield at the end of the investment horizon.

**Step 4:** To obtain the semiannual horizon return, use the following formula:[8]

$$\left( \frac{\text{Total future dollars}}{\text{Purchase price of bond}} \right)^{1/h} - 1$$

**Step 5:** Since coupon interest is assumed to be paid semiannually, double the interest rate found in step 4. The resulting interest rate is the horizon return expressed on a bond equivalent basis. Alternatively, the horizon return can be expressed on an effective annual interest rate basis by using the following formula:

$$(1 + \text{Semiannual horizon return})^2 - 1$$

***Illustration 12.***   Suppose that an investor with a 3-year investment horizon is considering purchasing a 20-year, 8 percent coupon bond for $828.40. The yield-to-maturity for this bond is 10 percent. The investor expects that he can reinvest the coupon interest payments at an annual interest of 6 percent and that at the end of the investment horizon the 17-year bond will be selling to offer a yield-to-maturity of 7 percent. The horizon return for this bond is computed in Exhibit 6–8.

Objections to the horizon return analysis cited by some portfolio managers are that it requires them to make assumptions about reinvestment rates and future yields and forces a portfolio manager to think in terms of an investment horizon. Unfortunately, some portfolio managers find comfort in meaningless measures such as the yield-to-maturity because it is not necessary to incorporate any expectations. The horizon return framework enables the portfolio manager to analyze the performance of a bond based on different interest rate scenarios for reinvestment rates and future market yields. By investigating multiple scenarios, the portfolio manager can see how sensitive the bond's performance is to each scenario. There is no need to assume that the reinvestment rate will be constant for the entire investment horizon.

For portfolio managers who want to use the market's expectations of short-term reinvestment rates and the yield on the bond at the end of the investment horizon, implied forward rates can be calculated from the yield curve. Implied forward rates are explained in Chapter 9 and are calculated based on arbitrage arguments. A horizon return computed using implied forward rates is called an *arbitrage-free horizon return.*

---

[8] This formula is the same formula as given in the previous chapter for calculating the yield on an investment when there is only one cash flow and, as expected, for calculating the yield on a zero coupon bond given earlier in this chapter.

**EXHIBIT 6–8**
**Illustration of Horizon Return Calculation**

**Assumptions:**

Bond = 8% 20-year bond selling for $828.40 (yield-to-maturity is 10%)
Annual reinvestment rate = 6%
Investment horizon = 3 years
Yield for 17-year bonds at end of investment horizon = 7%

**Step 1:** Compute the total coupon payments plus the interest-on-interest assuming an annual reinvestment rate of 6%, or 3% every six months. The coupon payments are $40 every six months for 3 years or 6 periods (the planned investment horizon). The total coupon interest plus interest-on-interest is

Coupon plus interest on interest =

$$\$40\left[\frac{(1.03)^6 - 1}{.03}\right] = \$258.74$$

**Step 2:** The projected sale price at the end of 3 years, assuming that the required yield-to-maturity for 17-year bonds is 7%, is found by determining the present value of 34 coupon payments of $40 plus the present value of the maturity value of $1,000, discounted at 3.5%. The price can be shown to be $1,098.51.

**Step 3:** Adding the amount in steps 1 and 2 gives total future dollars of $1,357.25.

**Step 4:** Compute the following:

$$\left(\frac{\$1,357.25}{\$828.40}\right)^{1/6} - 1$$
$$= (1.63840)^{.16667} - 1$$
$$= 1.0858 - 1$$
$$= .0858, \text{ or } 8.58\%$$

**Step 5:** Doubling 8.58% gives a horizon return of 17.16% on a bond equivalent basis. On an effective annual interest-rate basis, the horizon return is

$$(1.0858)^2 - 1$$
$$= 1.1790 - 1$$
$$= .1790$$
$$= 17.90\%$$

## Applications of Horizon Analysis

In the remainder of this section, we demonstrate how horizon analysis can be applied.

### Comparing Coupon and Zero Coupon Bonds

For managers of tax-exempt portfolios who intend to hold a bond until maturity, there is an analytical technique for assessing the relative value of the coupon and zero coupon bond. The technique is best presented by means of an illustration.[9]

Suppose that a portfolio manager is considering the following two 12-year bonds of the same quality rating: (1) a 12.6 percent coupon bond selling at par and (2) a zero coupon bond selling at 24.98 (per $100 par value). Both bonds are intended to be held to the maturity date, and therefore the investment horizon is 12 years. The yield-to-maturity for the zero coupon bond is 11.9 percent. Since no reinvestment of coupon payments is required, the horizon return is 11.9 percent. The horizon return for the 12.6 percent coupon bond will depend on the rate at which the coupon payments can be reinvested. We can determine the reinvestment rate that will produce the same total future dollars from both investments. This rate is called the *break-even reinvestment rate*.

Suppose that instead of investing $100 in the 12.6 percent coupon bond, the portfolio manager decides to invest in the zero coupon bond. The semi-annual yield-to-maturity is 5.95 percent; the $100 invested in the zero coupon bond will grow to $400 at the end of 24 periods (12 years).[10] If the portfolio manager places $100 in the 12.6 percent coupon bond, he will be indifferent between the zero coupon bond and the 12.6 percent bond if the latter produces total future dollars of $400. The total future dollars from holding an investment to maturity will be equal to the sum of (1) the coupon payments, (2) the maturity value, and (3) the interest-on-interest from reinvesting the coupon payment.

For the 12.6 percent coupon bond, the portfolio manager knows that for each $100 invested, $151.20 will be received from coupon payments (24 × $6.30) plus the maturity value of $100. Therefore, $251.20 ($151.20 + $100) will be received. For this bond to produce $400, interest-on-interest must equal $148.80 ($400 − $251.20). Alternatively, the coupon interest plus the interest-on-interest must equal $300. The future value of an annuity formula given above can be used to calculate the coupon plus interest-on-interest that will be realized from reinvesting the coupon payments at some reinvestment rate. The formula is as follows:

$$\text{Semiannual coupon} \left[ \frac{(1 + r)^h - 1}{r} \right]$$

In our illustration, we know that the semiannual coupon payment is $6.30 and the interest-on-interest should equal $300. Substituting these values into the above formula and a value of 24 for $h$, we have

---

[9] The reason we have focused on a tax-exempt portfolio is that there is a tax disadvantage for taxable zero coupon bonds. A taxable investor must pay taxes on accrued interest on a zero, even though no cash payment is made by the issuer until maturity. See Chapter 4.

[10] $100 (1.0595)^{24} = $400

$$300 = 6.30 \left[ \frac{(1 + r)^{24} - 1}{r} \right]$$

By trial and error, we can find the value for $r$ that will make the right side of the formula equal to $300. The semiannual break-even reinvestment rate would be 5.53 percent. Therefore, if the portfolio manager believes he or she can realize at least an 11.06 percent (2 × 5.53%) reinvestment rate, the 12.6 percent coupon bond will provide more future dollars than the zero coupon bond. If he or she expects to reinvest the coupon payments at a rate less than 11.06 percent, the zero coupon bond is a better investment since it will provide a higher horizon return.

The break-even reinvestment rate can be generalized to compare two coupon bonds with the same maturity.

### Comparing Municipal and Corporate Bonds

The conventional methodology for comparing the relative value of a tax-exempt municipal bond and a taxable corporate bond is to compute the *taxable equivalent yield*. The taxable equivalent yield is the yield that must be earned on a taxable bond in order to produce the same yield as a tax-exempt municipal bond. The formula is

$$\text{Taxable equivalent yield} = \frac{\text{Tax-exempt yield}}{1 - \text{Marginal tax rate}}$$

For example, suppose an investor in the 28 percent marginal tax bracket is considering a 10-year municipal bond with a yield-to-maturity of 7.2 percent. The taxable equivalent yield is

$$\frac{7.2\%}{1 - .28} = 10\%$$

If the yield-to-maturity offered on a comparable quality corporate bond with 10 years to maturity is more than 10 percent, those who use this approach would recommend that the corporate bond be purchased. If instead, a yield-to-maturity of less than 10 percent on a comparable corporate bond is offered, the investor should invest in the municipal bond.

What's wrong with this approach? The tax-exempt yield of the municipal bond and the taxable equivalent yield suffer from the same limitations that we discussed with respect to yield-to-maturity. Consider the difference in reinvestment opportunities for a corporate and a municipal bond. For the former, coupon payments will be taxed; therefore, the amount to be reinvested is not the entire coupon payment but an amount net of taxes. In contrast, since the coupon payments are free from taxes for a municipal bond, the entire coupon can be reinvested.

The horizon return framework can accommodate this situation by allowing us to explicitly incorporate the reinvestment opportunities. There is another advantage to the horizon return framework as compared to the conventional taxable equivalent yield approach. Changes in tax rates (either because the investor expects his or her tax rate to change or the tax structure to change) can be incorporated into the horizon return framework.

### Comparing Treasury Securities and Mortgage Pass-Through Securities

In Chapter 13, mortgage pass-through securities will be discussed. The difficulty with determining the yield for these securities is the uncertainty of cash flows because of prepayments. All yield measures for pass-through securities depend on the projected prepayments from the underlying pool of mortgages. Although we are running ahead of our game plan at this point, we can point out the problems with all of the yield measures for these securities. They assume that (1) the security is held until the last mortgage in the pool is paid off, (2) the cash flows (both coupon interest and principal repayment) can be reinvested at the yield calculated, and (3) the prepayments over the life of the security will be as projected. These assumptions are unrealistic, as is the resulting yield number. However, this meaningless yield number is then compared to the yield on a "comparable" Treasury security to determine the relative value of a pass-through and Treasury security. A better way to analyze pass-through securities is to calculate their expected horizon return. This requires a projection of prepayments over the investment horizon — a far less difficult task than projecting prepayments over the entire life of the security.

The application of the horizon (total) return framework to pass-through securities is provided in Chapter 27.

### Evaluating Potential Bond Swaps

Portfolio managers commonly swap an existing bond in a portfolio for another bond. Bond swaps can be categorized as follows: (1) pure yield pickup swaps, (2) substitution swaps, (3) intermarket spread swaps, and (4) rate anticipation swaps. Horizon return analysis can be used to assess the potential return from a swap.

1. *Pure yield pickup swap:* Switching from one bond to another that has a higher yield is called a pure yield pickup swap. The swap may be undertaken to achieve either higher current coupon income or higher yield to maturity, or both. No expectation is made about changes in interest rates, yield spreads, or credit quality.
2. *Rate anticipation swap:* A portfolio manager who has expectations about the future direction of interest rates will use bond swaps to position the

portfolio to take advantage of the anticipated interest rate move. These are known as rate anticipation swaps. If rates are expected to fall, for example, bonds with a greater price volatility will be swapped for existing bonds in the portfolio with lower price volatility (to take advantage of the larger change in price that will result if interest rates do in fact decline). The opposite will be done if rates are expected to rise.

3. *Intermarket Spread Swap* These swaps are undertaken when the portfolio manager believes that the current yield spread between two bonds in the market is out of line with its historical yield spread and that the yield spread will realign by the end of the investment horizon. Yields spreads between bonds exist for the following reasons: (1) there is a difference in the credit quality of bonds (for example, between Treasury bonds and double-A rated public utility bonds of the same maturity), or (2) there are differences in the features of corporate bonds that make them more or less attractive to investors (for example, callable and noncallable bonds, and putable and nonputable bonds).

4. *Substitution swap:* In a substitution swap a portfolio manager swaps one bond for another bond that is thought to be identical in terms of coupon, maturity, price sensitivity to interest rate changes, and credit quality but that offers a higher yield. This swap depends on a capital market imperfection. Such situations sometimes exist in the bond market because of temporary market imbalances. The risk that the portfolio manager faces is that the bond purchased may not be identical to the bond for which it is exchanged. For example, if credit quality is not the same, the bond purchased may be offering a higher yield because of higher credit risk rather than because of a market imbalance.

Horizon return analysis can be used to evaluate a substitution swap, as the following illustration demonstrates.

*Illustration 13.* Suppose that a tax-exempt pension portfolio includes a single-A rated, 10 percent, 18-year corporate bond selling at par. We'll call this bond A. Also suppose that the portfolio manager has the opportunity to swap into another bond, Bond B, that is also a single-A rated corporate bond but is selling at 100.41 to yield 10.2 percent. Bond B is a 10.25 percent coupon bond with 18.5 years to maturity. The portfolio manager believes that Bond B is cheap because it is offering a yield higher (10.2%) than Bond A (10%), a comparable quality corporate bond. The portfolio manager has an investment horizon of six months and expects that Bond B will fall into line with other single-A rated bonds by the end of the investment horizon. Let's assume that the next coupon payment for both bonds is exactly six months from now so that we need not consider reinvestment income.

Exhibit 6–9 shows the horizon return for both bonds for three assumed interest rate environments existing at the investment horizon (that is, six months from now): stable, falling 100 basis points, and rising 100 basis points.[11] For each interest rate environment, four yield spreads are shown. For the first, the yield spread is unchanged at 20 basis points (10.2% − 10%). The second yield spread is zero (i.e., Bond B's yield spread has moved in the direction anticipated by the portfolio manager). The third yield spread assumes a narrowing of the yield spread to 10 basis points, which represents a partial adjustment rather than the full adjustment anticipated by the portfolio manager. Finally, the last yield spread assumes that the yield spread widens to 30 basis points rather than narrowing as expected.

Under all interest rate environments, when the yield spread narrows, Bond B will outperform Bond A. However, if the yield spread widens, Bond A will outperform Bond B. Even if the spread is unchanged, Bond B will outperform Bond A.

Since we analyzed this swap from the perspective of a pension fund, the tax implications of selling Bond A are not considered because a pension fund is tax-exempt. Managers of taxable entities would have to undertake a more comprehensive analysis that takes into account any tax implications such as a realized gain or loss from the sale of Bond A.

## SUMMARY

In this chapter, the pricing of bonds and the calculation of various yield measures have been described. The price of a bond is equal to the present value of the cash flow expected. For bonds with embedded options, the cash flow is difficult to estimate. The required yield used to discount the cash flow is determined by the yield offered on comparable securities.

The two most popular yield measures cited in the bond market are the yield-to-maturity and yield-to-call. Both yield measures consider the coupon interest and any capital gain (or loss) at the maturity date or call date in the case of the yield-to-call. The coupon interest and capital gain (or loss), however, are only two of the three components of potential dollar return from owning

---

[11] Since there are no coupon payments to reinvest, the horizon return for both bonds can be computed as follows:

$$\frac{\text{Price six months from now at assumed yield} - \text{Initial price} + \text{Semiannual coupon}}{\text{Initial price}}$$

The semiannual coupon for Bond A is $5 and for B $5.125.

## EXHIBIT 6–9
## Analysis of a Substitution Swap

Held in Portfolio (Candidate for Sale): Bond A
 A single-A rated corporate, 10%, 18-year, selling at 100.00 to yield 10%

Candidate for Purchase: Bond B
 A single-A rated corporate, 10.25%, 18.5-year, selling at 100.41 to yield 10.2%

Investment Horizon: 6 months

Expectations:
 The buy candidate is currently mispriced (underpriced).
 The spread between the bond held in the portfolio and the buy candidate will be zero at the horizon date.

| | Bond A (Sell) | | | Bond B (Buy) | | |
|---|---|---|---|---|---|---|
| Spread (in basis points) | Yield (%) 10.0 | Price 100.00 | Horizon Return (%)* | Yield (%) 10.2 | Price 100.41 | Horizon Return (%)* |
| *Rates Stable* | | | | | | |
| Spread = 20 | 10.0 | 100.00 | 5.00 | 10.20 | 100.41 | 7.10 |
| Spread = 0 | 10.0 | 100.00 | 5.00 | 10.00 | 102.07 | 6.76 |
| Spread = 10 | 10.0 | 100.00 | 5.00 | 10.10 | 101.23 | 5.92 |
| Spread = 30 | 10.0 | 100.00 | 5.00 | 10.30 | 99.59 | 4.29 |
| *Falling Rates* | | | | | | |
| Spread = 20 | 9.0 | 108.73 | 13.73 | 9.20 | 109.15 | 13.81 |
| Spread = 0 | 9.0 | 108.73 | 13.73 | 9.00 | 111.04 | 15.69 |
| Spread = 10 | 9.0 | 108.73 | 13.73 | 9.10 | 110.09 | 14.74 |
| Spread = 30 | 9.0 | 108.73 | 13.73 | 9.30 | 108.23 | 12.89 |
| *Rising Rates* | | | | | | |
| Spread = 20 | 11.0 | 92.30 | −2.70 | 11.20 | 92.71 | −2.56 |
| Spread = 0 | 11.0 | 92.30 | −2.70 | 11.00 | 94.17 | −1.11 |
| Spread = 10 | 11.0 | 92.30 | −2.70 | 11.10 | 93.44 | −1.84 |
| Spread = 30 | 11.0 | 92.30 | −2.70 | 11.30 | 91.99 | −3.28 |

* Since there are no coupon payments to reinvest, the horizon return for both bonds can be computed as follows:

 *(Price 6 months from now at assumed yield − Initial price + Semiannual coupon) + Initial price*

The semiannual coupon for Bond A is $5 and for Bond B $5.125.

a bond until it matures or is called. The other component is the reinvestment of coupon income, commonly referred to as the interest-on-interest component. This component can be as large as 80 percent of a bond's total dollar return. The yield-to-maturity assumes that the coupon payments can be reinvested at the calculated yield-to-maturity. The yield-to-call assumes that the coupon payments can be reinvested at the calculated yield-to-call.

A better measure for measuring the potential return from holding a bond over a predetermined investment horizon is the horizon return measure. This measure considers all three sources of potential dollar return and can be used to analyze bond swaps.

# CHAPTER 7

---

# PRICE VOLATILITY
# CHARACTERISTICS OF
# FIXED INCOME SECURITIES

---

*Frank J. Fabozzi, Ph.D., CFA*
*Visiting Professor of Finance*
*Sloan School of Management*
*Massachusetts Institute of Technology*
*and*
*Editor, The Journal of Portfolio Management*

*Mark Pitts, Ph.D.*
*Senior Vice President*
*Lehman Brothers*

*Ravi E. Dattatreya, Ph.D.*
*Senior Vice President*
*Sumitomo Bank Capital Markets, Inc.*

---

To effectively employ fixed income portfolio strategies, it is necessary to understand the price volatility and convexity of bonds.[1] The purpose of this chapter is to explain and illustrate these concepts. First, we explain the characteristics of a bond that affect its price volatility. Second, we describe several measures of bond price volatility—price value of a basis point, yield value of 1/32, and duration. We then look at how the convexity of a bond affects its price volatility and show how to use these concepts in a typical application. Finally, we extend the concepts of duration and convexity to callable bonds.

---

[1] For convenience, this discussion focuses on bonds. However, in most cases the discussion applies to fixed income securities in general.

# PRICE/YIELD RELATIONSHIP
# FOR OPTION-FREE BONDS

A fundamental principle of an option-free bond (that is, a bond that does not have an embedded option) is that the price of a bond changes in the opposite direction of the change in the yield of the bond. This principle follows from the fact that the price of an option-free bond is equal to the present value of its expected cash flows. An increase (decrease) in the yield decreases (increases) the present value of its scheduled cash flows, and, therefore, the bond's price. Exhibit 7–1 illustrates this property for the following four bonds: (1) a 9 percent coupon bond with 5 years to maturity, (2) a 9 percent coupon bond with 20 years to maturity, (3) a 5 percent coupon bond with 5 years to maturity, and (4) a 5 percent coupon bond with 20 years to maturity.

If the price/yield relationship for any option-free bond is graphed, it would exhibit the shape shown in Exhibit 7–2. Notice that, as the yield rises, the price of the option-free bond declines. However, the relationship is not linear (that is, it is not a straight line). The shape of the price/yield relationship for any option-free bond is referred to as *convex,* meaning that it is bowed toward the origin. As we shall see, convexity implies that prices rise at an increasing rate as yields fall and that prices decline at a decreasing rate as yields rise. Obviously, with other factors equal, convexity is a positive attribute of a fixed income security.

Keep in mind that a given price/yield relationship may be appropriate only at a given point in the life of the bond. As a bond moves

**Exhibit 7–1**
**Price/Yield Relationship for Four Hypothetical Bonds**

| | Price at Given Yield | | | |
| | Coupon/Maturity | | | |
| Yield | 9%/5yr | 9%/20yr | 5%/5yr | 5%/20yr |
|---|---|---|---|---|
| 6.00% | 112.7953 | 134.6722 | 95.7349 | 88.4426 |
| 7.00 | 108.3166 | 121.3551 | 91.6834 | 78.6449 |
| 8.00 | 104.0554 | 109.8964 | 87.8337 | 70.3108 |
| 8.50 | 102.0027 | 104.7693 | 85.9809 | 66.6148 |
| 8.90 | 100.3966 | 100.9267 | 84.5322 | 63.8593 |
| 8.99 | 100.0396 | 100.0921 | 84.2102 | 63.2626 |
| 9.00 | 100.0000 | 100.0000 | 84.1746 | 63.1968 |
| 9.01 | 99.9604 | 99.9081 | 84.1389 | 63.1311 |
| 9.10 | 99.6053 | 99.0865 | 83.8187 | 62.5445 |
| 9.50 | 98.0459 | 95.5592 | 82.4132 | 60.0332 |
| 10.00 | 96.1391 | 91.4205 | 80.6957 | 57.1023 |
| 11.00 | 92.4624 | 83.9539 | 77.3871 | 51.8616 |
| 12.00 | 88.9599 | 77.4306 | 74.2397 | 47.3380 |

**EXHIBIT 7–2**
**Price/Yield Relationship**

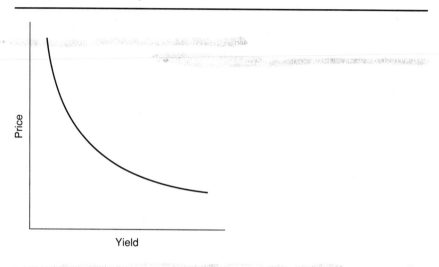

toward maturity, two factors influence the price of any option-free bond. First, the bond's price changes as the yield changes, as we previously discussed. Second, for discount and premium bonds, the bond's price changes even if yields remain the same. In particular, with yields held constant, the price of a discount bond increases as it moves toward maturity, reaching par value at the maturity date; for a premium bond, the bond's price will decrease as it moves closer to maturity, finally declining to the par value at the maturity date.

## BOND PRICE VOLATILITY

Although the prices of all option-free bonds move in the opposite direction of the change in yields, neither dollar price changes nor percentage price changes are the same for all bonds. For our four hypothetical bonds, this can be seen in Exhibit 7–3. The top panel of the exhibit shows the dollar price change and the bottom panel shows the percentage price change for various changes in the yield assuming that the initial yield for all four bonds starts at 9 percent. Note from Exhibit 7–3 that for a given bond the absolute dollar price change and the absolute percentage price change are not the same for an equal increase and decrease in the yield, except for very small changes in the yield. Even for a small change in yield, the absolute dollar price change is less symmetric than the percentage price change. In general, the dollar price and percentage price increases when

**EXHIBIT 7–3**

**Instantaneous Dollar and Percentage Price Changes for Four Hypothetical Bonds**

Four hypothetical bonds, priced initially to yield 9%:

9% coupon, 5 years to maturity, price  = 100.0000
9% coupon, 20 years to maturity, price = 100.0000
5% coupon, 5 years to maturity, price  =  84.1746
5% coupon, 20 years to maturity, price =  63.1968

*Dollar Price Change Per $100 Par*

| Yield Change to | Change in Basis Points | Coupon/Maturity | | | |
|---|---|---|---|---|---|
| | | 9%/5yr | 9%/20yr | 5%/5yr | 5%/20yr |
| 6.00% | −300 | $12.7953 | $34.6722 | $11.5603 | $25.2458 |
| 7.00 | −200 | 8.3166 | 21.3551 | 7.5088 | 15.4481 |
| 8.00 | −100 | 4.0554 | 9.8964 | 3.6591 | 7.1140 |
| 8.50 | −50 | 2.0027 | 4.7693 | 1.8063 | 3.4180 |
| 8.90 | −10 | 0.3966 | 0.9267 | 0.3576 | 0.6625 |
| 8.99 | −1 | 0.0396 | 0.0921 | 0.0356 | 0.0658 |
| 9.01 | 1 | −0.0396 | −0.0919 | −0.0357 | −0.0657 |
| 9.10 | 10 | −0.3947 | −0.9135 | −0.3559 | −0.6523 |
| 9.50 | 50 | −1.9541 | −4.4408 | −1.7614 | −3.1636 |
| 10.00 | 100 | −3.8609 | −8.5795 | −3.4789 | −6.0945 |
| 11.00 | 200 | −7.5376 | −16.0461 | −6.7875 | −11.3352 |
| 12.00 | 300 | −11.0401 | −22.5694 | −9.9349 | −15.8588 |

the yield declines are greater than the dollar price and percentage price decreases when the yield increases.

These two observations—the absolute and percentage price change not being equal for all bonds, and the asymmetry in the absolute and percentage price change for equal changes in yield—are explained by the characteristics of the bond that determine the shape of the price/yield relationship depicted in Exhibit 7–2. The remainder of this section will explain the characteristics that account for the first observation. Later in this chapter, we'll provide an explanation for the second observation. Now, as the following sections show, there are two characteristics of an option-free bond that are the primary determinants of its price volatility: coupon and term-to-maturity.[2]

---

[2] The time to the first coupon payment as well as the frequency of payments (monthly, semiannual, or annual) also have a small effect.

**EXHIBIT 7–3—Continued**

| Yield Change to | Change in Basis Points | Percentage Price Change Coupon/Maturity | | | |
|---|---|---|---|---|---|
| | | 9%/5yr | 9%/20yr | 5%/5yr | 5%/20yr |
| 6.00% | −300 | 12.80% | 34.67% | 13.73% | 39.95% |
| 7.00 | −200 | 8.32 | 21.36 | 9.92 | 24.44 |
| 8.00 | −100 | 4.06 | 9.90 | 4.35 | 11.26 |
| 8.50 | −50 | 2.00 | 4.77 | 2.15 | 5.41 |
| 8.90 | −10 | 0.40 | 0.93 | 0.42 | 1.05 |
| 8.99 | −1 | 0.04 | 0.09 | 0.04 | 0.10 |
| 9.01 | 1 | −0.04 | −0.09 | −0.04 | −0.10 |
| 9.10 | 10 | −0.40 | −0.91 | −0.42 | −1.03 |
| 9.50 | 50 | −1.95 | −4.44 | −2.09 | −5.01 |
| 10.00 | 100 | −3.86 | −8.58 | −4.13 | −9.64 |
| 11.00 | 200 | −7.54 | −16.05 | −8.06 | −17.94 |
| 12.00 | 300 | −11.04 | −22.57 | −11.89 | −25.09 |

## Volatility in Terms of Percentage Price Change

First, let's look at bond price volatility in terms of *percentage* price change for a change in yields.

For a given term to maturity and initial market yield, the percentage price volatility of a bond is greater the lower the coupon rate. This property can be seen by comparing the 9 percent and 5 percent coupon bonds with the same maturity (see the second panel of Exhibit 7–3). For example, if the initial market yield for the two 20-year bonds is 9 percent and the yield rises to 11 percent (that is, a 200 basis point increase), the 9 percent coupon bond will fall in price from 100 to 83.9539, a decline of 16.05 percent. However, the 5 percent 20-year bond will fall by 17.94 percent, from 63.1968 to 51.8616.

The second characteristic of a bond that affects its price volatility is its term-to-maturity. For a given coupon rate and initial yield, the longer the term-to-maturity, the greater the price volatility in terms of percentage price change.[3] This can be seen in the lower panel of Exhibit 7–3 by comparing the 5-year bonds to the 20-year bonds with the same coupon. For example, if the yield increases 200 basis points from 9 percent to 11 percent, the 9 percent 20-year bond's price will fall by 16.05 percent (100 to 83.9539), whereas the 9 percent 5-year bond will fall by only 7.54 percent (100 to 92.4624).

---

[3] There are rare exceptions for certain deep-discount, long-term coupon bonds.

## Volatility in Terms of Dollar Price Change

Do the same properities hold if volatility is measured in terms of dollar price change rather than percentage price change? The first panel of Exhibit 7–3 demonstrates that holding all other factors constant, the dollar price change is greater the longer the term-to-maturity. However, the first characteristic concerning the effect of the coupon rate is not true when volatility is measured in terms of dollar price change instead of percentage price change. In terms of dollar price change for a given maturity and initial market yield, the lower the coupon rate the smaller the dollar price change.

## The Effects of Yield-to-Maturity

We cannot ignore the fact that due to credit considerations different bonds trade at different yields, even if they have the same coupon and maturity. How, then, holding other factors constant, does the yield-to-maturity affect a bond's price volatility? As it turns out, an increase in yield decreases the percentage price change and the absolute dollar price change. To see this, we can compare a 9 percent 20-year bond initially selling at a yield of 9 percent, and a 9 percent 20-year bond initially selling at a yield of 14 percent. The former is initially at a price of 100, and the latter carries a price of 66.6707. Now, if the yields on both bonds increase by 100 basis points, the first bond trades down by 8.5795 points (8.5795%). After rates increase, the second bond will trade at a price of 62.2168, for a price decline of only 4.4540 (or 6.6805%). Thus, we see that the bond that trades at lower yields is more volatile in both percentage price changes and absolute price changes, as long as the other bond characteristics are the same.

A possibly more relevant comparison of bond price volatility is that of comparing bonds that trade at different yields but starting them all on the same footing (e.g., by comparing only bonds trading at par). For par bonds trading at different yields but with the same maturity, the lower yielding bonds still exhibit both greater percentage price changes and absolute price changes for a given change in yield.

## MEASURES OF BOND PRICE VOLATILITY

Money managers, arbitrageurs, and traders need to have a way to measure a bond's price volatility to implement hedging and trading strategies. Three measures that are commonly employed are (1) price value of a basis point, (2) yield value of a price change, and (3) duration.

## Price Value of a Basis Point

The *price value of a basis point (PVBP)*, also referred to as the *dollar value of an 01 (DV01)*, is the change in the price of the bond if the yield changes by 1 basis point. Typically, the price value of a basis point is expressed as the absolute value of the change in price; consequently, the greater the price value of a basis point, the greater the dollar price volatility. As we saw earlier in this chapter, price changes are almost symmetric for small changes in yield. Thus, it does not make a great deal of difference whether we increase or decrease yields to calculate the price value of a basis point.

We will illustrate the calculation of the price value of a basis point using the four bonds in Exhibits 7–1 and 7–3. For each bond, the initial price, the price after increasing the yield by 1 basis point (from 9% to 9.01%) and the price value of a basis point (the difference between the two prices) are shown in Exhibit 7–4.

Similarly, if we decrease the yield by 1 basis point, from 9 percent to 8.99 percent, we would find approximately the same price value of a basis point for the four bonds, as shown in Exhibit 7–5.

Some investors calculate the price value of more than 1 basis point. The principle of calculating the price value of any number of basis points is the same. For example, the price value of 10 basis points is found by computing the difference between the initial price and the price if the yield changed by 10 basis points. From the first panel of Exhibit 7–3, we can see that the price value of 10 basis points for the 5-year 9 percent coupon bond is 0.3947 per $100 par when the yield increases from 9 percent to 9.10 percent because the price decreases from 100 to 99.6053. Notice that the relationship is still nearly symmetric for a 10 basis point change in yield up or down and that the price value of 10 basis points is approximately equal to 10 times the price value of 1 basis point. However, for larger changes in yield, there will be a difference between the price value of a basis point if the yield is increased or decreased,

**EXHIBIT 7–4**
**Price Value of a Basis Point for Four Hypothetical Bonds**

| Bond | Initial Price 9% Yield* | Price at 9.01% Yield* | Price Value of a Basis Point[†] |
|---|---|---|---|
| 5-year 9% coupon | 100.0000 | 99.9604 | 0.0396 |
| 20-year 9% coupon | 100.0000 | 99.9081 | 0.0919 |
| 5-year 5% coupon | 84.1746 | 84.1389 | 0.0357 |
| 20-year 5% coupon | 63.1968 | 63.1311 | 0.0657 |

\* Price per $100 par to four decimal places.
† Absolute value per $100 of par value.

**EXHIBIT 7–5**
**Price Value of a Basis Point for Four Hypothetical Bonds**

| Bond | Initial Price 9% Yield | Price at 8.99% Yield | Price Value of a Basis Point |
|------|------------------------|----------------------|------------------------------|
| 5-year 9% coupon | 100.0000 | 100.0396 | 0.0396 |
| 20-year 9% coupon | 100.0000 | 100.0921 | 0.0921 |
| 5-year 5% coupon | 84.1746 | 84.2102 | 0.0356 |
| 20-year 5% coupon | 63.1968 | 63.2626 | 0.0658 |

and the price change for a large number of basis points no longer approximates the multiple times 1 basis point. Most investors who derive the price values of a basis point by calculating price changes for large movements in yields (such as 100 basis points), will average the PVBPs for an up move and a down move to get the final PVBP.

## Yield Value of a Price Change

Another measure of the price volatility of a bond used by many investors is the change in the yield for a specified price change. This is done by first calculating the bond's current yield to maturity, and then recalculating the yield if the bond's price is increased by $X$ dollars. Then the difference between the initial yield and the new yield is the yield value of an $X$ dollar price change. The lower is the yield value of an $X$ dollar price change, the greater is the dollar price volatility. The reason for this is that it would take a smaller change in yield to produce a price change of $X$ dollars.

As Treasury notes and bonds are quoted in 1/32 of a percentage point of par, investors in these markets usually let $X$ equal 1/32 of a percentage point of par and calculate the *yield value of a 32nd*. The yield values of a 32nd for the two 9 percent coupon bonds are shown in Exhibit 7–6, assuming that the price is decreased by 1/32.

**EXHIBIT 7–6**
**Yield Values of a 32nd for Two 9% Coupon Bonds**

| Bond | Initial Price − 1/32* | Yield at New Price | Initial Yield | Yield Value of 1/32 |
|------|------------------------|---------------------|----------------|---------------------|
| 5-year 9% coupon | 99.96875 | 9.0079% | 9.0000% | 0.0079% |
| 20-year 9% coupon | 99.96875 | 9.0034 | 9.0000 | 0.0034 |

*Initial price of 100 minus 1/32 of 1%

**EXHIBIT 7–7**
**Yield Values of an 8th for Two 9% Coupon Bonds**

| Bond | Initial Price−1/8* | Yield at New Price | Initial Yield | Yield Value of 1/8 |
|---|---|---|---|---|
| 5-year 9% coupon | 99.8750 | 9.032% | 9.000% | 0.032% |
| 20-year 9% coupon | 99.8750 | 9.014 | 9.000 | 0.012 |

*Initial price of 100 minus 1/8 of 1%

Notice that the yield value of a 32nd for the 20-year bond is lower than the 5-year bond. This agrees with our statement that the lower the yield value of an $X$ dollar price change, the greater the dollar price volatility.

Corporate bonds and municipal bonds are traded in 1/8 increments of a percentage point of par. Consequently, investors in these markets might be more concerned with the *yield value* of an 8th. The calculation of the yield value of an 8th for the two 9 percent coupon bonds is shown in Exhibit 7–7, assuming that price is decreased by 1/8.

## Duration

Another measure of the price volatility of fixed income securities is *duration*. First formulated by Frederick Macaulay in 1938,[4] duration is a weighted average term-to-maturity of the security's cash flows. The weights are the present values of each cash flow as a percent of the present value of all cash flows (i.e., the weights are the present value of each cash flow as a percent of the bond's full price). As we shall see, the greater the duration of a bond, the greater its percentage price volatility.

Mathematically, Macaulay duration *on a coupon date* is computed as follows:

$$\text{Macaulay duration (in years)} =$$

$$\sum_{t=1}^{n} \frac{t \times \text{PVCF}_t}{k \times \text{PVTCF}}$$

or

$$\frac{1 \times \text{PVCF}_1 + 2 \times \text{PVCF}_2 + 3 \times \text{PVCF}_3 + \ldots + n \times \text{PVCF}_n}{k \times \text{PVTCF}}$$

---

[4] Frederick Macaulay, *Some Theoretical Problems Suggested by the Movement of Interest Rates, Bond Yields, and Stock Prices in the U.S. Since 1856* (New York: National Bureau of Economic Research, 1938).

where

| | | |
|---|---|---|
| $k$ | = | number of periods, or payments, per year (such as $k = 2$ for semiannual pay bonds, $k = 12$ for monthly pay bonds, and so on) |
| $n$ | = | number of periods until maturity (specifically, number of years to maturity times $k$) |
| $t$ | = | the period when the cash flow is expected to be received ($t = 1,\ldots, n$) |
| $PVCF_t$ | = | the present value of the cash flow in period $t$ discounted at the yield-to-maturity |
| $PVTCF$ | = | the total present value of the cash flow of the bond where the present value is determined using the yield-to-maturity. This is simply the price of the bond |

For an option-free bond on a coupon date with semiannual payments, the cash flow for periods 1 through $n - 1$ is one-half the annual coupon interest. The cash flow in period $n$ is the semiannual coupon interest plus the maturity value. The formula can be easily extended to fractional periods when a bond is not on its coupon date.

For a bond selling on its coupon date, the total present value of the cash flows is simply the quoted price (or flat price) of the bond. For a bond not selling on a coupon date, the total present value of the cash flows is the bond's quoted price plus accrued interest. The presence of $k$ in the denominator is to adjust for the frequency of payments per year.

Exhibit 7–8 shows the details involved in calculating the Macaulay duration for the 9 percent 5-year bond selling at 100 to yield 9 percent. The Macaulay duration for the four bonds is given in Exhibit 7–9, assuming a yield to maturity of 9 percent for each.

As can be seen from Exhibit 7–9, the Macaulay duration of a coupon bond is less than its maturity. For a zero coupon bond, the Macaulay duration is equal to its maturity. With other factors held constant, the lower the coupon rate, the greater the duration of the bond.

Notice the consistency between the properties of percentage price volatility discussed earlier and the properties of duration. We showed that with all other factors constant, the longer the maturity, the greater the percentage price volatility. A property of duration is that with all other factors constant, the greater the maturity, the greater the duration will normally be.[5] We also showed that the lower the coupon rate, all other factors constant, the greater will be the percentage price volatility. As we just noted, generally the lower the coupon rate, the greater will be the duration. It appears that duration is telling us something about bond price volatility.

---

[5] This property does not necessarily hold for long-maturity, deep-discount coupon bonds.

**EXHIBIT 7–8**
**Calculation of Duration for 9% 5-Year Bond**

Coupon rate = 9.00%
Term (years) = 5
Yield-to-maturity = 9.00%
Price = 100

| Period (t) | Cash Flow* | PV of $1 at 4.5% | PVCF$_t$ | t×PVCF$_t$ |
|---|---|---|---|---|
| 1 | $ 4.50 | 0.956937 | 4.306220 | 4.30622 |
| 2 | 4.50 | 0.915729 | 4.120785 | 8.24156 |
| 3 | 4.50 | 0.876296 | 3.943335 | 11.83000 |
| 4 | 4.50 | 0.838561 | 3.773526 | 15.09410 |
| 5 | 4.50 | 0.802451 | 3.611030 | 18.05514 |
| 6 | 4.50 | 0.767895 | 3.455531 | 20.73318 |
| 7 | 4.50 | 0.734828 | 3.306728 | 23.14709 |
| 8 | 4.50 | 0.703185 | 3.164333 | 25.31466 |
| 9 | 4.50 | 0.672904 | 3.028070 | 27.25262 |
| 10 | 104.50 | 0.643927 | 67.290443 | 672.90442 |
| Total | | | 100.000000 | 826.87899 |

$$\text{Macaulay duration} = \frac{826.87899}{2(100)} = 4.13$$

*Cash flow per $100 of par value.

The relationship between Macaulay duration and bond price volatility is[6]

$$\text{Percentage change in price} =$$

$$\frac{-1}{\left(1 + \dfrac{\text{Yield}}{k}\right)} \times \text{Macaulay duration} \times \text{Yield change} \times 100$$

The relationship is exact for infinitesimal changes in yields, but is only approximate for larger changes.

Generally, the first two expressions on the right-hand side in this equation are combined into one term and called *modified duration;* that is,

$$\text{Modified duration} = \frac{\text{Macaulay duration}}{\left(1 + \dfrac{\text{Yield}}{k}\right)}$$

[6] Mathematically, the relationship is obtained by taking the first derivative of the price function then dividing it by price. See Frank J. Fabozzi, *Fixed Income Mathematics* (Chicago: Probus Publishing, 1988), Appendix A.

**EXHIBIT 7–9**
**Macaulay Duration for the Hypothetical Sample Bonds**

| Coupon | Maturity | Macaulay Duration |
|--------|----------|-------------------|
| 9% | 5 years | 4.13 years |
| 9% | 20 years | 9.61 years |
| 5% | 5 years | 4.43 years |
| 5% | 20 years | 10.87 years |

The relationship can then be expressed as follows:

Percentage price change $= -$Modified duration $\times$ Yield change $\times$ 100

To illustrate the relationship consider the 5 percent 20-year bond selling at 63.1968 to yield 9 percent. The Macaulay duration for this bond is 10.87 years. Modified duration is 10.40, as shown here:

$$\text{Modified duration} = \frac{10.87}{(1 + \frac{.09}{2})} = 10.40$$

If yields increase instantaneously from 9.00 percent to 9.10 percent, a yield change in decimal form of $+0.0010$, the formula above indicates that the percentage price change is

$$-10.40 \times (+.0010) \times 100 = -1.04\%$$

Notice from the second panel of Exhibit 7–3 that the actual percentage price change is $-1.03$ percent. Similarly, if yields decrease instantaneously from 9.00 percent to 8.90 percent (a 10 basis point decrease), the formula indicates that the percentage change in price would be $+1.04$ percent. From the second panel of Exhibit 7–3, the actual percentage price change would be $+1.05$ percent. This example illustrates that for small changes in yield, duration provides a good approximation of the percentage price change.

Instead of a small change in yield, let's assume that yields increase by 200 basis points, from 9 percent to 11 percent (a yield change of $+0.02$). The percentage change in price estimated using duration would be

$$-10.40 \times (+0.02) \times 100 = -20.80\%$$

How good is this approximation? As can be seen from the second panel of Exhibit 7–3, the actual percentage change in price is only $-17.94$ percent. Moreover, if the yield decreased by 200 basis points from 9 percent to 7 percent, the approximate percentage price change based on duration would be $+20.80$

percent, compared to an actual percentage price change of $+24.44$ percent. Thus, not only is the approximation off, but we can see that duration estimates a symmetric percentage change in price that, as we pointed earlier in this chapter, is not a property of the price/yield relationship for most fixed income securities.

Notice that for a 100 basis point change in yield, the formula tells us that the percentage price change will be equal to the bond's modified duration. While modified duration shows percentage price change, *dollar duration* shows the dollar price change of a bond and is calculated by multiplying modified duration by the bond's price.

The various measures of bond price volatility and their relationships to one another are summarized in Exhibit 7–10.

**EXHIBIT 7–10**

**Measures of Bond Price Volatility and Their Relationships to One Another**

*Notation:*

$D$ = Macaulay duration
$D^*$ = modified duration
PVBP = price value of a basis point
YV32 = yield value of a 32nd
$y$ = yield-to-maturity in decimal form
$Y$ = yield-to-maturity in percentage terms ($Y = 100 \times y$)
$P$ = price of bond
$k$ = number of coupons per year

*Relationships*

$D^* = \frac{D}{(1+y/k)}$      by definition

$\frac{\Delta P/P}{\Delta y} \approx D^*$      to a close approximation for small $\Delta y$

$\Delta P/\Delta Y \approx$ slope of price/yield curve      to a close approximation for small $\Delta Y$

$PVPB \approx \Delta P/(\Delta Y \times 100)$      to a close approximation for small $\Delta Y$

$PVBP \approx \frac{D^* \times P}{10000}$      to a close approximation (also called *dollar duration*)

$YV32 \approx \frac{1}{3200 \times PVBP}$      to a close approximation (when the yield is in percentage terms)

$PVBP \approx \frac{1}{3200 \times YV32}$      to a close approximation (when the yield is in percentage terms)

*For bonds at or near par:*

$PVBP \approx D^*/100$      to a close approximation

$D^* \approx \Delta P/\Delta Y$      to a close approximation for small $\Delta Y$

## CONVEXITY

We're now ready to tie together the price/yield relationship and several of the properties of bond price volatility discussed in this chapter. Recall the shape of the price/yield relationship, as shown in Exhibit 7–2. We referred to that shape as convex.

In Exhibit 7–11, a tangent line is drawn to the price/yield relationship at yield $y^*$. The tangent shows the rate of change of price with respect to a change in interest rates at that point (yield level). The slope of the tangent line is closely related to the price value of a basis point. Consequently, for a given starting price, the tangent (which tells us the rate of absolute price changes) is closely related to the duration of the bond (which tells us about the rate of percentage of price changes). The steeper the tangent line, the greater the duration; the flatter the tangent line, the lower the duration. Thus, for a given starting price, the tangent line and the duration can be used interchangeably and can be thought of as one and the same method of estimating the rate of price changes.

Notice what happens to duration (steepness of the tangent line) as yield changes: As yield increases (decreases), duration decreases (increases). This property holds for all option-free bonds.

**EXHIBIT 7–11**
**Line Tangent to the Price/Yield Curve**

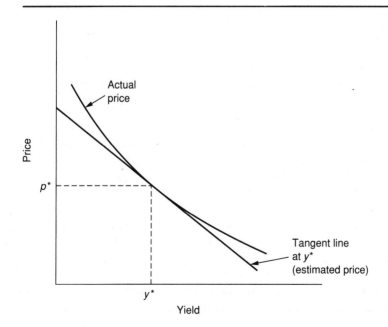

**EXHIBIT 7–12**
**Price Approximation Using Duration**

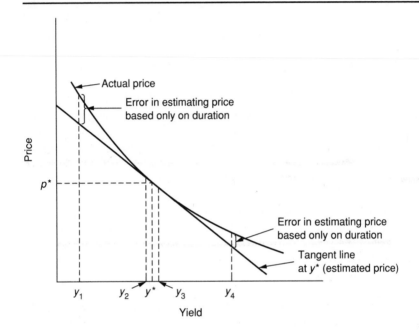

If we draw a vertical line from any yield (on the horizontal axis), as in Exhibit 7–12, the distance between the horizontal axis and the tangent line represents the price approximated by using duration starting with the initial yield $y^*$. The approximation will always understate the actual price. This agrees with what we demonstrated earlier about the relationship between duration (and the tangent line) and the approximate price change. When yields decrease, the estimated price change will be less than the actual price change, thereby underestimating the actual price change. On the other hand, when yields increase, the estimated price change will be greater than the actual price change, resulting in an overestimate for the actual price change and an underestimate of the actual price.

For small changes in yield, the tangent line and duration do a good job in estimating the actual price. However, the further away from the initial yield $y^*$, the worse the approximation. It should be apparent that the accuracy of the approximation depends on the convexity of the price/yield relationship for the bond.

The convexity of an option-free fixed income security *on a coupon date* can be calculated using the following formula:

$$\text{Convexity (in years)} = \frac{1}{(1 + \text{yield}/k)^2} \sum_{t=1}^{n} \frac{t \times (t + 1)\text{PVCF}}{k \times k \times \text{PVTCF}}$$

or

$$\frac{1 \times 2 \times \text{PVCF}_1 + 2 \times 3 \times \text{PVCF}_2 + \ldots + n \times (n + 1) \times \text{PVCF}_n}{(1 + \text{yield}/k)^2 \times (k \times k \times \text{PVTCF})}$$

where

| | | |
|---|---|---|
| $k$ | $=$ | number of periods, or payments, per year ($k = 2$ for semiannual pay bonds, $k = 12$ for monthly pay bonds, etc.) |
| $n$ | $=$ | number of periods until maturity (specifically, number of years to maturity times $k$) |
| $t$ | $=$ | the period when the cash flow is expected to be received ($t = 1,\ldots, n$) |
| $\text{PVCF}_t$ | $=$ | the present value of the cash flow in period $t$ discounted at the yield-to-maturity |
| $\text{PVTCF}$ | $=$ | the total present value of the cash flow of the bond where the present value is determined using the yield-to-maturity. This is the price of the bond. |

In Exhibit 7–13, we show the detailed calculations for the convexity of the 9 percent 5-year bond selling at 100 to yield 9 percent. The convexity for the four bonds in Exhibit 7–1 is summarized in Exhibit 7–14.

Duration provides a first approximation to the percentage price change. Convexity provides a second approximation, based on the following relationship.[7]

Approximate percentage price change due to convexity =

$$\tfrac{1}{2} \times \text{Convexity} \times (\text{Yield change})^2 \times 100$$

Here the formula gives only an approximation of that part of the price change that is due solely to the curvature of the price/yield relationship.

For example, for the 5 percent coupon bond maturing in 20 years, the approximate percentage price change due solely to convexity if the yield increases from 9 percent to 11 percent (+0.02 yield change) is

$$\frac{1}{2} \times 160.86 \times (0.02)^2 \times 100 = 3.22\%$$

---

[7] Mathematically this is derived from the second term of the Taylor series for the price function. See Appendix A in Fabozzi, *Fixed Income Mathematics*.

**EXHIBIT 7–13**
**Calculation of Convexity for 9% 5-Year Bond**

Coupon rate = 9.00%
Term (years) = 5
Yield-to-maturity = 9.00%
Price = 100

| Period (t) | $t(t + 1)$ | Cash Flow* | $PVCF_t$ | $t \times (t + 1) \times PVCF_t$ |
|---|---|---|---|---|
| 1 | 2 | $ 4.50 | 4.306220 | 8.6124 |
| 2 | 6 | 4.50 | 4.120785 | 24.7242 |
| 3 | 12 | 4.50 | 3.943335 | 47.3196 |
| 4 | 20 | 4.50 | 3.773526 | 75.4700 |
| 5 | 30 | 3.40 | 3.611030 | 108.3300 |
| 6 | 42 | 4.50 | 3.455531 | 145.1310 |
| 7 | 56 | 4.50 | 3.306728 | 185.1752 |
| 8 | 72 | 4.50 | 3.164333 | 227.8296 |
| 9 | 90 | 4.50 | 3.028070 | 272.5290 |
| 10 | 110 | 104.50 | 67.290443 | 7,401.9440 |
| Total | | | 100.000000 | 8,497.0650 |

$$\text{Convexity} = \frac{8,497.065}{(1.045)^2(2)(2)(100)} = 19.45$$

*Cash flow per $100 of par value.

If the yield decreases from 9 percent to 7 percent ($-0.02$ yield change) the approximate percentage price change due solely to convexity would also be 3.22 percent.

The approximate total percentage price change based on both duration and convexity is found by simply adding the two estimates. For example, if yields change from 9 percent to 11 percent, the approximate percentage price change would be:

**EXHIBIT 7–14**
**Convexity of the Four Hypothetical Sample Bonds**

| Coupon | Maturity | Convexity |
|---|---|---|
| 9% | 5 years | 19.45 |
| 9% | 20 years | 131.34 |
| 5% | 5 years | 21.38 |
| 5% | 20 years | 160.86 |

$$\text{Duration} = -20.80\%$$
$$\text{Convexity} = \underline{+3.22\%}$$
$$\text{Total} = -17.58\%$$

Recall that the actual percentage price change was $-17.94$ percent. For a decrease of 200 basis points, from 9 percent to 7 percent the approximate percentage price change would be as follows:

$$\text{Duration} = +20.80\%$$
$$\text{Convexity} = \underline{+3.22\%}$$
$$\text{Total} = +24.02\%$$

The actual percentage price change was $+24.44$ percent. Consequently, for large yield movements, a better approximation for bond price movement is obtained using both duration and convexity.

What is convexity measuring? It is measuring the rate of change of duration as yields change. For all option-free fixed income securities, duration increases as yields decline. This is a positive attribute of an option-free fixed income security because as yields decline, price appreciation accelerates. When yield increases, the duration for all option-free bonds will decrease. Once again, this is a positive attribute because as yields decline, this feature will decelerate the price depreciation. This is the reason why the absolute and percentage price change is greater when yields decline compared to when they increase by the same number of basis points. Thus, an option-free fixed income security is said to have *positive convexity*.

Although we have focused on the percentage price change due to convexity, a dollar price change can also be calculated. This is called *dollar convexity* and is found by multiplying convexity by the dollar price of the bond.

## AN APPLICATION

In this section, we shall apply the concepts discussed so far in this chapter to a typical swap strategy: a dumbbell-bullet strategy.

A *dumbbell* is a combination or a portfolio of two bonds. In this analysis we select the bonds and their holdings such that the dollar duration of the dumbbell is equal to that of a third bond, known as the *bullet*. We want to compare the relative attractiveness of the dumbbell and the bullet.

There are two unknowns in the creation of a dumbbell: the par holdings of each of the two bonds that compose the dumbbell. We need two conditions to determine these two unknowns. The first condition is that the total dollar duration of the dumbbell equals that of the bullet. By equating the dollar durations, we equate the initial interest rate risk of the two positions. A common second condition is that the total market value of the dumbbell equals that of the bullet. This ensures that the proceeds from the sale of the bullet (or dumbbell) can be used to purchase the dumbbell (bullet) with no cash left over.

Comparing the yield-to-maturity of the bullet to the weighted average yield-to-maturity of the dumbbell to determine whether a portfolio manager can enhance portfolio performance poses several problems. First, the yield for a portfolio is not simply the weighted average of the yields of the bonds in the portfolio. Instead, it is the internal rate of return of the cash flows of the portfolio. Second, the yield-to-maturity measure is a poor measure of the relative value because it assumes that the bonds will be held to maturity and that the coupon payments will be reinvested at the yield-to-maturity. Finally, bond price performance depends not only on duration but convexity. The following illustration demonstrates these points.

Exhibit 7–15 compares a dumbbell consisting of a 5-year 8.5 percent bond and a 20-year 9.5 percent bond blended in the ratio of 50.2 percent and 49.8 percent to a bullet of 10-year maturity and 9.25 percent coupon. All bonds are initially priced at par.

The yield-to-maturity of the bullet is 9.25 percent. The weighted average yield-to-maturity of the dumbbell is 9 percent. A naive analysis would suggest that there is a yield pickup of 25 basis points by buying the bullet and selling the dumbbell. However, while the dollar durations for the bullet and dumbbell are equal, the dollar convexities of the two are not. The dumbbell has higher dollar convexity. Thus, while there is a yield-to-maturity pickup by investing in the bullet, there is a convexity giveup by investing in the bullet. The yield giveup can be viewed as the cost of improving convexity. Furthermore, if the yield on the dumbbell is properly computed based on the cash flow from the two bonds, there is a much smaller yield pickup by investing in the bullet (6.3 basis points).

We're not yet finished with this story. We still have not properly assessed whether the bullet or dumbbell is more attractive because the yield—whether computed as a weighted-average yield or cash-flow yield—is not a complete measure of potential return. To assess the relative value, a horizon return must be computed over some holding period.

Exhibit 7–16 shows the horizon return for the performance of the bullet and dumbbell over a 6-month horizon for a parallel shift in the yield curve (i.e., the yield for all maturities changes by an equal number of basis points). The first column of the exhibit shows the change in yield. Since the strategy under consideration is to sell the dumbbell and buy the bullet, the second column shows the difference in the total dollars at the end of 6 months. The third column provides the same information based on horizon return rather than total dollars.

Our horizon analysis suggests that if yields change by more than 100 basis points, the dumbbell will outperform the bullet. This would generate a loss if we pursued a strategy of buying the bullet and selling the dumbbell. In contrast,

**EXHIBIT 7–15**
**Dumbbell-Bullet Analysis**

Three bonds used in analysis

| Bond | Coupon | Maturity (Years) | Price Plus Accrued | Yield | Dollar Duration | Dollar Convexity |
|------|--------|------------------|--------------------|-------|-----------------|------------------|
| A | 8.50 | 5 | 100 | 8.50% | 4.00544 | 19.8164 |
| B | 9.50 | 20 | 100 | 9.50 | 8.88151 | 124.1702 |
| C | 9.25 | 10 | 100 | 9.25 | 6.43409 | 55.4506 |

**Bullet**: Bond C

**Dumbbell**: Bonds A and B

Composition of dumbbell: 50.2% of bond A; 49.8% of bond B

Dollar duration of dumbbell =
$.502 \times 4.00544 + .498 \times 8.88151 = 6.434$

Average yield of dumbbell =
$.502 \times 8.50 + .498 \times 9.5 = 8.998$

*Strategy:* Sell the dumbbell and buy the bullet

*Analysis based on average yield*

Yield pickup = Yield on bullet − Average yield of dumbbell
= $9.25 - 8.998 = .252$, or 25.2 basis points

*Analysis based on duration, convexity, and average yield*

Dollar convexity of dumbbell =
$.502 \times 19.8164 + .498 \times 124.1702 = 71.7846$

Yield pickup = Yield on bullet − Average yield of dumbbell
= $9.25 - 8.998 = .252$, or 25.2 basis points

Convexity giveup = Convexity of dumbbell − Convexity of bullet
= $71.7846 - 55.4506 = 16.334$

*Analysis based on duration, convexity, and cash-flow yield*

Cash-flow yield of dumbbell* =

$$\frac{(8.5 \times .502 \times 4.00544) + (9.5 \times .498 \times 8.88151)}{6.434} = 9.187$$

Yield pickup = Yield on bullet − Cash-flow yield
= $9.25 - 9.187 = .063$, or 6.3 basis points

Convexity giveup = Convexity of dumbbell − Convexity of bullet
= $71.7846 - 55.4506 = 16.334$

---

* The calculation shown is actually a dollar-duration-weighted yield, a very close approximation to cash flow yield.

## EXHIBIT 7–16

## Dumbbell-Bullet Analysis Based on Horizon Analysis: Bullet Minus Dumbbell

| Yield | Parallel Shift | | Nonparallel Shift* | | Nonparallel Shift† | |
|---|---|---|---|---|---|---|
| | Dollar Return | Horizon Return | Dollar Return | Horizon Return | Dollar Return | Horizon Return |
| −5.000 | −3.59613 | −7.19 | −5.34489 | −10.69 | −1.94264 | −3.89 |
| −4.750 | −3.13782 | −6.28 | −4.80478 | −9.61 | −1.56223 | −3.12 |
| −4.500 | −2.72030 | −5.44 | −4.30917 | −8.62 | −1.21906 | −2.44 |
| −4.250 | −2.34103 | −4.68 | −3.85538 | −7.71 | −0.91076 | −1.82 |
| −4.000 | −1.99764 | −4.00 | −3.44084 | −6.88 | −0.63511 | −1.27 |
| −3.750 | −1.68787 | −3.38 | −3.06316 | −6.13 | −0.39002 | −0.78 |
| −3.500 | −1.40960 | −2.82 | −2.72005 | −5.44 | −0.17349 | −0.35 |
| −3.250 | −1.16081 | −2.32 | −2.40937 | −4.82 | 0.01635 | 0.03 |
| −3.000 | −0.93962 | −1.88 | −2.12906 | −4.26 | 0.18126 | 0.36 |
| −2.750 | −0.74421 | −1.49 | −1.87721 | −3.75 | 0.32293 | 0.65 |
| −2.500 | −0.57291 | −1.15 | −1.65201 | −3.30 | 0.44291 | 0.89 |
| −2.250 | −0.42410 | −0.85 | −1.45173 | −2.90 | 0.54271 | 1.09 |
| −2.000 | −0.29628 | −0.59 | −1.27475 | −2.55 | 0.62373 | 1.25 |
| −1.750 | −0.18802 | −0.38 | −1.11954 | −2.24 | 0.68729 | 1.37 |
| −1.500 | −0.09798 | −0.20 | −0.98465 | −1.97 | 0.73464 | 1.47 |
| −1.250 | −0.02489 | −0.05 | −0.86872 | −1.74 | 0.76695 | 1.53 |
| −1.000 | 0.03245 | 0.06 | −0.77046 | −1.54 | 0.78534 | 1.57 |
| −0.750 | 0.07518 | 0.15 | −0.68864 | −1.38 | 0.79086 | 1.58 |
| −0.500 | 0.10434 | 0.21 | −0.62213 | −1.24 | 0.78448 | 1.57 |
| −0.250 | 0.12095 | 0.24 | −0.56984 | −1.14 | 0.76714 | 1.53 |
| 0.000 | 0.12596 | 0.25 | −0.53074 | −1.06 | 0.73970 | 1.48 |
| 0.250 | 0.12025 | 0.24 | −0.50387 | −1.01 | 0.70300 | 1.41 |
| 0.500 | 0.10466 | 0.21 | −0.48834 | −0.98 | 0.65780 | 1.32 |
| 0.750 | 0.07999 | 0.16 | −0.48327 | −0.97 | 0.60484 | 1.21 |
| 1.000 | 0.04698 | 0.09 | −0.48786 | −0.98 | 0.54479 | 1.09 |
| 1.250 | 0.00632 | 0.01 | −0.50136 | −1.00 | 0.47830 | 0.96 |
| 1.500 | −0.04132 | −0.08 | −0.52305 | −1.05 | 0.40598 | 0.81 |
| 1.750 | −0.09533 | −0.19 | −0.55225 | −1.10 | 0.32839 | 0.66 |
| 2.000 | −0.15512 | −0.31 | −0.58834 | −1.18 | 0.24606 | 0.49 |
| 2.250 | −0.22015 | 0.44 | −0.63071 | −1.26 | 0.15949 | 0.32 |
| 2.500 | −0.28991 | −0.58 | −0.67881 | −1.36 | 0.06916 | 0.14 |
| 2.750 | −0.36391 | −0.73 | −0.73212 | −1.46 | −0.02450 | −0.05 |
| 3.000 | −0.44169 | −0.88 | −0.79012 | −1.58 | −0.12109 | −0.24 |
| 3.250 | −0.52285 | −1.05 | −0.85237 | −1.70 | −0.22020 | −0.44 |
| 3.500 | −0.60698 | −1.21 | −0.91843 | −1.84 | −0.32149 | −0.64 |
| 3.750 | −0.69370 | −1.39 | −0.98788 | −1.98 | −0.42462 | −0.85 |
| 4.000 | −0.78268 | −1.57 | −1.06035 | −2.12 | −0.52927 | −1.06 |
| 4.250 | −0.87358 | −1.75 | −1.13548 | −2.27 | −0.63515 | −1.27 |
| 4.500 | −0.96611 | −1.93 | −1.21292 | −2.43 | −0.74198 | −1.48 |
| 4.750 | −1.05997 | −2.12 | −1.29237 | −2.58 | −0.84952 | −1.70 |
| 5.000 | −1.15491 | −2.31 | −1.37352 | −2.75 | −0.95752 | −1.92 |

* Change in yield for bond C. Nonparallel shift as follows:

    Yield change bond A = Yield change bond C + 25 basis points

    Yield change bond B = Yield change bond C − 25 basis points

† Change in yield for bond C. Nonparallel shift as follows:

    Yield change bond A = Yield change bond C − 25 basis points

    Yield change bond B = Yield change bond C + 25 basis points

a gain would be produced if yields change by 100 basis points or less. The better performance of the dumbbell for large changes in yield is due to its better convexity.

While we have restricted our analysis thus far to a parallel shift in the yield curve, Exhibit 7–16 also shows the relative performance for nonparallel shifts. In the fourth and fifth columns, we assumed that if the yield on bond C (the intermediate-term bond) changes, bond A (the short-term bond) will change by the same amount plus 25 basis points, whereas bond B (the long-term bond) will change by the same amount less 25 basis points. Under this scenario, the dumbbell will always outperform the bullet. In the last two columns, the nonparallel shift assumes that for a change in bond C's yield, the yield on bond A will change by the same amount less 25 basis points, whereas that on bond B will change by the same amount plus 25 basis points. In this case, the bullet would outperform the dumbbell so long as the yield on bond C does not rise by more than 250 basis points or fall by more than 325 basis points.

Thus, horizon analysis tells us that looking at measures such as yield (yield-to-maturity, average-weighted yield, or cash-flow yield), duration, and convexity can be misleading because the performance of a security or a portfolio of securities depends on the magnitude of the change in yields over some investment horizon and how the yield curve changes.

## DURATION AND CONVEXITY
## FOR CALLABLE BONDS

Many corporate bonds are callable prior to the maturity date at the option of the issuer. Mortgage pass-through securities may be repaid in whole or part by the homeowner prior to the maturity of the mortgage loan. Thus, mortgage pass-through securities will exhibit price/yield characteristics similar to callable corporate bonds. For convenience, we will therefore focus our attention only on callable corporate bonds.

Exhibit 7–17 shows the price/yield relationship for both a noncallable bond and the same bond if it is callable. The convex curve a-a' is the price/yield relationship for the noncallable (option-free) bond. The unusual shaped curve denoted by a-b is the price/yield relationship for the callable bond.

The reason for the shape of the price/yield relationship for the callable bond is as follows: When the prevailing market yield for comparable bonds is much higher than the coupon rate on the bond, it is unlikely that the issuer will call the bond. For example, if the coupon rate on a bond is 8 percent and the prevailing yield on comparable bonds is 16 percent, it is highly improbable that the issuer will call in an 8 percent bond so that it can issue a 16 percent bond. In option terminology, the call option is deep out-of-the-money. Since the bond is unlikely to be called when it is deep out-of-the-money, a callable

**EXHIBIT 7–17**
**Noncallable and Callable Bond Price/Yield Relationship**

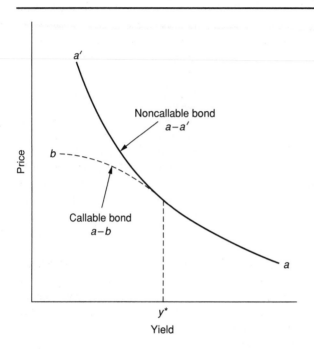

bond will have roughly the same price/yield relationship as a noncallable bond. However, even when the option is near-the-money (the coupon rate is near the market yield) investors will not pay the same price for the bond if it is callable because there is still the chance the market yield may drop further, making it beneficial for the issuer to call the bond.

As yields in the market decline, the likelihood increases that the issuer will benefit from calling the bond. We may not know the exact yield level at which investors begin to view the issue likely to be called, but we do know that there is some level. In Exhibit 7–17, at yield levels below $y^*$, the price/yield relationship for the callable bond departs significantly from the price/yield relationship for the noncallable bond. Consider, for example, a bond that can be called at 104 in a market in which a similar noncallable bond would sell for 109. Investors would obviously not pay 109 for the callable bond. If they did and the bond is called, investors would receive 104 (the call price) for a bond they purchased for 109. Consequently, for a range of yields below $y^*$, there is significant price compression—that is, there is limited price appreciation as yields decline.

To understand the price volatility and the potential performance of callable bonds over some investment horizon, it is necessary to understand the components of the callable bond. A callable bond is a bond in which the bondholder has sold the issuer a call option[8] that allows the issuer to repurchase the bond.

Effectively, the owner of the callable bond enters into two separate transactions. First, he or she buys a noncallable bond from the issuer, for which he pays some price. Then, he sells the issuer a call option for which he receives the option price from the issuer. Therefore, we can summarize the position of a callable bondholder as follows:

Long a callable bond = Long a noncallable bond + Short position in call

or equivalently,

Callable bond = Noncallable bond − Call option

The minus sign in front of the call option means that the bondholder has sold (written) the call option.

In terms of price, the price of a callable bond is therefore equal to the price of the two components parts. That is,

Callable bond price = Noncallable bond price − Call option price

The call option price is subtracted from the price of the noncallable bond because, when the bondholder sells a call option, he or she receives the option price. Graphically this can be seen in Exhibit 7–17. The difference between the price of the noncallable bond and the callable bond at a given yield is the price of the embedded call option.

The price of a call option increases when the expected price volatility of the underlying instrument increases. Since the price of a call option on a bond depends on interest rate volatility, the price of a callable bond will depend on expected interest rate volatility.

The duration of a callable bond after adjusting for a call option is commonly referred to as the *call-adjusted (modified) duration* and is discussed further in Chapter 36. It depends on three factors: (1) the duration of the underlying noncallable bond, (2) the ratio of the price of the noncallable bond to the callable bond, and (3) the sensitivity of the price of the call option to the change in the price of the underlying noncallable bond. The last factor is commonly referred to as the *delta*[9] of the option and measures how the option price will change if the price of the underlying noncallable bond changes by $1.

For a callable bond in which the coupon rate is substantially above the current market rate, the call-adjusted duration will be close to 0. In contrast, the call-adjusted duration for a callable bond in which the coupon rate is substantially

---

[8] Call options are the subject of Chapter 32.

[9] The delta of an option and the exact calculation of the duartion of a callable bond is explained in Chapter 33.

lower than the current market rate, is essentially the same as the duration of the noncallable bond. Thus, the call-adjusted duration for a callable bond will range between 0 and the duration of the noncallable bond.

The call-adjusted convexity of a bond can also be computed. It will depend on the same three factors that determine call-adjusted duration plus (1) the convexity of the noncallable bond and (2) the convexity of the call option. Call-adjusted convexity is discussed further in Chapter 36.

Recall that convexity measures the rate of change of duration. For an option-free bond, convexity is always positive. Duration, which is related to the slope of the tangent to the price/yield relationship, increases when yield decreases, and decreases when yield increases. As can be seen in Exhibit 7–17 the slope of the line tangent to the price/yield relationship for a callable bond flattens when yield decreases. Thus, duration gets smaller as yield decreases. This feature of a callable bond is referred to as *negative convexity* and causes the price compression that we referred to earlier.

## SUMMARY

In this chapter we reviewed the price volatility characteristics of option-free bonds and offered a quick overview of bonds with an embedded call option. Several convenient measures, including price value of a basis point, duration, dollar duration, and convexity, were shown to summarize the important attributes of price volatility. The limitations of these measures were illustrated.

# CHAPTER 8

## THE DETERMINANTS OF INTEREST RATES ON FIXED INCOME SECURITIES

*Frank J. Jones, Ph.D.*
*First Vice President &*
*Associate Director of Research*
*Merrill Lynch Capital Markets*

*Benjamin Wolkowitz, Ph.D.*
*Managing Director*
*Morgan Stanley & Co.*

This chapter discusses the determination of interest rates on fixed income securities. In discussing the determination of interest rates, first the determination of the general level of interest rates at a specific time and then the factors that cause differences in interest rates at a specific time are considered. The interest rates on securities issued by the U.S. Department of the Treasury (hereafter Treasury) are commonly accepted as the benchmark interest rates in the U.S. economy and, typically, in the world.

The interest rates on Treasury securities are commonly accepted as reflective of the general level of interest rates because there are more Treasury securities outstanding than any other securities in the world, the Treasury issues securities of every maturity spectrum on a regular basis, and Treasury securities have virtually no credit risk. The next chapter discusses the primary and secondary markets for Treasury securities.

The discussion of interest-rate determination presented in this chapter is structured so that the conceptual analysis is followed by applications of the conceptual conclusions. Most of these applications use Treasury securities as the basis for comparison. The first part of this discussion considers the determination of the general level of interest rates, which can be considered "the" interest rate.[1] The three major rationales or theories for interest-rate determination—liquidity preference, loanable funds, and inflation and the real rate of interest—are discussed. A synthesis of these approaches is also provided. A fourth rationale, the "tone of the market," is also reviewed and shown to have an impact on interest rates in the short term.

The second part of the discussion on interest-rate determination examines the factors that cause differences among interest rates at a specific time (i.e., why all interest rates are not equal to the general level of interest rates). There are three such factors, or reasons, for differences among interest rates.

The first factor is maturity. The impact of maturity on a security's interest rate is considered in the context of three hypotheses: the liquidity hypothesis, the expectations hypothesis, and the segmentation hypothesis.

Second, differences among interest rates on securities at a specific time also occur due to differences in credit risk. Investors respond to a risk-return tradeoff in that the greater the risk associated with a particular security, that is, the less creditworthy the issuer, the greater the required return. A third important reason for differences among interest rates on securities is taxability.

The chapter concludes with an overview of interest-rate determination, which combines all the concepts introduced and demonstrates how they interact to determine market interest rates. This synthesis of theory and actual experience relies on Treasury issues as a basis for comparison.

## RATIONALE FOR INTEREST-RATE DETERMINATION

In a broad sense, the economy can be conceived of as being composed of two sectors—the real sector and the financial sector. The real sector is involved with the production of goods and services with physical resources—labor and cap-

---

[1] This chapter discusses interest rates as though the interest rates on securities were directly comparable. Interest rates on all securities, however, are not, without adjustment, directly comparable. Typically, market makers refer to the value of securities in terms of their prices, not their interest rates. The interest rates on the securities are then calculated from their prices. Interest rates are important because they provide a common basis for comparing the returns on securities of different maturities and of different principal values. For these reasons, interest rates are always calculated on an annual basis, typically for $100 of maturity value. However, in calculating interest rates from prices, different assumptions are used for different securities. Thus, within the general term *interest rate* are included the returns on several types of securities that are calculated according to different assumptions and are called, alternatively, discount return, yield, bond equivalent yield, repo equivalent yield, and other measures of return. Thus, in comparing interest rates on different securities, adjustments must often be made so that the interest rates compared are calculated on the basis of the same assumptions. However, the magnitudes of the differences among interest rates calculated on the basis of different assumptions are in most cases small. This chapter ignores the effect of different assumptions used in calculating interest rates and uses the term *interest rate* as though the returns on all securities were comparable.

ital. Important examples of components of the real sector include automobile production, steel production, and housing construction. The financial sector is concerned with the transfer of funds from lenders to borrowers. Important examples of components of the financial sector include commercial banks, insurance companies, and securities dealers.

In the financial sector, equilibrium is attained when the demand for borrowed funds equals the supply of loanable funds, as discussed below. The interest rate is the variable that causes this equality, or equilibrium.

To an individual deciding whether to currently consume an amount of funds or abstain from consumption and supply the funds to the financial sector (i.e., "save"), the interest rate can be viewed as compensation for abstaining from current consumption. For example, an individual with $100 of disposable income when the interest rate is 10 percent must decide between consuming the $100 today or saving it for one year, after which the individual would have $110 to consume. The $10 of added consumption is in effect a reward for abstaining from current consumption. The greater the reward (i.e., the higher the interest rate), the more a saver should be willing to supply loanable funds. In the aggregate, the supply of loanable funds is directly related to the interest rates, which are reflected in the upward-sloping supply curve of Exhibit 8–1.

The steepness of this curve depends on the saver's preference for future consumption relative to present consumption. The greater this preference for savings, the flatter the supply curve—the more willing a saver is to save. In this case there is a greater increase in savings for a given increase in interest rates.

To a borrower of funds, the interest rate represents a cost. In the context of the preceding example, at an interest rate of 10 percent, borrowing $100 for one year will cost the borrower $10 in interest. To a business borrower,

**EXHIBIT 8–1**
**The Supply and Demand of Loanable Funds**

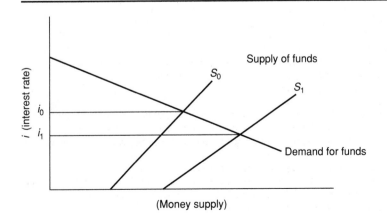

this $10 interest expense is the cost of borrowing to improve capital plant and equipment. If a business borrower can make operations sufficiently more efficient and consequently more profitable as a result of becoming more capital intensive, then borrowing should occur. The higher the interest rate, however, the greater must be the profitability associated with an investment for it to pay off. Since more investments will pay off at low interest rates than at high interest rates, the demand for funds by borrowers will decline as interest rates rise. For this reason, the demand for funds curve in Exhibit 8–1 is downward sloping.

The catalyst for achieving equality between the aggregate supply of funds and the aggregate demand for funds in the financial system is the interest rate. The financial sector is not, however, one uniform market. Rather the financial sector is composed of a number of financial institutions and markets that, although distinct, are interrelated. Each of these specific components of the financial sector is specialized, attracting funds from specific types of savers and making funds available to specific types of borrowers. There is, however, some substitution in which savers and/or borrowers who usually borrow or lend in one part of the financial sector may switch to a different part because of a change in relative interest rates.

Interest rates bring the supply and demand for funds into equality in each part of the financial system and operate in the same way to bring the total, or aggregate, supply and demand for funds in the financial system into equality.

Interest rates are not constant; rather, they vary over time. Understanding what affects interest rates and why they are variable is key to understanding the operations of the financial sector. The determination of the general level and variability of interest rates is explainable by several different theories, or frameworks. The three major theories, liquidity preference, loanable funds, and inflation and the real rate of interest, are described below. In addition to a general conceptual discussion of the theories, a discussion of how these theories can be practiced is provided. The focus in this section is on the general level of interest rates, not on any particular interest rate.

## Liquidity Preference

*Liquidity preference* is synonymous with the "demand for money." And, as is the case with the demand for other financial assets and liabilities, the demand for money is dependent on the level of interest rates.

The relationship between the demand for money and interest rates can be explained in two ways. The first relies on a Keynesian construction called the "speculative demand for money." In this approach, it is assumed that the investor is, as investment alternatives, either holding cash, which has a zero return and no risk, or holding a bond that has two forms of return: a coupon return and a potential capital gain or loss. If the capital loss on bonds is large enough to exceed the coupon return, the total return on bonds will be negative, and holding money, even at a zero return, would be preferable.

Since the prices of and interest rates on fixed income securities move inversely, bonds incur a capital loss when interest rates rise and a capital gain when interest rates fall. Thus, when interest rates are low, there will typically be an expectation that they will rise, thus resulting in a capital loss on bonds. In anticipation of such a capital loss, holding cash is preferable. Conversely, if interest rates are presently high, they will typically be expected to decline so that a capital gain on bonds is anticipated and holding bonds is preferable.

Interest rates affect the relative demand for money and bonds as illustrated by a downward-sloping demand curve shown in Exhibit 8–2. The demand for money increases as the current interest rate decreases because the lower the present interest rate, the more it is expected to rise; thus, the greater the expected capital loss and the more investors are inclined to hold money. With respect to Exhibit 8–2, as the interest rate rises from $i_2$ to $i_1$, the quantity of money demanded decreases from $Q_2$ to $Q_1$.

A second way to explain the relationship between interest rates and the demand for money is to conceive of the interest rate as the foregone return for holding money instead of an interest-bearing asset. Consequently, the higher the rate of interest, the greater is the return foregone by holding money, and the less money is held. In other words, according to Exhibit 8–2 as interest rates rise, the cost of holding money rather than an interest-earning asset rises. Consequently, as interest rates rise a smaller amount of money is held.

According to either explanation, the liquidity preference theory of interest rates explains the level of the interest rate in terms of the supply and demand for

**EXHIBIT 8–2**
**The Supply and Demand of Money**

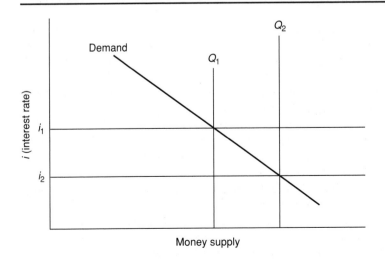

money. Thus, if the Fed increases (decreases) the supply of money and there is no change in the demand relationship, the interest rate will decrease (increase). Again referring to Exhibit 8–2, increasing the supply of money from $Q_1$ to $Q_2$ while leaving the demand relationship unchanged results in a lower equilibrium interest rate. In general, an increase in the supply or a decrease in the demand for money will cause interest rates to decline, whereas a decrease in supply or an increase in demand will cause interest rates to rise.

The liquidity preference theory of interest-rate determination can be used for determining both short-term and long-term changes in interest rates.

A partial, short-term analysis of interest-rate determination is based solely on tracking and analyzing short-term movements in the money supply. Since the Fed has the primary responsibility for determining the money supply, there has developed a school of interest-rate analysts, commonly known as "Fed watchers," who continually monitor and interpret the Fed's activities to infer from these activities the Fed's intentions regarding future activities that will affect the money supply and, consequently, interest rates. The weekly money supply statistics announced by the Fed on Thursday afternoons and widely disseminated by the financial press are carefully examined for indications of changes in Fed policy that could affect interest rates. An additional discussion of how the Fed's money supply data are interpreted is provided below.

In addition to watching and interpreting the market money supply data, the Fed's open-market operations and their effect on the federal funds rate are continuously monitored. As an example, the following discussion appeared in *The Wall Street Journal* (January 20, 1982):

> Some specialists said the recent rise in the funds rate reflected an apparently tougher stance adopted by the Fed late last month in supplying reserves to the banking system. And many contend the recent surge in the money supply will force the Fed to get even tougher.

A longer term application of the liquidity preference theory is based on the relationship between the money supply and the level of Gross National Product (GNP). This relationship is formally expressed by the equation: $M \times V = P \times Y$ (called the "quantity theory of money"), where $V$ is the velocity of money, $P$ is the price level, and $Y$ is real gross national product. The product of $P$ and $Y$, $P \times Y$, is nominal GNP, referred to simply as GNP.

According to this theory, if the level of the money supply over some future time period is less (greater) than the actual amount needed to support the expected level of GNP, then the level of interest rates is likely to rise (fall). Because of this relationship, economic forecasters go through the complex exercise of predicting GNP, the money supply, and their interrelationship in order to provide forecasts of interest rates.[2]

---

[2] See Chapter 60 for a thorough discussion of interest rate forecasting.

Predicting GNP and money supply relationships is usually conducted in the context of large econometric models of the U.S. economy. These multiequation models attempt to capture the complex interactions in the economy that result in the determination of interest rates, GNP, and money supply. The results of such models are frequently the basis for long-range financial planning by corporations and others.

## Loanable Funds

The *loanable funds theory* of interest-rate determination is based on the reasoning related to the supply and demand for loanable funds provided at the beginning of this section. This theory of interest-rate determination depends on the supply of funds available for lending by savers and the demand for such loanable funds by borrowers. As indicated above, as the return to lending rises (as interest rates rise), the supply of loanable funds increases. Conversely, when interest rates decline, the return to lenders declines, as does the supply of such funds.

Since interest rates represent a cost to borrowers, the opposite relationship applies to borrowers: As interest rates rise, borrowers' demand for funds decreases, and as interest rates decline, borrowers' demand for funds increases. These relationships are illustrated by Exhibit 8–3.

In Exhibit 8–3, the equilibrium level of interest rates is $r_0$, and the quantity of funds lent and borrowed at that rate is $E_{LF}$. If the interest rate were initially higher than $r_0$ (e.g., $r_1$), then the supply of funds, $S_{LF}$, would exceed the demand, $D_{LF}$, at that rate. This excess supply of funds would exert downward pressure on interest rates causing them to decrease to $r_0$, the point at which

**EXHIBIT 8–3**
**The Supply and Demand of Loanable Funds**

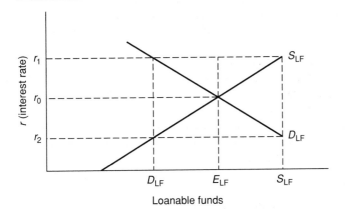

supply and demand would be in equilibrium. Alternately, if rates were below the equilibrium level (e.g., at $r_2$), then the demand would exceed the supply. Market pressures in this case would cause interest rates to increase again to the equilibrium level, $r_0$.

The loanable funds theory of interest-rate determination applies to aggregate borrowing and lending in the economy. If, at a given interest rate, intended aggregate borrowing is greater than intended aggregate lending, then interest rates will rise. Then the actual measured levels of borrowing and lending at the higher level of interest rates will be equal. If intended aggregate borrowing is less than intended aggregate lending, interest rates will decline until the actual measured levels of borrowing and lending will be equal at the lower level of interest rates.

To apply the loanable funds theory, aggregate borrowing and lending is typically divided into its components or sectors. Even though some borrowers and lenders can shift among types and maturities of sources and uses of funds and some cannot, a structure or taxonomy can be used in either case for determining aggregate borrowing and lending. This structure is useful for summarizing actual, measured aggregate borrowing and lending for past years.

As explained in Chapter 60, the structure is also useful for forecasting interest rates. For this purpose, an estimate is developed of the expected or intended levels of borrowing and lending of each type over a period of time. Then the sum of all types of borrowing (aggregate borrowing) is compared with the sum of all types of lending (aggregate lending). If the former is greater than the latter, interest rates are forecast to increase. And because of the increase in interest rates, actual borrowing would be less than expected borrowing and actual lending would be greater than expected lending. Then, ex post facto, actual measured borrowing and lending would be equal.

Often, instead of developing as complete a taxonomy of borrowing and lending as described above, analysts focus on only the major types of borrowing and lending such as federal government borrowing, business borrowing, and mortgage borrowing. Then by forecasting increases or decreases in these types of borrowing, analysts assess whether there will be upward or downward pressures on the interest rate.

A popularization of the application of the loanable funds theory on a sectorial basis is referred to as "crowding out." Large federal deficits require the U.S. Department of the Treasury to increase the amount of debt it has outstanding; and the issue of Treasury debt is alleged to compete with private-sector borrowing, assuming a fixed supply of available credit. Thus, an increase in the demand for funds by the Treasury causes interest rates to increase and forces out the private-sector issues. An example of the crowding out application of the loanable funds theory appeared in *The Wall Street Journal* (1981):

> Many dealers said they continue to be concerned about the size of the Treasury's financing needs. Traders also expressed nervousness over recent increases in short-

term interest rates. But many said they remain confident that bond prices will rebound early next year, mainly because they anticipate further evidence of erosion in the economy.

And another example appeared in a *New York Times* story (1981):

Unusually heavy year-end Government borrowings continued to weigh on the money market last week, raising short-term rates a point on average and reducing prices of longer-term coupon securities as much as two points, or $20 for each $1,000 of face value.

Thus, the crowding out concept derives from the loanable funds theory but focuses only on Treasury borrowing. Most applications of loanable funds use an intermediate approach between a complete taxonomy of sources and uses of funds and only a single use of funds; they consider a few major uses of funds and perhaps changes in the aggregate supply of funds.

## Inflation and the Real Rate of Interest

Interest rates represent a rate of return for lenders and a cost to borrowers. To be a meaningful representation of cost or return, however, interest rates should be related to the rate of price change. Consider a saver who has placed $5,000 in a money market fund earning a return of 12 percent per year. At the end of a year the saver has $5,600, a 12 percent increase in purchasing power. If, however, the price level had increased by 10 percent per year, then the net increase in purchasing power of the savings would be only 2 percent.

The 12 percent return on the savings is referred to as the "nominal rate of interest" since it measures the percent increase in the nominal number of dollars earned or paid over a period of time. The measure of change in purchasing power of 2 percent is referred to as the "real rate of interest" since it measures the real change in purchasing power. The difference between these two rates is the rate of inflation. Thus, the real rate of interest equals the nominal rate of interest minus the rate of inflation.

From the lender's perspective, the real rate of interest represents the increase in real purchasing power resulting from foregone consumption—savings. From the borrower's perspective, the real rate of interest represents the real cost of borrowing. The inflation component of the nominal rate of interest the borrower pays on the borrowed funds represents a deterioration of the principal of the loan (often described as paying back in cheap dollars) not a real cost of borrowed funds. A business should as a rule continue to borrow and invest until the real rate of return on investments equals the real rate of interest paid on borrowing.

Thus, there are two major determinants of the real rate of interest. The first is the return on investment—the return to capital. If a business can improve its efficiency of operations and earn a higher rate of return from investment, it will be inclined to pay a higher real rate of return on borrowed funds. The other influence is the preference of consumers. The more consumers want to consume currently rather than forgo consumption, the higher the real rate of return will have to be to induce them to alter their plans and save.

Then the real rate of interest and the rate of inflation jointly determine the nominal rate of interest. The effect of the rate of inflation on the nominal rate of interest is to cause the nominal rate to change so that the real rate is unaffected by the rate of inflation. Lenders, unless subject to a "dollar illusion," are concerned with the return of the real purchasing power on their savings rather than the nominal return. Such concern causes consumers to negotiate for nominal rates that keep their real rate of return at least constant. Thus, to the extent their savings are sensitive to the real rate of interest, an increase in inflation without corresponding increase in the real rate of interest will cause a decrease in savings. Consequently, there is upward pressure on the nominal rate of interest during periods of inflation, which prevents the real rate of interest from decreasing below its original level. To prevent savings from decreasing requires an increase in the nominal rate equal to the increase in the rate of inflation.

Inflation has a somewhat similar effect on the willingness of borrowers to pay a higher nominal rate of interest for funds. Inflation affects the return on investment by affecting the prices of goods and services produced. An investment earning a given amount net of the interest on borrowings will earn a higher nominal amount after inflation because the value of the goods and services produced by the investment have been inflated. If the interest payments on the borrowings do not increase as well, then the real rate of return on investment will also increase. Presumably, under such circumstances, borrowers will continue to increase their demand for funds until the nominal cost of borrowing has increased such that the real cost is at its preinflation level.

Over time, however, the real rate of interest may change for two reasons. First, the real rate of interest, since it is the real return on capital, may decrease during recessions because of a substantial amount of unused capital and a low return to the used capital. Similarly, it may increase during periods of economic growth because all capital is productively employed.

The second reason for changes in the real rate relates to *unexpected* changes in the rate of inflation. The nominal interest rate on a security at any time should reflect the *expected* average rate of inflation over the maturity of the security. If the financial markets *expect* a higher rate of inflation in the future, nominal interest rates should increase to reflect these expectations. However, if inflation changes unexpectedly, the initial nominal rate of interest will not correctly reflect the change, and the actual real rate of interest over the period will be different from the normal level of the real rate in the opposite direction of the unexpected change in the rate of inflation.

Consider the following example. Between times $T_0$ and $T_1$ the nominal rate of interest is 8 percent, the rate of inflation is 5 percent, and the real rate of interest is 3 percent. Assume that these are the normal levels.

Assume that at $T_1$ the rate of inflation *unexpectedly* increases to 6 percent. Since the change is unexpected, the nominal rate does not change, and thus the real rate of interest decreases to 2 percent. Assume that by $T_2$ the financial markets recognize the change in the rate of inflation and the nominal rate of interest increases to 9 percent, restoring the real rate of interest to 3 percent.

At $T_3$ the rate of inflation *unexpectedly* decreases to its original level of 5 percent. Because the change is unexpected, the nominal rate remains at 9 percent, so the real rate increases to 4 percent. By $T_4$ the financial market recognizes the change in the rate of inflation, the nominal rate of interest decreases to 8 percent, and the real rate of interest decreases to its original normal level of 3 percent. Thus, although expected changes in the rate of inflation should have no effect on the real rate of interest, unexpected changes in inflation will cause the real rate of interest to change in the opposite direction.

Typically, interest rates are referred to in nominal terms. Similarly, interest-rate determination models relate to the nominal rate of interest. As discussed above, the nominal rate of interest and the rate of inflation are directly related. Since the nominal rate of interest is, by definition, equal to the real rate of interest plus the rate of inflation, the rate of inflation is a major component of the level of the nominal rates of interest. In fact, given the levels of inflation and interest rates that have been observed during the last decade, changes in the nominal rate of interest have been due in greater measure to changes in inflation than to changes in the real rate of interest.

Calculations of the real rate of interest can be made from different measures of the rate of inflation and different interest rates, although in concept the measure of the inflation rate used should be the expected inflation rate over the maturity of the security whose interest rate is used. The interest rate can be either a short-term or a long-term interest rate. Very often the inflation rate used is based on an average over several previous periods or a projection of the trend of the past inflation rate into the future.

Since 1965, there has been considerable variation in the real rate of interest, the difference between the interest rate and the inflation rate. These changes in the real rate have been due both to changes in the strength of the economy and errors in inflationary expectations.[3] Although the correlation is less than perfect, the real rate of interest tends to be low during recessions and high during periods of economic strength.

To summarize, in models of the determination of the nominal rate of interest, the factors that affect the rate of inflation and the real rate of interest should be considered separately. Since there has been even greater volatility in the rate

---

[3] Some observers claim that the real rate of interest has been high in recent years because the real rate contains a risk premium to account for the increased volatility of interest rates since October 1979, when the Fed announced that it would devote more attention to controlling the money supply and less to controlling the interest rate.

of inflation than in the real rate of interest, an accurate determination of the rate of inflation is an important part of an accurate determination of the nominal rate of interest.

## Synthesis

The three different theories or rationales of the level of interest rates that were described in this section are not exclusive but, rather, are compatible and complementary ways of considering interest-rate determination. The liquidity preference theory, which considers the supply and demand for money, and the loanable funds theory, which considers the supply and demand for loanable funds, are equivalent ways of considering interest-rate determination. A model that includes both money and loanable funds would show that these two theories would determine the same interest rate. By introducing the effect of inflation to either the impact of the inflation and the real rate of interest theory on the level of interest rates is complementary to the other two explanations. Thus, the three theories described in this section should be viewed as a unified approach to interest-rate determination.

## Tone of the Market

The factors discussed above that affect interest rates—the supply and demand for money, the supply and demand for funds, and the inflation rate—are objective in nature. These fundamental factors undoubtedly determine the level of interest rates after some lag. But there is another type of influence on interest rates that responds very quickly—within hours, or even minutes, and at times includes subjective as well as objective factors. This type of influence is called the *tone of the market*.

The tone of the market determines the very short-run direction and volatility of interest rates and is due to actions by professionals in the interest-rate markets, mainly dealers in government securities, corporate bonds, and municipal bonds and also large institutional investors in these securities. The professionals continually monitor the nation's and the world's economic, political, and social condition and quickly assess their likely impacts on interest rates. In particular, they watch for changes in the condition of the nation's economic goals, inflation, unemployment, economic growth, balance of payments, economic policies, monetary policy, and fiscal policy. Even more specifically, they monitor the volume of new issues of Treasury, corporate, and municipal debt that will be brought to the market in the next few days and weeks, and the Fed open-market operations and monetary policy.

By monitoring and quickly assessing the likely impact of these factors on interest rates, the professionals are able to rapidly alter their portfolio strategies in view of new information. If dealers and portfolio managers expect interest rates to increase, they reduce the size of their portfolio to avoid losses, thus lowering the demand for securities and increasing interest rates. In response to the same expectations, they may reduce their holdings of long-term securities but increase their holdings of short-term securities, thus increasing long-term rates relative to short-term rates, a normal phenomenon during times of rising interest rates. Through these portfolio activities, the expectation that interest rates will rise actually causes interest rates to rise, at least for a short period of time. If interest rates are expected to decrease, the opposite will occur.

At times, professionals may respond not only to recent information but to expectations or anticipations of future information. Operating on the basis of future information is more subjective than operating after the release of new information. And at times the psychology of the market may contradict the fundamental factors: Professionals may expect future information that will reverse interest-rate trends based on recently available data.

The tone of the market, whether determined by objective (fundamental) or subjective (psychological) factors, affects interest rates very quickly. And activities by professionals that set the tone of the market by quickly translating new information or expectations of future information into present interest-rate changes add to the efficiency of the financial markets.

The following quotation from *The Wall Street Journal* indicates the nature and importance of the tone of the market:

> Bond prices swung widely as speculators stepped up their involvement in the credit markets.
>
> The Treasury recently offered $8\frac{3}{8}$ percent bonds of 2008, for example opened at $99\frac{22}{32}$ bid, $99\frac{24}{32}$ asked, traded as high as 100 bid, $100\frac{4}{32}$ asked only to finish the session at their opening levels.
>
> The earlier firming came as dealers purchased inventory for possible markups in any subsequent resumption of the strong price rally of the past two weeks.

## THE STRUCTURES OF INTEREST RATES

It is often asked what determines or affects "the" interest rate, as if there were a single interest rate. However, from the financial markets it is obvious that not one but several interest rates exist. And although these interest rates may move, in general, in the same direction at the same time, the amounts of their movements and at times even the direction of their movements may differ substantially. Thus, the spreads, or differences, between interest rates vary.

This section discusses the factors that tend to differentiate interest rates. These factors are often the basis for the "structures" of interest rates. There are three different structures of interest rates, and, even if securities are identical in every other respect, their interest rates may differ because of maturity, credit risk, and taxability.

## Maturity Structure (Term Structure) of Interest Rates

This subsection considers the relationship between a security's interest rate and its term-to-maturity. This relationship is usually referred to as the *maturity structure* or *term structure* of interest rates. A common analytical construct in this context is the yield curve (or term-structure curve), which illustrates the relationship between the interest rate and the maturity of securities that are identical in every way except maturity.

There are three distinct explanations of the relationship between the maturities of securities and their interest rates.

### *Liquidity Hypothesis*
Although there are several aspects to a security's liquidity, the major aspect is the security's potential for capital gain or loss, often called market risk. The major determinant of a security's market risk is its maturity because the longer the security's maturity, the greater the price change for a given change in its interest rate. For example, the prices of Treasury bonds are more volatile than the prices of Treasury bills.

Since there is a trade-off between the risk and the return on a security, investors typically require a higher return to invest in a security with higher risk. Because a security with a longer maturity has greater market risk and, for this reason, less liquidity, interest rates should increase with maturity as a compensation to investors. This relationship between the level of interest rates and the maturity of a security is called the *liquidity preference hypothesis* and is illustrated in Exhibit 8–4. This hypothesis does not purport to be a complete explanation of the term structure of interest rates but only a complement to the other explanations described below.

### *Expectations Hypothesis*
The *expectations hypothesis* begins with a premise considered in a preceding section, that lenders desire to maximize their return from providing funds and borrowers desire to minimize their cost of borrowing funds. However, unlike the preceding discussion, the expectations hypothesis explicitly considers how lenders and borrowers attain their objectives over a period of time rather than just at any moment in time.

To evaluate the temporal aspect of maximizing investment return and minimizing borrowing cost and how these decisions affect the relationship between interest rates and maturities, consider a two-period planning horizon. Consider each period to be one year, although it could be any other discrete period of time. A lender choosing a strategy over this two-period planning horizon has two alternatives—either to purchase a security with a maturity equal to the two periods or purchase a security with a one-period maturity with the intention of reinvesting for an additional period at the end of the first period. The lender's

**EXHIBIT 8–4**

**Liquidity Preference: The Relationship between the Level of Interest Rates and Maturity**

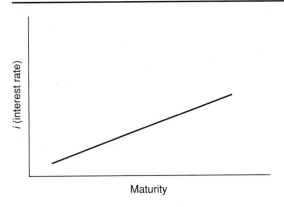

decision will depend on a comparison of the currently available two-period interest rate with the average of the currently available one-period rate and the expected one-period rate, one period hence. Obviously, the lender will select the strategy with the higher anticipated return. [4]

The borrower who is planning over the same two-period horizon is also faced with two alternatives—either to issue a security with a two-period maturity or to issue a one-period security with the intention of issuing another one-period security, one period hence. The borrower's decision will be based on the total cost of funds over the two periods. If the two-period interest rate is less than the average of the current one-period rate and the one-period rate expected one period hence, then the borrower will issue a two-period security. Otherwise, the borrower will sequentially issue two, one-period securities.

The decisions made separately by lenders and borrowers will affect the relative interest rates over the two-period horizon. For example, if the two-period interest rate exceeds the average of the one-period rate and the expected one-period rate one period hence, then all lenders would choose to invest for two periods and all borrowers would sequentially issue two, one-period securities. As a consequence, there would be an excess supply of funds in the two-period market, causing the two-period interest rate to decrease, and an excess demand for funds in the one-period market, causing the one-period interest rate to increase. According to the expectations hypothesis, the interest rates will continue to change until the current two-period rate equals the effective rate for two

---

[4] For a more detailed discussion of this subject, see Chapters 9 and 56.

sequential one-period securities. Under this circumstance, both borrowers and lenders will be indifferent between a single two-period transaction and two sequential one-period transactions, and thus interest rates will be in equilibrium.

The expectations hypothesis is also applicable to a larger number of periods. However, the basic conclusion that the current long-term rate should equal the average of the current and expected future short-term rates remains the same. As a result, borrowers and lenders will be indifferent between relying on a long-term security or a series of short-term securities.

The expectations hypothesis does not imply that all interest rates will be equal, only that the average of the observed and anticipated short-term rates will equal the long-term rate. If interest rates are expected to remain stable, however, so that future short-term rates are expected to equal the currently observed short-term rate, then current interest rates across all maturities will be equal, as illustrated by the yield curve shown in Exhibit 8–5. This is a "flat" yield curve.

If rates are expected to increase, the shape of the yield curve will be different. With an anticipated increase in interest rates, lenders will purchase short-term securities so that they can earn the higher anticipated rate after their initial short-term-maturity security matures and they subsequently reinvest in another short-term security at a higher rate, and also so that they avoid the capital losses that longer term securities would incur when interest rates rise. Borrowers, on the other hand, would be induced to issue long-term securities in order to lock in the currently low rates for a long period of time, thereby eliminating the need for issuing new securities at the higher rates. These actions of lenders and borrowers would result in an excess supply of short-term funds,

**EXHIBIT 8–5**
**Flat Yield Curve**

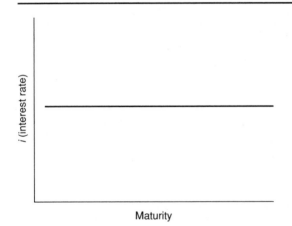

Maturity

causing short-term rates to decrease, and an excess demand for long-term funds, causing short-term rates to increase. These pressures on short- and long-term interest rates would produce an upward-sloping yield curve as illustrated in Exhibit 8–6.

According to the expectations hypothesis, these pressures on interest rates will continue until, again, the current long-term interest rate equals the average of the current and expected short-term rates. For example, if the current one-year rate is 12 percent, the expected one-year rate one year hence is 13 percent, and the expected one-year rate two years hence is 14 percent, then the current two-year rate would be 12.5 percent, and the current three-year rate should be the average of these three one-year rates, or 13 percent.[5] Thus, the yield curve based on the current one-year, two-year, and three-year rates would be upward-sloping.

The explanation is similar if interest rates are expected to decrease in the future. In this case, lenders would purchase only long-term securities in an attempt to lock in currently high interest rates before rates decrease and to reap the capital gain that would result from the decrease. Borrowers, on the other hand, would issue only short-term securities, thereby paying currently high rates for a short period of time with the expectation of subsequently issuing longer term securities when rates decrease. Consequently, there would be an excess supply of funds in the long-term market and an excess demand for funds in the short-term market, which would cause long-term interest rates to decrease and short-term interest rates to increase. These pressures on interest rates would

**EXHIBIT 8–6**
**Upward Sloping Yield Curve**

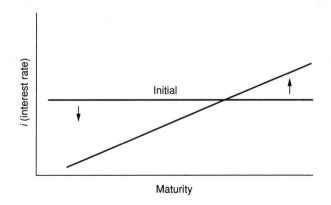

---

[5] This example ignores the effect of compound interest.

result in a downward-sloping, or inverted, yield curve as illustrated in Exhibit 8–7.

As indicated above, the liquidity hypothesis is not intended to be a complete explanation of the term structure of interest rates. Rather it is intended to supplement the expectations hypothesis. The combined effects of the liquidity hypothesis and the expectations hypothesis are shown in Exhibit 8–8.

The expectations hypothesis produces a horizontal yield curve when interest rates are normal, an upward-sloping yield curve when interest rates are low, and a downward-sloping yield curve when interest rates are high. Supplementing the expectations hypothesis with the liquidity hypothesis, which always predicts an upward-sloping yield curve, provides an upward bias to a yield curve based only on the expectations hypothesis. Indeed upward-sloping yield curves have historically been the most frequently observed, and for this reason upward-sloping yield curves are frequently referred to as normal yield curves. During recessionary periods, when interest rates are low and are expected to increase, the yield curve has a steep upward slope. However, when the economy is strong, credit is tight, and interest rates are high, downward-sloping yield curves are observed. Both observations are consistent with the expectations hypothesis.

### Segmentation Hypothesis
The basis for the *segmentation hypothesis* is the antithesis of the basis for the expectations hypothesis. Whereas the expectations hypothesis assumes that both borrowers and lenders are able to alter the maturity structure of their portfolios, each group shifting among the maturities of their respective borrowings or investments, the segmentation hypothesis assumes that both borrowers and lenders

**EXHIBIT 8–7**
**Downward-Sloping Yield Curve**

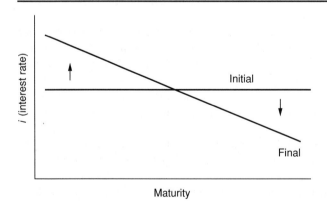

**EXHIBIT 8–8**
**Expectations Hypothesis plus Liquidity Hypothesis**

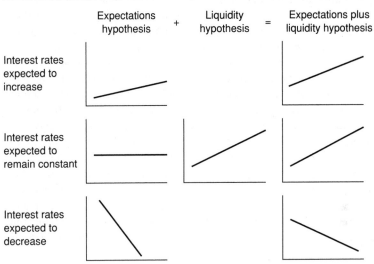

are constrained to particular segments of the maturity spectrum for institutional and legal reasons. For such market participants, shifting among maturities is not feasible, and therefore various maturity securities are not considered to be substitutes for one another, independent of the levels of the various interest rates.

In practice, there are numerous financial market participants whose borrowings or investments are, for a variety of reasons, constrained to only one portion of the maturity spectrum. For example, pension fund managers and insurance companies have a relatively small amount of their investments in short-maturity securities, whereas commercial banks have a relatively small amount of their investments in long-term bonds.

If indeed the market is segmented so that borrowers and lenders active in the market for one maturity are unlikely to be active in the market for any other maturity, then the interest rate associated with a particular maturity would have to be the result of the supply and demand pressures for only that maturity. Consequently, a change in supply and demand factors in one maturity will affect the interest rate for only that maturity and have no impact on the interest rate for any other maturity.

The segmentation hypothesis and the expectations hypothesis are competing, incompatible explanations of the relationship between interest rates and maturities on securities. For technical reasons, resolving which is the more correct explanation of the relationship is an intractable problem. In reality, there are probably some elements of both theories that are correct, although neither one is completely correct in explaining the relationship. In particular, it is unlikely that all borrowers and lenders are locked into one portion of the available maturity structure and unable to switch to another when interest rates dictate. Alternatively, there are undoubtedly some market participants who are restricted to particular segments of the maturity structure.

Either hypothesis could provide correct conclusions without the hypothesis holding in its extreme version. For example, for the expectations hypothesis to apply, not all borrowers and lenders have to be able to shift among maturities on the basis of relative interest rates, only enough to affect the relative interest rates. Similarly, for the segmentation hypothesis to apply, not all borrowers and lenders have to be restricted to particular segments of the maturity range, only enough so that the interest rates associated with each maturity segment are influenced by different supply-and-demand considerations. Observers of debt markets have noted characteristics supportive of both hypotheses in their less-than-extreme versions. However, most observers tend to support the expectations hypothesis complemented by the liquidity hypothesis as the dominant explanation for the observed relationship between interest rates and maturity.

The expectations-hypothesis/liquidity-hypothesis description of the maturity structure of interest rates can be applied to the actual behavior of the financial markets. The conclusions that can be drawn from this combination are that when the level of interest rates is normal the yield curve will have a slight upward slope—the long-term rates will be slightly greater than short-term rates. When the general level of interest rates is low, the term structure will have a steeper upward slope. Finally, when the level of interest rates is high, the term structure will have a downward slope. Pragmatically, the segmentation hypothesis adds nothing that either contradicts or supports this observation.

Empirical observations support conclusions derived from the expectations and the liquidity hypotheses.

## Credit Risk

The two major characteristics of a security are return and risk. In turn, there are two major types of risk: market risk and credit risk. Market risk refers to the volatility of the price of a security due to changes in the general level of interest rates. The market risk of a security is thus determined primarily by its maturity, since the longer the maturity, the greater the price change of the security for a given magnitude of interest rate change in the opposite direction. Thus, the term structure of interest rates relates to the market risk of a security. This section considers the other type of risk, credit risk.

The credit risk of a security is a measure of the likelihood that the issuer of the security, the borrower, will be unable to pay the interest or principal on the security when due. Credit risk thus measures the creditworthiness of the security's issuer. Federal securities, that is, issues of the U.S. Department of the Treasury, have the lowest credit risk. Federal agencies are perceived to have the next lowest credit risk because they are backed by the federal government. Corporate securities are rated lower than federal agencies with respect to credit risk. The relative credit risks of long-term corporate securities are rated by several private financial corporations. Exhibit 8–9 describes the rating categories of the two major ones—Moody's and Standard & Poor's.

Although the creditworthiness of different issuers of bonds affect the bonds' credit risk, even different bonds of the same issuer can have different credit risk depending on the characteristics of the specific bond. For example, a debenture (an unsecured bond) may have a higher credit risk than a bond that is collateralized by real or financial assets or a sinking-fund bond of the same issuer.

Some money market instruments are also rated by private financial corporations.[6] Both Standard & Poor's and Moody's rate commercial paper issues. For example, the grades usually acceptable to commercial paper investors are Standard & Poor's A–1, A–2, and A–3 and Moody's Prime–1, Prime–2, and Prime–3. However, other money market instruments, such as domestic bank negotiable certificates of deposit (CDs), are not rated by these agencies.

Interest rates are higher for securities with greater credit risk because investors have to be compensated for the additional risk. Consequently, the interest rate on a Treasury security is less than that on a AAA corporate security, which is in turn less than that on an A corporate security, all with the same maturity. These spreads tend to widen when interest rates are high and to narrow when interest rates are low. This is consistent with a "flight to quality," an increased preference by investors for low credit-risk instruments when interest rates are high and investors perceive low credit-risk borrowers as vulnerable. Money market spreads similarly show a widening when interest rates are high and a narrowing when interest rates are low (i.e., a flight to quality at high interest rates).

The credit-risk structure of interest rates explains variations in the interest rates on various securities of the same maturity due to differences in the credit risk of the issuers and issues. In addition, the size of the spreads between securities with high credit risk and low credit risk varies with the level of interest rates.

## Taxability Structure

There are three aspects of taxability that cause interest rates on different securities to differ at a specific time.

---

[6] Money market instruments are described in Chapter 11.

**EXHIBIT 8–9**
**Corporate Bond Rating Categories***

| Standard & Poor's Rating Categories† | Description |
| --- | --- |
| AAA (Aaa) | Bonds rated AAA have the highest rating assigned by Standard & Poor's to a debt obligation. Capacity to pay interest and repay principal is extremely strong. |
| AA (Aa) | Bonds rated AA have a very strong capacity to pay interest and repay principal and differ from the highest rated issues only in small degree. |
| A (A) | Bonds rated A have a strong capacity to pay interest and repay principal, although they are somewhat more susceptible to the adverse effects of changes in circumstances and economic conditions than bonds in higher rated categories. |
| BBB (Baa) | Bonds rated BBB are regarded as having adequate capacity to pay interest and repay principal. Whereas they normally exhibit adequate protection parameters, adverse economic conditions or changing circumstances are more likely to lead to a weakened capacity to pay interest and repay principal for bonds in this category than for bonds in higher rated categories. |
| BB (Ba)<br>B(B)<br>CCC (CCa)<br>CC(Ca) | Bonds rated BB, CCC and CC are regarded, on balance, as predominantly speculative with respect to capacity to pay interest and repay principal in accordance with the terms of the obligation. BB indicates the lowest degree of speculation and CC the highest degree of speculation. While such bonds will likely have some quality and protective characteristics, these are outweighed by large uncertainties or major risk exposures to adverse conditions. |
| C | The rating C is reserved for income bonds on which no interest is being paid. |
| D | Bonds rated D are in default, and payment of interest and/or repayment of principal is in arrears. |
| Plus (+) or minus (−) | The ratings from AA to B may be modified by the addition of a plus or minus sign to show relative standing within the major rating categories. |

* These Standard & Poor's corporate bond rating categories also apply to municipal bonds.
† The ratings in parentheses refer to the corresponding ratings of Moody's Investor's Service, Inc.
  Source: Standard & Poor's Corporation

## Tax-Exempt Municipals

The coupon payments on Treasury and corporate bonds are subject to federal income tax. Consequently, the after-tax yield on Treasury and corporate bonds is less than the coupon yield by an amount determined by the bondholder's tax bracket. The federal government does not tax the coupon payment on state and local securities.[7]  Since municipal securities are tax-exempt, their after-tax yield is the same as their pretax yield. Because investors are concerned with after-tax rather than pretax yields, municipal securities can be issued with lower coupons than the coupons on similar Treasury or corporate securities. For example, to an investor in the 30 percent tax bracket, a 7 percent municipal security selling at par has the same after-tax yield as a 10 percent Treasury or corporate security.

Thus, municipal bond interest rates differ from the interest rates on Treasury and corporate bonds because of the difference in taxability. The yield spread is always positive; that is, the yield on Treasury bonds is higher than the yield on municipal bonds.

The magnitude of the spread changes over the interest-rate cycle for two reasons. First, municipal bonds have a higher credit risk than Treasury bonds, and the phenomenon related to the flight to quality discussed in the previous section is applicable. Here, the flight to quality is from municipals to Treasuries when interest rates are high. In this case, however, since the rate on Treasury bonds is higher than the rate on municipal bonds, the flight to Treasury bonds during times of high interest rates tends to narrow the spread.

In addition, the spread between Treasury and municipal bond yields changes over the interest-rate cycle for reasons of taxability. The spread is the absolute difference between the Treasury and the municipal bond interest rates. However, the tax rate as it is applied to the coupon on Treasury securities has a relative or proportional effect. For example, to an investor in the 50 percent tax bracket, a 4 percent municipal security has the same after-tax yield as an 8 percent Treasury security, for a spread of 4 percent. However, a 6 percent municipal security has the same after-tax yield as a 12 percent Treasury security, for a spread of 6 percent. Similarly, an 8 percent municipal security has the same after-tax yield as a 16 percent Treasury security, for a spread of 8 percent. Because of the proportional nature of the federal income tax structure, the absolute spread between Treasury and municipal bonds varies over the interest-rate cycle, being larger when interest rates are high and smaller when interest rates are low.

Overall, because of the flight to quality, the spread between Treasury and

---

[7] State and local governments cannot tax the coupon payments of federal securities, but this exemption is not as important as the federal exemption on state and local government securities because the income tax rates of state and local governments are lower than federal income tax rates.

municipal bonds narrows when interest rates are high, and, because of the proportional nature of the income tax, the spread widens when interest rates are high. Consequently, the two effects are countervailing. Based on the historical Treasury bond/municipal bond interest rate spreads, the latter effect of interest rates on the spread dominates the former effect.

The spread between municipal and Treasury bonds may also vary structurally due to changes in tax legislation that affect the level of the personal income tax and the attractiveness of other tax shelters that compete with municipal securities as tax-reducing investments.

### Level of Coupon

Prior to the repeal of the preferential tax treatment of capital gains, there was a second aspect of taxability that caused interest rates among different securities, even of the same issuer and maturity, to differ *for bonds issued on or before July 18, 1984*. This aspect was the magnitude of the coupon of the security.

Although coupon payments on Treasury and corporate bonds are taxed at the ordinary income tax rate, prior to the 1986 tax act capital gains were taxed at a preferential tax rate. If a bond was acquired after July 22, 1984 and held for more than six months, the long-term capital gains tax, which was 40 percent of the personal income tax rate, applied. The holding period to qualify for a long-term capital gain for a bond purchased on or before July 22, 1984 was more than one year. For a bond issued on or before July 18, 1984 and held to maturity, therefore, the after-tax value of 1 percent of pretax coupon return was less to an investor than the after-tax value of 1 percent of pretax capital gains. This did not apply to bonds issued after July 18, 1984 that were held to maturity.

The yield-to-maturity of a bond, as it is commonly calculated, includes both the coupon return and the return due to capital gain or loss (the difference between the current market price and the par value of the bond) on an annual basis as if the security were held to maturity. If, for example, a 30-year security with an $80 coupon is selling for $1,000, its 8 percent yield-to-maturity is entirely due to the coupon return. If another 30-year security with a $60 coupon issued on or before July 18, 1984, was initially selling for $773.77 for an 8 percent yield-to-maturity, its yield-to-maturity consisted of a 7.75 percent coupon return, and the remainder was due to the capital gain over the 30-year life. Since this low-coupon "discount security" (a security selling for less than its maturity value of $1,000) had a portion of its return due to capital gains, which was taxed at a lower rate, the after-tax return on the low-coupon discount bond was greater than that of the high-coupon bond selling at "par" (its maturity value of $1,000). Therefore, the price of the discount bond was bid up, and the yield-to-maturity at its new actual trading price was somewhat less than the 8 percent yield on the par bond. The lower yield on the discount bond was to compensate for its more favorable tax treatment.[8]   Thus, low-coupon discount bonds normally sold at a yield somewhat lower than high-coupon bonds selling at par or at a premium (at a price greater than its maturity value) or even at a smaller discount because of this tax advantage. The yield spread, almost without exception, was positive (the yield on the high-coupon bond is greater than the yield on the low-coupon bond).

While at the time of this writing, capital gains are not granted preferential tax treatment, the reader should be aware of this effect should Congress pass a capital gains tax bill.

### Flower Bonds

Several Treasury bonds issued during the 1950s and early 1960s exhibit an attractive tax feature. These bonds, known as *flower bonds,* are acceptable *at par* in payment of federal estate taxes when owned by the decendent at death. These bonds were issued with low coupons. Because of this tax advantage, the (pretax) yields on these bonds are lower than on other Treasury bonds without the estate-tax eligibility provision.

## Interest Rate Structure: A Summary

Factors that affect one interest rate tend to affect all interest rates in generally the same way. For this reason, discussions of the determinants of interest rates often seem as if they are treating a single interest rate. This section provides the transition from the consideration of a single interest rate to the actual multiplicity of interest rates observed in the financial world.

There are three major structures of interest rates that contribute to the multiplicity of interest rates observed: the maturity structure, the credit-risk structure, and the taxability structure. There are other factors that cause differences in interest rates. One such factor is the liquidity of the security, often measured by the size of the bid/ask spread (the smaller the spread, the more liquid the security). The liquidity of a security may depend on the size of the original issue or the time since the original issue. Securities tend to be less liquid if the original-issue size was small and as the time since original issue increases. These aspects of liquidity supplement the market-risk aspect discussed above.

The fundamental factors that affect these three structures and the changes in the relationships among interest rates on the basis of these structures over the interest-rate cycle are discussed in this section.

---

[8] If the bond had been issued after July 22, 1984, the entire appreciation realized at maturity would have been treated as ordinary income.

## SUMMARY

Four potentially mutually exclusive rationales for determining the level of "the" interest rate—liquidity preference, loanable funds, inflation and the real rate of interest, and the tone of the market—have been discussed. The focus was on the factors that affect the general level of interest rates at a specific time, not on the differences among various interest rates at a specific time. We then discussed the structures of interest rates, the factors that tend, given the general level of interest rates, to affect the differences among specific interest rates at a specific time. As discussed, the three major factors are the maturity, the credit risk, and the taxability of the specific security. Now we shall integrate these various perspectives on interest-rate determination.

Most models of interest-rate behavior, whether used for explaining past interest-rate behavior or forecasting future interest-rate behavior, and whether they are judgmental or econometric models, incorporate elements of the liquidity preference, loanable funds, and inflation and the real rate of interest rationales. Thus, these three rationales are viewed as complementary rather than competitive as explanations for interest-rate behavior. There are, however, some differences in the applicability of these three rationales and also the tone of the market rationale, depending on whether the short-run or long-run responses of interest rates are being considered and whether short-term or long-term interest rates are being considered.

Liquidity preference is an important explanation of very short-run changes in interest rates, particularly changes in short-term interest rates in response to changes in the money supply. Money supply announcements made by the Federal Reserve Bank of New York every week are closely watched, and the financial markets respond quickly to them.

The nature of the response of interest rates, particularly short-term interest rates, to money supply announcements has changed significantly during the last decade. If it had been announced 15 years ago that money supply had increased significantly, interest rates would have declined and vice versa, as expected by the liquidity preference rationale. However, today when an announcement is made that money supply has increased significantly, interest rates usually increase rather than decrease, and vice versa. There are two reasons for this change in response.

First, since the mid-1970s the Federal Reserve System has, as an important part of its implementation of monetary policy, set ranges for future money supply growth. It then conducts monetary policy so that the actual money supply growth fits within these ranges. Thus, an announcement of a large increase in the money supply is now interpreted by the markets as requiring the Federal Reserve System to subsequently tighten money supply growth to keep it within the announced ranges. The markets, anticipating a subsequent decline in money supply growth, respond by making interest rates increase in response to the expected tightening.

Here again the liquidity preference rationale is operable, but now the market responds to expectations of subsequent money supply growth rather than to the announcement of the past money supply growth.

The second reason for the change in response is that inflation has become a more important force in determining interest rates. In view of the quantity theory of money, there is an important relationship between money supply and inflation. Thus, an announcement of a high growth in the money supply often causes market participants to conclude that inflation will accelerate, at least if this money supply growth rate continues, thus causing interest rates to increase due to the inflation and real rate of interest rationale. For both of these reasons, interest rates now often increase rather than decrease when there is an announcement of an increase in the money supply.

Essentially, all explanations of the level of interest rates include some measure of the money supply as a determinant, particularly for short-term interest rates and short-run changes. The liquidity preference rationale, however, is also used for determining the level of interest rates on a longer term basis. This use is implemented, as discussed above, in the context of the quantity theory of money: $M \times V = P \times Y$. By forecasting a likely growth in the money supply, $M$, and a likely range of increases in real GNP, $Y$, an assumption about the likely range of inflation, $P$, can be made from the quantity theory. From this rate of inflation and an assumption about the real rate of interest, the nominal rate of interest can be determined. This conceptual construction obviously relies jointly on the liquidity preference and the inflation and real rate of interest rationales of interest-rate determination.

The loanable funds rationale is typically used to explain and forecast interest rates on a long-term basis and applies, in general, to both long- and short-term interest rates. By developing a taxonomy of the likely sources and uses of funds over a period of time, as provided above, and by including an assumption about changes in the money supply, a forecast of potential imbalances between the supply and demand for funds can be made. Projected imbalances of supply over demand are then used as the basis for forecasting a decrease in interest rates and of demand over supply for forecasting an increase in interest rates.

It is in this context that crowding out (borrowing by the federal government sector, which makes borrowing by the private sector more expensive or impossible) is considered. In addition, increased borrowing by the business or consumer sectors put upward pressures on interest rates, and vice versa. In the loanable funds context, short- and long-term sources and uses of funds are typically aggregated, thus implicitly assuming substitutability among securities of various maturities.

With the higher levels of inflation seen in the late 1970s and early 1980s, the inflation and real rate of interest rationale has become very important in explaining the nominal level of interest rates. As discussed, although they are attributable both to variations in inflation and variations in the real rate of interest, variations in the nominal rate of interest are more attributable to the former than the latter. Thus, the real rate of interest might vary over a range of from $-1$ percent to 4 percent, and inflation might vary over a range of 5 percent to 15 percent. Therefore, including a measure of inflation in an explanation for the general level of interest rates is essential.

However, it is more difficult to include an accurate measure of the determinants of the real rate of interest. In general, the real rate of interest tends to vary over the business cycle, being high during periods of prosperity and low during periods of recession. Most explanations of the general level of interest rates include inflation explicitly but do not consider the real rate of interest explicitly.

Thus, most explanations of the general level of interest rates include elements of the liquidity preference, loanable funds, and the inflation and real rate of interest rationales, although there are some differences in emphasis depending on whether short-term or long-term interest rates and whether short-term changes or long-term changes in the rates are being considered. The tone of the market rationale should also be considered in determining interest rates, although typically only for very short-run changes and mainly in the short-term interest rates. Therefore, models that forecast quarterly interest rates often do not include the tone of the market.

Having determined the general level of interest rates, or "the" interest rate, by the methods summarized above, consideration can be given to determining specific interest rates on specific securities. To make this determination (given the general level of interest rates), the maturity, the identity of the issuer, and the taxability of the specific security must be considered—that is, the interest rate on the specific security must be considered with respect to the three structures of interest rates discussed above. In relating a specific interest rate to the general level of interest rates, two issues must be considered: (1) the normal spread between the specific interest rate and an interest rate reflective of the general level of interest rates, such as the 91-day Treasury bill rate or the long-term Treasury bond rate and (2) variations in the magnitude in this spread over the interest-rate cycle.

The conclusions of the three maturity structures of interest rates are as follows. When the level of interest rates is low, interest rates increase with maturity (the term structure of the interest-rate curve has a positive slope). And when the level of interest rates is high, interest rates decrease with maturity (the term structure of the interest rate curve has a negative slope). Thus, short-term interest rates vary through a much wider range than the long-term interest rates, as illustrated in Exhibit 8–10. And thus the spread between short-term and long-term interest rates (long term minus short term) varies considerably over the interest-rate cycle and becomes less positive (or more negative) as interest rates increase.

With respect to the identity of the issuer, the greater the credit risk of the issuer, the higher the interest rate on the security. It is in this regard that Treasury

**EXHIBIT 8–10**
**Interest Rate Variability by Maturity**

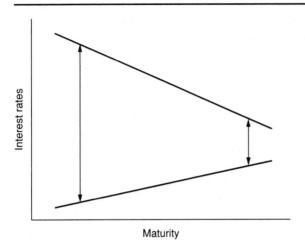

securities are the benchmark for interest rates. The Treasury has the lowest credit risk of any issuer, and Treasury securities have the lowest adjustment for credit risk. Different issues of the same issuer may also have different credit risks due to the nature of the securities. The spread between high credit-risk interest rates and low credit-risk interest rates (high credit risk minus low credit risk) increases with the level of interest rates because of a flight to quality when interest rates are high.

Finally, the taxability of the issue must be considered. The most important aspect of taxability relates to municipal securities whose coupons are exempt from federal income tax. Due to this tax exemption, actual pretax interest rates on municipals are lower than those on Treasury and corporate securities. Because taxes are on a relative or proportionate basis, the spread between Treasury and municipal securities (Treasury rate minus municipal rate) widens (narrows) as the level of interest rates increases (decreases).

Prior to the repeal of the preferential capital gains tax, another aspect of taxability was related to the magnitude of the coupon, which determines the degree of the discount or the premium of a security, since coupon income was taxed as ordinary income and capital appreciation as capital gains. Thus, the higher the coupon on a security, the higher was its interest rate to compensate for the greater tax liability. Finally, flower bonds have lower yields due to their estate-tax advantages.

Overall, the determination of interest rates occurs in two steps. First, the general level of interest rates is determined by the eclectic combination of the methods described above. Second, the appropriate spread between the interest rate on the specific security being considered and the general level of interest rates is determined by considering the factors that affect the structures of interest rates. The benchmark interest rate used in such spread analysis is typically the interest rate on a U.S. Treasury debt security.

# PART 2

# TREASURY, AGENCIES, AND MONEY MARKET INSTRUMENTS

# CHAPTER 9

## TREASURY AND STRIPPED TREASURY SECURITIES

*Frank J. Fabozzi, Ph.D., CFA, CPA*
*Visiting Professor of Finance*
*Sloan School of Management*
*Massachusetts Institute of Technology*
*and*
*Editor, The Journal of Portfolio Management*

*T. Dessa Fabozzi, Ph.D.*
*Vice President*
*Client Analytics*
*Merrill Lynch Capital Markets*

In this chapter, we discuss the Treasury securities market and the stripped Treasury securities market. We will also describe the Treasury yield curve, its implications, and theories of the term structure of interest rates.

## TREASURY SECURITIES

U.S. Treasury securities are backed by the full faith and credit of the U.S. government. Consequently, they are viewed by market participants as having *no credit risk*. Interest rates on Treasury securities are the benchmark interest rates used throughout the U.S. economy as well as in international capital markets. Market participants talk of yields on non-Treasury securities as trading above (or below) a particular Treasury security.

Two factors account for the prominent role of Treasury securities: volume (in terms of dollar value outstanding) and liquidity. The U.S. Department of the

Treasury is the largest single issuer of debt in the world, with Treasury securities accounting for $2 trillion (consisting of over 200 Treasury note and bond issues and 30 Treasury bill issues). In contrast, the entire U.S. corporate bond market accounts for about $900 billion and over 10,000 issues; the U.S. municipal bond market similarly accounts for about $760 billion, with more than 70,000 separate issuers and millions of individual issues. The large volume of total debt and the large size of any single issue have contributed to making the Treasury market the most active and hence most liquid market in the world. The spread between bid and ask prices is considerably narrower than other sectors of the bond market, and more issues can be readily purchased. In contrast, many issues in the corporate and municipal markets are illiquid and cannot be readily traded.

There are two categories of goverment securities—discount and coupon securities. The fundamental difference between these two types of securities is the form in which the holder receives interest and, as a result, the prices at which they are issued. Coupon securities pay interest every six months. Discount securities do not make periodic interest payments. Instead, the security holder receives interest at the maturity date, the interest being the difference between the amount received at the maturity date (called the *maturity*, *par*, or *face value*) and the purchase price.

The current practice of the Treasury is to issue all securities with maturities of one year or less as discount securities. These securities are called *Treasury bills*. All securities with maturities longer than one year are issued as coupon securities. Treasury coupon securities issued with original maturities between 2 and 10 years are called *notes*; those with original maturities greater than 10 years are called *bonds*. While there is therefore a distinction between a Treasury note and bond, in this chapter, we shall refer to both as simply a bond.

Although Treasury notes are not callable, many outstanding Treasury bond issues are callable within five years of maturity. Since February 1985, the Treasury no longer issues callable bonds.

Treasury securities are available in book-entry form at the Federal Reserve Bank. This means that the investor receives only a receipt as evidence of ownership instead of an engraved certificate. An advantage of book-entry is ease in transferring ownership of the security. Treasury bills are available only in book-entry form. Treasury coupon securities issued after January 1, 1983 are required to be in book-entry form.

Interest income from Treasury securities is subject to federal income taxation but is exempt from state and local income taxes.

## The Primary Market

Treasury securities are typically issued on an auction basis. There are regular cycles in which the Treasury auctions and issues securities of specific maturities. Three-month and six-month Treasury bills are auctioned every Monday; the amounts to be auctioned are ordinarily announced in the afternoon of the

Tuesday prior to the auction. One-year (52-week) Treasury bills are auctioned on the third week of every month, with announcement on the preceding Friday. When the Treasury is temporarily short of cash, it issues *cash management bills*. The maturity of cash management bills coincides with the length of time that the Treasury anticipates the shortfall of funds. Thus, cash management bills have maturities ranging from a few days to six months.

The Treasury regularly issues coupon securities with the following maturities: 2 years, 3 years, 4 years, 5 years, 7 years, 10 years, and 30 years.[1] Exhibit 9–1 summarizes the months that Treasury coupon securities are issued. At the beginning of the second month of each calendar quarter (February, May, August, and November), the Treasury conducts its regular refunding operations. At this time, it auctions 3-year, 10-year, and 30-year Treasury securities. The Treasury announces on the Wednesday of the preceding month (1) the amount that will be auctioned, (2) what portion of that amount is to replace maturing Treasury debt, (3) what portion of that amount is to raise new funds, and (4) the estimated cash needs for the balance of the quarter and how it plans to obtain the funds. During the second half of each calendar quarter, the Treasury conducts its "mini-refunding" and issues four-year and seven-year Treasury notes. A description of these cycles for all Treasury securities is provided in more detail in Exhibit 9–2.

## EXHIBIT 9–1
## Treasury Coupon Securities Auctioned by Month

| Month | Number of Years to Maturity | | | | | | |
|---|---|---|---|---|---|---|---|
| | 2 | 3 | 4 | 5 | 7 | 10 | 30 |
| January | x | | | | | | |
| February | x | x | | x | | x | x |
| March | x | | x | | x | | |
| April | x | | | | | | |
| May | x | x | | x | | x | x |
| June | x | | x | | x | | |
| July | x | | | | | | |
| August | x | x | | x | | x | x |
| September | x | | x | | x | | |
| October | x | | | | | | |
| November | x | x | | x | | x | x |
| December | x | | x | | x | | |

x = auctioned in indicated month

[1] Prior to April 1986, the Treasury also issued 20-year bonds.

**EXHIBIT 9–2**
**Treasury Auction Cycles**

*Discount Securities*

| | |
|---|---|
| Three-month (91-day) Treasury bills | Auctioned every Monday; issued on the following Thursday. |
| Six-month (182-day) Treasury bills | Same auction and issue cycle as for three-month Treasury bills (auctioned on Monday, issued on Thursday). Thus, 182-day Treasury bills eventually trade in consonance with 91-day Treasury bills. |
| Fifty-two week (364-day) Treasury bills | Auctioned every fourth Tuesday; issued on the following Thursday. Thus, 364-day Treasury bills eventually trade in consonance with 182-day and then 91-day Treasury bills. |

*Coupon Securities*

| | |
|---|---|
| Two-year | Two-year Treasury notes are auctioned every month, normally near the end of the month, for settlement on the last business day of the month, and may mature on the last business day of the month two-years hence. |
| Five-year | Five-year Treasury notes are auctioned on a quarterly cycle near the end of February, May, August, and November, months for settlement at the beginning of the March, June, September, and December months. These issues mature on the 15th of the February, May, August, and November, months approximately five years and two months after their settlement date (these notes are, thus, five-year, two-month notes, and their first coupon is a long coupon; that is, the first coupon represents approximately eight months interest). |
| Mini-Refunding (Four-year/seven-year) | The mini-refunding is a quarterly cycle issue of, typically, a four-year note, and a seven-year note. These issues are announced at the same time, typically during the middle of the month. They are then typically auctioned on consecutive business days late during the March, June, September, and December months for settlement at the beginning of the January, April, July, and October months. The four-year note matures on the last business day of the March, June, September, and December months four years after settlement; the seven-year note matures on the 15th day of the January, April, July, and October months seven years after settlement. |

The auction for Treasury bills and Treasury coupon securities is conducted on a yield basis.[2]  Competitive bids for Treasury bills must be submitted on

---

[2] Prior to 1974, the Treasury conducted auctions for coupon securities on the basis of price rather than yield.

**EXHIBIT 9–2**
**Treasury Auction Cycles—*Continued***

| | |
|---|---|
| Refunding (Three-year/ten-year/ thirty-year) | The refunding cycle is a quarterly cycle issue of notes and bonds that are issued on the 15th day of the February, May, August, and November quarterly cycle months and are typically auctioned on the Tuesday, Wednesday, and Thursday prior to the issue. Each refunding typically contains three issues: (1) a three-year note, (2) a ten-year note, and (3) a thirty-year bond. These issues mature on the 15th day of the February, May, August, or November months, the appropriate number of years (3, 10, or 30) after their issue. The issues in the refunding cycle have, however, been subject to some variations. |
| *Summary of maturity schedule* | 15th day of February, May, August, and November months: three-year, five-year, ten-year, and thirty-year.<br><br>15th day of January, April, July, and October: seven-year.<br><br>End of Month: two-year (monthly), four-year (March, June, September, and December). |

Source: Sharmin Mossavar-Rahmani, Frank J. Fabozzi, Frank J. Jones, and Benjamin Wolkowitz, "The Cash Market for U.S. Treasury Securities," Chapter 2 in Frank J. Fabozzi (ed.), *The Handbook of Treasury and Agency Securities* (Chicago: Probus Publishing, 1990).

a bank discount basis (explained below). For Treasury coupon securities, the bidder submits a bid based on the yield-to-maturity that he or she is willing to accept. Noncompetitive tenders may also be submitted for up to $1 million face amount. Such tenders include no bid yield, only a quantity. The price awarded to noncompetitive bidders is the average price determined by the competitive bidders.

The auction results are determined by first deducting the total noncompetitive tenders from the total securities being auctioned. The remainder is the amount to be awarded to the competitive bidders. The lowest yield bidders are awarded their securities at their bid price. Successively, higher yielding bidders are awarded securities at their bid price until the total amount offered (less noncompetitive tenders) is awarded. The highest yield at which securities are awarded is known as the "stop," and bidders at that price are awarded a percentage of their total tender. The difference between the average yield of all the bids accepted by the Treasury and the stop is called the "tail."

For example, the results of the one-year Treasury bill auction on June 23, 1989 was as follows:

| | | |
|---|---|---|
| Total issue | = | $9.00 billion |
| Less noncompetitive bids | = | 0.64 |
| Less Federal Reserve | = | 2.80 |
| Left for competitive bidders | = | $5.56 |

Total competitive bids received were as follows:

| $ Amount (billions) | Bid |
|---|---|
| $0.20 billion | 7.55 (highest price) |
| 0.26 | 7.56 |
| 0.33 | 7.57 |
| 0.57 | 7.58 (average price) |
| 0.79 | 7.59 |
| 0.96 | 7.60 |
| 1.25 | 7.61 |
| 1.52 | 7.62 (stop, or lowest, price) |

The Treasury would allocate to competitive bidders from the low-yield bid yield (i.e., highest price) to the highest yield bid (the lowest price) until $5.56 billion is distributed. Those who bid no more than 7.61 would be awarded the entire amount for which they bid. The total that would be awarded to these bidders is $4.36 billion, leaving $1.2 billion to be awarded. Each of the bidders at 7.62 would be awarded 79 percent (1.2/1.52) of his or her bid. The results of the auction would show 7.55 high, 7.58 average, and 7.62 the stop, with 79 percent awarded at the stop. Bidders higher in yield than 7.62 "missed" or were "shut out." This auction would have a tail of .04 (7.62 − 7.58).

### Role of Primary Dealers

Any firm can deal in government securities. In implementing its open market operations, the Federal Reserve will deal directly only with dealers that it designates as *primary*, or *recognized*, dealers. The Federal Reserve has established criteria for a firm to become a primary dealer. Basically, the Federal Reserve wants to be sure that the firm requesting status as a primary dealer has adequate capital relative to the positions in Treasury securities it assumes and does a reasonable volume of trading in Treasury securities (at least 1% of Treasury market activity). When a firm requests status as a primary dealer, the Federal Reserve will first request that the applying firm informally report its positions and trading volume. If these are acceptable to the Federal Reserve, it will then give the firm status as a *reporting dealer*. This means that the firm will be put on the Federal Reserve's regular reporting list. After some time as a reporting dealer, the Federal Reserve will elevate the firm to the status of primary dealer if it is convinced that the firm will continue to meet the criteria established.

The auction process relies on the participation of the primary government securities dealers. The primary dealers are expected to participate in every auction and typically bid for about 3 percent of every issue auctioned. The primary dealers subsequently redistribute the issue, at a profit or a loss, to both nonprimary dealers and institutional investors. The primary dealers are also expected to maintain a certain level of trading activity in the secondary market.

## The Secondary Market

The secondary market for Treasury securities is an over-the-counter market in which a group of U.S. government securities dealers continually provide bids and offers on outstanding Treasuries.[3] The secondary market is the most liquid financial market in the world.

In the secondary market, the most recently auctioned Treasury issues for each maturity are referred to as "on-the-run," or "current coupon" issues. Issues auctioned prior to the current coupon issues are typically referred to as "off-the-run" issues and are not as liquid as on-the-run issues. By "liquid," in this case, we mean the size of the bid-ask spread: the bid-ask spread is larger for off-the-run issues relative to on-the-run issues.

Dealers continuously provide bids and offers on specific outstanding Treasury securities. Dealer profits are generated from one or more of the following three sources: (1) the bid-ask spread, (2) appreciation in the securities held in inventory or depreciation in the securities sold short, and (3) the difference between the interest earned on the securities held in inventory and the cost of financing that inventory. The last source of profits is referred to as *carry* and depends on the shape of the yield curve. Where do dealers obtain the funds to finance an inventory position? That's another topic we'll cover shortly.

Another component of the Treasury secondary market is the "when-issued market," or "WI market," wherein Treasury securities are traded prior to the time they are issued by the Treasury. The when-issued trading for both Treasury bills and Treasury coupon issues extends from the day the auction is announced until the issue date. All deliveries on when-issued trades occur on the issue day of the Treasury security traded.

### Role of Brokers

Treasury dealers trade with the investing public and with other dealer firms. When they trade with each other, they trade through intermediaries known as government bond brokers. Dealers leave firm bids and offers with brokers, who display the highest bid and lowest offer in a computer network tied to each trading desk and displayed on a monitor. The dealer responding to a bid or offer by "hitting" or "taking" pays a commission to the broker. The size and prices of these transactions are highly visible to all dealers at once.

---

[3] Actually, some trading of Treasury coupon securities does occur on the New York Stock Exchange. However, the volume of these exchange-traded transactions is very small when compared to over-the-counter transactions.

Brokers are used by dealers because of the speed and efficiency with which trades can be accomplished. Brokers never trade for their own account and keep confidential the names of the dealers involved in trades. Five major brokers handle about 50 percent of the daily trading volume. They include Fundamental Brokers, Inc., RMJ Securities Corporation, Garban, Ltd., Cantor, Fitzgerald Securities Corporation, and Chapdelaine & Company Government Securities, Inc. These five brokers service the primary government dealers and a dozen or so other large government dealers aspiring to be primary dealers. Cantor, Fitzgerald Securities Corporation also serves as a broker for about 200 nonprimary dealers.

### Bid and Offer Quotes on Treasury Bills

Bid and offers in the dealer market for Treasury bills are computed in a special way. They are computed on a bank discount basis (in basis points) not on a price basis. The yield on a bank discount basis is computed as follows:

$$Y_D = \frac{D}{F} \times \frac{360}{t}$$

where

$Y_D$ = yield on a bank discount basis
$D$ = dollar discount, which is equal to the difference between the face value and the price
$F$ = face value
$t$ = number of days remaining to maturity

For example, a Treasury bill with 100 days to maturity, a face value of $100,000, and selling for $97,569 would be quoted as 8.75 percent on a bank discount basis:

$$D = \$100,000 - \$97,569$$
$$= \$2,431$$

Therefore,

$$Y_D = \frac{\$2,431}{\$100,000} \times \frac{360}{100}$$
$$= 8.75\%$$

Given the yield on a bank discount basis, it is simple to find the price of a Treasury bill. The price is found by first solving the above equation for the dollar discount ($D$), as follows:

$$D = Y_D \times F \times \frac{t}{360}$$

The price is then as follows:

$$\text{Price} = F - D$$

For our 100-day Treasury bill with a face value of $100,000, if the yield on a bank discount basis is quoted as 8.75 percent, $D$ is calculated as follows:

$$D = .0875 \times \$100,000 \times \frac{100}{360}$$

$$= \$2,431$$

Therefore,

$$\text{Price} = \$100,000 - \$2,431$$
$$= \$97,569$$

The quoted yield on a bank discount basis is not a meaningful measure of the return from holding a Treasury bill, for two reasons. First, the measure is based on a face value investment rather than the actual dollar amount invested. Second, the yield is annualized based on a 360- rather than a 365-day year, making it difficult to compare the yield with Treasury coupon securities that pay interest on a 365-day basis.

Despite its shortcomings as a measure of return, this is the way that dealers in the market have elected to quote Treasury bills. However, on many dealer quote sheets and some reporting services, two other yield measures that attempt to make the yield comparable to a coupon bond and other money market instruments are shown.

The measure that seeks to make the Treasury bill quote comparable to a coupon bond is called the *bond equivalent yield*.[4] This yield measure takes into consideration (1) the price rather than face value in computing yield, (2) a 365-day year rather than a 360-day year, and (3) the reinvestment opportunities available on a coupon security with more than 182 days (six months) to maturity. The formula for the bond equivalent yield for a Treasury bill depends on whether there are six months (182 days) or less to maturity, or more than six months to maturity. The reason for this is that, to compare a Treasury bill with a coupon security, it is necessary to take into consideration the fact that, on a coupon security with more than six months to maturity, there is an opportunity to reinvest the coupon payment. The formula for computing the bond equivalent yield for a Treasury bill with 182 days (six months) or less is as follows:

$$\frac{\text{Bond equivalent yield}}{(\text{for } t \le 182)} = \frac{365\,(Y_D)}{360 - t\,(Y_D)}$$

---

[4] As explained in Chapter 6, the bond equivalent yield is found by doubling the semiannual interest rate that equates the present value of the cash flow to the price of the bond.

The formula for the bond equivalent yield when there is more than 182 days follows:[5]

$$\text{Bond equivalent yield} \atop \text{(for } t > 182) = \frac{-(2t/365) + 2\sqrt{(t/365)^2 - [(2t/365) - 1][1 - (1/p)]}}{(2t/365) - 1}$$

where $p$ is the price of the Treasury bill that will produce \$1 of face value at maturity.

The *CD equivalent yield* (also called the *money market equivalent yield*) makes the yield on a Treasury bill more comparable to the way yields are quoted on money market instruments that pay interest on a 360-day basis, taking into consideration the price of the Treasury bill rather than its face value. (Money market instruments are the subject of Chapter 11.)

The formula for the CD equivalent yield is as follows:

$$\text{CD equivalent yield} = \frac{360 Y_D}{360 - t\,(Y_D)}$$

The top part of Exhibit 9–3 shows quotes on three Treasury bills on April 5, 1988, as reported by the Knight-Ridder MoneyCenter. The first quote is the yield

**EXHIBIT 9–3**
**Treasury Bill and Bond Notes from Knight-Ridder**

| Bills | Bid | Ask | Bond Equivalent | | C.D. Equivalent | |
|---|---|---|---|---|---|---|
| 3Mo 7/07/88 | 6.00− | 98+ | 6.178− | 6.162 | 6.093− | 6.078 |
| 6Mo 10/06/88 | 6.20 | −18+ | 6.490− | 6.474 | 6.402− | 6.386 |
| 1Yr 3/16/89 | 6.55+ | −54 | 6.976− | 6.959 | 6.993− | 6.976 |

| Coupons | Bid | Ask | Fed | | SIA | | Effective | |
|---|---|---|---|---|---|---|---|---|
| 73/83/90 | 99.20 | −21+ | 7.582− | 7.556 | 7.581− | 7.555 | 7.581− | 7.555 |
| 73/82/91 | 98.31 | −00+ | 7.784− | 7.765 | 7.779− | 7.760 | 7.779− | 7.760 |
| 77/83/92 | 99.16+ | −18 | 8.019− | 8.005 | 8.019− | 8.005 | 8.019− | 8.005 |
| 75/85/93 | 97.23 | −25 | 8.180− | 8.165 | 8.177− | 8.162 | 8.167− | 8.152 |
| 85/81/95 | 100.24+ | −26 | 8.747− | 8.465 | 8.470− | 8.461 | 8.470− | 8.461 |
| 81/82/98 | 96.17+ | −19 | 8.653− | 8.645 | 8.650− | 8.643 | 8.650− | 8.643 |
| 93/82/06 | 103.28+ | −30 | 8.935− | 8.930 | 8.933− | 8.928 | 8.916− | 8.911 |
| 87/88/17 | 100.07 | −08+ | 8.854− | 8.849 | 8.852− | 8.848 | 8.846− | 8.841 |

Source: Knight-Ridder MoneyCenter

[5] Marcia Stigum, *Money Market Calculations* (Homewood, IL: Dow Jones-Irwin, 1981), pp. 33–34.

on a bank discount basis, followed by the bond equivalent and CD equivalent yields.

### Bids and Offer Quotes on Treasury Coupon Securities

Prior to being auctioned, a new Treasury coupon issue is traded on a yield-to-maturity basis (e.g., 8.52 or 11.23). The auction process determines the coupon rate, and thereafter the issue trades on dollar price basis in price units of 1/32 of 1 percent of par (par is taken to be $100). For example, a quote of 92–14 refers to a price of 92 and 14/32. Thus, on the basis of $100,000 par value, a change in price of 1 percent is equal to $1,000 and 1/32 is equal to $31.25. A *plus* sign following the number of 32nds means that a 64th is added to the price. For example, 92–14+ refers to a price of 92 and 29/64, or 92.453125 percent, of par value.

On quote sheets and screens, the price quote is followed by some yield-to-maturity measure. Yield quotes can be shown based on the "Street" or "Treasury" method. The difference between these two yield measures is the procedure used to discount the first coupon payment when it is not exactly six months away. This occurs for two reasons. First, when the Treasury issues certain securities, the first coupon payment may be more or less than six months away. This situation is referred to as an "odd," or "irregular," first coupon payment. When the first coupon payment is more than six months away, it is said to have a long first coupon.[6] When the first coupon payment is less than six months from the date of issuance, the Treasury security is said to have a short first coupon.[7] A second situation in which an investor faces the prospect of receiving the next coupon payment in less than six months is when a security is purchased between coupon payment dates.

The difference in the Street and Treasury practice for computing yield is the procedure for discounting over a long first coupon period and over a fractional six-month period.[8] The Treasury method (also called the "Fed" method) assumes simple interest over the period from the valuation date to the next coupon payment. The Street method (also called the Securities Industry Associ-

---

[6] The 5-year Treasury note is an example of a Treasury security usually issued as a long first coupon security. The first coupon payment for the 5-year Treasury note is approximately eight months after the issuance date.

[7] The Treasury issues a security with a short first coupon when the auction date is the 15th or end of the month but that day falls on a weekend or holiday. In such cases, the Treasury issues the security on the next business day but pays the first coupon on the 15th or end of month six months later. Thus, the first coupon payment is less than six months.

[8] For a further discussion of the Fed yield and effective, or Street, yield, see Sharmin Mossavar-Rahmani, "Measuring Risk and Reward in the Treasury Market," Chapter 3 in Frank J. Fabozzi (ed.) *The Handbook of Treasury and Agency Securities* (Chicago, IL: Probus Publishing, 1990).

ation, or "SIA," method) assumes compound interest over the period from the valuation date to the next coupon payment date.[9]   From a practical point of view, once a security is issued and traded in the secondary market, investors and traders use the Street method.

Exhibit 9–3 shows the bid-ask price, Fed (Treasury) yield, and SIA (Street) yield for the current (on-the-run) Treasury coupon issues on April 5, 1988.

The invoice price that the buyer pays is equal to the agreed upon price plus accrued interest. Accrued interest is based on the actual number of days that the security is held. (This is referred to as "actual over actual" basis.) The accrued interest is determined as follows:

$$\frac{\text{Annual coupon}}{2} \times \frac{\text{Actual number of days held}}{\text{Actual number of days in coupon period}}$$

### Financing Dealer Positions

Suppose that a government dealer has purchased $10 million of a particular Treasury security. Where does the dealer obtain the funds to finance that position? Of course, the dealer can finance the position with his own funds. Typically, however, the dealer will use the repurchase agreement, or *repo* market, to obtain financing. In the repo market, the dealer can use the Treasury security purchased as collateral for a loan. The term of the loan and the interest rate that the dealer agrees to pay (called the *repo rate*) are specified. When the term of the loan is one day, it is called an *overnight repo*; a loan for more than one day is called a *term repo*.

The transaction is referred to as a repurchase agreement because it calls for the sale of the security and its repurchase at a future date. Both the sale price and the purchase price are specified in the agreement. The difference between the purchase (repurchase) price and the sale price is the dollar interest cost of the loan.

Let's illustrate the repurchase agreement with our dealer who needs to finance $10 million of a Treasury bond that he purchased and plans to hold overnight. Suppose that a customer of the dealer has excess funds of $10 million.

---

[9] For example, suppose that the next coupon payment is $X$ days from the valuation date and $W$ is the number of days between the issuance date and the first coupon date. Letting $K$ denote the ratio of $X$ to $W$, the discounting of a semiannual coupon payment, $c$, for both methods for a semiannual yield-to-maturity, $y$, is, for simple interest over the period (Treasury method),

$$\frac{c}{(1 + Ky)}$$

and, for compound interest over the period (Street method),

$$\frac{c}{(1 + y)^K}$$

The dealer would agree to deliver ("sell") $10 million of the Treasury bond to the customer the next day for an amount determined by the repo rate and buy ("repurchase") the same Treasury security from the customer the next day for $10 million. Suppose that the overnight repo rate is 6.5 percent. Then, as will be explained below, the dealer would agree to deliver the Treasury bonds for $9,998,194 and repurchase the same bonds for $10 million the next day. The $1,806 difference between the sale price of $9,998,194 and the repurchase price of $10 million is the dollar interest on the financing. From the customer's perspective, the same agreement is called a *reverse repo*.

The following formula is used to calculate the dollar interest on a repo transaction:

$$\text{Dollar interest } = \text{ (Dollar principal)} \times \text{(Repo rate)} \times \left( \frac{\text{Repo term}}{360} \right)$$

Notice that the interest is computed on a 360-day basis. In our example, for a repo rate of 6.5 percent and a repo term of one day (overnight), the dollar interest is $1,806, as shown below:

$$\text{Dollar interest } = \$10,000,000 \times .065 \times \frac{1}{360}$$
$$= \$1,806$$

What are the advantages of using the repo market for the dealer borrowing on a short-term basis and for the customer lending funds on a short-term basis? For the dealer, the repo rate is less than the cost of bank financing. From the customer's perspective, the repo market offers an attractive yield on a short-term, secured transaction that is highly liquid. In Chapter 12, the repo rate is discussed in more detail.

Although we have focused on financing a government dealer's long position, the repo market can also be used by government dealers to cover a short position. For example, suppose that a government dealer sold $10 million of Treasury securities two weeks ago and must now cover the position. The dealer can do a reverse repo (agree to buy the securities and sell them back).

Trading and arbitrage strategies involving cash market Treasury securities and Treasury futures rely on dealer financing in the repo market. For example, suppose that a dealer can purchase Treasury bonds with funds financed with a 30-day term repo. Suppose also that the dealer can enter into an agreement at the same time to sell the Treasury bonds for a specified price 30 days from now. If the cost of financing the position (the repo rate) is less than the rate that the dealer would earn holding the Treasury bonds and selling them 30 days from now, then an arbitrage profit will be realized. How can the dealer lock in a price now for the sale (or delivery) of the Treasury bonds 30 days from now? As explained in Chapter 32, this can be done in the Treasury bond futures market. Thus, there is a relationship between the repo rate, the Treasury bond price and the futures price. If the repo rate is such that the dealer can finance the Treasury bond and sell it in the futures market so as to earn a return higher than the repo rate, arbitrage profits are available. The actions of dealers and other market participants will ensure that these arbitrage profits are short-lived. Dealers, in fact, calculate the break-even rate that will eliminate any arbitrage profits. This is called the *implied repo rate*. When the implied repo rate and the actual repo rate differ, arbitrage opportunities may be available.

## STRIPPED TREASURY SECURITIES

As we explained in Chapter 6, the yield-to-maturity measure assumes that the coupon payments can be reinvested at the calculated yield-to-maturity. The risk that the investor will be forced to reinvest the coupon payments at a lower rate is called *reinvestment risk*. The lower is the coupon rate, the less is the reinvestment risk associated with a bond. To eliminate reinvestment risk, an investor would have to purchase a zero-coupon bond. This is a bond where an investor does not receive periodic interest payments. Instead, as in the case of Treasury bills, the investor purchases the bond below its maturity value, the difference between the maturity value and purchase price representing interest.

The Treasury does not issue zero-coupon notes or bonds. However, in August 1982, both Merrill Lynch and Salomon Brothers synthetically created zero-coupon Treasury receipts. Merrill Lynch marketed these Treasury receipts as "Treasury Income Growth Receipts" (TIGRs) and Salomon Brothers marketed its Treasury receipts as "Certificates of Accrual on Treasury Securities" (CATS). The two investment banking firms did this by purchasing long-term Treasury bonds and depositing them in a bank custodian account. They then issued receipts representing an ownership interest in each coupon payment on the underlying Treasury bond in the account and a receipt on the underlying Treasury bond's maturity value. This process of separating each coupon payment, as well as the principal (called the "corpus"), and selling securities against them is referred to as "coupon stripping."[10] Although the receipts created from the coupon stripping process were not issued by the U.S. Treasury, the underlying bond deposited in the bank custody account is a debt obligation of the U.S. Treasury; thus, the cash flow from the underlying security is certain.

To illustrate the process, suppose that $100 million of a Treasury bond with a 20-year maturity and a coupon rate of 12.5 percent is purchased to create zero coupon Treasury securities. The cash flow from this Treasury bond is 40 semiannual payments of $6.25 million each ($100 million times .125 divided

---

[10] The profits that government dealer firms can obtain from coupon stripping and the effect of coupon stripping on the pricing of Treasury securities is explained later in this chapter.

by 2) *and* the repayment of principal (corpus) of $100 million, 20 years from now. This Treasury bond is deposited in a bank custodian account. Receipts are then issued, each with a single payment claim on the bank custody account. Since there are 41 different payments that will be made by the Treasury in our example, a receipt representing a single payment claim on each dollar payment will be issued, which is effectively a zero coupon bond. The maturity value for a receipt on a particular Treasury payment, coupon or corpus, will be equal to the amount of the payment to be made by the Treasury on the underlying Treasury bond. In our example, 40 coupon receipts will each have a maturity value of $6.25 million and one receipt, the corpus, will have a maturity value of $100 million. The maturity dates for the receipts will coincide with the corresponding payment dates by the Treasury.

Other investment banking firms followed suit by creating their own receipts.[11]  These receipts, as well as CATs and TIGRs, are referred to as *trademark* zero-coupon Treasury securities since they are associated with a particular firm.[12]  Because receipts of one firm were rarely traded by competing dealers, the secondary market was not liquid for any one trademark. In addition, the investor was exposed to the risk—as small as it may be—that the custodian bank might go bankrupt.

To broaden the market and improve liquidity of these receipts, a group of primary dealers in the government market agreed to issue generic receipts that would not be directly associated with any of the participating dealers. These generic receipts are referred to as "Treasury Receipts" (TRs). Rather than representing a share of the trust as the trademarks do, TRs represent ownership of a Treasury security. However, the problem with the trademark and generic receipts is that settlement requires physical delivery, which is often cumbersome and inefficient.

Prior to June 1982, the Treasury was not a supporter of coupon stripping. In fact, a strongly worded letter from the Federal Reserve Bank of New York to primary government dealers stated, "In our view trading in Treasury securities stripped of coupons, or trading in the detached coupons themselves, is not a desirable market practice and should be discouraged."[13] The Treasury's objection was that taxpayers were able to undertake transactions involving stripped Treasuries that resulted in a lower tax liability. In June 1982, the Treasury withdrew

---

[11] For example, Lehman Brothers offered "Lehman Investment Opportunities Notes" (LIONs); E.F. Hutton offered "Treasury Bond Receipts" (TBRs); and Dean Witter Reynolds offered "Easy Growth Treasury Receipts" (ETRs). There were also GATORs, COUGARs and—you'll like this one—DOGS ("Dibbs on Government Securities").

[12] They were also referred to as "animal products" for obvious reasons.

[13] See Thomas J. Kluber and Thomas Stauffacher, "Zero Coupon Treasury Securities," Chapter 11 in Frank J. Fabozzi (ed.), *The Handbook of Treasuries* (Chicago: Probus Publishing, 1987).

its objections to coupon stripping when provisions were incorporated into the Tax Equity and Fiscal Responsibility Act of 1982 to eliminate such tax abuses.

Although the Treasury indirectly benefited from coupon stripping through the heightened demand for its securities by dealer firms, in February 1985, the Treasury announced its Separate Trading of Registered Interest and Principal of Securities (STRIPS) program to facilitate the strippping of designated Treasury securities. Specifically, all new Treasury bonds and all new Treasury notes with maturities of 10 years and longer are eligible for stripping through this program.[14] The zero coupon Treasury securities created under the STRIPS program are direct obligations of the U.S. government. Moreover, the securities clear through the Federal Reserve's book-entry system.[15]

As a result of the STRIPS program, the origination of trademarks and generic receipts has stopped. By December 1988, 65 percent of the zero-coupon Treasury market consisted of those created under the STRIPS program, about 14 percent were TRs, and the balance were trademarks (with CATs and TIGRs having the "lion's" share—8% and 13%, respectively).[16]

## ANALYSIS OF THE TREASURY YIELD CURVE

The graphical depiction of the relationship between the yield on Treasury securities for different maturities is known as the *yield curve*. Exhibit 9–4 shows four hypothetical yield curves. While a yield curve is typically constructed based on observed yields and maturities, the term structure of interest rates is the relationship between the yield on zero-coupon Treasury securities and their maturities. Any noncallable security can be thought of as a package of zero coupon securities. That is, each zero coupon security in the package has a maturity equal to its coupon payment date and, in the case of the principal, the maturity date. The value of the security should equal the value of all the component zero coupon securities. If this does not hold, it is possible to realize arbitrage profits. To determine the value of each zero coupon security, it is necessary to know the yield on the zero coupon Treasury security corresponding to that maturity. This yield is called the *spot rate*, and the graphical depiction of the relationship between the spot rate and its maturity is called the *spot rate curve*.

In this section, we explain how the theoretical spot rate curve is constructed from the yield curve. The theoretical spot rate plays a key role in the pricing of

---

[14] By December 1988, 23 percent of those securities eligible for stripping under the STRIPS program were stripped.

[15] In 1987, the Treasury permitted the conversion of stripped coupons into book-entry form under its Coupons Under Book-Entry Safekeeping (CUBES) program.

[16] Monte Shapiro and Carol E. Johnson, "Overview of Government Zero Market and Investment Strategies," Chapter 5 in *The Handbook of Treasury and Agency Securities*.

**EXHIBIT 9–4**
**Four Hypothetical Yield Curves**

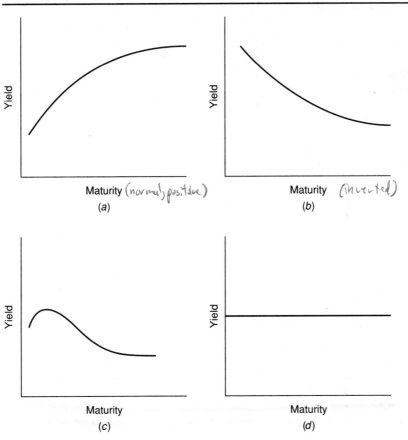

Maturity (normal, positive)
(a)

Maturity (inverted)
(b)

Maturity
(c)

Maturity
(d)

all financial instruments because all securities can be viewed as a package of zero coupon securities and options. However, the cash flows on non-Treasury securities are not risk free. The interest rate used to discount a risky cash flow will be equal to the interest rate on a theoretical zero coupon Treasury security with a maturity equal to the time of receipt of the risky cash flow plus a spread that reflects credit risk.

## Constructing the Theoretical Spot Rate Curve

It is possible to construct a theoretical spot rate curve from the observed yields on Treasury bills and Treasury coupon securities. To see how this is done, we'll use the hypothetical price, yield (yield-to-maturity) and maturity for the 20 Treasury securities shown in Exhibit 9–5.

**EXHIBIT 9–5**
**Maturity and Yield-to-Maturity for 20 Hypothetical Treasury Securities**

| Maturity | Coupon | Yield-to-Maturity | Price |
|---|---|---|---|
| 0.50 | 0.0000 | 0.0800* | 96.15 |
| 1.00 | 0.0000 | 0.0830* | 92.19 |
| 1.50 | 0.0850 | 0.0890 | 99.45 |
| 2.00 | 0.0900 | 0.0920 | 99.64 |
| 2.50 | 0.1100 | 0.0940 | 103.49 |
| 3.00 | 0.0950 | 0.0970 | 99.49 |
| 3.50 | 0.1000 | 0.1000 | 100.00 |
| 4.00 | 0.1000 | 0.1040 | 98.72 |
| 4.50 | 0.1150 | 0.1060 | 103.16 |
| 5.00 | 0.0875 | 0.1080 | 92.24 |
| 5.50 | 0.1050 | 0.1090 | 98.38 |
| 6.00 | 0.1100 | 0.1120 | 99.14 |
| 6.50 | 0.0850 | 0.1140 | 86.94 |
| 7.00 | 0.0825 | 1.1160 | 84.24 |
| 7.50 | 0.1100 | 0.1180 | 96.09 |
| 8.00 | 0.0650 | 0.1190 | 72.62 |
| 8.50 | 0.0875 | 0.1200 | 82.97 |
| 9.00 | 0.1300 | 0.1220 | 104.30 |
| 9.50 | 0.1150 | 0.1240 | 95.06 |
| 10.00 | 0.1250 | 0.1250 | 100.00 |

*On a bond equivalent basis.

The basic principle is that the value of a Treasury coupon security should be equal to the value of a package of zero-coupon Treasury securities. Consider first the 6-month Treasury bill in Exhibit 9–5. Since a Treasury bill is a zero coupon instrument, its yield of 8 percent is equal to the spot rate. Similarly, for the one-year Treasury, the yield of 8.3 percent is the one-year spot rate. Given these two spot rates, we can compute the spot rate for a 1.5-year zero-coupon Treasury. The value or price of a 1.5-year zero-coupon Treasury should equal the present value of the three cash flows from the 1.5-year coupon Treasury, where the yield used for discounting is the spot rate corresponding to the cash flow. Using $100 as par, the cash flow for the 1.5-year coupon Treasury is as follows:

| | | |
|---|---|---|
| 0.5 years | .085 × $100 × .5 | = $ 4.25 |
| 1.0 years | .085 × $100 × .5 | = $ 4.25 |
| 1.5 years | .085 × $100 × .5 + 100 | = $ 104.25 |

The present value of the cash flow is given as

$$\frac{4.25}{(1 + y_1)^1} + \frac{4.25}{(1 + y_2)^2} + \frac{104.25}{(1 + y_3)^3}$$

where

$y_1$ = one-half the six-month theoretical spot rate
$y_2$ = one-half the one-year theoretical spot rate
$y_3$ = one-half the 1.5-year theoretical spot rate

Since the six-month spot rate and one-year spot rate are 8.0 percent and 8.3 percent, respectively, then

$$y_1 = .04 \text{ and } y_2 = .0415$$

Therefore, the present value of the 1.5-year coupon Treasury security is

$$\frac{4.25}{(1.0400)^1} + \frac{4.25}{(1.0415)^2} + \frac{104.25}{(1 + y_3)^3}$$

Since the price of the 1.5-year coupon Treasury security is $99.45, the following relationship must hold:

$$99.45 = \frac{4.25}{(1.0400)^1} + \frac{4.25}{(1.0415)^2} + \frac{104.25}{(1 + y_3)^3}$$

We can now solve for the theoretical 1.5-year spot rate as follows:

$$99.45 = 4.08654 + 3.91805 + \frac{104.25}{(1 + y_3)^3}$$

$$91.44541 = \frac{104.25}{(1 + y_3)^3}$$

$$(1 + y_3)^3 = 1.140024$$

$$y_3 = .04465$$

Doubling this yield we obtain the bond equivalent yield of .0893, or 8.93 percent, which is the theoretical 1.5-year spot rate.

Given the theoretical 1.5-year spot rate, we can obtain the theoretical two-year spot rate. The cash flow for the two-year coupon Treasury in Exhibit 9–5 is given below:

| | | |
|---|---|---|
| 0.5 years | .090 × $100 × .5 | = $ 4.50 |
| 1.0 years | .090 × $100 × .5 | = $ 4.50 |
| 1.5 years | .090 × $100 × .5 | = $ 4.50 |
| 2.0 years | .090 × $100 × .5 + 100 | = $ 104.50 |

The present value of the cash flow is as follows:

$$\frac{4.50}{(1 + y_1)^1} + \frac{4.50}{(1 + y_2)^2} + \frac{4.50}{(1 + y_3)^3} + \frac{104.50}{(1 + y_4)^4}$$

where $y_4$ equals one-half the two-year theoretical spot rate. Since the six-month spot rate, one-year spot rate, and 1.5-year spot rate are 8.0, 8.3, and 8.93 percent, respectively,

$$y_1 = .04 \qquad y_2 = .0415 \qquad \text{and } y_3 = .04465$$

Therefore, the present value of the two-year coupon Treasury security is

$$\frac{4.50}{(1.0400)^1} + \frac{4.50}{(1.0415)^2} + \frac{4.50}{(1.04465)^3} + \frac{104.50}{(1 + y_4)^4}$$

Because the price of the two-year coupon Treasury security is $99.64 the following relationship must hold:

$$99.64 = \frac{4.50}{(1.0400)^1} + \frac{4.50}{(1.0415)^2} + \frac{4.50}{(1.04465)^3} + \frac{104.50}{(1 + y_4)^4}$$

We can now solve for the theoretical two-year spot rate as follows:

$$99.64 = 4.32692 + 4.14853 + 3.94730 + \frac{104.50}{(1 + y_4)^4}$$

$$87.21725 = \frac{104.50}{(1 + y_4)^4}$$

$$(1 + y_4)^4 = 1.198158$$

$$y_4 = .046235$$

Doubling this yield we obtain the theoretical two-year spot rate bond equivalent yield of 9.247 percent.

We can then use the theoretical two-year spot rate and the 2.5-year coupon Treasury in Exhibit 9–5 to compute the 2.5-year theoretical spot rate. In fact, the same methodology can be used to determine the theoretical spot rate for each hypothetical Treasury security shown in Exhibit 9–5. The theoretical spot rates are presented in Exhibit 9–6 and represent the term structure of interest rates.

Earlier in this chapter, we discussed stripped Treasury securities that are zero coupon Treasury securities created by dealer firms. It would seem logical that the observed yield on stripped Treasury securities can be used to construct an actual spot rate curve rather than go through the procedure we just described. There are two problems with using the observed yields on stripped Treasury securities to construct the term structure of interest rates. First, the liquidity of the stripped Treasury market is not as great as that of the Treasury coupon market. Thus,

**EXHIBIT 9–6**
**Theoretical Spot Rates**

| Maturity | Yield-to-Maturity | Theoretical Spot Rate |
|---|---|---|
| 0.50 | 0.0800 | 0.08000 |
| 1.00 | 0.0830 | 0.08300 |
| 1.50 | 0.0890 | 0.08930 |
| 2.00 | 0.0920 | 0.09247 |
| 2.50 | 0.0940 | 0.09468 |
| 3.00 | 0.0970 | 0.09787 |
| 3.50 | 0.1000 | 0.10129 |
| 4.00 | 0.1040 | 0.10592 |
| 4.50 | 0.1060 | 0.10850 |
| 5.00 | 0.1080 | 0.11021 |
| 5.50 | 0.1090 | 0.11175 |
| 6.00 | 0.1120 | 0.11584 |
| 6.50 | 0.1140 | 0.11744 |
| 7.00 | 0.1160 | 0.11991 |
| 7.50 | 0.1180 | 0.12405 |
| 8.00 | 0.1190 | 0.12278 |
| 8.50 | 0.1200 | 0.12546 |
| 9.00 | 0.1220 | 0.13152 |
| 9.50 | 0.1240 | 0.13377 |
| 10.00 | 0.1250 | 0.13623 |

the observed yields on stripped Treasury securities reflect a premium for liquidity (in the sense of marketability). Second, there are maturity sectors of the stripped Treasury securities market that attract specific investors who may be willing to trade off yield in exchange for an attractive feature associated with that particular maturity sector, thereby distorting the term-structure relationship. For example, unlike domestic taxable entities, certain foreign governments may grant investors preferential tax treatment on zero coupon Treasuries. As a result, these foreign investors invest heavily in long-maturity stripped Treasury securities, driving down yields in that maturity sector.

The methodology demonstrating how the theoretical spot rate curve can be constructed from observed yields, although useful, is in practice more complex for several reasons. First, there may be more than one Treasury issue with the same maturity selling at different yields. This reflects other factors that affect yield: difference in coupon and the presence of a call feature. Second, there is not a current Treasury issue for every possible maturity so that a continuous yield curve cannot be constructed using the procedure we just illustrated. Several methodologies have been suggested to statistically estimate the term structure. These are discussed in Chapters 56 and 58.

## Stripped Treasury Securities and the Term Structure of Interest Rates

The potential profitability for a dealer to undertake the creation of zero coupon Treasury securities depends on the actual yields on Treasury securities and the theoretical spot rate curve. To see how a government dealer can realize a profit from coupon stripping (creating zero coupon Treasury securities), consider a 10-year, 12.5 percent coupon Treasury selling at par (offering a yield-to-maturity of 12.5 percent). Suppose that a government dealer buys the issue at par and strips the issue, expecting to sell the zero coupon Treasury securities at the yields indicated for the corresponding maturity shown in Exhibit 9–5.

Exhibit 9–7 shows the price that would be received for each zero coupon Treasury security created. The price of the Treasury coupon security is just the total present value of all the cash flows from the stripped Treasury securities each discounted at the yield corresponding to its maturity (from Exhibit 9–5). The proceeds received from selling the zero-coupon Treasury securities would

**EXHIBIT 9–7**
**Profit Opportunity from Coupon Stripping Using Observed Yield for the Maturity**

| Maturity | Cash Flow | Present Value at 12.5% | Yield-to-Maturity | Present Value at Yield-to-Maturity |
|---|---|---|---|---|
| 0.50 | 6.25 | 5.8824 | 0.0800 | 6.0096 |
| 1.00 | 6.25 | 5.5363 | 0.0830 | 5.7618 |
| 1.50 | 6.25 | 5.2017 | 0.0890 | 5.4847 |
| 2.00 | 6.25 | 4.0942 | 0.0920 | 5.2210 |
| 2.50 | 6.25 | 4.6157 | 0.0940 | 4.9676 |
| 3.00 | 6.25 | 4.3442 | 0.0970 | 4.7040 |
| 3.50 | 6.25 | 4.0886 | 0.1000 | 4.4418 |
| 4.00 | 6.25 | 3.8481 | 0.1040 | 4.1663 |
| 4.50 | 6.25 | 3.6218 | 0.1060 | 3.9267 |
| 5.00 | 6.25 | 3.4087 | 0.1080 | 3.6938 |
| 5.50 | 6.25 | 3.2082 | 0.1090 | 3.4863 |
| 6.00 | 6.25 | 3.0195 | 0.1120 | 3.2502 |
| 6.50 | 6.25 | 2.8419 | 0.1140 | 3.0402 |
| 7.00 | 6.25 | 2.6747 | 0.1160 | 2.8384 |
| 7.50 | 6.25 | 2.5174 | 0.1180 | 2.6451 |
| 8.00 | 6.25 | 2.3693 | 0.1190 | 2.4789 |
| 8.50 | 6.25 | 2.2299 | 0.1200 | 2.3210 |
| 9.00 | 6.25 | 2.0987 | 0.1220 | 2.1528 |
| 9.50 | 6.25 | 1.9753 | 0.1240 | 1.9930 |
| 10.00 | 106.25 | 31.6046 | 0.1250 | 31.6046 |
| Total | | 100.0000 | | 104.1880 |

be $104.1880 per $100 of par value of the Treasury issue purchased by the dealer. This would result in a profit of $4.1880 per $100 purchased.

To understand why the government dealer has the opportunity to realize this profit, look at the third column of Exhibit 9–7. That column shows how much the government dealer paid for each of the cash flows by buying the entire package of cash flows (i.e., by buying the bond). For example, consider the $6.25 coupon payment in four years. By buying the 10-year Treasury bond priced to yield 12.5 percent, the dealer pays a price based on 12.5 percent (6.25% semiannual) for that coupon payment, or, equivalently, $3.8481. However, under the assumptions in this illustration, investors were willing to accept a lower yield, 10.4 percent (5.2% semiannual) to purchase a zero coupon Treasury security with four years to maturity. Thus, investors were willing to pay $4.1663. On this one coupon payment, the government dealer realizes a profit equal to the difference between $4.1663 and $3.8481 (or $.3182). From all the cash flows, the total profit is $4.1880. Coupon stripping is a good example of where the "the sum of the parts is greater than the whole."

Suppose that instead of the observed yield-to-maturity from Exhibit 9–5, the yields that investors want is the same as the theoretical spot rates shown in Exhibit 9–6. Exhibit 9–8 demonstrates that, in this case, the total proceeds from the sale of the zero coupon Treasury securities would be approximately equal to $100, making coupon stripping uneconomic. If the actual spot rate curve is different from the theoretical spot rate curve, coupon stripping may be profitable.

It is the process of coupon stripping that will cause the actual spot rate curve on zero coupon Treasuries not to depart significantly from the theoretical spot rate curve. As more stripping is done, forces of demand and supply will cause rates to move towards their theoretical spot rate levels. This is, in fact, what has happened in the Treasury market.

## Implied Forward Rates

We have just seen how the theoretical spot rate curve can be constructed from the yield curve. But there may be more information contained in the yield curve. Specifically, can we use the yield curve to infer the market's expectations of future interest rates? Let's explore this possibility.

Suppose that an investor has a one-year investment horizon and is faced with the following two alternatives:

*Alternative 1*: Buy a one-year Treasury bill

*Alternative 2*: Buy a six-month Treasury bill and when it matures in six months buy another six-month Treasury bill

The investor will be indifferent between the two alternatives if they produce the same yield or the same number of dollars per dollar invested over the one-

**EXHIBIT 9–8**
**Profit Opportunity from Coupon Stripping Using Theoretical Spot Yield Curve**

| Maturity | Cash Flow | Present Value at 12.5% | Theoretical Spot Yield | Present Value at Spot Yield |
|---------|-----------|------------------------|------------------------|------------------------------|
| 0.50 | 6.25 | 5.8824 | 0.08000 | 6.0096 |
| 1.00 | 6.25 | 5.5363 | 0.08300 | 5.7618 |
| 1.50 | 6.25 | 5.2017 | 0.08930 | 5.4824 |
| 2.00 | 6.25 | 4.9042 | 0.09247 | 5.2163 |
| 2.50 | 6.25 | 4.6157 | 0.09468 | 4.9595 |
| 3.00 | 6.25 | 4.3442 | 0.09787 | 4.6923 |
| 3.50 | 6.25 | 4.0886 | 0.10129 | 4.4227 |
| 4.00 | 6.25 | 3.8481 | 0.10592 | 4.1360 |
| 4.50 | 6.25 | 3.6218 | 0.10850 | 3.8850 |
| 5.00 | 6.25 | 3.4087 | 0.11021 | 3.6553 |
| 5.50 | 6.25 | 3.2082 | 0.11175 | 3.4367 |
| 6.00 | 6.25 | 3.0195 | 0.11584 | 3.1801 |
| 6.50 | 6.25 | 2.8419 | 0.11744 | 2.9766 |
| 7.00 | 6.25 | 2.6747 | 0.11991 | 2.7660 |
| 7.50 | 6.25 | 2.5174 | 0.12405 | 2.5343 |
| 8.00 | 6.25 | 2.3693 | 0.12278 | 2.4092 |
| 8.50 | 6.25 | 2.2299 | 0.12546 | 2.2217 |
| 9.00 | 6.25 | 2.0987 | 0.13152 | 1.9861 |
| 9.50 | 6.25 | 1.9753 | 0.13377 | 1.8266 |
| 10.00 | 106.25 | 31.6046 | 0.13623 | 28.4426 |
| Total | | 100.0000 | | 100.0010 |

year investment horizon. The investor knows the spot rate on the six-month Treasury bill and the one-year Treasury bill. However, he does not know what yield will be available on a six-month Treasury bill purchased six months from now. The yield on a six-month Treasury bill six months from now is called the *forward rate*. Given the spot rate for the six-month Treasury bill and the one-year Treasury bill rate, the forward rate on a six-month Treasury bill that will make the investor indifferent to the two alternatives can be determined as described below.

By investing in the one-year Treasury bill, the investor will receive the maturity value at the end of one year. Suppose that the maturity value of the one-year Treasury bill is $100. The price (cost) of the one-year Treasury bill would be as follows:

$$\frac{100}{(1 + y_2)^2}$$

where $y_2$ is one-half the bond equivalent yield of the theoretical one-year spot rate.

Suppose that the investor purchased a six-month Treasury bill for $P$ dollars. At the end of six months, the value of this investment would be

$$P(1 + y_1)$$

where $y_1$ is one-half the bond equivalent yield of the theoretical six-month spot rate.

Let $f$ be one-half the forward rate on a six-month Treasury bill available six months from now. Then the future dollars available at the end of one year from the $P$ dollars invested would be given by

$$P(1 + y_1)(1 + f)$$

Suppose that today we wanted to know how many $P$ dollars the investor must invest in order to get $100 one year from now. This can be found as follows:

$$P(1 + y_1)(1 + f) = 100$$

Solving we get,

$$P = \frac{100}{(1 + y_1)(1 + f)}$$

The investor will be indifferent between the two alternatives confronting him if he makes the same dollar investment and receives $100 from both investments at the end of one year. That is, the investor will be indifferent if

$$\frac{100}{(1 + y_2)^2} = \frac{100}{(1 + y_1)(1 + f)}$$

Solving for $f$, we get

$$f = \frac{(1 + y_2)^2}{(1 + y_1)} - 1$$

Doubling $f$ gives the bond equivalent yield for the six-month forward rate.

To illustrate this, we will use the theoretical spot rates shown on Exhibit 9–6. We know that:

Six-month bill spot rate $= .080$; therefore $y_1 = .0400$

One-year bill spot rate $= .083$; therefore $y_2 = .0415$

Substituting into the equation, we have

$$f = \frac{(1.0415)^2}{1.0400} - 1$$

$$= .043$$

The forward rate on a six-month security, quoted on a bond equivalent basis, is 8.60 percent (.043 × 2).

Let's confirm our results. The price of a one-year Treasury bill with a $100 maturity value is

$$\frac{100}{(1.0415)^2} = 92.19$$

If 92.19 is invested for six months at the six-month spot rate of 8 percent, the amount at the end of six months would be

$$92.19(1.0400) = 95.8776$$

If 95.8776 is reinvested for another six months in a six-month Treasury offering 4.3 percent for six months (8.6% annually), the amount at the end of one year is

$$95.8876(1.043) = 100$$

Both alternatives will have the same $100 payoff if the six-month Treasury bill yield six months from now is 4.3 percent (8.6% on a bond equivalent basis). This means that if an investor is guaranteed a 4.3 percent yield (8.6% bond equivalent basis) on a six-month Treasury bill six months from now, he will be indifferent between the two alternatives.

Since we used the theoretical spot rates to compute the forward rate, the resulting forward rate is called the *implied forward rate*.

While we have restricted our example to the calculation of the implied six-month forward rate six months from now, we can follow the same methodology to determine the implied forward rate six months from now for an investment for a period longer than six months. That is, the yield curve or, more specifically, the spot rate curve generated from the yield curve can be used to construct an implied forward rate six months from now for one-year investments, 1.5-year investments, two-year investments, 2.5-year investments, etc.

We can even take this one step further. It is not necessary to limit ourselves to implied forward rates six months from now. The yield curve can be used to calculate the implied forward rate for any time into the future for any investment horizon. As examples, the following can be calculated:

- The two-year implied forward rate five years from now
- The six-year implied forward rate ten years from now
- The seven-year implied forward rate three years from now

How is this done? To demonstrate how, we must introduce some notation. We will continue to let $f$ represent the forward rate. But now we must identify two aspects of the forward rate. First, we want to denote when the forward rate begins. Second, we want to denote the length of time of the forward rate. To identify these two aspects of the forward rate, we will use the following notation:

$$_n f_t = \text{the forward rate } n \text{ periods from now for } t \text{ periods}$$

Remember that in our examples each period is equal to six months. The following examples will illustrate this notation. Consider first our earlier example of the six-month forward rate six months from now. In this case, since we are looking at a forward rate six months from now, this is equal to one period from now. Thus, $n$ is 1. Since the length of the forward rate is six months, $t$ is equal to 1. Consequently, the six-month forward rate six months from now is denoted by $_1f_1$. The six-month forward rates can then be expressed as follows:

$_2f_1$ = six-month forward rate one year (two periods) from now

$_3f_1$ = six-month forward rate 1.5 years (three periods) from now

$_4f_1$ = six-month forward rate two years (four periods) from now, etc.

For forward rates four years (eight periods) from now, we would have the following:

$_8f_1$ = six-month forward rate four years (eight periods) from now

$_8f_2$ = one-year (two periods) forward rate four years (eight periods) from now

$_8f_3$ = 1.5-year forward rate four years (eight periods) from now, etc.

Now let's see how the spot rates can be used to calculate the implied forward rate. We shall assume in the illustration that there are zero coupon Treasury securities available.[17]  Suppose that an investor has a five-year investment horizon and is faced with the following two alternatives:

*Alternative 1*: Buy a five-year (10-period) zero coupon Treasury security

*Alternative 2*: Buy a three-year (6-period) zero coupon Treasury security and when it matures in three years buy a two-year Treasury security.

The investor will be indifferent between the two alternatives if they produce the same yield or same number of dollars per dollar invested over the five-year investment horizon. The investor knows the spot rate on the five-year Treasury security and the three-year Treasury security. However, she does not know what yield will be available on a two-year Treasury security purchased three years from now. That is, the investor does not know the two-year forward rate three years from now. In terms of our notation, the unknown is $_6f_4$.

The price of the five-year zero coupon Treasury security with a maturity value of $100 would be

$$\frac{100}{(1 + y_{10})^{10}}$$

---

[17] The existence of the zero coupon Tresury securities is not necessary for the determination of the implied forward rates. The assumption just simplifies the presentation.

where $y_{10}$ is one-half the bond equivalent yield of the theoretical five-year spot rate.

Suppose that the investor purchased a three-year zero coupon Treasury security for $P$ dollars. At the end of three years, the value of this investment would be

$$P(1 + y_6)^6$$

where $y_6$ is one-half the bond equivalent yield of the theoretical three-year spot rate. Let $_6f_4$ be the semiannual two-year forward rate three years from now. Then the future dollars available at the end of five years from the $P$ dollars invested is

$$P(1 + y_6)^6 \ (1 +_6 f_4)^4$$

Suppose that today we wanted to know how many $P$ dollars the investor must invest in order to get $100 one year from now. This can be found as follows:

$$P(1 + y_6)^6 \ (1 +_6 f_4)^4 = 100$$

Solving we get,

$$P = \frac{100}{(1 + y_6)^6 \ (1 +_6 f_4)^4}$$

The investor will be indifferent between the two alternatives confronting her if she makes the same dollar investment and receives $100 at the end of five years from both alternatives. That is, the investor will be indifferent if

$$\frac{100}{(1 + y_{10})^{10}} = \frac{100}{(1 + y_6)^6(1 +_6 f_4)^4}$$

Solving for $_6f_4$, we get

$$_6f_4 = \left[ \frac{(1 + y_{10})^{10}}{(1 + y_6)^6} \right]^{1/4} - 1$$

Doubling $_6f_4$ gives the bond equivalent yield for the two-year forward rate three years from now.

To illustrate this, we will use the theoretical spot rates shown on Exhibit 9–6. We know that:

$$\text{Three-year spot rate} = .09787; \text{ therefore } y_6 = .048935$$
$$\text{Five-year spot rate} = .11021; \text{ therefore } y_{10} = .055105$$

Substituting into the equation, we have

$$_6f_4 = \left[ \frac{(1.055105)^{10}}{(1.048935)^6} \right]^{1/4} - 1$$

$$= \left[ \frac{1.709845}{1.331961} \right]^{1/4} - 1$$

$$= .0644$$

The forward rate on a two-year Treasury security three years from now, quoted on a bond equivalent basis, is 12.88% (.0644 × 2). Let's confirm our results. The price of a five-year zero coupon Treasury security with a $100 maturity value is

$$\frac{100}{(1.055105)^{10}} = 58.48$$

If 58.48 is invested for three years at the three-year spot rate of 9.878 percent, the amount at the end of six periods would be

$$58.48(1.048935)^6 = 77.8931$$

If 77.8931 is reinvested for another two years (four periods) at 6.44 percent (12.88% annually), the amount at the end of the fifth year is

$$77.8931(1.0644)^4 = 100$$

Both alternatives will have the same $100 payoff if the two-year Treasury rate three years from now is 6.44 percent (12.88% on a bond equivalent basis).

In general, the formula for the implied forward rate is

$$_nf_t = \left[ \frac{(1 + y_{n+t})^{n+t}}{(1 + y_n)^n} \right]^{1/t} - 1$$

where $y_n$ is a semiannual spot rate. Doubling $_nf_t$ gives the implied forward rate on a bond equivalent basis.

To illustrate how to apply the formula, consider our earlier example where we sought the six-month forward rate six months from now. That is, we sought $_1f_1$. Since $n$ is equal to 1 and $t$ is equal to 1, the previous formula becomes

$$_1f_1 = \left[ \frac{(1 + y_{1+1})^{1+1}}{(1 + y_1)^1} \right]^{1/1} - 1$$

or

$$= \frac{(1 + y_2)^2}{(1 + y_1)} - 1$$

This agrees with our earlier formula.

In our previous example, we sought the two-year forward rate three years from now. If we substitute 6 for $n$ and 4 for $t$ in the general formula, we would obtain the same formula we used to compute the forward rate we derived earlier.

## Relationship Between Long Spot Rates
## and Short-Term Implied Forward Rates

While we have shown that there is a relationship between the implied forward rate and two spot rates, we can also demonstrate that there is a relationship between a spot rate and the implied short-term forward rates. To demonstrate this relationship, suppose our investor purchases a five-year zero coupon Treasury security for $58.48 with a maturity value of $100. The investor instead could buy a six-month Treasury bill and reinvest the proceeds every six months for five years. The number of dollars that will be realized will depend on the six-month forward rates. Suppose that the investor can actually reinvest the proceeds maturing every six months at the implied six-month forward rates. Let's see how many dollars would accumulate at the end of five years. The implied six-month forward rates were calculated for the yield curve given in Exhibit 9–5. The semiannual implied forward rates from Exhibit 9–6 are:

$$_1f_1 = .043000$$

$$_2f_1 = .050980$$

$$_3f_1 = .051005$$

$$_4f_1 = .051770$$

$$_5f_1 = .056945$$

$$_6f_1 = .060965$$

$$_7f_1 = .069310$$

$$_8f_1 = .064625$$

$$_9f_1 = .062830$$

By investing the $58.48 at the six-month spot rate of 4 percent (8% on a bond equivalent basis) and reinvesting at the above forward rates, the number of dollars accumulated at the end of five years would be

$$\$54.48(1.04)(1.043)(1.05098)(1.051005)(1.05177)(1.056945)$$

$$(1.060965)(1.06931)(1.064625)(1.06283) = \$100$$

Therefore, we see that if the implied forward rates are realized, the $54.48 investment will produce the same number of dollars as an investment in a five-year zero coupon Treasury security at the five-year spot rate. From this illustration, we can see that the five-year spot rate is related to the current six-month spot rate and the implied six-month forward rates.

In general, the relationship between a $t$-period spot rate, the current six-month spot rate, and the implied six-month forward rates is as follows:

$$y_t = [(1 + y_1)(1 +_1 f_1)(1 +_2 f_1)(1 +_3 f_1) \cdots (1 +_t f_1)]^{1/t} - 1$$

## Theories of the Term Structure of Interest Rates

In Exhibit 9–4 we presented four hypothetical yield curves. Panel A shows an upward-sloping yield curve; that is, yields rise as maturity increases. This shape is commonly referred to as a "normal," or "positive," yield curve. Panel B shows a downward-sloping, or "inverted," yield curve in which yields decline as maturity increases. Panel C shows a "humped" yield curve. Finally, Panel D shows a "flat" yield curve. Historically, all four yield curves have been observed at different points in the business cycle.

Two theories have evolved to explain the observed shapes of the yield curve: the expectations theory and the market segmentation theory. Each theory is explained below.

### Expectations Theory

According to the expectations theory, the shape of the yield curve is determined by market participants' (borrowers' and lenders') expectations of future interest rates. That is, the shape is determined by expected forward interest rates. There are two forms of the expectations theory: the pure expectations theory and the biased expectations theory.

Proponents of the *pure expectations theory*, also called the *unbiased expectations theory*, argue that the shape of the yield curve is determined *only* by expected forward interest rates. When interest rates are expected to rise, the yield curve will be normal, or positive; when they are expected to fall, the yield curve will be inverted, or negative. A flat yield curve suggests that interest rates are not expected to change. To understand why, consider first the case where market participants expect interest rates to rise in the future. Let's look at the actions of three groups of market participants with these expectations: investors, speculators, and issuers of securities.

Investors who want to invest in Treasury securities but expect rates to rise will not want to invest in longer term issues. The reason is that by investing in longer term issues now they will be locked into a lower interest rate if interest rates subsequently rise. Investors owning longer term Treasury issues will sell them and invest the proceeds received in short-term Treasury securities. The sale of longer term issues will drive down the price of these securities, thereby driving up their yields. The purchase of short-term Treasury securities will increase prices in the short-term sector of the yield curve and thereby drive down short-term yields. This will result in longer term yields rising above the yield on short-term Treasury securities.

Speculators who expected interest rates to rise will attempt to capitalize on this by selling (shorting) longer term Treasury securities. (Should interest rates rise as expected, the price of longer term Treasury securities will fall. Since the speculator sold Treasury issues and can then purchase them at a lower price to cover the short sale, a profit will be earned.) The proceeds received from the shorting of longer term Treasury securities would be invested in short-term

Treasury issues. Selling longer term Treasury issues and purchasing short-term Treasury issues will drive up yields on the former and drive down yields on the latter.

Issuers of securities who expected interest rates to rise would benefit if their expectations are realized by selling longer term issues in order to avoid paying the higher interest rates anticipated in the future. The supply of shorter term securities offered by borrowers will decline because of the higher anticipated interest cost of rolling over the issues when they mature. The increase in supply of longer term issues will drive up yields in this sector of the yield curve. In the short-term sector of the yield curve, the decline in supply will drive down yields.

Now consider the actions taken by these same three groups if interest rates are expected to fall.

Investors who want to invest in Treasury securities will want to invest in longer term issues. The reason is that by investing in longer term issues now they will be locking in a higher interest rate if interest rates subsequently fall. Investors owning shorter term Treasury issues will sell them and invest the proceeds received in longer term Treasury securities. The sale of shorter term issues will drive down the price of these securities thereby driving up their yields. The purchase of longer term Treasury securities will increase prices in the long-term sector of the yield curve and thereby drive down yields. This will result in an inverted yield curve.

Speculators who expected interest rates to fall will attempt to capitalize on this by buying longer term Treasury securities. (Should interest rates fall as expected, the price of longer term Treasury securities will rise, producing a profit for the speculator.) Typically speculators who borrow the proceeds to purchase Treasury securities will obtain those funds in the short-term sector of the yield curve. Buying longer term Treasury issues and borrowing in the short-term sector of the market will drive down yields in the longer term sector of the yield curve while driving up yields in the shorter term sector.

Issuers of securities who expected interest rates to fall would capitalize on these expectations by selling shorter term rather than longer term issues in order to benefit from the lower interest rates. The amount of longer term securities issued will decline to avoid locking in a higher interest cost. The increase in supply of shorter term issues will drive up yields in this sector of the yield curve. In the longer term sector of the yield curve, the decline in supply will drive down yields.

If the pure expectations theory holds, the implied forward rates that we discussed earlier will be the market's unbiased estimate of the yields expected in the future. Also, as we explained at the end of our discussion of implied forward rates, the current spot rate for any time period depends on the current six-month spot rate and the implied six-month forward rates. The pure expectations theory then asserts that the current spot rate depends on the current six-month (short-term) spot rate and the six-month (short-term) forward rates.

The pure expectations theory assumes that investors and borrowers are willing to shift between maturity sectors if there are opportunities from extending or shortening maturity. In contrast, the *biased expectations theory* asserts that the shape of the yield curve is determined by *both* expectations of future interest rates and a premium demanded (in terms of higher yield demanded) by investors and borrowers for shifting from one maturity sector to another. There are two variants of the biased expectations theory: the liquidity premium theory and the preferred habitat theory.

First let's look at the *liquidity premium theory*. As explained in Chapter 6, the longer the maturity is, the greater the bond price volatility is. Investors (lenders), according to this theory, prefer to invest or lend on a short-term basis because they are exposed to higher price risk (referred to by proponents of this theory as liquidity risk) when investing in longer term securities. To induce investors (lenders) to extend maturity or invest longer term, they must be offered a "liquidity premium." Consequently, forward rates embody both interest rate expectations and a liquidity premium. According to this theory, implied forward rates will not be an unbiased estimate of the market's expectations of future interest rates because they embody a liquidity premium. An upward-sloping yield curve may reflect either (1) expectations that interest rates in the future will rise or (2) expectations that interest rates in the future will fall but a high enough liquidity premium will force the yield curve to be upward-sloping.

The *preferred habitat theory* asserts that the premium demanded or paid for extending maturity reflects more than the associated liquidity. Prudent asset /liability management requires that the maturity (or duration) of investments is dictated by the nature of liabilities. Borrowers also have requirements that dictate in which maturity sector they should raise funds. Since investors, as well as borrowers, have preferences for investing in certain maturity sectors, this theory is referred to as the preferred habitat theory. To illustrate this preference for maturity sectors, consider a life insurance company that has issued a five-year guaranteed investment contract. The insurance company will not want to invest in six-month instruments because of the associated reinvestment risk. As another example, consider a thrift that has borrowed funds at a fixed rate for one year from the issuance of a one-year certificate of deposit. The thrift is exposed to price (or interest-rate) risk if the borrowed funds are invested in 20-year Treasury bonds. For either of these institutions, there is a risk of shifting out of their preferred maturity sector. The preferred habitat theory asserts that investors (as well as borrowers) will shift maturities only if they can be compensated for the associated risks. Thus, the shape of the yield curve is determined by both expectations of future interest rates and a risk premium to induce market participants to shift out of their preferred habitat. Thus, a positive-sloping, negative-sloping, flat, or humped yield curve are possible according to this theory.

*Market Segmentation Theory*

The market segmentation theory also postulates that the shape of the yield curve depends on asset/liability management constraints (either regulatory or self-imposed) and/or creditors (borrowers) restricting their lending (financing) to specific maturity sectors. The shape of the yield curve according to this theory is determined by supply and demand for securities within the specific maturity sector. The market segmentation theory differs from the preferred habitat theory in that it assumes that neither investors nor borrowers are willing to shift from one maturity sector to another to take advantage of opportunities concerning future interest rates.

## SUMMARY

The U.S. Treasury market is closely watched by all participants in the financial markets because interest rates on Treasury securities are the benchmark interest rates throughout the world. The Treasury issues three types of securities: bills, notes, and bonds. Treasury bills have initial maturities of one year or less, are sold at a discount from par, and do not make periodic interest payments. Treasury notes and bonds are coupon securities.

Treasury securities are issued on a competitive bid auction basis, with the Treasury establishing a regular auction cycle for the issuance of its securities. The auction process relies on the participation of primary government securities dealers. These are dealers with whom the Federal Reserve will deal directly. The secondary market for Treasury securities is an over-the-counter market. Dealers trade with the general investing public and with other dealers. Government brokers are used to facilitate transactions between government dealers. In the secondary market, Treasury bills are quoted on a bank discount basis; Treasury coupon securities are quoted on a price basis. Treasury dealers finance their position in the repo market.

While the Treasury does not issue zero coupon securities, government dealers have created these instruments by a process called coupon stripping. Zero coupon Treasury securities include trademarks (for example, TIGRs and CATS), Treasury Receipts, and STRIPS. The creation of the first two types of zero coupon Treasury securities has ceased; STRIPS now dominate the market. The advantage of zero coupon Treasury securities is that they eliminate reinvestment risk.

The yield curve is a graphical depiction of the relationship between the yield-to-maturity on Treasury securities and their maturity. The term structure of interest rates is represented by the theoretical spot rate curve, or the relationship between the yield on zero coupon Treasuries and maturity. The theoretical spot rate curve can be constructed from the yield curve. Implied forward rates can also be calculated from the spot rates. When the prices of Treasury securities are not the same as the prices based on the theoretical spot rate curve, coupon stripping (i.e., the creation of zero coupon Treasury securities) may be profitable.

Four types of yield curves have been observed: normal or positive, negative or inverted, flat, and humped. Theories of the term structure attempt to explain why we observe these shapes. There are two theories: the expectations theory and the market segmentation theory. The pure expectations theory asserts that the term structure is determined solely by expectations of future interest rates. If this theory is accepted, the implied forward rates are the market's unbiased estimate of future interest rates. Normal, inverted, and flat yield curves are consistent with this theory. There are two other theories that fall under the expectations theory—the liquidity premium theory and the preferred habitat theory. These theories are referred to as biased expectations theories because they assert that both interest rate expectations and a premium for risk associated with liquidity for extending maturity (in the case of the liquidity premium theory) or a risk premium associated with the risks of extending or shortening maturity from a market participant's preferred maturity sector (in the case of the preferred habitat theory) determine the term structure of interest rates. The market segmentation theory asserts that market participants are reluctant to depart from the maturity sector of the market that is consistent with their asset/liability or funding goals. As a result, the relative supply and demand in a maturity sector determine the interest rate in that sector.

# CHAPTER 10

## FEDERALLY SPONSORED AGENCY SECURITIES

*Laurie S. Goodman, Ph.D.*
*Vice President*
*Eastbridge Capital*

*Judith Jonson*
*Senior Associate*
*Citicorp*

*Andrew Silver, Ph.D.*
*Senior Analyst*
*Moody's Investors Service*

For a variety of policy reasons, the federal government has deemed it desirable to reduce the cost of capital for some of its constituencies. For the most part, these have included farmers, homeowners, and students. To aid these relatively small borrowers, a series of legislative acts has created a network of federally sponsored financial intermediaries that provide credit to these borrowers at a lower cost than would otherwise be available.

The federally sponsored agencies issue securities in large blocks in the open market. The proceeds are then lent once again to intermediaries who distribute loans to targeted borrowers.

Though there are no explicit or implicit federal guarantees of most of the securities issued by the federally sponsored agencies,[1] the general market per-

---

[1] The securities issued by the Farm Credit Financial Assistance Corporation are the exception to this rule.

ception that the government would ultimately "cover" any defaults causes all federally sponsored securities to come to market at yields that are below those on most corporate securities, though slightly above the Treasury's cost of funding.

In this chapter, we make a distinction between federal agencies and federally *sponsored* agencies. Federal agencies are direct arms of the U.S. government. Since 1973, they have not issued debt; their funds have been raised by the Treasury and passed through the Federal Financing Bank.[2] The amounts they owed at the end of November 1989 were (in millions of dollars) as follows:

| | |
|---|---:|
| Defense Department | $ 7 |
| Export-Import Bank | 10,990 |
| Federal Housing Administration | 308 |
| Government National Mortgage Assn. | 0 |
| Postal Service | 6,445 |
| Tennessee Valley Authority | 18,105 |
| U. S. Railway Association | 0 |
| Federal Agency Total | $35,855 |

Since the federal agencies currently do not issue debt, we will not discuss them further in this chapter.

The federally sponsored agencies are privately owned, publicly chartered entities that raise funds in the market place. Their outstanding debt is as follows:[3]

| | |
|---|---:|
| Farm Credit Financial Asst. Corp. | $ 847 |
| Financing Corporation | 8,170 |
| Federal Home Loan Banks | 138,229 |
| Federal Home Loan Mortgage Corp. | 27,018 |
| Federal National Mortgage Assoc. | 115,774 |
| Farm Credit Banks | 54,131 |
| Resolution Funding Corporation | 4,522 |
| Student Loan Marketing Assoc. | 27,688 |
| Federally Sponsored Agency Total | $376,379 |

---

[2] Prior to 1973, each of the federal agencies did issue its own debt securities. Since these issues were generally small and illiquid, they commanded a significant spread over Treasury securities. The Federal Financing Bank was organized in 1973 to address this problem.

[3] All amounts are as of November 1989. Data was obtained from the *Federal Reserve Bulletin,* March 1990.

## MAJOR ISSUERS AND
## SECURITY CHARACTERISTICS

We will first examine the structure of the major federally sponsored agencies and look at the characteristics of their securities. As can be seen from the breakdown of the amounts owed, agriculture and home ownership have been the largest beneficiaries of the federally sponsored agency system. Therefore, we will examine them by those classifications. The only federally sponsored agency that issues securities and does not serve the agricultural or housing areas is the Student Loan Marketing Association (SLMA or Sallie Mae). It is smaller than those discussed below but still has a noticeable market presence. SLMA issues short-term floating-rate notes on a monthly basis and longer term bonds periodically throughout the year.

### Agricultural Agencies
### (The Federal Farm Credit Bank System)

Beginning in 1916, a series of congressional legislative acts created three federally sponsored agencies that were designed to serve the nation's agricultural community. Together these three agencies formed the Federal Farm Credit Bank System (FFCBS): the Federal Land Banks (FLBs), created by the 1916 Federal Farm Loan Act; the Federal Intermediate Credit Banks (FICBs), organized under the Agricultural Credit Act of 1923; and the Banks for Cooperatives (BCoops), formed by passage of the Farm Credit Act of 1933.

There were originally an FLB, FICB, and BCoop in each of twelve U.S. districts (as well as a Central Bank for Cooperatives). The FLBs, FICBs, and BCoops had their own administrative and regulatory functions and issued debt separately to obtain funding to carry out their lending objectives: The FLBs extended first mortgage loans on agricultural properties, the FICBs made short-term loans, primarily for seasonal agricultural needs, and the BCoops provided loans to cooperative associations owned by farmers and assisted farmers in obtaining operating capital and fixed assets.

In 1979, the FLBs, FICBs, and BCoops began to issue debt on a consolidated basis as "joint and several obligations" of the entire Federal Farm Credit Bank System. Their other functions were maintained separately until 1987, when the Agricultural Credit Act of 1987 reorganized the FFCBS. As a result of this law, as of January 1, 1989, ten of the BCoops (as well as the Central Bank for Cooperatives) were consolidated into a single National Bank for Cooperatives, and eleven FLBs and FICBs were merged as partners by district into eleven Farm Credit Banks. (The twelfth FLB based in Jackson, Mississippi, went into receivership; therefore, the FICB of Jackson, without an entity with which to merge, has retained its original structure.)

The Farm Credit Banks, the National Bank for Cooperatives, the two remaining district BCoops (based in Springfield, Massachusetts, and St. Paul, Minnesota) and the FICB of Jackson now jointly issue three types of securities to fund agricultural loans to farmers and to agricultural associations within the system:

1. Discount notes with maturities from 5 to 270 days, auctioned daily
2. Short-term bonds with maturities of three to nine months, auctioned monthly
3. Longer term bonds with maturities of 1–10 years

In the early to mid-1980s, the FFCBS came under intense financial pressure due to nonperforming loans in the agricultural sector. The situation was caused initially by high interest rates and was exacerbated by depressed farm product prices and land values as the farm sector experienced a recession. The 1987 Agricultural Credit Act, in addition to reorganizing the FFCBS, attempted to address the FFCBS's financial crisis through a recapitalization of the system. For this purpose, the 1987 act created the Farm Credit Financial Assistance Corporation (FACO) and granted to it federally sponsored agency status. FACO is currently authorized to issue $4 billion in debt to aid the FFCBS.

To date, the agency has issued bonds with final maturities of 15 years, with some of the debt callable in 10 years. These FACO bonds are Treasury-backed; further, the U.S. Treasury will actually make full interest payments on the securities for the first five years and partial interest payments in the second five years (these amounts will be lent to the Farm Credit System).

## Home Mortgage Intermediaries

The first residential mortgage agency, created in 1932, was the Federal Home Loan Bank (FHLB) System. It was comprised of twelve regional FHLBs, with a governing body—the Federal Home Loan Bank Board (FHLBB)—located in Washington, D.C. Though its responsibilities were curtailed considerably in late 1989, the FHLB System was originally responsible for regulating and providing advances to this country's savings and loan associations (S&Ls, or "thrifts").

Currently, the main task of the FHLBs is to lend funds to thrift associations so that they can supply mortgages at low rates. To obtain the funding for this purpose, the FHLBs issue securities in the open market. These are backed by collateral of government securities, insured mortgages, or secured advances to the S&Ls; they are not guaranteed by the federal government, though a $4 billion credit line with the U.S. Treasury is in place. As in the case of Farm Credit securities, interest earned on the securities is taxed at the federal but not state or local levels. Types of securities issued include discount notes (with less than one year to maturity) and mostly noncallable bonds (with maturities of 3 months to 10 years).

Until recently, the FHLBB was authorized to oversee the Federal Savings and Loan Insurance Corporation (FSLIC), which provided insurance on deposits up to $100,000 for the nation's S&Ls. Supervision of this insurance function was removed from the purview of the FHLBB as a provision of the Financial Institutions Reform, Recovery and Enforcement Act (FIRREA) of 1989. FIRREA was the second legislative attempt to "bail out" a thrift industry that has become increasingly beleaguered over the last decade. The "thrift crisis" has led to the issuance of two new types of agency securities—FICO and REFCORP bonds.

Over the course of the 1980s, many thrifts ran into solvency problems, due at first to the high interest rates of the early 1980s, which plagued all financial institutions. However, as the decade progressed, nonperforming loans, mismanagement, risky investments, and in some cases, outright fraud, were increasingly being blamed for the insolvency. There was widespread concern that the FSLIC did not have a large enough asset base to uphold its responsibility of insuring the deposits of growing numbers of troubled thrift institutions.

The Competitive Equality and Banking Act (CEBA) of 1987 contained provisions that constituted the first response of Congress to the thrift crisis—the recapitalization of the FSLIC and creation of a new source of funding for it. Title III of CEBA created and granted full federally sponsored agency status to the Financing Corporation (FICO), at the same time authorizing FICO to issue up to $10.8 billion in long-term debt. Beginning in October 1987, FICO began to issue 30-year noncallable bonds, the principal of which is guaranteed by zero-coupon Treasuries.

Even as the CEBA legislation was passed in August 1987, there was criticism that it was not comprehensive enough to rescue the thrift industry. Indeed, by August of 1989, Congress was forced to address the issue again. This time the result was the FIRREA, which constituted a complete restructuring of the savings and loan industry and a dismantling of the Federal Home Loan Bank Board, though the regional FHLBs remained intact as entities. FIRREA shifted the authority for regulation of the thrift industry to a newly created Office of Thrift Supervision and moved the FSLIC insurance mechanism to a Savings Association Insurance Fund under the management of the Federal Deposit Insurance Corporation. Finally, the oversight of advances made by FHLBs to thrift institutions was given over to a Federal Housing Finance Board, which reports to the Department of Housing and Urban Development.

Another key element of FIRREA was the establishment of the Resolution Trust Corporation, whose directive is to liquidate or bail out insolvent savings institutions. Funding for the Resolution Trust Corporation is to be provided by the Resolution Funding Corporation (REFCORP). REFCORP has been authorized to issue $30 billion of long-term debt, again with principal guaranteed by the purchase of zero coupon Treasury bonds. ($20 billion more is to be raised directly by the U.S. Treasury.) To date, REFCORP has issued $9.5 billion in 30- and 40-year bonds.

Both FICO and REFCORP bonds are exempt from state and local taxes, as are most federally sponsored agency issues. This places them at an advantage over corporate bonds, those issued by FNMA and FHLMC, and those guaranteed by GNMA. Further, FICO and REFCORP issues to date range from 30 to 40 years in maturity. This is an attractive maturity range for some investors (e.g., index funds) since there is not a large supply of high-credit, long-term debt other than Treasuries—much corporate debt is callable, unlike FICO and REFCORP issues.

In 1938, the federal government created the Federal National Mortgage Association (commonly referred to as FNMA or Fannie Mae), the first federally sponsored agency whose primary purpose is to encourage the maintenance of an active secondary market for mortgages. A second agency with a similar purpose, the Federal Home Loan Mortgage Corporation (FHLMC or Freddie Mac), was created in 1970.[4] Fannie Mae and Freddie Mac purchase mortgages for sale to the secondary market and issue securities.

Both are owned by private stockholders but have credit lines with the U.S. Treasury of $2.25 billion (FHLMC) and $4 billion (FNMA). Fannie Mae issues short-term discount notes, and coupon-bearing securities as far out as 30 years, some of which are callable.

Though Freddie Mac still issues discount notes to fund its day-to-day operations, it has issued very few longer term securities since late 1986, instead concentrating its term activities in the pass-through market.

Unlike the other federally sponsored agencies we have discussed so far, Fannie Mae and Freddie Mac securities are not exempt from state and local taxation. They are taxed at the federal, state, and local levels.

## PRIMARY AND SECONDARY MARKETS

Agencies come to the market continuously to issue short-term discount notes for their day-to-day operational needs. They set the rates on those notes daily to reflect market conditions and their maturity preferences.

Intermediate and long-term coupon-bearing securities are sold through subscription offerings (i.e., through a syndicate of commercial banks and broker-dealers). The agencies do not issue longer term securities on as regular a schedule as does the Treasury, and the maturities are considerably more flexible.

---

[4] The Government National Mortgage Association (GNMA or Ginnie Mae) is a full federal agency, does not issue debt, and will not be included in our discussion. A discussion of securities guaranteed by GNMA is found in Chapter 27.

Intermediate-term bonds are offered on a more or less monthly basis, and longer term bonds several times per year. Exhibit 10–1 lists, by agency, the approximate maturities and amounts of coupon-bearing debt issued in 1988.

Agency securities, like the rest of the fixed income market, generally trade at a yield spread above Treasuries. Though federal sponsorship ensures fairly low credit spreads, agency liquidity is not as high as in the Treasury market. The total amount of agency debt is currently about $375 billion, compared to about $1.9 trillion in the Treasury market. An average-sized agency debt issue is $500 million, whereas Treasury issues are often as large as $8–10 billion. Because the lesser liquidity of the agency market causes larger transaction costs, investors require a yield premium to invest in this market.

**EXHIBIT 10–1**

**Federally Sponsored Agency Coupon-Bearing Security Issuance in 1988** (in Millions of Dollars)

|        | Maturity | Amount   |
|--------|----------|----------|
| FFCB   | 3 month  | $10,534  |
|        | 6 month  | 15,191   |
|        | 1 year   | 4,585    |
|        | 2 year   | 1,270    |
|        | 3 year   | 550      |
| FHLB   | 3 month  | 1,000    |
|        | 1 year   | 15,797   |
|        | 2 year   | 5,820    |
|        | 3 year   | 6,996    |
|        | 4 year   | 1,550    |
|        | 5 year   | 5,155    |
|        | 7 year   | 1,530    |
|        | 10 year  | 500      |
| FHLMC  | 6 month  | 1,500    |
| FICO   | 30 year  | 2,250    |
| FNMA   | 3 year   | 1,600    |
|        | 4 year   | 2,300    |
|        | 5 year   | 2,850    |
|        | 7 year   | 1,200    |
|        | 10 year  | 2,400    |
|        | 30 year  | 200      |
| SLMA   | 6 month  | 4,350    |
|        | 3 year   | 800      |
|        | 4 year   | 300      |
|        | 5 year   | 500      |
|        | 10 year  | 250      |
|        | 12 year  | 200      |

The yields on agency securities are generally highly correlated with yields on Treasuries. This is illustrated in Exhibits 10–2 and 10–3. Exhibit 10–2 shows the yield on a five-year Farm Credit Bank security compared to that of a comparable Treasury. The correlation during the period shown was .95. Exhibit 10–3 plots the yields on a 10-year FNMA issue and Treasury, where the correlation is .99.

In a "normal," or upward-sloping, yield-curve environment, the agency yield curve is usually more steeply sloped than the Treasury yield curve. To see this, consider Exhibit 10–4, showing active issues on both yield curves on February 1, 1988. In the Treasury market, the total spread between the 2-year and 10-year active issues is 81 basis points. For the agency market, it is 130 basis points. The difference between the two is compensation for less liquidity and slightly higher credit risk.

Computation of yield-to-maturity and accrued interest on agency securities is similar to the method used for Treasuries, but there are some important differences. These are discussed in the next section.

**EXHIBIT 10–2**
**Yield Levels: 5 Yr Treasury vs. FFCB 7.55 of 4/22/91** (Daily yields: 4/20/87 to 2/1/88)

Mean of spread:  .28               Minimum spread:  .03
Standard deviation of spread:  .13      Maximum spread:  .54

**EXHIBIT 10–3**
**Yield Levels: 10 Yr Active Treasury vs. FNMA 8s of 7/10/96** (Daily Yields: 4/20/87 to 2/1/88)

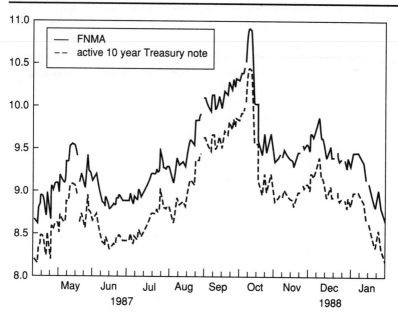

Within the agency market, spreads between different issues of the same agency seem to be based on factors like those in the Treasure market under normal circumstances. The most recently issued securities are the most active and therefore trade at lower yields than their more seasoned counterparts. Different agencies tend to trade at similar yields unless there is concern about the financial health of a particular agency. In this case, yields move upward to reflect concern about the possibility of default. It should be noted that though Fannie Mae securities are taxed at the state and local levels, these securities do generally have lower yields than other comparable-maturity agencies. The reasons are probably that (1) Fannie Mae is currently perceived to have slightly stronger credit quality than most other agencies, and (2) there are enough states without state and local taxes and enough bondholders who are nontaxable for these investors to set the price.

## CALCULATING YIELD AND ACCRUED INTEREST

As explained in Chapter 6, a yield-to-maturity calculation is an iterative process that gives the rate of discounting necessary to arrive at the market price. The

**EXHIBIT 10–4**
**Yield to Curve of Active Issues** (Date: 2/1/88)

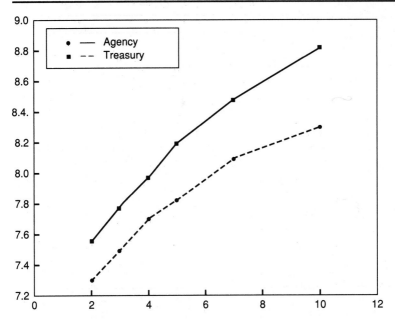

yields of the agencies are calculated on what is known as a "30/360 basis"—that is, assuming there are 30 days in each month and (therefore) 360 days per year. Treasuries, on the other hand, use an "actual/actual" method—that is, the actual number of days per month is counted, giving a 365-day year (or 366 in leap years). This affects the calculation of yield-to-maturity and the accrued interest on a security.

For example, consider an agency security, the FHLB 11¾ of 9/25/91. Its price for settlement on January 9, 1987, was 118:10 (i.e., 118 and $^{10}$⁄₃₂nds), its yield was 7.102, and the accrued interest was 3.394 on a coupon of 5.875. If this had been calculated by the method used for Treasuries with the same price, the yield would have been 7.099, with accrued interest of 3.441. This is because of the day-count difference in calculating the partial semiannual period between settlement and the next coupon date.

Using a 30/360 method, there are always 180 days between each coupon, whereas the actual method result ranges from 181 to 184 (this is known as the "basis"). So, in our example, the basis would be 180 for the FHLB security and for a comparable Treasury it would be 181 (the number of days between 9/25/86 and 3/25/87). Further, in computing the number of days between the settlement date of a transaction and the next coupon date, we find that the agency method produces 76 days and the Treasury method 75 days, as shown below.

| Agency Method (Assuming 30 Days in Every Month) | | Treasury Method (Counting Actual Days) | |
|---|---|---|---|
| Jan 9–end of Jan. | 21 | Jan 9–31 | 22 |
| February | 30 | February | 28 |
| March 1–25 | 25 | March 1–25 | 25 |
| Total | 76 | Total | 75 |

Therefore there is 76/180 (.4222) of a partial period when using the agency method and 75/181 (.4144) when using the Treasury method. The difference in the size of the fraction is small but enough to cause differences in yields.

A similar situation exists in calculating accrued interest. This time we need to look at the day-count difference in computing the number of days between the previous coupon and settlement:

| Agency Method (Assuming 30 Days in Every Month) | | Treasury Method (Counting Actual Days) | |
|---|---|---|---|
| September 25–30 | 5 | September 25–30 | 5 |
| October | 30 | October | 31 |
| November | 30 | November | 30 |
| December | 30 | December | 31 |
| January 1–9 | 9 | January 1–9 | 9 |
| Total | 104 | Total | 106 |

The basis remains the same—180 for the agency and 181 for a comparable Treasury. This means that 104/180 (.5778) of a 5.875 coupon is due if calculating with the agency method and 106/181 (.5856) if using the Treasury method.

## TRADING STRATEGIES

Agency securities have long been popular among buy-and-hold investors because of their yield premium over Treasury securities. However, for portfolio managers who trade more actively, there are also some good trading opportunities available in the agency market. Consider the following:

- The agency yield curve looked very steep in late October 1987, relative to the Treasury yield curve. If an investor had (1) purchased a 10-year agency security and sold a 7-year agency security and (2) purchased a 7-year Treasury and sold a 10-year Treasury to take advantage of this, the investor could have made over $150,000 on a $10 million trade for eight days.

- Farm Credit securities traded very cheaply relative to other agencies and to Treasuries during their crisis period in 1985. If an investor had purchased certain Farm Credit securities and sold Treasuries in the five-year area, the investor could have made more than 1 ½ points in a six-week period. This type of opportunity arises from time to time.
- Agency securities that are just outside of "preferred maturity" ranges often appreciate in value relative to securities that are already in those ranges. For example, in December 1987 an investor could have earned more than two points in less than two months by buying a 5 ½-year agency (the 11.70 FHLB of 7/26/93) and selling a 5-year (the 11.10 FHLB of 11/25/92), profiting as the 5 ½-year security "slid" closer to the preferred 5-year range.

Each of these profit opportunities represents a different type of trade—what we call "yield curve," "agency credit," and "individual issue" trades, respectively. In this section, we discuss each of these trading strategies.

## Yield Curve Strategies

Many trades involving agency securities arise from anticipated movements in the agency yield curve. For those expected agency movements that simply reflect shifts similar to those in the Treasury yield curve, investors are probably better off positioning themselves in the more liquid Treasury market, where bid-ask spreads are lower. However, the spreads between agencies and Treasuries of similar maturities are quite variable. As a result, profits can be made by correctly anticipating these shifts and positioning accordingly.

The particular positions that should be established depend on whether the investor anticipates a change in the agency-Treasury spread in a particular sector of the yield curve or whether he or she expects a general steepening or flattening of the agency yield curve relative to the Treasury curve, without a view about which end of the curve is going to move. In addition, the positions depend on whether the investor expects both curves to shift, or just the agency curve.[5]

## Agency Credit Quality Trade

Experienced players in the agency market have found that some of their best trading has involved taking advantage of the market's perception of the credit

---

[5] For illustrations of each trading strategy, see Laurie S. Goodman, Judith Jonson, and Andrew Silver, "Trading and Investment Opportunities with Agency Securities," and Chapter 11 in Frank J. Fabozzi (ed.), *The Handbook of Treasury and Government Agency Securities* (Chicago: Probus Publishing, 1990).

quality of a particular agency. In general, the market does not seem to react to the deteriorating financial condition of an agency until it receives extensive attention (by, for example, a newspaper article). Therefore, it has been possible to profit by acting on a judgment about an agency's underlying economic condition before media attention focuses on it. Furthermore, once this "crisis" has become the center of attention, additional opportunities exist for outguessing the market on the resolution of the problem. In the past, the market has tended to overreact to negative publicity, at least in retrospect; recent crises have been resolved in such a way that spreads soon returned to more normal levels. In addition, it is interesting to note that when a particular agency is perceived as weak, the credit spreads for other agencies widen as well, offering additional trading opportunities.[6]

## Individual Securities Trades

The agency market does not have quite the depth that characterizes the Treasury market. As a result, there are often opportunities for trades involving individual securities. However, these opportunities tend to be transitory and require active involvement in the market in order to take advantage of them.

A type of trade that appears on a more regular basis is one that takes advantage of the "hills and valleys" in the agency yield curve that are produced by investors' maturity preferences. The agency market is less efficient than the Treasury market in that agency investors are generally less willing to move out of certain preferred maturity ranges to pick up yield. As a result, there are often opportunities for other investors who are less constrained in their maturity preferences to take advantage of these yield differentials. Furthermore, as time passes and the securities "slide down the yield curve" into the preferred maturity ranges, demand picks up and prices rise. Thus, if investors can identify a security that is just outside of a preferred maturity range, they can put on a trade to take advantage of the expected relative appreciation of that security as it moves into the preferred range.

For example, many investors prefer to invest in securities with maturities of five years or less. Thus, the yield differential between securities with less than 5 years to maturity and those with more than, say, 5 ½ years to maturity is often much larger than that implied by the general slope of the yield curve. For example, in mid-December of 1987, the FHLB 11.10s of 11/25/92 had almost five years to maturity and was yielding 9.02%. At the same time, the FHLB 11.70 of 7/26/93 was yielding 9.42 percent. Therefore, by extending maturity by seven months beyond five years in securities of the same agency with similar

---

[6] Case histories from the Farm Credit and Fannie Mae crises are given in Goodman, Jonson, and Silver, "Trading and Investment Opportunities with Agency Securities."

**EXHIBIT 10–5**
**Sliding Down the Yield Curve**

| | December 15, 1987 (Settlement:/December 16, 1987) | | | February 2, 1988 (Settlement:/February 3, 1988) | | | |
|---|---|---|---|---|---|---|---|
| | Yield | Price plus Accrued Interest | Value of Position | Yield | Price plus Accrued Interest | Value of Position | Change in Value of Position |
| 11.70 FHLB of 7/26/96 (buy) | 9.42 | $114.30 | $10,000,000 | 8.22 | $121.17* | $10,601,050 | $601,050 |
| 11.10 FHLB of 11/25/92 (sell) | 9.02 | $108.77 | −$10,000,000 | 8.13 | 113.69 | −10,452,331 | −452,331 |
| $154,260 | .40 | −$ 5.53 | −$ 0 | .09 | $ 7.48 | $ 148,719 | $148,719 |
| Net financing cost (3/8% for 49 days) | | | | | | | $ 5,104 |
| Net profit | | | | | | | $143,615 |

*Includes receipt of coupon on 1/26/88.

coupons, investors could have picked up 40 basis points. Thus, a buy-and-hold investor holding the 11.10s could have sold the 11.10s, bought the 11.70s, paid a round-trip bid-ask spread of, say, $\frac{4}{32}$nds (which is equivalent to about 3 basis points per year on a 5-year security) and picked up a net 37 basis points (i.e., 40-3) per year.

Alternatively, active traders could have positioned themselves to take advantage of relative price changes as the 11.70s approached the five-year maturity range and started to trade more like other securities within the five-year range. For example, by early February 1988, the spread between the 11.10s and the 11.70s had narrowed to 9 basis points. If investors had bought $10 million of the 11.70s, sold short the 11.10s in mid-December, and unwound the positions in early February, they would have earned a net $143,615, as Exhibit 10–5 indicates.

# CHAPTER 11

## COMMERCIAL PAPER, MEDIUM-TERM NOTES, BANKERS' ACCEPTANCES, AND CDs

*Frank J. Fabozzi, Ph.D., CFA, CPA*
*Visiting Professor of Finance*
*Sloan School of Management*
*Massachusetts Institute of Technology*
*and*
*Editor, The Journal of Portfolio Management*

Historically, the money market has been defined as the market for assets maturing in less than one year. The assets traded in this market include Treasury bills, commercial paper, medium-term notes, bankers' acceptances, federal agency discount paper, short-term municipal obligations, certificates of deposit, repurchase agreements, floating-rate instruments, federal funds, and futures and options contracts in which the underlying instrument is a money market instrument. Although several of these assets have maturities greater than one year, they are still classified as part of the money market.

Treasury bills and federal agency discount paper were discussed in the previous two chapters. Repurchase agreements are covered in the next chapter. Floating-rate notes and short-term municipal obligations are discussed in Chapters 14 and 23, respectively. Chapter 32 covers futures and options.

In this chapter, we will cover commercial paper, medium-term notes, bankers' acceptances, and certificates of deposit. Although medium-term notes have maturities ranging from nine months to 30 years, the amount of medium-

The author thanks Barbara Laico and Mike Coppola of Merrill Lynch Money Markets for their helpful comments.

term notes maturing in less than two years is large. Federal funds are obligations traded between banks and cannot be acquired by nonbank entities; therefore, they will not be covered in this chapter.

## COMMERCIAL PAPER

An economic entity that needs long-term funds can raise those funds in either the equity or bond market. For example, a manufacturing firm that needs $175 million to build a plant can issue equity or long-term bonds or a combination of both. A municipality that needs funds to build a hospital can acquire those funds by issuing bonds in the municipal bond market. If, instead, an economic entity needs short-term funds, it may attempt to acquire those funds via bank borrowing. For example, a manufacturing firm that needs $20 million to purchase inventory but expects that the proceeds from the sale of that inventory will be received in three months may obtain a three-month bank loan. A state government that needs to meet a $50 million payroll but expects in one month to receive tax proceeds sufficient to cover the payroll may seek a one-month bank loan.

The issuance of commercial paper is an alternative to bank borrowing for large corporations (nonfinancial and financial) and municipalities with a strong credit rating. Commercial paper is a short-term unsecured promissory note issued in the open market that represents the obligation of the issuing entity.

Although the commercial paper market was limited to entities with strong credit ratings, in recent years some lower credit rated corporations have issued commercial paper by obtaining credit enhancements or other collateral to allow them to enter the market as issuers. Some lower rated companies have issued commercial paper without credit enhancements or collateral. Such issues are popularly referred to as *high-yield commercial paper*. At one time, the largest dealer of high-yield commercial paper was Drexel Burnham Lambert. Issuers of commercial paper are not restricted to U.S. corporations. Foreign corporations and sovereign issuers also issue commercial paper.

Although the original purpose of commercial paper was to provide short-term funds for seasonal and working capital needs, this instrument has been issued for other purposes in recent years. It has been used more often for "bridge financing." For example, suppose that a corporation needs long-term funds to build a plant or acquire equipment. Rather than raising long-term funds immediately, the issuer may elect to postpone the offering until more favorable capital market conditions prevail. The funds raised by issuing commercial paper are used until longer term securities are sold. Commercial paper has been used as bridge financing for corporate takeovers. Commercial paper has also been used as an integral part of an interest-rate swap transaction. In Chapter 53 interest-rate swaps are discussed.

The maturity of commercial paper is typically less than 270 days.[1] The reason for this is that the Securities Act of 1933 requires that securities be registered with the SEC; however, special provisions in the 1933 act exempt commercial paper from registration if maturity does not exceed 270 days. The most common maturity range for commercial paper is 30 to 50 days or less.

Issuers generally roll commercial paper over and use the proceeds to pay off holders of the maturing paper. The risk that the investor faces is that the issuer will be unable to issue new paper at maturity. As a safeguard against this, commercial paper is typically backed by unused bank credit lines. Rating companies such as Moody's, Standard & Poor's, Duff & Phelps, Fitch Investors Service, and McCarthy, Crisanti & Maffei assign ratings to commercial paper. These ratings are shown in Exhibit 11–1.

The commercial paper market has grown from $124 billion in December 1980 to $523 billion in December 1989. Since 1988, the size of the commercial paper market has exceeded that of the Treasury bill market. The investors in commercial paper are institutional investors. Money market mutual funds purchase roughly one third of all the commercial paper issued. Pension funds, commercial bank trust departments, state and local governments, and nonfinancial corporations seeking short-term investments purchase the balance. The minimum round-lot transaction is $100,000. Some issuers will sell commercial paper in denominations of $25,000.

## Issuers of Commercial Paper

As of 1988, there were 1,350 entities issuing commercial paper.[2] Corporate issuers of commercial paper can be divided into financial companies and nonfi-

**EXHIBIT 11–1**
**Commercial Paper Ratings**

| | | Commercial Rating Company | | |
|---|---|---|---|---|
| Moody's | S&P | Duff & Phelps | Fitch | McCarthy, Crisanti & Maffei |
| Prime-1 (P-1) | A-1/A-1 + | Duff-1 (D-1) | F-1 | MCM 1 |
| Prime-2 (P-2) | A-2 | Duff-2 (D-2) | F-2 | MCM 2 |
| Prime-3 (P-3) | A-3 | Duff-3 (D-3) | F-3 | MCM 3 |
| Prime-4 (P-4) | | | | MCM 4 |

Note: The ranking is from highest to lowest credit rating assigned.

---

[1] *Money Market Instruments* (New York: Merrill Lynch Money Marrkets, Inc., 1989), p. 16.

[2] *Handbook of Securities of the United States Government and Agencies* (New York: First Boston Corporation, 1988), p. 140.

nancial companies. Of the $508 billion of commercial paper outstanding as of October 1989, $387 billion was issued by financial companies.

There are three types of financial companies: captive finance companies, bank-related finance companies, and independent finance companies. Captive finance companies are subsidiaries of equipment manufacturing companies. Their primary purpose is to secure financing for the customers of the parent company. For example, the three major U.S. automobile manufacturers have captive finance companies: General Motors Acceptance Corporation (GMAC), Ford Credit, and Chrysler Financial. GMAC is by the far the largest issuer of commercial paper in the United States. A bank holding company may have a subsidiary that is a finance company providing loans to individuals and businesses to acquire a wide range of products. Independent finance companies are those that are not subsidiaries of equipment manufacturing firms or bank holding companies.

While the issuers of commercial paper are typically those with high credit ratings, as explained earlier, smaller and less well-known companies with lower credit ratings have been able to issue paper in recent years. They have been able to do so by means of credit support from a firm with a high credit rating (such paper is called *credit-supported commercial paper*) or by collateralizing the issue with high-quality assets (such paper is called *asset-backed commercial paper*). An example of credit-supported commercial paper is one supported by a letter of credit. The terms of a letter of credit specify that the bank issuing it guarantees that, if the issuer fails to pay off the paper when it comes due, the bank will do so. The bank will charge a fee for the letter of credit. From the issuer's perspective, the fee enables it to enter the commercial paper market and obtain funding at a lower cost than bank borrowing. Paper issued with this credit enhancement is referred to as *LOC paper*. The credit enhancement may also take the form of a surety bond from an insurance company.

### Directly Placed versus Dealer-Placed Paper

Commercial paper is classified as either "direct paper" or "dealer paper." Direct paper is sold by the issuing firm directly to investors without using a securities dealer as an intermediary. These issuing entities generally require continuous funds. As a result, they find it cost effective to establish a sales force to sell their commercial paper directly to investors.

With dealer-placed commercial paper, the issuer uses the services of a securities firm to sell its paper. Commercial paper sold in this way is referred to as dealer paper. Roughly 60 percent of the commercial paper outstanding at the end of 1989 was dealer paper. In recent years, competition in the dealer-placed commercial market has reduced the underwriting fees.

Historically, the dealer market was dominated by large investment banking firms because commercial banks were prohibited from underwriting commercial paper by the Glass-Stegall Act. However, in June 1987, the Fed granted subsidiaries of bank holding companies permission to underwrite commercial paper.[3] The lower underwriting fees brought about by competitive pressure forced Salomon Brothers in October 1987 to eliminate their commercial paper operations. While investment banking firms still dominate the dealer market, commercial banks are making inroads. This seems natural because, for the most part, the funds being raised in the commercial paper market represent those previously raised via short-term bank loans. At the end of 1989, the four largest commercial paper dealers were Merrill Lynch, Goldman Sachs, Shearson Lehman Hutton, and First Boston. The three largest commercial banks that underwrite commercial paper are Bankers Trust, Citicorp, and Morgan Guaranty.

In 1983, Merrill Lynch began to offer commercial paper programs in which the payments could be denominated in a currency other than U.S. dollars. Merrill Lynch called this program *multicurrency commercial paper*. The investor could select the foreign currency in which the commercial paper would repay. In October 1986, Goldman Sachs started a similar program, which it called *universal commercial paper*.[4] From an investor's perspective, the programs offered by Goldman Sachs and Merrill Lynch permit foreign-exchange rate speculation.[5]

## The Secondary Market

Despite the fact that the commercial paper market is larger than other money market instruments, secondary trading activity is much smaller. Typically, an investor in commercial paper is an entity that plans to hold it until maturity. This is understandable since an investor can purchase commercial paper with the specific maturity desired. Should an investor's economic circumstances change such that there is a need to sell the paper, it can be sold back to the dealer, or, in the case of directly placed paper, the issuer will repurchase it.

## Yields on Commercial Paper

Commercial paper is typically a discount instrument but can be issued as an interest-bearing instrument. That is, it is sold at a price less than its maturity value. The difference between the maturity value and the price paid is the interest earned by the investor. For commercial paper, a year is treated as having 360 days. Commercial paper is quoted on a discount basis, as are Treasury bills.

---

[3] Bankers Trust first attempted to underwrite commercial paper in 1978.

[4] Before getting out of the commercial paper business, Salomon Brothers offered a program denominated in U.S. dollars but indexed to a foreign-exchange rate.

[5] The issuer will agree to pay the principal in U.S. dollars. The dealer, Goldman Sachs or Merrill Lynch, make the payment in the foreign currency selected by the investor. The dealer usually protects itself by using a currency swap.

The yield offered on commercial paper tracks that of other money market instruments. The commercial paper rate is higher than that on Treasury bills for three reasons. First, the investor in commercial paper is exposed to credit risk. Second, interest earned from investing in Treasury bills is exempt from state and local income taxes. As a result, commercial paper has to offer a higher yield to offset this tax advantage of Treasury bills. Finally, the liquidity of commercial paper is less than that of Treasury bills. However, the liquidity premium demanded is probably small because, as stated earlier, investors typically follow a buy-and-hold strategy with commercial paper and so are less concerned with liquidity. The rate on commercial paper is higher by a few basis points than that on certificates of deposit, which we will discuss later in this chapter. The yield advantage of commercial paper is due to the higher liquidity of certificates of deposit.

## MEDIUM-TERM NOTES

A medium-term note is a corporate debt instrument. The unique characteristic of medium-term notes is that they are continuously offered to investors over a period of time by an agent of the issuer. Maturities range from nine months to 30 years. Investors select from the following maturity bands: nine months to one year, more than 1 year to 18 months, more than 18 months to two years, etc. The reason we discuss medium-term notes in a chapter on money market instruments is that a large portion of these instruments have short maturities. Medium-term notes are registered with the Securities and Exchange Commission under Rule 415 (the shelf registration rule). Registering under Rule 415 gives the issuer the maximum flexibility for issuing securities on a continuous basis.

The yield offered on a medium-term note depends on (1) the particular maturity selected by the investor, (2) the Treasury yield curve at the time of offering, and (3) the credit-risk premium demanded by the market. In other words, the medium-term note will be priced at a spread to the Treasury yield curve at the time of the offering. Medium-term notes are typically issued at par.

The medium-term note was pioneered by Merrill Lynch in 1981 to provide a funding gap between commercial paper and long-term bonds.[6] The first medium-term note issuer was Ford Motor Credit Company. By 1983, GMAC and Chrysler Financial used Merrill Lynch as an agent to issue medium-term notes. The subsequent growth of the domestic medium-term note market and its importance as a funding source can be seen by comparing it to the amount of domestic

---

[6] Actually, in 1972 GMAC first used medium-term notes to fund automobile loans with maturities of five years and less. The medium-term notes were issued directly to investors, without the use of an agent or benefit of a secondary market.

public debt issued.[7] In 1982, the first full year of medium-term notes issuance, $3.8 billion was offered. This was less than 10 percent of the $36.8 billion of domestic public debt issued. In sharp contrast, by 1989 the amount of domestic medium-term notes issued exceeded the issuance of domestic public debt: $118.4 billion versus $108.7 billion. In that year, 24.1 percent, or $28.5 billion, of the medium-term notes issued had maturities from nine months to two years; 50.1 percent, or $59.3 billion, of medium-term notes issued had maturities between two years and five years.

As of December 31, 1989, the amount of medium-term notes outstanding was $339 billion. Of this amount, $261 billion was issued through Merrill Lynch.[8] Issuers in the market include finance companies, bank or bank holding companies, industrial companies, thrifts, utilities, and sovereign or government agencies. As of December 1989, finance companies offered the largest number of programs, followed by bank or bank holding companies and then industrials.[9]

The system used by commercial rating companies to rate medium-term notes is the same as that used for long-term debt. Usually the rating matches the rating of the long-term debt of the corporate issuer with the same seniority level. Consequently, unsecured medium-term notes will usually carry the same rating as the corporate issuer's unsecured long-term debt; secured medium-term notes will typically carry the same rating as the corporate issuer's secured long-term debt. The medium-term note market, as with the commercial paper market, has been opened up to lower rated issuers by the use of credit enhancements such as letters of credit or guarantees or by the collateralization of the issue with high-quality assets.

## Types of Medium-Term Note Programs Offered

As an example of the types of medium-term note programs offered, we shall discuss those offered by Merrill Lynch. As of February 1990, Merrill Lynch had the following programs: (1) fixed-rate MTNs, (2) floating-rate MTNs, (3) credit-supported MTNs, (4) collateralized MTNs, (5) amortizing notes, and (6) multicurrency MTNs.[10]

---

[7] This includes nonconvertible, dollar-denominated debt, excluding junk bonds, mortgage-backed securities, and asset-backed securities. The information was obtained from IDD Information Services.

[8] This information was taken from "A History of Leadership," in *Money Market Instruments*, published by Merrill Lynch.

[9] The source of this information is "Medium-Term Note Issuer Profile: 1982-1989," in *Money Market Instruments*.

[10] The information about these programs is given in *Medium-Term Notes: An Investment Opportunity* (New York: Merrill Lynch Money Markets, Inc.) and *Money Market Instruments*.

Fixed-rate MTNs pay interest semiannually, on a 30/360 basis, just as other corporate bonds. As noted above, the yield offered is a spread to a comparable maturity Treasury security.

Floating-rate MTNs can be selected with daily, weekly, monthly, quarterly, or semiannual reset periods. There are a wide variety of indexes that the investor can select from, including LIBOR, commercial paper composite rate, Treasury bills, or prime rate. The spread that is added to or subtracted from the index selected will depend on the credit rating of the issuer and market conditions.

Credit-supported MTNs are backed by either an irrevocable letter of credit or some other guarantee. The rating of a credit-supported MTN will depend on the rating of the entity furnishing the credit support. Some medium-term note issuers such as thrifts have issued collateralized MTNs where the collateral supporting the issue is mortgage-backed securities.[11] Despite the lower credit rating of thrifts, overcollateralization has resulted in these issues receiving the highest credit rating.

Amortized notes offer an investor equal periodic dollar payments over the life of the issue. The payments include both principal and interest and are structured such that the note is fully repaid when the final payment is made. Thus, an amortized note is structured similar to a mortgage loan.[12] Amortized notes are typically unsecured corporate obligations. An advantage of this form of medium-term note is that the principal exposure of the investor declines as each payment is made by the issuer.

Multicurrency MTNs are nondollar-denominated securities. The investor can choose from more than 10 foreign currencies. The investor will be paid in U.S. dollars, however, based on the exchange rate prevailing at the time of payment. A designated exchange rate agent converts the interest and principal payments from the foreign currency to U.S. dollars.

## BANKERS' ACCEPTANCES

Simply put, a banker's acceptance is a vehicle created to facilitate commercial trade transactions. They are called bankers' acceptances because a bank accepts the responsibility to repay a loan to the holder of the vehicle created in a commercial transaction. Using bankers' acceptances to finance a commercial transaction is referred to as "acceptance financing."

The transactions in which bankers' acceptances are created are (1) the importing of goods into the United States, (2) the exporting of goods from the United States to foreign entities, (3) the storing and shipping of goods between

---

[11] Mortgage-backed securities are discussed in Chapters 27–30.
[12] See Chapter 26.

two foreign countries, in which neither the importer nor the exporter is a U.S. firm,[13]   and (4) the storing and shipping of goods between two entities in the United States.

As of October 1989, the amount of bankers' acceptances outstanding was $63 billion.[14]  Of this amount, $16 billion was created from transactions involving the importing of goods into the United States, $14 billion from the exporting of goods from the United States, and the balance, $33 billion, mostly includes transactions involving the storing and shipping between two foreign countries. Little use is made of acceptance financing by two parties within the United States.

Unlike the commercial paper and medium-term note markets, the banker's acceptance market has been shrinking since 1984, when it reached a peak of $78 billion. The banker's acceptance market has declined because alternative means for raising funds to finance transactions have been developed.

Bankers' acceptances are sold on a discounted basis, just as Treasury bills and commercial paper are. The major investors in bankers' acceptances are money market mutual funds and municipal entities.

***The Creation of a Banker's Acceptance.***    The best way to explain the creation of a banker's acceptance is by an illustration. The following entities will be involved in our transaction:

- Car Imports Corporation of America (Car Imports), a firm in New Jersey that sells automobiles
- West Germany Autos (WGA), a manufacturer of automobiles in West Germany
- Hoboken Bank of New Jersey (Hoboken Bank), a commercial bank in Hoboken, New Jersey
- West Berlin National Bank (Berlin Bank), a bank in West Germany
- High Caliber Money Market Fund, a mutual fund in the United States that invests in money market instruments

The following commercial transaction is being considered by Car Imports and WGA. Car Imports wants to import 15 cars manufactured by WGA. WGA is concerned with the ability of Car Imports to make payment on the 15 cars when they are received.

Acceptance financing is suggested as a means for facilitating this commercial transaction. Car Imports offers $300,000 for the 15 cars. The terms of the sale stipulate that the payment is to be made to WGA 60 days after it ships the 15 cars to Car Imports. WGA determines whether it is willing to accept

---

[13] The bankers' acceptances created from these transactions are called *third country acceptances*.
[14] *Federal Reserve Bulletin*, February 1990.

the $300,000. In considering the offering price, WGA will calculate the present value of the $300,000 because it will not be receiving the payment until 60 days after shipment. Suppose that WGA agrees to these terms.

Car Imports arranges with its bank, Hoboken Bank, to issue a letter of credit. The letter of credit indicates that Hoboken Bank will make good on the payment of $300,000 sixty days after shipment that Car Imports must make to WGA. The agreement to pay $300,000 sixty days after shipment is called a time draft. The letter of credit will be sent by Hoboken Bank to WGA's bank, Berlin Bank. Upon receipt of the letter of credit, Berlin Bank will notify WGA, who will then ship the 15 cars. After the cars are shipped, WGA presents the shipping documents to Berlin Bank and receives the present value of $300,000. WGA is now out of the picture.

Berlin Bank presents the time draft and the shipping documents to Hoboken Bank. The latter will then stamp "accepted" on the time draft. By doing so, Hoboken Bank has created a bankers' acceptance. This means that Hoboken Bank agrees to pay the holder of the bankers' acceptance $300,000 at the maturity date. Car Imports will receive the shipping documents so that it can procure the 15 cars once it signs a note or some other type of financing arrangement with Hoboken Bank.

At this point, the holder of the bankers' acceptance is the Berlin Bank. It has two choices. It can retain the bankers' acceptance as an investment in its loan portfolio, or it can request that Hoboken Bank make a payment of the present value of $300,000. Let's assume that Berlin Bank requests payment of the present value of $300,000.

Now the holder of the bankers' acceptance is Hoboken Bank. It has two choices: retain the bankers' acceptance as an investment as part of its loan portfolio or sell it to an investor. Suppose that Hoboken Bank chooses the latter and that High Caliber Money Market Fund is seeking a high quality investment with the same maturity as that of the bankers' acceptance. Hoboken Bank sells the bankers' acceptance to the money market fund at the present value of $300,000. Rather than sell a banker's acceptance directly to an investor such as High Caliber Money Market Fund, Hoboken Bank could sell it to a dealer. The dealer would then find an investor such as a money market fund to resell the banker's acceptance. In either case, at the maturity date, the money market fund presents the banker's acceptance to Hoboken Bank, receiving $300,000.

## The Accepting Banks

The banks that create bankers' acceptances (i.e., accepting banks) can be classified into four groups. First are the money center banks—banks that raise most of their funds from the domestic and international money markets and rely less on depositors for funds. The major money center banks that issue bankers' acceptances are Bankers Trust, Bank of America, Chase Manhattan, Citibank, and Morgan Guaranty. They maintain their own sales force to sell bankers' acceptances rather than use the services of a dealer.

The second group of accepting banks are some of the larger regional banks such as Harris Trust and Pittsburgh National Bank. A regional bank is one that relies primarily on deposits for its funding and makes less use of the money markets to obtain funds. The larger regional banks will maintain their own sales force to sell the bankers' acceptances but will use dealers to unload those they cannot sell.

Japanese banks are the third group of accepting banks. Japanese banks are classified as one of the following: city banks, local banks, long-term credit banks, trust banks, and mutual banks.[15] City banks are the most powerful financial institutions in Japan. The 13 city banks hold approximately 20 percent of all deposits in Japan. Japanese city banks are now the major issuers of bankers' acceptances. In April 1988, for example, there were approximately $32 billion of Japanese bankers' acceptances outstanding.[16] In 1988, the banker's acceptance market was approximately $67 billion. The largest issuer of Japanese bankers' acceptances is Daichi Kango Bank.[17] Because they do not have the sales force to distribute the bankers' acceptances they create directly to investors, Japanese accepting banks use the services of dealers.

The fourth group of accepting banks are Yankee banks. Included in this group are non-Japanese branches of foreign banks. Algemene, Credit Lyonnais, and Deutsche Bank are examples. The amount of bankers' acceptances issued by Yankee banks is small. For example, First Boston Corporation estimates that in April 1988 the amount of foreign bankers' acceptances (Japanese and Yankee) outstanding was $35 billion and that the amount of Japanese bankers' acceptances outstanding was $32 billion. Therefore, Yankee bankers' acceptances outstanding was only $3 billion.

*Credit Risk.* Investing in bankers' acceptances exposes the investor to credit risk. This is the risk that the accepting bank will not be able to pay the principal due at the maturity date.

*Eligible Banker's Acceptance.* An accepting bank that has decided to retain a banker's acceptance in its portfolio may be able to use it as collateral for a loan at the discount window of the Federal Reserve. The reason we say it

---

[15] For a discussion of these different institutions, see Noboru Honjo and Lisa J. Turbessi, "Participants in the Japanese Bond Markets," in Frank J. Fabozzi (ed.), *The Japanese Bond Market* (Chicago: Probus Publishing, 1990).

[16] *Handbook of Securities of the United States Government and Agencies*, p. 130.

[17] Marcia Stigum, *The Money Market* (Homewood, IL: Dow Jones-Irwin, 1990), p. 1015.

may be able to use it is that bankers' acceptances must meet certain eligibility requirements established by the Federal Reserve. One requirement for eligibility to discount is its maturity. With few exceptions, the maturity cannot exceed six months. Although the other requirements for eligibility are too detailed to review here, the basic principle is simple.[18] The banker's acceptance should be financing a self-liquidating commercial transaction.

Eligibility is also important because the Federal Reserve imposes a reserve requirement on funds raised via bankers' acceptances that are ineligible. The bankers' acceptances sold by an accepting bank are potential liabilities of the bank. However, no reserve requirements are imposed for eligible bankers' acceptances. Consequently, most of the bankers' acceptances satisfy the eligibility criteria. Finally, the Federal Reserve has also imposed a limit on the amount of eligible bankers' acceptances that may be issued by a bank. It may not exceed 150 percent of a bank's capital and surplus.

*Rates Charged on Bankers' Acceptances.* The rate that a bank will charge a customer for issuing a banker's acceptance is determined as follows. The bank will determine the rate that it can sell its banker's acceptance in the open market. To this rate it will add a commission. Here, competition from Japanese banks has significantly affected the banker's acceptance business. Japanese banks are willing to accept a lower commission than U.S. banks. For example, for a high credit rated customer, a commercial bank may charge 25 to 30 basis points, while a Japanese bank may charge 10 to 15 basis points.[19] In the case of ineligible bankers' acceptances, a bank will also add an amount to offset the cost of the reserve requirements imposed.

## Dealers

As explained above, banks may sell their bankers' acceptances directly to investors, or they may sell all or part to dealers, When the banker's acceptance market was growing in the early part of the 1980s, there were over 25 dealers. By 1989, the decline in the amount of bankers' acceptances issued drove many one-time major dealers such as Salomon Brothers out of the business. Today, the major dealer is Merrill Lynch. Shearson Lehman Hutton is another dealer in bankers' acceptances. The other key dealers are commercial banks such as Bankers Trust and Morgan Guaranty.

As in the case of Treasury securities, there are brokers who broker transactions between dealers. Two government brokers also broker bankers' acceptances: Fundamental Brokers, Inc. (FBI) and Garban, Ltd.

---

[18] The eligibility requirements are described in Jean M. Hahr and William C. Melton, "Bankers' Acceptances," *Quarterly Review*, Federal Reserve Bank of New York, Summer 1981.

[19] Stigum, *The Money Market*, p. 1007.

## CERTIFICATES OF DEPOSIT

Certificates of deposit (CDs) are issued by banks and thrifts to raise funds for financing their business activities. There is no limit on the denomination of a CD. CDs issued by banks covered by the Federal Deposit Insurance Corporation are insured for amounts up to $100,000. Our focus in this chapter is on negotiable CDs. These are CDs that are issued in denominations of $100,000 or more and can be sold in a secondary market. Subsequent references to a CD will imply a negotiable CD.

The largest investor group in CDs are investment companies. Money market funds make up the bulk of investment companies that invest in CDs. At a distant second are banks and bank trust departments, followed by municipal entities and corporations.

CDs can be classified into four types, based on the issuing bank. First are the domestic CDs. These are issued by domestic banks. Second are CDs that are denominated in U.S. dollars but are issued outside of the United States. These CDs are called Eurodollar CDs, or Euro CDs. A third type of CD is the Yankee CD, which is a CD denominated in U.S. dollars and issued by foreign banks with branches in the United States. Finally, thrift CDs are those issued by savings and loan associations and savings banks.

Money center banks and large regional banks are the primary issuers of domestic CDs. While there is no limit on the maximum maturity for a CD, the minimum maturity for a domestic CD is seven days. This is a restriction imposed by the Federal Reserve. Most CDs are issued with a maturity of less than one year. Those issued with a maturity greater than one year are called *term CDs.*

Unlike Treasury bills, commercial paper, and bankers' acceptances, yields on domestic CDs are quoted on an interest-bearing basis. For CDs with a maturity of one year or less, interest is paid at maturity. For purposes of calculating interest, a year is treated as having 360 days. For term CDs, interest is normally paid semiannually, again with 360 days representing a year.

Euro CDs are U.S. dollar-denominated CDs, issued primarily in London by U.S., Canadian, European, and Japanese banks. Branches of large U.S. banks were the major issuers of Euro CDs. In 1982, of the $93 billion Euro CDs issued, $50 billion was issued by branches of U.S. banks.[20] Since 1982, however, the share of Euro CDs issued by branches of U.S. banks has declined. Japanese banks have now become major issuers of Euro CDs.

As in the case of domestic CDs, interest on Euro CDs with maturities of one year or less is paid at maturity. For Euro CDs with a maturity of more than one year (i.e., term Euro CDs), interest is paid annually rather than semiannually, as in the case of domestic term CDs.

---

[20] As reported in *Quarterly Bulletin* published by the Bank of England.

## Floating-Rate CDs

A floating-rate CD (FRCD) is one in which the coupon interest rate on the CD changes periodically in accordance with a predetermined formula.[21] The predetermined formula indicates the spread (or margin) above some index that the coupon will reset periodically. There are FRCDs that reset the coupon daily, weekly, monthly, quarterly, or semiannually. Typically FRCDs have maturities from 18 months to five years.

When FRCDs were first issued, they were indexed to the Federal Reserve CD composite rate. Today, there are FRCDs that are indexed to one of several rates, including the London Interbank Offered Rate (LIBOR), the Treasury bill bond equivalent yield, the CD composite rate, the commercial paper composite rate, the federal funds rate, and the prime rate. LIBOR represents the global banking system's cost of obtaining short-term funds because it is a posted rate at which prime banks offer to make Eurodollar deposits available to other prime banks. Consequently, LIBOR is the most commonly used index for a floating-rate CD. When LIBOR is used as the index, the rate is determined in one of three ways. It is either (1) the rate reported on the LIBOR page of Reuters' News Service, (2) the rate set by a single reference bank, or (3) a rate set by a group of reference banks.

There are other features that may be included in a FRCD. For example, a FRCD may be callable by the issuer. It could also have a specified interest-rate ceiling or floor.

## Yields on CDs

The yields posted on CDs vary depending on the following three factors: (1) the credit rating of the issuing bank, (2) the maturity of the CD, and (3) the supply and demand for CDs. With respect to the third factor, banks and thrifts issue CDs as part of their liability management strategy. The supply of CDs will be driven by the demand for bank loans and the cost of alternative sources of capital to fund these loans. Moreover, bank loan demand will depend on the cost of alternative funding sources such as commercial paper. When loan demand is weak (strong), CD rates decline (rise). The effect of maturity depends on the shape of the yield curve. We will discuss the first factor below.

*Credit risk.*  At one time, domestic CDs issued by money center banks traded on a no-name basis. However, the financial crises that have occurred in the banking industry have caused investors to take a closer look at issuing

---

[21] In 1977 the initial issuers of FRCDs in the U.S. market were Japanese banks. For a history of the FRCD market, see David Muntner and Sara Kelly Fields, "Floating Rate Certificates of Deposit," Chapter 6 in Frank J. Fabozzi (ed.) *Floating Rate Instruments* (Chicago: Probus Publishing, 1986).

banks. Prime CDs (those issued by high-rated banks) of domestic banks trade at a lower yield than nonprime CDs (those issued by lower rated banks) of domestic banks. Because of the unfamiliarity investors have with foreign banks, generally Yankee CDs trade at a higher yield than domestic CDs.

Euro CDs offer a higher yield than domestic CDs. There are three reasons for this. First, there are reserve requirements imposed by the Federal Reserve on CDs issued by U.S. banks in the United States. There are no such requirements on issuers of Euro CDs. The reserve requirement effectively raises the cost of funds to the issuing bank because it cannot invest all the proceeds received from the issuance of a CD. The amount that must be kept as reserves will not earn a return for the bank. Since it will earn less on funds raised by selling domestic CDs, an issuing bank will pay less than a Euro CD. Second, the bank issuing the CD must pay an insurance premium to the FDIC, unlike funds raised from the issuance of a Euro CD. The insurance premium raises the cost of funds. Finally, Euro CDs are dollar obligations that are payable by an entity operating under a foreign jurisdiction. As a result, a portion of the spread between the yield offered on Euro CDs and domestic CDs reflects what can be termed a sovereign risk premium. This premium varies with the degree of confidence in the international banking system.

CD yields are higher than yields on Treasury securities of the same maturity. The spread is due mainly to the credit risk that a CD investor is exposed to and the fact that CDs offer less liquidity.[22] The spread due to credit risk will vary with economic conditions and confidence in the banking system. The spread will increase when there is a flight to quality or when there is a crisis in the banking system.

---

[22] The spread between Treasury bills and Eurodollar CDs is referred to as the "TED spread."

# CHAPTER 12

## REPURCHASE AGREEMENTS

*Oskar H. Rogg*
*Vice President*
*Liability Management*
*The First Boston Corporation*

Repurchase agreements are a very important, but often poorly understood, money market instrument. This chapter will present the basics of repurchase agreements, the nature of the market, and the mechanics of the instrument, as well as specials repo, the recent legal history of the market, Federal Reserve participation in the market, and finally, future trends in the market.

## THE BASICS

A *repurchase agreement* (*repo* for short) is the simultaneous sale and repurchase of a security for different settlement dates. From an economic standpoint, it resembles a collateralized loan. Securities market participants enter into repo transactions because they have cash and want a short-term investment or because they have securities and want to borrow short-term funds.

The latter transaction (the customer borrows short-term funds against securities) is often called a *reverse repo*, or *resale*. The terms repo and reverse repo describe the same transaction from different points of view; the purchaser's repo (sale/repurchase) is the seller's reverse repo (purchase/resale). To avoid confusion, we will avoid this terminology and instead refer to buying and selling collateral.

The following two examples illustrate a repo and reverse repo.

Suppose a customer wants to invest $10 million for three days. The dealer sells $9.5 million Treasury notes $9\frac{1}{8}$ of 9-30-91 to the customer for settlement today versus $10 million (market value). Simultaneously, the dealer buys back

$9.5$ million Treasury notes $9\frac{1}{8}$ of 9-30-91 from the customer for settlement three days hence versus $10 million plus interest (9.60% $\times$ $10 million $\times$ 3 days/360). The result is that the customer has invested $10 million for three days at 9.60 percent. This is the general market interest rate for a three-day repo. It is independent of the coupon, market price, and maturity of the specific collateral security.

Now suppose a customer owns $10 million Treasury notes $8\frac{1}{4}$ of 2-15-93 and wants to borrow funds overnight. The dealer buys $10 million Treasury notes $8\frac{1}{4}$ of 2-15-93 from the customer for settlement today versus $9.8 million (market value). Simultaneously, the dealer sells $10 million Treasury notes $8\frac{1}{4}$ of 2-15-93 back to the customer for settlement tomorrow versus $9.8 million plus interest (9.65% $\times$ 9.8 million $\times$ 1 day/360). The result is that the customer has borrowed $9.8 million for one day at 9.65 percent.

The preceding examples demonstrate the basic principle of a repo: A repo is a simultaneous purchase and sale of the *same* security for *different* settlement dates. From an economic standpoint, the purchaser does not care what the market price of the security is, whether it goes up or down, or what coupon the security carries. The market risk of the collateral is completely borne by the seller. The purchaser receives a fixed rate of interest on a short-term investment. The relative value of the collateral affects the purchaser from a credit standpoint only. On a trade date basis, neither party's securities positions are affected. Only on a settlement date basis does the transaction affect positions.

## FEATURES OF THE REPO MARKET

### Collateral

United States Treasury and agency issues, mortgage-backed pass-throughs and certain money market securities may be used for repo collateral. Although nonexempt securities such as corporate bonds can be used as collateral, Federal Reserve Regulation T places the restrictions on the extension of credit to non-broker-dealers, requiring margin requirements of up to 50 percent on these instruments. This limits the attractiveness of repos as a financing vehicle for these securities.

### Rate

The repo market provides both an attractive instrument for money market investors and a relatively inexpensive financing alternative for holders of securities. Market levels are based on competition between repos and other short-term instruments (Treasury and agency securities, commercial paper, and certificates of deposit) for the attention of buyers, and on the rate differential between repos and alternative funding sources (such as bank loans) available to sellers.

Repo rates depend on the type of collateral used. In general, the higher the credit quality of the collateral and the easier the security is to deliver and hold (e.g., wireable versus physical, semiannual coupon versus monthly pay), the lower the repo rate. Thus, mortgage-backed security repos trade at higher levels than federal agency repos, which in turn trade at higher levels than Treasury repos. If the Treasury collateral matures in one year or less, the repo will have an even lower rate, because the collateral is perceived as safer still. The more restrictions the buyer imposes with respect to the collateral, the lower the rate received. Of course, spread relationships are flexible and depend on the supply-and-demand status and the perceived credit quality of the specific type of collateral.

## Term

Repos can be executed for maturities of between one day and one year (occasionally longer under special circumstances). The vast majority of repos have maturities of three months or less. One-day transactions are called *overnight repos*. Longer transactions are called *term repos*. An *open repo* is an overnight repo that rolls over automatically until terminated by either party.

## Credit

Because the market value of the collateral changes constantly, both parties in a repurchase transaction may experience credit exposure. In addition, any margin given on a transaction increases the credit exposure for the party providing it. Although repo market participants can limit their credit exposure by requiring margin collateral and by regularly marking term transactions to market, there is no substitute for a thorough credit review of repo counterparties prior to initiation of repurchase transactions. This review typically includes analysis of the entity's financial statements and of its legal and corporate authority to enter into repurchase transactions. In addition, attention must be paid to the specifics of the transaction, including collateral, term, size, and margin.

## Market Participants

A wide variety of institutions participate in the repo market:

> *Net Sellers of Collateral*
> > thrifts
> > bank portfolios
> *Net Buyers of Collateral*
> > bank trust departments

money market funds

municipalities

corporations

*Spread Traders*

insurance companies and pension funds

bank security lending areas

Many sophisticated institutions will be involved in more than one area of the repo market; for example, a corporation might invest its short-term funds in repos and also reverse its government securities portfolio to lock in a spread.

## Matched Books

Securities dealers use repos both to finance their own positions and to execute matched book activities. In a matched book, the dealer would buy collateral from one customer, perhaps a thrift, and sell it to another customer, such as a money market fund, at a lower rate. In a perfectly matched book, the maturities of both transactions would be equal and the dealer would not have any rate risk. In practice, the dealer may mismatch the maturities to profit from anticipated market movements.

As an example, suppose a dealer predicts that interest rates will fall over the next 90 days. To take advantage of this projected decline, he buys $100 million worth of collateral from a thrift for three months at 10 percent. He then sells it to a money market fund, one week at a time, initially at 9.90 percent. If the dealer has guessed correctly, subsequent weekly rollovers will be at lower rates. Thus, the dealer will receive a high fixed rate from the thrift for the entire 90 days but pay declining floating rates to the money market fund over the life of the transaction.

It is important to include the value of compounding into this analysis. If rates stay at 9.90 percent, the dealer will not make 10 basis points. Instead, he will lose 2.5 basis points, because he is receiving interest quarterly and paying interest weekly, albeit at a lower rate.[1]

In practice, a dealer would seldom be able to match its book perfectly, even if it wanted to, because the buyers and sellers of collateral are unlikely to want the same trade maturity. To manage the mismatch risk, many matched-book traders hedge their interest-rate exposure through the use of financial futures and options.

---

[1] The equation is as follows:

$$\frac{1}{\left[1+\frac{0.10}{4}\right]^4} = \frac{1}{\left[1+\frac{.09875}{52}\right]^{52}} \text{ (approximately)}$$

## MECHANICS OF REPURCHASE AGREEMENTS

If market prices go down during the life of the repo, the collateral will be worth less than the principal amount of the trade. This leaves the purchaser exposed if the seller defaults, files for bankruptcy, or is placed in receivership by the applicable regulatory authority. If market prices rise, the seller is similarly exposed.

As an example, suppose a school district enters into a $10 million, 30-day repurchase agreement with a thinly capitalized securities dealer. The dealer delivers $10,050,000 face of the Treasury bond $8\frac{7}{8}$ 8-15-91 with a market value of $10 million. Unfortunately, during the life of the repurchase agreement, the dealer sustains dramatic trading losses and is forced into bankruptcy. Because the bankrupt dealer is in no position to repurchase the bond pursuant to the agreement, the school district sells the collateral in the open market to get its money back. Unfortunately, it quickly discovers that the market has dropped and the bonds are worth only $9,800,000. The district is forced to stand in line with the other unsecured creditors of the bankrupt dealer for the remaining $200,000.

### Margin

Repo market participants often require margin to limit their credit exposure. Margin is collateral in excess of the principal of the trade. Typical margin ranges between 1 percent and 3 percent of the trade principal but may be 10 percent or more for illiquid securities or weak credits.

For example, suppose a customer buys a repo for $10 million with 2 percent margin. The dealer delivers $9,690,000 Treasury notes $9\frac{1}{8}$ of 9-30-91 (market value = $10,200,000) versus $10 million and agrees to repurchase the security subsequently for the same $10 million plus interest.

### Mark to Market

Another way to limit credit exposure on term repos is to mark the collateral to market regularly. The collateral is valued at current market levels and the trade is adjusted accordingly, either through a margin call or a repricing. If the market price has risen, the seller requests an adjustment; if the market price has declined, the purchaser requests the adjustment.

For example, suppose a dealer delivers $9,690,000 Treasury notes $9\frac{1}{8}$ of 9-30-91 worth $10,200,000 to the customer versus $10 million (2 percent original margin). Several days later the market drops and the Treasuries are worth $9,950,000. The dealer and the customer agree to one of two options:

1. *Margin call*: The dealer sends the customer additional collateral with a market value of $250,000, restoring the margin to the original 102 percent.
2. *Repricing:* The principal amount of the transaction is changed to $9,755,000, restoring the 102 percent margin. The dealer wires the difference ($245,000) to the customer.

Interest is paid on the principal amount outstanding. If the trade is repriced, interest will be paid on the $10 million until the repricing and on $9,755,000 thereafter. If margin collateral is delivered, the principal of the trade remains at $10 million and interest is paid on that amount.

## Substitution

During the term of the repo, the seller of the collateral may need the specific collateral for delivery to another customer. The seller may then request a substitution, involving the delivery of other securities of equal market value, with the purchaser returning the original collateral. For example, suppose the seller delivers $9,690,000 Treasury notes $9\frac{1}{8}$ of 9-30-91 versus $10 million for a seven-day repo. Three days later, the seller requests a substitution. The purchaser returns the $9\frac{1}{8}$ notes to the seller, who replaces them with $9 million Treasury notes $9\frac{1}{2}$ of 10-15-94 as collateral. The principal amount of the trade remains $10 million.

Substitution provisions should be agreed upon at the time of the trade.

## Principal and Interest Payments

Even though the purchaser owns the collateral during the term of the repo, the seller is entitled to any principal or interest received. The purchaser is responsible for wiring to the seller any such funds received while holding the collateral.

## Delivery

There are several delivery alternatives for the repo collateral.

*Delivery*: The seller delivers the securities to the purchaser versus the principal of the trade. At the maturity of the repo, the purchaser returns the securities versus the trade principal plus financing interest.

*Safekeeping*: The seller holds the securities for the purchaser. The purchaser receives confirmations for the transaction but the collateral is held in a segregated customer account by the seller; this is also known as "hold in custody" repo or "letter" repo.

*Third Party*: Collateral is delivered to the purchaser's custodial account at the seller's clearing bank. Because collateral moves within the bank, this arrangement has the operational advantages of safekeeping while still accomplishing delivery.

## Repo Trading Practices

Nearly all repo trading is done on a cash (same day) settlement basis. This greatly reduces the tolerance for clerical and operational errors and necessitates close contact between the repo desk and the government securities clearance area.

In addition, cash settlement tends to compress the repo market activity into an 8–10 A.M. window to allow trades to be processed and cleared. This contributes to the volatility of the market because positions must be covered or traded quickly and participants often cannot "wait out" perceived shortages of money or collateral.

Repo rates are quoted on an actual/360 basis, which understates the true yield. It is important to adjust the yield accordingly when comparing repos to instruments that trade on a different basis.

A round lot in the repo market is $25 million. Because of the short-term nature of the market, operational costs can greatly affect rates on smaller pieces of collateral.

## SPECIALS REPOS

Our discussion of repurchase agreements thus far has assumed that the underlying collateral is generic. There is also a market for *specials repos*, where the underlying security is the salient feature of the transaction. The buyer of the repo will use the collateral to make delivery on a security that he has sold short.

To illustrate a specials repo, suppose a dealer sells $25 million Treasury notes $7\frac{7}{8}$ of 11-15-99 to a customer in the normal course of market-making activities. Guessing that the market price of the security will decline over the following week because of technical factors, he elects not to cover his short immediately. Instead, he enters into a repurchase agreement with another dealer under which he receives $25 million $7\frac{7}{8}$ of 11-15-99 as collateral. He turns around and uses that collateral to effect delivery on his outright sale. He will continue to cover his short in the repo market until he buys back the issue. Though he receives interest on the money he invested in the repurchase agreement, clearly his primary concern is receiving the specific collateral required to make delivery on his sale.

The short seller takes great pains in borrowing securities to make deliveries because market rules make failures to deliver very expensive. If a seller of a security fails to deliver it on the scheduled settlement date, she loses interest on the proceeds until she makes delivery (the buyer is entitled to the coupon on the settlement date but does not need to pay for the security until delivery is made). Thus, if the seller can obtain the security as repo collateral at any rate above 0 percent, it is less expensive than failing to make delivery on the outright sale.

To illustrate this, suppose the dealer commits to deliver $25 million $7\frac{7}{8}$ of 11-15-99 for $25 million principal plus $97,089.04 accrued interest. If she fails to deliver the security on the settlement date, she must still deliver it for $25,097,089.04 the following day, even though the security now carries an extra $5,393.83 of accrued interest. The buyer gets credit for paying for the Treasury note on the settlement date even though he had an extra day's use of his money. In effect, the seller has extended an interest-free loan to the buyer when she fails to make delivery. It goes without saying that intelligent buyers cry all the way to the bank over delivery failures and that sellers do their level best to avoid them.

Issues that are in demand by dealers who need to make deliveries on short sales are called "specials." Collateral becomes special when it is in high demand by government securities dealers who must make deliveries to customers. The interest rate that dealers are willing to receive when bidding on these issues can be several hundred basis points less than the rate for generic collateral, although only a handful of securities trade more than 30 basis points below the generic rate at any given time.

For example, suppose a customer owns $10 million Treasury notes $9\frac{1}{2}$ of 10-15-94 and wants to borrow cash for four days. The interest rate bid for generic collateral is 9.65 percent. However, this particular security is special. In all likelihood, traders have sold the issue short in anticipation of the seven-year Treasury auction and need to borrow securities to make deliveries. The dealer purchases the $10 million Treasury notes $9\frac{1}{2}$ of 10-15-94 on repo at 6.25 percent for four days. The result is that the customer pays 6.25 percent interest on borrowed funds, 340 basis points less than the general market, because of high demand for the specific collateral.

Conversely, after the dealer has covered his short, the security has value to him only as generic collateral and he would bid no lower than 9.65 percent. Because of this, the specials trading brings to mind a farmer's market—issues that are quite valuable at 9:30 A.M. trade like rubbish at 2:00 P.M.

In practice, dealers cover their own short sales in this manner and also run specials matched books, buying and selling collateral for various terms based on their expectations of tightness in specific issues and on their overall interest rate outlook.

## SECURITIES LENDING

Securities dealers also borrow securities needed to make deliveries. These loans are collateralized by other securities of equal value or cash. If the loan is collateralized by securities, the borrower pays the lender a fee. If the securities loan is collateralized by cash, the borrower receives a below-market interest rate on the money. The fee or rate differential is determined by how special the security is (its relative availability) and can range from 10 to several hundred basis points.

Securities loans are generally done on an open basis (terminable at the option of the lender or borrower) but may have specific maturities.

Many entities prefer to lend securities instead of reversing them because securities loans appear as a footnote to the balance sheet, but repurchase transactions increase assets and liabilities. In addition, pension plans subject to ERISA (the Employee Retirement Income Security Act) may only lend, not reverse repo, their securities.

As an example, suppose a dealer borrows $3 million FHLBs 7.70 of 6-26-89. In return for the FHLBs, she delivers Treasury notes with an equal market value for collateral. Because this security is not very special, the dealer pays the customer 35 basis points on the market value of the FHLB while the loan is outstanding.

## RECENT LEGAL EVENTS IN THE REPO MARKET

Legal aspects of the repo market have become more clearly defined during the 1980s, when large losses resulting from the failures of a few small government securities dealers forced market participants to focus on the credit risks of repo. Prior to the default of Drysdale Government Securities in 1982, repo collateral was valued on a principal-only basis because of operational considerations. The entity that borrowed securities in this fashion and sold them short generated cash because it received principal and interest on the sale. Drysdale engaged in such transactions and invested the cash to earn additional income.

Unfortunately, in a bull market, the firm lost money on its short sales and was unable to remit the coupons to the owners of the borrowed securities, triggering default. In the wake of this imbroglio, the Public Securities Association (PSA) issued guidelines for repurchase agreements that mandated the recognition of accrued interest when valuing collateral securities.

Complicating the Drysdale mess was the fact that money center banks had acted as *agents for an undisclosed third party* (i.e., Drysdale). Many repo market participants who had never heard of the firm suddenly found that Drysdale was the actual counterparty to their repurchase agreements. Although the banks eventually honored their obligations, chastened market participants began to review more closely the financial stability and legal status of their counterparties.

Central to the perceived safety of a repurchase transaction is the ability of the buyer to liquidate the collateral if the seller defaults. When Lombard-Wall Inc., another small securities firm, failed in 1982, the bankruptcy judge in the case issued a stay that prevented Lombard-Wall's repo counterparties from liquidating collateral. To prevent this situation from recurring, an amendment to the Bankruptcy Act was passed in 1984 that specifically exempted repo collateral from the automatic stay provisions of the bankruptcy code. Coverage under the amendment is limited to repurchase agreements of one year or less for collateral consisting of government, agency, and certain money market securities. In addition, the amendment did not preclude the Securities Investor Protection Corporation (SIPC) from preventing liquidation of repo collateral in a default situation.

Subsequent to the passage of the bankruptcy amendment, the failures of Lion Capital, RTD Securities Inc., ESM Government Securities Inc., and Bevill Bressler and Schulman Inc. resulted in losses on the part of their repurchase agreement counterparties. This time the villain was dealer safekeeping, otherwise known as hold-in-custody repo. To minimize operational costs and pay incrementally higher rates, the dealers in question held the repo collateral instead of delivering it to their customers. Unfortunately, when default occurred, the customers found that the collateral listed on their repo confirmations had been pledged to other parties as well.

Many of the injured parties were small municipalities and school districts across the nation. The resulting uproar prompted passage of the Government Securities Act of 1986. This act required greater disclosure in the repo markets and an executed repurchase agreement as a prerequisite for hold-in-custody transactions. The Public Securities Association also promulgated a form of repurchase agreement in an effort to further standardize the market.

## REPO PRODUCTS AND STRATEGIES

### Flex Repos

A flexible repo (flex repo) is a term repurchase agreement that provides for principal drawdowns prior to its final maturity. These transactions have proven particularly popular for structured municipal financings, which require a fixed reinvestment rate even though there is substantial cash-flow uncertainty.

To illustrate a flex repo, suppose a state housing finance agency issues $100 million in tax-exempt bonds to stimulate homeownership. Bond proceeds will eventually be expended to finance below-market-rate mortgages. However, the bond proceeds need to be invested until the mortgages are originated. The investment earnings are used to meet the interest payments on the tax-exempt issue.

The actual origination schedule can only be estimated; therefore, fixed-term investments are impractical because they introduce market and reinvestment risk. Instead, the housing agency and a securities dealer enter into a flex repo that allows for drawdowns of principal as needed, not on a preset schedule. In return for accepting increased risk by granting this flexibility, the dealer pays a lower rate on this repo than on an equivalent term transaction.

## Indexed Repos

An indexed repo is a term repo with the interest rate reset periodically as a function of the federal funds rate, LIBOR, the Treasury bill discount, or a similar short-term rate. The investor can again draw down (and in some cases add to) the principal as needed. Indexed repos are an attractive reinvestment vehicle for issuers of floating-rate securities who wish to "match their book" of assets and liabilities.

For example, suppose a hospital issues variable-rate debt to finance construction of a new wing. Pending expenditure of the proceeds, they are invested in an indexed repurchase agreement. Six months later, interest rates rise and the hospital's debt payments increase. However, since the repurchase agreement rate is indexed, investment earnings also rise. By matching their asset/liability book, the hospital has largely insulated this financing from interest-rate moves during construction.

## Spread Trades

Customers who own Treasury securities can often realize yield by executing spread trades—selling Treasury collateral on repo and purchasing mortgage-backed security collateral with the proceeds. This takes advantage of the higher repo rates often available for mortgage-backed collateral. However, following the thrift bailout and other changes in the repurchase market, opportunities for profitable spread trades are becoming few and far between.

For example, suppose a customer owns $10 million Treasury notes $8\frac{1}{4}$ of 2-15-93. He sells this collateral for seven days at 9.65 percent versus $9,800,000. The customer then reinvests the $9,800,000 in a seven-day repo collateralized by FHLMC 9s of 2-01-16 at 9.78 percent. The customer pays interest at 9.65 percent and receives interest at 9.78 percent, netting 13 basis points.

Commercial paper, time deposits, certificates of deposit, and other money market instruments also provide effective reinvestments for spread trades.

### Reverse-to-Maturity Transactions

Owners of short Treasury and agency securities can often realize a substantial yield pickup by reversing (selling on repo) these securities to maturity and reinvesting the proceeds. This transaction is appropriate for investors who are unable to sell the security as part of a swap because of accounting concerns.

The following example illustrates a reverse to maturity transaction. Suppose a customer owns $10 million of 12-29-88 Treasury bills. He reverses the issue to maturity with a dealer at a rate of 7.65 percent. The customer reinvests the proceeds in mortgage-backed security repo until 12-29-88 at a rate of 8.65 percent. The customer picks up 100 basis points of incremental yield. At maturity (12-29-88), the proceeds of the reverse and interest at 7.65 percent are paired off against the maturing principal of the bill.

The dealer is able to bid far below the normal reverse rate to reverse the Treasury bill because it will sell the security outright. The 7.65 percent rate represents the bid side yield on the bill (converted to a money market basis) plus a spread.

To do this transaction, the customer must:

- Be able to execute a reverse repo
- Own Treasury or Agency securities with a money market equivalent bid side yield that is less than the reinvestment rate
- Be unwilling or unable to actually sell the security as part of a swap into a higher yielding security

## THE OTHER REPO MARKET PARTICIPANT— FEDERAL RESERVE OPEN-MARKET ACTIVITY

The Federal Reserve (the Fed) influences short-term interest rates by adding and subtracting funds from the financial markets through open-market activities. Long-term interest rates are also influenced because the financing costs of holding securities are affected. The Fed may embark on open-market operations to move short-term rate levels or to maintain them in the face of technical factors such as settlement periods or tax deposits that would affect the supply of and demand for funds. Open-market activities generally take place between 11:35 A.M. and noon and are closely followed by short-term market participants. The most common open-market activities are as follows:

- *Customer Repo*: The Fed buys collateral on behalf of customers (foreign central banks). This adds cash to the financial system and can exert downward pressure on interest rates, although small amounts of customer repo may have no affect whatsoever on rate levels.
- *System Repo*: The Fed buys collateral on repo for its own account, adding cash to the system. This exerts a downward pressure on short-term rates.
- *Matched Sales*: The Fed sells securities for its own account and commits to repurchase them subsequently for a price that reflects financing interest (in effect a repo). This subtracts cash from the system and exerts upward pressure on rates.
- *Coupon Pass/Bill Pass*: The Fed buys Treasury notes and bonds (or bills) outright, instead of on repo. This adds reserves to the system on a longer term basis than system repo, pushing rates downward.

## FUTURE OF THE REPURCHASE
## AGREEMENT MARKET

There are several trends significantly affecting the repo market. Many ailing thrift institutions have long financed underwater mortgage-backed securities positions in the repo market rather than selling them and recording a loss. The government bailout of the thrift industry provides that many of these portfolios be liquidated and the losses recognized. These securities are being sold—either in their current form or repackaged into derivative products such as collateralized mortgage obligations—primarily to institutions that do not finance their portfolios in the repo market. A growing amount of mortgage-backed security collateral will no longer be available to the repo market.

The conversion of Federal Home Loan Mortgage Corporation (FHLMC) and Federal National Mortgage Association (FNMA) pass-through certificates to the Federal Reserve book-entry system and the establishment of Participants Trust Company (PTC) as a depository for Government National Mortgage Association (GNMA) securities have significantly reduced the operational problems of mortgage-backed security repo, thereby broadening its appeal to investors. Combined with the shrinking pool of collateral discussed above, this continuing immobilization of physical mortgage-backed securities will tighten the spread between Treasury and mortgage-backed repo rates.

In the specials market, the increasing number of institutions willing to lend or reverse specific securities has severely affected fees. Many institutions that were unwilling to lend securities for less than 50 basis points several years ago have been forced to accept 5 to 25 basis points in order to stay in the market. In this declining spread environment, market intermediaries, such as commercial bank securities lending areas, may find their market shares diminished as dealers bypass them to go directly to the owners of collateral.

# PART 3

# SENIOR CORPORATE SECURITIES, MUNICIPAL BONDS, AND GICs

# CHAPTER 13

## CORPORATE BONDS

*Frank J. Fabozzi, Ph.D., CFA, CPA*
*Visiting Professor of Finance*
*Sloan School of Management*
*Massachusetts Institute of Technology*
*and*
*Editor, The Journal of Portfolio Management*

*Richard S. Wilson*
*Managing Director*
*Research Products and Services*
*Fitch Investors Service, Inc.*

*Harry C. Sauvain, D.S.C.*
*University Professor Emeritus of Finance*
*Indiana University*

*John C. Ritchie, Jr., Ph.D.*
*Professor of Finance*
*Temple University*

A corporate bond is a debt instrument setting forth the obligation of the issuer to satisfy the terms of the agreement. Essentially an *I.O.U.*, it can be quite a complex instrument although the essential features may be relatively simple. The maker, or issuer, agrees to pay a certain amount or a percentage of the face, or principal, value (also known as par value) to the owner of the bond, either periodically over the life of the issue or in a lump sum upon the bond's retirement or maturity. Failure to pay the principal and/or interest when due (and to meet other of the debt's provisions) in accordance with the terms of the instrument constitutes legal default and court proceedings can be instituted to enforce the contract. Bondholders, as creditors, have a prior legal claim over common and preferred stockholders as to both income and assets of the corporation for the principal and interest due them and may have a prior claim over other creditors if liens or mortgages are involved. It is important to recognize, however, that a superior legal status will not prevent bondholders from suffering financial loss when the ability of a corporation to generate cash flow adequate to pay its obligations is seriously eroded.

Bond prices can and do undergo sizeable changes as the general level of interest rates changes, reflecting changing supply-and-demand conditions for loanable funds. Bonds can be acquired for income, emphasizing the relative sureness and attractiveness of periodic interest receipts and tending to ignore price fluctuations. On the other hand, fixed income securities can be among the most speculative investment vehicles available when bought on margin or when a low-quality issue is purchased.

Corporate bonds are usually issued in denominations of $1,000 and multiples thereof. In common usage, a corporate bond is assumed to have a par value of $1,000 unless otherwise explicitly specified. A security dealer who says he or she has five bonds to sell means five bonds each of $1,000 principal amount. If the promised rate of interest (coupon rate) is 6 percent, the annual amount of interest on each bond is $60 and the semiannual interest is $30.

While there may be technical differences between bonds, notes and debentures, we will use Wall Street convention and call fixed income debt by the general term—*bonds*.

## THE CORPORATE TRUSTEE

The promises of corporate bond issuers and the rights of investors who buy them are set forth in great detail in contracts generally called *indentures*. If bondholders were handed the complete indenture, some may have trouble understanding the legalese and have even greater difficulty in determining from time to time if the corporate issuer is keeping all the promises made. These problems are solved for the most part by bringing in a *corporate trustee* as a third party to the contract. The indenture is made out to the corporate trustee as a representative of the interests of bondholders; that is, the trustee acts in a fiduciary capacity for investors who own the bond issue.

A corporate trustee is a bank or trust company with a corporate trust department and officers who are experts in performing the functions of a trustee. This is no small task. The corporate trustee must, at the time of issue, authenticate the bonds issued—that is, keep track of all the bonds sold and make sure that they do not exceed the principal amount authorized by the indenture. It must then be a watchdog for the bondholders by seeing to it that the issuer complies with all the covenants of the indenture. These covenants are many and technical, and they must be watched during the entire period that a bond issue is outstanding. We will describe some of these covenants in subsequent pages.

It is very important that corporate trustees be competent and financially responsible. To this end, there is a federal statute known as the Trust Indenture Act, which requires that for all corporate bond offerings in the amount of more than $5 million sold on interstate commerce there must be a corporate trustee. The indenture must include adequate requirements for performance of the trustee's duties on behalf of bondholders; there must be no conflict between the trustee's interest as a trustee and any other interest it may have, especially if it is also a creditor of the issuer; and there must be provision for reports by the trustee to bondholders. If a corporate issuer fails to pay interest or principal, the trustee may declare a default and take such action as may be necessary to protect the rights of bondholders. If the corporate issuer has promised in the indenture to always maintain an amount of current assets equal to two times the amount of current liabilities, the trustee must watch the corporation's balance sheet and see that the promise is kept. If the issuer fails to maintain the prescribed amounts, the trustee must take action on behalf of the bondholders. However, it must be emphasized that the trustee is paid by the debt issuer and can only do what the indenture provides. The indenture may contain a clause stating that the trustee undertakes to perform such duties and only such duties as are specifically set forth in the indenture, and no implied covenants or obligations shall be read into the indenture against the trustee. Also, the trustee is usually under no obligation to exercise the rights or powers under the indenture at the request of bondholders unless it has been offered reasonable security or indemnity. The trustee is not bound to make investigations into the facts surrounding documents delivered to it, but it may do so if it sees fit.

The terms of bond issues set forth in bond indentures are always a compromise between the interests of the bond issuer and those of investors who buy bonds. The issuer always wants to pay the lowest possible rate of interest and to be tied up as little as possible with legal convenants. Bondholders want the highest possible interest rate, the best security, and a variety of covenants to restrict the issuer in one way or another. As we discuss the provisions of bond indentures, keep this opposition of interests in mind and see how compromises are worked out in practice.

## SOME BOND FUNDAMENTALS

Bonds can be classified by a number of characteristics, which we will use for ease of organizing this section.

## Bonds Classified by Issuer Type

The five broad categories of corporate bonds sold in the United States based on the type of issuer are public utilities, transportations, industrials, banks and finance companies, and international or Yankee issues. Finer breakdowns are often made by market participants to create homogeneous groupings. For example, public utilities are subdivided into telephone or communications, electric companies, gas distribution and transmission companies, and water companies. The transportation industry can be subdivided into airlines, railroads, and trucking companies. Like public utilities, transportation companies often have various degrees of regulation or control by state and/or federal government agencies. Industrials are a catchall class, but even here, finer degrees of distinction may be needed by analysts. The industrial grouping includes manufacturing and mining concerns, retailers and service-related companies. Even the Yankee or international borrower sector can be more finely tuned. For example, one might classify the issuers into categories such as supranational borrowers (International Bank for Reconstruction and Development and the European Investment Bank), sovereign issuers (Canada, Australia, United Kingdom), and foreign municipalities and agencies.

Exhibit 13–1 shows the volume of new corporate bond issuance in the 1973 through 1988 period.

## Corporate Debt Maturity

A bond's maturity is the date on which the issuer's obligation to satisfy the terms of the indenture are satisfied. On that date the principal is repaid with any premium and accrued interest that may be due. However, as we shall see later when discussing debt redemption, the final maturity date as stated in the issue's title may or may not be the date when the contract terminates. Many issues can be retired prior to maturity.

Thus, while we often talk about long-term and short-term bonds, our long-term holdings may turn out to be relatively short. Also, investors' perceptions of what constitutes short- and long-term maturity for bonds has undergone considerable change over time. A half century ago some experts viewed bonds with maturities of 5 to 15 years as short-term issues and those with maturities from 15 to 40 years as intermediate-term paper. Such is not the case today. Issues maturing within a year are usually viewed as the equivalent of cash items. Debt maturing more than one year from the reference date to five years later is generally thought of as short-term. Intermediate-term debt matures in 5 to 12 years, whereas long-term debt obviously matures in more than twelve years. These are not hard and fast classifications. Some think short-term bonds mature within two to three years and intermediate-term issues not longer than 8 to 10 years.

**EXHIBIT 13–1**

**Public Financing in the Taxable Bond Markets by Issuer Classification, 1973–1988**

(Nonconvertible Bond Offerings—Par Value [$ Millions])

| Year | Total | Communications | Electrics | Gas and Water | Industrials | Finance | Banks and Thrifts | Transportation | International |
|---|---|---|---|---|---|---|---|---|---|
| 1988 | $ 98,867 | $ 638 | $ 7,653 | $2,512 | $45,104 | $22,949 | $13,616 | $2,480 | $3,915 |
| 1987 | 104,634 | 2,495 | 12,283 | 2,848 | 42,056 | 24,329 | 13,945 | 1,593 | 5,085 |
| 1986 | 142,562 | 10,231 | 21,893 | 2,825 | 60,364 | 22,837 | 15,644 | 3,750 | 5,018 |
| 1985 | 80,118 | 3,210 | 6,354 | 1,566 | 32,161 | 19,817 | 9,638 | 1,427 | 5,945 |
| 1984 | 48,890 | 830 | 5,000 | 825 | 19,510 | 10,223 | 8,255 | 1,247 | 3,000 |
| 1983 | 35,697 | 1,965 | 5,400 | 1,470 | 9,391 | 5,927 | 6,758 | 896 | 3,890 |
| 1982 | 44,168 | 720 | 7,170 | 1,665 | 14,281 | 8,373 | 5,217 | 1,062 | 5,680 |
| 1981 | 40,655 | 3,820 | 6,425 | 1,640 | 12,729 | 7,175 | 1,975 | 1,316 | 5,575 |
| 1980 | 36,695 | 5,975 | 6,418 | 1,000 | 12,257 | 5,310 | 2,025 | 1,445 | 2,265 |
| 1979 | 24,941 | 3,700 | 4,760 | 555 | 6,114 | 3,236 | 2,200 | 991 | 3,385 |
| 1978 | 20,799 | 2,880 | 4,708 | 170 | 3,287 | 4,140 | 630 | 734 | 4,250 |
| 1977 | 25,929 | 2,625 | 5,306 | 302 | 4,472 | 5,723 | 1,520 | 873 | 5,108 |
| 1976 | 30,165 | 2,200 | 5,012 | 1,058 | 7,635 | 5,510 | 1,185 | 1,270 | 6,295 |
| 1975 | 34,918 | 3,035 | 6,932 | 1,319 | 14,100 | 2,538 | 920 | 967 | 5,107 |
| 1974 | 26,663 | 3,396 | 7,642 | 752 | 7,853 | 2,125 | 2,325 | 920 | 1,650 |
| 1973 | 13,315 | 3,149 | 4,757 | 449 | 1,235 | 1,923 | 555 | 522 | 725 |
| Total | $809,016 | $ 50,869 | $117,713 | $20,956 | $292,549 | $152,135 | $86,408 | $21,493 | $66,893 |

Derived from *Moody's Bond Survey*, various issues.

Source: Richard S. Wilson and Frank J Fabozzi, *The New Corporate Bond Market* (Chicago: Probus Publishing Company, 1990).

Prior to the Great Depression, there were a number of long-term bond issues with maturities of 100 or more years. Many were issued by railroads and others came out of corporate reorganizations. In a few cases, maturities were as long as 999 years from the date of issue. Today, only a few such issues are around. Investors prefer bonds to mature within their lifetime, not during the lifetime of some progeny centuries away.

Since the early 1970s, the average maturity of domestically issued new corporate debt shortened distinctly (see Exhibit 13–2). Investor preference for shorter maturities is attributed to the increased volatility of bond prices caused by higher interest rates. All other things being the same, shorter maturity means reduced price risk. However, the shorter maturity structure of corporate debt increases pressures on corporate financial managers. It becomes more difficult to

**EXHIBIT 13–2**
**Average Maturity of New Issue Investment-Grade Corporate Bonds, 1974–1988**

| Year | New Issue |
|------|-----------|
| 1988* | 11.05 |
| 1987[†] | 12.54 |
| 1986[‡] | 15.79 |
| 1985 | 12.86 |
| 1984 | 9.87 |
| 1983 | 15.37 |
| 1982 | 12.90 |
| 1981 | 15.70 |
| 1980 | 18.42 |
| 1979 | 22.01 |
| 1978 | 23.10 |
| 1977 | 22.83 |
| 1976 | 20.39 |
| 1975 | 17.99 |
| 1974 | 19.93 |

* For comparative purposes, the 1988 average maturity for speculative-grade debt was 10.34 years.

[†] 1987 average maturity for speculative-grade debt was 10.42 years.

[‡] 1986 average maturity for speculative-grade debt was 11.33 years.

Source: Richard S. Wilson and Frank J. Fabozzi, *The New Corporate Bond Market* (Chicago: Probus Publishing Company, 1990).

match long-lived assets with long-term liabilities. Years ago, a matching of assets and liabilities was deemed the proper course for corporations to follow. Now, that isn't necessarily so. The more frequent refinancings necessary to replace a heavier volume of maturing debt also add to the burden of the corporate financial officer and to the pressures on the corporate bond market. More of a company's cash flow might have to be directed to paying off these obligations as they become due.

## Interest Payment Characteristics

The three main interest payment classifications of domestically issued corporate bonds are straight coupon bonds, zero coupon bonds, and floating-rate, or variable-rate, bonds. Floating-rate issues are discussed in Chapter 14 and the other two types are examined below.

However, before we get into interest-rate characteristics, let us briefly discuss bond types. We refer to the interest rate on a bond as the coupon. This is technically wrong, as bonds issued today do not have coupons attached. Instead, bonds are represented by a certificate, similar to a stock certificate, with a brief description of the terms printed on both sides. These are called *registered bonds*. The principal amount of the bond is noted on the certificate, and the interest paying agent or trustee has the responsibility of making payment by check to the registered holder on the due date. Years ago, bonds were issued in *bearer*, or *coupon*, form with coupons attached for each interest payment. However, the registered form is considered safer and entails less paperwork. As a matter of fact, the registered bond certificate is on its way out as more and more issues are sold in *book-entry* form. This means that only one master or global certificate is issued. It is held by a central securities depositary that issues receipts demonstrating interests in this global certificate. U.S. Treasury issues are sold in this form.

Straight coupon bonds have an interest rate set for the life of the issue, however long or short that may be; they are also called *fixed-rate* bonds. Most fixed-rate bonds pay interest semiannually and at maturity. For example, a bond with an interest rate of 9 percent maturing on June 15, 2000 will pay $45 per $1,000 par amount each June 15 and December 15, including June 15, 2000. Of course, at maturity the par amount is also paid. Bonds with interest payable once a year are uncommon among domestic issues but are the norm for issues sold overseas. From time to time, investors may encounter bonds with other payment patterns such as quarterly or even monthly.

Interest payments due on Sundays or holidays are normally paid on the next business day without additional interest for the extra day or two the company has use of the monies. Interest on corporate bonds is based on a year of 360 days made up of twelve 30-day months. It does not matter whether the month is February, April, or May; all months for this purpose are of the same length.

The 9 percent bond pays interest of $90 per year per $1,000 face value. Interest accrues at the rate of $7.50 a month, or $0.25 per day. The corporate calendar day count convention is referred to as *30/360*.

Most fixed-rate corporate bonds pay interest in a standard fashion. However, there are some variations of which you should be aware. Most domestic bonds pay interest in U.S. dollars. However, starting in the early 1980s, issues were marketed with principal and interest payable in other currencies such as the Australian, New Zealand, or Canadian dollar or the European Currency Unit (ECU). Generally, interest and principal payments are converted from the foreign currency to U.S. dollars by the paying agent unless it is otherwise notified. The bondholders bear any costs associated with the dollar conversion. Foreign currency issues provide investors with another way of diversifying a portfolio, but not without risk. The holder bears the currency, or exchange, risk in addition to all of the other risks associated with debt instruments.

There are a few issues of bonds that can participate in the fortunes of the issuer over and above the stated coupon rate. These are called *participating bonds*, as they share in the profits of the issuer or the rise in certain assets over and above certain minimum levels. Another type of bond rarely encountered today is the *income bond*. These bonds promise to pay a stipulated interest rate, but the payment is contingent on sufficient earnings and is in accordance with the definition of available income for interest payments contained in the indenture. Repayment of principal is not contingent. Interest may be cumulative or noncumulative. If payments are cumulative, unpaid interest payments must be made up at some future date. If noncumulative, once the interest payment is past, it does not have to be repaid. Failure to pay interest on income bonds is not an act of default and is not a cause for bankruptcy. Income bonds have been issued by some financially troubled corporations emerging from reorganization proceedings.

Zero coupon bonds are, just as the name implies, bonds without coupons or an interest rate. Essentially, zero coupon bonds pay only the principal portion of a complete bond at some future date. These bonds are issued at discounts to par; the difference constitutes the return to the bondholder. The difference between the face amount and the offering price when first issued is called the *original-issue discount* (OID). The rate of return depends on the amount of the discount and the period over which it accretes. For example, a five-year zero coupon bond yielding 9 percent on a semiannual basis must be priced at 64.39 percent of par. If due in seven years, the price would be 59 percent; in ten years, 41.46 percent; and in 15 years, only 26.70 percent.

Zeros were first publicly issued in the corporate market in the spring of 1981 and were an immediate hit with investors. The rapture only lasted a couple of years because of changes in the income tax laws that made ownership more costly on an after-tax basis. Also, these changes reduced the tax advantages to issuers. However, tax deferred investors, such as pension funds, could still take advantage of zero coupon issues. One important risk is eliminated in a zero coupon investment—the reinvestment risk. Because there is no coupon to reinvest, there isn't any risk. Of course, although this is beneficial in declining interest-rate markets, the reverse is true when interest rates are rising. The investor will not be able to reinvest an income stream at rising reinvestment rates. Investors tend to find zeros less attractive in lower interest-rate markets because compounding is not as meaningful as when rates are higher. Also, the lower the rates are, the more likely that they will rise again, making a zero coupon investment worth less in the eyes of potential holders.

In bankruptcy, a zero coupon bond creditor can claim the original offering price plus accrued and unpaid interest to the date of the bankruptcy filing, but not the principal amount of $1,000. Zero coupon bonds have been sold at deep discounts and the liability of the issuer at maturity may be substantial. The accretion of the discount on the corporation's books is not put away in a special fund for debt retirement purposes. There are no sinking funds on most of these issues. One hopes that corporate managers properly invest the proceeds and run the corporation for the benefit of all investors so that there will not be a cash crisis at maturity. The potentially large balloon repayment creates a cause for concern among investors. Thus, it is most important to invest in higher quality issues so as to reduce the risk of a potential problem. If one wants to speculate in lower rated bonds, then that investment should throw off some cash return.

Finally, a variation of the zero coupon bond is the deferred-interest bond (DIB), also known as a zero/coupon bond. These bonds have generally been subordinated issues of speculative-grade issuers, also known as *junk* issuers. Most of the issues are structured so that they do not pay cash interest for the first five years. At the end of the deferred-interest period, cash interest accrues, generally between 13 percent and 18 percent, and is paid semiannually until maturity, unless the bonds are redeemed earlier. The deferred-interest feature allows newly restructured, highly leveraged companies and others with less than satisfactory cash flows to defer the payment of cash interest over the early life of the bond. Hopefully, when cash interest payments start, the company will be able to service the debt. If it has made excellent progress in restoring its financial health, the company may be able to redeem or refinance the debt rather than have high interest outlays.

An offshoot of the deferred-interest bond is the pay-in-kind (PIK) debenture. With PIKs, cash interest payments are deferred at the issuer's option until some future date. Instead of just accreting the original-issue discount as with DIBs or zeros, the issuer pays out the interest rate in additional pieces of the same security. The option to pay cash or in-kind interest payments rests with the issuer, but in many cases the issuer has little choice because provisions of other debt instruments often prohibit cash interest payments until certain indenture or loan tests are satisfied. The holder just gets more pieces of paper, but these at least can be sold in the market without giving up one's original investment;

PIKs, DIBs and zeros do not have provisions for the resale of the interest portion of the instrument. An investment in this type of bond, because it is issued by speculative-grade companies, requires careful analysis of the issuer's cash-flow prospects and ability to survive.

## SECURITY FOR BONDS

Shylock demanded a pound of flesh as his security. Investors who buy corporate bonds don't go quite that far, but they do like some kind of security. Either real property (using a mortgage) or personal property may be pledged to offer security beyond that of the general credit standing of the issue. In fact, the kind of security or the absence of a specific pledge of security is usually indicated by the title of a bond issue. However, the best security is a strong general credit that can repay the debt from earnings.

### Mortgage Bond

If you are a reader of *The Wall Street Journal*, you may have seen an advertisement for "$50,000,000 issue of Metropolitan Edison, First Mortgage Bonds, 9 percent Series, due December 1, 2008." That title tells you several things about this bond issue.

It tells you that the issuer has granted the bondholders a first-mortgage lien on substantially all of its properties. That is good from the viewpoint of bondholders. But in return the issuer got a lower rate of interest on the bonds than if the issue were unsecured. A debenture issue (i.e., unsecured debt) of the same company might have carried an interest rate of 9.25 percent to 9.375 percent. A *lien* is a legal right to sell mortgaged property to satisfy unpaid obligations to bondholders. In practice, foreclosure of a mortgage and sale of mortgaged property is unusual. If a default occurs, there is usually a financial reorganization on the part of the issuer, in which provision is made for settlement of the debt to bondholders. The mortgage lien is important, though, because it gives the mortgage bondholders a very strong bargaining position relative to other creditors in determining the terms of a reorganization.

Often first-mortgage bonds are issued in series with bonds of each series secured equally by the same first mortgage. The title of the bond issue mentioned above includes "9 percent Series," which tells you that the issue is one of a series. Many companies, particularly public utilities, have a policy of financing part of their capital requirements continuously by long-term debt. They want some part of their total capitalization in the form of bonds because the cost of such capital is ordinarily less than that of capital raised by sale of stock. So, as a principal amount of debt is paid off, they issue another series of bonds under the same mortgage. As they expand and need a greater amount of debt capital, they can add new series of bonds. It is a lot easier and more advantageous to issue a series of bonds under one mortgage and one indenture than it is to create entirely new bond issues with different arrangements for security. This arrangement is called a *blanket mortgage*. When property is sold or released from the lien of the mortgage, additional property or cash may be substituted or bonds may be retired in order to provide adequate security for the debtholders.

When a bond indenture authorizes the issue of additional series of bonds with the same mortgage lien as those already issued, the indenture imposes certain conditions that must be met before an additional series may be issued. Bondholders do not want their security impaired; these conditions are for their benefit. It is common for a first-mortgage bond indenture to provide that property acquired by the issuer subsequent to the granting of the first mortgage lien shall be subject to the first-mortgage lien. This is termed the *after-acquired clause*. Then the indenture usually permits the issue of additional bonds up to some specified percentage of the value of the after-acquired property, such as 60 percent. The other 40 percent, or whatever the percentage may be, must be financed in some other way. This is intended to ensure that there will be additional assets with a value significantly greater than the amount of additional bonds secured by the mortgage. Another customary kind of restriction on issue of additional series is a requirement that earnings in an immediately preceding period must be equal to some number of times the amount of annual interest on the new series and that interest on all outstanding series must be earned. For this purpose, *earnings* are usually defined as earnings before income tax. The number of times interest must be earned may be one and a half, two, or some other number. Still another common provision is that additional bonds may be issued to the extent that earlier series of bonds have been paid off.

You seldom see a bond issue with the term *second mortgage* in its title. The reason is that this term has a connotation of weakness. Sometimes companies get around that difficulty by using such words as *first and consolidated*, *first and refunding*, or *general and refunding mortgage bonds*. Usually this language means that a bond issue is secured by a first mortgage on some part of the issuer's property but by a second or even third lien on other parts of its assets. A general and refunding mortgage bond is generally secured by a lien on all of the company's property *subject* to the prior lien of first mortgage bonds.

## Collateral Trust Bonds

Some companies do not own fixed assets or other real property and so have nothing on which they can give a mortgage lien to secure bondholders. Instead, they own securities of other companies; they are *holding companies* and the other companies are *subsidiaries*. To satisfy the desire of bondholders for security, they pledge stocks, notes, bonds, or whatever other kind of obligations they own. These assets are termed *collateral* (or personal property), and bonds secured by such assets are *collateral trust bonds*. Some companies own both real property and securities. They may use real property to secure mortgage bonds and use securities for collateral trust bonds.

The legal arrangement for collateral trust bonds is much the same as that for mortgage bonds. The issuer delivers to a corporate trustee under a bond indenture the securities pledged, and the trustee holds them for the benefit of the bondholders. When voting common stocks are included in the collateral, the indenture permits the issuer to vote the stocks so long as there is no default on its bonds. This is important to issuers of such bonds because usually the stocks are those of subsidiaries, and the issuer depends on the exercise of voting rights to control the subsidiaries.

Indentures usually provide that, in event of default, the rights to vote stocks included in the collateral are transferred to the trustee. Loss of the voting right would be a serious disadvantage to the issuer because it would mean loss of control of subsidiaries. The trustee may also sell the securities pledged for whatever prices they will bring in the market and apply the proceeds to payment of the claims of collateral trust bondholders. These rather drastic actions, however, are not usually taken immediately on an event of default. The corporate trustee's primary responsibility is to act in the best interests of bondholders, and their interests may be served for a time at least by giving the defaulting issuer a proxy to vote stocks held as collateral and thus preserve the holding company structure. It may also defer the sale of collateral when it seems likely that bondholders would fare better in a financial reorganization than they would by sale of collateral.

Collateral trust indentures contain a number of provisions designed to protect bondholders. Generally, the market or appraised value of the collateral must be maintained at some percentage of the amount of bonds outstanding. The percentage is greater than 100 so that there will be a margin of safety. If collateral value declines below the minimum percentage, additional collateral must be provided by the issuer. There is almost always provision for withdrawal of some collateral provided other acceptable collateral is substituted.

Collateral trust bonds may be issued in series in much the same way that mortgage bonds are issued in series. The rules governing additional series of bonds require that adequate collateral must be pledged, and there may be restrictions on the use to which the proceeds of an additional series may be put. All series of bonds are issued under the same indenture and have the same claim on collateral.

## Equipment Trust Certificates

The desire of borrowers to pay the lowest possible rate of interest on their obligations generally leads them to offer their best security and to grant lenders the strongest claim on it. Many years ago, the railway companies developed a way of financing purchase of cars and locomotives, called *rolling stock*, in a way that enabled them to borrow at just about the lowest rates in the corporate bond market.

Railway rolling stock has for a long time been regarded by investors as excellent security for debt. This equipment is sufficiently standardized that it can be used by one railway as well as another. And it can be readily moved from the tracks of one railroad to those of another. There is generally a good market for lease or sale of cars and locomotives. The railroads have capitalized on these characteristics of rolling stock by developing a legal arrangement for giving investors a legal claim on it that is different from, and generally better than, a mortgage lien.

The legal arrangement is one that vests legal title to railway equipment in a trustee, which is better from the standpoint of investors than a first-mortgage lien on property. A railway company orders some cars and locomotives from a manufacturer. When the job is finished, the manufacturer transfers the legal title to the equipment to a trustee. The trustee leases it to the railroad that ordered it and at the same time sells *equipment trust certificates* (ETCs) in an amount equal to a large percentage of the purchase price, normally 80 percent. Money from sale of certificates is paid to the manufacturer. The railway company makes an initial payment of rent equal to the balance of the purchase price, and the trustee gives that money to the manufacturer. Thus, the manufacturer is paid off. The trustee collects lease rental money periodically from the railroad and uses it to pay interest and principal on the certificates. These interest payments are known as dividends. The amounts of lease rental payments are worked out carefully so that they are enough to pay the equipment trust certificates. At the end of some period of time, such as 15 years, the certificates are paid off, the trustee sells the equipment to the railroad for some nominal price, and the lease is terminated.

Railroad ETCs are usually structured in serial form; that is, a certain amount becomes payable at specified dates until the final installment. For example, a $15 million ETC might mature $1 million on each June 15, from 1990 through 2004. Each of the 15 maturities may be priced separately to reflect the shape of the yield curve, investor preference for specific maturities, and supply-and-demand considerations. The advantage of a serial issue from the investor's point of view is that the repayment schedule matches the decline in the value of the equipment used as collateral. Hence, principal repayment risk is reduced. From the issuer's side, serial maturities allow for the repayment of the debt periodically over the life of the issue, making less likely a crisis at maturity due to a large repayment coming due at one time.

The beauty of this arrangement from the viewpoint of investors is that the railroad does not legally own the rolling stock until all the certificates are paid. In case the railroad does not make the lease rental payments, there is no big legal hassle about foreclosing a lien. The trustee owns the property and can take it back because failure to pay the rent breaks the lease. The trustee can lease the equipment to another railroad and continue to make payments on the certificates from new lease rentals.

This description emphasizes the legal nature of the arrangement for securing the certificates. In practice, these certificates are regarded as obligations of the railway company that leased the equipment and are shown as liabilities in its balance sheet. In fact, the name of the railway appears in the title of the certificates. In the ordinary course of events, the trustee is just an intermediary who performs the function of holding title, acting as lessor, and collecting the money to pay the certificates. It is significant that even in the worst years of depression, railways have paid their equipment trust certificates, though they did not pay bonds secured by mortgages. Although railroads have issued the largest amount of equipment trust certificates, airlines have also utilized this form of financing.

## Debenture Bonds

After all the emphasis upon security, you might think that Shylock-minded investors would not buy bonds without something to secure them. But not so! Investors often buy large issues of unsecured bonds just as they buy first-mortgage bonds. These unsecured bonds are termed *debentures*. As a matter of fact, with the exception of the utility industry and specifically structured special purpose financings, nearly all other corporate debt sold is unsecured.

Debentures are not secured by a specific pledge of designated property, but that does not mean that they have no claim on property of issuers or on their earnings. Debenture bondholders have the claim of general creditors on all assets of the issuer not pledged specifically to secure other debt. And they even have a claim on pledged assets to the extent that these assets have value greater than necessary to satisfy secured creditors. In fact, if there are no pledged assets and no secured creditors, debenture bondholders have first claim on all assets along with other general creditors.

These unsecured bonds are sometimes issued by companies that are so strong financially and have such a high credit rating that to offer security would be gilding the lily. Such companies can simply turn a deaf ear to investors who want security and still sell their debentures at relatively low interest rates. But debentures are sometimes issued by companies that have already sold mortgage bonds and given liens on most of their property. These debentures rank below the mortgage bonds or collateral trust bonds in their claim on assets, and investors may regard them as relatively weak. This is the kind that bears the higher rates of interest.

Even though there is no pledge of security, the indentures for debenture bonds may contain a variety of provisions designed to afford some protection to investors. Frequently the amount of a debenture bond issue is limited to the amount of the initial issue. This limit is to keep issuers from weakening the position of debenture holders by running up additional unsecured debt. Sometimes additional debentures may be issued, provided that the issuer has earned its bond interest on all existing debt plus the additional issue, a specified number of times in a recent accounting period. If a company has no secured debt, it is customary to provide that debentures will be secured equally with any secured bonds that may be issued in the future. This is known as the *negative pledge clause*. Some provisions of debenture bond issues are intended to give the corporate trustee early warning of deterioration in the issuer's financial condition. The issuer may be required to always maintain a specified minimum amount of net working capital—the excess of current assets over current liabilities— equal to not less than the amount of debentures outstanding. The corporate trustee must watch the issuer's balance sheets and, on failure to maintain the required amount of net working capital, take whatever action is appropriate in the interest of debenture holders. Another common restriction is one limiting the payment of cash dividends by the issuer. Another limits the proportion of current earnings that may be used to pay dividends. However, the trend in recent years, at least with investment-grade companies, is away from indenture restrictions.

## Subordinated and Convertible Debentures

You might think that debenture bonds have about the weakest possible claim on the assets and earnings of a corporate issuer, but that is not so. Many companies have issued *subordinated debenture bonds*. The term *subordinated* means that such an issue ranks after secured debt, after debenture bonds, and often after some general creditors in its claim on assets and earnings. Owners of this kind of bond stand last in line among creditors when an issuer fails financially.

Because subordinated debentures are weaker in their claim on assets, issuers would have to offer a higher rate of interest unless they also offer some special inducement to buy the bonds. The inducement can be an option to convert bonds into stock of the issuer at the discretion of bondholders. If the issuer prospers and the market price of its stock rises substantially in the market, the bondholders can convert bonds to stock worth a great deal more than what they paid for the bonds. This conversion privilege may also be included in the provisions of debentures that are not subordinated. Convertible securities are discussed in Chapter 15.

The bonds may be convertible into something other than the common stock of the issuer. For example, the convertible subordinated debentures of Hi-G, Inc., $13\frac{1}{2}$s due 4/15/2001, are convertible into shares of its subsidiary, Computer Magnetics. The Sun Company, Inc., subordinated exchangeable debentures $10\frac{3}{4}$s due 4/1/2006 are exchangeable into common stock of Becton, Dickinson and Company. Sun had acquired 32 percent of Becton in 1978. There are also issues indexed to silver or its cash equivalent at the time of maturity or redemption. Sunshine Mining Company has sold four such offerings.

## Guaranteed Bonds

Sometimes a corporation may guarantee the bonds or another corporation.[1] Such bonds are referred to as guaranteed bonds. The guarantee, however, does not mean that these obligations are free of default risk. The safety of a guaranteed bond depends upon the financial capability of the guarantor to satisfy the terms of the guarantee, as well as the financial capability of the issuer. The terms of the guarantee may call for the guarantor to guarantee the payment of interest and/or repayment of the principal. A guaranteed bond may have more than one corporate guarantor. Each guarantor may be responsible for not only its pro rata share but also the entire amount guaranteed by the other guarantors. The debentures of Exxon Pipeline Company due 2004 are unconditionally guaranteed by Exxon Corporation and as such carry the triple-A rating of its guarantor. The joint venture of Gulf Oil and Texaco, called Pembroke Capital Company, is guaranteed by the two partners. The offering of $200 million, which represented the first public offering of a project-financed venture, initially received a triple-A rating because of its guarantors. (This issue has since been downgraded due to the credit deterioration of the guarantors.) Guaranteed bonds in which the guarantor is another corporation are prevalent in the railroad field. In order to lease the road of another company, a railroad company may have to agree to guarantee the debt of the company from which it is leasing the road.

## PROVISIONS FOR PAYING OFF BONDS

What would you pay for a bond that promises to pay interest in the amount of $50 or $60 a year from now to eternity but never promises to repay the principal? The right to receive interest in perpetuity may very well be worth $1,000, depending upon the current level of interest rates in the market, but investors generally dislike the absence of a promise to pay a fixed amount of principal on some specified date in the future; therefore, there is no such thing as a "perpetual bond" in the U.S. financial markets.

### Call and Refund Provisions

One important question in the negotiation of terms of a new bond issue is whether the issuer shall have the right to redeem the bonds prior to maturity, either as a whole or in part. Issuers generally want to have this right, and investors do not want them to have it. Both sides think that at some time in the

---

[1] There are debt obligations in which the guarantor is a federal agency. For example, certain mortgage-backed issues, discussed in Chapter 27, are guaranteed by a federal agency.

future the general level of interest rates in the market may decline to a level well below that prevailing at the time bonds are issued. If so, issuers want to redeem all of the bonds outstanding and replace them with new bond issues at lower interest rates. But this is exactly what investors do not want. If bonds are redeemed when interest rates are low, investors have to take their money back and reinvest it at a low rate.

The usual practice is a provision that denies the issuer a right to redeem bonds during the first 5 or 10 years following the date of issue if the proceeds from the redemption are from lower cost funds obtained with issues ranking equally with or superior to the debt to be redeemed. This type of redemption is called *refunding*. However, although most long-term issues have these refunding bars, or prohibitions, they are usually immediately callable, in whole or in part, if the source of funds is not lower interest cost money. Such sources may include retained earnings, the proceeds from a common stock sale, or funds from the disposition of property. While the redemption price is often at a premium, there are many cases where the call price is 100 percent of par.

Many short- to intermediate-term bonds and notes are not callable for the first three to seven years (in some cases, not callable for the life of the issue). Thereafter, they may be called for any reason. Bond market participants often confuse refunding protection with call protection. Call protection is much more absolute in that bonds cannot be redeemed for any reason. Refunding restrictions only provide protection against one type of redemption, as mentioned above. Failure to recognize this difference has resulted in unnecessary losses for some investors.

Long-term industrial issues generally have 10 years of refunding protection but are immediately callable. Electric utilities most often have 5 years of refunding protection although, during times of high interest rates, issues with 10 years of refunding protection have been sold. Long-term debt of the former members of the Bell Telephone System has five years of call protection.

As a rule, corporate bonds are callable at a premium above par. Generally, the amount of the premium declines as the bond approaches maturity. The initial amount of the premium may be as much as one year's interest or as little as interest for half a year. When less than the entire issue is called, the specific bonds to be called are selected randomly or on a pro rata basis. If the bonds selected on a random basis are bearer bonds, the serial numbers of the certificates are published in *The Wall Street Journal* and major metropolitan dailies.

## Outright Redemptions

For lack of a better term, we will use *outright redemptions* to describe the call of debt at general redemption prices. In the spring of 1973, Bristol-Myers Company called for redemption at 107.538 one-third, or $25 million, of its $8\frac{5}{8}$ percent debentures due 1995. Trading as high as 111 in 1972 and about 108–

109 when the call was announced, there were obviously some losses involved. Some market participants were confused by the call as they did not know the difference between nonrefundable and currently callable.

In 1977, NCR Corporation redeemed $75 million of its $9\frac{3}{4}$ percent debentures due 2000 at 107.88. The bonds were trading at $111-111\frac{1}{2}$. The company was in a strong cash position and projected cash flow was substantially in excess of expected capital spending plans. Thus, NCR took action to improve its balance sheet and to reduce leverage through the call of this debt.

In 1983, a good example of an industrial redemption was Archer Daniels Midland Company 16 percent sinking-fund debentures due May 15, 2011. The bonds were sold May 12, 1981 at $99\frac{1}{2}$ and had the standard redemption/refunding provisions (i.e., currently callable but nonrefundable prior to May 15, 1991). On June 1, 1983, the company announced the call of the bonds for August 1 at 113.95 plus accrued interest. On May 31, the bonds traded at 120. The source of the funds, according to the company, was from the two common stock offerings in January and June. While bondholders brought legal action, the court allowed the redemption to proceed. On August 6, 1984, Archer Daniels Midland sold $100 million of 13 percent sinking-fund debentures due 8/1/2014 at 97.241, for a yield of 13.375 percent. The financial press reported that the investor reception was lukewarm. Would you like to guess one of the reasons for this?

## Sinking-Fund Provision

Term bonds may be paid off by operation of a *sinking fund*. Those last two words are often misunderstood to mean that the issuer accumulates a fund in cash, or in assets readily sold for cash, that is used to pay bonds at maturity. It had that meaning many years ago, but too often the money supposed to be in a sinking fund was not all there when it was needed. In modern practice, there is no fund, and *sinking* means that money is applied periodically to redemption of bonds before maturity. Corporate bond indentures require the issuer to retire a specified portion of an issue each year. This kind of provision for repayment of corporate debt may be designed to liquidate all of a bond issue by maturity date, or it may be arranged to pay only a part of the total by the end of the term. If only a part is paid, the remainder is called a *balloon maturity*.

The issuer may satisfy the sinking-fund requirement in one of two ways. A cash payment of the face amount of the bonds to be retired may be made by the corporate debtor to the trustee. The latter then calls the bonds by lot for redemption. Bonds have serial numbers, and numbers may be randomly selected for redemption. Owners of bonds called in this manner turn them in for redemption; *interest payments stop at the redemption date*. Alternatively, the issuer can deliver to the trustee bonds with a total face value equal to the amount that must be retired. The bonds are purchased by the *issuer* in the open market. This option is elected by the issuer when the bonds are selling below par. A few corporate bond indentures, however, prohibit the open-market purchase of the bonds by the issuer.

Many electric utility bond issues can satisfy the sinking-fund requirement by a third method. Instead of actually retiring bonds, the company may certify to the trustee that it has utilized unfunded property credits in lieu of the sinking fund. That is, it has made property and plant investments that have not been utilized for issuing bonded debt. For example, if the sinking-fund requirement is $1 million, it may give the trustee $1 million in cash to call bonds; it may deliver to the trustee $1 million of bonds it purchased in the open market; or it may certify that it made additions to its property and plant in the required amount, normally $1,667 of plant for each $1,000 sinking-fund requirement. In this case, it could satisfy the sinking fund with certified property additions of $1,667,000.

The issuer is granted a special call price to satisfy any sinking-fund requirement. Usually, the sinking-fund call price is the par value if the bonds were originally sold at par. When issued at a price in excess of par, the sinking-fund call price generally starts at the issuance price and scales down to par as the issue approaches maturity.

There are two advantages of a sinking-fund requirement from the bondholder's perspective. First, default risk is reduced due to the orderly retirement of the issue before maturity. Second, if bond prices decline as a result of an increase in interest rates, price support may be provided by the issuer or its fiscal agent, since it must enter the market on the buy side in order to satisfy the sinking-fund requirement. However, the disadvantage is that the bonds may be called at the special sinking-fund call price at a time when interest rates are lower than rates prevailing at the time of issuance. In that case, the bonds will be selling above par but may be retired by the issuer at the special call price that may be equal to par value.

Usually, the periodic payments required for sinking-fund purposes will be the same for each period. Gas company issues often have increasing sinking-fund requirements. However, a few indentures might permit variable periodic payments, where the periodic payments vary based upon prescribed conditions set forth in the indenture. The most common condition is the level of earnings of the issuer. In such cases, the periodic payments vary directly with earnings. An issuer prefers such flexibility; however, an investor may prefer fixed periodic payments because of the greater default risk protection provided under this arrangement.

Many corporate bond indentures include a provision that grants the issuer the option to retire double the amount stipulated for sinking-fund retirement. This *doubling option* effectively reduces the bondholder's call protection because, when interest rates decline, the issuer may find it economically advantageous to exercise this option at the special sinking-fund call price to retire a substantial portion of an outstanding issue.

With the exception of finance companies, industrial issues almost always include sinking-fund provisions. Finance companies, on the other hand, almost always do not. The inclusion or absence of a sinking-fund provision in public utility debt obligations depends upon the type of public utility. Pipeline issues almost always include sinking-fund provisions, whereas telephone issues do not. Electric utility companies have varying sinking-fund provisions. There can be a mandatory sinking fund where bonds have to be retired or, as mentioned above, a nonmandatory sinking fund in which it may utilize certain property credits for the sinking-fund requirement. If the sinking fund applies to a particular issue it is called a *specific* sinking fund. There are also nonspecific sinking funds (also known as funnel, tunnel, blanket, or aggregate sinking funds) where the requirement is based upon the total bonded debt outstanding of an issuer. Generally, it might require a sinking-fund payment of one percent of all bonds outstanding as of year end. The issuer can apply the requirement to one particular issue or to any other issue or issues. Again, the blanket sinking fund may be mandatory (bonds have to be retired) or nonmandatory (whereby it can utilize unfunded property additions). Companies with blanket sinking funds include Alabama Power Company, Georgia Power Company, Consumers Power Company, and Pacific Gas and Electric Company, among others. In some years, they might actually retire bonds, whereas in other years they may certify unfunded property additions. The blanket sinking fund of Baltimore Gas and Electric Company is mandatory.

## Maintenance and Replacement Funds

Calls under maintenance and replacement fund (M&R) provisions first occurred in 1977/78. They shocked bondholders, as calls were thought to be unlikely under these provisions, which were little known and used. However, due to the steep decline in interest rates in 1985 and early 1986, some electric utility companies decided to make use of the M&R calls again. Now investors recognize this type of redemption, but since the calls were around the par level and the bonds with above market level coupons were trading at higher prices, the results still hurt.

Florida Power & Light Company retired $63.7 million out of $125 million of its $10\frac{1}{8}$ percent bonds due March 1, 2005 at 100.65 on September 2, 1977 through the M&R provisions. The regular redemption price at the time was 110.98 and the issue was well within the refunding period, which expired on February 28, 1980 (call price starting March 1, 1980 was 109.76).

In 1977 and 1978, Carolina Power & Light deposited nearly $79 million with its trustee under the M&R fund provisions. The company, on June 2, 1978, called $46 million of its privately held $11\frac{1}{8}$ percent bonds due 1994 and $32.7 million of the public 11 percent bonds of 1984 at the special redemption price of par. The company's announcement stated the following:

The funds deposited were derived at the time from cash flow; however, if it is assumed that the eventual result is the replacement of the interest cost of the bonds to be redeemed with bonds at a probable interest cost of about 9 percent for 30 years, it is apparent that there will be a significant reduction of interest costs with an attendant improvement in fixed-charge coverages. The security of the total body of bondholders is improved and the maturities lengthened. These debt management actions are a positive demonstration to customers, stockholders and regulators that the management of the company continues to exercise appropriate cost control measures.

Of course, some bondholders objected to the retirements, claiming that, as the calls were within the refunding protected periods, the companies were barred from these special debt redemptions. They also claimed that the prospectuses and offering statements were unclear. However, a *careful* reading of the prospectuses revealed that the debt could be redeemed at the special redemption prices for the replacement fund or from certain other deposited cash. The general redemption prices applied to other redemptions, provided that none of the bonds could be redeemed *at the general redemption price* prior to the end of the refunding protected period if such redemption was for the purpose or in anticipation of refunding the bonds through the use of borrowed funds at a lower interest cost. The M&R provisions were allowed exceptions, and the courts have upheld companies' rights to redeem bonds in accordance with their terms.

Not all electric utility companies provide maintenance and replacement fund requirements for all of their mortgage debt. Some of the more recent issues lack the M&R provisions, although, as long as some of the older issues are still outstanding with these clauses, the M&R provisions apply. A number of issues subject to M&R clauses may be retired at the higher general redemption price and not the lower special call price. Others are protected from M&R redemption through the end of the refunding protected period, and in some cases certain property credits *must* be used before cash could be deposited with the trustee.

## Redemption through the Sale of Assets and Other Means

Because mortgage bonds are secured by property, we want the integrity of the collateral to be maintained. We would not want a company to sell a plant (which has been pledged as collateral) and then to use the proceeds for a distribution to shareholders. Therefore, release and substitution of property clauses are found in most bond indentures.

Wisconsin Michigan Power retired $9.9 million of its $9\frac{1}{4}$ percent bonds due 2000 on February 28, 1977, through the release of property clause at a redemption price of 100.97. On June 30, 1976, the company sold its gas business for $16,920,000 to an affiliate, Wisconsin Natural Gas. Of the proceeds, $16,520,000 was deposited with the trustee under the mortgage per the release and substitution of property clause, and a portion of these funds was released to the company against certified property additions. The balance was used to redeem the $9\frac{1}{4}$s as interest rates dropped to a level where the company thought it was to its advantage to retire high-coupon debt.

On December 7, 1983, Virginia Electric and Power Company said it would redeem its $100 million $15\frac{3}{4}$ percent bonds due April 1, 1989 (the highest public coupon) with the proceeds (so-called release moneys) from the sale of ownership interests in some nuclear facilities. Property sales are not unusual for electric utility companies and a number have been negotiated in recent years.

Many utility bond issues contain provisions regarding the confiscation of assets by a governmental body through the right of eminent domain or the disposition of assets by order of or to any governmental authority. In a number of cases, bonds *must* be redeemed if the company receives more than a certain amount in cash. Washington Water Power Company must apply the proceeds of $15 million or more to the retirement of debt in the case of government takeover of its property. The redemption price may be either the special or regular, depending on the issue. In 1984, Pacific Power & Light Company sold an electric distribution system to the Emerald People's Utility District for $25 million. It applied these proceeds to the redemption of half of the outstanding $14\frac{3}{4}$ percent mortgage bonds due 2010 at the special redemption price of 100. This issue was not the highest-coupon bond outstanding in the company's capitalization. There were some 18s of 1991, but these were exempt from the special provisions for the retirement of bonds with the proceeds from property sold to governmental authorities. More recently, in April 1988, Utah Power & Light company retired some 13 percent bonds due 2012 with funds obtained from the condemnation of some of its property in Kaneb, Utah, and the sale of electric assets to a couple of other cities.

On December 13, 1983, InterNorth, Inc., announced the call on February 1, 1984, of $90.5 million out of $200 million of its $17\frac{1}{2}$ percent debentures due August 1, 1991, at the regular redemption price of 112.32. The refunding protected period expired September 30, 1988. However, the proceeds were obtained from the sale of its Northern Propane Gas Co. unit. Because these are unsecured debentures and not mortgage bonds, there was no release and substitution of property clause and no special call price. On October 1, 1984, it redeemed another $23,875,000 of these $17\frac{1}{2}$ percent debentures at 109.86 with funds obtained from the December 1983 sale of two tanker ships.

## SOURCES OF INFORMATION ABOUT CORPORATE BOND OFFERINGS

For a new corporate bond offering, an investor can obtain a prospectus. The prospectus is a statement filed by the issuer with the Securities and Exchange Commission and containing all of the pertinent information about the security being offered and the company offering the security.

Summary information about a new offering is provided in *Moody's Bond Survey*. This service is published weekly and provides information on the business of the issuer, how the issuer will use the proceeds, the quality rating of the issue as assigned by Moody's, denominations available, the form of the security (registered or bearer), exchange options, security for the bonds, guarantees, call provisions, sinking-fund requirements, restrictions on management, and statistical highlights about the issuer. This service provides information not only on new offerings but also on proposed offerings. *CreditWeek*, published weekly by Standard & Poor's, provides similar information. These weekly publications are usually carried by local libraries.

For seasoned issues, major contractual provisions are provided in *Moody's Manuals* or Standard & Poor's *Corporation Records*. To obtain basic information about a seasoned corporate issue, the investor can check the monthly publication by either Moody's (*Moody's Bond Record*) or Standard & Poor's (*Standard & Poor's Bond Guide*).

## PROMISED YIELDS ON CORPORATE BONDS AND BOND RATINGS

At any one time, the yields that investors obtain by purchasing bonds in the market vary according to how investors estimate the uncertainty of future payment of dollar amounts of interest and principal exactly as set forth in bond indentures. This uncertainty is often called *financial risk* because it depends upon the financial ability of issuers to make those payments. If an issuer can pay, it will. Failure by a company to pay usually means intervention of a court of law on behalf of bondholders and court supervision of the conduct of the business. In any event, a default is a disaster for an issuer.

Professional bond investors have ways of analyzing information about companies and bond issues to estimate the uncertainty of future ability to pay. These techniques are explained in Chapter 17. However, most individual bond investors and some institutional bond investors make no such elaborate studies. In fact, they rely largely upon bond ratings published by several organizations that do the job of bond analysis and express their conclusions by a system of ratings. The five nationally recognized statistical rating organizations (NRSROs) in the United States are Duff & Phelps, Inc. (D&P); Fitch Investors Service, Inc. (Fitch); McCarthy, Crisanti & Maffei, Inc. (MCM); Moody's Investors Service, Inc. (Moody's); and Standard & Poor's Corporation (S&P). These ratings are used by market participants as a factor in the valuation of securities on account of their independent and unbiased nature.

Rating definitions are released by these firms in their various publications. Investors are urged to read these definitions. It should be remembered that they are not "buy," "hold," or "sell" indicators. They do not state whether an issue is "cheap" or "dear" among the multitude of preferred issues. They do not point to the direction of the market. While only a guide to the issuer's ability and willingness to meet the terms of the issue, they are a very important factor in the bond investment decision.

The rating systems use similar symbols, as shown in Exhibit 13–3. The bonds in the four highest rating categories are known as *high-grade*, or

**EXHIBIT 13–3**
**Summary of Rating Symbols and Definitions**

| Moody's | S&P | Fitch | D&P | MCM | Brief Definition |
|---------|-----|-------|-----|-----|------------------|
| *Investment Grade—High Creditworthiness* | | | | | |
| Aaa | AAA | AAA | AAA | AAA | Gilt edge, prime, maximum safety |
| Aa1 | AA+ | AA+ | AA+ | AA+ | |
| Aa2 | AA | AA | AA | AA | Very high grade, high quality |
| Aa3 | AA− | AA− | AA− | AA− | |
| A1 | A+ | A+ | A+ | A+ | |
| A2 | A | A | A | A | Upper medium grade |
| A3 | A− | A− | A− | A− | |
| Baa1 | BBB+ | BBB+ | BBB+ | BBB+ | |
| Baa2 | BBB | BBB | BBB | BBB | Lower medium grade |
| Baa3 | BBB− | BBB− | BBB− | BBB− | |
| *Distinctly Speculative—Low Creditworthiness* | | | | | |
| Ba1 | BB+ | BB+ | BB+ | BB+ | |
| Ba2 | BB | BB | BB | BB | Low grade, speculative |
| Ba3 | BB− | BB− | BB− | BB− | |
| B1 | B+ | B+ | B+ | | |
| B2 | B | B | B | B | Highly speculative |
| B3 | B− | B− | B− | | |
| *Predominantly Speculative—Substantial Risk or in Default* | | | | | |
| | CCC+ | | | | |
| Caa | CCC | CCC | CCC | | Substantial risk, in poor standing |
| | CCC− | | | | |
| Ca | CC | CC | | | May be in default, extremely speculative |
| C | C | C | | | Even more speculative than those above |
| | CI | | | | CI = Income bonds—no interest is being paid |
| | | DDD | | | Default |
| | | DD | | DD | |
| | D | D | | | |

Source: Richard S. Wilson and Frank J. Fabozzi, *The New Corporate Bond Market* (Chicago: Probus Publishing Company, 1990).

*investment-grade*, meaning that financial risk is relatively low and the probability of future payment relatively high. Lower rated bonds have speculative elements, and the repayment of principal and interest in accordance with the terms of the issue are not ensured.

Both Moody's and Standard & Poor's publish yield indexes on long-term corporate bonds by issuer type and rating classification. These indexes show lower yields for the more creditworthy issues and higher yields as credit quality decreases and speculative elements become increasingly greater. Exhibit 13–4 presents the Moody's average promised yields [2] by rating category from 1976 through 1989.

These data on bond yields provide the empirical evidence that bond investors demand to obtain higher promised rates of return for high levels of financial risk. The differences in average yields between rating categories are measures of how much more they demand. The principle is that investors are averse to risk; they can be induced to take a little more risk only by the probability of a little more return on investment.

There is also empirical evidence that the yields actually realized by investors in corporate bonds over long periods of time vary in size according to rating categories. The classic study of realized yields to maturity on bonds was

**EXHIBIT 13–4**

**Average Promised Yields on Corporate Bonds by Quality Rating: 1976–1989***

| Year | Aaa | Aa | A | Baa |
|------|------|------|------|------|
| 1976 | 8.43% | 8.75% | 9.09% | 9.75% |
| 1977 | 8.02 | 8.24 | 8.49 | 8.97 |
| 1978 | 8.73 | 8.92 | 9.20 | 9.49 |
| 1979 | 9.63 | 9.94 | 10.20 | 10.69 |
| 1980 | 11.94 | 12.50 | 12.89 | 13.67 |
| 1981 | 14.17 | 14.75 | 15.29 | 16.04 |
| 1982 | 13.79 | 14.41 | 15.43 | 16.11 |
| 1983 | 12.04 | 12.42 | 13.10 | 13.55 |
| 1984 | 12.71 | 13.26 | 13.74 | 14.19 |
| 1985 | 11.37 | 11.82 | 12.28 | 12.72 |
| 1986 | 9.02 | 9.47 | 9.95 | 10.39 |
| 1987 | 9.38 | 9.68 | 9.99 | 10.58 |
| 1988 | 9.71 | 9.94 | 10.23 | 10.83 |
| 1989 | 9.26 | 9.46 | 9.74 | 10.18 |

\*  The annual yields are the average of the monthly averages as reported in *Moody's Bond Record.*

[2] Recall from Chapter 4 the difference between promised yields and realized yields

made a long time ago for the period 1900 through 1943. The study included issues in initial amounts of $5 million or more publicly offered during that period. It showed that realized yields on bonds rated in the first three rating categories at the time of issue were approximately 5 percent, but yields on triple-B bonds averaged 5.7 percent; for even lower rated bonds, yields rose to higher levels.[3] The flatness of the curve for the three highest rating categories may be attributed chiefly to defaults on even highly rated bonds during the Great Depression of the 1930s. For the past several decades, there have been relatively few defaults on bonds initially rated in the first three rating categories, which means that yields at time of issue have been approximately realized.

## APPROACHES TO EVALUATING CALLABLE CORPORATE BONDS

The holder of a callable corporate bond has given the issuer the right to call the issue prior to the maturity date. This results in two disadvantages to the bondholder. First, an issuer will call a bond when the yield on bonds in the market is lower than the issue's coupon rate. For example, if the coupon rate on a callable corporate bond is 13 percent and prevailing market yields are 7 percent, the issuer may find it economical to call the 13 percent issue and refund it with a 7 percent issue. From the investor's perspective, the proceeds received will have to be reinvested at a lower interest rate. Thus, callable bonds expose bondholders to reinvestment risk.

Second, as explained in Chapter 7, the price appreciation potential for a bond in a declining interest rate environment is limited when it is callable. The price of the callable bond will remain near its call price rather than rising to a higher price that would result for an otherwise comparable noncallable bond. This phenomenon for a callable bond is referred to as *price compression*, or *negative convexity*.

Given these disadvantages, why would any investor want to own one? If the investor receives sufficient compensation in the form of higher potential yield (lower price for the bond), an investor willing to accept call risk will be willing to hold a callable corporate bond.

As explained in Chapter 6, when a corporate bond is callable, the practice has been to calculate a yield-to-call as well as a yield-to-maturity. The smaller of these two yields is then considered to be a conservative estimate of the bond's potential return. In Chapter 6, however, it was explained that the yield-to-call assumes that (1) the investor will hold the bond to the assumed call date and (2)

---

[3] W. Braddock Hickman, *Statistical Measures of Corporate Bond Financing Since 1900* (Princeton, NJ.: National Bureau of Economic Research, 1960) pp. 394, 579, and 580.

the issuer will call the bond on that date. These assumptions are often unrealistic and the resulting yield-to-call offers little information about the bond's potential return.

To develop an analytical framework for assessing relative value and evaluating the potential performance of callable bonds over some investment horizon, it is necessary to understand the components of the bond owned. A callable corporate bond is a bond in which the bondholder has sold the issuing corporation a call option that allows the issuer to repurchase the contractual cash flows of the bond from the time the bond is first callable until the maturity date.

It is not the purpose of this chapter to review the approaches to valuing callable corporate bonds. Here we will just mention the two main approaches: the *options approach* and the *option-adjusted spread* approach. The former approach is explained in Chapter 36 and the latter in Chapter 37.

## EVENT RISK

In recent years, one of the more talked about topics among corporate bond investors is *event risk*. Over the last couple of decades, corporate bond indentures have become less restrictive, and corporate managements have been given a free rein to do as they please without regard to bondholders. Management's main concern or duty is to enhance shareholder wealth. As for the bondholder, all a company is required to do is to meet the terms of the bond indenture including the payment of principal and interest. With few restrictions and the optimization of shareholder wealth of paramount importance for corporate managers, it is no wonder that bondholders became concerned when merger mania and other events swept the nation's boardrooms. Events such as decapitalizations, restructurings, recapitalizations, mergers, acquisitions, leveraged buyouts, and share repurchases, among other things, often caused substantial changes in a corporation's capital structure, namely, greatly increased leverage and decreased equity. Bondholders' protection was sharply reduced and debt quality ratings lowered, in many cases to speculative-grade categories. Along with greater risk came lower bond valuations. Shareholders were being enriched at the expense of bondholders.

In reaction to the increased activity of corporate raiders and mergers and acquisitions, some companies incorporated "poison puts" in their indentures. These are designed to thwart unfriendly takeovers by making the target company unpalatable to the acquirer. The poison put provides that the bondholder can require the company to repurchase the debt under certain circumstances arising out of specific designated events such as a change in control. Poison puts may not deter a proposed acquisition but could make it more expensive. In some cases if the board of directors approves the change in control—a "friendly" transaction (and all takeovers are friendly if the price is right)—the poison but provisions will not become effective. The designated event of change in control generally means either that continuing directors no longer constitute a majority of the board of directors or that a person, including affiliates, becomes the beneficial owner, directly or indirectly, of stock with at least 20 percent of the voting rights. Many times, in addition to a designated event, a rating change to below investment grade must occur within a certain period for the put to be activated. Some issues provide for a higher interest rate instead of a put as a designated event remedy.

Event risk has caused some companies to include other special debt retirement features in their indentures. An example is the *maintenance of net worth clause* included in the indentures of some lower rated bond issues of the 1980s. In this case, an issuer covenants to maintain its net worth above a stipulated level, and, if it fails to do so, it must begin to retire its debt at par. Usually the redemptions affect only part of the issue and continue periodically until the net worth recovers to an amount above the stated figure or the debt is retired. In other cases, the company is only required to *offer to redeem* a required amount. An offer to redeem is not mandatory on the bondholders' part; only those holders who want their bonds redeemed need do so. In a number of instances in which the issuer is required to call bonds, the bondholders may elect not to have bonds redeemed. This is not much different from an offer to redeem. It may protect bondholders from the redemption of the high-coupon debt at lower interest rates. However, if a company's net worth declines to a level low enough to activate such a call, it would probably be prudent to have one's bonds redeemed.

Protecting the value of debt investments against the added risk caused by recent corporate management activity is not an easy job. Investors should carefully analyze the issuer's fundamentals to determine if the company may be a candidate for restructuring. Attention to news and equity investment reports can make the task easier. Also, review the indenture to see if there are any protective features. However, even these can often be circumvented by sharp legal minds. Toward this end, some of the debt rating services issue commentary on indenture features of corporate bonds, noting the degree of protection against event risk. Of course, large portfolios can reduce risk with broad diversification among industry lines, but price declines do not always affect only the issue at risk; they also can spread across the board and take the innocent down with them. This happened in the Fall of 1988 with the leveraged buyout of RJR Nabisco, Inc. The whole industrial bond market suffered as buyers and traders withdrew from the market, new issues were postponed, and secondary market activity came to a standstill. This can be seen in Exhibits 13–5 and 13–6. Exhibit 13–5 shows the impact of the initial leveraged buyout bid announcement on yield spreads for RJR Nabisco's debt. The yield spread to a benchmark Treasury increased from about 100 basis points to 350 basis points. The RJR transaction showed that size was not an obstacle. Therefore, other large firms that investors previously thought were unlikely candidates for a leveraged buyout were fair game. To see the spillover effect, look at Exhibit 13–6, which shows how event risk fears caused yield spreads to widen for three large firms.

**EXHIBIT 13–5**
**RJR Nabisco—The Impact of the Initial LBO Bid Announcement
on Yield Spreads**

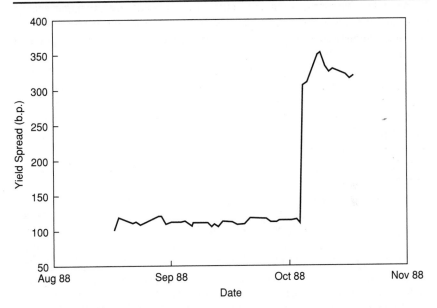

Source: N.R. Vijayarghavan and Randy Snook, "Takeover Event Risk and Corporate Bond Portfolio
Management," in Frank J. Fabozzi (ed.) *Advances and Innovations in Bond and Mortgage Markets*
(Chicago: Probus Publishing, 1989), p. 55.

## THE BOND MARKETS

It is easy to buy bonds. The minimum you need to know is the telephone number
of a broker-dealer firm with whom you have established an account. It is better,
though, if you know something about the bond markets and how they operate.
Familiarity with markets may affect your choice of bond issues and enable you
to minimize the cost of buying and selling.

Billions of dollars of new corporate bonds are sold each year in the primary
market—the market for new issues. As soon as a new bond issue is publicly
offered, investors begin to buy and sell in the secondary market—the market
for outstanding issues.

The secondary market for bonds is a big one. You may not hear as much
about it as about the stock markets, but there are more corporate bond issues
listed on the New York Stock Exchange (NYSE) than there are stock issues. The
dollar value of daily bond trading on the exchanges and in the over-the-counter
market appears to be not too much less than the value of trading in stocks on
the exchanges. The reason the bond market is inconspicuous to the public is that

**EXHIBIT 13–6**

**Anheuser Busch, Sara Lee & Union Pacific—Event Risk Fears and Widening Yield Spreads**

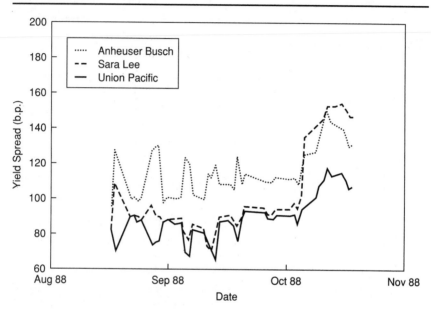

Source: N.R. Vijayarghavan and Randy Snook, "Takeover Event Risk and Corporate Bond Portfolio Management," in Frank J. Fabozzi (ed.) *Advances and Innovations in Bond and Mortgage Markets* (Chicago: Probus Publishing, 1989), p. 55.

it is mostly an institutional market wherein life insurance companies, pension funds, and savings institutions quietly buy and sell large amounts of bonds with little or no publicity.

There are really two bond markets. One is the *exchange market*, where certain members make a market in listed issues. The other is the *over-the-counter market*, which is a market made by dealer firms in their offices. The exchange market for bonds is chiefly the New York Stock Exchange. The over-the-counter market is chiefly in New York City, but there are many firms all over the country who buy and sell securities as dealers.

In discussing the bond markets, one must differentiate clearly between brokers and dealers. Brokers execute orders for accounts of customers; they are agents and get a commission for their services. Dealers buy and sell for their own accounts. When they buy, they take the risk of reselling at a loss. Dealers "make a market" when they quote a bond continuously. A *quote* is a bid and an offer. The *bid* is the price a dealer will pay for bonds of an issue to whoever may want to sell to the dealer; and the *offer* is the price at which a dealer will sell bonds to whoever may want to buy from the dealer. The offer is always higher than the bid; that is, the dealer buys at a lower price than that at which he or she sells, and so makes a profit. The difference between bid and offer prices is the dealer's *spread*.

## The Exchange Market

If you look only at the number of bond issues listed on the New York Stock Exchange—about 3,106 at the end of 1988—and at the market value of listed bonds—approximately $1.56 trillion—you would conclude that the exchange market is the big market. In fact, it is not. A very large percentage of all bond trading, including listed issues, is over the counter. In 1988, average daily volume on the NYSE for corporate debt transactions was only $30.4 million. Corporate activity in the over-the-counter market averaged more than $13.1 billion in 1988 according to data from the Securities Industry Association.

The difference between the size of the two markets is partly a matter of historical development and partly of adaptation to the requirements of institutional investors. The organized security markets developed chiefly as stock markets because, during a long period of history, there was a broad public interest in stocks. However, it has long been the custom for the larger corporate bond issues to be listed on the New York Stock Exchange. Dealers in the over-the-counter market have developed a larger and broader market chiefly because they have the capital required to assume the risk of buying and selling large amounts of bonds for their own accounts. They have benefitted by the great growth in bond investment by institutional investors during the past several decades.

The New York Stock Exchange assists bond trading by requiring that member firms execute customers' orders for nine bonds or fewer on the floor of the exchange unless a better price can be obtained off the floor. The exchange market has also been aided by the installation of the Automated Bond System, which provides quotes on all listed issues to broker-dealer firms that subscribe to the service. Leading newspapers publish daily a record of prices at which NYSE-listed bond issues were traded on the preceding business day. Examination of this information is a good way to learn more about the bond market. Exhibit 13–7 shows part of the record of trading in NYSE bond issues on a randomly selected day.

The first task is to identify corporate issuers. Most of us can read "ATT" to mean American Telephone and Telegraph Company. The particular bond issue is indicated by the interest rate and year of maturity; thus, "ATT 7s01" means an issue bearing interest at 7 percent and due in the year 2001. In the next column, reading from left to right, is the current yield on the issue. *Notice that*

**EXHIBIT 13–7**

**Excerpt from *The Wall Street Journal* Showing New York Exchange Bonds**

## CORPORATION BONDS
**Volume, $44,550,000**

| Bonds | Cur Yld | Vol | Close | Net Chg. |
|---|---|---|---|---|
| AL Lb 7¾14 | cv | 22 | 107½ | − 1 |
| Advst 9s08 | cv | 18 | 84½ | + ½ |
| AlaBn 9s99t | 9.1 | 5 | 98⅝ | + ⅛ |
| AlaP 10⅞05 | 10.5 | 7 | 103⅜ | + ⅛ |
| AlaP 8⅞06 | 9.2 | 10 | 96⅜ | − ¾ |
| AlaP 8¾07 | 9.1 | 13 | 96 | ... |
| AlaP 9⅝08 | 9.5 | 14 | 100⅞ | + ⅝ |
| AlaP 12⅝10 | 11.9 | 42 | 106⅜ | ... |
| vjAlgl 10.4s02f | ... | 64 | 21 | + 3 |
| vjAlgl 9s89mf | ... | 20 | 25⅞ | + 1⅞ |
| AlldC zr92 | ... | 63 | 79 | + ½ |
| AlldC zr98 | ... | 24 | 47¼ | − ¾ |
| AlldC zr2000 | ... | 10 | 38⅝ | − ¾ |
| AlldC zr9 | ... | 5 | 73 | ... |
| AlldC zr95 | ... | 5 | 63 | + 1⅜ |
| AlldC zr05 | ... | 10 | 25 | ... |
| AlldC zr07 | ... | 20 | 20⅜ | − 1⅛ |
| AldSig 9⅞97 | 9.7 | 53 | 101½ | + ¼ |
| Alcoa 9s95 | 8.9 | 10 | 100¾ | ... |
| AMAX 14¼90 | 14.2 | 41 | 100½ | − 2 |
| AMAX 14½94 | 12.4 | 40 | 117 | ... |
| AmBas 14⅞98 | 16.3 | 465 | 91½ | + ½ |
| Amdur 5½93 | cv | 41 | 64 | − 4 |
| AForP 5s30 | 9.3 | 4 | 53½ | + ½ |
| ABrnd 9⅛16 | 9.7 | 15 | 93¾ | ... |
| vjACM 6¾911 | cv | 22 | 31½ | + 1½ |
| ACyan 8⅜06 | 9.1 | 25 | 92⅜ | − 1⅝ |
| AmMed 8¼08 | cv | 1 | 51½ | + 1 |
| AmMed 11s98 | 12.6 | 3 | 87½ | − 1⅛ |
| ATT 5½97 | 6.6 | 5 | 83⅝ | + ¼ |
| ATT 6s00 | 7.2 | 79 | 82⅞ | + ⅝ |
| ATT 5⅛01 | 6.8 | 32 | 75⅜ | − ⅞ |
| ATT 8¾00 | 8.8 | 266 | 99⅝ | + ⅛ |
| ATT 7s01 | 8.0 | 137 | 87⅜ | ... |
| ATT 7⅛03 | 8.1 | 65 | 87½ | − ¼ |
| ATT 8.80s05 | 8.9 | 229 | 99⅛ | ... |
| ATT 8⅝s07 | 8.9 | 61 | 97⅛ | − ⅜ |
| ATT 8⅝26 | 9.1 | 89 | 95 | + ½ |
| Ames 7½14 | cv | 73 | 71 | − 2½ |
| Amoco 9.2s04 | 9.1 | 10 | 101¼ | ... |
| Amoco 8⅜05 | 8.6 | 37 | 96⅞ | ... |
| Amoco 7⅞07 | 8.5 | 10 | 93⅛ | ... |
| AmocoCda 7⅜13 | 6.3 | 51 | 117½ | + ½ |
| ArizP 10⅝00 | 10.4 | 60 | 102½ | ... |
| Asar 9¾2000 | 9.8 | 10 | 99½ | − ¾ |
| AshO 11.1s04 | 10.8 | 9 | 102¾ | − ¼ |
| ARch 9½96 | 9.3 | 60 | 102 | + ¼ |
| ARch 9¼93 | 9.0 | 20 | 102⅞ | ... |
| ARch 9⅞16 | 9.1 | 52 | 108⅝ | − 1⅞ |
| BPNA 10s00 | 9.9 | 5 | 101 | ... |

| Bonds | Cur Yld | Vol | Close | Net Chg. |
|---|---|---|---|---|
| ChryF 9¼91 | 9.3 | 50 | 100 | + ⅜ |
| ChryF 8⅜97 | 9.2 | 25 | 91½ | + ½ |
| ChryF 8⅛94 | 8.6 | 25 | 94⅞ | ... |
| CirclK 8¼05 | cv | 15 | 36½ | ... |
| CirclK 12¾97 | 21.3 | 229 | 59⅞ | + ⅞ |
| CirclK 7¼06 | cv | 81 | 42¼ | + ¼ |
| CirclK 13s97 | 28.3 | 1 | 46 | ... |
| Citicp 8.45s07 | 9.2 | 59 | 91¾ | ... |
| Citicp 8⅛07 | 9.1 | 10 | 89¼ | + ¼ |
| Citicp 11⅞95 | 11.8 | 25 | 100½ | ... |
| Clmt zrD90 | ... | 4 | 91¼ | ... |
| Clmt zrD05 | ... | 2 | 24¾ | + 2¼ |
| Claytn 7¾01 | cv | 1 | 99 | ... |
| ClevEl 8¾05 | 9.2 | 2 | 95¼ | + 1 |
| ClevEl 9.85s10 | 9.9 | 10 | 99⅛ | − 1⅛ |
| Coastl 11¼96 | 10.8 | 70 | 104 | ... |
| Coastl 11¾06 | 11.1 | 141 | 105½ | − ¼ |
| Coastl 8.48s91 | 8.7 | 663 | 97¾ | − ⅜ |
| Coastl 11⅛98 | 10.9 | 25 | 102⅜ | − ⅛ |
| ColuG 9⅛95 | 9.2 | 4 | 99½ | ... |
| Cmdis 9.65s02 | 10.0 | 5 | 96⅛ | ... |
| CmwE 8¾05 | 9.2 | 10 | 95 | + 1 |
| CmwE 9⅜04 | 9.4 | 5 | 99¼ | + ⅛ |
| CmwE 8⅛07J | 9.1 | 27 | 89½ | + 1⅜ |
| CmwE 8⅛07D | 9.1 | 5 | 89 | + ⅛ |
| CmwE 9⅛08 | 9.4 | 56 | 96¾ | + ¼ |
| CmwE 11⅛10 | 10.4 | 5 | 107⅜ | − ¼ |
| CmwE 11¾15 | 10.6 | 5 | 111¼ | + 2¼ |
| Compq 6½13 | cv | 7 | 137 | ... |
| Consec 12¾97 | 14.9 | 136 | 85½ | − ¼ |
| ConEd 4⅝93 | 5.3 | 4 | 87⅞ | + ⅜ |
| ConEd 9⅜00 | 9.2 | 5 | 101⅝ | ... |
| ConEd 7.9s01 | 8.6 | 4 | 92⅛ | − ⅞ |
| ConEd 7¾03 | 8.5 | 10 | 91¼ | + ¼ |
| ConEd 8.4s03 | 8.7 | 7 | 97 | + ¼ |
| ConEd 9⅛04 | 9.1 | 1 | 100 | + ⅛ |
| CnNG 7¾98 | 8.2 | 5 | 95 | + ⅛ |
| CnPw 6⅝98 | 7.9 | 4 | 84¼ | − ½ |
| CnPw 8⅛01 | 9.0 | 4 | 90⅝ | ... |
| CnPw 9¾06 | 9.8 | 5 | 100 | + ⅜ |
| CnPw 9s06 | 9.4 | 1 | 96 | ... |
| CnPw 8⅞07 | 9.2 | 14 | 96 | + ⅜ |
| CtlDat 12¾91 | 12.7 | 363 | 100½ | − ¾ |
| CtlDat 8½11 | cv | 20 | 87 | + 2 |
| CoopCo 10⅝05 | cv | 25 | 68¼ | + ¼ |
| Copwld 9.92s08 | cv | 2 | 100 | + 1 |
| Crane 7s93 | 7.6 | 4 | 92¼ | + ⅛ |
| Crane 7s94 | 7.6 | 10 | 92 | + ¾ |
| CrayRs 6⅛11 | cv | 31 | 74 | − 2 |
| Crstwd 6¼91 | cv | 5 | 93⅛ | ... |
| CritAc 13⅛14 | 12.7 | 3 | 103½ | + ⅜ |
| CritAc 11¼15 | 10.9 | 3 | 103 | ... |
| Dana dc5⅞06 | cv | 26 | 81 | + 2 |

## Quotations as of 4 p.m. Eastern Time
## Monday, January 8, 1990

**Volume $44,810,000**

**SALES SINCE JANUARY 1**
(000 omitted)

| 1990 | 1989 | 1988 |
|---|---|---|
| $199,848 | $135,312 | $158,642 |

| | Domestic Mon. | Domestic Fri. | All Issues Mon. | All Issues Fri. |
|---|---|---|---|---|
| Issues traded | 625 | 609 | 630 | 612 |
| Advances | 239 | 233 | 243 | 235 |
| Declines | 239 | 240 | 240 | 241 |
| Unchanged | 147 | 136 | 147 | 136 |
| New highs | 18 | 20 | 20 | 21 |
| New lows | 11 | 3 | 11 | 3 |

## Dow Jones Bond Averages

| 1989 High | 1989 Low | 1990 High | 1990 Low | | 1990 Close | 1990 Chg. | 1990 %Yld | 1989 Close | 1989 Chg. |
|---|---|---|---|---|---|---|---|---|---|
| 94.15 | 87.35 | 93.04 | 92.89 | 20 Bonds | 92.89 | −0.04 | 9.35 | 88.35 | −0.05 |
| 95.26 | 86.95 | 94.48 | 94.31 | 10 Utilities | 94.35 | +0.04 | 9.27 | 88.00 | +0.06 |
| 93.26 | 87.60 | 91.60 | 91.43 | 10 Industrials | 91.43 | −0.13 | 9.44 | 88.70 | −0.16 |

| Bonds | Cur Yld | Vol | Close | Net Chg. |
|---|---|---|---|---|
| GMA 9¼93 | 9.2 | 40 | 101 | + ⅜ |
| GMA 8½91 | 8.5 | 20 | 100½ | + ¼ |
| GMA 8⅞96 | 8.9 | 1062 | 99¾ | + ¼ |
| GMA 8s96 | 8.4 | 5 | 95½ | − ½ |
| GMA 8⅛92 | 8.2 | 7 | 99¼ | ... |
| GMA 8s93J | 8.2 | 140 | 98 | ... |
| GMA 8s93O | 8.2 | 100 | 97⅞ | − ⅛ |
| GMA 7¼90 | 7.3 | 100 | 99 | ... |
| GMA 8s94 | 8.2 | 26 | 97½ | + ⅜ |
| GMA 7⅛92i | 7.3 | 5 | 97⅛ | − ⅛ |
| GMA 7⅞97 | 8.3 | 75 | 95 | + ⅞ |
| GM 8⅝s05 | 9.0 | 15 | 95½ | − ½ |
| Gene 14¼94 | 13.8 | 20 | 103 | + ⅞ |
| Genrad 7¼11 | cv | 112 | 60 | + 1 |
| GaPw 8⅝04 | 9.3 | 12 | 92⅞ | − ½ |
| GaPw 11¾05 | 11.3 | 40 | 104 | + ⅛ |
| GaPw 9⅞06 | 9.8 | 5 | 100⅞ | ... |
| GaPw 9⅝08 | 9.7 | 1 | 99⅜ | − ¼ |
| GaPw 9¾08 | 9.8 | 50 | 100 | ... |
| GaPw 10½09 | 10.2 | 8 | 102½ | − ⅛ |
| GaPw 11s09 | 10.6 | 6 | 104¼ | + 1 |
| GaPw 13⅛12 | 12.4 | 14 | 105½ | ... |
| GaPw 10s16A | 9.9 | 15 | 101¼ | + ⅜ |
| GibFn 9¼08f | cv | 12 | 2 1/16 | + 11/16 |
| GdNgF 13¼95 | 14.4 | 100 | 92¼ | ... |

| Bonds | Cur Yld | Vol | Close | Net Chg. |
|---|---|---|---|---|
| LomF 7s11f | cv | 27 | 21 | ... |
| LomF 10¾93f | ... | 25 | 26 | ... |
| LglsLt 11⅞15 | 11.1 | 5 | 106¾ | − ¼ |
| LglsLt 11.7s93 | 11.0 | 3 | 106 | ... |
| LglsLt 11½14 | 11.0 | 15 | 104¼ | ... |
| Loral 7¼10 | cv | 7 | 91½ | − ¼ |
| Lorilld 6⅞93 | 7.4 | 38 | 92⅞ | ... |
| LouGs 9¼00 | 9.1 | 14 | 101¼ | + ¼ |
| vjLykes 7½94N f | ... | 100 | 15 | + 1 |
| vjLykes 7½94f | ... | 193 | 16⅞ | + 3 |
| vjLykes 11s00f | ... | 57 | 15 | − ½ |
| MGMUA 13s96 | 15.1 | 28 | 86 | ... |
| MfrH 8⅛04 | 9.4 | 20 | 86 | + ⅞ |
| MfrH 8⅛07 | 9.7 | 10 | 84 | − ½ |
| Manvl 12s92 | 11.8 | 14 | 101⅝ | + ⅛ |
| Mapco 10¾99 | 10.6 | 2 | 101⅛ | − 1¾ |
| MarO 8.5s06 | 9.7 | 61 | 88 | + 1 |
| MarO 9½94 | 9.5 | 408 | 100½ | + ¼ |
| MarkIV 13⅜99 | 13.5 | 16 | 99 | ... |
| Masco 5¼12 | 6.6 | 15 | 79¾ | − ¼ |
| Mattel 11⅝03 | 11.7 | 73 | 99⅝ | + ⅛ |
| Maxus zr04 | ... | 4 | 39 | − ½ |
| McCro 6½92 | cv | 1 | 69½ | ... |
| McCro 7½94 | 13.4 | 5 | 56⅛ | ... |
| McCro 7¾95 | 13.5 | 4 | 57½ | − 3 |

*this is not the yield-to-maturity*. In some instances you find the letters *cv* instead of current yield. The letters mean that the bond is *convertible*. The conversion option affects market price and distorts current yield. Sometimes the letter *f* appears in the column for current yield. This means that the bond is *traded flat*; that is, a purchaser does not have to pay a seller accrued interest from the bond's last interest payment date to the date of purchase. All other bonds are traded with accrued interest. Bonds traded flat are in default, or, for some other reason the next interest payment is particularly uncertain. Moving to the right, you see a number that indicates the total volume of trading in an issue during the day. Scan that column and you see that trading in some issues has involved only 5 or 10 bonds. Then you come to the closing prices for the day. In the last column is the net change in closing price on the day of the report relative to the closing price on the most recent previous day the bond issue was traded.

## The OTC Market

The over-the-counter (OTC) market is hard to describe in precise language because it does not exist in a particular place, it has no listed issues, and there is no published information about the prices at which bonds are traded or about the volume of trading. Any dealer can make a market for a bond issue without having to be a member of an exchange or even a member of the National Association of Securities Dealers (the organization to which most broker-dealer firms belong).

The heart of the over-the-counter market is a group of perhaps one dozen large dealer firms located in New York City that make *wholesale* markets in large numbers of bond issues. Their market is called wholesale because for the most part they deal only with other wholesalers and with broker-dealer firms that have *retail* orders from their own customers to execute as brokers. Wholesalers also deal directly with large institutional investors, who buy and sell in large lots, such as 100 bonds or more.

Some years ago, the National Association of Securities Dealers (NASD)— which is both a trade association and a governing organization—developed a computerized system by which dealers may enter their bids and offers for issues in which they make a market; subscribers can read these quotations on terminals in their offices. The system is called *NASDAQ* (for National Association of Security Dealers Automated Quotation service). A broker-dealer firm with an order to execute for a customer can learn instantly the highest bid and lowest offer for the issue in which he or she is interested and then execute the order by telephone. This is much more efficient than the old system of telephoning around to several dealers for quotes.

## DIFFERENCES IN THE QUALITY
## OF MARKETABILITY

Any bond that is quoted continually by a dealer is a *marketable bond*; there is a market for it. But sophisticated investors want to know much more than that; they want to know how good the market is. It may be inferred that a bond quoted by only one dealer in Kansas City has a poor market and that one quoted by half a dozen large wholesalers in New York City has an excellent market. There are gradations between poor and excellent. It is useful to recognize differences in the quality of markets for different bond issues.

The principal basis for grading securities in marketability is the size of the spread between dealers' bid and asked prices. A narrow spread—say, one fourth to one half of 1 percent—indicates an excellent market. A wide spread—such as 2 or 3 percent—means a poorly marketable issue. The principal determinant of the size of spread is not so much the number of dealers, as suggested above, but the usual volume of trading in an issue. The number of dealers is more or less proportionate to the volume of trading. If there is a lot of business in a bond issue, there are more dealers seeking the business. The size of the spread is also related to the volume of trading. A large volume of trading and a large number of dealers make a highly competitive market in which spreads narrow. In the actively traded issues, dealers take less risk when they buy bonds and carry them in inventory. Usually, price changes in any short period are small, and a dealer who wishes to do so can unload bonds. In addition, active trading distributes the dealer's costs over many transactions.

The reason for differentiating between bond issues in grades of marketability is that high marketability costs money. Other things being equal, investors prefer the highly marketable issues and accordingly will pay slightly more for them. A slightly higher price means a slightly lower yield. An investor who buys in the bond market and expects to sell in the market after some period of time needs high marketability. Only by trading in highly marketable issues can the investor minimize transaction costs. Consider, for example, the cost of buying and selling a bond that is usually quoted with a spread of one half of 1 percent. The cost of a *round trip*—that is, a purchase and a sale—is only 1 percent for the dealer. In addition, a broker's commission on a round trip is likely to be about one half of 1 percent. The sum is about 1.5 percent. In comparison, the cost of a round trip in a poorly marketable issue might be twice as much.

Many investors do not need high marketability. They buy new corporate bond issues when they are first offered to the public at the public offering price. The cost of public distribution is paid by the issuer. Then they usually hold bonds until they are redeemed at par or a premium over par when bonds are called before maturity. Thus, they pay no dealer's spread and no commission. The round trip is free. On exceptional occasions such investors elect to sell bonds in the market and have to pay for a one-way trip back.

There is also another category of corporate bond investors, which includes those who buy in the secondary market and seek to realize capital gains by sale in the market at a higher price; there is speculation in bonds just as there is in stocks. Clearly this category of investors needs highly marketable issues in order to minimize the transaction costs.

## SUMMARY

The category of securities described by the term *corporate bonds* includes a great variety of investment instruments. Under this heading, you find bond issues generally regarded as bearing very little risk of payments in dollar amounts and others that are distinctly speculative. You find a wide range of obligations in length of the period to maturity—from those due within a few days to issues that may have as many as 30 to 40 years to maturity. There are bonds secured by first mortgages on issuers' plant and equipment and those that have no specific pledge of security. There are obligations designed for particular categories of issuers such as equipment-trust obligations for transportation companies and collateral-trust bonds for holding companies. Provisions for redemption vary widely. There are bonds that are not callable before maturity and those that are callable at any time after a specified period of notice. Most, but not all, corporate bonds have sinking funds to retire bonds from time to time during the period to maturity.

It is not surprising, then, that corporate bonds of all these varieties appeal to investors of many varieties. Life insurance companies buy more corporate obligations than any other category of investors, but other institutions, such as pension funds, trust funds, mutual funds, and casualty insurance companies, are important on the demand side of the market. Although financial institutions make up the principal market, many individuals find corporate issues of one kind or another suitable for their personal investment portfolios.

# CHAPTER 14

## DOMESTIC FLOATING-RATE AND ADJUSTABLE-RATE DEBT SECURITIES

Richard S. Wilson
*Managing Director*
*Research Products and Services*
*Fitch Investors Service, Inc.*

This chapter discusses the many varieties of *floating-rate* and *adjustable-rate* debt. It reviews the market for domestic instruments, which have coupons or interest rates that adjust periodically over their stated life span, with adjustments occurring as often as once a week to as infrequently as every 11 years.

### CLASSIFICATION OF FLOATING-RATE DEBT INSTRUMENTS AND SUMMARY OF TERMS

Floating-rate notes (FRNs) is a phrase that embraces different types of securities with a similar feature—a coupon or interest rate that is adjusted periodically due to changes in a base or benchmark rate.[1] While the jargon of the investment world will continue to utilize this term to cover all manner of variable-rate debt issues (although there are more than 85 phrases and acronyms describing the

---

[1] The U.S. Government issues a form of floating-rate debt, namely the Series EE Savings Bonds. The semiannual interest rate is determined each May and November, and it is based on 85 percent of the average market return for the preceding six months for five-year Treasury bonds with a constant maturity. If held at least five years, the minimum rate will be 6 percent. If held for less than five years, interest is earned on a fixed, graduated scale, rising from 5.5 percent after one year to the guaranteed minimum at five years.

different types of debt, ranging from annual adjustable-rate notes to yield-curve notes), they could very well be classified in two very broad, and at times, overlapping categories.

Thus, floating-rate notes are those instruments with coupons based on a short-term rate index (such as the prime rate or the three-month Treasury bill) and reset more than once a year.

Adjustable-rate notes or variable-rate notes (or debentures, bonds, and the like) are debt securities with coupons based on a longer-term index. Coupons are usually redetermined no more than once a year, but often a longer time elapses between changes in the interest rates. For example, the base rate might be the two-year Treasury yield, and the coupon would then change every two years to reflect the new level of the Treasury security.

## HISTORICAL OVERVIEW

Floating-rate notes originated in Europe and made their appearance in this country in the early 1970s. To the best of our knowledge, the first publicly offered issue was $15 million Mortgage Investors of Washington Floating Rate (8% to 12% ) Senior Subordinated Notes due November 1, 1980, offered on November 1, 1973. This was quickly followed by $20 million First Virginia Mortgage and Real Estate Investment Trust with similar terms.

The big impetus to the market was the Citicorp (a bank holding company) $650 million floating-rate notes issued July 30, 1974. The offering was originally structured with the individual investor in mind (Citicorp would be obligated to repurchase any notes offered to it every six months after issuance), and the initial demand was such that it probably could have sold close to $1 billion of the notes. However, opposition from the thrift industry, Congress, and others caused Citicorp to modify the proposed terms so that the date of the first put [2] was June 1, 1976, and semiannually thereafter. It also reduced the size of the final offering. The interest rate on the notes was to be redetermined or readjusted each June and December at 1 percent higher than the Treasury bill rate, except that the minimum rate for the first year was 9.7 percent. The Treasury bill rate at the date of the offering was 7.7 percent.

Citicorp's offering was followed quickly by an issue of Chase Manhattan Corporation. Other corporate borrowers flocked to the trough over the next few months—by year-end 13 issues were outstanding, amounting to $1.36 billion. Issuance of floaters disappeared as rapidly as they made their mark on the

---

[2] A put is a provision of the debt instrument that gives the holder the right to require the issuer to repurchase the security at certain prices (generally 100 percent of face value) at specific dates prior to the stated maturity.

investment community, and not one issue was offered for the next three years. Again, in mid-1978, Citicorp tapped the market with a $200 million, 20-year note issue. This time it did not give the holder the right to put the notes back to the company, and the interest rate was set at a spread above the six-month Treasury bill rate.

In 1979, 18 issues similar to Citicorp's (except that some could be converted into long-term fixed-rate debt) were sold. This was followed by only six offerings for $912 million over the next two years. However, increased market volatility and high interest rates whetted investors' appetites for variable-rate securities, and the market started to mushroom in 1982; now they are an accepted part of the market. The issues range in quality from triple-A down to single-D (the issuer is in default). While most are tied in one way or another with various interest-rate bases, several have been linked to nonfinancial benchmarks, such as the price of West Texas crude oil or the share volume on the New York Stock Exchange. There have also been a few issues convertible into common shares.

## SIZE OF THE MARKET

Banks and financial service companies have been the largest issuers of those securities accounting for 71.9 percent of the number of issues and 66.4 percent of the total amount. This is understandable, due to the floating-rate nature and turnover of their financial assets. In effect, they are trying to provide a matching of floating-rate assets with floating-rate liabilities. Exhibit 14–1 shows the distribution by type of issue:

Exhibit 14–2 shows volume details for the approximately 440 variable-rate debt offerings sold publicly through the end of 1988 by the basis of coupon adjustment. The largest amount—$21.67 billion, or 29.9 percent of the total—is based on the Treasury constant maturity (TCM)[3] or a rate determined by the issuer. Following closely in second place with $20.5 billion, or 28.3 percent, of the total are issues based on the U.S. Treasury bill rate, either the weekly auction rate or the yield based on secondary market transactions. Somewhat more than $15 billion, or 20.7 percent, of the offerings are based on one or another of the London InterBank Offering Rates (LIBOR).[4] Just over 11 percent of the

---

[3] The Treasury constant-maturity series is described in the Federal Reserve Statistical Release H. 15(519). Yields on Treasury securities at constant maturity are estimated from the Treasury's daily yield curve. This curve, which relates the yield on a security to its time to maturity, is based on the closing market bid yields on actively traded Treasury securities. The constant-yield values are read from the yield curve at fixed maturities, currently 1, 2, 3, 4, 5, 7, 10, and 30 years. This method permits estimation of the yield for a 10-year maturity, for example, even if no outstanding security has exactly 10 years remaining to maturity.

[4] LIBOR is the rate at which the major banks in London lend Eurodollar deposits of specific maturities.

**EXHIBIT 14–1**

**Offerings of Variable-Rate Securities by Issuer Classification (Par Value Dollars in Millions-Number of Issues)**

| YEAR | Banks & Thrifts | No. of Issues | Finance & Related | No. of Issues | Inter-national | No. of Issues | Industrial, Transportation & Others |
|---|---|---|---|---|---|---|---|
| 1988 | $3,695.0 | 19 | $6,889.7 | 31 | – | – | $2,691.0 |
| 1987 | $1,825.0 | 15 | $1,031.6 | 5 | – | – | $1,516.0 |
| 1986 | $3,768.6 | 19 | $2,514.2 | 16 | – | – | $1,436.3 |
| 1985 | $3,934.8 | 38 | $4,425.0 | 31 | $553.5 | 4 | $7,630.6 |
| 1984 | $5,295.0 | 42 | $3,315.0 | 26 | $2,500.0 | 5 | $5,052.0 |
| 1983 | $3,710.0 | 20 | $1,025.0 | 9 | $100.0 | 1 | $300.0 |
| 1982 | $350 | 3 | $1,890.0 | 13 | – | – | $775.0 |
| 1981 | $250.0 | 1 | $25.0 | 1 | – | – | $85.0 |
| 1980 | $250.0 | 1 | $250.0 | 1 | – | – | $52.0 |
| 1979 | $2,041.5 | 14 | $250.0 | 2 | – | – | $400.0 |
| 1978 | $200.0 | 1 | – | – | – | – | – |
| 1974 | $1,160.0 | 8 | $10.0 | 1 | – | – | $157.5 |
| 1973 | – | – | $35.0 | 2 | – | – | – |
| Total | $26,479.9 | 181 | $21,660.5 | 138 | $3,153.5 | 10 | $20,095.4 |
| % of Total | 36.54% | 40.77% | 29.89% | 31.08% | 4.35% | 2.25% | 27.73% |

| YEAR | Total No. of Issues | % of Total Utilities | % of Total No. of Issues | Total, $ Million | No. of Issues | Amount Issued | Number of Issues |
|---|---|---|---|---|---|---|---|
| 1988 | 19 | – | – | $13,275.7 | 69 | 18.32% | 15.54% |
| 1987 | 9 | $125.0 | 1 | $4,497.6 | 30 | 6.21% | 6.76% |
| 1986 | 8 | – | – | $7,719.1 | 43 | 10.65% | 9.68% |
| 1985 | 22 | $575.0 | 5 | $17,118.9 | 100 | 23.62% | 22.52% |
| 1984 | 30 | $275.0 | 3 | $16,437.0 | 106 | 22.68% | 23.87% |
| 1983 | 4 | $100.0 | 1 | $5,235.0 | 35 | 7.22% | 7.88% |
| 1982 | 7 | – | – | $3,015.0 | 23 | 4.16% | 5.18% |
| 1981 | 1 | – | – | $360.0 | 3 | 0.50% | 0.68% |
| 1980 | 1 | – | – | $552.0 | 3 | 0.76% | 0.68% |
| 1979 | 2 | – | – | $2,691.5 | 18 | 3.71% | 4.05% |
| 1978 | | – | – | $200.0 | 1 | 0.28% | 0.23% |
| 1974 | 2 | – | – | $1,327.5 | 11 | 1.83% | 2.48% |
| 1973 | | – | – | $35.0 | 2 | 0.05% | 0.45% |
| Total | 105 | $1,075.0 | 10 | $72,464.3 | 444 | | |
| % of Total | 23.65% | 1.48% | 2.25% | | | | |

Note: Excludes those issues convertible into common stock or certificates of deposit and those offered on a best-efforts or continuous-offering basis.

market is comprised of issues which float off the prime, commercial paper, and other short-term rates.

Some of the issues provide the holder with the option of putting the debt back to the borrower at par at certain dates prior to maturity. Generally, to exercise a put option, the holder must notify the issuer or its trustee some time prior to the put date (usually notice of 30 to 60 days is required). Often the put,

**EXHIBIT 14–2**

**Offerings of Variable-Rate Securities by Basis of Coupon Adjustment (Par Value Dollars in Millions-Number of Issues)**

| YEAR | Prime, C/P, M/M, Auction, and Other | No. of Issues | LIBOR | No. of Issues | Treasury Bills | No. of Issues | TCM[a] or Rate Determined by Issuer | No. of Issues |
|---|---|---|---|---|---|---|---|---|
| 1988 | $4,579.0 | 22 | $1,200.0 | 6 | $1,700.0 | 7 | $2,585.0 | 10 |
| 1987 | $1,025.0 | 11 | $825.0 | 5 | – | – | $1,395.0 | 6 |
| 1986 | $300.0 | 1 | $1,400.0 | 10 | $2,185.0 | 8 | $2,160.0 | 11 |
| 1985 | $290.0 | 4 | $8,237.4 | 42 | $2,803.5 | 19 | $5,476.0 | 30 |
| 1984 | $2,000.0 | 3 | $2,950.0 | 26 | $5,012.0 | 34 | $6,050.0 | 41 |
| 1983 | $100.0 | 1 | $400.0 | 2 | $3,585.0 | 23 | $1,150.0 | 9 |
| 1982 | – | – | – | – | $1,000.0 | 7 | $2,015.0 | 16 |
| 1981 | – | – | – | – | – | – | $335.0 | 2 |
| 1980 | – | – | – | – | $250.0 | 1 | $250.0 | 1 |
| 1979 | – | – | – | – | $2,441.5 | 17 | $250.0 | 1 |
| 1978 | – | – | – | – | $200.0 | 1 | – | – |
| 1974 | $7.5 | 1 | – | – | $1,320.0 | 10 | – | – |
| 1973 | $35.0 | 2 | – | – | – | – | – | – |
| Total | $8,336.5 | 45 | $15,012.4 | 91 | $20,497.0 | 127 | $21,666.0 | 127 |
| % of Total | 11.50% | 10.14% | 20.72% | 20.50% | 28.29% | 28.60% | 29.90% | 28.60% |

| YEAR | Kiwi & ANZAC[b] | No. of Issues | Stepped-Up Coupons | No. of Issues | Miscellaneous | No. of Issues | Total | No. of Issues |
|---|---|---|---|---|---|---|---|---|
| 1988 | $65.7 | 1 | – | – | $3,146.0 | 23 | $13,275.7 | 69 |
| 1987 | $187.6 | 3 | $140.0 | 1 | $925.0 | 4 | $4,497.6 | 30 |
| 1986 | $497.8 | 6 | $400.0 | 4 | $776.3 | 3 | $7,719.1 | 43 |
| 1985 | – | – | – | – | $312.0 | 5 | $17,118.9 | 100 |
| 1984 | – | – | – | – | $425.0 | 2 | $16,437.0 | 106 |
| 1983 | – | – | – | – | – | – | $5,235.0 | 35 |
| 1982 | – | – | – | – | – | – | $3,015.0 | 23 |
| 1981 | – | – | – | – | $25.0 | 1 | $360.0 | 3 |
| 1980 | – | – | – | – | $52.0 | 1 | $552.0 | 3 |
| 1979 | – | – | – | – | – | – | $2,691.5 | 18 |
| 1978 | – | – | – | – | – | – | $200.0 | 1 |
| 1974 | – | – | – | – | – | – | $1,327.5 | 11 |
| 1973 | – | – | – | – | – | – | $35.0 | 2 |
| Total | $751.0 | 10 | $540.0 | 5 | $5,661.3 | 39 | $72,464.2 | 444 |
| % of Total | 1.04% | 2.25% | 0.75% | 1.13% | 7.81% | 8.78 | | |

Note: Excludes those issues convertible into common stock or certificates of deposit and those offered on a best-efforts or continuous-offering basis.

[a] TCM = Treasury Constant Maturity

[b] Kiwi and ANZAC issues are denominated in the Australian or New Zealand dollar.

once exercised, is irrevocable; but a few of the note indentures make it possible for one to withdraw the notification of redemption. This is usually found in issues for which a company might wish to forestall early redemptions by increasing the interest rate above what is determined by the interest-rate-setting mechanism.

For example, an issuer might wish to delay or prevent the early redemption of the debt if it has determined that it needs the funds for business activities. By doing so, it will not have to borrow the funds from other sources, thus possibly eliminating expenses associated with another borrowing.

Also, call provisions[5] are not constant among the issues. Some are not optionally redeemable by the issuer for the life of the notes, while other issues can be called two or three years after sale. In some cases, the call provision applies to only part of the time that the issue is outstanding.

Denominations vary among the issues, ranging from a minimum of $1,000 to as large as $100,000, with increments of $1,000 to $100,000. In cases of large minimum denominations where a put is provided, it may be exercised in whole or in part, and, if the latter, the remaining outstanding holding must be at least equal to the required minimum denomination.

There are also some issues that are exchangeable either automatically at a certain date (often five years after issuance) or at the option of the issuer into fixed-rate securities. Many of these issues carry bond ratings below investment grade and must be considered to have speculative elements according to the rating definitions. Generally, the fixed-rate note that is issued on exchange will mature no later than five years after the exchange, or, in some cases, at the maturity date of the variable-rate note. The fixed-rate notes will bear interest based on a premium to the comparable Treasury constant maturity.

In 1984, Chrysler Financial Corporation issued subordinated exchangeable variable-rate notes due in 1994 which were exchangeable, at Chrysler's option, into fixed-rate notes maturing August 1, 1994. The interest rate on the fixed-rate notes was based on a rate equal to 124 percent of the ten-, seven-, or five-year Treasury constant maturity, depending on when the exchange occurred, but no later than August 1, 1989. The company exchanged the variable-rate notes in 1986 for 9.30% fixed-rate notes with the coupon rate based on the 10-year TCM benchmark.

## DETERMINATION OF THE COUPON

Since financial engineers have created debt instruments with a variety of terms, market participants should carefully review the prospectuses and offering documents of issues in which they are interested.

As was mentioned above, the coupons or interest rates of floaters are based on various benchmarks ranging from short-term rates, such as the prime rate and one-month commercial paper, to one-year and longer Treasury rates, as well as

---

[5] Call provisions are included in bond contracts to allow the issuer to retire the debt at its convenience. This usually occurs when the general level of interest rates is below the coupon of the subject debt security.

nonfinancial determinants. There are also issues where the rates are arbitrarily set by the issuer, and others where the interest rate is determined by a Dutch auction procedure. In many cases, the basic data can be obtained quite easily, with few calculations required. Federal Reserve Release H.15(519)—"Selected Interest Rates"—is one important source of this needed data. For other issues, the coupon-setting data are more difficult to obtain, and the investor must rely on the trustee or agent bank to announce the rates. The revised rates are often published in a newspaper of general circulation in New York City. However, many note agreements do not require the publication of the new rates but state only that such notice be mailed to the registered holder of the security.

Most of the issues sold in the United States are payable in U.S. dollars. But there are also issues denominated in the European Currency Unit (ECU) and Australian and New Zealand dollars (also called ANZAC or Kiwi issues). In most cases, the interest rate is set at a certain premium to the base or benchmark rate. For issues based on the Treasury constant maturity, it might be at a minimum percentage of the base rate (and may be set higher at the issuer's discretion). An example is Primerica Corporation's Extendible Notes due August 1, 1996, which were scheduled for an interest rate change on August 1, 1987. The coupon was 13.25 percent, but because interest rates were considerably lower, the company set the rate for the period from August 1, 1987 through July 31, 1992, at 8.4 percent, about 105 percent of the five-year Treasury constant maturity of 8 percent. The minimum percentage under the indenture was 102.5 percent. Apparently this rate was not satisfactory to the holders; many notes were put back to the company during the first two weeks of July or the holders threatened to do so. In any event, several days prior to the commencement of the new rate and interest period, a notice appeared in *The Wall Street Journal* announcing that the company "is exercising its option under the terms of the extendible notes due 1996 to establish an interest rate higher than the rate previously announced. . . . " The rate was increased to 8.875 percent, equal to 110.9 percent of the Treasury constant maturity. The notice further stated, "Holders of the Notes who have previously elected repayment of their Notes may revoke such election (and thereby become entitled to receive the increased interest rate)" by notice "to the company or the Trustee no later than 5:00 P.M., New York City time on the first business day following publication of this Notice."

In other cases, the rate might be set at a certain number of basis points above or below the base rate. Many three-month LIBOR-based issues have the rate set at LIBOR Plus $\frac{1}{8}$ or $\frac{1}{4}$ of 1 percent (12.5 or 25 basis points), while some three-month Treasury bill based issues are spread from 100 basis points to as much as 450 basis points over the base rate. The spread over the base rate tends to be higher for relatively low-yielding indexes and lower for higher yielding ones, all other things being equal. In some issues, the spread may be a discount from the base rate. In general, the progression of the benchmark rates from the lowest spread to the highest starts with the prime rate, followed by LIBOR, federal funds, commercial paper, certificates of deposit, the 11th District cost of funds, and finally Treasury bills, which often have the widest spreads. The 11th District index is a weighted average of interest costs for thrift liabilities in the 11th district of the Federal Home Loan Bank System.

Some issues provide for a change in the spread from the base rate at certain intervals over the life of the floater. For instance, the coupon for Citicorp's floater due September 1, 1998 was based on the interest yield equivalent of the market discount rate for six-month Treasury bills plus 120 basis points from March 1, 1979 through August 31, 1983 and then 100 basis points over the base rate to August 31, 1988. It is currently 75 basis points over until maturity. Step-down floaters have the same characteristic of a lower spread as maturity approaches. Chemical Banking Corporation's two-year step-down floating-rate notes due July 18, 1990 have a 25 basis point premium to the one-month commercial paper index for the first year, declining to a 20 basis point premium in the second year. Some issues are on an either or basis. One such example is BarclaysAmerican Corporation floating-rate subordinated notes due November 1, 1990. Interest is payable quarterly and calculated monthly at the higher of (1) the prime rate minus 125 basis points or (2) the 30-day commercial paper rate plus 25 basis points. Other issues have their coupon rates determined through a Dutch auction procedure or remarketing process, with the applicable interest rate the one at which all sell orders and all buy orders are satisfied.

One usually expects that as interest rates rise, the coupon on the floater will increase, and, as rates fall, the coupon will decrease. This makes sense to most people but there are some issues that might be confusing. With yield-curve notes, the interest rate is reset and payable twice a year based on a certain percentage rate (depending on the issue) minus the six-month LIBOR rate. For example, the General Motors Acceptance Corporation's yield-curve notes due April 15, 1993, are based on 15.25 percent minus six-month LIBOR. If LIBOR is at 8 percent, the rate on the notes would be 7.25 percent. If LIBOR increases to 10 percent, the yield-curve note drops to 5.25 percent, and if LIBOR falls to 6 percent, the yield-curve note would have a rate of 9.25 percent. It appears that only those investors who are bullish on the direction of interest rates would care for these issues. Another type of issue for interest rate bulls are the maximum reset notes and debentures. The two issues (one of each), which came to market in late 1985, were not warmly received by investors. The initial coupon rates were 10.625 percent. Interest is adjusted and payable semiannually, and if, at the interest determination date, six-month LIBOR exceeds 10.50 percent, then the interest rate for the period will be reduced from 10.625 percent by the amount of the excess, with the minimum rate being zero percent. With LIBOR at 12 percent, the rate on these notes would decline to 9.125 percent. At least if LIBOR exceeds $21\frac{1}{8}$ percent the holder will not have to pay the issuer anything.

Some of the issues have floors below which the interest rate cannot go. A number of the LIBOR-based issues have minimum rates of 5.25 percent. Others have declining minimums such as the Citicorps due September 1, 1998. The minimum rate is 7.50 percent through August 31, 1983, then 7 percent through August 31, 1988, and then 6.50 percent to maturity. Certain issues have ceilings or maximum rates, often because of state usury laws. For many issues, the maximum rate is 25 percent (due to New York State's usury law), but holders of $2.5 million or more of an issue are exempt from this ceiling. In 1974, Crocker National Corporation sold $40 million of floating-rate notes due 1994 with a 10 percent maximum rate due to uncertainties with California law. For several years, the coupon rate was below the ceiling but in 1979 interest rates shot up, restricting the coupon to 10 percent. As the notes had a put feature, many investors put the bonds back to the company and reinvested the proceeds in more attractive instruments. Had there been no put option, those investors would have been out of pocket for a number of years.

Several floating-rate issues have both a floor and a ceiling, which together are called collars. Baltimore Gas & Electric Company issued a couple of floaters in 1985 with collars. Based on the 91-day Treasury bill auction rate (bond equivalent basis) the spreads are 110 basis points for one and 112.5 basis points for the other. The collars are 8 percent and 12 percent, and 7.90 percent and 11.90 percent, respectively. These appear to be relatively narrow bands within which the interest rate may vary, but the lower ceiling is offset to some extent by the higher floor.

## LOOKING AT YIELDS—EVALUATION METHODS

Bonds with coupons that remain constant to the next put date should be looked at on a yield-to-put basis, whether the put is five months or five years away. Instead of using the maturity date in the calculations, the optional put date is used. This method takes into account any premium or discount amortized or accreted over the remaining term to the put.

More complex are those issues where the coupon varies over the time to put or maturity. There are numerous calculations used by investors in evaluating the relative attractiveness, and we will briefly discuss several of them. It is important when comparing issues to make sure that they have similar coupon redetermination *bases* and to be consistent with the method used so as to reduce distortions that could occur if issues with dissimilar features are analyzed. Comparing a weekly certificate of deposit-based floater with quarterly interest payments to a six-month Treasury bill secondary market-based floater paying interest semiannually would not be acceptable, nor would using one method of calculation for issue A and another for issue B be Valid, in our opinion. The issue used in this discussion is a hypothetical one, and the terms and results are shown in Exhibit 14–3. It should be noted that there are cases where one bond might appear to be the more attractive value under one method or set of assumptions and less attractive under another method and circumstances. Market participants will have to live with these complications.

The current-yield method (current interest rate divided by market price) is not a satisfactory measurement for floaters, in our view, because it only reflects the present point in time, assuming that both the coupon and the price remain unchanged. When comparing two similar issues with each other, the current yield would not provide much help in determining relative values, especially when there are different coupon reset dates involved. However, if we were to readjust or reset the coupon as of the present time we would get a better guide to the relative attractiveness (all other things being equal). Thus, the simple current yield for issue A is 9.34 percent, and the adjusted reset current yield is 9.08 percent.

While the contractual reset spread to the base rate is plus 100 basis points, the notes are selling at a discount and we are really getting a greater spread or margin. Subtracting the assumed reset rate (7.75 percent) from the adjusted reset current yield (9.08 percent) gives us the adjusted spread to base 133 basis points. If the notes were selling at par, the adjusted reset spread would be 100 basis points (8.75 percent–7.75 percent).

## EXHIBIT 14–3
## Hypothetical Issue A

| | |
|---|---|
| Coupon/maturity | 9.00% September 1, 1999 |
| Coupon reset and payment dates | March 1 & September 1 |
| Reset spread | +100 basis points (1.00%) |
| Base rate | 6-month U.S. Treasury bill, interest yield equivalent of the secondary market rate |
| Price | 96.375 |
| Today's assumed base rate | 7.75% |
| Adjusted reset coupon | 8.75% |
| Time remaining to maturity (assuming today is 12/1/89) | 9.667 years |
| Simple current yield | 9.34% |
| Adjusted reset current yield | 9.08% |
| Adjusted spread to base | 133 basis points |
| Zero coupon basis—spread from base | 138 basis points |
| Simple or positive margin | 143 basis points |
| Reset or adjusted yield-to-maturity | 9.32% |
| Spread or reset yield-to-maturity over base rate | 157 basis points |

However, floating-rate notes are not perpetual securities, as are preferred stocks. For issues selling below par, we pick up the discount at maturity (or put date), and for issues selling above par we lose the premium. Therefore, other calculations are used to analyze floaters. For example, one can view the bond as a zero coupon issue, obtain the yield-to-maturity on that basis and add it to the reset spread to arrive at the zero coupon basis-spread from base measurement. Of course, in relative value analysis, the investor must take into consideration the quality of the debt as well as other factors such as call, sinking-fund, and subordination provisions, if any.

## MARKET COMMENT

The first series of floating-rate notes issued in 1974 met with good investor reception. The two-year delay until the put feature became operative was a small negative, but it was used to mollify the thrift interests that feared an outflow of deposits to these new securities. From the investor's viewpoint, they were, at worst, two-year instruments and then six-month instruments once the puts became effective. Price volatility was relatively modest because of the put. Investors also flocked to the second round of floaters, which came to market in 1979. Many did not care that the new generation of floating-rate paper did not have any puts. They thought that as long as the coupon rate was adjusted every six months the bonds would naturally stay around par. However, there was nothing to keep them trading around par when all others around them were changing. The spread was fixed at market levels that existed at the time the issues were originally offered. They did not have puts and, as interest-rate movements became increasingly more volatile later in the year, their prices sank. These new issues were just intermediate-to longer-term securities with a coupon that happened to fluctuate. If the credit quality of the issue deteriorated, prices would be reduced. Because of rapid movements in interest rates, the coupon rates, when reset, were often below market rates. Prices had to adjust for this gap between the floater rate and the market rate. The semiannual coupon change did not provide the needed support. In the January 1980 to June 1981 period, based on end-of-week prices on the New York Stock Exchange, Citicorp's June 1, 1989, floater with a put had a price range of only 96 to $103 \frac{1}{4}$. In comparison, floaters without puts had wider price fluctuations. Manufacturers Hanover's floating-rate notes of May 1987 moved between $86 \frac{1}{4}$ and $101 \frac{1}{2}$, while Chase Manhattan's due in 2009 had a low of 82 and a high of $100 \frac{1}{2}$.

In early 1980, interest rates fell sharply. The floaters that were hurt the most in the preceding few months moved rapidly from the low 80s and 90s to the par area. For example, Chase Manhattan's 2009s went from 86 to about 100 in 15 weeks. But restraining some prices were the investors who wanted to get even; they wanted to get rid of an investment that had not measured up to their initial unreal performance expectations. After the rally, prices tumbled again as rates rose once more. This history shows how important the put feature can be. Of course, it also helps to know the risks and rewards of the various instruments one happens to be investing in.

Many floating-rate note investors are financial institutions with floating-rate liabilities of one sort of another. Other investors use floaters as substitutes for money market instruments, although those without put features are not perfect substitutes for short-dated instruments. Money market funds are large buyers of floaters with puts within one year. They have been used as hedges against rising interest-rate markets. If interest rates are thought to be on the increase, floaters with frequent resets should provide increasing income. Their defensive characteristics ought to lend them price stability. A mismatched floater might be suitable. Resetting weekly to increasingly higher levels with interest payable quarterly or semiannually, the holder is not locked into one rate for three or six months. LIBOR has historically been at higher levels than Treasury bill rates and the relationship between the two should be analyzed prior to investing. If the spread between the two is relatively narrow and one's interest-rate outlook is cautious, then LIBOR-based floaters might be considered so as to take advantage of a possible widening of the spread relationship.

Investors looking for a decline in interest rates may prefer floaters with less frequent resets (such as extendible notes) and deferred resets (so as to maintain the higher coupon for as long as possible). Of course, large investors don't have to limit themselves to just what is available in the domestic market; the supply of floating-rate paper in the foreign markets is considerable. The major investment firms with their worldwide trading capabilities participate in these markets 24 hours a day.

# CHAPTER 15

## CONVERTIBLE SECURITIES AND WARRANTS

*John C. Ritchie, Jr., Ph.D.*
*Professor of Finance*
*Temple University*

A bond or preferred stock may have warrants attached or offer a conversion privilege. In either case, the holder has the right to acquire the common stock of the issuing corporation under specified conditions rather than by direct purchase in the market. One can, however, pay what later proves to be an excessive price for the privilege conferred.

This chapter clarifies the nature of each of these securities, discusses their advantages and disadvantages, and develops an analytical framework aimed at assessing the desirability of acquiring either security by an investor. The investor's point of view, rather than that of the issuer, is emphasized.

### CONVERTIBLE SECURITIES

The holder of a convertible bond or preferred stock can exchange the security, at his or her option, for the common stock of the issuer in accordance with terms set forth in the bond indenture. The option to convert is solely at the discretion of the holder and will only be exercised when and if the holder finds such an exchange desirable.[1]

---

[1] We will later discuss the possibility of the corporation forcing conversion by exercising a call privilege.

Convertible bonds are typically subordinated debentures; this means that the claims of "senior" creditors must be settled in full before any payment will be made to holders of subordinated debentures in the event of insolvency or bankruptcy. Senior creditors typically include all other long-term debt issues and bank loans. Subordinated debentures do, of course, have a priority over common and preferred stock. Convertible preferred stocks are equity securities with a priority to dividend payments over common stock that offer the opportunity to share in corporate growth.

Although our discussion will consistently refer to convertible bonds, the comments and the approach to analysis of such securities is in general equally applicable to convertible preferred stocks.

## Who Issues Convertibles?

The issuers of convertible bonds are classified in Exhibit 15–1 in terms of broad groupings commonly used by bond analysts and the rating services such as Standard and Poor's Corporation. It is interesting to note that while utility issues account for a large portion of total bond issues outstanding in the United States, they chose to issue practically no convertibles during the late 1970s, and offered a relatively small proportion of new convertible issues in the 1980s. Industrial corporations have been the main issuers of convertible bonds.

New cash offerings of convertibles tend to be greater during periods of rising stock prices, such as in 1972, 1975–76, 1980–81, 1983, and 1985–87. For example, the rapid rise in common stock prices beginning in 1985 and peaking in October 1987 (before the sharp break in stock prices) fueled a sharp increase in the amount of convertibles issued. The right to share in future price rises for the common stock is likely to be most highly valued during a period of bullish expectations for common stocks, allowing corporations to issue conversion securities on favorable terms.

Convertible securities are often employed as deferred common stock financing. The issuing companies expect them to be converted in the future. For example, a smaller and more speculative firm may issue subordinated convertible debenture bonds. The company incurs less dilution in earnings per share both at issue and typically in the future, thus benefitting existing owners. This occurs because the conversion price of a convertible issue typically exceeds the issuing price that could be realized on a sale of common stock. Conversion can later be forced through call, assuming company success, thus allowing the issuer to sell common stock at a higher price than could have been realized through an immediate issue. This point is illustrated in the discussion of advantages and disadvantages of convertibles that follows. Moreover, cost is lowered while the convertible issue remains outstanding.

**EXHIBIT 15–1**
**Convertible Bond Issues 1972–88 (Billions of Dollars)**

| Issuing Classification | 1972 | 1975 | 1978 | 1980 | 1982 |
|---|---|---|---|---|---|
| Utility (including communications) | 0.1 | 0.0 | 0.0 | 0.2 | 0.5 |
| Industrial (including transportation) | 1.4 | 0.8 | 0.3 | 3.4 | 2.0 |
| Finance | 0.8 | 0.5 | 0.1 | 0.5 | 0.5 |
| Total convertible issues | 2.3 | 1.3 | 0.4 | 4.1 | 3.0 |
| Calls | −0.2 | −0.2 | −0.1 | −0.4 | −0.2 |
| Mergers. exch. bonds for stocks | | | | | +1.6 |
| Conversions | −1.8 | −0.8 | −0.5 | +0.6 | −1.3 |
| Net increase in convertibles | 0.3 | 0.3 | −0.2 | 4.3 | 3.1 |
| Net increase in coporate bonds | 18.9 | 34.0 | 34.0 | 39.3 | 53.8 |
| Convertible issues as a percent of increase in coporate issues based on: | | | | | |
|    Total convertible issues | 12.17% | 3.82% | 1.45% | 10.18% | 5.58% |
|    Net increase in convertibles | 1.59% | 0.88% | NM | 10.69% | 5.76% |

| Issuing Classification | 1983 | 1984 | 1985 | 1986 | 1987E | 1988P |
|---|---|---|---|---|---|---|
| Utility (including communications) | 0.8 | 0.2 | 1.4 | 0.1 | 0.4 | 0.6 |
| Industrial (including transportation) | 5.0 | 3.3 | 7.5 | 9.1 | 10.1 | 4.8 |
| Finance | 0.7 | 0.5 | 3.1 | 1.9 | 0.9 | 1.0 |
| Total convertible issues | 6.5 | 4.0 | 12.0 | 11.1 | 11.5 | 1.0 |
| | | | | | | 6.4 |
| Calls | −6.1 | −1.2 | −2.2 | −5.8 | −3.3 | −2.5 |
| Mergers exch. bonds for stocks | +0.6 | +1.4 | +0.4 | +0.9 | +0.5 | +0.3 |
| Conversions | −1.2 | −1.6 | −1.4 | −1.2 | −5.5 | −1.5 |
| Net increase in convertibles | −0.2 | 2.6 | 8.8 | 5.0 | 3.2 | 2.7 |
| Net increase in coporate bonds | 49.7 | 92.0 | 114.7 | 110.8 | 106.2 | 94.1 |
| Convertible issues as a percent of increase in coporate issues based on: | | | | | | |
|    Total convertible issues | 13.08% | 4.35% | 10.46% | 10.02% | 10.83% | 6.80% |
|    Net increase in convertibles | NM | 2.83% | 7.67% | 4.51% | 3.01% | 2.87% |

NM = Not meaningful

Source: 1982–1988 from Henry Kaufman, Jeffrey Hanna, and R. S. Salomon, Jr., *Prospects for Financial Markets in 1988* (New York: Salomon Brothers Inc., December, 1987). Earlier dates are from earlier issues.

## Advantages and Disadvantages to Issuing Firms

Convertible issues offer two basic potential advantages to the issuer. First, a lower interest cost is incurred and generally less restrictive covenants need be included in the indenture than for a nonconvertible bond issue. In other words, the investor pays for the privilege of speculating on future favorable price changes in the underlying common stock by accepting a lower interest return and a less restrictive debt agreement.

The required yield to sell a convertible relative to that of a nonconvertible issue varies over time and with the issuer. A nonconvertible issue might require a yield-to-maturity that could range from 50 basis points (one half of 1 percent) to 4 percent (or more) higher than that offered by a convertible issue.[2] Convertible bonds, moreover, are typically subordinated debt issues. The rating agencies, therefore, have usually rated convertible issues one class below that of a straight debenture issue.[3] This would suggest even higher relative interest-cost savings than suggested by the differentials noted above. The interest-cost savings to a firm will, of course, be highly related to market expectations for the common stock.

Second, a firm may be able to sell common stock at a better price through a convertible bond than by a direct issue. To illustrate, assume a firm is currently earning $5 a common share and that the common stock is selling at $50 per share. The firm believes it can utilize new capital effectively and that it would be preferable to raise equity rather than debt capital. The firm foresees, however, a potential fall in earnings per share if common stock is sold directly because it will take time to bring the new facilities, acquired with the funds raised, on stream. The market might well also fear potential dilution of earnings per share and might not be as optimistic as management about the future of the planned investments. For these reasons, the firm might have to sell new common stock at less than $50 a share. On the other hand, the firm might be able to sell a convertible bond issue at par that can be converted into 20 shares of the firm's common stock. The required interest rate might result in less dilution in earnings per share currently than would a direct stock issue, since the number of shares outstanding would not increase. Further assume that the bonds would be callable at 105 ($1,050 per bond).

If the new capital investments raised earnings per share to $6.50 two years hence, the price of the common stock in the market would increase to $65 a share, assuming that a price-earnings ratio of 10 continued to exist. The firm could then call the bonds, forcing conversion. The value of stock received in conversion is $1,300 ($65 per share times 20 shares), which is greater than the cash ($1,050) that would be received by allowing the issuer to call the stock. In effect, the firm sold stock for $50 a share, less issuance costs, through the convertible bonds. The firm, therefore, received a greater price per share than by a direct issue of common stock at that time, since the market price for a direct issue is expected to be lower and the issuance cost of a common issue is typically higher than for a convertible bond issue. The firm, in other words, would have

---

[2] For example, see Eugene F. Brigham, "An Analysis of Convertible Debentures Theory and Some Empirical Evidence," *Journal of Finance*, March 1966, pp. 35–54.

[3] George E. Pinches and Kent A. Mingo, "A Multivariate Analysis of Industrial Bond Ratings," *Journal of Finance*, March 1973, pp. 1–18.

to issue fewer common shares to raise a given amount by selling convertibles and forcing conversion than by directly selling common stock. Also, interest cost is lowered, sometimes substantially, by offering the conversion privilege.

Convertible securites do have possible disadvantages to the issuer. If the underlying common stock does increase markedly in price, the issuer might have been better off had the financing been postponed and a direct issue made. Moreover, if the price of the common stock drops after the issue of the convertible instrument, conversion cannot be forced and will not occur. The firm, therefore, cannot be sure it is raising equity capital when a convertible issue is made.

## Advantages to the Investor

An investor purchasing a convertible security supposedly receives the advantages of a senior security: the safety of principal in terms of a prior claim to assets over equity security holders and relative income stability at a known rate. Furthermore, if the common stock of the issuer rises in price, the convertible instrument will usually also rise to reflect the increased value of the underlying common stock. Upside potential can be realized through sale of the convertible bond, without conversion into the stock. On the other hand, if the price of the underlying common stock declines in the market, the bond can be expected to decline only to the point where it yields a satisfactory return on its value as a straight bond. A convertible offers the downside protection that bonds can offer during bad economic times, while allowing one to share in the upside potential for the common stock of a growing firm.

In terms of their yield, convertible bonds also typically offer higher current yield than do common stocks. If the dividend yield on the underlying common stock surpassed the current yield on the convertible bond, conversion would tend to be attractive.

Convertible bonds may have special appeal for financial institutions, notably commercial banks. Commercial banks are not permitted to purchase common stocks for their own account and, therefore, lose the possibility of capital gains through participation in corporate earnings growth. In 1957, approval was given for the purchase of eligible convertible issues by commercial banks if the yield obtained is reasonably similar to nonconvertible issues of similar quality and maturity and they are not selling at a significant conversion premium. Admittedly, commercial banks hold relatively few convertibles, and convertibles typically do sell at a conversion premium.

Convertible bonds have good marketability, as shown by active trading in large issues on the New York Exchange, whereas nonconvertible issues of similar quality are sometimes difficult to follow, since they are traded over the counter.

## Disadvantages to the Investor

The investor pays for the conversion privilege by accepting a significantly lower yield-to-maturity than that currently offered by nonconvertible bonds of equivalent quality. Also a call clause can lessen the potential attractiveness of a convertible bond because the firm may be able to force conversion into the common stock, as previously discussed. The possibility of forced conversion limits the speculative appeal.

If anticipated corporate growth is not realized, the purchaser will have sacrificed current yield and may well see the market value of the convertible instrument fall below the price paid to acquire it. A rise in the price of the underlying common stock is necessary to offset the yield sacrifice. For example, prices of convertible bonds rose to very high levels in 1965, but in 1966, when both stock and bond markets declined, many convertible issues declined even more than the stocks into which they were convertible. It appears a speculative premium was built into the price of convertibles in 1965, and the market no longer believed this premium was justified in 1966.

Investor risk can be markedly heightened by purchasing convertibles on margin. If interest rates rise after purchase, bondholders may receive margin calls, reflecting falling prices of convertible bonds, as happened during the 1966–70 period. Many bonds had to be sold, depressing the market further than purchasers had thought possible based on their estimate of a floor price at which the bonds would sell on a pure yield or straight investment basis.

## Analysis of Convertible Bonds

The following factors must be considered when evaluating convertible securities:

1. The appreciation in price of the common stock that is required before conversion could become attractive. This is measured by the *conversion premium ratio*.
2. The prospects for growth in the price of the underlying stock.
3. The downside potential in the event that the conversion privilege proves valueless.
4. The yield sacrifice required to purchase the convertible.
5. The income advantage offered through acquiring the convertible bond, rather than the number of common shares that would be obtained through conversion.
6. The quality of the security being offered.
7. The number of years over which the conversion premium paid to acquire the convertible will be recouped by means of the favorable income differential offered by the convertible relative to the underlying common stock. This is the *break-even time*.

The discussion that follows will concentrate on calculations typically used by analysts to evaluate points 1, 3, 4, 5, and 7. Valuation of convertibles will also be briefly discussed. The grading of bonds in terms of quality, both by the rating agencies and in terms of financial analysis, is discussed in Chapters 17 and 19. Assessing the prospects for growth in the price of the underlying common stock is the work of fundamental analysis. The techniques of fundamental analysis are reviewed in several well-accepted books.[4]

## Convertible Securities: An Illustrative Analysis

Exhibit 15–2 contrasts the 7% convertible debentures issued by Boise Cascade that mature in the year 2116 with the $3.625 convertible preferred stock issued by Inland Steel. Pertinent calculations contained in the exhibit are explained below.

A few basic definitions are in order before we begin to discuss Exhibit 15–2. The convertible security contract will either state a conversion ratio or a conversion price. A *conversion ratio* directly specifies the number of shares of the issuing firm's common stock that can be obtained by surrendering the convertible security. Alternatively, the conversion rate may be expressed in terms of a *conversion price*—the price paid per share to acquire the underlying common stock through conversion. The conversion ratio may then be determined by dividing the stated conversion price into the par value of the security:

$$\text{Conversion ratio} = \frac{\text{Par of security}}{\text{Conversion price}}$$

For example, if the conversion price were $20, a holder of such a bond would receive 50 shares of common stock in conversion, assuming a typical par value of $1,000 for the bond.

In some cases, the security contract may provide for changes in the conversion price over time. To illustrate. a conversion price of $20 might be specified for the first five years, $25 for the next five years, $30 for the next five years, and so on. This, of course, means that a holder of the instrument will be able to obtain fewer shares through conversion each time the conversion price increases. For example, 50 shares can be obtained when the conversion price is $20, but only 40 shares when the conversion price rises to $25. Such a provision forces investors to emphasize early conversion if they intend to convert, and the provision would be reasonable if corporate growth generally leads to a rising value for the common stock over time.

---

[4] For example, see John C. Ritchie, Jr., *Fundamental Analysis: A Back-to-the-Basics Investment Guide to Selective Quality Common Stocks* (Chicago, IL: Probus Publishing, 1989) or Frank K. Reilly, *Investment Analysis and Portfolio Management*, 3rd ed. (Chicago, IL: The Dryden Press), 1989, Chapters 9 and 12–15.

**EXHIBIT 15–2**

**Comparative Data For Two Convertible Securities Early May 1989**

| | Boise Cascade 7s 2016 | Inland Steel 3.625 Preferred |
|---|---|---|
| *Known Data* | | |
| Conversion ratio | 22.84 | 1.667 |
| Market price of convertible | $1095.00 | 65.00 |
| Market price of common stock | $45.63 | 38.75 |
| Dividend per share—common | $1.40 | 1.40 |
| Call price | $1049 | NCB |
| First call date | Immediately | 4/30/90 |
| Yield-to-maturity for equivalent quality nonconvertible[1] | 9.50% | 10.00% |
| *Calculated Data* | | |
| Market conversion price[2] | $47.94 | 38.99 |
| Conversion premium per share | $2.31 | .24 |
| Conversion premium ratio[3] | 5.06% | .62% |
| Current yield—convertible | 6.39% | 5.58% |
| Yield-to-Maturity—convertible | 6.20% | NM |
| Dividend yield—common | 3.07% | 3.61% |
| Yield sacrifice on convertible[4] | 3.30% | 4.42% |
| Income differential—total[5] | 38.02 | 1.29 |
| Income differential—per share | 1.66 | .77 |
| Break-even time | 1.39 years | .31 years |
| Estimated floor price[6] | $762.70 | $36.25 |

NCB = No call before

NM = Not meaningful

[1] The average yield-to-maturity for bonds or preferred stocks of companies of equivalent quality, coupled with the writer's judgment.

[2] Market price of the convertible instrument divided by the conversion ratio.

[3] The conversion premium per common share divided by the market price of the common stock.

[4] The yield-to-maturity offered by equivalent nonconvertible securities less the yield offered by the convertible security.

[5] The interest income paid by the converting instrument less the annual dividend income that would be received by converting into the underlying common shares. This figure expresses the income advantage in holding the convertible bond, rather than the equivalent number of shares of the underlying common stock.

[6] The price at which the convertible would have to sell to offer the yield currently being offered by nonconvertible securities of equivalent risk.

### Conversion Premium

The *market conversion price* of a convertible instrument represents the cost per share of the common stock if obtained through the convertible instrument, ignoring commissions. For example, the market conversion price of $47.94 calculated for the Boise Cascade convertible bond is obtained by dividing the market price of the convertible bond ($1095) by the number of common shares that could be obtained by converting that bond (22.84 shares). Since the market conversion price per common share is higher than the current market price of a common share, the bond is selling at a *conversion premium*, represented by the excess cost per share to obtain the common stock through conversion.

The *conversion premium ratio* shows the percentage increase necessary to reach a *parity price* relationship between the underlying common stock and the convertible instrument. *Conversion parity* is that price relationship between the convertible instrument and the common stock at which neither a profit nor a loss would be realized by purchasing the convertible, converting it, and selling the common shares that were received in conversion, ignoring commissions. At conversion parity, the following conditions would exist:

$$\frac{\text{Par of security}}{\text{Conversion price}} = \frac{\text{Market price of the convertible}}{\text{Market price of the common}}$$

When the price of the common stock exceeds its conversion parity price, one could feel certain that the convertible security would fluctuate directly with changes in the market price of the underlying common stock. In other words, gains in value of the underlying common stock should then be able to be realized by the sale of the convertible instrument, rather than conversion and sale of the stock itself. The market conversion price, incidentally, is the parity price for a share of common stock obtainable through the convertible instrument.

At the time of this comparative analysis, both instruments sold at a premium, but the premium on the Boise Cascade convertible bonds was substantially greater in both relative and absolute terms. If one assumes that the appreciation potentials of the common stocks of both companies were equal (a feeling the market appeared not to hold), the Inland Steel Preferred had a substantial advantage. An increase of only 0.62 percent in the common stock of Inland Steel was needed to ensure that further increases in the underlying common would be reflected in the price of the convertible instrument. Boise Cascade common stock, however, would have to rise 5.06 percent before the conversion had an ensured value.

There is usually, although not always, some conversion premium present on convertible instruments, which reflects the anticipation of a possible increase in the price of the underlying common stock beyond the parity price. Professional arbitrageurs are constantly looking for situations in which the stock can be obtained more cheaply (allowing for commissions) by buying the convertible instrument than through direct purchase in the market. For example, assume that a bond is convertible into 20 shares and can be purchased for $1,000. If the common stock was currently selling at $55 a share, an arbitrageur would buy the convertible and simultaneously short sell the common stock. The arbitrageur would realize a gross profit (before transaction costs) of $100 calculated as follows:

| | |
|---|---|
| Short sale of 20 shares at $55/share | $1,100 |
| Less purchase cost of bond | 1,000 |
| | $ 100 |

The demand by arbitrageurs for the convertible would continue until the resultant rise in price of the convertible no longer made such actions profitable.

### Yield Sacrifice

At the time of this analysis, nonconvertible bonds of equivalent quality to the convertible issued by Boise Cascade offered a yield of 9.50 percent, or 330 basis points higher than the yield-to-maturity offered by the convertible. The yield sacrifice would have to be overcome by a rise in the price of the underlying common stock, or the investor would have been better off to purchase the nonconvertible instrument. The yield sacrifice required by the Inland Steel preferred was significantly higher than that for the Boise Cascade bonds, thereby requiring more appreciation potential for its common stock during the holding period to make the convertible attractive. Although the Boise Cascade instrument offered an advantage in terms of the lower yield sacrifice required, this could have been offset by a more attractive price appreciation potential for the common stock of Weyerhaeuser, if that was in fact the case.

### Downside Risk Potential

The floor price for a convertible is estimated as that value at which the instrument would sell in the market to offer the yield of an equivalent nonconvertible instrument. Boise Cascade bonds were rated AA by Standard and Poor's Corporation at the time of this analysis, and the average yield paid by AA bonds was used as the required market yield to represent the yield on a nonconvertible bond if issued by Boise Cascade. An Atlantic Richfield nonconvertible preferred, felt to be of equivalent quality to the Inland Steel issue, yielded 10 percent.

The floor price of the Inland Steel convertible was calculated, therefore, by dividing the annual dividend ($3.625) by 10 percent. Present-value calculations were used to determine the price ($762.70) at which the Boise Cascade Corporation bond would have to sell to yield 9.5 percent to maturity.

The analysis suggests a 9.5 greater downside risk for Inland Steel Corporation convertible bonds than for the Boise Cascade convertible.

One should not place too much emphasis on the estimated floor prices, however. The calculations assume that current-yield levels will continue, and this may well not be correct. On the one hand, if yields rise to even higher levels and the conversion privilege proves worthless, the price of the bonds could fall below the estimated floor price. On the other hand, if yield levels fall, the loss will not be as great as suggested. More importantly, one should not be purchasing convertibles (remember the yield sacrifice) unless one believes the probability is relatively high that the market price of the underlying common will rise and eventually exceed the parity price for that common stock.

### Break-Even Time

Break-even time represents the number of years it will take for the favorable income differential over the common stock offered by the convertible instrument to equal the total dollar conversion premium paid to acquire that convertible instrument. For example, the break-even time for the Boise Cascade bonds is 1.39 years, calculated as follows:

| | |
|---|---:|
| Interest paid on each $1,000 bond at 7 percent | $70.00 |
| Dividend income offered by 22.84 shares into which each bond is convertible (22.84 shares × 1.40/share) | 31.98 |
| Favorable bond income differential | 38.02 |
| Favorable income differential per common share (38.02 ÷ 22.84 shares) | $ 1.66 |
| Break-even time equals the conversion premium per share divided by the favorable income differential per share (2.31/1.66) | 1.39 years |

Professional investors in convertible bonds consider break-even times of three years or less as desirable and question longer payback times. Break-even times up to five years, calculated by the method illustrated above, can be acceptable where justified by strong expectations for favorable growth in the underlying common and a favorable yield differential while holding the convertible. Both convertible instruments offer a highly favorable break-even time.

Of course, the decision to buy a convertible cannot be based solely on break-even time. The prospects for the common, the conversion premium, and call and other risks must also be considered.

## Dilution of the Conversion Privilege

A large common stock split or stock dividend could markedly dilute the value of the conversion privilege, unless adjustment of the number of shares received in conversion is made. For example, assume that a bond is convertible into 20 shares and that the company undergoes a two-for-one stock split. Recognizing this, the conversion privilege is typically protected by terms in the bond indenture providing for a pro rata adjustment of the conversion price and/or the conversion ratio so that the exchange ratio would increase to 40 shares after the stock split.

## Valuation of Convertibles

An investor in a convertible security owns a fixed income security and a call option on the firm's common stock. In essence, the investor is promised a contractually stated stream of future cash payments for a variable and uncertain claim on earnings and the residual value of the firm.

A bond value that establishes a lower boundary, or floor, to the price of a convertible can be calculated by determining the present value of the future cash-flow stream offered by the convertible instrument. For example, consider a 4 percent coupon, $1000 per bond maturing in 5 years and paying interest semiannually. If current conditions require a yield of 6 percent for instruments of equivalent risk, the bond value can be calculated as follows:

$$\text{Bond value} = \sum_{t=1}^{10} \frac{20}{(1 + .03)^t} + \frac{1000}{(1 + .03)^{10}} = \$914.70$$

Since interest is paid semiannually, the cash flows are discounted at one-half the annual rate and the number of payment periods are doubled.[5] This is the floor price previously discussed. Admittedly, the floor value could change over time as interest rates change. A convertible, however, will never sell for less than its conversion value, measured as the number of shares that would be received in conversion times the current market price of the common stock. The conversion value of the Boise Cascade bond was, accordingly, $1042.19 (45.63 × 22.84). This conversion value will rise as the value of the common stock rises, as shown by the line representing conversion value in Exhibit 15–3.

There are, therefore, two lower bounds to the price of any convertible bond: (1) the instrument's bond value and (2) its conversion value. The heavy line in the figure shows the combined effect of these two lower boundaries. The conversion value will exceed the bond value when the firm is doing well and the value of the underlying stock exceeds the value as a straight bond. However, the straight bond value will be the lower boundary when it exceeds the value of the stock received in conversion. When the firm is doing poorly, the straight bond value becomes the lower boundary for valuation purposes.

Since convertible security holders can wait and benefit from hindsight rather than make an immediate decision on conversion, a convertible will always have a higher market value than its lower boundary, except when the instrument is maturing or the market is convinced the firm has no future. The actual selling price of the convertible can, therefore, be represented by a line like the dashed line in Exhibit 15–3. The difference between the lower boundary and the dashed line is the value of the call option on the firm.

---

[5] For detailed illustration of the calculations involved, see Chapter 6.

**EXHIBIT 15–3**

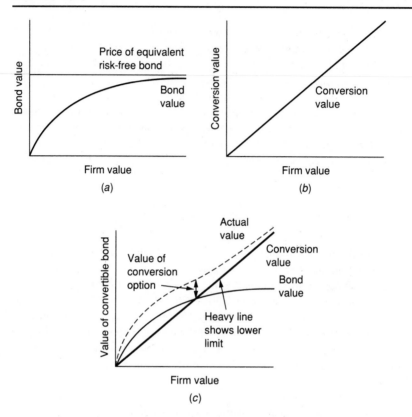

Source: Richard A. Brealey and Stewart C. Myers, *Principles of Corporate Finance* (New York: McGraw-Hill Book Company, 1988), p. 529.

The Black-Scholes option valuation framework might be used for a quick approximation of the convertibles noncallable warrant value.[6]   Unfortunately, this approach entails a number of unrealistically simple assumptions regarding dividend policy, the stock's volatility, and the possibility of call. A straight-forward model, known as the binomial model, has been developed, which copes with the callability issue and generates a tree of future stock prices that can be used to estimate the value of the call.[7]

---

[6] Luke Knecht and Mike McCowin, "Valuing Convertibles Securities," in Frank J. Fabozzi, ed., *Advances and Innovations in the Bond and Mortgage Markets*, (Chicago, Il.: Probus Publishing, 1989), pp. 107–108.

[7] J. Cox, S. Ross, and M. Rubinstein, "Option Pricing: A Simplified Approach," *Journal of Financial Economics*, September 1979, pp. 229–263.

Four basic generalizations concerning the value of convertibles are:

1. The more volatile the underlying stock, the greater the warrant or option value will be.
2. The value of holding your equity exposure in warrant form and keeping the bulk of your funds invested (e.g., Treasury bills) increases as interest rates rise and decreases as interest rates fall. This has a direct influence on option and warrant valuation.
3. Convertibles with greater call protection (i.e., longer options) are worth more than equivalent securities with less call protection. Time value is a powerful component of an option's value.
4. The greater the disparity between the dividend rate on the underlying common stock and the convertible, the greater the current value will be.[8]

## When Should a Convertible Be Converted or Sold?

If the prospects for favorable growth in the underlying common stock or the relative prices and yields of the convertible security and the common stock change significantly, a sale or conversion may be suggested. For example, the dividend obtainable by converting into the common stock of AT&T from the $4 convertible preferred rose to $4.20 a share during 1977. A conversion was then desirable, assuming the investor still wished to retain a claim on the further potential growth of AT&T, since current yield would be increased through conversion by 20 cents per share.

## SUMMARY OF CONVERTIBLES

Some fixed income securities are convertible into common stock, offering the basic advantages of a senior security (bond or preferred stock) while allowing the holder to participate in potential corporate growth. The investor pays for the conversion privilege by accepting a significantly lower yield than could be obtained by purchasing nonconvertible bonds or preferred stocks. A convertible, moreover, usually sells at a premium over the value of the underlying common stock. If the anticipated growth in the value of the common stock is not realized, the purchaser will have sacrificed yield and may well also see the value of the convertible instrument fall sharply.

There are three distinct areas of analysis that should be undertaken when evaluating a convertible security:

---

[8]Luke Knecht and Mike McCowin, pp. 108–109. These generalizations follow from the basic principles of option theory.

1. The quality of the security should be assessed in the same way as for other nonconvertible senior securities. This requires assessing the ability of the issuing company to meet the fixed charges mandated by the issue under reasonably conceivable adverse economic circumstances.
2. The growth potential for the underlying common stock must be evaluated, since that growth potential offers the basis for generating the added yield necessary to offset the yield sacrifice incurred at the time of purchase and provides a return that makes purchase attractive.
3. Special calculations developed in the illustrative analysis in this chapter should be used to assess the relative attractiveness of the many convertible securities available in the market.

Conversion should be considered when the annual total dividends that would be received from the common shares obtained through conversion exceed the annual coupon payments offered by the convertible bond. Sale of the convertible security should also be considered when the price of that security exceeds the estimated value of the underlying stock into which it is convertible and/or the prospects for favorable growth in the underlying common stock deteriorate.

## COMMON STOCK WARRANTS

A warrant is usually a long-term option, at least when issued, that conveys to the holder the privilege of buying a specified number of shares of the underlying common stock at a specified exercise price at any time on or before an expiration date. The typical warrant originates by attachment to a bond or preferred stock issue, with the intent to lower the cost of capital for the issuing firm and/or make an issue more attractive to investors, thereby improving its marketability. Warrants may also be added to make possible the sale of a marginal-quality issue. In addition, warrants may be issued to corporate employees under a bonus plan or could even be offered as security for a direct sale.

A warrant that is attached to a bond or preferred stock can only be exercised by the holder of that financial instrument. Such warrants, however, may typically be detached as of a particular date and subsequently traded on their own merits. A number of warrants are now listed by the New York Stock Exchange, and trading in warrants can be expected to increase in volume in the years ahead.[9]

---

[9] The first warrant to be listed on the NYSE was an AT&T warrant that expired April 1975. Other warrants have since been listed. Most existing warrants, however, trade over the counter or are listed on the American or Pacific Coast Stock Exchanges.

## Warrants and Stock Rights Distinguished

Stock purchase rights are created by corporations that issue them to existing common stockholders when making a privileged subscription offering. Stock rights typically allow subscription to new shares on a pro rata basis at a price below the current market price for the common stock, and warrants at the time of issue offer the holder the option to buy the common stock at a price substantially *above* the current market price. Warrants, however, have a long life, often exceeding five years, and stock rights usually have a life of one month or less.

The value of a warrant is usually defined in terms of the probabilities that the future price of the common stock will exceed the exercise price. The value of stock rights, on the other hand, is measured in terms of the dollar savings per right that can be realized by purchasing the common stock at the preferential price, which is below the current market price.

## Warrants and Call Options Distinguished

A call option gives the buyer the right to purchase the underlying common stock from the option seller at a fixed price within a given period. Therefore, it is similar to a warrant. Call options also trade independently from the common stock, as do warrants.

However, call options are written by investors, who will purchase and deliver already outstanding shares of common stock if the option is exercised. Warrants, on the other hand, are issued by business corporations, and the corporation utilizes the instrument as a means of selling a new issue and thereby raising additional capital. Also, warrants may well have a life of many years, but a call option typically expires within nine months. Finally, warrants are often attached to bonds (or other financial instruments) to make them more attractive when being initially sold.

## Leverage and Minimum Values

The price of a warrant is usually quite small in comparison with the current market price of the common stock of the issuer. A given percentage increase in the common stock's price, therefore, may have a magnified percentage effect on the price of the warrant.

For example, assume that the common stock of company X is now selling for $50 a share, and an investor expects the price to rise to $100 a share within a few years. Further assume that a warrant giving the holder the right to buy a share of common stock of company X for $65 a share at any time during the next 10 years is outstanding. A warrant currently sells for $10.

An investor who bought the common stock at $50 a share would realize a 100 percent gain (ignoring commissions) plus any dividend income received if the stock rose to $100 in a year. The *minimum value of the warrant* when the stock rises to $100, however, is about $35 ($100−$65), the saving that can be realized by acquiring the stock through exercise of the warrant rather than by direct purchase. If it were much less than this, arbitrageurs would buy the warrant and short sell the stock to take advantage of the ensured gain, thereby forcing the price of the warrant to the minimum value.[10] An investor who had bought a warrant at $10 and sold it at $35 would have realized a gain of 250 percent, substantially exceeding the gain offered by direct purchase of the common stock. Actually, the warrant is likely to be selling for more than $35 when the stock reaches $100 per share because of the speculative enthusiasm such a price would tend to generate.

But the value of the warrant may fall sharply, even to zero, if the common stock does not rise in value. Notice that, at any price below $65 a share for the common stock, the warrant has no ensured minimum value. Suppose the price of the common stock merely stayed at $50 a share, and reduced expectations for future growth in the market reduced the price of a warrant to $5. An investor in the warrants would have lost 50 percent of his or her capital, but an investor in the stock would have no potential current loss and would receive any dividend income paid by the corporation. Furthermore, if the stock does not rise above $65 a share before expiration, the warrant will be worth $0.

Like any leveraged situation, the potential return is increased by purchasing warrants, but risk is also increased.

## Valuation Models for Warrants

The financial literature suggests that, like convertible bonds, the Black-Scholes option pricing model[11] could be used to estimate the value for a warrant that has no unusual features and where the common stock does not pay a dividend. Many stocks do, however, pay dividends and the current holder does not receive those dividends while holding the warrant. In effect, a warrant holder loses when a cash dividend is paid to common stockholders, since payment of that dividend lowers the value of the firm. A warrant holder must recognize that a higher return might be realized by exercising the warrant and becoming a stockholder entitled to dividends rather than by continuing to hold the warrant. Early exercise would only be attractive, however, where the dividend payment is larger than the interest that can be earned by investing the exercise price.

---

[10] In the event a warrant entitles the holder to purchase more or less than one share, the formula for calculating the minimum value is $N(MP − EP)$, where $N$ is the number of shares that can be purchased through exercise of the warrant, MP is the market price of a share of common stock, and EP is the exercise price, or price at which a share of the common stock can be acquired through the warrant.

[11] Fischer Black and Myron Scholes, "The Pricing of Options and Corporate Liabilities," *Journal of Political Economy*, May/June 1973, pp. 637–659.

As with convertibles, a binomial model of development, which is beyond the scope of this chapter, can be used to estimate the value of the warrant.[12] This model does cope with the dividend problem. Dilution can also be a complicating factor.[13]

## Warrant Premiums

Warrants tend to sell at a premium over a minimum value, reflecting expectations of future increases in the price of the common stock and the leverage potential. The speculative leverage possibilities diminish, however, as the price of the underlying stock rises relative to the exercise price of the warrant and/or as the warrant approaches expiration. This is because the expectation of further substantial gains in the price of the common stock is likely to become less probable in terms of market expectations, leading to lower leverage potential that may not seem worthwhile when one realizes that direct purchase of the common stock would generate dividend income that will not be realized through purchase of the warrant.

The factors affecting the size of the warrant premium have been explored in the financial literature and are briefly summarized below:

1. The most important factor, of course, is the market's expectations regarding the future price of the underlying common stock. The greater the growth expectations, the larger the premium will be, other things being equal.
2. The longer the warrant has to go before reaching the expiration date, the higher the premium is likely to be. Once the life of a warrant exceeds five years, however, it has less chance of further increasing the premium paid.
3. A higher dividend yield offered by the underlying common stock will tend to lower the premium paid, since the sacrificed dividend yield makes purchase of the warrant less attractive.
4. Empirical studies suggest that warrants trading on organized exchanges tend to have higher premiums than those trading over the counter. For similar reasons, the warrants of small companies or those of companies whose stocks are inactively traded tend to have smaller premiums.
5. As the expiration date of the warrant nears, the premium tends to shrink, and the price of the warrant approaches minimum value or zero, whichever is the lower boundary.

---

[12] For the development of and an illustrated use of the model, see Richard A. Brealey and Stewart C. Myers, *Principles of Corporate Finance* (New York: McGraw-Hill Book Company, 1988), Chapter 21.

[13] Brealey and Myers also suggest and illustrate a method for handling this problem on pages 523–527 of their text referred to in footnote 12.

## SUMMARY OF WARRANTS

The purchase of a warrant, essentially a means of obtaining a call on a common stock, offers attractive leverage possibilities. A warrant typically sells at a premium over the value represented by acquiring the common stock through exercise. If the expected appreciation is not realized on the common stock, an investor in warrants may lose a greater percentage of the capital invested than would have been lost by direct investment in the common stock. On the other hand, investment in warrants may produce a greater percentage gain on the capital committed, when the stock does increase in value, than could have been realized by direct investment in the underlying common stock.

# CHAPTER 16

# NONCONVERTIBLE PREFERRED STOCK

Richard S. Wilson
*Managing Director*
*Research Products and Services*
*Fitch Investors Service, Inc.*

This chapter reviews fixed-rate and variable-rate nonconvertible preferred stock. Preferred stock that is convertible into common shares is discussed in Chapter 15.

## THE ESSENTIAL NATURE OF PREFERRED STOCKS

Preferred stock is a class of stock that entitles the holder to certain preferences over the common stock of the issuer. It is an equity-type security and not a debt instrument. These preferred equity instruments can be traced back to the mid-16th century in England and to before 1850 in the United States. However, they first came into prominence in the 1890s during the formation of the giant trusts and industrial combinations. At first, preferences concerned dividend rights, but later other provisions were added giving the shares additional features and priorities over the common equity. Preferred shares have some of the characteristics of debt securities (although ranking below debt in the capital structure of a corporation) including priority over common shares in liquidation of the issuer. For the sake of convenience, the term *preferred* will refer to all classes of senior equity securities unless specifically noted.

**319**

## PROFILE OF THE PREFERRED STOCK MARKET

Fixed-dividend, adjustable-rate, and auction market and remarketed preferreds are the three main types of nonconvertible preferred stocks. More will be said later about the specifics of these issues; we will review in this space the size and makeup of the public nonconvertible preferred market.

### Issue Types and Issuers

One of the major structural changes in the preferred stock market over the last 10 years is characterized by the trend away from fixed-rate dividends toward variable-rate dividends. Although the total volume of nonconvertible preferred stock issuance in the public markets is greater than a decade ago, the growth has come in variable-rate issues, not the conventional preferreds. Before 1982, the only dividend a public preferred had was fixed-rate, i.e., the same dividend applied throughout the life of the issue. In May of that year, Chemical Bank issued the first adjustable-rate preferred stock (ARPS) in the public market. The private market had a few variable-rate issues such as AMAX Inc.'s LIBOR-based stock issued in 1978 and Citibank and Chemical New York Corporation's three-year adjustable-rate shares.

The market's romance with adjustable-rate preferreds did not last long as a better, less volatile mousetrap was invented. Two years later, in 1984, Dutch auction market preferreds appeared. The next year, ARPS issuance started its descent and auction market and remarketed preferreds became the new hot items. So while before 1982 the public market was 100 percent fixed-dividend issues, in 1982 only 45 percent of the volume was conventional preferreds. In 1984, less than 13 percent of the dollar volume was in fixed-rate shares, and in 1986 only 26 percent. In 1988, straight-dividend preferreds accounted for less than 16 percent of total issuance. Exhibit 16–1 shows the new issue nonconvertible preferred stock financing volume by type of issue for 1982 through 1988.

The second major structural change of the 1980s has been the shift in the industrial classification of the issuers. Historically, utility companies have been the largest issuers of preferred stock. Prior to 1982, electric, gas, water, and telephone companies accounted for well over half of any one year's volume, and, in some cases, nearly all. However, in 1982 the pattern changed as less than 44 percent of the dollar volume came from utility issuers. Due to the lower financing needs of utilities, issuance fell off on an absolute and relative basis. In 1985, utility preferred stock issuance amounted to $655 million, or only 10 percent out of some $6.5 billion of preferred offerings. In 1987, utility volume was 29 percent of the total, and in 1988 only 10.8 percent.

Of the more than $45 billion raised in the nonconvertible public preferred market during the 1982 to 1988 period, some 59 percent was from financially oriented companies—banks, thrifts, finance, and insurance companies. A num-

**EXHIBIT 16–1**
**Preferred Stock Financing Volume by Issuer Type, 1982–1988**

| Type of Issue | Total ($ Million) (# of issues) | 1988 | 1987 | 1986 | 1985 | 1984 | 1983 | 1982 |
|---|---|---|---|---|---|---|---|---|
| Fixed dividend | $11,726.47 | $1,122.50 | $2,896.50 | $2,259.63 | $1,066.60 | $463.00 | $1,609.50 | $2,308.74 |
| # of issues | 199 | 18 | 41 | 36 | 10 | 11 | 33 | 50 |
| Adjustable-rate | $13,354.90 | $457.46 | $991.06 | $513.00 | $1,561.34 | $2,632.89 | $4,375.94 | $2,823.21 |
| # of issues | 147 | 5 | 8 | 10 | 19 | 33 | 48 | 24 |
| Auction market | $16,761.50 | $3,510.50 | $3,344.50 | $5,559.50 | $3,797.00 | $550.00 | -- | -- |
| # of issues | 236 | 58 | 48 | 69 | 54 | 7 | -- | -- |
| Remarketed | $3,345.00 | $2,010.00 | $990.00 | $220.00 | $125.00 | -- | -- | -- |
| # of issues | 40 | 19 | 15 | 4 | 2 | -- | -- | -- |
| Total volume | $45,187.87 | $7,100.46 | $8,222.06 | $8,552.13 | $6,549.94 | $3,645.89 | $5,985.44 | $5,131.95 |
| Total Issues | 622 | 100 | 112 | 119 | 85 | 51 | 81 | 74 |

ber of these were structured, asset-related transactions of special purpose, bulletproof, bankruptcy remote issuer subsidiaries of thrift institutions. This type of issuer is new to the 1980s. In that seven-year period, utilities accounted for 22.6 percent, and industrial companies a little less than 13 percent. Exhibit 16–2 shows the financing volume by industry type in the 1982 to 1988 period.

At the beginning of 1989, the public nonconvertible preferred stock market consisted, in round numbers, of some 1,000 fixed-dividend issues with a par or stated value of $29 billion. There were about 130 adjustable-rate preferred stock issues with a par or stated value of $11 billion, and 240 or so variable-rate issues with close to $17 billion outstanding. In total, the preferred market approximated 1,370 issues with a par value of close to $57 billion. In comparison, the Federal Reserve System reported that the amount of U.S. corporate bonds outstanding at the end of 1988 was $1.3 trillion. U.S. Treasury debt outstanding was $2.1 trillion. Thus, the preferred market is only a mole hill compared with other financial sectors of the economy.

## PREFERRED STOCK RATINGS

A preferred stock rating is an indicator or assessment of the issuer's ability to meet the terms of the issue including dividend payments and sinking-fund requirements, if any, in accordance with the appropriate legal document authorizing such shares. These documents include the certificate of incorporation, the certificate of designation, or the charter, among others. At the end of 1989, preferred stock ratings were issued by five nationally recognized statistical rating organizations (NRSROs). The five NRSROs are Duff & Phelps, Inc., Fitch Investors Service, Inc., McCarthy, Crisanti & Maffei, Inc., Moody's Investors Service, Inc., and Standard & Poor's Corporation. These are agencies whose ratings are generally accepted by the vast majority of investment professionals and by regulatory authorities.

Rating agencies help to bridge the gap between issuers and investors by issuing credit rating opinions. Because of their independent and unbiased nature, ratings are used by market participants as a factor in the valuation of securities. Investors should be cautioned that while some agencies' preferred stock ratings may have symbols similar to their debt rating symbols, preferred ratings should be viewed within the universe of preferred equity, separate and distinct from debt.

Ratings are defined by these firms in their various publications. Investors are urged to read these definitions. It should be remembered they are not "buy," "hold," or "sell" indicators. They do not state whether or not an issue is "cheap" or "dear" among the multitude of preferred issues. They do not point to the direction of the market. Although only a guide to the issuer's ability and willingness to meet the terms of the issue, they are a most important factor in the preferred stock investment decision.

**EXHIBIT 16–2**
**Preferred Stock Financing Volume by Industry Type, 1982–1988**

| Industry Type | Total ($ Million) (# of issues) | 1988 | 1987 | 1986 | 1985 | 1984 | 1983 | 1982 |
|---|---|---|---|---|---|---|---|---|
| Banks | $10,736.17 | $872.46 | $1,721.06 | $1,732.50 | $1,588.84 | $727.36 | $2,246.95 | $1,847.00 |
| # of issues | 114 | 7 | 20 | 18 | 20 | 10 | 23 | 16 |
| Financial | $4,293.25 | $1,975.50 | $1,076.50 | $315.00 | $150.00 | $225.00 | $551.25 | - - |
| # of issues | 59 | 27 | 16 | 5 | 2 | 3 | 6 | - - |
| Savings & loan | $8,876.23 | $1,135.00 | $1,985.00 | $3,290.00 | $1,334.50 | $997.70 | $134.03 | - - |
| # of issues | 113 | 14 | 23 | 45 | 19 | 11 | 1 | - - |
| Insurance | $2,775.21 | $17.00 | $206.50 | $380.00 | $1,185.50 | $235.00 | $200.00 | $551.21 |
| # of issues | 29 | 1 | 3 | 5 | 13 | 2 | 2 | 3 |
| Electric/gas | $10,222.34 | $763.50 | $2,063.00 | $1,649.60 | $655.00 | $874.25 | $2,003.25 | $2,213.74 |
| # of issues | 206 | 16 | 37 | 32 | 13 | 18 | 42 | 48 |
| Telecommunications | $520.04 | - - | $345.00 | - - | - - | $145.04 | - - | $30.00 |
| # of issues | 9 | - - | 5 | - - | - - | 3 | - - | 1 |
| Industrial | $5,835.69 | $1,005.00 | $675.00 | $1,185.03 | $1,636.10 | $441.54 | $493.02 | $400.00 |
| # of issues | 68 | 15 | 6 | 14 | 18 | 4 | 6 | 5 |
| Transportation | $596.94 | - - | $150.00 | - - | - - | - - | $356.94 | $90.00 |
| # of issues | 4 | - - | 2 | - - | - - | - - | 1 | 1 |
| Mutual funds | $1,332.00 | $1,332.00 | - - | - - | - - | - - | - - | - - |
| # of issues | 20 | 20 | - - | - - | - - | - - | - - | - - |
| Total | $45,187.87 | $7,100.46 | $8,222.06 | $8,552.13 | $6,549.94 | $3,645.89 | $5,985.44 | $5,131.95 |
| # of issues | 622 | 100 | 112 | 119 | 85 | 51 | 81 | 74 |

## THE TERMS OF THE BARGAIN WITH INVESTORS

The agreement or authorizing document between a corporate issuer and the preferred shareowners has numerous provisions governing the rights and duties of the two parties. Similar to a bond indenture, the preferred stock document sets forth the terms and dividend preferences, redemption and sinking-fund provisions, and rights in liquidation, among other things.

### Preferred Stock Terms and Features

The chief difference between preferred and common stock lies with the treatment of dividends. Preferred stock dividends either are fixed-rate or variable-rate. As mentioned before, the total public preferred market is now about evenly divided between fixed-rate and variable-rate issues. Fixed-rate preferred stock is entitled to dividends at a predetermined rate based on the par value, stated value, or fixed dollar amount per share annually before any dividend can be paid on the issuer's common stock. For example, such dividend may be stated as $2.50 per share ($25.00 par or stated value) or 10.00 percent based on some predetermined value. In the latter case, if the par value were $25.00 the annual dividend would amount to $2.50 per share; if the par value were $50.00 per share, the annual dividend would be $5.00, and if the par value were $100.00 per share then the annual dividend would be $10.00. Dividends on fixed-rate shares are normally paid quarterly although there are a few issues with semiannual dividend payments. The amount of the dividend on straight preferred stock is ordinarily limited to that fixed amount or rate of dividend stated in the description of the issue. It is as though the preferred stockholders say to the common stockholders, "Let us have dividends up to the stipulated amount per share before you receive dividends, and, regardless of whether you receive them, we will agree that our dividends shall be limited to the stipulated amount per share. You common shareholders can have dividends in an amount only limited by the financial ability of the company to pay them."

Most fixed-rate shares pay their dividends in cash. However, a feature of the speculative 1980s is the appearance of preferreds paying dividends in kind. They are known as *PIKs*. This printing press paper dividend is a device used by weak companies to conserve their limited cash resources to pay higher ranked security holders. Although some advocates say that PIKs resemble compounding instruments—shares issued on shares—compounding can work in reverse. After all, if the issuer doesn't succeed, the investor will take a greater loss without having received any cash. True, the PIK dividends can be sold, but this is certainly not the same as a cash dividend. Taxable investors also have to pay income taxes on these paper dividends. If the issuer succeeds, the shares get called and the promoters get the gravy. Also the number of shares received as dividends is calculated on the par or stated value, not the market value of the preferred. If the preferred shares decline in price, the dividend will be worth less. If this were a cash dividend-paying security and the market for the shares declined, an investor, having confidence in the outlook for the company, would at least be able to reinvest the dividends at the reduced market price for a greater number of shares. In the opinion of many observers, investors in speculative-grade securities would do better receiving a cash return, not funny money.

In contrast to fixed-dividend preferreds, there are adjustable-rate preferred stocks (ARPS). In general, these issues have dividends that are adjusted or reset quarterly at a fixed spread (dividend reset spread) above, at, or below the highest of three points on the Treasury yield curve. These benchmark rates are (1) the per annum market discount rate for three-month Treasury bills, (2) the 10-year Treasury constant maturity, and (3) the 20-year or 30-year Treasury constant maturity (TCM), as the case may be. The Treasury constant maturity yields are calculated by the Federal Reserve and relate the yield on a government bond to its maturity. This dividend-setting structure has an advantage as it is not tied to either a short-term or long-term rate. A fixing based on only one rate could prove to be a disadvantage when the shape or slope of the yield curve changes. Most of the dividends are subject to minimum levels called *collars*. The maximum rate is the cap and the minimum rate is the floor.

ARPS are neither money market instruments nor substitutes for short-dated securities. They possess more of the characteristics of equities than of debt. They do not enjoy the "magical drawing power," or "magnetism," of an approaching maturity as is the case with floating-rate debt. Preferred stock investors needing an investment in a money market type of equity are advised to turn to remarketed preferred stock or auction market preferred, described below.

Some market participants might be under the impression that ARPS should trade around the par level at the dividend adjustment date, no matter what the direction of interest rates is. However, it should be remembered that the dividend determination spreads were set in place when the shares were first issued. Interest-rate levels, the creditworthiness of the issuer, and/or the tax laws could change with the result that investors may demand a different relationship to the base rate. Securities do not trade in a vacuum but in the marketplace, which constantly scrutinizes relative values. Values are placed on securities, taking into account many factors including the terms of the particular issue, other alternative investments, market conditions, and investors' perceptions of quality and liquidity, among others.

Auction preferred stock (*APS*), an offshoot of adjustable-rate preferred stock, was first publicly issued in 1984, when the American Express Company offered $150 million of Money Market Preferred Stock (*MMP*). This evolution in the preferred market was warmly received by market participants. From 1984 through 1988, slightly more than 59 percent of the preferred new issue volume was comprised of auction preferred stock and its cousin, remarketed preferred stock. Investment bankers have given proprietary names and acronyms to the many issue varieties. The instrument is designed for corporate cash managers seeking tax-advantaged money market type income. Most of the shares or units of trading are priced at $100,000. A few issues even have shares with stated values as high as $500,000 or even $1 million each. The dividends, most of which are payable every seven weeks (there are some exceptions) and determined by auction bids from current holders and potential buyers, are reflective of current money market conditions (both taxable and tax-exempt) and perceived credit risks.

In addition to auction preferred shares, there are remarketed preferred stocks (*RP*) which have the dividend rate determined by a remarketing agent. The dividend is set at a rate designed to enable the agent to remarket all of the tendered shares at the original offering price. The remarketed preferred offers the holder the choice of dividend resets and payments every seven days or every 49 days. In some cases, other dividend periods may also be offered. The portfolio manager of "temporarily" idle corporate funds should find these auction and remarketed issues attractive alternatives to money market debt instruments including short-term tax-exempts and other types of preferred stocks.

The more frequent dividend-setting mechanism of APS and RP shares, plus the fact that the rate is determined through an auction or remarketing process as opposed to being fixed at a predetermined spread from a base rate as is the case with adjustable-rate preferreds, allows the dividends (subject to certain minimum and maximum rates) to be based on the current credit standing and perceptions of the issuer as well as conditions in the marketplace. Thus, the price of auction and remarketed preferred shares does not normally fluctuate as all purchases and sales conducted through the auction or remarketing are at the original issue price. Therefore, an important difference between ARPS and APS/RP stock involves principal protection. ARPS do not provide it while APS/RPs do. The latter issues are designed so that the issuer, not the investor, generally bears the credit risk as well as the risks associated with supply imbalances.

## Nonparticipating Preferred Stock

Almost all preferred stocks in today's public market are nonparticipating. This means that the owners of preferred are entitled to no more than the rate or amount of dividend stipulated in the legal provisions describing the class of stock. A company may become very profitable and realize earnings many times the amounts necessary to pay the regular preferred dividend. However, this does preferred stockholders little good except to perhaps boost the rating for the shares. The big earnings over and above those needed for preferred dividends go to the common stockholders to be reinvested in the firm or to be distributed as common dividends.

In the history of preferreds, there have been instances of participating preferred stocks. The terms have varied, but the general idea may be illustrated by a single provision: After the preferred has received its stipulated dividend and the common has received the same amount of dividend per share as the preferred, funds remaining available for dividend payments are distributed in equal amounts per share between both the common and preferred stocks. From the standpoint of corporate management, such an arrangement is too good for preferred stock because it permits preferred stockholders to have their cake and eat it too. Their cake is the preference to dividends; the eating of it is participation with common in larger dividends per share.

## Cumulative Preferred Stock

A lopsided deal in favor of corporate management is noncumulative preferred stock. The language would say, in effect, "If the issuer does not pay the preferred dividend in any dividend period, you just forget about it because you are not going to get paid." That would be a very weak preference because management could skip a dividend payment at its discretion. In our financial history, there have been few noncumulative preferred stocks of this type, and most of these have probably been the result of corporate reorganizations.

An example of noncumulative preferred stock was Wabash Railway's 5 percent Series A shares. Between 1915 and 1926, no dividends (or less than the stated amount) were paid even though earnings were available for payment at times. The company reinvested earnings in plant and equipment. When the Board of Directors later wanted to pay dividends on the Series B preferred and the common shares, the Series A holders brought legal action to obtain back and unpaid dividends, as they were earned even though not paid. In 1930, the Supreme Court decided in favor of the company, holding that, as the earnings were reinvested in plant and equipment and as no dividends were declared, the preferred holders had no right to receive a share of the earnings. Some state statutes (New Jersey for one) provide that preferred dividends are cumulative if there are earnings and no dividends are declared.

There have been a few more issues of noncumulative preferreds where the dividends are paid *only* if earned; if the company records a loss for a year, the dividend is not paid and it is not made up or left to accumulate for payment in future years. The right to the dividend is gone forever and the company has no obligation to make future payment. These are known as *cumulative-to-the-extent-earned* preferreds.

However, although there have been few noncumulative preferreds, they reappeared in 1988 when The Bank of New York Company, Inc., issued a couple of series of fixed/adjustable-rate noncumulative preferreds. Investors thought this relic of the past had gone the way of the dodo bird, but someone saw the need for it. *Barron's* financial weekly, in its April 18, 1988 issue, refers to this type of preferred as "a relic of the horse-and-buggy era, a device of the robber barons." These preferred shares are contingently convertible into common stock with a market value equal to the preferreds' stated value in the event of a dividend omission or a downgrading below investment grade. However, this contingent conversion feature doesn't provide full principal protection, as there is a maximum number of common shares that can be issued for each preferred share. If the common gets low enough in price, the preferred shareholder could take a hit. Of course, the pricing of the shares theoretically takes into account the noncumulative and contingent conversion features, at least at the initial offering.

*Cumulative* means that when a preferred dividend is not paid (whether or not earned) it accumulates and no dividend may be paid on shares ranking on a parity with or junior to the preferred until all dividend arrearages have been paid on the particular preferred issue. The prohibition of dividend payments on common stock when dividends on preferred stock are in arrears is a serious restriction. Common stockholders like their dividends and, when common dividends are stopped and cannot be resumed until preferred dividend arrearages are paid, they can direct some very sharp questions to management. This dissatisfaction is also expressed in the stock market by lower share prices.

Usually failure to pay preferred dividends results in other financial restrictions on management. It is common to provide that while preferred dividends are in arrears the issuer may not redeem any shares of stock junior to the preferred. Generally, the terms of preferred stocks also provide that when dividends are in arrears sinking-fund payments on the preferred and on any junior preferred are suspended and no money may be used to redeem preferred or common stock. The company may not purchase any shares of the preferred except through a purchase offer made to all preferred shareholders. Consumers Power Company is an exception because its corporate charter does not contain any restrictions on the repurchase or redemption of its preferred and preference shares while there are arrearages of dividends on such stock.

A thorough study of preferred stock includes an examination of the terms of any bond issues and bank loans of the issuer and of any class of preferred senior to the one being studied. Sometimes these senior securities have provisions prohibiting payment of dividends on junior securities when the issuer's financial condition falls below standards set in these agreements such as a minimum current ratio or a minimum amount of surplus available for the payment of dividends. In 1984, Long Island Lighting Company, as part of its revolving credit agreement with fourteen banks, agreed to suspend the declaration of preferred stock dividends payable on and after October 1, 1984. Dividends were resumed in 1989 after reaching agreement with the authorities over rate matters and the disposition of the politically sensitive Shoreham nuclear generating plant.

In early 1985, the LTV Corporation sought approval from the holders of its 5 percent subordinated debentures due January 15, 1988 to the declaration and payment of regular quarterly cash dividends to January 15, 1988 on its preferred stock then outstanding or to be outstanding. The indenture under which the debentures were issued prohibited the payment of dividends and certain other distributions to the aggregate of $15 million plus LTV's accumulated net income subsequent to December 31, 1966. Due to asset write-downs, losses, and expected losses, there would be a deficiency in retained earnings under this provision, which would preclude the payment of dividends. Declaration of dividends due for payment in the first quarter of 1985 was deferred.

In the proxy statement sent to debentureholders, the Company stated:

> The Board of Directors and management of the Company strongly recommend that Debentureholders give their approval [to pay cash dividends on the preferred stock]. The Company believes that such approval is in the best interests of Debentureholders and the Company because it would enhance the Company's ability to refinance existing debt and raise additional capital in the market place. The ability to pay preferred dividends will also enhance the Company's ability to issue additional preferred stock instead of debt, which, under certain circumstances, may be more beneficial to both the Company and its debentureholders.

On February 6, 1985, the debentureholders approved the company's request and received a payment of $2.50 per $100 principal amount of debentures outstanding. Preferred dividends were declared on February 7 for payment on March 1; regular declaration and payments continued thereafter on the normal quarterly schedule until they were again omitted in the fall of the year. In July 1986, LTV sought protection from creditors under Chapter 11 of the bankruptcy laws.

## Preference to Assets

At the time a preferred stock is issued, hardly anyone thinks about the possibility that the issuing corporation may be liquidated or reorganized, except perhaps, the lawyers who draw up the terms of security issues. They write in provisions about what happens to a preferred stock in the event the issuer is liquidated either voluntarily or involuntarily in financial failure. A simple preference is that preferred stockholders are entitled to receive, after settlement has been made with creditors and holders of any senior issue of preferred, the par, stated, or liquidation value of the preferred before any distribution is made to common stock or to any junior preferred issue. In the case of stock without par value, an amount per share is stipulated. Sometimes preferred holders are entitled to a larger amount in voluntary liquidation than in involuntary liquidation.

For example, Detroit Edison's 15.68 percent series cumulative preferred has an involuntary liquidation value of $100 per share and a voluntary liquidation value of the amount equal to the optional redemption price applicable at the time of liquidation. In the case of Consumers Power Company's $7.76 preference stock, the involuntary liquidation value is $100 per share and the voluntary liquidation value $101.43 a share (the initial offering price).

There are some issues that may participate with the common stock in the event of liquidation. Public Service Electric & Gas Company had a $1.40 cumulative dividend preference common entitling the holder to receive, upon the Company's liquidation, twice the amount per share distributed on each share of common. Holders of Southern California Edison's 5 percent original cumulative participating preferred stock, par value $8 $\frac{1}{3}$, were entitled to the par value in the event of liquidation before payment on preferred, preference, or common stock. It was also entitled to participate with the common stock in any balance remaining after the preferred and preference shares have been paid in full (including dividends) and par ($4$\frac{1}{6}$) had been paid on the common. Finally, Southern California Gas Co. has an issue of 6 percent, $25 par value preferred with asset participation rights. In liquidation or dissolution of the company, holders of the outstanding preferred stock would be entitled to receive no more than the par value for their shares and any accrued dividends. However, the subject preferred will receive the $25 par value and accrued and unpaid dividends; then it shall participate on a pro rata basis with the common in the remaining assets after the par value has been paid on the common.

Seldom are corporations voluntarily liquidated, but City Investing Company is one such exception. On June 28, 1985, it called for redemption at the liquidation values plus accrued dividends three series of publicly issued convertible preference stock. Two of the issues were converted by their holders into common shares as the conversion values were substantially in excess of the redemption price. However, holders of the third issue—$2.875 convertible/exchangeable preference series E—turned their shares in for the $25 redemption price because the conversion worth was only about $17.50 a share.

Wickes Companies and its subsidiary, Gamble-Skogmo, Inc., emerged from reorganization in early 1985. Wickes $8.75 Series A preferred, $100 par value, received 7.459 shares of the new company's common stock. The new common shares were worth $3.53125 per share, or a total of $26.34 per share of old preferred. Gamble-Skogmo's $1.75 preferred ($40 par value) received 4.321 shares of the new Wickes common and the $1.60 preferred ($35 par value) received 3.779 shares. The total market values of these two distributions were $15.26 and $13.34 a share, respectively. If the company had liquidated instead of reorganizing, the distribution to all security holders probably would have been smaller.

Another example of a distribution to preferred holders of a company coming out of bankruptcy proceedings is Itel Corporation. Itel had an issue of $1.44 preferred with a liquidation price of $15.00 per share. Each 100 shares of preferred (total liquidation value of $1,500) received 38.7 shares of common stock of the newly reorganized company. With the new common initially valued at

$7.25 a share, the holder received $280.58 worth of stock, or about 18.70 percent of the claim.

## Voting Rights

Preferred stock issuers are inclined toward the view that as long as preferred shareholders receive their dividends regularly, there is no need for them to have voting rights. Generally, preferred shares do not carry standard voting privileges, but in some cases each preferred share has the same voting rights as the common equity. Southern California Edison's preferred issues have varying degrees of voting power; some issues have three votes per share and other issues one vote per share.

However, when preferred dividends have been in arrears for a certain period (usually four or six dividend payments), it is common practice to give nonvoting stock the right to elect some number of directors. This is *contingent voting stock*; the voting right is contingent upon the preferred stockholders' lack of dividends. The most common kind of contingent voting right involves the right of owners of a class of preferred stock to vote as a class so as to elect two directors. Thus, preferred holders are assured of representation on the board of a company experiencing financial difficulties. This kind of provision has become common because the New York Stock Exchange requires it as a condition for listing nonvoting preferred stocks. Another kind of contingent voting provision gives preferred stockholders one vote per share, the same as common stock, when dividends are in arrears. When arrears of dividends on contingent voting stock have been paid or settled, the conditional voting right ceases. In 1985, preferred holders elected members to the Board of Directors of Eastern Air Lines and Public Service Company of New Hampshire. In Eastern's case, they elected two members of the Board. In the case of Public Service Company of New Hampshire the preferred stockholders, voting as a class, elected seven members to serve on the Board while the common shareholders elected six.

The terms of some preferreds state that certain corporate acts must be approved by preferred shareholders voting as a class whenever dividends have been in arrears for some period of time. For example, agreement by two-thirds of the preferred stock voting as a class may be required for approval of such management proposals as (1) increasing the authorized amount of any class or series of stock that ranks ahead of the preferred as to dividends or as to assets upon liquidation, (2) altering the provisions of the issuer's articles of incorporation, or (3) merging or consolidating with another company in such manner as to adversely affect the rights and preferences of the preferred stock. Preferred stock with such a provision is called vetoing stock because it can veto action proposed by management. The power to veto ceases when dividend arrears are paid.

## Redemption Provisions

Circumstances often change while a preferred stock is outstanding, and a time may come when an issuer finds it desirable to eliminate the shares from its capitalization. Preferred stock voting rights might present an obstacle for control of a corporation by its common shareholders. Or it may become economical to refund a preferred stock with bonds to increase earnings for the common stock. Interest is a deductible expense in calculating corporate income subject to income taxes, but preferred dividends are not. Such a refunding would change a nondeductible expense (preferred dividends) to a tax-deductible expense (bond interest). Or an issuer might want to restructure its capitalization. In 1985, Pacficorp and Atlantic Richfield Co. redeemed preferreds for these reasons. The most important reason for a senior security to be redeemed is that financing costs have declined, thereby making it possible for the issuing company to save money through the replacement of high-cost issues with lower cost issues. Virtually all issuers of preferred stock make provisions for (1) periodic redemption by a sinking fund, (2) redemption of stock in whole or in part by call, or (3) conversion into common stock.

Preferreds without any redemption provisions are quite rare. These are truly perpetual issues because there is no way other than through reorganization that the issuer can retire the stock against the will of the owner. Of course, it could make open-market purchases or ask for tenders of the shares, but the stock can not be involuntarily lost by the investor. There are a few other issues that do not appear to be callable, but they contain sinking-fund features that provide for the periodic retirement of the shares.

Nearly all preferreds are redeemable in one way or another. A majority of the outstanding public issues are currently callable at any time, in whole or in part, at the option of the issuer and at preset prices plus accrued and unpaid dividends up to the call date. Generally, the initial call price is par or the offering price plus the annual dividend or rate. The call price is then reduced periodically to par or the initial offering price. For example, Duke Power Company's 7.12 percent Series Q preferred stock ($100 par value) is callable at $107.12 for its first five years through March 15, 1992, then at $104.75 for the next five years, then at $102.38 for the next five years, and finally at $100.00 on and after March 16, 2002. A few other issues have redemption schedules with call prices declining each year by generally equal amounts.

Most new issues provide some type of deferred call or redemption provision. Some might not be callable under any circumstance for the first 5 to 10 years, while others might be currently callable but protected against lower cost refunding for a certain period. This is similar to provisions found in corporate debt issues. Noncallable is far more absolute than nonrefundable, and yet many investors are confused and treat refunding protection the same as call protection. This could prove to be costly.

To make the distinction clear, many currently callable issues cannot be called for a certain period if the company sells debt or equity securities ranking equal or superior to the preferred at a lower cost of capital than the outstanding preferred. This is refunding protection; it does not allow the issuer to take advantage of lower money costs on senior issues for a certain number of years following the initial public offering of the stock. However, if the issuer sells junior preferred or common equity prior to the expiration of the refunding protected period, the proceeds may be used to retire or refund the higher cost preferred.

Commonwealth Edison Company issued 1 million shares of 9.44 percent cumulative prior preferred stock in June 1970. Less than two years later, it redeemed the shares at $110; just prior to the redemption announcement, the stock was trading at about $119 to $120 a share. The funds for the redemption came from the sale of common stock and common stock purchase warrants, clearly junior securities. The preferred prospectus stated:

> Prior to August 1, 1980, none of the shares ... may be redeemed through refunding, directly or indirectly, by or in anticipation of the incurring of any debt or the issuance of any shares of the Prior Preferred Stock or of any other stock ranking prior to or on a parity with the Prior Preferred Stock, if such debt has an interest cost ... or such shares have a dividend cost ... less than the dividend cost ... of the 9.44 percent ... Stock.

The company was sued by some institutional holders, but the judge decided the redemption provision did not prohibit redemption directly out of an issue of common shares. Since then, other companies have done similar redemptions.

In the decision concerning the Florida Power & Light Company's maintenance and replacement fund redemption,[1] the judge stated:

> The terms "redemption" and "refunding" are not synonymous. A "redemption" is simply a call of bonds. A "refunding" occurs when the issuer sells bonds in order to use the proceeds to redeem an earlier issue of bonds. ... The refunding bond issue being sold is closely linked to the one being redeemed by contractual language and proximity in time so that the proceeds will be available to pay for the redemption. Otherwise, the issuer would be taking an inordinate risk that market conditions would change between the redemption of the earlier issue and the sale of the later issue.

This principle can also be applied to preferred stock redemptions.

Sinking-fund provisions for preferred stocks are similar to those of bonds. They provide for the periodic retirement of stock, usually on an annual basis. Often commencing on or after the call or refunding protected period has expired, there are instances where the sinking fund operates prior to such expiration. A

---

[1] Lucas et al. v. Florida Power & Light Company, Final Judgement, paragraph 77.

specific number of shares or a certain percentage of the original issue is specified for retirement periodically. Often it will amount to about 2 to 8 percent of the original number of shares, with 5 percent being the more common requirement. Commonwealth Edison had an issue of $10.875 preference stock that required all of the shares to be retired at one time at par through the sinking fund on November 1, 1989, the date the call protected period terminated. Thus, this issue had another feature that most bonds have—that is, a maturity of sorts. Most sinking funds have provisions allowing the issuer the noncumulative option to increase payments (usually to double the amount at any one time). Sinking-fund payments may be made in shares of stock purchased in the open market or by the call of the required number of shares at the sinking-fund call price, normally par or stated value. There are instances in which a company wishing to retire an entire issue of sinking-fund preferred will call the maximum number of shares allowed for the sinking fund at the lower sinking-fund redemption price and redeem the balance at the normal call price. Failure to make sinking-fund payments is not an act of default as it would be in the case of debt; the company cannot be placed in bankruptcy.

Many preferred stock market participants refer to issues without sinking funds as perpetual preferreds but this is a misuse of that term. Non-sinking-fund issues need not be perpetual, yet they do not have a date at which they must be retired. Sinking-fund operations can provide some measure of market support if the issuer can come into the open market and purchase stock at less than the redemption price. However, in periods of lower interest and dividend rates and higher preferred prices, a call below market prices can result in capital losses to investors. Shares to be redeemed for the sinking fund are usually selected randomly by lot and not pro rata, or in proportion, to one's holdings.

An important consideration for property and casualty insurance companies is a rule by the National Association of Insurance Commissioners allowing qualifying sinking-fund preferred stocks to be valued on the books at cost rather than to be marked to the current market price. This accounting or valuation treatment, at least for regulatory or reserve purposes, reduces the impact of market fluctuations on the company's portfolio to the extent that it utilizes sinking-fund preferreds.

Some preferred issues have purchase funds. These are, to some extent, optional on the part of an issuer because it will have to use its best efforts to retire a portion of the shares periodically if such shares can be purchased in the open market, or through tender, at less than the redemption or liquidation price. If the stock is selling above the applicable price, the purchase fund cannot be put into operation. Again, the purchase fund may provide some market support to the issue in a higher dividend rate environment, but when rates are lower it is inoperative. In the case of Occidental Petroleum's $15.50 cumulative preferred stock issued in connection with the acquisition of Cities Service Company in 1982, Occidental was required to use its best efforts to purchase shares in the open market at or below the liquidation value with the proceeds derived from certain asset sales in excess of $100 million. Any shares so purchased would then be credited against any sinking-fund payments when the sinking fund became operational.

It is important to read prospectuses carefully. Although preferreds are not bonded securities, unlike mortgage debt with its release and substitution of property clauses, there have been instances of preferred stock retirement prior to the end of the refunding protected period because of asset sales. A case in point is Crown Zellerbach Corporation's $3.05 cumulative preferred stock, Series B, issued May 19, 1982 at $20 per share. It was protected against refunding prior to April 15, 1987 and had the normal call schedule starting immediately at $23.05 and declining to $20 a share in 1997. However, it also had a special provision for its retirement prior to April 15, 1997 if the company sold certain assets aggregating at least $100 million in any 12-month period. The redemption premium under this circumstance was one-half the regular redemption premium. It started at $21.52 per share and declined to $20 in 1997. On May 20, 1983, Crown Zellerbach redeemed this stock at the special redemption price of $21.42 a share; the regular call price at that time was $22.85. The proceeds came from the sale of its interests in Crown Zellerbach Canada Ltd. and a small steamship company. In late October, 1982, it announced it had a preliminary agreement for the sale of these assets; the use of the proceeds for share redemption should not have come as any surprise to the preferred holders. The shares sold at $21\frac{7}{8}$ at the end of December and rose as high as $23\frac{7}{8}$ in 1983 prior to the retirement of the stock.

## MULTIPLE ISSUES OF ONE CLASS OF PREFERRED

Some companies may have multiple classes of preferred stock. The terms of the two or more classes are determined separately at the times of their respective issuance. When there is more than one class, investors may wonder which stock is senior to another in claim to dividends and assets upon liquidation. A senior preferred may receive dividends whereas a junior preferred does not. Other rights and limitations of the two or more classes of preferred may differ. Generally speaking, preferred shares are senior to preference shares. Some companies have only one class of senior equity outstanding, while others might have two classes with different priorities. Consolidated Edison has only preferred shares, while Consumers Power and a number of other utilities have preferred and preference shares.

Companies using preferred stocks in their capitalizations usually authorize a class of preferred stock with a defined preference as to dividends. This class may be issued in series from time to time; there may be Series A, Series B, and so on, with each series of the same class ranking equally with each other as to dividend preference. It is not uncommon for public utility companies to have six, eight, or more series of one class of preferred outstanding. One series may have one stipulated rate of dividends and another series a different rate. For example, Texas Utilities Electric Company has more than 25 series of straight preferred stock with dividends ranging upwards from $4.00 per share (three series of $4.00 preferred) of $100 stated value. Also, the company has two series of adjustable-rate shares and one issue of fixed-rate shares that may become Dutch auction rate stock in 1992.

Just as with bonds, the other terms of a class of preferred stock may differ among the series. One series may be voting and another nonvoting. The terms for sinking-fund redemption and for redemption in whole or in part may vary. One series may be convertible and another not. Each series is tailored to conditions in the securities markets at the time of issue.

In the early 1970s, electric utility companies made increased use of preference stock. Some companies were unable to issue preferred shares because of restrictions contained in their bond indentures; they simply could not meet the required earnings tests for issuance of additional preferred stock. As there are usually no similar restrictions on the issuance of shares junior to the preferred, classes of preference shares were authorized and issued. Also, many corporate charters restricted preferred shares to $100 par or stated value. To broaden the market for their stock, some utilities offered preference stock with lower par values such as $10, $20, and $25. The lower prices appealed to many individual and less sophisticated investors because they could buy round lots of 100 shares each instead of odd lots of 1 to 99 shares. Although primarily of psychological value only to the small investor (100 shares at $25 is the same as 25 shares at $100 each), this allowed companies to take advantage of a pool of capital that was previously not too interested in preferred stocks.

Another device used by some issuers to bring the price of their shares down to a level at which individual investors would buy them is the depositary preferred share. The depositary share represents a fractional interest in a whole preferred share that has been deposited with a bank under legal depositary agreements. It entitles the holder proportionately to all of the rights and preferences of the underlying preferred stock. For example, in 1989 Household International, Inc., issued 3 million depositary shares at $25 each representing an interest in one quarter share of $100 stated value $9\frac{1}{2}$ percent cumulative preferred stock. In 1985, Harnischfeger Corporation issued 3 million shares of Series B $3.402 depositary preferred shares at $25.00 a share. Each represented a one-fiftieth ownership in the Series B sinking-fund exchangeable preferred stock (60,000 shares deposited with the depositary bank). The company used this financing method because it did not have enough authorized shares of preferred stock to permit a broad distribution. Only 132,500 shares of authorized but unissued stock were available.

## TAXABILITY OF PREFERRED STOCK DIVIDENDS

Tax laws should always be considered when making investment decisions, and preferred stock is no different. Currently a corporation may exclude from gross income 70 percent of the qualified dividends received from other *domestic* corporations subject to federal income taxes. It does not matter whether the dividends are from preferred, preference, or common stock. This exclusion is justified on the ground that it mitigates double taxation of dividends paid by one company to another and then paid to the stockholders of the second company. Dividends by one company are paid after its earnings have been taxed under the federal corporate income tax. Then when received by a second company they would be taxed again as income to that company. This 70 percent exclusion, or dividends received deduction (*DRD*), leaves only 30 percent to be taxed in the hands of a corporate owner of preferred stock. This rule only applies to preferreds of banks, utility holding companies, railroads, and industrial and financial concerns. Dividends from registered investment companies are treated differently, depending on the source of the income used to pay dividends. For utility operating companies, the deduction is applicable to "new money" issues—those preferreds sold after October 1, 1942 for purposes other than refunding. Preferreds sold prior to that date and those issued afterwards for debt and preferred refunding purposes are "old money" issues, with the dividends received deduction only 58.82 percent. There are only about 125 utility old money issues and 28 "partly new money" issues out of nearly 1,000 or so fixed-dividend preferred stock issues outstanding. Partly new money issues are those where only a portion of the proceeds are used for refunding purposes.

In order to qualify for the dividends received deduction, a corporation must hold the preferred shares at least 46 days. Days on which the stock is held after the dividend is received, as well as prior to its receipt, are counted for purposes of this minimum holding period. The deduction is increased to 80 percent for investors holding at least 20 percent of a dividend paying corporation (by the dividend payer's voting power and value). Also, the deduction may be reduced in the case of "debt-financed portfolio stock." This is stock acquired or carried with indebtedness that is directly attributable to the investment in such shares.

The effective tax rate on dividends for qualified investors in the 34 percent marginal corporate tax bracket and a 70 percent dividends received deduction is 10.2 percent (.30 x .34). Taxes are paid on only 30 percent of the dividends with the investor keeping 89.8 percent of the dividend. Exhibit 16–3 summarizes the intercorporate dividends received deduction for new money and old money stock for corporations in the 34 percent tax bracket.

Exhibit 16–4 shows the pretax and the after-tax yields at the 34 percent corporate tax rate for preferred stocks and fully taxable alternative investments

**EXHIBIT 16–3**
**Summary of Intercorporate Dividends Received Deduction**

|  | New Money | Old Money |
|---|---|---|
| Dividends received | $1,000.00 | $1,000.00 |
| Dividend exclusion: | | |
| Percent | 70.00% | 58.82% |
| Amount | $ 700.00 | $ 588.20 |
| Amount subject to taxes | $ 300.00 | $ 411.80 |
| Marginal tax rate | 34% | 34% |
| Taxes paid | $ 102.00 | $ 140.01 |
| Effective tax rate | 10.20% | 14.00% |
| Dividends retained: | | |
| Percent | 89.80% | 86.00% |
| Amount | $ 898.00 | $ 859.99 |

such as commercial paper, certificates of deposit, and corporate debts, as well as the pretax yields needed on alternative fully taxable investments in order to equal the preferred's after-tax return. Thus, a preferred with a dividend of 8.00 percent will provide an after-tax yield of 7.18 percent under current tax rates and the new money dividends received deduction. In order to equal these yields, a fully taxable investment must yield 10.88 percent (after-tax preferred yield divided by 1 minus the tax rate, or 7.18/.66). A fully taxable instrument with an 8.00 percent nominal rate yields only 5.28 percent to a corporate investor in the 34 percent tax bracket.

Yields on preferreds and most debt instruments are calculated using a day count basis of a 360-day year as the denominator and either the actual number of days or 30-day months as the numerator. When comparing after-tax yields with most other investments, the second column of Exhibit 16–4 is the appropriate one to use. However, some tax-exempt short-term instruments such as variable-rate demand obligations (VRDOs) and unit priced demand adjustable tax-exempt securities (UPDATES) have yields calculated on the basis of the actual number of days per month and actual number of days per year. This basis is called "actual/actual" and overstates the yield for comparison purposes. The auction market and remarketed preferred yields are understated in comparison to these short-term municipals. Therefore, adjustments have to be made to the auction preferred yield to put it on the same footing as the comparable short-term tax-exempt investment.

Instead of multiplying the nominal preferred yield by 89.8 percent to get the after-tax return, the preferred yield should be multiplied by 91 percent to get the adjusted after-tax basis equivalent for VRDO/UPDATES comparisons. The nominal preferred yield must be grossed up yield to account for the actual

**EXHIBIT 16–4**
**Comparison of New Money Preferred Stock and Other Yields**

| | Preferred Stock After-Tax Yield Comparison to: | | After-Tax Yield on a Fully Taxable Investment | Pretax Yield Needed to Equal After-Tax Return on Preferred | |
|---|---|---|---|---|---|
| Nominal Yield | Taxable & Other Debt 30/360 | Short-term Tax-exempts Actual/Actual | | Taxable Securities | Tax-exempt Securities |
| 4.00% | 3.59% | 3.64% | 2.64% | 5.44% | 3.59% |
| 4.50 | 4.04 | 4.10 | 2.97 | 6.12 | 4.04 |
| 5.00 | 4.49 | 4.55 | 3.30 | 6.80 | 4.49 |
| 5.50 | 4.94 | 5.01 | 3.63 | 7.48 | 4.94 |
| 6.00 | 5.39 | 5.46 | 3.96 | 8.16 | 5.39 |
| 6.50 | 5.84 | 5.92 | 4.29 | 8.84 | 5.84 |
| 7.00 | 6.29 | 6.37 | 4.62 | 9.52 | 6.29 |
| 7.50 | 6.74 | 6.83 | 4.95 | 10.20 | 6.74 |
| 8.00 | 7.18 | 7.28 | 5.28 | 10.88 | 7.18 |
| 8.50 | 7.63 | 7.74 | 5.61 | 11.57 | 7.63 |
| 9.00 | 8.08 | 8.19 | 5.94 | 12.25 | 8.08 |
| 9.50 | 8.53 | 8.65 | 6.27 | 12.93 | 8.53 |
| 10.00 | 8.98 | 9.10 | 6.60 | 13.61 | 8.98 |
| 10.50 | 9.43 | 9.56 | 6.93 | 14.29 | 9.43 |
| 11.00 | 9.88 | 10.01 | 7.26 | 14.97 | 9.88 |
| 11.50 | 10.33 | 10.47 | 7.59 | 15.65 | 10.33 |
| 12.00 | 10.78 | 10.92 | 7.92 | 16.33 | 10.78 |

365-day count instead of 360 days. Thus, an 8.00 percent dividend is multiplied by the fraction 365/360 resulting in $8 \times 1.0139$, or 8.1111. This adjusted pretax yield is then multiplied by 89.8 to obtain the adjusted after-tax yield, which in this case is 7.28 percent, or 91 percent of the 8 percent nominal rate. These adjusted after-tax yields are found in the table's third column.

The break-even or indifference level between preferreds and the pretax yield needed from a fully taxable instrument to match the preferred's net yield is 73.5 percent. As long as the preferred's pretax yield is greater than 73.5 percent of the required return from a fully taxable investment, the preferred shares are the more attractive. When it is less than the break-even rate percent, the alternate investment will provide a greater yield.

Our discussion to this point has centered on corporations and the dividends received deduction. Of interest is the recent broadening of the preferred market with the issuance of *American Depositary Shares* (*ADS*), representing preference shares of British and Irish companies. Dividends paid by these companies to American shareholders, whether corporations or individuals, while not eligible for the dividends received deduction, are considered dividends for federal income tax purposes. Under the income tax treaties between the United Kingdom (or Ireland) and the United States, the dividend payments carry an imputed tax credit, which in 1989 equalled one third of the nominal dividend. In the United Kingdom, it is called the advance corporation tax (ACT). Eligible corporate U.S. holders receive an effective after-tax equivalent of 88 percent of the nominal dividend as compared with 89.8 percent for qualified dividends subject to the DRD. Individual investors in the 28 percent tax bracket effectively keep 96 percent of the nominal dividend, and those in the 33 percent bracket retain 89.3 percent. The ACT payment or imputed tax credit is designed to lessen the burden of double taxation on qualified holders. Exhibit 16–5 shows how the effective tax rates are calculated for dividends received from British corporations. The United Kingdom imposes a 15 percent withholding tax on the sum of the nominal dividend and the ACT, while Ireland presently does not impose withholding taxes on preference share dividends.

## THE MARKET FOR PREFERREDS

Publicly distributed preferred stocks are marketable in the sense that they may be traded on the stock exchanges and in the over-the-counter market. There is usually a dealer or a stock exchange specialist willing to quote a bid price (what he or she will pay if you want to sell) and an offered price (what he or she will sell it for if you want to buy). But there are marked differences in the marketability of preferred stocks, and these differences are important to investors who buy and sell these stocks.

**EXHIBIT 16–5**

**Comparison of Dividends with Imputed Tax Credits Received from United Kingdom Corporations**

|     |                                                                                           | Corporation | Individual | |
| --- | ----------------------------------------------------------------------------------------- | ----------- | ---------- | ----- |
|     | *Marginal Tax Rate*                                                                       | 34%         | 33%        | 28%   |
| (a) | Nominal dividend                                                                          | $ 9.00      | $ 9.00     | $ 9.00 |
| (b) | Plus imputed tax credit (1/3 of nominal)                                                  | 3.00        | 3.00       | 3.00  |
| (c) | Total dividend and ACT credit                                                             | $12.00      | $12.00     | $12.00 |
| (d) | Less 15% U. K. withholding tax on (c) above                                               | 1.80        | 1.80       | 1.80  |
| (e) | Dividend paid to eligible U. S. holder                                                    | $10.20      | 10.20      | 10.20 |
| (f) | Cash tax outlay to the IRS on (c) above (marginal income tax rate less tax credit for the 15% U. K. withholding tax) | 2.28        | 2.16       | 1.56  |
| (g) | Net after-tax dividend to U. S. holder                                                    | $ 7.92      | $ 8.04     | $ 8.64 |
| (h) | Effective tax-free dividend rate (g)/(a)                                                  | 88%         | 89.3%      | 96%   |

Less than half of the publicly issued preferred shares are listed on the New York or the American Stock Exchanges; the rest trade in the over-the-counter market. This is similar to the situation with corporate bonds. While the normal unit of trading is 100 shares on the major stock exchanges, some issues trade in round lots of 10 shares. Investors who wish to buy or sell odd lots (i.e., less than the standard unit of trading) will pay a fraction more or receive a fraction less per share than a round lot transaction. These 10-share issues are indicated in the stock exchange transaction tables with the letter $z$ next to the trading volume.

Exchange listings generally improve an issue's marketability but other factors include the size and the quality ratings. Larger unlisted issues might be more marketable and trade in greater volume than smaller listed issues. The better marketability of larger and higher rated issues is attributed to the fact that many preferred investors are restricted to what they can hold in their portfolios. There are generally more buyers for shares with these characteristics and trades can take place far easier than for small and noninvestment-grade issues. The spread between the bid and the ask prices are often smaller for highly marketable securities because the volume of trading is greater and the trader or specialist will usually have little trouble in selling the shares to a willing buyer at market prices close to the price at which the shares just previously traded. If it looks as though the trader would experience difficulty in quickly moving the shares, the bid price would likely be lower and the ask price would likely be higher.

## SOURCES OF INFORMATION
## ABOUT PREFERRED STOCKS

The best source of information about a specific preferred stock is the prospectus published at the time it is first issued. Prospectuses contain fairly complete information about the terms of the new preferred issues; however, in many cases (but not all), the information about the operations of the issuers leaves much to be desired. This is due to the shortened prospectus form used by many corporations under the streamlined shelf registration procedures introduced by the Securities and Exchange Commission in 1982.

You can get information about preferred stocks from many of the sources for common stocks and bonds. Manuals issued by financial publishers provide detailed information about corporate issuers and their securities. They are particularly useful for information about the provisions of preferred stocks such as we have been discussing. They also publish monthly guides to senior securities, which contain condensed information about many preferred stock issues. You can compare a number of preferreds quickly by using them. They provide in abbreviated form the ratings of the issues, information about the principal terms, current and historical price data, and shares outstanding, among other things. Also, corporate annual reports will often contain valuable information. In addition, a number of investment brokers also provide research about individual issues and issuers as well as statistical publications.

The major daily and weekly financial newspapers have stock tables that include trading and dividend data on common and preferred shares. One newspaper, *Investors Daily*, has a separate table for listed preferred stocks, which is quite a convenience for preferred stock investors.

## SUMMARY

A preferred stock is a peculiar kind of security. It is senior to common stock and junior to debt. While preferred may have many features similar to debt, it is not debt. Preferred stock is a right of ownership in a company. There are many possible variations in the terms of the different preferred issues. They are distinctly unlike common stock in that dividends not paid usually accumulate and generally must be paid before dividends may be paid on the common. But unlike bonds, failure to pay dividends on preferred is not a default as is failure to pay bond interest. Although not a default, dividend omissions may result in the imposition of serious financial restrictions upon the issuer. Like bonds, many preferred issues have no voting power as long as dividends are being paid, but they usually gain some limited voting power when dividends are in arrears. A company may have one class of preferred stock and issue it in series with different terms for different series of stock. Preferred stock is peculiar because it has some of the characteristics of bonds and some of the characteristics of common equity. It is also peculiar because the exclusion from taxable income of most of the amount of preferred dividends received by corporations from qualified issuers causes it to be owned very largely by corporate investors rather than individuals.

# CHAPTER 17

## CREDIT ANALYSIS
## FOR CORPORATE BONDS*

*Jane Tripp Howe, CFA*
*Senior Credit Analyst*
*Pacific Investment*
*Management Company*

Traditionally, credit analysis for corporate bonds has focused almost exclusively on the default risk of the bond. That is, what is the chance that the bondholder will not receive the scheduled interest payments and/or principal at maturity. This one-dimensional analysis concerned itself primarily with straight ratio analysis. This approach was deemed appropriate during the time when interest rates were stable and investors purchased bonds with the purpose of holding them to maturity. In this scenario, fluctuations in the market value of the bonds due to interest-rate changes were minimal, and fluctuations due to credit changes of the bonds were mitigated by the fact that the investor had no intention of selling the bond before maturity. During the past decade, however, the purpose of buying bonds has changed dramatically. Investors still purchase bonds for security and thereby forgo the higher expected return of other assets such as common stock. However, an increasing number of investors buy bonds to actively trade them with the purpose of making a profit on changes in interest rates or in absolute or relative credit quality. The second dimension of corporate bond credit analysis addresses the latter purpose of buying a bond. What is the likelihood of a change in credit quality that will affect the price of the bond? This second dimension of corporate bond analysis deals primarily with the ratios

---

*I wish to thank Richard S. Wilson, Fitch Investors Service, Inc., for his helpful comments and suggestions.

and profitability trends, such as return on equity, operating margins, and asset turnover, generally associated with common stock analysis. In practice, both dimensions of analysis should be applied in corporate bond analysis. In a sense, both dimensions are addressing the same issue—default or credit risk. However, only by using both dimensions of credit analysis will the analyst address the dual purpose of bond holding: security of interest and principal payments and stability or improvement of credit risk during the life of the bond.

Historically, common stock and bond research areas have been viewed as separate. However, with the development of options theory, the two disciplines are beginning to be viewed as complementary.

The value of the option is a direct function of the company's aggregate equity valuation. As the market value of a company's stock increases, the value of the option increases. Conversely, as the market value of a company's stock declines, so does the value of the option. The practical implication of this theory for corporate bonds analysis is that the perceptions of both markets should be compared before a final credit judgment is rendered. For the analyst who believes that there is a higher level of efficiency in the stock market than in the bond market, particular attention should be paid to the stock price of the company being analyzed. Of interest will be those situations in which the judgment of the two markets differ substantially.

For example, in early 1981 the market to book values of the major chemical companies ranged from .77 to 2.15. The bond ratings of these same companies ranged from Baa/BBB to Aaa/AAA. The interesting point is not the range of either the market to book values or bond ratings, but rather the fact that although there was some correlation between the market/book ratios and bond ratings, there were instances in which there was little or no correlation. Options theory would suggest that there should be more of a relationship between the two. When the relative valuation of the bond as measured by the rating is low compared with the equity valuation as measured by market/book, one or both markets may be incorrectly valuing the company. Given the evidence that bond-rating changes generally lag market moves, it is likely in this case that the bond market is undervaluing the company.

Although there are numerous types of corporate bonds outstanding, three major issuing segments of bonds can be differentiated: industrials, utilities, and finance companies. This chapter will primarily address industrials in its general description of bond analysis and then discuss the utility and finance issues.

## INDUSTRY CONSIDERATIONS

The first step in analyzing a bond is to gain some familiarity with the industry. Only within the context of an industry is a company analysis valid. For example, a company growing at 15 percent annually may appear attractive. However, if the industry is growing at 50 percent annually, the company is competitively weak. Industry considerations can be numerous. However, an understanding of the following eight variables should give the general fixed income analyst a sufficient framework to properly interpret a company's prospects.

## Economic Cyclicality

The economic cyclicality of an industry is the first variable an analyst should consider in reviewing an industry. Does the industry closely follow GNP growth, as does the retailing industry, or is it recession resistant but slow growing, as is the electric utility industry? The growth in earnings per share (EPS) of a company should be measured against the growth trend of its industry. Major deviations from the industry trend should be the focus of further analysis. Some industries may be somewhat dependent on general economic growth but be more sensitive to demographic changes. The nursing home industry is a prime example of this type of sensitivity. With the significant aging of the U.S. population, the nursing home industry is projected to have above average growth for the foreseeable future. Other industries, such as the banking industry, are sensitive to interest rates. When interest rates are rising, the earnings of banks with a high federal funds exposure underperform the market as their loan rates lag behind increases in the cost of money. Conversely, as interest rates fall, banking earnings outperform the market because the lag in interest change works in the banks' favor.

In general, however, the earnings of few industries perfectly correlate with one economic statistic. Not only are industries sensitive to many economic variables, but often various segments within a company or an industry move counter-cyclically, or at least with different lags in relation to the general economy. For example, the housing industry can be divided between new construction and remodeling and repair. New construction historically has led GNP growth, but repair and remodeling has exhibited less sensitivity to general trends. Therefore, in analyzing a company in the construction industry, the performance of each of its segments must be compared with the performance of the subindustry.

## Growth Prospects

A second industry variable related to that of economic cyclicality is the growth prospects for an industry. Is the growth of the industry projected to increase and be maintained at a high level, such as in the nursing industry, or is growth expected to be stable? Each growth scenario has implications for a company. In the case of a fast-growth industry, how much capacity is needed to meet demand, and how will this capacity be financed? In the case of slow-growth industries, is there a movement toward diversification and/or a consolidation within the industry, such as in the trucking industry? A company operating within a fast-growing industry often has a better potential for credit improvement than does a company whose industry's growth prospects are below average.

## Research and Development Expenses

The broad assessment of growth prospects is tempered by the third variable—the research and development expenditures required to maintain or expand market position. The technology field is growing at an above-average rate, and the companies in the industry should do correspondingly well. However, products with a high-technological component can become dated and obsolete quickly. Therefore, although a company may be well situated in an industry, if it does not have the financial resources to maintain a technological lead or at least expend a sufficient amount of money to keep technologically current, its position is likely to deteriorate in the long run. In the short run, however, a company whose R&D expenditures are consistently below industry averages may produce above-average results because of expanded margins.

## Competition

Competition within an industry also directly relates to the market structure of an industry and has implications for pricing flexibility. An unregulated monopoly is in an enviable position in that it can price its goods at a level that will maximize profits. Most industries encounter some free market forces and must price their goods in relation to the supply and demand for their goods as well as the price charged for similar goods. In an oligopoly, a pricing leader is not uncommon. General Motors Corporation, for example, performs this function in the automobile industry. A concern arises when a small company is in an industry that is trending toward oligopoly. In this environment, the small company's costs of production may be higher than those of the industry leaders, and yet it may have to conform to the pricing of the industry leaders. In the extreme, a price war could force the smaller companies out of business. This situation is present now in the brewing industry. For the past two decades, as the brewing industry has become increasingly concentrated, the leaders have gained market share at the expense of the small, local brewers. Many small, local brewers have either been acquired or have gone out of business. These local brewers have been at a dual disadvantage: They are in an industry whose structure is moving toward oligopoly, and yet their weak competitive position within the industry largely precludes pricing flexibility.

## Sources of Supply

The market structure of an industry and its competitive forces have a direct impact on the fifth industry variable—sources of supply of major production components. A company in the paper industry that has sufficient timber acreage to supply 100 percent of its pulp is preferable to a paper company that must buy all or a large percentage of its pulp. A company that is not self-sufficient in its factors of production but is sufficiently powerful in its industry to pass along increased costs is also in an enviable position. RJR Nabisco is an example of the latter type of company. Although RJR Nabisco has major exposure to commodity prices for ingredients, its strong market position has enabled it to pass along increased costs of goods sold.

## Degree of Regulation

The sixth industry consideration is the degree of regulation. The electric utility industry is the classic example of regulation. Nearly all phases of a utility's operations are regulated. The analyst should not be as concerned with the existence or absence of regulation per se but rather with the direction of regulation and the effect it has on the profitability of the company. For the electric utility industry, regulation generally places a cap on earned returns. Other industries, such as the drug industry, also have a high though less pervasive degree of regulation. In the drug industry, however, the threat of increased regulation has been a negative factor in the industry for some time.

## Labor

The labor situation of an industry should also be analyzed. Is the industry heavily unionized? If so, what has been the historical occurrence of strikes? When do the current contracts expire, and what is the likelihood of timely settlements? The labor situation is also important in nonunionized companies, particularly those whose labor situation is tight. What has been the turnover of professionals and management in the firm? What is the probability of a firm's employees, such as highly skilled engineers, being hired by competing firms? The more labor intensive an industry, the more significance the labor situation assumes.

## Accounting

A final industry factor to be considered is accounting. Does the industry have special accounting practices such as those in the insurance industry or the electric utility industry? If so, an analyst should become familiar with industry practices before proceeding with a company analysis. Also important is whether a company is liberal or conservative in applying the generally accepted accounting principles. The norm of an industry should be ascertained, and the analyst should be sure to analyze comparable figures.

## FINANCIAL ANALYSIS

Having achieved an understanding of an industry, the analyst is ready to proceed with a financial analysis. The financial analysis should be conducted in three phases. The first phase consists of traditional ratio analysis for bonds. The second phase, generally associated with common stock research, consists of analyzing the components of a company's return on equity (ROE). The final phase considers such nonfinancial factors as management and foreign exposure and includes an analysis of the indenture.

### Traditional Ratio Analysis

There are numerous ratios that can be calculated in applying traditional ratio analysis to bonds. Of these, eight will be discussed in this section. Those selected are the ratios with the widest degree of applicability. In analyzing a particular industry, however, other ratios assume significance and should be considered. For example, in the electric utility industry, allowance for funds used in construction as a percent of net income is an important ratio that is inapplicable to the analysis of industrial or financial companies.

*Pretax Interest Coverage.* Generally, the first ratio calculated in credit analysis is pretax interest coverage. This ratio measures the number of times interest charges are covered on a pretax basis. Fixed-charge coverage is calculated by dividing pretax income plus interest charges by total interest charges. The higher the coverage figure, the safer the credit. If interest coverage is less than 1X, the company must borrow or use cash flow or sale of assets to meet its interest payments. Generally, published coverage figures are pretax as opposed to after-tax because interest payments are a pretax expense. Although the pretax interest coverage ratio is useful, its utility is a function of the company's other fixed obligations. For example, if a company has other significant fixed obligations, such as rents or leases, a more appropriate coverage figure would include these other fixed obligations. An example of this is the retail industry, in which companies typically have significant lease obligations. A calculation of simple pretax interest coverage would be misleading in this case because fixed obligations other than interest are significant. The analyst should also be aware of any contingent liabilities such as a company's guaranteeing another company's debt. For example, there has been a dramatic increase in the insurance industry's guaranteeing of other company's debt. Today, this guaranteed debt exceeds the debt of the industry. Although the company being analyzed may never have to pay interest or principal on the guaranteed debt, the existence of the guarantee diminishes the quality of the pretax coverage. In addition, the quality of the guaranteed debt must be considered.

Once pretax interest coverage and fixed-charge coverage are calculated, it is necessary to analyze the ratios' absolute levels and the numbers relative to those of the industry. For example, pretax interest coverage for an electric utility of 4.5X is consistent with an AAA rating, whereas the same coverage for a drug company would indicate a lower rating.

Standard & Poor's 1986–1988 median ratios of pretax interest coverage ranges for the senior debt of industrial companies were as follows:

| Rating Classification | Pretax Interest Coverage |
| --- | --- |
| AAA | 13.52 |
| AA | 8.98 |
| A | 5.25 |
| BBB | 3.69 |

*Leverage.* A second important ratio is *leverage,* which can be defined in several ways. The most common definition, however, is long-term debt as a percent of total capitalization. The higher the level of debt, the higher the percentage of operating income that must be used to meet fixed obligations. If a company is highly leveraged, the analyst should also look at its margin of safety. The margin of safety is defined as the percentage that operating income could decline and still be sufficient to allow the company to meet its fixed obligations. Standard & Poor's 1986–1988 median ratios of leverage for the senior debt of industrial companies were as follows:

| Rating Classification | Long-Term Debt/Capitalization |
| --- | --- |
| AAA | 12.4 |
| AA | 18.8 |
| A | 30.1 |
| BBB | 37.7 |

The most common way to calculate leverage is to use the company's capitalization structure as stated in the most recent balance sheet. In addition to this measure, the analyst should calculate capitalization using a market approximation for the value of the common stock. When a company's common stock is selling significantly below book value, leverage will be understated by the traditional approach.

The degree of leverage and margin of safety varies dramatically among industries. Finance companies have traditionally been among the most highly leveraged companies, with debt to equity ratios of 10:1. Although such leverage is tolerated in the finance industry, an industrial company with similar leverage would have a difficult time issuing debt.

In addition to considering the absolute and relative levels of leverage of a company, the analyst should evaluate the debt itself. How much of the debt has a fixed rate, and how much has a floating rate? A company with a high component of debt tied to the prime may find its margins being squeezed as interest rates rise, if there is no compensating increase in the price of the firm's goods. Such a debt structure may be beneficial during certain phases of the interest-rate cycle, but it has the disadvantage of precluding a precise estimate of what interest charges for the year will be. In general, a company with a high percentage of floating-rate debt is less preferable than a similarly leveraged company with a small percentage of floating-rate debt.

The maturity structure of the debt should also be evaluated. What is the percentage of debt that is coming due within the next five years? As this debt is refinanced, how will the company's embedded cost of debt be changed? In this regard, the amount of original-issue discount (OID) debt should also be considered. High-quality OIDs were first issued in sizable amounts in 1981, although lower quality OIDs have been issued for some time. This debt is issued with low or zero coupons and at substantial discounts to par. Each year the issuing company expenses the interest payment (coupon times the total principal amount due at maturity) as well as the amortization of the discount. At issuance, only the actual bond proceeds are listed as debt on the balance sheet. However, as this debt payable will increase annually, the analyst should consider the full face amount due at maturity when evaluating the maturity structure and refinancing plans of the company.

*Cash Flow.*   A third important ratio is cash flow as a percent of total debt. Cash flow is often defined as net income from continuing operations plus depreciation, depletion, amortization, and deferred taxes. In calculating cash flow for credit analysis, the analyst should also subtract noncash contributions from subsidiaries. In essence, the analyst should be concerned with cash from operations. Any extraordinary sources or uses of funds should be excluded when determining the overall trend of cash-flow coverage. Cash dividends from subsidiaries should also be questioned in terms of their appropriateness (too high or too low relative to the subsidiary's earnings) and also in terms of the parent's control over the upstreaming of dividends. Is there a legal limit to the upstreamed dividends? If so, how close is the current level of dividends to the limit? Standard & Poor's 1986–1988 Median Ratios of Funds From Operations/Long-Term Debt for the senior debt of industrial companies were as follows:

| Rating Classification | Funds From Operations/<br>Long-Term Debt |
|---|---|
| AAA | 110 |
| AA | 84 |
| A | 48 |
| BBB | 37 |

*Net Assets.* A fourth significant ratio is net assets to total debt. In analyzing this facet of a bond's quality, consideration should be given to the liquidation value of the assets. Liquidation value will often differ dramatically from the value stated on the balance sheet. At one extreme, consider a nuclear generating plant that has had operating problems and has been closed down and whose chance of receiving an operating license is questionable. This asset is likely overstated on the balance sheet, and the bondholder should take little comfort in reported asset protection. At the other extreme is the forest products company whose vast timber acreage is significantly understated on the balance sheet. In addition to the assets' market value, some consideration should also be given to the liquidity of the assets. A company with a high percentage of its assets in cash and marketable securities is in a much stronger asset position than a company whose primary assets are illiquid real estate.

The wave of takeovers, recapitalizations, and other restructurings has increased the importance of asset coverage protection. Unfortunately for some bondholders, a merger or takeover has decimated their asset coverage by adding layers of debt to the corporate structure that is senior to his holdings. While the analyst would find it difficult to predict takeovers, it is incumbent upon the analyst to evaluate the degree of protection from takeovers and other restructurings that the bond indenture offers.

Standard & Poor's offers some assistance in this regard through its Event Risk Covenant Rankings, which assess the protection offered by the indenture to such restructurings. Standard & Poor's ranks this protection on a scale of E-1 (strong protection) to E-5 (little or no protection). The analyst must be mindful that indenture protection will vary significantly among the bonds of the same issuer.

In addition to the major variables discussed above, the analyst should also consider several other financial variables including intangibles, unfunded pension liabilities, the age and condition of the plant, and working capital adequacy.

*Intangibles.* Intangibles often represent a small portion of the asset side of a balance sheet. Occasionally, particularly with companies that have or have had an active acquisition program, intangibles can represent a significant portion of assets. In this case, the analyst should estimate the actual value of the intangibles and determine if this value is in concert with the balance sheet valuation. A carrying value significantly higher than market value indicates a potential for a write-down of assets. The actual write-down may not occur until the company actually sells a subsidiary with which the intangibles are identified. However, the analyst should recognize the potential and adjust capitalization ratios accordingly.

*Unfunded Pension Liabilities.* Unfunded pension liabilities can also affect a credit decision. Although a fully funded pension is not necessary for a high credit assessment, a large unfunded pension liability that is 10 percent or more of net worth can be a negative. Of concern is the company whose unfunded pension liabilities are sufficiently high to interfere with corporate planning. For example, a steel company with high unfunded pension liabilities might delay or decide against closing an unprofitable plant because of the pension costs involved. The analyst should also be aware of a company's assumed rate of return on its pension funds and salary increase assumptions. The higher the assumed rate of return, the lower the contribution a company must make to its pension fund, given a set of actuarial assumptions. Occasionally, a company having difficulty with its earnings will raise its actuarial assumption and thereby lower its pension contribution and increase earnings. The impact on earnings can be dramatic. In other cases, companies have attempted to "raid" the excess funds in an overfunded retirement plan to enhance earnings.

*Age and Condition of Plant.*   The age of a company's plant should also be estimated, if only to the extent that its age differs dramatically from industry standards. A heavy industrial company whose average plant age is well above that of its competitors is probably already paying for its aged plant through operating inefficiencies. In the longer term, however, the age of net plant is an indication of future capital expenditures for a more modern plant. In addition, the underdepreciation of the plant significantly lowers inflation-adjusted earnings.

The Financial Accounting Standards Board Statement Number 33 requires extensive supplementary information from most companies on the effect of changing prices. This information is generally unaudited and there is still no consensus on the best presentation of such data. However, the supplementary information provision does give the analyst an indication of the magnitude of the effects of inflation on a given company. The effects differ dramatically from industry to industry. At one extreme are the high-technology and financial firms, where the effects are nominal. At the other extreme are the capital intensive industries, where the effects are major.

*Working Capital.*   A final variable in assessing a company's financial strength concerns the strength and liquidity of its working capital. Working capital is defined as current assets less current liabilities. Working capital is considered a primary measure of a company's financial flexibility. Other such measures include the current ratio (current assets divided by current liabilities) and the acid test (cash, marketable securities, and receivables divided by current liabilities). The stronger the company's liquidity measures, the better it can weather a downturn in business and cash flow. In assessing this variable, the analyst should consider the normal working capital requirements of a company and industry. The components of working capital should also be analyzed. Although accounts receivable are considered to be liquid, an increase in the average days a receivable is outstanding may be an indication that a higher level of working capital is needed for the efficient running of the operation.

## Analysis of the Components of Return on Equity

Once the above financial analysis is complete, the bond analyst traditionally examines the earnings progression of the company and its historical return on equity (ROE). This section of analysis often receives less emphasis than the traditional ratio analysis. It is equally important, however, and demands equal emphasis. An analysis of earnings growth and ROE is vital in determining credit quality because it gives the analyst necessary insights into the components of ROE and indications of the sources of future growth. Equity analysts devote a major portion of their time examining the components of ROE, and their work should be recognized as valuable resource material.

A basic approach to the examination of the components of return on equity is presented in a popular investment textbook by Jerome B. Cohen, Edward D. Zinbarg, and Arthur Zeikel.[1]  Their basic approach breaks down return on equity into four principal components: pretax margins, asset turnover, leverage, and one minus the tax rate. These four variables multiplied together equal net income/stockholders' equity, or return on equity.

$$\left( \frac{\text{Nonoperating pretax income}}{\text{Sales}} + \frac{\text{Operating pretax income}}{\text{Sales}} \right) \times \frac{\text{Sales}}{\text{Assets}} \times \frac{\text{Assets}}{\text{Equity}}$$

$$\times (1 - \text{Tax rate}) = \text{Net Income/Equity}$$

In analyzing these four components of ROE, the analyst should examine their progression for a minimum of five years and at least through a business cycle. The progression of each variable should be compared with the progression of the same variables for the industry, and deviations from industry standards should be further analyzed. For example, perhaps two companies have similar ROE's, but one company is employing a higher level of leverage to achieve its results, whereas the other company has a higher asset-turnover rate. As the degree of leverage is largely a management decision, the analyst should focus on asset turnover. Why have sales for the former company turned down? Is this downturn a result of a general slowdown in the industry, or is it that assets have been expanded rapidly and the company is in the process of absorbing these new assets? Conversely, a relatively high rise in asset-turnover rate may indicate a need for more capital. If this is the case, how will the company finance this growth, and what effect will the financing have on the firm's embedded cost of capital?

---

[1] *Investment Analysis and Portfolio Management* (Homewood, Ill.: Richard D. Irwin, 1977).

The analyst should not expect similar components of ROE for all companies in a particular industry. Deviations from industry norms are often indications of management philosophy. For example, one company may emphasize asset turnover, and another company in the same industry may emphasize profit margin. As in any financial analysis, the trend of the components is as important as the absolute levels.

In order to give the analyst a general idea of the type of ratios expected by the major rating agencies for a particular rating classification, Standard & Poor's medians of key ratios for 1986–1988 by rating category are outlined in Exhibit 17–1. The analyst should only use this table in the most general applications, however, for two reasons. First, industry standards vary considerably. Second, financial ratios are only one part of an analysis.

For analysts interested in financial ratios for specific industries, Standard & Poor's CreditStats Service should be consulted. This service, introduced in October 1989, presents key financial ratios organized into 53 industry groups as well as ratio analysis by long-term rating category for utility companies.

**EXHIBIT 17–1**
**Three-Year (1986-1988) Medians of Key Ratios by Rating Category**

|  | AAA | AA | A | BBB | BB | B |
|---|---|---|---|---|---|---|
| Pretax interest coverage (x) | 13.52 | 8.98 | 5.25 | 3.69 | 2.42 | 1.32 |
| Pretax interest coverage including rents (x) | 5.23 | 5.14 | 3.18 | 2.21 | 1.78 | 1.26 |
| Pretax funds flow interest coverage (x) | 16.15 | 12.00 | 7.62 | 5.52 | 4.19 | 2.18 |
| Funds from operations/total debt (%) | 109.5 | 83.9 | 47.7 | 37.1 | 23.4 | 9.5 |
| Free operating cash flow/ total debt (%) | 46.2 | 16.8 | 10.2 | 7.4 | 0.8 | (4.2) |
| Pretax return on permanent capital employed (%) | 24.2 | 22.1 | 17.1 | 14.4 | 12.8 | 9.9 |
| Operating income/sales (%) | 21.2 | 16.3 | 13.5 | 12.1 | 13.1 | 9.8 |
| Long-term debt/ capitalization (%) | 12.4 | 18.8 | 30.1 | 37.7 | 50.5 | 66.1 |
| Total debt/capitalization including short-term debt(%) | 19.5 | 25.6 | 35.0 | 39.5 | 53.7 | 69.1 |
| Total debt/capitalization including short-term debt (including 8X rents) (%) | 33.8 | 36.5 | 49.1 | 55.4 | 63.8 | 75.1 |

Note: These are not meant to be minimum standards.

Source: Standard & Poor's Corporation, 1989.

## Nonfinancial Factors

After the traditional bond analysis is completed, the analyst should consider some nonfinancial factors that might modify the evaluation of the company. Among these factors are the degree of foreign exposure and the quality of management. The amount of foreign exposure should be ascertainable from the annual report. Sometimes, however, specific country exposure is less clear because the annual report often lists foreign exposure by broad geographic divisions. If there is concern that a major portion of revenue and income is derived from potentially unstable areas, the analyst should carefully consider the total revenue and income derived from the area and the assets committed. Further consideration should be given to available corporate alternatives should nationalization of assets occur. Additionally, the degree of currency exposure should be determined. If currency fluctuations are significant, has management hedged its exposure?

The quality and depth of management is more difficult to evaluate. Earnings progress at the firm is a good indication of the quality of management. Negative aspects would include a firm founded and headed by one person who is approaching retirement and has made no plan for succession. Equally negative is the firm that has had numerous changes of management and philosophy. On the other hand, excessive stability is not always desirable. If one family or group of investors owns a controlling interest in a firm, they may be too conservative in terms of reacting to changes in markets. Characteristics of a good management team should include depth, a clear line of succession if the chief officers are nearing retirement, and a diversity of age within the management team.

## INDENTURE PROVISIONS

An indenture is a legal document that defines the rights and obligations of the borrower and the lender with respect to a bond issue. An analysis of the indenture should be a part of a credit review in that the indenture provisions establish rules for several important spheres of operation for the borrower. These provisions, which can be viewed as safeguards for the lender, cover such areas as the limitation on the issuance of additional debt, sale and leasebacks, and sinking-fund provisions.

The indentures of bonds of the same industry are often similar in the areas they address. Correlation between the quality rating of the senior debt of a company and the stringency of indenture provisions is not perfect. For example, sometimes the debt test is more severe in A securities than in BBB securities. However, subordinated debt of one company will often have less restrictive provisions than will the senior debt of the same company. In addition, more restrictive provisions are also generally found in private placement issues. In analyzing a company's indenture, the analyst should look for the standard industry provisions. Differences in these provisions (either more or less restrictive) should be examined more closely. In this regard, a more restrictive nature is not necessarily preferable if the provisions are so restrictive as to hinder the efficient operation of the company.

Outlined below are the provisions most commonly found in indentures. These provisions are categorized by industry because the basic provisions are fairly uniform within an industry. A general description of the indenture is found in a company's prospectus. However, notification is generally given that the indenture provisions are only summarized. A complete indenture may be obtained from the trustee who is listed in the prospectus.

## Utility Indentures

*Security.*   The security provision is generally the first provision in a utility indenture. This provision specifies the property upon which there is a mortgage lien. In addition, the ranking of the new debt relative to outstanding debt is specified. Generally, the new bonds rank equally with all other bonds outstanding under the mortgage. This ranking is necessary, but it has created difficulty for the issuing companies because some mortgage indentures were written more than 40 years ago. Specifically, because all bondholders must be kept equal, companies must often retain antiquated provisions in their indentures. Often these provisions hinder the efficient running of a company due to structural changes in the industry since the original writing of the indenture. Changes in these provisions can be made, but changes have occurred slowly because of the high percentage of bondholders that must approve a change and the time and expense required to locate the bondholders.

*Issuance of Additional Bonds.*   The "Issuance of Additional Bonds" provision establishes the conditions under which the company may issue additional first mortgage bonds. Often this provision contains a debt test and/or an earnings test. The debt test generally limits the amount of bonds that may be issued under the mortgage to a certain percentage (often 60 percent) of net property or net property additions, the principal amount of retired bonds, or deposited cash. The earnings test, on the other hand, restricts the issuance of additional bonds under the mortgage unless earnings for a particular period cover interest payments at a specified level.

Although both of these tests may appear straightforward, the analyst must carefully study the definitions contained in the tests. For example, net property additions may be defined as plant that has operating licenses. Over the past decade, although there has been a great deal of nuclear construction, few operating licenses have been granted. Therefore, there is a significant backlog of construction work in progress (CWIP) that has had to be financed and yet may not be operational for some time. This situation can present problems for the company whose indenture requires net plant additions to be licensed and/or used and useful assets. In the extreme case, a company with a heavy nuclear construction program may find itself unable to issue bonds under its mortgage agreement.

In a similar circumstance, a company whose regulatory commission requires a substantial write-down related to nuclear construction may find itself unable to meet a debt test for several years if the write-down is taken in one quarter.

The potential for such write-downs has become more visible since the implementation of SFAS 90. SFAS 90 requires utilities to record a loss against income for any portion of an investment in an abandoned plant for which recovery has been disallowed. It further requires all costs disallowed for ratemaking purposes to be recognized as a loss against income as soon as it becomes probable with respect to disallowances of new plant costs resulting from a "cap" on expenditures. These losses may be reported by either restating financial statements for prior fiscal years or by recording the cumulative loss the year SFAS 90 is adopted.

*Maintenance and Replacement Fund.*   The purpose of a maintenance and replacement fund (M&R) is to assure that the mortgaged property is maintained in good operating condition. To this end, electric utility indentures generally require that a certain percentage of gross operating revenues, a percentage of aggregate bonded indebtedness, or a percentage of the utility's property account be paid to the trustee for the M&R fund. A major portion of the M&R requirement has historically been satisfied with normal maintenance expenditures. To the extent there is a remaining requirement, the company may contribute cash, the pledge of unbonded property additions, or bonds.

The rapid escalation of fuel costs during the 1970s has greatly raised the required levels of many M&R funds that are tied to operating revenues. This situation precipitated a number of bond calls for M&R purposes. Bonds can still be called for this purpose, but investors are more cognizant of this risk and are less likely to pay a significant premium for bonds subject to such a call. Furthermore, M&R requirements are slowly being changed toward formulas that exclude the large portion of operating income attributable to rises in fuel costs. Finally, a number of companies have indicated that they have no intention of using M&R requirements for calling bonds because of the original intent of the provision and also because of the disfavor such an action would generate among bondholders. However, the intent of companies in this regard would certainly be secondary if a call for M&R requirements were ordered by a commission.

*Redemption Provisions.*   The redemption, or call, provision specifies during what period and at what prices a company may call its bonds. Redemption provisions vary. Long-term bonds are generally currently callable but nonrefundable for five years. Exceptions are the longer term issues of the AT&T System, which are noncallable for five years. In the case of intermediate- and short-term issues, the noncall provisions generally extend to a year or two prior to maturity. Refunding is an action by a company to replace outstanding bonds with another debt issue sold at a lower interest expense. (Refunding protection does not protect the bondholder from refunding bonds with equity or short-term debt.) The refunding protection is a safeguard for bondholders against their bonds being refunded at a disadvantageous time.

*Sinking Fund.*   A sinking fund is an annual obligation of a company to pay the trustee an amount of cash sufficient to retire a given percentage of bonds. This requirement can often be met with actual bonds or with the pledge of property. In general, electric utilities have 1 percent sinking funds that commence at the end of the refunding period. However, there are several variations of the sinking-fund provision with which the analyst (and bondholder) should be familiar in that they could directly affect the probability of bonds being called for sinking-fund purposes. Some companies have nonspecific, or funnel, sinkers. This type of sinker often entails a 1 or $1\frac{1}{2}$ percent sinking fund applicable to all outstanding bonds. The obligation can be met by the stated percentage of each issue outstanding, by cash, or by applying (or funneling) the whole requirement against one issue or several issues.

*Other Provisions.*   In addition to the provisions discussed above, the indenture covers the events of default, modification of the mortgage, security, limitations on borrowings, priority, and the powers and obligations of the trustee. In general, these provisions are fairly standard. However, differences occur that should be evaluated.

## Industrial Indentures

Many of the provisions of an industrial indenture are similar to those of a utility's indenture, although specific items may be changed. For example, sinking-fund and redemption provisions are part of an industrial indenture. However, refunding protection for an industrial is generally 10 years (as opposed to 5 years for an electric utility), and sinking funds often have the option to double or more than double their requirements on an annual basis at the option of the company.

In general, there are five indenture provisions that have historically been significant in providing protection for the industrial bondholder.

***Negative Pledge Clause.*** The negative pledge clause provides that the company cannot create or assume liens to the extent that more than a certain percentage of consolidated net tangible assets (CNTA) is so secured without giving the same security to the bondholders. This provision is important to the bondholders because their security in the specific assets of the company establishes an important protection for their investment. The specific percentage of CNTA that is exempted from this provision is referred to as exempted indebtedness, and the exclusion provides some flexibility to the company.

***Limitation on Sale and Lease-Back Transactions.*** The indenture provision limiting sale and lease-back parallels the protection offered by the negative pledge clause, except that it provides protection for the bondholder against the company selling and leasing back assets that provide security for the debtholder. In general, this provision requires that assets or cash equal to the property sold and leased back be applied to the retirement of the debt in question or used to acquire another property for the security of the debtholders.

***Sale of Assets or Merger.*** The sale of assets or merger provision protects the debtholder in the event that substantially all of the assets of the company are sold or merged into another company. Under these circumstances, the provision generally states that the debt be retired or be assumed by the merged company.

***Dividend Test.*** The dividend test provision establishes rules for the payment of dividends. Generally, it permits the company to pay dividends to the extent that they are no greater than net income from the previous year plus the earnings of a year or two prior. Although this provision allows the company to continue to pay dividends when there is a business decline, it assures the debtholders that the corporation will not be drained by dividend payments.

***Debt Test.*** The debt test limits the amount of debt that may be issued by establishing a maximum debt/assets ratio. This provision is generally omitted from current public offerings. However, there are numerous indentures outstanding that include this provision. In addition, private placements often include a debt test. When present, the debt test generally sets a limit on the amount of debt that can be issued per dollar of total assets. This limitation is sometimes stated as a percentage. For example, a 50 percent debt/asset limit restricts debt to 50 percent of total assets.

## Financial Indentures

***Sinking-Fund and Refunding Provisions.*** Similar to industrial indentures, indentures for finance issues specify sinking-fund and refunding provisions. In general, finance issues with a short maturity are noncallable, whereas longer issues provide 10-year call protection. Occasionally, an issue can be called early in the event of declining receivables. Sinking funds are not as common in finance issues as they are in industrial issues, although they are standard for some companies.

*Dividend Test.* Perhaps the most important indenture provision for a debtholder of a finance subsidiary is the dividend test. This test restricts the amount of dividends that can be upstreamed from a finance subsidiary to the parent and thereby protects the debtholder against a parent draining the subsidiary. This provision is common in finance indentures, but it is not universal. (One notable exception is International Harvester Credit, now Navistar.)

*Limitation on Liens.* The limitation on liens provision restricts the degree to which a company can pledge its assets without giving the same protection to the bondholder. Generally, only a nominal amount may be pledged or otherwise liened without establishing equal protection for the debtholder.

*Restriction on Debt Test.* The debt test limits the amount of debt the company can issue. This provision generally is stated in terms of assets and liabilities, although an earnings test has occasionally been used.

## UTILITIES

Utilities are regulated monopolies. These companies generally operate with a high degree of financial leverage and low fixed-charge coverage (relative to industrial companies). These financial parameters have been historically accepted by investors due to the regulation of the industry and the belief that there is minimal, if any, bankruptcy risk in those securities because of the essential services they provide. The changing structure of the electric utility industry brought about by increasing investment in nuclear generating units and their inherent risk has changed this belief. Initially, the faltering financial position of General Public Utilities precipitated by the Three Mile Island nuclear accident and the regulatory delays in making a decision regarding the units highlighted the default risk that does exist in the industry. More recently, the defaults of several Washington Public Power Supply System issues and the bankruptcy of of Public Service Company of New Hampshire reemphasized the default risk. In addition, the industry is faced with the acid rain issue and increased uncertainty in construction costs and growth rates. In 1985, Standard & Poor's developed more conservative financial benchmarks for a given rating to reflect the increased risk in the industry.

## Segments within the Utility Industry

There are three major segments within the utility industry: electric companies, gas companies, and telephone companies. This chapter will deal primarily with the electric utilities. This segment encompasses most of the variables affecting the industry in general.

## Financial Analysis

There are four major financial ratios that should be considered in analyzing an electric utility: leverage, pretax interest coverage, cash flow/spending, and cash flow/capital.

Leverage in the electric utility industry is high relative to industrial concerns. This degree of leverage is accepted by investors because of the historical stability of the industry. The expected ranges for AAA, AA, A, BBB, and BB companies are outlined below:

| Rating Classification | Debt Leverage |
| --- | --- |
| AAA | Less than 41% |
| AA | 39–46% |
| A | 44–52% |
| BBB | 50–58% |
| BB | Greater than 56% |

In calculating the debt leverage of an electric utility, long-term debt/capitalization is standard. However, the amount of short-term debt should also be considered because this is generally variable-rate debt. A high proportion of short-term debt may also indicate the possibility of the near-term issuance of long-term bonds. In addition, several companies guarantee the debt of subsidiaries (regulated or nonregulated). The extent of these guarantees should be considered in calculating leverage.

Fixed-charge coverage for the electric utilities is also low relative to coverage for industrial companies. Standard & Poor's expected ranges for coverage are as follows:

| Rating Classification | Expected Pretax Fixed-Charge Coverage |
| --- | --- |
| AAA | Greater than 4.5X |
| AA | 3.5–5.0X |
| A | 2.5–4.0X |
| BBB | 1.5–3.0X |
| BB | Less than 2.0X |

These ranges are accepted by investors because of the stability of the industry. However, due to the changing fundamentals of the industry discussed above, perhaps less emphasis should be placed on the exact coverage figures and more on the trend and quality of the coverage.

The utility industry is unique in that its earnings include allowance for funds used during construction (AFUDC). AFUDC is an accounting treatment that allows utilities to recognize income (at a rate determined by individual regulatory commissions) on the amount of funds employed in construction. The percentage that AFUDC represents of total earnings varies significantly from almost zero to well in excess of 70 percent of earnings. Currently, AFUDC generates more than 50 percent of industry earnings. Obviously, the higher the percentage that AFUDC represents of net earnings, the lower the quality of earnings. This becomes evident when the cash flow of a utility is calculated. Often, the cash flow of a utility with substantial AFUDC is less than the dividend requirements of the company. In this instance, the company is returning the capital of the shareholders!

In calculating fixed-charge coverage, the analyst should calculate two sets of coverage figures—fixed-charge coverage including AFUDC and fixed-charge coverage excluding AFUDC, with the latter being more important.

A third important ratio is cash flow/spending. This ratio should be approximated for three years (the general range of an electric company's construction forecast). The absolute level as well as the trend of this ratio gives important insights into the trend of other financial parameters. An improving trend indicates that construction spending is probably moderating, whereas a low cash flow/spending ratio may indicate inadequate rates being approved by the commissions and a heavy construction budget. Estimates for construction spending are published in the company's annual reports. Although these are subject to revision, the time involved in building a generating unit makes these forecasts reasonably reliable. In 1985, Standard & Poor's deemphasized this ratio primarily due to its volatility. Although it will still be considered, Standard & Poor's now emphasizes cash flow/capital as a preferable indicator of cash flow adequacy.

Standard & Poor's ranges for cash flow/spending (suspended in January 1985) and its expected ranges for net cash flow/permanent capital are as follows:

| Rating Classification | Expected Cash Flow/ Spending | Net Cash Flow/ Permanent Capital |
|---|---|---|
| AAA | — | Greater than 7% |
| AA | More than 40% | 5–8% |
| A | 20–50% | 3–6% |
| BBB | Less than 30% | Less than 4% |

In calculating cash flow, the standard definition outlined above should be followed. However, AFUDC should also be subtracted, and any cash flow from nonregulated subsidiaries should be segregated and analyzed within the total context of the company. The regulatory commissions take divergent views on nonutility subsidiaries. Some commissions do not regulate these subsidiaries at all, whereas other commissions give inadequate rate relief to an electric utility with a profitable nonutility subsidiary under the premise that the company should be looked at as a whole. In the extreme, the latter view has encouraged companies to sell or spin off some subsidiaries.

## Nonfinancial Factors

Although financial factors are important in analyzing any company, nonfinancial factors are particularly important in the electric utility industry and may alter a credit assessment. The five nonfinancial factors outlined below are of particular importance to the utility industry. These are in addition to the nonfinancial factors discussed earlier.

Regulation is perhaps the most important variable in the electric utility industry. All electric companies are regulated. Most are primarily regulated by the state or states within which they operate. If a company operates in more than one state, the analyst should weigh the evaluation of the regulatory atmosphere by revenues generated in each state. In addition, the Federal Energy Regulatory Commission (FERC) regulates interstate operations and the sale of wholesale power. Currently, FERC regulation is considered to be somewhat more favorable than that of the average state regulatory commission.

Utilities that are constructing or operating nuclear reactors are also subject to the regulation of the Nuclear Regulatory Commission (NRC). The NRC has broad regulatory and supervisory jurisdiction with respect to the construction and operation of nuclear reactors. Importantly, the NRC approves licensing of nuclear reactors.

Regulation by state commissions, FERC, and the NRC is most visible. However, regulation by congressional action also has potential financial impact. For example, passage of acid rain legislation appears likely. Such legislation would likely mandate the reduction of sulfur dioxide and nitrogen oxide emissions. In order to reduce these emissions, utilities can either install scrubbers or switch to low-sulfur coal. Either option is costly.

Regulation is best quantified by recent rate decisions and the trend of these decisions. Although a company being analyzed may not have had a recent rate case, the commission's decisions for other companies operating within the state may be used as a proxy. Regulatory commissions are either appointed or elected. In either case, the political atmosphere can have a dramatic effect on the trend of decisions.

The regulators determine innumerable issues in a rate decision, although analysts often mistakenly focus only on the allowed rate of return on equity or the percentage of request granted. In particular, the commissions determine how much of construction work in progress (CWIP) is allowed into the rate base. A company may appear to have a favorable allowed ROE but be hurt by the fact that only a small portion of the company's capital is permitted to earn that return, while the CWIP earns nothing. Due to the high construction budgets for nuclear generating plants and the length of time these plants are under construction, allowance of CWIP in the rate base is of critical importance. Some companies have more than half of their capital in CWIP that is not permitted to earn a return.

The importance of whether CWIP is allowed in the rate base is highlighted by the financial distress and January 1988 bankruptcy filing of Public Service Company of New Hampshire (PSNH). PSNH's Seabrook Nuclear Unit I was virtually complete in 1986. However, licensing delays and New Hampshire's statutory prohibition of CWIP in the rate base were major contributing factors in the bankruptcy filing.

In addition, regulators have a high degree of control over the cash flow of a company through the allowance or disallowance of accounting practices and the speed with which decisions are made on cases.

The source of a company's energy is a second important variable. Currently, a company with a heavy nuclear construction budget is viewed negatively relative to a company with coal units under construction. Not only are the lead times for nuclear construction much longer than for other generating plants, but the risk of delays in licensing and going on line are significant in nuclear construction. The energy source variable relates to a third variable—the growth and stability of the company's territory. Although above-average growth is viewed positively in an industrial company, it may be viewed negatively with respect to an electric utility. An electric utility with above-average growth must necessarily have a high construction budget. To the extent that CWIP is disallowed or only partially allowed in the company's rate base, the company is likely to have declining financial parameters until the unit is operational.

Slow growth is not necessarily positive if it places a utility in a position of excess capacity. The increase in co-generation and the mergers of utilities in order to better match supply and demand can place a utility at risk. This could result if Utility A were selling power to Utility B. If the expiration of the contract coincides with Utility B's ability to purchase power for less and results in Utility B's nonrenewal of the contract, Utility A could be negatively affected unless it can sell the power to a third utility.

A fourth variable, whether or not a company is a subsidiary of a holding company, should also be considered. Holding company status permits non-utility subsidiaries, but it is not universal that these subsidiaries (if successful) will improve the overall credit quality of the company. This depends on the regulatory atmosphere. Furthermore, when there are several electric utility subsidiaries, the parent is more likely to give relatively large equity infusions to the relatively weak subsidiaries. The stronger subsidiary may have to "support" the other subsidiaries. Finally, holding companies should be analyzed in terms of consolidated debt. Although a particular subsidiary may have relatively strong financial parameters, off-balance sheet financing may lower the overall assessment.

A final nonfinancial factor is the rate structure of a utility. An electric utility with a comparatively low rate structure is generally in a stronger position politically to request rate increases than one with rates higher than national averages, and particularly one with rates higher than regional averages.

## FINANCE COMPANIES

Finance companies are essentially financial intermediaries. Their function is to purchase funds from public and private sources and to lend them to consumers and other borrowers of funds. Finance companies earn revenue by maintaining a positive spread between what the funds cost and the interest rate charged to customers. The finance industry is highly fragmented in terms of type of lending and type of ownership. This section will briefly outline the major sectors in the industry and then discuss the principal ratios and other key variables used in the analysis of finance companies.

### Segments within the Finance Industry

The finance industry can be segmented by type of business and ownership. Finance companies lend in numerous ways in order to accommodate the diverse financial needs of the economy. Five of the major lending categories are (1) sales finance, (2) commercial lending, (3) wholesale or dealer finance, (4) consumer lending, and (5) leasing. Most often, companies are engaged in several of these lines rather than one line exclusively. Sales finance is the purchase of third-party contracts that cover goods or services sold on a credit basis. In most cases, the sales finance company receives an interest in the goods or services sold. Commercial finance is also generally on a secured basis. However, in this type of financing, the security is most often the borrower's accounts receivable. In factoring, another type of commercial lending, the finance company actually purchases the receivables of the company and assumes the credit risk of the receivables.

Dealer or wholesaler finance is the lending of funds to finance inventory. This type of financing is secured by the financed inventory and is short-term in nature. Leasing, on the other hand, is intermediate to long-term lending—the lessor owns the equipment, finances the lessee's use of it, and generally retains the tax benefits related to the ownership.

Consumer lending has historically involved short-term, unsecured loans of relatively small amounts to individual borrowers. In part because of the more lenient bankruptcy rules and higher default rates on consumer loans, consumer finance companies have dramatically expanded the percentage of their loans for second mortgages. The lower rate charged to individuals for this type of loan is offset by the security and lower default risk of the loan.

There are numerous other types of lending in addition to those described above. Among these are real estate lending and export/import financing.

The ownership of a finance company can significantly impact evaluation of the company. In some instances, ownership is the most important variable in the analysis. There are three major types of ownership of finance companies: (1) captives, (2) wholly owned, and (3) independents.

Captive finance companies, such as General Motors Acceptance Corporation and J. C. Penney Financial, are owned by the parent corporation and are engaged solely or primarily in the financing of the parent's goods or services. Generally, maintenance agreements exist between the parent and the captive finance company under which the parent agrees to maintain one or more of the finance company's financial parameters, such as fixed-charge coverage, at a minimum level. Because of the overriding relationship between a parent and a captive finance subsidiary, the financial strength of the parent is an important variable in the analysis of the finance company. However, captive finance companies can have ratings either above or below those of the parent.

A wholly owned finance company, such as Associates Corporation of North America, differs from a captive in two ways. First, it primarily finances the goods and services of companies other than the parent. Second, maintenance agreements between the parent and the subsidiary are generally not as formal. Frequently, there are indenture provisions that address the degree to which a parent can upstream dividends from a finance subsidiary. The purpose of these provisions is to prevent a relatively weak parent from draining a healthy finance subsidiary to the detriment of the subsidiary's bondholders.

Independent finance companies are either publicly owned or closely held. Because these entities have no parent, the analysis of this finance sector is strictly a function of the strengths of the company.

## Financial Analysis

In analyzing finance companies, several groups of ratios and other variables should be considered. There is more of an interrelationship between these ratios and variables than for any other type of company. For example, a finance company with a high degree of leverage and low liquidity may be considered to be of high investment quality if it has a strong parent and maintenance agreements. No variable should be viewed in isolation but rather within the context of the whole finance company/parent company relationship.

*Loan Loss.* The most important ratio in analyzing a finance company is the relationship of the company's loan loss experience and related variables. Net loan losses are defined as loans deemed uncollectible and therefore written off less recoveries of loans previously written off. The importance of this ratio is twofold. First, the net loan loss is a major and unpredictable expense variable. Second, a company with an above-average loan loss record has the necessary business expertise to create a loan portfolio of above-average quality. A related variable that should also be evaluated is the company's provision for these losses. A company whose loss provisions are consistently inadequate should be further explored for other indications of liberal accounting.

In evaluating the company's loan loss experience, the analyst must also necessarily consider the quality of the portfolio. Diversification is one measure of portfolio quality. Is the portfolio diversified across different types of loans? If the company is concentrated in or deals exclusively in one lending type, is there geographic diversification? A company that deals exclusively in consumer loans in the economically sensitive Detroit area would not be as favorably viewed as a company with broad geographic diversification. Accounting quality is also an important factor in assessing portfolio quality. The more conservative the accounting for recognition of income, revenue, and loan losses, the better. The security for the loans is also an important variable in portfolio quality. The stronger the underlying security, the higher the loan quality. The analyst should be primarily concerned with the level of loans compared with levels of similar companies and the risk involved in the type of lending. For example, the expected loan loss from direct unsecured consumer loans is higher than for consumer loans secured by second mortgages. However, the higher fees charged for the former type of loan should compensate the company for the higher risk.

*Leverage.* Leverage is a second important ratio used in finance company analysis. By the nature of the business, finance companies are typically and acceptably more highly leveraged than industrial companies. The leverage is necessary to earn a sufficient return on capital. However, the acceptable range of leverage is dependent on other factors such as parental support, portfolio quality, and type of business. The principal ratio to determine leverage is total debt to equity, although such variations as total liabilities to equity may additionally be used. In a diversified company with high portfolio quality, a leverage ratio of 5 to 1 is acceptable. On the other hand, a ratio of 10 to 1 is also acceptable for a captive with a strong parent and maintenance agreements. The analyst should always view the leverage of a finance company in comparison with similar companies.

*Liquidity.* The third important variable in finance company analysis is liquidity. Because of the capital structure of finance companies, the primary cause of bankruptcies in this industry is illiquidity. If for some reason a finance company is unable to raise funds in the public or private market, failure could quickly result. This inability to raise funds could result from internal factors, such as a deterioration in earnings, or from external factors such as a major disruption in the credit markets. Whatever the cause, a company should have some liquidity cushion. The ultimate liquidity cushion, selling assets, is only a last resort because these sales could have long-term, detrimental effects on earnings. The traditional liquidity ratio is cash, cash equivalents, and receivables due within one year divided by short-term liabilities. The higher this ratio, the higher the margin of safety. Also to be considered are the liquidity of the receivables themselves and the existence of bank lines of credit to provide a company with short-term liquidity during a financial crisis. In general, the smaller and weaker companies should have a higher liquidity cushion than those companies with strong parental backing, who can rely on an interest-free loan from the parent in times of market stress.

*Asset Coverage.* A fourth important variable in the analysis of finance companies that is related to the three variables discussed above is the asset coverage afforded the bondholder. In assessing asset protection, the analyst should consider the liquidation value of the loan portfolio.

*Earnings Record.* The fifth variable to be considered is the finance company's earnings record. The industry is fairly mature and is somewhat cyclical. The higher the annual EPS growth, the better. However, some cyclicality should be expected. In addition, the analyst should be aware of management's response to major changes in the business environment. The recent more lenient personal bankruptcy rules and the fact that personal bankruptcy is becoming more sociably acceptable have produced significantly higher loan losses in direct, unsecured consumer loans. Many companies have responded to this change by contracting their unsecured personal loans and expanding their portfolios invested in personal loans secured by second mortgages.

*Size.* A final factor related to the finance company or subsidiary is size. In general, the larger companies are viewed more positively than the smaller companies. Size has important implications for market recognition in terms of selling securities but also in terms of diversification. A larger company is more easily able to diversify in terms of type and location of loan than is a smaller company, and thereby to lessen the risk of the portfolio.

In addition to an analysis of the financial strength of the company according to the above variables, the analyst must incorporate the net effect of any affiliation the finance company has with a parent. If this affiliation is strong, it may be the primary variable in the credit assessment. The affiliation between a parent company and a finance subsidiary is straightforward; it is captive, wholly owned, or independent. However, the degree to which a parent will support a finance subsidiary is not as straightforward. Traditionally, the integral relationship between a parent and a captive finance subsidiary has indicated the highest level of potential support. However, it is becoming increasingly clear that a wholly owned finance subsidiary can have just as strong an affiliation. For example, General Electric Credit Corporation (GECC) finances few or no products manufactured by its parent, General Electric Company. However, General Electric receives substantial tax benefits from its consolidation of tax returns with GECC. Additionally, General Electric has a substantial investment in its credit subsidiary. Therefore, although there are no formal maintenance agreements between General Electric and GECC, it can be assumed that General Electric would protect its investment in GECC if the finance subsidiary were to need assistance. In other instances, it may be that the affiliation and maintenance agreements are strong but that the parent itself is weak. In this case, the strong affiliation would be discounted to the extent that parent profitability is below industry standards.

In addition to affiliation, affiliate profitability, and maintenance agreements, the analyst should also examine any miscellaneous factors that could affect the credit standing of the finance company. Legislative initiatives should be considered to determine significant changes in the structure or profitability or the industry.

## THE RATING AGENCIES AND BROKERAGE HOUSES

There is no substitute for the fundamental analysis generated by the fixed income analyst. The analyst has many sources of assistance, however. The major sources of assistance are the public rating agencies and brokerage houses that specialize in fixed income research.

### Rating Agencies

Five rating agencies provide public ratings on debt issues: Standard & Poor's Corporation, Moody's Investors Service, Fitch Investors Service, Duff & Phelps, Inc., and McCarthy, Crisanti & Maffei, Inc, (MCM).

Standard & Poor's (S&P) and Moody's are the most widely recognized and used of the services, although Duff & Phelps and Fitch are frequently cited. Fitch was revitalized in 1989 by a new investor group. S&P and Moody's are approximately the same size, and each rates the debt securities of approximately 2,000 companies. If a company desires a rating on an issue, it must apply to the rating agency. The agency, in turn, charges a one-time fee of generally $5,000 to $20,000. For this fee, the issue is reviewed periodically during the life of the issue, and at least one formal review is made annually.

Four of the rating agencies designate debt quality by assigning a letter rating to an issue. Standard & Poor's ratings range from AAA to D, with AAA obligations having the highest quality investment characteristics and D obligations being in default. In a similar fashion, Moody's ratings extend from Aaa to

C, and Fitch's from AAA to D. Duff & Phelps, historically, assigned numerical ratings from 1 to 17, with 1 analogous to a AAA.

In June 1989, Duff & Phelps changed its ratings to match the scales used by Moody's and Standard & Poor's. Duff & Phelps' ratings currently extend from AAA to CCC.

Public ratings are taken seriously by corporate managements because a downgrade or an upgrade by a major agency can cost or save a corporation thousands of dollars in interest payments over the life of an issue. In the event of downgrade below the BBB− or Baa3 level, the corporation may find its bonds ineligible for investment by many institutions and funds, either by legal or policy constraints. Corporations therefore strive to maintain at least an investment-grade rating (Baa3 or higher) and are mindful of the broad financial parameters that the agencies consider in deriving a rating.

Many factors promote the use of agency ratings by investors, bankers, and brokers. Among these strengths are the breadth of companies followed, the easy access to the ratings, and the almost universal acceptance of the ratings. On the other hand, the ratings are criticized for not responding quickly enough to changes in credit conditions and for being too broad in their classifications.

The slow response time of the agencies to changes in credit conditions is certainly a valid criticism. There are few instances in which the lag is significant in terms of a dramatic change, but the market generally anticipates rating changes. The rating agencies have become increasingly sensitive to this criticism and have been quicker to change a rating in light of changing financial parameters. On the other hand, the agencies recognize the financial impact of their ratings and their obligation to rate the long-term (as opposed to the short-term) prospects of companies. They therefore have a three- to five-year perspective and purposefully do not change a rating because of short-term fluctuations.

Standard & Poor's has addressed this criticism directly by creating *Creditwatch,* a weekly notice of companies whose credit ratings are under surveillance for rating changes. These potential rating changes can be either positive or negative. The basis for potential change can emanate from a variety of sources, including company and industry fundamentals, changes in the law, and mergers. Duff & Phelps also has a "Watch List" of companies that are potential upgrades or downgrades. Additionally, subscribers to the agencies' services have access to agency analysts to discuss individual companies or industries.

Investors who are concerned that the ratings are too broad in their classifications have several options among the brokerage-house services that offer more continuous ratings.

## Brokerage-House Services

Numerous brokerage houses specialize in fixed income research. Generally, these services are available only to institutional buyers of bonds. The strength of the research stems from the in-depth coverage provided, the statistical techniques employed, and the fine gradations in rating. On the other hand, the universe of companies that these firms follow is necessarily smaller than that followed by the agencies.

In spite of the numerous services available, the market continues to demand more fixed income research. To partially satisfy this demand, many independent analysts are evaluating segments of the market previously not covered or inadequately covered. This research is frequently supplied by specialists in independently originated research such as Autranet.

## CONCLUSION

This chapter has emphasized a basic methodology in analyzing corporate bonds. A format for analysis is essential. However, analysis of securities cannot be totally quantified, and the experienced analyst will develop a second sense about whether to delve into a particular aspect of a company's financial position or to take the financial statements at face value. All aspects of credit analysis, however, have become increasingly important as rapidly changing economic conditions and increasingly severe business cycles change the credit quality of companies and industries.

# CHAPTER 18

## HIGH-YIELD BONDS

*Robert D. Long, CFA*
*Managing Director*
*The First Boston Corporation*

As the name implies, high yield is a relative notion. The simplest definition of a high-yield bond is a security with a promised return (coupon) in excess of that available from a risk-free asset class. The higher yield compensates investors for assuming various risks, which for corporate bonds is primarily risk of default but may also include price volatility, liquidity, or uncertainty regarding maturity.

In a book on fixed income securities, a chapter on high-yield securities is not entirely at home. Although the majority of the market is composed of bonds with fixed coupons, the high-return characteristics and generally junior position in the capital structure makes this security class much closer to equity than traditional fixed income securities.

In the 1970s, most high-yield bonds were fallen angels—originally investment-grade bonds, BBB or better, that had been downgraded because of deteriorating financial results. Steel, auto, and other industrial products companies made up much of the universe. In the 1980s, the market grew dramatically from new issues, many of which represented mezzanine financing in leveraged acquisitions. Financing techniques of recent years have developed a variety of instruments including bonds with equity interests, variable payments depending on operating results or commodity indexes, extendible maturities, resettable coupons, automatic conversion to equity, and other esoteric features that further blurs the traditional distinction between bonds and stocks.

The boundaries of the high-yield market stretch from an arbitrary cutoff point at the upper end of bonds rated less than BBB by one of the two leading rating agencies to nonrated issues with no current coupon. The lower end resembles equity, particularly if a variable-return component is included. Perhaps the only real difference between high-yield and equity is that there is always a layer of equity with voting rights, junior to the high-yield securities.

## MAJOR SECURITY CLASSES

While high-yield securities have been a part of the U.S. capital market for over a hundred years, private placements have historically been a large part of the market. During the 1980s, however, new underwritings of public high-yield debt exploded, as the market grew from $2.6 billion in 1977 to $227.8 billion by the end of 1989 (see Exhibit 18–1). Of this total, eight major security classes can be identified:

*Fixed-Cash Coupon.* This is the largest segment accounting for 69 percent of the market at the end of 1989. A fixed-cash coupon and a fixed maturity are the main characteristics, with a wide range of call/put features, sinking-fund variations, and maturities available. The seniority also varies from the most senior secured position to the most subordinated issues in a given capital structure.

**EXHIBIT 18–1**
**The Evolution of the High-Yield Market, 1977–1989: Innovative Security Types Have Been Developed**

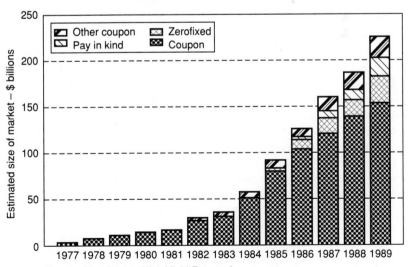

Source: First Boston High Yield Research

*Zero Coupon.* The second largest sector is a fixed-maturity obligation with a zero coupon. Within this category, the majority of issues have a combination of a zero coupon for an initial period of three to seven years, followed by a cash coupon for the remaining life of the security. While most of these are subordinated issues, a number of senior zeros exist. The use of zero or zero/fixed coupons was developed to provide an initial period of additional liquidity for newly formed leveraged acquisitions. During the zero coupon period, a company has time to develop asset sales plans or operating improvements to enhance cash flows to levels that would ultimately support higher interest payments. Unfortunately, this flexibility can also be used to finance higher prices for acquisitions that ultimately may not be able to accommodate the accreting interest charges.

*Pay-In-Kind Coupon (PIK).* A variation of the zero coupon is the pay-in-kind feature, which allows the coupon payments to be made in units of the security itself. For example, a 14 percent PIK bond would deliver 14 percent annually in additional "baby" bonds rather than cash. At the end of the PIK period, an investor would own a larger number of securities, but the cash flow would be identical to a zero coupon investment of the same maturity.

*Step Coupons.* These are a variation of the zero/fixed coupon in which the initial rate is set at a lower coupon than the rate in a subsequent period. They are used for the same purpose as zero/fixed issues, but offer the advantage of some cash income to investors during the initial period.

*Extendible Reset Notes.* Instead of having a fixed maturity, an extendible note can have an optional extension, usually at the option of the issuer but occasionally at the option of the holder. Extendible notes are usually accompanied by a feature that resets the coupon so that the security trades at par or 101 percent. While this reset feature was designed to provide a cushion to prevent the bond price from deteriorating at the end of a period, the issuer effectively assumes a large refinancing risk in doing so, particularly if there is no maximum or cap on the reset rate. For high-yield securities, the reset feature also contains the risk that the higher coupon required could not be supported by the credit and would increase the likelihood of a default, even if cash flow remains stable. Therefore, reset securities are most likely to be practical when an asset sale or other source of cash is likely to be sufficient to retire the issue at the reset date.

*Increasing-Rate Notes.* These are cash-paying instruments in which the coupon payment automatically escalates annually or quarterly. While the stated maturity may be ten years or more, the rising coupon increases the probability of early retirement. These have been widely used as public bridge facilities, where a more permanent vehicle is ultimately put in place.

*Floating-Rate Coupons.* Floating-rate high-yield debt is only a small part of the high-yield universe. In general, the rates are tied to a widely followed fixed income index but in some cases may be tied to commodity prices such as copper or oil.

*Preferred Stock.* The high-yield market includes issues of preferred stock with mandatory redemption. The majority of recent issues also have PIK features. The use of preferred stock has been encouraged by senior bank lenders with a desire to see a larger equity cushion in leveraged transactions. However, most of the issues were created in exchange for common stock rather than in underwritings and often trade at large discounts to face value.

As the market has grown, it has become more diverse. Exhibit 18–2 shows the industries that were represented at the end of 1989. Consumer manufacturing (10.3%) was the largest single category, followed by general industrial (7.9%) and food and drug distribution (7.8%). These are all industries with relatively stable cash flows, which are better suited to financial leverage. The breakdown by rating (Exhibit 18–3) shows that 55 percent of the market is single-B rated, with CCC/Split CCC the second largest category. Within each rating category, the yields vary dramatically between different credits. This suggests that the rating categories are much less useful in differentiating between the credit quality of high-yield bonds than they are in the investment-grade market.

## RISK AND RETURN

While high-yield bonds experience some degree of price volatility, the most important risk faced by investors is that of default. This can be through a failure to pay interest and principal, usually accompanied by a bankruptcy proceeding, or through the attempt to restructure outside of a bankruptcy filing through a distressed exchange offer. As this chapter will show, the yield spread of the high-yield universe over the "risk-free" Treasury bond during the 1980s has substantially exceeded the loss to investors from default experience. While the returns of any individual bonds are likely to be dramatically negative in a default, this specific security risk is similar in the equity market, and is the reason that diversification reduces risk in high-yield portfolios. This is the basis for the need to diversify a high-yield portfolio. In 1989, however, a combination of adverse market developments led, sparked by enactment of legislation by Congress requiring thrifts to sell all high yield holdings, to a price decline far greater than the default losses. This performance underscores the need for fixed income investors to understand price volatility risk as well as credit risk.

**EXHIBIT 18–2**
**First Boston High Yield Index (Weighting by Industry)**

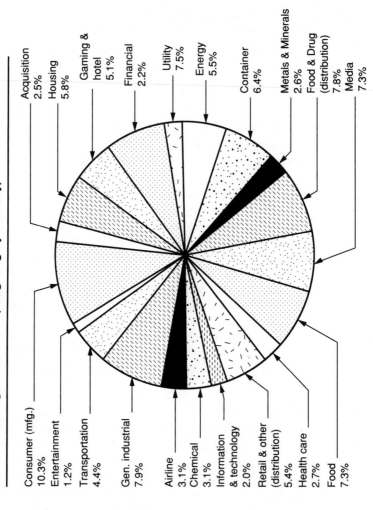

Acquisition 2.5%
Housing 5.8%
Gaming & hotel 5.1%
Financial 2.2%
Utility 7.5%
Energy 5.5%
Container 6.4%
Metals & Minerals 2.6%
Food & Drug (distribution) 7.8%
Media 7.3%

Consumer (mfg.) 10.3%
Entertainment 1.2%
Transportation 4.4%
Gen. industrial 7.9%
Airline 3.1%
Chemical 3.1%
Information & technology 2.0%
Retail & other (distribution) 5.4%
Health care 2.7%
Food 7.3%

**EXHIBIT 18–3**
**First Boston High Yield Index (Weighting by Rating)**

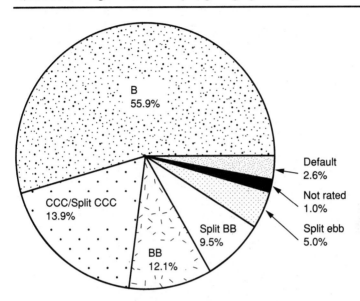

For the nine years from 1981 through 1989, the First Boston High Yield Index[1] posted a return of 14.15 percent compounded annually. This compares with 12.89 percent for the 10-year U.S. Treasury bond (see Exhibit 18–4). For the period, the high-yield market outperformed the government market by 126 basis points annually. Because the index return includes the effect of defaults, this spread represents the amount by which high-yield investors have been over-compensated, relative to a risk-free rate. This outperformance for the decade is impressive considering the unusually wide divergence of 1600 basis points between the high-yield and Treasury returns in 1989 (see Exhibit 18–4). During the same period, the equity market returned 15.94 percent as measured by the S&P 500 but only 9.42 percent annually as measured by the OTC composite, which underscores the substantial volatility of the equity market and the variation in returns of different equity sectors.

## Default Losses

To estimate the effect of defaults on returns, the First Boston default study calculated the loss to investors from every high-yield default since 1977. Whereas

---

[1] The First Boston High Yield Index is a market-weighted index of high-yield public securities encompassing different types of securities such as cash pay, zero/fixed, and defaulted securities.

**EXHIBIT 18–4**
**Comparison of 9-Year Total Returns and Volatility: 1981–1989**

| Index | Annual Total Return* | | | | | | | | |
|---|---|---|---|---|---|---|---|---|---|
| | 1981 | 1982 | 1983 | 1984 | 1985 | 1986 | 1987 | 1988 | 1989 |
| First Boston High Yield Index™ | 8.96% | 36.57% | 13.91% | 10.69% | 24.93% | 15.63% | 6.54% | 13.65% | 0.38% |
| 10-Year Treasury | 4.85 | 32.02 | 3.50 | 12.93 | 26.31 | 20.15 | –2.79 | 6.11 | 16.57 |
| Shearson/Lehman Govt./ Corp. Index | 2.95 | 39.20 | 9.27 | 16.62 | 24.05 | 16.52 | 2.55 | 7.59 | 14.23 |
| Salomon Brothers Mortgage PT Index | 1.18 | 41.35 | 10.86 | 15.76 | 25.72 | 13.44 | 4.06 | 8.83 | 15.18 |
| Shearson/Lehman Govt. Agency Index | 9.36 | 27.75 | 7.39 | 14.50 | 20.43 | 15.31 | 2.20 | 7.04 | 14.57 |
| S&P 500 | –5.00 | 21.60 | 22.60 | 6.20 | 31.70 | 18.60 | 5.23 | 16.44 | 31.50 |
| OTC Composite | –3.21 | 18.67 | 19.87 | –11.22 | 31.36 | 7.36 | –5.26 | 15.42 | 19.26 |

**EXHIBIT 18–4**—*Continued*

| | 9-Year Comparison | | | |
| Index | Value of $100 Inv't | 9-Year Compounded Growth Rate | Return Spread vs HY Index | Volatility of Annual Returns |
| --- | --- | --- | --- | --- |
| First Boston High Yield Index™ | $329.43 | 14.16% | 0 | 10.03% |
| 10-Year Treasury | 297.88 | 12.89 | −126 | 10.69 |
| Shearson/Lehman Corp. Index | 332.68 | 14.29 | 12 | 10.86 |
| Salomon Brothers Mortgage PT Index | 341.43 | 14.62 | 45 | 11.44 |
| Shearson/Lehman Govt. Agency Index | 298.99 | 12.94 | −122 | 7.30 |
| S&P 500 | 378.54 | 15.94 | 177 | 11.64 |
| OTC Composite | 224.81 | 9.42 | −474 | 13.37 |

*Measured by the Standard Deviation of Annual Returns

Source: First Boston High Yield Research

most studies of default have focused on the amount of issues as a percentage of the universe (default rate), the First Boston study measures the losses investors have experienced from price declines and loss of coupons. Actual prices have been used to measure the loss to investors. Our study also includes the negative impact of distressed exchange offers, which has been a popular alternative to an outright default or Chapter 11 filing. The results show that default losses have been much smaller than the yield spread of high-yield bonds over Treasury securities.

Our study shows the market-weighted average default loss rate from 1977 through 1989 to be 1.86 percent, including all distressed exchange offers and fallen angels (Exhibit 18–5). When fallen angels are excluded, the rate drops to 1.49 percent. Fallen angels account for nearly one third of the par value of defaulting issues but only 20 percent of the total loss to investors. The lower loss rate can be attributed to Texaco's strategic default in 1987. Its bonds suffered an average total loss of only 18.5 percent (12.8% excluding coupon loss). The weighted-average principal loss over the 13-year period is 49.6 percent. From 1977–89, a total of 381 bonds of 167 companies defaulted or announced exchange offers.

Over $7 billion of public debt defaulted or was involved in a distressed exchange offer during 1989, resulting in a default loss rate of 2.49 percent. This figure is based on an average amount of high-yield debt outstanding (as

**EXHIBIT 18–5**
**Default Loss Rates: 1977–1989**

| Year | High-Yield Straight-Debt Universe* (Millions) | Defaulted Principal Amount† (Millions) | Dollar Principal Loss (Millions) | Principal Loss | Total Loss Including Coupon (Millions) | Default Loss Rates | Without FA Debt |
|---|---|---|---|---|---|---|---|
| 1977 | $8,479.0 | $585.4 | $288.9 | 49.35% | $308.5 | 3.64% | 2.74% |
| 1978 | 9,401.0 | 265.2 | 83.5 | 31.48 | 92.6 | 0.99 | 0.64 |
| 1979 | 10,675.0 | 126.5 | 17.1 | 13.51 | 22.8 | 0.21 | 0.08 |
| 1980 | 15,125.0 | 257.1 | 149.3 | 58.08 | 162.1 | 1.07 | 0.60 |
| 1981 | 17,362.0 | 349.7 | 115.7 | 33.09 | 131.1 | 0.76 | 0.09 |
| 1982 | 18,536.0 | 1,038.3 | 622.7 | 59.97 | 670.7 | 3.62 | 0.70 |
| 1983 | 28,233.0 | 379.4 | 133.1 | 35.09 | 155.0 | 0.55 | 0.44 |
| 1984 | 41,700.0 | 408.9 | 184.2 | 45.05 | 207.3 | 0.50 | 0.34 |
| 1985 | 59,178.0 | 2,055.8 | 796.8 | 38.76 | 920.0 | 1.55 | 1.55 |
| 1986 | 92,985.0 | 4,319.0 | 2,210.7 | 51.19 | 2,254.4 | 2.64 | 2.22 |
| 1987 | 121,827.0 | 7,485.0 | 1,833.0 | 24.49 | 2,286.0 | 1.88 | 1.13 |
| 1988 | 163,618.0 | 3,661.2 | 1,955.6 | 53.41 | 2,173.7 | 1.33 | 0.96 |
| 1989 | 215,202.0 | 7,298.4 | 4,967.6 | 68.06 | 5,444.8 | 2.53 | 2.49 |
| Totals | | $28,230.0 | $13,358.2 | | $15,028.9 | | |

*Weighted Averages*

| | 1977–1989 | Without FA Debt |
|---|---|---|
| Default Loss Rate | 1.87% | 1.51% |
| Principal Loss | 49.50% | 54.98% |

* Mid-year figures
† Includes distressed exchange offers

Source: First Boston, S&P, and Moody's for 1977–86

**EXHIBIT 18–6**
**Excess Premiums vs. Default Losses** (1978–1990)

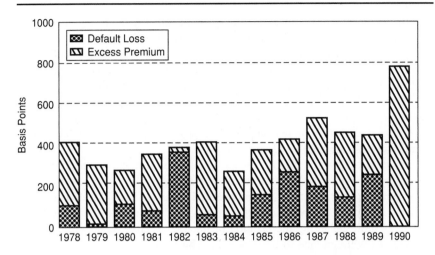

of June 30th) of $215.2 billion. The 2.49 percent rate is higher than the historical experience of 1.86 percent over the 13 years from 1977–1989. This is due primarily to a more severe principal loss of 68.3 percent for 1989 compared with the historical weighted-average loss of 54.3 percent, not including Texaco. The onslaught of negative news confronting the high-yield market during the last four months of the year fostered widespread fear that a recession would result in a massive wave of defaults and restructurings. This accentuated the difference between strong and suspect credits and hit distressed securities particularly hard, resulting in the higher principal loss number. In fact, the 1989 principal loss is not that far from the recession-plagued 1982 experience of 60.0 percent.

The spread over Treasuries relative to default losses, or excess premium, is shown in Exhibit 18–6. The premium is calculated as the spread between the yield on the high-yield market at the beginning of the year and the rate on the 10-year U.S. Treasury, which is closest to the average life of the high-yield universe. The default loss rate for each year is compared against the spread. In no year since 1977 has the default loss rate reached the spread between the two markets. The average excess premium since 1977 has been 249 basis points. The First Boston High Yield Index on December 31, 1989 was a record 790 basis points. Although the default rate may remain high in 1990, it could triple from 1989 levels and still leave some excess premium. This clearly shows that investors have been more than compensated for assuming the default risk of high-yield bonds.

## CONCLUSION

Much attention has been paid to the negatives of the high-yield market. It is certainly not an appropriate security class for all investors, any more than commodity futures would be. However, there has been a consistent negative slant in much of the published commentary about the market, particularly in the public media. It is a market that many observers love to hate. Such a bias is obviously inconsistent with the returns for the decade of the 1980s and is one of the reasons that spreads widened to record levels at the end of 1989. Other reasons for the market weakness have been the higher default rates of 1989, expectations of a higher rate in 1990, as well as a general contraction of liquidity in both the high-yield and equity markets.

Looking toward the 1990s, several points are clear. First, the high-yield market growth will slow from the breakneck speed of the 1980s, as is typical for any market after a year of sharp underperformance. Second, regulatory decisions regarding S&L and insurance company holdings of high-yield securities as well as those regarding the taxation of interest expense versus dividends of corporations will continue to be important. Third, the degree of economic stability in the United States will have a direct impact on default rates and the performance of the sectors, as will interest rates in general. Finally, the wide spreads available should continue to generate demand for the security class. One new area of demand has been created from structured finance vehicles, primarily collateralized bond obligations (CBOs). These represent the application of existing structures for asset-backed securities to new financing vehicles in which the collateral is a diversified portfolio of high-yield securities.[2] By offering different tranches of a structured financing vehicle, different investors can assume varying degrees of risk participation and return from the sector, just as the fixed income markets have learned with other asset classes such as credit card receivables (which have a higher default rate) and auto loans. In summary, the rising yields in the high-yield market will eventually generate enough buying interest to bring supply and demand into better balance which will also bring yield spreads closer to the average levels experienced in the 1980s.

---

[2] Asset-backed securities are discussed in Chapter 31.

# CHAPTER 19

## CREDIT CONSIDERATIONS IN EVALUATING HIGH-YIELD BONDS

*Jane Tripp Howe, CFA*
*Senior Credit Analyst*
*Pacific Investment*
*Management Company*

## INTRODUCTION

Many analysts shy away from the analysis of high-yield bonds. Perhaps their reticence is a function of the security's lack of a rating or of a rating that is "below investment grade" and therefore publicly documented as having varying degrees of investment risk or elements of speculation. Although the comfort of an investment-grade rating is missing or its assignment is often enough to prohibit the security's inclusion in a portfolio, the potential rewards of this area of credit analysis are well worth the time invested.

The analysis of high-yield bonds, or junk bonds as they are unfortunately nicknamed, is similar to the complete analysis of any other corporate bond, but the emphasis of the analysis must change. Both high-yield and junk bonds are securities that trade primarily on their creditworthiness, as opposed to the level of interest rates. However, an important difference exists between junk and high-yield securities. Both classifications generate high yields. Although the yield of junk bonds reflects the poor quality of the underlying issuer, the yield of many high-yield securities reflects a variety of circumstances such as the small size of a firm or the lack of a credit history. While rating agencies often penalize such a firm by giving it a low rating, the firm may exhibit good credit quality in many areas. It is this difference that presents the challenge to the credit analyst.

The recent expansion of the high-yield market presents an opportunity for the analyst to identify the quality in issues that the majority of analysts have ignored. This process involves in-depth research. Because many high-yield bonds have short histories, the analyst must necessarily make more projections. Overall, the analysis will be heavily weighted to the second dimension of credit analysis discussed in Chapter 17—those aspects that are most commonly associated with the analysis of common stock. In addition, the analyst is often faced with innovative characteristics of the security such as options exercisable only under certain circumstances. These features must be evaluated within the context of the total valuation process.

The artificial differentiation between bonds and the associated technique of credit analysis stem perhaps from some investors' segmentation of the market, whereby the bond portion is the "safe" area in which no risk should be taken. In this framework, potential rewards from bonds are probably not considered. Recent academic papers and numerous studies generated by the securities industry show the fallacy of such reasoning. In a Wharton study, Blume and Keim have shown that from January 1982 to May 1984, a diversified portfolio of high-yield bonds produced higher returns than diversified portfolios of either high-grade bonds or equities.[1] During this period, the lower quality bonds generated an annual return of 20.3 percent. During the same period, A-rated bonds generated 16.6 percent annually, AAA-rated bonds 15.0 percent annually, and equities even less.

If this is the case, why have these credits been historically so carefully ignored by most analysts? There are four major reasons for this inefficient behavior. First, institutional and legal constraints are often imposed on money managers, confining investments to "investment-grade" securities (i.e., those rated BBB − or higher by the rating agencies). Interestingly, these same money managers often buy the equity of a company whose debt they would not buy. Second, the high-yield market has been well developed for only a few years. Previously, the high-yield market lacked liquidity and stability. Portfolio managers hesitated to invest in this market for portfolios that required liquidity. Third, diversification in the low-grade market has historically been difficult. Until recently, the market has been heavily weighted in the railroad industry, as potential issuers relied primarily on bank financing and private placements. Finally, the lack of significant buyers restricted young growth companies from issuing public debt. High-yield securities were therefore associated with junk securities and the behavior was reinforced. A further discussion of these points is given in Chapter 45, along with a history of the high-yield market.

The analysis of high-yield bonds is essentially the same as the complete analysis of investment-grade bonds. However, because of the nature of the company, more time will generally be involved. Extensive market projections are

---

[1] Marshall E. Blume and Donald B. Keim, "Risk and Return Characteristics of Lower-Grade Bonds" (Philadelphia: Rodney L. White Center for Financial Research, 1984) pp. 3–4.

often required as well as possible explanations for inconsistencies in growth patterns. In addition, the commitment involved in the analysis of high-yield bonds cannot be made to merely analyze a single credit or even several credits. Because the prices of high-yield bonds change more as a function of changes in creditworthiness (nonmarket risk) than as a function of interest-rate changes (market risk), any commitment to high-yield bonds must be made within the context of a portfolio in order to help it benefit from diversification and lowering of specific risk. The analyst must be familiar with a number of industries to accomplish this.

The importance of diversification and its ability to increase expected return per unit of risk is an accepted tenet of portfolio management. Even portfolio managers who invest solely in high-grade securities will lower their risk by diversifying across industries, coupons, and maturities. The addition of a diversified portfolio of high-yield bonds may add more to a portfolio than the generally perceived higher rate of return. The study by Blume and Keim found that lower quality bonds experienced less volatility or risk than high-grade bonds or equities over the period studied, when risk was defined as the standard deviation of monthly returns.[2] Blume and Keim suggest that this result may be explained by the fact that much of the risk associated with high-yield bonds is nonmarket or firm specific and can therefore be eliminated by diversification.

The implications of this result are far reaching. Many investors, particularly institutional investors, are leery of the high-yield bonds because of the added risk they attribute to these bonds. This avoidance behavior is reinforced by the occasional well-publicized default or bankruptcy. The evidence shows, however, that the investor would be better off in terms of return and possible reduction of risk by including a diversified portfolio of high-yield bonds in a total portfolio. The avoidance behavior may in fact enhance yields. It is unfortunate that well-intentioned bureaucrats occasionally seek to "protect" the public by trying to legislate that certain types of high-yield securities be avoided. They may be increasing the rewards to the investors who do participate in the high-yield market.

Similar to any other bond analysis, the analyst's purpose here is to determine the value of the security. Will the issuing company be able to meet its interest and principal payments? Will the credit quality of the bond change over the life of the issue?

The progression of analysis for a high-yield bond should also be the same as that for any bond as discussed in Chapter 17. The analysis must be rigorous, however, as the margin of safety is generally more narrow. In addition, several areas of analysis should be expanded.

---

[2] Blume and Keim, "Risk and Return Characteristics of Lower-Grade Bonds," p. 4.

## Competition

The size of a company has important credit implications. It is well known that many "small" firms file for bankruptcy each year. It should be noted, however, that these firms are not the same "small" firms that are issuing high-yield debt. The firms labeled small by investors are generally small only in relation to the giants of the industry. As the rating agencies favor the very large, well-established firms, the "small" firms suffer by comparison.

In an industry where the leader or leaders can set pricing, a small firm could be at a significant disadvantage. In the scenario where the pricing is set, the small firm must have unit costs approaching, equal, or lower than the pricing leaders. The small firm that is inefficient could not withstand a prolonged pricing war. The leaders in this case could launch a pricing war to gain market share and effectively drive the inefficient producers out of business. In certain circumstances, the small firm may be able to differentiate its product and thereby control a certain segment of the market. However, there is always the threat of competition. The company with a market niche must be monitored to ensure that the niche remains the domain of the company in question.

## Cash Flow

One of the most important elements in analyzing a high-yield security is cash flow. In such an analysis, cash flow/long-term debt is not as important as cash flow/total cash requirements. Does the company have enough cash flow to meet its interest payments and to fund necessary research and growth? Does the company have sufficient cash flow to tide it over during a period of weak economic activity? What borrowing capacity is available? The ability to borrow enabled several large firms such as Chrysler and Ford Motor to meet their debt obligation when these companies were producing significant losses. As a result, the companies were granted time to reformulate products and reposition themselves for an upturn in the economy and industry. The smaller firm may not have this advantage. On the other hand, the larger firms, which often have the luxury of expanding borrowings during weak markets, may be trading on their market name long after their credit quality has deteriorated.

The analyst must particularly focus on cash flow in certain leveraged buyout situations. Although the purchaser may have a specific plan for selling assets to reduce debt and related payments, time may be critical. Can the company meet its cash obligations if the sale of assets is delayed? How liquid are the assets that are scheduled for sale? Are the appraised values of these assets accurate? What financial flexibility does the company have in terms of borrowing capacity? Are indenture covenants being met?

## Net Assets

In analyzing a bond, the liquidation value of the assets must be ascertained or at least approximated. Are these assets properly valued on the balance sheet? Of particular interest may be real estate holdings. For example, in analyzing the gaming companies, a market assessment of land holdings should be included. On the other hand, one should also consider the likelihood of those assets being available for liquidation, if necessary. To whom do they belong? Are they mortgaged or being used as collateral? Assets are occasionally spun off to the equity owners of the company. In such a circumstance, the bondholders may experience a sudden and dramatic deterioration of credit quality. Other bondholders are secured by specific assets such as railroad cars or a nuclear power station. In these circumstances, the value and marketability of the collateral must be ascertained. Collateral by definition must be specific and so must be the analysis. Ten railroad engines may appear to be secure until it is discovered that the engines are not only obsolete but have not been maintained for a number of years.

Particular attention must be paid to the asset protection in a takeover situation. In this instance, assets that originally provided protection for your holdings could be used to secure new debt senior to your holding.

The analyst must also focus on the location of the assets. If the assets are in a foreign country, the analyst should be familiar with that country's laws regarding expatriation of funds. In the extreme case, the analyst should be familiar with that country's laws regarding bankruptcy proceedings.

## Management

Management is a critical element in the assessment of any firm. Given enough time, poor management can bankrupt the most prosperous firm. Conversely, good management is essential to the long-term survival of all firms. Many successful firms were started by employees of the leaders in an industry. The high-technology area is an example of this. Often, employees decide to start their own firms for personal profit. Very often the firms are founded by some of the leading engineers or salesmen. While the creative talents and profit motive in these firms may be high, the whole management team must be evaluated. Is there a strong financial manager? Is there a strong marketing manager? Where are the controls? Start-up operations provide high incentives for success. The ownership of a significant portion of the company by management is generally positive. Too often employees of a large firm relate only to their personal paychecks and not to the overall profitability of the firm.

## Leverage

Companies that issue high-yield bonds are generally highly leveraged. Leverage per se is not harmful and in many circumstances is beneficial to growth. However, the degree of leverage should be evaluated in terms of its effect on the financial flexibility of the firm. As pointed out in Chapter 17, leverage should be calculated on absolute and market-adjusted bases. The most common approach to market adjustment is to calculate a market value for the equity of the firm. To the extent that the common stock is selling below book value, leverage will be understated by a traditional approach. Some firms also adjust the market value of debt in calculating leverage. While this approach is interesting, a consistent approach must be employed when convertibles are considered in the equity equation. The benefit of adjusting the equity side of the leverage equation is clear. As the market values a company's equity upward, the market is indicating a willingness to support more leverage. A similar increase in the market adjustment of a firm's debt may indicate an upward appraisal of creditworthiness or an overall lowering of interest rates. In either case, the company would probably have the opportunity to refinance at a lower cost and thereby increase profitability.

## SPECIAL TYPES OF HIGH-YIELD SECURITIES

In addition to the special circumstances involved in analyzing a high-yield security, the analyst is faced with nontraditional forms of financing. This is not surprising. Over the past ten years, the high-yield market has provided the majority of innovative financing. A thorough understanding of the type of security is necessary to complete an evaluation. Some modifications of the security have important implications for the analysis. The modifications and refinements to high-yield securities have been numerous. Several of these modifications are outlined below.

### Exchangeable Variable-Rate Notes (EVRNs)

EVRNs are subordinated, intermediate-term obligations that pay interest quarterly. The interest rate is fixed for a short period. This period is called the "teaser," since the fixed rate is generally set above the rate dictated by the formula. After the fixed-rate period, the rate is adjusted quarterly and is tied to certain benchmarks such as the prime rate or 90-day Treasury bills. Generally, the issuer has the option to exchange the notes for fixed-rate notes with predetermined features such as maturity, call price, etc. Generally the issuer must exchange the securities after five years.

## Usable Bonds

Usable bonds are securities that are issued with a warrant to purchase the issuing company's common stock. When the warrants are exercised, the bonds can be used at par in lieu of cash. (These bonds are also called synthetic convertibles when they are considered with their respective warrants.) The market value of these securities is sometimes highly correlated to the value of the company's stock and amount of usable bonds outstanding in relation to the amount required for exercise of the warrants.

## Springing Issues

Springing securities are issues that will change one or more of their characteristics if a certain event occurs. One such issue was a note offering with springing warrants that would be exercisable only if someone tried to acquire the issuer. Another springing security was originally issued as subordinated debt but would become senior indebtedness when an old outstanding debenture had been discharged as long, as the issuing company was able to create the additional senior indebtedness without violating any covenants of a third outstanding issue. In evaluating springing issues, the analyst must determine the likelihood of the issue's changing form and the value of the change.

## Pay-in-Kind Securities

Pay-in-kind securities (PIKs) give the issuer the option to pay interest in either cash or additional securities for a specified period of time. This option gives the issuer flexibility in terms of its cash-flow management. The PIK market has grown significantly in recent years.

In evaluating PIK securities, the analyst must use a discounted cash-flow technique if the security is trading at either a discount or a premium. This approach is required because the value of the payments-in-kind are equal to the current market value of the security.

## Other Issues

In recent years, the assortment of high-yield securities has proliferated. Issues that offer a share of the firm's profits in addition to a stated interest rate as well as issues backed by commodities have been floated. Other firms have issued private placements with registration rights.

The variety of financing alternatives is likely to continue to expand. The analyst must evaluate the characteristics of each issue to determine how much, if any, value it adds to the credit. The analysis of low-grade securities often requires additional work. The investor is rewarded for this effort in two ways. The first benefit is enhanced yield. This yield advantage has been significant. Historically, low-grade securities have yielded 300 to 500 basis points more than comparable Treasury issues. The yield advantage versus high-grade corporates has almost been as great. When this advantage is compounded annually, the performance benefit to individuals as well as institutional investors is significant. The advantage is only slightly reduced when default risk is considered. The second benefit of high-yield credit analysis is the likelihood of identifying credits that are improving. These credits will not only provide enhanced yield but also capital appreciation relative to the market. This benefit is familiar to the credit analyst who views his job as identifying improving as well as deteriorating credits.

## PERFORMANCE OF HIGH-YIELD SECURITIES AND DEFAULT RISK

Historically, defaults and bankruptcies have been nominal in relation to out-standing U.S. debt. W. Braddock Hickman's study, *Corporate Bond Quality and Investor Experience*, concluded that, on average, during the period 1900–1943, 1.7 percent of all straight public and private debt defaulted.[3] More recent studies have found historic default rates of only approximately .5 percent annually, with several years producing no defaults.

Recently, several default studies have been published. These studies address various time frames between 1970 and 1987. Although the studies vary in their methodologies and definitions of default, the consensus annual default figure is approximately 2–3 percent of all high-yield issues outstanding.

Drexel Burnham produced a study in 1988 that tracked the annual high-yield default rates on a cumulative basis. The results of this study are presented in Exhibit 19–1.

Any study of defaults must pay particular attention to the industry source of the default. When defaults are analyzed by industry, it becomes evident that close to 50 percent of the high-yield defaults during 1977–1987 were in the oil and steel industries. This fact clearly emphasizes the potential reward of credit research.

Regardless of how low default rates are in a given year, investors who own defaulted issues will be greatly impacted if the defaulted issues represent a significant portion of their portfolios. A portfolio must be well diversified to avoid such a negative scenario.

---

[3] W. B. Hickman, *Corporate Bond Quality and Investor Experience* (Princeton University Press and the National Bureau of Economic Research, 1958).

**EXHIBIT 19–1**
**Cumulative Annual High-Yield Default Rate**
**(1977–1987)**

| Year | Cumulative Annual Rate |
|------|------------------------|
| 1977 | 0% |
| 1978 | 0 |
| 1979 | 0.27 |
| 1980 | 0.86 |
| 1981 | 0.60 |
| 1982 | 0.81 |
| 1983 | 0.71 |
| 1984 | 0.80 |
| 1985 | 1.39 |
| 1986 | 2.01 |
| 1987 | 2.03 |

Source: Drexel Burnham Lambert, "1988 Annual High Yield Market Report," p. 21.

In spite of careful analysis, the investor may be faced with a default or bankruptcy. In such a circumstance, analysis must continue. There have been situations where a defaulting issuer has subsequently resumed payments or issued stock to debt holders that eventually was worth more than the original debt.

The potential for defaults in the high-yield area has discouraged some investors from participating in this market. For some investors, this may not have been a rational decision. To fully evaluate the decision whether to participate in the high-yield market, potential investors must balance the potential for default with the potential for gain. The potential for gain for high-yield versus high-grade bonds is illustrated in Exhibit 19–2.

## BROKERAGE HOUSES AND THE RATING AGENCIES

As with high-grade securities, there is no substitute for sound fundamental analysis. The rating agencies can provide some help. More in-depth research in this area is being generated by the brokerage houses. The backruptcy of Drexel Burnham Lambert has generated increased research efforts at other brokerage houses that are trying to fill the void created by Drexel's bankruptcy. Currently, several firms are active in the high-yield area.

**EXHIBIT 19–2**
**Total Returns of High-Yield versus High-Grade Bonds (1980–1988)**

| Year | High-Yield Bonds | High-Grade Bonds |
|------|------------------|------------------|
| 1980 | −1.3% | 0.9% |
| 1981 | 4.7 | 2.9 |
| 1982 | 33.1 | 36.6 |
| 1983 | 17.5 | 7.4 |
| 1984 | 7.9 | 16.0 |
| 1985 | 23.7 | 25.3 |
| 1986 | 13.1 | 16.9 |
| 1987 | 8.1 | 1.2 |
| 1988 | 14.4 | 9.4 |

Source: Merrill Lynch Pierce Fenner & Smith Capital Markets.

## CONCLUSION

Analysts often classify themselves according to the type of security they analyze. This classification is misleading. An analyst who understands the principles of accounting and credit analysis should feel equally comfortable with high- or low-grade securities. Analysis will never be a rote process. It is only the good analyst who knows when to delve into a specific area exhaustively and when to quickly assess other areas of a company. This intuitive aspect of credit analysis is particularly important in analyzing low-grade credits. It can usually be developed with experience.

# CHAPTER 20

## INVESTING IN CHAPTER 11 AND OTHER DISTRESSED COMPANIES*

*Jane Tripp Howe, CFA*
*Senior Credit Analyst*
*Pacific Investment*
*Management Company*

Investors and analysts often shy away from distressed and Chapter 11 companies. On the surface, this hesitancy is understandable. Most investors would not willingly invest in bankrupt companies, which the Random House Dictionary defines as "at the end of one's resources" or in the state of "utter ruin, failure, depletion, or the like." Most analysts believe that analysis directed at healthy companies is more likely to be profitable. This avoidance of bankrupt and distressed companies is not wise for several reasons. First, investing in Chapter 11 companies can be highly profitable. Many companies use the bankruptcy process to reorganize. Often, the reorganization process gives companies a new start that can provide rewarding investment opportunities. The key to success is to differentiate between the companies that are truly depleted and those that will reorganize successfully. Secondly, a total avoidance of bankrupt companies may result in an investor selling a holding of a bankrupt company at its lowest price. The prices of securities of companies that have filed for Chapter 11 often plummet when the filing is made. These prices often recover somewhat with time. Investors who immediately sell their securities upon news of a filing will often suffer a more significant loss than would occur if they had been patient.

Historically, most investors who owned companies in bankruptcy did so by default. Today, many investors actively invest in companies in reorganization.

* I wish to thank George Putnam III, publisher of *Bankruptcy Datasource,* for his helpful comments and suggestions.

These investors intend to profit by taking advantage of the substantial inefficiencies in this market. This chapter gives the investor an understanding of the bankruptcy process and outlines a method for evaluating securities in bankruptcy.

The methodology outlined here can also apply to companies that are distressed but have not filed for bankruptcy. In the case of distressed companies, the analyst should value the company as an ongoing business as well as a business that has filed for bankruptcy. With these two valuations in hand, the analyst will be able to weigh the potential benefit/cost of investing in the security.

## THE IMPORTANCE OF A BASIC UNDERSTANDING

Most investors believe that they will never have to deal with a company that has filed for protection under the Bankruptcy Code. Although this may be true for the majority of investors, as long as there are bankruptcies, there will be investors who own the securities of the bankrupt companies. The possibility of your owning the securities of one of these companies is increasing as the number of companies filing for protection under the Bankruptcy Code has been increasing in recent years. A basic understanding of bankruptcy analysis is also important in order to evaluate the potential rewards of this market.

## OVERVIEW OF BANKRUPTCY

There are two types of investors who deal with the securities of companies in bankruptcies. The first type is the investor who owns the security by default. This investor purchases the security with the intention of profiting from a healthy company. The second type of investor buys the securities of bankrupt companies after the company has filed for protection. Regardless of how you came to own the security, the analysis of the holding is similar.

Investors who analyze their investment holdings carefully are unlikely to be surprised if one of their investments petitions for bankruptcy protection. The decline of a company into bankruptcy generally takes several years and is often the result of illiquidity and deteriorating operating performance. Although most bankruptcies can be predicted in advance with sound credit analysis, occasionally companies file for protection that are financially sound. For example, Johns Manville was profitable when it declared bankruptcy in August 1982. Manville filed for bankruptcy because of the contingent liabilities arising from claims of individuals suffering from asbestos-related diseases as well as claims from property owners who incurred costs for the removal of asbestos materials from their property. Although bankruptcy filings for nonfinancial reasons are less easy to predict, they should not be complete surprises. For example, sometime in the future, tobacco companies could be faced with a similar situation regarding their contingent liabilities for illnesses caused by smoking. The astute analyst should always be mindful of footnotes that outline contingent liabilities.

All companies that file for bankruptcy are governed by the Bankruptcy Reform Act of 1978, which then-President Carter signed into law on November 6, 1978. The Act became law on October 1, 1979. The purpose of the law is twofold: (1) to provide consistency to the companies filing for protection under the law and (2) to provide a framework under which a company can either reorganize or liquidate in an orderly fashion. Perhaps the most important facet of bankruptcy law is the protection it affords companies in distress. Filing for protection triggers the automatic stay provisions of the Code. This provision precludes attempts of creditors to collect prepetition claims from the debtor or otherwise interfere with its property or business. This provision gives the debtor breathing room to formulate a plan of reorganization or to formulate a plan for orderly liquidation. Creditors are necessarily discouraged from racing to the court to dismember the debtor.

The current Bankruptcy Code consists of 15 chapters. Each chapter deals with a different facet and/or type of bankruptcy. For most investors, an understanding of Chapters 7 and 11, which deal with corporate liquidation and corporate reorganization, respectively, are sufficient.

## When a Company Files for Protection

When a company files for protection under the bankruptcy law, it can do so either voluntarily or involuntarily. A voluntary petition is filed by the company declaring bankruptcy. In an involuntary bankruptcy, the petition is filed by the creditors of the company.

When a company files for bankruptcy, the filing may include only the parent company and exclude one or more subsidiaries. For example, when Southmark filed for protection in July 1989, several of its subsidiaries were not included in the filing. These nonfiling subsidiaries included NACO Finance, Thousand Trails, Southmark California (Carlsberg Corp.), and Servico. In a similar manner, when Lomas Financial filed for Chapter 11 in September 1989, many of its operating subsidiaries were not included. In an effort to educate the investing public as to which of its subsidiaries filed and which did not file, it placed a full page advertisement in the New York Times to outline the difference.

When a company files for bankruptcy, it files in the appropriate circuit and the appropriate district within that circuit. (There are 11 circuits and 93 districts.) The "appropriate" court cannot necessarily be predicted. Appropriate can mean the court with jurisdiction over the company's headquarters location or perhaps the court with jurisdiction over its principal place of business. Companies have some flexibility in their choice of geographic location for filing. Eastern Airlines, for instance, filed in New York even though its corporate headquarters is Miami. The airline stated it filed in New York because it has substantial operations in

New York, and its financial efforts and lawyers are there. Many of Eastern's creditors are also in New York, which will facilitate meetings.

When a company petitions for protection, its petition is accompanied by several items, including basic administrative information and a listing of the 20 largest creditors. These creditors will be contacted by the court and called for a meeting. Other financial information is required within 15 days of filing. Sometimes, the financial information accompanies the filing. Other times, it is delayed. Included in this financial information is a listing of assets and liabilities as of the petition date. This listing represents the company's best estimate of its assets and liabilities. Often, this listing of assets and liabilities can cover several hundred pages.

Significant adjustments are often made to the assets and liabilities by the time a company completes its reorganization process. These adjustments are noticeable when assets are sold during the reorganization process and also when the asset values are compared with estimates of the liquidation value of the assets. This is principally because the values are based on the company as an ongoing business in its prepetition form. Revco's February 1989 sale of 113 sites exemplifies the discrepancy between listed asset values and realizable value. In its February 1989 sale, Revco was enabled (with bankruptcy court approval) to sell 14 sites. What is more significant, however, is the fact that no bids were made on several sites. The difference between listed market value of assets and the liquidation value of these assets can be even more dramatic. For example, in its September 5, 1989, Second Amended Plan of Reorganization, Cardis Corporation estimated that its inventory would be discounted by 52 percent. Cardis further estimated that its net plant, property, and equipment would be discounted by 23 percent in a liquidation. In fact, the only asset that will not suffer a discount will be cash.

Although the assets and liabilities filed with the Bankruptcy Court are not precise, they are useful in that they give an indication of the overall picture of the company. For example, when Manville filed for protection in 1982, it had more assets than liabilities and was a profitable company. On the other hand, when Worlds of Wonder filed on December 22, 1987, it listed $271.6 million in debts and $222.1 million in assets.

Once a company files for protection under the Bankruptcy Code, the company becomes a "debtor-in-possession." As such, the company continues to operate its business under the supervision of the court. Usually, the debtor-in-possession needs to obtain court approval only for major and unusual transactions (such as the sale of property). Generally, the United States Trustee for the particular district is assigned to the proceeding. The U.S. Trustee's duties are essentially administrative. The appointment of the U.S. Trustee has become fairly standard.

The increasing complexity of bankruptcies has resulted in the increased frequency of a second appointment to a bankruptcy case. This appointment is usually an examiner but can also be a trustee. The requirements for the appointment of an examiner are fairly broad. An examiner can be appointed if the appointment serves the interests of the creditors, equity holders, or other interests. For example, an examiner was appointed in the case of A. H. Robbins because management had shown an inability to follow the bankruptcy rules. An examiner was also appointed in the case of Eastern Airlines, whose slide into bankruptcy was at least partially caused by striking unions. Shortly after Eastern Airlines filed for protection, the unions petitioned the court to have a trustee appointed to run the Company. Eastern management petitioned the court to have an examiner appointed rather than a trustee so that it would have more flexibility in running its business. The federal bankruptcy judge in the Eastern case ordered the appointment of a "powerful" examiner, who was given a broad mandate to end the strike. Sometimes, if there are allegations of negligence or mismanagement, then an examiner will be appointed to investigate the allegations and report to the court. Occasionally, a trustee will be appointed by the court to take control of the business if there is gross negligence or mismanagement. This is relatively unusual. A recent case where a trustee was appointed was Sharon Steel, where there were allegations of fraud.

## Proceeding Toward a Plan

The purpose in filing for protection under the Bankruptcy Code is to give the debtor time to decide whether it should reorganize or liquidate and time to formulate a plan for the chosen action. The intent generally is to successfully reorganize. The first step in formulating a plan of reorganization is the appointment of committees. Generally, only a committee of unsecured creditors is appointed by the U.S. Trustee. Frequently, this committee is comprised of an elected subcommittee of the 20 largest creditors. The committee represents a particular class of claimants. Its principal function is to help formulate a plan of reorganization that is equitable to all classes and that will be confirmed (approved) by the court and the claimants. The committee approach is necessary because plans are negotiated.

Although only one committee is usual, there has been a growing incidence of multiple committees, each representing a different class of creditors. For example, in the Revco D.S. bankruptcy, there are two committees—the Noteholders Committee and the Unsecured Creditors Committee. In the Allegheny bankruptcy, there were four committees: the Equity Holders Committee, the Secured Creditors Committee, the Unsecured Creditors Committee, and the Sunbeam Corporation Creditors Committee. Often, the existence of multiple committees slows the bankruptcy process as factions can develop that undermine the spirit of cooperation necessary to formulate a plan. Cooperation is necessary because plans of reorganization rarely work under the premise of absolute priority; that is, the most senior classes are paid in full before a less senior class receives anything. The negotiation process inherent in a reorganization generally grants all classes some token distribution in order to obtain their acceptance of the plan. This is the reason why shareholders often receive some percent of the equity of the reorganized company. (The percentage distributed to the equity holders varies considerably. In recent plans of reorganization, equity holders of Po Folks are proposed to receive 0%, while equity holders of Allis Chalmers are proposed to receive 19%.)

After the committee of unsecured creditors has been appointed, the debtor generally makes specific decisions whether to assume or to reject its executory contracts (contractual commitments entered prior to bankruptcy for the provision of future goods or services). In many bankruptcies, the rejection of high-priced contracts has been beneficial to the debtor. For example, when LTV declared bankruptcy, it was able to reject several high-priced contracts for raw materials. Several debtors also rejected high-priced labor contracts. For example, in 1984, a bankruptcy judge upheld Continental Airline's decision to break its labor agreements with its pilots union. The laws have changed for the rejection of labor contracts. Currently, collective bargaining agreements cannot be rejected so easily. Although many executory contracts can be rejected, specific rules may apply to the rejection of certain contracts. For example, Chapter 11 companies may reject leases with the approval of the Bankruptcy Court, only after they have made efforts to sell the sites. This was the case with Revco. After Revco had held an auction for 113 of its sites, the Bankruptcy Court was likely to grant Revco permission to reject the leases of sites for which no bids were received.

## Formulation of a Plan

Once the committee(s) are in place, the formulation of a plan begins. The debtor has the exclusive right to file a plan of reorganization for 120 days. The length of the exclusive period is determined by the court and can be extended or shortened. (Generally, the exclusive period tends to be longer than 120 days.) No other plan from interested parties can be filed during this period. However, this exclusive period does not stop other parties from formulating plans. In the case of Allegheny International, the unsecured creditors formulated a plan during the exclusive period (which had been repeatedly extended) because of their frustration with what they perceived to be lack of progress in the Allegheny bankruptcy. Generally, the first plan of reorganization is not the final plan. It is common to see the first amended and second amended plans of reorganization. (During August 1989, Allegheny International filed its Sixth Amended Plan of Reorganization.) Sometimes, even the debtor knows that its first formulation of a plan is not its final formulation. For instance, Allegheny actually labeled its August 30, 1988 Disclosure Statement "Preliminary." It is important to remember that a plan is commonly amended at least once before it is confirmed. Amended plans often entail significant changes in the funding of the plan, terms of the reorganization securities, and distributions to classes. Investors must be certain that they are working with the most recent plan of reorganization.

Investors must also be aware of plans of reorganization filed by others. For example, in September 1989, four plans of reorganization were filed for Public Service Company of New Hampshire. These plans were filed by (1) Public Service Company of New Hampshire (the debtor), (2) New England Power Company on behalf of itself and New England Electric System, (3) The United Illuminating Company, and (4) Northeast Utilities Service Company. A potential investor in Public Service Company of New Hampshire's securities would have to be familiar with each of these plans.

There are several ways to ensure that the investor is working with the most recent plan. One way is to keep in contact with the debtor. A second way is to keep in contact with the court in which the petition was filed. A third way is to subscribe to a bankruptcy service such as *Bankruptcy Datasource* in Boston, which has the advantage of being timely and convenient.

In filing a plan of reorganization, a debtor with one or more subsidiaries must decide if the plan will incorporate substantive consolidation of the subsidiaries. Under substantive consolidation, all of the assets and liabilities of the entities in question are pooled and used collectively to pay debts. Substantive consolidation must be approved by the court. The approval is not granted lightly. In order for substantive consolidation to be granted, proponents must prove that the parent and the subsidiaries in question operated as a single unit. This can be proved by such means as intercompany guarantees and transfers of assets. The issue of substantive consolidation can have important ramifications for the investor. For example, in the case of LTV, the aerospace/defense subsidiary was profitable and had assets in excess of its liabilities. On the other hand, the steel subsidiary was unprofitable at the time of filing and had liabilities significantly in excess of its assets. If LTV is reorganized without substantive consolidation, investors owning the securities guaranteed by the aerospace/defense subsidiary will receive generous distributions. On the other hand, if substantive consolidation is granted, the distributions to these investors will be decreased as the assets of the aerospace/defense subsidiary will be pooled to pay the debts of the entire corporation.

## Disclosure Statement

Once a plan of reorganization has been finalized (and generally has been informally approved by the major creditors), the debtor produces and files for approval a disclosure statement about the plan with the court. The disclosure statement provides enough information to allow reasonable investors to make informed judgments. The court does not approve a disclosure statement unless the judge is satisfied that the information presented is accurate and helpful to the impaired classes. A disclosure statement summarizes the plan. It also contains fairly detailed financial information about the debtor including the company's five-year pro forma statements, which are required by statute. It also presents a liquidation analysis of the company that supports the company's contention that creditors will receive a higher distribution under the plan than they would if the debtor were to be liquidated. The disclosure statement also provides a brief history of the company, including reasons for filing and significant events since filing. The disclosure statement is generally more understandable and readable than the legal plan.

If the court approves the disclosure statement, the plan and the disclosure statement are mailed to the impaired classes for approval. Holders of claims that are not impaired (i.e., claims that are paid in full or whose interests are not adversely affected by the proceeding) are not entitled to vote because unimpaired classes are conclusively presumed to have accepted the plan. Classes that are entitled to vote are generally given 30 days to do so.

In order for a plan to be accepted, at least two thirds of the amount and more than one half of the number of claims allowed for voting purposes of each impaired class and at least two thirds of the outstanding shares of each class of interests must accept the plan. If the plan is approved by the voting classes, it is sent to the court for confirmation. When the court confirms the plan, it approves the transactions specified in the plan and a date for the reorganization to take effect.

## Cram-Down

It is interesting to note that a plan can be confirmed under the cram-down provisions even if the required number of creditors do not approve the plan. The confirmation of a plan under the cram-down provisions must meet several specific requirements. First, the plan must be shown not to discriminate unfairly against any impaired class. Such a determination includes the requirement that no class shall receive more than 100 percent of the amount of its claim. In addition, each dissenting class must receive as much as they would be entitled to receive under a liquidation. Often, plans state that the Bankruptcy Court will confirm the plan under the cram-down provisions if all the requirements are met except for the requirement that each class has accepted the plan. Second, a plan must be shown to be fair and equitable to a nonaccepting class. Under the Bankruptcy Code, a plan is fair and equitable to a nonaccepting class if, among other things, it provides that the nonaccepting class either (a) receives property of a present value equal to the allowed amount of such claims, or (b) if the class is to receive property of any lesser value, no class junior to the nonaccepting class receives or retains any property under the plan.

# ANALYSIS OF COMPANIES IN REORGANIZATION

There are several different approaches that can be used to invest in the bankruptcy market. Large and aggressive investors buy a substantial block of the debtor's bonds and try to become a significant factor in the reorganization plan. Often these investors pool their resources in "vulture funds," which invest in the securities of bankrupt companies. Such funds often operate by acquiring large blocks of a particular class of securities and use their leverage in the reorganization process to formulate a plan favorable to their position. All such strategies are not profitable. In one case, a vulture fund acquired a large percentage of the subordinated debentures of a Chapter 11 company, hoping that it would receive a controlling equity interest in the reorganized company. Unfortunately for the vultures, more than 90 percent of the equity in the reorganized company was distributed to secured creditors.

## Investing in Individual Securities

Another approach to investing in Chapter 11 companies, more suited to individual investors, is to buy specific securities in a bankrupt company. This approach has the advantage of not requiring a large investment, thereby allowing investors to diversify their investments. It does require, however, a significant commitment to analysis of the company but has the potential of being extremely profitable.

In buying the securities of a bankrupt company, the investor has the choice of investing for a general improvement in the overall condition of the company or of investing in situations (such as secured bonds) where the return is more quantifiable because of the assets.

## Selecting the Universe

Selection of a universe of potential acquisition candidates is the initial step in investing in bankrupt securities. Thousands of corporations file Chapter 11 petitions yearly. However, many of these filings represent corporations whose securities are inappropriate for individual investment because the securities are not publicly traded or because the corporations are very small. In these cases, the individual investor could have difficulty obtaining sufficient financial information for analysis or purchasing the securities if analysis could be accomplished. Individual investors should confine their universe to companies that are publicly traded and have assets of at least $25 million. Potential candidates fitting this description can be collected from a variety of sources. An individual investor will probably find a sufficient universe from which to select simply by consulting the business section of newspapers. All listed bankruptcies are identified by a symbol. All bankruptcies listed on the New York, American, and the

National Association of Securities Dealers Automated Quotations system's over-the-counter have a "vj" preceding the name of the stock. For example, BASIX Corporation was listed on the New York Stock Exchange Composite Transactions as of September 26, 1989, as vjBasix. The NASDAQ National Market Issue listings include an additional indication of bankruptcy. These listings are identified by a four- or five-letter symbol. The fifth letter indicates the issues that are subject to restrictions or special conditions. Securities that are in bankruptcy have a "Q" as the fifth letter of their symbol. For example, American Carriers was listed on the NASDAQ National Market Issues as of April 6, 1989, as vjAmCarriers ACIXQ. A reading of the business section of a major newspaper should keep investors current on recent bankruptcy listings.

## Obtaining Financial Information

Perhaps the most difficult aspect of investing in Chapter 11 companies is obtaining financial information. Trading in the securities of small companies that have filed for bankruptcy can present problems if the companies are delisted. (If a company is delisted, its price can often be found on the National Daily Quotation Service "Pink Sheets," published by the National Quotation Bureau. The Pink Sheets also provide potential market makers for the issues listed on the sheets.) More importantly, financial information can be difficult to obtain after a filing. Although SEC filing requirements are not suspended for Chapter 11 companies, filing requirements are often neither strictly observed nor enforced. Therefore, a potential investor may want to limit his or her universe of investment candidates to those Chapter 11 companies whose filings are current. This is not always necessary, however, if the investor uses other sources of information and invests only in those securities that are clearly undervalued, employing alternative methods of evaluation.

Once a list of potential candidates has been selected, the collection of financial information should begin. For each company, the investor should obtain the most recent annual report, 10-K, and quarterly report. In addition, the investor should obtain the 8-K that reports on the bankruptcy because this document may have useful facts about the filing. These documents will give the investor some indication of how the company has performed historically and perhaps why it declared bankruptcy. (Old copies of *Value Line* are also useful for obtaining historical perspectives on companies.) The investor should also collect information on the company's publicly traded securities. For stock, such data would include current shares outstanding, par value, and current price.

The information that should be gathered for bonds is more substantial. Bond data should include a complete description of the bond, the amount of bonds outstanding including the amount of original-issue discount, price, and security (i.e., the specific assets supporting the bond). If the value of the security is known or can be estimated, this should also be listed. All bonds should be listed in order of seniority. Sometimes the securities data is found in the 10-K. More often, the investor needs to consult the appropriate *Moody's Manual* (industrial, public utility, etc). These are found in most libraries.

It is also important to stay current on the news items that affect each of the companies being considered. An easy way to accomplish this is to use a computer news retrieval service such as the Dow Jones News Retrieval, which lists all news stories from the past 90 days from the Dow Jones News Service (the Broad Tape), *The Wall Street Journal,* and *Barron's.* Finally, one should attempt to be placed on the mailing list of the companies being considered. This is sometimes difficult, particularly for those who do not own any securities.

## Investing without a Plan of Reorganization

Perhaps the most important documents for the analysis of bankrupt securities are the most recent plan of reorganization and the accompanying disclosure statement. These documents specify what each class of claimants (including each class of security holders) will receive in a reorganization. If a plan of reorganization has not been filed, investors must speculate on the distributions to the classes. Because it does not lend itself to thorough analysis, investing without a plan of reorganization is not generally recommended for the individual investor. Although investors can make intelligent decisions regarding some of the more senior debt of the Chapter 11 company, the inability to analyze thoroughly causes trouble in the area of common stock. An analysis of distributions for numerous bankruptcies quickly reveals the variance of distributions for similar classes of claimants. This is most noticeable in the distributions made to holders of common equity interests who have received from zero percent to a major portion of the equity in the reorganized company.

Potential distributions to common stockholders can be further complicated if the "new value" principle is applied. This principle contends that the equity holders who contribute new money and management expertise to the reorganization should receive a substantial equity position in the reorganized company. Unfortunately for the holders of subordinated debt, the increased distribution to equity holders translates into a decreased equity distribution to them. Although this principle has been applied in some small bankruptcies, it is infrequently applied in the larger cases. This may change. Revco has filed a preliminary proposal that grants 55 percent of the new Revco stock to its stockholders in exchange for $150 million. Under the proposal, secured creditors would be paid in full, but subordinated debt holders would only receive stock and bonds valued at 25 percent of their claims.

The valuation of the securities of a debtor that has not filed a plan of reorganization is similar to a liquidation analysis with one important exception. The company is assumed to be an ongoing business, and therefore no substantial discount is applied to the value of its assets. Under this approach, the assets of the company are totaled and the liabilities are systematically subtracted from this total to give an approximation of how many assets are available to repay each class of claimants. Each class is subtracted in order of seniority. For example, the fully secured claims will be among the first to be subtracted. Although this approach is a quick valuation technique, it is imprecise. It can, however, be used even with somewhat dated financials. Further, this methodology can be usefully applied to both a full and a liquidation value of the company. This application would serve to bracket the value of the company with a worst case (liquidation value) as well as an optimistic case (full valuation). The application of this technique is outlined below.

**Estimated Valuations of Securities**

| | | |
|---|---|---:|
| Total Assets | | $xxx |
| Less: | Collateralized debt | |
| | Banks | – xxx |
| | Other | – xxx |
| Equals: | Amount remaining for distribution to other creditors | xxx |
| Less: | Amount due to other creditors (in order of seniority) | – xxx |

This approach is generally not applicable to the valuation of the common stock simply because the assets are depleted before the common stock holders are eligible for a distribution. In order to estimate a value for common stock holders, one must make assumptions regarding a plan of reorganization and what percentage of the equity of the reorganized company the old shareholders will receive. If this approach is used, the valuation of the common stock should follow the methodology presented under "Investing With a Plan of Reorganization."

## Secured Bonds

A major exception to the premise that investors should generally wait until a plan of reorganization is filed relates to secured bonds. When a company petitions for protection, it is subject to the automatic stay provisions of the Bankruptcy Code. These provisions generally disallow the accrual of interest during bankruptcy, except in the case of secured bonds. Secured claims are allowed to accrue postpetition interest during bankruptcy to the extent of the value of the collateral. (Although post-petition interest is accrued, the Code does not generally require that it be paid.) Given these provisions, an astute investor could conceivably purchase a secured bond whose collateral exceeds the principal amount of the bond at a substantial discount to par, knowing that eventually the bond will either be reinstated or be paid off at par plus post-petition interest. An example of how this provision of the Bankruptcy Code could have been beneficial to investors is provided by the LTV bankruptcy. When LTV filed for bankruptcy on July 1, 1986, all of its securities declined significantly. The overall decline overlooked the intrinsic value of the Youngstown Sheet & Tube First Mortgage bonds, whose collateral exceeded the value of the bonds. These bonds, therefore, were entitled to the continuation of their interest.

An additional exception relates to certain equipment trust financing. Much airline equipment debt and railroad equipment debt is exempt from the automatic stay provisions of the Code and the power of the court to repossess the equipment due to §§1110 and 1168 of the Bankruptcy Code, respectively. Instead, the court gives the debtor 60 days to reaffirm the lease on the equipment or return the equipment to the lessor. The debtor is unlikely to cancel the lease because the equipment represented by the lease is the operating asset of the company, without which the company cannot operate. Airlines cannot operate without airplanes! Generally, in cases of §1110 equipment trusts, the debtor assumes the lease and resumes current interest payments, including interest payable during the 60-day period. Recent examples of §1110 equipment trusts are Eastern Air Lines' 16.125 percent Secured Equipment Trust Certificates due 10/15/02 and Eastern's 17.5 percent Secured Equipment Certificates, Series A, due 1/1/98, and Series B, due 7/1/97. The fact that a particular equipment certificate is covered under §1110 is not part of the general description of the certificate. The investor must refer to the "Events of Default, Notice and Waiver" section of the prospectus or indenture of a given issue to ensure that a particular trust certificate is covered.

## Fraudulent Conveyance

Investors cannot rely blindly on the secured status of particular bonds. In some instances, the issue of fraudulent conveyance or transfer may become an issue. If fraudulent conveyance is proved, the seniority of debt may be reordered.

Fraudulent conveyance can become an issue when a company is restructured and security interests are granted in the stock or assets of a company. For example, assume that company A acquires company B in a leveraged buyout for $550 million. Prior to the buyout, company B's capital structure consisted of equity and $300 million in subordinated debt.

Assume further that the transaction was financed by $50 million in equity and $500 million in debt secured by the assets of company B. Company A subsequently filed for bankruptcy within six months of the LBO. At first glance, one would assume that the secured bonds issued by company A would be paid in full with company B's bonds receiving a share in the remaining assets. In fact, company B's bonds could be deemed senior to company A's bonds if it can be proved that a fraudulent conveyance occurred. Fraudulent conveyance can be proven if fraud was involved. It can also be proved if, at the time of the transfer, company B received less than fair or less than reasonably equivalent value for the transfer and either (1) was insolvent or rendered insolvent by the transfer, (2) its remaining unencumbered property constituted unreasonably small capital, or (3) it is believed that it incurred debts beyond its ability to pay as such debt matured.

## Investing with a Plan of Reorganization

The analysis of companies in bankruptcy that have filed plans of reorganization should be approached in the same systematic way that the analysis of any security is approached. However, there are two important differences. First, the analyst must place more emphasis on pro formas and place less emphasis on historical results. This emphasis is mandated because a reorganized company is generally significantly different from the company that filed for protection. Second, the analyst must be a combination equity/fixed income securities analyst. It is not always clear which of the securities of the reorganized debtor are the most attractive. Often, the relative rates of return among old securities are substantially reordered under the plan. The analyst must therefore be willing to value all securities of the debtor and purchase those that offer the highest potential returns.

## Evaluation of the Plan

The first step in analyzing a company in bankruptcy that has filed a plan is to carefully read the plan and determine the distribution each class will receive upon reorganization. This effort should be conducted on a per share or per bond basis. Terms of new securities that are to be issued under the plan should be examined carefully so that they be valued properly. Often, securities issued in reorganization have unique characteristics. For example, the senior notes proposed under Texas International's April 28, 1989 Plan of Reorganization provided for an initial coupon payment 39 months after issuance. The notes proposed under Delta US's May 1989 plan provide that interest and principal repayments can be deferred for a specific period if cash flow and rig count, respectively, are below certain levels. Furthermore, an increasing number of issues proposed under plans of reorganization are bonds whose interest may be paid in kind at the option of the reorganized debtor.

    The analysis of a plan should begin with a listing of each class of creditor, the amount of the claim, the proposed distribution, the proposed distribution per security—where applicable—and the value of the distribution. This part of the analysis could take the form for the hypothetical ABC, Incorporated, shown in Exhibit 20–1.

    Frequently, there are only a total of 6 to 12 classes of creditors. These can be individually listed. Sometimes, as in the case of Allegheny International, there are over 50. In these instances, it is wise to itemize only the relevant classes or consolidate the classes to make them more manageable. The classes that should be listed are those classes that contain publicly traded securities

**EXHIBIT 20–1**
**Plan of Reorganization — ABC, Incorporated**

| Class | Amount of Claim | Total Distribution | Distribution per Security | Valuation per Security |
|---|---|---|---|---|
| 1st mortgage bonds | $100 million | $100 million plus pre- and post- petition interest in cash | 100% | 100% |
| Debentures | $100 million | $100 million face value of debentures of reorganized debtor | 100% | 90%* |

* The amount of discount attributable to the new debentures is a function of coupon, credit considerations, etc.

---

or classes that receive securities to be publicly traded. By consolidating the proposed distribution in this manner, the investor can easily focus on the relevant securities.

It is also advisable at this point to chart the proposed equity ownership per class. This chart allows the investor to quickly convert changes in the valuation of the company into tangible values. A chart of equity ownership could take the form shown in Exhibit 20–2.

Western Company of North America's equity ownership is fairly straight-forward. The only dilution that has to be considered is that from the possible exercise of employee options. Frequently, the distribution of equity in plans of reorganization are more complex, with warrants and options affecting the fully diluted stock ownership of several classes. In such cases, it is helpful to include additional columns that outline the fully diluted common stock ownership. This chart could take the form of Exhibit 20–3, which outlines the equity ownership proposed under Heck's Second Amended Plan.

## Determining a Price Per Share for the Debtor

Once the specifics of the plan of reorganization are known, including potential dilution, the valuation of the company can proceed. In this chapter, Cardis Corporation will be used for our analysis.

Cardis Corporation filed for bankruptcy on May 25, 1988. It has been engaged in the wholesale and retail distribution of automotive parts, supplies, tools, and accessories since 1917. Cardis also owns Tune-Up Masters, which operates 242 company-owned service centers principally in the western and southwestern United States.

**EXHIBIT 20–2**

**Distribution of New Common Stock of Western Company of North America: Second Amended Plan of Reorganization**

| Class | Number of Shares | % of Common |
|---|---|---|
| Senior unsecured claims | 8,750,000 | 70.00 |
| Senior subordinated claims | 1,285,438 | 10.28 |
| Junior subordinated claims | 1,120,812 | 8.97 |
| Old preferred stock | 562,500 | 4.50 |
| Old common stock | 406,250 | 3.25 |
| Management incentive compensation plan | 375,000 | 3.00 |
| Total | 12,500,000 | 100.00 |
| Reserved for employee option plans | 956,250 | 7.1 |

Source: Western Company of North America's Second Amended Plan of Reorganization and Disclosure Statement dated January 19.1989, *Bankruptcy Datasource*, Boston, MA.

**EXHIBIT 20–3**

**Proposed Equity Ownership of Heck's**

| | Number of Shares | % of Common | Fully Diluted Number of Shares | % of Common |
|---|---|---|---|---|
| Unsecured claims and PNB | 2,000,000 | 79% | 2,000,000 | 68% |
| Shareholder actions | 22,222 | 1 | 22,222 | 1 |
| Old common | 200,000 60,000 warrants | 8 | 260,000 | 9 |
| Key employees | 225,000 warrants | 0 | 225,000 | 7 |
| Hallwood | 294,967 147,484 warrants | 12 | 442,451 | 15 |
| Total | 2,517,189 shares | 100% | 2,949,673 | 100% |

Source: Heck's Second Amended Joint Plan of Reorganization and Disclosure Statement dated March 24, 1989, *Bankruptcy Datasource*, Boston, MA.

Cardis's Second Amended Plan of Reorganization and Disclosure Statement were filed on August 11, 1989. The plan is premised on the sale of Tune-Up Masters (TUM) and the reorganization of the company around its remaining warehouse distribution centers and 29 retail stores. Importantly, however, the plan may be confirmed without the sale. Under the Second Amended Plan of Reorganization, Security Pacific National Bank (SPNB) will receive $15 million in cash, a $29 million seven-year secured note, a $20 million secured revolving credit note, and $8 million from the sale of stock or assets of TUM. The plan provides that if TUM is not sold within three months of the confirmation date, the debtor will issue 80,000 shares of new preferred stock to SPNB with a face amount of $8 million. The reorganized debtor will then convey its right and interests to the TUM stock to a trust for the benefit of SPNB and the reorganized debtor. The general unsecured creditors will receive 65 percent of the stock of reorganized Cardis, debenture holders will receive 15 percent of the stock, old equity holders will receive 10 percent of the stock, and a final 10 percent of the stock will be reserved for management. This allocation of common stock is presented in Exhibit 20–4.

The analysis of Cardis should begin with the debtor's pro forma income statements, balance sheets, and cash-flow statements, which are provided in the disclosure statement. Care should be taken to evaluate the debtor's assumptions in formulating these pro formas. Modifications should be made to the pro formas where the assumptions look doubtful. After the pro formas have been adjusted, an estimate of the company's value (in terms of price per share) should be calculated. One way of approaching this task is to apply valuation multiples. The

**EXHIBIT 20–4**

**Proposed Equity Ownership of Cardis: Second Amended Plan of Reorganization**

| Class | Number of Shares | Percent of Common* |
|---|---|---|
| Unsecured creditors | 7,540,000 | 65% |
| Subordinated debentures | 1,740,000 | 15 |
| Present equity security holders | 1,160,000 | 10 |
| Reserved for management | 1,160,000 | 10 |
| Total | 11,600,000 | 100 |

* The percentages are subject to a potential dilution of 13 percent if the reorganized debtor exercises its right under certain circumstances to put 1,800,691 common shares in exchange for the new preferred stock.

Source: Cardis Corporation's Second Amended Plan of Reorganization and Disclosure Statement dated August 11, 1989, *Bankruptcy Datasource*, Boston, MA.

analyst should estimate what range of multiples the stock should command in terms of earnings, sales, book value, and cash. The analyst can use the traditional approach of averaging the appropriate multiples of comparable companies and then applying these multiples to the company being analyzed.

In the case of Cardis, the analyst must first determine the market multiples of the auto parts (replacement) industry. To estimate the auto parts industry multiples, one should first select an industry sample of companies. In this case, SPX Corp., Echlin, Federal Mogul, and Genuine Parts are used as the representative sample. These four companies were selected in part because they are all followed by *Value Line,* and therefore consistent projections of earnings, sales, book value and cash flow were readily available. Once the sample was selected, *Value Line's* estimates for 1992–1994 for each of the companies was listed. These estimates are listed in Exhibit 20–5.

Once the estimates of these values have been logged, the range of valuations relative to price/share can be calculated for each of the sample companies by dividing each estimate by the estimated prices. Because *Value Line* gives a range for estimated prices, it is necessary to divide the appropriate per share figure by both the high and the low price estimates. Once these calculations are made, the numbers should be averaged to generate an average range of valuations for the industry, as shown below.

| | |
|---|---|
| Price $\overline{\text{Sales/Share}}$ | .69 to .92 |
| Price $\overline{\text{BV/Share}}$ | 2.09 to 2.78 |
| Price $\overline{\text{Earning/Shares}}$ | 11.59 to 15.68 |
| Price $\overline{\text{Cash/Share}}$ | 8.37 to 11.28 |

To arrive at an estimated value for the common stock of Cardis, multiply the above multiples (or, more realistically, some discount of the multiples so as to reflect the problems associated with the debtor) times the appropriate variable for Cardis. When these valuations are multiplied times the pro forma estimates of Cardis' sales/share, book value/share, EPS, and cash/share, a value of $.54 to $9.56 per share is estimated for Cardis. If the multiples are discounted by 50 percent to reflect problems associated with Cardis, the valuation declines to $.27 to $4.78. This looked attractive versus a September 1989 price of $0.06. However, this price assumes that each old share of Cardis will own the same proportionate share of the new company. In fact, Cardis' August 1989 Plan of

**EXHIBIT 20–5**
**Auto Parts (Replacement) Industry (1992–1994 *Value*
*Line* Estimates)**

|  | Price Range | Sales/ Share | BV/ Share | EPS | Cash/ Share |
|---|---|---|---|---|---|
| Cardis* |  | 10.43 | .26 | .16 | .45 |
| Echlin | 20–31 | 32.75 | 13.50 | 1.80 | 2.75 |
| Federal Mogul | 40–48 | 73.90 | 18.95 | 3.70 | 6.30 |
| Genuine Parts | 56–72 | 60.00 | 18.80 | 3.85 | 4.25 |
| SPX Corp. | 46–64 | 69.65 | 25.95 | 4.65 | 6.90 |

* Company estimates from the disclosure statement.

Reorganization provides that each old share will receive the equivalent of .20 new shares. Therefore, these prices must be discounted by a factor that reflects that a share purchased at current prices may only be worth .20 shares if the plan is confirmed. When the estimated valuation is discounted by 80 percent as required, the estimated value declines to $.05 to $.96. At these levels, the stock is valued at the low end of the projections. The projected prices must be discounted once more, however, to reflect the potential dilution of 13 percent should reorganized Cardis exercise its put. If this potential dilution is considered, the projected range for Cardis becomes $.04 to $.83.

Once the valuation of the debtor's stock is complete, the analyst should proceed to investigate the other securities of the debtor, if any, to determine if another security is attractive. Frequently, this is where value is found.

Cardis has outstanding $25.16 million (as of 4/30/88) 12.5% Senior Subordinated Debentures due 6/30/97. To determine if the bonds are undervalued or overvalued, the relationship between the current price of each bond and the valuation of its proposed distribution must be compared. In the case of Cardis, debenture holders are proposed to receive 69.6 shares per $1000 of face value of debenture. The analyst must value these distributions to see if the debentures represent an undervalued or an overvalued situation. If the valuation of Cardis common stock outlined above is used, then the debentures should be worth between $2.78 and $57.77 per bond. This compares with a market estimate of $15 per bond. The bonds appear to be within the same relative range as the common (i.e., at the low end of the projections).

Both the common stock and the debentures of Cardis appear to have more upside potential than downside risk. The risk/reward trade-off will be a function of the price the investor actually pays for the securities. Frequently, securities of bankrupt companies are thinly traded and the offering price of a security may differ substantially from the most recent quotation.

## CONCLUSION

The analysis of bankrupt securities involves several variables. The investor must analyze both the plan of reorganization as well as the pro forma projections of the reorganized company. The analysis should not stop once these two analyses are complete, however. Companies should be monitored in order to keep current on changes in the plan as well as on company prospects. Changes in this market can occur quickly and be significant. The likelihood of these changes must be factored into the analysis. They also signal the need for diversification in bankruptcy investing. The time element must also be factored into the analysis. Most bankrupt securities do not accrue interest during reorganization. Therefore, the investor must estimate when the company will emerge from bankruptcy to fully estimate (and discount) values. Because most bankrupt companies take at least a year to reorganize and some have taken over seven years (Manville), the time element can be significant.

# CHAPTER 21

## MUNICIPAL BONDS

Sylvan G. Feldstein, Ph.D.
Vice President
Municipal Bond Research Department
Merrill Lynch Capital Markets

Frank J. Fabozzi, Ph.D., CFA, CPA
Visiting Professor of Finance
Sloan School of Management
Massachusetts Institute of Technology
and
Editor, The Journal of Portfolio Management

Municipal bonds are securities issued by state and local governments and their creations such as "authorities" and special districts. Most recent available information indicates that approximately 37,000 different states, counties, school districts, special districts, towns, and other public issuing bodies have issued municipal bonds. Although some investors buy municipal bonds as a way of supporting public improvements such as schools, playgrounds, and parks, the vast majority buy them because interest income from such bonds generally is exempt from federal income taxes. Consequently, municipal bonds are purchased by those who are in high marginal tax brackets, because on an after-tax basis they offer a yield that is greater than comparable bonds that are fully taxable. Because of the tax-exempt feature of municipal bonds, the yield on municipal bonds is less than that on Treasuries with the same maturity. The ratio of municipal yields to Treasury yields is not constant, but changes as a result of changes in tax rates and economic conditions.

The major buyers of municipal bonds are individuals (which includes households and mutual funds), property and casualty insurance companies, and commercial banks. Although these three investor categories have dominated the market since the mid-1950s, the relative participation of each category has changed. The factors that have caused shifts in the relative participation of each group include (1) changes in the tax law affecting marginal tax rates, (2) changes in the tax law affecting the deductibility of interest to purchase municipal bonds for commercial banks, and (3) improvements or deterioration of taxable income in the case of property and casualty insurance companies. The most recent significant tax legislation to affect the municipal bond market was the 1986 Tax Reform Act.[1]

Municipal bonds come in a variety of types, with different redemption features, credit risks, and marketability. Consequently, the holder of municipal bonds is exposed to the same risks as the holder of corporate and Treasury bonds: interest-rate risk, reinvestment risk, and call risk. Moreover, the holder of a municipal bond, like the holder of a corporate bond, faces credit risk.

In this chapter, we describe the basic characteristics of municipal bonds as well as the municipal bond industry. In Chapters 22 and 23, a framework for evaluating the creditworthiness of municipal securities is presented.

## TYPES OF MUNICIPAL OBLIGATIONS

### Bonds

In terms of municipal bond security structures, there are basically two different types. The first type is the general obligation bond, and the second is the revenue bond.

General obligation bonds are debt instruments issued by states, counties, special districts, cities, towns, and school districts. They are secured by the issuer's general taxing powers. Usually, a general obligation bond is secured by the issuer's unlimited taxing power. For smaller governmental jurisdictions such as school districts and towns, the only available unlimited taxing power is on property. For larger general obligation bond issuers such as states and big cities, the tax revenues are more diverse and may include corporate and individual income taxes, sales taxes, and property taxes. The security pledges for these larger issuers such as states are sometimes referred to as being *full faith and credit obligations*.

Additionally, certain general obligation bonds are secured not only by the issuer's general taxing powers to create monies accumulated in the general fund

---

[1] For a discussion of the impact of the 1986 act on individuals, property and casualty insurance companies, and commercial banks, see Sylvan G. Feldstein and Frank J. Fabozzi, *The Dow Jones-Irwin Guide to Municipal Bonds* (Homewood, IL: Dow Jones-Irwin, 1987), Appendix A.

but also from certain identified fees, grants, and special charges, which provide additional revenues from outside the general fund. Such bonds are known as being *double barreled* in security because of the dual nature of the revenue sources.

Also, not all general obligation bonds are secured by unlimited taxing powers. Some have pledged taxes that are limited as to revenue sources and maximum property tax millage amounts. Such bonds are known as *limited tax general obligation bonds*.

The second basic type of security structure is found in a revenue bond. Such bonds are issued for either project or enterprise financings in which the bond issuers pledge to the bondholders the revenues generated by the operating projects financed. Below are examples of the specific types of revenue bonds that have been issued over the years.

*Airport Revenue Bonds.* The revenues securing airport revenue bonds usually come from either traffic-generated sources—such as landing fees, concession fees, and airline apron-use and fueling fees—or lease revenues from one or more airlines for the use of a specific facility such as a terminal or hangar.

*College and University Revenue Bonds.* The revenues securing college and university revenue bonds usually include dormitory room rental fees, tuition payments, and sometimes the general assets of the college or university.

*Hospital and Nursing Home Revenue Bonds.* The security for these bonds is dependent on federal and state reimbursement programs (such as Medicaid and Medicare), third-party commercial payers (such as Blue Cross, HMOs, and private insurance), and individual patient payments.

*Single-Family Mortgage Revenue Bonds.* Single-family mortgage revenue bonds are usually secured by the mortgages and mortgage loan repayments on single-family homes. Security features vary but can include Federal Housing Administration (FHA), Federal Veterans Administration (VA), or private mortgage insurance.

*Multifamily Revenue Bonds.* These revenue bonds are usually issued for multifamily housing projects for senior citizens and low-income families. Some housing revenue bonds are usually secured by mortgages that are federally insured; others receive federal government operating subsidies, such as under section 8, or interest-cost subsidies such as under section 236; and still others receive only local property tax reductions as subsidies.

*Industrial Development and Pollution Control Revenue Bonds.* Bonds have been issued for a variety of industrial and commercial activities that range from manufacturing plants to shopping centers. They are usually secured by payments to be made by the corporations or businesses that use the facilities.

*Public Power Revenue Bonds.*  Public power revenue bonds are secured by revenues to be produced from electrical operating plants. Some bonds are for a single issuer, who constructs and operates power plants and then sells the electricity. Other public power revenue bonds are issued by groups of public and private investor-owned utilities for the joint financing of the construction of one or more power plants. This last arrangement is known as a *joint power* financing structure.

*Resource Recovery Revenue Bonds.*   A resource recovery facility converts refuse (solid waste) into commercially saleable energy, recoverable products, and a residue to be landfilled. The major revenues for a resource recovery revenue bond usually are (1) the "tipping fees" per ton paid by those who deliver the garbage to the facility for disposal; (2) revenues from steam, electricity, or refuse-derived fuel sold to either an electric power company or another energy user; and (3) revenues from the sale of recoverable materials such as aluminum and steel scrap.

*Seaport Revenue Bonds.*  The security for seaport revenue bonds can include specific lease agreements with the benefitting companies or pledged marine terminal and cargo tonnage fees.

*Sewer Revenue Bonds.*  Revenues for sewer revenue bonds come from hookup fees and user charges. For many older sewer bond issuers, substantial portions of their construction budgets have been financed with federal grants.

*Sports Complex and Convention Center Revenue Bonds.*  Sports complex and convention center revenue bonds usually receive revenues from sporting or convention events held at the facilities and, in some instances, from earmarked outside revenues such as local motel and hotel room taxes.

*Student Loan Revenue Bonds.*  Student loan repayments under student loan revenue bond programs are sometimes 100 percent guaranteed either directly by the federal government—under the Federal Insured Student Loan program (FISL) for 100 percent of bond principal and interest—or by a state guaranty agency under a more recent federal insurance program, the Federal Guaranteed Student Loan program (GSL). In addition to these two federally backed programs, student loan bonds are sometimes secured by the general revenues of the specific colleges involved.

*Toll Road and Gas Tax Revenue Bonds.*  There are generally two types of highway revenue bonds. The bond proceeds of the first type are used to build such specific revenue-producing facilities as toll roads, bridges, and tunnels. For these pure enterprise-type revenue bonds, the pledged revenues usually are the monies collected through the tolls. The second type of highway bond is one in which the bondholders are paid by earmarked revenues outside of toll collections such as gasoline taxes, automobile registration payments, and driver's license fees.

*Water Revenue Bonds.*    Water revenue bonds are issued to finance the construction of water treatment plants, pumping stations, collection facilities, and distribution systems. Revenues usually come from connection fees and charges paid by the users of the water systems.

## Hybrid and Special Bond Securities

Though having certain characteristics of general obligation and revenue bonds, there are some municipal bonds that have more unique security structures as well. They include the following.

*Federal Savings and Loan Insurance Corporation-Backed Bonds.*    In this security structure, the proceeds of a bond sale were deposited in a savings and loan association that, in turn, issued a certificate of deposit (CD). The CD was insured by the Federal Savings and Loan Insurance Corporation (FSLIC) up to a limit of $100,000 of combined principal and interest for each bondholder. The savings and loan association used the money to finance low- and moderate-income rental housing developments. While these bonds are no longer issued, there are billions of dollars of these bonds in the secondary market.

*Insured Bonds.*    These are bonds that, in addition to being secured by the issuer's revenues, also are backed by insurance policies written by commercial insurance companies. The insurance, usually structured as a surety-type insurance policy. is supposed to provide prompt payment to the bondholders if a default should occur.

*Lease-Backed Bonds.*    Lease-backed bonds are usually structured as revenue-type bonds with annual rent payments. In some instances the rental payments may only come from earmarked tax revenues, student tuition payments, or patient fees. In other instances, the underlying lessee governmental unit is required to make annual appropriations from its general fund.

*Letter of Credit-Backed Bonds.*    Some municipal bonds, in addition to being secured by the issuer's cash-flow revenues, also are backed by commercial bank letters of credit. In some instances the letters of credit are irrevocable and, if necessary, can be used to pay the bondholders. In other instances, the issuers are required to maintain investment-quality worthiness before the letters of credit can be drawn upon.

*Life Care Revenue Bonds.*   Life care bonds are issued to construct long-term residential facilities for older citizens. Revenues are usually derived from initial lump-sum payments made by the residents.

*"Mello-Roos" Bonds.*   These are bonds issued in California to finance public facilities in developing areas. The bond security is usually dependent on the commerical success of the specific development involved.

*Moral Obligation Bonds.*   A moral obligation bond is a security structure for state-issued bonds, indicating that, if revenues are needed for paying bondholders, the state legislature involved is legally authorized, though not required, to make an appropriation out of general state tax revenues.

*Municipal Utility District Revenue Bonds.*   These are bonds that are usually issued to finance the construction of water and sewer systems as well as roadways in undeveloped areas. The security is usually dependent on the commercial success of the specific development project involved, which can range from the sale of new homes to the renting of space in shopping centers and office buildings.

*New Housing Authority Bonds.*   These bonds are secured by a contractual pledge of annual contributions from HUD. Monies from Washington are paid directly to the paying agent for the bonds, and the bondholders are given specific legal rights to enforce the pledge. These bonds can no longer be issued.

*Tax Allocation Bonds.*   These bonds are usually issued to finance the construction of office buildings and other new buildings in formerly blighted areas. They are secured by property taxes collected on the improved real estate.

*"Territorial" Bonds.*   These are bonds issued by United States territorial possessions such as Puerto Rico, the Virgin Islands, and Guam. The bonds are tax-exempt throughout most of the country. Also, the economies of these issuers are influenced by positive special features of the U.S. corporate tax codes that are not available to the states.

*"Troubled City and State" Bailout Bonds.*   There are certain bonds that are structured to appear as pure revenue bonds but in essence are not. Revenues come from general purpose taxes and revenues that otherwise would have gone to a state's or city's general fund. Their bond structures were created to bail out underlying general obligation bond issuers from severe budget deficits. Exam-

ples are the New York State *Municipal Assistance Corporation for the City of New York Bonds (MAC)*; the State of Illinois *Chicago School Finance Authority Bonds*; and, more recently, the Louisiana Recovery District *Sales Tax Bonds*.

*Refunded Bonds.* These are bonds that may originally have been issued as general obligation or revenue bonds but are now secured by an "escrow fund" usually consisting entirely of direct U.S. government obligations that are sufficient for paying the bondholders. *They are among the safest of all municipal bonds if the escrow is properly structured.*

## Notes

Tax-exempt debt issued for periods ranging not beyond three years is usually considered to be short-term in nature. Below are descriptions of some of these debt instruments.

*Tax, Revenue, Grant, and Bond Anticipation Notes: TANs, RANs, GANs, and BANs.* These are temporary borrowings by states, local governments, and special jurisdictions. Usually, notes are issued for a period of 12 months. TANs and RANs (also known as TRANs) are issued in anticipation of the collection of taxes or other expected revenues. These are borrowings to even out the cash flows caused by the irregular flows of income into the treasuries of the states and local units of government. BANs are issued in anticipation of the sale of long-term bonds.

*Tax-Exempt Commercial Paper.* This short-term borrowing instrument is issued for periods ranging from 30 to 270 days. Generally the tax-exempt commercial paper has backstop commercial bank agreements, which can include an irrevocable letter of credit, a revolving credit agreement, or a line of credit.

In this chapter, we shall refer to both municipal bonds and municipal notes as simply municipal bonds.

## Newer Market-Sensitive Debt Instruments

Municipal bonds are usually issued with one of two debt retirement structures or a combination of both. Either a bond has a "serial" maturity structure (wherein a portion of the loan is retired each year), or a bond has a "term" maturity (wherein the loan is repaid on a final date). Usually term bonds have maturities ranging from 20 to 40 years and retirement schedules (which are known as sinking funds) that begin 5 to 10 years before the final term maturity.

Because of the upward-sloping yield curve that existed in the municipal bond market between 1979 and 1990, many investment bankers introduced innovative financing instruments priced at short or intermediate yield levels. These debt instruments are intended to raise money for long-term capital projects at reduced interest rates. Below are descriptions of some of these more innovative debt structures.

***Put or Option Tender Bonds.*** A "put" or "option tender" bond is one in which the bondholder has the right to return the bond at a price of par to the bond trustee prior to its stated long-term maturity. The put period can be as short as one day and as long as 10 years. Usually, put bonds are backed either by commercial bank letters of credit in addition to the issuer's cash-flow revenues or entirely by the cash-flow revenues of the issuer.

***Super Sinkers.*** A "super sinker" is a specifically identified maturity for a single-family housing revenue bond issue to which all funds from early mortgage prepayments are used to retire bonds. A super sinker has a long-stated maturity but a shorter, albeit unknown, actual life. Because of this unique characteristic, investors have the opportunity to realize an attractive return when the municipal yield curve is upward sloping on a bond that is priced as if it had a maturity consideration longer than its anticipated life.

***Variable-Rate Notes.*** Variable-rate notes have coupon rates that change. When a variable-rate note has a put feature, it is called a *variable-rate demand obligation*, which may be exercised after one day, seven days, quarterly, semi-annually, annually, or longer. The coupon rate is tied to one of various indexes. Specific examples include percents of the prime rate, the J. J. Kenney Municipal Index, the Merrill Lynch Index, or a percent of the 90-day Treasury bill rate. A bank letter of credit is usually required as liquidity backup for variable-rate demand obligations.

A variation of variable-rate obligations is one in which the investor in advance selects the interest rate and interest payment date from 1 up to 90 or 180 days. The security may have a nominal 30-year maturity. Such a bond has a put feature of a variable-rate demand obligation and the maturity flexibility of tax-exempt commercial paper. One version of this investment vehicle is called UPDATES (Unit Priced Demand Adjustable Tax-Exempt Securities).

***Zero Coupon Bonds.*** A zero coupon bond is one in which no coupon interest payments are paid to the bondholder. Instead, the bond is purchased at a very deep discount and matures at par. The difference between the original-issue discount price and par represents a specified compounded annual yield. In the municipal bond market, there is also a variant of the zero coupon bond called a "municipal multiplier," or "compound interest bond." It is a bond that is issued at par and *does* actually have interest payments. However, the interest payments are not distributed to the holder of the bond until maturity. Rather, the issuer agrees to reinvest the undistributed interest payments at the bond's yield-to-maturity when it was issued. For example, suppose that a 10 percent, 10-year bond with a par value of $5,000 is sold at par to yield 10 percent.

Every six months, the maturity value of the bond is increased by 5 percent of the maturity value of the previous six months. So at the end of 10 years, the maturity value of the bond will be equal to $13,267 [= $5,000 $\times (1.05)^{20}$]. In the case of a 10-year zero coupon bond priced to yield 10 percent, the bond would have a maturity value of $5,000 but sell for $1,884 when it is issued.[2]

## THE LEGAL OPINION

Municipal bonds have legal opinions. The relationship of the legal opinion to the safety of municipal bonds for both general obligation and revenue bonds is threefold. First, bond counsel should check to determine if the issuer is indeed legally able to issue the bonds. Second, bond counsel is to see that the issuer has properly prepared for the bond sale by having enacted the various required ordinances, resolutions, and trust indentures and without violating any other laws and regulations. This preparation is particularly important in the highly technical areas of determining if the bond issue is qualified for tax exemption under federal law and if the issue has not been structured in such a way as to violate federal arbitrage regulations. Third, bond counsel is to certify that the security safeguards and remedies provided for the bondholders and pledged either by the bond issuer or by third parties, such as banks with letter-of-credit agreements, are actually supported by federal, state, and local government laws and regulations.

The popular notion is that much of the legal work done in a bond issue is boilerplate in nature, but from the bondholder's point of view the legal opinions and document reviews should be the ultimate security provisions. The reason is that if all else fails, the bondholder may have to go to court to enforce his or her security rights. Therefore, the integrity and competence of the lawyers who review the documents and write the legal opinions that usually are summarized and stated in the official statements are very important.[3]

## THE COMMERCIAL CREDIT RATING
## OF MUNICIPAL BONDS

Of the municipal bonds that were rated by a commercial rating company in 1929 and plunged into default in 1932, 78 percent had been rated double-A or better, and 48 percent had been rated triple-A. Since then the ability of rating

---

[2] Variations on the zero coupon bond were introduced to allow municipal issuers to circumvent restrictions on the amount of par value that they were legally permitted to issue.

[3] For specific studies on problems with legal opinions, see Chapter 11 in Feldstein and Fabozzi, *Dow Jones-Irwin Guide to Municipal Bonds*.

agencies to assess the creditworthiness of municipal obligations has evolved to a level of general industry acceptance and respectability. In most instances, they adequately describe the financial conditions of the issuers and identify the credit-risk factors. However, a small but significant number of recent instances have caused market participants to reexamine their reliance on the opinions of the rating agencies.

As an example, the troubled bonds of the Washington Public Power Supply System (WPPSS) should be mentioned. Two major commercial rating companies—Moody's and Standard & Poor's—gave their highest ratings to these bonds in the early 1980s. Moody's gave the WPPSS Projects 1, 2, and 3 bonds its very highest credit rating of Aaa and the Projects 4 and 5 bonds its rating of A1. This latter investment-grade rating is defined as having the strongest investment attributes within the upper medium grade of creditworthiness. Standard & Poor's also had given the WPPSS Projects 1, 2, and 3 bonds its highest rating of AAA and Projects 4 and 5 bonds its rating of A+. While these high-quality ratings were in effect, WPPSS sold over $8 billion in long-term bonds. By 1990, over $2 billion of these bonds were in default.

In fact, since 1975 all of the major municipal defaults in the industry initially had been given investment-grade ratings by these two commercial rating companies. Of course, it should be noted that in the majority of instances ratings of the commercial rating companies adequately reflect the condition of the credit. However, unlike 25 years ago when the commercial rating companies would not rate many kinds of revenue bond issues, today they seem to view themselves as assisting in the capital formation process.[4] The commercial rating companies now receive fairly substantial fees from issuers for their ratings, and they are part of large, growth-oriented conglomerates. Moody's is an operating unit of the Dun & Bradstreet Corporation and Standard & Poor's is part of the McGraw-Hill Corporation.

Today, many institutional investors, underwriters, and traders rely on their own in-house municipal credit analysts for determining the creditworthiness of municipal bonds. However, other investors do not perform their own credit-risk analysis, but, instead, rely upon credit-risk ratings by Moody's and Standard & Poor's. In this section, we discuss the rating categories of these two commercial rating companies.

## Moody's Investors Service

The municipal bond rating system used by Moody's grades the investment quality of municipal bonds in a nine-symbol system that ranges from the highest

---

[4] See Victor F. Zonana and Daniel Hertzberg, "Moody's Dominance in Municipals Market is Slowly Being Eroded," *The Wall Street Journal*, November 1, 1981, pp. 1 and 23; and Peter Brimelow, "Shock Waves from Whoops Roll East," *Fortune*, July 25, 1983, pp. 46–48.

**EXHIBIT 21–1**
**Moody's Municipal Bond Ratings**

| Rating | Definition |
|--------|------------|
| Aaa | Best quality; carry the smallest degree of investment risk. |
| Aa | High quality; margins of protection not quite as large as the Aaa bonds. |
| A | Upper medium grade; security adequate but could be susceptible to impairment. |
| Baa | Medium grade; neither highly protected nor poorly secured—lack outstanding investment characteristics and sensitive to changes in economic circumstances. |
| Ba | Speculative; protection is very moderate. |
| B | Not desirable investment; sensitive to day-to-day economic circumstances. |
| Caa | Poor standing; may be in default but with a workout plan. |
| Ca | Highly speculative; may be in default with nominal workout plan. |
| C | Hopelessly in default. |

investment quality, which is Aaa, to the lowest credit rating, which is C. The respective nine alphabetical ratings and their definitions are found in Exhibit 21–1.

Municipal bonds in the top four categories (Aaa, Aa, A, and Baa) are considered to be of investment-grade quality. Additionally, bonds in the Aa through B categories that Moody's concludes have the strongest features within the respective categories are designated by the symbols Aa1, A1, Baa1, Ba1, and B1, respectively. Moody's also may use the prefix *Con.* before a credit rating to indicate that the bond security is dependent on (1) the completion of a construction project, (2) earnings of a project with little operating experience, (3) rentals being paid once the facility is constructed, or (4) some other limiting condition. Moody's applies numerical modifiers 1, 2, and 3 in each generic rating classification from Aa through B to municipal bonds that are issued for industrial development and pollution control. The modifier 1 indicates that the security ranks in the higher end of its generic rating category; the modifier 2 indicates a midrange ranking; and the modifier 3 indicates that the bond ranks in the lower end of its generic rating category.

The municipal note rating system used by Moody's is designated by four investment-grade categories of Moody's Investment Grade (MIG), as shown in Exhibit 21–2.

Moody's also provides credit ratings for tax-exempt commercial paper. These are promissory obligations (1) not having an original maturity in excess of nine months and (2) backed by commercial banks. Moody's uses three

**EXHIBIT 21–2**
**Moody's Municipal**
**Note Ratings**\*

| Rating | Definition |
|---|---|
| MIG 1 | Best quality |
| MIG 2 | High quality |
| MIG 3 | Favorable quality |
| MIG 4 | Adequate quality |

\* A short issue having a "demand" feature (i.e., payment relying on external liquidity and usually payable upon demand rather than fixed maturity dates) is differentiated by Moody's with the use of the symbols VMIG1 through VMIG4.

designations, all considered to be of investment grade, for indicating the relative repayment capacity of the rated issues, as shown in Exhibit 21–3.

## Standard & Poor's

The municipal bond rating system used by Standard & Poor's grades the investment quality of municipal bonds in a 10-symbol system that ranges from the highest investment quality, which is AAA, to the lowest credit rating, which is D. Bonds within the top four categories (AAA, AA, A, and BBB) are considered by Standard & Poor's as being of investment-grade quality. The respective 10 alphabetical ratings and definitions are shown in Exhibit 21–4.

Standard & Poor's also uses a plus (+) or minus (−) sign to show relative standing within the rating categories ranging from AA to BB. Additionally, Stan-

**EXHIBIT 21–3**
**Moody's Tax-Exempt Commercial Paper**
**Ratings**

| Rating | Definition |
|---|---|
| Prime 1 (P–1) | Superior capacity for repayment |
| Prime 2 (P–2) | Strong capacity for repayment |
| Prime 3 (P–3) | Acceptable capacity for repayment |

**EXHIBIT 21–4**
**Standard & Poor's Municipal Bond Ratings**

| Rating | Definition |
| --- | --- |
| AAA | Highest rating; extremely strong security. |
| AA | Very strong security; differs from AAA in only a small degree. |
| A | Strong capacity but more susceptible to adverse economic effects than two above categories. |
| BBB | Adequate capacity but adverse economic conditions more likely to weaken capacity. |
| BB | Lowest degree of speculation; risk exposure. |
| B | Speculative; risk exposure. |
| CCC | Speculative; major risk exposure. |
| CC | Highest degree of speculation; major risk exposure. |
| C | No interest is being paid. |
| D | Bonds in default with interest and/or repayment of principal in arrears. |

dard & Poor's uses the letter $p$ to indicate a provisional rating that is intended to be removed upon the successful and timely completion of the construction project. A double dagger (‡) on a mortgage-backed revenue bond rating indicates that the rating is contingent upon receipt by Standard & Poor's of closing documentation confirming investments and cash flows. An asterisk (*) following a credit rating indicates that the continuation of the rating is contingent upon receipt of an executed copy of the escrow agreement.

The municipal note rating system used by Standard & Poor's grades the investment quality of municipal notes in a four-symbol system that ranges from highest investment quality, SP−1+, to the lowest credit rating, SP−3. Notes within the top three categories (i.e., SP−1+, SP−1, and SP−2) are considered by Standard & Poor's as being of investment-grade quality. The respective ratings and summarized definitions are shown in Exhibit 21–5.

Standard & Poor's also rates tax-exempt commercial paper in the same four categories as taxable commercial paper. The four tax-exempt commercial paper rating categories are shown in Exhibit 21–6.

## How the Rating Agencies Differ

Although there are many similarities in how Moody's and Standard & Poor's approach credit ratings, there are certain differences in their respective approaches as well. As examples, we shall present below some of the differences in approach between Moody's and Standard & Poor's when they assign credit ratings to general obligation bonds.

**EXHIBIT 21–5**
**Standard & Poor's Municipal Note Ratings**

| Rating | Definition |
|--------|------------|
| SP–1 | Very strong or strong capacity to pay principal and interest. Those issues determined to possess overwhelming safety characteristics will be given a plus (+) designation. |
| SP–2 | Satisfactory capacity to pay principal and interest. |
| SP–3 | Speculative capacity to pay principal and interest. |

The credit analysis of general obligation bonds issued by states, counties, school districts, and municipalities initially requires the collection and assessment of information in four basic categories. The first category includes obtaining information on the issuer's debt structure so that the overall debt burden can be determined. The debt burden usually is composed of (1) the respective direct and overlapping debts per capita as well as (2) the respective direct and overlapping debts as percentages of real estate valuations and personal incomes. The second category of needed information relates to the issuer's ability and political discipline for maintaining sound budgetary operations. The focus of attention here is usually on the issuer's general operating funds and whether or not it has maintained at least balanced budgets over the previous three to five years. The third category involves determining the specific local taxes and intergovernmental revenues available to the issuer, as well as obtaining historical information on both tax collection rates, which are important when looking at property tax levies, and on the dependency of local budgets on specific revenue sources, which is important when looking at the impact of state and federal revenue sharing monies. The fourth and last general category of information necessary to the credit analysis is an assessment of the issuer's overall socioeconomic environment. Economic indexes that must be determined include the local employ-

**EXHIBIT 21–6**
**Standard & Poor's Tax-Exempt**
**Commercial Paper Ratings**

| Rating | Definition |
|--------|------------|
| A–1+ | Highest degree of safety |
| A–1 | Very strong degree of safety |
| A–2 | Strong degree of safety |
| A–3 | Satisfactory degree of safety |

ment distribution and composition, population growth, and real estate property valuation and personal income trends, among others.

Although Moody's and Standard & Poor's rely on these same four informational categories in arriving at their respective credit ratings of general obligation bonds, what they emphasize among the categories can result at times in dramatically different credit ratings for the same issuer's bonds. The objective here is to outline what these differences between Moody's and Standard & Poor's actually are. Furthermore, although the rating agencies have stated in their publications what criteria guide their respective credit-rating approaches, the conclusions here about how they go about rating general obligation bonds are not only derived from these sources, but also from reviewing their credit reports and rating decisions on individual bond issues.

***How do Moody's and Standard & Poor's Differ in Evaluating the Four Basic Informational Categories?*** Simply stated, Moody's tends to focus on the debt burden and budgetary operations of the issuer, whereas Standard & Poor's considers the issuer's economic environment as the most important element in its analysis. Although in most instances these differences of emphasis do not result in dramatically split credit ratings for a given issuer, there are at least two recent instances in which major differences in ratings on general obligation bonds have occurred.

The general obligation bonds of the Chicago School Finance Authority are rated only A by Moody's, but Standard & Poor's rates the same bonds AA. In assigning the credit rating of A, Moody's bases its rating on the following debt- and budget-related factors: (1) The deficit-funding bonds are to be retired over a 30-year period, an unusually long time for such an obligation; (2) the overall debt burden is high; and (3) the school board faces long-term difficulties in balancing its operating budget because of reduced operating taxes, desegregation program requirements, and uncertain public employee union relations.

Standard & Poor's credit rating of AA appears to be based primarily upon the following two factors: (1) Chicago's economy is well diversified and fundamentally sound; and (2) the unique security provisions for the bonds in the opinion of the bond counsel insulate the pledged property taxes from the school board's creditors in the event of a school-system bankruptcy.

Another general obligation bond wherein split ratings have occurred is the bond issue of Allegheny County, Pennsylvania. Moody's rates the bonds A, whereas the Standard & Poor's rating is AA.

Moody's A credit rating is based primarily upon four budget-related factors: (1) above-average debt load with more bonds expected to be issued for transportation related projects and for the building of a new hospital, (2) continued unfunded pension liabilities, (3) past unorthodox budgetary practices of shifting tax revenues from the county tax levy to the county institution district levy, and (4) an archaic real estate property assessment system.

Standard & Poor's, higher credit rating of AA also appears to be based upon four factors: (1) an affluent, diverse, and stable economy with wealth variables above the national medians, (2) a good industrial mix with decreasing dependence on steel production, (3) improved budget operations having accounting procedures developed to conform to generally accepted accounting principles, and (4) a rapid debt retirement schedule that essentially matches anticipated future bond sales.

*How do the Credit-Rating Agencies Differ in Assessing the Moral Obligation Bonds?* In more than 20 states, state agencies have issued housing revenue bonds that carry a potential state liability for making up deficiencies in their one-year debt service reserve funds (backup funds), should any occur. In most cases if a drawdown of the debt reserve occurs, the state agency must report the amount used to its governor and the state budget director. The state legislature, in turn, may appropriate the requested amount, though there is no legally enforceable obligation to do so. Bonds with this makeup provision are the so-called moral obligation bonds.

Below is an example of the legal language in the bond indenture that explains this procedure.

> In order to further assure the maintenance of each such debt service reserve fund, there shall be annually apportioned and paid to the agency for deposit in each debt service reserve fund such sum, if any, as shall be certified by the chairman of the agency to the governor and director of the budget as necessary to restore such fund to an amount equal to the fund requirement. The chairman of the agency shall annually, on or before December first, make and deliver to the governor and director of the budget his certificate stating the sum or sums, if any, required to restore each such debt service reserve fund to the amount aforesaid, and the sum so certified, if any, shall be apportioned and paid to the agency during the then current state fiscal year.

Moody's views the moral obligation feature as being more literary than legal when applied to legislatively permissive debt service reserve makeup provisions. Therefore, it does not consider this procedure a credit strength. Standard & Poor's, to the contrary, does. It views moral obligation bonds as being no lower than one rating category below a state's own general obligation bonds. Its rationale is based upon the implied state support for the bonds and the market implications for that state's own general obligation bonds should it ever fail to honor its moral obligation.

Several municipal bonds that have split ratings as a result of these two different opinions of the moral obligation. As examples, in mid-1990 the Nonprofit Housing Project Bonds of the New York State Housing Finance Agency, and the General Purpose Bonds of the New York State Urban Development Corporation had the Moody's credit rating of Ba, which is a speculative investment category. Standard & Poor's, because of the moral obligation pledge of the state of New York, gave the same bonds a credit rating of BBB, which is an investment-grade category.

***How do the Credit Rating Agencies Differ in Assessing the Importance of Withholding State Aid to Pay Debt Service?*** Still another difference between Moody's and Standard & Poor's involves their respective attitude toward state-aid security-related mechanisms. Since 1974, it has been the policy of Standard & Poor's to view as a very positive credit feature the automatic withholding and use of state aid to pay defaulted debt service on local government general obligation bonds. Usually the mechanism requires the respective state treasurer to pay debt service directly to the bondholder from monies due the local issuer from the state. Seven states have enacted security mechanisms that in one way or another allow certain local government general obligation bondholders to be paid debt service from the state-aid appropriations, if necessary. In most instances the state-aid withholding provisions apply to general obligation bonds issued by school districts.[5]

Although Standard & Poor's does review the budgetary operations of the local government issuer to be sure there are no serious budgetary problems, the assigned rating reflects the general obligation credit rating of the state involved, the legal base of the withholding mechanism, the historical background and long-term state legislative support for the pledged state aid program, and the specified coverage of the state aid monies available to maximum debt-service requirements on the local general obligation bonds. Normally, Standard & Poor's applies a blanket rating to all local general obligation bonds covered by the specific state-aid withholding mechanism. The rating is one or two notches below the rating of that particular state's general obligation bonds. Whether the rating is either one notch below or two notches below depends on the coverage figures, the legal security, and the legislative history and political durability of the pledged state-aid monies involved. It should also be noted that, although Standard & Poor's stated policy is to give blanket ratings, a specified rating is only granted when an issuer or bondholder applies for it.

Although Moody's recognizes the state-aid withholding mechanisms in its credit reviews, it believes that its assigned rating must in the first instance reflect the underlying ability of the issuer to make timely debt-service payments. Standard & Poor's, to the contrary, considers a state-aid withholding mechanism that provides for the payment of debt service equally as important a credit factor as the underlying budget, economic, and debt-related characteristics of the bond issuer.

---

[5] The states involved are Indiana, Kentucky, New Jersey, New York, Pennsylvania, South Carolina, and West Virginia.

*What is the Difference in Attitudes toward Accounting Records?*   Another area of difference between Moody's and Standard & Poor's concerns their respective attitudes toward the accounting records kept by general obligation bond issuers. In May 1980, Standard & Poor's stated that if the bond issuer's financial reports are not prepared in accordance with generally accepted accounting principles (GAAP) it will consider this a "negative factor" in its rating process. Standard & Poor's has not indicated how negative a factor it is in terms of credit rating changes but has indicated that issuers will not be rated at all if either the financial report is not timely (i.e., available no later than six months after the fiscal year-end) or is substantially deficient in terms of reporting. Moody's policy here is quite different. Because Moody's reviews the historical performance of an issuer over a three- to five-year period, requiring GAAP reporting is not necessary from Moody's point of view, although the timeliness of financial reports is of importance.

## MUNICIPAL BOND INSURANCE

Municipal bond insurance is a contractual commitment by an insurance company to pay the bondholder any bond principal and/or coupon interest that is due on a stated maturity date but that has not been paid by the bond issuer. Once issued, this municipal bond default insurance usually extends for the term of the bond issue, and it cannot be canceled by the insurance company. A one-time insurance premium (generally paid at the time of original bond issuance) is paid for the insurance policy and is nonrefundable.

The bondholder or trustee who has not received payments for bond principal and/or coupon interest on the stated due dates for the insured bonds must notify the insurance company and surrender to it the unpaid bonds and coupons. Under the terms of the policy, the insurance company is usually obligated to pay the paying agent sufficient monies for the bondholders. These monies must be enough to cover the face value of the insured principal and coupon interest that was due but not paid. Once the insurance company pays the monies, the company becomes the owner of the surrendered bonds and coupons and can begin legal proceedings to recover the monies that are now due it from the bond issuer.

### The Insurers

Municipal bond insurance has been available since 1971. Some of the largest and financially strongest insurance companies in the United States have been participants in this industry, as well as smaller monoline insurance companies. By 1990, approximately 25 percent of all new municipals were insured. The following monoline companies are major municipal bond insurers as of 1990:

AMBAC Indemnity Corporation (AMBAC)

Capital Guaranty Insurance Company (CGIC)

Financial Guaranty Insurance Company (FGIC)

Municipal Bond Investors Assurance (MBIA)

## Market Pricing of Insured Municipal Bonds

In general, although insured municipal bonds sell at yields lower than they would without the insurance, they tend to have yields substantially higher than Aaa/AAA-rated noninsured municipal bonds.

## EQUIVALENT TAXABLE YIELD

An investor interested in purchasing a municipal bond must be able to compare the promised yield on a municipal bond with that of a comparable taxable bond. The following general formula is used to determine the equivalent taxable yield for a tax-exempt bond:

$$\text{Equivalent taxable yield} = \frac{\text{Tax-exempt yield}}{(1 - \text{Marginal tax rate})}$$

For example, suppose an investor in the 28 percent marginal tax bracket is considering the acquisition of a tax-exempt bond that offers a tax-exempt yield of 6 percent. The equivalent taxable yield is 8.33 percent, as shown below.

$$\text{Equivalent taxable yield} = \frac{.06}{(1 - .28)} = .0833$$

When computing the equivalent taxable yield, the traditionally computed yield-to-maturity is not the tax-exempt yield if the issue is selling below par (i.e., selling at a discount) because only the coupon interest is exempt from federal income taxes. Instead, the yield-to-maturity after an assumed capital gains tax is computed and used in the numerator of the formula.

The yield-to-maturity after an assumed capital gains tax is calculated in the same manner as the traditional yield-to-maturity. However, instead of using the redemption value in the calculation, the net proceeds after an assumed tax on any capital gain is used.

There is a major drawback in employing the equivalent taxable yield formula to compare the relative investment merits of a taxable and tax-exempt bond. Recall from the discussion in Chapter 6 that the yield-to-maturity measure assumes that the entire coupon interest can be reinvested at the computed yield. Consequently, taxable bonds with the same yield-to-maturity cannot be compared because the total dollar returns may differ from the computed yield. The same problem arises when attempting to compare taxable and tax-exempt bonds, especially since only a portion of the coupon interest on taxable bonds can be reinvested, although the entire coupon payment is available for reinvestment in the case of municipal bonds. The horizon return framework that should be employed to compare taxable and tax-exempt bonds is discussed in Chapter 6.[6]

## STATE AND LOCAL TAX TREATMENT[7]

The tax treatment of municipal bonds varies by state. There are three types of tax that can be imposed: (1) an income tax on coupon income, (2) a tax on realized capital gains, and (3) a personal property tax.

A majority of the states levy an individual income tax, as does the District of Columbia. Several of these states exempt coupon interest on *all* municipal bonds, whether the issue is in state or out of state. Coupon interest from obligations by in-state issuers is exempt from state individual income taxes in most states. A few states levy individual income taxes on coupon interest whether the issuer is in state or out of state.

State taxation of realized capital gains is often ignored by investors when making investment decisions. In many states, a tax is levied on a base that includes income from capital transactions (i.e., capital gains or losses). In many states where coupon interest is exempt if the issuer is in state, the same exemption will not apply to capital gains involving municipal bonds.

Approximately 20 states levy a personal property tax. Of these, only 11 apply this tax to municipal bonds. The tax resembles more of an income tax than a personal property tax. For example, in Kansas, Michigan, and Ohio, personal property taxes are measured on the annual income generated by a bond.

In determining the effective tax rate imposed by a particular state, an investor must consider the impact of the deductibility of state taxes on federal income taxes. Moreover, in about 13 states, *federal* taxes are deductible in determining state income taxes.

---

[6] See also Martin L. Leibowitz, "Total Aftertax Bond Performance and Yield Measures for Tax-Exempt Bonds Held in Taxable Portfolios," in *The Municipal Bond Handbook*, Vol. I, Frank J. Fabozzi, Sylvan G. Feldstein, Irving M. Pollack, and Frank G. Zarb (eds.) (Homewood, Ill.: Dow Jones-Irwin, 1983).

[7] The source of information for this section is from Steven J. Hueglin, "State and Local Tax Treatment of Municipal Bonds," Chapter 4 in *The Municipal Bond Handbook*, Vol. I, Frank J. Fabozzi, et al. (eds.).

# YIELD RELATIONSHIPS WITHIN THE MUNICIPAL BOND MARKET

## Differences within an Assigned Credit Rating

Bond buyers primarily use the credit ratings assigned by the commercial rating companies, Standard & Poor's and Moody's, as a starting point for pricing an issue. The final market-derived bond price is composed of the assigned credit rating and adjustments by investors to reflect their own analysis of creditworthiness and perception of marketability. For example, as we noted earlier, insured municipal bonds tend to have yields that are substantially higher than noninsured superior-investment-quality municipal bonds even though most insured bonds are given triple-A ratings by the commercial rating companies. Additionally, many investors have geographical preferences among bonds, in spite of identical credit quality and otherwise comparable investment characteristics.

## Differences between Credit Ratings

With all other factors constant, the greater the credit risk perceived by investors, the higher the return expected by investors. The spread between municipal bonds of different credit quality is not constant over time. Reasons for the change in spreads are (1) the outlook for the economy and its anticipated impact on issuers, (2) federal budget financing needs, and (3) municipal market supply-and-demand factors. During periods of relatively low interest rates, investors sometimes increase their holdings of issues of lower credit quality in order to obtain additional yield. This narrows the spread between high-grade and lower-grade credit issues. During periods in which investors anticipate a poor economic climate, there is often a "flight to quality" as investors pursue a more conservative credit-risk exposure. This widens the spread between high-grade and lower-grade credit issues.

Another factor that causes shifts in the spread between issues of different quality is the temporary oversupply of issues within a market sector. For example, a substantial new-issue volume of high-grade state general obligation bonds may tend to decrease the spread between high-grade and lower grade revenue bonds. In a weak market environment, it is easier for high-grade municipal bonds to come to market than for weaker credits. Therefore, it is not uncommon for high grades to flood weak markets at the same time there is a relative scarcity of medium- and low-grade municipal bond issues.

## Differences between In-State and General Market

Bonds of municipal issuers located in certain states (for example, New York, California, Arizona, Maryland, and Pennsylvania) usually yield considerably less than issues of identical credit quality that come from other states that trade in the "general market." There are three reasons for the existence of such spreads. First, states often exempt interest from in-state issues from state and local personal income taxes, and interest from out-of-state issues is generally not exempt. Consequently, in states with high income taxes (e.g., New York and California), strong investor demand for in-state issues will reduce their yields relative to bonds of issues located in states where state and local income taxes are not important considerations (e.g., Illinois, Florida, and New Jersey). Second, in some states, public funds deposited in banks must be collateralized by the bank accepting the deposit. This requirement is referred to as pledging. Acceptable collateral for pledging will typically include issues of certain in-state issuers. For those issues qualifying, pledging tends to increase demand (particularly for the shorter maturities) and reduce yields relative to nonqualifying comparable issues. The third reason is that investors in some states (e.g., South Carolina) exhibit extreme reluctance to purchase issues from issuers outside of their state or region. In-state parochialism tends to decrease relative yields of issues from states in which investors exhibit this behavior.

## Differences between Maturities

One determinant of the yield on a bond is the number of years remaining to maturity. As explained in Chapters 8 and 9, the yield curve depicts the relationship at a given point in time between yields and maturity for bonds that are identical in every way except maturity. When yields increase with maturity, the yield curve is said to be *normal* or have a *positive slope*. Therefore, as investors lengthen their maturity, they require a greater yield. It is also possible for the yield curve to be "inverted," meaning that long-term yields are less than short-term yields. If short-, intermediate-, and long-term yields are roughly the same, the yield curve is said to be *flat*.

In the taxable bond market, it is not unusual to find all three shapes for the yield curve at different points in the business cycle. However, in the municipal bond market the yield curve is typically normal or upward sloping. Consequently, in the municipal bond market, long-term bonds offer higher yields than short- and intermediate-term bonds.

## THE PRIMARY AND SECONDARY MARKETS

### The Primary Market

A substantial number of municipal obligations are brought to market each week. A state or local government can market its new issue by offering them publicly to the investing community or by placing them privately with a small group of investors. When a public offering is selected, the issue is usually underwritten by investment bankers and municipal bond departments of commercial banks. Public offerings may be marketed by either competitive bidding or direct negotiations with underwriters. When an issue is marketed via competitive bidding, the issue is awarded to the bidder submitting the lowest best bid.

Most states mandate that general obligation issues be marketed via competitive bidding; however, this is generally not required for revenue bonds. Usually state and local governments require that a competitive sale be announced in a recognized financial publication such as *The Bond Buyer*, which is the trade publication of the municipal bond industry. *The Bond Buyer* also provides information on upcoming competitive sales and most negotiated sales as well as the results of the sales of previous weeks.

When an underwriter purchases a new bond issue, it relieves the issuer of two obligations. First, the underwriter is responsible for the distribution of the issue. Second, the underwriter accepts the risk that investors might fail to purchase the issue at the expected prices within the planned time period. The second risk exists because the underwriter may have incorrectly priced the issue and/or because interest rates rise, resulting in a decline in the value of unsold issues held in inventory. The underwriter spread (i.e., the difference between the price it paid the issuer for the issue and the price it reoffered the issue to the public) is the underwriter's compensation for undertaking these risks as well as for other services it may have provided the issuer.[8]

An official statement describing the issue and issuer is prepared for new offerings.

## The Secondary Market

Although municipal bonds are not listed and traded in formal institutions, as are certain common stocks and corporate bonds on the New York and American stock exchanges, there are very strong and active billion-dollar secondary markets for municipals that are supported by hundreds of municipal bond dealers across the country. Markets are maintained on local credits by regional brokerage firms, local banks, and by some of the larger Wall Street firms. General market names are supported by the larger brokerage firms and banks, many of whom have investment banking relationships with the issuers. Buying and selling decisions are often made over the phone and through municipal bond brokers. For a small fee, these brokers serve as intermediaries in the sale of large blocks of municipal bonds among dealers and large institutional investors. These brokers are primarily located in New York City. In addition to these brokers and the daily offerings sent out over *The Bond Buyer*'s "munifacts" teletype system,

---

[8] For example, in the case of negotiated offerings, there is the value of the origination services provided by the underwriter. Origination services represent the structuring of the issue and planning activities surrounding the offering.

many dealers advertise their municipal bond offerings for the retail market in what is known as *The Blue List*. This is a 100+-page booklet that is published every weekday by the Standard & Poor's Corporation. In it are listed municipal bond and note offerings and prices.

In the municipal bond market, an odd lot of bonds is $25,000 (five bonds) or less in par value for retail investors. For institutions, anything below $100,000 in par value is considered an odd lot. Dealer spreads—the difference between the dealer's bid and ask prices—depend on several factors. For the retail investor, the dealer spread can range from as low as one quarter of one point ($12.50 per $5,000 of par value) on large blocks of actively traded bonds to four points ($200 per $5,000 of par value) for odd lot sales of an inactive issue. The average spread for retail investors seems to be around two points ($100 per $5,000 of par value). For institutional investors, the dealer spread rarely exceeds one half of one point ($25 per $5,000 of par value).

## REGULATION OF THE MUNICIPAL SECURITIES MARKET[9]

As an outgrowth of abusive stock market practices, Congress passed the Securities Act of 1933 and the Securities Exchange Act of 1934. The 1934 act created the Securities and Exchange Commission (SEC), granting it regulatory authority over the issuance and trading of *corporate* securities. Congress specifically exempted municipal securities from both the registration requirements of the 1933 act and the periodic-reporting requirements of the 1934 act. However, antifraud provisions did apply to offerings of or dealings in municipal securities.

The reasons for the exemption afforded municipal securities appear to have been due to (1) the desire for governmental comity, (2) the absence of recurrent abuses in transactions involving municipal securities, (3) the greater level of sophistication of investors in this segment of the securities markets (i.e., institutional investors dominated the market), and (4) the fact that there were few defaults by municipal issuers. Consequently, from the enactment of the two federal securities acts in the early 1930s to the early 1970s, the municipal securities market can be characterized as relatively free from federal regulation.

In the early 1970s, however, circumstances changed. As incomes rose, individuals participated in the municipal securities market to a much greater extent. As a result, public concern over selling practices occurred with greater frequency. For example, in the early 1970s, the SEC obtained seven injunctions

---

[9] This discussion is drawn from Thomas F. Mitchell, "Disclosure and the Municipal Bond Industry," Chapter 40 and Nancy H. Wojtas, "The SEC and Investor Safeguards," Chapter 42 in *The Municipal Bond Handbook*, Vol. I, Fabozzi, et al. (eds.).

against 72 defendants for fraudulent municipal trading practices. According to the SEC, the abusive practices involved both disregard by the defendants as to whether the particular municipal bond offered to individuals were in fact appropriate investment vehicles for the individuals to whom they were offered and misrepresentation or failure to disclose information necessary for individuals to assess the credit risk of the municipal issuer, especially in the case of revenue bonds. Moreover, the financial problems of some municipal issuers, notably New York City, made market participants aware that municipal issuers have the potential to experience severe and bankruptcy-type financial difficulties.

Congress passed the Securities Act Amendment of 1975 to broaden federal regulation in the municipals market. The legislation brought brokers and dealers in the municipal securities market, including banks that underwrite and trade municipal securities, within the regulatory scheme of the Securities Exchange Act of 1934. In addition, the legislation mandated that the SEC establish a 15-member Municipal Securities Rule Making Board (MSRB) as an independent, self-regulatory agency, whose primary responsibility is to develop rules governing the activities of banks, brokers, and dealers in municipal securities.[10] Rules adopted by the MSRB must be approved by the SEC. The MSRB has no enforcement or inspection authority. This authority is vested with the SEC, the National Association of Securities Dealers, and certain regulatory banking agencies such as the Federal Reserve Bank.

The Securities Act Amendment of 1975 does *not* require that municipal issuers comply with the registration requirement of the 1933 act or the periodic-reporting requirement of the 1934 act. There have been, however, several legislative proposals to mandate financial disclosure. Although none has been passed, there is clearly pressure to improve disclosure. Even in the absence of federal legislation dealing with the regulation of financial disclosure, underwriters began insisting upon greater disclosure as it became apparent that the SEC was exercising stricter application of the antifraud provisions. Moreover, underwriters recognized the need for improved disclosure to sell municipal securities to an investing public that has become much more concerned about credit risk by municipal issuers.

On June 28, 1989, the Securities and Exchange Commission formally approved the first bond disclosure rule, effective January 1, 1990. The following paragraphs summarize its contents.

The rule applies to all new issue municipal securities offerings of $1 million or more. Exemptions have been added for securities offered in denominations of $100,000 or more, if such securities

---

[10] For a detailed discussion of the MSRB, see Frieda K. Wallison, "Self-Regulation of the Municipal Securities Industry," Chapter 41 in *The Municipal Bond Handbook*, Vol. I, Fabozzi, et al. (eds.).

- Are sold to no more than 35 "sophisticated investors," or
- Have a maturity of 9 months or less; or
- Are variable-rate demand instruments.

Prior to bidding or purchasing an offering, underwriters must obtain and review official statements that are deemed final by the issuer, with the omission of no more than the following information:

- Offering price;
- Interest rate;
- Selling compensation;
- Aggregate principal amount;
- Principal amount per maturity;
- Delivery dates; and
- Other terms or provisions required by an issuer of such a security to be specified in a competitive bid, ratings, other terms of the securities depending on such matters, and the identity of the underwriters.

The underwriters shall contract with an issuer or its designated agent to receive within seven business days after any final agreement to purchase, offer, or sell any offering and in sufficient time to accompany any confirmation that requests payment from any customer, copies of a final official statement.

Except for competitively bid offerings, the underwriters shall send, no later than the next business day, to any potential customer, on request, a single copy of the most recent preliminary official statement, if any.

Underwriters will be required to distribute the final official statement to any potential customer, on request, within 90 days, or 25 days if the final official statement is available from a repository.

## THE NATURE OF THE MUNICIPAL BOND INDUSTRY

By the late 1980s, there were three characteristics of the municipal bond industry that distinguished it from what it was in 1960, 1970, and even as recently as 1980. First, municipal bond and note volume increased along with the volatility of interest rates—regardless of the maturity, credit quality, or type of financing structure involved. Second, new financing techniques emerged resulting in more diverse, complex, and changing bond and note security structures. Third, there was growing reliance on retail investors and on those institutional buyers, such as bond funds, that catered primarily to individuals.

### Increased Volume and Interest-Rate Volatility

A characteristic of the municipal bond industry by the late 1980s was that it had become a major capital market. As an example, according to *The Bond*

*Buyer*, tax-exempt state and local government long-term debt outstanding by year-end 1960 was only $66 billion, whereas by year-end 1989 it was over $750 billion.[11] This represented over a 1,000 percent increase over 25 years.

Even the traditional institutional buyers of municipal bonds, such as property and casualty insurance companies, had begun to maintain quasi-trading positions in municipals. An increasing number of investors also began to "buy and trade" municipals, discarding the traditional "buy and hold" investment strategy.

One corollary of this broadening base of market participation was that there were more transitory and speculative forces in the marketplace than in the past. These forces may help explain the volatility of interest rates that characterize the municipal bond and note markets almost on a daily basis, as well as the relative lack of sustained trading patterns in many sectors of the market. It should be noted that the dramatic moves in the business cycle and changing Federal Reserve Board monetary strategies have also been overall contributing factors.

## New Financing Techniques

Along with the increased municipal bond volume, issuers and investment bankers have been using new financing techniques and security structures. Additionally, as inflation and U.S. government borrowing increased in the early 1980s, many traditional private sector borrowers began to look to tax-exempt securities—and particularly revenue bonds—as more economical financing vehicles. For instance, in 1970 only 33.5 percent, or $5.959 billion, of the total amount of municipal bonds issued in that year were revenue bonds; in 1989, 65.6 percent, or $68.58 billion, of all municipals issued were revenue bonds.[12] By 1990, revenue bonds were being used to raise capital for hospitals, water and sewer projects, airports, seaports, single-family home mortgage lenders, electric utilities, and builders of multifamily housing, among others. Revenue bonds have also been used to provide capital for loans to students and small businesses.

Because of the availability of various federal aid and taxation benefits, many municipal revenue bonds have elaborate bond security structures that could be subject to future adverse congressional actions and IRS interpretations.[13] Housing bonds backed by future federal "Section 8" appropriations and

---

[11] These data are derived from *The Bond Buyer*.

[12] These data are derived from the Merrill Lynch Fixed Income Strategy Report, First Quarter 1990, p. 22.

[13] As an example of the potential role of the IRS, in June of 1980 the Battery Park City Authority sold $97.315 million in construction loan notes, which at the time received legal comfort from bond counsel that interest on the notes was exempt from federal income taxation. In November of 1980, however, the IRS held that interest on such notes was not exempt. The issue was not resolved until September 1981 when the Authority and the IRS signed a formal agreement by which the Authority agreed to pay annually to the IRS the arbitrage gains, and the IRS, in turn, agreed that the interest paid on the notes was not taxable.

leveraged lease resource recovery revenue bonds incorporating certain tax benefits for the plant vendors are but two examples. Additionally, because of the dramatic changes that occurred in the early 1980s in the U.S. tax code and in specific federal aid programs as the result of Reaganomics, the "state of the art" in structuring revenue bonds has been undergoing constant change. Even state and local government general obligation bond issuers, because of their dependency on numerous intergovernmental aid and revenue sharing programs, developed more complex financial structures.

In addition to the greater reliance on revenue bonds, it should also be noted that investor fears of inflation have eroded confidence in long 20- to 30-year municipals regardless of the particular security structure used. Unlike the U.S. Treasury market, where an inverted yield curve existed for much of the late 1970s and 1980s, the municipal bond market was characterized by having a very steep yield curve — where the yield differentials between 1-year notes and 30-year bonds of equal creditworthiness were at times as wide as 500 basis points.

Because of the widespread investor resistance to buying long municipals, investment bankers introduced several new financing techniques. These included "put" bonds, variable coupon rate bonds, "super sinkers," and "zero" coupon bonds, all described earlier in this chapter. Commercial banks used tax-exempt commercial paper, lines of credit, and letters of credit in structuring new municipal bond and note financings. Government bond dealers and investment bankers incorporated "collateralized" repurchase agreements (repos) into several bond and note security structures. The goal of these various innovative structures was either to attract investors to long-term municipal debt instruments and/or to reduce the financing costs for the borrowers.

## Increased Importance of the Retail Investor

With the growth of confiscatory federal, state, and local government taxes on personal incomes in the 1960s and 1970s, individuals — particularly upper-income as well as middle-income wage earners — looked to municipal securities as a convenient way to shelter nonearned incomes. The increased bond volume and reduced commercial bank and casualty insurance company earnings, which decreased their traditional robust appetites for tax-exempt bonds, made municipal yields very attractive for retail investors. As an example, in September of 1982 short-term ready-access municipal note funds offered investors federal tax-free yields of over 6.5 percent compared to 5.5 percent in taxable passbook savings accounts.

Because of the strong demand by retail investors for tax-exemption, certain anomalies in yield relationships began to occur by the early 1980s. During one week in the spring of 1982, Dade County, Florida, sold general obligation bonds due in 25 years at a yield of 14 percent. The bonds were rated A-1 by Moody's and A by Standard & Poor's. During the same week New York City sold 25-year general obligations as well. Its bonds—at the time rated Ba-1 by Moody's and BBB by Standard—sold at a yield of only 14.5 percent. This narrow yield spread of 50 basis points resulted from the higher tax burden on individuals in New York. High personal income taxes created strong demands for local municipal bonds, which are tax-exempt from state of New York, New York City, and federal income taxes.

Municipal bond funds—which sell primarily to individuals—also became major institutional forces in the marketplace. These institutional buyers, unlike many insurance companies and banks, were "yield" buyers who bought long-term, A-rated revenue bonds for their relatively high yields. This preference by the bond funds for A-rated paper along with the weaker market for the high grades (i.e., AA- and AAA-rated bonds) brought about some other very unusual yield relationships. As an example, in 1982 the state of Florida sold 20-year high-investment-grade, AA-rated general obligations at a yield of 13.90 percent. At the same time, the North Carolina Eastern Municipal Power Agency sold 20-year A-rated revenue bonds at a yield of 13.25 percent. As a result of the increased role of retail buyers and the weaker demand by banks and insurance companies for high grades, by the 1980s the market at times priced retail-type weaker credit quality bonds at comparable or lower yields than it did higher quality bonds.

# CHAPTER 22

## GUIDELINES IN THE CREDIT ANALYSIS OF GENERAL OBLIGATION AND REVENUE MUNICIPAL BONDS

*Sylvan G. Feldstein, Ph.D.*
*Vice President*
*Municipal Bond Research Department*
*Merrill Lynch Capital Markets*

### INTRODUCTION

Although historically the degree of safety of investing in municipal bonds has been considered second only to that of U.S. Treasury bonds, beginning in the 1970s there has developed among many investors and underwriters ongoing concerns about the potential default risks of municipal bonds.

### The First Influence: Defaults and Bankruptcies

One concern resulted from the well-publicized, billion-dollar general obligation note defaults in 1975 of New York City. Not only were specific investors threatened with the loss of their principal, but also the defaults sent a loud and clear warning to the municipal bond investors in general. That warning was that regardless of the supposedly ironclad legal protections for the bondholder, when issuers, such as large cities, have severe budget-balancing difficulties, the political hues, cries, and financial interest of public employee unions, vendors, and community groups may be dominant forces in the initial decision-making process.

This reality was further reinforced by the new federal bankruptcy law, which took effect on October 1, 1979, and which makes it easier for municipal bond issuers to seek protection from bondholders by filing for bankruptcy. One by-product of the increased investor concern is that since 1975 the official statement, which is the counterpart to a prospectus in an equity or corporate bond offering and which is to contain a summary of the key legal and financial security features, has become more comprehensive. As an example, prior to 1975 it was common for a city of New York official statement to be only 6 pages long, whereas for a bond sale in 1990 it was close to 100 pages long.

## The Second Influence: Strong Investor Demand for Tax Exemption

The second reason for the increased interest in credit analysis was derived from the changing nature of the municipal bond market. For most of the decade of the 1970s, the municipal bond market was characterized by strong buying patterns by both private investors and institutions. The patterns were caused in part by high federal, state, and local income tax rates. Additionally, as inflation pushed many investors into higher and higher income tax brackets, tax-exempt bonds increasingly became an important and convenient way for sheltering income. One corollary of the strong buyers' demand for tax exemption has been an erosion of the traditional security provisions and bondholder safeguards that had grown out of the default experiences of the 1930s. General obligation bond issuers with high tax and debt burdens, declining local economies, and chronic budget-balancing problems had little difficulty finding willing buyers. Also, revenue bonds increasingly were rushed to market with legally untested security provisions, modest rate covenants, reduced debt reserves, and weak additional-bond tests. Because of this widespread weakening of security provisions, it has become more important than ever before that the prudent investor carefully evaluate the creditworthiness of a municipal bond before making a purchase.

In analyzing the creditworthiness of either a general obligation or revenue bond, the investor should cover five categories of inquiry. They are questions related to (1) legal documents and opinions, (2) politics/management, (3) underwriter/financial advisor, (4) general credit indicators and economics, and (5) red flags, or danger signals.

The purpose of this chapter is to set forth the general guidelines that the investor should rely upon in asking questions about specific bonds.

## THE LEGAL OPINION

The popular notion is that much of the legal work done in a bond issue is boilerplate in nature, but from the bondholder's point of view the legal opinions and document reviews should be the ultimate security provisions because, if all else fails, the bondholder may have to go to court to enforce his or her security rights. Therefore, the integrity and competency of the lawyers who review the documents and write the legal opinions that usually are summarized and stated in the official statements are very important.

The relationship of the legal opinion to the analysis of municipal bonds for both general obligation and revenue bonds is threefold. First, the lawyer should check to determine if the issuer is indeed legally able to issue the bonds. Second, the lawyer is to see that the issuer has properly prepared for the bond sale by having enacted the various required ordinances, resolutions, and trust indentures and without violating any other laws and regulations. This preparation is particularly important in the highly technical areas of determining if the bond issue is qualified for tax exemption under federal law and if the issue has not been structured in such a way so as to violate federal arbitrage regulations. Third, the lawyer is to certify that the security safeguards and remedies provided for the bondholders and pledged either by the bond issuer or by third parties, such as banks with letter-of-credit agreements, are actually supported by federal, state, and local government laws and regulations.

## General Obligation Bonds

General obligation bonds are debt instruments issued by states, counties, towns, cities, and school districts. They are secured by the issuers' general taxing powers. The investor should review the legal documents and opinion as summarized in the official statement to determine what specific *unlimited* taxing powers, such as those on real estate and personal property, corporate and individual income taxes, and sales taxes, are legally available to the issuer, if necessary, to pay the bondholders. Usually for smaller governmental jurisdictions, such as school districts and towns, the only available unlimited taxing power is on property. If there are statutory or constitutional taxing power limitations, the legal documents and opinion should clearly describe how they impact the security for the bonds.

For larger general obligation bond issuers, such as states and big cities that have diverse revenue and tax sources, the legal opinion should indicate the claim of the general obligation bondholder on the issuer's general fund. Does the bondholder have a legal claim, if necessary, to the first revenues coming into the general fund? This is the case with bondholders of state of New York general obligation bonds. Does the bondholder stand second in line? This is the case with bondholders of state of California general obligation bonds. Or are the laws silent on the question altogether? This is the case for most other state and local governments.

Additionally, certain general obligation bonds, such as those for water and sewer purposes, are secured in the first instance by user charges and then by the general obligation pledge. (Such bonds are popularly known as being double barreled.) If so, the legal documents and opinion should state how the bonds are secured by revenues and funds outside the issuer's general taxing powers and general fund.

## Revenue Bonds

Revenue bonds are issued for either project or enterprise financings that are secured by the revenues generated by the completed projects themselves, or for general public-purpose financings in which the issuers pledge to the bondholders tax and revenue resources that were previously part of the general fund. This latter type of revenue bond is usually created to allow issuers to raise debt outside general obligation debt limits and without voter approvals. The trust indenture and legal opinion for both types of revenue bonds should provide the investor with legal comfort in six bond-security areas:

1. The limits of the basic security
2. The flow-of-funds structure
3. The rate, or user-charge, covenant
4. The priority-of-revenue claims
5. The additional-bonds test
6. Other relevant covenants

*Limits of the Basic Security.*   The trust indenture and legal opinion should explain what the revenues for the bonds are and how they realistically may be limited by federal, state, and local laws and procedures. The importance of this is that although most revenue bonds are structured and appear to be supported by identifiable revenue streams, those revenues sometimes can be negatively impacted directly by other levels of government. As an example, the Mineral Royalties Revenue Bonds that the state of Wyoming sold in December 1981 had most of the attributes of revenue bonds. The bonds had a first lien on the pledged revenues, and additional bonds could only be issued if a coverage test of 125 percent was met. Yet the basic revenues themselves were monies received by the state from the federal government as royalty payments for mineral production on federal lands. The U.S. Congress was under no legal obligation to continue this aid program. Therefore, the legal opinion as summarized in the official statement must clearly delineate this shortcoming of the bond security.

*Flow-of-funds Structure.*   The trust indenture and legal opinion should explain what the bond issuer has promised to do concerning the revenues received. What is the order of the revenue flows through the various accounting funds of the issuer to pay for the operating expenses of the facility, to provide for payments to the bondholders, to provide for maintenance and special capital improvements, and to provide for debt-service reserves. Additionally, the trust indenture and legal opinion should indicate what happens to excess revenues if they exceed the various annual fund requirements.

The flow of funds of most revenue bonds is structured as *net revenues* (i.e., debt service is paid to the bondholders immediately after revenues are paid to the basic operating and maintenance funds, but before paying all other expenses). A *gross revenues* flow-of-funds structure is one in which the bondholders are to be paid even before the operating expenses of the facility are paid. Examples of gross revenue bonds are those issued by the New York Metropolitan Transportation Authority. However, although it is true that these bonds legally have a claim to the fare-box revenues before all other claimants, it is doubtful that the system could function if the operational expenses, such as wages and electricity bills, were not paid first.

*Rate or User-charge Covenants.* The trust indenture and legal opinion should indicate what the issuer has legally committed itself to do to safeguard the bondholders. Do the rates charged only have to be sufficient to meet expenses, including debt service, or do they have to be set and maintained at higher levels so as to provide for reserves? The legal opinion should also indicate whether or not the issuer has the legal power to increase rates or charges of users without having to obtain prior approvals by other governmental units.

*Priority of Revenue Claims.* The legal opinion as summarized in the official statement should clearly indicate whether or not others can legally tap the revenues of the issuer even before they start passing through the issuer's flow-of-funds structure. An example would be the Highway Revenue Bonds issued by the Puerto Rico Highway Authority. These bonds are secured by the revenues from the Commonwealth of Puerto Rico gasoline tax. However, under the commonwealth's constitution, the revenues are first applied to the commonwealth government's own general obligation bonds if no other funds are available for them.

*Additional-bonds Test.* The trust indenture and legal opinion should indicate under what circumstances the issuer can issue additional bonds that share equal claims to the issuer's revenues. Usually, the legal requirement is that the maximum annual debt service on the new bonds as well as on the old bonds be covered by the projected net revenues by a specified minimum amount. This can be as low as one times coverage. Some revenue bonds have stronger additional-bonds tests to protect the bondholders. As an example, the state of Florida Orlando-Orange County Expressway Bonds have an additional-bonds test that is twofold. First, under the Florida constitution the previous year's *pledged historical revenues* must equal at least 1.33 times maximum annual debt service on the outstanding and to-be-issued bonds. Second, under the original trust indenture, *projected revenues* must provide at least 1.50 times the estimated maximum annual debt service on the outstanding and to-be-issued bonds.

*Other Relevant Covenants.*   Lastly, the trust indenture and legal opinion should indicate if there are other relevant covenants for the bondholder's protection. These usually include pledges by the issuer of the bonds to insure the project (if it is a project-financing revenue bond), to have the accounting records of the issuer annually audited by an outside certified public accountant, to have outside engineers annually review the condition of the capital plant, and to keep the facility operating for the life of the bonds.

In addition to the above aspects of the specific revenue structures of general obligation and revenue bonds, two other developments over the recent past make it more important than ever that the legal documents and opinions summarized in the official statements be carefully reviewed by the investor. The first development involves the mushrooming of new financing techniques that may rest on legally untested security structures. The second development is the increased use of legal opinions provided by local attorneys who may have little prior municipal bond experience. (Legal opinions have traditionally been written by experienced municipal bond attorneys.)

## Legally Untested Security Structures and New Financing Techniques

In addition to the more traditional general obligation bonds and toll road, bridge, and tunnel revenue bonds, there are now more nonvoter-approved, innovative, and legally untested security mechanisms. These innovative financing mechanisms include lease-rental bonds, moral obligation housing bonds, take-and-pay power bonds with step-up provisions requiring the participants to increase payments to make up for those that may default, commercial bank-backed letter-of-credit "put" bonds, and tax-exempt commercial paper. What distinguishes these newer bonds from the more traditional general obligation and revenue bonds is that they have no history of court decisions and other case law to firmly protect the rights of the bondholders. For the newer financing mechanisms, the legal opinion should include an assessment of the probable outcome if the bond security were challenged in court. Note, however, that most official statements do not provide this to the investor.

## The Need for Reliable Legal Opinions

For many years before the 1980s, concern over the reliability of the legal opinion was not as important as it is now. As the result of the numerous bond defaults and related shoddy legal opinions in the 19th century, the investment community demanded that legal documents and opinions be written by recognized municipal bond attorneys. As a consequence, over the years a small group of primarily Wall Street-based law firms and certain recognized firms in other financial centers dominated the industry and developed high standards of professionalism.

In the 1980s, however, more and more issuers began to have their legal work done by local law firms, a few of whom had little experience in municipal bond work. This development along with the introduction of more innovative and legally untested financing mechanisms has created a greater need for reliable legal opinions. An example of a specific concern involves the documents the issuers' lawyers must complete so as to avoid arbitrage problems with the Internal Revenue Service. On negotiated bond issues, one remedy has been for the underwriters to have their own counsels review the documents and to provide separate legal opinions.

## THE NEED TO KNOW WHO *REALLY* IS THE ISSUER

Still another general question to ask before purchasing a municipal bond is just what kind of people are the issuers? Are they conscientious public servants with clearly defined public goals? Do they have histories of successful management of public institutions? Have they demonstrated commitments to professional and fiscally stringent operations? Additionally, issuers in highly charged and partisan environments in which conflicts chronically occur between political parties and/or among factions or personalities within the governing bodies are clearly bond issuers to scrutinize closely and possibly to avoid. Such issuers should be scrutinized regardless of the strength of the surrounding economic environment.

### For General Obligation Bonds

For general obligation bond issuers, focus on the political relationships that exist on the one hand among chief executives, such as mayors, county executives, and governors, and on the other hand their legislative counterparts. Issuers with unstable political elites are of particular concern. Of course, rivalry among political actors is not necessarily bad. What is undesirable is competition so bitter and personal that real cooperation among the warring public officials in addressing future budgetary problems may be precluded. An example of an issuer that was avoided because of such dissension is the city of Cleveland. The political problems of the city in 1978 and the bitter conflicts between Mayor Kucinich and the city council resulted in a general obligation note default in December of that year.

### For Revenue Bonds

When investigating revenue bond issuers, it is important to determine not only the degree of political conflict, if any, that exists among the members of the bond-issuing body but also the relationships and conflicts among those who make the appointments to the body. Additionally, the investor should determine whether the issuer of the revenue bond has to seek prior approval from another governmental jurisdiction before the user-fees or other charges can be levied. If this is the case, then the stability of the political relationships between the two units of government must be determined.

An important example involves the creditworthiness of the water and electric utility revenue bonds and notes issued by Kansas City, Kansas. Although the revenue bonds and notes were issued by city hall, it was the six-member board of public utilities, a separately elected body, that had the power to set the water and electricity utility rates. In the spring of 1981, because of political dissension among the board members caused by a political struggle between a faction on the board of public utilities and the city commissioners (including the city's finance commissioner), the board refused to raise utility rates as required by the covenant. The situation only came under control when a new election changed the makeup of the board in favor of those supported by city hall.

In addition to the above institutional and political concerns, for revenue bond issuers in particular an assessment of the technical and managerial abilities of the staff should be made. The professional competency of the staff is a more critical factor in revenue bond analysis than it is in the analysis of general obligation bonds. The reason is that, unlike general obligation bonds, which are secured in the final instance by the full faith and credit and unlimited taxing powers of the issuers, many revenue bonds are secured by the ability of the revenue projects to be operational and financially self-supporting.

The professional staffs of authorities that issue revenue bonds for the construction of nuclear and other public power-generating facilities, apartment complexes, hospitals, water and sewer systems, and other large public works projects, such as convention centers and sports arenas, should be carefully reviewed. Issuers who have histories of high management turnovers, project cost overruns, or little experience should be avoided by the conservative investor, or at least considered higher risks than their assigned commercial credit ratings may indicate. Additionally, it is helpful, although not mandatory, for revenue bond issuers to have their accounting records annually audited by outside certified public accountants so as to ensure the investor of a more accurate picture of the issuer's financial health.

## ON THE FINANCIAL ADVISOR AND UNDERWRITER

Shorthand indications of the quality of the investment are (1) who the issuer selected as its financial advisor, if any, (2) its principal underwriter if the bond sale was negotiated, and (3) its financial advisor if the bond issue came to market competitively. Additionally, since 1975 many prudent underwriters will not bid on competitive bond issues if there are significant credit-quality concerns.

Therefore, it is also useful to learn who was the underwriter for the competitive bond sales as well.

Identifying the financial advisors and underwriters is important for two reasons.

## The Need for Complete, Not Just Adequate, Investment Risk Disclosures

The first reason relates to the quality and thoroughness of information provided to the investor by the issuer. The official statement, or private placement papers if the issue is placed privately, is usually prepared with the assistance of lawyers and a financial advisor or by the principal underwriter. There are industry-wide disclosure guidelines that are generally adhered to, but not all official statements provide the investor with complete discussions of the risk potentials that may result from either the specific economics of the project or the community settings and the operational details of the security provisions. It is usually the author of this document who decides what to either emphasize or downplay in the official statement. The more professional and established the experience of the author is in providing the investor with unbiased and complete information about the issuer, the more comfortable the investor can be with information provided by the issuer and in arriving at a credit-quality conclusion.

## The Importance of Firm Reputation for Thoroughness and Integrity

By itself, the reputation of the issuer's financial advisor and/or underwriter should not be the determinant credit-quality factor, but it is a fact the investor should consider, particularly the case for marginally feasible bond issues that have complex flow-of-funds and security structures. The securities industry is unique as compared with other industries, such as real estate, in that trading and investment commitments are usually made verbally over the phone with a paper trail following days later. Many institutional investors, such as banks, bonds funds, property and casualty insurance companies, have learned to judge issuers by the "company" they keep. Institutions tend to be conservative, and they are more comfortable with financial information provided by established financial advisors and underwriters who have recognized reputations for honesty. Individual investors and analysts would do well to adopt this approach as well.

## GENERAL CREDIT INDICATORS AND ECONOMIC FACTORS IN THE CREDIT ANALYSIS

The last analytical factor is the health or viability of the economics of the bond issuer or specific project financed by the bond proceeds. The economics cover a variety of concerns. When analyzing general obligation bond issuers, one should look at the specific budgetary and debt characteristics of the issuer as well as the general economic environment. For project-financing, or enterprise, revenue bonds, the economics are primarily limited to the ability of the project to generate sufficient charges from the users to pay the bondholders. These are known as pure revenue bonds.

For those revenue bonds that rely not on user charges and fees but instead on general purpose taxes and revenues, the analysis should take basically the same approach as for the general obligation bonds. For these bonds, the taxes and revenues diverted to the bondholders would otherwise have gone to the state's or city's general fund.

As examples of such bonds, both the New York State Municipal Assistance Corporation for the City of New York Bonds (MAC), secured by general New York City sales taxes and annual state-aid appropriations, and the state of Illinois Chicago School Finance Authority Bonds, secured by unlimited property taxes levied within the city of Chicago, are bonds structured to appear as pure revenue bonds; but in essence they are not. They both incorporate bond structures created to bail out the former, New York City, and the latter, Chicago's board of education, from severe budget deficits. The creditworthiness of these bonds is tied to that of their underlying jurisdictions, which have given or have had portions of their taxing powers and general fund revenues diverted to secure the new revenue-type bail-out bonds. Besides looking at the revenue features, the investor therefore must look at the underlying jurisdictions as well.

## For General Obligation Bonds

For general obligation bonds, the economics include asking questions and obtaining answers in four specific areas: debt burden, budget soundness, tax burden, and the overall economy.

*Debt Burden.* In relation to the debt burden of the general obligation bond issuer, some of the more important concerns include the determination of the total amount of debt outstanding and to be issued that is supported by the general taxing powers of the issuer as well as by earmarked revenues.

For example, general obligation bonds issued by school districts in New York State are general obligations of the issuer and are also secured by state-aid to education payments due the issuer. If the issuer defaults, the bondholder can go to the state comptroller and be made whole from the next state-aid payment due the local issuer. An example of another earmarked-revenue general obligation bond is the State of Illinois General Obligation Transportation, Series A Bond. For these state general obligations, debt service is secured by gasoline taxes in the state's transportation fund as well.

The debt of the general obligation bond issuer includes, in addition to the general obligation bonds outstanding, leases and "moral obligation" commitments, among others. Additionally, the amount of the unfunded pension liabilities should be determined. Key debt ratios that reveal the burden on local taxpayers include determining the per capita amount of general obligation debt as well as the per capita debt of the overlapping or underlying general obligation bond issuers. Other key measures of debt burden include determining the amounts and percentages of the outstanding general obligation bonds as well as the outstanding general obligation bonds of the overlapping or underlying jurisdictions to real estate valuations. These numbers and percentages can be compared with most recent year medians, as well as with the past history of the issuer, to determine whether the debt burden is increasing, declining, or remaining relatively stable.

***Budgetary Soundness.*** Concerning the budgetary operations and budgetary soundness of the general obligation bond issuer, some of the more important questions include how well the issuer over at least the previous five years has been able to maintain balanced budgets and fund reserves. How dependent is the issuer on short-term debt to finance annual budgetary operations? How have increased demands by residents for costly social services been handled? That is, how frugal is the issuer? How well have the public-employee unions been handled? They usually lobby for higher salaries, liberal pensions, and other costly fringe benefits. Clearly, it is undesirable for the pattern of dealing with the constituent demands and public-employee unions to result in raising taxes and drawing down nonrecurring budget reserves. Last, another general concern in the budgetary area is the reliability of the budget and accounting records of the issuer. Are interfund borrowings reported? And who audits the books?

***Tax Burden.*** Concerning the tax burden, it is important to learn two things initially. First, what are the primary sources of revenue in the issuer's general fund? Second, how dependent is the issuer on any one revenue source? If the general obligation bond issuer relies increasingly upon either a property tax, wage and income taxes, or a sales tax to provide the major share of financing for annually increasing budget appropriations, taxes could quickly become so high as to drive businesses and people away. Many larger northern states and cities with their relatively high income, sales, and property taxes appear to be experiencing this phenomenon. Still another concern is the degree of dependency of the issuer on intergovernmental revenues, such as federal or state revenue sharing and grants-in-aid, to finance its annual budget appropriations. Political coalitions on the state and federal levels that support these financial transfer programs are not permanent and could undergo dramatic change very quickly. Therefore, a general obligation bond issuer that currently has a relatively low tax burden but receives substantial amounts of intergovernmental monies should be carefully reviewed by the investor. If it should occur that the aid monies are reduced, as has been occurring under many federal legislative programs, certain issuers may primarily increase their taxes, instead of reducing their expenditures to conform to the reduced federal grants-in-aid.

*Overall Economy.* The fourth and last area of general obligation bond analysis concerns the issuer's overall economy. For local governments, such as counties, cities, towns, and school districts, key items include learning the annual rate of growth of the full value of all taxable real estate for the previous 10 years and identifying the 10 largest taxable properties. What kinds of business or activity occur on the respective properties? What percentage of the total property tax base do the 10 largest properties represent? What has been the building permit trend for at least the previous five years? What percentage of all real estate is tax-exempt, and what is the distribution of the taxable ones by purpose such as residential, commercial, industrial, railroad, and public utility? Last, who are the five largest employers? Concerning the final item, those communities that have one large employer are more susceptible to rapid adverse economic change than communities that have more diversified employment and real estate bases. For additional information that reveals either economic health or decline, one must determine whether the population of the community over the previous 10 years has been increasing or declining by age, income, and ethnicity and how the monthly and yearly unemployment rates compare with the national averages as well as with the previous history of the community.

For state governments that issue general obligation bonds, the economic analysis should include many of the same questions applied to local governments. In addition, the investor should determine on the state level the annual rates of growth for the previous five years of personal income and retail sales and how much the state has had to borrow from the Federal Unemployment Trust Fund to pay unemployment benefits. This last item is particularly significant for the long-term economic attractiveness of the state, since under current federal law employers in those states with large federal loans in arrears are required to pay increased unemployment taxes to the federal government.

## For Revenue Bonds

*Airport Revenue Bonds.*  For airport revenue bonds, the economic questions vary according to the type of bond security involved. There are two basic security structures.

The first type of airport revenue bond is one based upon traffic-generated revenues that result from the competitiveness and passenger demand of the airport. The financial data on the operations of the airport should come from audited financial statements going back at least three years. If a new facility is planned, a feasibility study prepared by a recognized consultant should be reviewed. The feasibility study should have two components: (1) a market and demand analysis to define the service area and examine demographic and airport utilization trends and (2) a financial analysis to examine project operating costs and revenues.

Revenues at an airport may come from landing fees paid by the airlines for their flights, concession fees paid by restaurants, shops, newsstands, and parking facilities, and from airline apron and fueling fees.

Also, in determining the long-term economic viability of an airport, the investor should determine whether or not the wealth trends of the service area are upward; whether or not the airport is either dependent on tourism or serves as a vital transfer point; whether or not passenger enplanements and air cargo handled over the previous five years have been growing; whether or not increased costs of jet fuel would make such other transportation as trains and automobiles more attractive in that particular region; and whether or not the airport is a major domestic hub for an airline, which could make the airport particularly vulnerable to route changes caused by schedule revisions and changes in airline corporate management.

The second type of airport revenue bond is secured by a lease with one or more airlines for the use of a specific facility such as a terminal or hangar. The lease usually obligates them to make annual payments sufficient to pay the expenses and debt service for the facility. For many of these bonds, the analysis of the airline lease is based upon the credit quality of the lessee airline. Whether or not the lease should extend as long as the bonds are outstanding depends on the specific airport and facility involved. For major hub airports, it may be better not to have long-term leases, since without leases fees and revenues can be increased as the traffic grows regardless of which airline uses the specific facility. Of course, for regional or startup airports, long-term leases with trunk (i.e., major airline) carriers are preferred.

***Highway Revenue Bonds.*** There are generally two types of highway revenue bonds. The bond proceeds of the first type are used to build specific revenue-producing facilities such as toll roads, bridges, and tunnels. For these pure enterprise revenue bonds, the bondholders have claims to the revenues collected through the tolls. The financial soundness of the bonds depend on the ability of the specific projects to be self-supporting. Proceeds from the second type of highway revenue bond generally are used for public highway improvements, and the bondholders are paid by earmarked revenues such as gasoline taxes, automobile registration payments, and driver's license fees.

Concerning the economic viability of a toll-road, -bridge, or -tunnel revenue bond, the investor should ask a number of questions.

1. What is the traffic history, and how inelastic is the demand? Toll roads, bridges, and tunnels that provide vital transportation links are clearly preferred to those that face competition from interstate highways, toll-free bridges, or mass transit.

2. How well is the facility maintained? Has the issuer established a maintenance reserve fund at a reasonable level to use for such repair work as road resurfacing and bridge painting?
3. Does the issuer have the ability to raise tolls to meet covenant and debt-reserve requirements without seeking approvals from other governmental actors such as state legislatures and governors? In those few cases where such approvals are necessary, the question of how sympathetic have these other power centers been in the past in approving toll-increase requests should be asked.
4. What is the debt-to-equity ratio? Some toll-road, -bridge, and -tunnel authorities have received substantial nonreimbursable federal grants that have helped to subsidize their costs of construction. This, of course, reduces the amount of debt that has to be issued.
5. What is the history of labor-management relations, and can public-employee strikes substantially reduce toll collections?
6. When was the facility constructed? Generally, toll roads financed and constructed in the 1950s and 1960s tend now to be in good financial condition because the cost of financing was much less than it is today. Many of these older revenue bond issuers have been retiring their bonds ahead of schedule by buying them at deep discounts to par in the secondary market.
7. If the facility is a bridge that could be damaged by a ship and made inoperable, does the issuer have adequate "use and occupancy" insurance?

Those few toll-road and -bridge revenue bonds that have defaulted have done so because of either unexpected competition from toll-free highways and bridges, poor traffic projections, or substantially higher than projected construction costs. An example of one of the few defaulted bonds is the West Virginia Turnpike Commission's Turnpike Revenue Bonds issued in 1952 and 1954 to finance the construction of an 88-mile expressway from Charleston to Princeton, West Virginia. The initial traffic-engineering estimates were overly optimistic, and the construction costs came in approximately $37 million higher than the original budgeted amount of $96 million. Because of insufficient traffic and toll collections, between 1956 and 1979 the bonds were in default. By the late 1970s with the completion of various connecting cross-country highways, the turnpike became a major link for interstate traffic. Since 1979 the bonds have become self-supporting in terms of making interest coupon payments.

Concerning the economics of highway revenue bonds that are not pure enterprise type but instead are secured by earmarked revenues, such as gasoline taxes, automobile registration payments, and driver's license fees, the investor should ask the following questions.

1. Are the earmarked tax revenues based on either state constitutional mandates, such as the state of Ohio's Highway Improvement Bonds, or are

they derived from laws enacted by state legislatures, such as the state of Washington's Chapters 56, 121, and 167 Motor Vehicle Fuel Tax Bonds? A constitutional pledge is usually more permanent and reliable.

2. What has been the coverage trend of the available revenues to debt service over the previous 10 years? Has the coverage been increasing, stable, or declining?

3. If the earmarked revenue is gasoline tax, is it based either on a specific amount of cents per gallon of gasoline sold or as a percentage of the price of each gallon sold? With greater conservation and more efficient cars, the latter tax structure is preferred because it is not as susceptible to declining sales of gasoline and because it benefits directly from any increased gasoline prices at the pumps.

***Hospital Revenue Bonds.***    Two unique features of hospitals make the analysis of their debt particularly complex and uncertain. The first concerns their sources of revenue, and the second concerns the basic structure of the institutions themselves.

During the past 20 years, the major sources of revenue for most hospitals have been (1) payments from the federal (Medicare) and combined federal-state (Medicaid) hospital reimbursement programs and (2) appropriations made by local governments through their taxing powers. It is not uncommon for hospitals to receive at least two thirds of their annual revenues from these sources. How well the hospital management markets its service to attract more private-pay patients, how aggressive it is in its third-party collections, such as from Blue Cross and HMO's, and how conservatively it budgets for the governmental reimbursement payments are key elements for distinguishing weak from strong hospital bonds.

Particularly for community-based hospitals (as opposed to teaching hospitals affiliated with medical schools), a unique feature of their financial structure is that their major financial beneficiaries, physicians, have no legal or financial liabilities if the institutions do not remain financially viable over the long term. An example of the problems that can be caused by this lack of liability is found in the story of the Sarpy County, Nebraska, Midlands Community Hospital Revenue Bonds. These bonds were issued to finance the construction of a hospital three miles south of Omaha, Nebraska, that was to replace an older one located in the downtown area. Physician questionnaires prepared for the feasibility study prior to the construction of the hospital indicated strong support for the replacement facility. Many doctors had used the older hospital in downtown Omaha as a backup facility for a larger nearby hospital. Unfortunately, once the new Sarpy hospital opened in 1976, many physicians found that the new hospital could not serve as a backup because it was 12 miles further away from the major hospital than the old hospital had been. With these physicians not referring their patients to the new Sarpy hospital, it was soon unable to make bond principal payments and was put under the jurisdiction of a court receiver.

The above factors raise long-term uncertainties about many community-based hospitals, but certain key areas of analysis and trends reveal the relative economic health of hospitals that already have revenue bonds outstanding. The first area is the liquidity of the hospital as measured by the ratio of dollars held in current assets to current liabilities. In general, a five-year trend of high values for the ratio is desirable because it implies an ability by the hospital to pay short-term obligations and thereby avoid budgetary problems. The second indicator is the ratio of long-term debt to equity, as measured in the unrestricted end-of-year fund balance. In general, the lower the long-term debt to equity ratio, the stronger the finances of the hospital. The third indicator is the actual debt-service coverage of the previous five years as well as the projected coverage. The fourth indicator is the annual bed-occupancy rates for the previous five years. The fifth is the percentage of physicians at the hospital who are professionally approved (board certified), their respective ages, and how many of them use the hospital as their primary institution.

For new or expanded hospitals, much of the above data is provided to the investor in the feasibility study. One item in particular that should be covered for a new hospital is whether or not the physicians who plan to use the hospital actually live in the area to be served by the hospital. Because of its importance in providing answers to these questions, the national reputation and experience of the people who prepare the feasibility study is of critical concern to the investor.

***Housing Revenue Bonds.***   For housing revenue bonds, the economic and financial questions vary according to the type of bond security involved. There are two basic types of housing revenue bonds—each with a different type of security structure. One is the housing revenue bond secured by *single-family* mortgages, and the other is the housing revenue bond secured by mortgages on *multifamily* housing projects.

Concerning single-family housing revenue bonds, the strongly secured bonds usually have four characteristics.

1. The single-family home loans are insured by the Federal Housing Administration (FHA), Federal Veterans Administration (VA), or an acceptable private mortgage insurer. If the individual home loans are not insured, then they should have a loan-to-value ratio of 80 percent or less.
2. If the conventional home loans have less than 100 percent primary mortgage insurance coverage, an additional 5–10 percent mortgage-pool insurance policy would be required. The private mortgage insurer should be of high quality in terms of company capitalization and in terms of conservative underwriting standards and limits.
3. In addition to a debt reserve with monies equal at least to six months of interest on the single-family housing revenue bonds, there is a mortgage reserve fund that has an amount equal at least to 1 percent of the bond issue outstanding.

4. The issuer of the single-family housing revenue bonds is in a region of the country that has either stable or strong economic growth as indicated by increased real estate valuations, personal income, and retail sales, as well as low unemployment rates and relatively low state and local government overall tax burdens.

In the 1970s, state agency issuers of single-family housing revenue bonds assumed certain prepayment levels in structuring the bond maturities. In recent years, most issuers have abandoned this practice but investors should review the retirement schedule for the single-family mortgage revenue bonds to determine whether or not the issuer has assumed large, lump-sum mortgage prepayments in the early year cash-flow projections. And if so, how conservative are the prepayment assumptions, and how dependent is the issuer on the prepayments to meet the annual debt-service requirements?

It should be noted that single-family housing revenue bonds issued by local governments, such as towns, cities, and counties usually have conservative bond-retirement schedules that have not included any home mortgage prepayment assumptions. Single-family housing revenue bonds issued by states did use prepayment assumptions. This positive feature of local government-issued bonds is balanced somewhat by the facts that the state-issued bonds generally no longer include prepayment assumptions and usually are secured by home mortgages covering wider geographic areas. Additionally, the state issuing agencies usually have professional in-house staffs that closely monitor the home mortgage portfolios, whereas the local issuers do not. Finally, state issuing agencies have accumulated substantial surplus funds over the years that can be viewed as an additional source of bondholder protection.

For multifamily housing revenue bonds, there are four specific, though overlapping, security structures. The first type of multifamily housing revenue bond is one in which the bonds are secured by mortgages that are federally insured. Usually the federal insurance covers all but the difference between the outstanding bond principal and collectible mortgage amount (usually 1 percent), and all but the *nonasset* bonds (i.e., bonds issued to cover issuance costs and capitalized interest). The attractiveness of the federal insurance is that it protects the investor against bond default within the limitations outlined. The insurance protects the bondholders regardless of whether or not the projects are fully occupied and generating rental payments.

The second type of multifamily housing revenue bond is one in which the federal government subsidizes under the federal Section 8 program all annual costs, including debt service, of the project not covered by tenant rental payments. Under Section 8, the eligible low-income and elderly tenants pay only 15 to 30 percent of their incomes for rent. Since the ultimate security comes from the Section 8 subsidies, which escalate annually with the increased cost of living in that particular geographic region, the bondholder's primary risks concern the developer's ability to complete the project, find tenants eligible under the federal guidelines to live in the project, and then maintain high occupancy rates for the life of the bonds. The investor should carefully review the location and construction standards used in building the project, as well as the competency of the project manager in selecting tenants who will take care of the building and pay their rents. In this regard, state agencies that issue Section 8 bonds usually have stronger in-house management experience and resources for dealing with problems than do the local development corporations that have issued Section 8 bonds. It should be noted that the federal government has eliminated new appropriations for the Section 8 program, and there is little new issuance of tax-exempt debt supported by this subsidy program.

The third type of multifamily housing revenue bond is one in which the ultimate security for the bondholder is the ability of the project to generate sufficient monthly rental payments from the tenants themselves to meet the operating and debt-service expenses. Some of these projects may receive governmental subsidies (such as interest-cost reductions under the federal Section 236 program and property tax abatements from local governments), but the ultimate security is the economic viability of the project. Key information includes the location of the project, its occupancy rate, whether large families or the elderly will primarily live in the project, whether or not the rents necessary to keep the project financially sound are competitive with others in the surrounding community, and whether or not the project manager has proven records of maintaining good services and of establishing careful tenant selection standards.

A fourth type of multifamily housing revenue bond is one that includes some type of private credit enhancement to the underlying real estate. These credit enhancements can include guarantees by an insurance company, the Federal National Mortgage Association (FNMA), or a bank letter of credit.

Other financial features desirable in all multifamily housing bonds include a debt-service reserve fund, which should contain an amount of money equal to the maximum annual debt service on the bonds, a mortgage reserve fund, and a capital repair and maintenance fund.

Still another feature of many multifamily housing revenue bonds, and particularly of those issued by state housing agencies, is the state moral obligation pledge. Several state agencies have issued housing revenue bonds that carry a potential state liability for making up deficiencies in their one-year debt-service reserve funds, should any occur. In most cases if a drawdown of the debt reserve occurs, the state agency must report the amount used to its governor and state budget director. The state legislature, in turn, may appropriate the requested amount, though there is no legally enforceable obligation to do so. Bonds with this makeup provisions are the so-called moral obligation bonds.

The moral obligation only provides a state legislature with permissive authority—*not mandatory authority*—to make an appropriation to the troubled state housing agency. Therefore, the analysis should determine (1) if the state has the budgetary surpluses for subsidizing the housing agency's revenue bonds; and

(2) if there is a consensus within the executive and legislative branches of that particular state's government to use state general fund revenues for subsidizing multifamily housing projects.

*Industrial Revenue Bonds.* Generally, industrial revenue bonds are issued by state and local governments on behalf of individual corporations and businesses. The security for the bonds usually depends on the economic soundness of the particular corporation or business involved. If the bond issue is for a subsidiary of a larger corporation, one question to ask is whether or not the parent guarantees the bonds. Is it only obligated through a lease, or does it not have any obligation whatsoever for paying the bondholders? If the parent corporation has no responsibility for the bonds, then the investor must look very closely at the operations of the subsidiary in addition to those of the parent corporation. Here the investor must also determine whether the bond is guaranteed by the company or is a lease obligation.

For companies that have issued common stock that is publicly traded, economic data is readily available either in the annual reports or in the 10-K reports that must be filed annually with the Securities and Exchange Commission. For privately held companies, financial data are more difficult to obtain.

In assessing the economic risk of investing in an industrial revenue bond, another question to ask is whether the bondholder or the trustee holds the mortgage on the property. Although holding the mortgage is not an important economic factor in assessing either hospital or low-income, multifamily housing bonds where the properties have very limited commercial value, it can be an important strength for the holder of industrial development revenue bonds. If the bond is secured by a mortgage on a property of either a fast-food retailer, such as McDonalds, or an industrial facility, such as a warehouse, the property location and resale value of the real estate may provide some protection to the bondholder, regardless of what happens to the company that issued the bonds. Of course, the investor should always avoid possible bankruptcy situations regardless of the economic attractiveness of the particular piece of real estate involved. The reason is that the bankruptcy process usually involves years of litigation and numerous court hearings, which no investor should want to be concerned about.

*Lease-rental Bonds.* Lease-rental bonds are usually structured as revenue bonds, and annual rent payments, paid by a state or local government, cover all costs including operations, maintenance, and debt service. The public purposes financed by these bond issues include the construction of public office buildings, fire houses, police stations, university buildings, mental health facilities, and highways, as well as the purchase of office equipment and computers. In some instances, the rental payments may only come from student tuition, patient fees, and earmarked tax revenues, and the state or local government is not legally obligated to make lease-rental payments beyond the amount of available earmarked revenues. However, for many lease-rental bonds the underlying lessee state, county, or city is required to make annual appropriations from its general fund. For example, the Albany County, New York, Lease Rental South Mall Bonds were issued to finance the construction of state office buildings. Although the bonds are technically general obligations of Albany County, the real security comes from the annual lease payments made by the state of New York. These payments are annually appropriated. For such bonds, the basic economic and financial analysis should follow the same guidelines as for general obligation bonds.

*Public Power Revenue Bonds.*  Public power revenue bonds are issued to finance the construction of electrical generating plants. An issuer of the bonds may construct and operate one power plant, buy electric power from a "wholesaler" and sell it "retail," construct and operate several power plants, or join with other public and private utilities in jointly financing the construction of one or more power plants. This last arrangement is known as a joint-power financing structure. Although there are revenue bonds that can claim the revenues of a federal agency (e.g., the Washington Public Power Supply System's Nuclear Project No. 2 Revenue Bonds, which if necessary can claim the revenues of the Bonneville Power Administration) and many others that can require the participating underlying municipal electric systems to pay the bondholders whether or not the plants are completed and operating (i.e., the Michigan Public Power Agency Revenue Bonds), the focus here is how the investor determines which power projects will be financially self-supporting without these backup security features.

There are at least five major questions to ask when evaluating the investment soundness of a public power revenue bond.

1. Does the bond issuer have the authority to raise its electric rates in a timely fashion without going to any regulatory agencies? This is particularly important if substantial rate increases are necessary to pay for either new construction or plant improvements.
2. How diversified is the customer base among residential, commercial, and industrial users?
3. Is the service area growing in terms of population, personal income, and commercial/industrial activity so as to warrant the electrical power generated by the existing or new facilities?
4. What are the projected and actual costs of power generated by the system, and how competitive are they with other regions of the country? Power rates are particularly important for determining the long-term economic attractiveness of the region for those industries that are large energy users.

5. How diversified is the fuel mix? Is the issuer dependent on one energy source such as hydro dams, oil, natural gas, coal, or nuclear fuel?

Concerning electrical generating plants fueled by nuclear power, the aftermath of the Three Mile Island nuclear accident in 1979 has resulted in greater construction and maintenance reviews and costly safety requirements prompted by the Federal Nuclear Regulatory Commission (NRC). The NRC oversees this industry. In the past, although nuclear power plants were expected to cost far more to build than other types of power plants, it was also believed that, once the generating plants became operational, the relatively low fuel and maintenance costs would more than offset the initial capital outlays. However, with the increased concern about public safety brought about by the Three Mile Island accident, repairs and design modifications are now expected to be made even after plants begin to operate. This of course increases the ongoing costs of generating electricity and reduces the attractiveness of nuclear power as an alternative to the oil, gas, and coal fuels. For ongoing nuclear plant construction projects, the investor should review the feasibility study to see that it was prepared by experienced and recognized consulting engineers and that it has realistic construction, design schedule, and cost estimates.

*Resource Recovery Revenue Bonds.*   A resource recovery facility converts refuse (solid waste) into commercially salable energy, recoverable products, and a residue to be landfilled. The major revenues for a resource recovery bond usually are the "tipping fees" per ton paid by those who deliver the garbage to the facility for disposal; revenues from steam, electricity, or refuse-derived fuel sold to either an electric power company or another energy user; and revenues from the sale of recoverable materials such as aluminum and steel scrap.

Resource recovery bonds are secured in one of two ways or a combination thereof. The first security structure is one in which the cost of running the resource recovery plant and paying the bondholders comes from the sale of the energy produced (steam, electricity, or refuse-derived fuel) as well as from fees paid by the haulers, both municipal and private, who bring the garbage to the facility. In this financing structure, the resource recovery plant usually has to be operational and self-supporting for the bondholders to be paid. The second security structure involves an agreement with a state or local government, such as a county or municipality, that contractually obligates the government to haul or to have hauled a certain amount of garbage to the facility each year for the life of the facility and to pay a tipping fee (service fee) sufficient to operate the facility. The tipping fee must include amounts sufficient to pay bondholders whether or not the resource recovery plant has become fully operational.

When deciding to invest in a resource recovery revenue bond, one should ask the following questions. First, how proven is the system technology to be used in the plant? *Mass burning* is the simplest method, and it has years of proven experience. In mass burning, the refuse is burned with very little processing. Prepared fuels and shredding, the next most proven method, requires the refuse to be prepared by separation or shredding so as to produce a higher quality fuel for burning. More innovative and eclectic approaches require the most detailed engineering evaluations by qualified specialists. Second, how experienced and reliable are the construction contractors and facility operators (vendors)? Third, are there adequate safeguards and financial incentives for the contractor/vendor to complete and then maintain the facility? Fourth, what are the estimated tipping fees that will have to be charged, and how do they compare with those at any available nearby landfills? One way for a state resource recovery revenue bond issuer to deal with the latter concern occurred with the Delaware Solid Waste Authority's Resource Recovery Revenue Bonds, Series 1979. The state of Delaware enacted a law requiring that all residential garbage within a specified geographic region be hauled to its plant. Fifth, is the bondholder protected during the construction stage by reserves and by fixed-price construction contracts? Sixth, are the prices charged for the generated energy fixed, or are they tied to the changing costs of the fuel sources such as oil and gas in that particular market place?

Because of the uniqueness of the resource recovery technology, there are additional questions that should be asked. First, even if the plant-system technology is a proven one, is the plant either the same size as others already in operation or a larger scale model that would require careful investor review? Second, if the system technology used is innovative and eclectic, is there sufficient redundancy, or low-utilization assumptions in the plant design to absorb any unforeseen problems once the plant begins production? Last, in addition to the more routine reserves—such as debt, maintenance, and special capital improvement reserves—and covenants—such as covenants that commercial insurance be placed on the facility and that the contractor (or vendor) pledge to maintain the plant for the life of the bonds—there should also be required yearly plant reviews by independent consulting engineers. The vendor should be required to make the necessary repairs so that the facility will be operational for the life of the bonds.

For resource recovery revenue bonds that have a security structure involving an agreement with a local government, additional questions for the investor to ask are the following: Is the contractual obligation at a fixed rate, or is the tipping fee elastic enough to cover all the increasing costs of operations, maintenance, and debt service? Would strikes or other *force majeure* events either prevent the contract from being enforceable or preclude the availability of an adequate supply of garbage? Last, the investor should determine the soundness of the budgetary operations and general fund reserves of the local government that is to pay the tipping or service fee. For these bonds, the basic economic analysis should follow the same guidelines as for general obligation bonds.

*Student Loan Revenue Bonds.* Student loan revenue bonds are usually issued by statewide agencies and are used for purchasing either new guaranteed student loans for higher education or existing guaranteed student loans from local banks.

The student loans are 100 percent guaranteed. They are either guaranteed directly by the federal government—under the Federal Insured Student Loan (FISL) program for 100 percent of principal and interest—or by a state guaranty agency—under a more recent federal insurance program, the Federal Guaranteed Student Loan (GSL) program. This latter program provides federal reimbursement for a state guaranty agency on an annual basis for 100 percent of the payment on defaulted loans up to approximately 5 percent of the amount of loans being repaid, 90 percent for claims in excess of 5 percent but less than 9 percent, and 80 percent for claims exceeding 9 percent. The federal commitments are not dependent on future congressional approvals. Loans made under the FISL and GSL programs are contractual obligations of the federal government.

Although most student loans have federal government support, the financial soundness of the bond program that issues the student loan revenue bonds and monitors the loan portfolio is of critical importance to the investor because of the unique financial structure of a student loan portfolio. Although loan repayments from the student or, in the event of student default, repayments from the guaranty agency are contractually insured, it is difficult to precisely project the actual loan repayment cash flows. The reason is that the student does not begin repaying the loan until he or she leaves college or graduate school and all other deferments, such as military service, have ended. Before the student begins the loan repayments, the federal government pays the interest on the loans under prescribed formulas. Therefore, the first general concern of the investor should be to determine the strength of the cash-flow protection.

The second general concern is the adequacy of the loan guaranty. Under all economic scenarios short of a depression, in which the student loan default rate could be 20 percent or greater, the GSL, sliding federal reinsurance scale of 100–90–80 should provide adequate cash-flow and bond default protection as long as the student loan revenue bond issuer effectively services the student loan repayments, has established and adequately funded loan-guaranty and debt-reserve funds, employs conservative loan-repayment assumptions in the original bond-maturity schedule, and is required to call the bonds at par if the student loan repayments are accelerated. This latter factor presents a reinvestment risk for the bondholder.

There are eight specific questions for the investor to ask. (1) What percentage of the student loans are FISL and GSL backed, respectively? (2) Has a loan-guarantee fund been established and funded? Usually a fund that is required to have an amount at least equal to 2 percent of the loan principal outstanding is desirable. (3) Is the issuer required to maintain a debt-reserve fund? Usually, for notes, a fund with at least six-months interest, and for bonds a fund with a one-year maximum annual debt-service are desirable. (4) If the bond issuer has purchased portfolios of student loans from local banks, are the local lenders required to repurchase any loans if there are either defaults or improperly originated loans? (5) What in-house capability does the issuer have for monitoring and servicing the loan repayments? (6) What is the historical loan-default rate? (7) How are the operating expenses of the agency met? If federal operating subsidies are received under the "Special Allowance Payment Rate" program, what are the rate assumptions used? In this program the issuer receives a supplemental subsidy, which fluctuates with the 91-day U.S. Treasury bill rate. (8) If a state agency is the issuer, is it dependent on appropriations for covering operating expenses and reserve requirements?

*Water and Sewer Revenue Bonds.* Water and sewer revenue bonds are issued to provide for a local community's basic needs and as such are not usually subject to general economic changes. Because of the vital utility services performed, their respective financial structures are usually designed to have the lowest possible user changes and still remain financially viable. Generally, rate covenants requiring that user charges cover operations, maintenance, and approximately 1.2 times annual debt-service and reserve requirements are most desirable. On the one hand, a lower rate covenant provides a smaller margin for either unanticipated slow collections or increased operating and plant maintenance costs caused by inflation. On the other hand, rates that generate revenues in excess of 1.2 times could cause unnecessary financial burdens on the users of the water and sewer systems. A useful indication of the soundness of an issuer's operations is to compare the water or sewer utility's average quarterly customer billings to those of other water or sewer systems. Assuming that good customer service is given, the water or sewer system that has a relatively low customer billing charge generally indicates an efficient operation and therefore strong bond-payment prospects.

Key questions for the investor to ask include the following. (1) Has the bond issuer through local ordinances required mandatory water or sewer connections? Also, local board of health directives against well water contaminations and septic tank usage can often accomplish the same objective as the mandatory hookups. (2) In regard to sewer revenue bonds in particular, how dependent is the issuer on federal grants either to complete ongoing construction projects or to supplement the cost of future expansions of the sewer system? The level of dependence is particularly important in light of efforts in Congress to reduce the multibillion dollar federal sewage treatment grant program for states and local governments. (3) What is the physical condition of the facilities in terms of plant, lines, and meters, and what capital improvements are necessary for maintaining the utilities as well as for providing for anticipated community growth? (4) For water systems in particular, it is important to determine if the system has water supplies in excess of current peak and projected demands. An operating system at less than full utilization is able to serve future customers and bring in revenues without having to issue additional bonds to enlarge its facilities. (5) What is the operating record of the water or sewer utility for the previous five years? (6) If the bond issuer does not have its own distribution system but instead charges other participating local governments that do, are the charges or fees either based upon the actual water flow drawn (for water revenue bonds) and sewage treated (for sewer revenue bonds) or upon gallonage entitlements? (7) For water revenue bonds issued for agricultural regions, what crop is grown? An acre of oranges or cherries in California will provide the grower with more income than will an acre of corn or wheat in Iowa. (8) For expanding water and sewer systems, does the issuer have a record over the previous two years of achieving net income equal to or exceeding the rate covenants, and will the facilities to be constructed add to the issuer's net revenues? (9) Has the issuer established and funded debt and maintenance reserves to deal with either unexpected cash-flow problems or system repairs? (10) Does the bond issuer have the power to place tax liens against the real estate of those who have not paid their water or sewer bills? Although the investor would not want to own a bond for which court actions of this nature would be necessary before the investor could be paid, the legal existence of this power usually provides an economic incentive for water and sewer bills to be paid promptly by the users.

Additional bonds should only be issued if the need, cost, and construction schedule of the facility have been certified by an independent consulting engineer and if the past and projected revenues are sufficient to pay operating expenses and debt service. Of course, for a new system that does not have an operating history, the quality of the consulting engineer's report is of the uppermost importance.

## RED FLAGS FOR THE INVESTOR

In addition to the areas of analysis described above, certain red flags, or negative trends, suggest increased credit risks.

### For General Obligation Bonds

For general obligation bonds, the signals that indicate a decline in the ability of a state, county, town, city, or school district to function within fiscally sound parameters include the following:

1. Declining property values and increasing delinquent taxpayers.
2. An annually increasing tax burden relative to other regions.
3. An increasing property tax rate in conjunction with a declining population.

4. Declines in the number and value of issued permits for new building construction.
5. Actual general fund revenues consistently falling below budgeted amounts.
6. Increasing end-of-year general fund deficits.
7. Budget expenditures increasing annually in excess of the inflation rate.
8. The unfunded pension liabilities are increasing.
9. General obligation debt increasing while property values are stagnant.
10. Declining economy as measured by increased unemployment and declining personal income.

## For Revenue Bonds

For revenue bonds, the general signals that indicate a decline in credit quality include the following:

1. Annually decreasing coverage of debt service by net revenues.
2. Regular use of debt reserve and other reserves by the issuer.
3. Growing financial dependence of the issuer on unpredictable federal and state-aid appropriations for meeting operating budget expenses.
4. Chronic lateness in supplying investors with annual audited financials.
5. Unanticipated cost overruns and schedule delays on capital construction projects.
6. Frequent or significant rate increases.
7. Deferring capital plant maintenance and improvements.
8. Excessive management turnovers.
9. Shrinking customer base.
10. New and unanticipated competition.

# CHAPTER 23

## ANALYZING THE CREDITWORTHINESS OF SHORT-TERM MUNICIPAL OBLIGATIONS

*Sylvan G. Feldstein, Ph.D.*
Vice President,
Municipal Bond Research Department
Merrill Lynch Capital Markets

*Frank J. Fabozzi, Ph.D., C.F.A.*
Visiting Professor of Finance
Sloan School of Management
Massachusetts Institute of Technology
and
*Editor, The Journal of Portfolio Management*

This chapter provides a basic framework for analyzing the various short-term municipal investments available. They include tax, revenue, grant, and bond anticipation notes; repurchase agreements; and tax-exempt commercial paper.

## TAX, REVENUE, GRANT, AND BOND ANTICIPATION NOTES

These notes are temporary borrowings by states, local governments, and special jurisdictions to finance a variety of activities. Notes are issued for a period of 12 months, although it is not uncommon for notes to be issued for periods as short as three months and for as long as three years. There are two general purposes for which notes are issued—to even out cash flows and to temporarily finance capital improvements. Each reason is explained below.

First, many states, cities, towns, counties and school districts, as well as special jurisdictions, borrow temporarily in anticipation of collection of taxes or other expected revenues. Their need to borrow occurs because, although payrolls, bills, and other commitments have to be paid starting at the beginning of the fiscal year, property taxes and other revenues such as intergovernmental grants are due and payable after the beginning of the fiscal year. These notes, identified as Tax Anticipation Notes (TANs), Revenue Anticipation Notes (RANs), or Grant Anticipation Notes (GANs), are usually used to even out the cash flows that are necessitated by the irregular flows of income into the treasuries of the states and local units of government. In some instances, combination Tax and Revenue Anticipation Notes (TRANs) are issued, which usually are payable from two sources. An example would be the TRANs issued by the state of New York.

Notes are also issued in anticipation of the sale of long-term bonds. Such notes are known as Bond Anticipation Notes (BANs). There are three major reasons why capital improvements are initially financed with BANs.

First, because the initial cost estimates for a large construction project can vary from the construction bids actually submitted, and since better terms are sometimes obtained on a major construction project if the state or local government pays the various contractors as soon as the work begins, BANs are often used as the initial financing instrument. Once the capital improvement is completed, the bills paid, and the total costs determined, the BANs can be retired with the proceeds of a final bond sale.

Second, issuers such as states and cities that have large, diverse, and on-going capital construction programs will initially issue BANs, and later retire them with the proceeds of a single long-term bond sale. In this instance, the use of BANs allows the issuer to consolidate various, unrelated financing needs into one bond sale.

Lastly, BANs are sometimes issued in relation to market conditions. By temporarily financing capital improvements with BANs, the issuer has greater flexibility in determining the timing of its long-term bond sale and possibly avoiding unfavorable market conditions.

## Evaluating Tax, Revenue, and Grant Anticipation Notes

Tax Anticipation Notes (TANs) are usually secured by the taxes for which they were issued. Counties, cities, towns and school districts, usually issue TANs for expected property taxes. Some governmental units go so far as to establish escrow accounts for receiving the taxes, and use the escrowed monies to pay the noteholders.

Revenue Anticipation Notes (RANs) or Grant Anticipation Notes (GANs) are also usually secured by the revenues for which they were issued— intergovernmental capital construction grants and aid, as well as local taxes other than property taxes. In one extreme case, resulting from the New York City note default in 1975, RANs issued by New York City for expected educational aid from the state of New York provided for the noteholder to go directly to the state comptroller before monies were sent to the city's treasury, if that was necessary to remedy a default. Most RANs just require the issuer itself to use the expected monies to pay the noteholders once they are in hand.

Most TANs, RANs, and GANs issued by states, counties, cities, towns, and school districts are also secured by the "general obligation pledge," which is discussed later in this chapter.

Before recommending purchase of TAN, RAN, or GAN, an analyst should obtain information in five areas. These are in addition to what is required if long-term bonds were being considered for purchase. The five areas are the following:

1. Determining the reliability of the expected taxes, revenues, or grants.
2. Determining the degree of dependency of the note issuers on the expected monies.
3. Determining the soundness of the issuers' budgetary operations.
4. Determining the problem of "rollovers."
5. Determining the historical and projected cash flows by month.

Each area is discussed below.

***Reliability of the Expected Taxes and Revenues.***    If a TAN is issued in anticipation of property taxes, the analyst should investigate the tax collection rates over the previous five years. Tax collection rates below 90 percent usually indicate serious tax collection problems. Additionally, if the issuer is budgeting 100 percent of the tax levy but collecting substantially less, serious problems can be expected.

In the case of a RAN or GAN issued in anticipation of state or federal grant monies, the first question to ask is if the grant has been legislatively authorized and committed by the state or federal government. Some RAN issuers (including New York City prior to its RAN defaults in 1975) would issue RANs without having all the anticipated grants committed by the higher levels of government. Other local governments, hard-pressed to balance their budgets, may still follow this practice in order to obtain quick cash through the sale of RANs. As a safeguard, the analyst should make sure the issuer has in its possession a fully signed grant agreement prior to the RAN or GAN sale.

***Dependency on Expected Monies.***    One measure of the creditworthiness of the TAN or RAN issuer is its degree of dependency on the temporarily borrowed monies. Some jurisdictions, for example, limit the amount of TANs that can be issued in anticipation of property taxes to a percentage of the prior year's levy that was actually collected. The state of New Jersey, which has one of the more fiscally conservative local government regulatory codes in the country, limits the annual sale of TANs and RANs by county and municipal governments to no more than 30 percent of the property taxes and various other revenues actually collected in the previous year. School districts may not exceed one half of current expenses. Many other states are more permissive and allow local governments to issue TANs and RANs up to 75 to 100 percent of the monies previously collected or even expected to be received in the current fiscal year.

*Soundness of Budgetary Operations.*   Another critical element is the issuer's history of overall prudent and disciplined financial management. The analyst should determine how well the issuer has maintained end-of-year fund balances in its major operating funds over the previous five fiscal years.

*The Problems of "Rollovers."*   Retiring TANs or RANs with the proceeds of new issues or issuing TANs or RANs to be retired in a fiscal year following the one in which they were originally issued are indications of fiscal problems. Such practices, known as "rollovers," are sometimes used by hard-pressed issuers to disguise chronic operating budget deficits. To leave no doubt as to the soundness of their budgetary operations, many states, local governments, and special jurisdictions have established, either by statute or by administrative policy, that all TANs and RANs issued in one fiscal year must be retired before the end of that fiscal year. Although such a policy reduces the issuer's flexibility in dealing with unexpected emergencies, it helps provide protection to the noteholders against TANs and RANs ever being used for hidden deficit financing. In some circumstances, RANs and GANs can be properly issued for periods greater than 12 months, providing the granting agency has established a reimbursement schedule that matches the maturity of the note.

*Historical and Projected Cash Flows.*   The TAN, RAN, or GAN issuer's cash-flow history and projections can provide valuable information on creditworthiness. A monthly accounting going back over the previous fiscal year, showing the beginning fund balances, revenues, expenditures, and end-of-month fund balances is required. The analyst should determine how well the issuer has met its fiscal goals by maintaining at least a balanced budget and meeting all liabilities, including debt-service payments.

Cash-flow tables on the projected monthly cash flows for the fiscal year in which the TANs or RANs are to be issued should be examined. Of particular importance are whether or not the issuer has included in the projections sufficient revenues to retire the TANs, RANs, or GANs, including interest payments, and whether or not the estimated revenues and expenditures amounts are realistic in light of the prior fiscal year's experience.

**EXHIBIT 23–1**

**City of Buffalo Cash Receipts and Disbursements** (Combined City and Board of Education General Funds)

| | July 1, 1981–June 30, 1982 (Actual) (000's Omitted) | | | | | |
|---|---|---|---|---|---|---|
| | July 1981 | Aug 1981 | Sept 1981 | Oct 1981 | Nov 1981 | Dec 1981 |
| Beginning Cash and Investments | $23,378 | $27,661 | $24,879 | $21,334 | $65,262 | $50,112 |
| Cash Receipts: | | | | | | |
| Property Taxes (1) | 25,445 | 17,023 | 1,443 | 1,461 | 1,646 | 12,008 |
| State and Federal Aid (2) | 4,805 | 867 | 2,866 | 14,044 | 682 | 6,171 |
| Erie County Sales Tax (3) | 1,537 | 2,049 | 2,030 | 4,847 | 2,191 | 2,138 |
| Other Income | 1,854 | 3,593 | 4,534 | 3,392 | 4,431 | 3,391 |
| Temporary Loans | | | | 50,000 | | |
| Total Cash Receipts | $33,641 | $23,532 | $10,873 | $73,744 | $8,950 | $23,708 |
| Cash Disbursements: | | | | | | |
| Operations | $21,026 | $26,314 | $14,418 | $29,816 | $24,100 | $29,715 |
| To Capital Debt Service Fund | 8,332 | | | | | 4,893 |
| Temporary Loans Repaid | | | | | | |
| Total Cash Disbursements | $29,358 | $26,314 | $14,418 | $29,816 | $24,100 | $34,608 |
| Ending Cash and Investments | $27,661 | $24,879 | $21,334 | $65,262 | $50,112 | $39,212 |

(1)  Property taxes received in fiscal year 1981-82 exceed those projected to be received in fiscal year 1982-83 mainly due to the amount of taxes in arrears, including demolition assessments, paid by the City to the City Treasurer in 1981-82 as a result of acquisition of property by the City through "in rem" foreclosure proceedings.

(2)  State and Federal Aid received in fiscal year 1981-82 is less than that projected to be received in

Exhibit 23–1 is a historic monthly cash flow summary for RANS that were issued by Buffalo, New York. Exhibit 23–2 is a projected monthly cash flow summary for the RANS issued by Buffalo, New York.

## Evaluating Bond Anticipation Notes

BANs are secured principally by the issuer's access to the municipal bond market (i.e., its ability to issue long-term bonds, the proceeds of which will be used to

| | July 1, 1981—June 30, 1982 (Actual) (000's Omitted) | | | | | |
| --- | --- | --- | --- | --- | --- | --- |
| Jan 1982 | Feb 1982 | March 1982 | April 1982 | May 1982 | June 1982 | Totals |
| $39,212 | $49,854 | $43,622 | $34,166 | $18,291 | $27,240 | |
| 25,556 | 1,402 | 3,567 | 1,348 | 1,468 | 467 | 92,844 |
| 4,578 | 16,084 | 3,872 | 1,694 | 26,529 | 57,111 | 139,303 |
| 3,538 | — | 5,772 | 6,336 | 556 | 2,204 | 33,198 |
| 2,888 | 6,278 | 6,240 | 4,154 | 3,892 | 10,435 | 55,082 |
| | 19,000 | | | | | 69,000 |
| $36,570 | $42,764 | $19,451 | $13,532 | $32,445 | $70,217 | $389,427 |
| $25,928 | $23,996 | $28,907 | $29,407 | $23,496 | $28,873 | $305,996 |
| | | | | | | 13,225 |
| | 25,000 | | | | 44,000 | 69,000 |
| $25,928 | $48,996 | $28,907 | $29,407 | $23,496 | $72,873 | $388,221 |
| $49,854 | $43,622 | $34,166 | $18,291 | $27,240 | $24,584 | |

fiscal year 1982-83 as a result of $13.7 million of overburden aid due in June 1982 but received on July 2, 1982, plus $9 million of additional aid to education expected to be received in fiscal year 1982-83.

(3)   Erie County Sales Tax receipts are lower in fiscal year 1982-82 than projected for fiscal year 1982-83 as a result of a payment of approximately $3.0 million expected to be received in June 1982 but actually received in July 1982.

retire the BANs). Most BANs issued by states, counties, cities, towns and school districts are also secured by the general obligation pledge, which is discussed later in this chapter.

The analyst should obtain information in the following two areas because they help to determine the ability of the issuer to gain market access:

1. The creditworthiness of the issuers.

2. Expected future market conditions and the flexibility of the issuers.

Each is discussed below.

**EXHIBIT 23–2**

**City of Buffalo Cash Receipts and Disbursements** (Combined City and Board of Education General Funds)

*July 1, 1982—August 31, 1982 (Actual)*
*September 1, 1982—June 30, 1983 (Projected)*
*(000's Omitted)*

|  | July 1982 | Aug 1982 | Sept 1982 | Oct 1982 | Nov 1982 | Dec 1982 |
|---|---|---|---|---|---|---|
| Beginning Cash and Investments | $24,584 | $39,547 | $36,991 | $26,553 | $77,680 | $63,131 |
| Cash Receipts: | | | | | | |
| Property Taxes (1) | 19,526 | 23,114 | 1,302 | 1,302 | 1,475 | 11,194 |
| State and Federal Aid (2) | 20,574 | 1,133 | 3,380 | 14,437 | 3,953 | 3,838 |
| Erie County Sales Tax (3) | 4,839 | 2,237 | 2,147 | 5,138 | 2,287 | 2,252 |
| Other Income | 833 | 5,218 | 4,235 | 3,147 | 2,938 | 5,333 |
| Temporary Loans | | | | 60,000 | | |
| Total Cash Receipts | $45,772 | $31,702 | $11,064 | $84,024 | $10,653 | $22,617 |
| Cash Disbursements: | | | | | | |
| Operations | $22,262 | $34,258 | $21,502 | $32,897 | $25,202 | $34,097 |
| To Capital Debt Service Fund | 8,547 | | | | | 4,808 |
| Temporary Loans | | | | | | |
| Total Cash Disbursements | $30,809 | $34,258 | $21,502 | $32,897 | $25,202 | $38,905 |
| Ending Cash and Investments | $39,547 | $36,991 | $26,553 | $77,680 | $63,131 | $46,843 |

(1) Property taxes received in fiscal year 1981-82 exceed those projected to be received in fiscal year 1982-83 mainly due to the amount of taxes in arrears, including demolition assessments, paid by the City to the City Treasurer in 1981-82 as a result of acquisition of property by the City through "in rem" foreclosure proceedings.

(2) State and Federal Aid received in fiscal year 1981-82 is less than that projected to be received in fiscal year 1982-83 as a result of $13.7 million of overburden aid due in June 1982

*Creditworthiness.* Because outstanding BANs are retired with the proceeds of long-term bond sales, the creditworthiness of the BANs is directly related to the creditworthiness of the underlying issuer. The analyst must obtain the same credit information used for analyzing long-term bonds. In general, the stronger the bond credit quality, the greater is the ability of the BAN issuer to complete long-term bond sales.

Besides determining the credit quality of the underlying bonds, the analyst should also determine the issuer's probable market access and acceptance. That is, in the past how well have the bonds of the issuer been received in the

|  |  | July 1, 1982–August 31, 1982 (Actual) | | | |  |
|  |  | September 1, 1982–June 30, 1983 (Projected) | | | |  |
|  |  | (000's Omitted) | | | |  |
| Jan 1983 | Feb 1983 | March 1983 | April 1983 | May 1983 | June 1983 | Totals |
|---|---|---|---|---|---|---|
| $46,843 | $55,206 | $51,410 | $40,019 | $23,945 | $32,730 |  |
| 23,863 | 1,302 | 3,297 | 1,215 | 1,302 | 867 | 89,759 |
| 3,395 | 13,948 | 6,324 | 2,662 | 28,872 | 73,609 | 176,125 |
| 3,730 | 3,906 | 2,182 | 6,686 | 563 | 2,344 | 38,311 |
| 3,155 | 2,828 | 6,386 | 3,138 | 3,828 | 5,249 | 46,288 |
|  |  |  |  |  |  | 60,000 |
| $34,143 | $21,984 | $18,189 | $13,701 | $34,565 | $82,069 | $410,483 |
| $25,780 | $25,780 | $29,580 | $29,775 | $25,780 | $33,880 | $340,793 |
|  |  |  |  |  |  | 13,355 |
|  |  |  |  |  | 60,000 | 60,000 |
| $25,780 | $25,780 | $29,580 | $29,775 | $25,780 | $93,880 | $414,148 |
| $55,206 | $51,410 | $40,019 | $23,945 | $32,730 | $20,919 |  |

but received on July 2, 1982, plus $9 million of additional aid to education expected to be received in fiscal year 1982-83.

(3)   Erie County Sales Tax receipts are lower in fiscal year 1982-82 than projected for fiscal year 1982-83 as a result of a payment of approximately $3.0 million expected to be received in June 1982 but actually received in July 1982.

marketplace? Has the issuer had to pay interest costs substantially higher than other bond issuers of similar creditworthiness? How many bids were received for a competitively bid issue? Has the issuer attempted to sell a similar amount of bonds in previous years? Answers to these questions will determine the credit risks involved in the purchase of BANs.

*Future Market Conditions.*   BAN investors cannot know in advance what the condition of the market will be when their BANs come due. If the issuer's creditworthiness is at least of investment-grade quality, however, there should be a market for that issuer's bonds. Of course, the weaker the credit quality and the larger the amount of BANs to be retired, the higher the rate of interest would have to be.

If the BANs come due at a time when interest rates in the municipal bond market are rising, the BAN issuer should have the flexibility to retire the maturing BANs with a new BAN issue, rather than long-term bonds. Most state and local government finance regulations recognize this need by allowing BANs to be retired from new BAN issues. The ability of the issuer to do so is directly related to the credit quality of the issuer.

Unlike most TANs, RANs and GANs, BANs can be refunded (i.e., rolled over into new BANs). However, prudent issuers are usually limited by local laws to having their BANs outstanding for no longer than five to eight years. If there is no limit as to how long the BANs can be outstanding, the temptation is great for the BAN issuer to avoid funding-out the BANs with a bond issue.

In order to strengthen credit quality and improve marketability, some issuers will use a credit agreement with a nationally reputable banking institution that requires the bank, under certain conditions, to pay the noteholders any outstanding principal and interest due at maturity. The bank would usually issue refunding notes with a specified maturity schedule at that time.

*The General Obligation Pledge.*  Many TANs, RANs and GANs issued by states, cities, towns, counties, and school districts are secured by the general obligation pledge. This means that the issuers are legally obligated to use their full taxing powers and available revenues to pay the noteholders. Therefore, if a city's tax anticipation note is secured by property taxes as well as by the general obligation pledge and if the city's property tax collection rate that particular year does not generate sufficient taxes to pay the noteholder, the city must use other resources to make the noteholder whole, including available monies in its general fund. Of course, the importance of the general obligation pledge is directly related to the diversification of the issuer's revenue base and lack of dependence on note sales, as well as on the soundness of its budgetary operations.

Many BANs are also secured by the general obligation pledge of the issuer. If the overall credit quality, revenue structure, and market image of the underlying general obligation issuer are stronger than those of the agency or department that has issued the BANs, then the general obligation pledge would be a positive factor, strengthening the issuer's market access for either rolling over the BANs or retiring them with the proceeds of a long-term bond sale.

## EVALUATING REPURCHASE AGREEMENTS

A repurchase agreement (or "repo") is a contractual agreement between a municipal issuer (or its bank trustee) and a commercial bank, investment banking firm, or other government bond dealer. In the transaction, the repo issuer (e.g., a government bond dealer) receives cash and, in turn, usually provides interest-bearing U.S. government securities to a municipal issuer as collateral for the cash, with the contractual commitment to repurchase the securities at predetermined dates and prices. Construction loan note proceeds, and even cash-flow revenues, are often invested through repos until the money is needed to pay either debt-service or construction expenses associated with the specific projects. Over the years, investment bankers and municipal issuers have found repos to be attractive short-term investment vehicles because they can match the maturity of the repo to their specific cash-flow needs.

Repos were not generally recognized as pressing credit concerns until the summer of 1982, when a few modestly capitalized government bond dealers that had repos outstanding—Drysdale Securities Corporation, Comark Securities, Inc., and Lombard-Wall, Inc.—experienced severe financial stress. On August 12, 1982, Lombard-Wall filed for court protection under the Federal Bankruptcy Code. Under the automatic-stay provisions of section 362 (a) of the code, as well as a temporary restraining order issued on August 17, no note trustee could sell the collateral securing a Lombard-Wall repo without court approval. In effect, the collateral was frozen.

As an example of the severity of this freeze on individual creditworthiness, one hospital bond issuer had $43.34 million, or 37 percent of its bond proceeds, invested with Lombard-Wall. Another issuer had its total debt-reserve fund invested with Lombard under a 30-year repo. Several construction loan note issuers also had whole note issue proceeds invested with Lombard-Wall.

The credit risks for the holders of the notes involved were substantially increased because

- The bankruptcy court's restraining order on August 17 prevented the sale or disposition of securities received from Lombard-Wall under repurchase or investment agreements without court approval;
- Several of the note issuers were dependent upon these securities to finance construction and related activities; and
- It was not possible to determine future court actions in these areas.[1]

In September 1982, the bankruptcy judge, in an oral opinion concerning an issuer in Pennsylvania, held that the repo collateral belonged to Lombard-Wall.[2] That is, the court considered the collateral used in the repos to be "secured

---

[1] This is based on observations at the time of the court proceedings, as well as on interviews with various lawyers involved in the litigations.

[2] "Sale Barred of Lombard-Wall Bonds Used in Repo for Hospital Authority," *American Banker*, September 20, 1982, p. 2. According to the counsel for Dauphin, before the judge's oral decision was typed and signed, the parties involved settled their dispute. Interview with James A. Moyer, Esq., of LeBoeuf, Lamb, Leiby and Macrae, October 4, 1982.

loans" to Lombard-Wall. Before the collateral could be liquidated, the judge would have to agree on the terms of the liquidation and who was to receive the proceeds. It should be noted that on July 10, 1984, the President signed into law the Amendments Bankruptcy Act, which exempts repos with a maturity of one year or less, or on demand, from the automatic stay provisions of the U.S. Bankruptcy Code.

In the Lombard-Wall case, the judge also refused to release the collateral Lombard-Wall borrowed from a third party. At least three Texas bond issuers — the Lubbock Housing Finance Corporation, the Abilene Housing Finance Corporation, and the Baytown Housing Finance Corporation — received approval to sell only two thirds of their collateral, as the other third had been borrowed by Lombard-Wall from a third party.[3]

Although the great bull bond markets of August and September 1982 helped to bail out Lombard-Wall, at the time over 50 municipal note issuers faced serious financial problems as the result of the bankruptcy. If repos are used in financial transactions, an analyst should consider the following seven factors.

1. Are construction funds, any other proceeds, or project enterprise revenues invested through repos? If so, to what extent is the note issuer dependent on the repo monies? Clearly, construction loan note proceeds, debt-reserve funds, mortgage loan repayments, and grant receipts invested in repos are of greater concern than idle funds.

2. Are the repos with well-capitalized, established government bond dealers, investment banking firms, or banking institutions? Repos should not be with undercapitalized government securities arbitrage and trading firms. Inclusion on a trading list approved by the Federal Reserve Bank is not sufficient evidence of creditworthiness.

3. Are the repos fully secured with collateral that is in negotiable form and in the possession and control of the municipality or trustee? Title to the collateral should at all times be with the trustee.

4. The collateral should only include (a) direct general obligations of the United States or obligations unconditionally guaranteed by the United States; (b) bonds, debentures, or notes issued by certain agencies including the Federal Home Loan Banks, Federal Financing Bank, and Federal Home Loan Mortgage Corporation (including participation certificates); and (c) public housing bonds, temporary notes, or preliminary loan notes fully secured by contracts with the United States.

---

[3] After the court decision, the trustee for the three bond issues used its own resources to remedy the losses resulting from the Lombard-Wall investments. "3 Texas Agencies Will Be Repaid Lombard Funds," *The Bond Buyer*, September 9, 1982, p. 3. It should also be noted that it was reported that the third party involved was the Trust Department of Bankers Trust (*The Bond Buyer*, September 7, 1982, p. 1).

5. Because the vagaries of the bond market impose the risk that the fair market value of the collateral may substantially decline at any time, the collateral should be valued at least monthly; the fair market value of the securities, as stated in the repo agreements, should mean the bid prices as they appear in the "Composite Closing Quotations for Government Securities," published by the Federal Reserve Bank of New York.

6. If the value of the collateral decreases below the level agreed upon under the repurchase agreement and is not replenished immediately after notice, then the note trustees should have the right to sell the respective securities. If the repo issuer defaults in an interest payment, after one business day's notice, the bank trustee should have the option to declare the repo agreement terminated.

7. The repo agreement should state that third parties are not owners of any collateral and that the collateral is free of all liens.

## EVALUATING TAX-EXEMPT COMMERCIAL PAPER[4]

This short-term, tax-exempt borrowing instrument is used for periods ranging from 30 to 270 days. Generally, tax-exempt commercial paper has "backstop" commercial bank agreements, which can include an irrevocable letter of credit, a revolving credit agreement, or a line of credit. If the security does not include a credit backstop for the benefit of the investor, the credit-risk analysis would follow the guidelines discussed above in regard to tax, revenue, grant, and bond anticipation notes.

The irrevocable letter of credit is the strongest type of investor comfort. It requires the bank to pay necessary amounts to the limits of the letter. Of course, the analyst should review the terms of the agreement carefully so as to determine whether the letter of credit extends only to defaulted note principal or also includes principal and interest through the date of default on the note.

A revolving credit agreement could have the same creditworthiness as the irrevocable letter of credit. However, the analyst must examine the agreement to see if there are circumstances under which the bank may be released from responsibility. A line-of-credit agreement is generally the weakest backstop because it usually has a number of release clauses that allow a bank to avoid providing funds when required. In all the commercial bank supports, the monies are usually provided as a remedy for a default. The investor or trustees must present a claim after the default in order to benefit from the backstop.

---

[4]This discussion is drawn from James J. Goodwin II, "Tax-Exempt Commercial Paper," in Sylvan G. Feldstein, Frank J. Fabozzi, and Irving M. Pollack eds., *The Municipal Bond Handbook*, Volume II (Homewood, Ill.: Dow Jones-Irwin, 1983).

## The Preference Problem

Current bankruptcy law is unclear as to whether or not a paper holder could be forced to repay the trustee if the tax-exempt commercial paper issuer files in bankruptcy and the holder had had a maturity of 90 days or less from such a filing and was "paid" via a rollover of the paper. This could occur even though the investor did not know of the impending bankruptcy of the issuer. Needless to say, the analyst should determine the underlying creditworthiness of the tax-exempt commercial paper issuer, in addition to the commercial bank credit support.

## SUMMARY

In this chapter, we have discussed the basic security features of different types of municipal short-term investments. These investments range from well-secured instruments with little or no credit risk to those of substantially weaker creditworthiness. While we have indicated the guidelines in evaluating the specific instruments, we have only indicated the basic questions to ask. A review of a specific instrument would require even greater investigation by the analyst.

# CHAPTER 24

## EUROCAPITAL MARKETS*

*Hung Q. Tran\*\**
Director
*Fixed Income Research, New York*
*Deutsche Bank*

*Larry Anderson*
*Head of Fixed Income Research, London*
*Deutsche Bank*

*Ernst-Ludwig Drayss*
*First Vice President, Frankfurt*
*Deutsche Bank*

Europe has occupied a central position in the global supply and demand of capital throughout history. Until the world wars, Europe was, on balance, a net supplier of funds to the rest of the world in need of capital to develop its industrial infrastructure. In the postwar years, Europe itself needed a large influx of capital for reconstruction. Consequently, many European countries developed large and persistent balance-of-payment deficits on their current accounts, which required external financing—a trend aggravated by the sharply rising commodity prices of the 1970s.

*This chapter is adapted from a chapter with the same title that appeared in Robert Lawrence Kuhn (ed.) *International Finance and Investing*, vol. 6 in The Library of Investment Banking (Homewood, IL: Dow Jones-Irwin, 1990). The data has been updated.

**The following members of the Deutsche Bank Fixed Income Research Department contributed to this chapter: Patrick Paradiso (New York); Yvona Fierlinger (London); Eva-Maria Mann, Dieter Ritter, and Reiner Back (Frankfurt).

## RECENT HISTORY OF EUROPEAN FINANCE

### Europe in the Global Supply and Demand of Funds

In recent years, many large European countries have significantly improved their external payment positions, resulting in current account surpluses for this group; thus once again these countries have become suppliers of capital to the world. Certain countries in this group—such as West Germany, the United Kingdom, the Netherlands, and Switzerland—have accumulated a net external asset position of about $300 billion, roughly comparable to that of Japan in mid-1988. This makes these European countries important players in the global financial markets.

In addition to being a collection of direct borrowers and lenders, Europe has also performed the important function of international intermediation (i.e., channeling the savings from one group of countries to another through financial centers in London and elsewhere on the Continent and via the Euromarket). During the 1970s, the Eurocredit market was critical in the smooth recycling of the petrodollars from oil-producing countries. Since the early 1980s, the Euro-market has helped finance the U.S. current account deficit through substantial Eurobond issuance by U.S. corporations and through net inflows into the U.S. banking system.

The intermediation function of Europe can also be highlighted by the professional management of investible funds being performed in centers like London, Switzerland, Luxembourg, and the like. Investment management services have attracted significant funding from institutional and individual investors world-wide, which they are investing on an increasingly global basis.

### Europe as an Alternative to the U.S. Dollar and Yen Blocs

Given the need for diversification, both in borrowing and investing activities, the European capital markets should be viewed as a single entity, and as an alternative to the U.S. dollar and yen blocs.

*Relative Size.*   First, in terms of relative size, the European bond and stock markets taken together are comparable to the U.S. and Japanese markets. In 1988, Europe accounted for about 28 percent of the world bond market and nearly 29 percent of the world government bond market (see Exhibits 24-1*a* and 24-1*b*).

*Stable Exchange Rates.*   Second, thanks to the European Monetary System (EMS) and the convergence of economic policies and performances, exchange rates have been kept much more stable within Europe than without. In fact,

**EXHIBIT 24–1***a*
**World Bond Market Capitalization** (All Bonds)*

|  | 1986 | 1988 |
|---|---|---|
| US$ bloc (US$, C$, A$, NZ$) | 48.84% | 47.54% |
| Yen | 20.14 | 22.51 |
| DM bloc (DM, Dfl, Ffr, Dkr, £) | 17.62 | 17.63 |
| Rest of Europe (Lit, Sfr, Bfr, Pta, Asch, ECU) | 10.07 | 10.10 |
| Others (Skr, Nkr, I£, FM) | 3.33 | 2.22 |
|  | 100.00% | 100.00% |

*Legend*

| | |
|---|---|
| US$ = U. S. dollar | Lit = Italian lira |
| C$ = Canadian dollar | Sfr = Swiss franc |
| A$ = Australian dollar | Bfr = Belgian franc |
| NZ$ = New Zealand dollar | Pta = Spanish peseta |
| Yen = Japanese yen | Asch = Austrian schilling |
| DM = German mark | ECU = European Currency Unit |
| Dfl = Dutch guilder | Skr = Swedish krona |
| Ffr = French franc | Nkr = Norwegian krone |
| Dkr = Danish krone | I£ = Irish punt |
| £ = U. K. pound | FM = Finnish markka |

* Expressed in US$ terms.

**EXHIBIT 24–1***b*
**World Bond Market Capitalization**
(Government Bonds Only)*

|  | 1986 | 1988 |
|---|---|---|
| US$ bloc | 37.99% | 38.41% |
| Yen | 28.60 | 30.31 |
| DM bloc | 16.01 | 15.33 |
| Rest of Europe | 14.40 | 13.35 |
| Others | 3.00 | 2.60 |
|  | 100.00% | 100.00% |

* Expressed in US$ terms.

against the U.S. dollar and the yen, the European currencies have moved more or less in a bloc and within a relatively narrow band of fluctuation.

*Single Internal Market.* Third, the current plan by the European Economic Community (EEC) to achieve a single internal market in Europe by 1992 should foster even more stability in intra-European exchange rates and an integration of its capital markets.

*Financial Liberalization.* Fourth, the process of financial liberalization in recent years has opened up the European capital markets to foreign participation.

## Europe as a Key Link in a
## 24-Hour Trading Environment

As the globalization of financial markets progresses, 24-hour trading has become more popular. Consequently, Europe, and particularly London, is becoming a key link in such a continuous trading environment. Of particular interest is the trading in London of vital international securities such as U.S. Treasuries, Japanese government bonds, and major U.S. equities.

Because of the above-mentioned reasons, an understanding of the European capital markets is very important for participants in today's financial markets. This chapter will describe the Euromarket centered in London.

## HISTORY AND DEVELOPMENT OF THE
## EUROCAPITAL MARKET

### Formation of the Eurodollar Deposit Market

In the early 1950s, the U.S. dollar emerged as the major international currency, with Europe becoming an important center for the intermediation of the currency. This was due to the following factors:

- U.S. dollars were made available in the form of aid programs for the reconstruction of Western Europe after the Second World War.
- The currency was considered relatively stable and secure and therefore was held by central banks as part of their foreign currency reserves.
- U.S. companies increased their direct investment overseas by setting up manufacturing units abroad.
- For political reasons, certain countries preferred to deposit dollars in Europe after the war rather than in the United States.

With the establishment of a large pool of U.S. dollars in Europe, banks took on the task of intermediating and developing an efficient wholesale market in dollar deposits.

## Development of the Euromoney Market

As the Euromarket grew, it offered a number of profitable opportunities to both banks and their clients. Many U.S. banks took the defensive step of following their customer base overseas in order to utilize their existing system more profitably and to offer domestic customers a wider range of services and multinational customers a fully-integrated banking package. As a result, banks developed new techniques and products to meet an increasingly competitive environment. Additionally, European banks had access to attractive Eurocurrency funding and could build up new portfolio assets, diversifying away from purely domestic business.

The Euromarkets also offered the opportunity to arbitrage with the domestic market. London emerged as the center of the burgeoning Euromarket. London already offered established financial institutions, related services, and an international language; this was enhanced by incentives and concessions from the U.K. authorities such as the relaxation of exchange controls in the U.K. in December 1958 for nonsterling currencies.

These actions encouraged federal- and state-supervised U.S. banks, which were restricted from expanding domestically by regulatory constraints (e.g., 1933 Glass-Steagall Act, restrictions on interstate banking, and Regulation Q) and by structural constraints (e.g., fragmentation) to establish branches in London. In addition, London provided relatively easy access to all the time zones in the United States, Europe, the Middle East, and Africa. Finally, London had already developed the expertise and facilities for international finance, due to the worldwide role of its currency as the complement to the growing importance of the U.S. dollar.

As competition in the Eurocurrency market increased, banks broke out of their traditional role of using Eurodollar funds for short-term interbank lending in order to develop a syndicated loan market lending funds over longer periods to governments and multinational corporations. Additionally, wider services were offered to clients in an increasing number of currencies, and gradually more products were developed in allied sectors such as in foreign exchange, forward transactions, and eventually the bond market.

## Founding of the Eurocapital Markets

In the early 1960s, New York was the most easily accessible market in which corporations could raise capital at attractive rates of interest. Therefore, international companies came to New York to issue U.S. dollar Yankee bonds.

When banks started to lend to international companies out of Europe, they issued bonds in New York and placed them with European investors who had accumulated surplus dollar funds. These banks developed expertise in managing bond issues and built up an investor base of European clients. Gradually, they began to issue bonds domestically. However, European borrowers were inhibited by the higher rates of interest required in European currencies.

The impetus for the development of a European issue market was the U.S. restrictions implemented to reduce the rapid outflow of capital due to large holdings of U.S. assets overseas—which itself was exacerbated by foreign issues offered in the United States. In July 1963, in order to reduce foreign borrowings in the United States, the government imposed an interest equalization tax (IET) on Yankee bond issues. The tax, levied on the purchase price of Yankee bonds for U.S. citizens, was aimed at eliminating the interest-rate differential between the higher interest rates on European and lower ones on U.S. dollar bonds. As a result, European borrowers had little incentive to issue in the U.S. capital market rather than in their own domestic markets. The tax was estimated to have increased the effective cost to foreigners of issuing in the United States by one full percentage point. As a result, the Yankee bond market was effectively closed to all borrowers with the exception of those borrowers with tax-free status such as the World Bank. The tax, originally proposed as temporary, was extended and even raised in 1967 to add 150 basis points to borrowing costs.

As the European market developed and gained depth, even after the IET was withdrawn in June 1974, borrowers did not rush back to the Yankee market. European institutions and subsidiaries of U.S. banks developed extensive relationships with borrowers and investors in the domestic markets. Since the initial pioneers were generally the most respected and established banks and issuing houses, the market was aided by the confidence inspired by the participants. Therefore, the Eurobond market developed in the early years to 1974 by establishing a firm base and becoming self-perpetuating as the repayment of Eurobonds by borrowers gave money back to investors who could reinvest in other new Eurobonds and provide permanent capital to borrowers.

## Brief Historical Review of the Eurocapital Market

Exhibit 24–2 depicts the development of the Eurobond market. It shows the year-by-year increase in size from US$ 75 million in 1963 to an annualized US$ 219 *billion* by 1989. The relative and shifting importance of the various currencies is also evident.

*1960s.* The market began to develop in 1963, as a natural progression from the Euromoney market and for the aforementioned reasons. Activity was largest in the U.S. dollar bond sector stimulated by the imposition of the interest equalization tax (IET) and the growing awareness by borrowers and investors of

**EXHIBIT 24-2**
**Eurobond Issues By Currency: 1963–1990** (US$ Million Equivalent)

| Currency | 1963 Volume | 1963 % Market | 1964 Volume | 1964 % Market | 1965 Volume | 1965 % Market |
|---|---|---|---|---|---|---|
| U. S. dollar | 30.0 | 40.0 | 495.5 | 81.1 | 525.5 | 76.6 |
| Deutschemark | 0.0 | 0.0 | 91.3 | 14.9 | 91.3 | 13.3 |
| Composite/dual | 31.0 | 41.0 | 24.0 | 3.9 | 55.0 | 8.0 |
| Australian dollar | 0.0 | 0.0 | 0.0 | 0.0 | 0.0 | 0.0 |
| Canadian dollar | 0.0 | 0.0 | 0.0 | 0.0 | 0.0 | 0.0 |
| U. K. sterling | 0.0 | 0.0 | 0.0 | 0.0 | 0.0 | 0.0 |
| Japanese yen | 0.0 | 0.0 | 0.0 | 0.0 | 0.0 | 0.0 |
| Other currencies | 14.0 | 18.7 | 0.0 | 0.0 | 14.0 | 2.0 |
| Total | 75.0 | 100.0 | 610.8 | 100.0 | 685.8 | 100.0 |

| Currency | 1966 Volume | 1966 % Market | 1967 Volume | 1967 % Market | 1968 Volume | 1968 % Market |
|---|---|---|---|---|---|---|
| U. S. dollar | 833.5 | 77.7 | 1,591.3 | 88.3 | 2,303.0 | 73.7 |
| Deutschemark | 146.2 | 13.6 | 158.7 | 8.8 | 760.1 | 24.3 |
| Composite/dual | 93.6 | 8.7 | 39.2 | 2.2 | 62.0 | 2.0 |
| Australian dollar | 0.0 | 0.0 | 0.0 | 0.0 | 0.0 | 0.0 |
| Canadian dollar | 0.0 | 0.0 | 0.0 | 0.0 | 0.0 | 0.0 |
| U. K. sterling | 0.0 | 0.0 | 0.0 | 0.0 | 0.0 | 0.0 |
| Japanese yen | 0.0 | 0.0 | 0.0 | 0.0 | 0.0 | 0.0 |
| Other currencies | 0.0 | 0.0 | 12.2 | 0.7 | 0.0 | 0.0 |
| Total | 1,073.3 | 100.0 | 1,801.4 | 100.0 | 3,125.1 | 100.0 |

| Currency | 1969 Volume | 1969 % Market | 1970 Volume | 1970 % Market | 1971 Volume | 1971 % Market |
|---|---|---|---|---|---|---|
| U. S. dollar | 1,632.5 | 57.4 | 1,718.0 | 63.4 | 2,138.0 | 61.0 |
| Deutschemark | 1,116.7 | 39.3 | 514.6 | 19.0 | 830.4 | 23.7 |
| Composite/dual | 60.0 | 2.1 | 104.0 | 3.8 | 251.5 | 7.2 |
| Australian dollar | 0.0 | 0.0 | 0.0 | 0.0 | 0.0 | 0.0 |
| Canadian dollar | 0.0 | 0.0 | 0.0 | 0.0 | 0.0 | 0.0 |
| U. K. sterling | 0.0 | 0.0 | 0.0 | 0.0 | 0.0 | 0.0 |
| Japanese yen | 0.0 | 0.0 | 0.0 | 0.0 | 0.0 | 0.0 |
| Other currencies | 33.2 | 1.2 | 371.8 | 13.7 | 285.9 | 8.2 |
| Total | 2,842.4 | 100.0 | 2,708.4 | 100.0 | 3,505.8 | 100.0 |

**EXHIBIT 24–2—***Continued*

| | 1972 | | 1973 | | 1974 | |
| --- | --- | --- | --- | --- | --- | --- |
| Currency | Volume | % Market | Volume | % Market | Volume | % Market |
| U. S. dollar | 2,978.0 | 56.2 | 1,943.0 | 56.0 | 767.0 | 47.8 |
| Deutschemark | 1,251.7 | 23.6 | 964.6 | 27.8 | 203.4 | 12.7 |
| Composite/dual | 30.0 | 0.6 | 189.7 | 5.5 | 222.2 | 13.8 |
| Australian dollar | 36.5 | 0.7 | 0.0 | 0.0 | 0.0 | 0.0 |
| Canadian dollar | 0.0 | 0.0 | 0.0 | 0.0 | 58.0 | 3.6 |
| U. K. sterling | 26.1 | 0.5 | 0.0 | 0.0 | 0.0 | 0.0 |
| Japanese yen | 0.0 | 0.0 | 0.0 | 0.0 | 0.0 | 0.0 |
| Other currencies | 980.9 | 18.5 | 370.4 | 10.7 | 355.5 | 22.1 |
| Total | 5,303.2 | 100.0 | 3,467.8 | 100.0 | 1,606.1 | 100.0 |

| | 1975 | | 1976 | | 1977 | |
| --- | --- | --- | --- | --- | --- | --- |
| Currency | Volume | % Market | Volume | % Market | Volume | % Market |
| U. S. dollar | 2,749.5 | 41.7 | 8,635.0 | 66.6 | 10,086.0 | 63.5 |
| Deutschemark | 1,815.1 | 27.5 | 2,095.7 | 16.2 | 3,936.9 | 24.8 |
| Composite/dual | 585.8 | 8.9 | 102.2 | 0.8 | 33.0 | 0.2 |
| Australian dollar | 0.0 | 0.0 | 18.7 | 0.1 | 11.3 | 0.1 |
| Canadian dollar | 575.0 | 8.7 | 1,389.0 | 10.7 | 656.0 | 4.1 |
| U. K. sterling | 0.0 | 0.0 | 0.0 | 0.0 | 216.0 | 1.4 |
| Japanese yen | 0.0 | 0.0 | 0.0 | 0.0 | 91.2 | 0.6 |
| Other currencies | 867.7 | 13.2 | 722.4 | 5.6 | 845.7 | 5.3 |
| Total | 6,593.1 | 100.0 | 12,963.1 | 100.0 | 15,876.0 | 100.0 |

| | 1978 | | 1979 | | 1980 | |
| --- | --- | --- | --- | --- | --- | --- |
| Currency | Volume | % Market | Volume | % Market | Volume | % Market |
| U. S. dollar | 5,516.4 | 45.0 | 9,712.9 | 66.0 | 12,934.2 | 65.8 |
| Deutschemark | 4,940.5 | 40.3 | 2,572.3 | 17.5 | 3,015.8 | 15.3 |
| Composite/dual | 198.7 | 1.6 | 387.7 | 2.6 | 96.3 | 0.5 |
| Australian dollar | 30.6 | 0.3 | 17.1 | 0.1 | 49.8 | 0.3 |
| Canadian dollar | 0.0 | 0.0 | 424.2 | 2.9 | 279.6 | 1.4 |
| U. K. sterling | 288.5 | 2.4 | 248.1 | 1.7 | 916.0 | 4.7 |
| Japanese yen | 79.4 | 0.6 | 115.9 | 0.8 | 256.3 | 1.3 |
| Other currencies | 1,199.6 | 9.8 | 1,244.0 | 9.5 | 2,120.1 | 10.8 |
| Total | 12,253.7 | 100.0 | 14,722.2 | 100.0 | 19,668.1 | 100.0 |

## EXHIBIT 24–2—*Continued*

| Currency | 1981 Volume | 1981 % Market | 1982 Volume | 1982 % Market | 1983 Volume | 1983 % Market |
|---|---|---|---|---|---|---|
| U. S. dollar | 21,684.1 | 81.4 | 39,133.6 | 81.4 | 35.047.2 | 75.2 |
| Deutschemark | 1,235.4 | 4.6 | 3,987.9 | 8.3 | 4,343.1 | 9.3 |
| Composite/dual | 663.0 | 2.5 | 772.2 | 1.6 | 1,727.1 | 3.7 |
| Australian dollar | 0.0 | 0.0 | 0.0 | 0.0 | 220.1 | 0.5 |
| Canadian dollar | 646.8 | 2.4 | 1,238.2 | 2.6 | 1,121.9 | 2.4 |
| U. K. sterling | 538.6 | 2.0 | 802.0 | 1.7 | 1,986.2 | 4.3 |
| Japanese yen | 364.4 | 1.4 | 473.7 | 1.0 | 276.6 | 0.6 |
| Other currencies | 1,522.1 | 5.7 | 1,691.4 | 3.5 | 1,905.6 | 4.1 |
| Total | 26,654.4 | 100.0 | 48,099.1 | 100.0 | 46,627.8 | 100.0 |

| Currency | 1984 Volume | 1984 % Market | 1985 Volume | 1985 % Market | 1986 Volume | 1986 % Market |
|---|---|---|---|---|---|---|
| U. S. dollar | 61,837.2 | 77.5 | 93,747.6 | 69.8 | 114,050.0 | 61.8 |
| Deutschemark | 5,194.7 | 6.5 | 9,709.1 | 7.2 | 17,059.9 | 9.2 |
| Composite/dual | 2,721.5 | 3.4 | 6,839.7 | 5.1 | 6,882.8 | 3.7 |
| Australian dollar | 322.1 | 0.4 | 3,126.6 | 2.3 | 3,062.8 | 1.7 |
| Canadian dollar | 2,015.3 | 2.5 | 2,876.3 | 2.1 | 5,217.8 | 2.8 |
| U. K. sterling | 4,091.0 | 5.1 | 5,804.5 | 4.3 | 10,502.7 | 5.7 |
| Japanese yen | 1,208.3 | 1.5 | 6,970.8 | 5.2 | 18,642.7 | 10.1 |
| Other currencies | 2,362.9 | 3.0 | 5,187.6 | 3.9 | 9.132.2 | 4.9 |
| Total | 79,753.1 | 100.0 | 134,262.3 | 100.0 | 184,550.7 | 100.0 |

| Currency | 1987 Volume | 1987 % Market | 1988 Volume | 1988 % Market | 1989 Volume | 1989 % Market |
|---|---|---|---|---|---|---|
| U. S. dollar | 60,516.2 | 42.1 | 73,643 | 40.8 | 121,605 | 55.5 |
| Deutschemark | 14,685.6 | 10.2 | 23,777 | 13.2 | 15,930 | 7.3 |
| Composite/dual | 7.524.4 | 5.2 | 11,283 | 6.3 | 13,870 | 6.3 |
| Australian dollar | 9,190.2 | 6.4 | 8.166 | 4.5 | 6,794 | 3.1 |
| Canadian dollar | 5,992.9 | 4.2 | 13,233 | 7.3 | 12,541 | 5.7 |
| U. K. sterling | 14,895.6 | 10.4 | 24,670 | 13.7 | 20,508 | 9.4 |
| Japanese yen | 22,747.7 | 15.8 | 16,656 | 9.2 | 16,262 | 7.4 |
| Other currencies | 8,347.0 | 5.8 | 8,931 | 5.0 | 11,639 | 5.3 |
| Total | 143,899.6 | 100.0 | 180,359 | 100.0 | 219,149 | 100.0 |

**EXHIBIT 24–2—Continued**

| Currency | 1990 (Jan–March) Volume | % Market |
|---|---|---|
| U. S. dollar | 16,939 | 36.5 |
| Deutschemark | 7,473 | 16.1 |
| Composite/dual | 5,869 | 12.6 |
| Australian dollar | 1,095 | 2.4 |
| Canadian dollar | 679 | 1.5 |
| U. K. sterling | 6,074 | 13.1 |
| Japanese yen | 5,949 | 12.8 |
| Other currencies | 2,340 | 5.0 |
| Total | 46,418 | |

Note: Volume figures rounded to the nearest tenth; market share may not add due to rounding.

the advantages of the Eurobond market. In 1963, a total of seven Eurobonds were issued, three of which were in Eurodollars. Gradually, other currency markets developed as authorities lifted controls and restrictions, while the dollar sector grew more rapidly with the continued supply of dollars in Europe and increasing acceptance of bonds in the market.

Throughout the 1960s, although U.S. dollar bonds accounted for 80 percent of market issuance activity, the Deutschemark (DM) Eurobond market sector grew steadily. This was aided by the imposition of a 25 percent withholding tax on domestic DM bonds held by nonresidents, introduced to stem the strong currency inflows into Germany. The fear of domestic inflation as the money supply was expanded to maintain fixed exchange rates led to the tax differential treatment on new DM bond issues. Foreign issues in DM bonds were exempted so that overseas investors were attracted to DM bonds issued by nonresident borrowers, spurring the growth of the Euro-DM market. Whereas in 1963 no DM bonds were issued, in 1968 this sector claimed 24 percent of the new issue market.

In 1967, a Euro-French franc issue was launched, followed in 1969 by a Euro-Dutch guilder bond. This increased the breadth and attraction of the Eurobond market by allowing issuers to diversify currency risks and seize favorable opportunities in different markets. Between 1963 and 1969, the total volume of Eurobonds grew 38-fold, still dominated by issues in U.S. dollars, but followed by DM-denominated bond issues. Other currency sectors were insignificant. Many nondollar areas were still controlled by national authorities, restricting the volume of domestic currency overseas in line with domestically-targeted exchange rate and monetary policies.

Additionally, the size and timing of Eurobond issues in some currencies were tightly controlled by the authorities. The growth of the Eurodollar sector was aided by further restrictions on direct investment overseas by U.S. companies in 1968 to reduce the outflow of dollars from the United States. This encouraged U.S. companies to raise capital in the Euromarkets to finance overseas operations, and 1968 became a particularly attractive year for Eurobond issuance activity, with a total volume of $3.1 billion.

In 1969, increasing short-term interest rates, particularly U.S. rates, prompted investors to switch to the shorter end. As a result, new issue volume in the Eurobond market fell for the first time to $2.8 billion, a decline in US$ bond issuance contributing significantly. Investors turned to strong currencies such as the DM in anticipation of currency fluctuation, and the volume of DM Eurobonds offered rose to account for 39 percent of the total market in 1969.

*1970s.* The end of the 1960s and the beginning of the 1970s was a difficult time for the Eurobond market. The upward pressure on the DM, as U.S. inflation rose, led investors to switch from holding Eurodollar to DM-denominated bonds. Following the devaluation of the U.S. dollar in October 1969, investors temporarily retreated from the DM sector and new DM issue volume halved in 1970 to $514 million. Following the 1971 Smithsonian Agreement, new parities for currency exchange rates were established, restoring some stability to the bond markets.

Altogether, the early 1970s were difficult years for the major economies; persistent U.S. balance-of-payment deficits and increasing short-term dollar interest rates acted as a disincentive to borrowers in the Eurobond market. This was combined with the fourfold increase in oil prices and the collapse of a number of banks, increasing market uncertainty. In 1974, a total volume of $1.6 billion was launched in the Eurobond markets, compared with $3.5 billion in 1973.

The second half of the decade enjoyed considerable growth in the Eurobond market as the large dollar surpluses amassed by oil exporters flooded the Euromarket. The primary market more than doubled between 1975 and 1979, while the volume of US$ Eurobonds grew almost fourfold. However, the increase in volume can also be attributed to the considerable increase in the rate of inflation during the 1970s, which necessitated larger financings by corporations and governments. Total borrowings in the Eurobond market for the years 1975–80 exceeded that for 1965–70 by 7 percent. Corporate borrowings grew by 5 percent, sovereign and state-guaranteed by 8 percent. A large part of the latter increase was attributable to the financing of balance-of-payment deficits due to higher oil prices in the 1970s.

*1980s.*   The early 1980s were characterized by high and volatile interest rates, appreciation of the U.S. dollar, and increasing U.S. trade deficits. Many of the Third World countries, who had amassed large borrowings to help pay for the higher-priced oil, were now facing larger interest costs and reduced exports to the developed economies, compounding concern over debt repayment.

Countries that previously had access to the bond market directly now raised funds through traditional bank borrowings. Whereas in the late 1970s Central and Latin American nations were active in issuing bonds, rising to a high of 12 percent of primary bond issuance in 1978, there have rarely been any issues since 1983 by borrowers from these geographical sectors. This has contributed to the trend in the tiering of borrowers, whereby those considered lesser quality by the market have turned back to syndicated loans for their funding needs.

The U.S. dollar remained the primary currency of issue in this period, followed by the DM. The relatively high value of the dollar in the early 1980s attracted investors to this market. More recently, however, we witnessed the opposite trend as increasing U.S. balance-of-payment deficits and a declining confidence in the U.S. economy caused investors to move towards other hard currency sectors.

This period saw the emergence of the Japanese investor as a major force in international finance. Japanese fund managers, especially, have diversified holdings from U.S. dollar bonds to the DM and ECU sectors. The 1980s also saw a tremendous growth in Euroyen bond issues; constituting only 1.3 percent of new issue activity in 1980, it climbed to 15.5 percent in 1987 (the second largest sector after U.S. dollar bonds).

Finally, there has been a specific increase in demand for securitized instruments as investors take a cautious approach to liquidity and credit risk, enhancing the disintermediation process in the global financial markets. This has added to the attraction of the bearer nature of Eurobonds.


## FIXED-RATE DEBT INSTRUMENTS IN THE EUROMARKETS

### Straight Bonds

Traditionally, straight (or fixed-rate) bonds have been the mainstay of Eurocapital market financing. Throughout the 25-year history of these markets, fixed-rate bonds and notes have accounted for far more than 50 percent of total new issue volume each year. The years 1984 and 1985 were exceptions to this rule, however, due to a surge in the volume of floating-rate notes that were launched in this period. Exhibit 24–3 shows the size of the fixed-rate Eurobond market in 1989 by currency (approaching US$ 115 billion).

**EXHIBIT 24–3**
**Issue Volume by Currency: Fixed-Rate Eurobonds** (US$ Million Equivalent)

| Currency | 1989 |
|---|---|
| U. S. dollar | 47,465 |
| Japanese yen | 15,479 |
| Deutschemark | 9,401 |
| U. K. pound | 10,446 |
| Australian dollar | 6,700 |
| ECU | 13,299 |
| Canadian dollar | 10,740 |
| Dutch guilder | 1,174 |
| Danish krone | 216 |
| Total | 114,920 |

Straights in the Euromarket are almost exclusively bearer instruments, although some sovereign borrowers have floated large denomination-registered bonds for tax reasons. Euro-straights pay interest annually as compared with most other government bond markets (except continental Europe) and foreign bond markets, such as Yankee and Bulldog, where coupons are paid semiannually.

The fact that investors receive half of the coupon payment six months earlier on bonds paying interest semiannually than on Eurobonds means that an investor should be indifferent between a higher yield Eurobond and a semiannual bond. The calculation of the equivalent yield on a Eurobond that would be necessary to equal the yield on a semiannual bond is given by the equation below:

$$E = r(1 + r/400),$$

where

$E$ = annual equivalent yield

$r$ = semiannual yield (percent)

For example, to be equivalent to a bond paying interest annually and yielding 10 percent per annum to redemption, a Eurobond would have to yield 10.25 percent.

A significant volume of straight bonds in the past have been issued with attached warrants representing a securitized call or, in some instances, put options for currencies, commodities, debt, or equities. Equity warrants will be covered in the next major section.

## Debt Warrants

Beginning in 1983, many issues of straight debt were floated with attached warrants allowing the holder to purchase further debt of the borrower at a fixed price. These warrants were basically equivalent to long-term interest-rate call options. They were primarily used for U.S. dollar bonds but were also used extensively in the Euro-DM sector. The high yields in the U.S. dollar sector made them attractive for investors since the perceived trend of interest rates was down and the call options offered a highly leveraged instrument that produced spectacular returns.

Another motivation for investors to buy the warrants was a protection against a drop in the value of the U.S. dollar on the foreign-exchange market, while at the same time participating in the rally on the U.S. dollar bond market. Through the warrant, which usually cost US\$ 50 to 100, a much larger bond position could be assumed and any gain would be made on the entire bond position, while any foreign exchange loss would be limited to the smaller amount paid for the warrant.

A typical debt warrant issue would be structured as follows: US\$ 200 million, 10 years, $13\frac{1}{2}$ percent at par, callable in 2 years at 102 percent, with warrants allowing the holder to purchase a bond with the same maturity bearing a $12\frac{1}{2}$ percent coupon at par.

This structure allowed borrowers to automatically refinance their debt at lower rates of interest, should yields decline. The call option on the host bond was utilized, and since the warrant was deeply in the money it would be exercised at expiration or before. The coupon on the new debt, the back bond, is significantly lower than on the host bond.

Rather than employing theoretical option pricing models (e.g., Black-Scholes), traders of debt warrants in the Euromarkets rely on break-even yields to determine value. For example, a US\$ 45 warrant with a life of two years that is exercisable into a 10-year, 10 percent bond at par (US\$ 1,000) implies an eight-year bond yield of 9.18 percent (AIBD yield basis) in two years. At this yield the warrant will be worth US\$ 45 at expiration. The 9.18 percent will be compared with the present yield on eight-year bonds to judge the warrant's value.

A variation to the above structure, which was popular for a time in the mid-1980s, was the concept of "harmless" warrants. One of the major disadvantages of normal debt warrants is that their exercise could, if the host bond does not have the corresponding call rights, result in an increase in outstanding debt of the borrower. This would result in a deterioration of balance sheet positions and ratios and perhaps a downgrading of credit quality.

The harmless warrant is intended to avoid these difficulties by providing for exercise of the warrants only by exchanging the host bond for the underlying back bond during the first half of the warrants' life. Only during the second half of the warrants' life can the warrants be exercised against cash, but during this period the borrower has a call right for the host bonds. The harmless warrant thus represents the securitization of the call right on the host bond. Through these conditions, the outstanding volume of debt can be maintained at a constant level.

## Currency Warrants

The issuance of currency warrants in connection with the flotation of a Eurobond is usually an arbitrage operation. The borrower, and hence the writer of the currency option, is able to secure a higher premium on the options he is selling than the premium he has to pay for his hedge to cover his exposure.

A net gain is only possible if there is some reason why investors cannot directly purchase the options used as the hedge. It may be that large denominations make the OTC options unattractive for retail investors who may nevertheless be attracted to the warrants either as a hedge or as a leveraged investment instrument. Also, some institutional investors are prohibited by law or by their own internal rules from purchasing securities that are not listed on an exchange. Listed warrants would consequently satisfy this requirement and the borrower can earn a profit in doing so.

## Commodity Warrants

Two commodities have been used as the basis for warrant issues in the Euromarket: gold and oil. Gold warrants attached to a fixed-rate bond offer a particularly attractive package since the return on the package should be protected against inflation by the inclusion of the call options for gold.

The borrower, on the other hand, faces the problem of hedging risk. Some issues of gold warrants are naturally hedged because they have been issued by gold mining companies that would profit from a gold price increase.

Other borrowers, however, unless they are prepared to accept the unlimited risk of an open position, must purchase a hedge that would cost less than the warrants attached to the bond issue.

## Other Fixed-Rate Debt Instruments

Besides these innovations, dual-currency, partly-paid, and indexed bonds have been floated on the Euromarkets.

*Dual-Currency Bonds.* Dual-currency bonds pay interest in one currency while the bonds are redeemed in a different currency. They therefore resemble a portfolio of annuity and zero coupon bonds in two different currencies. The composition of the portfolio is determined by the conditions of the bond at issuance. Since it should be possible to replicate the cash flows in the different currencies, there are obvious arbitrage possibilities that can be exploited. The most commonly used variety on the Euromarkets in recent years has been a bond that pays interest in yen and is redeemed in U.S. dollars. The structure resembles that of indexed bonds whose redemption is a function of exchange rates. Other indexed bonds, primarily in the yen sector, have been linked to yields in the U.S. Treasury market.

*Partly-Paid Bonds.*   Partly-paid bonds have played only a limited role in the Euromarket and only in certain situations. The partly-paid structure proved attractive in the mid-1980s when the dollar began to decline in the foreign-exchange market and U.S. dollar yields fell from very high levels. The partly-paid structure represents a call option that will profit from lower interest rates, while the absolute exposure to U.S. dollar foreign-exchange-rate risk is kept at a low level.

## VARIABLE-RATE DEBT INSTRUMENTS IN THE EUROMARKETS

Variable-rate debt instruments in the Euromarket include capital market instruments (floating-rate notes) as well as money market instruments (Euronotes and Eurocommercial paper) with long facility lives.

### Floating-Rate Notes

Floating-rate notes (FRNs) are typically long-term variable-rate bonds linked to interest rates in the money markets and issued primarily by banks, sovereign borrowers, U.S. savings and loan associations, and U.K. building societies. Exhibit 24–4 shows the size of the floating-rate note Eurobond market in 1989 by currency (over US$ 20 billion). Normally, coupons on FRNs in the Euromarket are based upon one of the London interbank rates (LIBOR, LIMEAN, or LIBID), but other base rates have been used, including the following: rates on U.S. Treasury bills, the Japanese prime rate, and an average yield on short-term French government bonds. The following innovative structures have been used with Euro-FRNs: mismatched, capped, and perpetual.

*Mismatched FRNs.*   Mismatched floaters exploit an investment technique to allow the issuer to achieve a reduction in the coupon paid. If the yield curve has a positive slope—its normal shape—financing a FRN with shorter-dated money than the coupon reset period will result in an increase in the return on the bond.

For example, if a FRN has a coupon of six-month LIBOR reset semiannually, then financing the FRN position with three-month money will produce

**EXHIBIT 24–4**
**Issue Volume by Currency: Floating-Rate Notes Eurobonds** (US$ Million Equivalent)

| Currency | 1989 |
|---|---|
| U. S. dollar | 8,978 |
| Japanese yen | 1,074 |
| U. K. pound | 8,255 |
| New Zealand dollar | 0 |
| French franc | 176 |
| Australian dollar | 92 |
| Deutschemark | 2,368 |
| Total | 20,943 |

a pickup in return. Assume that at the coupon fixing, six-month LIBOR is 8 percent, while three-month LIBOR is $7\frac{7}{8}$ percent. The one-eighth percentage point differential between six-month and three-month money can be used to increase the return by financing at $7\frac{7}{8}$ percent for three months and then rolling forward. The investor must accept that three-month LIBOR in three months may be above the 8 percent coupon, thus reducing the return and perhaps producing a loss.

A mismatched FRN would pay, for example, six-month LIBOR but the coupon would be reset every three months. This would consequently reduce the risk an investor bears since only when the interest-rate structure is inverted does the financing with three-month money reduce the return. Borrowers are able to reduce the coupons on their FRN accordingly. Naturally, mismatched FRNs are popular in times of very steep yield curves.

*Capped FRNs.* A capped FRN has a maximum coupon beyond which the adjustment to higher base rates no longer takes place. This is conceptually equal to a put option on the coupon at the capped rate. The bond investor is the writer of the option and must be compensated for the risk by a higher return on this type of FRN compared with a conventional one. The issuer of the FRN can then either hold the option or sell it to a third party, thus reducing the total cost of financing. Numerous FRNs in the Euro-DM sector have been capped.

*Perpetual FRNs.* Beginning in 1985 and continuing into 1986, a large volume of FRNs without a redemption date were launched by U.K., Canadian, and U.S. banks. These FRNs were structured in order to meet the guidelines of the respective central banks to be considered as part of the issuing banks' primary capital. In numerous cases, the coupons were linked in some manner to the dividend on the bank's stock. In all cases, the FRNs were subordinated debt. All told, about US$ 15 billion of undated FRNs had been offered in the Euromarket by the latter half of 1986.

As of early 1988, prices in this sector of the FRN market experienced a major deterioration as investors became concerned about the liquidity of their assets and sold large quantities of bonds to the market makers. Prices declined to exceptionally large discounts and, even at these low prices, there was no significant investor interest. The primary market for perpetual FRNs had been effectively closed.

## Euronotes and Eurocommercial Paper

Note issuance facilities (NIFs) are credit facilities with long maturities (five to seven years usually) in which the borrower can obtain funds up to a maximum amount by issuing short-term money market paper over the life of the facility. The first facility of this kind was arranged for New Zealand in 1981, but the real growth in this sector began in 1984.

Exhibit 24–5 shows the size and relative composition of the Euromarket short-term financing facilities market in 1988–89. In 1989 Eurodollar commercial paper and certificates of deposit were US$ 46 billion, Euro medium-term notes over $15 billion, note issuance facilities about $7 billion, and sterling commercial paper and certificates of deposit $740 million.

NIFs have been given a variety of other names to reflect small differences in their organization (e.g., revolving underwriting facilities [RUFs], transferrable underwriting facilities [TRUFs]) but they all have the same basic structure: A banking consortium is required either to take up notes issued or to provide a credit to the borrower. Often the function of placing agents (those banking

**EXHIBIT 24–5**
**Euromarket Short-Term Financing**
**Facilities** (US$ Million Equivalent)

|                         | 1988   | 1989   |
| ----------------------- | ------ | ------ |
| Euro$ CP and CD         | 45,733 | 45,502 |
| Euro MTNs               | 17,850 | 15,239 |
| Note issuance facilities | 15,250 |  6,657 |
| Sterling CP and CD      |  1,008 |    740 |
| Total                   | 79,841 | 68,138 |

and taking the paper) and underwriters (those banks providing credit) is divided among different banks. A tender panel is also sometimes used to bid for the notes and to provide a market element in determining the price.

The fact that the standby credits involved in NIFs represent off-balance-sheet contingent risks for banks caused regulatory authorities to begin requiring provisions to be made for these risks with primary capital, thus decreasing the attractiveness of this instrument for both the banks and the borrowers. Some quality borrowers were capable of doing without the standby credit—the risk being small that their paper would not find demand (the programs developed along these lines were similar to the U.S. commercial paper facilities). Growth in these nonunderwritten facilities accelerated between 1986 and 1988, and the trend is clearly to utilize Eurocommercial paper rather than NIFs.

## EQUITY WARRANT AND CONVERTIBLE ISSUES IN THE EUROMARKETS

### Fixed-Rate Bonds with Equity Warrants

Fixed-rate bonds with equity warrants attached have been very popular in the Euromarkets beginning in the middle 1980s. The long period of rising stock prices meant that investors preferred the leverage provided by the securitized call options to the downside protection offered by convertible bonds. Issuers found equity warrant issues attractive because of the low cost of debt—at times 500 to 600 basis points below capital market yields—and the advantageous swaps that these issues produced.

For swap purposes, the equity warrant instrument is preferable to the convertible. The end maturity of the debt is known because the warrants can be separated from the bond and traded—or exercised—separately. The currency of choice for equity-linked Eurobonds is still the U.S. dollar. See Exhibit 24–6, which also indicates the size of the equity-linked Euromarket in 1989 (over US$ 71 billion).

### Bonds with Ex Warrants

The bond "ex warrants" often offer yields significantly higher than straight bonds in the same currency because the market perceives the liquidity of "ex bonds" to be limited. They are, therefore, available to produce attractive floating-rate assets, either through a conventional asset swap or as repackaged FRNs in which the bonds are used as collateral.

**EXHIBIT 24–6**
**Issue Volume by**
**Currency: Equity-**
**Linked Eurobonds**\*
(US$ Million Equivalent)

| Currency | 1989 |
| --- | --- |
| U. S. dollar | 65,372 |
| U. K. pound | 1,640 |
| Deutschemark | 3,934 |
| Dutch guilder | 504 |
| ECU | 69 |
| Australian dollar | 0 |
| Total | 71,519 |

\* Excluding repackaged debt

## Convertibles

Convertibles have been used in the Euromarket almost from its inception, with U.S. corporations making extensive use of this instrument. Maturities on convertibles are usually longer than equity warrant issues, with 15 years being a very common maturity. Convertibles are popular in the pound sterling sector, where equity warrant issues have been scarce.

## EUROEQUITY MARKET

In 1986 and 1987, the placement of equity via the Euromarket accelerated substantially. The development of a Euroequity market was seen as a normal continuation of the growth of the Euromarkets and also as a welcome replacement for a drop in both profitability and volume in the Eurobond primary market.

The reason for the development of a Euroequity market—which represents the simultaneous placement of a company's equity in several different countries, with or without listing on a stock exchange in that country—was to enable a large volume of business that would not have been possible in a single market without disruption. The enormous privatization issues conducted by the United Kingdom and France during this period were greatly simplified by this worldwide placement.

# BORROWING IN THE EUROMARKET

## Rationale

In surveying the international markets, a prospective borrower is faced with the problem of deciding where capital should be raised. This decision is based on three fundamental criteria: (1) cost effectiveness, (2) diversification effects, and (3) wider-ranging goals.

*Cost-Effectiveness.* The cost-effectiveness of floating a Eurobond is to be judged relative to the cost of a bond issued either in the domestic or in the respective foreign bond market. In some currencies, there is no distinction between the Euromarket and the foreign bond market (e.g., DM sector) or there is no Euromarket for that currency (e.g., Swiss franc). For the largest sector—the Eurodollar bond market—the cost advantage will be determined by comparing the cost of issues of a bond offered in the U.S. market and of a dollar bond placed in the Japanese market with that of a Eurodollar bond.

There is no hard and fast rule as to which market will offer the more attractive terms and conditions, since the markets are quite often so volatile that the cheapest market can change daily. Statistical analysis of bond yields on the Euromarket indicates a significant influence of the foreign-exchange market on yield differentials between the Euromarket and U.S. Treasury yields.

*Diversification Effects.* In times of a weak U.S. currency, spreads between these two markets widen; conversely, a strong dollar usually results in smaller spreads. Eurodollar financings will consequently be most favorable when the dollar is rising. The U.S. domestic or Yankee market will probably offer more attractive yields for borrowers in periods of dollar weakness.

The cost will also be a function of the maturity of financing being sought. Only rarely is the Euromarket open to issues with maturities beyond 10 years; longer-dated offerings are usually more advantageous on the domestic or foreign bond market.

Another consideration, which may even outweigh a cost disadvantage of a Eurofinancing, is the possibility of opening new financing sources for the borrower. Quite often, Eurocommercial paper programs are established to complement rather than to replace existing US$ programs. The retail nature of a number of the Euromarkets makes it imperative that a borrower's name be widely known if attractive terms are to be achieved.

*Wider-Ranging Goals.* Finally, the decision to issue a Eurobond or another financing vehicle in the Euromarket may be in furtherance of a more far-reaching strategy. Corporate borrowers may utilize the launching of a Eurobond to hold roadshows in the countries of the underwriting banks. This may aid considerably the subsequent flotation and listing of its shares in that country. Similarly, supranational organizations may have it as their policy to tap as many different markets as possible to increase their visibility and diversify their balance sheets.

## Underwriting and Syndication

In the Eurobond market, as it has evolved, the bought deal predominates. This means that the complete terms of a new issue are agreed upon between the lead managers and the borrower prior to launching. This contrasts with most other bond markets where the issue price is left open during the subscription period. Terms on equity and equity-linked financings in the Euromarket are, however, usually left open during the subscription period.

It is clear that the bought deal increases the risk that underwriting banks must bear in the market, and this is reflected in the fee structure. In the U.S. domestic market, the gross spread (i.e., total fees, including management, underwriting, and selling) is significantly lower than on Eurobond issues. For 10-year issues, for example, total fees on a Eurodollar bond issue are usually around 250 basis points, while on a comparable US$-denominated security, total fees of 60 to 80 basis points are common. Another feature of syndication in the Euromarket is the lack, quite often, of a separate selling group, with the underwriting banks accomplishing the selling and distribution of new issues.

The so-called club deal has also been utilized on numerous occasions in the Euromarket. In this form of syndication a management group accomplishes all three functions necessary in a bond flotation: management, underwriting, and placement.

## Borrower Profiles

*Overall Trends.*   Exhibits 24–7 and 24–8 illustrate the transforming profile of borrowers on the Euromarkets. Two different profiles are presented—by borrower category (i.e., corporates, sovereigns, etc., in Exhibit 24–7), and by borrower geographic region (i.e., Europe, the Americas, Asia, etc., in Exhibit 24–8)—during three time periods (1975, 1980, 1989). Regarding borrower category, note the relative increase in corporate borrowing (46 percent in 1975 to 74 percent in 1989) and relative decrease in sovereign and state-guaranteed borrowing (see Exhibit 24–7). Regarding borrower geographic region, note the relative decrease in European borrowing and the relative increase in Asian borrowing (see Exhibit 24–8). (It is interesting that the American percentage increased between 1975 and 1980 and then came back down.)

**EXHIBIT 24–7**

**Borrowers on the Euromarkets** (by Market Share)

| Category | 1975 | 1980 | 1989 |
|---|---|---|---|
| Corporates | 46.4 | 55.5 | 74.2 |
| State-guaranteed | 27.8 | 21.6 | 12.7 |
| Sovereign | 20.4 | 14.0 | 6.2 |
| Supranationals | 5.4 | 8.9 | 6.9 |
| Total | 100.0 | 100.0 | 100.0 |

Relative size, however, is probably less important than absolute size. It is critical to appreciate the enormous increase in the absolute size of the Euromarkets—from US$ 6.59 billion in 1975 to US$ 19.66 billion in 1980 to US$ 219.15 billion in 1989. Consequently, a percentage decrease in *relative* market share between 1975 and 1989 would still mean a very large increase in absolute size.

*Corporate Borrowers.* In the formative years, 1965 to 1975, corporate borrowers dominated the Eurobond markets, issuing up to 75 percent of total new issue volume. By 1975, however, the combination of sovereign and state-guaranteed borrowing together with a significant amount of new issues for supranational borrowers (e.g., World Bank, Inter-American Development Bank) had reduced the market share of corporate borrowers to below 50 percent. During the next 10 years, however, the percentage amount of new corporate debt increased again.

*Sovereign Borrowers.* One reason for this increase was the decline in the market share accounted for by sovereign borrowers. The debt crisis in the early

**EXHIBIT 24–8**

**Borrowers on the Euromarkets by Geographic Region** (by Market Share)

| Region | 1975 | 1980 | 1989 |
|---|---|---|---|
| Europe | 53.1 | 47.4 | 37.2 |
| Americas | 18.6 | 32.1 | 11.6 |
| Asia | 11.8 | 7.8 | 40.7 |
| Supranationals | 5.5 | 8.9 | 6.9 |
| Others | 11.0 | 3.8 | 3.6 |
| Total | 100.0 | 100.0 | 100.0 |

1980s had a strong impact on the market since numerous countries, which had previously tapped the Euromarket, were no longer in a position to launch bond issues. Also, the improvement in the trade balance of a number of European countries, which had been financing their trade shortfall through Eurobond issues, meant that the supply of sovereign debt no longer grew at the rapid rates of the late 1970s and early 1980s.

*Privatization.* The other part of public sector borrowing in the Euromarket—public-owned enterprises—also fell relative to the total market. This reflected the privatization of government-owned industry and banks in the 1980s; there were fewer companies that could be granted a government guarantee and that in turn financed their capital needs in the Euromarket.

*Declining Offering Size.* Geographically, the most striking development is the decline of the relative size of European borrowings. There were two major reasons for this. Much of the European borrowing in the 1970s and early 1980s was associated with sovereign borrowing to finance current account deficits. With the improvement in the current account situation of these countries later in the 1980s, the amount of new debt floated by these countries has declined.

*Japanese Borrowers.* More important, however, was the strong rise of the share accounted for by Asian borrowers, reflecting the increasing importance of Japan on the world capital markets. Japanese banks have greatly increased their operations in many national and international sectors, and this opened the way for Japanese companies to tap more sources of capital. In the Eurodollar sector alone, Japanese borrowers floated equity-warrant and convertible issues worth US$ 31 billion between 1985 and the end of 1987.

## INVESTING IN THE EUROMARKET

### Investor Base

Investors in the Euromarkets can be divided into three general categories: private individuals (usually referred to as retail investors), institutional clients (pension funds, central banks, etc.), and corporate investors. The relative importance of each of these different types of investors depends upon the currency sector in question.

*Retail Investors.* Some, such as the Australian and New Zealand dollar markets, are predominantly retail markets, with institutional involvement minimal. Retail markets are almost always characterized by high nominal coupons, which appeal to investors in countries with low interest rates.

*Professional Investors.* The U.S. dollar sector, on the other hand, is mainly used by professional investors who value Eurodollar bonds, based on two considerations: the yield spread to the U.S. Treasury market and the liquidity of the issue.

*Issue Size.* Issue size, although an important consideration, is primarily a function of the willingness on the part of banks to make markets in the issue. This is a consequence of the fact that in the Euromarket the volume of business transacted on the telephone dwarfs that conducted on exchanges.

## Clearing Systems

In the early years of the Eurocapital markets, settlement of trades was done by physical delivery of securities and payment by check. This system was inherently costly, risky, and, as trading volumes rapidly increased, impractical.

Consequently, in the late 1960s, two clearing systems for the Euromarket were established: Euroclear (1968) in Brussels and Cedel (1970) in Luxembourg. These two systems transact with themselves and with the various national clearing systems — for example, the Kassenvereine in Germany, Sicovam in France, Sega in Switzerland, and the Depository Trust Company in the United States. These systems accept a wide variety of securities, both domestic and international.

The Euroclear and Cedel systems provide the following services:

1. *Custodial Services.* Securities are deposited for safekeeping and clearing purposes; both primary and secondary market activities are offered. Coupon payments and redemptions are handled.
2. *Settlement of Trades.* Euromarket and national markets.
3. *Banking Services.* Money transfer and credit facilities.
4. *Primary Market Distribution.*
5. *International Equities.* Settlement of primary and secondary market transactions.
6. *Securities Lending and Borrowing.*

## NATIONAL MARKETS IN EUROPE

Europe as an economic entity can be compared with the United States and Japan. The gross national product of Europe is comparable with that of the United States. From an economic point of view, Europe has been united in the European Economic Community. The European Monetary System, which combines the major European currencies, has as its purpose the maintenance of stable currency exchange rates.

Various economic and political relations are reflected in the close cooperation between the European governments and central banks. Efforts for further integration have been given impetus by the plan to create a single internal market in Europe by 1992. Besides being viewed as a major economic entity, the European capital market can also be seen as a bloc in competition with the U.S. and Japanese markets.

The world bond market can be divided into three large blocs: the US$ bloc with a share of 48 percent; the European bloc with 28 percent; and the Yen bloc with 23 percent (see Exhibit 24–1). With respect to the stock markets, the percentages are as follows: Japan 38 percent, U.S. 35 percent, Europe 22 percent, and the remainder 5 percent (as of October 1987).

In 1988, the four leading national markets in Europe accounted for more than two thirds of the European bond market (Germany, 26 percent; Italy, 19.6 percent; U.K., 9.9 percent; France, 13.4 percent—see Exhibit 24–9a). When only government bonds are considered, although the overall big four percentage is higher at more than 75% of the market, there is a significant re-allocation among them (Italy, 35 percent; U.K., 17 percent; Germany, 15 percent; France, 9 percent—see Exhibit 24–9b).

**EXHIBIT 24–9a**
**1988 European Market Capitalization: All Bonds** (US$ Million Equivalent)

|  | Volume | %
Market |
| --- | --- | --- |
| Germany | 730 | 26.4 |
| Italy | 543 | 19.6 |
| United Kingdom | 274 | 9.9 |
| France | 371 | 13.4 |
| Belgium | 95 | 3.4 |
| Denmark | 160 | 5.8 |
| Sweden | 140 | 5.1 |
| Switzerland | 144 | 5.2 |
| Netherlands | 134 | 4.8 |
| Austria | 54 | 2.0 |
| ECU | 41 | 1.5 |
| Spain | 79 | 2.9 |
| Total | 2,765 | 100.0 |

**EXHIBIT 24–9b**
**1988 European Bond Market Capitalization: Government Bonds Only** (US$ Million Equivalent)

|  | Volume | %
Market |
| --- | --- | --- |
| Germany | 176 | 14.6 |
| Italy | 420 | 34.7 |
| United Kingdom | 207 | 17.1 |
| France | 112 | 9.3 |
| Belgium | 67 | 5.6 |
| Denmark | 44 | 3.6 |
| Sweden | 51 | 4.2 |
| Switzerland | 7 | 0.6 |
| Netherlands | 80 | 6.6 |
| Austria | 9 | 0.7 |
| Spain | 36 | 3.0 |
| Total | 1,209 | 100.0 |

# CHAPTER 25

## GUARANTEED INVESTMENT CONTRACTS*

*Kenneth L. Walker*
President
*T. Rowe Price Guaranteed Asset Advisors, Inc.*

*Klaus O. Shigley, FSA*
Vice President
*The John Hancock Mutual Life Insurance Company*

## WHAT IS A GIC?

The term "guaranteed return" has enabled the life insurance industry to develop a major asset class with characteristics unique unto itself and unmatched by any competing asset class. The buyer of a GIC obtains an investment that provides a nonfluctuating principal value as interest rates rise and fall.

The term *GIC* is generally defined as a *guaranteed investment contract*. It sometimes is also referred to as a *guaranteed income contract*, *guaranteed interest contract*, or *guaranteed insurance contract*. Whatever term is used, the instrument implies the same meaning—a guarantee of principal and a predetermined rate of interest to be credited over the investment's life.

The stability of returns is provided through the GIC's valuation basis. Unlike stocks and bonds, which are valued at fair market, GICs are valued for financial reporting purposes in defined contribution plans at book or par value. Pursuant to FASB 87, defined benefit plans may be required to value GICs at their fair value, a term generally meant to include a valuation based on current market yields.

---

*This chapter represents a compilation of excerpts from *Guaranteed Investment Contracts: Risk Analysis and Portfolio Strategies*, published by Business ONE-Irwin.

The term "guarantee" implies that the insurer is guaranteeing the principal and the interest rate. In actuality, the guarantee only applies to the interest rate (or formula) and expense schedule. Though the guarantee may imply the protection of principal, that guarantee is only as good as the insurer's claims-paying ability.

It is often argued that the insurer's payback ability is equivalent to a corporate debenture. Although it is not legally accurate, an analogy can be drawn between the two instruments. A debtholder enjoys a lien position as a general creditor, as dictated in the corporate indenture. A corporate debt issue's payback ability is supported by its earnings power and may be collateralized by specific assets.

A GIC owner becomes a policyholder of the insurer. In most states, policyholders enjoy a senior lien over the general creditors of the insurer. In an insurance company bankruptcy, the policyholder generally ranks ahead of the general creditors.

## THE GENERAL ACCOUNT, SEPARATE ACCOUNT, AND SUBSIDIARIES

Insurance companies provide pooled investment products in two ways: through the general account and through separate accounts. GICs and annuities are predominantly issued through the general account, become liabilities of the issuing company, and enjoy the full backing of the issuer. Sometimes GICs are issued through a separate account. The concern becomes whether or not equivalent payback protection is provided for GICs issued through the separate account. Generally, when GICs are issued through a separate account, the backing of the general account is afforded to the policyholders.

The general account is the portfolio of unpledged assets of the insurance company. These assets meet the general obligations of the insurer without any priority on those obligations and with no separate identification of assets for any particular policy. Investments are made primarily in bonds, common and preferred stocks, mortgage loans, real estate, private placement issues, and other eligible investments.

The separate account is an account established by the insurer to hold assets of a determinable group of policyholders. Stock, bond, real estate, and money market funds are typically issued through a separate account. When GICs are issued through the separate account, it is usually done to allow the insurer the ability to better account for the amount of GICs outstanding, including the allocation of supporting assets from the investment department, the management of the asset/liability structure of the guaranteed instruments from other product lines, and better allocation of associated expenses. The use of the GIC separate account becomes one of management and bookkeeping convenience.

In recent years, a number of insurance companies have created pension subsidiaries. Many have done so for the segmentation and issuance of pension investment products and/or for tax-related reasons. In this parent/subsidiary relationship, the financial strength of the subsidiary may or may not be as solid as that of the parent. The subsidiary may be undercapitalized, with the parent maintaining minimum statutorily required capital and surplus. Many subsidiaries' incomes are derived from single product lines, something that no analyst likes to see. Pyramiding of surplus can result from one dollar of true surplus in the subsidiary company being shown in each and every parent company in the pyramid of companies forming the corporate structure. Evaluation of reinsurance activities can compound the quality assessment since the parent can provide surplus relief through an internal letter of credit. In buying from the pension subsidiary, the purchaser must assess the level of protection provided by the parent company.

## Who Are the Buyers?

Who are the buyers of qualified GICs? At the plan sponsor level, those who desire to provide a conduit for a perceived relative risk-free investment and whose returns do not fluctuate use GICs. As shown in Exhibit 25–1, GICs are an integral component of the investment structure of defined contribution plans.

When the participant is given the right to select among several investment options, the GIC option is often the most popular choice, as shown in Exhibit 25–2. Over one third of all 401(k) assets are committed to GICs.

Defined benefit plans typically have not had interest in GICs when yields are below double digits. In addition, their usage is primarily yield spread driven. Many who bought in the late 1970s and early 1980s dropped out of the market for new purchases when yields declined in 1982. Over intervals of a complete market rate cycle, the yield premium provided by the equivalent "private-placement" GIC yield spreads varies, as illustrated in Exhibit 25–3. At higher rate levels, the spread tends to widen on a relative basis. At lower rate levels, the spread tends to narrow on a relative basis. (Note the exception to this general rule for the year 1986.)

In the early 1980s, GIC yields approximated the returns expected from the traditional equity and bond markets. If investors had asked their equity managers at that time what the projected annualized total returns would have been over the upcoming three to five years, most managers would have responded with a figure in the 14–16 percent range. Total returns of 12–14 percent were typically projected for bond portfolios. It is no wonder that when a guaranteed annualized compounded return of 14 percent could be negotiated for a five-year period, many pension plans bought GICs.

Those pension funds that have always used GICs as a part of the investment portfolio have done so for a number of reasons. First, they may have wanted to protect an overfunded status for actuarial purposes. Second, some plan sponsors like to maintain downside protection for a percentage of the portfolio. Third, there has been a shift in focus among many plan sponsors toward a more pas-

**EXHIBIT 25–1**
**How Asset Mix Varies with Type of Plan**

| Type of Investment | Pension Plans | All Defined Contributions Plans | Profit Sharing Plans | Savings and Thrift Plans | 401(k) Plans | Combined Plans |
|---|---|---|---|---|---|---|
| *Common Stocks* | | | | | | |
| Active | 38.6% | 11.1% | 11.5% | 6.7% | 13.9% | 12.5% |
| Company stock | 0.7 | 26.0 | 29.3 | 21.2 | 28.5 | 27.1 |
| Passive | 12.5 | 4.7 | 4.5 | 4.7 | 5.7 | 3.7 |
| Total domestic stocks | 51.9 | 41.8 | 45.3 | 32.6 | 48.1 | 43.2 |
| *International Stocks* | | | | | | |
| Active | 4.6 | 0.6 | 0.9 | 0.1 | 0.1 | 0.7 |
| Passive | 0.4 | 0.1 | * | 0.0 | 0.0 | 0.2 |
| Total international stocks | 5.0 | 0.7 | 0.9 | 0.1 | 0.1 | 0.8 |
| *Bonds* | | | | | | |
| Active | 17.1 | 6.3 | 11.2 | 1.6 | 2.5 | 7.8 |
| Immunized or dedicated | 4.8 | 0.1 | 0.1 | * | 0.1 | 0.1 |
| Other passive | 2.9 | 0.5 | 0.5 | 0.1 | 0.3 | 0.5 |
| Total bonds | 24.7 | 6.9 | 11.8 | 1.7 | 2.9 | 8.4 |
| *Other* | | | | | | |
| Guaranteed investment contracts | 2.6 | 41.2 | 25.4 | 59.2 | 38.4 | 39.4 |
| Equity real estate | 5.0 | 1.0 | 1.3 | * | 0.2 | 1.3 |
| Cash and short-term securities | 6.5 | 6.7 | 13.0 | 3.8 | 8.0 | 5.3 |
| Other | 3.5 | 1.8 | 2.2 | 2.6 | 2.6 | 1.4 |

Source: Greenwich Associates: "Large Corporate Pensions 1989, Report to Participants."

**EXHIBIT 25–2**
**How Asset Mix of 401(k) Plans Varies with Plan Assets**

| Type of Investment | Total Companies | Over $500 Million | $201–500 Million | $50–200 Million | Under $50 Million |
|---|---|---|---|---|---|
| | | *Common Stocks* | | | |
| Active | 9.8% | 9.1% | 8.5% | 15.6% | 14.2% |
| Company stock | 23.7 | 23.6 | 33.3 | 15.6 | 18.0 |
| Passive | 6.3 | 6.9 | 4.3 | 4.3 | 5.5 |
| Total domestic stocks | 39.8 | 39.6 | 46.1 | 35.4 | 37.7 |
| | | *International Stocks* | | | |
| Active | 0.5 | 0.6 | * | 0.1 | 0.0 |
| Passive | * | 0.0 | * | 0.0 | 0.0 |
| Total international stocks | 0.5 | 0.6 | 0.1 | 0.1 | 0.0 |
| | | *Bonds* | | | |
| Active | 2.7 | 2.2 | 2.2 | 5.1 | 8.7 |
| Immunized or dedicated | * | 0.0 | 0.1 | 0.3 | 0.0 |
| Other passive | 0.6 | 0.7 | 0.3 | 0.5 | 0.3 |
| Total bonds | 3.3 | 2.9 | 2.5 | 5.9 | 9.0 |
| | | *Other* | | | |
| Guaranteed investment contracts | 47.6 | 49.4 | 39.7 | 44.8 | 39.0 |
| Equity real estate | 0.5 | 0.6 | 0.3 | * | 0.0 |
| Cash and short-term securities | 6.3 | 5.7 | 5.4 | 11.3 | 9.2 |
| Other | 1.9 | 1.1 | 6.0 | 2.5 | 5.0 |

Mean is dollar-weighted. Projected to the Greenwich Associates universe of large corporations.

Source: Greenwich Associates, "Large Corporate Pensions 1989, Report to Participants."

sive form of management through the use of immunization programs, portfolio dedication, indexed funds, and GICs.

Defined contribution profit sharing and money purchase plans have historically used GICs for different reasons. Defined contribution plan usage is primarily driven by the principal guarantee and book value withdrawal features. The buyers in these plans incorporate GICs as a method of smoothing the volatility of returns from one year to the next. Since most defined contribution plans provide at least annual statements of account balances to the participants, the last thing a plan sponsor wants is to answer questions from participants about negative returns. Hence the use of GICs provides a complementary hedging

**EXHIBIT 25–3**
**GIC Yield Spreads** (Three-Year Maturity)

|      | High Rate | Low Rate | High Spread | Low Spread |
|------|-----------|----------|-------------|------------|
| 1982 | 16.25%    | 11.17%   | 1.86        | 0.71       |
| 1983 | 12.14     | 10.57    | 1.78        | 0.39       |
| 1984 | 13.56     | 10.75    | 0.82        | 0.06       |
| 1985 | 11.46     | 8.57     | 0.64        | 0.18       |
| 1986 | 8.84      | 7.14     | 1.02        | 0.27       |
| 1987 | 9.52      | 6.99     | 0.68        | −0.13      |
| 1988 | 9.12      | 7.54     | 0.34        | −0.13      |
| 1989 | 9.85      | 8.01     | 0.65        | −0.02      |

Assumes a $1 million deposit. Spread denotes yield spread over Treasuries.

Source: GIC yields obtained from The Laughlin Group, Portland, Oregon, and T. Rowe Price GIC Index.

strategy to other asset classes in the portfolio by providing downside principal protection.

With the explosive growth of the 401(k) marketplace in the early 1980s, the asset allocation process was rewritten. When the plan sponsor had the opportunity to shift the burden of asset allocation to the participant via employee directed plans, the sponsor was only too happy to do so. All the employer had to do was provide investment choices covering a spectrum of risk-return trade-offs with distinct characteristics: an equity fund, and a bond, money market, or GIC fund. Most chose to combine the equity and GIC options.

## TYPES OF GIC INSTRUMENTS

### Bullet Contracts

Bullet contracts are the largest single GIC vehicle. They are attractive investments because of their simple terms: a lump sum deposit, a preset simple or compound rate of interest, and a lump sum payment at maturity. Interest can either be reinvested at the contract rate or be paid periodically to the contractholder. Bullet contracts can be negotiated on a benefit-responsive basis to provide for the plan's liquidity needs.

Maturities range from one to twenty years. Many carriers have introduced short-term bullet GICs to compete in the short-term cash markets. It is not uncommon to see 30-day to 1-year issues being offered at substantial premiums over other short-term cash equivalents, thus allowing the use of short-term GICs in short-term oriented accounts.

An interesting facet of shorter term GICs is the periods when they are most often offered: usually at quarter-ends and predominantly during the months of September through November. Carriers often use these contracts as a financing tool, a bridge loan equivalent to finance the investments being purchased to back the underwriting of next year's window contracts.

## Window Contracts

A window GIC is designed to accept recurring deposits, usually from 3 to 12 months following issue. At the contract negotiation, a rate is committed for the deposits during the window period and continues to be credited throughout the holding period. Window GICs are utilized primarily for annual cash flows in 401(k) plans because they allow the plan sponsor to communicate a definite rate to plan participants.

The attractiveness of the window is its ability to provide a specific rate for plan-year deposits. This attractiveness, however, has its price. Because of the risks associated with the many unknowns of the window (e.g., timing and amounts of deposits and withdrawals, transfers to competing plan investment options, and interest-rate volatility risks), the carrier incorporates risk-contingency charges to cover these potential risks.

## Floating-Rate Contracts

The most revolutionary GIC to emerge in recent years is the floating-rate GIC, a contract whose rate changes periodically and is tied to a preestablished market benchmark, usually an established corporate or Treasury bond index. Some are tied to the short end of the yield curve, some to the longer end. Some are open-ended with predefined "advance notice" contract termination language (an equivalent "put" option); others have negotiated maturities.

The floater provides excellent upside potential in periods when interest rates are expected to rise. Most are benefit-responsive and accept recurring deposits. Those whose rate formulas are based on a percentage of the longer end of the yield curve often provide rates equivalent to intermediate three- and four-year fixed-rate investments.

Floating-rate GICs provide an excellent opportunity to hedge the market (i.e., position all or part of the portfolio to take advantage of upward movements in interest rates). If a percentage of the portfolio is committed to floaters, the balance invested in fixed-rate instruments provides protection against the downside movement in interest rates.

## Participating Contracts

Participating contracts provide participation in the actual investment experience of the insurer's supporting assets. Originally introduced decades ago as an open-ended arrangement (i.e. Deposit Administration and Immediate Participation Guarantee contracts), the latest generation has evolved into set maturity contracts.

Participating contracts can provide competitive returns, particularly in declining interest rate environments, where a positive total return in excess of the coupon yield occurs as the price of the supporting assets appreciate in value. As with other non-fixed rate guaranteed instruments, participating contracts provide a suitable hedge to declining rate movements.

## Derivatives/Synthetics

Look-alike GIC instruments are evolving, as investment advisors and investment bankers seek ways to replicate the GIC to compete directly with the insurers. Investment programs have been developed where the derivative or synthetic instrument is designed with the same underlying characteristics as the GIC. Strategies including interest rate SWAPs and reverse SWAPs, portfolios of mortgage-backed securities, and immunization programs are being introduced as a way for the buyer to 1) have greater control over the supporting assets, particularly from a credit/quality perspective and 2) to potentially realize returns over the life of the investment in excess of current spot GIC fixed rates. The true test is whether these alternatives that are not involved with a bank or insurance wrap will qualify for book value accounting treatment (which has yet to be tested as this chapter is written).

## Bank Investment Contracts

An important development in the GIC marketplace has been the introduction of Bank Investment Contracts. Although banks and savings and loans have been offering investment certificates to investment portfolios for years, the interest and availability of these instruments has increased tremendously in the past several years.

A BIC is the generic term for a deposit obligation. Unlike certificates of deposit (CDs) most BICs are issued as modified time deposit obligations. Time deposits issued to qualified retirement plans can provide for benefit liquidity, unlike CDs which can only provide for early termination, subject to withdrawal penalties. An active secondary market exists for CDs. None exists for time deposits. FDIC insurance is currently provided at the participant level, treating them as an equivalent depositor.

Whereas banks use a liability-based strategy, they approach the BIC as a deposit to support their lending activities. As such, their availability is subject to overall loan demand.

## "If" and "But" Contracts

Although their name may seem confusing, "if" and "but" contracts do exactly what the name implies. The contract can be a bullet or window contract. Its lump-sum book value maturity is provided only if the carrier is unwilling to renew or exceed the rate guarantee following the expiration of the initial terms (an equivalent call provision). But if the renewal rate is equal to or greater than the expiring rate, the contractholder is locked into a new contract whose terms are usually the same as the original guarantee period except for the guaranteed rate.

The long-term risk of this contract is that the new rate may not be competitive in a future rate environment and may in fact be only marginally higher than the previous rate. For buyers of GICs who like to know the maturity date in advance, use of these contracts may not provide that opportunity as holding them could develop into a perpetual relationship. A known maturity is only guaranteed in a declining interest-rate environment.

## Pooled GIC Funds

Pooled, or collective, GIC funds were introduced in the early 1980s. Designed primarily to accommodate smaller deposits through a pooling arrangement of many plans, their popularity was immediate, often providing more liberal underwriting terms and better yields than smaller plans could negotiate on an individual basis. Both closed-ended and open-ended funds have been developed, all with unique design formats. Most provide book value benefit withdrawals at the participant level and market value withdrawals at the plan level.

Open-ended pooled GIC funds provide a flexible investment conduit for those desiring a rate that coincides with general levels of interest rates. They provide diversification of carrier and maturity and offer the benefit of aggressive management by experienced investment professionals. Most funds provide instant liquidity for benefit withdrawals. Their yield generally exceeds short-term market rates, often providing longer term yields for shorter term funds.

For those seeking to arbitrage interest rates to take advantage of the higher yielding alternatives, pooled GIC funds provide that opportunity because of the lag effect of the investment yield. As rates decline, the lag effect produces rates that are higher than the current rates because the portfolio contains older, higher yielding contracts. Conversely, as rates move upward, the lag effect often produces yields that are below current rates.

Closed-ended funds are offered in two types: those that accept recurring deposits and those that accept lump-sum deposits. The former is similar to a window contract in that a rate is negotiated in advance for future, recurring deposits. The latter is similar to a bullet contract, accepting a one-time deposit that is held to the maturity of the fund.

The window fund is the most popular of the closed-ended funds. Plan sponsors who desire a known rate for future deposits or who wish to communicate a rate to the participants for future cash flow find the window fund to be an attractive depository.

## INVESTMENT CONSIDERATIONS OF THE INSURER

The insurance industry is in the liability management business. Every policy written creates a liability for the issuing carrier. It must manage this liability so as not to jeopardize the company's net worth.

A fundamental objective of the industry is to avoid the unknown risks (i.e., events that can undermine the product's pricing structure). In an effort to manage these unknown risks, insurance companies can employ various stringent actuarial and investment disciplines.

Exhibit 25–4 presents a menu of business strategies. Along one axis, or dimension, the insurer selects from a spectrum of interest-rate risks. Along the other dimension, the insurer selects from a spectrum of credit risks. Each location in the matrix represents a different business strategy. The lower right-hand box, for example, represents a business strategy characterized by an investment policy of large interest-rate bets and large credit bets. The objective becomes judging under what conditions the risks might be acceptable.

**EXHIBIT 25–4**
**Matrix of Business Strategies**

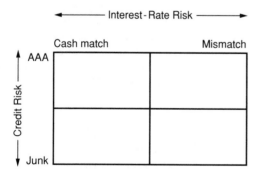

Which of these business strategies is best employed in the management of GIC contracts? Why are there such large differences in the guaranteed rates provided by otherwise similar insurance carriers? Why is the relationship between asset and liability duration so important?

To answer these questions, an understanding of how interest-rate risks are managed is important. Exhibit 25–5 illustrates five methods of managing the interest-rate risk. At one extreme, the interest rate risk can be managed by deliberate mismatching. This was the prevailing strategy for many financial institutions prior to 1980—most notably thrifts and savings banks, but also certain accounts maintained by insurance companies. At the other extreme, interest-rate risk can be managed by removing risk completely by matching each liability outflow with an asset inflow.

Between these two extremes, different degrees of exposure to interest-rate volatility can be selected. One strategy is to make limited bets on the direction of the general level of interest rates. This strategy is labeled as tactical interest-rate betting to distinguish the strategy from indiscriminate betting.

A more conservative strategy on the risk spectrum is to accept the exposure due to a change in the shape of the yield curve but not to changes in the general level of rates. This is referred to as duration matching.

A still more conservative strategy is to avoid exposure to most of the change in the shape of the yield curve as well as the general level of rates by matching both duration and convexity.

The motive for mismatching is to generate higher gross investment rates. An illustrative Treasury yield curve (see Exhibit 25–6) shows that an additional 148 basis points can be obtained if funds are invested in 10-year bonds to cover a 3-month liability. The investor can borrow funds for 3 months at a cost of 5.65 percent and invest them in 10-year instruments at the rate of 7.13 percent. (The adjustments over Treasuries are ignored.)

It is important to understand both the risks and the implications of mismatching. Exhibit 25–7 illustrates the risk of mismatch. The vertical axis rep-

**EXHIBIT 25–5**

**Managing Interest-Rate Risk**

- Mismatch
- Tactical Interest-Rate Bets
- Duration Matching
- Duration/Convexity Matching
- Cash Match

**EXHIBIT 25–6**

**Treasury Yield Curve (March 5, 1987)**

| Maturity | Yield | Spread vs. 3 Months |
|----------|-------|---------------------|
| 3 months | 5.65% | 0% |
| 6 months | 5.76 | .11 |
| 1 year | 5.88 | .23 |
| 5 years | 6.68 | 1.03 |
| 10 years | 7.13 | 1.48 |

**EXHIBIT 25–7**
**Asset/Liability Mismatch (Inefficient Exercise)**

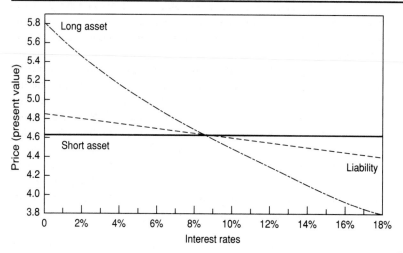

resents price; the horizontal axis represents interest rates. The three curves are the responses of the prices of a long- and short-maturity asset and an intermediate-term fixed liability to interest-rate changes.

The price function of the long-term asset has the greatest "slope," or price-per-unit change, in interest rate. The slope of a price function is a measure of its price volatility with respect to interest rates. This measure is more generally called duration.

The short-term asset has virtually no price volatility as indicated by its straight-line price function. Its duration (or the slope of its price function) is approximately zero. These price functions are graphical representations of the well-known fact that long-term fixed income assets have greater price risk (or volatility) than short-term fixed income assets. This illustration of price functions is useful for two reasons. First, it shows the potential consequence of a mismatch. Consider, for example, the gap between the liability curve and the long-term asset curve when rates rise and there is a duration mismatch (if the slopes of the price functions are not equal). Second, the exhibit illustrates how to use a specific weighted combination of a long- and a short-term asset to create a portfolio whose price function matches the slope (or price volatility) of an intermediate-term liability. This commonly used portfolio management technique is called barbelling.

The objective in matching the duration of liabilities and assets is to immunize surplus from interest-rate changes. If assets and liabilities have the same duration, they have equal price volatility (i.e., the relationships between assets and liabilities will be invariant if interest rates change). One should be cautioned at this point that the argument above has been oversimplified. Duration is merely the first-order term in an approximation for price volatility. The approximation is improved when the second-order term is added, commonly referred to as convexity—a measure of the curvature of the price function. Matching convexity as well as duration gives a better approximation of future price if the shape of the yield curve changes.

Why does anyone care what strategy an insurer uses to manage the interest risk? If it is believed that interest rates behave randomly (or that no one can correctly predict interest rates more than 50 percent of the time), then a strategy other than cash matching is a gamble. This is illustrated in Exhibit 25–8.

The greater the duration mismatch, the greater the gamble. A duration mismatch of two years, for example, carries with it a 2 percent probability of losing 4.92 percent of the net worth of an insurance company. Illustrated another way, if the insurer's equity is 4.92 percent of its liability, a strategy of a two-year duration mismatch has a 2 percent probability of insolvency, if the insurer sells only GICs. It should be noted that there is also a statistically symmetrical probability of earning 4.92 percent rather than losing it.

The statistical assertions above assume that interest rates behave randomly, and the changes in rates have a standard deviation of 15 percent. That is, if interest rates are initially at 8 percent, then 67 percent (or one standard deviation in either direction from the mean) of interest-rate outcomes next year will lie between 9.2 percent and 6.8 percent (i.e., $8\% \pm 1.2\%$, where 1.2% is 15% of 8%). This does not mean that such a bet is inherently unsound. It does mean that the insurer must have enough net worth to survive a losing bet. If the insurance company does not have sufficient resources, there is a residual probability labeled "insolvency probability target" that the plan sponsor will have to provide the needed funds.

If the insurer wishes to mismatch, then it must be prepared to risk more or less surplus, depending on the degree of confidence it has in the outcome. In general, most insurers operate at least at the 98 percent confidence level.

**EXHIBIT 25–8**
**Capital Requirements for Mismatch**

|  |  | Duration Mismatch in Years | | | |
|---|---|---|---|---|---|
|  |  | .5 | 1 | 2 | 5 |
| Probability of Insolvency | .33 | .26% | .53% | 1.06% | 2.64% |
|  | .10 | .77 | 1.54 | 3.07 | 7.68 |
|  | .05 | .98 | 1.97 | 3.94 | 9.84 |
|  | .02 | 1.43 | 2.46 | 4.92 | 12.30 |

Assumes: Parallel shifts, Interest rate: 8%, Standard deviation: 15%

The other dimension of risk is the credit risk. As indicated in Exhibit 25–9, there has been a significant spread over Treasuries for investing in junk bonds. The exhibit illustrates what happened in 1986. Spreads between junk bonds and Treasuries ranged from about 300 basis points to as much as 450 basis points.

The downside to this buying opportunity is the increased probability of default, which is indicated in Exhibit 25–10. As is illustrated in column 4, net default rates between 1970 and 1985 were as high as 11 percent.

It is fair to say that most insurance company managements aim to survive not merely the recession scenarios but also the depression scenarios. This implies that a portfolio must be supported by at least an 11 percent equity base.

For the purpose of supporting guarantees with junk bond portfolios, there is not much relevance to the average default rate of only 1.3 percent or 2.2 percent (depending on which observation period shown in Exhibit 25–10 is chosen). Merely providing for average default is not a real life, real answer solution. That would be analogous to walking off Anthony's Pier 4 into Boston Harbor and over to George's Island on the strength of the statistical observation that the average depth of Boston Harbor is five feet! To be viable as a strategy, investing in junk bonds carries with it the obligation not only to provide for average default but also to maintain sufficient capital to survive the disaster scenarios.

The focus thus far has been on the statistical consequences of aggressive business strategies. Have these potentially disastrous consequences deterred all

**EXHIBIT 25–9**

**Morgan Stanley Core Portfolio of Junk Bonds (Yield Spread vs. Treasury 13$\frac{1}{8}$s of 2001)**

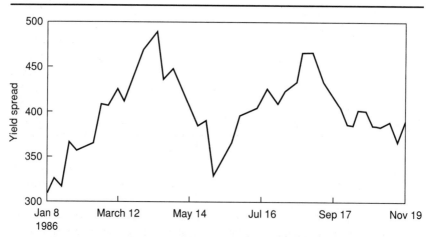

Note: Pronounced volatility of the spread between high-yield core issues and governments reflects the markets' short-term independence and provides profit opportunities for sector arbitrage.

**EXHIBIT 25–10**
**Historical Default Rates—Low-rated, Straight Debt Only**
**($ Millions)**

| Year | Par Value Outstanding with Utilities | Par Value Defaulted | Default Rate |
|------|------|------|------|
| 1985 | $59,078 | $992.10 | 1.679% |
| 1984 | 41,700 | 344.16 | 0.825 |
| 1983 | 28,233 | 301.08 | 1.066 |
| 1982 | 18,536 | 577.34 | 3.115 |
| 1981 | 17,362 | 27.00 | 0.155 |
| 1980 | 15.126 | 244.11 | 1.482 |
| 1979 | 10,675 | 20.00 | 0.187 |
| 1978 | 9,401 | 118.90 | 1.265 |
| 1977 | 8,479 | 380.57 | 4.488 |
| 1976 | 8,015 | 29.51 | 0.368 |
| 1975 | 7,720 | 204.10 | 2.644 |
| 1974 | 11,101 | 122.82 | 1.106 |
| 1973 | 8,082 | 49.07 | 0.607 |
| 1972 | 7,106 | 193.25 | 2.719 |
| 1971 | 6,643 | 82.00 | 1.234 |
| 1970 | 6,996 | 796.71 | 11.388 |
| Average default rate—1970 to 1985 | | | 2.205% |
| Average default rate—1974 to 1984 | | | 1.518 |
| Average default rate—1975 to 1985 | | | 1.570 |
| Average default rate—1978 to 1985 | | | 1.340 |

Source: Morgan Stanley, "High Yield Bonds: A Buying Opportunity."

the players from engaging in these strategies? No. As illustrated in Exhibit 25–11, financial institutions have positioned themselves all over the matrix.

Investment bankers for the most part deal in high-quality assets and hedge most of their interest risk. Savings banks have characteristically held short-term assets and made long-term loans, creating a mismatch. Commercial banks are for the most part match-funded but retain significant credit risk. Finance companies and leasing companies have assumed a good deal of both kinds of risks.

At first glance, it looks as though the financial service industry is an accident waiting to happen. Fortunately, two fundamental principles help to stabilize the industry.

The first principle is that, in order to generate similar comfort levels, capital markets will demand greater amounts of capital from financial service companies engaged in riskier strategies. Investment bankers are engaged in the least-risky strategy (except for their own accounts) and have capital on the order of 2 to 4 percent of liabilities. Commercial banks have approximately 7 percent.

**EXHIBIT 25–11**
**Matrix of Financial Institutions**

| | Cash match | Mismatch |
|---|---|---|
| **AAA** | Investment bankers | Savings banks |
| **Junk** | Commercial banks | Finance companies |

Interest-Rate Risk →
Credit Risk (AAA ↑ ... Junk ↓)

AAA finance and leasing companies normally have between 10 percent and 15 percent.

The second principle is that higher rated financial institutions will hold more equity than lower rated institutions. For companies engaged in similar strategies, those with more capital will get higher ratings from the major rating agencies.

How does all this explain the issue raised earlier about the large variation in GIC guarantees among otherwise similar insurance companies? The answer lies in the determination of the cost of capital and the capital allocation decision.

Exhibit 25–12 shows how return on equity is calculated for a spread-lending business such as the management of GICs. The basic idea (which is illustrated

**EXHIBIT 25–12**
**Return on Equity (ROE) Equation**

$$\frac{PM\% \cdot L + RIE\% \cdot E}{E} = ROE\% \text{ before tax}$$

$$\frac{.5\% \cdot \$100 + 9\% \cdot \$5}{\$5} = \frac{\$.95}{5} = 19\%$$

$$\frac{(1 - TR)(PM\%L + RIE\% \cdot E)}{E} = ROE\% \text{ after tax}$$

PM = Profit Margin
RIE = Return on Invested Equity
L  = Liability
E  = Equity
TR = Tax Rate

in the middle equation) is that, with $5 of capital, $100 of someone else's money can be borrowed, which can be invested at a spread of 50 basis points (or .5%). If the $5 is invested at 9 percent, then the total return on the $5 investment is 19 percent pretax. If $1000 were borrowed with $5 of capital and invested at a 50-basis-points spread, the return on investment would be 109 percent. It is unlikely, however, that a lender would loan $1000 to support a venture capitalized at $5 unless there were very little risk of failure.

Exhibit 25–13 illustrates where all this is leading. The exhibit shows the required profit margins for both 10 percent and 15 percent after-tax ROE targets for various capital allocations. A 15 percent after-tax ROE objective requires a net spread of 140 basis points between net investment income and the net guarantee to support a 10 percent capital allocation to the business.

Exhibit 25–13 also presents a sorting of capitalization ratios. Insurance companies are shown as being capitalized at 10 percent in contrast to the conventional perception that they are capitalized at 6 or 7 percent. This recognizes the reality that regulations force them to maintain redundant reserves.

Why are there such big differences in GIC guarantees? Part of the answer lies in a difference of opinion about the appropriate capital allocation for various risk strategies. For example, a 4 percent capital allocation for a large mismatch or risky credit strategy is clearly inappropriate—that is, too low. If 4 percent is the capital allocation used to determine the cost of capital, and thus used in setting the price, and the remaining investment spread is passed into the guarantee, then guarantees will be too high. If the "correct" capital allocation is 10 percent, then expenses (i.e., cost of capital) are understated by 39 basis points (6.4% − .25%) for a 10 percent after-tax ROE objective, and 84 basis points (1.40% − .56%) for a 15 percent after-tax ROE objective.

**EXHIBIT 25–13**
**Required Profit Margins**

|  | Capital Allocation | After-Tax ROE | |
|---|---|---|---|
|  |  | 10% | 15% |
| Investment banks | 2% | .13% | .28% |
| Savings banks | 4 | .25 | .56 |
| Commercial banks | 7 | .45 | .98 |
| Insurance companies | 10 | .64 | 1.40 |
| Finance companies | 15 | .96 | 2.11 |

Assumes: ROE = 9%, TR = 35%

# SPECIFIC UNDERWRITING RISKS
# FOR GICS

Exhibit 25–14 shows transfers among various investment options made between 1981 and 1984 in the profit sharing plan of a large bank. All transfers to and from GICs were done at book value. Although most insurance companies no longer issue GICs to plans that permit unencumbered transfers to competing money market options, this exhibit clearly illustrates the problems faced by GIC underwriters.

This plan has a money market option as well as a guaranteed interest option. The cash flows evidence the effective utilization of the option granted by the GIC issuer. When yield curves were inverted (1981), funds flowed from the GIC to the money market option. When interest rates declined in 1983, funds flowed from the money market option to the higher composite-rate GIC option.

In 1983, the $5 million of transfers from the money market fund to the GIC were roughly equal to ongoing contributions directed to the GIC option. In this case, contributions to the GIC after interest rates fell were double the expected contributions. This exhibit of cash flows is a dramatic example of the more general phenomenon of written options inside GIC contracts.

Exhibit 25–15 illustrates the price function of a put option. In typical GIC applications, the option is owned by the plan participant. The participant has the right to sell (put) the participation in the GIC back to the insurance company at a fixed price. This right increases in value as interest rates rise. Thus, the insurance company's liability increases as interest rates rise. Note the contrast between the behavior of this liability and the behavior of a conventional asset, which declines as interest rates rise. Other examples of plan features that trigger the use of this option are excessive withdrawals at book value as rates rise, switches to money market or other competing funds, and redirection of contributions to more attractive investment options.

**EXHIBIT 25–14**
**Breakdown of Flows**

|  | Transfers | | | |
|---|---|---|---|---|
|  | 1981 | 1982 | 1983 | 1984 |
| GIC | (1,674,028) | (187,122) | 5,454,985 | 3,271,486 |
| Stocks and bonds | (313,569) | (1,576,928) | 322,235 | (2,593,420) |
| RE | (20,239) | 139,913 | 113,577 | (61,638) |
| Money market | 2,023,565 | 1,664,305 | (5,248,710) | 626,258 |
| C.S. | (15,729) | (40,168) | (642,087) | (1,210,674) |
| Commercial paper % | 18.50% | 13.25% | 8.63% | 10.0% |

**EXHIBIT 25–15**
**Written Put Option**

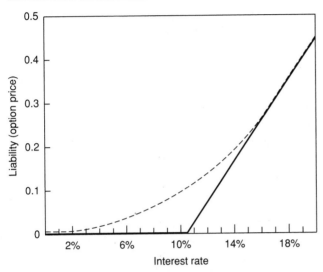

- Excessive withdrawals at book value when yields rise
- Redirection of contributions
- Switches to money market or other competing funds, in-service withdrawals

Exhibit 25–16 illustrates the price function of a call option. In the GIC application, this option is owned by the plan participant. The participant can buy an additional piece of GIC from the insurer at a fixed price (at par). This right (or option) increases in value as interest rates decline. In this event, the participant can increase deposits into a high-rate contract after rates have declined. The participant can also move money from other investment options into the GIC. The price function of a liability with such an option will grow faster than the otherwise similar asset as rates decline.

Insurance companies respond to the potential financial effect of these options by imposing risk charges and underwriting restrictions, such as caps and floors, or by refusing to underwrite at all. For pricing, this translates into pricing an out-of-the-money option at a fraction of its real cost. The residual cost for the put option under various assumptions is illustrated in Exhibit 25–17.

## MANAGING A GIC PORTFOLIO

GIC portfolio management is one form of fixed income management where a passive buy-and-hold strategy is usually employed. This buy-and-hold strategy

**EXHIBIT 25–16**
**Written Call Option**

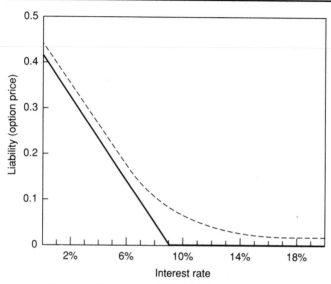

- Excessive deposits into GIC after yields have dropped
- Switches from employer stock, money market, or other competing funds into GIC
- Redirection of contributions from other funds into GIC

is necessary because no active trading or secondary markets exist for GICs. Ongoing investment decisions, as in any fixed income portfolio, focus on the slope of the yield curve and yield spreads. Emphasis, too, is placed on absolute yield and quality with the return controlled by the reinvestment of the coupon, maturing proceeds, and cash-flow patterns from the plan.

The portfolio should be diversified to protect against the credit risk of individual issuers. It should be designed to defend against adverse changes in interest rates, including reinvestment risks and an inverted yield curve. The lack of liquidity, a limited universe of issuers, limited types of contracts, and an inconsistency in contractual terms place constraints on the portfolio manager that are not normally found in other fixed income portfolios. In order to compensate for these constraints, the manager must adopt techniques from the other investment markets.

Because of the instrument's nonmarketability, the portfolio must be structured with a long-term orientation. Six basic objectives are paramount:

1. Safety and stability of principal
2. Yields concurrent with market rates
3. Positive inflation-adjusted returns over an interest-rate cycle

**EXHIBIT 25–17**
**Written Put Option (Inefficient Exercise)**

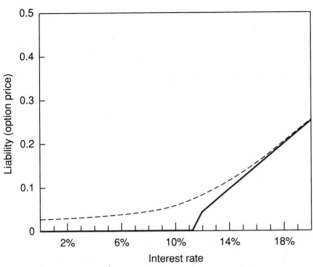

- Options not always exercised when financially advantageous
- Restrictive plan provisions, unsophisticated participants, inertia
- Corridor and smaller slope

4. Adequate liquidity
5. Issuer and reinvestment diversification
6. Adherence to portfolio management standards

Using these overall goals as a guide, the portfolio manager develops working rules to govern the investment management of the portfolio. The manager must determine which fixed income techniques are employed. Two choices are prevalent—a market-timing strategy or a baseline approach.

Market-timing strategies utilize interest-rate forecasting as their key premise. Investment decisions are governed by the manager's near-term and long-term outlook for interest rates. On the short end, the outlook influences the manager's decision as to the appropriate time to invest—today, next week, or next month. The manager attempts to select the time when near-term rates will offer the greatest rate of return. In the long-term perspective, the manager determines the optimum holding period for the contract. Market timing requires an innate skill and foresight in the determination of future interest rates.

The baseline approach is a more conservative strategy in managing GIC portfolios. This strategy recognizes more fully the nonmarketability of the GIC and places less emphasis on long-term market-timing strategies. The manager attempts to minimize the portfolio's reinvestment risk by laddering the maturing proceeds in a regular pattern over some course of time.

The structure of a baseline portfolio is determined more by the requirements and investment objectives of the portfolio than by prevailing and anticipated future market rates. These requirements evolve from a clear statement of the objectives of the portfolio. Plan design, cash-flow requirements, corporate philosophy, and investment performance goals are the fundamental issues that must be analyzed and planned for in the ensuing strategy. A well-defined plan incorporates these factors in a written policy.

## Plan Design

In structuring the GIC portfolio, attention to plan design and administrative requirements is critical. It is important to coordinate the investment aspects with the plan design aspects. A trade-off occurs in designing the benefit plan. The portfolio manager wants to provide the most flexible plan possible while recognizing the illiquid nature of the instrument. The portfolio manager also wants to provide competitive returns. In the GIC investment option, the challenge is to obtain the best of both worlds.

In the bidding process, the underwriter looks for potential risk. When risks are identified, charges are assessed. The greater the risk to the carrier, the less attractive the plan becomes to the underwriter. Some insurers will decline to quote, some will add restrictive contract provisions, and some will charge heavily for the perceived risks through lower quoted rates.

## Cash-Flow Requirements

Planning for cash-flow needs is dependent on the type of benefit plan. Defined benefit plan cash flows are generally known.

Defined contribution plans have many uncertain and highly variable cash flows. Portfolio design is dependent to a great extent on the plan provisions. The ability to redirect future contributions or transfer existing balances to other investment funds, the opportunity to make in-service withdrawals or loans, and the flexibility of payout at termination or layoff influence the stability of the portfolio. Since these events cannot be controlled, the contracts must be negotiated to cover the plan design characteristics and requirements.

Cash outflows from a portfolio can be satisfied in two basic fashions. They can be paid from current inflows and/or cash reserve balances, or they can be paid from existing contracts negotiated with a benefit-responsive feature.

Portfolios that make payments from current cash inflows or a cash reserve fund pose less risk to the carrier when these funds are utilized as the first source for benefit payments. Contractual risk charges are lower and hence earnings are higher. If an excessively large cash reserve is maintained, the total fund return may suffer since cash reserves traditionally earn lower rates (i.e., lower than GIC rates). The portfolio manager must determine if the lower earnings on the cash portion justify avoiding the approximate 20-basis points, benefit-responsive charge.

## Corporate Philosophy

Corporate philosophy governs the environment in which the plan must function on an ongoing basis. Actions initiated by the corporate entity often have a far-reaching impact on the employee benefit program. The portfolio manager must anticipate the impact of corporate actions and include contractual features that maintain the integrity of the fund during transition periods.

Acquisitions, divestitures, restructurings, and cost reduction efforts affect large numbers of employees and their balances. Unfortunately none of these events nor their impacts can be predicted.

GICs must serve three masters when these situations occur—the carrier, the contractholder, and the participant. The carrier must protect the integrity of the investments in the general account. The contractholder must ensure that the contract facilitates the activities required under the terms of the plan. Participants must be protected against potential market value penalties.

If the corporate culture encompasses changing business focuses, the GIC portfolio manager must anticipate the impact of these events and build safeguards into the portfolio design through contract negotiation. The manager must isolate the risks and develop a strategy that mediates their impact between the fund and the carrier.

## Performance Goals

The plan sponsor must develop an appropriate performance perspective for the GIC fund in order for the GIC portfolio manager to implement the investment strategy and communicate it to the participants. If the fund is intended to look like a money market fund, the portfolio's return needs to be responsive to market interest rates.

The guaranteed fund is structured and marketed as a safe-harbor alternative with protection of principal and an earnings rate guaranteed by the insurer. Announced rates of return for current deposits and long-term holding periods encourage the participants to view the option as a lockup vehicle much like a certificate of deposit.

Since each portfolio has target characteristics based on the representations made of it, the portfolio manager must develop a strategy to make the fund "behave" accordingly. More importantly, surrogate performance benchmarks can be used as objective evaluation measures, as illustrated in Exhibit 25–18 and Exhibit 25–19. Benchmarks for a "money market" GIC portfolio may require

**EXHIBIT 25–18**
**GIC Rates Compared to Money Market Rates**

|      | GIC Average Rates (Two-Year Maturity) | | | Money Market Yields | Average |
|------|-------|-------|---------|---------------------|---------|
|      | High  | Low   | Average |                     |         |
| 1982 | 16.40% | 10.67% | 14.00% | 12.23% | 1.77 |
| 1983 | 11.86 | 9.95  | 10.85 | 8.58  | 2.27 |
| 1984 | 13.23 | 10.26 | 11.94 | 10.04 | 1.90 |
| 1985 | 11.02 | 8.01  | 9.58  | 7.71  | 1.87 |
| 1986 | 8.43  | 6.10  | 7.30  | 6.26  | 1.04 |
| 1987 | 9.17  | 6.58  | 7.55  | 6.12  | 1.43 |
| 1988 | 8.88  | 7.07  | 7.95  | 7.11  | 0.84 |
| 1989 | 9.73  | 7.73  | 8.63  | 8.87  | −0.24 |

Assumes a $1 million deposit invested at average market yields.

Sources: GIC rate data obtained from The Laughlin Group, Portland, Oregon and T. Rowe Price GIC Index. Money market yields obtained from Donoghue's Money Market Fund Averages/All Taxable.

returns of at least 1.5 percent above a recognized money market composite. The portfolio's target duration may be between 0.5 and 0.75 years. A "stable-value" GIC portfolio may have a target duration benchmark between 1.5 and 3.5 years. A return goal of 1.0 percent above the yield-to-maturity on an equivalent-maturity U.S. Treasury obligation may be established.

As the growth of the GIC marketplace has spiraled in recent years, institutional investors have searched for ways to quantify the investment performance aspects of their GIC portfolios. Because of the unique characteristics associated with the GIC, no quantifiable basis has existed to provide the absolute or relative performance comparisons provided by the equity, bond, and money markets.

The investor using GICs should incorporate continuing performance reviews in the management process, as would be done with any other asset class. The review should be at two levels—the first level being the continuing review of the viability of the GIC as an investment alternative and the second level being the review of the investment returns generated over some defined time period.

The first order of review includes the assessment of how well the GIC fund/portfolio is meeting its intentions within the overall framework of the plan. When used in an employee choice plan, is its return meeting the reasonable expectations of participants? If GICs are used as a component in the asset-allocation process of defined benefit or defined contribution profit sharing or money purchase plans, where the plan sponsor is making the asset-allocation decision, are they providing the risk-adjusted returns needed to offset their illiquid nature?

**EXHIBIT 25–19**
**GIC Returns Compared to Bond Returns**

| | Shearson Lehman Intermediate Government/Corporate Index | | GIC Average Rates (Four-Year Maturity) | | |
|------|--------|-------|-------|-------|---------|
| Year | Return | Yield | High | Low | Average |
| 1982 | 26.11% | 12.03% | 16.53% | 11.52% | 14.31% |
| 1983 | 8.60 | 10.93 | 12.37 | 10.83 | 11.69 |
| 1984 | 14.37 | 11.33 | 13.87 | 11.09 | 12.56 |
| 1985 | 18.00 | 10.64 | 11.80 | 8.84 | 10.40 |
| 1986 | 13.13 | 9.29 | 9.11 | 7.39 | 8.03 |
| 1987 | 3.66 | 8.70 | 9.87 | 7.35 | 8.34 |
| 1988 | 6.67 | 9.17 | 9.28 | 7.84 | 8.59 |
| 1989 | 12.77 | 8.81 | 9.33 | 8.13 | 8.89 |

Table illustrates the comparative returns between the government/corporate yields and returns and the yields generated from GICs. Assumes a $1 million deposit invested at average market yields.

Source: GIC rate data obtained from the Laughlin Group, Portland, Oregon and the T. Rowe Price GIC Index.

On the second level, plan sponsors establish specific objectives for the absolute, relative, and comparative goals of the GIC portfolio. On an absolute basis, the investor should be concerned that the portfolio's return is meeting specific or inflation-adjusted return investment expectations. On a relative basis, the investor should be concerned that the portfolio is competitive over time with external current market yields. On a comparative basis, one GIC manager can be evaluated against another—as long as objectives and the timing of manager funding is the same. The absolute basis is the most quantifiable; the relative basis is the most difficult, since the portfolio's return is directly related to available interest rates at the point in time in which the assets were purchased. A GIC portfolio constructed in a 10 percent environment will outperform one constructed in an 8 percent environment.

Comparisons of GIC portfolios with existing outside performance benchmarks have proved inadequate. A bond index does not provide an equivalent benchmark. It factors into the return equation the price function of the assets. The appreciation or depreciation of the underlying assets, when added to the accrued income (expressed as a percent of the original investment) produces the total return for the period being measured. The total return for the GIC is simply the current yield because the asset is valued at par or book value with no underlying appreciation or depreciation in the asset's value.

Money market indexes produce a more comparable basis, as the investments that make up the money market portfolio are normally carried at book value. The durations, however, are relatively short—six months or less—versus the typical GIC portfolio, whose durations are normally in the two-to three-year range.

Hence, the user of GICs is presented with a dilemma. There is the need to continually evaluate the portfolio's return to ensure that the portfolio is meeting the intended investment objectives and to ensure that the returns generated are in fact competitive. Notwithstanding this need, there are few resources available to assist in the review.

## THE FUTURE

Complementing the acceptance of GICs as a fixed income equivalent and as a manageable asset class has been the proliferation of the instrument into the synthetic and derivative markets. Alternative uses of the instrument are emerging that are similar to other areas within the fixed income markets: the use of swaps in managing interest-rate reinvestment risk exposure, the development of "look-alike" derivative GIC instruments built around bond immunization programs, and the entry of the banks. Each represents the growing sophistication of the marketplace and the demands being placed by the larger plan sponsors, consultants, and managers to create more flexible funding arrangements.

To draw an analogy to other fixed income markets, a comparison can be made to the bond markets of the late 1960s and early 1970s, where the typical buy-and-hold approach changed to more aggressive investment management strategies. A similar comparison can be made to the cash markets of the late 1970s and early 1980s, where the emphasis became yield maximization. GICs have become a recognized asset class.

# PART 4

# MORTGAGE-BACKED AND ASSET-BACKED SECURITIES

# CHAPTER 26

## MORTGAGES

*Dexter Senft*
*Managing Director,*
*Fixed Income Research*
*The First Boston Corporation*

*Frank J. Fabozzi, Ph.D., CFA, CPA*
*Visiting Professor of Finance*
*Sloan School of Management*
*Massachusetts Institute of Technology*
*and*
*Editor, The Journal of Portfolio Management*

In order to understand and analyze mortgage-related securities, it is necessary to understand how mortgages operate. In this chapter, we examine several types of mortgage loans, their cash flow, and certain other aspects relevant to the analysis of pass-through securities.

## WHAT IS A MORTGAGE?

By definition, a mortgage is a "pledge of property to secure payment of a debt." Typically, property refers to real estate, which is often in the form of a house; the debt is the loan given to the buyer of the house by a bank or other lender. Thus, a mortgage might be a "pledge of a house to secure payment of a bank loan." If a homeowner (the *mortgagor*) fails to pay the lender (the *mortgagee*), the lender has the right to foreclose the loan and seize the property in order to ensure that it is repaid.

The form that a mortgage loan takes could technically be anything the borrower and lender agree upon. Traditionally, however, most mortgage loans have been structured similarly. There has been a fixed rate of interest on the loan for its entire term, and the loan has been repaid in monthly installments of principal and interest. Each loan has been structured in such a way that the total payment each month (the sum of the principal and interest) has been equal, or *level*. We shall refer to this type of loan arrangement as a traditional mortgage loan. (There is a growing trend away from this traditional structure, but this is getting ahead of the story.) In a traditional mortgage loan, the terms to be negotiated are the interest rate and the period to maturity. Interest rates vary with the general economic climate, and maturities range from 12 to 40 years, depending on the type of property involved. Most mortgages on single-family homes carry 30-year maturities.

Exhibit 26–1 illustrates the breakdown of monthly payments between principal and interest on a 30-year, 10 percent traditional mortgage. At first, the mortgage payment is mostly interest. The principal portion increases over time until, at maturity, the payment is almost entirely principal. At all times, however, the sum of the principal and interest payments is the same. Notice that over the course of the loan the borrower pays more dollars as interest than as principal—in fact, total interest is more than twice total principal in this example.

**EXHIBIT 26–1**

**Monthly Mortgage Payments—Interest/Principal (30-Year 10 Percent Conventional Loan)**

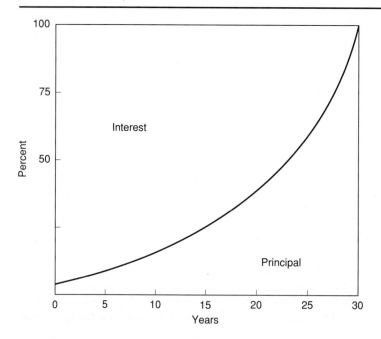

The principal portion of each monthly payment is used to reduce the amount of the loan outstanding. In mortgage terms, the loan is *amortized* over 30 years, and the principal payments each month are known as amortization payments. The amount of the loan that is outstanding at any time is known as the *mortgage balance*. In any month, the interest payment equals the interest rate (expressed monthly) times the mortgage balance at the beginning of the month (see Exhibit 26–2). Often the mortgage balance is expressed as a ratio or percentage of the original loan amount, in which case the mortgage balance runs from 1 (or 100 percent) initially to 0 at maturity. Exhibit 26–3 shows how the mortgage balance for several possible loans would decline over time. Another way to view the mortgage balance is as the amount of the house value the home buyer does not yet own. The amount of a home's value that is owned is referred to as the homeowner's *equity*. Equity can be defined as the difference between the current value of the home and the mortgage balance; as the mortgage balance declines, the equity rises. Equity also increases if the current value of the home increases because of home improvements, inflation, and so on.

Sometimes a mortgagor may want to make a monthly payment that is greater than the amount actually due, with the idea of applying the excess payment to further reduce the loan. Such excess principal payments are called *prepayments* and may be made for several reasons. (These reasons will be discussed in detail later). Prepayments result in a direct reduction of the mortgage balance and a direct increase in the amount of equity. Another way to define mortgage balance is that it equals the original loan amount less the total amount of amortization and prepayments to date.

A mortgagor who fails to make a mortgage payment is said to be *delinquent*. Delinquences can have a variety of causes—the homeowner may have died, become unemployed, bounced a check, or simply forgotten to make the payment. The mortgagee then reminds the homeowner that the payment is overdue and attempts to collect the money. If the matter is not resolved quickly, the mortgagee may assess the mortgagor with a late payment charge. Sometimes there is no quick solution, and the mortgagor may become more than one month in arrears. Although most lenders are willing to allow a borrower a few months leeway, in extreme cases it may be necessary for the bank to foreclose the loan, in which case the property is taken from the mortgagor and sold in order to pay off the loan.

## QUALIFYING FOR A MORTGAGE

Borrowers who are interested in obtaining mortgage loans must meet certain standards set by the lender in order to be considered creditworthy. The first thing a lender checks is whether or not the borrower has any other loans or obligations outstanding; if so, these will diminish the borrower's ability to make

**EXHIBIT 26–2**

**Sample Payment Schedule: Traditional Mortgage
(10 Percent Interest Rate, 30-Year [360-Month] Term)**

| Month | Mortgage Balance Dollars | Decimal | Monthly Payment | Interest | Principal |
|---|---|---|---|---|---|
| 0 | 50000.00 | 1.00000 | | | |
| 1 | 49977.88 | .99956 | 438.79 | 416.67 | 22.12 |
| 2 | 49955.58 | .99911 | 438.79 | 416.48 | 22.30 |
| 3 | 49933.09 | .99866 | 438.79 | 416.30 | 22.49 |
| 4 | 49910.41 | .99821 | 438.79 | 416.11 | 22.68 |
| 5 | 49887.55 | .99775 | 438.79 | 415.92 | 22.87 |
| 6 | 49864.49 | .99729 | 438.79 | 415.73 | 23.06 |
| 7 | 49841.24 | .99682 | 438.79 | 415.54 | 23.25 |
| 8 | 49817.80 | .99636 | 438.79 | 415.34 | 23.44 |
| 9 | 49794.16 | .99588 | 438.79 | 415.15 | 23.64 |
| 10 | 49770.33 | .99541 | 438.79 | 414.95 | 23.83 |
| — | — | — | — | — | — |
| 100 | 46567.88 | .93136 | 438.79 | 388.48 | 50.30 |
| 101 | 46517.16 | .93034 | 438.79 | 388.07 | 50.72 |
| 102 | 46466.02 | .92932 | 438.79 | 387.64 | 51.14 |
| 103 | 46414.45 | .92829 | 438.79 | 387.22 | 51.57 |
| — | — | — | — | — | — |
| 200 | 38697.88 | .77396 | 438.79 | 323.44 | 115.34 |
| 201 | 38581.57 | .77163 | 438.79 | 322.48 | 116.30 |
| 202 | 38464.30 | .76929 | 438.79 | 321.51 | 117.27 |
| 203 | 38346.05 | .76692 | 438.79 | 320.54 | 118.25 |
| — | — | — | — | — | — |
| 300 | 20651.61 | .41303 | 438.79 | 174.30 | 264.48 |
| 301 | 20384.93 | .40770 | 438.79 | 172.10 | 266.69 |
| 302 | 20116.01 | .40232 | 438.79 | 169.87 | 268.91 |
| 303 | 19844.86 | .39690 | 438.79 | 167.63 | 271.15 |
| — | — | — | — | — | — |
| 355 | 2140.13 | .04280 | 438.79 | 21.31 | 417.47 |
| 356 | 1719.18 | .03438 | 438.79 | 17.83 | 420.95 |
| 357 | 1294.72 | .02589 | 438.79 | 14.33 | 424.46 |
| 358 | 866.72 | .01733 | 438.79 | 10.79 | 428.00 |
| 359 | 135.16 | .00870 | 438.79 | 7.22 | 431.56 |
| 360 | 0.00 | .00000 | 438.79 | 3.63 | 435.16 |

Note: Each month, the interest payment is $\frac{1}{12}$ of 10 percent of the mortgage balance. The principal payment is the total payment less the interest due. The principal balance is reduced by the amount of the principal payment.

**EXHIBIT 26–3**
**Examples of Mortgage Balances for Various Loans**

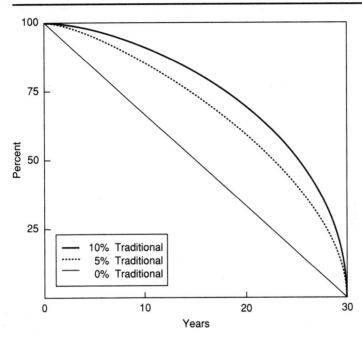

mortgage payments. Next the lender determines the income and net worth of the borrower. Many mortgage lenders use these classical rules of thumb to determine whether or not a borrower's income is adequate for the mortgage:

1. The total mortgage payment (principal and interest) should not exceed 25 percent of the borrower's total income less any payments owed for other obligations.
2. Total mortgage payments plus other housing expenses should not exceed 33 percent of the borrower's income less payments for other obligations. Other housing expenses include such items as taxes, insurance, utilities, and normal maintenance costs.

Of course, these percentages may vary depending on the lender and the circumstances. In particular, borrowers with relatively high net worth and/or liquid assets will find lenders to be more flexible. Also, in times of high interest rates and tight money, lenders have been known to bend these rules in order to maintain a certain level of business.

The buyer is usually required to make a down payment on the property in order to qualify for the mortgage. The down payment might range anywhere from 5 to 25 percent of the purchase price. The reason for requiring a down payment is that in the event the lender is forced to foreclose the loan and sell the property, the mortgage balance will be more easily recovered. In other words, there is room for error if the property is sold—even if it cannot bring the original purchase price on the market, there can still be enough to cover the debt. Lenders use the term *loan-to-value ratio*, or LTV, to express the amount of protection on the mortgage. LTV is calculated as the ratio of the mortgage balance to the market value of the property and is expressed as a percentage. The lower the LTV, the less the loan amount relative to the property value, and the greater the safety.

The LTV ratio tends to decrease over time. For example, if a buyer makes a 10 percent down payment on a property and mortgages the rest, the LTV is initially 90 percent. Over time, the mortgage balance declines from amortization and prepayments, while the property value tends to increase owing to inflation. Both of these changes serve to lower the LTV.

As with income requirements, down payment and LTV requirements depend on certain circumstances. These include not only the net worth of the borrower but the condition and marketability of the property and the availability of credit. Higher LTV ratios are associated with newer, more marketable properties and with easier credit and lower interest rates.

An important (if not obvious) conclusion about qualifying for a mortgage is that it becomes harder when interest rates rise. Because of the income and LTV requirements, smaller mortgage balances are affordable when rates rise, and yet this is also the time when inflation and therefore home purchase prices are rising. As a consequence, all but those buyers with large amounts of cash or equity are squeezed from the market.

## MORTGAGE INSURANCE

There are two types of mortgage insurance that may be used when borrowers obtain mortgage financing. One type is originated by borrowers and the other by lenders. Although both have a beneficial effect on the creditworthiness of the borrowers, the latter is of greater importance from the lender's point of view.

The first type of mortgage insurance is taken out by the borrower, usually with a life insurance company. The policy provides for the continuing payment of the mortgage after the death of the insured person, thus enabling the survivors to continue living in the house. In the sense that the mortgage might just as well have been paid off with part of the proceeds of ordinary life insurance, this form of mortgage insurance is really only a special form of life insurance. It is cheaper than ordinary life insurance, however, because the death benefit, which is equal to the mortgage balance, declines over time.

The other type of mortgage insurance is taken out by the lender, although borrowers pay the insurance premiums. This policy covers some percentage of the loan amount and guarantees that in the event of a default by the borrower the insurance company will pay the amount insured or pay off the loan in full.

An example of how this type of mortgage insurance works is shown in Exhibit 26–4. Suppose that a borrower finances $60,000 of property with a $5,000 down payment and a $55,000 mortgage. The initial LTV ratio is fairly high (91.7%), so mortgage insurance is obtained in the amount of $11,000 (20% of the loan). Suppose that the borrower defaults after five years (the mortgage balance having been paid down to $52,000 by then). Suppose further that the property has deteriorated in condition (or perhaps has been partially destroyed), and its market value falls to $50,000. The bank then turns to the insurance company.

Several options are open to the insurance company, perhaps the simplest of which is that it can assist the borrower financially so that the amount in arrears can be paid and no foreclosure is necessary. Assuming that this fails, there are two other alternatives. First, the insurance company could pay the claim of $11,000 and let the bank foreclose. The bank, which gets $50,000 for the property and $11,000 insurance, actually makes a profit of $9,000 over the mortgage balance outstanding. A better alternative for the insurance company, however, is to pay off the mortgage balance ($52,000), take title of the property, and sell it (for $50,000). The insurance company thereby loses only $2,000, instead of $11,000. Of course, the insurer could hold the property or even make improvements to it in hope of making a future gain instead of selling it immediately.

The net effect of mortgage insurance from the lender's standpoint is to reduce its risk. The exposure of a lender to loss equals the amount loaned less property value and mortgage insurance. In a sense, the insurance has an effect similar to having a higher down payment because both reduce the lender's exposure to loss. Mortgage insurance is advantageous to borrowers who do not have enough money for a large down payment but who can afford enough down payment and insurance to satisfy the lender.

The cost of the insurance can be passed on to the borrower in several ways. Traditionally, the cost was added to the mortgage rate as an extra one-eighth percent or one-fourth percent, depending on the amount of coverage. As mortgage rates escalated, however, increasing the rate further became less attractive. (In a sense, the insurance company would be increasing the chance of the default it was insuring against.) It has become increasingly common to pay for mortgage insurance in one lump sum at the time of mortgage origination.

It is not necessary to have mortgage insurance in effect for the entire term of a loan. Because the mortgage balance amortizes and the LTV tends to fall

**EXHIBIT 26–4**

**How Mortgage Insurance Works in the Event of a Default**

Situation initially:

$$LTV = \frac{55,000}{60,000} = 91.7\%$$

$11,000 mortgage
insurance obtained

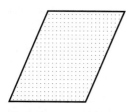

Mortgage:    $55,000
Down payment    5,000
Total    $60,000

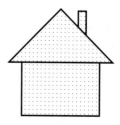

Property value: $60,000

Situation after 5 years:
Borrower defaults
Property value falls

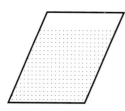

Mortgage balance:
$52,000

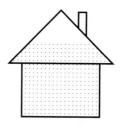

Property value: $50,000

Option 1: Insurance company pays claim

    Lender has

| | | |
|---|---|---|
| | $50,000 | Property |
| | 11,000 | Insurance |
| | (52,000) | Bad debt |
| | $ 9,000 | Net profit |

    Insurance company has    ($11,000)  Loss

Option 2: Insurance company takes title to property

    Lender has

| | | |
|---|---|---|
| | $52,000 | From insurer |
| | (52,000) | Bad debt |
| | 0 | Net profit |

    Insurance company has

| | | |
|---|---|---|
| | $50,000 | Property |
| | (52,000) | Payment to lender |
| | (2,000) | Net loss |

over time, the lender may deem mortgage insurance to be unnecessary when the mortgage balance has declined to some predetermined level. At that point, the policy is either cancelled or allowed to expire.

## SERVICING

Among the jobs that mortgage lenders must perform in order to ensure that borrowers make timely and accurate payments are sending payment notices, reminding borrowers when payments are overdue, recording prepayments, keeping records of mortgage balances, administering escrow accounts for payment of property taxes or insurance, sending out tax information at year-end, and initiating foreclosure proceedings. These functions are collectively known as *servicing* the loans. Many times the original lender is the one who services the loan, but this is not always the case. Sometimes the mortgage is sold to someone else, and the servicing of the loan may or may not go along with the mortgage.

In the event that one party owns a mortgage and another services it, the servicer receives a fee (the *servicing fee*) for the trouble. Servicing fees usually take the form of a fixed percentage of the mortgage balance outstanding. Although the percentage may vary from one servicer to the next, it is usually in the area of .25 percent to .50 percent. Small servicing fee percentages are usually associated with larger commercial property loans, and larger percentages with smaller residential loans. From the point of view of the owner of the mortgage, the servicing fee comes out of the interest portion of the mortgage payment. For example, if party A owns a 10 percent mortgage being serviced by party B for a three eights of 1 percent fee, then A is really earning $9^5/8$ percent (10% minus three eighths of 1%) on the loan.

In addition to servicing fees, there are occasionally other fees that the servicer may keep. For example, some servicers are entitled to keep late-payment penalties paid by the borrower, foreclosure penalties, and certain other penalty fees. The specific types and amounts of fees that servicers are entitled to receive are set forth in a servicing agreement between the mortgage owner and the servicer.

## MORTGAGE ORIGINATION

The original lender of mortgage money is called the *mortgage originator*. Exhibit 26–5 shows the originators of residential mortgages. The single largest originating group is the savings and loan industry. Savings and loans, together with savings banks and credit unions, constitute the "thrift industry"—so-called because its funds come from the savings accumulated by its thrifty depositors. Regulatory and tax considerations encourage thrifts to invest in mortgages (or mortgage-related securities). As a consequence, many thrifts retain the mortgages they originate for inclusion in their portfolios.

Commercial banks make up the second largest group of originators, and like thrift institutions, the money they put into mortgages comes primarily from deposits. Again, many of the loans originated by commercial banks are held for investment.

The third major originator of mortgage loans is the mortgage company sector, or "mortgage bankers." Unlike thrifts and commercial banks, mortgage banks do not have depositors. They are in the business of finding other sources of mortgage money, such as thrifts or insurance companies, and making it available for housing construction and ownership; mortgage bankers' profits come from servicing the loans they originate, plus any profit that can be made from buying and selling the mortgages. Mortgage bankers are rarely mortgage investors; the loans they originate are typically sold to other more permanent investors.

The lesser originators are also shown in Exhibit 26–5.

## Overview of The Mortgage Origination Process

A potential home buyer who wants to borrow funds to purchase a home will apply for a loan from a mortgage originator. The process begins with the completion of an application form that provides financial information about the applicant and the payment of an application fee. The mortgagor originator then performs a credit evaluation of the applicant. The two primary factors in determining whether or not the funds will be lent are the (1) payment-to-income (PTI) ratio and (2) the loan-to-value (LTV) ratio, which were discussed earlier.

If the lender decides to loan the funds, a commitment letter will be sent to the applicant. This letter commits the lender to loan funds to the applicant. The length of time of the commitment varies between 30 and 60 days. At the time of the commitment letter, the lender will require that the applicant pay a commitment fee. The applicant loses the commitment fee if the applicant decides not to purchase the property or if the applicant uses an alternative source of funds to purchase the property. Thus, the commitment letter states that for a fee the applicant has the right but not the obligation to require the lender to provide funds at a certain interest rate and with certain terms.

At the time the application is submitted for approval, the mortgage originator will give the applicant a choice of mortgage types and rates. The various types of mortgages are discussed later in this chapter. Usually, the choice is between a fixed-rate mortgage or an adjustable-rate mortgage. In the case of a fixed-rate mortgage, the lender typically gives the applicant a choice of when the interest rate on the mortgage will be determined. The choices may be (1) at

**EXHIBIT 26–5**
**Origination of Residential Mortgage Loans** (Millions of Dollars)

| | Thrifts | Commercial Banks | Mortgage Bankers | Life Insurance Companies | Pension Funds | Federal Credit Agencies* | State & Local Credit Agencies | Total |
|---|---|---|---|---|---|---|---|---|
| 1986 | 229,950 | 115,789 | 138,800 | 7,537 | 123 | 4,415 | 8,308 | 504,922 |
| 1987 | 230,545 | 132,851 | 112,502 | 6,756 | 50 | 4,010 | 7,811 | 494,525 |
| 1988:Q1 | 36,570 | 18,788 | 18,522 | 767 | 22 | 919 | 486 | 76,074 |
| 1988:Q2 | 55,980 | 28,904 | 25,012 | 1,826 | 39 | 988 | 532 | 113,281 |

* Consists primarily of activities of the Farmers Home Administration. Also includes Federal Land Banks and the Federal Housing and Veterans Administrations.

Source: The U.S. Department of Housing and Urban Development, Survey of Mortgage Lending Activity.

the time the loan application is submitted, (2) at the time a commitment letter is issued to the borrower, or (3) at the closing date (i.e., the date that the property is purchased).

The mortgage rate that the originator will set on the loan will depend on the mortgage rate required by investors who purchase mortgages. There will usually be different mortgage rates for delivery at different times (30 days, 60 days or 90 days in the future).

## Mortgage Securitization

Mortgage originators can either (1) hold a new mortgage in their portfolio, (2) sell the mortgage to an investor or conduit, or (3) use the mortgage as collateral for the issuance of a security. When a mortgage is used as collateral for the issuance of a security, the mortgage is said to be *securitized*. In the next chapter, the securities created are discussed.

When a mortgage originator intends to sell the mortgage, it will obtain a commitment from the potential buyer. Two federally sponsored credit agencies and several private companies buy mortgages. Since these agencies and private companies pool these mortgages and sell them to investors, they are called *conduits*.

The two agencies, the Federal Home Loan Mortgage Corporation (FHLMC, or "Freddie Mac") and the Federal National Mortgage Association (FNMA, or "Fannie Mae"), purchase only certain kinds of mortgages, known as *conforming* mortgages. A conforming mortgage is simply one that meets their underwriting standards. Three of the major underwriting standards established by these agencies in order to qualify as a conforming mortgage are (1) a maximum PTI, (2) a maximum LTV, and (3) a maximum loan amount. If an applicant does not satisfy these underwriting standards, the mortgage is called a *nonconforming* mortgage. Loans that exceed the maximum loan amount and therefore do not qualify as conforming mortgages are called *jumbo* loans.

Examples of private conduits are Citimae, Inc. (a subsidiary of Citicorp), Collateralized Mortgage Securities Corporation (a subsidiary of First Boston), Bear Stearns Mortgage Capital Corporation, Residential Funding Corporation (a subsidiary of Salomon Brothers), Sears Mortgage Securities Corporation, and Shearson Lehman Hutton Mortgage Corporation. Private conduits typically will securitize both conforming and nonconforming mortgages.

## WHAT TYPES OF PROPERTIES ARE MORTGAGED?

Virtually all forms of real estate have been mortgaged, but these properties fall into several categories. First, property (and the mortgage on it) can be classified as either residential or nonresidential, depending on whether or not people use the property primarily for living. Residential properties include houses, apartments, condominiums, cooperatives, and mobile homes. These do not necessarily have to be someone's primary residence—for example, summer homes and skiing condominiums are classified as residential properties. Residential properties are subdivided into one- to four-family dwellings and multifamily dwellings for the purposes of Federal Reserve statistics.

Nonresidential properties are subdivided into commercial properties and farm properties. The commercial category encompasses a wide variety of properties such as office buildings, shopping centers, hospitals, and industrial plants.

## NONTRADITIONAL MORTGAGES

The decade of the 1970s saw the advent of many new and different varieties of mortgages. Unlike traditional mortgages, most of these alternative mortgage instruments (AMIs) do not have level monthly payments, but employ some other (often complicated) scheme. One AMI even provides a way for the homeowner to continually take cash out of equity, as opposed to continually putting cash into it.

What was the impetus for the creation of AMIs, and in what ways are they superior to traditional mortgages? The answers to these questions are related to the level and behavior of mortgage interest rates. In the 15 years ending in 1979, mortgage rates doubled from roughly 6 percent levels to 12 percent levels, and by 1981 they had almost tripled. More importantly, the volatility of these rates increased tremendously. Moves of 1 percentage point between the time a loan application was made and the time the loan was closed were not unheard of in 1979. The interest climate resulted in a great deal of risk to both borrower and lender that the rate that seemed plausible one week might be out of line the next week (not to mention the next 30 years). High interest rates combined with the rapid inflation in housing prices to make home financing difficult in general and all but impossible for the first-time buyer. AMIs were created as a way of coping with these problems.

There are literally dozens of different types of AMIs, each with its own peculiar twist. We will discuss the more common ones and those that will probably become more popular in the future.

### Graduated-Payment Mortgages (GPMs)

The only essential differences between the GPM and the traditional mortgage is that the payments on a GPM are not all equal. Graduated payment refers to the fact that GPM payments start at a relatively low level and rise for some number of years. The actual number of years that the payments rise and the percentage increase per year depend on the exact type or plan of the GPM. The five major GPM plans work as illustrated in Exhibit 26–6.

At the end of the graduation period, the monthly payment is held at its existing level for the remainder of the mortgage term. Exhibit 26–7 shows the payment schedule on a $50,000, 10 percent, Plan III GPM.

The attraction of a GPM is the small payment in its early years. A first-time home buyer who might not be able to afford payments on a traditional mortgage might be able to afford the smaller payments of the GPM, even if both loans were for the same principal amount. Eventually, when the graduation period has ended, homeowners with GPMs make up the difference by paying larger monthly amounts than the traditional mortgages require. The originators of GPMs reason that most home buyers, particularly young, first-time home buyers, have incomes that will increase at least as rapidly as the mortgage payments increase. Thus, they should always be able to afford their monthly payments. Exhibit 26–8 compares the initial and final payments of a traditional mortgage with the five GPM plans, assuming all mortgages have a $50,000 balance and a 10 percent interest rate. Notice that the lowest initial payment is on the Plan III GPM, and in this example it is about $100 less per month than the traditional mortgage in the first year. The Plan III GPM is the only plan to offer a 7.5 percent graduation rate; this is the maximum graduation rate that federally chartered banks can currently offer.

The first three GPM plans qualify for inclusion in certain types of mortgage pass-through securities discussed in the next chapter. The majority of the GPMs underlying certain types of pass-through securities are Plan III graduated-payment mortgages because, as can be seen from Exhibit 26–8, Plan III has the lowest initial monthly mortgage payment. Within a pool of mortgages that are collateral for a mortgage pass-through security, GPMs from all three plans may be found. However, analysts typically assume all GPMs are of the Plan III type.

Because GPMs have smaller initial payments than do traditional mortgages, they do not pay down their mortgage balances as quickly. The interesting feature

**EXHIBIT 26–6**
**The Five Major GPM Plans**

| Plan | Term-to-Maturity (Years) | Years that Payments Rise | Percentage Increase per Year |
|------|------|------|------|
| I | 30 | 5 | 2.5% |
| II | 30 | 5 | 5.0 |
| III | 30 | 5 | 7.5 |
| IV | 30 | 10 | 2.0 |
| V | 30 | 10 | 3.0 |

**EXHIBIT 26–7**
**Mortgage Pay-**
**ment Schedule**
**for a $50,000 Plan**
**III GPM (30-Year**
**Term, 10 Percent**
**Mortgage Rate)**

| Year(s) | Monthly Payment |
|---------|-----------------|
| 1 | $333.52 |
| 2 | 358.53 |
| 3 | 385.42 |
| 4 | 414.33 |
| 5 | 445.40 |
| 6-30 | 478.81 |

Note: Plan III GPMs call for monthly payments that increase by 7.5 percent at the end of each of the first five years of the mortgage.

of GPMs is that in their early years they do not pay down any principal at all—in fact their mortgage balances actually *increase* for a short period of time. Technically, we say that they experience "negative amortization" at the outset. To see how this works consider the first-month payment on the GPM in Exhibit 26–7.

**EXHIBIT 26–8**
**Comparison of Initial and Final**
**Payments: Traditional Mort-**
**gages versus GPMs ($50,000,**
**10 Percent, 30-Year Mortgages)**

| Loan Type | Initial Payment | Final Payment |
|-----------|-----------------|---------------|
| Traditional | $438.79 | $438.79 |
| GPM Plan I | 400.29 | 452.88 |
| GPM Plan II | 365.29 | 466.22 |
| GPM Plan III | 333.29 | 478.81 |
| GPM Plan IV | 390.02 | 475.43 |
| GPM Plan V | 367.29 | 493.60 |

Interest due for month one is 10 percent per year for one-twelfth year on $50,000 balance. The negative amortization can be calculated as follows:

$$\$50,000 \times 1/12 \times 10/100 = \$416.67$$
$$\text{Payment on GPM} = \$333.52$$
$$\text{Principal paid} = \$333.52 - \$416.67 = -83.15$$
$$\text{New mortgage balance} = \$50,000 - (-83.15) = \$50,083.15$$

Another way of viewing this situation is as follows: The amount paid on the mortgage ($333.52) was insufficient to cover even the interest due on the loan ($416.67), so the shortfall ($83.15) is lent to the mortgagor. Thus, the new mortgage balance is the sum of the original balance plus the new loan:

$$\$50,000 + \$83.15 = \$50,083.15$$

Of course, the mortgage balance must eventually be reduced to zero. The annual increases in the mortgage payment eventually catch up to and overtake the amount of interest due, and at that time the mortgage balance begins to decrease. In Exhibit 26–9, the mortgage balances (expressed as ratios to the original loan amount) are shown at the end of each year for all five GPM plans as well as for a traditional mortgage. Notice that a Plan III GPM has a balance that rises through the end of the fourth year, at which point it declines to zero over the next 26 years. It is interesting to note that the mortgage balance does not go below 1.0 until some time in the 10th year. Exhibit 26–10 is a graph of the mortgage balances for a traditional mortgage and a Plan III GPM.

## Growing Equity Mortgages

A growing equity mortgage (GEM) is another fixed-rate mortgage whose monthly payments increase over time. However, unlike a GPM there is no negative amortization. The initial monthly mortgage payment is the same as for a level-payment fixed-rate mortgage. By increasing the monthly mortgage payments, more of the mortgage payments are applied to paying off the principal. As a result, the principal amount of the GEM is repaid faster. For example, a $50,000 GEM loan at a rate of 10 percent might call for an initial monthly payment of $438.79 (the same as a traditional 10% 30-year mortgage). However, the GEM payment would gradually increase, and the GEM might be fully paid in only 15 years.

## Adjustable-Rate Mortgages

An adjustable-rate mortgage (ARM) is a mortgage in which the interest rate on the loan is reset periodically. The interest rate may change every six months,

**EXHIBIT 26–9**

**Graduated-Payment Mortgage (GPM) Factor Comparison for 10 Percent, 30-Year Loans**

| Year-End Factors | Ordinary Mortgage | Plan I 5-Year 2.5 % | Plan II 5-Year 5.0 % | Plan III 5-Year 7.5 % | Plan IV 5-Year 2.0 % | Plan V 10-Year 3.0 % |
|---|---|---|---|---|---|---|
| 0 | 1.00000 | 1.00000 | 1.00000 | 1.00000 | 1.00000 | 1.00000 |
| 1 | .99444 | 1.00412 | 1.01291 | 1.02090 | 1.00670 | 1.01241 |
| 2 | .98830 | 1.00615 | 1.02258 | 1.03769 | 1.01214 | 1.02335 |
| 3 | .98152 | 1.00582 | 1.02845 | 1.04949 | 1.01614 | 1.03258 |
| 4 | .97402 | 1.00281 | 1.02987 | 1.05526 | 1.01853 | 1.03985 |
| 5 | .96574 | .99678 | 1.02612 | 1.05383 | 1.01909 | 1.04484 |
| 6 | .95660 | .98734 | 1.01640 | 1.04385 | 1.01759 | 1.04725 |
| 7 | .94649 | .97691 | 1.00567 | 1.03282 | 1.01376 | 1.04669 |
| 8 | .93533 | .96539 | .99381 | 1.02064 | 1.00732 | 1.04277 |
| 9 | .92300 | .95266 | .98071 | 1.00719 | .99796 | 1.03504 |
| 10 | .90938 | .93860 | .96623 | .99233 | .98532 | 1.02299 |
| 11 | .89433 | .92307 | .95025 | .97591 | .96902 | 1.00606 |
| 12 | .97771 | .90591 | .93258 | .95777 | .95101 | .98736 |
| 13 | .85934 | .88696 | .91307 | .93773 | .93111 | .96670 |
| 14 | .83906 | .86602 | .89151 | .91559 | .90913 | .94388 |
| 15 | .81665 | .84289 | .86770 | .89113 | .88484 | .91867 |
| 16 | .79189 | .81733 | .84140 | .86412 | .85802 | .89082 |
| 17 | .76454 | .78910 | .81233 | .83427 | .82838 | .86005 |
| 18 | .73432 | .75792 | .78023 | .80130 | .79564 | .82606 |
| 19 | .70094 | .72347 | .74477 | .76488 | .75948 | .78851 |
| 20 | .66407 | .68541 | .70559 | .72464 | .71953 | .74703 |
| 21 | .62333 | .64336 | .66230 | .68019 | .67539 | .70120 |
| 22 | .57833 | .59692 | .61449 | .63108 | .62663 | .65058 |
| 23 | .52862 | .54561 | .56167 | .57684 | .57277 | .59466 |
| 24 | .47370 | .48892 | .50332 | .51691 | .51326 | .53288 |
| 25 | .41303 | .42631 | .43885 | .45071 | .44752 | .46463 |
| 26 | .34601 | .35713 | .36764 | .37757 | .37491 | .38924 |
| 27 | .27197 | .28071 | .28897 | .29678 | .29468 | .30595 |
| 28 | .19018 | .19629 | .20207 | .20752 | .20606 | .21394 |
| 29 | .09982 | .10303 | .10606 | .10892 | .10816 | .11229 |
| 30 | .00000 | .00000 | .00000 | .00000 | .00000 | .00000 |

**EXHIBIT 26–10**
**Comparison between Plan III GPM and a Traditional Mortgage**

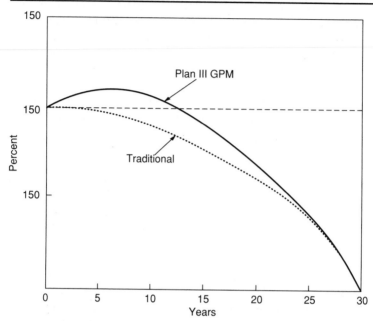

one year, two years, or three years. The interest rate at the reset date is equal to a reference or base index plus a spread, or "margin."

The base index is typically either a market yield (e.g., Treasury securities, prime rate) or a calculated measure such as a thrift cost of funds index or a moving average of mortgage rates. The two most popular indexes for ARMs are the one-year constant maturity Treasury rate (CMT) and the 11th District Cost of Funds (COF). COF is a calculated figure based on the monthly weighted average interest cost for liabilities of thrifts in the 11th Federal Home Loan Bank District.[1]

The index will have an important impact on the performance of an ARM. Historically, the 11th District Cost of Funds (1) exhibits less volatility than the one-year Treasury rate and (2) has a tendency to lag behind movements of the one-year Treasury rate. We observe these two characteristics for the 11th District

---

[1] This district includes the states of California, Arizona, and Nevada. The cost of funds is calculated by first computing the monthly interest expenses for all thrifts included in the 11th District. The interest expenses are summed and then divided by the average of the beginning and ending monthly balance.

COF because of the manner in which it is calculated. The index is a composite cost of funds that includes both historical and current costs. When interest rates are rising, the composite interest cost will include the lower historical cost and the higher current costs. The average will therefore be lower than the current cost. The opposite is true when interest rates are falling. The implication is that when interest rates are falling (rising), an ARM indexed off the 11th District COF will pay a higher (lower) rate than an ARM indexed off the one-year Treasury rate.

The frequency with which the mortgage rate resets varies. For ARMs indexed to the one-year CMT, the mortgage rate is generally reset once a year. The monthly mortgage payments for the subsequent year are then based on the new indexed mortgage rate. For an 11th District COF-based ARM, the mortgage rate typically adjusts monthly.

ARMs have been popular with lenders because they shift interest-rate risk from the lender to the borrower. Thrifts prefer to hold ARMs in their portfolios rather than fixed-rate mortgages because ARMs often provide a better match with their liabilities, which tend to be short-term. Since liabilities are closely tied to the calculated cost of funds index, many thrifts prefer ARMs benchmarked to the 11th District Cost of Funds.

To encourage borrowers to use ARMs rather than fixed-rate mortgages, mortgage originators frequently offer an initial mortgage rate that is less than the prevailing market rate. This below market initial mortgage rate is commonly referred to as a *teaser rate*. At the reset date, the benchmark index plus the margin determines the new mortgage rate. For example, suppose that one-year ARMs are typically offering a 100 basis point margin over the one-year Treasury rate. Suppose also that the current one-year Treasury rate is 6.5 percent, so that the initial mortgage rate should be 7.5 percent. The mortgage originator might set an initial teaser rate of 6.75 percent, a rate 75 basis points below the current index rate plus the margin.

The basic ARM is one that resets periodically and has no other terms that affect the monthly mortgage payment. Typically, however, ARMs do have other terms that affect the monthly mortgage payment, and, hence, an investor's cash flow. These include (1) periodic caps and (2) lifetime rate caps and floors.

*Periodic Caps.*   There are two types of periodic caps: rate caps and payment caps. Rate caps limit the amount that the mortgage interest rate may increase or decrease at a reset date. The rate cap is expressed in percentage points. The most common rate cap on annual reset loans is 2 percent. There is no negative amortization in an ARM with a rate cap. Payment caps limit the change in the monthly mortgage payment at a reset date. The payment cap is expressed as a percentage of the payment; for example, the monthly payment may be allowed to increase 7.5 percent at most. Thus, while there is no restriction on how much the mortgage rate may change, there is a restriction on the amount that the monthly mortgage payment may change. With a payment cap, there can be negative amortization because the cap on the monthly mortgage payment may result in a payment that is not sufficient to cover the higher mortgage interest.

The impact of the two types of periodic caps on the cash flow and mortgage balance is illustrated in Exhibit 26–11.[2] The first ARM in the table is based on a 2 percent rate cap structure while the second ARM is based on a 7.5 percent payment cap structure. The underlying mortgage for both ARMs is a 30-year, $100,000 mortgage with a spread of 200 basis points over the index rate. The initial index rate is 8.5 percent, which means that the initial mortgage rate should be 10.5 percent. In the illustration, it is assumed that the initial rate for both mortgages is a teaser of 8.5 percent, the mortgage rate and monthly mortgage payment reset annually, and the rate cannot exceed 13.5 percent. The second column in the table shows the assumed index rate for each year. In the first year, the monthly mortgage payment and the end of year mortgage balance are identical for both mortgages. In the second year, the index rate is assumed to increase to 9.5 percent. In the absence of any rate cap, the mortgage rate would be 11.5 percent. Because of the 2 percent rate cap, the mortgage rate for the first ARM in the second year is restricted to 10.5 percent, an increase of only 200 basis points over the initial mortgage rate. With the 7.5 percent payment cap, the mortgage rate increases to 11.5 percent. To amortize the mortgage balance at the end of the first year at an 11.5 percent mortgage rate, the monthly mortgage payment would have to increase from $768.91 (the first year monthly mortgage payment at an 8.5 percent mortgage rate) to $986.80. However, the 7.5 percent payment cap restricts the monthly mortgage payment to $826.58 (1.075 times $768.91). Interest alone for the first month of the second year on the existing mortgage balance is $951.09 ($99,244 × 0.115/12). The difference of $124.51 between the interest for that month of $951.09 and the new monthly mortgage payment of $826.58 is added to the mortgage balance. That is, the 7.5 percent payment cap has resulted in negative amortization for this ARM. In the second month of the second year, the interest is greater than $951.09 because the mortgage balance has increased. Thus, more than $124.51 would be added to the mortgage balance in that month. At the end of the second year, the mortgage balance is $100,819. Eventually, the payment on the second ARM will rise to a level where the mortgage balance is paid down. Some ARMs with payment caps also provide for a maximum amount of permitted negative amortization, thereby ensuring that the monthly payments will eventually "catch up."

---

[2] This illustration is taken from Bella S. Borg and Andrew Carron, "The Valuation of Adjustable Rate Mortgages," Chapter 29 in Frank J. Fabozzi (ed.), *The Handbook of Mortgage-Backed Securities: Revised Edition* (Chicago, IL: Probus Publishing, 1988).

**EXHIBIT 26–11**
**Rate Cap Structure versus Payment Cap Structure***

| | | | Rate Cap Structure | | | Payment Cap Structure | | |
| Year | Index Rate | Index Plus Margin | Mortgage Rate | Beginning Balance | P&I Payment | Mortgage Rate | Beginning Balance | P&I Payment |
|---|---|---|---|---|---|---|---|---|
| 1 | 8.50% | 10.50% | 8.50% | $100,000 | $768.91 | 8.50% | $100,000 | $768.91 |
| 2 | 9.50 | 11.50 | 10.50 | 99,244 | 912.39 | 11.50 | 99,244 | 826.58 |
| 3 | 10.50 | 12.50 | 12.50 | 98,690 | 1,060.63 | 12.50 | 100,819 | 888.57 |
| 4 | 12.50 | 14.50 | 13.50 | 98,275 | 1,135.87 | 13.50 | 102,874 | 955.21 |
| 5 | 11.50 | 13.50 | 13.50 | 97,888 | 1,135.87 | 13.50 | 105,455 | 1,026.86 |
| 6 | 9.00 | 11.00 | 11.50 | 97,446 | 990.51 | 11.00 | 107,492 | 1,053.54 |
| 7 | 7.00 | 9.00 | 9.50 | 96,729 | 853.90 | 9.00 | 106,631 | 974.53 |
| 8 | 4.00 | 6.00 | 7.50 | 95,624 | 728.07 | 6.00 | 104,445 | 901.44 |
| 9 | 5.00 | 7.00 | 7.00 | 94,004 | 698.85 | 7.00 | 99,767 | 833.83 |
| 10 | 6.00 | 8.00 | 8.00 | 92,139 | 755.93 | 8.00 | 96,646 | 792.91 |

*$100,000 original principal balance. 30-year original term, and a ceiling of 13.5%.

Source: Bella S. Borg and Andrew S. Carron, "The Valuation of Adjustable Rate Mortgages," Chapter 29 in Frank J Fabozzi (ed.), *The Handbook of Mortgage-Backed Securities: Revised Edition* (Chicago, IL: Probus Publishing, 1988), p. 800.

*Lifetime Caps and Floors.* Most ARMs have an upper limit on the mortgage rate that can be charged over the life of the loan. This lifetime loan cap is expressed in terms of the initial rate, the most common lifetime cap being 5 percent to 6 percent. For example, if the initial mortgage rate is 7 percent and the lifetime cap is 5 percent, the maximum interest rate that the lender can charge at any time is 12 percent. Many ARMs also have a lower limit, or "floor," on the interest rate that can be charged.

*Convertible ARMs.* There are some ARMs that can be converted into fixed-rate mortgages. These are called *convertible ARMs*. The new rate could be either (1) a rate determined by the lender or (2) a market-based rate. The latter rate could be some interest rate spread over the mortgage commitment rates established by FHLMC or FNMA. The trend is toward a market-determined rate. A borrower is typically able to convert at any time between the first and fifth dates at which the mortgage rate is reset. The lender charges a nominal fee for conversion.

## RISKS ASSOCIATED WITH INVESTING IN MORTGAGES

The principal investors in mortgages are thrifts and commercial banks. Pension funds and life insurance companies also invest in mortgages, but their ownership is small compared to banks and thrifts. Exhibit 26–12 shows the net funds provided by investor category for both (unsecuritized) mortgage loans and mortgage securities. By "net funds," it is meant the total amount of mortgage originations and purchases, less the amount of sales.

These investors are exposed to four main risks by investing in whole loans: (1) interest-rate risk, (2) prepayment risk, (3) credit risk, and (4) liquidity risk.

### Interest-Rate Risk

As explained in Chapter 7, interest-rate risk is the risk of loss in the event that general market rates change. Since a mortgage is a debt instrument, its price will decline when interest rates rise, and vice versa.

### Prepayment Risk

As we explained earlier in this chapter, the borrower has the right to pay off all or part of the mortgage balance at any time. Effectively, someone who invests in a mortgage has granted the borrower an option to prepay the mortgage. The uncertainty associated with the cash flow as a result of this embedded option

**EXHIBIT 26–12**

**Sources of Credit for Mortgage Originations: Net Funds Provided by Investors** (Millions of Dollars)

| | Thrifts | Commercial Banks | Pension Funds | Life Insurance Companies | Other[†] | Total |
|---|---|---|---|---|---|---|
| *Net Acquisitions of Mortgage Loans*[*] | | | | | | |
| 1986 | 124,124 | 78,714 | 741 | 6,901 | 27,584 | 238,064 |
| 1987 | 158,581 | 104,643 | 959 | 6,451 | (398) | 270,236 |
| 1988:Q1 | 25,626 | 12,911 | 286 | 701 | (5,891) | 33,633 |
| *Net Acquisitions of Mortgage-Related Securities*[‡] | | | | | | |
| 1986 | 79,428 | 60,761 | 22,224 | 22,488 | 146,355 | 330,256 |
| 1987 | 63,430 | 35,132 | 52,802 | 17,528 | 133,382 | 302,274 |
| 1988:Q1 | 799 | 7,581 | 10,294 | 4,243 | 22,643 | 45,560 |
| *Total Sources of New Housing Credit*[§] | | | | | | |
| 1986 | 202,552 | 139,475 | 22,965 | 29,389 | 173,939 | 568,320 |
| 1987 | 222,011 | 139,775 | 53,761 | 23,979 | 132,984 | 572,510 |
| 1988:Q1 | 26,425 | 20,492 | 10,580 | 4,944 | 16,752 | 79,193 |

[*] The net acquisitions figure is the sum of mortgage originations and purchases less sales.
[†] Others include mortgage bankers, households, corporations, and other insurance companies.
[‡] Net acquistions of mortgage-related securities equal purchases less sales.
[§] Technically, total sources of new housing credit should equal total originations; here they do not because purchases exceed sales. This reflects statistical problems in the HUD data (see appendix, *Secondary Mortgage Markets*, February 1984).

is called *prepayment risk*. In the next chapter this risk is discussed in more detail. For now, it is sufficient to say that, by holding an individual mortgage, an investor is exposed to substantial prepayment risk. This risk can be reduced somewhat by holding a diversified portfolio of mortgages.

## Credit Risk

The credit risk is the risk of loss due to a homeowner/borrower default. For FHA-insured and VA-guaranteed mortgages, this risk is minimal because the credit of FHA and VA stand behind such loans. For privately insured mortgages, the risk can be gauged by the credit rating of the private insurance company that has insured the mortgage. For conventional mortgages without private insurance, the credit risk depends on the borrower. The risk exposure can be roughly gauged by the LTV.

## Liquidity Risk

Liquidity risk is the risk of loss in the event that the investment must be sold quickly. It is typically measured by the bid-ask spread in the marketplace for the investment. Most mortgage securities are highly liquid and therefore have minimal liquidity risk. While there is an active secondary market for whole loans which we shall discuss further below, the fact is that bid-ask spreads are large compared to other debt instruments.

## THE DEVELOPMENT OF THE CURRENT MORTGAGE MARKET

### The Primary Mortgage Market

Historically, the predominant suppliers of mortgage funds were thrifts. Thrifts initially provided mortgages only for local citizens and obtained their funds from local depositors. Thus, the demand for funds came from local citizens who needed mortgages and the supply of funds came from the same local citizens who deposited funds in a local thrift. But the supply and demand for mortgage funds did not, except by accident, match. When the demand for mortgage funds was less than the supply of funds, thrifts would invest in other types of sources such as government or corporate securities. When the demand for mortgage funds was greater than the supply, there were not many opportunities for thrifts to obtain funds to satisfy the additional demand.

The obvious drawback of a mortgage origination mortgage market structured in this way is that it relies on local supply and demand. As a result, in one region of the country there might be excess demand for mortgages resulting in high mortgage rates, while in another part of the country supply may exceed demand resulting in low mortgage rates. This is the highly segmented mortgage market that existed in the United States for the two decades that followed World War II.

Because of the imbalance between local supply and demand, a new participant entered the mortgage market—the mortgage banker that we discussed earlier in this chapter. Unlike thrifts and commercial banks, mortgage bankers did not provide funds from deposit taking. Instead, they originated mortgages and sold them to life insurance companies and/or thrifts in other parts of the country. They provided a *brokerage function*. The introduction of mortgage bankers brought mortgage rates throughout the country closer and reduced the shortage of mortgage money available in high-demand regions.

While the mortgage market operated this way through the late 1960s, it had a major pitfall—it was dependent on the availability of funds from thrifts and banks, whether local or national. Prior to 1986, the maximum interest rate that thrifts and commercial banks were permitted to pay was regulated by the federal government. When market interest rates were less than the maximum interest rates that banks and thrifts were allowed to pay on deposits, there was a steady flow of funds into these institutions to provide mortgage financing. However, when market interest rates exceeded the maximum interest rates these institutions were permitted to pay, depositors withdrew their funds and invested in other instruments that paid market rates. This process is called *disintermediation*. As a result, mortgage funds dried up and mortgage rates rose substantially.[3]

What was needed was a mortgage market that was less dependent on deposit-taking institutions. This could be accomplished by developing a strong secondary mortgage market to which financial institutions in addition to deposit-taking institutions and life insurance companies would find it attractive to supply funds. This was accomplished by the development of a secondary mortgage market.

## The Secondary Mortgage Market

The foundations for the secondary mortgage market can be traced back to the Great Depression and the congressional legislation that followed. Prior to the mid-1930s, the only type of mortgage that was available was a balloon mortgage. With a balloon mortgage, the homeowner must either pay off the mortgage balance with cash or refinance the mortgage by borrowing once again from the thrift. Thrifts had lines of credit with commercial banks so that they could obtain funding for mortgages. During the Great Depression, all financial institutions faced a liquidity squeeze. As a result, commercial banks cut off the line of credit and, in turn, S&Ls could no longer provide funding to refinance balloon mortgages that were coming due. The result was a substantial number of defaults.

Congress' response to the Great Depression and its adverse consequences for financial markets was to establish several public-purpose agencies. The Federal Reserve provided better liquidity for commercial banks through the Federal Reserve discount window. Liquidity for thrifts was provided by the creation of the Federal Home Loan Banks (FHLBs). FHLBs were granted the right to borrow from the Treasury, thereby providing this agency with liquidity.

Another creation of Congress, the Federal Housing Administration (FHA), addressed the problems with the balloon mortgage. It was the FHA that developed and promoted the long-term self-amortizing mortgage we described earlier in this chapter. In addition, the FHA reduced credit risk for investors by offering insurance against mortgage defaults. Not all mortgages could be insured,

---

[3] Such "credit crunches" were exacerbated by the existence of low usury ceilings (e.g., 10%) in many states.

however. To be insured, the mortgage applicant had to satisfy the underwriting standards established by FHA. By doing so, FHA was the first to standardize mortgage terms. While this may be taken for granted today, this standardization was essential for the development of a secondary mortgage market. In the early 1940s the Veteran's Administration guaranteed qualified mortgages.

But who was going to buy (invest) in these mortgages? Thrifts could do so, but they often needed liquidity. Congress tackled that problem when it created another government-sponsored agency, the Federal National Mortgage Association (FNMA). This agency, popularly known as "Fannie Mae," was charged with the responsibility to create a liquid secondary market for mortgages. It tried to accomplish this objective by buying and selling mortgages. Basically, Fannie Mae provided a *dealer function*. Unlike mortgage bankers, Fannie Mae held an inventory of mortgages. The value of that inventory could rise or fall, depending on whether interest rates decreased or increased. This is the same situation faced by a dealer in U.S. Treasury securities, who has an inventory of government securities.[4] Fannie Mae needed a funding source in case it faced a liquidity squeeze. Congress provided this by giving Fannie Mae a credit line with the Treasury.[5]

Despite the presence of Fannie Mae, the secondary mortgage market did not fully develop. During periods of tight money, Fannie Mae could do little to mitigate the housing crisis. In 1968, Congress divided Fannie Mae into two organizations: (1) the current Fannie Mae, and (2) the Government National Mortgage Association (popularly known as "Ginnie Mae"). Ginnie Mae's function is to use the "full faith and credit of the U.S. government" to support the FHA and VA mortgage market. Two years later in 1970, the Federal Home Loan Mortgage Corporation (popularly known as "Freddie Mac") was created by Congress to provide additional support for conventional mortgages (i.e., those not insured by the FHA or VA).

Ginnie Mae accomplished its objective by guaranteeing securities issued by private entities who pooled mortgages together and then used these mortgage pools as collateral for the security sold. Freddie Mac and Fannie Mae purchased mortgages, pooled these mortgages, and then issued securities themselves using the pool as collateral. The securities sold are called *mortgage pass-through securities*. They are purchased by many types of investors who had previously shunned investing in the mortgage market. In the 1980s, private issuers of mortgage pass-through securities who did not use the backing of the three agencies but instead used some form of private credit enhancement began issuing these securities backed by conventional single-family mortgages and commercial real estate mortgages.

---

[4] Except that Fannie Mae was always *long*.
[5] Fannie Mae also issued debt directly.

This process of converting individual mortgages into pools and selling them to investors is called *securitization*. Currently there are agency conduits and private conduits. Fannie Mae, Freddie Mac, and the private conduits also perform the dealer function in the secondary mortgage market.

## SUMMARY

This chapter described the U.S. mortgage market and the mortgage origination process. The major originators of mortgage loans are thrifts, commercial banks, and mortgage bankers.

The various types of mortgages and their cash-flow characteristics were Explained. These included the traditional level-payment fixed-rate mortgages, graduated-payment mortgages, growing equity mortgages, and adjustable-rate mortgages.

The uncertainty associated with investing in any of these mortgages is related to, because of prepayments, uncertain cash flows. The uncertainty associated with the cash flow is called prepayment risk. In addition, by investing in mortgages an investor faces liquidity risk and interest-rate risk and may be exposed to credit risk. The major investors are thrifts and banks.

The mortgage market at one time was primarily a market in which local citizens made deposits in local thrifts and these thrifts loaned the funds to local citizens who wanted to purchase a home. Because of the imbalance between local supply and demand, mortgage bankers smoothed out the imbalance by making funds available from regions of the country with surplus funds to regions of the country that needed funds. This system, however, was dependent on regulated deposits at thrifts and banks. A secondary market developed in which public and private conduits securitized mortgages, thereby allowing other investors to supply funds to the mortgage market.

# CHAPTER 27

## MORTGAGE PASS-THROUGH SECURITIES

Linda Lowell
*Vice President*
*Mortgage Investment Strategies*
*Smith Barney*

Pass-throughs are the predominant form of mortgage-related security, so much so that the terms "mortgage-backed security," "MBS," and "pass-through" have become interchangeable in common usage. The importance of MBSs extends, as well, to structured mortgage securities such as CMOs, REMICs, and Strips, for which pass-throughs are the most common form of collateral.

The pass-through market has achieved dramatic growth in the 1980s. Pass-throughs have fostered an extensive and stable secondary market for housing debt and, in recent years, spurred the securitization of other receivables such as automobile and credit card loans. By the end of 1988, there were approximately $722 billion of agency pass-throughs outstanding; by comparison, the size of the high-grade corporate bond market was over $800 billion and the marketable Treasury security market about $1.9 billion.[1] Burgeoning investor interest has been a key factor spurring this tremendous growth. Pass-through securities are extensively held by every class of institutional investor, including commercial banks and savings institutions, insurance companies, mutual funds, and pension plans.

This growth has been fostered by the federal government's concern for the availability of housing and of mortgage credit. The involvement of three

---

[1] Taken from the Federal Reserve and Drexel Burnham Lambert's Fixed Income Research Analytics databases.

government-sponsored agencies has lent the market the stability, credit support, and standardization necessary to attract investors traditionally committed to the corporate and Treasury sectors of the debt market, as well as to encourage the participation of private guarantor/issuers.

The pass-through structure has proved to be an excellent vehicle for securitizing many different types of mortgage instruments available to home buyers. As a result, in addition to the standard-level payment mortgage, large amounts of adjustable-rate mortgages and graduated-payment mortgages have been securitized.

This chapter is intended to provide a brief overview of the variety of pass-through types and an introduction to the general structure and analysis of level-payment pass-throughs, the largest and most frequently traded form of MBSs. The discussion then moves to the features of pass-throughs that distinguish them from noncallable corporate or Treasury debt instruments and that give them their market properties. The chapter concludes with a discussion of the economic or total rate of return performance of pass-throughs in various interest-rate scenarios and a relative value analysis of these securities.

## WHAT IS A MORTGAGE PASS-THROUGH SECURITY?

Pass-through securities are created when mortgages are pooled together, and undivided interests or participations in the pool are sold. The originator or another institution that purchases this right continues to service the mortgages, collecting payments and "passing through" the principal and interest, less the servicing, guarantee, and other fees, to the security holders. The security holders receive pro rata shares of the resultant cash flows. A portion of the outstanding principal is paid each month according to the amortization schedules established for each individual mortgage. In addition, and this is a critical feature of mortgage pass-through securities, the principal on individual mortgages in the pool can be prepaid without penalty in whole or in part at any time before the stated maturity of the certificate. This characteristic has important implications for the price and yield of the certificate, as will be explored in detail later.

Mortgage originators (savings and loans, commercial banks, and mortgage bankers) are among the most active in pooling mortgages and issuing pass-throughs. In many cases, the originator obtains the guarantee of one of three federally sponsored agencies, GNMA (the Government National Mortgage Association, or "Ginnie Mae"), FNMA (the Federal National Mortgage Association, or "Fannie Mae") and FHLMC (the Federal Home Loan Mortgage Corporation, or "Freddie Mac"). A significant volume of mortgages are directly purchased, pooled, and securitized by the agencies as well. A smaller amount of mortgages are securitized directly by private issuers.

## AGENCY PASS-THROUGH SECURITIES

The vast majority of regularly traded pass-throughs, then, are issued and/or guaranteed by federally sponsored agencies. Differences between the agencies—the nature of their ties to the U.S. Government, their stated role in national housing policy, and so forth—have important consequences for the relative value and performance of their pass-throughs. In addition, considerable diversity exists within each agency's pass-through programs. Some of the differences between programs also influence the investment characteristics of the securities. For this reason, the agencies and their major programs are discussed in some detail. A summary of the terms and features of the more widely traded types of agency pass-throughs is included in Exhibit 27–1.

**EXHIBIT 27–1**
**Features of Mortgage Pass-Through Securities**

|  | GNMA I | GNMA II |
| --- | --- | --- |
| *Number of Lenders in Pool* | Single | Single & multiple |
| *Mortgages* | FHA, VA, FMHA | FHA, VA, FMHA |
| *Pool Types*[1] | Single-family level payment (SF), graduated payment (GP), and growing equity mortgages (GA, GD), mobile home (MH), construction (CL), project (PL), and buydown loans (BD) | Same as GNMA I except includes adjustable-rate mortages, or ARMs (AR), and excludes PL, CL, and BD pools. (Buydown mortgages can be included in SF pools.) |
| *Pool Terms* | Separate programs for SF and GP series with 15- and 30-year terms; MH 12- (A), 15- (B), 18- (C), 20-year (D) terms; GA and GD terms vary | AR pools have 30-year terms |
| *Mortgage Seasoning* | Only new mortgages (less than 24 months) | (less than 24 months) |
| *Mortgage Coupon Range* | 0.5% over security rate (approximately 3.5% above for mobile home) | 0.5%–1.5% over security rate (approximately 3.5% above for mobile homes) |
| *Guaranty* | Full and timely payment of principal and interest (backed by full faith and credit of U. S. Govt.) | Full and timely payment of principal and interest (backed by full faith and credit of U. S. Govt.) |

## EXHIBIT 27–1—*Continued*

|  | FHLMC Regular PC | FHLMC Swap | FNMA MBS |
|---|---|---|---|
| *Number of Lenders in Pool* | Multiple | Single & multiple | Multiple |
| *Mortgages* | Conventional and seasoned FHA and VA | Conventional and seasoned FHA and VA | Conventional and seasoned FHA and VA |
| *Pool Types*[1] | FHA/VA (15), conventional 30-year (16, 17); conventional 15-year (20), multifamily Plan B (22, 49), ARM (35, 41) | FHA/VA (14), conventional 30-year (18, 25, 27, and 28 guarantee the timely payment of interest, 26 the timely principal and interest), multifamily (23, 24), conventional 15-year (21), multi-family variable interest rate, or VIRs (31). | Conventional long-term level pay (CL), intermediate (CI), conventional long-term fully assumable (CA), conventional short-term (CS), FHA/VA long-term (GL), FHA long-term project loans (MA), and growing equity (GEM) |
| *Pool Terms* | FHA/VA and ARM securities have 30-year terms. Multifamily pool terms vary with series: 22 series have 15-year terms, 49 series have 10-year terms | Unless defined otherwise, these series' have 30-year terms. | Long-term is 30 years, intermediate 15 years, and short-term 7 years. GEM series have 15-year terms, MA 40 years |
| *Mortgage Seasoning* | No limit on seasoning | No limit on seasoning | No limit on seasoning |
| *Mortgage Coupon Range* | No restrictions[2] | 0.5%–2.5% above the pass-through rate[2] | 0.5%–2.5% above the pass-through rate[3] |
| *Guaranty* | Timely payment of interest and eventual payment of principal. Mortgages insured by eligible insurers | Timely payment of interest; certain series guarantee timely payment of principal and interest | Full and timely payment of principal and interest |

## Government National Mortgage Association Pass-Through Securities

The largest and best-known group of pass-through securities is guaranteed by GNMA, a wholly owned U.S. government corporation within the Department of Housing and Urban Development (HUD). The mortgage pools underlying GNMA pass-through securities are made up of FHA-insured or VA-guaranteed mortgage loans. GNMA pass-throughs are backed by the full faith and credit of the U.S. government.

Furthermore, the GNMA pass-through security is what is known as a *fully*

## EXHIBIT 27–1 — *Continued*

|  | GNMA I | GNMA II | FHLMC Regular PC | FHLMC Swap | FNMA MBS |
|---|---|---|---|---|---|
| Payment Delay | 45 stated 15 actual | 50 stated 20 actual | 75 stated 45 actual | 75 stated 45 actual | 55 stated 25 actual |
| Assumability | Yes | Yes | No | No | No |
| Minimum Pool size | $1 million | $1 million[4] | $50 million | $1 million[5] | $1 million[6] |
| Maximum Mortgage Amount | $124,875[7] | $124,875[7] | $187,600[8] | $187,600[8] | $187,600[8] |

[1] Series types or prefixes are given in parentheses.

[2] After June 1, 1987, mortgage rates on regular or cash PC pools may be 0.0 to 2.0 percent above the security rate, but the range between maximum and minimum mortgage rates in the pool may not exceed 1.0 percent; the range between maximum and minimum mortgage rates for guarantor pools may not exceed 1.0 percent.

[3] The range between maximum and minimum mortgage rates in the FNMA pool may not exceed 2.0 percent.

[4] $1 million minimum pool size for SF pools; $500,000 for GP, GT, GA, GD, AR, or AZ pools; $350,000 for MH pools.

[5] A series of "mini" FHLMC swap securities was established in 1986 with pool minimum of $250,000 and backed by 30-year (43 timely interest, 46 timely principal and interest); 15-year (44 timely interest and 47 timely principal and interest); and FHA/VA (45 timely interest and 48 timely principal and interest). These securities are not considered good for delivery in generic trades.

[6] The FNMA "majors" program has a minimum pool size of $250,000.

[7] Maximum FHA loan in high-cost region is $124,875 (e. g., New York, Los Angeles, etc.); maximum VA loan $144,000 (current December 1, 1989).

[8] FHLMC and FNMA loan limits range from $187,600 for single-family unit to $360,450 for four-family units. In Alaska, Guam, and Hawaii, the loan maximums ranges from $281,400 to $540,675 (effective December 1, 1989).

*modified* pass-through security, which means that regardless of whether or not the mortgage payment is made, the holder of the security will receive full and timely payment of principal and interest. Among MBSs, GNMA is considered to be of the best credit quality, since it is backed directly by the U.S. government.

GNMA administers two primary pass-through programs, the original GNMA program (GNMA I), in existence since 1970, and GNMA II, established in 1983. The GNMA I and II programs are further divided into a variety of subprograms depending on the type of mortgages that make up the underlying pool. A variety of different types of mortgage pools are eligible for GNMA guarantee. The most commonly held and traded of all pass-through securities represents pools of 30-year maturity, fixed-rate level-payment mortgages on single-family residential homes (SF). GNMA SFs are guaranteed by both the GNMA I and GNMA II programs. Single-family mortgages with original maturities of 15 years are part of the same SF pool type; the pools are traded as GNMA "Midgets" and differ from the 30-year securities only in stated maturity.

GNMA securities are based on other types of single-family mortgages as well, including graduated-payment (GPM), growing equity (GEM), buydown (BD), and adjustable-rate (ARM) loans. Markets for these securities are smaller and less liquid than for the traditional GNMA SFs, and the differences between the underlying mortgages have important consequences for analysis of the securities' characteristics. Mobile home loans and project loans are also securitized. Project loan securities are normally backed by a single FHA-insured loan for multifamily housing, hospitals, and similar public-benefit housing-related projects.

GNMA pools are the most homogeneous among pass-throughs. All mortgages in a pool must be of the same type and be less than 12 months old. Ninety percent of the pooled mortgages backing 30-year pass-throughs must have original maturities of 20 or more years. The mortgage interest rates of GNMA I pools must all be the same and the mortgages must be issued by the same lender. The changes introduced with GNMA II include the ability to assemble multiple issuer pools, thereby allowing for larger and more geographically dispersed pools as well as securitization of smaller portfolios. Also, a wider range of coupons is permitted in a GNMA II pool (the excess yield over the lowest rate is retained by the issuer or servicer as servicing income and is not passed through). Issuers are permitted to take greater servicing fees, ranging from 50 to 150 basis points. GNMA I's and II's also differ in permitted payment delay; GNMA I payments are received with a 15-day delay, while GNMA II's have an additional 5-day delay passing through principal and interest payments because issuer payments are consolidated by a central paying agent. Finally, GNMA II requires a larger minimum pool size—$7 million principal value in contrast to the $1 million required for GNMA I pools.

## Conventional Mortgage-Backed Securities

Pass-throughs most generally fall into two groups: those guaranteed by GNMA and those guaranteed by FHLMC and FNMA. Those of the latter group are often referred to as conventional pass-throughs, since they are not government-insured or assumable. The nature of the guarantee made by the conventional agencies is different as well. FHLMC and FNMA are not really agencies of the U.S. government; rather they are government-sponsored entities (GSEs). Nonetheless, their securities, like Treasury securities, presently are not rated by the rating agencies. The market perceives a difference in credit quality from GNMAs and, as a consequence, requires a higher risk premium for conventional pass-throughs. Normally, this translates into a higher yield, with all else equal. The vigorous participation of FNMA and FHLMC in the MBS derivative market, as issuers of CMOs and Strips, has helped to bid up these securities relative to GNMAs. In coupon classes that are unlikely to be used as CMO collateral or when market conditions temporarily halt CMO creation, perceived differences in credit quality result in wider price differentials.[2]

Conventional loans backing FHLMC and FNMA pass-throughs are due on sale in contrast to FHA and VA loans, which can be assumed by the buyer. This is one of the features which leads to notable differences in the prepayment characteristics of FHLMC and FNMA securities on the one hand, and GNMA securities on the other. Other fundamental differences between conventional and FHA/VA mortgages include the fact that FHA and VA loans provide implicit housing subsidies to middle income persons and veterans, and rates tend to be below those for conventional mortgages. Similarly the ceiling on FHA loans is lower than that on the conventional loans pooled in FHLMCs. In general, it is inferred that people with conventional mortgages are wealthier and more mobile than those with FHA and VA mortgages. Any conventional home mortgage loans that meet the documentation and other requirements of the guaranteeing agency and the specific program may be included in a pool.

*Federal Home Loan Mortgage Corporation Participation Certificates.* FHLMC was created in 1970 to promote an active national secondary market for conventional residential mortgages and has been issuing mortgage-backed securities since 1971. At its creation, FHLMC was governed as an entity within the Federal Home Loan Bank System, with stock held by member thrift institutions. The 1989 Financial Institutions Reform, Recovery, and Enforcement Act (FIRREA) restructured FHLMC to give it a market-oriented corporate structure similar to that of FNMA under the regulatory control of the Department of Housing and Urban Development (HUD). The agency pools a wide variety of fixed- and adjustable-rate mortgages under its Cash and Guarantor programs. The largest of these pass-through programs are the single-family, fixed-rate 15- and 30-year Participation Certificates (PCs). Under the Cash program, FHLMC purchases conventional one-to-four family mortgage loans and participations from originators, pools them (minimum pool size is $50 million), and sells undivided interest in them as PCs. The Guarantor program was originally established to provide liquidity to the thrift industry by allowing originators to swap pooled mortgages (minimum pool size $1 million) for PCs in those same pools (hence these are sometimes called swap PCs). The certificates can be held, used as collateral for short- and long-term borrowings, or sold. This program quickly

---

[2] Since 1984, the creation of derivative mortgage-backed securities has proceeded at such a brisk pace that the supply of many pass-through securities has been sharply reduced. As of the end of 1989, almost 50 percent of the outstanding principal amount of conventional pass-throughs with half or whole coupons (the more liquid of the tradable coupon classes) has been pledged to CMOs or strips and can no longer trade. By contrast only about 20 percent of the outstanding amount of frequently traded GNMA coupon classes has been pledged to structured products.

became popular with nonthrift mortgage originators as well and now accounts for the bulk of FHLMC pass-through production.

In June 1990, FHLMC announced a major change in its pass-through programs. In particular, securities issued beginning in September 1990 will have a shorter payment delay and, in many programs, a stronger guarantee. Historically, in the larger programs, FHLMC guaranteed the *timely* payment of interest and the *eventual* payment of principal. (Such securities are "modified" in contrast to GNMAs which are fully "modified," as they guarantee the timely payment of both interest and principal.) A number of smaller programs provided fully modified pass-throughs as well. The new Gold PCs are fully modified. Pass-throughs issued prior to September had 75-day stated payment delays; under the new program the stated delay is shortened to 45 days.

Mortgages underlying both the FHLMC regular and swap PCs are permitted to have original maturities of not less than 15 or more than 30 years. Seasoned mortgages (mortgages outstanding for some time) are also permitted. Consequently, the actual life of the investment may differ significantly from the stated maturity of the security. Coupons also vary much more widely within a pool than with GNMA securities, but in this feature there are important differences between regular and swap PCs. Coupons of mortgages in swap pools must be above the pass-through rate and may be as much as 250 basis points above the pass-through rate. In contrast, regular PC pools contain mortgages with rates up to 200 basis points above the pass-through rate, but the range between the highest and lowest mortgage rate may not exceed 100 basis points. Mortgages even may have interest rates below the coupon on the pool. This wide dispersion of interest rates can have a significant impact on the prepayment risk of the resulting security.

FHLMC regular and swap securities also are issued with 15-year maturities. (The shorter maturity regular PC is known as a "Gnome," the swap as a "non-Gnome.") These mortgages have original maturities of not less than 10 years. In addition, FHLMC has both cash and guarantor FHA/VA programs, normally containing FHA/VA loans too seasoned for inclusion in GNMA pools. FHLMC also offers FHA/VA, ARM, and multifamily-backed securities, generally under both the cash and guarantor programs.

*Federal National Mortgage Association Mortgage-Backed Securities.* The Federal National Mortgage Association is the newest agency player in the pass-through market; the first FNMA MBSs were issued in 1981. The agency was established to promote a secondary market for conventional and seasoned FHA/VA single- and multifamily mortgages. FNMA is, in effect, a quasi-private corporation. While a number of federal constraints on its activities exist, it does not receive a government subsidy or appropriation, its stock is traded on the New York Stock Exchange, and it is taxed at the full corporate rate. In addition to holding loans purchased from originators in its portfolio, FNMA also may securitize and sell the mortgages. FNMA pools mortgages from its purchase programs and issues MBSs through a swap program similar to FHLMC's. Like GNMA, FNMA guarantees the timely payment of principal and interest for all securities it issues. Similarly, its securities are not rated by the rating agencies.

The 30-year conventional security, FNMA CL, is based on level-payment mortgages fully amortizing in 16 to 30 years. FNMA also issues securities based on conventional mortgages amortizing in 8 to 15 years, FNMA CIs or "Dwarfs." The agency also has played a significant role in issuing adjustable- and variable-rate mortgage pass-throughs. In addition, it administers programs to securitize FHA and VA 30-year loans and FHA-insured project loans.

Pool size starts at $1 million and more than one originators may join to form pools. FNMA pools may contain seasoned or aged mortgages and coupons are permitted to vary in a range of 200 basis points, from 0.5 percent to 2.5 percent above the pass-through rate.

### Private Pass-through Securities

Conventional mortgage pass-throughs are also issued by private entities such as commercial banks, thrifts, homebuilders, and private conduits. The supply of these securities, roughly $5–$6 billion a year, is very small in comparison to that of agency pass-throughs. These securities are not guaranteed or insured by any government agency. Instead, their credit is normally enhanced by pool insurance, letters of credit, guarantees, or subordinated interests. The great majority of private pass-throughs issued have received a rating of "AA" or better.

The primary role of private issuers is to provide a secondary market for conventional loans that do not qualify for FHLMC and FNMA programs. Normally, it is more profitable for originators of conforming loans (i.e., loans that do qualify for an agency security) to use the agency programs. There are a number of reasons why conventional mortgage loans may not qualify, but the chief one is that the principal balance exceeds the maximum allowed by the government (these are called "jumbo" loans in the market). Another significant difference from agency conventional pass-throughs is that there is no limitation by private issuers on the range of underlying mortgage rates above the pass-through coupon, nor on servicing and guarantee fees. These features will influence the prepayment characteristics of private pass-throughs.

## MORTGAGE AND PASS-THROUGH CASH FLOWS

The investment characteristics and performance of pass-throughs cannot be evaluated without a thorough understanding of what cash flows are received by the investor. Analysis of the cash-flow pattern begins with the simplest case, the payment stream of the underlying mortgage, assuming level payments and no prepayment of principal. Following that, the effects of payment delays, servicing fees (the amount retained by a servicer reduces the cash flow to pass-through holders), and prepayments are incorporated into the analysis.

Standard residential fixed-rate mortgages are repaid in equal monthly installments of principal and interest (hence, the term *level payment*). In the early years, most of the monthly installment consists of interest. Over time, the interest portion of each payment declines as the principal balance declines until, near maturity, almost all of each payment is principal.

Given the assumption that all of the mortgages have the same coupons and maturities, the scheduled cash-flow pattern from a mortgage pool is consistent with that of an individual mortgage. Exhibit 27–2 shows the scheduled cash-flow pattern for a $1 million pool of identical 10 percent, 30-year mortgages without prepayments. Because there is a fixed rate of interest on the loan and no prepayments occur, the total mortgage cash flow is level over all periods. When the assumption that all the mortgages in the pool are identical is relaxed, the scheduled principal and interest payment cannot be calculated with absolute accuracy unless they are determined for each individual mortgage and then aggregated. By treating the pool like a single mortgage and calculating principal and interest payments using the weighted average coupon (WAC) and maturity (WAM) for

**EXHIBIT 27–2**
**Scheduled Mortgage Pool Cash Flows ($1 Million Pool of 10 Percent 30-Year Mortgages)**

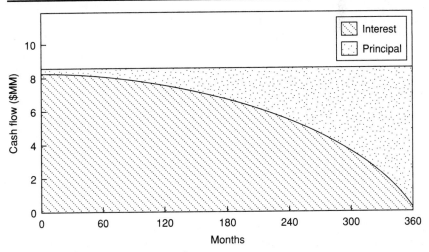

Note: Assumes no prepayments.

the pool[3] it is possible to project the payments with reasonable accuracy when pools are fairly homogeneous, as GNMA pools are. (The discrepancy arises from the fact that amortization is not a "linear" function. Individual loans will be paying principal and interest at different rates depending on the age and term of the loan.) The accuracy of projected amortization schedules using WAC and WAM statistics is somewhat less when a wide range of coupons, maturities, and seasonings are permitted in a pool.

The cash flow from a pass-through certificate is similar but not identical to the cash flow from the underlying pool of mortgages. The differences arise from the deduction of servicing fees and a delay in the receipt of payments. While the total scheduled monthly cash flow from the mortgage pool is level, the cash flow from the corresponding pass-through is not. The servicing fee is a percentage of the outstanding principal, and thus the dollar amount of servicing fee decreases as principal declines. As a consequence, the total cash flows to pass-through owners increase slightly over the term. The cash flow from a passthrough certificate with a 9.5 percent coupon (the difference between the 10 percent WAC and a 0.5 percent servicing fee) is presented in Exhibit 27–3. The

**EXHIBIT 27–3**

**Scheduled Mortgage-Backed Security Cash Flows ($1 Million Pool of 10 Percent, 30-Year Mortgages and a 9.5 Percent Pass-through Certificate)**

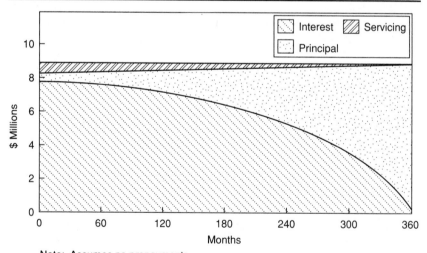

Note: Assumes no prepayments.

---

[3] The WAC and WAM are computed using as weights the principal amount outstanding.

graph shows that the decline in servicing fees leads to slightly increasing cash flow over time.

The delay does not alter the level of payments, but it does affect their timing. In effect, it pushes the stream of payments further out in time and effectively lowers the present value of the payment stream. There are two sources of payment delay in pass-throughs. Mortgage payments are made in arrears; that is, the first mortgage payment is due from the homeowner at the beginning of the second month after origination. Secondly, as a result of processing the payment, the holder of the corresponding pass-through does not receive this payment until later. An investor in a GNMA single-family pass-through, for example, does not receive payment until the 15th day of the second month. A GNMA trader will express that 15-day actual delay as a 45-day delay so as to include the normal mortgage delay of the preceding 30-day month. FNMA securities have a stated delay of 55 days, which means the first payment takes place on the 25th day of the second month. FHLMC securities have a 75-day delay.

Delay decreases the present value of the stream of payments: the greater the delay, the lower the price for a given cash-flow yield. Similarly, for a given yield and payment stream, yield declines as delay increases. Yield and cash flows held equal, GNMA securities with lower delays will trade at higher prices than FNMAs or FHLMCs, and FNMAs will trade higher than FHLMCs. The effect of delay on the price and yield of a 10 percent coupon pass-through is indicated in Exhibit 27–4.

Analysis of the cash flows from pass-through securities would end here if individual loans in the pool could not prepay at any time prior to their stated maturities. The possibility of prepayments means that cash flows cannot be predicted with certainty. Assumptions concerning the likely prepayment pattern must be made in order to estimate the cash flows.

**EXHIBIT 27–4**
**The Effect of Payment Delay on Pass-Through Yield and Price**

| Stated Delay | Yield | Change | Price | Change (%) |
|---|---|---|---|---|
| 30 | 9.59 |  | 99  8/32 |  |
| 45 | 9.54 | −.05 | 98 27/32+ | −0.39 |
| 50 | 9.53 | −.06 | 98 23/32+ | −0.52 |
| 55 | 9.51 | −.08 | 98 19/32 | −0.66 |
| 75 | 9.45 | −.14 | 98  2/32 | −1.20 |

Note: Assumes 9.5 coupon, 99 $\frac{8}{32}$ price, 9.59 yield and no pre-payments.

Exhibit 27–5 depicts the cash-flow patterns for the pass-through when pre-payments are introduced. The cash-flow pattern shown in the diagram is based on the assumption that a constant fraction of the remaining principal is prepaid each month (in this case, at a constant prepayment rate of 0.5% per month). The cash flow is no longer level in each month over the period. Instead, it declines each month as both prepayments and scheduled principal payments reduce the remaining principal balance of the pool.

The interest rate and age of a mortgage (or WAC and WAM of the underlying loans in mortgage pool) determine the rate at which scheduled principal is paid to the investor. In general, for the same principal amount and term, the higher the mortgage rate is, the greater the interest payments and, accordingly, the lower the principal payments in the early years of the mortgage are. A look at any of the cash-flow figures should make apparent the effect of age on cash flows. All other things being equal, age affects the cash flow by establishing the amount of principal included in a given monthly payment and the number of payments remaining. As the security ages, a greater proportion of the payments will be principal. For pass-throughs purchased at a discount, older pass-throughs will have higher yields—more principal is returned sooner at par. Age has the

**EXHIBIT 27–5**

**Scheduled and Unscheduled Mortgage-Backed Security Cash Flows ($1 Million Pool of 10 Percent, 30-Year Mortgages and a 9.5 Percent Pass-through Certificate)**

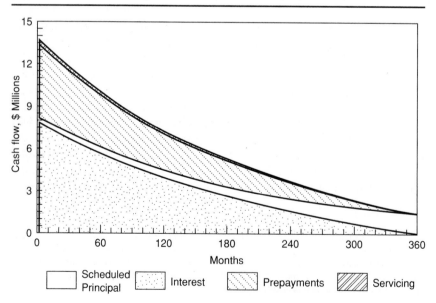

opposite impact on premium securities; at the same price and coupon older pass-throughs have lower yields, since less principal is outstanding for shorter periods of time to earn high coupon income while principal is coming back to the investor at par. In either case, the further the price of the security is from par, the greater the impact of seasoning on the yield. The yields for securities that are near par are not significantly affected.

The issue date or stated maturity often does not give a complete idea of the seasoning of the underlying mortgages, particularly in the case of securities issued by FNMA and FHLMC, which can contain mortgages already seasoned at the time of issue. A weighted-average maturity statistic is available for many pass-through programs but will not always be useful for determining the degree of seasoning in the pool, since original maturities may vary by as much as 20 years for 30-year securities and five years for 15-year securities. Because of this ambiguity, it is possible to significantly misestimate a pool's scheduled principal payments. Moreover, when the historical scheduled principal payments are misstated, the calculation of experienced prepayments can also be in error.[4]

The cash flows from pass-throughs, particularly as they reflect monthly amortization, delays, and the likelihood of prepayments, give rise to the major differences between pass-throughs on the one hand and Treasury and corporate bonds on the other. Other important differences among these instruments are summarized in Exhibit 27–6.

## DETERMINANTS OF PREPAYMENT RATES

The causes of prepayments generally fall under two headings—refinancing and mobility. Following the decline of mortgage rates and resultant surge of prepayments experienced in 1986, the market focused considerable attention on the refinancing component of prepayments. Homeowners tend to refinance when the current market mortgage rate is far enough below the rate on their existing mortgage to lower their monthly payment significantly. The difference in payments must be at least great enough to permit the homeowner to recover the loan fees and other costs of refinancing over some reasonable horizon. A common rule of thumb puts this lower mortgage rate at 200 basis points below the existing mortgage's rate. Because the future level of interest rates is hard to predict, the resulting prepayments are also difficult to predict. Refinancings are a negative

---

[4] Total principal payments are determined using the pool's factor, a statistic provided by the guarantor agency and indicating the fraction of original principal amount still outstanding for the pool. The drop between two consecutive factors measures the amount of total principal paid down over a single period. The amount of prepayments is estimated by subtracting estimated scheduled principal payments from total principal payments.

**EXHIBIT 27–6**

**Features of Pass-Through, Government, and Corporate Securities Compared**

|  | Pass-Throughs | Treasuries |
|---|---|---|
| Credit Risk | Generally high grade; range from government guaranteed to A (private pass-throughs) | Government guaranteed |
| Liquidity | Good for agency issued/guaranteed pass-through | Excellent |
| Range of Coupons (Discount to Premium) | Full range | Full range |
| Range of Maturities | Medium- and long-term (fast-paying and seasoned pools can provide shorter maturities than stated) | Full range |
| Call Protection | Complex prepayment pattern; investor can limit through selection variables such as coupon, seasoning, and program | Noncallable (except certain 30-year bonds) |
| Frequency of Payment | Monthly payments of principal and interest | Semiannual interest payment |
| Average Life | Lower than for bullets of comparable maturity; can only be estimated due to prepayment risk | Estimate only for small number of callable issues; otherwise, known with certainty |
| Duration/Interest-Rate Risk | Function of prepayment risk; can only be estimated; can be negative when prepayment risk is high | Unless callable, a simple function of yield, coupon, and maturity; is known with certainty |
| Basis for Yield Quotes | Cash-flow yield based on monthly payments and a constant CPR assumption | Based on semiannual coupon payments and 365-day year |
| Settlement | Once a month | Any business day |

**EXHIBIT 27–6—*Continued***

|  | Corporates | Stripped Treasuries |
| --- | --- | --- |
| *Credit Risk* | High grade to speculative | Backed by government guarantees |
| *Liquidity* | Generally limited | Fair |
| *Range of Coupons (Discount to Premium)* | Full range for a few issuers | Zero coupon (discount securities) |
| *Range of Maturities* | Full range | Full range |
| *Call Protection* | Generally callable after initial limited period of five to ten years | Noncallable |
| *Frequency of Payment* | Semiannual interest (except Eurobonds, which pay interest annually) | No payments until maturity |
| *Average Life* | Minimum average life known, otherwise a function of call risk | Known with certainty |
| *Duration/Interest-Rate Risk* | Function of call risk; can be negative when call risk is high | Known with certainty; no interest-rate risk if held to maturity |
| *Basis for Yield Quotes* | Based on semiannual coupon payments and 360-day year of twelve 30-day months | Bond equivalent yield based on either 360- or 365-day year, depending on sponsor |
| *Settlement* | Any business day | Any business day |

event for pass-through investors since they are triggered by a fall in market rates and the returned principal will be reinvested at lower yields. Investors who purchase their high-coupon pass-throughs at a premium may experience additional losses, since the principal is repaid at par and must remain outstanding.

Mobility refers to the fact that at any time, in any mortgage rate environment, homeowners sell their homes and move. (The due-on-sale clause, now enforceable by federal law, ensures this kind of prepayment. Notice that GNMA pools, made up of assumable mortgages, experience this form of prepayment at a lower rate.) The link between prepayments and interest-rate levels also is important for loans with below-market coupons. In this case, high interest rates may work as a disincentive to homeowners who might otherwise move, while falling interest rates will be associated with increased prepayments. Related causes include terminations due to divorce, default, and disasters such as floods, fires, and the borrower's death. More affluent homeowners are generally thought to be more mobile. This is one of the reasons normally advanced to explain the slower prepayments of GNMA pass-throughs, where FHA or VA insurance in effect lowers the mortgage rate charged the borrower.

It should be apparent that pass-throughs with different coupons or, more to the point, with different WACs on the underlying loans, have different degrees of prepayment risk. The farther below current mortgage rates a pool's WAC is, the slower the pool is expected to prepay. Likewise prepayments are faster for pools with above-market-rate WACs. Generally, pass-throughs with higher coupons prepay faster than pools with lower coupons; this fundamental characteristic of prepayment behavior has resulted in the grouping of pass-throughs within the various programs into different coupon classes with different trading characteristics depending on the market's perception of their prepayment risk.

It is important to remember that the pass-through coupon is less than the interest rate on the underlying mortgages by the amount of servicing (and guarantee fees) retained. The mortgage rate, not the coupon, determines whether or not it makes economic sense to refinance. In the case of GNMA I securities, the coupon precisely indicates the underlying mortgage rate since every mortgage must have the same rate and the issuer strips off 50 basis points of servicing from that income stream. With other pass-throughs, there is considerable room for variation in underlying mortgage rates. For this reason, it is important to consider the weighted average coupon (WAC) of the underlying mortgages in any analysis of FNMA and FHLMC securities.

The age or seasoning of a pool is another key determinant of prepayment behavior. Normally, some months or years elapse after a mortgage is closed before the borrower is willing or able to go to the effort and expense of moving or refinancing. As a result, prepayment rates increase from a very low level during the early years of a pass-through's life to level off some time after 20 to 65 months (depending on program and coupon, among other factors). As a result newly issued pass-throughs will demonstrate low prepayment rates, but high rates of increase from month to month. Likewise the prepayment rates of fully seasoned ("seasoned" means that monthly prepayment rates have stopped increasing) securities will be relatively stable. For instance, more affluent homeowners are generally thought to be able to move or refinance sooner so that conventional pass-throughs season more quickly and level off at higher prepayment rates than GNMAs, which are backed by government-insured loans.

Considerable attention has been given to identifying the factors underlying prepayment activity in mortgage pass-throughs so that econometric models describing this activity can be formulated and used to predict prepayments. The spread between current mortgage rates and the underlying mortgage rates is typically modeled as the primary determinant of prepayment activity. The weighted average age of the pool is another important factor. Some models also attempt to capture the tendency for pools to become less sensitive to refinancing opportunities, or to "burnout," after sustaining very high prepayment rates for significant periods of time. Seasonality, that is, the tendencey of homeowners to be more mobile in the spring and summer months, may also be modeled.

## Measuring Prepayments

The market has evolved a variety of conventions for quantifying prepayments intended to facilitate trading and investment in mortgage-backed securities. The oldest and simplest of these was the prepaid life assumption employed by secondary market traders of whole loan mortgages. At one time the 12-year prepaid life assumption was the industry standard for quoting mortgage yields. Under this convention, the first 12 years of cash flows consist entirely of amortized principal and interest in each of the mortgages in the pool (based on a 360-month maturity). At the end of the 12th year, the remaining principal balance is assumed to be paid in full. In other words, the entire pool is treated like a single mortgage prepaying in the 12th year of its life. The yield-to-maturity (or IRR) calculated for a given price and the cash flows derived from a 12-year prepaid life assumption was termed the "mortgage yield." (Mortgage yields were also calculated for other prepaid lives—for instance, 7-year prepaid life—but the 12-year assumption was the standard.) During the 1970s, however, increases in the level and volatility of interest rates led in turn to substantial increases in the level and volatility of prepayment rates. The 12-year prepaid life assumption could not be adjusted for the wide differences in coupon, maturity, seasoning, and other security characteristics prevalent in today's market.

Recognizing the problems with the prepaid life assumptions, traders and investors began using the termination experience [5] collected on FHA-insured mortgages issued since 1970 to model expected prepayments. This distribution of prepayments over the life of a pool is easily adapted to express faster or slower prepayment speeds by using a multiple of the base table. For instance, "0 percent of FHA" means no prepayments, "100 percent of FHA" refers to the average rate, and "200 percent of FHA" means twice the FHA rate. Another application of FHA experience was to fix the age and outstanding balance of a security and determine the multiple of FHA experience indicated by the pool's factor at that age. Assuming that the pool continues to prepay at the same percent of FHA experience over its remaining life, a cash-flow yield is calculated given the current market price.

Unfortunately, FHA experience is defined on a single parameter: age of the mortgage. By averaging individual mortgage data, it ignores the critical

---

[5] This data is published periodically by HUD in the form of a table of 30 numbers indicating the probability of survival of a mortgage at any given year up to maturity. Prepayment rates are implicit in these survivorship rates.

link between coupon and prepayments. Furthermore, the underlying data are from assumable FHA and VA mortgages and can be misleading when applied to conventional pass-throughs. Other disadvantages of using FHA experience to evaluate mortgage securities include the fact that it does not incorporate variables such as the level of interest rates and economic activity known to influence prepayment activity. Finally, FHA experience did not provide a consistent standard because a new series is published each year or so, often based upon different statistical manipulations of the underlying data.[6]   For instance in 1986, investors could conceivably be pricing MBSs based on 1981, 1983, 1984, or 1985 FHA statistics.

*Conditional Prepayment Rates.*   The FHA prepayment standard(s) gave way in the mid-1980s to the conditional prepayment rate (CPR). This measure has become the principal means traders and investors employ to quantifying prepayment activity in pass-throughs. This convention assumes that a fraction of the remaining principal is prepaid each month (or year), which implies that each individual mortgage in the pool is equally likely to prepay. The CPR measures prepayments based ("conditional") on the previous month's remaining balance (thus it can represent an average or compound rate over many periods or a single-period rate) the resulting rate sometimes is expressed as an annualized percentage. This simple quantification is intuitive and easy to incorporate into pricing and yield formulas. In calculating yields or prices, investors may employ a single CPR assumption across the term of the investment or a series of varying CPR assumptions reflecting historical experience or prepayment expectations derived from formal prepayment forecast models. When an internal rate of return is calculated using realistic CPR assumptions over the life of the security, the result is termed "cash-flow yield" (in contrast to the outmoded "mortgage yield" based on a prepaid life assumption).

*The PSA Prepayment Standard Model.*   The Public Securities Association (PSA) introduced a Standard Prepayment Model to replace the FHA experience tables for the purpose of valuing collateralized mortgage obligation (CMO) issues. The PSA standard was intended to simplify the comparison and analysis of CMO yield tables but is also occasionally used as a prepayment measure for pass-throughs. It is not really a model; more correctly, it is a measurement standard expressed as a monthly series of annual conditional prepayment rates.

---

[6] For instance, prior to FHA 83, all mortgages back to 1957 were included; subsequently all mortgages prior to 1970 were excluded. Extrapolation was used to a greater degree to derive "experience" for years not covered by actual data. Similarly, through 1981, each year's data was equally weighted; starting in 1982, mortgages issued in the 1980s were given additional weight.

It begins at 0.2 percent per year in the first month and increases by 0.2 percent per year in each successive month until month 30, when the series levels out at 6 percent per year until maturity. Prepayments are measured as simple linear multiples of this schedule. For instance, 200 percent PSA is 0.4 percent per year in the first month, 0.8 percent per year in the second month, and 12 percent per year after month 30. This is unrealistic in the sense that prepayments in fast-paying pools do not increase proportionately in each month or year over the term of the pool. Exhibit 27–7 depicts both the PSA standard and the 1985 FHA series for comparison.

One advantage of the PSA CPR series is that it does reflect the increase in CPRs that occurs as the pool ages. This effect is also captured by the FHA series, but the PSA CPRs do not display the random fluctuation in prepayment rates found in the FHA tables. Finally, it should be noted that, beyond month 30, using the PSA is equivalent to applying a static CPR over the remaining life of the pool.

## EVALUATING PASS-THROUGH SECURITIES— YIELD, AVERAGE LIFE, AND DURATION

In order to make trading and investment decisions, participants in the pass-through market require some means of evaluating the risks and rewards in individual investment opportunities and of comparing a variety of possible invest-

**EXHIBIT 27–7**
**PSA vs. FHA CPR Series**

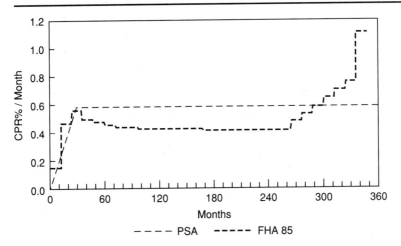

ments. The price of a pass-through is the present value of the projected cash flows discounted at the current yield required by the market given the specific risk and cash-flow characteristics of the security in question. Likewise, yield at a given market price is employed by the market as the basis for determining if the anticipated investment return is adequate and for identifying relative value. Using yield as a prospective measure of performance, however, has the same disadvantages for pass-through evaluation as it has for other interest-paying obligations. With pass-throughs, yield measures have the added difficulty of being sensitive to the prepayment assumptions used to project the cash flows from which the yield is calculated.

As explained and illustrated in Chapter 6, yield is a poor predictor of any bond's performance because it assumes that (1) all cash flows are reinvested at an interest rate equal to the yield and (2) the security is held to maturity. Deviations from the first assumption are particularly significant for pass-throughs owing to their monthly principal repayments, since interest on these payments compounds monthly in the yield calculation instead of semiannually as with Treasury and corporate bonds.[7]

Exhibit 27–8 demonstrates how much the yield can vary when reinvestment rates different from the yield-to-maturity are used to project the total cash flows to be received from a pass-through. The second assumption is equally unrealistic. If an investment is not held to maturity, the realized yield will be affected by any capital gain or loss on the remaining cash flows, as market yields and prices are likely to have changed since the initial investment was made.

If the pass-through is priced at par, changes in prepayment speeds do not affect the yield calculation.[8] No matter when the principal is returned, the security will continue to yield its coupon rate on the remaining principal. The earlier receipt of principal offsets the loss of coupon income at faster speeds, and additional coupon income offsets the additional delay in return of principal at slower speeds. However, if the security is purchased at a premium, faster prepayments

---

[7] The difference in payment timing between pass-throughs and bonds also means their yields are not directly comparable in making relative value assessments. The greater frequency of payments increases the value of a pass-through of a given coupon compared to traditional corporate or government debt. Interest compounds monthly. This monthly compounding gives pass-through securities an advantage over other securities of the same coupon. Quoted cash-flow yields, however, do not reflect the advantage. For instance, a 10.00 percent cash-flow yield is equivalent to a 10.21 percent bond yield. In order to compare pass-through yields to yields on other securities, it is necessary to adjust the mortgage yield upward to its bond equivalent yield (BEY). Basically, the monthly coupons are treated as if they are collected and reinvested at the cash-flow yield rate until the end of each semiannual or other period. The accumulated (compounded) amount is larger than the sum of the face amount of six monthly coupons.

[8] Actually, the yield does not change if the security was purchased at its **parity price** (slightly less than 100), which adjusts par for the payment delay. The delay lowers yield price by moving the cash flows further out into the future.

**EXHIBIT 27–8**

**Effect of Reinvestment Rate on Realized Yield from Monthly Payments on a 9.5% Pass-Through Priced at 99 8/32 to Yield 9.54%**

| Reinvestment Rate (%) | Realized Cash-Flow Yield (%) | Change from Expected Yield (%) |
|---|---|---|
| 4 | 5.93 | −37.84 |
| 6 | 7.16 | −24.95 |
| 8 | 8.48 | −11.11 |
| 10 | 9.87 | 3.46 |
| 12 | 11.33 | 18.76 |
| 14 | 12.84 | 34.59 |
| 16 | 14.41 | 51.05 |

Note: Assumes 0.50 percent service fee and no prepayments.

than expected will reduce the yield: Prepayments shorten the amount of time principal remains outstanding to earn above market coupon payments, thereby lowering the total cash flows. In a similar fashion, the yield of a discount security increases with faster prepayments as the time required to earn the discount is shortened. Principal purchased at, say, 90 percent of its value, is returned at 100 percent. The effect of prepayments on yield for securities purchased close to, above, or below par is shown in Exhibit 27–9.

**EXHIBIT 27–9**

**Effect of Different Prepayment Rates on the Cash-Flow Yield of Discount, Current and Premium Coupon Pass-Throughs***

| CPR (%/yr) | Price | | |
|---|---|---|---|
| | 89 20/32 | 99 28/32 | 105 4/32 |
| 2 | 8.78 | 9.57 | 10.67 |
| 4 | 8.97 | 8.58 | 10.57 |
| 6 | 9.18 | 9.58 | 10.46 |
| 8 | 9.39 | 9.59 | 10.35 |
| 10 | 9.62 | 9.60 | 10.23 |
| 12 | 9.85 | 9.62 | 10.11 |
| 18 | 10.58 | 9.65 | 9.74 |
| 24 | 11.37 | 9.68 | 9.33 |

*$7\frac{1}{2}$%, $9\frac{1}{2}$%, and $11\frac{1}{2}$% coupons, respectively.

A fundamental measure of the risk in any investment is its term, or longevity. Because the principal is returned throughout the pass-through's life, maturity is not a good measure of the longevity of this form of debt. The likelihood of prepayments amplifies this deficiency. For these reasons, a preferred measure for mortgage-backed securities, including pass-throughs, is the average elapsed time until the principal is fully returned. The commonly used measure, *average life*, is the weighted average time to principal repayment, with the amount of the principal paydowns (both scheduled and unscheduled) as the weights. Average life expresses the average number of years that each principal dollar will be outstanding. Clearly the higher the prepayment rate, the sooner the principal is returned and hence the shorter the average life. It should also be apparent from the definition that average life declines as a security ages. Average life also is affected by coupon rate. For a given prepayment assumption, average life increases with coupon rates because, at higher interest rates, a larger proportion of the payment is interest in early years, in effect slightly delaying the repayment of principal. However, if prepayments are allowed to vary with interest rates so that they reflect increasing or decreasing incentives to refinance, or mobility, they will swamp the coupon effect in premium coupon securities.

Another measure of an investment's longevity used in the early years of the MBS market was *half-life*. A pass-through's half-life is the length of time required for half of the principal to be repaid.

In recent years, *duration* has become more important for the evaluation of pass-throughs than average life. As explained in Chapter 7, duration is the weighted average time to receipt of the present value of both principal and interest cash flows. Duration is appealing because it can be used to measure the price sensitivity of a bond. That is, "modified" duration expresses the amount the price (present value) will change given a small change in the yield used to discount the cash flows. Thus, duration has important applications as a measure of interest-rate risk. As with yield and average life calculations, both Macaulay and modified duration are highly sensitive to the prepayment assumptions used to project the cash flows. As a result, duration can significantly misestimate the actual price change of pass-throughs when interest rates decline. More importantly, a pass-through's duration changes as the expected prepayment rates used to calculate it change in response to changes in the general level of interest rates. Pass-through duration shortens in a bull market and lengthens in a bear market. As a result, a pass-through's price declines more quickly for a small change in interest rates as the general level of interest rates rises. Similarly, pass-through prices increase more slowly for successive declines in the general level of interest rates. As explained in Chapter 7, this characteristic of a pass-through's price behavior is generally referred to as "negative convexity."

## Relative Value Analysis

A crucial ingredient in the analysis of mortgage-backed securities is the ability to compare these investments to other fixed income securities. The variety of MBS programs and the broad range of coupons within programs gives additional impetus to relative value analysis. Market participants have evolved various quantitative frameworks within which under and overvalued securities can be identified and rational investment decisions made.

In simplest terms, relative value analysis seeks to compare securities of equivalent risk. Various attempts have been made to capture all aspects of pass-throughs' interest-rate risk in a manner that allows comparison to Treasury securities.

Once the yield spread to an appropriate Treasury security is determined, that spread should be comparable to the spread provided by another fixed income security of similar risk. The earliest attempts at relative value analysis matched maturities or average lives. This approach failed to account for the great difference between the cash-flow patterns of Treasuries and MBSs.

A sounder comparison is made using the duration calculated with a reasonable prepayment assumption. By matching durations, a point on the pass-through yield curve is compared to a point on the Treasury curve that should respond in a similar fashion to small changes in interest rates. The next step is to determine the required yield spread over the Treasury at which investors are willing to invest in mortgage-backed securities. This premium compensates investors for the prepayment risk as well as differences in credit quality, liquidity, and the additional reinvestment risk arising from monthly payments. Cheap securities would be those trading at a greater spread to the equivalent risk Treasury than required; rich securities would be trading at a lower spread than required. Taking another approach, an investor can examine the entire pass-through yield curve in comparison to Treasuries in an attempt to identify those MBSs where the spread is widest and indicates the greatest value relative to other pass-throughs.

The success of relative value analysis depends on correctly identifying Treasury securities of equivalent interest-rate risk. Unfortunately, as noted above, duration cannot correctly summarize the price sensitivity of pass-throughs, because it cannot account for the variation in prepayment experience as interest rates change. Actual price movements of pass-throughs in response to interest-rate changes differ significantly from those predicted by their duration both in magnitude and direction. That is, certain pass-throughs experience price declines during periods of falling interest rates (negative duration) because lower interest rates translate into higher prepayments, which in turn translate into capital losses and unrealized earnings. Consequently, the market demands a higher risk premium for those coupons perceived to have increased prepayment risk.

Similarly, cash-flow yield calculations do not reflect the likelihood that prepayment behavior can change from assumptions used at pricing. As a consequence, a new generation of analytic tools has been developed that treats the pass-through as a composite security consisting of a long position in mortgages and a short position in call options (each borrower's right to call a piece of the pool away from the investor). A larger discussion of the theory behind such models and how they are formulated is beyond the scope of this chapter. In brief, their objective is to explicitly evaluate the option to prepay given the current yield environment, a process for modeling likely changes in interest rates for realistic levels of interest-rate volatility, and a prepayment model which links prepayment activity to interest-rate levels. Different analytic techniques may be used to arrive at such models, but the basic outputs will include option-adjusted measures of yield, and yield spread over Treasuries, as well as option-adjusted measures of price sensitivity or duration. Rich-cheap analysis is conducted using these measures in the same way as with older techniques—investments with similar risk characteristics are compared to identify superior value. The difference is that the investor has the advantage of being able to compare a theoretical value to the actual market spread to make a better-informed investment decision.

## Total Return Analysis

Yield is not commonly used to describe the historical investment performance of a pass-through. Instead, the total rate of return is used. The actual or economic return received by an investor is the sum of interest and principal payments as well as any reinvestment income received over a holding or measurement period, plus any capital gain or loss if the bond is sold at the end of the period. If the bond is not sold, the total return calculation takes into account any appreciation or depreciation in market price as of the end of the period.

Total returns can also be projected to support trading and investment decisions. Such analysis, if performed with adequate care, overcomes many of the shortcomings of yield. For one thing, assumptions about interest-rate and prepayment scenarios can be used to project principal and interest payments and reinvestment income over the period, as well as market prices at the end of the measurement horizon. Care is required, in particular, in determining terminal prices for pass-throughs because the yield spreads investors require for securities reflect their perception of prepayment and other risks. Since interest-rate shifts alter the magnitude of these risks as well as their impact on cash flows, it is not necessarily reasonable to assume that the required yield spread for a particular security would be the same at the end of the horizon as at the beginning. An approach which adjusts for this problem would be to use the yield spread earned by an otherwise similar pass-through that has the same average life at the outset as the security in question does at the end of the horizon. (Matching durations would involve an iterative search because average life is simply a function of principal paydowns and time, while duration is a function of yield as well). In other words, if a 9 percent GNMA single-family 30-year pass-through shortens to a three-year average life in a down-100-basis-points scenario, its terminal price can be calculated from the yield found by adding the spread of the GNMA single-family 30-year security that today has an average life closest to three years to the yield of the three-year Treasury less 100 basis points. Another approach prices the remaining cash flows at the same option-adjusted spread to Treasuries as demonstrated by the security at the beginning of the period. This approach has the advantage of incorporating a mathematical expectation rather than a point estimate of required spreads.

Projected returns for discount, current, and premium coupon FNMA securities are depicted in Exhibit 27–10. A constant spread to Treasuries is used to determine asset prices at the end of the horizon, and the Smith Barney Prepayment Model is used to project the cash flows and terminal values. Readers should note the differences in projected total return performance between pass-throughs from different coupon sectors of the market. The greatest variability is displayed by the FNMA 12. This pass-through displays significant negative convexity as rates decline, prepayments accelerate, and principal purchased at a high premium is returned at par. On the other hand, as interest rates rise and refinancing incentives disappear, prepayments rapidly slow down. As the security's duration lengthens, its performance dominates that of the discount and current coupon securities. This reflects the impact of high coupon income, as principal remains outstanding longer. The discount MBS, a FNMA 8, display the opposite return pattern—as prepayments increase, more principal is returned at a gain, generating returns far in excess of those displayed by the current and premium pass-throughs. On the downside, as the duration of the discount pass-through extends, its market value drops more sharply, contributing to its low returns in the more bearish environments.

**EXHIBIT 27–10**
**One-Year Return (%)**

|  |  | FNMA 8 | FNMA 10 | FNMA 12 |
|---|---|---|---|---|
|  | −200 | 18.48 | 13.89 | 9.50 |
|  | −150 | 16.39 | 13.19 | 9.73 |
| Interest | −100 | 14.01 | 12.35 | 10.16 |
| Rate | −50 | 11.68 | 11.52 | 10.24 |
| Shift | 0 | 9.89 | 10.04 | 9.76 |
| (Basis | 50 | 7.62 | 8.32 | 8.79 |
| Points) | 100 | 5.41 | 6.34 | 7.64 |
|  | 150 | 3.28 | 4.39 | 6.70 |
|  | 200 | 1.21 | 2.88 | 5.39 |

The security priced close to parity, the FNMA 10, displays a projected return pattern somewhere in the middle. More bullish scenarios induce rapid prepayments, which begin to erode performance beyond a 150 basis point decline in yields. On the downside, prepayment rates slow down at moderate pace, lengthening the time to receipt of principal and consequently increasing the security's price response to interest-rate increases.

Total return projections may also be employed in making relative value assessments. In this context, the investor would prefer the securities offering the greatest return advantage over comparable Treasuries.

## SUMMARY

In this chapter, the investment characteristics of mortgage pass-through securities are explained and the various tools for valuing them are briefly described. In the next chapter, investing in specific mortgage pools is explained. Chapters 29 and 30 describe CMOs and stripped mortgage pass-through securities, respectively.

# CHAPTER 28

## INVESTING IN SPECIFIED POOLS

*Chuck Ramsey*
*Senior Managing Director*
*Bear Stearns & Co., Inc.*

*J. Michael Henderson, CFA*
*Associate Director*
*Bear Stearns & Co., Inc.*

At the most elementary level, a trade in a specified pool is merely a transaction in which the pool number is known. This contrasts with a typical TBA (to be announced) transaction, in which pool information is not known at the time of the trade. For example, an investor may purchase $1 million GNMA 8's on a TBA basis and receive up to three pools, the pool numbers of which will be announced shortly before settlement date. On the other hand, the investor might ask to know the pool number prior to purchase. In this latter case, the investor has specified a minor distinction from TBA delivery and, in so doing, has entered into a specified trade at its most elementary level.

The degree of specification desired by the investor may also be more detailed. TBA offerings are generally for mortgage pools containing relatively recently issued mortgages maturing in approximately 30 years. Such an offering represents the norm, or generic type. Any departure from this norm, or TBA "good delivery," represents some degree of specificity. For example, the investor may request one pool per $1 million instead of the standard three pools per $1 million, or the investor may even request a single $10 million or a single $100 million pool. Perhaps the investor prefers a pool containing mortgages on which an average of 10 years have elapsed and on which 20 years of time remain until the maturity of the pool. The investor may request a pool of mortgages that has experienced a particular rapidity of prepayments over an extended period of time. Because the speed of prepayments has a major effect upon the yield and/or average life of the investment, the investor may attempt to employ such specificity in order to effect a greater degree of certainty concerning the yield and average life of the investment. Other examples of diversion from the TBA or generic norm will be discussed later in this chapter.

## HISTORICAL EVOLUTION OF THE SPECIFIED POOL MARKET

The initial creation of GNMA pools occurred in the early 1970s. Within a few years, FHLMC and FNMA followed with their own pools issuance. In the early years, GNMA pools of a particular coupon traded interchangeably, and there were no marginal distinctions to render the pools greatly different from the norm. As noted above, however, investors did deviate from TBA "good delivery" by specifying different pool sizes than were represented by a TBA offering.

With the passage of time, enterprising investors began to realize that although many mortgage pools might have been created equally, there could be rather dramatic differences in prepayment speeds of different mortgage pools. Because the prepayment speed affected the yield and/or average life of a mortgage security investment, the astute investment manager attempted to understand the yield and average life ramifications caused by various speeds upon a particular coupon at a particular dollar price.

Exhibit 28–1 is a price/yield table for FNMA pool 64 (coupon, 7.50; weighted average maturity, 7.05). At a dollar price of $88.25, assuming a constant prepayment percentage (CPP), or the interchangeably used constant prepayment rate (CPR), speed of 8 percent, the investor will earn a 10.27 bond equivalent yield and the average life will be about 7 years. In actuality, prepayments during the last year have occurred at 14.09 percent CPP, and this speed results in a yield of 11.05 and an average life of about 5 years. If there were never a prepayment on FNMA 64, then the yield would be 9.40 and the average life would be about 11 years. Hence, varying prepayment speeds may cause some rather dramatic differences in yield and average life for a particular pool.

**EXHIBIT 28–1**
**FNMA Pool 64 Price/Yield Matrix**

|  | 8.00% CPP | 14.09% CPP | 0.00% CPP |
|---|---|---|---|
| Avg. Life | 6.92 | 5.06 | 11.20 |
| Price |  |  |  |
| 88–08 | 10.27 | 11.05 | 9.40 |

In 1981, FHLMC began issuing mortgage pools under the guarantor, or "swap," program. Among the results of this program was the creation of an infinitely greater variety of mortgage paper. Whereas previously most issuance of pools was of current coupons with 30-year maturities, the swap program provided investors with a wide array of coupons in new pools of older mortgages. Because the universe of coupons and average lives had been so greatly expanded, many investors who formerly were uninterested in mortgage securities (because these investors had limited or no particular need for 10- to 12-year average life and/or current coupon paper with a final maturity of 30 years) now had reason to reexamine the possibilities available in the specified pool market. For example, deep-discount coupons of four or five with weighted average maturities (WAMs) of 5 to 10 years creating average lives of 2 to 5 years became available. An example of such a pool is presented in Exhibit 28–2.

As the variety of mortgage paper and the universe of potential investors increased, research staffs attempted to understand, quantify, and even predict what levels of prepayments might be appropriate for various combinations of coupons, WAMs, and weighted average coupons (WACs). Such analysis generally encompassed economic models. Analysts began to study the relationship between how rapidly mortgages prepaid and the geographical locations of the mortgages. For example, one may intuitively surmise that there are probably differences in prepayment speeds between pools with Los Angeles mortgages and pools with Houston mortgages. Investors began to try to quantify these relative differences in order to have a better understanding of prepayment speeds and, therefore, yields and average lives.

## INVESTOR RATIONALE UNDERLYING
## THE PURCHASE OF SPECIFIED POOLS

Investors are drawn to mortgage securities because they are often able to pick up yield and/or quality versus many other investment vehicles. Because there are few free lunches to be had in the investment arena, there must be some trade-offs associated with these advantages. The trade-off is that the investor takes on uncertainty. If an investor purchases a seven-year Treasury, he or she is certain to receive 14 equal interest payments on predetermined dates and the principal back in seven years. The investor is also certain at the outset about the yield he or she has purchased, although the yield realized will depend upon the rate and fashion in which he or she reinvests the interest payments.

With mortgage securities, however, the investor purchases an array of possibilities as to average life and yield. This variability is amply illustrated by FNMA 64, wherein there was approximately a 250-basis-point range between the yield earned at the three-month speed and the yield earned if there were never to be a prepayment on FNMA 64. Furthermore, the average lives under those two

**EXHIBIT 28–2**
**FHLMC Pool 183161**

| | | Price/Yield Matrix | | | | |
|---|---|---|---|---|---|---|
| Coupon: | 5.00% | | | | | |
| Servicing: | 0.625% | | | | | |
| Issue date: | 11/82 | 0.00% | 8.00% | 11.12% | 13.11% | 14.81% |
| Maturity: | 1/96 | CPP | CPP | CPP | CPP | CPP |
| | Avg. Life | 3.29 | 2.82 | 2.66 | 2.56 | 2.48 |
| Prepayment History: | Price | | | | | |
| 3 month: 14.81 CPP | | | | | | |
| 6 month: 13.11 CPP | | | | | | |
| 1 year: 11.12 CPP | | | | | | |
| Life: 7.58 CPP | 89–24 | 8.64 | 9.22 | 9.47 | 9.64 | 9.79 |

extreme circumstances varied from about 4 years to about 11 years. The variability of yield and average life is exacerbated by the fact that, whereas the investor in the seven-year Treasury note need only consider the effect of reinvestment rates upon the stream of interest payments, the mortgage security investor must also consider the effect of that reinvestment rate upon variable principal payments. The goal of the investor is to gather sufficient data concerning prepayment speeds so that he or she may quantify the range of possibilities and also predict the most likely range of average life and yield possibilities. If the investor is satisfied with a reasonable range of possible average lives and yields and this range offers sufficient yield and quality inducement versus other investment vehicles, then the investment in mortgage securities is suitable for inclusion in the investment manager's portfolio. Therefore, the major challenge confronting the investment manager is to surmise a reasonable prepayment speed to assume for a particular mortgage pool.

## SPECIFIED POOL ANALYSIS

Specified pool analysis begins with a look at the pool itself. Exhibit 28–3 presents a profile of FNMA pool 173.

FNMA 173 is an 8.50 coupon pool with a WAC of 9.301. The WAC is the average interest rate paid by the homeowner to the mortgage originator. The pool was issued in 1982, so the investor has the benefit of several years of prepayment history available in order to make a judgment concerning how well or how poorly the pool has prepaid. The pool has a WAM of 2–2007 and the longest mortgage in the pool has its final payment in 5–2011. Hence, FNMA 173 is an example of a pool that was issued about five years after the mortgages were created. The investor can readily see that the pool has experienced prepayments

**EXHIBIT 28–3**

**FNMA Pool 173–CL Conventional 30-Year Single Family Midwest Federal Savings & Loan Association, Minneapolis, MN**

| Coupon: | 8.50% |
| WAC: | 9.301% |

| Pool size: | 19,988,403.89 |
| Issue date: | 3/82 |
| Maturity: | 5/11 |
| WAM: | 2/07 |

*Price/Yield Matrix*

| | 0.00% CPP | 8.00% CPP | 12.87% CPP | 13.93% CPP | 15.57% CPP |
|---|---|---|---|---|---|
| Avg. Life | 12.58 | 7.34 | 5.64 | 5.34 | 4.92 |

| Price | | | | | |
|---|---|---|---|---|---|
| 92 | 9.78 | 10.35 | 10.74 | 10.84 | 10.98 |

*Prepayment History:*

| 1 month: | 12.04 CPP |
| 3 month: | 15.57 CPP |
| 6 month: | 13.93 CPP |
| 1 year: | 12.87 CPP |
| Life: | 8.32 CPP |

in excess of 8 percent CPP since issuance and has experienced considerably more rapid prepayment speeds within the past year. If the investor were to pay $92 for the pool, he or she would earn a 10.35 yield, assuming that the pool will prepay at 8 percent CPP in the future.

The investor should note that the pool is from Minneapolis. One Wall Street firm tracks prepayment tendencies by state. An examination of Exhibit 28–4 reveals that mortgages from Minnesota should prepay slightly more slowly than national prepayment speed norms. The same firm has a sample of 124 pools containing $633 million of mortgages from Minneapolis with coupons ranging from 8 percent to 10 percent. In the past year, the weighted average CPP of this sample of pools has been 13.23 percent. FNMA 173 has experienced prepayments of 12.87 percent CPP within the last year so it is very similar to the sample. However, since the range of coupons in the sample is from 8 percent to 10 percent, one might surmise that FNMA 8.50s, which are in the lower part of the range, might have prepaid at somewhat less than the weighted average of 13.23 percent CPP, so FNMA 173 might actually be slightly faster than the average 8.50 coupon from Minneapolis.

Further specific geographic investigation may be undertaken through the appraisal of economic conditions and trends in the Minneapolis area. Exhibit 28–5 presents the work of a regional economist employed by one Wall Street firm. Such analysis provides further economic information that has bearing upon

**EXHIBIT 28–4**
**Regional Prepayment Index**

| Geographical Breakdown of FNMA CL 000173 | | | | |
|---|---|---|---|---|
| State | Original Bal. Share | % Bal. | Loans | % Loans |
| Minnesota | 19,988,403.89 | 100.000 | 462 | 100.000 |

*Attention*

Regional Prepayment Index is calculated based on the *original* loan composition of the pool. The current loan composition is subject to change given unequal paydowns. This may be particularly true for seasoned pools where geography is widely dispersed.

RPI Index Rating: 95.163

RPI is based on a national average of 100. Values above 100 are expected to prepay faster than the national average while those below 100 are expected to be slower.

Assuming that unreported loans are generic, we project this pool will prepay 4.837% slower than generics.

State prepayment speeds are calculated from a large sample of pools.

*Any specific pool can deviate from the average.*

**EXHIBIT 28–5**
**FNMA Region Analysis**

*MN-WI, Minneapolis-St. Paul*

*Conditions*

Minneapolis-St. Paul's fortunes lie largely in high-tech and durable goods manufacturing and to a lesser extent agriculture. Due to its reliance on these areas, the MSA's economy, which also contains the state capital, is highly import sensitive and stagnated growth in its farming and goods-producing areas have recently slowed growth throughout much of the economy.

Manufacturing employment, 19.8% of the total (US = 18.7%), grew an average of 1.6% per year (1982–87, US = 0.3%) and rose by 0.9% in 1987 (US = 0.6%). Declining sectors include office and computing machinery, fabricated metals, pulp and paper products, and nonelectrical machinery. Growing sectors include commercial printing, chemical products, and transportation equipment.

Nonmanufacturing employment grew an average of 4.2% per year (1982–87, US = 3.2%) and gained 4.7% in 1987 (US = 2.9%). Every major sector continued to advance impressively in 1987 with construction and services leading the way at 9.1% and 5.5% respectively.

Despite the growing local economy, evidenced by 4.0% employment growth in 1987 (US = 2.5%), and only slightly above average population increase the unemployment rate rose somewhat from 4.2% to 4.3% during the 1986–87 period (US = 6.2%).

mortgage termination rates in the Minneapolis-St. Paul Metropolitan Statistical Area (MSA).

The investor should also take into account the fact that within the past year FNMA 173 has prepaid at a somewhat more rapid rate than FNMA 8.50s. In the last six-month, three-month, and one-month comparison, FNMA 173 has prepaid at a considerably more rapid rate. (This increasing prepayment divergence between FNMA 173 and all FNMA 8.50s will be examined and explained later in this chapter.)

Attention should also be turned to the payment consistency experienced by FNMA 173. Such consistency may be prized by the investor because returns are smoothed over shorter investment horizons. Part of the consistency may be explained by the fact that FNMA 173 is a fairly large pool of about $20 million original face amount. The likelihood of several mortgages terminating in any given month is greater than if the pool were, for example, $500,000. (In a $500,000 pool, if the mortgages average $30,000, there would be about 17 mortgages in the pool. If the WAM were 20 years, then there would be an average of only one mortgage termination every 14 months.) Hence, although the speed as measured by CPP might well be identical over an extended period of time, in the short run the less consistent pool might provide an extremely lesser or greater yield than the larger, more consistently prepaying pool.

Another area for analytical consideration is the prepayment speeds associated with various WAMs. One intuitively knows that homeowners typically do not move out of a house on which they have recently been granted a mortgage. The investor should attempt to include WAM evaluation in his or her overall analysis of a specific pool in an attempt to quantify the magnitude of differences of prepayment speeds among various WAMs. Exhibit 28–6 presents CPP speeds for one-year, six-month, three-month, and one-month time periods for all FNMA 8.50s sorted by WAM. This survey could be most helpful to the investor in his or her analysis of FNMA 173, a FNMA 8.50 with a WAM of 2007. The survey indicates that there was $15.2 billion original face of FNMA 8.50s outstanding on 9/14/87, of which 6.5 percent, or about $1 billion, was 8.50s with a 2007 WAM.

FNMA 8.50s with 2007 WAMS have prepaid at a CPP rate of 12.9 percent during the last year, 13.6 percent during the last six months and three months, and 11.1 percent in the latest month. Hence, FNMA 173 has prepaid at approximately the same speed in the last year and somewhat faster than 2007 8.50s in the other periods measured. As a discount coupon, the faster the prepayment speed, the higher the yield, since the collateral is prepaid at par. The reverse is true of premium coupon pools.

A further examination of Exhibit 28–6 exposes the fallacy of using averages of prepayment speeds by coupon when one is attempting to estimate prepayment speeds for a specific pool. Exhibit 28–6 shows that approximately 70 percent, or about $10.6 billion, of FNMA 8.50s was issued in 1986 and 1987 (WAMs of 2016 and 2017, respectively). This very large sample has prepaid at a much slower rate than the seasoned 2007 and similarly seasoned WAM paper. These different prepayment rates are what one would intuitively expect because, as was discussed above, homeowners with new mortgages are less likely to terminate their mortgages than homeowners who have had mortgages for several years. This intuitive observation has been captured in the sophisticated prepayment models that have been developed to project future speeds; it is referred to commonly as the pure aging effect.[1] Exhibit 28–3 indicates that FNMA 173 prepaid at a significantly more rapid rate than the average FNMA 8.50, but one may readily derive from Exhibit 28–6 the fact that average prepayment speeds are skewed dramatically downward because such a great portion of FNMA 8.50s is collateralized by new origination mortgages.

If the investor pays $92 for FNMA 173 and the pool prepays at 8 percent CPP in the future, he or she will earn a yield of 10.35. The 8 percent CPP assumption is nothing more than a benchmark, a point of comparison to other mortgage pools and other different sector investment vehicles. In this instance the investor is implicitly accepting 8 percent CPP as a reasonable and perhaps

---

[1] See R. Blaine Roberts, "The Consequences of the Pure Aging Effect on the Yields of Mortgage-Backed Securities," in Frank J. Fabozzi (ed.), *Mortgage-Backed Securities: New Strategies, Applications and Research* (Chicago, IL: Probus Publishing, 1987).

# EXHIBIT 28–6

| | Coupon | WAM Mat | Avg WAC | Pools Report | Total Pools | Out $MM | Orig $MM | 12 mo CPP | 6 mo CPP | 3 mo CPP | 12 mo PSA | 6 mo PSA | 3 mo PSA | Aug CPP | 1987 PSA |
|---|---|---|---|---|---|---|---|---|---|---|---|---|---|---|---|
| | | | | | | | | | | | | | | *FNMA CL 360 Prepayment Report* | |
| FNMA | 8.500 | 1991 | 9.000 | 1 | 1 | 1 | 1 | 18.9 | 16.3 | 18.7 | 315 | 272 | 312 | 14.5 | 241 |
| FNMA | 8.500 | 1992 | 9.000 | 1 | 1 | 1 | 2 | 16.8 | 15.8 | 26.1 | 280 | 263 | 435 | 44.3 | 738 |
| FNMA | 8.500 | 1993 | 9.000 | 1 | 1 | 2 | 2 | 8.5 | 11.1 | 8.3 | 141 | 185 | 138 | 16.8 | 279 |
| FNMA | 8.500 | 1994 | 9.001 | 4 | 4 | 4 | 5 | 21.1 | 20.9 | 21.0 | 352 | 349 | 351 | 4.9 | 82 |
| FNMA | 8.500 | 1995 | 9.118 | 4 | 5 | 3 | 7 | 8.5 | 7.1 | 6.0 | 141 | 118 | 100 | 1.7 | 29 |
| FNMA | 8.500 | 1996 | 9.086 | 9 | 9 | 12 | 15 | 10.7 | 10.6 | 9.6 | 178 | 176 | 160 | 10.9 | 182 |
| FNMA | 8.500 | 1997 | 9.003 | 7 | 7 | 12 | 15 | 9.4 | 7.5 | 9.6 | 157 | 125 | 160 | 1.8 | 30 |
| FNMA | 8.500 | 1998 | 9.152 | 17 | 17 | 31 | 43 | 10.7 | 10.3 | 9.2 | 178 | 172 | 153 | 5.7 | 95 |
| FNMA | 8.500 | 1999 | 9.041 | 16 | 16 | 46 | 61 | 10.9 | 12.1 | 13.7 | 181 | 202 | 229 | 12.1 | 201 |
| FNMA | 8.500 | 2000 | 9.085 | 17 | 17 | 30 | 43 | 10.4 | 11.6 | 9.4 | 174 | 193 | 157 | 6.7 | 111 |
| FNMA | 8.500 | 2001 | 9.174 | 31 | 32 | 114 | 180 | 13.0 | 14.0 | 13.7 | 216 | 234 | 228 | 9.9 | 165 |
| FNMA | 8.500 | 2002 | 9.188 | 47 | 48 | 87 | 125 | 12.2 | 11.9 | 8.4 | 204 | 199 | 141 | 7.4 | 123 |
| FNMA | 8.500 | 2003 | 9.130 | 45 | 45 | 165 | 241 | 12.2 | 12.4 | 13.3 | 203 | 206 | 222 | 13.8 | 231 |
| FNMA | 8.500 | 2004 | 9.223 | 65 | 65 | 247 | 343 | 11.0 | 11.6 | 11.9 | 183 | 193 | 199 | 10.4 | 173 |
| FNMA | 8.500 | 2005 | 9.234 | 72 | 72 | 397 | 636 | 12.6 | 12.9 | 12.9 | 210 | 214 | 216 | 11.6 | 194 |
| FNMA | 8.500 | 2006 | 9.246 | 121 | 121 | 989 | 1505 | 12.9 | 13.6 | 14.4 | 214 | 227 | 239 | 12.6 | 211 |
| FNMA | 8.500 | 2007 | 9.424 | 115 | 115 | 989 | 1591 | 12.9 | 13.6 | 13.6 | 214 | 226 | 226 | 11.1 | 185 |
| FNMA | 8.500 | 2008 | 9.682 | 60 | 60 | 732 | 1178 | 15.1 | 16.5 | 16.1 | 251 | 275 | 269 | 14.9 | 248 |
| FNMA | 8.500 | 2009 | 9.426 | 12 | 12 | 50 | 58 | 29.7 | 24.1 | 12.8 | 494 | 401 | 213 | 8.8 | 147 |
| FNMA | 8.500 | 2010 | 9.767 | 7 | 7 | 10 | 11 | 21.4 | 24.6 | 10.6 | 356 | 409 | 176 | 1.3 | 22 |
| FNMA | 8.500 | 2011 | 9.205 | 10 | 10 | 16 | 17 | N/A | 10.4 | 2.7 | N/A | 174 | 46 | 0.6 | 11 |
| FNMA | 8.500 | 2012 | 9.275 | 13 | 13 | 15 | 19 | 6.3 | 6.1 | 5.6 | 105 | 102 | 93 | 5.4 | 90 |
| FNMA | 8.500 | 2013 | 9.246 | 24 | 24 | 45 | 46 | 2.9 | 1.4 | 2.7 | 49 | 23 | 46 | 5.1 | 86 |
| FNMA | 8.500 | 2014 | 9.339 | 60 | 60 | 109 | 112 | 2.7 | 4.6 | 5.2 | 44 | 76 | 87 | 4.9 | 82 |
| FNMA | 8.500 | 2015 | 9.456 | 213 | 213 | 503 | 524 | 5.0 | 6.8 | 7.0 | 102 | 137 | 140 | 6.5 | 131 |
| FNMA | 8.500 | 2016 | 9.451 | 1102 | 1102 | 3870 | 3971 | 5.4 | 5.1 | 4.5 | 165 | 185 | 174 | 4.1 | 162 |
| FNMA | 8.500 | 2017 | 9.132 | 1652 | 1652 | 6734 | 6786 | N/A | 2.0 | 2.0 | N/A | 130 | 159 | 2.2 | 189 |
| FNMA | 8.500 | 2013 | 9.300 | 3606 | 3729 | 14937 | 17129 | 11.5 | 9.6 | 6.5 | 208 | 214 | 203 | 5.5 | 188 |
| Seasoned | | 2006 | 9.362 | 782 | 3729 | 4142 | 6288 | 13.0 | 13.6 | 13.5 | 216 | 227 | 225 | 11.7 | 195 |
| | | | | | | 15215 | 17536 | | | | | | | | |

Source: Bear, Stearns & Co.

conservative estimate of how rapidly the mortgages will prepay. Such an acceptance appears to be perfectly rational, considering the volume and quality of facts brought to bear in the investment decision.

In summary, FNMA 173 has had a long history of rapid and consistent prepayment. Prepayment speeds in Minneapolis are fairly rapid in relation to the universe of prepayments; this empirical data is bolstered by the qualitative and quantitative input of a regional economist concerning the economic health of the Minneapolis-St. Paul MSA. FNMA 173 has experienced prepayments perhaps slightly above the averages for the Minneapolis-St. Paul MSA. FNMA 173 has a WAM of 2007, and such WAMs have prepaid quite rapidly during the last year. Additionally, FNMA 173 compares quite favorably against the $1 billion sample of FNMA 8.50s with a 2007 WAM. This mass of data leaves the investor quite comfortable with the 8 percent CPP assumption.

If the Treasury yield curve is as follows,

$$5 \text{ year} = 8.90$$
$$7 \text{ year} = 9.15$$
$$10 \text{ year} = 9.33$$

then the investor who pays $92 in order to earn a 10.35 yield at the 8 percent CPP assumption will earn 120 basis points over the seven-year Treasury note. If the pick-up of 120 basis points over the Treasury yield curve is acceptable and compares favorably with the yields available in other sectors of the bond market, then mortgage securities in general, and FNMA 173 specifically, warrant a place in the investor's portfolio. Furthermore, all of the data concerning FNMA 173 prepayment speeds, as they relate to the economic climate in the Minneapolis-St. Paul MSA, and prepayment speeds of FNMA 8.50s with a 2007 WAM provide the investor with ample reason to anticipate that there might be prepayment speeds in excess of 8 percent CPP. For example, if FNMA 173 continued to prepay as it has within the past year, the investor would earn a 10.74 yield. This yield represents an absolute yield pick-up of another 39 basis points over the yield earned at the 8 percent CPP assumption. The spread increment is even greater since the faster speed shortens the average life to just over five years. The yield spread at the one-year speed over the five-year Treasury is 184 basis points. If there were never again a prepayment (such an occurrence would be historic) on FNMA 173, the yield would be 9.78, a 45 basis point pick-up over the 10-year Treasury.

## EXAMPLES OF OTHER TYPES OF SPECIFIED POOLS

Because of the large issuance of pools with older mortgages and because sufficient time has elapsed in order to view mortgage prepayment patterns over longer time periods, the specified pool market now offers a myriad of coupons, WAMs, WACs, and cash flows. Such a variety enables investment managers to find the cash flow they are seeking through careful analysis of specified pools.

Exhibit 28–7 presents a profile of FNMA pool 997. The most unique characteristic of FNMA pool 997 is that it has a WAC of 11.543 and a coupon of 9.50. This very high WAC coupled with the fact that the mortgages have been outstanding for a long time should result in a fairly short piece of paper. One Wall Street firm's prepayment model suggests that this pool, with its unique combination of coupon, WAM, and WAC, should prepay at a CPP speed of 11.18 percent when the prevailing mortgage rate is 10.75. The pool is from a geographical area that has prepaid very rapidly during the past year (25.76% CPP). Armed with this information, investment managers who add FNMA 977 to their portfolios at $97 are implicitly making the judgment that, although they may not know exactly how long the average life of the investment will be, they will receive a very enticing spread over the Treasury curve regardless of the prepayment speed. If the Treasury curve is as follows,

$$2 \text{ year} = 8.24$$
$$3 \text{ year} = 8.54$$
$$4 \text{ year} = 8.69$$
$$5 \text{ year} = 8.90$$
$$7 \text{ year} = 9.15$$

an investment manager would earn about 115 basis points over the seven-year at the prepayment model's estimated speed of 11.18 percent CPP, about 180 basis points over the four-year at the life speed of 18.55 percent CPP, and 250 basis points or more over the curve at the one-year, six-month, and three-month prepayment speeds. Such an investment would have a great appeal to many investment managers.

## EXHIBIT 28–7
## FNMA Pool 997

| | | | Price/Yield Matrix | | | | |
|---|---|---|---|---|---|---|---|
| Coupon: | 9.50% | | | | | | |
| Servicing: | 2.043% | | | | | | |
| Issue Date: | 12/82 | | 11.18% | 18.55% | 33.93% | 42.37% | 37.06% |
| Maturity: | 9/09 | | CPP | CPP | CPP | CPP | CPP |
| | | Avg. Life | 6.44 | 4.41 | 2.42 | 1.87 | 2.19 |
| *Prepayment History:* | | Price | | | | | |
| 3 month: | 37.06 CPP | | | | | | |
| 6 month: | 42.37 CPP | | | | | | |
| 1 year: | 33.93 CPP | | | | | | |
| Life: | 18.55 CPP | 97 | 10.29 | 10.49 | 10.97 | 11.28 | 11.08 |

Just as FNMA 997 offers the investment manager unique characteristics for achieving a very unusual combination of yield and average life possibilities, FHLMC 183161, previously presented in Exhibit 28–2, offers an equally unique but greatly different array of yield and average life characteristics. FHLMC 183161 has a 5 percent coupon and a 1993 maturity. Such a short maturity dramatically reduces the average life variability. At $89.75, the investor would earn a yield of 9.22 at 8 percent CPP, or 68 basis points above the three-year Treasury note shown above. At 8 percent CPP, the average life is 2.82 years. At the most rapid prepayment speed observed, the three-month speed of 14.81 percent CPP, the average life declines to only 2.48 years, and if there is never a prepayment the average life increases to only 3.29 years. Hence, as the WAM shortens, the average life variability declines and the investment manager's degree of certainty about the average life and yield is greatly increased. Of course, in this example the prepayment speeds during the last year, six months, and three months will add an additional 25, 42, and 57 basis points, respectively, to the yield. Many investors might employ FHLMC 183161 as a surrogate for very short-term notes because there may be a yield pick-up without a particularly wide range of average life variability.

## SUMMARY

Because mortgage securities have been issued for a number of years and because of the large issuance in the last few years of older mortgages in new pools, the variety of combinations of coupon, WAM, and WAC is extensive. Mortgage securities no longer consist of only 30-year generic prices, yields, and average lives. Because of a very diverse universe of pools and the resultant creation of large sophisticated databases (containing information about specific pools and the different prepayment speeds associated with varying geography, WAMs, and WACs), the investment manager is now able to include specified pools for a wide variety of cash-flow requirements. This wealth of research has enabled the investment manager to achieve the yield, average life, and issuer quality he or she desires along with a greater degree of confidence concerning the yield or total return and average life outcomes the mortgages will experience.

# CHAPTER 29

## COLLATERALIZED MORTGAGE OBLIGATIONS

Gregory J. Parseghian
*Managing Director*
*The First Boston Corporation*

Collateralized mortgage obligations (CMOs) are a dynamic innovation in the mortgage securities market. Since their introduction in June 1983, CMOs have grown into a $250 billion market. CMOs generally retain many of the yield and credit quality advantages of pass-throughs, while eliminating some of the administrative burdens imposed by the traditional mortgage-backed security. Each of the group of bonds issued in a CMO deal is referred to as a *tranche*. The shorter final maturity, enhanced call protection, and semiannual payments found on many CMO tranches make them suitable for some investors who cannot incorporate pass-throughs into their portfolios or strategies. As a result, the profile of participants in the CMO market differs from that of pass-through owners. The wide range of risk and return characteristics found within the universe of CMO securities gives them the potential to meet the needs of a broader investor group than can the more homogeneous pass-through market.

### THE CMO PRODUCT

CMOs are bonds that are collateralized by whole loan mortgages or mortgage pass-through securities. In addition to the security afforded by the fully dedicated collateral, some CMO issues also possess minimum reinvestment rate and minimum sinking-fund guarantees. The cash flows generated by the assets in the collateral pool are used to first pay interest and then pay principal to the CMO bondholders.

A key difference between traditional pass-throughs and CMOs is the mechanics of the principal payment process. In a pass-through, each investor receives a pro rata distribution of any principal and interest payments (net of servicing) made by the homeowner. Because mortgages are self-amortizing assets, a pass-through holder receives some return of principal each month. Complete return of principal and the final maturity of the pass-through, however, do not occur until the final mortgage in the pool is paid in full. This results in a large difference between average life and final maturity as well as a great deal of uncertainty with regard to the timing of principal return.

The CMO substitutes a principal paydown priority schedule among tranches for the pro rata process found in pass-throughs. In the early CMO structures, principal payments were made in a sequential basis, with all distributed principal going to one tranche until it was retired. The next tranche in the schedule then would become the exclusive recipient of principal payments. This pattern would be repeated until the final CMO tranche. Innovations in the CMO structure designed to create extremely stable average life tranches (see the section on PAC bonds) and to create floating-rate tranches (see the section on FRCMOs) have resulted in principal payments to multiple tranches simultaneously. The common denominator between the sequential-pay CMOs and those where multiple tranches receive principal payments simultaneously is that the guidelines governing principal return are stipulated in the prospectus of the deal. Further, it is possible to calculate the precise impact of shifting collateral prepayment rates on each CMO tranche.

The effect of the CMO innovation is to utilize cash flows of long maturity, monthly-pay collateral to create securities with short-, intermediate-, and long-final maturities and expected average lives. On the offering date of the first FHLMC(A) deal, for example, the final maturities of the tranches ranged from 5 years to 25 years and the expected average lives of the bonds ranged from 3 years to 21 years. The shorter classes clearly held more appeal than the underlying collateral for investors seeking low exposure to interest-rate risk. Since the shorter tranches had to be retired before longer tranches received principal payments, the longer tranches had a form of call protection. This feature appealed to investors who required less call and reinvestment risk than pass-through securities or whole loans carry.

CMOs are an important innovation because they broaden the range of investment objectives that can be achieved by using mortgage securities. Prior to the introduction of FHLMC CMO in June 1983, the mortgage securities market was dominated by 15- and 30-year final maturity pass-throughs. The inherent problem was that this structure did not meet the needs of the entire universe of fixed income investors. Hence, some market participants effectively were excluded from the major segment of the mortgage securities market. The shorter average life CMO tranches frequently meet the requirements of investors requiring lower duration and faster return of principal. The longer CMO classes offer a greater degree of protection against call and reinvestment risk. PAC tranches offer greater cash-flow stability at the expense of a small yield give-up. The conclusion is that a greater array of investors is able to participate in the mortgage market because of the introduction of CMOs. This is extremely important because investors have limited choices of high-quality fixed income securities with higher yields than Treasuries.

## THE BASIC CMO STRUCTURE

Exhibit 29–1 illustrates the structure of a typical CMO issue and demonstrates how cash flows get from the collateral to the bondholders. Interest is paid to each of the three tranches of bondholders. Cash flow generated by the collateral, in excess of that required to pay interest to all bondholders, is paid exclusively to the first tranche bondholders. In this example, it is assumed that monthly cash flows generated by the collateral are reinvested until the semiannual bond payment date. The inclusion of this reinvestment income means that the amount available for the semiannual distribution to bondholders exceeds the sum of the six monthly cash flows from the collateral. Exhibit 29–2 illustrates the effect on cash flows after the first class is retired. It shows that the second tranche then becomes the exclusive recipient of principal payments.

**EXHIBIT 29–1**
**Cash-Flow Diagram for a CMO at Origination of the CMO**

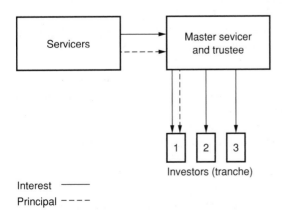

Interest ——
Principal ————

**EXHIBIT 29–2**
**Cash-Flow Diagram of a CMO After the First Tranche is Retired**

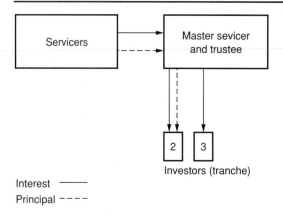

Interest ———
Principal ----

# EVOLUTION OF THE CMO

## Early Developments

A review of the history of CMO development demonstrates the innovations that have made CMOs an increasingly popular financing alternative and investment vehicle. From the viewpoint of an issuer, one objective is to tailor the cash flows due bondholders to closely resemble those produced by the mortgages. Deviations from this standard generally result in less proceeds at the time of the bond sale relative to the value of the collateral.

CMOs were further enhanced to better suit the requirements of investors. Methods of using whole loan collateral, GPMs, and conventional mortgages improved the yields that could be passed through to investors. The introduction of the accrual bond provided a uniquely call-protected mortgage security and enabled larger offerings of three-year and five-year final maturity tranches. The concentration on meeting the liquid asset requirements of thrifts and the needs of insurance companies to fund guaranteed investment contracts (GICs) and other intermediate liabilities had further effects on the CMO structure.

The original FHLMC CMO deal, co-managed by First Boston and Salomon Brothers in June 1983, was a three-tranche offering with a guaranteed minimum sinking fund. The collateral was level-pay whole loans, the credit of which was guaranteed by FHLMC. FHLMC's guaranteed sinking fund was structured to approximate a 100 percent FHA prepayment rate on the underlying collateral.

Pulte Homes, through its subsidiary Guaranteed Mortgage Corporation, issued the first private CMO in July 1983. ("Private" refers to the absence of any government agency acting as guarantor for the bonds; the security is publicly traded.) The collateral for the Pulte A deal, the first offering from the Pulte Guaranteed Mortgage Corporation I shelf, was GNMA level-pay (SFs) and graduated-payment mortgages (GPMs). In order to overcome the potential problem of insufficient cash-flow generation in the early years by the GPMs to service the bonds, Pulte set aside capital with a trustee to cover the greatest possible shortfall due to negative amortization. This fund, referred to as the debt-service reserve fund, is an innovation that enabled inclusion of GPM mortgages in the collateral pool.

Subsequent Pulte and American Southwest CMOs began to employ techniques that eliminated the need for the debt-service reserve fund. There were two innovations that enabled this to occur. The primary idea was the creation of the accrual bond: a bond that receives neither principal nor interest payments until all previous tranches are fully retired. The accrual bonds are designed to have negative amortization and hence absorb that created by the GPM collateral. Other means of absorbing negative amortization include coupon income from premium mortgages and unscheduled principal return from discount mortgages.

CMOs with semiannual payments to bondholders have a potential problem making coupon payments if large monthly flows of principal from the collateral must be reinvested in a low-interest-rate environment. The rating agencies stipulated that a reserve fund be set aside for this risk or that excess mortgages be put up to collateralize the bonds. The "calamity clause," introduced by Pulte Homes, eliminated the need for these measures by stipulating that prepayments beyond a specified rate could be passed through monthly to bondholders.

The next significant step in CMOs involved the collateral included in private deals. Most of the early private CMO deals utilized only GNMA, FNMA, and FHLMC guaranteed pass-throughs. Subsequent deals, however, included conventional mortgages insured by private entities such as MGIC, General Electric, and Aetna. CitiMac's CMO offering went several steps further. First, the credit guarantee on the conventional whole loans was provided by Citicorp and Citi-Mac, the issuer of the CMO. Second, CitiMac guaranteed a minimum sinking fund that approximates an SMM (Single Monthly Mortality), as opposed to an FHA prepayment rate on the collateral.

## SPECIAL FEATURES IN EARLY DEALS

The preceding section dealt with CMOs assumed to have the simplest possible structure. There are a large number of special features on various CMOs, however, that must be detailed in order to accurately evaluate the universe of CMO securities.

## Guaranteed Minimum Sinking Fund

The speed at which principal is retired on CMO bonds is highly dependent on the cash flow generated by the underlying collateral. Future cash flows from coupon income and amortization of the collateral are known. The rate of prepayments that will be received, however, cannot be predicted with certainty. Hence, the best cash flow that can be guaranteed to be generated by the mortgages is that assuming a zero percent prepayment rate on the collateral.

Some issuers, such as FHLMC and CitiMac, guarantee a minimum repayment schedule on the CMOs which exceeds that guaranteed to be generated by the collateral. If cash flow received from the underlying collateral is insufficient to meet the sinking-fund requirement, then the issuer is obligated to advance an amount sufficient to cover the shortfall. The amount guaranteed to be retired each semiannual period is expressed in the prospectus as a percentage of the remining principal balance of the CMO. The sinking-fund schedule generally reflects an approximation of a selected FHA or SMM prepayment rate on the underlying collateral. In subsequent periods, issuers generally can recover advances made to the extent that cash flow generated by the collateral exceeds the minimum amount guaranteed to the bondholders.

Exhibit 29–3 demonstrates the mechanics of the guaranteed minimum sinking-fund feature. In period 1, the sinking-fund guarantee is assumed to require a principal payment of at least $1,000. The collateral, however, generated cash flow sufficient for only $500 of principal payments, meaning that the issuer had to advance the other $500. In period 2, the collateral produced enough to cover the guarantee but no excess. In period 3, another $100 had to be advanced by the issuer, bringing the total advanced to $600. The collateral generated a $200 excess in period 4. Since advances must be repaid with excess before excess can be applied to retire more bond principal, the entire $200 was

**EXHIBIT 29–3**
**Guaranteed Minimum Sinking Fund**

| Period | [1] Principal Guaranteed to Bondholders | [2] Cash Flow Generated by Collateral in Excess of that Needed for Interest | [3] [2] − [1] Excess (+) or Shortfall (−) | [4] Advance Required by Issuer | [5] Return of Advances | [6] [3] − [5] Excess Paid to Bondholders |
|---|---|---|---|---|---|---|
| 1 | $1,000 | $ 500 | $ −500 | $500 | 0 | N/A |
| 2 | 900 | 900 | 0 | 0 | 0 | 0 |
| 3 | 800 | 700 | −100 | 100 | 0 | N/A |
| 4 | 700 | 900 | 200 | 0 | 200 | 0 |
| 5 | 600 | 2,000 | 1,400 | 0 | 400 | 1,000 |

retained by the issuer and used to reduce the $600 in advances outstanding to $400. In period 5, the first $400 of excess cash flow generated by the collateral is used to return the remaining advance outstanding. The remaining $1,000 of the $1,400 excess may then be used to retire more CMO principal. An additional wrinkle found on some CMOs is that the advance account accrues interest. For purposes of this example, we assumed no such accrual.

The effect of the minimum guaranteed sinking fund is to place a floor on the minimum pace of bond retirement above what can be guaranteed solely by cash flows from the collateral. This feature is particularly valuable in a rising-interest-rate environment, when prepayments tend to decline. A bond with no sinking-fund guarantee may experience a greater lengthening of its expected average life than will a bond with a minimum guaranteed sinking fund. This sinking-fund guarantee limits cash-flow and average life uncertainty and adds value to a CMO.

## Guaranteed Minimum Reinvestment Rate

In CMOs that make semiannual payments to bondholders, the monthly cash flows generated by the collateral must be reinvested until the payment date to bondholders. The rate earned on the cash flows reinvested can have a material effect on the amount available to pay bondholders and the average life of the CMO tranches. A guaranteed minimum reinvestment rate requires the guarantor (generally a triple-A bank or agency) to supplement the reinvestment income if it does not meet the minimum rate. The effect is to quicken the pace of bond retirement relative to what would be retired if there were no guarantee in periods of very low short-term interest rates.

## Credit Guarantee on Mortgages

The issuer of a CMO may establish a reserve fund to absorb some or all of the losses upon defaults of the whole loans or pass-throughs in the collateral pool. Generally, this type of guarantee exists only in CMOs such as CitiMac's that are backed by whole loans. In contrast, most bonds issued by home builders need no supplemental credit guarantees since the mortgages are insured by GNMA, FNMA, or FHLMC.

## Removal of Excess Cash Flow by Issuer

The issuer of a CMO is always required to pay interest on CMO bonds. In addition, the issuer must pay down enough CMO principal so that the outstanding CMO bonds remain fully collateralized. If cash available on a payment date to bondholders exceeds the sum of required principal and interest payments, then this amount is termed the excess. This excess also is referred to as the *CMO residual.*

There is wide variation among CMO deals on the method by which to calculate and distribute this excess. Some deals allow the issuer to retain the entire excess, while others stipulate that the entire amount be distributed to bondholders. Many CMO indentures contain a formula dividing the excess between CMO bondholders and the issuer.

It is clear that distribution of the excess to the bondholder shortens the expected average life of the CMO. Investors should not be alarmed, however, if the indenture provides that the issuer retains part or all of the excess. The yield table for each deal, which generally lists yields, timing of principal payments, final maturity, duration, and average life under a range of collateral prepayment rates, fully reflects the provisions relating to the handling of the excess. Hence, it is critical to scan the yield table in order to gain an understanding of how the various features of a particular CMO work together to influence cash flows.

## Special Reserve Fund for Negative Amortization Collateral

Some CMO offerings contain special reserve funds to supplement, if necessary, the cash flows from the portion of collateral that experiences negative amortization, such as would occur with GPMs. This feature is generally termed the "debt-service reserve fund." The effect of this feature is to bias upward the speed at which bonds are retired.

## Prepayment Reserve Fund

In a CMO that makes semiannual payments to bondholders, the issuer must pay coupon income on the entire principal balance outstanding at the beginning of the six-month period. This can pose difficulty if the reinvestment rate available on monthly principal return from the collateral is less than the coupon rate on the bonds. Some CMOs overcome this hurdle with a calamity clause that allows the issuer to make monthly principal payments to the bondholder.

CMOs without a calamity clause frequently have a prepayment reserve fund. This fund, which represents capital set aside by the issuer at the outset of the deal, is used to supplement the reinvestment income on monthly principal received from the collateral. This supplement may be required to make interest and principal payments to bondholders.

While it is easy at first glance to categorize the preceding special features as good and bad, these labels do not necessarily lead to an accurate assessment of the relative value of the particular CMO. For example, excess-income removal provisions frequently appear in combination with special reserve funds for negative amortization securities. Under close scrutiny, it becomes apparent that the approximate net effect of the provisions is to cancel out and generate cash flows to bondholders similar to those in more simply structured CMO offerings. The critical yardstick is the yield table, which enables the investor to scrutinize the cash-flow characteristics of the bonds under a range of prepayment assumptions on the collateral.

## IMPORTANCE OF THE ISSUER

All CMO offerings to date are backed by collateral that is held in trust exclusively for the benefit of bondholders. This means that bondholders retain possession of the collateral in the event of default of the CMO issuer. The credit quality of the CMO issuer is important only to the extent that promises made to bondholders cannot be satisfied by the collateral. Examples of this include guaranteed minimum sinking funds, guaranteed minimum reinvestment rates, and credit guarantees on the underlying collateral. A generalization that can be made is that CMOs issued by home builders tend to be structured to meet obligations to bondholders exclusively with cash flow from the collateral. In contrast, FHLMC, CitiMac, and other financial institutions that have issued CMOs more frequently have provisions that may result in bondholder reliance on the issuer to supplement cash flows generated by the collateral.

## LATER DEVELOPMENTS IN CMO EVOLUTION

All of the early CMO deals featured solely fixed-rate bonds with a sequential-pay principal retirement format. The primary economic rationale for CMO issuance was the creation of securities with the yield advantage and credit quality of mortgages and a range of expected final maturities and average lives broader than that available in the pass-through market.

Later developments in CMO structure featured the introduction of floating-rate CMOs (FRCMOs) and planned amortization classes (PACs). FRCMOs created the first significant availability of LIBOR-based assets with quality similar to agencies in the mortgage market. Deals featuring PAC and PAC-support bonds disproportionately allocate average life variability among tranches. PAC classes generally carry lower yield and lesser average life variability than the collateral, whereas support bonds most frequently have wider yield spreads to Treasuries but greater average-life variability compared to the collateral.

The recent innovations in CMOs have brought about an alphabet soup of PACs, TACs, jump Zs, and PAC-support bonds. While the original intent of the CMO process was to segment the average lives of mortgage-backed assets, many of the more recent developments were made to stratify the degree of cash-flow variability with respect to changes in prepayments on the underlying collateral. Portfolio managers now may tailor portfolios to reflect not only desired duration but also required convexity and exposure to prepayment trends.

As investment banks became the dominant issuer of CMOs, a market developed for the placement and trading of CMO residuals. Residuals are the cash flows generated by the collateral in excess of those required to pay bondholders and fees associated with the deal. A residual investor also assumes responsibility for absorbing any tax liability or credit caused by the difference between the taxable income generated by the collateral and the interest paid and expenses associated with the trust.

## SPECIAL TYPES OF CMO TRANCHES

### Accrual Bonds

Many CMO issues include one or more tranches that are accrual bonds. An accrual bond does not receive any cash payments of principal *or interest* until all tranches preceding it are retired. In effect, an accrual bond is a deferred-interest obligation, resembling a zero coupon bond, prior to the time that the preceding tranches are retired. The accrual bond, also termed the Z-bond, then receives cash payments representing interest and principal on the accrued amount outstanding. This amount is the original principal balance plus the compounded accrued interest. Accrual bonds are purchased most frequently by investors who require the greatest degree of protection against reinvestment and call risk or who seek the greater price leverage afforded by these classes.

Exhibit 29–4 demonstrates the effect of an accrual bond in a CMO structure. Interest accrues on, but is not paid to, the accrual bond (the fourth tranche

**EXHIBIT 29–4**
**Cash-Flow Diagram for a CMO with an Accrual Tranche**

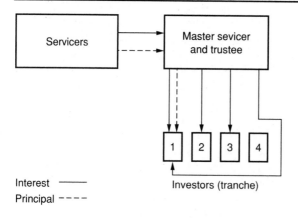

Interest ——
Principal – – – –

in this example) until the first three tranches are fully retired. The sequential payment of principal concept is not affected by the existence of an accrual bond. Since interest payments on this tranche are deferred, however, the payment of principal on the prior classes is accelerated by the amount of interest deferred on the accrual bond. Exhibit 29–5 shows that the second tranche in the sequence becomes the sole recipient of principal after the first tranche is retired. One should note that an accrual bond need not be the last class and that some deals have more than one accrual bond tranche.

## CMO Residuals

CMO residuals represent the "equity" interest in a CMO transaction. In general, the residual holder will receive the difference between the cash flows derived from the collateral and those applied to make payments to the bondholders and to pay trust expenses. Exhibit 29–6 graphically depicts the residual on a fixed-rate CMO with four tranches backed by $9\frac{1}{2}$ percent collateral.

The cash flows to the residual owner depend critically on the prepayment rate of the underlying collateral. When CMOs contain floating-rate tranches, the level of LIBOR also plays a key role in the cash flows to the residual holder. The value of a residual is based on the expected cash flows over a range of possible interest-rate scenarios, as well as consideration of factors such as liability for expenses and income tax consequences. Market participants typically project the pattern of yields or returns provided by a particular residual in order to determine its suitability to their investment needs and analyze both pretax and after-tax yields.

**EXHIBIT 29–5**
**Cash-Flow Diagram of a CMO After the First Tranche Is Retired**

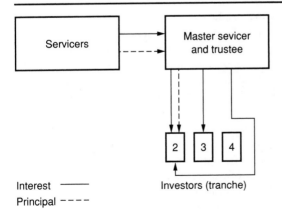

Interest ——
Principal ----

**EXHIBIT 29–6**
**CMO Residual**

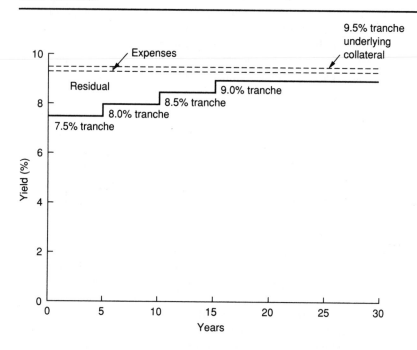

Exhibit 29–7 displays the expected yield on the residual of Morgan Stanley Trust Series 30, a bearish residual initially priced to yield 13.00 percent. Bearish residuals increase in yield as interest rates rise and decrease as rates decline. This kind of residual typically stems from a CMO structure where the mortgage collateral only backs fixed-coupon CMO tranches. The major factor influencing the yield and performance of the residual is the rate at which the collateral prepays. As depicted in the exhibit, the yield of the residual declines as interest rates fall and prepayments rise. Yield drops because the more rapid prepayments are applied to the shorter, lower coupon tranches, reducing the coupon spread between the CMO and the collateral and shortening the period over which the holder receives the residual cash flows. Conversely, in a rising rate environment, the yield of the residual rises, benefitting from a wider average coupon spread between the CMO bonds and the collateral and longer average life of the residual cash flows.

Other types of residuals include humped and stable residuals, whose names also are derived from their patterns of expected yields as interest rates change. These projections require assumptions on future LIBOR rates as well as the prepayment projections on the underlying collateral.

**EXHIBIT 29–7**
**Bearish Residual Expected Yield Analysis**

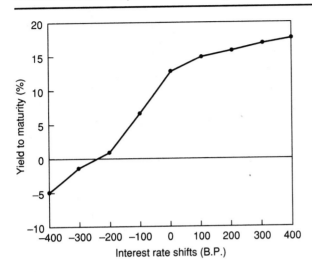

## Controlled Amortization Bonds:
## The PAC Structure

A PAC bond has two important features that distinguish it from a conventional CMO class. First, a PAC amortizes with a sinking fund that is predetermined as long as the prepayments on the underlying collateral remain within a broad range of speeds. Second, a PAC can make principal payments at the same time as some or all of the other CMO classes. Thus, unlike traditional CMO tranches, the PAC is not a "serial-pay" bond. It will receive its scheduled payments regardless of the status of its companion classes.

The most attractive feature of a PAC class to the CMO investor is its enhanced degree of cash-flow certainty. Except in extreme prepayment scenarios, the PAC bond can be expected to pay down principal according to its specified sinking fund. In a typical PAC backed by current coupon FNMAs, the investor can expect to receive the scheduled cash flow unless the prepayment speed on the underlying collateral slows to less than 50 percent PSA or increases beyond 350 percent PSA.

Due to the enhanced degree of cash-flow certainty, PAC bonds represent a significant value to the CMO buyer and especially to buyers who have avoided the mortgage market because of cash-flow uncertainty. Each PAC should be evaluated independently with respect to this specific cash-flow characteristic, but it is clear they should trade at a premium to comparable average life traditional CMO. PACs generally trade 10 basis points (b.p.) to 40 b.p. richer than comparable traditional CMO tranches of similar collateral and average life characteristics.

The cash-flow certainty of the PAC bond is facilitated by reallocating cash-flow uncertainty to other tranches of the CMO, often referred to as the non-PAC tranches. The extent to which these other tranches are affected depends upon the structure of the specific PAC. Investors considering the non-PAC tranches of a PAC CMO series should consult CMO yield tables and evaluate total return risk before making an investment decision. Total return and average life variability of non-PAC tranches is generally greater than traditional tranches in a CMO that contains no PACs.

***PAC Bond Impact.***    Assume that by the terms of the bond indenture, PAC investors are scheduled to receive $1 million per quarter beginning in two years and continuing for 10 years thereafter. This $1 million comes from the cash flow on the underlying collateral and the PAC class *receives priority* over all other tranches in receipt of principal. For example, if the collateral pays as expected at 175 percent PSA and generates $2 million in principal in a given quarter, $1 million goes to the PAC bond and the other $1 million goes to the CMO tranche that is currently receiving principal.

If, however, prepayment rates on the underlying collateral slow and only $1.5 million of principal is generated, the PAC still receives its scheduled $1 million, but the current CMO tranche receives only $500,000. Thus, the other CMO tranches provide a buffer for the PAC bond. If prepayments slow dramatically and only $750,000 of principal is generated, then the PAC bond receives the entire amount and no principal is passed through to the other tranches. In addition, the PAC has first call in future quarters on the $250,000 to which it was entitled but failed to receive; that is, the PAC has a cumulative right to its scheduled principal.

If prepayments on the underlying collateral increase, then the PAC continues to receive its scheduled $1 million, and all other principal received goes to pay down the current CMO tranche. As in the slow prepayment scenario, the other tranches absorb the cash-flow uncertainty. In cases of extremely fast prepayments, the other CMO tranches would be retired early. It is possible that the PAC (no longer cushioned) would then be forced to receive larger than scheduled principal payments, resulting in early retirement of the PAC.

***Effect of PAC on Other Tranches.***    The following example compares average life and total return sensitivity of a CMO with a PAC tranche to a traditionally structured CMO with no PACs under various interest-rate scenarios. The M.D.C. Mortgage Funding Corporation, Series M (MDC-M) CMO serves as the example of a structure containing a PAC bond. For purposes of analyzing the effect of a PAC bond within a CMO, a hypothetical MDC-M CMO with similar characteristics was structured without a PAC tranche. This hypothetical CMO will be referred to as "Ex-PAC."

The MDC-M CMO is comprised of five tranches, totaling $200.1 million at issue, backed by new FNMA $9\frac{1}{2}$s. The fourth tranche is a $60.6 million PAC and provides for a minimum mandatory sinking fund over 10 years beginning in 1988. The scheduled payments to the PAC tranches are provided below in Exhibit 29–8.

The Ex-PAC CMO is comprised of four tranches, also assumed to be backed by FNMA $9\frac{1}{2}$s. The first three tranches have the same average lives as those in the MDC-M CMO at the pricing speed of 175 percent PSA. The fourth tranche of the Ex-PAC CMO is an accrual bond with an average life marginally longer than the accrual tranches of the MDC-M CMO.

The PAC tranche receives priority on prepayments to meet the sinking-fund schedule. In periods of slow prepayment rates, prepayments on the underlying collateral would first be allocated to the PAC tranche, thus lengthening the average life of companion tranches.

In periods of fast prepayment rates, the PAC receives only the stipulated principal amounts set forth in the sinking-fund schedule. Under such a scenario, average lives of the surrounding tranches would shorten as excess principal flows are redirected around the PAC tranche.

*Average Life Analysis.* Exhibit 29–9 illustrates that the average life variability of the second and accrual tranches is significantly greater within the PAC structure than under the CMO that contains no PACs. To a lesser extent, the third tranche suffers more variability under the PAC structure, whereas the first tranche exhibits little difference between the two structures.

The second tranche under the PAC structure has a potential for lengthening to an 8.5-year average life versus 6.9 years for the second tranche in the hypothetical CMO with no PACs, assuming a +200 b.p. interest-rate rise. This may

**EXHIBIT 29–8**
**MDC–M CMO Scheduled PAC**
**Tranche Payments**

| Period | Quarterly Sinking-Fund Payment |
|---|---|
| 10/1/88–7/1/91 | $1,675,000 |
| 10/1/91–7/1/95 | 1,750,000 |
| 10/1/95–1/1/96 | 1,500,000 |
| 4/1/96–7/1/96 | 1,250,000 |
| 10/1/96–7/1/97 | 1,000,000 |
| 10/1/97–7/1/98 | 750,000 |

**EXHIBIT 29–9**
**Average Life Variability**

*MDC Mortgage Funding Corporation Series M CMO*
*(MDC-M)*

*Estimated Average Lives per Tranche*

| Interest-Rate Change | First Tranche | Second Tranche | Third Tranche | Accrual Tranche | PAC Tranche |
|---|---|---|---|---|---|
| +200 b.p. | 3.2 yrs | 8.5 yrs | 13.3 yrs | 21.8 yrs | 6.4 yrs |
| +100 | 2.9 | 7.3 | 12.5 | 21.1 | 6.4 |
| + 50 | 2.8 | 6.9 | 12.3 | 20.0 | 6.4 |
| Unchanged | 2.4 | 5.6 | 10.9 | 19.7 | 6.4 |
| − 50 | 1.9 | 4.1 | 8.3 | 17.5 | 6.4 |
| −100 | 1.5 | 3.0 | 5.4 | 14.7 | 6.4 |
| −200 | 1.0 | 2.0 | 3.0 | 4.4 | 6.0 |

*Hypothetical MDC Series M CMO*
*Without PAC Tranche*
*(Ex-PAC)*

*Estimated Average Lives per Tranche*

| Interest-Rate Change | First Tranche | Second Tranche | Third Tranche | Accrual Tranche |
|---|---|---|---|---|
| +200 b.p. | 2.9 yrs | 6.9 yrs | 12.8 yrs | 22.3 yrs |
| +100 | 2.7 | 6.4 | 12.1 | 21.7 |
| + 50 | 2.7 | 6.3 | 11.9 | 21.5 |
| Unchanged | 2.4 | 5.6 | 10.9 | 20.4 |
| − 50 | 2.1 | 4.6 | 9.1 | 18.1 |
| −100 | 1.7 | 3.7 | 7.2 | 14.9 |
| −200 | 1.2 | 2.5 | 4.5 | 9.5 |

be attributable to the similar average life assumptions at pricing of the second tranche (5.6 years) and the PAC tranche (6.4 years). The PAC tranche average life target under the pricing speed takes preference over any other tranche. Thus, slower prepayments render it difficult to realize both average life estimates, and the non-PAC tranche suffers accordingly.

Evaluating the second tranche at slower prepayment rates underscores its average life sensitivity in rising-interest-rate environments. The potential risk of diverting second tranche principal cash flows to the PAC tranche becomes more pronounced. This represents a very small potential change in average life variability for the early tranche; Exhibit 29–9 demonstrates, however, that it can have a more significant effect on the second tranche. In the MDC-M CMO, the PAC tranche's sinking fund does not commence for two years, allowing the first tranche a significant period during which it alone amortizes. Its average life variability is less than that of the second tranche.

In bull market scenarios, the MDC-M accrual tranche runs the risk of a dramatic shortening in average life versus the accrual tranche under a non-PAC structure. Under a yield curve shift of 200 b.p. decline, the MDC-M fourth tranche would have an expected average life of 4.4 years, as opposed to 9.5 years for the Ex-PAC. In the bear market scenarios, the average life variability is similar. The PAC tranche with its sinking fund may only receive a set amount of principal prepayment regardless of the speed at which the underlying collateral pays off. The excess prepayments are allocated to the earliest tranches, thereby shortening all tranches in falling rate environments.

The actual PAC tranche in the MDC-M CMO has an average life range of 6.0 to 6.4 years across all interest-rate environments examined. Clearly, companion tranches bear the burden of ensuring the average life or cash-flow certainty of the PAC tranche. Exhibit 29–10 summarizes estimated average life ranges for the PAC and Ex-PAC CMOs.

Non-PAC tranches within a PAC-structured CMO trade at significantly wider yield spreads to Treasuries than standard structure CMOs. The cash-flow uncertainty that is reallocated to these non-PAC tranches suggests that they should be priced at higher yields than otherwise comparable tranches in CMOs that contain no PACs.

As expected, PAC tranches with enhanced cash-flow certainty trade considerably richer than similar average life "plain vanilla" tranches. To analyze whether or not the yield sacrifice for less negative convexity is warranted, total return scenario analysis must be employed.

***Projected Total Returns.*** Comparative total return analysis indicates that the existence of a PAC tranche serves to transfer incremental negative convexity to the second and third tranches (Exhibits 29–11 and 29–12).

**EXHIBIT 29–10**
**Average Life Range** (MDC-M vs. MDC-M Ex-PAC)

| | *Average Life Range per Tranche (+/– 200 b.p.)* | | | | |
|---|---|---|---|---|---|
| | First Tranche | Second Tranche | Third Tranche | Accrual Tranche | PAC Tranche |
| Initial pricing assumption | 2.4 yrs | 5.6 yrs | 10.9 yrs | 19.7 yrs | 6.4 yrs |
| MDC-M | 1.0–3.2 | 2.0–8.5 | 3.0–13.3 | 4.4–21.8 | 6.0–6.4 |
| MDC-M Ex-PAC | 1.2–2.9 | 2.5–6.9 | 4.5–12.8 | 9.5–22.3 | — |

Exhibit 29–11 graphs the returns for second tranches under both the PAC and plain vanilla structures and the actual PAC tranche. The negative convexity of the second tranches under both structures (MDC-M2 and Ex-PAC) is obvious. The dotted line represents the expected returns of the PAC tranche itself and exhibits very slight positive convexity.

In comparing the MDC-M2 tranche under the Ex -PAC structure with the PAC bond itself, the PAC bond may be expected to outperform in a volatile interest-rate environment. Upward or downward yield curve shifts of more than 100 b.p. point to the superior return characteristics of the PAC bond. For yield changes in either direction of 100 b.p. or less, the traditional second tranche outperforms.

The effects of shifting cash-flow uncertainty under the PAC CMO to the second tranche were illustrated by Exhibit 29–9. The negative convexity of returns for the MDC-M2 tranche is more pronounced than that of the second tranche in the non-PAC CMO structure (MDC-M2 Ex-PAC). The MDC-M2 will underperform under virtually any rate scenario and only equal the return of its non-PAC counterpart in an unchanged to −50 b.p. rate environment.

**EXHIBIT 29–11**

**Total Return Curve Second and PAC Tranche Comparison (1-Year Holding Period)**

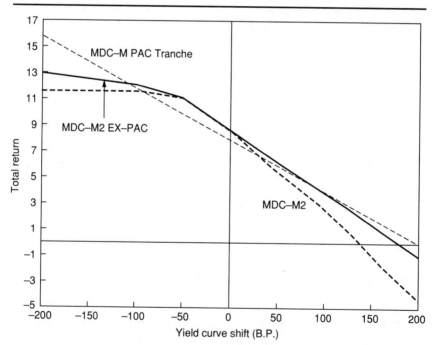

**EXHIBIT 29–12**
**Total Return Comparison Third Tranche Comparison (1-Year Holding Period)**

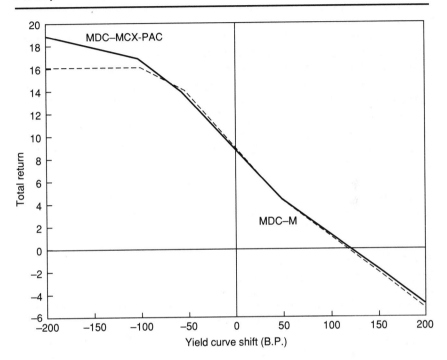

The results of the scenario analysis indicate that the PAC tranche outperforms only in the most volatile rate environments. This is clearly due to the superior convexity evidenced by a PAC tranche. Superior performance occurs in the extreme bull market case where the PAC returns 15.69 percent versus 12.71 percent for the hypothetical non-PAC second tranche. In the extreme bear market scenario, the PAC outperforms by only 1.20 percent in terms of total return.

In the simulation of total returns, the PAC tranche was priced 20 b.p. richer than a similar average life tranche in a plain vanilla structure. In cases where the sacrifice in yield for more favorable convexity characteristics exceeds 20 b.p., the total return profile of PAC bonds may not be as attractive.

Thus, a PAC tranche exhibits favorable convexity characteristics in comparison to a similar average life CMO tranche under a standard structure. However, in an environment of small net interest-rate changes, the standard structure CMO outperforms.

Exhibits 29–13 and 29–14 illustrate that the expected returns of first and accrual tranches are roughly equivalent under both the PAC and Ex-PAC struc-

**EXHIBIT 29–13**
**Total Return Comparison First Tranche Comparison (1-Year Holding Period)**

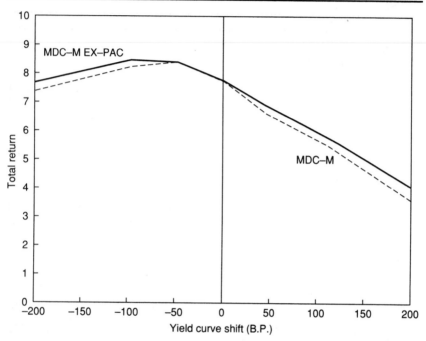

tures, although the Ex-PAC accrual tranche marginally outperforms under almost every interest-rate scenario.

Accrual tranche performance differs primarily in the case of an extreme bull market. The Ex-PAC accrual tranche does not shorten in duration to the extent of its PAC counterpart. Thus, the accrual tranche under the traditional structure outperforms the PAC accrual tranche in a −200 b.p. scenario by 40.4 percent to 32.6 percent in total return.

It appears that the first and accrual tranches in a PAC structure are less susceptible to the unfavorable effects of cash-flow uncertainty. The sinking fund of the PAC class does not begin for two years. During these two years, the first tranche may amortize substantially. The accrual tranche does not receive principal on a current basis until such time as the PAC and other tranches mature. Principal cash flows to the outer tranches, first and accrual, do not coincide with the operation of the sinking fund to the degree that the intermediate tranches (second and third) do. Hence, the first and accrual tranches bear less of the burden in ensuring the cash-flow certainty of the PAC tranche.

**EXHIBIT 29–14**
**Total Return Comparison Accrual Tranche Comparison (1-Year Holding Period)**

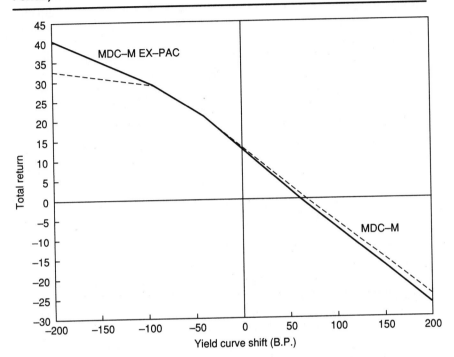

The investment conclusions are twofold:

1. Nonaccrual CMO tranches under an Ex-PAC structure outperform similar average life tranches of a CMO with a built-in PAC tranche in virtually all interest-rate environments. Correspondingly, intermediate tranches (second and third) in a PAC structure bear the primary burden of ensuring the cash-flow certainty of the PAC tranche.
2. An actual PAC tranche will equal or fall short of total return generated by a similar average life Ex-PAC tranche, given small net changes in interest rates; only in a volatile environment, ±100 b.p. or more, will a PAC tranche outperform.

## Floating-Rate CMOs

Another significant innovation in the CMO market is the floating-rate tranche, which was introduced in the fall of 1986 and has become an integral part of the CMO sector. Although floating-rate CMO volume has been low lately due to relatively high short-term rates, floaters have broadened the CMO market by attracting a large number of traditional investors in the non-mortgage related floating-rate securities. CMO floaters generally offer higher yields than comparable floating-rate notes and fixed-rate securities, without sacrificing credit quality.

As the volume of these securities has increased, so too has the complexity of analyzing each deal from an investor's point of view. The CMO floaters that have been issued have contained various quoted margins or spreads, coupon cap schedules, payment delays, gross-up provisions, and other features. The following discussion explores the various features of floating-rate CMOs and their impact on returns to investors.

*Quoted Margin or Spread.* The majority of CMO floaters issued have used the London InterBank Offered Rate (LIBOR) as the index. The term of the index has varied: one-, three-, and six-month LIBORs have been used. There is nothing to preclude the use of other indexes in the future, should investor interest exist.

The coupons on CMO floaters are reset at a fixed spread over the index rate. This spread is referred to as the quoted margin (or spread) and is usually expressed in basis points. The quoted spreads of CMO floaters have ranged from 25 to 70 b.p. The actual spread an investor will receive may differ from the quoted spread, depending upon the features of the issue.

The size of the quoted spread is based on several factors. The average life of the floating-rate tranche is one determinant of quoted spread. The longer the average life is, the greater the quoted spread will be. This is due to the ordinarily upward-sloping shape of the yield curve and investors' concerns over maturity extension and rate caps.

Maximum coupons, or caps, also impact the amount of quoted spread. CMO floaters issued to date have contained two types of caps: stepped caps and lifetime caps. Stepped caps are limits that are set initially (i.e., at 8% to 9%), increasing by a small increment each year (i.e., to 11% to 12%) after four to five years. This type of cap has been used in floaters with two- to three-year average lives. A lifetime cap is a coupon limit in effect over the bond's entire life. Lifetime caps have ranged from 11 percent to 13 percent and are generally present in floaters with longer average lives.

Factors that determine the level of coupon caps are the weighted average coupon rate of the fixed-rate classes in the CMO and the par amount and weighted average pass-through rate of the collateral (as more fully discussed later). Once an approximate cap schedule is determined, issuers set the quoted spread at an amount that is attractive to investors. Investors are compensated with higher quoted spreads for the risk of the coupon being capped out. In general, the amount of quoted spread has an inverse relationship to the level of the cap. Thus, a low cap would be indicative of a high quoted spread, and vice versa.

Another determinant of quoted spread is the type of collateral. As is the case with fixed-rate CMOs, floaters backed by FNMAs and FHLMCs yield more than floaters backed by GNMAs because of the preceived higher, government-guaranteed credit quality of GNMAs. To date, FNMA- and FHLMC-backed floaters have had mean quoted spreads of 47 b.p. and 48 b.p., respectively, versus a mean on GNMA-backed floaters of 35 b.p.

The amount of quoted spread is not necessarily the actual or effective spread that an investor will receive from a CMO floater. Coupon caps, coupon refix and payment frequencies, payment delays, and gross-up provisions may all have an effect on quoted spread that reduces the realized spread to the investor.

*Maximum Coupons or Caps.* All CMO floaters are backed by fixed-rate mortgages or mortgage-backed securities. Therefore, to ensure that the cash flow will always be sufficient to pay the coupon interest, there are caps on the floating interest rates. Most caps are set at a rate above the pass-through rate of the underlying collateral. This does not mean, however, that, if the coupon rate of the floater reached the cap, the cash flows from the collateral would not be sufficient to pay the bonds. Issuers have combined floating-rate tranches with fixed-rate tranches in CMOs and used over-collateralization to compensate for the notional shortfall. By combining floating- and fixed-rate tranches in a CMO, issuers limit the amount of coupon interest that would have to be paid under rising interest-rate scenarios. The effect of the floating-rate tranche reaching its maximum coupon under such a scenario is offset somewhat by the lower fixed coupons of the other classes. As long as the weighted average coupon on the bonds (assuming the floating tranche is at its maximum cap rate) is less than the weighted average pass-through rate on the collateral, the cash flows from the collateral will be sufficient to pay the required bond cash flows. For example, ML Trust V is a two-tranche CMO with a $375 million floating-rate first tranche and a $375 million 6 percent fixed-coupon second tranche. The floater has a coupon of 3-month LIBOR plus .5 percent, subject to a cap of 13 percent. The CMO is backed by $750 million par amount of 9.5 percent FHLMC certificates. Under a scenario where the coupon of the first class reaches the cap, the weighted average coupon of the CMO would be 9.5 percent [(375/750 × 13%) + (375/750 × 6%)]. Thus, the 9.5 percent FHLMC collateral could support the bonds in the event the floating-rate coupon reached the cap.

Another method of ensuring the supportability of the floating-rate CMOs in a rising interest-rate environment is over-collateralization. Over-collateralization entails backing either a CMO floater with fixed-rate mortgage or mortgage-backed securities with a higher principal amount than the principal amount of the bonds. The FBC Mortgage Securities Trust VII Series A CMO, for example, is a $240 million par amount single-tranche floating-rate CMO with a coupon of 3-month LIBOR plus .5 percent, subject to a lifetime cap of 11.5 percent. It is backed by $260 million par amount of FHLMC certificates with a weighted average pass-through rate of 10.51 percent. Under a scenario where the floating-rate coupon has reached the cap, the CMO would pay interest of 11.5 percent on a quarterly basis. The collateral pays a weighted average coupon of 10.51 percent on a monthly basis. In order to make the two rates comparable, it is necessary to express the monthly weighted average coupon of the collateral as a quarterly rate. The resulting quarterly rate is 10.60 percent $\{4 \times [(1 + 10.51\% /12)^3 - 1]\}$. Applying this rate to the $260 million par amount of the collateral gives approximately the same coupon income as the amount needed to pay interest on $240 million of bonds when they have a coupon of 11.5 percent ($260 million $\times$ 10.60% = $240 million $\times$ 11.50%).

***Coupon Refix and Payment Frequency.*** The coupon refix frequency of a CMO floater refers to the periodic reset of a floater's coupon to current market levels. CMO floating-rate coupons refix on monthly, quarterly, and semiannual bases. All else being equal, a shorter refix period reduces the likelihood that a coupon will vary from market levels. The benefit of a shorter refix period is not without a cost, however; the spreads between one-month LIBOR and three-month LIBOR and one-month LIBOR and six-month LIBOR have averaged approximately 5 b.p. and 15 b.p., respectively, over the past two years. Thus, an investor who bought a quarterly-pay, monthly-reset floater would earn less coupon income than one who bought a quarterly-pay, quarterly-reset floater, assuming that all else is constant.

The effect of a shorter refix period should not be analyzed without taking coupon payment frequency into account. CMO floaters offer monthly, quarterly, and semiannual payments. For the same nominal coupon rate, more frequent coupon payments will result in a higher effective yield, due to the reinvestment of cash flows.

The periodicity of the coupon refix and the reset index do not necessarily have to match. The period of the reset index can exceed the period of the coupon refix, and vice versa (although the latter case is rare). In a positively sloped yield curve environment, a refix period shorter than the index period provides two benefits: compounding of interest and the use of a higher index.

An example will help to illustrate the effects of coupon refix and payment frequency. For simplicity, assume the three hypothetical LIBOR scenarios shown in Exhibit 29–15. For each scenario, we have assumed that the spread among one-, three-, and six-month LIBOR conform to recent experience.

Exhibit 29–16 shows the effective spread over three-month LIBOR for four CMO floating-rate tranches when the nominal coupons are expressed on the consistent quarterly pay basis. FBC Mortgage Securities Trust VII Series B is a typical quarterly-pay, quarterly-refix tranche with a coupon of three-month LIBOR plus .4 percent. Its quoted spread and effective spread are the same. The GMAC Class B-1 floater is a monthly-pay, monthly-reset tranche with a coupon

**EXHIBIT 29–15**
**Hypothetical LIBOR Scenarios**

| | LIBOR | | |
| --- | --- | --- | --- |
| Scenario | One-Month | Three-Month | Six-Month |
| 1 | 6.05% | 6.10% | 6.20% |
| 2 | 6.55 | 6.60 | 6.70 |
| 3 | 7.05 | 7.10 | 7.20 |

of one-month LIBOR plus .25 percent. When viewed on a quarterly-pay basis, the effective spread of the GMAC-B1s is less than the quoted spread because the advantage of monthly compounding (3 to 4 b.p.) is offset by the negative spread between one-month and three-month LIBOR (5 b.p.). The Oxford A-1s have a monthly-pay, monthly-reset coupon of three-month LIBOR plus .5 percent. Since the coupon resets off three-month LIBOR, the effective spread is not negatively affected by the one-month to three-month LIBOR spread. The effect of monthly compounding adds 4 to 5 b.p. to the quoted spread. The FBC Mortgage Securities Trust IX Series A floater is the only semiannual-pay, semiannual-reset floater issued to date. When viewed on a quarterly basis, its effective spread is greater than its quoted spread because the positive spread between three-month and six-month LIBOR (10 b.p.) is more than enough to offset the negative impact of semiannual versus quarterly compounding (6 to 8 b.p.).

This example does not attempt to show what would happen in a changing interest-rate environment. In an increasing rate environment, the short refix period floaters could offer higher effective spreads, depending on the magnitude of interest-rate changes. The analysis above could be performed in conjunction with an investor's interest-rate forecast to determine more accurately the effects of coupon refix and payment frequency.

***Coupon Payment Delays.*** A coupon payment delay on a bond refers to a situation where the end of a coupon period does not correspond to the coupon payment date. A payment delay reduces effective yield because interest does not accrue between the end of the coupon period and the payment date. Payment delays on CMO floaters have ranged from 30 to 50 days, with most issues having no delay. At current rates, the delay may cost an investor up to 8 b.p. in yield. Exhibit 29–17 compares the effective spread over LIBOR of three CMO floating-rate tranches with payment delays of 0, 30, 50 days, using the LIBOR scenarios in Exhibit 29–16. The example shows that a 30-day delay reduces the quoted spread by 4 to 5 b.p., and a 50-day delay reduces the quoted spread by 6 to 8 b.p.

**EXHIBIT 29–16**
**Impact of Coupon Refix and Coupon Payment Frequency**

| Issuer and Series | Coupon Refix Frequency | Coupon Payment Frequency | Nominal Coupon | Nominal Coupons under 3 LIBOR Scenarios | Nominal Coupons as Quarterly Rate | Effective Spread over 3-Month LIBOR |
|---|---|---|---|---|---|---|
| FBC Mortgage Securities Trust VII Series B | Q | Q | 3-month LIBOR+.4% | 6.50% 7.00 7.50 | 6.50% 7.00 7.50 | .40% .40 .40 |
| GMAC Mortgage Securities Series B, Class B-1 | M | M | 1-month LIBOR+.25% | 6.30 6.80 7.30 | 6.33 6.84 7.34 | .23 .24 .24 |
| Oxford CMO Trust 1 Series A, Class A-1 | M | M | 3-month LIBOR+.5% | 6.60 7.10 7.60 | 6.64 7.14 7.65 | .54 .54 .55 |
| FBC Mortgage Securities IX Series A | S | S | 6-month LIBOR+.7% | 6.90 7.40 7.90 | 6.84 7.33 7.82 | .74 .73 .72 |

**EXHIBIT 29–17**
**Impact of Payment Delay**

| Issuer and Series | Tranche | Nominal Coupon | Nominal Coupons under 3 LIBOR Scenarios | Coupon Payment Delay | Effective Coupon after Impact of Delay | Effective Spread over LIBOR Index |
|---|---|---|---|---|---|---|
| TMAC CMO Trust 1986–2 | 2–A | 3-month LIBOR+.5% | 6.60% | 0 days | 6.60% | .50% |
| | | | 7.10 | | 7.10 | .50 |
| | | | 7.60 | | 7.60 | .50 |
| Dean Witter CMO Trust 1 | A | 3-month LIBOR+.5% | 6.60 | 30 | 6.56 | .46 |
| | | | 7.10 | | 7.06 | .46 |
| | | | 7.60 | | 7.55 | .45 |
| CMO Trust 13 | A | 1-month LIBOR+.5% | 6.55 | 50 | 6.49 | .44 |
| | | | 7.05 | | 6.98 | .43 |
| | | | 7.55 | | 7.47 | .42 |

*Gross-Up Provisions.* Another factor that affects returns from a CMO floater is the "gross-up" provision. These provisions relate to the payment day convention of a CMO floater. In general, the payment day convention of a CMO floater is not the same as that of LIBOR. LIBOR is quoted on an actual/360-day year basis, whereas CMOs typically pay interest on 30/360-day basis. In order to eliminate this discrepancy, some CMO floaters pay interest on an actual/360-day year payment basis. Others "gross up" LIBOR to the equivalent rate on a 30/360-day year payment basis. Example coupon calculations for three CMO floating-rate tranches will help to illustrate this point. Exhibit 29–18 shows hypothetical coupon calculations for American Pioneer CMO Trust 1-A, Ryland Acceptance Corp. Four 23-A, and N.W. Acceptance Corp. A-1 CMOs; three-month LIBOR remains constant at 6.25 percent and the three bonds have the same payment period. The American Pioneer tranche pays interest on a 30/360 day basis but contains a gross-up provision. The Ryland Acceptance tranche pays interest on an actual/360-day basis. The N.W. Acceptance tranche pays interest on a 30/360 day basis with no gross-up provision. The results of the hypothetical computation show that the American Pioneer and N.W. Acceptance tranches have roughly equivalent effective coupons and the Ryland Acceptance floating-rate tranche has an effective coupon greater than that of the N.W. Acceptance floating-rate tranche by 5 b.p. A comparison of the three floating-rate tranches without performing this analysis would lead one to believe that the coupon of the N.W. Acceptance tranche exceeded that of the other two by 10 b.p.

*Methodology for Comparing Returns of CMO Floaters.* Using the methods discussed above, it is possible to express the quoted spreads of CMO floaters on a consistent quarterly pay basis. The spreads so derived incorporate the effects of differing coupon refix and payment frequencies, coupon payment delays, and gross-up provisions. Expressing the spreads on a consistent basis will help to identify relative value among floating-rate CMO tranches.

## EVALUATING CMOs

The objective of most mortgage security analysis is to gain insight and create expectations of the cash-flow pattern in various market environments. A three-step process can be employed in applying this type of analysis to CMO securities. The first phase involves examination of the pass-throughs or whole loans that collateralize the offering. The second step is to review the process by which principal and interest received from the collateral flows through to the bondholders of various tranches. The third phase of the analysis involves a determination of the impact of other special features on the expected cash flows to bondholders. Taken together, the three steps in the analysis process seek to make a determination of the likely pace of cash flows to CMO bondholders under various market environments.

**EXHIBIT 29–18**
**Hypothetical Floating-Rate Coupon Computations**

| Issuer and Series | Tranche | 3-Month LIBOR | Gross-Up Factor | Quoted Spread | Floating-Rate Coupon* | Payment Basis | Interest Period 3/1/87-6/1/87 | Interest per $1,000 Bond | Effective Spread over 3-Mo LIBOR 30/360 | Actual/360 |
|---|---|---|---|---|---|---|---|---|---|---|
| American Pioneer CMO Trust 1 | 1-A | 6.25% | 365/360 | 40% | 6.74% | 30/360 | 90 days | $16.842 | .49% | .34% |
| Ryland Acceptance Corp. Series 23 | 23-A | 6.25 | N/A | 40 | 6.65 | Actual/ 360 | 92 | 16.994 | .55 | .40 |
| N. W. Acceptance Corp. Series A | A-1 | 6.25 | N/A | 50 | 6.75 | 30/360 | 90 | 16.875 | .50 | .35 |

*Computed as follows: LIBOR × gross-up factor + quoted spread

Generally, greater uncertainty surrounding the timing of cash flows is perceived to represent the risk in a mortgage security. The end result is to evaluate the sufficiency of the yield to compensate the investor for the risks undertaken.

## The Underlying Collateral

The following factors should be considered:

1. Average coupon and maturity
2. Range of coupons and maturities
3. Cash-flow pattern of mortgages
   a. Level pay
   b. Graduated payment
   c. Other
4. Geographic distribution
5. Due-on-sale provisions
6. Prepayment history if seasoned
7. Amount of collateral relative to amount of bonds

The average and range of coupons and maturities, in combination with the geographic distribution, due-on-sale provisions, and prepayment history, are needed to forecast prepayments on the underlying collateral. It is necessary to forecast prepayments under various scenarios because of the impact they have on the amount of cash flow generated by the collateral.

## Structure and Seasoning of a CMO

The amount of collateral backing the deal relative to the amount of CMO bonds outstanding is very significant. If a deal becomes over-collateralized, meaning that the amount of collateral exceeds that necessary to make payments to bond-holders under any market scenario, the remaining bonds will be paid relatively quickly. If, however, the issuer is empowered to retain excess cash flow generated by the collateral, the bonds would not enjoy as much benefit of expected shortening of average life produced by over-collateralization. A build-up in the amount of collateral relative to the quantity of bonds can be caused by a number of factors. If the reinvestment rate or prepayment rate experience is more favorable than the extremely conservative assumptions employed when constructing the asset pool, then over-collateralization is likely to occur. Another assumption frequently employed is that if premium bonds (above the need to pay interest to CMO bondholders) are used to retire additional bonds, then the remaining principal amount of collateral will be greater than the remaining principal amount of bonds.

The sequential-pay feature on CMOs makes the seasoning process even more significant for CMOs than for pass-throughs. As a first tranche is retired, for example, the holders of the second tranche move from no receipt of principal to an environment of rapid principal paydowns. Amortization and prepayments on the underlying collateral and retirements of CMO bond principal have an effect on both the long and short CMO tranches. Faster than anticipated retirement of the first tranche of bonds may shorten the final maturity and expected average life of not only the second tranche but also the longer tranches in the CMO offering. The yield tables, generally revised on the dates of prepayments to bondholders, reflect the effects of principal retirement and passage of time. Since actual prepayment speeds and expected amortization rates of the underlying collateral change over time, it is critical to use updated yield tables.

## Sensitivity to Prepayment Changes

The major risk inherent in a mortgage security is the uncertainty of timing of cash flows. The primary source of uncertainty in a CMO is the prepayment rate on the underlying collateral. In order to determine the likely price sensitivity of a particular CMO to changing prepayments, one must consider several factors.

1. *Yield Effect.* If the price of a CMO bond differs from par, then the rate of prepayments has an effect on yield. For CMOs trading at a discount, a higher prepayment rate connotes faster retirement of principal and higher yield. A CMO trading at a premium to par suffers a decline in yield if prepayments rise on the underlying collateral.

2. *Average Life Effect.* Changes in the prepayment rate on the collateral generally impact the average life and final maturity of a CMO bond. The extent to which this occurs depends upon the structure of the CMO offering.

3. *Yield-Spread Effect.* Most CMO bonds are quoted in terms of yield spread to the Treasury curve. Changes in the prepayment rate have a dual effect on this relationship. First, the CMO's yield may change if the price differs from par. Second, if the Treasury yield curve has a positive or negative slope, the reference yield on the Treasury curve may change from that originally assumed. A third factor must be considered for in-depth analysis. If prepayment rates rise and a CMO with an original average life assumption of seven years moves to an average life assumption of four years, then the required spread to the Treasury curve may change. Assuming that yield spreads should tighten as the expected average life shortens, this would exert upward pressure on a CMO's price.

4. *Special Features.* A change in prepayments may trigger a minimum guaranteed sinking fund. To the extent that this fund mitigates the effect of slower prepayments on cash flow to bondholders, it reduces the bond's sensitivity to changes in prepayment rates.

The net effect of the factors listed above determines the impact of changing prepayment rates on the price and return of CMOs. An investor must be aware of CMO yield, yield spread to Treasuries, and the comparison point on the Treasury yield curve in order to evaluate sensitivity to prepayments. The universe of CMO tranches has vastly differing sensitivities to prepayment rates on underlying collateral. To the extent that this sensitivity causes risk, the investor must be compensated in the form of yield.

## The Coupon Rate and Relationship of CMO Price to Par

These factors will determine the current yield and likely impact of increased prepayments on yields and returns. All else being equal, a CMO trading at par should have a greater yield spread to Treasuries than a CMO trading at a discount. As in all other fixed income sectors, the incremental call risk in a current coupon relative to a discount coupon requires incremental yield spread to represent fair value. It should be recognized, however, that the speed of retirements will be more dependent on the interest rates of the collateral pool than on the price of the CMO bonds.

# CHAPTER 30

## STRIPPED MORTGAGE PASS-THROUGH SECURITIES*

*Steven J. Carlson*
*Senior Vice President*
*Fixed Income Strategies*
*Shearson Lehman Hutton*

*Timothy D. Sears*
*Vice President*
*Mortgage Securities Research*
*Goldman Sachs & Co.*

The secondary mortgage market's response to the challenge of structuring mortgage cash flow to meet investor needs has been varied and innovative. Academicians refer to this process of carving up mortgage cash flow in order to allocate risk among different investors as "completing the market." Issuers call it "broadening the investor base." The fixed-rate 30-year mortgage may be an appealing instrument to homeowners, but the investor public that considers it an ideal portfolio asset is limited. Achieving the widest possible distribution of mortgage product, and therefore the best price, has sparked the creation of innovative ways to satisfy investors.

The latter half of 1986 saw the introduction of stripped mortgage pass-throughs. These were best exemplified by the 12 FNMA stripped mortgage-

---

*The authors acknowledge the assistance of Mary Parker in the preparation of this chapter.

backed securities (SMBS) issues, the earliest alphabet series, structured as "synthetic coupon" pass-throughs. This involved decoupling the mortgage principal and interest payments and recombining them in proportions that produced a coupon different from the underlying pass-through.

The strip market moved from partial stripping of principal and interest to the logical point of total stripping. Stripped mortgage pass-through securities are of two types: one that pays interest only (IO) and one that pays principal only (PO). By viewing mortgage pass-throughs this way, investors can see the advantages of stripping. First, stripped mortgages offer an efficient way to trade prepayment risk. As the mortgagor weighs the costs and benefits of a prepayment, the holders of the corresponding stripped mortgage-backed security can trade, and therefore control, the risk associated with the mortgagor's decision. The holder of a PO security benefits from the homeowner's decision to prepay, while the IO holder gains from a decision not to prepay. Second, since prepayments are highly correlated with interest-rate movements, holding varying proportions of IOs and POs gives investors control over the interest-rate exposure of their portfolios.

Viewing stripped mortgage pass-throughs as a recombined package of IOs and POs is more than just a useful analytical device. Stripping makes new positions available that are unattainable through standard pass-throughs or partially stripped mortgages. The stripped structure creates value by offering investors the greatest number of choices.

This chapter contains five sections. The first shows mortgage cash flow divided into its constituent parts and presents an intuitive discussion of the effect of prepayments on the timing and level of IO and PO cash flow.

The second section builds a simple model of mortgage security valuation to provide insight into trading relationships. It also supplies a graphic demonstration of the opportunities created by IO and PO securities.

A qualitative discussion of appropriate yield levels for IO and PO securities appears in the third section, including current pricing of stripped securities. Performance is covered next, with an analysis of total returns for IOs and POs under varying market scenarios. A snapshot assessment of performance is provided by an estimate of mortgage duration and convexity.

Portfolio uses for IO and PO securities are indicated in the fourth section, where two methods of hedging mortgage-backed securities are discussed. The first takes the interest-rate sensitivity of IOs and POs into account and demonstrates their utility as highly leveraged tools for asset/liability managers. The second shows how to use IOs and POs in hedging the prepayment risk of a standard mortgage pass-through.

The final section covers the conditions that will increase the liquidity in stripped mortgage pass-throughs, improving their utility as portfolio management tools.

## CASH FLOW FOR IO AND PO SECURITIES

To understand how IO and PO securities can enhance the opportunities in the mortgage market, it is necessary to gain an understanding of their trading relationships with respect to other securities. The first step is to achieve a clear perspective on how IO and PO cash flow is generated.

Scheduled principal and interest payments for a 9 percent mortgage pass-through are shown in Exhibit 30–1*a*. It shows the effects of amortization on principal and interest cash flow when there are no prepayments. Scheduled principal payments start out small since the majority of each monthly payment is allocated to interest on the outstanding balance. As principal is retired, less interest is owed and an increasing fraction of the payment can be devoted to paying down principal. Scheduled mortgage payments make the IO security appear to have a much shorter cash-flow average life than the PO security. This fact should be recognized only as a point of departure.

If the pass-through prepays at 8 percent CPR for the remainder of its life, the cash-flow profile in Exhibit 30–1*b* will result. It is clear that the timing of the principal cash flow has been rearranged dramatically. Principal payments are shifted strongly toward the near-term. At the same time, the total interest payment returned each month is greatly reduced. This exhibit points out an

**EXHIBIT 30–1***a*
**Scheduled Mortgage Cash Flow** ($100 Million Face; 9% Pass-Through)

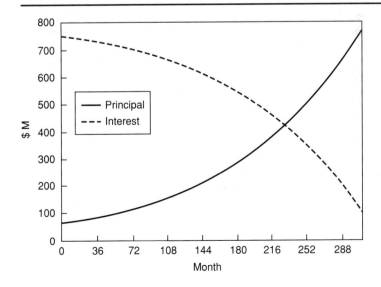

**EXHIBIT 30–1***b*
**Mortgage Cash Flow At 8% CPR** ($100 Million Face; 9% Pass-Through)

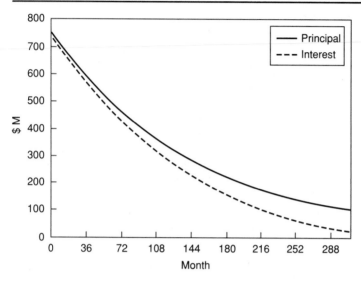

important fact about interest—it lives off principal. Risk associated with an IO security is related to the level of future cash flow. Any reduction in the outstanding balance reduces future interest cash flow. By contrast, principal cash flow must add up to the face value of the mortgage. Risk associated with principal payments comes from uncertainty about their timing.

Against this background, Exhibits 30–1*c* and 30–1*d* display the cash-flow profiles of principal and interest payments under different CPR assumptions. Even small increases in the prepayment rate can bring the half-life of the principal payments down to less than 15 years. Exhibit 30–1*c* illustrates that a 9 percent pass-through at 4 percent CPR has a half-life of 15 years. Exhibit 30–1*c* also depicts the diminishing marginal impact of changes in CPR on changes in the timing of principal cash flows. Congruently, Exhibit 30–1*d* shows that the first few percentage points of CPR have a large impact in reducing interest cash flow. A comparison of the two exhibits confirms the notion that interest is a residual income that depends on the existence of principal. If principal is repaid early, the total amount of expected interest payments is reduced.

An understanding of how cash flow is generated provides only the first step toward attaining an intuitive grasp of a security's performance. The next subsection explores how the value of IOs and POs reacts to changes in interest rates.

**EXHIBIT 30–1c**
**Principal Cash Flow At Various CPRs** ($100 Million Face; 9% Pass-Through)

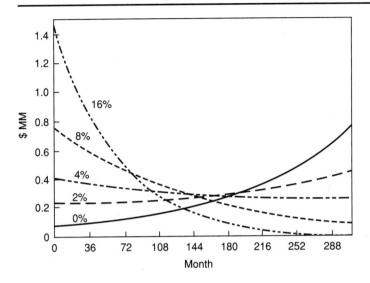

**EXHIBIT 30–1d**
**Interest Cash Flow At Various CPRs** ($100 Million Face; 9% Pass-Through)

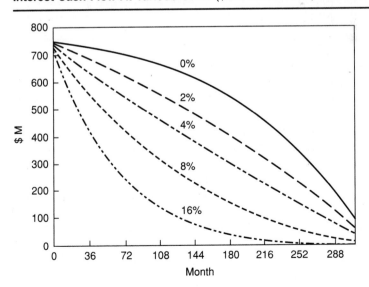

## The Price/Yield Relationship for Treasury and Mortgage Securities

The simplest price/yield relationship exists for a noncallable bond such as a Treasury security. Since cash flow for a Treasury security is immutable, calculating the price of the security at any given yield level is easy. For example, the price/yield relationship of a 10-year, 7 percent coupon Treasury bond is negatively sloped (see Exhibit 30–2a). The sensitivity of price to yield changes is given by the slope of the price/yield curve. The more "bullish" the bond is, the steeper the slope will be. At any given yield level, the popular volatility measure, modified duration, is the negative of the slope divided by the corresponding price. Finally, there is some positive convexity associated with this bond issue; that is, the ends of the price/yield curve curl up a bit. Thus, if market yields drop at a constant rate, the 10-year bond rallies at an increasing rate. When yields increase at a constant rate, the bond price falls at a decreasing rate. This convexity is valued positively by market participants because it offers some protection against volatile interest rates.

It would be convenient if mortgage performance could be expressed in such precise terms. However, discovering the price/yield relationship for mortgages is a considerably more complex task. Most Wall Street firms have developed complex valuation methods that take into account such factors as the shape

**EXHIBIT 30–2a**
**Price/Yield Relationship** (10-Year Treasury Security; 7% Coupon)

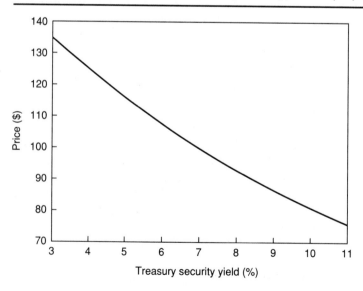

of the yield curve, interest-rate volatility, the level of projected prepayments, and their sensitivity to mortgage rates, among others. Despite these extensive research efforts, different dealers will generally agree only on the broad outlines of performance for most mortgage securities. However, some qualitative conclusions can still be drawn about IO and PO performance on the basis of a very simple mortgage pricing model. The model is based on the discounted value of mortgage cash flow. For example, for a 9 percent GNMA priced near par, the model projects an annual prepayment rate of 6.5 percent. Prepayment rates are assumed to be a deterministic, decreasing function of market yield levels. If rates drop, prepayments increase rapidly but cap-out near 50 percent CPR. If rates increase, prepayments slow gradually to 4.5 percent CPR. Price is obtained by discounting the projected cash flow at the yield on the current coupon pass-through. Where comparisons to Treasury securities are made, a constant 200-basis-point yield spread is assumed. This simple model is not useful for forecasting exact price behavior. However, it produces highly intuitive pricing comparisons — sufficient for the essentially qualitative conclusions drawn below.

Exhibit 30–2b illustrates the price/yield relationship for a 9 percent mortgage pass-through predicted by the model. As with the Treasury bond, the price/yield relationship is usually negatively sloped. In addition, mortgages have negative convexity because cash flow shifts adversely when market yields change; the effective duration of a mortgage-backed security lengthens as rates

**EXHIBIT 30–2b**
**Price/Yield Relationship** (Treasury and Pass-Through Securities)

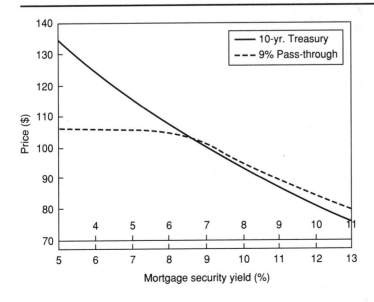

rise and shortens as rates fall. This effect hurts relative price performance when the market moves either way.

Another important determinant of the value of any fixed income security is the coupon rate. For a mortgage pass-through, the underlying mortgage rate is even more important because of its prime influence in determining the pre-payment rate of the collateral. The effect of the coupon rate on the mortgage security's price/yield relationship is shown in Exhibit 30–2c. A good way to interpret the graph is to follow the bull market of 1986 along the graph from right to left. The 1986 rally produced severe "price compression" among higher coupon pass-throughs. As rates fell, high-coupon mortgage securities began to cap-out, while the prices of lower coupons continued upward. Price compression began at a point not too far above par. When yields declined far enough, prices began to decrease as the effect of lower yields was outweighed by faster prepayments. Some high-coupon pass-throughs even began to exhibit negative price responses to lower interest rates. By contrast, a capping-out effect does not occur for the Treasury security price/yield profile.

## TRADING CHARACTERISTICS OF IOs AND POs

Carving up the cash flow of a mortgage pass-through into IOs and POs would produce two securities with their own unique price/yield relationship. Exhibit

**EXHIBIT 30–2c**
**Price/Yield Relationship** (7, 8, 9, 10 & 11% Pass-Through Securities)

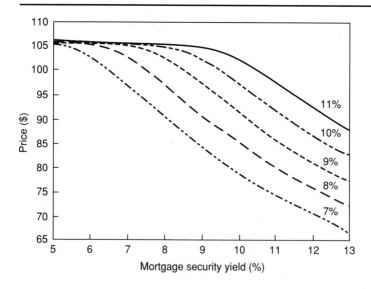

**EXHIBIT 30–3***a*
**Price/Yield Relationship** (MBS and Related IO, PO Securities)

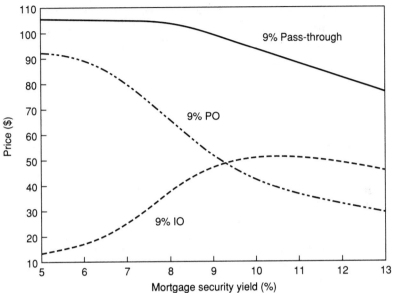

30–3*a* compares the relationship of a 9 percent mortgage pass-through with its corresponding IO and PO components.

In absolute terms, the IO and PO curves are both often steeper than the price/yield curve associated with the underlying pass-through. Thus, IO and PO securities will likely exhibit more price volatility than standard pass-throughs. In effect, the stripped securities are highly leveraged hedging or speculative vehicles.

It is important to note that complete stripping of mortgages does not preclude the formation of any portfolio that could be constructed with partially stripped mortgages. Any issue of partially stripped mortgages (or even the underlying pass-through itself) can be reconstructed using the appropriate combination of IOs and POs. Furthermore, partially stripped mortgages do not offer as wide a range of feasible portfolios as their completely stripped counterparts.

Exhibit 30–3*b* displays the price/yield relationship of the securities emerging from a partially stripped pool along with the corresponding IO and PO classes. The partially stripped structure allocates 50 percent of the principal to each piece but unequal amounts of interest. One class receives one-third of each month's interest payment, whereas the other class receives the remaining two-thirds. The price/yield relationship for the two partially stripped classes

**EXHIBIT 30–3***b*
**Portfolios of 9% IO and PO Securities** (9% MBS and Synthetic 6% and 12% Coupons)

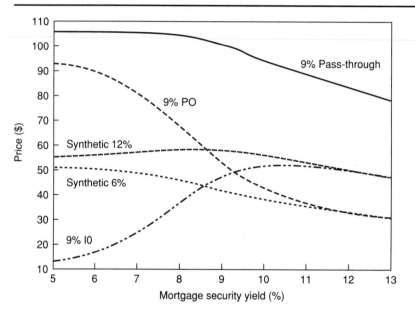

is reminiscent of the underlying pass-through. The performance profile of both classes lies between that of the corresponding IO and PO profiles when price is expressed as a percent of the par value of the underlying collateral. This should not be surprising since both partially stripped classes are, in essence, bundled portfolios of IOs and POs.

Viewing the price/yield relationships for the 9 percent IO and PO securities separately shows how different the components are. Depending on the level of interest rates, the IO class offers a play against interest rate volatility or a hedge against rising interest rates. In the latter case, it is appropriate to view the IO as having a negative mortgage duration. The IO security offers investors an asset that represents a short position in the market yet one which generates positive cash flow. In a higher yield environment, the 9 percent IO security becomes an interest rate volatility play. Investors are effectively short a straddle position on interest rates. They win if rates stay relatively stable and lose if rates rise or fall by a significant amount. A PO security performs differently. Its purchase always represents a bullish stance. Also, when the corresponding pass-through is near par, the PO security displays a substantial amount of positive convexity—a characteristic previously hard to find in the mortgage-backed sector. Exhibits 30–4*a* and 30–4*b* show the duration and convexity characteristics implied by the simple mortgage pricing model.

**EXHIBIT 30–4a***
**Mortgage Duration** (9% IO, PO and Pass-Through Securities)

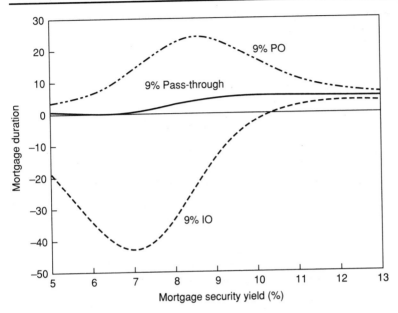

*Duration $= \frac{100}{P} \times \frac{dP}{dy}$,

## The Effect of Coupon on IO and PO Value

Just as the coupon rate influences the price/yield relationship for pass-throughs, it also shifts and shapes the price/yield relationship for IO and PO securities. A family of POs backed by a range of pass-through coupons is presented in Exhibit 30–5a. Several aspects of trading patterns can be observed. First, the higher the coupon, the more valuable the PO. Higher coupons have higher prepayment rates, so investors receive their principal earlier. Second, these instruments all display positive convexity over a significant trading range, much like deep discount issues in the pass-through market.

An IO security displays behavior that is quite different from a PO. Depicted in Exhibit 30–5b is a family of IOs with different coupon rates. At very high interest rate levels, all securities behave somewhat like Treasury bonds and characteristically follow the normal, negatively sloped price/yield relationship. At these yield levels, prepayments are slow and rather insensitive to interest rates. In a very high interest rate environment, even IOs can benefit from decreases in market yields. In a lower interest rate environment, however, prepayments begin to accelerate, quickly depriving the IO security holder of future cash flow. IOs

**EXHIBIT 30–4***b**^*

**Convexity** (9% IO, PO, and Pass-Through Securities)

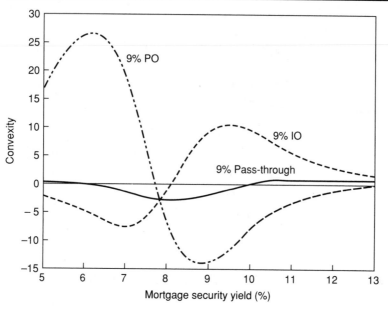

$$\text{Convexity} = \frac{100}{P} \cdot \frac{d^2P}{dy^2}$$

can respond quite positively to increases in interest rates when rates are low and prepayment rates are high. A bear market would extinguish the incentive to prepay. Coupons that slow down would generally experience an increase in IO value.

It is interesting to consider an investor's choice in a market populated by IOs and POs. The range of opportunities that would be available in a market environment like today's is illustrated by the 9 percent mortgage yield level shown in Exhibits 30–5*a*, and 30–5*b*. A security like the 7 percent PO offers substantial convexity with an effective duration of about nine years. The 8 percent and 9 percent POs offer longer mortgage duration and greater convexity. Finally, 10 percent and 11 percent POs offer roughly the same short-term price performance, as indicated by their parallel price/yield curves.

In the IO market, a varied array of choices emerges. The price behavior of a 7 percent IO is like that of a very short-duration bond, while the effective duration of an 8 percent IO is practically zero. Moving higher in coupon, an investor would view IOs as bearish instruments much like a mortgage servicing portfolio or a CMO residual. Adding a comparatively small amount of 10 percent IOs or 11 percent IOs to a portfolio would dramatically reduce its duration.

**EXHIBIT 30–5a**

**A Hypothetical PO Securities Market** (7, 8, 9, 10, & 11% Underlying Pass-Through Coupons)

**EXHIBIT 30–5b**

**A Hypothetical IO Securities Market** (7, 8, 9, 10 & 11 % Underlying Pass-Through Coupons)

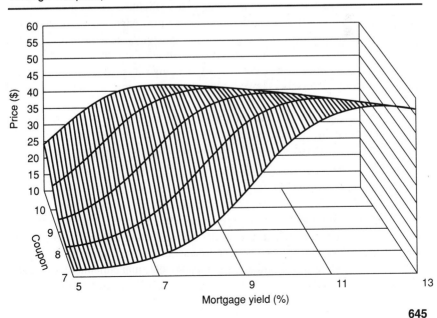

## PRICING AND PERFORMANCE

Discounting all cash flow at the same yield to produce the foregoing price/yield relationships was a tenuous assumption. Exact pricing of IO and PO securities is a problem for a more sophisticated pricing model, one that is beyond the scope of this chapter. However, a productive, if qualitative, discussion concerning the required yield for IO and PO securities can be based on an intuitive principle. Asymmetric returns influence yield. In many instances returns on IO and PO securities offer skewed returns. A security that offers a floor for returns along with upside potential ought to offer a relatively low yield. Conversely, a security that has limited upside potential but significant downside risk should offer a high yield.

Naturally, an increase in the required yield for a PO corresponds to an analogous decrease in the required yield for an IO. This point is helpful in cases where stronger statements about yield can be made for one of the securities than the other. This principle forms the basis for the discussion below. In the case of IOs and POs, the discussion centers mainly on the underlying collateral, whether it is a near-current, discount, or premium coupon pass-through.

*Near-current coupon collateral:*

- The yield of an IO security backed by near-current coupon collateral should be higher than the yield of the underlying collateral. Current coupon mortgages have no particular incentive to refinance and are therefore expected to prepay at a rate only slightly above discount collateral. For an IO security, this means that expected cash flow will not increase much in a high interest rate environment. On the other hand, cash flow would be severely diminished by a bond market rally. It seems reasonable to expect investors to be compensated for these adversely skewed returns by receiving a higher expected yield.
- The corresponding PO security reflects the same facts. Since prepayment rates are liable to increase in a rally, POs would perform extremely well. The downside risk is limited by the initially low prepayment rate. As a result, yield for this security is likely to be quite low.

*Discount collateral:*

- The required yield for the IO security will tend to be lower than that for a current coupon IO because of the call protection inherent in the underlying collateral. Returns are still vulnerable to a pick-up in prepayments, but this situation is less likely to occur. The discount collateral also implies that prepayments cannot slow down much, so there is not a substantial amount of upside potential.

- Consistent with the lower required yield for the IO security is a relatively higher yield for the companion PO. Investors necessarily expect to wait longer for the return of all the principal when the PO security is backed by discount collateral. Reduced upside potential may increase the required yield above that of a current coupon PO.

*Premium collateral:*

- In this case, IO securities have significant upside potential. If interest rates move up, the IO holder will gain value from reduced prepayment rates. Downside potential depends on whether prepayment rates can increase further. Potential returns are more symmetric. This advantage will tend to decrease the required yield below that of IOs based on discount and current coupon collateral.
- Once again the same forces that drive down the yield on the IO security drive up the yield on the PO. If the collateral is already prepaying fast when the PO security is purchased, then there is a risk that prepayments will slow down. Also, the upside potential of the security is that much more limited.

The foregoing discussion indicates that required yields for IOs and POs will likely vary from that of the underlying securities.

Pricing of IOs and POs is determined by a number of factors, including WAC, WAM, geographical distribution, and liquidity, among others. As a result, individual issues can have different prices even though they are backed by mortgages that would be considered good substitutes for each other.

At the time of this writing, the IO/PO market is almost three years old. As a result, we have had some chance to see price performance over time. Exhibit 30–6 shows the prices of the FNMA SMBS Trust 1 IOs and POs along with generic FNMA 9s. Most of the time, the IOs have been quite stable in price, while the POs have generally moved in line with collateral price. Over time, there has been a trend toward higher prices for the PO and lower prices for the IO. Three factors are at work here: (1) a modest rise in price for the underlying collateral, (2) a realignment of the market's perception of relative value between IOs and POs in late 1988, and (3) accretion toward par ($100 for the PO and $0 for the IO) that naturally occurs over time.

Projected performance based on Goldman Sachs' valuation model is presented in Exhibit 30–7. It shows yields under projected prepayments along with total rates of return over one year under various interest-rate scenarios. The highly leveraged and contrasting profiles are especially relevant to the next section.

**EXHIBIT 30–6**
**Weekly Prices for FNMA 9s and 9 Strips**
(Jan. 15, 1988–Nov. 10, 1989)

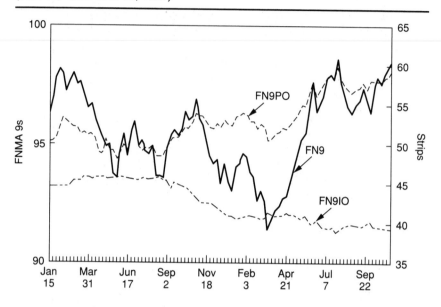

## OPPORTUNITIES FOR ASSET/LIABILITY MANAGERS

Unlike investors in noncallable fixed income securities, investors in mortgage-backed securities are exposed to two major sources of price risk. The first is market direction, or yield risk. The second comes from possible changes in the market's expectation about prepayment rates. These two risks are related because changes in interest rates often precipitate changes in the market's expectation about prepayment behavior. The simultaneous relationship between market movements and prepayments is perhaps the biggest problem faced by investors in mortgage pass-throughs. However, this relationship is not always perfectly coupled. For example, mortgage security prices move independently on days when monthly prepayment information is released. Because IOs and POs provide investors with highly leveraged investment vehicles, they can offer asset/liability (A/L) managers extremely efficient portfolio management tools to apply to these problems. In most cases, hedging objectives can be achieved with relatively small purchases of IOs and/or POs.

Financial institutions can employ IOs and POs to manage their duration gap. For example, institutions with an asset duration exceeding that of their lia-

**EXHIBIT 30–7**
**Mortgage Valuation Analysis for FNMA Stripped Securities**

| Security | Price 11/09/89 | WAC | Remaining Term | Projected PSA | Yield | Option Adjusted Duration | Scenario Return Profile | | | | |
|---|---|---|---|---|---|---|---|---|---|---|---|
| | | | | | | | −200 | −100 | 0 | 100 | 200 |
| *FNMA Principal-Only Trust, 30-Year Single-Family Collateral* | | | | | | | | | | | |
| 8.0% PO (T54) | 54–27 | 8.86 | 329 | 131 | 8.3 | 10.71 | 31.75 | 18.86 | 8.20 | −0.67 | −8.25 |
| 8.5% PO (T7) | 57–10 | 9.18 | 323 | 138 | 7.87 | 11.09 | 31.95 | 18.77 | 7.81 | −1.38 | −9.17 |
| 9.0% PO (T1) | 59–08 | 9.69 | 321 | 152 | 7.82 | 12.03 | 33.67 | 19.75 | 7.77 | −2.17 | −10.75 |
| 9.5% PO (T4) | 61–11 | 10.09 | 320 | 168 | 7.74 | 12.78 | 34.07 | 20.47 | 7.71 | −2.85 | −11.64 |
| 10.0% PO (T29) | 65–07 | 10.75 | 332 | 212 | 7.89 | 14.21 | 32.03 | 21.63 | 7.92 | −3.99 | −13.91 |
| *FNMA Interest-Only Trust, 30-Year Single-Family Collateral* | | | | | | | | | | | |
| 8.0% IO (T54) | 39–16 | 8.86 | 329 | 131 | 10.44 | −2.61 | −5.38 | 5.53 | 10.32 | 11.73 | 11.31 |
| 8.5% IO (T7) | 39–13 | 9.18 | 323 | 138 | 11.37 | −3.98 | −8.70 | 4.82 | 11.15 | 13.52 | 13.72 |
| 9.0% IO (T1) | 39–11 | 9.69 | 321 | 152 | 11.88 | −6.71 | −16.55 | 1.89 | 11.58 | 15.99 | 17.37 |
| 9.5% IO (T4) | 39–03 | 10.09 | 320 | 168 | 12.38 | −9.42 | −22.51 | −1.05 | 12.00 | 18.40 | 21.02 |
| 10.0% IO (T29) | 36–23 | 10.75 | 332 | 212 | 12.71 | −15.59 | −28.16 | −7.76 | 12.20 | 23.33 | 28.76 |
| *FNMA MBS, 30-Year Single-Family Collateral* | | | | | | | | | | | |
| 8.0% MBS | 94–11 | 9.00 | 330 | 133 | 9.14 | 5.01 | 16.63 | 13.23 | 9.08 | 4.69 | 0.31 |
| 8.5% MBS | 96–12 | 9.40 | 340 | 140 | 9.25 | 4.76 | 15.83 | 13.06 | 9.19 | 4.95 | 0.64 |
| 9.0% MBS | 98–13 | 9.81 | 352 | 150 | 9.36 | 4.54 | 14.88 | 12.85 | 9.32 | 5.17 | 0.86 |
| 9.5% MBS | 100–10 | 10.23 | 352 | 170 | 9.50 | 4.04 | 13.57 | 12.29 | 9.46 | 5.67 | 1.58 |
| 10.0% MBS | 101–30 | 10.68 | 350 | 209 | 9.61 | 3.37 | 12.27 | 11.55 | 9.57 | 6.34 | 2.55 |

bilities could purchase IOs and significantly reduce their exposure to an increase in interest rates. Because an IO's price increases when traditional fixed income assets decrease in value, its mortgage duration is negative. The price of the security would be extremely sensitive to interest rate changes and would move in the opposite direction from most fixed income securities.

Stripping regular mortgage pass-throughs into IOs and POs gives investors tools to hedge or exploit mortgage prepayment risk. Because the prices of the two securities react inversely to changes in prepayment rates, they can offer a means to control prepayment risk. As a result, mortgage investors have the ability to decompose their two principal risks into an interest rate component and a prepayment rate component, and address them separately. The following discussion describes how an investor in mortgage-backed securities, IOs, and POs can construct hedges to reduce prepayment risk.

Exhibit 30–8a depicts the market value of a $100 investment in 11 percent IO, PO, and pass-through securities as a function of prepayment rate, assuming that the securities' respective yields are kept constant. The analysis is based on 15 percent CPR as the pricing speed for all the securities. As shown, the pass-through and the IO decrease in value as the prepayment rate increases.

**EXHIBIT 30–8a**
**Value/CPR Relationship** (11% Pass-Through, IO, and PO Securities @ 15% CPR)

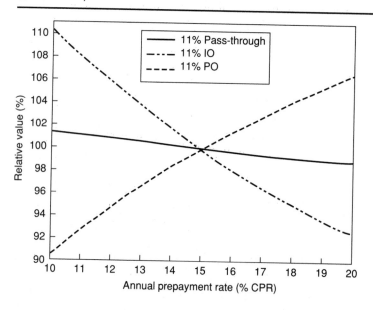

Conversely, the PO security increases in value as the prepayment rate rises making the PO security the one to buy when hedging the prepayment risk of a premium coupon pass-through.

This can be accomplished by constructing a portfolio that balances the price-weighted CPR sensitivity of the pass-through with that of the PO security. Such a portfolio would be insulated against the prepayment fluctuations that may occur even when interest rates remain constant. Exhibit 30–8*b* shows the change in value of the pass-through, PO, and hedged positions when the prepayment rate moves away from 15 percent CPR. To further illustrate this point, Exhibit 30–9 displays hedge ratio and projected profit/loss calculations for this transaction. The investor can hedge this particular pass-through by purchasing $0.30 worth of 11 percent POs for each $1 worth of 11 percent pass-throughs.

An analogous transaction could be performed for a discount pass-through. In this case, an IO security would be the appropriate hedging vehicle to balance a slowdown in prepayment rates. One caveat: in order to lock in the hedge, the investor must be assured that the speeds of the PO (or IO as the case may be) and the pass-through are closely linked. Practically speaking, IOs and POs need to be backed by large pools to ensure that their prepayment behavior approaches that of a generic pass-through.

**EXHIBIT 30–8***b*
**Hedging Prepayment Risk** (Premium Pass-Through)

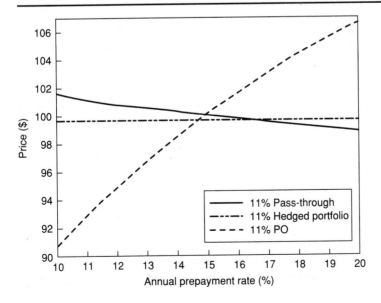

**EXHIBIT 30-9**
**Hedging Prepayment Risk** (Calculation Details)

*Direct CPR Hedge: Profit/Loss Analysis*
*Individual Securities*

|  | Price | | Face Value | | Beginning Market Value | 1% CPR Increase Profit (Loss) | 1% CPR Decrease Profit (Loss) |
|---|---|---|---|---|---|---|---|
| 11% GNMA | 108.125 | × | 92.486 | = | 100.00 | ($0.003) | $0.003 |
| 11% PO | 73.245 | × | 136.530 | = | 100.00 | 0.016 | (0.016) |

*Hedged Portfolio*

|  | Price | | Face Value | | Beginning Market Value | 1% CPR Increase Profit (Loss) | 1% CPR Decrease Profit (Loss) |
|---|---|---|---|---|---|---|---|
| 11% GNMA | 108.125 | × | 76.977 | = | 83.231 | ( 0.003) | 0.003 |
| 11% PO | 73.245 | × | 22.894 | = | 16.769 | 0.003 | ( 0.003) |
| Hedged portfolio Position |  |  | 99.831 |  | $100.00 | ($0.000) | $0.000 |

*Calculation Details*

|  | GNMA 11[‡] | 11% PO[‡] |
|---|---|---|
| Price | 108.04 | 73.08 |
| Modified duration | 3.8 | 4.3 |
| PVBP | 3.973 | 3.001 |
| E* | −0.329 | 1.631 |
| PVCPR[†] | −0.355 | 1.194 |
| Yield (CBE) | 8.92% | 6.48% |

CPR Market Value Hedge Ratio of MBS11 to MBSPO 11: 0.297 = −0.355/1.194

[*] E is equal to the percent change in price given an instantaneous one percent point change in CPR.
[†] PVCPR is equal to the price value of a one percent point change in CPR.
[‡] Both the GNMA 11 and 11% PO are assumed to have a WAM of 283 months.

# BUILDING LIQUIDITY IN THE STRIPPED MORTGAGE PASS-THROUGH MARKET

This chapter has outlined the benefits of stripped mortgage pass-throughs. For investors to achieve all the advantages, a liquid market is necessary. Most of the trading strategies discussed necessitate monitoring and adjusting the portfolio's composition over time. Liquidity in the market for strips corresponds to a narrower dealer spread, more accurate pricing, and increased attractiveness as portfolio management tools. Liquidity will not develop by accident. Issuers and investors need to consider carefully a number of factors that will foster trading in stripped pass-throughs.

Stripping large, homogeneous pools helps. As noted earlier, the value of IOs and POs is very dependent on prepayment rates. Purchasing strips based on a small pool entails bearing unnecessary prepayment risk. Stripping large pools ensures that the prepayment rate is close to the generic rate. Homogeneity in terms of coupon, maturity, and mortgage type makes stripped pass-throughs easier to value. This is true at issuance but even more important for secondary market trading. Typically, issuers do not report which individual loans have prepaid or other substitute pieces of information such as current weighted average coupon. Homogeneity reduces the impact of this problem. If securities are based on heterogeneous pools, secondary market trading is likely to be limited by the market's use of worst-case scenarios in evaluating the resulting IOs and POs. The degradation of market liquidity is more serious for stripped pass-throughs than for standard pass-throughs.

Liquidity is also promoted through the use of recombination features, especially for agency collateral. For example, many of the FNMA SMBS issues allow exchange of SMBS classes for the corresponding MBS certificate. Even though exercise of the option to recombine is unlikely, its existence ensures that the total value of the SMBS classes never falls below that of the underlying pass-through. If for some reason the value should fall, investors could purchase the SMBS classes, recombine them, and reap an arbitrage profit.

Liquidity in the strips market is promoted by a standardized structure. The IO/PO structure does predominate among strip structures used today. However, the synthetic discount/premium structure of the first strips continues to be issued occasionally, targeted to investors subject to specific accounting or investment requirements.

# CHAPTER 31

## ASSET-BACKED SECURITIES

*Andrew S. Carron*
*Director*
*Fixed Income Research*
*The First Boston Corporation*

Asset-backed securities (ABS) are supported by installment loans or leases or by revolving lines of credit. Although the structures of ABS deals have varied, all issues feature credit enhancements that lead to high credit ratings and limited investor exposure to the credit of the seller. This new generation of securities was introduced by First Boston in 1985, with the sale of lease-backed notes by Sperry Lease Finance Corporation. Since then, more than $50 billion in asset-backed securities have been issued, the majority supported by automobile loans and credit card receivables.

Investors are attracted to asset-backed securities for the following reasons:

- **Credit quality.** Asset-backed securities have high credit ratings, based on recourse provisions or third-party credit enhancements covering many times the historical loss rates on the underlying assets.
- **Yield.** Asset-backed securities offer investors yields that exceed those on bonds of comparable maturity and quality.
- **Liquidity.** Rapid market growth and large deal sizes have encouraged the development of a liquid secondary market, comparatively more liquid than that for corporate bonds.
- **Relatively predictable cash flows.** Most asset-backed securities carry some prepayment uncertainty, but, unlike mortgage securities, prepayments are virtually unaffected by changing market interest-rate levels.
- **Maturity.** The majority of asset-backed securities generally have final maturities ranging from five to six years at the time of issue, with the

average time to receipt of principal (average life) ranging from one to three years.

As a result of these favorable attributes, ABS have developed a diversified investor base. Asset-backed securities have been purchased by bank portfolios, trusts and investment advisors, thrift institutions, insurance companies, public and private pension funds, and corporations, both in the United States and internationally.

## MARKET DEVELOPMENT AND GROWTH

The asset-backed securities market has grown rapidly since its inception in late 1985. Cumulative issuance through the end of 1989 totaled $55 billion, with $15 billion issued during 1988 and a record $20 billion issued in 1989.[1]

Until early 1988, most asset-backed securities were supported by automobile loans. Since then the pattern has shifted strongly toward issues backed by credit card receivables. Auto ABS issuance, however, surged in the fourth quarter of 1989, as Ford Credit issued two deals totaling $5 billion. Exhibit 31–1 shows quarterly issuance of ABS from 1985 to 1989. The risk-based capital guidelines for commercial banks have provided a strong impetus for capital-constrained banks to sell assets such as credit card receivables, which have high risk weights.

The new capital requirements for banks and thrifts have made ABS less attractive for these institutions to hold than mortgage-backed securities. However, the decline in ABS purchases by depository institutions has been more than offset by increased participation of other investor categories. Many ABS are now eligible investments for pension funds governed by ERISA, and the funds have become substantial buyers of asset-backed securities. ABS are also being offered to the retail investor market.

Credit card asset-backed securities have principal payment lockout periods, which automobile-loan-backed securities do not; credit card issues tend to have longer average lives; and credit card deals were issued more recently, on average, than those backed by automobile loans. Therefore, credit card ABSs represent 56 percent of the market outstanding but only 38 percent of the issuance to date (see Exhibit 31–2). Issuance of new ABS is expected to remain strong because of the high turnover rate of the underlying assets and because of the continuing desire of ABS issuers to reduce their leverage.

---

[1] Data in this chapter exclude mortgage-related products, such as manufactured housing and home equity loans, that are occasionally included in ABS totals.

**EXHIBIT 31–1**

**ABS Issuance by Quarter through December 31, 1989**

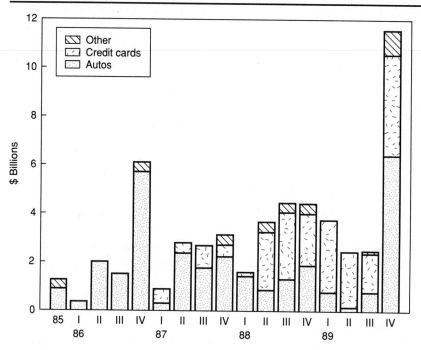

**EXHIBIT 31–2**

(a) **ABS Collateral Breakdown—Outstanding as of December 31, 1989 ($35.6 Billion Total);** (b) **Cumulative Issuance through December 31, 1989 ($54.8 Billion Total)**

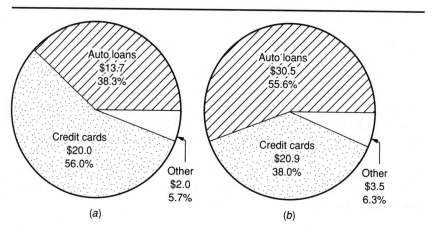

(a)                              (b)

Issuance of new ABS takes many forms. Most deals are triple-A rated, publicly offered, U. S. issues. There have been numerous private placements, and certain deals (in whole or in part) have been issued in Europe.

## STRUCTURE

While all asset-backed securities have many features in common, there are two distinct types of collateral that dictate security structure: installment contracts and revolving lines of credit. Installment loans, such as those made for the purchase of automobiles, trucks, recreational vehicles, and boats, have defined amortization schedules and fixed final maturity dates. Revolving loans, such as those extended to credit card holders, have no specific amortization schedule or final maturity date; they are extended and repaid repeatedly over time, more or less at the discretion of the borrower.

Most collateral behind asset-backed securities is subject to early repayment. However, most credit card securities are structured to provide more certain principal payment schedules than those of the underlying assets. Many issues have a "cleanup" call to alleviate the administrative burden associated with small security balances.

All asset-backed securities have one or more forms of credit enhancement to raise the quality of the security above that of the underlying loans. Credit enhancement can take many forms: yield spread (excess servicing), letter of credit, reserve fund, third-party guaranty, recourse to the issuer, overcollateralization or senior/subordinated structure. A letter of credit from a triple-A rated bank is the most prevalent credit enhancement.

Asset-backed securities are structured as a trust, similar to mortgage-backed securities. Under the Uniform Commercial Code, there is no need for a trustee to take physical possession of any account documents to perfect a security interest in the receivables, as is required with mortgage securities.

### Installment Contract ABSs

Typical installment contract ABS bears a close structural relationship to mortgage pass-through securities. ABS offer investors an undivided interest in a trust formed by the issuer. To establish the trust, the issuer pools installment sales contracts (loans) on automobiles, trucks, boats, or other assets. The installment sale agreements in the pool may have various final maturities, usually extending no more than five years from the date of issuance. Interest rates on the loan contracts exceed the pass-through rate of interest on the security. All contracts call for full amortization of principal over the term-to-maturity through virtually equal monthly payments.

Investors receive monthly interest on the outstanding balance. The securities generally have a payment delay comparable to that of GNMA pass-throughs; interest and principal for each month is remitted to investors on the fifteenth day of the following month. Investors receive a full month's interest on any prepayments. Each investor receives a pro rata portion of principal and interest each month. The amount of principal included in each payment will depend on the amortization and prepayment rate of the underlying collateral. Faster prepayments will shorten the average life of the issue.

The issuer generally continues to service the loans after the issuance of the ABS. Servicers are usually required to advance interest and scheduled principal for delinquent loans. Where a limited guaranty exists, the issuer may be required to repurchase defaulted receivables up to the stated maximum recourse level.

## Revolving Credit ABS

Credit card ABS are less like mortgage-backed securities than installment contract ABS. For a specified period (the revolving period), credit card ABS do not amortize principal. Instead, principal from the receivables is retained by the trustee to reinvest in additional receivables. Because of the high rate of principal paydowns on credit card debt, the length of the revolving period largely determines the average life of the issue.

Despite some differences, many similarities between mortgage securities and credit card ABS remain. The credit card ABS issuer continues to service the receivables. The receivables of a specified set of accounts are included in the transaction. Interest on the credit card ABS is generally paid monthly with a delay, usually on the fifteenth of the month. Most deals carry a fixed rate of interest, although there have been LIBOR-based floating-rate issues. Principal payments are distributed monthly with the interest payment during the amortization period, which follows the end of the revolving period. The amount of principal distribution is determined as cardholder payments are received.

There are four basic credit card ABS structures, differing in their method of principal return. The structure that most closely resembles corporate bonds is a bullet maturity payment, where a third party has provided a maturity guarantee that virtually eliminates extension risk. The "soft-bullet" structure is identical except for the maturity guarantee. The third structure features a controlled amortization or sinking-fund schedule. In the fourth structure, which provides the least repayment certainty, investors receive principal based on the actual payment rates of the collateral.

Credit card ABS are usually structured as a sale using certificates of ownership of the credit card receivables or as a borrowing that uses notes collateralized by receivables. In a sale of receivables, the receivables are sold either through a participation in the receivables or to a trust owned by the investors. Subsequently, all new receivables originated from the securitized portfolio of accounts are automatically sold at the time of their creation. Because of possible fluctuations in the total amount of receivables in the accounts, a second ownership class may be retained by the seller that increases or decreases in size to absorb the fluctuation. In a collateralized note offering, the issuer, either directly or through a special purpose corporation, issues notes secured by the receivables, which are general obligations of the issuer.

## CREDIT CONSIDERATIONS

Asset-backed securities are structured to insulate investors against most reasonably foreseeable events. Nevertheless, collateral quality remains important.

Automobile loans historically have had relatively low loss rates. Delinquency rates have averaged between 1.5 percent and 2.5 percent during the past 20 years. The actual amount of loss from these delinquencies has been less because of the ability to recover losses through automobile repossessions.

In recent years, loan losses have been trending upward, due in part to more aggressive lending practices. Higher new car prices and increased competition have caused the automobile finance companies to increase the risk in their portfolio by extending loan maturities. The average new car loan had a maturity in excess of 4.5 years in 1988 versus 3.7 years in 1983. Because longer term loans require more time for borrowers to build equity in their cars, loan losses can be expected to be higher than for shorter term loans. The lender, however, is compensated for this risk with a higher coupon on the loan.

Credit enhancement levels have been adjusted upward to compensate for increased collateral risk in automobile loan ABS. Most automobile loan ABS continue to receive triple-A ratings from Moody's and Standard & Poor's.

The credit quality of credit card ABSs is derived in part from the quality of the accounts from which the securitized receivables are drawn. Losses on credit card receivables tend to be higher and more variable than on automobile loans. Historical performance of the credit card portfolio can be used as a predictor of future loss rates. Credit support levels are then established to insulate investors from any reasonable risk of loss, so credit support is correspondingly greater on credit card ABS than on automobile-loan-backed securities. Excess servicing (yield spread) also provides an important source of credit enhancement.

Credit card securities are further protected by a unique feature known as "payout events." Payout events are possible events in the life of the transaction that, if allowed to continue, might tend to weaken the transaction and increase the risk of investor loss. When a trustee determines that a payout event has occurred, the security begins amortizing immediately, returning principal to the investor at par. Examples of payout events include the following:

1. A significant increase in loss rates on the underlying loan portfolio, which might exhaust the credit support.
2. A significant decrease in the share of the deal retained by the seller.
3. The bankruptcy or receivership of the card issuer, which could affect the quality of the loan servicing.
4. A reduction in yield on the underlying loan portfolio, which would lessen the money available to pay interest and other expenses on the security.
5. The trust is determined to be an investment company under the Investment Company Act of 1940.

For the investor, payout events are a two-edged sword. They provide investor protection against principal loss or delay in payment of amounts due on the credit card ABS. They also create the possibility that credit card ABS will be amortized much sooner than expected, which is positive if rates have risen since issue but negative if rates are lower. Payout events are unlikely, however, and because loss, delinquency, and other payout event characteristics change slowly, payout events should not occur unexpectedly.

All asset-backed securities are protected against loss by some form of credit enhancement. This credit support operates like insurance or guarantees against loss up to a stated maximum dollar amount. Typical coverage levels range from 8 percent to 15 percent of the original amount of the security for automobile asset-backed securities and from 8 percent to 20 percent for credit card asset-backed securities. Most ABS structures can withstand default rates on the underlying collateral of at least five to eight times the worst case historical experience.

## Types of Credit Support

Credit support for a particular issue is provided by one or two of the following methods:

*Yield Spread (Excess Servicing).* The note rate on the receivables underlying asset-backed securities is generally substantially greater than the coupon on the securities themselves. The difference between the two rates can be allocated to actual servicing costs and provision for losses, with the remainder being considered excess servicing. This amount would ordinarily revert to the seller as additional profit. However, it is available to make payments to bondholders in the event of higher than anticipated losses on the collateral receivables.

*Letter of Credit.* A third party, generally a highly rated bank, puts up a letter of credit equal to the maximum amount of credit support being provided. The LOC provider agrees to reimburse the trust for the amount of all receivables charged off up to the amount specified in the letter of credit. If the provider makes such a payment, the remaining LOC liability decreases by that amount.

In most cases, the LOC is replenished following a payment by diverting excess cash flows from the issuer to the LOC provider. In other cases, the amount of the LOC may be reduced over time as the security balance declines through amortization. Letters of credit are the most common form of credit enhancement in both automobile and credit card issues.

*Subordination.* A single loan portfolio backs two tranches: a senior tranche with a high rating that is sold to investors and a subordinated tranche that is often retained by the issuer. All losses are absorbed by the subordinated tranche until and unless it is completely exhausted. Unlike recourse (see below), the subordinated tranche is created at the time of issue, and the tranche will have residual value for the issuer if losses are not excessive. This method is unique in that it does not depend on the credit of a third party and thus eliminates one source of credit uncertainty. A small number of automobile and credit card issues have used a senior/subordinated structure.

*Guaranty.* A third party, generally an insurer, promises to reimburse the trust for losses up to a stated maximum dollar amount. In most other respects, guaranties operate very much like letters of credit. FSA and GECC have to date issued guaranties for automobile asset-backed securities.

*Recourse.* Bad loans may be put back to the issuer of the security. The issuer promises to reimburse the trust for losses up to a stated maximum dollar amount. This method enhances creditworthiness not only through access to the issuer's resources but also through giving the issuer a strong incentive to service the loan portfolio in a diligent manner. Recourse has been used in a number of automobile asset-backed securities, occasionally in combination with a letter of credit.

*Reserve Fund.* A cash reserve is created at issue to reimburse the trust for losses up to the amount of the reserve. A reserve fund may be used in combination with other methods of credit enhancement and may be a secondary form of support.

*Overcollateralization.* The face amount of the loan portfolio is larger than the security that it backs. The security will therefore amortize more quickly, and a buffer is created against losses. When the security matures, any remaining collateral reverts to the issuer.

## Default Protection

Credit support generally provides protection against default rates many times greater than historical experience. Exhibit 31–3 provides an example of default protection in an asset-backed security.

**EXHIBIT 31-3**
**Default Protection in Credit Card ABS ($ Thousands)**

| Month | Principal Balance | Available LOC Amount | Available LOC % | Cash Flow Available | | | Payments | | | | Investor Principal Payment (17.73% plus LOC Draw) |
|---|---|---|---|---|---|---|---|---|---|---|---|
| | | | | Receivables Yield (17.69%) | LOC Draw | Total | Servicing (2.00%) | Interest Payment (8.95%) | Default (27.4%) | Total | |
| 1 | $350,000 | $42,000 | 12.00% | $5,042 | $ 6,179 | $11,220 | $583 | $2,610 | $ 7,992 | $11,185 | $ 0 |
| 2 | 350,000 | 35,821 | 10.23 | 5,042 | 6,173 | 11,215 | 583 | 2,610 | 7,992 | 11,185 | 0 |
| 3 | 350,000 | 29,648 | 8.47 | 5,042 | 6,168 | 11,210 | 583 | 2,610 | 7,992 | 11,185 | 68,615 |
| 4 | 281,385 | 23,480 | 8.34 | 4,053 | 4,959 | 9,012 | 469 | 2,099 | 6,425 | 8,993 | 55,164 |
| 5 | 226,221 | 18,521 | 8.19 | 3,259 | 3,986 | 7,245 | 377 | 1,687 | 5,165 | 7,230 | 44,349 |
| 6 | 181,871 | 14,534 | 7.99 | 2,620 | 3,205 | 5,824 | 303 | 1,356 | 4,153 | 5,812 | 35,655 |
| 7 | 146,217 | 11,330 | 7.75 | 2,106 | 2,576 | 4,682 | 244 | 1,091 | 3,339 | 4,673 | 28,665 |
| 8 | 117,552 | 8,754 | 7.45 | 1,693 | 2,071 | 3,764 | 196 | 877 | 2,684 | 3,757 | 23,045 |
| 9 | 94,506 | 6,683 | 7.07 | 1,361 | 1,664 | 3,026 | 158 | 705 | 2,158 | 3,020 | 18,527 |
| 10 | 75,979 | 5,019 | 6.61 | 1,094 | 1,338 | 2,432 | 127 | 567 | 1,735 | 2,428 | 14,895 |
| 11 | 61,084 | 3,681 | 6.03 | 880 | 1,075 | 1,955 | 102 | 456 | 1,395 | 1,952 | 11,975 |
| 12 | 49,109 | 2,605 | 5.30 | 707 | 864 | 1,572 | 82 | 366 | 1,121 | 1,569 | 9,627 |
| 13 | 39,481 | 1,741 | 4.41 | 569 | 694 | 1,263 | 66 | 294 | 901 | 1,262 | 7,740 |
| 14 | 31,741 | 1,047 | 3.30 | 457 | 558 | 1,105 | 53 | 237 | 725 | 1,104 | 6,223 |
| 15 | 25,518 | 489 | 1.92 | 368 | 448 | 816 | 43 | 190 | 583 | 816 | 25,518 |
| | | | | | $41,960 | | | | $55,358 | | $350,000 |

Note: Payment of 1% annual LOC facility fee (not shown) is deducted from cash flow available.

The J.C. Penney 1989–B issue is a typical credit card ABS. It features a 12 percent letter of credit (LOC) from a third party, 2.34 percent of excess servicing at current loss rates that can be applied against losses, and provisions for early amortization. Recent loss experience on the portfolio has been 4.4 percent per annum. The monthly payment rate on the receivables is assumed to be 19.2 percent, which is allocated as 1.47 percent to interest (17.69 percent per annum) and 17.73 percent to principal. The bonds pay monthly interest at 8.95 percent per annum.

Exhibit 31–3 shows in detail the cash flows from the deal. An increase in defaults causes the portfolio yield to decline, triggering a payout event in the third month. The deal subsequently amortizes over a 15-month period. In the 15th month, the principal balance declines below 6 percent of the original amount, and the mandatory repurchase (clean-up) provision is exercised. Cash flows from the collateral, the LOC, and the excess servicing combine to support the bonds at a 27.4 percent annual loss rate, assuming the receivables yield and the principal repayment rate remain constant and that no payments are made on accounts that default. This loss rate is over six times the historical rate on the accounts in the deal.

Defaults can increase substantially above the rate implied by the 12 percent LOC and the 2.34 percent excess servicing because of the rapid repayment of principal after a payout event is triggered. Even with a 27.4 percent annual loss rate, only $54.4 million in defaults occur during the 15 months that the bonds are outstanding: 15.5 percent of the original bond balance. Default protection remains strong even if portfolio yield or principal repayments rates decline substantially.

## CASH-FLOW CHARACTERISTICS OF ABS

In general, the cash-flow characteristics of the loans and contracts underlying asset-backed securities determine the cash-flow characteristics of the securities themselves. Automobile asset-backed securities tend to mirror the performance of the collateral fairly closely. Credit card asset-backed securities substantially modify the cash-flow characteristics of the underlying loans in order to provide more stable cash flows to investors.

Automobile loans amortize principal over their term-to-maturity but may be paid off in advance of scheduled maturity. In fact, most such loans are prepaid, usually at the option of the borrower. When a loan prepayment occurs, the principal is passed through on a pro rata basis to the certificate holders, retiring that portion of their principal that is attributable to the loan that has prepaid. Unexpectedly high prepayments will make the average life of a security shorter than expected, whereas prepayments lower than anticipated will have the opposite effect. Thus, it is necessary to understand and predict the rate of prepayments in order to evaluate the securities.

Automobile loan prepayments generally result from the sale, repossession, or loss of the vehicle. Other causes include voluntary prepayment (when the obligor decides to retire the obligation with cash), refinancing, death of the obligor, or repurchase of the contract from the pool by the servicer. (Such repurchases are relatively uncommon, and result from breach of warranty, renegotiation of contracts, and administrative convenience.)

Because of the relatively short maturity and small balance of the typical automobile loan receivable, refinancing of a high interest rate obligation by a lower rate one is less common in the automobile market than in the mortgage market. (Refinancing of a fixed-rate mortgage normally occurs when interest rates fall significantly.) The incentive to refinance an automobile installment sale contract is not strong because monthly payment savings are minimal. Also, loan rates are higher on used cars than on the new cars that back automobile ABS, which also discourages refinancing of new car loans. Lower refinancing activity works to the advantage of the security holder, since a large drop in market interest rates does not produce the massive prepayments that most mortgage securities would experience. First Boston has validated these observations through analysis of actual prepayment rates on automobile loan receivables.[2]

Credit card loans do not have an amortization schedule, although they do require a minimum monthly payment expressed as a percentage of the outstanding balance. Actual monthly payment rates are in the range of 10 percent to 20 percent. Thus, a typical portfolio would pay down very quickly.

Credit card asset-backed securities are structured with a lockout period. That is, no principal will be returned to investors for a specified period following issuance. This is accomplished by purchasing new receivables from the same accounts as the original loans are paid down, thereby maintaining the original balance. Since credit card holders periodically borrow and repay against their line of credit, the new loans added to a pool will derive from the same card holder accounts as the original loans that were paid down. Typical lockout periods range from 18 months to as long as 10 years. Following the lockout date, the security enters the amortization period during which new charges are no longer purchased by the trust and the loans paid down are passed through to holders of the security. The card holder monthly payment rate determines the speed at which credit card ABS amortize. Although this rate varies across the industry and over time, the prepayment rate on a given portfolio tends to remain within a fairly narrow range and does not vary with market interest rates. As a result, the length of the amortization period is predictably short.

Typical cash-flow patterns for a premium mortgage-backed security and for automobile and credit card asset-backed securities are shown in Exhibit 31–4.

---

[2] See *Prepayment Rates on Automobile Receivables* (New York: First Boston, March 1986).

**EXHIBIT 31–4**
**Annual Principal Cash Flow per $1,000 Original Balance**

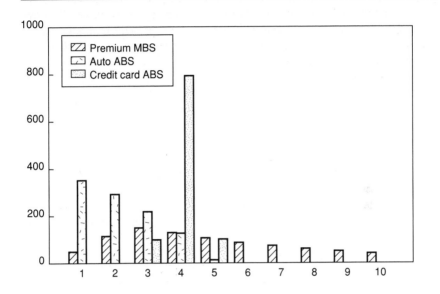

While the pattern for the credit card issue is more stable than that for the automobile issue, the variation between the two ABS issues is relatively small, especially in comparison with mortgage-backed securities.

## VALUATION OF ASSET-BACKED SECURITIES

Asset-backed securities are valued on the basis of the timing and certainty of the cash flows compared to similar average life investments. This involves an evaluation of the security's credit quality, principal payment patterns, and prepayment rate.

Unlike mortgage-backed pass-through securities, which perform very differently from traditional bonds, asset-backed securities closely resemble noncallable bonds in terms of price changes relative to interest-rate changes. There is a slight difference in cash-flow predictability between ABS and term bonds. This justifies a slight yield premium for ABS over term bonds of comparable quality, although this spread is not nearly as great as that between many mortgage-backed securities and high-quality term bonds.

Spreads of ABS to Treasuries have moved within a fairly narrow range as the ABS market has matured. In the two-year average life sector, the yield spread of ABS to Treasuries has rarely been less than 65 basis points or more than

95 basis points. Because they provide somewhat less cash-flow predictability, automobile ABSs generally trade up to 5 basis points wider than credit card ABS.

Asset-backed securities have historically provided excellent relative value versus corporate issues of comparable maturity. Investor interest in ABS should remain strong because of their yield advantage, high credit quality, short and predictable maturities, and excellent liquidity.

# PART 5

# OPTIONS
# AND FUTURES

# CHAPTER 32

## FIXED INCOME OPTIONS AND FUTURES MARKETS

*Mark Pitts, Ph.D.*
*Senior Vice President*
*Lehman Brothers*

*Frank J. Fabozzi, Ph.D., CFA*
*Visiting Professor of Finance*
*Sloan School of Management*
*Massachusetts Institute of Technology*
*and*
*Editor,* The Journal of Portfolio Management

With the advent of options, futures, and forwards on interest-rate instruments, proactive fixed income risk management, in its broadest sense, assumes a new dimension. Investment managers and traders can achieve new degrees of freedom. It is now possible to alter the interest-rate sensitivity of a fixed income portfolio economically and quickly. *Derivative contracts,* known as such because they derive their value from an underlying instrument, offer investment managers and traders risk and return patterns that were previously either unavailable or too costly.

The purpose of this chapter is fourfold. First, we explain the basic characteristics of options, futures, and forward contracts. Second, we review the most actively traded and most representative over-the-counter (OTC) and listed contracts. Third, we explain how to determine the theoretical price of a futures contract (the theoretical price of an options contract is much more difficult to determine; the determinants of the price of an option are reviewed in Chapter 33 and discussed in more detail in Chapter 34.) Finally, we provide an overview of how futures can be employed in portfolio management. We omit from our discussion the use of futures for hedging; this topic will be explained in more detail in Chapter 49. An overview of strategies employing options is provided in Chapter 33.

## BASIC CHARACTERISTICS
## OF DERIVATIVE CONTRACTS

### Futures Contracts

A *futures contract* is an agreement between a buyer (seller) and an established futures exchange or its clearing house in which the buyer (seller) agrees to take (make) delivery of a specific amount of a valued item such as a commodity, stock, or bond at a specified price at a designated time. For some futures contracts, settlement at expiration is in cash rather than actual delivery.

When an investor takes a position in the market by buying a futures contract, the investor is said to have a *long position in* or *be long the futures*. If, instead, the investor's opening position is the sale of a futures contract, the investor is said to have a *short position in* or *be short the futures*.

Futures contracts based on a financial instrument or a financial index are known as *financial futures*. Financial futures can be classified as (1) interest rate futures, (2) stock index futures, or (3) currency futures. This chapter focuses on interest rate futures and includes a description of the most important interest rate futures contracts currently traded.

To illustrate how financial futures work, suppose that $X$ buys a futures contract and $Y$ sells a futures contract on an 8 percent five-year Treasury note for settlement one year from now. Suppose also that the price at which $X$ and $Y$ agree to transact one year from now is $100. This is the futures price. This means that one year from now $Y$ must deliver an 8 percent 5-year Treasury note and will receive $100. $X$ will take delivery of an 8 percent 5-year Treasury note and will pay $100.

The profit or loss realized by the buyer or seller of a futures contract depends on the price and interest rate on the delivery date. For example, if the market price of an 8 percent 5-year Treasury note at the settlement date is $110, because rates have declined, the buyer of the futures profits, paying $100 for a security that is worth $110. In contrast, the seller loses, because an instrument worth $110 must be delivered in exchange for $100. If interest rates rise on 8 percent 5-year Treasury notes so that the market price is $90, the seller of the futures contract profits and the buyer loses.

When the investor first takes a position in a futures contract, he or she must deposit a minimum dollar amount per contract as specified by the exchange. Futures brokers can, and often do, ask for more than the exchange minimums. As the price of the futures contract fluctuates, the value of the investor's equity in the position changes. At the close of each trading day, any market gain results in an increase in the investor's equity, whereas any market loss results in a decrease. This process is referred to as *marking to market*. Should an investor's equity position fall below an amount determined by the exchange, the investor must provide additional margin. On the other hand, if an investor's equity increases, he or she may withdraw funds. Consequently, a futures position frequently involves substantial cash flows prior to the delivery date. Margin is described in more detail later in this chapter.

## Forward Contracts

A *forward contract* is much like a futures contract. A forward contract is an agreement for the future delivery of some amount of a valued item at a specified price at a designated time. Futures contracts are standardized agreements that define the delivery date (or month) and quality and quantity of the deliverable. Futures contracts are traded on organized exchanges. A forward contract is, in contrast, usually nonstandardized, and is traded over the counter by direct contact between buyer and seller.

Although both futures and forward contracts set forth terms of delivery, futures contracts are not intended to be settled by delivery. In fact, generally less than 2 percent of outstanding futures contracts are delivered or go to final settlement. However, forward contracts *are* intended to be held to final settlement. Many of the most popular forward contracts, however, settle in cash rather than actual delivery.

Forward contracts are not typically marked to market. Consequently, there is no interim cash flow on forwards.

Finally, both parties in a forward contract are exposed to credit risk, because either party may default on its obligation. In contrast, credit risk for futures contracts is minimal, because the clearing corporation associated with the exchange guarantees the other side of each transaction.

## Options

An *option* is a contract in which the seller of the option grants the buyer of the option the right to purchase from, or sell to, the seller a designated instrument at a specified price within a specified period of time. The seller (or *writer*), grants this right to the buyer in exchange for a certain sum of money called the *option price* or *option premium*.

The price at which the instrument may be bought or sold is called the *exercise* or *strike price*. The date after which an option is void is called the *expiration date*. An *American option* may be exercised any time up to and including the expiration date. A *European option* may be exercised only on the expiration date.

When an option writer grants the buyer the right to purchase the designated instrument, it is called a *call option*. When the option buyer has the right to sell the designated instrument to the writer, the option is called a *put option*. The buyer of an option is said to be *long the option;* the writer is said to be *short the option*.

Consider, for example, an option on an 8 percent 5-year Treasury note with one year to expiration and an exercise price of $100. Suppose that the option price is $2 and the current price of the Treasury note is $100 with a yield of 8 percent. If the option is a call option, then the buyer of the option has the right to purchase an 8 percent 5-year Treasury note for $100 within one year. The writer of the option must sell the Treasury note for $100 to the buyer if he or she exercises the option. Suppose that the interest rate on the Treasury note declines and its price rises to $110. By exercising the call option the buyer realizes a profit, paying $100 for a Treasury note that is worth $110. After considering the cost of buying the option, $2, the net profit is $8. The writer of the option loses $8. If, instead, the market interest rate rises and the price of the Treasury note falls below $100, the call option buyer will not exercise the option, losing the option price of $2. The writer will realize a profit of $2. Thus, the buyer of a call option benefits from a decline in interest rates (a rise in the price of the underlying fixed income instrument) and the writer loses.

If the option is a put rather than a call, and the interest rate on Treasury notes declines and the price rises above $100, the option buyer will not exercise the option. The buyer will lose the entire option price. If, on the other hand, the interest rate on Treasury notes rises and the note's price falls below $100, the option buyer will profit by exercising the put option. In the case of a put option, the option buyer benefits from a rise in interest rates (a decline in the price of the underlying fixed income instrument) and the option seller loses.

The maximum amount that an option buyer can lose is the option price. The maximum profit that the option writer (seller) can realize is the option price. The option buyer has substantial potential upside return, whereas the option writer has substantial downside risk. The risk/reward relationship's for option positions are investigated in Chapter 33.

Option can be written on cash instruments or futures. The latter are called *futures options* and are traded only on the exchanges. Options on cash instruments are also traded on the exchanges, but have been much more successfully traded over the counter. These *OTC,* or *dealer, options* are tailor-made options on specific Treasury issues, mortgage securities, or interest-rate indices. Option contracts are reviewed later in this chapter.

## Differences between Option and Futures (or Forward) Contracts

Unlike a futures or forward contract, an option gives the buyer the *right* but not the *obligation* to perform. The option seller has the obligation to perform. In the case of a futures or forward contact, both the buyer and seller are obligated to perform. In addition, the buyer of a futures or forward contract does not pay the seller to accept the obligation, whereas in the case of an option, the buyer pays the seller an option premium.

Consequently, the risk/reward characteristics of the two contracts also differ. In a futures or forward contract, the long position realizes a dollar-for-dollar gain when the price of the futures or forward increases and suffers a dollar-for-dollar loss when the price of the futures or forward decreases. The opposite holds for a short position. Options do not provide such a symmetric risk/reward relationship. The most that a long position may lose is the option premium yet the long retains all the upside potential. However, the gain is always reduced by the price of the option. The maximum profit that the short position may realize is the option price, but the short position has substantial downside risk.

## SPECIFICATIONS OF REPRESENTATIVE FUTURES CONTRACTS

This section highlights some of the more interesting aspects of the most important and most representative listed fixed income futures contracts. Additional details on these contracts are presented in Exhibit 32–1. The exchange that trades a given contract will provide more detailed information.

The primary exchange-traded interest-rate futures contracts can be divided into two groups: those based on long- and intermediate-term instruments, and those based on short-term instruments. In the former category, the most important contracts are the Treasury bond futures contract, the 10-year Treasury note futures contract, and the municipal bond futures contract. In the latter category, the most important contracts are the Eurodollar time deposit futures contract and the Treasury bill futures contract. There are significant similarities between the contract specifications among the intermediate- and long-term contracts and among the short-term contracts. Furthermore, the long- and intermediate-term contracts are traded on the Chicago Board of Trade (the Board or CBOT), and the short-term contracts are traded on the International Monetary Market (IMM) of the Chicago Mercantile Exchange (the Merc or CME). There are also liquid contracts on 5-year notes traded on the CBOT and the Financial Instrument Exchange, FINEX (a division of the New York Cotton Exchange). The specifications for the 5-year contracts are shown in Exhibit 32–1, but are not discussed here.

There are also important foreign exchanges that trade dollar-denominated interest-rate futures contracts. Most notable are the London International Financial Futures Exchange (LIFFE) and the Singapore International Monetary Exchange (SIMEX). These exchanges trade interest-rate futures contracts similar to their American counterparts. In fact, in the case of the IMM Eurodollar contract, there is an automatic offset when one trades the Eurodollar contract

**EXHIBIT 32–1**
**Selected Futures and Futures Options Contracts***

| | Futures Contracts | | |
| --- | --- | --- | --- |
| | *IMM*<br>*90-Day T-bills* | *IMM*<br>*Eurodollars Futures* | *CBOT*<br>*5-Year T-notes* |
| *Trading Months* | March, June, September, and December | March, June, September, and December | March, June, September, and December |
| *Trading Unit* | U.S. T-bills with a face value of $1,000,000 | $1,000,000 3-month Eurodollar time deposit | U.S. T-notes with a face value of $100,000 |
| *Deliverable Grade* | U.S. T-bills maturing 90, 91, or 92 days from the delivery date. | (Actual delivery not allowed) | Any of the four most recently auctioned five-year T-notes. Specifically, U.S. T-notes that have an original maturity of not more than 5 1/4 years and not less than 4 1/4 years, as of the first day of the delivery month. |
| *Price Quotation* | Index (100 minus annualized discount rate) in minimum increments of .01 or one basis point or $25.00 (Example 100 − 8.00 = 92.00) | Index (100 minus annualized interest rate) in minimum increments of .01 or one basis point or $25.00 (Example 100 − 8.00 = 92.00) | Percentage of par in minimum increments of one-half of one thirty-second of a point, or $15.625. |
| *Last Trading Day* | Business day preceding the 1st day of the contract month on which a 13-week T-bill is issued and a one-year T-bill has 13 weeks remaining to maturity. | 2nd London business day before 3rd Wednesday of contract month. | The eighth to last business day of the delivery month. |
| *First Delivery Date* | First business day following the last day of trading. | (Actual delivery not allowed) | First business day of the delivery month. |
| *Last Delivery Date* | First business day following the last day of trading. | (Actual delivery not allowed) | Last business day of the delivery month. |

on SIMEX. Thus, one can buy in Chicago in the morning, sell the identical contract in Singapore at night, and no positions will remain on the books.

## The Treasury Bond Futures Contract

The T-bond futures contract is the most successful interest-rate (or commodity) futures contract. Prices and yields on the T-bond futures contract are quoted in terms of a (fictitious) 20-year 8 percent Treasury bond, but the CBOT allows many different bonds to be delivered in satisfaction of a short position in the contract. Specifically, any Treasury bond with at least 15 years to maturity or

**EXHIBIT 32–1—Continued**

| | Futures Contracts | | |
|---|---|---|---|
| | FINEX<br>5-Year T-notes | CBOT<br>10-Year T-notes | CBOT<br>30-Year T-notes |
| Trading Months | March, June, September, and December | March, June, September, and December | March, June, September, and December |
| Trading Unit | U.S. T-notes with a face value of $100,000 | U.S. T-notes with a face value of $100,000 | U.S. T-bonds with a face value of $100,000 |
| Deliverable Grade | U.S. T-notes with original maturity of 4 1/2 to 5 1/2 years, and a maturity of 4 1/4 to 5 1/2 years at delivery. | U.S. T-notes that mature no less than 6 1/2 and no more than 10 years from the first day of the delivery month. | U.S. T-notes that mature at least 15 years from the delivery date or, if callable, not callable for at least 15 years from the first day of the delivery month. |
| Price Quotation | Percentage of par in minimum increments of one-half of one thirty-second of a point, or $15.625. | Percentage of par in minimum increments of one thirty-second of a point or $31.25 per "tic." | Percentage of par in minimum increments of one thirty-second of a point or $31.25 per "tic." |
| Last Trading Day | The eighth to last business day of the delivery month. | The eighth to last business day of the delivery month. | The eighth to last business day of the delivery month. |
| First Delivery Date | First business day of the delivery month. | First business day of the delivery month. | First business day of the delivery month. |
| Last Delivery Date | Last business day of the delivery month. | Last business day of the delivery month. | Last business day of the delivery month. |

to first call, if callable, qualifies for delivery. Consequently, there are usually at least 20 outstanding bonds that constitute good delivery.

The T-bond futures contract calls for the short (i.e., the seller) to deliver $100,000 face value of any one of the qualifying Treasury bonds. However, because the coupons and maturities vary widely, the price that the buyer pays the seller depends on which bond the seller chooses to deliver. The rule used by the Chicago Board of Trade is one that adjusts the futures price by a conversion factor that reflects the price the bond would sell for at the beginning of the delivery month if it were yielding 8 percent. Using such a rule, the conversion factor for a given bond and a given delivery month is constant through time and is not affected by changes in the price of the bond or the price of the futures contract.

To illustrate, consider the delivery price for the Treasury 12 percent bonds of 8/15/13, callable 8/15/08, if they had been delivered on the June 1988 contract. At the beginning of June 1988 this bond had 20 years, $2\frac{1}{2}$ months to call. To calculate the conversion factor, the term-to-call is rounded down to the nearest quarter year, in this case giving an even 20 years to call. Because a 20-year 12 percent bond yielding 8 percent sells for 139.59, the conversion factor for the

**EXHIBIT 32–1—Continued**

|  | Options Contracts | | |
| --- | --- | --- | --- |
|  | Options on IMM Eurodollar Futures | Options on CBOT 10-Year Treasury Note Futures | Options on CBOT Treasury Bond Futures |
| Trading Months | March, June, September, and December | March, June, September, and December | March, June, September, and December |
| Trading Unit | $1,000,000 3-month Eurodollar time deposit futures | $100,000 face value 10-year T-note futures contract | $100,000 face value T-bond futures contract |
| Delivery | Underlying futures contract | Underlying futures contract | Underlying futures contract |
| Price Quotation | In basis points at a value of $25/basis points | Premiums are quoted in terms of percent of par in minimum increments of one sixty-fourth (1/64 of 1 percent of $100,000 face value, or $15.625 rounded upwards to the nearest penny). | Premiums are quoted in terms of percent of par in minimum increments of one sixty-fourth (1/64 of 1 percent of $100,000 face value, or $15.625 rounded upwards to the nearest penny). |
| Last Trading Date | Second London business day before the 3rd Wednesday of contract month | Friday that precedes the 1st business day of the contract month by at least 5 business days. | Friday that precedes the 1st business day of the contract month by at least 5 business days. |
| Exercise | Any day except last trading results in a futures contract. Exercise on last trading day results in cash settlement. | Any day up to and including last trading day. Exercise results in a position in futures. | Any day up to and including last trading day. Exercise results in a position in futures. |

* Contract specifications are subject to change without notice.

12 percent bond for the June 1988 contract was 1.3959 (i.e., 139.59 divided by 100).

The seller has the right to choose which qualifying bond to deliver and when during the delivery month delivery will take place. When the bond is delivered, the buyer is obligated to pay the seller the futures price times the appropriate conversion factor, plus accrued interest on the delivered bond.

Paradoxically, the success of the CBOT Treasury bond contract can in part be attributed to the fact that the delivery mechanicism is not as simple as it may first appear. There are several options implicit in a position in bond futures. First, the seller chooses which bond to deliver. Thus, the seller has an option to swap between bonds. If the seller is holding bond A for delivery, but Bond B becomes cheaper to deliver, he can swap Bond B for Bond A and make a more profitable delivery. Second, within some guidelines set by the CBOT, the seller decides when during the delivery month delivery will take place. He thus has a timing option which can be used to his advantage. Finally, the short retains the possibility of making the "wild card" play. This potentially profitable situation arises from the fact that the seller can give notice of intent to deliver for several hours after the exchange has closed and the futures settlement price has been fixed. In a falling market the seller can use the wildcard option to profit from the fixed delivery price.

The seller's options tend to make a contract a bit more difficult to understand, but at the same time they make the contract more attractive to speculators, arbitrageurs, dealers, and anyone else who believes he understands the contract better than other market participants. Thus, in the case of the Treasury bond futures contract, complexity has helped provide liquidity.

## The 10-Year Treasury Note Futures Contract

The CBOT Treasury note contract was modeled after the CBOT Treasury bond contract and resembles it in many respects. The Treasury note contract allows delivery of any note that has a maturity of $6\frac{1}{2}$ to 10 years on the first delivery day of the month. To qualify for delivery the instrument must have been issued as a Treasury note; thus, old Treasury bonds with a remaining life of $6\frac{1}{2}$ to 10 years do not qualify.

The Treasury note futures contract offers the seller the same flexibility that the Treasury bond futures contract offers. By giving proper notice, the seller can deliver at almost any point he chooses during the delivery month. He also chooses which of the qualifying notes to delivery and receives an amount equal to the futures price times the conversion factor for the delivered note (also based on an 8 percent yield), plus accrued interest. There has not, however, been as much of a play in the most deliverable issue for the Treasury note futures contract as there has been for the Treasury bond futures contract. It has more frequently been obvious well in advance which note (or when-issued note) would be delivered by the seller. The note futures contract offers the seller the same wildcard play that is offered by the bond futures contract.

## The Treasury Bill Futures Contract

The IMM's futures contract on Treasury bills was the first contract on a short-term debt instrument and has been the model for most subsequent contracts on short-term debt. The contract is based on three-month Treasury bills with a face value of $1,000,000.

The contract is quoted and traded in terms of a futures "price," but the futures price is, in fact, just a different way of quoting the futures interest rate. Specifically, the futures price is the annualized futures rate subtracted from 100. For example, a futures price of 92.25 means that Treasury bills are trading in the futures market at a rate of 7.75 percent. The actual price that the buyer pays the seller is calculated using the usual formula for Treasury bills:

$$\text{Invoice price} = \$1,000,000 \times [1 - \text{Rate} \times (\text{Days to maturity}/360)]$$

where the rate is expressed in decimal form. As this formula shows, each basis point change in the interest rate (or each .01 change in the futures price) leads to a $25 change in the invoice price for a 90-day bill. Consequently, the value of a .01 change in the futures contract is always $25.

The Treasury bill futures contract is considerably simpler than the T-bond and T-note futures contracts. First, because all Treasury bills of the same maturity are economically equivalent, there is effectively only one deliverable issue, namely, Treasury bills with three months to maturity. The fact that the three-month bills may be either new three-month bills or older bills that currently have three months of remaining life makes little difference because the new and old issues will trade the same in the cash market. Thus, all the subtleties surrounding conversion factors and most deliverable issues are absent from the Treasury bill futures market. Furthermore, there is little uncertainty or choice involved in the delivery date, because delivery must take place during a very narrow time-frame, usually a three-day period. The rules of the exchange make clear well in advance the exact dates on which delivery will take place. Finally, because there are no conversion factors, there is no wildcard play in the Treasury bill futures market.

Although the Treasury bill futures contract is simple and thus may not provide as many speculative and arbitrage opportunities as the more complex long- and intermediate-term futures contracts, it does provide a straightforward means of hedging or speculating on the short end of the yield curve. Because the Treasury bill rate is a benchmark off which other short-term rates may be priced, the bill contract fills a well-defined need of many market participants.

## The Eurodollar Time Deposit Futures Contract

As the Eurodollar and LIBOR sectors of the fixed income market have grown substantially in recent years, so has volume in the IMM's Eurodollar time deposit futures contract. Unlike most other fixed income futures contracts, the Eurodollar contract does not allow actual delivery. Instead, settlement is made in cash. The final settlement price is determined by the three-month Eurodollar deposit rate when trading on the contact is concluded. Although this mechanism does not allow delivery of an actual instrument, the cash flow from a futures position is such that the contact provides a very good vehicle for hedging or speculating on short-term Eurodollar and LIBOR-based debt.

Like the Treasury bill contract, the quoted futures price for Eurodollar time deposits is equal to 100 minus the annualized yield. Also, each .01 change in the futures price (1 basis point change in yield) carries a value of $25. Settlement on Eurodollar futures takes place on a single day during the delivery month.

The yield on the Eurodollar futures contract is quoted in terms of an add-on, or simple, interest rate. Rates on Eurodollar contracts are thus directly comparable to the rates on domestic CDs or interbank deposits. However, to compare the Eurodollar rate to the Treasury bill rate, one of the rates must be converted so that both rates will be in the same terms.

The Eurodollar futures contract is one of the most heavily traded contracts. It is frequently used to trade the short end of the yield curve, and many hedgers have found the Eurodollar contract to be the best hedging vehicle for a wide range of hedging situations.

## The Municipal Bond Futures Contract

Because there are risks unique to the municipal bond market, the Treasury bond futures contract has not been particularly effective in managing the risk of municipal bonds. Proposed and actual changes in tax laws, and changing economic conditions that might be expected to increase the likelihood of defaults are examples of factors that might affect the municipal bond market but not the Treasury market. The CBOT's municipal bond futures contract was designed to give participants in the municipal bond market a more effective means of controlling such risks.

The municipal bond futures contract is based on the value of the Bond Buyer Index (BBI). The BBI consists of 40 actively traded general obligation and revenue bonds. To be included in the BBI, the rating of the issue must be at least single A and the size of the term portion of the issue must be at least $50 million ($75 million for housing issues). No more than two bonds of the same issuer are included in the BBI. In addition, for an issue to be considered, it must meet the following three conditions: It must have (1) at least 19 years remaining to maturity, (2) a first call date between 7 and 16 years, and (3) at least one call at par prior to redemption.

The Bond Buyer serves as the index manager for the contract and prices each issue in the index based on prices received daily from five dealer-to-dealer brokers. After dropping the highest and lowest price obtained for each issue, the average of the three remaining prices is computed. The average price is then multipled by a conversion factor designed to equate the bond to an 8 percent issue, just as in the cases of the Treasury bond and note futures contracts. This gives an average converted price for each bond in the BBI. These prices are then summed and divided by 40, giving an average converted price for the BBI.

The BBI is revised bimonthly when new issues are added and older issues, or issues that no longer meet the criteria for inclusion in the index, are dropped. A smoothing coefficient is calculated on the index revision date so that the value of the BBI will not change merely because of the change in its composition.[1]    The average converted price for the BBI is multiplied by this coefficient to get the value of the BBI for a particular date.

## Mechanics of Futures Trading

*Types of Orders.*    When a trader wants to buy or sell a futures contract, the price and conditions under which the order is to be executed must be communicated to the futures brokers. The simplest type of order, yet potentially the most perilous from the trader's perspective, is the *market order.* When a market order is placed, it is executed at the best price available as soon as the order reaches the trading pit, the area on the floor of a futures exchange where all transactions for a specific contract are made. The danger of market orders is that an adverse move may take place between the time the trader places the order and the time the order reaches the trading pit.

To avoid the dangers associated with market orders, the trader can place a *limit order* (or *resting order*) that designates a price limit for the execution of the transaction. A *buy limit order* indicates that the futures contract may be purchased only at the designated price or lower. A *sell limit order* indicates that the futures contract may be sold at the designated price or higher.

The danger of a limit order is that there is no guarantee that it will be executed at all. The designated price may simply not be obtainable. Even if the contract trades at the specified price, the order may not be filled because the market does not trade long enough at the specified price (or better) to fill all outstanding orders. Nevertheless, the dangers of a limit order may be fewer than those of a market order. The trader has more control with a limit order, because the price designated in the limit order can be revised based on prevailing market prices so long as the order has not already been filled.

The limit order is a conditional order: It is executed only if the limit price or a better price can be obtained. Another type of conditional order is the *stop order.* A stop order specifies that the order is not to be executed until the market reaches a designated price, at which time it becomes a market order. A *buy stop order* specifies that the order is not to be executed until the market rises to a designated price (i.e., trades at or above, or is bid at or above, the designated price). A *sell stop order* specifies that the order is not to be executed until the market price falls below a designated price (i.e., trades at or below, or is offered at or below, the designated price). A stop order is useful when a futures trader already has a position on but cannot watch the market constantly. Profits can be preserved or losses minimized on open positions by allowing market movements

---

[1] The coefficient adjustment does have implications for trading and hedging of municipal bonds. See: Jane Sachar Brauer, "The Bond Buyer Municipal Index Coefficient," in Frank J. Fabozzi (ed.) *Advances and Innovations in the Bond and Mortgage Markets* (Chicago: Probus Publishing, 1989).

to trigger a closing trade. In a sell (buy) stop order the designated price is less (greater) than the current market price of the futures contract. In a sell (buy) limit order the designated price is greater (less) than the current market price of the futures contract.

There are two dangers associated with stop orders. Because futures markets sometimes exhibit abrupt price changes, the direction of the change in the futures price may be very temporary, resulting in the premature closing of a position. Also, once the designated price is reached, the stop order becomes a market order and is subject to the uncertainty of the execution price noted earlier for market orders.

A *stop-limit order*, a hybrid of a stop order and a limit order, is a stop order that designates a price limit. Thus, in contrast to the stop order, which becomes a market order if the stop is reached, the stop-limit order becomes a limit order if the stop is reached. The order can be used to cushion the market impact of a stop order. The trader may limit the possible execution price after the activation of a stop. As with a limit order, the limit price may never be reached after the order is activated, and therefore the order may not be executed. This, of course, defeats one purpose of the stop order—to protect a profit or limit a loss.

A trader may also enter a *market-if-touched order*. A market if touched order is like a stop order in that it becomes a market order if a designated price is reached. However, a market-if-touched order to buy would become a market order if the market *falls* to a given price, whereas a stop order to buy becomes a market order if the market *rises* to a given price. Similarly, a market-if-touched order to sell becomes a market order if the market rises to a specified price, whereas the stop order to sell becomes a market order if the market falls to a given price. One may think of the stop order as an order designed to exit an existing position at an acceptable price (without specifying the exact price), and the market-if-touched order as an order designed to enter a position at an acceptable price (also without specifying the exact price).

Orders may be placed to buy or sell at the open or the close of trading for the day. An *opening order* indicates that a trade is to be executed only in the opening range for the day, and a *closing order* indicates that the trade is to be executed only within the closing range for the day.

Futures brokers may be given freedom to try to get the best possible price for their clients. The *discretionary order* gives the broker a specified price range in which to fill the order. For example, a discretionary order might be a limit order that gives the broker a one tic (i.e., one basis point or one 32nd) discretion to try to do better than the limit price. Thus, even if the limit price is reached and the order could be filled at that limit, the broker can wait for a better price. However, if it turns out that the market goes in the wrong direction, the broker must fill the order but at no worse than one tic from the limit price. A *not held order* gives the broker virtually full discretion over the order. The not held order may be placed as any of the orders mentioned so far (market, stop, limit, etc.), but if the broker believes that filling the orders is not advisable, he or she need not fill it.

A client may enter orders that contain order cancellation provisions. A *fill-or-kill* order must be executed as soon as it reaches the trading floor or it is immediately cancelled. A *one-cancels-other order* is a pair of orders that are worked simultaneously, but as soon as one order is filled the other is automatically cancelled.

Orders may designate the time period for which the order is effective—a day, week, or month, or perhaps by a given time within the day. An *open order,* or *good-til-cancelled order,* is good until the order is specifically cancelled. If the time period is not specified, it is usually assumed to be good only until the end of the day. For some orders, like the market order, a specific time period is not relevant, because they are executed immediately.

Upon execution of an order, the futures broker is required to provide confirmation of the trade. The confirm indicates all the essential information about the trade. When the order involves the liquidation of a position, the confirm shows the profit or loss on the position and the commission costs.

***Taking and Liquidating a Position.***   Once an account has been opened with a broker, the futures trader may take a position in the market. If the trader buys a futures contract, he is said to have a long position. If the trader's opening position is the sale of the futures contract, the trader is said to have a short position.

The futures trader has two ways to liquidate a position. To liquidate a position prior to the delivery date, he or she must take an offsetting position in the same contract. For a long position this means selling an identical number of contracts; for a short position this means buying an identical number of contracts.

The alternative is to wait until the delivery date. At that time the investor liquidates a long position by accepting delivery of the underlying instrument at the agreed upon price, or liquidates a short position by delivering the instrument at the agreed upon price. For those interest-rate futures contracts that do not call for actual delivery (e.g., Eurodollar and municipal bond futures), settlement is in cash at the settlement price on the delivery date.

***The Role of the Clearing Corporation.***   When an investor takes a position in the futures market, there is always another party taking the opposite position and agreeing to satisfy the terms set forth in the contract. Because of the *clearing corporation* associated with each exchange, the investor need not worry about the financial strength and integrity of the party taking the opposite side of the contract. After an order is executed, the relationship between the two parties is severed. The clearing corporation interposes itself as the buyer for every sale and the seller for every purchase. Thus the investor is free to liquidate a position without involving the other party to the original transaction and without worry that the other party may default. However, the investor *is* exposed to default on the part of the futures broker through which the trade is placed. Thus, each institution should make sure that the futures broker (and specifically the *subsidiary* that trades futures) has adequate capital to ensure that there is little danger of default.

*Commissions.* Commissions on futures contracts have been fully negotiable since 1974. Futures commissions are usually quoted on the basis of a "round-turn," meaning a price that includes the opening and closing out of the futures contract. In most cases, the commission is the same regardless of the maturity date or type of the underlying instrument traded.

Commissions for institutional accounts vary enormously, ranging from a low of about $11 to a high of about $30. Like any service, the price that a broker charges a particular client is based on many factors, including (1) volume of business, (2) amount of value added by the broker, (3) strength of the relationship (or desire to create a relationship), (4) cost of providing the service, and (5) related transactions. To create a good working relationship for both parties, an account manager should consider all of these factors when negotiating commissions.

*Margin Requirements.* When first taking a position in a futures contract, an investor must deposit a minimum dollar amount per contract as specified by the exchange. (A broker may ask for more than the exchange minimum, but may not require less than the exchange minimum.) This amount is called the *initial margin* and constitutes a "good faith" deposit. The initial margin may be in the form of Treasury bills. As the price of the futures contract fluctuates, the value of equity in the position changes. At the close of each trading day, the position is marked to market, so that any gain or loss from the position is reflected in the equity of the account. The price used to mark the position to market is the settlement price for the day.

*Maintenance margin* is the minimum level to which an equity position may fall as a result of an unfavorable price movement before additional margin is required. The additional margin deposited, also called *variation margin,* is simply the amount that will bring the equity in the account back to its initial margin level. Unlike original margin, variation margin must be in cash. If there is excess margin in the account, that amount may be withdrawn.[2]

---

[2] Although there are initial and maintenance margin requirements for buying stocks and bonds on margin, the concept of margin differs for futures. When securities are bought on margin, the difference between the price of the security and the initial margin is borrowed from the broker. The security purchased serves as collateral for the loan and interest is paid by the investor. For futures contracts, the initial margin, in effect, serves as good faith money, indicating that the investor will satisfy the obligation of the contract. No money is borrowed by the purchaser. Similarly, the seller of futures borrows neither money nor securities.

If variation margin is required, the institution is contacted by the brokerage firm and informed of the additional amount that must be deposited. A margin notice is sent as well. Even if futures prices subsequently move in favor of the institution such that the equity increases above the maintenance margin, the variation margin must still be supplied. Failure to meet a request for variation margin within a reasonable time will result in the closing out of a position.

Margin requirements vary by futures contract and by the type of transaction; that is, whether the position is an outright long or short, or a spread (a long together with a short), and whether the trade is put on as a speculative position or as a hedge. Margins are higher for speculative positions than for hedging positions and higher for outright positions than for spreads. Margin requirements also vary between futures brokers. Exchanges and brokerage firms change their margin requirements as contracts are deemed to be more or less risky, or as it is felt that certain types of positions (usually speculative positions) should be discouraged.

## SPECIFICATIONS OF REPRESENTATIVE FUTURES OPTIONS CONTRACTS

Although futures contracts are relatively straightforward financial instruments, options on futures (or *futures options*, as they are commonly called) deserve extra explanation. Options on futures are very similar to other options contracts. Like options on cash (or spot) fixed income securities, both put and call options are traded on fixed income futures. The buyer of a call has the right to buy the underlying futures contract at a specific price. The buyer of a put has the right to sell the underlying futures contract at a specific price. If the buyer chooses to exercise the option, the option seller is obligated to sell the futures in the case of the call, or buy the futures in the case of the put.

An option on the futures contract differs from more traditional options in only one essential way: The underlying instrument is not a spot security, but a futures contract on a security. Thus, for instance, if a call option buyer exercises his option, he acquires a long position in futures instead of a long position in a cash security. The seller of the call will be assigned the corresponding short position in the same futures contract. For put options the situation is reversed. A put option buyer exercising the option acquires a short position in futures, and the seller of the put is assigned a long position in the same futures contract. The resulting long and short futures positions are like any other futures positions and are subject to daily marking to market.

An investor acquiring a position in futures does so at the current futures price. However, if the strike price on the option does not equal the futures price at the time of exercise, the option seller must compensate the option buyer for the discrepancy. Thus, when a call option is exercised, the seller of the call must pay the buyer of the call the current futures price minus the strike price. On the other hand, the seller of the put must pay the buyer of the put the strike price minus the current futures price. (These transactions are actually accomplished by establishing the futures positions at the strike price, then immediately marking to market.) Note that, unlike options on spot securities, the amount of money that changes hands at exercise is only the difference between the strike price and the current futures price, not the whole strike price. Of course, an option need not be exercised for the owner to take his gains; he can simply sell the option instead of exercising it.

We now turn to the options contracts themselves. We describe two of the most important contracts, the CBOT's option on the long-term bond futures contract and the IMM's option on the Eurodollar contract. There are also options on the 5-year and 10-year note futures contracts, but because they are both very similar in structure to options on Treasury bond futures, they are not included in this section. Details on all the liquid futures options contracts are given in Exhibit 32–1.

## Options on Treasury Bond Futures

Options on CBOT Treasury bond futures are in many respects simpler than the underlying futures contracts. Usually, conversion factors, most deliverables, wildcard plays, and other subtleties of the Treasury bond futures contract need not concern the buyer or seller of options on Treasury bond futures. Although these factors affect the fair price of the futures contract, their impact is already reflected in the futures price. Consequently, they need not necessarily be reconsidered when buying or selling an option on the futures.

The option on the Treasury bond futures contract is in many respects an option on an index, the "index" being the futures price itself, that is, the price of the fictitious 20-year 8 percent Treasury bond. Like the futures contract, the nominal size of the contract is $100,000. Thus, for example, with futures prices at 95, a call option struck at 94 has an intrinsic value of $1,000, and a put struck at 100 has an intrinsic value of $5,000.

The premiums for options on Treasury bond futures are quoted in terms of points and 64ths of a point. Thus, an option premium of 1-10 implies a price of 1 10/64 percent of face value, or $1,156.25 (from $100,000 × 1.15625% ). Minimum price fluctuations are also 1/64th of 1 percent.

Though an option on the Treasury bond futures contract is hardly identical to an option on a Treasury bond, it serves much the same purpose. Because spot and futures prices for Treasury bonds are highly correlated, hedgers and speculators frequently find that options on bond futures provide the essential characteristics needed in an options contract on a long-term fixed income instrument.

## Options on Eurodollar Futures

Options on Eurodollar futures fill a unique place among exchange-traded hedging products. These options are currently the only liquid listed option contracts based on a short-term interest rate.

Options on Eurodollar futures (traded on the IMM) are based on the quoted Eurodollar futures price (i.e., 100 minus the annualized yield). Like the underlying futures, the size of the contract is $1,000,000 and each .01 change in price carries a value of $25. Likewise, the option premium is quoted in terms of basis points. Thus, for example, an option premium quoted as 20 (or .20) implies an option price of $500; a premium of 125 or (1.25) implies an option price of $3,125.

Like other debt options, buyers of puts on Eurodollar futures profit as rates move up and buyers of calls profit as rates move down. Consequently, institutions with liabilities or assets that float off short-term rates can use Eurodollar futures options to hedge their exposure to fluctuations in short-term rates. Consider first those institutions that have liabilities that float off short-term rates. These include banks and thrifts that issue CDs and/or take deposits based on money market rates. Also included are industrial and financial corporations that issue commercial paper, floating-rate notes, or preferred stock that floats off money market rates. Likewise, those who make payments on adjustable-rate mortgages face similar risks.[3]  In each instance, as short-term rates increase, the liability becomes more onerous for the borrower. Consequently, the issuers of these liabilities may need a means of capping their interest-rate expense. Although options on Eurodollar futures do not extend as far into the future as many issuers would like, they are effective tools for hedging many short-term rates over the near term. Consequently, an institution with floating-rate liabilities can buy an interest-rate "cap" by buying puts on Eurodollar futures. As rates move up, profits on the put position will tend to offset some or all of the incremental interest expense.

On the other side of the coin, and facing opposite risks, are the purchasers of floating-rate instruments—that is, investors who buy money market deposits, floating-rate notes, floating-rate preferred stock, and adjustable-rate mortgages. Investors who roll over CDs or commercial paper face the same problem. As rates fall, these investors receive less interest income. Consequently, they may feel a need to buy interest-rate "floors," which are basically call options. As rates fall, calls on debt securities increase in value and will offset the lower interest income received by the investor.

---

[3] To the extent that the interest-rate payment on an adjustable-rate mortgage has an upper and lower bound, the risk to issuers and investors is limited by the very nature of the instrument.

In conclusion, options on Eurodollar futures can be used to limit the risk associated with fluctuations in short-term rates. This is accomplished by buying puts if the exposure is to rising rates, or by buying calls if the exposure is to falling rates.

## Mechanics of Trading Futures Options

To take a position in futures options, one works with a futures broker. The types of orders that are used to buy or sell futures options are generally the same as the orders discussed for futures contracts. The clearing house associated with the exchange where the futures option is traded once again stands between the buyer and the seller. Furthermore, the commission costs and related issues that we discussed for futures also generally apply to futures options.

There are no margin requirements for the buyer of futures options, but the option price must be paid in full when the option is purchased. Because the option price is the maximum amount that the buyer can lose regardless of how adverse the price movement of the underlying futures contract, there is no need for margin.

Because the seller has agreed to accept all of the risk (and no reward other than the option premium) of the position in the underlying instrument, the seller is generally required to deposit not only the margin required for the underlying futures contract but, with certain exceptions, the option price as well. Furthermore, subsequent price changes adversely affecting the seller's position will lead to additional margin requirements.

## OTC CONTRACTS

There is a substantial over-the-counter market for fixed income options and forwards. (Forward contracts are the over-the-counter equivalent of futures contracts.) For example, in the OTC market, one can easily buy or sell options on LIBOR, commercial paper, T-bill, and prime rates. One can buy and sell options on virtually any Treasury issue. One can buy and sell options on any number of mortgage securities. One can buy and sell options with expirations ranging from as short as 1 day to as long as 10 years. In the OTC market one can easily take forward positions in 3- and 6-month LIBOR going out to about 2 years.

In the options market in particular, a natural division has evolved between the OTC market and the listed market. Given the relatively small number of futures contracts, the exchanges' need for standardization, and the synergy created by the futures options contract trading side by side with the underlying futures contract, the exchanges have been most successful with options on futures contracts. Because off-exchange options on futures are prohibited, futures options cannot be traded over-the-counter. On the other hand, because the OTC market is very good at creating flexible structures and handling a diversity of terms, the OTC market has been more successful than the exchanges in trading options on cash securities and options on cash market interest rates.

In the following sections we discuss the structure of the OTC fixed income derivative markets and their advantages and disadvantages relative to the exchange-traded markets. We also discuss the most important contracts traded in the OTC market. These are (1) options on mortgage securities, (2) options on cash Treasuries, (3) caps and floors on LIBOR, and (4) forward rate agreements on LIBOR.

## The Structure of the OTC Market

Like other OTC markets, there is no central marketplace for OTC fixed income options and forward contracts. A transaction takes place whenever a buyer and seller agree to a price. Unlike an exchange transaction, the terms, size, and price of the contract generally remain undisclosed to other market participants. Accordingly, the OTC market is much less "visible" than the exchange markets and it is more difficult to ascertain the current market price for a given option or forward contract. Two groups, however, help to alleviate this problem. First there are the OTC market makers. Market makers in OTC fixed income options and forwards are typically large investment banks and commercial banks. A market maker, by definition, stands ready to either buy or sell a given option or forward contract to accommodate a client's needs. To be effective, the market maker must be willing and able to handle large orders and must keep his bid-ask spreads reasonably narrow.

The other group that helps bring order to the OTC market is the brokers. The sole job of the brokers is to bring together buyers and sellers; it is not the brokers' job to take positions in option and forward contracts. The buyers and sellers that the brokers bring together can be market makers or the end-users of the contracts. To do their job, the brokers must distribute information about the prices where they see trades taking place and the prices at which they believe further trades can be completed. This information is distributed to potential buyer and sellers over the phone and over publicly available media such as Telerate pages.

Because there is no central market for OTC fixed income options and forwards, there can be no clearing house. Consequently, those who position OTC contracts may have to give considerable weight to the creditworthiness of their counterparty. For example, entities that sell options or position forward rate agreements (FRAs) can have potential liabilities equal to several times their net worth. Furthermore, there is no guarantee that these counterparties have ef fective hedges against their positions, or in fact, that they are hedging at all. Furthermore, financial problems on the part of the counterparty can jeopardize the ability or willingness of the counterparty to make good on the terms of a contract even if it is hedged. Consequently, unlike the exchange-traded markets where one neither knows nor cares who is on the other side of a trade, in the OTC market it is usually very important to know who is on the other side. Creditworthiness can be one of the most important considerations in the trade.

The potential credit problems associated with OTC trades are mitigated in a number of ways. First, some institutions will not buy options from or take either side of an FRA contract with any party other than a major entity with a sound credit rating. Secondly, some institutions require their counterparty to post collateral immediately after the transaction is completed. This collateral serves much the same purpose as initial margin in the futures and futures options market. Finally, some institutions reserve the right to call for additional collateral from their counterparties if the market moves against the counterparty. This is analogous to variation margin in the exchange-traded markets. Although these provisions may not be as good as a central clearing house, they are apparently good enough for a very large number of institutions and good enough for a very large market to develop.

Liquidity, in terms of being able to easily close out an existing position, can be a constraint in the over-the-counter market. OTC options and forwards are generally not assignable transactions. Thus, for example, if one sells an option, the contingent liability associated with that option cannot be transferred to a third party without the express permission of the option buyer. If an option seller wants to cover his short option position, often the best strategy is to buy a similar option from a third party to offset the risks of the original option. However, if the credit of the offsetting party is in question, or the offsetting option is not identical, risks will remain for the option seller. The option buyer can face similar problems if closing out the option before expiration. Credit considerations and/or the fact that the option buyer may not be able to sell an identical option to offset the first option make it more difficult to effectively close out the long option position. Because FRAs involve contingent liabilities for both sides of the transaction, similar problems exist for both buyers and sellers of FRAs.

Some of the problems associated with the OTC market arise from the fact that the contracts are not standardized. However, nonstandardization leads to many benefits as well. As indicated above, OTC contracts can be specified in virtually any terms that are acceptable to both buyer and seller. A potential buyer or seller can thus approach a market maker with whatever structure is needed and in many (but certainly not all) cases obtain the desired structure at a reasonable price. Compared to the very rigid structure of the exchange-traded markets, this is a remarkable advantage.

## The OTC Contracts

*Options on Mortgages.*   The over-the-counter market for options on fixed income instruments began in the mid 1970s with *standby* commitments. Standbys were essentially put options on mortgages that allowed the holder (usually a mortgage banker) to sell mortgages at a given price during a given period of time. Although standbys were popularized by the Federal National Mortgage Association, other institutions soon got into the business of selling options. Thrift institutions in particular soon became sellers of puts, as well as calls, on mortgages. The thrift would typically sell out-of-the-money puts (struck at a yield that seemed attractive relative to current yields) and out-of-the-money calls (often struck at the thrift's cost of the underlying securities). Until the early 1980s there were no real market makers in the OTC mortgage options market. Thus, a trade typically did not occur until an end-user who wanted to buy an option could be paired with an end-user who wanted to sell the very same option. The intermediary who stood in between these two parties was usually not willing to position one side without the other.

Today, the market for options on mortgages includes many more participants, although the original standby commitments no longer exist. Investment banks and commercial banks now play a major role in the mortgage options market. Many of the large investment and commercial banks are now willing to position mortgage options without having the other side of the trade. This makes the market much more liquid and flexible than it otherwise would be. The end-users of options on mortgages have not changed greatly, but the number of users has increased greatly. Mortgage bankers continue to buy puts on mortgages. Thrifts continue to sell both puts and calls. As some thrifts now play the role of mortgage banker, they too have become buyers of puts on mortgages. Money managers have also become a part of the market, usually as sellers of call options against mortgages in their portfolios.

The market for mortgage options today is composed almost entirely of options on the standard agency pass-through mortgage securities. Options on CMO tranches, IOs, POs, and the like are not a significant part of the OTC mortgage options market. The majority of the options traded are on 30-year mortgages, but options on 15-year products are also readily available. In terms of expiration, trading in mortgage options tends to be concentrated in the shorter expirations, with most of the options expiring within 60 days, and the vast majority expiring within 1 year. In terms of strike price, most of the trading is in at-the-money and out-of-the-money options.

Given the willingness of OTC market makers to position options, a client can easily trade options on $25 million of underlying securities with little or no prior notice. Some firms will position $100 million or more of mortgage options on the wire. Thus, the OTC options market can be as liquid as the exchange-traded options markets.

*Options on Treasury Securities.* Although not as old as the OTC options market for mortgages, the OTC options market for Treasury securities is now just as large and liquid. As in the mortgage options market, investment banks and commercial banks play major roles as market makers, frequently standing ready to buy or sell options on $100 million (or more) of Treasury securities. Most of the action is in options expiring within 60 days, written at-the-money or out-of-the-money. Options on Treasuries are concentrated in the on-the-run issues, with most of the remaining business being done in the once-off-the-run issues.

Except for the mortgage bankers, who have considerably less interest in options on Treasuries, the end-users of options on Treasuries mirror the market for options on mortgages. Thrifts tend to be writers of out-of-the-money puts and calls, and money managers and mutual funds tend to be covered call writers.

*Caps and Floors on LIBOR.* The primary OTC options covering the short end of the yield curve are the caps and floors on 3- and 6-month LIBOR. A cap on LIBOR is, in essence, a series of puts on LIBOR-based debt, whereas a floor on LIBOR is, in essence, a series of calls on LIBOR-based debt.

The buyer of a cap or floor holds most of the rights in the contract, just like other options. The seller of a cap or floor will of course receive an options premium from the buyer, but is then obligated to perform on the contract.

To illustrate how these contracts work, let's take a 5-year, $100 million cap on 3-month LIBOR struck at 11 percent. Such a contract will specify specific reset dates occuring every 3 months for a total of 20 resets. The first reset will usually occur immediately or within a couple of weeks of the trade date, and the last reset will usually be about 3 months before the stated maturity of the contract. To determine what the payoff to the cap buyer will be, on every reset date one compares 3-month LIBOR (taken from a predetermined source) to the 11 percent strike rate. If 3-month LIBOR is at or below 11 percent, nothing is owed to the cap buyer. If, however, 3-month LIBOR is above 11 percent, the cap seller must pay the cap buyer the monetary value of the amount by which 3-month LIBOR exceeds 11 percent. In this case, for a 90-day interest accrual period, the value of each basis point is $2,500 (from .0001 × $100,000,000 × 90/360). Thus, for example, if 3-month LIBOR on a particular reset date is 11.50 percent, the cap seller owes the cap buyer $125,000 for that reset. If, on the next reset date, 3-month LIBOR is 13 percent, the cap seller owes the cap buyer $500,000 for that reset. If, on the next reset date, 3-month LIBOR is 10.50 percent, the cap seller owes nothing to the cap buyer for that reset. In most cases, the cap seller pays the cap buyer the amount of money owed for a particular reset at the end of the interest accrual period, in this case, 3 months after the reset date.

The mechanics of floors are similar, except that the payoff comes when rates fall below a given level, instead of when they rise above a given level.

For example, if one buys a $25 million 7-year 6.50 percent floor on 6-month LIBOR, there are a total of 14 reset dates. On each of these reset dates, one compares 6-month LIBOR to 6.50 percent. If 6-month LIBOR is above 6.50 percent, nothing is owed to the buyer of the floor for that reset. If, however, 6-month LIBOR is below 6.50 percent, for a 180-day interest accrual period the floor seller owes the floor buyer $1,250 for every basis point that 6-month LIBOR is below 6.50 percent (from .0001 × $25,000,000 × 180/360).

Like other OTC options markets, the cap and floor market is composed of market makers, end-users, and brokers. The market makers are once again the large investment banks and commercial banks. However, there are fewer market makers and generally wider spreads in the cap and floor market than there are in the options market for mortgages or Treasury securities. Nonetheless, there is an active market out to 10 years, particularly for out-of-the-money caps, and to a lesser degree, out-of-the-money floors.

The end-user buyers of caps and floors are primarily institutions with risks that they need to cover. For example, institutions that fund short and lend long will tend to have losses as short-term rates rise. Similarly, businesses that fund by rolling over short-term obligations such as commercial paper or by bank borrowings tied to LIBOR or the prime rate will tend to have losses as short-term rates rise. These institutions, which include many thrifts, banks and finance companies, as well as industrial and construction companies, can protect themselves against rising short-term rates by buying caps. End-user buyers of floors tend to be those firms that face losses if rates fall. Such a case might occur, for example, if an institution borrows at a floating rate with a built-in floor. Such an institution may be structured so that floating rates, per se, pose no problem; the problem arises when the floating rate at which they borrow is no longer really floating because the floor has been hit. This institution may buy a floor so that it will receive monetary compensation from the floor seller whenever the floating rate falls below the floor rate, thus covering the risks of lower rates.

The sellers of caps and floors, other than the market makers, are quite varied. In some cases, sellers sell caps or floors outright to bring in premium income. Others sell caps and/or floors to smooth out the cash flows on other fixed income instruments, such as certain derivative mortgage products. In other cases, sellers only implicitly sell the caps or floors. The following example illustrates both kinds of sellers.

When the cap market was developing, it quickly became obvious that there were many natural buyers of caps, but few natural sellers of caps. One successful effort to create sellers of caps occurred when investment bankers, who had many potential buyers of caps, realized that caps could be created as a derivative of the floating-rate note (FRN) market. Issuers of FRNs routinely issue notes reset off LIBOR. Furthermore, there were known buyers of *capped* FRNs; but of course, capped FRNs must have a higher coupon than uncapped FRNs to compensate the FRN buyer for the cap risk. If an issuer sells capped floating-rate notes, the issuer, in effect, buys a cap on LIBOR from the buyer of the FRN. This cap can then be sold to the investment banker, who in turn sells it to his cap-buying clients. The deals that took place took exactly this form. The investment bankers underwrote capped FRNs for certain FRN issuers who agreed to make cap-like payments to their investment banker. The banker then sold caps to another client but did not incur any market risks, because the two sets of potential payments offset one another. Using part of the proceeds of the sale of the cap, the investment bank agreed to make payments to the issuer to bring the cost of the floating-rate debt down to a level below that of uncapped floating-rate notes. Thus the investment bankers, the issuers of the FRNs, the buyers of the FRNs, and the ultimate cap-buying clients all walked away with a satisfactory transaction.

Such a transaction illustrates how creative financing can be used to create a seller of an instrument when no obvious seller exists. In this example, the issuers of the FRNs are willing to sell caps, given the fact that they, in turn, find someone willing to sell the caps to them. The ultimate seller of caps is the buyer of the capped FRNs. The buyers of the FRNs are, however, only "implicit" sellers of caps in the sense that they never explicitly have a position in caps on their books.

This example, which is just one of dozens, shows how market makers explicitly and implicitly induce end-users of financial products to buy or sell the instruments that allow the market makers to cover their positions in the OTC market. This is not to say that the market makers are taking advantage of the other parties to their trades. As is often the case, all parties to a transaction can come out ahead.

*Forward Rate Agreements (FRAs).* The FRA market represents the over-the-counter equivalent of the exchange-traded futures contracts on short-term rates. FRAs are a natural outgrowth of the interbank market for short-term funds. However, unlike the interbank market, virtually any creditworthy entity can buy or sell FRAs.

The liquid and easily accessible sector of the FRA market is for 3- and 6-month LIBOR. Rates are widely quoted for settlement starting one month forward, and settling once every month thereafter out to about six months forward. Thus, for example, on any given day forward rates are available for both 3- and 6-month LIBOR one month forward, covering, respectively, the interest period starting in one month and ending in four months, and the interest period starting in one month and ending in seven months. These contracts are referred to as 1×4 and 1×7 contracts. On the same day there will be FRAs on 3- and 6-month LIBOR for settlement two months forward. These are the 2×5 and 2×8 contracts. Similarly, settlements occur three months, four months, five months, and six months forward for both 3- and 6-month LIBOR. These contracts are also denoted by the beginning and end of the interest period that they cover.

On each subsequent day, contracts with the same type of structures are offered again, that is, contracts with one month, two months, and so on, to settlement date. Thus, although on any given day a relatively limited number of structures are widely quoted, new contracts with new settlement dates are offered at the beginning of each day. This is quite different from the futures market, where the same contracts with the same delivery dates trade day after day.

Like other OTC debt instruments, there are market makers and brokers who make the market work. However, unlike the other OTC derivative instruments, in the FRA market the commercial banks are clearly the dominant force among the market makers. This dominance is due to the ability of the banks to blend their FRA transactions into their interbank transactions and overall funding operations. Consequently, many banks are willing to quote on a much wider variety of structures than the standard structures explained above. One can choose maturities other than 3- and 6-month LIBOR, and one can choose many settlement dates other than at an even number of months in the future.

In most cases, FRAs are written so that no money changes hands until the settlement date. To determine the cash flows on the settlement date, LIBOR taken from some predetermined source is compared to the LIBOR rate specified in the FRA contract. The actual dollar amount that changes hands is the dollar value of the difference between the two rates, *present valued* for a period equal to the maturity of the underlying LIBOR, either 3 or 6 months. The rational behind present valuing is that if an FRA is used to hedge the rate on a deposit (or other short-term instrument), the loss (gain) due to a change in interest rates will be paid (saved) at the maturity of the deposit, not at the issue date. Thus, because cash payments on the FRA are made on the settlement date (which presumably is the same as the issue date of the deposit) the present value of the interest expense (or saving) on the deposit will equal the amount of money actually received or paid on the FRA.

Finally, one peculiarity of the FRA market deserves note. If one *buys* an FRA one profits from an *increase* in rates, and if one *sells* an FRA one profits from a *decline* in rates.

## PRICING AND ARBITRAGE IN THE INTEREST-RATE FUTURES MARKET

One of the primary concerns that most traders and investors have when taking a position in futures contracts is whether the futures price at which they transact will be a "fair" price. Buyers are concerned that the price may be too high and that they will be picked off by more experienced futures traders waiting to profit from the mistakes of the uninitiated. Sellers worry that the price is artificially low and that savvy traders may have manipulated the markets so that they can buy at bargain-basement prices. Furthermore, prospective participants frequently find no rational explanation for the sometimes violent ups and downs that occur in the futures markets. Theories about efficient markets give little comfort to anyone who knows of or has experienced the sudden losses that can occur in the highly leveraged futures markets.

Fortunately, the futures markets are not as irrational as they may at first seem; if they were, they would not have become so successful. The interest-rate futures markets are not perfectly efficient markets, but they probably come about as close as any market. Furthermore, there are both very clear reasons why futures prices are what they are and there are methods by which traders, investors, and borrowers can and will quickly eliminate any discrepancy between futures prices and their fair levels.

There are several different ways to price futures contracts. Fortunately, all lead to the same fair price for a given contract. Each approach relies on the "Law of One Price". This law states that a given financial asset (or liability) must have the same price regardless of the means by which one goes about creating that asset (or liability). In this section we will demonstrate one way in which futures contracts can be combined with cash market instruments to create cash flows that are identical to other cash securities.[4] The Law of One Price implies that the synthetically created cash securities must have the same price as the actual cash securities. Similarly, cash instruments can be combined to create cash flows that are identical to futures contracts. By the Law of One Price the futures contract must have the same price as the synthetic futures created from cash instruments.

## Pricing of Futures Contracts

To understand how futures contracts should be priced, consider the following example. Suppose that a 20-year, 100 par value bond with a coupon rate of 12 percent is selling at par. Also suppose that this bond is the deliverable for a futures contract that settles in three months. If the current 3-month interest rate at which funds can be loaned or borrowed is 8 percent per year, what should be the price of this futures contract?

Suppose the price of the futures contract is 107. Consider the following strategy:

Sell the futures contract at 107.

Purchase the bond for 100.

Borrow 100 for three months at 8 percent per year.

---

[4] For the other ways to price futures contracts, see Chapter 5 in Mark Pitts and Frank J. Fabozzi, *Interest Rate Futures and Options* (Chicago: Probus Publishing, 1990).

The borrowed funds are used to purchase the bond, resulting in no initial cash outlay for this strategy. Three months from now, the bond must be delivered to settle the futures contract and the loan must be repaid. These trades will produce the following cash flows:

*From settlement of the futures contract*:

| | | |
|---|---|---|
| Flat price of bond | = | 107 |
| Accrued interest (12% for 3 months) | = | 3 |
| Total proceeds | = | 110 |

*From the loan*:

| | | |
|---|---|---|
| Repayment of principal of loan | = | 100 |
| Interest on loan (8% for 3 months) | = | 2 |
| Total outlay | = | 102 |
| Profit | = | 8 |

This strategy will guarantee a profit of 8. Moreover, the profit is generated with no initial outlay because the funds used to purchase the bond are borrowed. The profit will be realized *regardless of the futures price at the settlement date*. Obviously, in a well-functioning market, arbitrageurs would buy the bond and sell the futures, forcing the futures price down and bidding up the bond price so as to eliminate this profit.

In contrast, suppose that the futures price is 92 instead of 107. Consider the following strategy:

Buy the futures contract at 92.

Sell (short) the bond for 100.

Invest (lend) 100 for 3 months at 8 percent per year.

Once again, there is no initial cash outlay. Three months from now a bond will be purchased to settle the long position in the futures contract. That bond will then be used to cover the short position (i.e., to cover the short sale in the cash market). The outcome in three months would be as follows:

*From settlement of the futures contract*:

| | | |
|---|---|---|
| Flat price of bond | = | 92 |
| Accrued interest (12% for 3 months) | = | 3 |
| Total outlay | = | 95 |

*From the loan*:

| | | |
|---|---|---|
| Principal received from maturing investment | = | 100 |
| Interest earned from the 3-month investment (8% for 3 months) | = | 2 |
| Total outlay | = | 102 |
| Profit | = | 7 |

The 7 profit is a pure arbitrage profit. It requires no initial cash outlay and will be realized regardless of the futures price at the settlement date.

There is a futures price that will eliminate the arbitrage profit, however. There will be no arbitrage if the futures price is 99. Let's look at what would happen if the two previous strategies were followed and the futures price were 99. First, consider the following strategy:

Sell the futures contract at 99.

Purchase the bond for 100.

Borrow 100 for 3 months at 8 percent per year.

In three months the outcome would be as follows:

*From settlement of the futures contract*:

| | | |
|---|---|---|
| Flat price of bond | = | 99 |
| Accrued interest (12% for 3 months) | = | 3 |
| Total proceeds | = | 102 |
| Repayment of principal of loan | = | 100 |
| Interest on loan (8% for 3 months) | = | 2 |
| Total outlay | = | 102 |
| Profit | = | 0 |

There is no arbitrage profit.

Next consider the following strategy:

Buy the futures contract at 99.

Sell (short) the bond for 100.

Invest (lend) 100 for 3 months at 8 percent per year.

The outcome in three months would be as follows:

*From settlement of the futures contract:*

| | | |
|---|---|---|
| Flat price of bond | = | 99 |
| Accrued interest (12% for 3 months) | = | 3 |
| Total outlay | = | 102 |

*From the loan:*

| | | |
|---|---|---|
| Principal received from maturing investment | = | 100 |
| Interest earned from the 3-month investment (8% for 3 months) | = | 2 |
| Total proceeds | = | 102 |
| Profit | = | 0 |

Thus neither strategy results in a profit. Hence the futures price of 99 is the equilibrium price, because any higher or lower futures price will permit arbitrage profits.

### Theoretical Futures Price Based on Arbitrage Model

Considering the arbitrage arguments just presented, the equilibrium futures price can be determined on the basis of the following information:

1. The price of the bond in the cash market.
2. The coupon rate on the bond. In our example, the coupon rate was 12% per annum.
3. The interest rate for borrowing and lending until the settlement date. The borrowing and lending rate is referred to as the *financing rate*. In our example, the financing rate was 8 percent per annum.

We will let

$r$ = financing rate (%)
$c$ = current yield, or coupon rate divided by the cash market price
$P$ = cash market price
$F$ = futures price
$t$ = time, in years, to the futures delivery date

and then consider the following strategy that is initiated on a coupon date:

Sell the futures contract at $F$.

Purchase the bond for $P$.

Borrow $P$ until the settlement date at $r$.

The outcome at the settlement date is

*From settlement of the futures contract*:

| Flat price of bond | $=$ | $F$ |
|---|---|---|
| Accrued interest | $=$ | $ctP$ |
| Total proceeds | $=$ | $F + ctP$ |

*From the loan*:

| Repayment of principal of loan | $=$ | $P$ |
|---|---|---|
| Interest on loan | $=$ | $rtP$ |
| Total outlay | $=$ | $P + rtP$ |

The profit will equal:

$$\text{Profit} = \text{Total proceeds} - \text{Total outlay}$$
$$\text{Profit} = F + ctP - (P + rtP)$$

In equilibrium the theoretical futures price occurs where the profit from this trade is zero. Thus, to have equilibrium, the following must hold:

$$0 = F + ctP - (P + rtP)$$

Solving for the theoretical futures price, we have

$$F = P + Pt(r - c) = P(1 + t(r - c)) \qquad (32\text{–}1)$$

Alternatively, consider the following strategy:

Buy the futures contract at $F$.

Sell (short) the bond for $P$.

Invest (lend) $P$ at $r$ until the settlement date.

The outcome at the settlement date would be

*From settlement of the futures contract*:

| Flat price of bond | $=$ | $F$ |
|---|---|---|
| Accrued interest | $=$ | $ctP$ |
| Total outlay | $=$ | $F + ctP$ |

*From the loan*:

| | | |
|---|---|---|
| Proceeds received from maturing of investment | = | $P$ |
| Interest earned | = | $rtP$ |
| Total proceeds | = | $P + rtP$ |

The profit will equal

$$\text{Profit} = \text{Total proceeds} - \text{Total outlay}$$
$$\text{Profit} = P + rtP - (F + ctP)$$

Setting the profit equal to zero so that there will be no arbitrage profit and solving for the futures price, we obtain the same equation for the futures price as equation (32–1).

Let's apply equation (32–1) to our previous example in which

$$r = .08$$
$$c = .12$$
$$P = 100$$
$$t = .25$$

Then the theoretical futures prices is

$$F = 100 + 100 \times .25(.08 - .12)$$
$$= 100 - 1 = 99$$

This agrees with the equilibrium futures price we derived earlier.

The theoretical futures price may be at a premium to the cash market price (higher than the cash market price) or at a discount from the cash market price (lower than the cash market price), depending on $(r - c)$. The term $r - c$ is called the *net financing cost* because it adjusts the financing rate for the coupon interest earned. The net financing cost is more commonly called the *cost of carry*, or simply *carry*. *Positive carry* means that the current yield earned is greater than the financing cost; *negative carry* means that the financing cost exceeds the current yield. The relationships can be expressed as follows:

| Carry | Futures Price |
|---|---|
| Positive $(c > r)$ | Will sell at a discount to the cash price $(F < P)$ |
| Negative $(c < r)$ | Will sell at a premium to the cash price $(F > P)$ |
| Zero $(r = c)$ | Will be equal to the cash price $(F = P)$ |

In the case of interest-rate futures, carry (the relationship between the short-term financing rate and the current yield on the bond) depends on the shape of the yield curve. When the yield curve is upward sloping, the short-term financing rate will generally be less than the current yield on the bond, resulting in positive carry. The futures price will then sell at a discount to the cash price for the bond. The opposite will hold true when the yield curve is inverted.

### A Closer Look at the Theoretical Futures Price
To derive the theoretical futures price using the arbitrage argument, we made several assumptions. We will now discuss the implications of these assumptions.

*Interim Cash Flows.*    No interim cash flows due to variation margin or coupon interest payments were assumed in the model. However, we know that interim cash flows can occur for both of these reasons. Because we assumed no variation margin, the price derived is technically the theoretical price for a forward contract (which are not marked to market at the end of each trading day). If interest rates rise, the short position in futures will receive margin as the futures price decreases; the margin can then be reinvested at a higher interest rate. In contrast, if interest rates fall, there will be variation margin that must be financed by the short position; however, because interest rates have declined, the financing can be done at a lower cost. Thus, whichever ways rates move, those who are short futures gain relative to those who are short forwards. Conversely, those who are long futures lose relative to those who are long forwards. These facts account for the difference between futures and forward prices.

Incorporating interim coupon payments into the pricing model is not difficult. However, the value of the coupon payments at the settlement date will depend on the interest rate at which they can be reinvested. The shorter the maturity of the futures contract and the lower the coupon rate, the less important the reinvestment income is in determining the futures price.

*The Short-Term Interest Rate (Financing Rate).*    In deriving the theoretical futures price it is assumed that the borrowing and lending rates are equal. Typically, however, the borrowing rate is greater than the lending rate.

We will let

$$r_B = \text{borrowing rate}$$
$$r_L = \text{lending rate}$$

Consider the following strategy:
Sell the futures contract at $F$.
Purchase the bond for $P$.
Borrow $P$ until the settlement date at $r_B$. The futures prices that would produce no arbitrage profit is

$$F = P + P(r_B - c) \qquad (32\text{--}2)$$

Now consider the following strategy:

Buy the futures contract at $F$.

Sell (short) the bond for $P$.

Invest (lend) $P$ at $r_L$ until the settlement date.

The futures price that would produce no profit is

$$F = P + P(r_L - c) \qquad (32\text{--}3)$$

Equations (32–2) and (32–3) together provide boundaries for the futures price equilibrium. Equation (32–2) provides the upper boundary and equation (32–3) the lower boundary. For example, assume that the borrowing rate is 8 percent per year, or 2 percent for three months, while the lending rate is 6 percent per year, or 1.5 percent for three months. Then, using equation (32–2) and the previous example, the upper boundary is

$$
\begin{aligned}
F(\text{upper boundary}) &= \$100 + \$100(.02 - .03) \\
&= \$99
\end{aligned}
$$

The lower boundary using equation (32–3) is

$$
\begin{aligned}
F(\text{lower boundary}) &= \$100 + \$100(.015 - .03) \\
&= \$98.50
\end{aligned}
$$

In calculating these boundaries, we assumed no transaction costs were involved in taking the position. In actuality, the transactions costs of entering into and closing the cash position as well as the round-trip transaction costs for the futures contract must be considered and do affect the boundaries for the futures contract.

***Deliverable Bond and Settlement Date Unknown.*** In our example we assumed that (1) only one bond is deliverable and (2) the settlement date occurs three months from now. As explained earlier in this chapter, futures contracts on Treasury bonds and Treasury notes are designed to allow the short position the choice of delivering one of a number of deliverable issues. Also, the delivery date is not known.

Because there may be more than one deliverable, market participants track the price of each deliverable bond and determine which is the cheapest to deliver, The futures price will then trade in relation to the bond that is cheapest to deliver. As we explained earlier in this chapter, the cheapest to deliver is the bond or note that will result in the smallest loss or the greatest gain if delivered by the short futures position.[5]

---

[5] An alternative procedure is to compute the implied (break-even) repo rate. This rate is the yield that would produce no profit or loss if the bond were purchased and a futures contract were sold against the bond. The cheapest-to-deliver bond is the one with the highest implied repo rate.

There are several reasons, in addition to the ones we have already discussed, why the actual futures price will diverge from the theoretical futures price based on the arbitrage model. First, there is the risk that while an issue may be the cheapest to deliver at the time a position in the futures contract is taken, it may not be the cheapest to deliver after that time. For example, 31 Treasury bond issues were deliverable against the June 1985 bond futures contract. For most of 1985 the 7 5/8s Treasury maturing on February 15, 2007 was cheapest to deliver. On January 23, 1985, however, the 10 3/8 Treasury maturing on November 15, 2012 was the cheapest to deliver. A change in the cheapest to deliver can dramatically alter the futures price.[6] Because of this, there will be a divergence between the theoretical futures price and the actual futures price. A second reason for this divergence is the other delivery options granted the short position. Finally, there are biases in the CBOT conversion factors.[7]

***Deliverable Is a Basket of Securites.*** The municipal index futures contract is a cash settlement contract based on a basket of securites. The difficulty in arbitraging this futures contracts is that it is too expensive to buy or sell every bond included in the index. Instead, a portfolio containing a smaller number of bonds may be constructed to track the index. The arbitrage, however, is no longer risk-free, because there is the risk that the portfolio will not track the index exactly. This is referred as *tracking error risk*. Another problem in constructing the portfolio so that the arbitrage can be performed is that the composition of the index is revised periodically. Therefore, anyone using this arbitrage trade must constantly monitor the index and periodically rebalance the constructed portfolio.

## APPLICATIONS TO PORTFOLIO MANAGEMENT

This section describes various ways in which a money manager can use interest-rate futures contracts.

---

[6] See Marcelle Arak, Laurie S. Goodman, and Susan Ross, "The Cheapest to Deliver on the Treasury Bond Futures Contract," *Advances in Futures and Options Research,* vol. 1, part B, (1986), pp. 49–74.

[7] For a further discussion, see Arak, Goodman, and Ross, "The Cheapest to Deliver on the Treasury Bond Futures Contract"; James F. Meisner and John W. Labuszewski, "Treasury Bond Futures Delivery Bias," *Journal of Futures Market,* winter 1984, pp. 569–572; and Laura F. Kodres, "Biases Toward the Cheapest to Deliver Bond," unpublished working paper, Northwestern University, 1984.

## Changing the Duration of the Portfolio

Money managers who have strong expectations about the direction of interest rates will adjust the duration of their portfolio to capitalize on their expectations. Specifically, if they expect interest rates to increase, they will shorten the duration of the portfolio; if they expect interest rates to decrease, they will lengthen the duration of the portfolio. Also, anyone using structured portfolio strategies must periodically adjust the portfolio duration to match the duration of some benchmark.

Although money managers can alter the duration of their portfolios with cash market instruments, a quick and less expensive means for doing so (especially on a temporary basis) is to use futures contracts. By buying futures contracts on Treasury bonds or notes, they can increase the duration of the portfolio. Conversely, they can shorten the duration of the portfolio by selling futures contracts on Treasury bonds or notes.

## Asset Allocation

A pension sponsor may wish to alter the composition of the pension fund's assets between stocks and bonds. An efficient means of changing asset allocation is to use financial futures contracts—interest-rate futures and stock index futures. This strategy is explained in Chapter 50.

## Creating Synthetic Securities for Yield Enhancement

A cash market security can be synthetically created by using a position in the futures contract together with the deliverable instrument. The yield on the synthetic security should be the same as the yield on the cash market security. If there is a difference between the two yields, it can be exploited so as to enhance the yield on the portfolio.

To see how, consider an investor who owns a 20-year Treasury bond and sells Treasury futures that call for the delivery of that particular bond three months from now. While the maturity of the Treasury bond is 20 years, the investor has effectively shortened the maturity of the bond to three months.

Consequently, the long position in the 20-year bond and the short futures position are equivalent to a long position in a 3-month riskless security. The position is riskless because the investor is locking in the price that he or she will receive three months from now—the futures price. By being long the bond and short the futures, the investor has synthetically created a 3-month Treasury bill. The return the investor should expect to earn from this synthetic position should be the yield on a 3-month Treasury bill. If the yield on the synthetic 3-month Treasury bill is greater than the yield on the cash market Treasury bill, the investor can realize an enhanced yield by creating the synthetic short-term security. The fundamental relationship for creating synthetic securities is as follows:

$$RSP = CBP - FBP \qquad (32\text{–}4)$$

where

$CBP$ = cash bond position
$FBP$ = bond futures position
$RSP$ = riskless short-term security position

A negative sign before a position means a short position. In terms of our previous example, $CBP$ is the long cash bond position, the negative sign before $FBP$ refers to the short futures position, and $RSP$ is the riskless synthetic 3-month security or Treasury bill.

Equation (32–4) states that an investor who is long the cash market security and short the futures contract should expect to earn the rate of return on a risk-free security with the same maturity as the futures delivery date. Solving equation (32–4) for the long bond position, we have

$$CBP = RSP + FBP \qquad (32\text{–}5)$$

Equation (32–5) states that a cash bond position equals a short-term riskless security position plus a long bond futures position. Thus, a cash market bond can be synthetically created by buying a futures contract and investing in a Treasury bill.

Solving equation (32–5) for the bond futures position, we have

$$FBP = CBP - RSP \qquad (32\text{–}6)$$

Equation (32–6) tells us that a long position in the futures contract can be synthetically created by taking a long position in the cash market bond and shorting the short-term riskless security. But shorting the short-term riskless security is equivalent to borrowing money. Notice that it was equation (32–6), that we used in deriving the theoretical futures price when the futures was underpriced. Recall that when the futures price was 107, the strategy to obtain an arbitrage profit was to sell the futures contract and create a synthetic long futures position by buying the bond with borrowed funds. This is precisely what equation (32–6) states. In this case, instead of creating a synthetic cash market instrument as we did with equations (32–4) and (32–5), we have created a synthetic futures contract. The fact that the synthetic long futures position was cheaper than the actual long futures position provided an arbitrage opportunity.

If we reverse the sign of both sides of equations (32–4), (32–5), and (32–6), we can see how a short futures position can be synthetically created.

In an efficient market the opportunities for yield enhancement should not exist very long. But even in the absence of yield enhancement, synthetic securities can be used by money managers to hedge a portfolio position that they find difficult to hedge in the cash market either because of lack of liquidity or because of other constraints.[8]

## Hedging

Hedging [9] with futures involves taking a futures position as a temporary substitute for transactions to be made in the cash market at a later date. If cash and futures prices move together, any loss realized by the hedger from one position (whether cash or futures) will be offset by a profit on the other position. When the net profit or loss from the positions are exactly as anticipated, the hedge is referred to as a *perfect* hedge.

In practice, hedging is not that simple. The amount of net profit will not necessarily be as anticipated. The outcome of a hedge will depend on the relationship between the cash price and the futures price when a hedge is placed and when it is lifted. The difference between the cash price and the futures price is called the *basis*. The risk that the basis will change in an unpredictable way is called *basis risk*.

In most hedging applications the bond to be hedged is not identical to the bond underlying the futures contract. This kind of hedging is referred to as *cross hedging*. There may be substantial basis risk in cross hedging. An unhedged position is exposed to price risk, the risk that the cash market price will move adversely. A hedged position substitutes basis risk for price risk.

A short (or sell) hedge is used to protect against a decline in the cash price of a fixed income security. To execute a short hedge, futures contracts are sold. By establishing a short hedge, the hedger has fixed the future cash price and transferred the price risk of ownership to the buyer of the futures contract. As an example of why a short hedge would be executed, suppose that a pension fund manager knows that bonds must be liquidated in 40 days to make a $5 million payment to the beneficiaries of the pension fund. If interest rates rise during the 40-day period, more bonds will have to be liquidated to realize $5 million. To guard against this possibility, the manager would sell bonds in the futures market to lock in a selling price.

A long (or buy) hedge is undertaken to protect against an increase in the cash price of a fixed income security. In a long hedge the hedger buys a futures

---

[8] For a more detailed discussion of synthetic securities, see Robert W. Kopprasch, Cal Johnson, and Armand H. Tatevossian, "Strategies for the Asset Manager: Hedging and the Creation of Synthetic Assets," in Frank J. Fabozzi and T. Dessa Garlicki (eds.),*Advanced in Bond Analysis and Portfolio Strategies* (Chicago, IL: Probus Publishing, 1987), and Robert P. Lecky, "Synthetic Asset Strategies," in Frank J. Fabozzi (ed) *Fixed Income Portfolio Strategies* (Chicago, IL: Probus Publishing, 1989).

[9] Hedging is discussed in more detail in Chapter 49.

contract to lock in a purchase price. A pension fund manager may use a long hedge when substantial cash contributions are expected and the manager is concerned that interest rates will fall. Also, a money manager who knows that bonds are maturing in the near future and expects that interest rates will fall can employ a long hedge to lock in a rate.

## Conclusion

In this chapter we have examined several of the most important and representative exchange-traded and OTC interest-rate futures and options contracts. We have also explored cash and futures arbitrage and equilibrium futures pricing. We've concluded with some of the most important uses of interest-rate futures contracts.

# CHAPTER 33

## OVERVIEW OF EXCHANGE-TRADED OPTIONS ON FIXED INCOME SECURITIES AND OPTION STRATEGIES

*Robert W. Kopprasch, Ph.D., CFA\**
*Managing Director*
*Hyperion Capital Management Inc.*

*Victor J. Haghani*
*Interest Rate Arbitrage Group*
*Salomon Brothers Inc*

Since the first options contract on Treasury bond futures was traded at the Chicago Board of Trade (CBOT) in October 1982, exchange-traded options on fixed income securities have come into wide use as a means of managing risk and expressing market views. The burgeoning trading volume and broadening variety of securities covered by options has made exchange-traded options on fixed income securities important instruments in their own right. Trading volume and month-end open interest has expanded rapidly. This growth in exchange-traded options volume comes in the wake of the success of other exchange-traded fixed income instruments such as Treasury bond futures (CBOT) and Eurodollar time deposit futures (CME).[1]

In addition to the increased liquidity of exchange-traded options, the variety of fixed income securities covered by options contracts has increased. Options on Treasury bonds, notes, and bills, as well as options on Treasury bond futures,

---

\* This chapter was written when Dr. Kopprasch was vice president at Salomon Brothers Inc.
[1] See Chapter 32 for a description of these contracts.

Treasury note futures, and Eurodollar time deposit rate futures, are traded on various exchanges.[2] Many patterns of risk and return are made possible by the existence of options at different strike prices and with a range of expiration dates for each underlying security.

The purpose of this chapter is to present a general overview of exchange-traded options, with attention paid to the basics of the option contract and some of the strategies that are possible. Detailed treatment of the valuation of fixed income contracts is not covered in this chapter. Chapter 34 is devoted to this important topic. Hedging with options is illustrated in Chapter 49.

## BASICS OF THE OPTION CONTRACT

There are two basic types or classes of options—puts and calls. A *call* option is the right (but not the obligation) to *buy* a particular security at a specified price (known as the strike price) and usually may be exercised any time until its expiration date. A *put* option is the right (but not the obligation) to *sell* a particular security at a specified price (known as the strike price) and also can normally be exercised until its expiration date. It is important to emphasize the optional nature of these contracts—the holder has the option to exercise the contract if it is in his or her best interest to do so. If not, the holder will let the option expire and will lose only the premium. On the other hand, the creator or writer of an option contract has an obligation to sell (in the case of a call) or buy (in the case of a put) the securities covered by the contract if the holder exercises the option.

The following are the five basic elements of any options contract:

- *The underlying security*—the security that may be purchased (in the case of a call) or sold (in the case of a put) by the option holder until the expiration date. Some option contracts require delivery of actual cash instruments, for instance the $9\frac{7}{8}$ percent coupon Treasury bond maturing 11/15/2015. These options are called options on actuals. Where the underlying security is a futures contract (for example, the options on Treasury bond futures), the option is known as an option on futures.
- *The strike price*—the price governing the transaction that takes place when an option is exercised.
- *The expiration date*—most exchange-traded options are American options and can be exercised up to and including the expiration date, after which they expire and become worthless. European options can only be exercised on the expiration date of the option, and not before.
- *The premium*—the price paid for the option.

---

[2] See Chapter 32 for a description of options on futures contract currently traded.

- *The size of the contract*—the amount (usually in par amount) that is covered by one contract.

## The Role of the Clearing Corporation

When a trade takes place on an options exchange, the details of the transaction (e.g., number of contracts, price) are agreed to by the actual trading parties or their agents. However, after the trade clears, the clearing corporation assumes the obligation to perform under the contract. At the same time, however, the investor who is short in the contract has an obligation to the clearing corporation. Thus, the clearing corporation stands between the two investors, and its guarantee of performance relieves the option buyer of the necessity of checking the credit of the individual seller of the contract. This is similar to the mechanism used in the futures markets and was patterned after the futures market system at the time that exchange-traded options on equities were first developed.

The standardized contract, when combined with the clearing corporation system, allows some interesting and useful investment features. First, because all trading must take place through the clearing corporation, trading can be (and is) accomplished without a certificate. The clearing corporation, through its members, maintains records of who is short and who is long, and no certificate is needed to verify this.

Second, when the clearing corporation mechanism is combined with the standardized contracts available on the options exchanges, it also creates the possibility of reversing one's position and negating the responsibility assumed when an options contract was created or sold short. Thus, if an investor wants to offset his position, he merely engages in the opposite transaction for the same option contract. When an investor becomes both short and long in a particular option contract (e.g., an "opening sale" is followed by a "closing purchase"), his position is effectively and contractually eliminated. This mechanism allows sellers to enter into option obligations without the fear of becoming locked into the position if the market moves adversely or if their market projections change. Similarly, option holders need not exercise their options, but can sell them in the secondary market and realize any price and tax benefits that may have accrued to their favor.

## The Intrinsic Value

An option contract's premium can be thought of as having two elements; the intrinsic value (which may be zero) and the time premium. The intrinsic value is merely the immediate exercise value of the option. For example, if a call option has a strike price of 80 and the security is currently selling for 84, the option has an intrinsic value of 4. The time premium is the difference between the option premium and intrinsic value, and its calculation is obvious. If the option described above were selling for 6, the time premium would be 2.

Determining what an option is "worth," rather than its market price, is more difficult. This estimate of true value will be considered again in the option valuation section in this chapter.[3] First we will concentrate on the intrinsic value of an option as if the option were held to expiration, because at expiration the time value is zero. At expiration, the actual price will closely approximate intrinsic value because of the arbitrages that would otherwise be possible if these values differed significantly.

## PUTS AND CALLS ON FIXED INCOME SECURITIES

### The Call Option

In order to illustrate the return patterns associated with a call option, the following example of an option on an actual cash security will be utilized. The analysis of an option on an interest-rate futures contract is largely analogous to the present example and will be discussed later in the chapter.

1. Underlying security—8 percent, 30-year bond.
2. Strike price—100.
3. Expiration date—December 19xx.

In option parlance, this option would be known as a December 100. The intrinsic value pattern of this option is shown in Exhibit 33–1. At all prices below 100, the option's intrinsic value is zero because the security can be purchased in the market for less than it can be purchased via exercising the option. At all prices above 100, the option's intrinsic value is simply the difference between the market price and the strike price of 100.

Remembering that the intrinsic value is the value that should prevail at or near an option's expiration date, we can also construct a profit chart for an investor if we know the price paid for the option. If an investor paid five points for this option, the resulting profit pattern would be as shown in Exhibit 33–2.

Several elements in Exhibit 33–2 are important. First, note that the maximum loss to the call option buyer is the premium; no matter how low the ultimate price of the bond, the buyer's loss is limited to five points. Second, the premium paid for the call option also determines the break-even price shown in Exhibit 33–2. At all prices above the break-even price, the investor shows a profit. This profit is equal to the intrinsic value at expiration less the premium paid for the option. (For ease of presentation, the foregone interest on the capital used to pay the premium is not included in the exhibits. The role of the short-term rate will be discussed later.)

In order to place these charts and concepts into a framework more familiar

---

[3] For more detail, see Chapter 34.

**EXHIBIT 33–1**
**The Intrinsic Value Pattern of a Call**

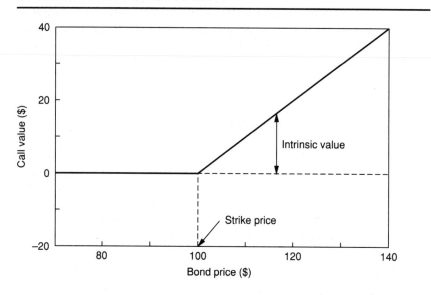

**EXHIBIT 33–2**
**The Intrinsic Value and Profit Patterns of a Call**

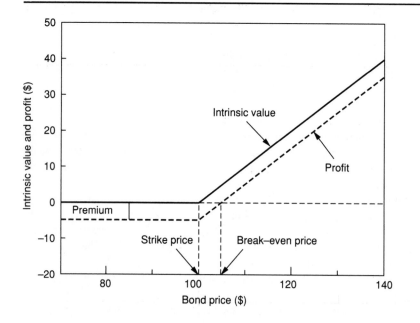

to the fixed income investor, they will be restated with yield instead of price as the horizontal axis. In Exhibit 33–3, we see the price-yield curve for the deliverable bond, which relates the price on the deliverable bond to its yield-to-maturity. (The values for this graph are determined with the option expiration date used as the settlement date.) With Exhibit 33–3 as a backdrop, it is easy to construct the intrinsic value of a call as a function of yield as is shown in Exhibit 33–4. The pattern shown illustrates a reversal of the pattern in Exhibit 33–2 because of the inverse relationship between yield and prices. The slight curvature shown in the intrinsic value line follows that of the price-yield curve shown in Exhibit 33–3. When the option is viewed in this way, we can translate the strike price into a strike yield as shown.

The profit pattern in Exhibit 33–2 is translated into a yield framework in Exhibit 33–5, illustrating the profit pattern of a call option versus the yield of the deliverable instrument at expiration. The break-even price in Exhibit 33–2 translates to a break-even yield in Exhibit 33–5. It can be seen that the break-even yield is a function of two factors: the premium, which determines how much outflow must be recovered, and the slope of the price-yield curve, which determines how much yield movement is necessary to recover that premium. The slope of the price yield curve is a function of the coupon, yield, maturity, and frequency of coupon payment.

*The Call Writer.* Let us now consider the other side of the call option transaction, that is, the seller or creator of the call. If the call writer has no

**EXHIBIT 33–3**
**Price-Yield Curve for 8 Percent, 30-Year Bond**

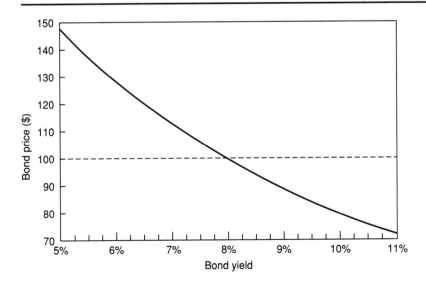

**EXHIBIT 33–4**
**Intrinsic Value of a Call versus Yield at Expiration**

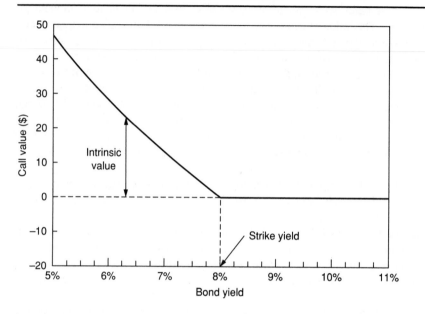

**EXHIBIT 33–5**
**Profit Pattern of a Call versus Yield at Expiration**

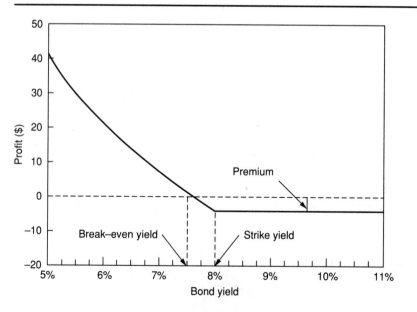

other position in the market, the resulting profit pattern is like that shown in Exhibit 33–6. We can see that if the yield at expiration is above the strike yield (which of course means that the price is below the strike price), the option holder will allow the option to expire and the call writer will have earned the premium. If, on the other hand, the yield at expiration is below the strike yield, the option will be exercised and the call writer will be forced to purchase the security in the marketplace at its now higher price and deliver it at the lower strike price. This will cause a loss of at least some of the premium and perhaps more than the premium. If the yield at expiration is below the break-even yield, the call writer will show an absolute loss.

The reader will note that Exhibit 33–6 is merely Exhibit 33–5 rotated around the horizontal zero line. This is not surprising, because the call buyer and the call writer are on the opposite sides of the transaction, and whoever "wins" does so at the expense of the other. (Except for transaction costs, option trading is a "zero sum" game.)

It is easy to see that the call writer who has no other position in the market is neutral to bearish, because only if yields remain approximately constant or move upward will the call writer show a profit. If yields decline below the strike yield, some of the premium will be eroded with absolute loss resulting. The call buyer shown in Exhibit 33–5, on the other hand, is obviously bullish because the buyer's profit comes when yields decline and prices rise.

An alternative approach for the call seller or call writer is to own the security

**EXHIBIT 33–6**
**The Call Writer's Profit Pattern ("Naked")**

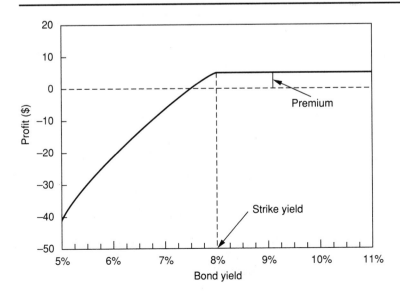

underlying the option when the option is sold. In this case, if yields decline and prices rise, the call seller will not suffer an economic loss in delivering the security to the call holder because he or she will already own it. (Of course, an opportunity loss occurs.) Only if the security declines in price by an amount sufficient to erode the premium will the call seller (who covers his position with the underlying security) show a real loss. In option terminology, such a call writer is known as a "covered" call writer; the writer who is uncovered is usually referred to as being "naked." Exhibit 33–7 shows that a security owner who is neutral to bearish on the security he or she holds can sell an option on it and thereby generate some protection for downward price moves. This protection, of course, is equal to the premium income received. Such a strategy may be employed when the holder is restricted from selling the security, due to regulatory or accounting rules, for example.

## The Put Option

A put option, as described earlier, is an option to sell a security at a specified price. A put option has value at expiration if the market price of the underlying security is *below* the strike price, allowing the put holder to buy the security in the market and "put" it to the put writer at the higher strike price. The intrinsic value at expiration is thus the difference between the strike price and the market price if the strike is above the market price, and zero otherwise.

**EXHIBIT 33–7**
**The Covered Call Writer's Profit Pattern**

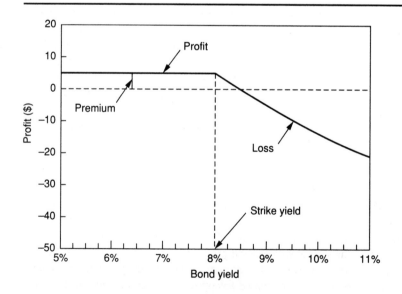

In order to illustrate the intrinsic value and profit patterns of a put, we will utilize a hypothetical put with terms identical to the call example used earlier.

1. *Underlying security*—8 percent, 30-year bond.
2. *Strike price*—100.
3. *Expiration date*—December 19xx.

A chart of the put's intrinsic value, analogous to Exhibit 33–2 for calls, is shown in Exhibit 33–8. Exhibit 33–9 translates this into the yield framework and adds a profit line that assumes that the put cost 5 points. The intrinsic value line is adapted directly from the right side of Exhibit 33–3 in which the price of the security lies below the strike price.

***The Put Writer.*** For every put option outstanding, there must be a seller, and that seller guarantees to buy the securities "put" to him or her if the option is exercised. The put seller therefore buys the security at a price higher than the market price whenever a put option is (rationally) exercised. If the strike price is higher than the market by more than the premium received for the option, the put seller suffers a loss. This is shown in Exhibit 33–10.

The put seller's profit pattern, shown in Exhibit 33–10, exhibits a striking similarity to the covered call writer's profit pattern, shown in Exhibit 33–7. This illustrates that there exist several paths to equivalent profit patterns when using options. (Several others will be described in later sections.) Furthermore, it suggests that put and call prices may be related to one another to prevent dominance of one return pattern over another. This will also be discussed later in the chapter.

***A Note on Options on Money Market Instruments.*** The intrinsic value and profit patterns shown in the preceding sections are based on a *long-term* fixed income security, the price of which is not a linear function of yield. This is the reason for the slight curvature in the patterns. Eurodollar time deposit futures and Treasury bills are quoted on a discount yield basis that relates price and yield in a linear fashion. Thus, the curvature of the figures shown above would disappear if the underlying securities were Eurodollar time deposit futures or Treasury bills (instead of bonds) and if the horizontal axis were shown as quoted discount yield.

## Options Strategies and Tactics

Investors who are familiar with the concepts of the past several sections have undoubtedly considered the "rate anticipation" uses of options. If rates are expected to decline, calls can be purchased and will generate profits if rates fall sufficiently. Similarly, puts will provide profits if purchased prior to a sufficient climb in rates. These approaches to options, as well as hedging (covered later), concentrate on the price movement of the option when profitable, but it is also

**EXHIBIT 33–8**
**The Intrinsic Value of a Put**

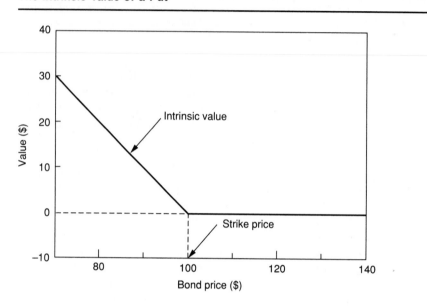

**EXHIBIT 33–9**
**Intrinsic Value and Profit Pattern of a Put versus Yield at Expiration**

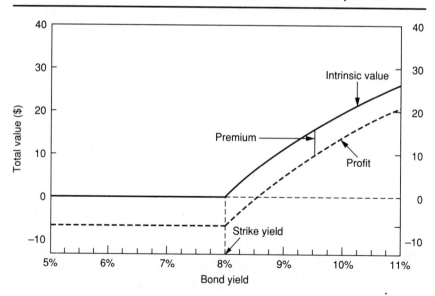

**EXHIBIT 33–10**
**The Put Writer's Profit Pattern ("Naked")**

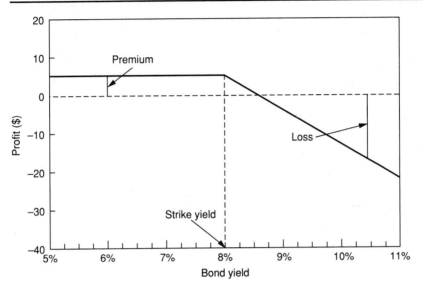

interesting and useful to consider the times when options expire with no intrinsic value. Several such cases are examined in the following sections.

Prior to studying these options strategies, however, a few notes on terminology may be helpful. When an option has a positive intrinsic value, it is said to be *in-the-money*. Thus, when a call is referred to as in-the-money, the implication is that the market price of the underlying security exceeds the strike price (i.e, the left side of Exhibit 33–4). An in-the-money put has a strike price that exceeds the market price of the underlying security. Options are referred to as *at-the-money* when the strike price and the market price of the underlying security are equal or nearly so. An option is *out-of-the-money* when the security must move in a favorable direction (up for calls, down for puts) just to reach the strike price. Thus, the December 100 call is out-of-the-money if the underlying bond is trading at 96, but the December 100 put on the same bond would be in the money. [4]

---

[4] The terminology is consistent with that used in the equity option market. In the debt market, where forward trading is more common, these terms are sometimes modified to reflect this "other market." Thus, we use the terms *at-the-money-spot* in the same way equity participants use *at-the-money*, as well as *in-*, *at-*, and *out-of-the-money-forward* to reflect comparisons of the strike price with the forward price of the underlying security, for settlement on the option exercise or exercise settlement date.

## Viewing Call Options as Alternative Investments[5]

Long-term fixed income investors will discover that call options offer a number of interesting strategies. One of these involves the purchase of calls as an alternative to investment in an equivalent par amount in the long-term sector, with the excess funds being invested in the short-term market. Although we normally think of purchasing calls as being beneficial when prices rise, a somewhat surprising result emerges from an analysis of this strategy.

First, let us consider the cash flows associated with the purchase at par of an 8 percent, 30-year bond (for which one-year put and call options are available). These cash flows consist of the 100 outflow, a semiannual inflow of 4, and a redemption of 100 at maturity (see Exhibit 33–11). To begin our comparative analysis, let us assume that short-term rates approximate 8 percent

**EXHIBIT 33–11**
**Cash Flows of an 8 Percent, 30-Year Bond.**

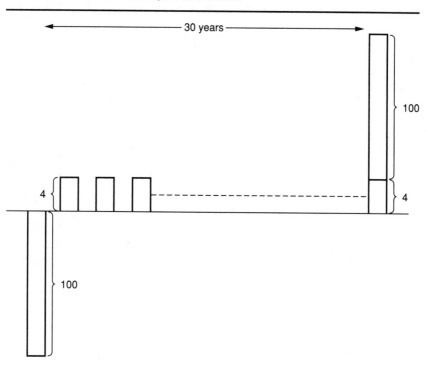

[5] This and the following section are based on a talk given by Martin L. Leibowitz at the Financial Analysts Federation Futures Conference, September 1981.

(i.e., the yield curve is flat) and that a one-year call with a strike price of 100 is available for 5 points.

Let us assume that, instead of buying a bond, the investor buys one call (with a strike of 100) for 5 and invests the remaining 95 in a one-year semiannual coupon instrument. If yields decline and the underlying long-term bond increases in price, the investor would exercise the option and buy the remaining income stream of the bond for 100. The cash flows associated with this approach are shown in Exhibit 33–12. Note that the first-year income stream is lower because only 95 is invested in the short-term security. The investor would receive 0.20 less semiannually, only 95 at maturity (end of year one), and then would pay 100 (the strike price) for the bond. The net difference between the cash flows in Exhibits 33–11 and 33–12 is shown in Exhibit 33–13. (Note that Exhibit 33–14 could also describe the situation in which the investor borrowed the money to pay the premium, paid periodic interest on it, and repaid the loan when the option expired.)

The important point of Exhibit 33–13 is that it shows that the option has a cost that is not offset by any benefits in the future. Now let us consider what happens if rates have increased 200 basis points to 10 percent. Naturally, the

**EXHIBIT 33–12**
**Cash Flows If Call Option Is Exercised**

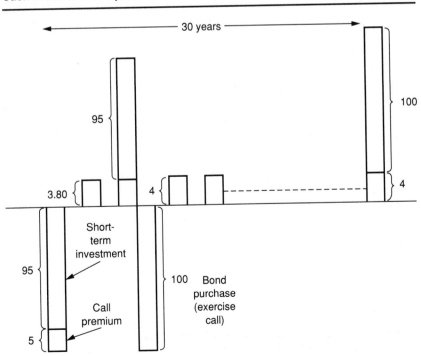

**EXHIBIT 33–13**
**The Cost of a Call: Premium and Forgone Interest**

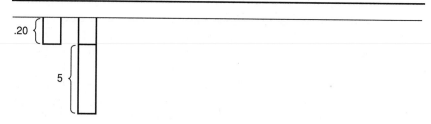

option will be allowed to expire, and if the investor buys a new par bond, the semiannual cash flows will be as shown in Exhibit 33–14.

When the cash flows of Exhibit 33–14 are compared to the base case shown in Exhibit 33–11, the difference takes on the pattern shown in Exhibit 33–15. The "extra" income results from the increase in yields and would be even higher if the yield increase had been greater. Thus it appears that the call options, when viewed as an alternative to a long bond purchase, actually provide an option on higher yields, even though calls are usually thought of as profitable when yields decline.[6]

This provides a convenient point at which to mention the effect of short-term rates on option premiums. Consider again the cash-flows diagrammed in Exhibits 33–11-13. If short-term rates were higher, the cash flows resulting from the short-term investment shown in Exhibit 33–12 would be higher, resulting in a lower net cost for the call than shown in Exhibit 33–13. Another way of looking at this is to say that the investor could pay more than five for the call but still have the same net cost.

If short-term rates were lower than long-term rates, the investor would pay not only the premium for the call, but would lose some yield on the remaining funds that were invested short term, thereby increasing the effective cost of the call. This effect is likely to lower the nominal dollar price that the investor would otherwise be willing to pay for the call. More discussion on this topic will be included in the Option Valuation section.

## Using Puts Protect Long Positions

The dramatic rise in rates and in rate volatility has made investors in long-term securities particularly vulnerable to large price swings. Hedging with futures

---

[6] Actually, it is the investment in the short-term security that provides the investor with funds to invest at higher rates (or lower rates) in the future. The role of the call option is to provide a floor on the rate at which the funds will be invested. Thus, it is the combined position (not the call alone) that provides an option on higher yields.

**EXHIBIT 33–14**
**Cash Flows If Call Is Not Exercised**

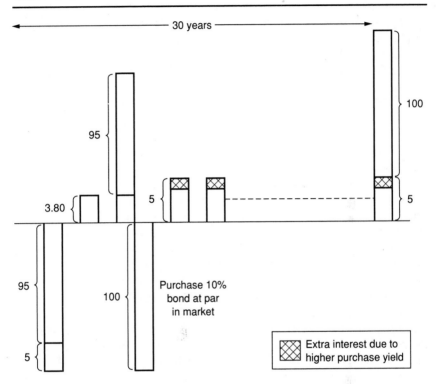

**EXHIBIT 33–15**
**Call's Cost Can Be Offset by Higher Future Interest**

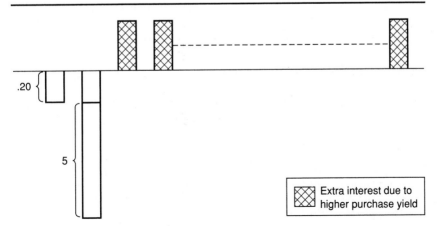

can reduce downside risk, but at the expense of losing upside potential. Fixed income puts also provide protection, but at a known cost, leaving any remaining upside profit intact.

Let us utilize the securities introduced in the previous section, namely, a 30-year, 8 percent bond (at par) and the associated one-year put, struck at par. By simultaneously purchasing a put and the bond, the investor has the right to sell the bond at par anytime over the next year. If yields decline over the year and the bond increases in price, the put will be allowed to expire worthless. But if yields increase and drive down the price of the bond, the investor will be able to sell the bond at par and reinvest the proceeds in new, higher coupon instruments at par.

To construct the cash flow pattern, let us assume the following: The put costs 4 points, the yield curve is flat at 8 percent, the investor borrows the funds for the premium, pays interest semiannually, and will repay the premium loan at expiration. If the option expires unexercised, the cash flow pattern of the long bond (Exhibit 33–11) will be altered by the flows shown in Exhibit 33–16. If the option is exercised, and the investor reinvests his funds in a higher paying bond, the long bond flows will be altered by the flows shown in Exhibit 33–17. This clearly indicates the advantage of the put when yields increase.

Of course, it is not necessary to borrow the put premium, and that construct was used only to demonstrate the resemblance of Exhibits 33–16 and 33–17 to Exhibits 33–13 and 33–15.

The similarity in these option-induced cash flows (Exhibit 33–15 and Exhibit 33–17) is another example of how nearly identical risk-return patterns can be constructed from various combinations of long and short positions in cash securities and options. In this case, protecting a long position with a put is nearly identical to protecting the absence of a long position with a call, shown in the last section.

## Options in the Portfolio Context

The sections above have described several applications of options to particular security positions. In addition to these specific security transactions, options can have broader use in the adjustment of the risk position (i.e., the rate sensitivity) of the entire portfolio. Active managers can effectively "lengthen" the portfolio (i.e., increase the bullish rate sensitivity or performance) by purchasing calls. The portfolio can be "shortened" by buying puts.

Recent pension fund activity has heightened the interest in contingent immunization,[7] and fixed income options can be used in the "active" and "near-

---

[7] See Martin L. Leibowitz and Alfred Weinberger, "Contingent Immunization." Salomon Brothers Inc, January 28, 1981.

**EXHIBIT 33–16**
**The Cost of a Put: Premium and Interest**

immunized" modes of operation. Any investor desiring to adjust the rate sensitivity of a portfolio should evaluate the potentially useful role of options.

## Equivalent Positions

Several examples have indicated that investors can achieve nearly identical profit patterns in alternative ways. For example, the put writer's profit pattern was shown to be similar to the covered call writer's profit pattern. In fact, there are a number of security positions that can be duplicated with options. The following presents several.

$$\text{Long position in underlying security} = \text{Long call} + \text{Short put} \qquad (33\text{–}1)$$

This can be demonstrated by remembering that higher prices result in profits on the long position and on the long call, and lower prices result in losses on the long position and on the short put. By rearranging the components, other relationships can be found.

**EXHIBIT 33–17**
**Put's Cost Can Be Offset by Higher Future Interest**

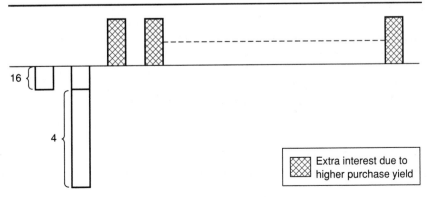

For example, if we add a short call to both sides of the equation (the long call and short call on the right cancel out), we have

$$\text{Long position in underlying security} + \text{Short call} = \text{Short put} \quad (33\text{--}2)$$

The left side is the covered call writer, and the right side is the put writer. (See again Exhibits 33–7 and 33–10.)

By adding a long put to each side, equation (33–1) becomes

$$\text{Long position} + \text{Long put} = \text{Long call} \quad (33\text{--}3)$$

By reversing the position of each component in equation (33–1), we get

$$\text{Short position in underlying security} = \text{Short call} + \text{Long put} \quad (33\text{--}4)$$

Adding a long call to each side of equation (33–4) yields

$$\text{Short position} + \text{Long call} = \text{Long put} \quad (33\text{--}5)$$

Note that the positions on either side of the equations may involve different cash outlays, and thus the higher outlay position must be financed, or the lower outlay position implicitly includes a short-term cash equivalent investment.

The equivalence of these positions can be demonstrated by combining the individual profit patterns of the components. The availability of these equivalent positions may prompt investors to move from one to the equivalent if it can be achieved at cheaper cost, or may invite arbitrage between equivalent positions.

For example, Equation (33–3) suggests that

$$\text{Long position} + \text{Long put} + \text{Short call} = 0,$$

that is, a riskless position. In fact, the position *is* riskless and will be described later in the section on Conversions.

## OPTION VALUATION

### Determinants of Value

The determination of "fair" price or value for an option *is* important to both purchasers and sellers of options, regardless of the strategy they may be employing. For most equity options, variations of the Black-Scholes model normally are used in the valuation process. Although such models may be adapted to certain fixed income options with some degree of success, there are significant differences between the assumptions of the Black-Scholes framework and the reality of the fixed income market. First, a bond option valuation model must take account of the fact that the underlying instrument is changing over time. To cite an extreme example, a five-year option on a ten-year bond begins its life as an option on ten-year bond but expires as an option on a five-year bond. It is clear that the price volatility of this security will change over time. Another requirement for a fixed income option valuation model is that it address the correlation of short-term interest rates and the yields that determine the price of the underlying security.

Although it is not our purpose to explain these pricing models in detail, it is useful to present the basic inputs to these models and the logic behind their impact on value. These determinants of option value are: strike price, expected volatility of the underlying security, time to expiration, the cash flows of the underlying security (if any), short-term rates, and the current price of the underlying security.

*The Strike Price.*   The strike price determines how far in- or out-of-the-money the option is when being valued. Other things being equal, an in-the-money option is worth more than one at-the-money, and the at-the-money option is worth more than one out-of-the-money. For a call option, this means the lower the strike price, the higher the premium; for a put option the higher the strike price, the higher the option value.

*Volatility of the Underlying Security.*   The expected volatility of the underlying security in the options valuation context refers to the expected variance of potential price moves of the underlying security.[8] Exhibit 33–18 is a probabilistic representation of two levels of expected volatility. From this illustration we will show why higher expected volatility translates to higher premiums on both puts and calls.

With Exhibit 33–18 as a point of reference, consider a call option with a strike price of 110, where the price of the underlying security is 100. All else constant, it is evident that there is a higher probability that the call option expires in-the-money if expected volatility is 20 percent than if expected volatility is 10 percent. The fact that there is also a higher probability of large negative price moves is of no concern to the call option holder, because any adverse price moves below the strike price represent zero intrinsic value at expiration, and no worse. The same argument can be made for an out-of-the-money put option; for instance, a put option struck at 90 is worth more if expected volatility is 20 percent rather than 10 percent.

---

[8] In debt option valuation, yield volatility is often the primary variable, and price volatility is derived from that.

**EXHIBIT 33–18**
**Expected Price of Underlying Security under Different Volatilities.**

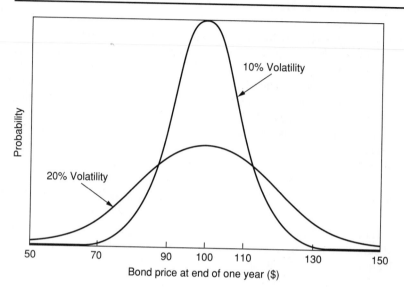

Bond price at end of one year ($)

Higher expected volatility also increases the option premium for in-the-money puts and calls. Perhaps the easiest way to make this argument is by referring to the earlier section discussing equivalent positions. Using the relationship that equates a long call position with a long put position plus a long position in the underlying, equation (33–3), it can be seen that if increased expected volatility raises the value of an out-of-the money call option, then the in-the-money put option on the right-hand side of the equation must also increase in value. The same argument shows that expected volatility and the price of an in-the-money call option are positively related.

Estimating the volatility of the underlying security is perhaps the most difficult task in the pricing of an option. It is the only variable affecting the option premium that is not directly observable in the market when the option is priced and is as elusive a quantity to predict as the future price of the underlying security itself. An estimation method that involves both a measure of historical volatility and the current level of expected volatility as implied by the price of options traded in the market can be used.

*Time to Expiration.* The time to expiration specifies the time constraint under which the volatility of the security operates and sets implicit limits to the range of potential prices likely to be realized. The time to expiration also determines the absolute dollar impact of the short-term rate and the cash flows of the underlying security on the price of the option. A longer time to expiration tends to increase the value of the option by extending the range of potential price movement, as does a higher volatility.[9]

***Cash Flows of the Underlying Security.*** Depending on the structure of the option contract, cash flows on the underlying security may have a major impact on the option value. For example, although a zero coupon bond can be expected to grow in price, even at a constant yield, a full coupon bond yielding its coupon rate will not. If the strike price is fixed, the lack of price growth of the full coupon bond (due to its return in the form of periodic cash flows) will lower the value of a call option versus a call on the growing security. The nature of the strike price is also important in this regard. Even the "nongrowing" (constant yield) par bond will grow in total price (including accrued interest) between coupon payments. If the option contract specifies purchase or sale at the quoted price plus accrued interest, the intercoupon growth will have little impact on value, because the strike price will rise along with accrued interest.

***The Short-Term Rate.***[10] The role of short-term rate has been mentioned earlier, in relation to financing the premium. Another look is provided in this section.

Let us consider the purchase, for 4 points, of a one-year call on a 30-year, 8 percent bond when the yield curve is flat at 8 percent. To compare this case with the purchase of the bond at par, assume that the call buyer will also put 96 in one-year CDs at 8 percent. Thus, both investments (call plus CD and long bond) have equal outlays. The dollar returns for the two strategies, including income (but ignoring reinvestment), are shown in Exhibit 33–19.

It is not difficult to see the impact that higher short-term rates would have if the premium remained constant at 4. If the short-term rate were 16 percent, for example, the total value of the CD (96 + interest) would exceed the bond's market value and earned interest, and the call + CD strategy would dominate the bond purchase; that is, the call + CD would be better for at least some possible yield levels at expiration and never worse. This is shown in Exhibit 33–20. All investors who were not prohibited by regulatory or other constraints would sell their bonds and buy CDs and calls. These actions would tend to drive call prices higher while reducing the yield spread between bonds and CDs until the dominance disappeared. Thus, higher short-term rates would raise the level of call premiums.

---

[9] For European options, it is possible to increase time to expiration and decrease the value of the option.

[10] The arguments presented here are based on market forces. Theoretical option valuation models incorporate the short-term rate in its effects on the present value of the strike price. This concept is considered in more detail in Chapter 34.

**EXHIBIT 33–19**
**Bond Purchase versus Call + CD Strategy**

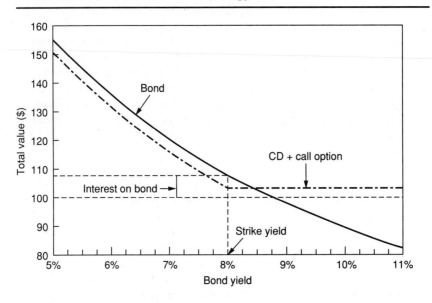

**EXHIBIT 33–20**
**Dominance of Bond by Call + CD**

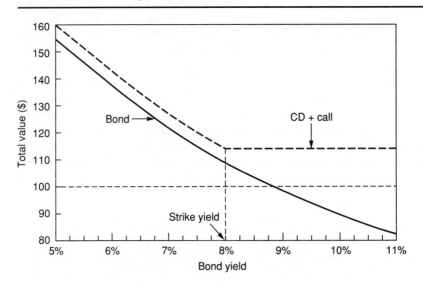

*Option Premiums and the Price of the Underlying Security.* The previous sections discussed the impact of a number of factors on option premiums. Most of these factors—such as volatility, short-term rates, time to expiration, and expected cash flows—do not change significantly from day to day. The time to expiration changes, of course, but when the time to expiration is long, the slight daily decline has almost no impact on premium. When the time to expiration is short, the time premium is usually small, and declines in the time premium itself are small on an absolute basis. This leaves price changes in the underlying security as the most important determination of changes in option premiums. In the discussion that follows, we will assume that all of the parameters other than price—namely volatility, short-term rates, expected cash flows, and time to expiration—remain constant, and we will examine the option premium for various prices of the underlying security.

If the option is very far out-of-the-money, relative to the volatility of the underlying security, the option will have little value, because the possibility of going in-the-money is remote. If the option is very deep in-the-money, it will sell for close to its intrinsic value, with little time premium. The reasons for this lie in the basic appeal of the option itself—leveraged gains and limited losses. A deep-in-the-money option must sell at a high price because of its high intrinsic value, thus exposing potential buyers to large losses if prices decline. In addition, the leverage is drastically reduced because of the high price paid for the option. Thus, while arbitrage will prevent the premium from falling below the intrinsic value by any appreciable amount, the lack of appeal to buyers and selling pressure from arbitrageurs (see the section on Early Exercises of Options) will prevent the premium from going much above the intrinsic value.

Somewhere between the extremes (deep in-the-money and deep out-of-the-money) previously described, the time value reaches its greatest level. This level usually is realized when the option is close to being at-the-money. With these general statements as background, let us examine Exhibit 33–21, which relates the premium of a call to the various yields and corresponding prices of the underlying security. The horizontal axis of the figure is the yield to maturity of the underlying security. The left vertical axis shows the price of the underlying security. The right vertical axis shows the value of the option.

When the option is deep out-of-the-money (toward the right), the value is small because a large move in the security is necessary just to reach the strike price. The premium increases as the price gets higher (moving to the left in the figure). As the option moves deep in-the-money, the premium approaches the intrinsic value.

A theoretical value of a put is developed in a like manner, except that the put increases in value as the underlying security declines in price. The pattern is similar otherwise, starting with a low value when out-of-the-money, and approaching the intrinsic value as the option becomes deeper in-the-money. This pattern is shown in Exhibit 33–22; note that the premium scale is inverted.

**EXHIBIT 33–21**
**Theoretical Value of a Call**

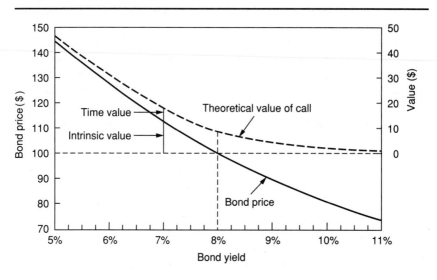

**EXHIBIT 33–22**
**Theoretical Value of a Put Relative to Bond Price**

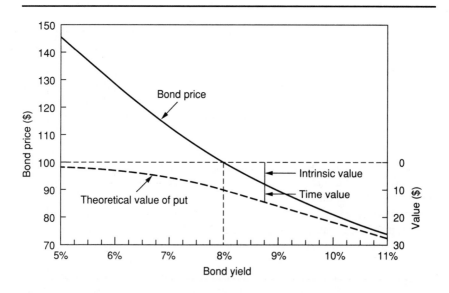

The put's theoretical value can also be viewed against the intrinsic value that was first shown in Exhibit 33–10, and this comparison is shown in Exhibit 33–23. (The values shown are for puts that can be exercised at any time prior to expiration.)

While the pattern shown in Exhibit 33–23 is upright, with larger values appearing higher on the chart, the presentation in Exhibit 33–22 is more useful when discussing hedging. Thus, both Exhibit 33–21 (for calls) and Exhibit 33–22 (for puts) will be the basis for the discussions on hedging that follow.

## Conversions and Reversals

A somewhat different approach considers the relationship of put and call prices to each other through processes known as conversion and reverse conversion. In a conversion, an investor (usually a member firm) buys both a put and the underlying security and sells a call with the same strike price as the put. As described in the next paragraph, the investor takes on no risk, and removes puts from and provides calls to the market, as shown in Exhibit 33–24. The investor creates conversions to earn the difference, if large enough, between the price of the call sold and the put purchased. This difference must cover the net cost of carry on the long security, based on the current yield of the long security and the rate to finance it; any excess is profit. Thus the short-term rate affects the spread in put and call premiums.

**EXHIBIT 33–23**
**Theoretical Value of a Put Relative to Intrinsic Value**

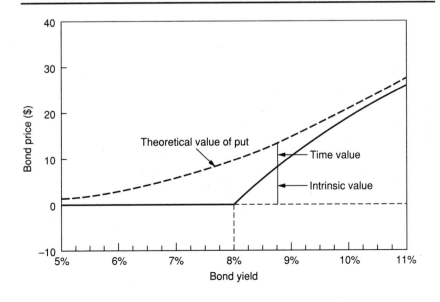

**EXHIBIT 33–24**
**The Conversion Process**

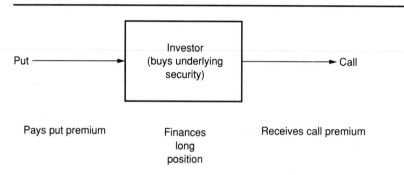

For example, assume that in June a December 100 put costs $5\frac{1}{2}$, the December 100 call sells for 6, and the underlying 8 percent bond is selling for 100. If the investor buys the bond, buys a put, and sells a call, he will be in a risk-free position. If the bond's price increases, it will be called away from him at 100, the price he paid for it. If the price declines, the investor will exercise his put and sell the bond for the strike price of 100. Thus, whether prices rally, decline, or remain constant, the investor will sell the bond for 100, the price paid. (Note that the number following the expiration month is the strike price, not the year of expiration. This might cause confusion if there is trading in December 92s, for example.)

Now let's examine the motivation for entering into conversion transactions. Assume that short-term financing rates are 8 percent. The calculations are shown in Exhibit 33–25.

The net dollar return is thus $0.52 per bond purchased on a risk-free basis. If the financing (short-term) rate were higher, the spread between put and call premiums would have to be wider to maintain this profit. If the financing rate were much higher, the profit would become a loss. In that case, the positions would be reversed to earn the difference.

Normally, conversions (and reverse conversions) are done by dealers who can arbitrage differences in premiums that would be too small to be profitable to public investors. This section was intended to describe the relationship between put and call prices as well as to provide further explanation on the role of short-term rates on put and call premiums, not to suggest an option-trading strategy for investors. It should also be noted that the conversion and reversal process previously described involves the use of options that will not be exercised before the expiration date of the option. Where early exercise of an option is likely, the conversion and reversal processes will not be risk-free.

**EXHIBIT 33–25**
**Calculation of Profit from Conversion**

| | | |
|---|---|---|
| Net Investment | | |
| Buy security | −100.00 | |
| Buy put | −  5.50 | |
| Sell call | +  6.00 | |
| | | −  99.50 |
| Net Cost of Carry | | |
| Finance charge | | |
| Amount × Rate × Time | | |
| 99 1/2 × 8 percent × 1/2 year  = | −  3.98 | |
| Current Return on Security | | |
| One coupon earned | +  4.00 | |
| | | +   0.02 |
| Total Cost of Investment | | −  99.48 |
| Sale Price of Investment | | |
| Whether put or called | | +100.00 |
| Profit per Bond | | +   0.52 |

## Early Exercises of Options

In general, most options are worth more alive than dead, because an option that is sold will generate the intrinsic value (if any) plus the time premium (if any). If an option is exercised, however, only the intrinsic value is recovered from the position. Because most fixed income option exercise transactions incorporate accrued interest added to the strike price, coupon dates cause few exercises. This is in contrast to the equity market, where dividend payments (ex-dates) can trigger exercises, because the price of the stock changes but the strike is not adjusted.

Nevertheless, several factors can cause early exercise of puts and calls. Those that are specific to particular option contracts are not discussed here. This section will present only one scenario to demonstrate that early exercise can be a rational action.

Consider a one-year call with a strike of 70 on an 8 percent bond currently trading at 100. The option is obviously deep (30 points) in-the-money. Suppose that the relevant short-term (one-year) rate for an investor is 8 percent. We will examine the covered write under these conditions, that is, buy the bond and sell the call.

Assume that the call sells for only its intrinsic value of 30. If the investor feels that there is little possibility that the bond will sell for less than 70 at the end of a year, this transaction is similar to a futures "cash and carry." The investor would buy the security for 100 and sell the call for 30, resulting in a net cost of 70 (which will also be the sale price one year hence). Over the next year, the investor will earn 8 (two coupons) on an investment of 70 for a return of over 11 percent. This is clearly an attractive proposition.

If the attractiveness of selling calls causes many investors to sell calls and put downward pressure on the call price, the price might dip below the intrinsic value. If this happens, and the options can be exercised immediately, arbitrageurs will buy the options, exercise them, and sell the underlying security to earn the difference between the market price and the intrinsic value. Thus, the options may be exercised early.

On the other hand, holders of the calls will find that they have an asset worth $30 that is not going to produce interest over the year, but that will be subject to price changes that are approximately equal to the changes on the underlying bond. Thus, because they have the market risk of a bond position already, they might as well invest $70 to exercise the call and earn 8 percent interest on the $100 face value of the bond. If they do not wish to take on the market risk of the bond, they can sell the call and earn interest on the resulting $30 inflow. This selling pressure will add to that previously described, and may introduce more arbitrage.

Most of the actions discussed above involve selling the option, which induces a downward move in price. The only likely buyers at the high level of premium are arbitrageurs who buy the options in order to exercise them. Thus, the situation is basically unstable, and the only stabilizing force results in exercising the options. If this happens, the cash and carry investor would not earn the two coupons, because the security would be called away long before the one-year holding period originally expected. In any case, it can be seen that a variety of forces can result in early exercise of options. Holders of options should be aware of this and evaluate the attractiveness of exercising. Writers of options should be aware of the possibility of receiving an exercise notice long before expiration.

## OPTIONS ON FUTURES

The highest volume of trading in debt options on the exchanges has been in options on futures contracts. These contracts include options on Treasury bond futures, Treasury note futures, and Eurodollar time deposit rate futures.

Although an option on a futures contract may seem like a complicated security, it is in many ways a simpler instrument to analyze and trade than an option on an actual cash instrument. This is because the impact of the cash flows of the cash security is already taken into account in the price of the futures contract and hence need not be addressed in the pricing of the option.

When the holder of a call option on a futures contract exercises the option, he or she is delivered the futures contract at the current market price. Whereas exercise of a call option on an actual cash instrument requires the buyer to pay the full price of the underlying security, exercise of an in-the-money call option on the futures contract requires the option writer to pay the option holder the difference between the current price of the futures contract and the strike price. Essentially, a futures trade takes place at the strike price and then both parties immediately are marked to market. In the case of exercise of a put option on a futures contract, the holder of the option is assigned a short futures position at the current market price, and the grantor of the option pays the holder the difference between the strike and the current futures price.

One way to think of the options on bond futures that captures the essence of the contract (though not the technicalities) is to view the futures contract as simply an index of government bond prices. Then the option can be thought of as a cash settlement option, where the seller of the option pays the holder the difference between strike and index value (market price) upon the exercise of an in-the-money option.[11]

The following example comparing an option on a cash bond and an option on the futures contract on that same cash bond illustrates the similarities between the two types of option contracts.

---

*Option on Actual*
Underlying security:        8 percent 30-year bond
Strike price:               100
Expiration date of option:  Dec 19xx

*Option on Futures*
Underlying security:        Futures contract on 8 percent 30-year bond
                            delivery Dec 19xx
Strike price:               100
Expiration date of option:  Dec 19xx

---

Exhibit 33–26 shows the value of the call option on the futures contract at expiration, that is, the intrinsic value of the option, together with the profit pattern. Because the expiration of the option contract coincides with the delivery date of the futures contract[12] the cash price of the 8 percent, 30-year bond will

---

[11] In the unlikely event of an exercise of an out-of-the-money option, the holder of the option would pay the option writer.

[12] In practice there may be a short time period between the expiration of the options contract and the delivery date of the futures contract.

**EXHIBIT 33–26**
**Intrinsic Value and Profit Pattern of a Call**
**versus Futures Price**

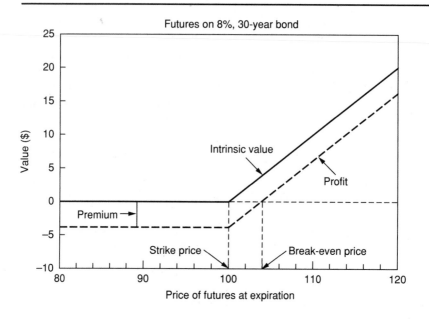

equal the price of the futures contract on the 8 percent, 30-year bond. Hence, the intrinsic value patterns of the option on the futures and the option on the cash bond are identical. This is an important observation, because if the buyer of the option is only concerned with the final payoff pattern of the option, he or she will be indifferent as to the option on the futures and the option on the actual security so long as the premiums for the two options are the same. As shown in Exhibit 33–27, if the price of the option on the actual is greater than the price of the option on the futures, the profit pattern of the options on the futures contract will always lie above the profit pattern for the option on the actual bond. This is an unstable situation in which selling of the option on the actual and buying of the option on the futures will realign the prices of the two options contracts.

In practice, there are certain forces that may cause the price of the option on the futures contract to be different from the price of an option on the corresponding cash security. First, the early exercise values for the two kinds of options will be different, because the price of the futures is usually different from the price of the cash security, reflecting the positive or negative cost of carry. Second, the multiple security delivery mechanism of the Treasury bond and Treasury note

**EXHIBIT 33–27**
**Dominance of Profit Pattern of Option on Futures over Option on a Cash Bond**

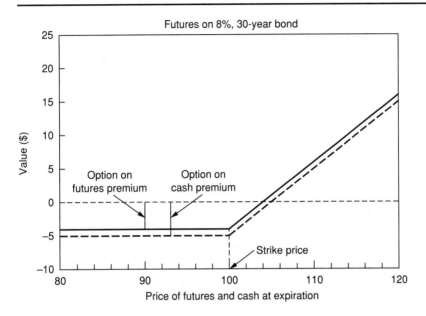

futures contracts on the CBOT often drives a wedge between the forward price of the relevant cash security and the price of the futures contract.[13,14]

## The Hedge Ratio (Delta)

In most option valuation models developed for equities, the "hedge ratio" that is provided is simply the ratio of the change of the theoretical value of the option to the change in the current price of the stock. Because we have chosen to present theoretical value as a function of yield instead of price, the hedge ratio will be calculated somewhat differently, but it will have the same meaning, namely, the change in the value of the option for a given change in the price of the underlying security.

---

[13] See Robert W. Kopprasch, Cal Johnson, Armand Tatevossian, "Strategies for the Asset Manager: Hedging and the Creation of Synthetic Assets," in Frank J. Fabozzi and T. Dessa Garlicki (eds.), *Advances in Bond Analysis & Portfolio Strategies* (Chicago: Probus Publishing, 1987).

[14] Although the preceding analysis was cast in terms of the options on bond and note futures contracts, the analysis of the option on the Eurodollar time deposit futures contract is basically the same.

The price sensitivity of the underlying bond is the slope of the price yield curve at the current yield level, sometimes referred to as the "price value of one basis point." In effect, it is the price change that would occur in response to a one-basis-point change in the yield. The same calculation can be applied to the option to determine its price sensitivity, and the reader can see from Exhibits 33–21 and 33–22 that the option's price move per basis point yield change is always lower than, or at most equal to, that of the bond. The hedge ratio (defined consistently with its meaning in the equity market) is the ratio of the price sensitivity of the option to the price sensitivity of the bond.

$$\text{Hedge ratio} = \frac{\text{Price value per basis point of option}}{\text{Price value per basis point of bond}}$$

The hedge ratio can be visualized in Exhibit 33–28, which enlarges a smaller section of Exhibit 33–21. The slopes of the two price curves are shown and the price response of the bond is greater. This is true for virtually all yield levels. However, when the option is deep-in-the-money, the price responses are nearly identical and the hedge ratio is approximately one, its largest possible value.

While the above definition is consistent with the equity market definition, it is somewhat unfortunate that the term *hedge ratio* has that meaning, because the same term is used in futures hedging to mean something entirely different.

**EXHIBIT 33–28**
**The Price Responses of Call and Bond to a Change in Yield**

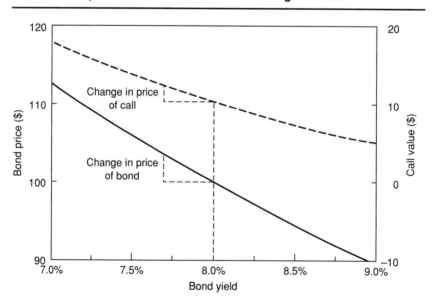

## SUMMARY

The market in fixed income options offers a variety of approaches and alternatives to fixed income investing. We have attempted to provide a background for the analysis of these financial instruments. After carefully studying the details of specific contracts that may be relevant to them, potential investors will find that options offer new opportunities and applications in investing, arbitrage, and hedging. Options can be combined in a variety of ways with cash instruments and financial futures to create synthetic securities that may be attractive in their own right.

# CHAPTER 34

# AN OVERVIEW OF FIXED INCOME OPTION MODELS

*Lawrence J. Dyer*
Vice President
Morgan Stanley

*David P. Jacob\**
Director of Fixed Income Research
J.P. Morgan Securities, Inc.

Fixed income option pricing has evolved from an esoteric specialty into an important analytic tool in the fixed income market. In addition to its obvious application in the large and expanding over-the-counter and exchange-traded fixed income options markets, option pricing theory has been successfully applied to a variety of fixed income securities and instruments with embedded options, including callable bonds, mortgage pass-throughs, and complex liability streams such as Single Premium Deferred Annuities (SPDAs) issued by insurers. Over time, researchers have developed increasingly complex option pricing models to represent the behavior of fixed income securities. This chapter provides a critical guide to option pricing models in the fixed income area. It reviews the theoretical basis of option pricing for fixed income securities and the appropriateness of commonly used option pricing models—modified Black-Scholes, binomial-on-yield, and yield-curve, or arbitrage-free models—for various practical option pricing situations. The comments on appropriateness of these models for option

---

*David P. Jacob was with Morgan Stanley when the first draft of this chapter was prepared.

pricing are equally valid for the measurement of the duration or the interest-rate sensitivity of an option.

Investors must choose the model they believe is appropriate for a given application. At a practical level, the choice of an option pricing model involves a trade-off between the degree to which the model approximates reasonable behavioral assumptions for fixed income securities and the costs of developing and using the model. Two criteria are used to judge a model. The first is how well the price process of the model matches historical and theoretical models of interest-rate behavior—for example, negative interest rates should be precluded or occur with negligible probability. The second is that the model should not allow risk-free arbitrage between option prices and security prices. The mathematical description of this condition may appear daunting. Its practical implication, however, is easy to understand: An option pricing model should not produce prices that allow the creation of an options position that will always produce a profit when hedged with an offsetting security position or vice versa.

The most advanced models yield results that exhibit the nonarbitrage principle throughout the life of the security underlying the option. This may require hundreds or even millions of calculations to ensure that the model does not allow arbitrage over the 30-year life of a long corporate bond or mortgage. Thus, while the most complex models require considerable resources to develop and use, they ensure that the results are reasonable. Using an inappropriate model can lead to incorrect value and duration estimates for the options under consideration. The cost of such errors can greatly exceed the cost of developing an appropriate model. Less complex models apply a more lenient standard for eliminating arbitrage opportunities, such as examining only a short-term and a long-term rate rather than the entire yield curve. This produces acceptable results in some cases, but not all.

For example, a Black-Scholes model modified to price short-term options on bond futures or coupon bonds provides option prices that, for practical purposes, are not significantly different from those derived from the more complex fixed income option pricing models that are available. Although these models may produce slightly different prices for similar assumptions, these differences probably would not allow a trader or investor to earn a profit consistently. However, a Black-Scholes-like fixed income option pricing model gives prices for long-term options on fixed income securities that are inaccurate. It assigns high prices to some types of options on fixed income securities that are easily shown to be worthless. Therefore, using such a model to value or hedge long-term options or securities with embedded long-term options, such as callable bonds, may lead to poor results.

This chapter reviews the fundamentals of option pricing and then discusses the assumptions and theoretical merits of various models that have been used in fixed income option pricing. The discussion is on a nontechnical level, relying on examples instead of equations to illustrate relevant points. The purpose of this chapter is to provide an overview of the various models and help practitioners decide which model is the most appropriate in a particular situation.

The next section reviews the basic components and principles common to all models. Three basic categories of models that have been used in pricing fixed income options are then discussed. The assumptions underlying each model are stated and their theoretical merits are compared. Then, the practical implications of those assumptions are addressed, and we answer the question, "Which model should we use?"

## THE BASICS OF OPTIONS PRICING[1]

In principle, finding the price of a fixed income option is a straightforward process. First, the price of the underlying security is projected forward to the expiration date of the option, and each price is assigned a probability of occurring based on a process that makes the expected returns from holding the bond equal to the risk-free interest rate. Then, the payoffs for the option at expiration are determined by the security's price, the type of option, and the option's strike price. Finally, the current value of the option is determined by calculating the expected present value of its payoffs at expiration. Alternatively, a self-financing, dynamically adjusted portfolio that combines a position in the underlying security and either borrowing or lending at the risk-free rate of interest may be used to determine the value of the option.

Options come in a variety of flavors. Call options give their owner a payoff equal to the larger of the difference between the price of a bond and the option's strike price or zero. Exhibit 34–1 shows the value of a call option with a strike price of 100 at expiration and one month and three months to expiration for various bond prices. Put options also give their owner a payoff equal to the larger of the difference between the strike price of the option and the bond's price or zero. Exhibit 34–2 shows the value of a put option with a strike of 100 at expiration and one month and three months to expiration for various bond prices. In addition, an option may be a European-style option that cannot be exercised before maturity, an American-style option that may be exercised at any time before its expiration, or some combination of the two.

In practice, fixed income securities present a number of complications that must be carefully examined if an option pricing model is to provide reasonable values. For example, the discounting rate used to find the present value of an

---

[1] For a more detailed introduction to fixed income options, see Lawrence J. Dyer and David P. Jacob, "Guide to Fixed Income Option Pricing Models," in Frank J. Fabozzi (ed.), *The Handbook of Fixed Income Options* (Chicago: Probus Publishing, 1989).

**EXHIBIT 34–1**
**Value of an American Call Option with a Strike Price of 100**

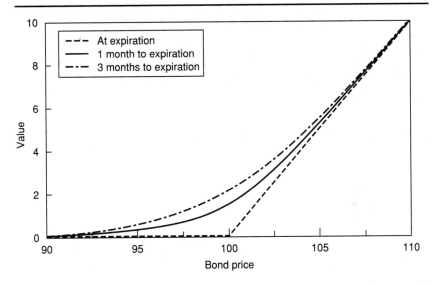

**EXHIBIT 34–2**
**Value of an American Put Option with a Strike Price of 100**

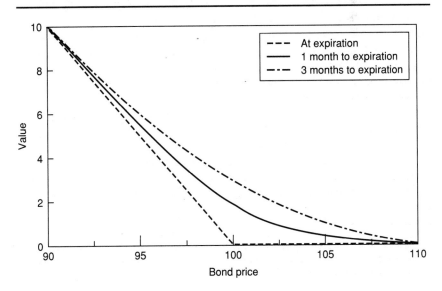

option on a fixed income security and the interest rate of the bond underlying the option ought to be correlated. This correlation significantly increases the complexity of finding the present value of a fixed income security's payoffs and is ignored in many option pricing models. So, if the short-term rate is fixed at 10 percent, and this rate is always above the return from holding a security in the model, then the pricing process provides no incentive for investors to hold long-term securities. These models result in option prices that would allow riskless profits if they were available in the marketplace. Eliminating this problem requires specifying the short- and long-term rates in the model carefully and thus introducing a correlation between them. Another complication is that a model may incorrectly define a process that drives a security price, for example, by allowing negative interest rates. In this case, the model may provide option prices that appear reasonable—for example, they would satisfy put-call parity—but it will systematically misprice options.

The first part of this section discusses the principle of arbitrage pricing, which is the basis of analytical option valuation techniques. This principle states that if two different investments or investment strategies have identical cash flows, they must be assigned the same value by the market. The option models discussed here use this principle to find the cost of a dynamic, self-financing investment strategy that replicates the payoff of an option; the value of the option must be the expected cost of executing the strategy. The second part of this section discusses the importance of correctly modeling the stochastic process governing the behavior of security prices when constructing an option pricing model.

## Arbitrage Pricing

If two investments produce identical cash flows with identical risks, then investors should assign them the same price. If this is not the case, a rational investor will simultaneously buy the cheap security and short the expensive security. Because the future payoffs for the two securities exactly offset each other, such an investor will earn the difference between the securities' prices without incurring risk or investing any cash. Of course, we have ignored many practical factors such as taxes, liquidity, and transaction costs that can cause prices to diverge between two otherwise identical investments. Including these factors results in a null zone where the prices of the securities may differ, but either the difference is too small to allow a profit to be locked in or institutional factors fully account for the price difference. If the price difference were to move outside this zone, arbitrage would be possible.

The following example illustrates how arbitrage arguments are applied to determine the price of an option. This approach is based on the insight that the value of an option may be hedged over a range of prices by following a particular trading strategy. With this strategy, the option is hedged by an offsetting position in the underlying security. This position is chosen in such a way that, for certain assumptions, it offsets the price change in the option for a given price change in the underlying security. This technique is also known as delta-neutral hedging. Though this technique mimics the price changes of an option due to changes in the underlying security's price, it must also include the effect of the leverage implicit in an option contract. This leverage, or borrowing, is designed to make the payoffs for a delta-neutral hedge exactly match those of the option. Because the payoff of the option is exactly matched at expiration, the cost of creating the hedge—that is, the cash investment required to set up the delta-neutral hedge—must be the value of the option for the assumptions in use.

Consider a security that has two possible future values: If state 1 occurs, the security is worth $100; if state 2 occurs, the security is worth $70. A risk-free security exists that costs $90 today and pays $100 in both future states. This translates into a risk-free rate of 11.11 percent. A call option on the security with a strike price of $80 is offered. The call would pay $20 in state 1 and $0 in state 2. Exhibit 34–3 finds the value of this option.

The first section of Exhibit 34–3 shows the equations that relate the option payoff in each future state to the payoff from a delta-neutral hedging strategy that combines holdings in the security and cash borrowed at the risk-free rate. The second section shows that holding two-thirds of a unit of the security and borrowing $42 in cash exactly replicates the option payoff. Note that the option replication strategy is independent of the probability of a particular state occurring and the current price of the security. The last section finds the value of the call option assuming that the current price of the security is $80. The value of the call option is the cost of the strategy that replicates its payoffs, namely $11.33.

The theory of modern finance requires that equilibrium prices among all securities not allow riskless arbitrage among securities.[2] The preceding example considered only the call option, the short-term rate, and the security underlying the call option. To eliminate arbitrage, a large number of securities must be examined. For example, a 30-year Treasury bond may be stripped into 59 coupon payments before maturity along with a coupon and principal payment at maturity. Each payment must be considered a separate security to rule out all arbitrage opportunities. Because of the large number of possible arbitrage situations, many

---

[2] For a complete discussion on arbitrage and option pricing, See Richard Bookstaber, David P. Jacob, and Joseph Langsam, "The Arbitrage Free Pricing of Options on Interest-Sensitive Instruments." *Advances in Futures and Options Research,* Vol. 1, Part A, 1986.

**EXHIBIT 34–3**

**Delta-Neutral Investment Strategy that Replicates the Performance of a Call Option with a Strike Price of $80**

---

**Section 1**

*The option payoffs replicate the security payoffs and borrowing.*

$$\text{State} \quad \substack{\text{security} \\ \text{payoff}} \times \substack{\text{Amount} \\ \text{of security}} - \text{Borrowing} \times (1 + \substack{\text{risk-} \\ \text{free} \\ \text{rate}}) = \text{Option payoff}$$

| 1 | $100 | × | Amount | − | Borrowing | × | (1.1111) | = | max (100 − 80, 0) | = | $20 |
| 2 | $ 70 | × | Amount | − | Borrowing | × | (1.1111) | = | max ( 70 − 80, 0) | = | $ 0 |

**Section 2**

*Holding 2/3 of a unit of the security and borrowing $42 replicates the option payoff.*

$$\text{State} \quad \substack{\text{security} \\ \text{payoff}} \times \substack{\text{Amount} \\ \text{of security}} - \text{Borrowing} \times (1 + \substack{\text{risk-} \\ \text{free} \\ \text{rate}}) = \text{Option payoff}$$

| 1 | $100 | × | 2/3 | − | $42 | × | (1.1111) | = | $20 |
| 2 | $ 70 | × | 2/3 | − | $42 | × | (1.1111) | = | $ 0 |

**Section 3**

*The value of the option is the cost of creating the replicating portfolio.*

$$\substack{\text{Current price} \\ \text{of security}} \times \text{Amount of security} - \text{Borrowing} = \text{Option value}$$

$$\$80 \quad \times \quad 2/3 \quad - \quad \$42 \quad = \$11.33$$

---

models in use do not rule out all arbitrage opportunities. This is acceptable in applications where the violations of arbitrage are not so severe as to warrant the added complexity of an arbitrage-free model.

The insights from arbitrage pricing are used in another option pricing technique. Exhibit 34–3 shows that the price of the option does not depend on the probability of the underlying security's price moving up or down and that the option's price is independent of the expected return of the bond. Therefore, the option's price is determined relative to the bond price solely by arbitrage considerations. The implication of this is that investors can value options as though they were risk-neutral. This technical consideration of financial theory implies that the option can be priced as if the expected return of the security underlying the option were equal to the risk-free rate, allowing the price of the option to be determined without solving the arbitrage equations.

## Volatility

Stated simply, volatility is a measure of how much a security's price is likely to move in a given unit of time.[3] By convention, volatility is quoted on an annualized percentage basis. This section discusses the effect of an increase in volatility on the value of an option and also discusses the effect of alternative processes on volatility.

Volatility affects the value of an option through its effect on the underlying security's distribution of payoffs. Volatility may also affect the discounting process in models that incorporate yield-curve dynamics. We will discuss the discounting process in the next part of this section as well as in our discussion of the various models.

An increase in volatility does not always cause the price of an option to rise, and a decrease does not always cause the price to fall. For example, the price of an in-the-money option may decrease as volatility increases because the increase in volatility increases the price range of the payoff distribution. If the new payoff distribution sufficiently increases the probability of the option expiring out-of-the-money, then the price of the option will fall. Volatility changes may also have nonobvious effects on fixed income securities or strategies with explicit or implicit price caps and/or floors. These include callable bonds, mortgages, and various options strategies (such as price spreads).

It is important to realize that intuition based on knowledge of traditional equity options pricing models can lead to false conclusions when dealing with the more complicated payoffs found in fixed income securities, such as those from interest-only or principal-only strips of mortgage-backed securities or options on CMOs.[4]

## Discounting Procedure

The risk-free rate used in the discounting procedures in the preceding examples expresses the time value of money, which is obviously essential in valuing cash flows that are to be received in the future. In the more advanced option pricing models this rate plays a central role in option pricing through its relationship to the nonarbitrage-pricing principle, because the replicating portfolio requires that some amount of money be borrowed or lent at the short-term riskless rate. If this risk-free rate is not specified carefully, then the model will allow arbitrage. In the context of fixed income option pricing, the proper handling of the risk-free rate is critical for the elimination of put/call parity arbitrage. This will be examined in detail in the next section.

---

[3] Volatility measures are discussed in the next chapter.

[4] Principal-only and interest-only strips are discussed in Chapter 30. CMOs are covered in Chapter 29.

To illustrate how the risk-free rate can affect the value of an option, we will examine the effect of a change in the risk-free rate in the example of Exhibit 34–3. The value of a call option on this security with a strike price of $80 and a riskless rate of 11.11 percent is $11.33. If we retain all the other assumptions, but raise the riskless rate of interest to 17.65 percent, then the value of the option would be $13.67, $2.34 higher than the price for the initial risk-free rate.

For options on fixed income securities, a change in one interest rate is likely to be accompanied by changes in the interest rates of other maturities. For example, a change in the short-term rate would be likely to cause a similar shift in the direction of longer term rates, and vice versa. Although modeling such interactions so that arbitrage opportunities are excluded is complex, it affects the pricing of options whose expiration dates are near the maturity dates of the underlying securities. For short-term options on long-term bonds, such careful modeling of the discount process leads to only minor changes in option prices; in this case, the extra precision in the model is not worth the extra effort.

## Representation of the Underlying Security's Price Process

In the preceding examples the security could achieve only two possible values at the end of each period. These examples provide little detail on the process driving the price of the security or the relationship between the price of the security and other investments. In practice, discrete representations such as binomial or multinomial lattices, as well as continuous representations of security price behavior, are used to model securities' price behavior. In these models, the process by which security prices change is carefully constructed though the different models may use different processes. While theorists search for the process that best represents reality, the practitioner should ask, "Are there simpler representations that will suffice in my situation?"

Obviously, a process that allows the yield curve to take on a multitude of shapes is more realistic than a simple binomial model of a bond's yield to maturity, where the yield of a security can move to only two possible levels from any point in time. However, the added complexity of a full yield-curve model will not result in any practical advantage in modeling a three-month option on a noncallable 30-year coupon bond when compared with simple models, because the effect of the bond's volatility will dominate the effect of any yield-curve reshaping. However, a more complicated option, such as one that pays off on the basis of the difference between two rates, may require a more complete model of yield-curve behavior or some other change in the modeling approach.

In the next section, we will show that many of the currently employed fixed income option models assume an interest-rate process rather than a price process for the underlying security. The reasons for this will become apparent later; however, it is obvious that this approach leads to a host of questions that are not addressed by the equity models. For example, can one assume the yield curve moves in a parallel fashion? Should all rates along the yield curve be assumed to be perfectly correlated? Do volatilities differ systematically along the yield curve? Do reasonable processes admit differently shaped yield curves? The answers to these questions will be discussed later in this chapter.

In evaluating alternative-option pricing models, our approach is to compare the results with an eye to the differences in the underlying processes of the models. Two similar processes should provide similar prices. Although it would seem puzzling if different processes that appeared to be reasonable representations of reality produced radically different option values or option characteristics, in theory such an effect can occur.

Recent work has examined the effect of different interest-rate processes on the pricing of callable bonds.[5] In essence, the results of this modeling show that the value of an option may be significantly affected by the underlying process, particularly if the process assumes that rates are mean reverting. Differences in the theoretical value assigned to an option for different distributions are not unexpected in this case, because mean reversion significantly reduces the probability of a large change in interest rates. The good news is that the relative value among bonds is far less affected than is the absolute value assigned to the embedded option.

## COMPARISON OF MAJOR MODELS

The Black-Scholes formula and its binomial counterpart, the Cox-Ross-Rubinstein binomial pricing model, have been well known among Wall Street quantitative analysts since their creation. Thus, it has been natural for analysts who find themselves involved in fixed income applications to use these models to price fixed income options. However, as the characteristics of fixed income options have become better understood, new models have been developed that more accurately represent the pricing process of fixed income securities.

This section discusses three basic categories of fixed income option models. The first category includes applications of variations of the Black-Scholes model for fixed income securities. The discussion of the chacteristics of Black-Scholes also applies to binomial models such as the Cox-Ross-Rubinstein binomial model that are based on the same assumptions. Next, we consider a binomial model based on yield-to-maturity of bonds. As we will see, the main reason for the development of this model was to address concerns about the applicability of the lognormal assumption for bond returns in Black-Scholes-like models. The final category of models is composed of what we call yield curve models. The common theme among these models is that, in one way or another, they spec-

---

[5] See M. Hogan and S. Breidbart, "The Long-Term Behavior of Interest Rates and Options Pricing," Morgan Stanley, New York, November 1989.

ify the interest-rate dynamics along the entire yield curve. These specifications restrict the changes in shape of the yield curve both over time and for different interest-rate movements, so that arbitrage opportunities in the model are eliminated. This increases the computational complexity and, thus, the cost of using such a model.

The discussion in this section centers on the major elements of each model and some of their relative strengths and weaknesses. The models' usefulness for valuing various types of options and securities will be discussed in the next section.

## Black-Scholes

Fischer Black and Myron Scholes were the first to derive an analytic solution for the price of a European option on a non-dividend-paying stock. Their solution showed that the value of an option on a stock was determined by arbitrage considerations rather than by an investor's risk preferences or expectations about the future performance of the stock. The value of an option depends on five parameters: (1) the stock price, (2) the exercise price of the option, (3) the volatility of the stock's return, (4) the time to expiration of the option, and (5) the continuously compounded short-term interest rate for borrowing and lending. Their solution assumed that the logarithm of the stock's returns followed a normal distribution. An example of the price distribution is shown in Exhibit 34–4; this model assumes that the distribution of security prices is skewed so that higher prices are more likely to occur than lower prices.

The following illustrates a number of ways in which this model breaks down when applied to options on fixed income securities and discusses some of the common "fixes" for these problems. While the fixes are appropriate in some circumstances, in others they are not.

*The Appropriate Price Volatility Changes over Time.* Blindly applying Black-Scholes can lead to trouble. Supposed that the formula is used to price a three-year European call option on a three-year zero coupon bond. Because the bond matures at the end of three years, its price at expiration must be $100; therefore, the value of this option must be the maximum of zero or the discounted value of par minus the strike price. Thus, its value depends only on the strike price. The option payoff in this case is independent of the process, volatility, short-term riskless rates, and current value of the security, because the price of the underlying security at the expiration of the option is known with certainty. The first two lines of Exhibit 34–5 show how the arbitrage value of this option differs from the Black-Scholes prices for different strike prices. What went wrong with Black-Scholes in this case?

The most obvious problem is the volatility assumption of Black-Scholes as it applies to bonds. Because bonds have a finite maturity, the price volatility

**EXHIBIT 34–4**
**Price Distribution Projected One Year Forward Based on an Initial Bond Price of 100 and a 10% Annual Price Volatility**

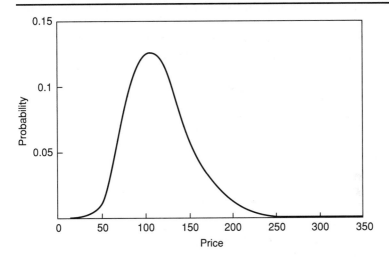

of a bond falls toward zero as time passes, whereas the Black-Scholes model assumes that price volatility is constant over time.[6]

Is there any way to correct this deficiency? Taking the limit of the Black-Scholes value as the volatility approaches zero, as shown in Exhibit 34–5, gives the same values as the arbitrage-based argument. Note that this example uses the correct riskless rate for the Black-Scholes model—the zero coupon bond rate corresponding to the expiration date of the option—not an overnight rate as is sometimes used. This approach does not, however, resolve the question of what volatility to use for other expiration dates.

***Possibility of Negative Interest Rates.*** Even with the available quick fixes and adjustments, problems remain with using Black-Scholes in the fixed income area. One of these problems can be demonstrated through the following example of an out-of-the-money call. Consider a five-year European call option on a 30-year zero coupon bond. If the five-year riskless rate is 8 percent annual and the yield of the 30-year zero is 6 percent annual, the bond is worth $17.41 today. Further, assume that the price volatility for this option is 25 percent and that the strike price is $102. The value of this option must be 0, because the

---

[6] Modifications of the model to allow for volatility changing as a function of the stock price were derived by John Cox and Stephen Ross, in "The Valuation of Options for Alternative Stochastic Processes," *The Journal of Financial Economics,* 1976.

**EXHIBIT 34–5**

**Value of a Three-Year Call Option on a Three-Year Zero Coupon Bond.**

| | | | Strike Price | | |
|---|---|---|---|---|---|
| | 80 | 90 | 100 | 110 | 120 |
| Arbitrage value* | $15.02 | $ 7.51 | $ 0.00 | $ 0.00 | $ 0.00 |
| Black-Scholes value[†] | 19.22 | 14.49 | 10.70 | 7.78 | 5.60 |
| Black-Scholes value as volatility goes to zero[‡] | 15.02 | 7.51 | 0.00 | 0.00 | 0.00 |

* Assumes that the three-year risk-free rate is 10% annual
[†] Assumes a 4% price volatility, risk-free rate of 10% annual and current bond price of 75.13
[‡] Assumes a risk-free rate of 10% and current bond price of 75.13

bond can never be worth more than $100 unless interest rates are negative. Yet, the Black-Scholes model assigns this option a value of $1.80. This is over 10 percent of the underlying bond's price of $17.41.

This error is due to the lognormal assumption for bond prices in Black-Scholes. Bonds have a minimum and a maximum price: The minimum price is 0 and the maximum price is the sum of the remaining cash flows associated with the bond (assuming interest rates are nonnegative). According to the lognormal price assumption, there is some probability that a bond will reach any positive price.

*Adjusting for Coupon Payments.* So far we have restricted our examples to zero coupon bonds; in reality, most bonds pay coupons. Black-Scholes must be adjusted to reflect the effects of both coupon payments and changes in accrued interest for the underlying bond over the life of an option. The modification of Black-Scholes used in this case is the same approximation that is used for stocks with known dividend payments.

This modification results in the replacement of the current bond price in the Black-Scholes model with the price of the bond less the present value of any coupons paid and its change in accrued interest from the settlement date to the expiration date. Consider a six-month European call option struck at par on a 30-year, 10 percent semi-annual coupon priced at par. The six-month riskless rate is 8 percent on a bond-equivalent basis. The price volatility is 10 percent. The present value of the coupon payment (before the option's expiration date) in six months given the riskless rate of 8 percent (BEY) is $4.81 ($5/1.04). The value of the underlying security in Black-Scholes is therefore $95.19 (100−4.81). Substituting this price in the Black-Scholes equation gives a call option value of $8.06. This technique also adjusts for the pull toward par of both premium and discount bonds. Premium bonds tend to fall in price and discount bonds tend to rise in price because they both will be priced at par when they mature. Note that we use the short-term rate to discount the interest effects; using the long-term rate would allow an investor to risklessly earn the long-term rate over a short-term period.

*American Options.*  The final issue with regard to the Black-Scholes model is what to do in the case of an American-style option. Recall that American options, in contrast to European options, permit exercise prior to their expiration. Many fixed income options fall into this category. The Black-Scholes model was developed for European options on non-dividend-paying stocks. While American-style calls on non-dividend-paying stocks have the same value as a European call, in general an American option is worth more than a European option. This is because it is often optimal to exercise an American option before expiration.

The binomial-option-pricing methodology allows American-type options to be valued. This method was first presented in Cox, Ross, and Rubinstein.[7] In contrast to the Black-Scholes model, which is a closed-form solution to the option pricing problem, the binomial model is a numerical method. This approach parallels the examples in our first section; however, the price movements of the underlying security are specified in such a way that, for large binomial lattices, they follow the same lognormal process as the Black-Scholes model. Moreover, the binomial model can be used to solve the problems for which the Black-Scholes model is inappropriate, such as American calls on a dividend-paying security or American-style put options. But because the assumptions for the price distribution in this model are the same as in Black-Scholes, the binomial model requires the same modifications previously discussed and is subject to the same criticisms. The next subsection contains a discussion of how a binomial model can be adapted to solve for option values when the yield of a bond is assumed to be lognormally distributed. This approach answers the main criticisms of the Black-Scholes model for pricing short-term options on bonds.

## Binomial Model Based on Yield to Maturity[8]

Exhibit 34–6a shows a lognormal yield distribution assuming a bond with an initial yield of 10 percent and an annual yield volatility of 10 percent after one year. The lognormal yield distribution is skewed; increases in yield are more

---

[7] John Cox, Stephen Ross, and Mark Rubinstein, "Option Pricing: A Simplified Approach," *Journal of Financial Economics,* September 1979, pp. 229–63.

[8] See R. P. Clancy, "Options on Bonds and Applications to Product Pricing," *Transactions,* Volume XXXVII, 1985.

likely than decreases, as shown by the tail to the right in Exhibit 34–6a. Exhibit 34–6b shows the price distributions that result from this yield distribution assuming bonds with a 10 percent coupon and 1, 10, and 30 years to maturity. Comparing these figures with Exhibit 34–4 shows how the lognormal yield process model differs from the lognormal price process in the Black-Scholes model. Though the lognormal price distribution results in prices for all bonds that are positively skewed, the lognormal yield process does not. When yields follow a lognormal distribution, the maximum price of a bond must be less than the sum of its cash flows, and the minimum price is zero. The shape of the price distribution is determined by the effects of the yield distribution, the difference between the maximum price and the current price of the bond, and the convexity of the bond. Exhibit 34–6b illustrates that the combination is likely to result in a negatively skewed price distribution for short maturity bonds that have a low maximum price and low convexity, and a positively skewed price distribution for long maturity bonds that have a higher maximum price and larger convexity.

The lognormal yield-to-maturity model offers a number of attractive characteristics relative to the Black-Scholes model. By definition, there is no possibility of negative interest rates, because the yields follow a lognormal distribution. Further, because the bond prices are calculated from a yield distribution for each period, they will reflect both the decrease in price volatility and the pull toward par as the bond ages. This was not true in the price volatility models discussed above.

The following example, shown in Exhibit 34–7, illustrates the binomial model based on yields. Consider a 1-year European call option on a 30-year zero coupon bond. In this example, both the 1- and 30-year interest rates are initially at 10 percent (BEY), and the yield volatility is 15 percent.[9] As with the other models discussed thus far, the option's price is determined by arbitrage: The payoffs of the option are replicated at each node with a portfolio containing the underlying security and borrowed money. This requires that the yield lattice be translated into a price lattice for the underlying bond. Section 2 of the exhibit shows the price lattice for the 30-year zero coupon bond in the example. Notice that the maturity of the bond decreases as the lattice progresses through time. The option price is found following the methods illustrated in the first section of this chapter. The last two sections of the exhibit show the value of an option at each node in the lattice assuming that the short-term rate is always 10 percent. In this case, the value of an at-the-money call option is $1.78 and that of a put is $0.78.

The advantages of the lognormal yield process for bond prices over the lognormal price process are obvious: There are no adjustments to the inputs of the model to rectify its shortcomings, as there were for price volatility and coupon

---

[9] See Dyer and Jacob, "Guide to Fixed Income Option Pricing Models," for a complete discussion of this example.

**EXHIBIT 34-6**
**(a) Yield Distribution Projected One Year Forward Based on an Initial Yield level of 10% and a 10% Annual Yield Volatility (b) Price Distribution Projected One Year Forward for Various Maturity Bonds with 10% Coupons Based on Yield Distribution in Exhibit 34-6a**

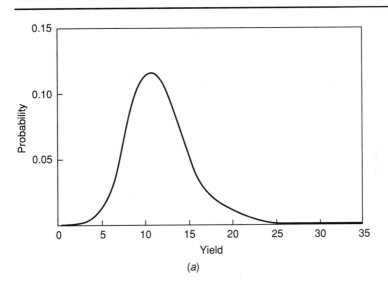

(a)

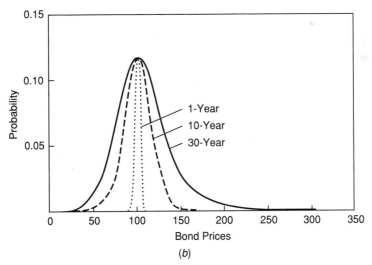

(b)

## EXHIBIT 34–7
## Binomial Model Based on Yield-to-Maturity

---

### Section 1

*Yield lattice for a 15% yield volatility*

| Years forward | 0 | 1 | 2 |
|---|---|---|---|

Projected yields: $10\%$ — $11.62\%$ — $13.50\%$ / $10.00\%$ ; $8.61\%$ — $10.00\%$ / $7.41\%$

Projected yields

| 0 | 1 | 2 |
|---|---|---|
| 10% | 11.62% | 13.50% |
|  | 8.61% | 10.00% |
|  |  | 7.41% |

### Section 2

*Price lattice for a 30-year zero coupon bond*

| Years forward<br>Remaining maturity | 0<br>30 | 1<br>29 | 2<br>28 |
|---|---|---|---|
| Projected<br>prices | $5.73 | $4.13 | $ 2.89 |
|  |  | $9.12 | $ 6.93 |
|  |  |  | $13.52 |

### Section 3

*Value of a call struck at $5.73 with the risk-free rate fixed at 10%*

| Years forward | 0 | 1 | 2 |
|---|---|---|---|
| Call<br>values | $1.78 | $0.45 | max ( 2.89 − 5.73, 0) = $0.00 |
|  |  | $3.91 | max ( 6.93 − 5.73, 0) = $1.20 |
|  |  |  | max (13.52 − 5.73, 0) = $7.79 |

### Section 4

*Value of a put struck at $5.73 with the risk-free rate fixed at 10%*

| Years forward | 0 | 1 | 2 |
|---|---|---|---|
| Put<br>values | $0.78 | $1.53 | max (5.73 − 2.89, 0) = $2.84 |
|  |  | $0.00 | max (5.73 − 6.93, 0) = $0.00 |
|  |  |  | max (5.73 − 13.52, 0) = $0.00 |

---

bonds in Black-Scholes. Moreover, this model can easily value American-style options by solving the lattice equations.[10]   In fact, the binomial lattice can handle the hybrid nature of options embedded in callable bonds, which are European during the call protection period and American thereafter.

---

[10] The American feature is handled by replacing the value of the option at each point by the larger of the values of the European option or of immediate exercise.

*Violation of Arbitrage-Free Pricing.* In the above example we assumed that the riskless rate was a constant. Aside from the lack of realism of this assumption, particularly over long periods of time, it may allow arbitrage opportunities between bonds and the riskless rate. If the riskless rate is not between the returns on the bond for the up and down lattice points, then arbitrage opportunities exist. It is sometimes difficult to avoid such arbitrage opportunities. For example, as a bond approaches maturity, the returns for up and down yield shifts approach the yield on the bond; this is an identity at maturity. If the risk-free rate is fixed while the yield on the bond varies for a long-term option such as a callable bond, there must eventually be an arbitrage between the risk-free rate and the bond's return at some of the states on the lattice. As a result, these models are usually designed to have the riskless rate move along with the yield of the underlying security in most applications of this model.

Exhibit 34–8 shows the values of the call and put in Exhibit 34–7, assuming that the risk-free rate is equal to the long-term rate in each period. This approach changes the values of both options slightly. The effect is larger for longer-term options and for higher volatilities. While this method adjusts the short-term rate in such a way that obvious arbitrage opportunities can be avoided, it does not produce an arbitrage-free lattice. The lattice, which is based on a flat term structure and parallel-yield shifts, may be shown to have arbitrage opportunities in two ways. Section 1 of Exhibit 34–9 shows that the European put and call values in Exhibit 34–8 violate put/call parity. Section 2 of Exhibit 34–9 shows that a duration-matched combination of a 1-year and a 30-year zero coupon bond

**EXHIBIT 34–8**
**Value of a Put and Call on the 30-Year Zero Coupon Bond in Exhibit 34–7 when the Bond Yield and Risk-Free Rate Move in Parallel.**

**Section 1**

*Value of a call struck at $5.73*

| Years forward | 0 | 1 | 2 |
|---|---|---|---|
| Call price | $1.76 | $1.46 / $3.85 | max ( 2.89 − 5.73, 0) = $0.00 / max ( 6.93 − 5.73, 0) = $1.20 / max (13.52 − 5.73, 0) = $7.79 |

**Section 2**

*Value of a put struck at $5.73*

| Period | 0 | 1 | 2 |
|---|---|---|---|
| Put price | $0.70 | $1.46 / $0.00 | max (5.73 −  2.89, 0) = $2.84 / max (5.73 −  6.93, 0) = $0.00 / max (5.73 − 13.52, 0) = $0.00 |

**EXHIBIT 34–9**
**Signs of an Arbitrage-Ridden Lattice.**

---

### Section 1

*Violation of a put/call parity for floating short-term rate in Exhibit 34–8*

Put/Call Parity Relationship

$$\frac{\text{Call}}{\text{price}} - \frac{\text{Put}}{\text{price}} = \frac{\text{Bond}}{\text{price}} - \frac{\text{Discounted}}{\text{strike price}}$$

Test for Parity

$$\$1.76 \; - \; \$0.70 \; \overset{?}{=} \; \$5.73 \; - \; \frac{\$5.73}{(1.1)^2}$$

$$\$1.06 \; \neq \; \$1.00$$

### Section 2

The return of a duration-matched combination of zero coupon bonds dominates the return of a single bond.

For parallel yield shifts in Exhibit 34–8, returns for a combination of 31% thirty-year and 69% one-year zero coupon bonds dominates a ten-year zero coupon bond.

|  | *Return for Bond* | | | |
|---|---|---|---|---|
|  | *One-Year* | *Ten-Year* | *Thirty-Year* | *Combination* |
| State 1 | 10.00% | (3.56%) | (27.9% ) | (2.31%) |
| State 2 | 10.00% | 23.34% | 59.16% | 25.24% |

will outperform an equal investment in a 10-year bond over the first period if only parallel shifts of this yield curve are possible. Similar results may be shown for the rest of the lattice. This arbitrage between bonds on the yield curve makes possible the violation of put/call parity. Another problem with this model is that the yield volatility on the lattice is constant over the life of the bond. This is reasonable for short time periods, but does not match the observed behavior of yields for different maturity bonds. One would prefer a model in which yield volatility decreases as maturity increases. This would match the observed historical behavior of yield volatilities.

We now turn to a discussion of a group of models that are internally consistent with regard to arbitrage between bonds of different maturities. Unfortunately, these models require considerably more work to define and apply than the models considered so far.

## Yield-Curve Models

The two previous subsections showed that modifying equity-option-pricing models to price options on fixed income securities leads to both practical and theoretical inconsistencies. The underlying cause of these difficulties has been discussed in a number of research papers[11] and can be summarized as follows: *A theoretically consistent fixed-income, option-pricing model must specify the dynamics of the yield curve in such a way that no security or combination of securities consistently provides a higher expected rate of return than another over a short period of time.* Practitioners have adopted various approaches to implementing this condition for arbitrage-free pricing.

This subsection contains a discussion of the three main methods used to build an arbitrage-free fixed income option pricing model. They should be considered different methods of solving the same arbitrage-free pricing problem and not different models of the pricing process. As such, they should provide the same answer to any given problem, provided they are based on the same set of assumptions. Each approach offers a different set of advantages and disadvantages that makes one method or another easier to implement in a given situation. As the basic characterics of these arbitrage-free, yield-curve models are similar, our discussion centers on their implementation in an arbitrage-free binomial model. This approach illustrates the important features of an arbitrage-free model in the most intuitive way. Two other methods commonly used to create an arbitrage-free yield-curve model, simulations of the yield-curve process and numerical solutions to the partial differential equation that describes the arbitrage-free pricing condition, are discussed briefly.

*Arbitrage-Free Binomial Model.* The arbitrage-free binomial model is based on a lattice of interest rates much like the binomial model based on yields discussed in the previous subsection. In this model the yields on the lattice represent a series of possible future short-term interest rates designed to satisfy conditions preventing changes in the yield curve that would permit arbitrage opportunities. The binomial model based on yield, in contrast, uses a lattice of the underlying security's yield that may allow arbitrage. Most of the arbitrage-free binomial models assume a multiplicative binomial process that approximates a lognormal yield distribution when making the lattice of short-term rates.

A yield lattice is designed so that the period between lattice points corresponds to a short-term rate. In a model based on 90-day interest rates, the lattice would consist of 3-month rates; in a model based on 30-day rates, the

---

[11] For example, see J. Harrison and D. Kreps, "Martingales and Arbitrage in Multiperiod Securities Markets." *Journal of Economic Theory,* Vol. 20, No. 3, June 1979; and Bookstaber, Jacob, and Langsam, op. cit.

lattice would consist of 1-month rates. The choice of the term is important because it determines the size and number of periods of the lattice. This, in turn, determines the accuracy and cost of running the model. This model will always produce an answer, but if the lattice is too small, the answer produced is likely to be wrong. A test that is frequently used to determine whether the size of a lattice is sufficient for a given type of problem is to check for significant option value changes when the lattice size is increased. If the lattice is sufficiently large for the type of problem under consideration, the value will not change significantly. Once the size of the lattice has been tested and found to be accurate for pricing a type of option, then it may be used to value similar types of options with confidence.

Exhibit 34–10 builds a two-period, arbitrage-free binomial lattice using one approach. Other methods may also be used to produce an arbitrage-free

**EXHIBIT 34–10**
**Constructing an Arbitage-Free Binomial Lattice.**

---

### Section 1

*Initial Zero Coupon Bond Yield Curve*

| Maturity (years) | 1 | 2 | 3 |
|---|---|---|---|
| Yield | 8.00% | 9.00% | 9.50% |

### Section 2

*Binomial lattice of one-period forward rates based on the initial 8% one-period rate and 10% yield volatility*

| Maturity (years) | 1 | 2 | 3 |
|---|---|---|---|
| One-period forward rate lattice | 8.00% | 8.84% / 7.24% | 9.77% / 8.00% / 6.55% |
| Yield curve from lattice | 8.00% | 8.02% | 8.06% |

### Section 3

*The lattice is adjusted to provide the initial yield curve*

| Maturity (years) adjusted | 1 | 2 | 3 |
|---|---|---|---|
| One-period forward rate lattice | 8.00% | 11.02% / 9.02% | 12.75% / 10.44% / 8.54% |
| Yield curve from lattice | 8.00% | 9.00% | 9.50% |

---

binomial lattice. The yield curve for the lattice is based on one-, two-, and three-period zero coupon bonds with yields of 8 percent, 9 percent, and 9.5 percent, respectively. Section 2 shows that the expected value of the yields from the conventional-binomial-lattice approach does not equal the initial-yield curve. But the lattice may be adjusted such that the short-term rate volatility is unchanged and the expected value of the lattice yields equals the initial yield curve.

Exhibit 34–11 solves for the option prices on the lattice. The put/call parity relationship holds for the two-year European put and call on the three-year zero coupon bond, as will be shown. As discussed in the first section of this chapter, for any European contingent claim that can be priced by arbitrage, the value of the claim can be found by computing the expected discounted value of its payoffs, provided that the model adjusts the expected return of the underlying security to be equal to the riskless rate for each period in the lattice. Because the arbitrage-free binomial lattice makes this adjustment, the values of the call and put in the exhibit can be computed in this manner. Alternatively, the lattice may be used to solve for the arbitrage portfolios that mimic the behavior of the option.

Section 1 of Exhibit 34–11 shows that the price lattice for values of the three-period zero coupon bond at the end of period two are 92.13, 90.56, and 88.70. The payoffs for the call and put are determined by these prices, as shown in sections 2 and 3. To value the option, these payoffs are discounted back to the beginning of the lattice, using the short-term rates for the state in section 3 of Exhibit 34–10. The expected values of the call and put are $0.69 and $0.27, respectively. If the lattice is arbitrage-free, put/call parity will hold and the difference betweeen the value of the call and the put will equal the difference between the value of the underlying bond and the discounted value of the strike price for the options.[12] The current value of the three-period zero coupon bond is 76.17, and the discounted value of the strike price is 75.70 ($90 \div 1.09^2$). Thus, the difference between these values is $0.42, the same as the difference between the call and the put: Put/call parity is satisfied.

At this point we would like to make several observations about the lattice and the procedure. The choice of the probability of rates going up, $p = 1/2$, was arbitrary. We could instead have chosen it to be 3/4. In this case, the adjustments to the lattice required for the nonarbitrage condition would differ, but the procedures would remain the same.[13]

One of the attractions of this method is that only one lattice needs to be created for a given volatility and yield curve. Once this is done, all securities, regardless of whether their payoffs are certain or uncertain, can be priced with

---

[12] For a discussion of put/call parity, see Bookstaber, Jacob, and Langsam, op. cit.

[13] However, in this case, to maintain the same volatility one would have to change the size of the up and down move.

**EXHIBIT 34–11**
**Arbitrage-Free Option Prices — Arbitrage-Free Price Lattice for Three-Period Zero Coupon Bond.**

### Section 1

| Years forward | 0 | 1 | 2 |
|---|---|---|---|

Bond prices

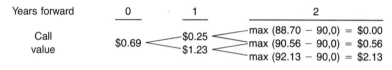

$76.17 —$80.73 — $88.70
$83.79 — $90.56
$92.13

### Section 2

*Value of a two-year call on the three-year bond struck at $90*

| Years forward | 0 | 1 | 2 |
|---|---|---|---|

Call value  $0.69 — $0.25 — max (88.70 − 90,0) = $0.00
$1.23 — max (90.56 − 90,0) = $0.56
max (92.13 − 90,0) = $2.13

### Section 3

*Value of a two-year put on the three-year bond struck at $90*

| Years forward | 0 | 1 | 2 |
|---|---|---|---|

Put value  $0.27 — $0.59 — max (90 − 88.70,0) = $1.30
$0.00 — max (90 − 90.56,0) = $0.00
max (90 − 90.13,0) = $0.00

the same lattice in a similar manner by discounting back along the lattice and computing expected values. Moreover, because it is a lattice model it easily handles American options.

Other than the extra work that is necessary to build the arbitrage-free binomial lattice, this model seems to have addressed all of the theoretical problems that we have encountered. Nevertheless, there are reasons to develop alternative models. Certain types of assets and liabilities have payoffs that depend not only on the interest rate at the time of payoff (this is the case for a European call or put) but also on the entire path of rates until the time of payoff — for example, a mortgage-backed security or a Single Premium Deferred Annuity issued by an insurance company.

Although the lattice of interest rates remains connected for these problems, the cash flows on the lattice depend on the path of interest rates. This results in a cash-flow lattice that is disconnected — the cash flows along every path through the lattice are different. This significantly increases the number of calculations needed to solve a problem on the lattice. For a connected lattice there are $n(n + 1)/2$ systems of equations that must be solved where $n$ is the number of periods in the lattice. Therefore, the solution for a 30-period lattice contains 465 equations. For a disconnected lattice, however, there are $2^n$ systems of equations to solve: The solution for a 30-period lattice contains a system of over one billion equations. In order to make the problem tractable, practitioners use sampling procedures that examine a limited number of paths through the payoff lattice. The sampling efficiency of these procedures may be increased by applying variance reduction techniques that improve the sampling efficiency.[14]

An alternative to sampling from the binomial lattice is the use of Monte Carlo simulation techniques to solve the continuous time model of the options-pricing equation. This technique is discussed in the following subsection, along with other numerical techniques.

***Monte Carlo Simulation.*** In practice, the Monte Carlo simulation technique works as follows. First, a large sample of short-term interest rate paths is generated from the current short-term rate; these short-term rates are generated in such a way that they follow a lognormal distribution. However, these interest rate paths will not, in general, price back to the current yield curve because their expected values are approximately the short-term rate. Therefore, the short-term rates are adjusted following a procedure similar to that illustrated in our discussion of the arbitrage-free binomial model. The adjustment makes the expected value of a zero coupon bond priced on the set of paths equal to the price for the bond from the current spot-rate curve. The adjustments should also maintain the volatility of the changes in the short-term rate. Given a set of arbitrage-free paths, any security or option with payoffs that can be defined on the interest-rate paths may be valued by first determining the payoffs associated with the instrument along each of the paths and then discounting these payoffs back along the paths at the short-term rates. The initial yield curve should, however, be appropriate for the security being priced. This requires an adjustment to the Treasury yield curve, usually made by adding a spread to the curve. The spread that provides the market's price for a security is called an option-adjusted spread.

Monte Carlo simulation has been particularly useful for valuing mortgage-backed securities. The payoffs for a mortgage-backed security will, in general, have different values along each path and at each point in time.[15]   The ad-

---

[14] For a description of this technique, see David P. Jacob, Graham Lord, and James Tilley, "A Generalized Framework for Pricing Interest-Sensitive Cash Flows," *Financial Management,* Winter 1987.

[15] For a description of the mortgage-backed example, see David P. Jacob and Alden L. Toevs, "An Analysis of the New Valuation, Duration and Convexity Models for Mortgage-Backed Securities," in Frank J. Fabozzi (ed.), *The Handbook of Mortgage-Backed Securities: Revised Edition* (Chicago: Probus Publishing, 1988).

vantage of this method over a binomial model for valuing mortgages is that a large number of different paths are generated. In contrast, all of the sample paths from the binomial model share one of two nodes in the first period, one of three nodes in the second period, and so on. This reduces the number of unique states at a given point in time, and thus decreases the accuracy of the mortgage price estimated along the paths.

*Differential Equation Approach.* In some cases the value of the payoff can be obtained by numerically solving a differential equation. The techniques are beyond the scope of this chapter, but they are fairly standard and can be found in any good book on numerical methods. This method applies a more rigorous mathematical approach to the valuation of an option and, therefore, reduces its computational complexity. One should be aware, however, that even with this approach adjustments are made to the projected yields in the model so that bonds are priced in accordance with their market values.

This approach offers a significant advantage in some applications relative to the Monte Carlo method: It readily values American-style options. Monte Carlo simulation is not well suited to valuing these options because they allow early exercise. As discussed in the first section of this chapter, valuing an American option requires that both the value of a European option and the value of immediately exercising the American option be computed. This requires that the value of an additional option be calculated at each point where there is a possibility of early exercise. These extra computations quickly make Monte Carlo simulation impractical for calculating the value of American options. An alternative approach that applies a rule of thumb to determine early exercise could be used, but would be unlikely to provide arbitrage-free pricing.

## WHICH MODEL SHOULD BE USED?

None of the option pricing models described is perfect for all situations. Users must choose between those models that are easy to implement but do not capture all of the special characteristics of fixed income securities and those that adhere to arbitrage-free pricing principles but are expensive to build and cumbersome to use. One might think that the added accuracy would always be worth the extra expense. However, some of the yield-curve models require large amounts of computer resources and take a great deal of time to produce results. Obviously, a trader who must manage a position's risk exposure in a rapidly changing market would be willing to sacrifice some theoretical nicety in favor of speed.

In other circumstances, such as pricing complex securities, the results from a model must be judged relative to the realities of the marketplace. Frequently, the markets for such securities do not fully reflect the assumptions of perfect liquidity, no transaction costs, and perfect information made in the pricing models.

Under these circumstances, no model can be used to risklessly arbitrage mispricing, but a model may provide reasonable indications of value. The choice in a specific situation ought to be dictated by the performance of the models available for the application. If two models lead to the same investment or trading decisions from the user's perspective, then the approach that is easier to use and/or most cost effective is the logical choice.

In this section we summarize our views on which model or models appear to provide reasonable performance in specific situations. We begin by discussing the relative merits of the models for pricing short-term fixed income options; we then discuss long-term fixed income options.

## Options with Short Terms to Expiration

Short-term options on fixed income securities trade both in the over-the-counter market and on the futures exchanges. These options typically have one year or less to expiration.

*Options on Fixed Income Securities and Futures Contracts.* In practice, options on fixed income securities are priced by a modified version of the Black-Scholes model, its binomial equivalent, or a binomial model on yields. Options on fixed income futures contracts are usually priced by the Black commodity model, which is a modification of the Black-Scholes model, though a binomial model in yield may be adapted to this case. Options on money market instruments, such as Eurodollar futures, are usually priced with a Black commodity model modified to represent a securities yield instead of its price. Of course, one could use an arbitrage-free binomial model to evaluate short-term options on any of these securities, but the results from this complex model would be unlikely to be worth the extra work.

One would expect both the Black-Scholes and binomial yield models to produce similar results for European options with short terms to expiration on long maturity bonds and notes that are nearly in-the-money. This conclusion is based both on the similarity of the long-term bond price distributions for the Black-Scholes model and the binomial model in yield (discussed in the previous section) and on the assumption that the differences in discounting procedures between these models should not have a significant effect on the resulting option prices, due to the short time to expiration. However, the differences in the distributions may affect the pricing of out-of-the money options.

Many practitioners prefer the binomial model based on yields for these options because Black-Scholes may neither produce reliable results for American-style options nor reliably price options on securities with short terms to maturity. In Exhibits 34–4 and 34–6 the differences in the skewness of the price distributions for these models illustrate the potential for mispricing.

The binomial-yield model has an additional advantage in that the yield volatilities of a bond are comparable over time. In contrast, the price volatilities used in Black-Scholes models are sensitive to changes in the bond's duration, which, in turn, is sensitive to yield changes, coupon effects, and aging. Therefore, price volatilities may not be comparable over time for bonds and notes. This is particularly true for bond and note futures where changes in the cheapest to deliver bond may significantly change the duration of the contract. Consequently, yield volatilities are a better measure of the market's volatility and, therefore, the relative value of options. In our view, they should be used as relative historical volatility measures even if options are priced and hedged based on the Black-Scholes model.

The distinction between pricing options on cash bonds and pricing options on futures is of limited importance because of the close tracking of prices between the cash and the futures markets. One should also remember that the price of a futures contract reflects financing considerations whereas the price of a cash bond does not. This may cause some confusion. For example, an at-the-money call option on a futures contract would be an in-the-money call on a cash security in a positively sloped yield curve. The exception to this is when the cheapest-to-deliver bond is likely to change as rates change. In this case there may be a significant change in the duration of the bond or note contract that would not be measured by the models discussed here.[16] Modeling this effect is possible using a binomial yield lattice, but is beyond the scope of this chapter.

The preceding comments refer to using the models to determine the value of short-term fixed income options, but for many applications hedging an option is equally important. Although we believe that the Black-Scholes model may leave something to be desired in measuring value, it offers some advantages over the other models in hedging applications. Because the Black-Scholes model is continuous, the prices and risk measures for options, such as delta, kappa, theta, and so on, change smoothly. For the binomial model, numerical differences due to the coarseness of the lattice can make the risk measures coarse. This causes the risk measure to change in an abrupt and therefore unnatural way. An approach that smooths these values uses a series of lattices measuring different options parameters to compute a price curve, and then uses analytic approximations to facilitate the calculation of the derivatives. Alternatively, larger lattices may be used to increase the accuracy of the binomial approach.

***Short-Term Options on Mortgage-Backed Forwards.*** Options on mortgage-backed forwards are often evaluated using Black's commodity model. However, this approach will tend to overstate the true value of calls and understate the true value of puts, unless the volatility input is adjusted for the negative convexity of the mortgage. The embedded prepayment feature of the mortgage-backed security is the source of this effect. Although a more complex approach

---

[16] The effect of such a change is discussed in the *Financial Futures Handbook,* Morgan Stanley, February 1989.

(such as a technique based on a yield-curve model) can be created to incorporate this effect, such a model would be much more expensive than the Black commodity model. Alternatively, a binomial model may be created that incorporates the effect of price compression on the pricing of mortgage options.[17] It is interesting to note that the Black commodity model is the standard model used in this market.

## Long-Term Options

Recently, the attention of Wall Street analysts has focused on the pricing of long-term options. This is because of the rapid development of the mortgage market and the effect of volatile interest rates on callable corporate debt. The nearly universal conclusion is that consistent pricing for long-term options can only be obtained through an arbitrage-free, yield-curve model.

*Callable and Putable Bonds.* Corporate bonds are frequently issued with a call feature. For example, telephone bonds are issued with maturities as long as 40 years and with a call option that is, typically, European for the first five years and American thereafter. Further, the call price declines over time according to a schedule. Originally many practitioners used the binomial model based on yields to value these options, but this model sometimes produced values for the options that did not make sense. To a large extent, this was due to the arbitrary nature of the risk-free rate chosen for the model. Changes in this rate could produce very different conclusions on the value of these options. Unfortunately, this model could not provide a method for determining a reasonable risk-free rate. More recently, arbitrage-free models that provide appropriate discount rates have been used to value these securities. These models specify the risk-free, or discounting, rate over the life of the option, which allows more consistent valuations of these securities.

However, these models do not guarantee the user a profit when they suggest that a particular option is cheap or rich. To extract the profit implied by the model, an investor would have to purchase or sell the callable bond and then effectively hedge it dynamically for the life of the option, or until the market reaches a "fair value" for the option. Therefore, the performance of the model must be tested under real market conditions. The same test should be applied to any option-trading strategy.

*Mortgage-Backed Securities.* Another major area where yield-curve models have been applied and proved their worth is the evaluation of mortgage-

---

[17] For more information, see David P. Jacob and M. Sitte, "Price Compression and the Pricing of Options on Mortgage-Backed Securities," Morgan Stanley, March 1989.

backed securities. The embedded option for these securities is the interest-sensitive prepayment component of the mortgage. This makes the cash flows for these securities quite dependent on the path of interest rates. Because of the path dependence of the cash flows and long term of the securities, Black-Scholes and binomial models on yields are not well suited for analyzing these securities. Therefore, a yield-curve model is necessary to obtain consistent option values.

Most practitioners favor the Monte Carlo simulation approach because of its flexibility and relative simplicity, as discussed in the previous section. However, numerical solutions to differential equations or the arbitrage-free binomial lattice may also be used.

When creating a mortgage model, remember that the prepayment function is very important in determining the option's characteristics. If it is estimated on unrepresentative data (for example, you believe that homeowners have changed their prepayment behavior relative to the history used in an estimate) or if it is estimated over a small amount of data, its results should be treated with suspicion. As with callable bonds, those who understand the assumptions realize that the mispricings suggested by the model are usually not arbitrageable without risk. However, the results of empirical tests of this approach show that the model is quite useful in discerning relative value.[18]

***Other Applications.*** Yield-curve models have been applied extensively to the analysis of interest-sensitive insurance company liabilities. In fact, some of the earliest theoretical work on these models was done to evaluate insurance company liabilities such as Single Premium Deferred Annuities.[19] These liabilities are similar to mortgage-backed securities in that their cash flows are interest-sensitive with a large degree of path dependence. Therefore, most analysts favor a simulation approach in modeling these instruments. The pricing of these securities may depend on the slope of the yield curve, because of investor and competing insurer's behavior, a two-factor model may represent this process better than a one-factor model.

## Closing Thoughts

At this point we would like to look forward to the next generation of models and then summarize our view of practical option pricing.

---

[18] See David P. Jacob, Gary Latainer, and Alden L. Toevs, "Value and Performance of Mortgage-Backed Securities," Morgan Stanley, 1987.

[19] See Peter D. Noris and Sheldon Epstein, "Finding the Immunizing Investment for Insurance Liabilities: The Case of the SPDA," in Frank J. Fabozzi (ed.), *Fixed Income Portfolio Strategies: State-of-the-Art Technologies and Innovations* (Chicago: Probus Publishing, 1989).

***What Will the Next Generation of Models Look Like?***   Despite the time and effort expended to develop the option pricing models discussed above, the future will probably produce new, more complex models. This is because more complex securities and strategies will be developed. For example, an investor may desire an option that provides a payoff based on the difference between the 90-day Treasury bill rate and the yield on the long bond. In this situation, one might build a model that allows some independence between the different parts of the yield curve. The arbitrage-free models currently available have nearly perfect correlation between the short-term and long-term rates. However, as long as the option does not depend on the difference between two rates, one might want first to test to see how well a nonarbitrage-free model works before attempting a two-factor model.

As we mentioned earlier, the appropriateness of distributional and volatility assumptions used in the model may come under more study. Though the history of the levels of interest rates and the shape of the yield curve is frequently studied, the historical behavior of volatility is not. Given the importance of these parameters in valuing securities with embedded options, more empirical work would be useful.

***The Real Test of Option Pricing Models.***   The true test of a model— whether it works in practice—is an important point that is often missed in the quest for "better" models. If a model does not accomplish what you want, then all of its complexity is worthless. It should therefore be tested to see how well it can reproduce the payoffs that it promises. This is accomplished by dynamically adjusting a hedge portfolio recommended by the model. If the hedge's ability to reproduce the option's payoffs is poor, the model is not going to be useful for arbitrage. On the other hand, it may still be useful for answering relative value questions or as an indication of a security's duration and convexity; these aspects should be tested as well.

In some situations, one may have to work with models that provide prices that have relatively large confidence intervals. For example, some of the derivative mortgage-backed securities, such as interest-only and principal-only strips, have cash flows that are extremely sensitive to the path of interest rates; thus, imperfections in the prepayment model used to generate the mortgage's cash flows are magnified. Moreover, there is very little price history with which to test a model's usefulness. In this case, one must be cautious in the application of the technology. However, one should not be deluded into believing that by ignoring the problems and using a simpler model more useful answers can be obtained. In summary, users should work with the most cost-effective model that has been successfully tested for their particular application. In situations where testing is not feasible, they should go with the most theoretically correct model that their resources permit.

**EXHIBIT 34-12**
**Summary and Recommended Applications for the Models**

| Model | Recommended Application | Advantages | Disadvantages | Caveats |
|---|---|---|---|---|
| Black-Scholes/ Cox-Ross-Rubinstein Binomial Models | Short-term options on bonds, notes, and interest rates<br><br>Short-term options on futures<br><br>Short-term options on mortgage-backed forwards | Easy to implement<br><br>Low cost<br><br>"Standard model" | Does not model early exercise for American-style options<br><br>The short-term rate in the model is fixed<br><br>Adjustments are required for interest payments and accrual price volatility changes over the life of an option<br><br>The mortgages' price volatility must be adjusted to reflect convexity | Inappropriate for long-term options and, potentially, short-term options on short-term bonds |
| Binomial in Yield | Short-term options on bonds, notes, and interest rates<br><br>Short-term options on futures | Better model of price, yield, and pull-to-par process for bonds and notes<br><br>Prices American-style options<br><br>Allows floating short-term rate | Violates put/call parity<br><br>More expensive to run than Black-Scholes | May be used for long-term options such as callable bonds but the results should be carefully checked for reasonableness |
| Yield Curve Models | Long-term options on bonds, notes, and interest rates<br><br>Callable bonds<br><br>Mortgage-backed securities<br><br>Complex assets and liabilities, e.g., Single Premium Deferred Annuities for insurance companies | Satisfies put/call parity<br><br>Better model of long-term interest rate behavior<br><br>Can price American-style options (binomial and numerical solution of differential equations)<br><br>Yield volatility behavior is consistent with empirical observations, i.e., short-term rate volatility is greater than long-term rate volatility | Most expensisve models to develop and run | Highly correlated short- and long-term rates make this inappropriate for options on the difference between two rates<br><br>Differences between market value and models value for long-term options may not be realizable through arbitrage trading due to transactions costs and mistracking<br><br>Accuracy of mortgage model depends on prepayment rate estimates |

## CONCLUSION

The characteristics of fixed income securities differ from those of equities. Therefore, the option pricing models designed for stocks are inappropriate for valuing and analyzing the characteristics of fixed income securities in many situations. But we have shown that the basic principles of pricing via arbitrage and the ability to replicate the payoffs of an option that are the basis of the equity models can be applied to fixed income securities. Given the added complexity and costs associated with the best theoretical answer, it is interesting to note that it is not required for all applications.

In some situations, such as with short-term European options on bonds or futures, one can (and from a cost standpoint, probably should) consider models that, though not theoretically pure, produce results that are close enough to those produced with the more complex models. In other situations, such as pricing mortgage-backed securities, more complicated models are usually necessary. Exhibit 34–12 summarizes our recommendations and offers caveats for the models for a variety of applications. The most important point is that all models should be tested with real data before being adopted. This will provide the only true indication to practitioners as to how useful a model can be.

# CHAPTER 35

## BEHAVIOR OF VOLATILITY AND TRADING CHARACTERISTICS OF FIXED INCOME OPTIONS

*Nicholas C. Letica*
*Assistant Vice President*
*BT Securities Corporation*

*William J. Curtin*
*Senior Vice President*
*Lehman Brothers*

*Andrew Lawrence*
*Vice President*
*Greenwich Capital Markets*

*John Drastal*
*Vice President*
*Lehman Brothers*

Many fixed income securities, such as callable corporates and mortgage-backed securities (MBSs), are a combination of two elements: a long position in a noncallable bond and an implicit or explicit long or short options position.[1] Therefore, to address the value of such a security properly, investors must address the option component. Volatility has a very strong influence on the option component and thus becomes a very important parameter when analyzing

---

[1] This is discussed in more detail in Chapter 36.

the composite security. The purpose of this chapter is to describe the behavior of volatility and its effect on the trading characteristics of fixed income options. We also explain the various ways that volatility can be measured.

## EFFECTS OF VOLATILITY ON OPTION PRICING

Evaluating the impact of volatility on the option component (and therefore the security) is simply a matter of basic options theory. Although it is beyond the scope of this chapter to delineate a comprehensive options pricing theory, it is useful to review two of the essential parameters involved in the pricing of embedded options.[2]

First, as volatility increases, the value of a given option rises. Investors that are long options have limited liability: The greatest loss they can incur is the option fee. Conversely, the upside potential is theoretically limitless. A long options position performs well when volatility rises, as the likelihood that the underlying security moves past the strike price increases. Thus, an investor is willing to pay more for an option where the underlying security is volatile, due to the possibility of unlimited profit without a similar increase in losses. The relationship between option value and volatility is displayed in Exhibit 35–1 for a call that is at-the-money (ATM), out-of-the-money (OTM), and in-the-money (ITM). A short options position, on the other hand, performs poorly when volatility increases. Option sellers demand more of a premium when the underlying security is volatile, in order to compensate for the greater risk exposure. Option buyers (sellers) are volatility buyers (sellers), hoping that volatility will increase (decrease), resulting in increased (decreased) option value.

The second important rule to remember is that as the time to expiration declines, the value of a given option falls (time decay). The longer the time to expiration, the greater the likelihood that the underlying price will move past the strike price.

The effect of time to expiration on call value is shown in Exhibit 35–2. As the time to expiration lengthens, the influence of volatility on the value of an option increases exponentially. The impact of volatility at varying lengths of time to expiration is shown in Exhibit 35–3. Note that the slope of the line is steeper when there is a greater amount of time to expiration. As time passes, time decay and volatility compete with each other. Rising volatility acts to increase the option's value whereas time decay serves to decrease it.

---

[2] Fixed income option pricing models are discussed in the previous chapter.

**EXHIBIT 35–1**
**Call Option Value vs. Percent Price Volatility (Three Calls: At-the-Money,
1 Point In-the-Money, 1 Point Out-of-the-Money; Three Months from
Expiration).**

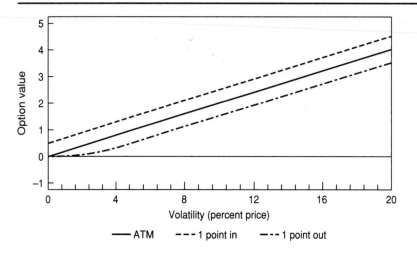

**EXHIBIT 35–2**
**Call Option Value vs. Underlying Security Price (Call Struck at Par with
One and Three Months to Expiration).**

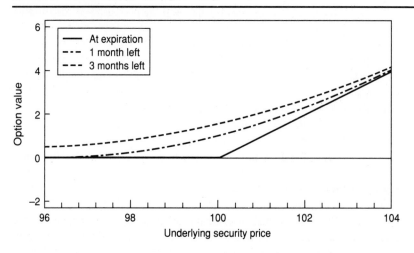

**EXHIBIT 35-3**
**Call Option Value for Different Times to Expiration with Changing Volatility.**

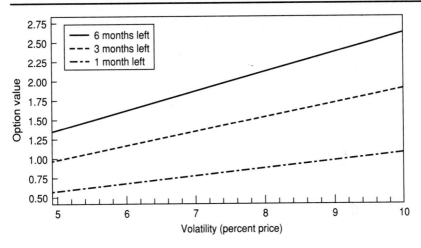

## WHAT IS VOLATILITY?

Statistically, volatility is a measure of the dispersion or spread of observations around the mean of the set of observations. If volatility seems strangely like a standard deviation, then you remember your statistics. When people speak of volatility, all they really are talking about is a standard deviation.

For fixed income securities, volatility is expressed in yield or price units, either on a percentage or on an absolute basis. Price volatilities can be computed for any security. Yield volatilities should be computed only for those securities with a consistent method for computing yield. Given the complexity of calculating a yield on a MBS and the variation of results, the predominant volatility measure in the MBS market is price volatility. The government bond market, where yields are easily calculated, favors yield volatility.

## TYPES OF VOLATILITY

### Empirical Volatility

Empirical volatility is the actual, historical market volatility of a specific security. These numbers are typically calculated for varying time periods (10 days, 30 days, 360 days) and are usually annualized (for this chapter, all volatilities are annualized).[3] Calculating an empirical volatility is nothing more than calculating the standard deviation of a time series. Thus, an absolute volatility is the annualized standard deviation of daily price or yield changes, assuming a normal distribution. A sample volatility calculation for GNMA 10 percent mortgage-backed securities can be found in Appendix A. The distribution of daily yield changes of the 30-year, constant maturity Treasury bond from 1982 to 1988 is displayed in Exhibit 35–4. This distribution is fairly normal, with a slight bias toward negative changes. This bias is primarily due to the bull market that dominated during this interval.

Percentage volatility is the annualized standard deviation of the daily change in the log of prices or yields, assuming a lognormal distribution of prices or yields. Exhibit 35–5 shows the distribution of the logs of daily yield changes of the 30-year, constant maturity Treasury from the beginning of 1982 to the

**EXHIBIT 35–4**

**30-Year Constant Maturity Treasury, Distribution of 1-Day Absolute Yield Changes (BP), 1/82–1/88.**

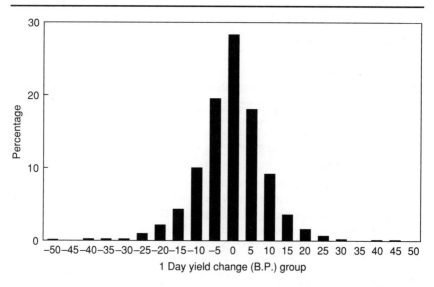

---

[3] When annualizing a volatility certain assumptions are inherent to the calculation. To convert from daily to yearly volatility, for example, the daily volatility is multiplied by the square root of the number of business days in the year, approximately 250. The various assumptions that are made when converting to an annual volatility and the way to derive this number are shown in Appendix B.

beginning of 1988. Similar to the daily absolute yield changes (Exhibit 35–4), the logs of the daily yield changes have a slight bias toward lower yields. The intuitive approach to calculate a percentage volatility is to find the standard deviation of daily *returns*, assuming a normal distribution. This approach is equivalent to the lognormal assumption as long as the distribution can be characterized as being equally normal and lognormal and the changes in prices are taken on a small interval, such as daily. Appendix A provides more complete explanation and an example of the lognormal calculation.

As previously mentioned, empirical volatility can be measured over varying time periods. The most common interval on which the standard deviation is taken is 30 days; other common interval are 10 days and 360 days. The choice of interval determines how quickly and to what degree an empirical volatility responds to deviations. As the time period shortens, volatility increasingly reflects current conditions, but is more unstable as each sample asserts greater influence in the deviation. Conversely, as the interval increases, more of a lag and a smoothing are introduced into the calculation. The effect of using different intervals when calculating volatility on the 10-year Treasury is displayed in Exhibit 35–6. The optimal sampling interval for analyzing empirical volatility depends on the application. When pricing an option on an MBS, for example,

**EXHIBIT 35–5**
**30-Year Constant Maturity Treasury, Distribution of 1-Day Percentage Yield Changes (% ), 1/82–1/88.**

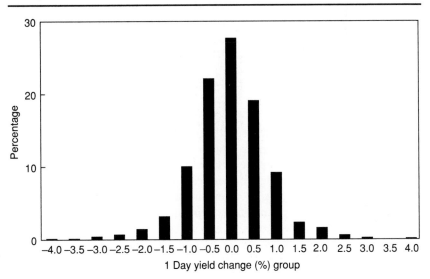

**EXHIBIT 35–6**
**10-Day vs. 30-Day Volatility on 10-Year Constant Maturity Treasury.**

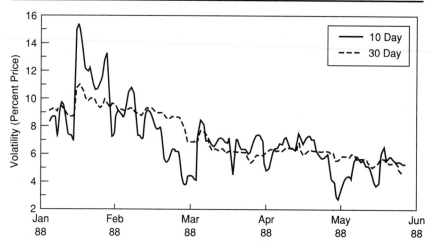

the interval used to calculate an empirical volatility should be chosen to match the length of the option contract. This provides the investor with an indication of how volatile the underlying security has been recently and how this relates to the volatility employed to price the option.

With no industry standard for volatility units, converting between the price and yield expression of absolute or percentage volatility is a useful skill. The path to follow to convert from one unit to the next is shown in Exhibit 35–7. The modified duration of a security provides the link between price and yield volatilities. Modified duration is defined as the percentage change in price divided by the absolute change in yield.[4]

## Implied Volatility

Implied volatility is merely the market's expectation of future volatility over a specified time period. Because an option's price is a function of the volatility employed, where an option's price is known the implied volatility can be derived. Although it sounds straightforward, calculating an implied volatility is far more complicated than calculating an empirical volatility, because expectations cannot be observed directly. An option pricing model along with a mathematical

---

[4] Modified duration is explained in Chapter 7.

method to infer the volatility must be employed. The result of this calculation is a percentage price volatility that can be converted to the various types of volatility measures discussed previously (see Exhibit 35–7).

Owing to the existence and liquidity of fixed income options, proxies for implied volatilities can be derived from Treasuries. The bond futures market on the Chicago Board of Trade (CBOT) is one of the most liquid markets for fixed income options and provides the information necessary to calculate an implied volatility. The resultant implied volatility provides a good indication of the market's expected volatility for the Treasuries with maturities similar to that of the particular bond futures contract in question. The implied volatility on the 20-year bond futures contract for example, is a useful proxy for the market's expected volatility on long-term Treasury securities.

Exhibit 35–8 shows implied percentage prices and absolute yield volatilities for calls and puts on the bond futures contract of March 1990 over a range of strike prices. Exhibit 35–9 provides a specific example of how an implied percentage price volatility can be converted into an implied absolute yield volatility (from Exhibit 35–8). In particular, the absolute yield volatility for calls on the March 1990 bond contract with a strike price of 92 is derived from this option contract's percentage price volatility.

**EXHIBIT 35–7**
**Converting Volatility Measures.**

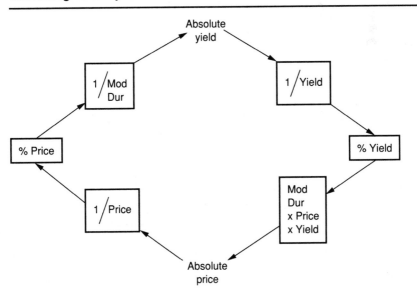

**EXHIBIT 35–8**

**Implied Volatilities for Options on Bond Futures**
(Based on Closing Prices for January 18, 1990)

*March 1990 Bond Contract Closing @ 95 8/32*
*(Modified Duration = 8.61)*

|  | Strike Price* | | | |
| --- | --- | --- | --- | --- |
|  | 92 | 94 | 96 | 98 |
| Closing call option price | 3:21 | 1:45 | 0:38 | 0:12 |
| Closing put option price | 0:07 | 0:27 | 1:21 | 2:59 |
| *Percentage Price Volatilities* | | | | |
| Implied call volatility | 9.28 | 9.34 | 8.90 | 9.82 |
| Implied put volatility | 9.71 | 8.94 | 8.78 | 9.76 |
| *Absolute Yield Volatilities* | | | | |
| Implied call volatility | 108 | 109 | 103 | 114 |
| Implied put volatility | 113 | 104 | 102 | 113 |

* Option prices are quoted in points and 64ths (i.e., 3:21 = 3.00 + 21/64).

# THE RELATIONSHIP BETWEEN EMPIRICAL AND IMPLIED VOLATILITY

Comparing empirical and implied volatilities can be characterized as running forward but looking backward. An implied volatility is the market's view of future volatility, whereas empirical volatility is a measure of what volatility

**EXHIBIT 35–9**

**Sample Calculation of Converting from Percentage Price Volatility to Absolute Yield Volatility for Bond Futures Calls Struck at 92**

$$\text{Modified duration} = \frac{\%\ \text{Change in price}}{100\ \text{b.p. change in yield}} \quad (35\text{–}1)$$

$$\text{Absolute yield volatility} = \text{Percentage price volatility} \times \frac{1}{\text{Modified duration}} \times 100.0 \quad (35\text{–}2)$$

$$\text{Absolute yield volatility} = 9.28 \times \frac{1}{8.61} \times 100 = 107.8\ \text{basis points} \quad (35\text{–}3)$$

**EXHIBIT 35–10**
**Actual Volatility (30-Year Constant Maturity) vs. CBOT Implied Volatility**
(30-Day Actual Volatility; Daily Implied Volatility).

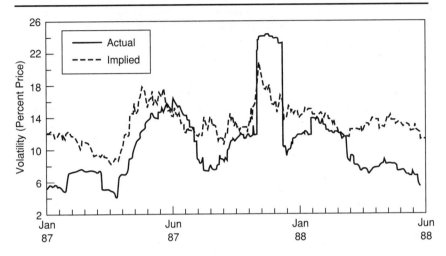

has been. The empirical volatility on the 30-year, constant maturity Treasury is plotted against implied volatility on the CBOT bond futures contract for the past two years in Exhibit 35–10. Several characteristics of the relationship become clear from an examination of the graph. First, the two volatilities trend together. Second, implied volatility tends to be a smoothed function of empirical volatility. Third, implied volatility, over time, generally is higher than empirical volatility.

The fixed income market can be described as an unstable equilibrium that is put into disequilibrium by unforeseen events. This description is consistent with the shapes of empirical volatility curves, where levels generally move in a saw-toothed, gradual fashion that is occasionally interrupted by large, spiked movements. Implied volatility seldom shows the kind of large deviations from the current mean that actual volatility exhibits. The effect of a single event does not usually have as great an influence on implied volatility as it does on empirical volatility because the perspective is different. Implied volatility is a long-term estimate that is not likely to be drastically changed owing to a single event. The same reasoning also explains why implied volatility recovers more quickly from large deviations than does empirical. Implied volatility is an "instantaneous" measure of investor sentiment that does not have the lag effect inherent in a standard deviation of actual observations.

## THE APPLICATIONS OF IMPLIED
## AND EMPIRICAL VOLATILTY

Implied and empirical volatility are the measures most commonly used to price explicit options or securities with embedded options. Properly evaluating any option requires the determination of a distribution of prices in the future. Given the current value of a security and its volatility, a price distribution can be constructed. The price for the option is then determined by taking a probability-weighted average of the results at each point in the distribution.

For example, the pricing of most mortgage-related securities requires a model that evaluates the embedded option component. Constructing a distribution of MBS prices in the future is really a function of finding a distribution of interest rates. Because implied volatility represents the market's view of expected volatility, it is the most applicable volatility measure available. The implied volatility derived from bond futures on the CBOT can be used to generate a distribution of future interest rates.

Pricing an over-the-counter (OTC) option on the specific security also requires an estimate of volatility, but in this case it is of the underlying security. Estimating the volatility of an MBS for pricing an option typically involves a number of volatility considerations. To start, the recent empirical volatility of the security is considered. The empirical volatility for any fixed income security depends on its maturity and/or coupon. For MBSs, empirical volatility tends to be higher for lower coupons. In addition to the empirical volatility for the security, option investors also evaluate current estimates of implied volatility. If implied volatility is rising, the volatility level at which an OTC option is priced would probably be increased by some proportional amount above the empirical volatility. If determining a fair level of volatility for pricing options seems vague, it reflects the nature of the science. Although the implied and empirical volatility data are the most important determinants of a fair volatility level, intangibles such as supply and demand considerations and bid/ask spreads also influence the level of volatility employed.

## IMPACT OF VOLATILITY
## ON FIXED INCOME SECURITIES

Owing to the effect volatility has on securities with embedded options, investors should incorporate their opinion of the future direction of volatility when considering which fixed income securities to purchase or sell. A matrix of interest-rate direction and volatility direction is used in Exhibit 35–11 to identify some appropriate securities for various environments. The securities listed in each quadrant are appropriate given the respective expected volatility and interest-rate envi-

**EXHIBIT 35–11**
**Yield/Volatility Quadrant Analysis.**

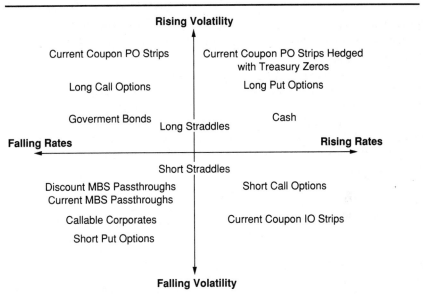

ronment. If interest rates and volatility are expected to rise, for example, long put options or long straddles provide good returns. In an environment of falling interest rates coupled with rising volatility, owning principal-only strips (POs)[5] or long call options   enhances returns. All of the securities above the horizontal axis in Exhibit 35–11 are relatively better choices in rising volatility environments because they are either long options or (at the minimum) are not short options. POs, which benefit from prepayments, thrive in a falling rate environment. Government bonds, even those with call provisions, trade like noncallables. Treasuries are not explicitly long an option position, but when volatility is rising they are better to own than securities that have short option components. Conversely, positions that are short options and benefit from lower volatility lie below the horizontal axis. Callable corporates and MBS passthroughs benefit as volatility declines because the value of the embedded (short) option falls.

Changes in the level of implied volatility traditionally have had a strong influence on the value of MBSs relative to Treasuries. The effect of volatility on the spread of MBSs to Treasuries is well documented. When volatility increases,

---

[5] These securities are the topic of Chapter 30.

the embedded short options for MBSs tend to appreciate, causing the MBS to cheapen (and the spread to widen) relative to Treasuries. Thus, these securities typically underperform Treasuries in this environment. This relationship is illustrated in Exhibit 35–12 by examining the spread between both the current coupon GNMA and the constant maturity, 10-year Treasury against the CBOT implied volatility.

## APPENDIX A. PERCENTAGE VOLATILITIES AND THE LOGNORMAL DISTRIBUTION: A SAMPLE CALCULATION OF ABSOLUTE AND PERCENTAGE VOLATILITY

One could compute a percentage price volatility by finding the standard deviation of daily price returns, assuming a normal distribution, and then annualizing. Daily returns would be computed as follows:

$$R = (P_2/P_1) - 1, \qquad (35 - 1)$$

where $P_1$ is the price on the first day and $P_2$ is the price on the next consecutive business day. A better way to compute the percentage volatility is to assume a lognormal distribution of prices and find the standard deviation of the logs of the daily price quotients, that is, $\ln(P_2/P_1)$. For the lognormal assumption to be

**EXHIBIT 35–12**
**Implied Volatility vs. GNMA to Treasury Yield Spread.**

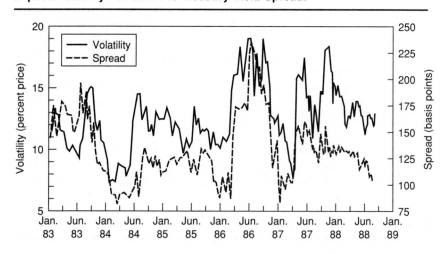

accurate, the log of the daily price quotient and the daily return should be equal. This condition holds true if the price quotient is near 1, or

$$\ln(P_2/P_1) = (P_2/P_1) - 1; \qquad (35 - 2)$$

where $P_2/P_1 \approx 1$. For one-day price movements, this assumption is valid even on the most volatile days. For example, if a bond starts at par ($P_1 = 100$) and moves five points in one day ($P_2 = 95$), the price quotient $P_2/P_1 = 95/100 = 0.95$. The log of the price quotient $\ln(0.95)$ is $-0.051$, and the return $R = 0.95 - 1 = -0.05$. Exhibit 35–5 shows the distribution of daily percentage changes of yields on the 30-year constant maturity calculated by $\ln(P_2/P_1)$. The lognormal method may be computed more quickly by taking advantage of the properties of logs ($\ln(P_2/P_1) = \ln P_2/P_1$) and makes the price quotients equivalent to a continuously compounded return.

This is clearly illustrated in Exhibit 35–13, in which a sample volatility calculation is presented for GNMA 10 percent pass-through securities. The volatility is calculated over a 10-day period in 1989 from October 13 to October 27. Both percentage and absolute price volatility are derived, with percentage volatility being derived in two ways: by direct calculation of daily returns and by calculation of daily percentage changes in price assuming a lognormal distribution. As can be seen from the exhibit, based on the given sample, one would expect the price of GNMA 10s to vary by 2.76 percent on an annual basis.

**EXHIBIT 35–13**

**10-Day Absolute and Percentage Price Volatilities for GNMA 10% MBS** (From 10/13/89 to 10/27/89)

| Date | Price (% Par) | Percentage Volatilities | | Absolute Volatilities |
|---|---|---|---|---|
| | | $P_2/P_1 - 1$ | $LN(P_2) - LN(P_1)$ | $P_2 - P_1$ |
| 13 OCT 1989 | 102.18750 | | | |
| 16 OCT 1989 | 102.03125 | −0.1529% | −0.1530% | −0.15625 |
| 17 OCT 1989 | 102.00000 | −0.0306 | −0.0306 | −0.03125 |
| 18 OCT 1989 | 101.93750 | −0.0613 | −0.0613 | −0.06250 |
| 19 OCT 1989 | 102.12500 | 0.1839 | 0.1838 | 0.18750 |
| 20 OCT 1989 | 101.90625 | −0.2142 | −0.2144 | −0.21875 |
| 23 OCT 1989 | 102.15625 | 0.2453 | 0.2450 | 0.25000 |
| 24 OCT 1989 | 102.43750 | 0.2753 | 0.2749 | 0.28125 |
| 25 OCT 1989 | 102.50000 | 0.0610 | 0.0610 | 0.06250 |
| 26 OCT 1989 | 102.43750 | −0.0610 | −0.0610 | −0.06250 |
| 27 OCT 1989 | 102.28125 | −0.1525 | −0.1526 | −0.15625 |
| Standard deviation of one-day price changes | | 0.1744 | 0.1743 | 0.17803 |
| Annualized volatility (X = 250) | | 2.7568 | 2.7557 | 2.81491 |

On an absolute price basis, one would expect an annual maximum deviation of 2.81 points.

The results from the two methods of calculating percentage price volatility are almost identical. The standard deviation of the daily returns $(P_2/P_1 - 1)$ is 0.1744 percent whereas the standard deviation of the daily changes in the natural logs of the prices $\ln(P_2) - \ln(P_1)$ is 0.1743 percent. On an annualized basis, this is a difference of only 0.0011 percent, an insignificant number.

## APPENDIX B. ANNUALIZING VOLATILITY

A standard deviation is based on variance, a measure of the dispersion in squared units of the observations.

$$\text{Var}(X, Y) = \text{Var}(X) + \text{Var}(Y) + 2 \times \text{Cov}(XY) \qquad (35 - 6)$$

where Var = variance and Cov = covariance. The standard deviation is the square root of the variance, which returns the measure to the original units of the observations. The daily variance is annualized by multiplying by the number of business days in the year, typically 250. Therefore, the standard deviation is annualized by multiplying by the square root of 250. For the conversion to be valid, we assume that there is no correlation between daily changes, that is, that the covariance is zero. Also, we assume no volatility on weekends or holidays. This assumption is reasonable because volatility over weekends or holidays does not appear to be greater than day-to-day volatility between weekdays.

# PART 6

# ANALYSIS OF BONDS WITH EMBEDDED OPTIONS

# CHAPTER 36

## APPROACHES TO THE VALUATION OF CALLABLE CORPORATE BONDS

*Ravi E. Dattatreya, Ph.D.*
Senior Vice President
Sumitomo Bank Capital Markets, Inc.

*Frank J. Fabozzi, Ph.D., CFA*
Visiting Professor of Finance
Sloan School of Management
Massachusetts Institute of Technology
and
Editor, The Journal of Portfolio Management

Most of the longer corporate and agency bonds issued today contain call features that can often have a significant impact on their prices as well as on their performance in changing interest-rate environments. Callability is attractive to issuers as it gives them flexibility in controlling financing costs if and when interest rates move downward. Investors in turn are compensated by means of higher coupon rates when the bonds are issued. The call feature, along with credit risk, is the major factor in the perceived yield spread between corporate and Treasury bonds. Because of the trade-off between the coupon rate or yield and flexibility, proper evaluation of the call feature is important to investors. In as much as different market segments such as corporate callable bonds and Treasuries exert influence on one another, a good understanding of how callable bonds behave and can be valued is helpful even if there is no intention to deal directly with them.

Because the analysis of callable bonds can be complex, market participants have developed some simple procedures to determine value. These procedures, which could perhaps be justified in the stable, calm markets of decades ago, seem almost arbitrary in the volatile interest-rate environment of today.

Several approaches are currently in use for the valuation of callable bonds. The *classical approach* takes an all-or-none view, assuming that the bond will be called or not called depending upon certain market parameters. The *option approach* attempts to analyze the callable bond by explicitly estimating the value of the embedded option in the bond. This estimation is done using option pricing models modified to handle some additional complexities, as discussed later in this chapter. The *option-adjusted spread approach* does not value the embedded option directly. We will return to this approach later in this chapter. It is discussed in detail in the next chapter.

The goal of this chapter is to clarify the issues involved in the three approaches to the analysis of callable bonds. Unfortunately, there is no standardization of terminology and technique in this area. Therefore, it is best to examine the underlying assumptions before relying on any valuation model.

## CLASSICAL ANALYSIS

Because of the call feature, the effective maturity of a callable bond can be anywhere between the first call date and its stated maturity. This uncertainty in the maturity of the bond defeats the popular measure of value, yield-to-maturity (or simply, yield), which requires a fixed maturity for computation. To accomodate this requirement, traditionally, callable bonds are evaluated by assuming that the bond will be called if the price of the bond is above a certain threshold value and that it will not be called otherwise. Presumably, if the bond price is high and interest rates are low, this increases the likelihood of call; if the bond price is low and rates are high, then there is a lower probability of call. Once the effective maturity is assumed fixed, the yield can then be easily computed. Depending upon whether the call is assumed or not, we get the yield-to-call (YTC) or yield-to-maturity (YTM).

The threshold price used is usually par or the first call price. Sometimes a value known as the *crossover price*[1] is used. This is the price above which the yield-to-maturity is greater than the yield-to-call. The implication is that the issuer will behave, with respect to calling the bond, in such a way that the investor receives the minimum yield—hence the name *minimum yield method* for this approach. Even though the crossover yield or minimum yield analysis appears reasonable on the surface, it breaks down totally under several common

---

[1] The crossover price can be easily computed: First, we compute the crossover yield, which is the yield at which the price of the bond on the first call date is the call price. Crossover price is the price of the bond today computed at the crossover yield.

situations, indicating that its application is not appropriate except under extreme circumstances.

For example, consider an inverted yield curve environment,[2] where the 5-year rate is at 16 percent and the 30-year rate is 12 percent. Suppose that a 30-year, 12.25 percent coupon bond callable in 5 years at $105\frac{7}{8}$ is priced at a slight discount to par at $98\frac{2}{32}$, with a YTM of 12.50 percent. The YTC is 13.65 percent, so the YTM is below the YTC. An investor, using the minimum yield method would ignore the call, treating the bond as a straight 30-year bond. That is, he would compare the yield-to-maturity of the callable bond to the long end of the yield curve to determine value. The bond price looks reasonable until we observe that the YTC itself is 234 basis points below the five-year rate. We can therefore do better by simply purchasing a straight five-year bond at a yield of 16 percent.

There are subtle theoretical problems as well with the minimum yield method. The yield or horizon return computed to call and to maturity are very different in sensitivity to interest-rate changes, the level of uncertainty, or variability in the actual returns obtained, etc. and thus are not directly comparable; nor is there an acceptable procedure to make them so.[3] When the magnitude of the difference between the yields computed to call and to maturity is large, the two yields will imply vastly different reinvestment rates for the same coupon stream. This again is commonly ignored in bond research, but can be handled by using a fixed reinvestment rate and computing the horizon return rather than the yield.

The usual methods are flawed even when the yield curve is not inverted. They imply an abrupt change at the crossover point, when the assumption of call switches over to no-call. One of the reasons for these drawbacks is that these methods use the price (or yield) of the callable bond itself for valuation, whereas the bond, in fact, is responding to changes in the market levels. Therefore, market variables should be used to drive any viable model for callable bonds. The likelihood of call does not depend on whether the callable bond is selling above par or the call price or even the crossover price but at what rate the redemption can be financed (i.e., on the new issue market). For example, consider a bond that is callable at par immediately. In this case, we do not expect the bond to trade above the call price, and the minimum yield method will treat the bond as noncallable.

---

[2] Unless otherwise stated, the yield curve represents yield levels of noncallable bonds of the appropriate credit. This can be obtained by adding quality spreads to the Treasury yield curve.

[3] However, such direct comparisons between yields to different maturities are deeply entrenched in fixed income analysis. For example, as explained in Chapter 6, the average yield is typically used in dumbbell-bullet analysis even though the maturities of the three bonds involved are disparate. Because of such widespread usage, we do not expect the discrepancy mentioned here to be objectionable to but a few.

Some practitioners improve upon the basic YTM/YTC analysis by making additional adjustments to reflect call. This adjustment, in practice, is usually arbitrary. When a bond is callable immediately, the method breaks down completely, as the YTC is then undefined. Even computing the actual yield realizable under various investment rate assumptions provides only a marginal improvement over the standard analysis and still retains the major problems.

A better procedure, perhaps, than the minimum yield method is what can be called the *maximum yield method*. Here, the investor demands that the yield computed to any possible call date is higher than the corresponding call-free yield. How much higher the yield should be is still the unknown factor.

The intention of the examples presented above is not to say that such gross errors are made frequently but only that there is a potential for their occurrence. Most market participants can be expected to make amendments, though not scientific, in the traditional methods as they realize the possibility of mispricing. What is required is a systematic method to determine the price of callable bonds, the development of which is the goal of this chapter.

## MARKET RESPONSE OF CALLABLE BONDS

We can obtain useful insight into the valuation of a callable bond by estimating its price behavior in the market. In this context, it helps to view the callable bond as responding to changes in the noncallable yield levels rather than treating the yield (or price) of the callable bond as a fundamental, independent variable. Let us therefore look first at the price behavior of a noncallable bond as a function of interest rates. For simplicity of exposition, we assume a flat yield curve in this section.

Exhibit 36–1 shows the price-yield curve of a 30-year, 10.75 percent noncallable bond. The horizontal axis represents the change in the yield of the bond and the vertical axis the corresponding prices.

A shorter maturity bond is shown in Exhibit 36–2. Specifically, the bond is a five-year, 10.75 percent noncallable bond. This is a normal bond, except that at maturity it pays 105 instead of the usual 100.[4]  The price-yield curve for this bond has the same fundamental characteristics as the one for the 30-year bond. The curve is not as steep (i.e., the dollar duration is smaller). Also, this slope changes less as the yield is varied (i.e., the convexity is smaller). For high yield levels, the long bond price is less than the price of the shorter bond. For lower yield levels, the short bond price is lower.

Consider now a 30-year, 10.75 percent bond, callable in year 5 at 105. In year 5, if the rates are low, the issuer may decide to call the bond leaving the

---

[4] The reason for selecting a maturity payment not equal to par will become clear shortly.

**EXHIBIT 36–1**

**10.75%, 30-Year Noncallable Bond Price-Yield Relationship**

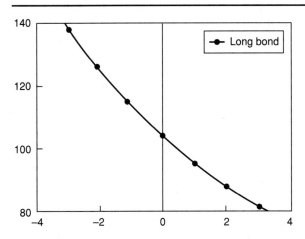

investor with the unattractive task of investing the proceeds in low-coupon (or low-yielding) bonds. Thus, the callable bond is less attractive to an investor than the noncallable long bond, which will continue to pay the 10.75 percent coupon even if rates drop.

Similarly, the callable bond is less attractive to an investor than the short maturity bond of Exhibit 36–2 because, if rates rise, the bond will not

**EXHIBIT 36–2**

**Price-Yield Relationship for a 10.75%, 5-Year Noncallable Bond (Short Bond)**

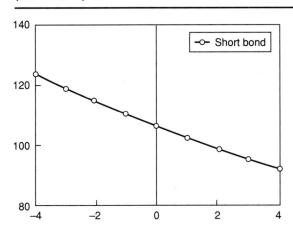

be called, and the investor loses the opportunity to invest in high-coupon (or high-yielding) bonds. On the other hand, the short bond matures, providing the attractive reinvestment opportunity.

Thus, the callable bond is worth less than both the long bond and the short bond. Therefore, we can obtain an upper bound on the price of the callable bond by looking at the lower of the prices of the long and short bonds. This upper bound is shown in Exhibit 36–3. Sometimes this upper bound is called the price-to-worst, and the corresponding yields are called yield-to-worst. However, these are only bounds, and the actual value of the callable bond is *below* the price-to-worst.

The price-yield curve for the callable bond, then, is a curve that is bounded above by the curves for the short and the long bonds. For very low yield levels, the likelihood of call is high, and investors would be willing to pay almost the same for either the short bond or the callable bond. Similarly, at very high yield levels, the likelihood of call is low, and we can expect the value of the callable bond to be close to that of the long bond. For intermediate yield levels, the curve represents a smooth, continuous transition from the long bond to the short bond. This is shown in Exhibit 36–4.

A few additional observations can be made. For very high yield levels, the callable bond behaves much like a long noncallable bond in terms of its duration and convexity. Again, for very low yield levels, the callable bond's behavior is close to that of the short bond in its duration and convexity. Thus, as rates fall, the duration of the callable bond falls from that of the long bond to that of the short bond (i.e., it decreases). This property is opposite to that of

**EXHIBIT 36–3**
**Upper Bound for the Value of a Callable Bond**

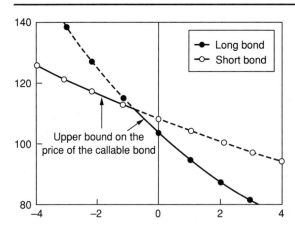

**EXHIBIT 36–4**
**Market Performance of a 30-Year, 10.75% Bond Callable at 105 Compared to a 30-Year Long Bond and a 5-Year Short Bond**

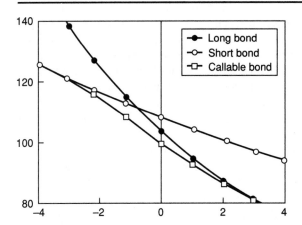

noncallable bonds, for which the duration increases as rates fall. The callable bond is therefore said to have *negative convexity*[5] in the intermediate-yield range.

Finally, the actual price is lower than the so-called price-to-worst, and the discrepancy is small only when the rate levels are in the extreme. In the normal operating range, the difference can be significant.

## THE OPTION APPROACH TO PRICING CALLABLE BONDS

The most natural way to analyze a callable bond is to treat it as a combination of a long position in a call-free bond and a short position in a call option on the same bond.[6] For example, consider our 10.75 percent, 30-year callable bond callable in 5 years at 105. The investor effectively owns a 30-year bond and has sold a call option that grants the issuer the right to call the bond in 5 years

---

[5] Geometrically, a curve is concave or negatively convex if it lies below the tangent drawn at that point.

[6] Compare this with the covered-call writing or "buy/write" technique, where the investor buys a bond and writes (sells) a call option on the same bond.

at an exercise price of 105. Therefore, the price of a callable bond is equal to the price of the call-free bond *minus* the value of the option. That is,

Callable bond price = Call-free bond price − Call option price

The reason for subtracting the call option price is that the bondholder has sold an option.

Notice that the higher the value of the option is, the lower the value of the callable bond is. Once the bond is thus divided, it can be valued as the sum of the two relatively simpler parts. The call-free portion can be priced easily; to value the option part, we could use an option pricing model. For now, let's assume that we have an option pricing model that can value the embedded option.

In our example, the corresponding call-free bond is the 10.75 percent, 30-year noncallable. Exhibit 36–5 shows, for a change in interest rates, the price of the call-free bond, the estimated call option price, and the callable bond price. Also shown is the price of the 10.75 percent, five-year bond. The callable bond price is found by subtracting the estimated call option price from the call-free bond price. Exhibit 36–6 graphs the relationships shown in Exhibit 36–5.

## CALL-ADJUSTED OR OPTION-ADJUSTED YIELD

Given the above relationship between the prices of the callable bond, the call option, and the call-free bond, there are many ways to determine if a bond is correctly priced. We can, for example, assume that the price of the call-free bond is correctly priced, determine the option price using an option pricing model, and impute the theoretical price of the callable bond. This price can then be compared with the market price of the callable bond. Alternatively, we can compare the theoretical price of the option with the market price of the option, obtained by subtracting the callable bond price from the assumed call-free bond price.

It is also possible to analyze the callable bond *without* assuming the price of the call-free bond. In this technique, we start with a trial value of the call-free bond price, compute the option price, and examine the market price of the callable bond; then the trial price of the call-free bond is changed and the steps are repeated. This iterative process is continued until the model-determined price of the callable bond is equal to the market price. The corresponding price of the call-free bond, thus, has been determined to match the market price of the callable bond and is therefore called the *implied* call-free bond price. The corresponding yield of the call-free bond is called the *call-adjusted*, or *option-adjusted yield*.

To illustrate the calculation of the call-adjusted yield, suppose that an 8 percent coupon callable corporate bond with 20 years to maturity and callable

**EXHIBIT 36–5**

**Prices for the Long Bond, Short Bond, Call Option, and Callable Bond for Changes in Interest Rates**

| Change in Interest Rates | Call-Free Bond | Price of Short Bond† | Call Option Price | Call-able Bond* |
|---|---|---|---|---|
| −5.000 | 129.945 | 129.945 | 45.409 | 175.354 |
| −4.750 | 128.629 | 128.629 | 41.192 | 169.821 |
| −4.500 | 127.329 | 127.330 | 37.248 | 164.577 |
| −4.250 | 126.045 | 126.047 | 33.558 | 159.603 |
| −4.000 | 124.769 | 124.780 | 30.110 | 154.879 |
| −3.750 | 123.503 | 123.530 | 26.887 | 123.503 |
| −3.500 | 122.218 | 122.295 | 23.903 | 146.121 |
| −3.250 | 120.930 | 121.075 | 21.127 | 142.057 |
| −3.000 | 119.585 | 119.872 | 18.600 | 138.185 |
| −2.750 | 118.211 | 118.683 | 16.283 | 134.494 |
| −2.500 | 116.783 | 117.509 | 14.188 | 130.972 |
| −2.250 | 115.279 | 116.349 | 12.330 | 127.609 |
| −2.000 | 113.744 | 115.205 | 10.652 | 124.396 |
| −1.750 | 112.137 | 114.074 | 9.186 | 121.323 |
| −1.500 | 110.468 | 112.958 | 7.916 | 118.383 |
| −1.250 | 108.778 | 111.855 | 6.791 | 115.568 |
| −1.000 | 107.054 | 110.766 | 5.817 | 112.871 |
| −0.750 | 105.292 | 109.691 | 4.993 | 110.285 |
| −0.500 | 103.525 | 108.628 | 4.279 | 107.804 |
| −0.250 | 101.761 | 107.579 | 3.662 | 105.423 |
| 0.000 | 100.000 | 106.543 | 3.136 | 103.136 |
| 0.250 | 98.240 | 105.520 | 2.697 | 100.937 |
| 0.500 | 96.506 | 104.509 | 2.316 | 98.823 |
| 0.750 | 94.796 | 103.510 | 1.992 | 96.789 |
| 1.000 | 93.115 | 102.524 | 1.715 | 94.830 |
| 1.250 | 91.466 | 101.549 | 1.478 | 92.944 |
| 1.500 | 89.845 | 100.587 | 1.280 | 91.125 |
| 1.750 | 88.268 | 99.636 | 1.105 | 89.372 |
| 2.000 | 86.720 | 98.696 | 0.960 | 87.681 |
| 2.250 | 85.215 | 97.69 | 0.833 | 86.048 |
| 2.500 | 83.749 | 96.852 | 0.723 | 84.471 |
| 2.750 | 82.316 | 95.946 | 0.632 | 82.948 |
| 3.000 | 80.925 | 95.051 | 0.551 | 81.476 |
| 3.250 | 79.571 | 94.167 | 0.481 | 80.052 |
| 3.500 | 78.251 | 93.294 | 0.423 | 78.674 |
| 3.750 | 76.971 | 92.431 | 0.370 | 77.340 |
| 4.000 | 75.725 | 91.578 | 0.324 | 76.049 |
| 4.250 | 74.512 | 90.735 | 0.286 | 74.798 |
| 4.500 | 73.334 | 89.903 | 0.251 | 73.586 |
| 4.750 | 72.189 | 89.080 | 0.221 | 72.410 |
| 5.000 | 71.074 | 88.267 | 0.195 | 71.270 |

* 30-year, 10.75% non-callable bond.
† 5-year, 10.75% non-callable bond, payment at maturity = 105.

**EXHIBIT 36–6**

**Market Performance of a Callable Bond: 30-Year, 10.75% Bond Callable at 105 in Year 5 Compared to Underlying Bond**

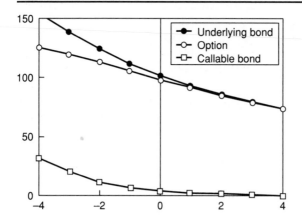

at 104 is selling at 102. Suppose that using an option pricing model, the call option is estimated to be 4.21. Then the implied call-free bond price is 102 (callable bond price) plus 4.21 (call option price), or 106.21. Since it is the *implied* call-free bond price, the cash flows would be those to maturity. In our illustration, it would be 40 payments of $4 (per $100 par) every six months plus $100 at the end of 40 six-month periods. The six-month yield (internal rate of return) that will make this cash flow equal to the implied call-free price of 106.21 is 3.7 percent. Doubling this yield gives a call-adjusted yield of 7.4 percent on a bond equivalent yield basis.

Once the call-adjusted yield has been determined, we can use the familiar methods of analysis applicable to simple, noncallable bonds. For example, we might compare this yield to that on a comparable maturity Treasury to get a feel for whether or not the bond is properly priced. If the call-free yield is determined to be reasonable, so will the price of the callable bond, by implication.

### Relationship to Option-Adjusted Method

Notice that in determining the implied call-adjusted yield, we change the trial values of the call-free yield. The value of the embedded option also changes correspondingly. In a way, we can think of the procedure as determining the credit spread at which the market price and model price are equal. In this manner, this approach resembles the option-adjusted spread method (described in the next chapter) where the net value of the callable bond (i.e., call-free value less the call option value) is estimated directly by changing the credit spread used.

If all of the assumptions match, then the option approach and the option-adjusted spread approach should provide substantially the same valuations. Then, the two approaches would differ just in the way the results are stated. Each method has its own advantages. However, we prefer the option approach for the following reasons:

1. It uses the full term structure so that the internal and external consistency conditions are satisfied. The internal consistency (or no-arbitrage) condition, requires that no *riskless profitable arbitrage* exist among fairly priced securities.[7] The external consistency condition requires that the valuation model be fine tuned or calibrated so that actual market prices and implied model values are in agreement.[8]
2. It provides additional parametric information such as duration adjusted for the embedded option (described in the next section), effortlessly. This facility makes the method useful in determining *suitability* of an investment as well as its valuation. The parametric information can also be used in hedging applications.
3. It can provide the results in dollars or in the normal yield-to-maturity terms, thus making the numbers more meaningful and the model itself less of a black box.[9]

## Call-Adjusted Duration and Convexity

The formulas we presented in Chapter 7 for duration and convexity assumed that the bond's cash flow is fixed, not depending on the level of interest rates. For callable bonds, the cash flow depends on the level of interest rates. Therefore, only under special circumstances to be described below should the formulas for duration and convexity presented in Chapter 7 be used for callable bonds.

Duration and convexity formulas can be adjusted to take into account the embedded option. When interest rates change, a chain of events takes place that affects the price of the callable bond. First, the price of the call-free bond changes. The sensitivity of the price of the call-free bond to interest-rate changes depends on its duration and convexity. Second, the change in the price of the call-free bond will change the price of the call option. The sensitivity of the

---

[7] For a further discussion of this condition, see Ravi E. Dattatreya and Frank J. Fabozzi, *Active Total Return Management of Fixed Income Portfolio* (Chicago: Probus Publishing, 1989), pp. 76–84.

[8] See Dattatreya and Fabozzi, *Total Active Return Management of Fixed Income Portfolios*, pp. 85–87.

[9] Black boxes, it is said, are found on crashed aircraft.

price of the option to changes in the price of the call-free bond will depend on the duration/delta and gamma/convexity[10] of the option.

*Call-Adjusted Duration.* The call-adjusted duration of a callable bond can be shown to be[11]

$$
\left( \frac{\text{Call-free bond price}}{\text{Callable bond price}} \right) \times \left( \begin{array}{c} \text{Duration of} \\ \text{call-free} \\ \text{bond} \end{array} \right) \times (1 - \text{delta})
$$

The call-adjusted duration depends on

- The ratio of the price of the call-free bond to the price of the callable bond. The difference between the two prices is the price of the call option. The greater (smaller) the price of the call option is the higher (lower) the ratio. Thus, we see that the call-adjusted duration will depend on the price of the call option.
- The duration of the call-free bond.
- The delta of the call option.

Consider the case of a callable corporate bond selling at a deep discount. The call option is deep out-of-the money (i.e., the coupon rate is substantially below the current market interest rate). The price of the call option would be small; therefore, the ratio of the call-free bond price to the callable bond price would be close to one. The delta of the call option would be close to zero (i.e., the price of the call option would not be sensitive to the change in the call-free bond price). Using the above formula, the call-adjusted duration for the callable bond would be equal to the duration of the call-free bond. Thus, it is under this extreme condition that the duration formula we presented in Chapter 7 can be used for a callable bond.

Suppose instead that the bond is currently callable and that the coupon rate is substantially above the current market interest rate. The delta of the call option would be equal to one. The formula tells us that the call-adjusted duration for this bond would be equal to *zero*.

Between these two extremes—a deep-discount callable bond and an immediately callable bond with a coupon rate substantially above the current market interest rate—the call-adjusted duration of a callable bond will fall.

While the call-adjusted duration formula above is cast in terms of the delta of the call option, it can also be expressed in terms of the call option's modified duration. The formula is then

---

[10] The delta and gamma of a call option are explained in Chapter 38.

[11] For the mathematical derivation, see Appendix A of Frank J. Fabozzi, *Fixed Income Mathematics* (Chicago: Probus Publishing, 1988).

$$\left(\frac{\text{Call-free bond price}}{\text{Callable bond price}}\right) \times \left(\begin{array}{c}\text{Duration of}\\ \text{call-free}\\ \text{bond}\end{array}\right) - \left(\frac{\text{Call option price}}{\text{Callable bond price}}\right) \times \left(\begin{array}{c}\text{Duration}\\ \text{of call}\\ \text{option}\end{array}\right)$$

*Call-Adjusted Convexity.*    The convexity of a callable bond can also be adjusted to account for the embedded option. The call-adjusted convexity is:[12]

$$\frac{\text{Call-free bond price}}{\text{Callable bond price}} \times$$

$$\left[\left(\begin{array}{c}\text{Convexity of}\\ \text{call-free}\\ \text{bond}\end{array}\right) \times (1 - \text{delta}) - \left(\begin{array}{c}\text{Price of}\\ \text{call-free}\\ \text{bond}\end{array}\right) \times \text{gamma} \times \left(\begin{array}{c}\text{Duration of}\\ \text{call-free}\\ \text{bond}\end{array}\right)^2\right]$$

The call-adjusted convexity depends on the same three factors that determine the call-adjusted duration, plus the convexity of the noncallable bond and the gamma of the call option. Gamma measures the convexity of the call option.

Since the gamma of a call option is positive and the delta is between 0 and 1, call-adjusted convexity will be less than the convexity of the noncallable bond. Unlike the convexity for an option-free bond which is always positive, the call-adjusted convexity may be negative. This is, as we explained earlier in this chapter, callable bonds may exhibit negative convexity. This may occur when the yield falls such that the call option moves in the money.

## VALUING THE EMBEDDED CALL OPTION

Some researchers have attempted to model the implicit option as a European option expiring on the first call date and have used the Black-Scholes model to determine its value. Unfortunately this approach substantially underestimates the option value and therefore is of little practical value because it leads to inconsistent results. For example, such a model would conclude incorrectly that a bond callable in one year is more valuable than an identical bond callable in two years. The reason is that the one-year European option is worth less than a two-year option. It also fails for bonds callable immediately.

The embedded option in a callable bond has many complexities in addition to those that are already present in the more standard, exchange-traded options on bonds. Only by including all of the complex features of the option can the

---

[12] The proof is given in Appendix A of Fabozzi, *Fixed Income Mathematics*.

call option be properly evaluated. While a discussion of option pricing models is beyond the scope of this chapter, the complexities associated with modeling embedded call options are briefly described below. In Chapter 34, fixed income option pricing models are explained, providing a more detailed explanation of the complexities associated with valuing embedded call options.

## Features of a Call Option

*European-American Effect.* The implicit option in callable bonds combines the exercise features of both European and American options by providing for a period of call protection, during which the option cannot be exercised. The bond is callable at any time after this period.

*Strike Price.* Usually, the strike price of an exchange-traded option is held constant until expiration. However, the call price for a typical callable bond starts at a price above par (usually around par plus half the coupon) and declines steadily year by year until it reaches par. Subsequently, the bond is callable at par until maturity. In addition, the costs associated with the call and perhaps the cost of financing the call by a new issue could be included in the strike price.

*Yield-Price Distribution.* To evaluate an option on a security, we have to make an assumption about the behavior of the price movement of the security. The popular stock option models assume that the price of the stock moves according to a lognormal distribution, which implies that the price of the security can increase or decrease indefinitely. Because a bond's price approaches par as it nears maturity, its price volatility eventually decreases, making this assumption inappropriate for describing bond price movements. It is relatively much easier to develop a consistent assumption for the movement of interest rates and then derive the price movement of bonds. This is the approach that should be taken. However, if the time to expiration of an option is significantly shorter than the time to maturity of the underlying bond, variations of the price-based stock option models (such as the modified Black-Scholes model) can be used to derive reasonable estimates of the option value.

*Volatility.* The value of an option depends on the way the underlying security moves. Option models usually define a property called volatility, which measures the rate and range of up and down movements of the price of the security. Usually, the standard deviation (or variance) of the assumed distribution is used as the volatility measure.

In general, the value of an option increases with volatility. An estimated volatility, admittedly an easier task to produce than a prediction of the market direction, nevertheless remains an opinion about the future. The uncertainty in this input variable, more than anything else, keeps option pricing something of an art. Most models assume that the (yield) volatility is constant throughout the life of the option, which in the case of a callable bond is its stated maturity. One can include in the model a varying volatility, making the model more complex. We feel that the additional precision gained, if any, is marginal in light of the relatively gross approximations made in other input variables. Furthermore, the user would then face the unenviable task of guessing how the volatility varies.

Each of the factors discussed above highlights a shortcoming of popular stock option models, such as the celebrated Black-Scholes model, in evaluating callable bonds. We recommend the more flexible binomial model with extensive modifications incorporating the factors discussed above as well as those below. Most modern option models, including the two mentioned here, are based on the same central concept. They price the option so as to remove any possible riskless arbitrage between the option and the underlying security, rather than use an expectation of how the market might move. This is the correct way to value options.[13]

*The Interest-Rate Process.* In stock models, we can assume without any internal contradiction, that the price of the stock is independent of the level of interest rates. This allows us complete freedom in selecting the stock price distribution and the interest-rate distribution. For simplicity, most stock models assume a constant interest rate. However, this degree of freedom is not available in bond option pricing models because interest-rate levels and bond prices are not independent. Behavior of short-term rates may influence the level of longer term rates. Any interest-rate process assumption will imply corresponding prices of various securities.

The interdependence of interest rates of different maturities results in the internal and external consistency conditions that must be satisfied by an assumed interest-rate process.[14] Both of the consistency conditions are extremely important in developing a viable model to value callable bonds. If the internal consistency condition is violated, we get meaningless, self-contradictory results. If the external consistency condition is not satisfied, many securities in the market can appear, incorrectly, cheap or rich.

---

[13] See Chapter 5 of Dattatreya and Fabozzi, *Active Total Return Management of Fixed Income Portfolios.*

[14] For the description of a consistent valuation procedure see Ravi E. Dattatreya and Frank J. Fabozzi, "A Simplified Model for the Valuation of Debt Options," Chapter 4 in Frank J. Fabozzi (ed.), *The Handbook of Fixed Income Options* (Chicago: Probus Publishing, 1989).

## PORTFOLIO AND ASSET/LIABILITY MANAGEMENT IMPLICATIONS

The price performance characteristics of callable bonds must be understood by portfolio managers in order to effectively implement any portfolio strategy. Several examples are given below.

### Indexing

An indexing strategy seeks to match the performance of a benchmark portfolio. Because of the large number of issues in a typical bond index, an indexed portfolio is constructed using a small subset of the issues in the index rather than all the issues. In the stratified sampling (or cell) approach, the index is partitioned into cells on the basis of features such as market sector, duration, quality, etc. Issues are then selected for each cell so as to match the characteristics of the index. Because the indexed portfolio is not identical to the index, the performance of the two will not be identical. The difference between the performance of the two is called *tracking error*. The objective is to construct a portfolio with minimum tracking error.

Constructing an indexed portfolio that matches the performance of the U.S. government bond sector is not difficult, because of the lack of a call feature for most issues in this sector.[15] For example, one study reports that for the two-year period 1984-1985, the average monthly tracking error of an optimal portfolio constructed to match the Treasury sector of the Salomon Brothers Investment-Grade Bond Index was two basis points, with a standard deviation of 5 basis points. The largest monthly tracking error was 5 basis points and the lowest was -1 basis point.[16]

In contrast to the small tracking error for Treasuries, the embedded option in callable corporate bonds makes it more difficult to construct a portfolio to track this sector. For example, the same study just cited found that the average monthly tracking error for the corporate bond sector was 9 basis points with a standard deviation of 17 basis points. The highest monthly tracking error was 40 basis points and the lowest was -26 basis points.

To reduce the likelihood of large tracking error for the corporate bond sector, the characteristics used to create the cells should include the duration and convexity of the issues in this sector. More specifically, the call-adjusted duration and call-adjusted convexity should be matched.

---

[15] Although there are some callable U.S. government bonds outstanding, the Treasury no longer issues callable bonds.

[16] As reported in Exhibit 5 of Sharmin Mossavar-Rahmani, "Understanding and Evaluating Index Fund Management," in Frank J. Fabozzi and T. Dessa Garlicki-Fabozzi (eds.), *Advances in Bond Analysis and Portfolio Stratgies* (Chicago, IL: Probus Published, 1987), pp. 443–449.

## Active Strategies: The Importance of the Benchmark

The performance of portfolio managers is evaluated relative to some benchmark index or bogey. The objective is to outperform the market in any interest-rate environment. The plan sponsor determines the benchmark index presumably based on its liability structure. Since the performance of the index will depend on its composition, particularly with respect to the proportion of noncallable to callable bonds, the portfolio manager must understand the performance characteristics of the benchmark index.

Typically, active bond portfolio managers hold a large portion of their portfolio in nongovernment bonds. The nongovernment bond sector is comprised primarily of corporates and mortgage-backed securities. The securities in these market sectors are characterized by issues that have embedded call options.

When interest rates are declining and volatility is increasing, callable corporate bonds (as well as mortgage-backed securities) will underperform U.S. government bonds because (1) negative convexity "kicks in" as interest rates decline sufficiently and (2) the value of the embedded call option increases, thereby decreasing the price of a callable bond as volatility increases. In an environment of increasing interest rates and decreasing volatility, callable bonds will outperform U.S. government bonds. A summary of the expected relative performance of callable bonds and noncallable bonds in various market environments is given in Chapter 40.

Active portfolio decisions, therefore, should be made on the basis of not only the anticipated direction of interest rates but also (1) the nature of the benchmark index and (2) expected interest-rate volatility.

## Immunization

Immunization strategies are discussed in Chapter 42. The objective of immunization is to lock in a target rate of return that will be sufficient to satisfy a liability stream. A necessary condition is that the dollar duration of the assets equals the dollar duration of the liabilities.

Typically, an immunized portfolio is constructed using corporate bonds. The theory of immunization is that as interest rates decline, the lower reinvestment income due to lower reinvestment rates would be more than offset by capital appreciation of the portfolio due to lower interest rates. In the case of callable corporate bonds, the offsetting capital appreciation is truncated due to their negative convexity. The standard duration of a bond portfolio that includes callable corporate bonds is not a good measure of its interest-rate sensitivity.

In addition, not only is there the requirement that the dollar duration of the assets and liabilities must be equal, but there is the requirement that the convexity of the assets should be greater than or equal to the convexity of the liabilities. It is the call-adjusted convexity that should be considered in satisfying this requirement.

To eliminate or mitigate call risk, the immunized portfolio can be restricted to only noncallable bonds. Or, if callable bonds are included, the universe can be restricted to deep-discount callable bonds (i.e., bonds where the call option is deep out-of-the-money). However, restricting the universe of acceptable bonds to noncallable bonds and/or deep-discount callable bonds raises the cost of an immunized portfolio because they offer a lower yield than callable bonds.

If there are no restrictions placed on callable bonds that may be included in the immunized portfolio, the optimization program used to create the portfolio should recognize the value of the embedded call option. After the initial portfolio is created, more frequent monitoring of the portfolio during declining interest-rate and high interest-rate volatility environments is essential. This will permit the swapping of any callable corporate bonds for other bonds before a substantial adverse impact on the immunized portfolio due to negative convexity is realized.

# CHAPTER 37

## OPTION-ADJUSTED SPREAD ANALYSIS*

*Lakhbir S. Hayre, D.Phil.*
Director
Financial Strategies Group
Prudential-Bache Capital Funding

*Kenneth Lauterbach*
Vice-President
Financial Strategies Group
Prudential-Bache Capital Funding

The proper valuation of debt securities is generally recognized as one of the central problems in quantitative financial analysis. It is particularly important for securities with interest-rate-dependent cash flows such as floating-rate instruments, callable corporate bonds and mortgage-backed securities (MBSs). The dramatic growth over the last few years in the size and diversity of the bond market and an increase in volatility and competitiveness has forced portfolio managers to focus more closely on the investment characteristics of such securities and to estimate their relative value within the spectrum of fixed income securities.

This chapter describes a valuation methodology that can be used to compare debt securities with widely differing cash-flow patterns. It differs from traditional bond valuation in two major ways. First, instead of using constant discount rates to calculate the present values of cash flows, it uses discount rates derived from

*\*Copyright:* Prudential-Bache Capital Funding. The authors would like to thank David Audley, Robert Samuel, Cyrus Mohebbi, and Vincent Pica for their assistance and helpful comments; and Gladys Cardona, Joseph Reel and Efren Alba for the preparation of this chapter.

the term structure of interest rates. Second, instead of assuming that interest rates remain at their current levels over the life of the security, the methodology evaluates a security based on the full range of interest-rate environments that could occur over the life of the security.

Interest-rate movements are described by means of a probabilistic model. There are several different mathematical means for describing and evaluating the effects of interest-rate changes; the approach used here is statistical, or "Monte Carlo," simulation by means of computer-generated random numbers.[1]   Monte Carlo simulation is used to generate a large number of random paths for interest rates in a way that is consistent both with the term structure of interest rates and historical interest-rate behavior. Security cash flows are then obtained along each path. A value of the security for each interest-rate path is obtained by calculating the present value of its cash flows using discount rates based on that path.

A key output in the analysis is a spread, usually referred to as the "option-adjusted" spread (OAS), which represents an incremental return or risk premium over Treasury securities. On-the-run (OTR) Treasuries are assumed to provide a "risk-free" rate of return, and the valuation model is calibrated so that all on-the-run Treasuries have an OAS of zero. For other securities, the OAS is the implied risk premium or extra return relative to on-the-run Treasuries.

The methodology was initially developed for evaluating the impact of the embedded options in MBSs and callable corporate bonds and hence is often referred to as option-adjusted analysis (OAA). It can be applied to any security, however, regardless of cash-flow structure or uncertainty.

In the chapter, we give a basic overview of OAA. The concept of an incremental return over the Treasury curve and the modeling of interest-rate variation are discussed first. Calibration of the interest-rate distribution against the Treasury curve is also described. Then we apply the methodology to mortgage pass-through securities and collateralized mortgage obligation (CMO) bonds; the OASs provide an indication of the relative prepayment risks of different MBSs. Analysis of callable corporate bonds follows. OAA is used to estimate the impact of call provisions on a bond's performance, to estimate effective durations and convexities and to obtain projected prices if interest rates change. Finally, we discuss the use of OAA in relative value analysis. By using a consistent means of valuing securities, OAA allows the portfolio manager to properly compare securities that may have widely differing cash-flow characteristics. This is illustrated by comparing a mortgage-backed pass-through with a regular agency

---

[1] The other main approaches are continuous time diffusion processes, which lead to differential equations, and binomial lattices. Our model uses statistical simulation since this seems to provide the most flexibility in dealing with complex securities such as MBSs, whose cash flows may depend on both the current and past values of several correlated interest rates.

debenture and by a rich/cheap analysis of off-the-run Treasuries. A risk/reward profile can also be obtained for different securities, or for a portfolio as a whole, by considering the frequency distribution of the values of the securities along the different interest-rate paths.[2]

# VALUATION OF A STREAM OF CASH FLOWS

## Traditional Methods

The standard method for valuing a security is to find the present value of its expected future cash flows using a chosen discount rate. The discount rate that equates the present value of the security to its market price is the yield-to-maturity (YTM). A security's extra return relative to Treasuries is obtained by comparing the security's YTM to the yield of a Treasury with a similar maturity. The difference in yields is the security's spread over the "comparable" Treasury. Interest-rate volatility is generally ignored in traditional analysis; securities are evaluated based on current interest-rate levels or in some cases by assuming a specified change in rates.

There are several problems in using traditional analysis to evaluate a security:

- In calculating the YTM, the same discount rate is used to calculate the present values of cash flows received at different points in time. This ignores the term structure of interest rates (exemplified, say, by the Treasury yield curve), which implies that the market assigns different discount rates to cash flows of differing maturities. In essence, the YTM is an averaged discount rate that does not fully utilize the information provided by the term structure about the market values of cash flows of different maturities.
- The choice of a comparable benchmark Treasury against which the security's yield is compared can be arbitrary and even misleading. For example, a zero coupon 10-year bond and a coupon-paying 10-year bullet bond both would be compared to the 10-year Treasury, although the cash-flow patterns of the two securities are very different. This problem is especially acute for securities with interest-rate-contingent cash flows such as MBSs and callable corporate bonds whose maturity may depend on the future course of interest rates.

---

[2] Historical analysis, which indicates that the use of OAS-based trading strategies can lead to significant increases in returns, is provided in Lakhbir S. Hayre and Kenneth Lauterbach, "Stochastic Valuation of Debt Securities," in Frank J. Fabozzi (ed.), *Managing Institutional Assets* (New York: Ballinger Publishing, 1990).

- The effect of interest-rate volatility on securities with interest-rate-contingent cash flows can obviously be critical but is typically ignored in standard fixed income analysis. This is a particularly relevant now since much of the recent growth in the fixed income sector has been in securities with contingent cash flows.

The valuation methodology described in this chapter and generally described as option-adjusted analysis (OAA), attempts to deal with the drawbacks of traditional analysis described above. It differs from traditional fixed income analysis in two fundamental ways:

- OAA introduces interest-rate volatility. Instead of assuming that interest rates remain at their current levels over the life of the security, OAA evaluates securities under the more realistic assumption that interest rates are likely to vary in an unpredictable manner over the life of the security.
- In OAA, each cash flow from the security is individually compared to a corresponding Treasury cash flow, and the security's higher return is in essence expressed as an incremental spread over the whole Treasury curve; the OAS measures the extra return the security provides relative to an investment in Treasuries (which is assumed to provide the risk-free rate of return).

## Calculation of Implied Risk Premium or OAS

Most investors are familiar with the concept of present value. If $R(1)$, $R(2)$, ... is a set of discount rates for time periods 1,2, ... then the present value of $1 to be received at time $t$ is

$$1/\{[1 + R(1)][1 + R(2)] \ldots [1 + R(t)]\}$$

Suppose that $R(1)$, $R(2)$, ... represent a risk-free rate (for example, a Treasury-bill rate). In practice, investors can, by incurring some extra degree of risk, obtain higher returns. If the appropriate discount rate for a particular investment or security is the riskless rate plus a risk premium $s$, then the present value of $1 to be received from this security at time $t$ is

$$1/\{[1 + R(1) + s][1 + R(2) + s] \ldots [1 + R(t) + s]\}$$

This gives the discount function applicable to a cash flow received from the security at time $t$, and we will label it $DISCF(t, s)$. If the security pays cash flows $CF(1)$, $CF(2)$, ... at time periods 1,2, ... then the value of the security is obtained by present valuing all the cash flows using the appropriate discount factors:

$$PV(s) = CF(1) * DISCF(1, s) + CF(2) * DISCF(2, s) + \ldots$$

This can be thought of as the value of the security corresponding to a particular set (or path) $R(1)$, $R(2)$, ... of riskless rates and a specified risk premium $s$ over the riskless rate. In practice, of course, when trying to value a security we do not know the path that interest rates will take over the term of the security. One approach in dealing with this uncertainty is to use statistical methods to generate a large number of possible interest-rate paths that can occur over the term of the security and calculate $PV(s)$, the value of the security, for each path. The average of the security values so obtained can be thought of as the true or "fair" value of the security:

$$\text{Value of Security} = \text{average of } PV(s) \text{ over all interest-rate paths}$$
$$= AVGPV(s) \tag{37-1}$$

This gives the fair value of a security for a given risk premium or spread $s$ over the riskless rate.

*Definition of the OAS.*   Equation (37-1) gives the fair value of a security assuming that its fair risk premium is $s$. Typically, however, we are more likely to know the market price of a security, and the question that the OAS answers is, what risk premium or incremental spread over the riskless rate does this security provide? The answer is obtained by finding the value of $s$ that makes the average present value of the security, calculated as described above, equal to the market price of the security:

$$\text{Price} = AVGPV(s) \tag{37-2}$$

The solution of this equation gives the security's implied spread or risk premium over the riskless rate and is what is typically termed the OAS. By definition, it follows that for any security providing the risk-free rate of return, the solution of Equation (37-2) is zero.

*Calibration Against Treasury Curve.*   The risk-free rate has been defined here as the return received by investing in OTR Treasuries. Hence, assuming that they are efficiently priced, each OTR should have a risk premium or OAS of zero. That is, the valuation model should be calibrated so that for each OTR,

$$\text{Market Price} = AVGPV(0) \tag{37-3}$$

where $AVGPV(s)$ is as defined in Equation (37-1). In practical terms, this involves making appropriate statistical adjustments to the sample of possible interest-rate paths used in calculating the OAS; the result, roughly speaking, is that the average or mean interest-rate path will correspond to the usual implied short-term Treasury forward rates. See the next section for more discussion on this and the appendix to Hayre and Lauterbach ("Stochastic Valuation"), for some technical details.

## Modeling Interest-Rate and Cash-Flow Uncertainty

The previous section gave a general description of the calculation of the OAS. The specific steps involved may be summarized as follows:

1. Model fluctuations in interest rates over the life of the security.
2. Obtain cash flows for the security along each interest-rate path.
3. For a chosen incremental spread over Treasuries, obtain present values for the cash flows along each possible interest-rate path by discounting by the short-term Treasury rates along the path plus the spread. The average of these present values over all possible interest-rate paths is the theoretical security value corresponding to the given spread or risk premium over Treasuries.
4. Calculate the incremental spread over Treasuries implied by the market price of the security. This is the *option-adjusted spread*.

Exhibit 37–1 gives a schematic representation of this process. Below, we discuss some of the details of these steps as implemented in the model used to analyze mortgage securities and callable corporates later in this chapter.

*Modeling Interest-Rate Fluctuations.*   As is fairly common in modeling interest-rate movements, we assume that percentage changes in interest rates have a bell-shaped or "normal" frequency curve.[3]  Computer-generated random numbers are used to obtain paths of interest rates, with the random numbers scaled so that the volatility displayed by the simulated interest-rate movements matches observed market volatilities. The number of possible interest-rate paths that could occur over the term of the security is theoretically infinite. Hence, a sufficient number of paths are chosen randomly so as to obtain an adequate statistical representation of the whole universe of possible paths.

*Cash Flows on Interest-Rate Paths.*   For noncallable Treasuries, agencies, or corporates, the cash flows are the same on all interest-rate paths. For interest-rate-contingent cash flows, such as MBSs or callable bonds, a method for generating cash flows (e.g., a prepayment model) as a function of the interest-rate path is needed. The next two sections provide details on MBSs and callable corporate bonds.

*Present Values on Interest-Rate Paths.*   As described above, the cash flows on each interest-rate path are discounted to the present by the risk-free discount

---

[3] The interest rate is said to be "lognormal." A "mean reversion" process is applied to stop the rates from going to abnormally high or low levels. The appendix to Hayre and Lauterbach, "Stochastic Valuation of Debt Securities," gives a more detailed description of the interest-rate generation process.

**EXHIBIT 37–1**
**Option-Adjusted Valuation of a Security**

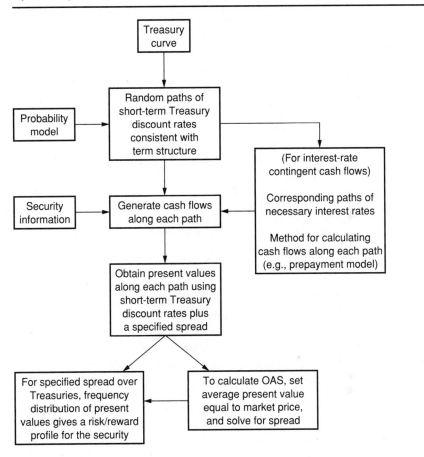

rates along the path plus a spread. If this spread is considered a "fair" risk premium over Treasuries for the security, then the present value on a path can be considered to be the fair or theoretical price for the security, *given this particular realization of interest rates*. Some interest-rate paths will affect positively the value of the security, while other interest-rate paths will affect adversely the present value of the security. The average of these present values can be considered the fair price corresponding to this particular spread over Treasuries.

As an illustration, Exhibit 37–2 shows the distribution of present values for an agency security for an incremental spread of 50 basis points; in other words, for each interest-rate path, the cash flows from the agency are discounted by the short-term rates on the path plus 50 basis points. A short-term rate volatility of

**EXHIBIT 37–2**

**Distribution of Present Values for the FNMA 9.35% Debenture of February 12, 1996**

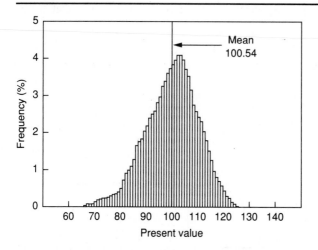

15 percent per year is assumed. The agency is the FNMA 9.35 percent debenture maturing on February 12, 1996. It is noncallable and hence its cash flows are fixed. Thus, variation in present values is caused by variation in the short-term Treasury discount rates. Since the coupon on the agency is fixed, low interest-rate paths lead to high present values for the security, while high interest-rate paths lead to low present values.

Also shown in Exhibit 37–2 is the average of the present values. For a spread of 50 basis points, the average is 100.54; this is the fair price if 50 basis points is considered to be a fair spread over Treasuries for this agency debenture.

The actual price of the FNMA debenture is 101.1875. Calculation of the OAS requires finding the spread that makes the average present value equal to this price.[4] An iterative solution method gives the OAS as being equal to 38 basis points; in other words, if a spread of 38 basis points is added to the short-term Treasury discount rates, the average of the resulting present values for the agency's cash flows is equal to 101.1875, the current price of the security.

---

[4] The spread is calculated by a process of iteration. An initial guess for the spread is chosen, then the average present value is calculated for this spread and compared with the specified price. The spread is then adjusted up or down repeatedly until the average present value is equal to the specified price.

## Comparison of the OAS and Traditional Yield Spreads

To summarize, it can be seen that the OAS differs from the traditional spread over Treasuries in two ways:

- The traditional spread is a spread off a single point on the current Treasury curve. The OAS can be viewed as an average spread over the whole Treasury curve.
- Interest-rate volatility is factored into the calculation by allowing random fluctuations in discount rates and, for interest-rate-contingent cash flows, calculating the security cash flows separately for each interest-rate path.

In financial terms, the OAS can be interpreted as the average extra return that is received for investing in a particular security instead of investing in the "safe" alternative of OTR Treasuries. To those who would ask, "which OTR?", the theoretically correct reply is that it does not matter, since the model has been calibrated so that all OTRs have a zero OAS, making us indifferent as to which OTR we invest in. In fact, however, there is a very strong connection between the OAS and the traditional Treasury yield spread. For securities with fixed (noninterest-rate-dependent) cash flows, the OAS is typically very close to the traditional Treasury yield spread. For securities with interest-rate-dependent cash flows, the effect of using a large sample of possible interest-rate paths and calculating a projected set of security cash flows for each path is to capture the impact of changing interest rates on the security. The resulting spread over Treasuries has hence been adjusted for the effects of embedded options, and thus the name OAS.

## MORTGAGE SECURITIES

The methodology described in the previous section was to a large extent motivated by the dramatic growth of the MBS market in recent years and the need to obtain a better understanding of mortgage securities. The investment characteristics of MBSs are influenced significantly by mortgage prepayment rates, which in turn are interest-rate dependent. This section describes the application of OAA to mortgage securities. Pass-throughs are analyzed first, followed by a discussion of CMO bonds.[5]

---

[5] For an application to the valuation of CMO residuals (a derivative mortgage security highly sensitive to changes in interest rates), see Hayre and Lauterbach, "Stochastic Valuation of Debt Securities."

## Obtaining Mortgage Cash Flows

The general steps involved in the OAA of MBSs are those shown in Exhibit 37–1. Obtaining MBS cash flows along interest-rate paths requires generating paths of mortgage rates and estimating prepayment rates along the paths.

*Generating Paths of Mortgage Rates.*    For each path of short-term Treasury rates, a corresponding path of mortgage rates is generated, with the relationship based on empirical analysis of historical interest-rate behavior.

Calibration against the Treasury curve introduces drifts or trends into the paths of short-term Treasury rates. For example, an upward-sloping yield curve gives an upward bias to the rates. The shape of the yield curve is determined by market expectations of interest-rate changes and by a variety of other factors, which collectively are called *term premia*. Both market expectations and term premia are factors in the term structure at almost all times, with their relative influences varying over time.[6]

In generating a mortgage-rate path that corresponds to a given short-rate path, an important question is what proportion of the drift in the short-term discount-rate paths to pass on to the mortgage rates. Trends in mortgage rates affect prepayment projections. For example, an upward trend in mortgage rates will cause projected prepayments to decline, which can have a marked effect on prepayment-sensitive securities such as CMO residuals and stripped MBSs.

The approach taken here is to divide the drift in the short-term discount rates into expectation and term premia components and pass only the expectation component through to the mortgage rates. The term premia component has been modeled as a function of term using historical market data.[7]

*Prepayment Rates along a Path.*    For a given path of mortgage rates, prepayment levels are obtained from the Prudential-Bache prepayment model.[8]   The model uses mortgage rates and security information, such as type, net and gross coupons, age, and past prepayment history to generate monthly prepayment projections for the specified mortgage-rate path. The prepayment rates then are used to obtain the monthly cash flows from the security. An important point to note is that mortgage prepayments are heavily dependent on past prepayments: a pool of mortgage holders exposed to attractive refinancing opportunities for the first time are likely to prepay much faster than mortgagees who have already gone

---

[6] See Chapters 9 and 56 of this book for a discussion of the term structure of interest rates.

[7] We are grateful to the Portfolio Management Group of The Prudential Insurance Company of America and to Russell Read in particular for sharing some of their findings with us.

[8] For a description of the model, and a discussion of the determinants of mortgage prepayments, see Hayre, Lauterbach and Mohebbi, "Prepayment Models and Methodologies," in Frank J. Fabozzi (ed.), *Advances and Innovations in the Bond and Mortgage Markets* (Chicago: Probus Publishing, 1989).

through a refinancing phase (this phenomenon is typically labelled "burnout"). This dependence on the past makes Monte Carlo simulation generally the only practical method for stochastic analysis of mortgage securities.

## Option-Adjusted Analysis of Pass-Throughs

Mortgage pass-throughs, like all fixed-rate securities (we only consider fixed-coupon pass-throughs in this section), are subject to interest-rate risk; the value of their coupon payments changes inversely to interest rates. In addition, pass-throughs are subject to prepayment risk, a form of call risk; mortgage holders generally have the right to prepay at any time all or part of their mortgages. Prepayment levels are dependent on interest rates, thus leading to interdependent changes in the value of a pass-through as interest rates change.

For MBSs, the OAS can be thought of as the average incremental return over Treasuries after factoring out the effects of interest-rate and prepayment-rate variation on cash flows. As such, it gives a better indication of the value of an MBS than the usual yield spread over a comparable Treasury. This latter spread is calculated assuming a fixed projected prepayment rate and thus ignores interest-rate and prepayment-rate volatility.

Exhibit 37–3 shows the regular spreads and OASs for several GNMA coupons.

Exhibit 37–3 shows that the GNMA 11 has a regular spread of 108 basis points, compared with a spread of 106 basis points for the GNMA 8, suggesting that the two securities provide very similar returns over comparable maturity Treasuries. However, once interest rates and prepayment volatility are considered, the GNMA 11 looks less attractive; the GNMA 11 has an OAS of 48

## EXHIBIT 37–3
### Yield Spreads and OASs for GNMAs

| Coupon | Price* | Rem. Term | Proj. PSA† | Yield | Avg. Life | Spread‡ | OAS § |
|--------|--------|-----------|------------|-------|-----------|---------|-------|
| GNMA  8 | 91–18 | 18–09 | 100 | 9.84 | 8.0 | 106 | 88 |
| GNMA  9 | 96–08 | 20–08 | 108 | 9.87 | 8.5 | 105 | 80 |
| GNMA 10 | 99–31 | 28–02 | 130 | 10.14 | 9.6 | 123 | 80 |
| GNMA 11 | 105–21 | 26–00 | 199 | 9.77 | 6.9 | 108 | 48 |
| GNMA 12 | 109–00 | 26–03 | 331 | 9.19 | 4.4 | 88 | 33 |
| GNMA 13 | 111–12 | 25–00 | 396 | 8.89 | 3.6 | 70 | 50 |

\* Prices and prepayment projections as of May 5, 1988.
† Projected prepayment rate is expressed as a percentage of the benchmark Public Securities Association (PSA) curve.
‡ Spread is the difference between the yield of the GNMA and the Treasury curve yield at the average life.
§ OAS is calculated using a short-rate volatility of 15 percent.

basis points, compared with 88 basis points for the GNMA 8. This results from the negative convexity of the GNMA 11. A drop in interest rates tends to lead to a marked increase in the prepayment rate of the premium GNMA 11, thus reducing the benefits of the higher coupon compared to lower discount rates, as well as returning the premium faster. On the other hand, if interest rates rise, the decline in the GNMA 11 prepayments is beneficial because the premium is returned at a slower rate; but it also means that the negative effect of the higher discount rates is increased, because of the higher outstanding principal balances.

In contrast, the GNMA 8 has low prepayment volatility. Interest rates would have to drop several hundred basis points before prepayments increase significantly. Hence, once interest-rate volatility is considered, the GNMA 8 offers better value than the GNMA 11. From Exhibit 37–3, it is clear that low-premium coupons, which not coincidently are the ones with the highest prepayment volatility and negative convexity, tend to be most affected by interest-rate volatility.

*Sensitivity of OASs to Changes in Volatility.* Interest-rate volatility changes also have the greatest effect on low-premium coupons. Exhibit 37–4 shows the OASs of the GNMA coupons in Exhibit 37–3 at annual interest-rate volatilities of 0 percent, 10 percent, 15 percent and 20 percent.

The OASs of all coupons are reduced by heightened interest-rate volatility, with the low-premium coupon most affected. In an options theory context, this can be explained by viewing an MBS as a noncallable bond minus a call option; the higher the volatility, the greater the value of the call option, and hence the lower the value of the MBS.

The difference between the OASs at zero volatility and at specified higher levels gives an indication of the impact of interest-rate volatility on various coupons and may be termed an "option cost." The option cost is relatively low for discounts, increases to a maximum for the high prepayment volatility

**EXHIBIT 37–4**
**Sensitivity of GNMA OASs to Volatility Changes**

|  | OAS at Volatility of | | | |
|---|---|---|---|---|
|  | 0% | 10% | 15% | 20% |
| GNMA  8 | 105 | 96 | 88 | 79 |
| GNMA  9 | 106 | 94 | 80 | 64 |
| GNMA 10 | 130 | 106 | 80 | 55 |
| GNMA 11 | 119 | 82 | 48 | 17 |
| GNMA 12 | 116 | 68 | 33 | 3 |
| GNMA 13 | 115 | 77 | 50 | 26 |

low premiums, and then starts decreasing for the high premiums, which, like discounts, have low prepayment volatility.

The negative impact of interest-rate volatility even on discount coupons can be explained by considering the effect of higher prepayments if interest rates drop. If there is a substantial drop in interest rates, the discount coupons gain from a faster return of principal, but this leaves a lower outstanding balance with which to benefit from the differences between the coupons and prevailing short-term rates.

As Exhibit 37–4 indicates, interest-rate volatility is a critical parameter in OAA. It is useful to look at the OASs at several volatility levels to obtain a clearer understanding of the option-adjusted value of the MBS. Not only do the OASs change as volatility changes, but also, to a lesser extent, even the *relative* values of different coupons can change. For example, from Exhibit 37–4, at an assumed volatility of 10 percent per year, the GNMA 10 has an OAS of 106 basis points, which is greater than the OAS of 94 basis points for the GNMA 9; however, at a volatility of 20 percent, the GNMA 9 has an OAS of 64 basis points compared with an OAS of 55 basis points for the GNMA 10, indicating that the GNMA 9 is a better value at the higher volatility level.

***Distribution of Present Values.*** Each computer-generated random path of interest rates represents a possible realization of the future. The present value of a security's cash flows on this path represents the outcome of investing in the security for this particular realization of interest rates. The dispersion and range of present values obtained from a large number of randomly generated interest-rate paths provides valuable insight into the risks and rewards of investing in the security.

Exhibit 37–5 shows the distribution of present values obtained from 2,000 simulations for a GNMA 7, GNMA 11, and GNMA 15. The present values were calculated using the OASs in the discounting; for ease of comparison, the present values are stated as a percentage of the current market price so that the average for each distribution is 100 percent.

The distribution of the GNMA 7, a deep-discount coupon, is only slightly skewed. Because of its substantial call protection (mortgage rates would have to drop to about 5 percent before it experiences very high prepayments), the properties of the GNMA 7 are somewhat comparable to those of a 10-year Treasury.

The GNMA 11 is a low-premium coupon with very high prepayment volatility at current mortgage-rate levels. This is reflected in the distribution of present values. The distribution is heavily skewed to the left. The chances of large upside gains are limited by prepayment risk; if interest rates decline, increasing prepayments cancel part of the gain in value from the lower rates. On the other hand, the distribution of present values is concentrated in a relatively narrow range; the fast principal paydown means that the GNMA 11 is basically a short-term security.

**EXHIBIT 37–5**

**Distribution of Present Values for a GNMA 7, GNMA 11, and GNMA 15**

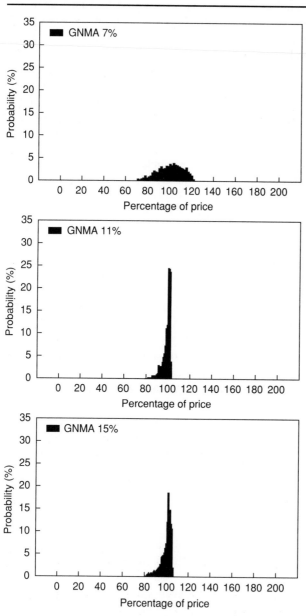

In terms of relative risk, as measured by the dispersion of present values, it is interesting to note that the GNMA 11 has a narrower range of present values than a 10-year Treasury. Thus, despite the fact that the GNMA 11 is a 30-year security and is subject to prepayment variability, it is possible to say that it has less investment uncertainty than the 10-year Treasury (assuming liquidity and credit quality are roughly comparable).

This emphasizes the points made in the previous section about the causes of uncertainty in the value of a security. For high-quality, liquid securities, there are generally two main reasons for this uncertainty: the value of the security's coupon payments relative to prevailing rates in the future, and, for callable securities, the impact of the call features. The 10-year Treasury suffers only from the first risk, whereas the GNMA 11 suffers from both. However, the first risk has more impact on the 10-year Treasury than on the GNMA 11 because the GNMA's principal is reduced over time, making its coupon payments relatively less important.

Finally, for the GNMA 15, the distribution of present values is less skewed. The GNMA 15 is a very high-premium security and its prepayment levels will not change significantly unless there is a substantial increase in prepayments. Thus, like the GNMA 7, the GNMA 15 has only limited prepayment volatility, and its investment profile is similar to that of a shorter maturity Treasury.

## CMO Bonds

A CMO segments mortgage cash flows in order to create a number of bonds of varying maturities. A basic or prototype CMO contains three to five sequential-pay bonds, with one often structured as an accrual class or "Z-bond." Although the last few years have seen the creation of a vast diversity of CMO structures including floating-rate classes, bonds with more or less guaranteed pay-down schedules ("PAC" bonds), and simultaneous-pay bonds, our attention is restricted, for illustrative simplicity, to the basic CMO structure described above. In practice, the OAA of a specific CMO bond requires using the exact paydown structure of that CMO issue.

As an example, a generic four-class "ABCZ" CMO (i.e., four sequential-pay classes with a Z-bond as the final class) is used. All principal paydowns from the collateral are paid to class A until it is retired, then to class B, and so on. The collateral is GNMA 9 pass-throughs. The par amounts of the bonds in each class are chosen so that the four classes have average lives of approximately 2, 5, 7, and 20 years, respectively. The bonds are assumed to be monthly pay, with a 30-day delay.

Exhibit 37–6 gives traditional and OAA for the four-class ABCZ CMO described above. Interest-rate volatility has a greater effect on the value of the CMO bonds than on the GNMA 9. The reason is that a given change in the prepayment rate on the GNMA 9 has a proportionately greater effect

**EXHIBIT 37–6**
**OASs for a GNMA 9 CMO**

| Class | Par Amt. ($) | Price* | Cpn. | Avg. Life (Yrs.) | B-E Yield | Treasury Spread | OAS at Volatility of 10% | 15% | 20% |
|---|---|---|---|---|---|---|---|---|---|
| GNMA 9† | | | | | | | | | |
| A | 100 | 92.65625 | 9.0 | 11 | 10.48 | 123 | 104 | 88 | 71 |
| B | 35.1 | 98.37792 | 8.0 | 2 | 9.10 | 100 | 67 | 48 | 21 |
| C | 19.0 | 95.50843 | 8.5 | 5 | 9.85 | 115 | 83 | 59 | 25 |
| Z | 18.0 | 94.74840 | 9.0 | 7 | 10.27 | 125 | 103 | 80 | 52 |
| | 27.9 | 80.99889 | 9.0 | 17 | 10.87 | 150 | 102 | 79 | 52 |

* All prices shown in decimal form.
† The GNMA 9 is assumed to have a remaining term of 28–00 years; the CMO is priced assuming a projected prepayment speed of 100 percent PSA.

on the CMO bond that is paying down at the time. For example, class A comprises about one third of the total issue; hence a 1 percent prepayment on the GNMA 9 means approximately a 3 percent prepayment for class A. This makes the OASs of the CMO bonds more sensitive to changes in interest-rate volatility and, hence, prepayment-rate volatility than the OAS of the GNMA 9.[9]

In terms of investment characteristics, class C is the bond most comparable to the underlying GNMA 9. In general, however, because of differing maturities, a direct comparison of CMOs and pass-throughs may not always be relevant. For example, investors in the short-maturity class A bonds would have different maturity needs than investors in the GNMA 9 pass-through, suggesting that the A bond should be compared to short-maturity corporate bonds or Treasuries rather than the GNMA.

## CALLABLE CORPORATE BONDS

Many corporate bonds have some type of call provision, allowing the issuer to redeem the bonds at stated times at specified prices. Typically, corporate bonds have a period of call protection, after which they become callable at any time. For example, a 10-year bond may have 5 years of call protection, and then be callable at par from year 5 onward. In some cases, there may be a call premium in the form of above-par call prices in the earlier part of the callable period; for example, a 15-year bond may have 7 years of call protection and is then callable at a call price that starts at 105 at year 7, declines to par by year 10, and is par from year 10 onwards.

The issuer's decision whether or not to exercise a call is largely (but not completely) driven by interest rates. Traditional analysis of callable bonds has tended to ignore the interest-rate-dependent nature of their investment characteristics. Typically, a YTM (assuming no call) and a yield-to-call (assuming that the bond is called at the earliest call date) are calculated. The lesser of these values is often termed the yield-to-worst. While these numbers provide some information, they tend to misstate the bond's value and do not allow for an accurate determination of the effective duration of the bond.

---

[9] In this sense, the CMO bonds can be said to have greater prepayment uncertainty than the GNMA 9. However, in terms of cash-flow uncertainty, the CMO bonds have less prepayment uncertainty than the GNMA 9, since, for a particular bond, the cash flows are concentrated in a smaller time period than the 30-year GNMA. A distinction thus has to be made between the effects of prepayment uncertainty on value and on cash-flow timing.

In this section, the methodology described in the first section is applied to the analysis of callable corporate bonds. The OAS of a corporate bond is calculated, and a method for calculating the effective duration of the bond is described. The methodology also allows us to obtain projected price paths if interest rates change.

## Bond Cash Flows on Interest-Rate Paths

While a corporation's decision to call a bond is largely interest-rate driven, the call option typically is not exercised in an efficient fashion. Transaction costs may mean that the bonds are not called until they are in-the-money by at least some minimum amount. Noneconomic considerations, such as the desire to preserve investor goodwill, may also inhibit the exercise of the call. Conversely, the desire to retire unwanted debt may encourage the exercise of the call. A distinction also has to be made between callability and refundability; while a bond may be callable after, say, five years, it may not be refundable until after, say, seven years. Calling the bond before the first refundable date will imply a "cash call" (i.e., the corporation would retire the debt without issuing new debt to cover the cost). In many cases, restrictions on refunding will tend to discourage the corporation from calling the bond.

The approach used here is similar to that for mortgage securities described in the previous section. An interest-rate-dependent "probability-of-call" function, equivalent to the prepayment model for mortgage securities, is used at each callable date to determine whether or not the bond is called. The function used here calls the bond if the present value of the remaining cash flows (to maturity) exceeds the call price by some "issuer premium." [10]

The issuer premium is the cost that the issuer would incur by redeeming the bond. It incorporates the factors discussed above such as the cost of reissuing the debt if it is a refunding, the current ability of the corporation to raise new funds, the cost of lost investor goodwill if the bonds are retired prior to maturity, the opportunity cost of not being able to wait for a more favorable market environment if the option is of the American type, the effect of a declining call price schedule, the transaction cost of retiring the bonds, and so on.

Obviously, there are a number of issues associated with modeling this premium, many of which are specific to the issuer but some of which can be treated generally. A fuller discussion of the issues involved in developing a corporate

---

[10] In a refunding context, this is basically equivalent to calling the bond if the savings in interest expenses exceed the issuer premium.

prepayment model is beyond the scope of this chapter.[11] The call decision rule used here, while a relatively simple (compared to mortgage prepayment models) version of a corporate probability-of-call model, which uses market data to estimate issuer premiums, gives results that are consistent with empirical experience.

## Option-Adjusted Spreads

As discussed in the first section, the OAS for a callable bond can be interpreted as the effective spread over Treasury rates after interest-rate volatility and the effect of the bond's call provisions have been factored out. Exhibit 37–7 shows OASs for three callable bonds.

Exhibit 37–7 shows that the call provisions affect the bonds to different degrees, depending on various factors. The ITT bond has a call that is already in-the-money and has less than one remaining year of call protection; hence, it is affected significantly by the call option. The Marriott and the GMAC bonds are affected to somewhat similar degrees by their call provisions. The Marriott has about four and one-half years of remaining call protection; the GMAC has no remaining call protection, but it has a lower coupon and a call premium in the form of a call price that is greater than par.

An interesting point is illustrated by the fact that the OAS of the ITT bond declines as volatility increases. The ITT bond, with a coupon of 10.80 percent, is likely to be called at the first call date (July 1, 1989) unless interest rates increase substantially. Hence, at first glance, it might be supposed that since a higher volatility decreases the chances of the bond being called,[12] then the bond would benefit from a higher volatility. However, the interest-rate realizations on which the bond will not be called are paths with high interest rates so that the cash flows, being discounted by higher rates, will have lower present values. In

---

[11] While many of the considerations involved in modeling mortgage prepayments also apply to corporates, it is worth noting that an important difference between mortgages and callable corporates is that prepayments on a mortgage security represent the actions of a large number of homeowners, whereas the decision to call a corporate bond is typically an all-or-nothing decision made by a single entity, namely, the corporation. Given information on interest rates and mortgage characteristics, it is possible to use statistical methods to predict the rate of prepayments on a large pool of mortgages with a fair degree of accuracy. On the other hand, because the decision of a corporation as to whether to call a bond will be made by one or two people (e.g., the CFO and the CEO), there will always be a degree of unpredictability about the call decision. Fortunately, however, while this is an important consideration in analysis for a single interest-rate realization, averaging over a large number of interest-rate realizations (as is done in OAA) reduces the importance of this problem.

[12] The average life of the bond, defined as the average over all interest-rate paths to the time until the bond is called, is 1.25 years at 10 percent volatility, 1.41 years at 15 percent volatility, and 1.50 years at 20 percent volatility.

**EXHIBIT 37-7**
**OASs for Callable Corporate Bonds**

| Issuer | S&P Rating | Maturity | Next Call Date | Next Call Price | Current Price | Cpn. (%) | YTM | Treasury Yield Spread | OAS at Volatility of | | |
|---|---|---|---|---|---|---|---|---|---|---|---|
| | | | | | | | | | 10% | 15% | 20% |
| ITT FIN | A | 07/01/92 | 07/01/89 | 100.00 | 101.58 | 10.800 | 10.27 | 168 | 57 | 30 | −4 |
| MARRIOT | A− | 02/01/96 | 02/01/93 | 100.00 | 99.59 | 9.625 | 9.70 | 85 | 65 | 50 | 37 |
| GMAC | AA− | 07/15/07 | Callable now | 104.00 | 84.19 | 8.000 | 9.86 | 82 | 71 | 54 | 41 |

Note: Based on closing prices and Treasury rates on September 20, 1988.

other words, while a higher volatility may reduce the call risk in some cases, it also increases the interest-rate risk (i.e., the chances of a reduction in the fixed-coupon bond's value due to higher interest rates is increased by higher volatility).

As would be expected when dealing with embedded options, volatility is generally a major determinant of the bonds' OASs. We discuss a precise method of measuring the cost of embedded options next.

## Cost of the Embedded Option

The cost of a bond's call provisions to the investor can be determined from OAA. This, in effect, values the call option that the investor has granted to the issuer.

The option cost is found by considering a noncallable bond that is otherwise identical to the callable bond. A simple (and frequently used) technique is to calculate the YTM of the noncallable bond, find the spread over a similar maturity Treasury, and call the difference between this spread and the OAS of the callable bond the option cost. However, this method ignores the fact that the regular spread and the OAS are not directly comparable. A more meaningful approach is to value the callable and noncallable bonds in a consistent way, and then consider the difference.

The approach is illustrated in Exhibit 37–8 for two of the bonds shown in Exhibit 37–7. The OAS of the callable bond is calculated first; this OAS is then used as the spread in finding the value of the noncallable bond. The difference between the values of the noncallable and callable bonds can be considered to

**EXHIBIT 37–8**
**Cost of Embedded Options**

| Volatility (%) | Callable OAS (b. p.) | Implied Noncallable Price | Option Cost ($) | Noncallable OAS (b. p.) | Option Cost (b. p.) |
|---|---|---|---|---|---|
| ITT: Price = 101.58, Coupon = 10.80%, Maturity 7/1/92, 1st Call date 7/1/89 |
| 10 | 57 | 105.06 | 3.48 | 167 | 110 |
| 15 | 30 | 105.94 | 4.36 | 167 | 137 |
| 20 | −4 | 107.07 | 5.49 | 167 | 171 |
| GMAC: Price = 84.19, Coupon = 8.000%, Maturity 7/15/07, Callable now, Current call price 104, Par in 2002 |
| 10 | 71 | 84.99 | 0.80 | 82 | 11 |
| 15 | 54 | 86.33 | 2.14 | 82 | 28 |
| 20 | 41 | 87.35 | 3.16 | 82 | 41 |

be the option cost in price terms. Similarly, if the OAS of the noncallable bond is calculated using the callable bond's price, we obtain an option cost in spread terms.

The ITT bond has a coupon of 10.80 percent, which is 200 to 300 basis points above current refunding rates, making it likely that the bond will be called next year unless rates rise substantially. Hence, the option cost is high, even at a 10 percent volatility. The GMAC, on the other hand, is a deep-discount bond with an out-of-the-money option. Hence, its option cost is relatively low at a 10 percent volatility but increases at higher volatilities, which increase the value of the embedded option.

## Price Behavior and Effective Duration

An important objective for the portfolio manager in evaluating any security is to determine its likely price behavior as interest rates change. In particular, it is necessary to estimate the duration of the security. The usual duration measures (Macaulay or modified) can be inaccurate for interest-rate-contingent cash flows such as mortgage securities or callable corporates.

OAA can be used to calculate an "effective" duration measure for bonds with contingent cash flows. Such a measure takes into account the effect of interest-rate changes on the bonds' cash flows. The effective duration is calculated by assuming that the OAS remains constant, and by moving the initial value of the short-term Treasury rate up and down by a small amount (50 basis points in this case) and calculating the new implied prices. These new prices also allow us to estimate convexity.

Exhibit 37–9 shows effective durations and convexities for the bonds discussed in Exhibits 37–7 and 37–8, as well as for noncallable but otherwise identical bonds. For noncallables, the effective duration is essentially the same as modified duration but is calculated in the same way as the callable bonds' durations.

The effect of a bond's call provision on its duration depends on a number of factors. One is the length of the remaining call-free period; the greater this period, the less the reduction in the bond's duration due to the call features. Another important variable is whether the embedded option is in-the-money or out-of-the-money. The GMAC bond, for example, is a deep-discount, and, even though it is immediately callable, the reduction in the duration due to the call is minor. The ITT bond has an option that is significantly in-the-money, and consequently its duration is substantially reduced because of the call.

The technique used for estimating effective duration can also be used for obtaining projected price paths as interest rates change. In other words, we calculate the OAS using the current price of the bond and current interest-rate levels and then assume that the OAS stays constant as interest rates change. This allows us to calculate an implied price for each new level of interest rates.

**EXHIBIT 37–9**
**Effective Duration and Convexity for Callable Corporate Bonds**

| Bond | Maturity | Next Call Date | Price | Effective Duration | | Convexity | |
|------|----------|-----------|-------|----------|-------------|----------|-------------|
| | | | | Callable | Noncallable | Callable | Noncallable |
| ITT FIN | 07/01/92 | 07/01/89 | 101.58 | 1.1 | 3.0 | −0.3258 | 0.1872 |
| MARRIOTT | 02/01/96 | 02/01/93 | 99.59 | 4.6 | 5.1 | 0.2135 | 0.5683 |
| GMAC | 07/15/07 | Callable now | 84.19 | 8.1 | 8.4 | 0.5328 | 1.6818 |

Note: Volatility assumption is 15 percent per annum.

Exhibit 37–10 shows projected price paths for the Marriott issue and for a noncallable but otherwise identical bond. Because the Marriott bond has four and one-half years of call protection remaining, there is relatively little difference in the two price paths at current-rate levels, but the difference increases as interest rates decline. Exhibit 37–11 shows projected price paths for the ITT bond and an identical noncallable bond.

The projected price path shows that the ITT bond has a high degree of negative convexity because of its call features and premium price. As interest rates decline, the price continues to increase (due to the high coupon and the remaining nine months of call protection), but there is substantial price compression since low interest rates mean that the bond investor is likely to receive the coupon interest only until the first call date. This indicates that the rate of price increase, or duration, is declining; in other words, the price path has negative convexity. This is illustrated in Exhibit 37–12, which shows the effective duration for the ITT bond as interest rates change, along with the effective duration of a hypothetical noncallable but otherwise identical bond.

The effective duration of the ITT bond decreases as rates decline, in contrast with the hypothetical noncallable bond, whose duration continues to increase. It is interesting to note that, as interest rates continue declining, the effective

**EXHIBIT 37–10**
**Projected Price Paths for the Marriott Bond**

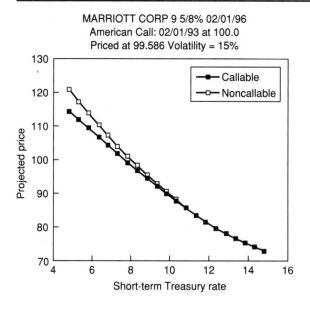

MARRIOTT CORP 9 5/8% 02/01/96
American Call: 02/01/93 at 100.0
Priced at 99.586 Volatility = 15%

**EXHIBIT 37–11**
**Projected Price Paths for the ITT Bond**

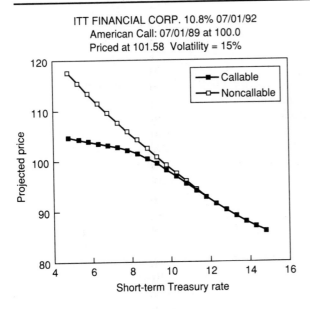

ITT FINANCIAL CORP. 10.8% 07/01/92
American Call: 07/01/89 at 100.0
Priced at 101.58  Volatility = 15%

**EXHIBIT 37–12**
**Effective Durations for the ITT Bond**

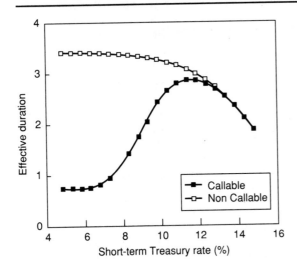

duration of the callable bond bottoms out; it is then basically the same as a 10.80 percent bond maturing on the first call date, since it is very likely to be called at the first call date.

## APPLICATIONS TO RELATIVE VALUE ANALYSIS

OAA can be a valuable tool for the portfolio manager. It allows consistent valuation of securities with widely differing cash-flow patterns and provides estimates of effective durations for these securities. It can help the portfolio manager to identify value in the market and is especially useful in this respect for complex securities with uncertain future cash flows. This section discusses the use of OAA for relative valuation. A historical analysis for MBSs showing that the OASs have been excellent indicators of relative value against comparable duration Treasuries and that OAS-based trades can significantly improve returns is presented elsewhere.[13]

The OAS provides a means of comparing securities that factors in interest-rate volatility, the shape of the yield curve, and the possible dependence of cash flows on interest rates. It is important to note that differences in liquidity and credit quality have not been incorporated into the analysis; in fact, the OAS may be interpreted as partially reflecting the lower liquidity and credit quality of a security relative to on-the-run Treasuries.[14] Although it is possible to incorporate these factors in a more general stochastic model, this model is not pursued in this chapter. Hence, possible liquidity and credit-quality differences should be kept in mind when comparing securities by means of their OASs.

Two examples are discussed below.

### Comparison of an Agency and a Mortgage Pass-Through

An agency pass-through and a regular comparable maturity debenture of the agency have identical credit quality and similar liquidity. Therefore, their OASs provide a good indication of their relative values.

As an example, a relatively new FNMA 9 percent pass-through is compared with the FNMA 9.35 percent debenture maturing on February 12, 1996, shown in Exhibit 37–2. At current prepayment projections, the pass-through has an effective duration of about five and one-half years, which is comparable to the duration of the agency security. Exhibit 37–13 compares the two securities.

---

[13] See Hayre and Lauterbach, "Stochastic Valuation of Debt Securities."

[14] It also reflects remaining cash-flow uncertainty (due to possibly incorrect interest-rate or call probability model assumptions), current demand and supply for the security, particular characteristics of the security (e.g., high or low coupon), and other relevant factors.

**EXHIBIT 37–13**
**Comparison of a Pass-through and an Agency**

| Security | Price | Rem. Term | Avg. Life | Effective Duration | Yield | Treasury Spread | OAS at Volatility | | |
|---|---|---|---|---|---|---|---|---|---|
| | | | | | | | 10% | 15% | 20% |
| FNMA 9% PT | 95-10 | 28.05 | 9.80 | 5.48 | 9.98 | 115 | 104 | 84 | 64 |
| FNMA 9.35% | 101-06 | 7.70 | 7.70 | 5.37 | 9.13 | 38 | 38 | 38 | 38 |

Note: Based on closing prices on June 29, 1988.

Exhibit 37–13 shows that even at a high volatility level of 20 percent, the MBS still provides an OAS advantage of about 25 basis points. At a 15 percent volatility assumption, which is closer to recent historical levels, the advantage for the MBS is about 45 basis points. The portfolio manager can decide whether or not this spread advantage compensates for the longer term of the MBS, its remaining cash-flow uncertainty due to possibly incorrect assumptions about interest-rate behavior and prepayment levels, and duration uncertainty.

Further insight into the relative rewards and risks of the two securities is provided by the frequency distribution of present values corresponding to different interest-rate paths. Exhibit 37–14 shows these distributions assuming 15 percent volatility.

The debenture has a fairly symmetric distribution, since its cash flows are fixed. The MBS shows the skewed present value distribution characteristic of callable securities; increasing prepayments reduce price appreciation as interest rates decline. The MBS also has a slightly lower dispersion (a standard deviation of about 9.7 percent for the distribution of present values, compared with 10.2 percent for the debenture); thus, in terms of investment uncertainty, the MBS is a slightly more conservative security.

### Rich/Cheap Analysis for Treasuries

As a second example, Exhibit 37–15 gives OASs for all Treasuries maturing in 1995, including the current on-the-run seven-year issue, the 8.375 percent maturing on April 15, 1995. By definition, the on-the-run Treasury has an OAS of zero.

Since the cash flows for the Treasuries are fixed, the OAS—the incremental return over the on-the-run Treasury curve—does not change very much if volatility changes. Thus, the OAS is essentially the spread over the implied forward short-term Treasury rates.

The OAS allows a clearer comparison of off-the-run Treasuries than YTM, since a consistent discount function is used for all securities. The −13 OAS of the 3 percent of February 15, 1995, for example, indicates the market's preference for discount securities. An interesting comparison can be made between the 11.25 percent and 12.625 percent coupons maturing on May 15, 1995; the 11.25s actually provide a higher OAS despite their lower coupon rate.

The analysis in Exhibit 37–15 can be combined with a history of OASs for these securities to determine if there have been any recent changes in their OASs.

### SUMMARY

The bond markets have undergone a major transformation in the last decade. Volatility has increased dramatically, increasing both the risks and rewards for

**EXHIBIT 37–14**

**Frequency Distributions of Present Values for a Pass-Through and an Agency**

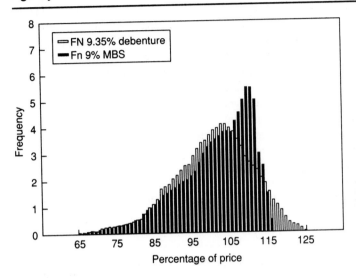

**EXHIBIT 37–15**

**OASs for Treasuries Maturing In 1995**

| | | | | OAS at Volatilities of | |
| | | | | --- | --- |
| Coupon | Maturity | Price | Yield | 0% | 15% |
| 8.625 | 1/15/95 | 99.74219 | 8.6760 | −1 | −1 |
| 3.000 | 2/15/95 | 71.78125 | 8.6877 | −13 | −13 |
| 10.500 | 2/15/95 | 108.98438 | 8.6846 | 3 | 3 |
| 11.250 | 2/15/95 | 112.64063 | 8.6963 | 5 | 5 |
| 8.375* | 4/15/95 | 98.31250 | 8.7049 | 0 | 0 |
| 10.375 | 5/15/95 | 108.68750 | 8.6678 | −1 | −1 |
| 11.250 | 5/15/95 | 112.87500 | 8.7174 | 5 | 5 |
| 12.625 | 5/15/95 | 120.26563 | 8.6493 | 1 | 1 |
| 10.500 | 8/15/95 | 109.27344 | 8.7218 | 3 | 4 |
| 9.500 | 11/15/95 | 104.10938 | 8.7294 | 1 | 1 |
| 11.500 | 11/15/95 | 115.08594 | 8.6839 | 0 | 0 |

Note: Closing prices on June 29, 1988.
* On-the-run Treasury.

bond investors. This has been accompanied by a tremendous expansion in the size and diversity of the market. Large sectors of the market now consist of securities, such as floating-rate instruments, MBSs, and callable corporates, which often have complex, interest-rate-dependent cash flows. These factors have combined to make it more difficult for the professional portfolio manager to identify value in the bond markets and assess the risk of a particular security.

Traditional bond valuation methods can be inadequate and even misleading, especially when dealing with interest-rate-contingent cash flows. This chapter has described option-adjusted analysis, a bond valuation methodology that attempts to improve upon traditional methods. It utilizes the term structure of interest rates in calculating the present values of cash flows, and it introduces interest-rate volatility into the analysis. All securities are valued relative to a base reference group, which in this chapter has been on-the-run Treasuries. This allows a consistent comparison of different securities including those with interest-rate-contingent cash flows. Historical analysis indicates that these new valuation methods can help the portfolio manager to improve returns significantly.

# CHAPTER 38

## THE VALUATION AND EXPOSURE MANAGEMENT OF BONDS WITH EMBEDDED OPTIONS*

*Richard Bookstaber, Ph.D.*
*Principal*
*Morgan Stanley & Company*

## INTRODUCTION

Many bonds have option-like features. Put bonds, bonds with bond warrants, and convertible bonds all include attached options to enhance their value. The call feature of corporate and Treasury bonds and the prepayment option in mortgage-backed securities represent a short call option position to the investor. Corporate debentures and other bonds with default risk are implicitly option-like instruments, having a payoff that is equal to a promised stream of payments or, if such payments are not made, a payoff that is equal to some claim on the underlying assets of the firm.[1]

---

*For complete citations, see **References** section at the end of the chapter.

[1] The treatment of corporate debentures as bonds with option positions is found in Merton (1974), Galai and Masulis (1976), in Chapter 5 of Bookstaber (1987), and in Chapter 7 of Cox and Rubinstein (1985). Such a bond can be viewed as a pure interest-rate vehicle combined with a short put option on the assets of the firm. The put option gives the issuer of the bond the right to put the assets of the firm to the bondholder in lieu of the promised payment. For high-quality credit, this option is not likely to be exercised, since the value of the firm is far above the payments due the bondholders. However, understanding this option feature leads to a number of important insights for pricing and controlling the risk of high-yield bonds. See, for example, Bookstaber and Jacob (1986a, 1986b).

Many other financial instruments share the characteristics of bonds with implicit options. In the insurance industry, Guaranteed Investment Contracts (GICs)[2] and Single Premium Deferred Annuities (SPDAs) often have early redemption features that, like a put option, allow the holder to cash in the policy prematurely at par. In the thrift industry, certificates of deposit often have a similar put option attached through an early redemption feature. An analysis of the option features of fixed income securities can be applied to these financial liabilities as well.

Bonds with embedded options can be viewed as a portfolio consisting of a pure bullet bond and an option. The techniques of fixed income analysis must be augmented by the use of option theory to effectively price and measure the exposure of these bonds.

For example, the conventional application of duration, the most popular measure of interest-rate sensitivity, is of limited value for bonds with implicit option positions. Since the price of an option does not move linearly with changes in the underlying bond's value, the convexity of any duration measure can become a severe problem. Also, a number of factors that are not important in determining bond pricing and interest-rate sensitivity, such as interest-rate volatility and the shape of the yield curve, are important for the valuation of the option.

The inability of most investors to successfully grapple with the pricing and exposure implications of these options leads to profit opportunities for those investors who can. The increased complexity that options add to the exposure measurement of fixed income instruments adds to their profit potential as well. Many investors are hesitant to take positions in bonds that are close to call or in mortgage-backed securities trading at a premium, since the impact of the option exercise is difficult to assess. Thus, there is relatively greater demand for discount callable bonds and for deep-discount mortgage-backed securities, where the call feature has less impact. The simple economics of supply and demand lead the bonds trading near or above par to trade at more attractive yields.

Other bonds with option features, such as put bonds, are often mispriced simply because investors in the fixed income market are not familiar with option pricing and trading methods. Most fixed income investors view the option implicit in put bonds as an attractive added feature but do not understand the trading methods for extracting the full value of the option.

The potential for mispricing can be illustrated by considering the conventions used in pricing callable bonds. Callable bonds conventionally are priced either to call or to maturity, depending on how imminent the call is thought to be. It is clear, however, that both prices are incorrect and in fact contain

---

[2] GICs are discussed in Chapter 25.

the upper and lower bounds on possible embedded option prices. A callable bond will never be worth as much as a similar noncallable bond, since there is always the possibility of interest rates dropping to the point that the call will be exercised.[3] Similarly, a callable bond will never have a value as low as it would appear when it is priced to call, since, until it is actually called, there is still some chance that rates will increase the make the exercise uneconomic.[4] Given the conventions in callable bond pricing, then, it is not surprising that many callable bonds will be either underpriced in the market because they are priced to call or overpriced because they are priced to maturity.

The knowledge gap in the market, both in exposure management and option pricing, has opened up profit opportunities for those who can deal with these embedded options. The purpose of this chapter is to lay out the pricing and exposure management issues and to point out the methods for bridging this gap.

## PRICING

A bond with an embedded option can be considered as a portfolio of two securities: a bullet bond without any option feature and an option. To price these bonds, we first price the value of the underlying bond using the usual discounted cash-flow methods of bond pricing and price the value of the option using option pricing theory. The net value of the bond will be the sum of the value of these two assets for a long option position, such as a put bond, or the value of the bullet less the value of the option for short option positions such as callable bonds. The principle of value additivity leads the value of the sum of a set of assets to equal the sum of their individual values.

### Yield Measurement for Bonds with Options: Adjusted Yield

Without adjustments, the yield of a bond with an attached option is not directly comparable to that of a pure bullet bond. We would clearly expect the yield on a callable bond to be higher than on a noncallable bond, since the call is to the detriment of the bondholder. Similarly, a bond with an attached warrant or a put

---

[3] The inaccuracies in pricing that arise from pricing a callable bond to maturity, thereby totally ignoring the negative impact of the call feature, are illustrated by considering the telephone issues, which often have 20 or more years of callability. No matter what the current interest-rate environment, it is hard to dismiss the value of an option with such a long time remaining to expiration.

[4] Furthermore, there may be internal issues in the firm that obviate the desirability to call an issue. For example, other issues with a higher coupon rate may be outstanding and may have a more pressing need to be called.

bond would be expected to have a lower yield than a pure bullet bond, since the long option position gives additional payoff potential. To compare the yield of these various bonds, an adjustment must first be made to net out these option features. The value additivity principle provides a natural means of comparing bonds with disparate option features.

Taking the price of a bond with an option position, we appeal to the additivity principal to separate out the option component by subtracting from the bond price the value of the option (in the case of a long option position), or adding back in the option component (in the case of a short option position).[5] The result will be the price of the remaining bullet bond after the attached option has been netted out at the theoretically fair price. The yield of the resulting bullet is then computed in the usual method. The result is called the *adjusted yield*.

In Exhibit 38–1, suppose that we want to compute the adjusted yield on a callable bond with 20 years to maturity and a 10 percent coupon. The bond is currently priced at par. First, we determine the price of the short call position. The bond is callable at 110 and has five years of call protection. Suppose that we price this call option, using an option pricing model, and find it to be worth $1.75. Since the bondholder is short this call option, that implies the value of the bullet is par value plus $1.75, or $101.75. The call-adjusted yield on this bond is then equal to the yield on a 10 percent coupon, 20-year noncallable bond priced at $101.75, which is 9.80 percent.

**EXHIBIT 38–1**
**Adjusted Yield**

*Assumptions*

> 20-year, 10 % coupon bond, callable after 5 years at 110
> Bond is priced at par to yield 10 %
> Option premium is priced at $1.75

*Calculation of Adjusted Yield*

|  |  |
|---|---|
| Price of callable bond | $100.00 |
| + Price of call option | 1.75 |
| Price of bullet bond | 101.75 |

*Adjusted Yield* = 9.80%

---

[5] Getting the option price requires the use of an option pricing model. Obviously, this pricing procedure will only be as accurate as the option model used. Furthermore, the value additivity principle will not be applicable in more complex bond structures, where there are a number of options that interact. For example, the analysis is less straightforward when a callable bond also contains sinking-fund provisions or when a convertible bond is also callable.

The same analysis would be done to compute the adjusted yield on a put bond or a bond with a bond warrant. The only difference would be that the value of the option would be subtracted out rather than added in.

## The Put/Call Parity Relationship for Bonds with Options

The pricing of the option component will obviously depend on the essential characteristics of the option position: whether the option is a put or a call and whether the option position is long or short. In classifying option positions, the distinction between long and short positions is more important than the distinction between put and call options. Using the put/call parity relationship, it is easy to transform a position in a put into a call position with identical payoff characteristics. Thus, we can look at a put bond, a bond with an attached put option, in the same way we look at a bond with an attached call warrant.

To see this, consider two bonds, one with a put option attached and the other with a call option attached. The first bond is a 10-year bullet, and the put option attached to it gives the holder the right to put the bond back to the issuer at par 5 years before the maturity date. The second bond is a bond with five years to maturity. It has the same par value and the same coupon payment schedule as the first bond. The call option attached to this bond has five years to expiration as well. It gives the holder the right, at its time of expiration in five years, to call a bond with five years of maturity and with coupon payments equal to the other two bonds. Both of these options are assumed to be European options, which means they can only be exercised at the time of expiration in five years.

Both bond-option packages will give the same coupon flow until year five, since they are assumed to have the same coupon rates and since the options offer no opportunities to alter the cash flows before that time. What happens at year five depends on the bond price that exists at that time.

Suppose that in five years bond yields have dropped, leading the bond prices to rise above par. The 10-year bond—which now has 5 years remaining to maturity—will not be put back to the issuer at par, since it is worth more than par. The put option will accordingly be left to expire unexercised, and the bondholder will end up with the bullet bond maturing in year 10. The bondholder with the call option package will see his five-year maturity bond mature and, since the bond underlying his call option is priced above par, will take the proceeds and exercise the call option to call a five-year maturity bond at par. The net result is that, if yields drop, both bondholders will have identical bullet bonds which mature in year 10.

Suppose now that rather than yields dropping at year five, they increase, leading the bond prices to drop below par. The holder of the 10-year bond will now exercise the put option to put the bond back to the issuer, since the resulting payoff of par will be greater than the value from continuing to hold the bond.

The holder of the five-year bond will let the call option expire unexercised, since it would be uneconomic to exercise the right to pay par for a bond that is priced below par in the marketplace. The net result in the case of rising yields will also be identical for both the put and the call holder. They will both end up with par at year five. The payoffs of these two bond packages are summarized in Exhibit 38–2.

Since the 10-year, bond-put option package gives the same payoff in all cases as the 5-year, bond-call option package, the two packages must be priced identically today. Otherwise there would be arbitrage opportunities available. The investor would only need to buy the cheaper and sell the more expensive of the two packages to lock in a riskless profit.[6]

**EXHIBIT 38–2**
**Put/Call Parity**

*Current Position*

A. Call on a 10-year bond with 5 years to expiration
   5-year bond
B. Put on a 10-year bond with 5 years to expiration
   10-year bond

*Position in Five Years*

| *Case 1*<br>*5-year Bond Priced*<br>*below Par* | *Case 2*<br>*5-year Bond Priced*<br>*above Par* |
|---|---|
| A. Let call expire<br>Bond matures | A. Exercise call<br>Pay for 5-year bond with<br>matured bond |
| B. Exercise put<br>Deliver bond | B. Let put expire<br>Retain 5-year bond |

*Net Result*

| Receive par value | Receive 5-year bond at par |
|---|---|

---

[6] The general formulation of the put/call parity relationship is:

$$B + P = C + E/(1 + r),$$

where $B$ is the current price of the underlying asset (in this case, a bullet bond), $P$ is the current value of a put option with exercise price $E$, and $C$ is the price of a call option on $B$ with the same exercise price and time to expiration. The discount factor $(1 + r)$ is for a time period equal to the time to expiration of the option. As this expression indicates, for a bond currently selling at par, a call and put option with an exercise price $E$ equal to par must have the same value. Further discussion of put/call parity for coupon-paying bonds is presented in Goodman (1985).

## The Payoff Profile of Bonds with Option Positions

We will illustrate the pricing of bonds with option positions using two examples—one with a short option position, callable bonds, and the second with a long option position, put bonds.

*Example 1: Callable Bonds.* The buyer of a callable bond is implicitly receiving a premium for the call option written to the issuer. This premium is paid out in the form of higher coupon payments and therefore higher yield for the bond. As with any option writer, the holder of the callable bond will be best off if the option expires worthless. However, since the bondholder is a covered call writer, she will lose from any decline in bond price as well. The ideal world, therefore, is for the bond price to stay exactly at the exercise price of the option. This will lead the option value to decay to zero, allowing the bondholder to keep all of the premium while preserving the greatest possible value for the underlying bond consistent with the zero value for the option. If the bond price moves above the exercise price, the bondholder will have to deliver the bond to the issuer and will need to reinvest the proceeds in a lower interest-rate environment. If the bond price moves down, the option will not be exercised, but the bond itself will generate a loss.

The payoff profile for a callable bond is shown in Exhibit 38–3. The underlying bond has 10 years to maturity and a coupon rate of 10 percent. There

**EXHIBIT 38–3**
**Callable Bond Payoff versus Bond without Option**

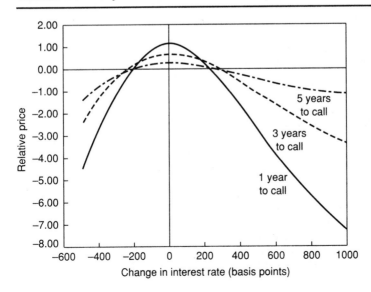

are five years to call at the time of issue. The exhibit shows the payoff as a function of bond yields when the option has one year to call, (top line), three years to call (middle line), and five years to call (bottom line). The closer the option comes to expiration, the greater the payoff in the event of no interest-rate changes. The curvature of the payoff profile also increases. The curvature tends to counteract the increasing peak of the profile so that the break-even point is nearly the same for all three curves. However, a sizable change in interest rates will lead to a far greater potential loss as the time to call approaches.

In option strategy analysis, this type of payoff is called a "negative gamma" payoff; it has a payoff that will be adversely affected by volatile swings in the price of the underlying bond.[7] The trade-off in a gamma strategy is between the time decay of the option premium and the volatility of prices. In the case of a negative gamma strategy, the time decay is favorable. Since the option loses value over time, the option writer finds that the payoff profile moves upward over time. On the other hand, volatility is undesirable. This payoff will be preferred by an investor who believes bond prices will be stable.

***Example 2: Put Bonds.*** The put bond sensitivity to interest-rate changes is opposite that of the callable bond. This would be expected, since, using put/call parity, a put bond can be restructured as a bond with a long call position, while a callable bond is obviously a bond with a short call position. If yields drop by the time the option expires, then the option will not be exercised. The bondholder will then have a longer maturity bond, which, in the lower yield environment, will be priced above par. If yields increase, the bond can be put at par and the proceeds reinvested at the higher prevailing interest rate. If yields remain unchanged, then the option gives no benefit over holding a bullet, and the cost of the option premium will lead to a net lower yield for the put bond. The put bond holder has the option to trade off between short- and long-term rates, depending on which is more desirable.

The payoff profile for a put bond is shown in Exhibit 38–4. This bond is a 15-year bond with a European put with 10 years to expiration. The bond has a 10 percent coupon rate.[8]

---

[7] The gamma of an option position is the second derivative of the option position value with respect to the underlying security price. That is, it is the change in the position delta with a change in the underlying security price. The gamma is thus a measure of the curvature of the payoff profile. It is a useful measure for delta neutral strategies, where the option position is unaffected by small changes in the value of the underlying security (i.e., where the position delta is zero).

[8] The put bonds issued domestically generally have European-style puts, meaning that these puts can only be exercised at the time of expiration. In contrast, the bonds with detachable bond warrants issued in Europe are American-style, in that they can be exercised any time before or at the time of expiration. This feature leads the maturity of the issue received upon exercise of the warrant to be a function of the time of exercise of the option. For example, if a seven-year warrant on a seven-year bond is exercised one year after issue, the holder will receive a bond with six years remaining to maturity. If it is exercised after three years, the holder will receive a bond with four years remaining to maturity.

**EXHIBIT 38–4**
**Put Bond Payoff versus Bond without Option**

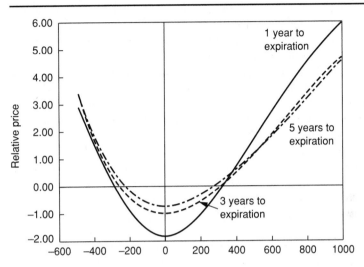

The payoff of this bond is as would be expected. The price is less than that of a comparable bullet if rates do not change. The price differential widens as the time to maturity of the bond and the time to maturity of the option approach. The top line shows the option with five years remaining to expiration, the middle line three years, and the bottom line one year. The time decay increases at an increasing rate as expiration approaches, so the drop in value is more significant as we move from five to three and then to one year to expiration. The curvature of the payoff profile also increases as expiration approaches. As a result, the break-even point does not move appreciably as time to expiration approaches, even though the gap in prices is increasing. A 250 basis point change in yield is necessary to break even.

This payoff profile is termed a *positive gamma* payoff in the option strategy literature. It benefits from increases in volatility but is hurt by time decay in the option premium. Since the investor is long option premium, the drop in value of the option over time diminishes the value of this position. This is indicated by the downward movement in the payoff profile. If the underlying bond is more volatile than was assumed in determining the initial price of the option, profits from the volatility will more than compensate for this decay.

## Taking Advantage of Mispricing

The objective in active bond management is to trade on yield differentials. Bonds with differentially higher yields are purchased, and those with differentially lower yields are sold. The returns from this strategy are immediately evident in the higher cash flow generated by the portfolio.

Bonds with options can be traded in the same way, using the adjusted yield to generate the trading signals. The difference from the usual active bond trading strategy is how the additional yield is realized in the portfolio. Higher adjusted yield does not immediately translate into higher cash flow. Adjusted yield may measure the mispricing of the option as well as of the bullet bond. If the option on a callable bond is overvalued, the adjusted yield will be higher. If the option on a put bond is overvalued, the adjusted yield will be lower. If the high adjusted yield is the result of the option being mispriced, profits from the mispricing rely on exploiting that option.

There are three ways to exploit the mispricing of a bond with an option.

First, as is done with equities and other misvalued securities, the bond can be purchased for sale once the market becomes aware of its value and corrects the price. Our empirical work has shown that, for many bonds, mispricing will correct over time. But, for some bonds with active option features, the poor understanding of the market may lead to continued misvaluation of the option. The mispricing will not then be captured through a recovery in the price.[9]

Second, as with any option, it is possible to create an arbitrage hedge to extract the profit. The arbitrage profit opportunity arises because an option can be replicated synthetically through a dynamic hedging strategy in the underlying security.[10] If the price of the option in the market is not the same as the cost of creating the option synthetically, then an arbitrage can be executed by buying the cheaper and selling the higher priced of the market and the synthetic option. Since the payoff of the two options will be the same, the position, and hence the profit from the transaction, is riskless.

While this methodology is used extensively in trading listed options, there are several impediments to using it with options on bonds. First, most options on bonds are not detachable. Therefore, to execute the strategy, the investor must also carry around the bond as extra baggage. Buying $1 million of mispriced options may require also holding $100 million of bonds. If the options are mispriced by 10 percent, capturing the mispricing amounts to only $\frac{1}{10}$ of 1 percent return on the total investment.

A second problem with the execution of a dynamic arbitrage strategy is the cost of trading in and out of the underlying bond. The dynamic trading strategy, as the name suggests, requires periodic adjustments in the position of the underlying security. Given the bid-ask spreads for many bonds, such adjustments could be costly. If the mispricing of the bond is expected to correct quickly and the hedge only needs to be executed over a short time period,

---

[9] The persistent undervaluation of put bonds is an example.

[10] The dynamic strategy as the basis for option pricing and for extracting profits from mispriced options is discussed in Bookstaber (1985, 1987) and in Cox and Rubinstein (1985).

these problems are less important. Then the hedge can be used to lock in the mispricing against unforeseen changes in interest rates.

A third method is to play off the volatility of the interest-rate market, a method called a gamma strategy. As the callable bond and put bond examples show, the bond position includes an implicit bet on the range of movement of interest rates. For a callable bond, the bet is that rates will be stable, whereas for the long option position of the put bond the bet is that interest rates will be more volatile. Just as a bullet bond position can be used to profit from beliefs in the direction component of interest rates, so the option feature allows the investor to take positions and profit off of the nondirectional or volatility-related interest-rate movements.

The price of the option will dictate the attractiveness of the gamma strategy. For example, the callable bond strategy shown in Exhibit 38–3 will look more attractive the cheaper the option is, since the payoff will then move upward and be profitable for a wider range of interest rates. If a bond is mispriced, this implicitly means that the trade-off between time decay and volatility, and the expected return from the gamma strategy, is extraordinarily favorable.

## EXPOSURE MANAGEMENT

It is conventional to relate the interest-rate sensitivity of a fixed income security to the zero coupon bond with the same interest-rate sensitivity. This relationship is expressed as the security's *duration*. The duration of a bond measures interest-rate sensitivity in units of years. A duration of five years means the bond has the same interest-rate sensitivity as a zero coupon bond with five years to maturity. Since the price of a zero coupon bond is a convex function of time to maturity, its derivative with respect to interest rates will be an increasing function of time to maturity. A larger duration will therefore imply a greater price sensitivity to interest rates. The interest sensitivity of a bond can be related to its duration through the following expression:[11]

$$D_B = -\frac{dP_B}{d(1+r)}\frac{(1+r)}{P_B} \tag{38–1}$$

where $D_B$ is the duration of the bond. Since duration is defined as the maturity of the zero coupon bond with interest-rate sensitivity equivalent to that of the bond under analysis, this relationship is definitional.

A coupon-paying bond can be reviewed as a portfolio of zero coupon bonds. Since the duration of each of these zero coupon bonds is immediately known,

---

[11] This expression shows duration to be the interest elasticity of the bond price.

the duration of a coupon-paying bond can be easily determined as the sum of the durations of each of the zero coupon bonds in the replicating portfolio, each weighted by its share of the market price of the coupon-paying bond. That is,

$$D_B = \sum_t w_t \times t \qquad (38\text{–}2)$$

where $w_t$ is the proportion of the market price of the coupon-paying bond attributed to the zero coupon bond maturing at date $t$.[12] This expression makes use of the additivity property of duration: The duration of a sum of cash flows is equal to the sum of the individual cash flows' durations.

## Changing Interest-Rate Sensitivity and the Convexity of Duration

The duration of a zero coupon bond of given maturity is the maturity of that zero and is therefore constant. The duration of other fixed income securities will vary with changes in interest rates and will also vary as the time to maturity of the security approaches. This can be seen from Equation (38–2) by recognizing that the weights are functions of both the interest-rate level and time and that the replicating portfolio itself will change as coupon payments are made. The mathematical term for the change in interest-rate sensitivity manifested through the change in duration, the second derivative of $P_B$ with respect to $r$, is the *convexity* of the bond.

While the convexity of zero coupon bonds is zero, the convexity of other bonds is not. This means that duration is only a linear approximation of their interest-rate sensitivity. In graphic terms, it only reflects the tangent line at a given interest rate and time to maturity of the price of the bond plotted as function of interest rates.

The convexity of duration places obvious limitations on its descriptive power. Despite the shortcomings that arise from duration being a linear approximation of interest-rate sensitivity, it still provides a highly intuitive and valuable tool for exposure measurement and asset/liability management. For bonds with option positions, however, the problems with convexity loom larger, and the value and intuitive appeal of duration weaken.

Options are linked to interest rates through the underlying asset. The option price is a function of the price of the underlying instrument, which in turn is a

---

[12] This equation assumes that yield curves are flat and shift in a parallel fashion. Such an assumption is inconsistent with basic arbitrage condition for yield-curve generation but is, nonetheless, a common assumption used in the professional finance literature. Other duration formulas have been developed based on more realistic yield-curve assumptions. See, for example, Bierwag, Kaufman, and Toesv (1983).

function of interest rates. The relationship of an option to the underlying bond is expressed by the option's *delta*.[13] A delta of .5 means that a one-point change in the price of the underlying bond will lead to a one-half-point change in the price of the option. The delta of a call option is positive, bounded by zero and one. The delta of a put option is negative and is bounded by negative one and zero.[14] The further an option is out-of-the-money, the closer the delta is to zero. As an option move far into-the-money, the option tends to move one-for-one with the underlying bond, and the delta approaches one for a call option and minus one for a put option.[15]

Options are also related to interest rates through the cost-of-carry of the option position. Options provide a leveraged position in the underlying asset; the cost of the option is far below the value of the claim the option gives. The option holder gets the right to claim the asset from the option writer without needing to hold the asset physically. The option premium will compensate the option writer for the carrying cost of holding the asset for possible delivery through the option premium. Just as with futures contracts, the option price will include an implied cost-of-carry. The option premium will be greater the higher the carrying cost and therefore the higher the interest rate. The interest-rate sensitivity of an option, then, expressed in terms of duration, includes two components—one for the effect of interest rates through the underlying asset and one for the effect of interest rates on carrying costs.[16]

---

[13] The delta is nothing more than the partial derivative of the option price with respect to the underlying bond price:

$$\Delta = \partial C / \partial P_B$$

[14] Since a put option pays off more the further the underlying asset drops below the exercise price, its price moves in the direction opposite that of the underlying asset. Although the delta of options is bounded by zero and one in absolute value terms, the absolute value of their percentage price changes will be bounded below by one. Since options are leveraged securities, their price will always change in percentage terms by more than the underlying asset. The percentage change in an option with a change in the underlying security can be measured by its price elasticity $(dC/dP_B)(P_B/C)$. This measure of the option's leverage is also called the option's lambda.

[15] A call option is out-of-the-money when the price of the underlying asset is less than the exercise price and is in-the-money when the price of the underlying asset is greater than the exercise price. A put option is out-of-the-money when the price of the underlying asset is greater than the exercise price and is in-the-money when the price of the underlying asset is less than the exercise price. That is, an option is out-of-the-money when it has no intrinsic value and is in-the-money when it has intrinsic value.

[16] The total derivative of the option price with respect to interest rates must include the impact of changing interest rates on the carrying cost of the option and on the present value of the terminal payment, as reflected in the discounting of the exercise price. The hedge ratio is conventionally expressed as the partial derivative of the option price with respect to the bond price. While the bond price will itself be determined by interest rates, this derivative does not take the impact of carrying cost changes into account.

$$dC/dr = [(\partial C/\partial P_B) \times (\partial P_B/\partial r)] + \partial C/\partial r$$
$$= (\Delta \times -[D_B/(1 + r)]P_B) + \partial C/\partial r \tag{38–3}$$

The additional link of the delta between the interest-rate sensitivity of the option and the duration of the underlying bond increases the potential range of movement in the option price for changes in the interest rate and therefore increases the potential slippage in the application of duration as a measure of the interest-rate sensitivity. Since the option is a leveraged security, the change in the bond price with a change in interest rates will be magnified in percentage terms in its impact on the option price.[17]

Since the option price is itself a convex function of the underlying bond price, the problems that convexity brings to the applicability of duration will likewise be magnified. The increased convexity of duration for options is intuitively apparent when it is realized that options will generally be more dissimilar to a zero coupon bond than will the bonds underlying the options.

The intuitive relationship between a coupon-paying bond and a zero coupon bond is strained when applied to options. An option cannot be so straightforwardly expressed as a portfolio of zeros; the option delta must be used as an intermediate input. While any instrument can be equated to the interest-rate sensitivity of a particular zero at any given point of time, if the relationship is unstable, it loses its explanatory value. For an option, the zero of equivalent interest-rate sensitivity is changing both because of the usual forces of convexity that relate to the underlying bond and further because of the changes in the delta of the option.

The duration of the option can be seen by rewriting Equation (38–3):

$$D_C = \frac{(D_B \times \Delta \times P_B}{C)} - \frac{\partial C}{\partial r}\left(\frac{1 + r}{C}\right)$$
$$= (D_B \times \lambda) - \rho \tag{38–4}$$

where $\lambda$, a measure of the leverage of the option, is the elasticity of the option price with respect to the underlying bond price, $\lambda = (dC/dP_B)(P_B/C)$, and $\rho$ is the elasticity of the option price with respect to interest-rate changes, $\rho = [\partial C/\partial r](1 + r)/C$.

---

[17] The leverage leads options to have unusually high values for duration. Durations on the order of 100 years are not uncommon. In the limit, options that are further out-of-the-money and therefore that have greater leverage resemble a forward contract, which has infinite duration. The possibility of very large, or even infinite, duration is merely an artifact of the way the duration measure is constructed. Since the duration divides the derivative of price with respect to interest rate by the price, a zero price will lead to an undefined duration. This, however, does not imply undefined interest-rate sensitivity.

Exhibit 38–5 illustrates the sequence of effects that leads to the option's duration. The top panel shows the duration of the underlying bond. The second panel shows the delta of the option as a function of the various interest rates, and the third shows the ratio of the price of the underlying bond to the price of the option. As shown by Equation (38–4), it is the product of these three that leads to the duration of the option, depicted in the last panel of the exhibit. The second term and the third term both contribute to the increased convexity of the options duration. It is the leverage of the option that leads to its high duration. Since lambda is always greater than one, the option will always have higher duration that the underlying bond. The leverage of an option, and therefore the duration of an option, increases as the option drops out-of-the-money.

***Example 1: Callable Bonds.*** The additivity of the duration measure allows us to express the duration of the callable bond as the sum of the duration of its parts. The callable bond will have a duration equal to the duration of the underlying bullet bond, $D_B$, less the duration of the short call position, $D_C$:

$$D = \alpha D_B - (1 - \alpha)D_C \qquad (38\text{–}5)$$

where $\alpha$ is the proportion of the callable bond value made up by the bullet, $\alpha = P_B/(P_B + C)$. Using Equation (38–4) for the duration of the call option, this can be rewritten as the simple expression

$$D = [\alpha - (1 - \alpha)\lambda]D_B + (1 - \alpha)\rho \qquad (38\text{–}6)$$

The duration of a callable bond will be bracketed by the duration of a bond with a time to maturity equal to the time to call, and a bond with a time to maturity equal to that of the bond itself. When the option is far out-of-the-money, the leverage of the option, $\lambda$, will be large and the duration of the option will be as well. However, the larger duration of the option will be more than countered by its reduced weight in the duration calculation, as determined by $(1 - \alpha)$. When the bond is out-of-the-money, the duration of the bond will therefore move closer to that of the underlying bond. As the bond moves toward a premium, the duration will move closer to that of a bond with a time to maturity equal to the time to call. The time to call will have an impact on the sensitivity of the duration to the call feature. Obviously, the more time there is remaining to the call date, the smaller the effect the call provision will have.

Exhibit 38–6 illustrates the duration features of a callable bond. The underlying bond has 10 years to maturity and a coupon rate of 10 percent. The bond initially has five years of call protection. For simplicity, we assume that the bond can then be called at par and that the call option is European. Exhibit 38–6 shows the duration of this bond with 10 years remaining to maturity and five years to call; with eight years remaining to maturity and three years to call; and with six years remaining to maturity and one year to call. The base interest rate

**EXHIBIT 38–5**

**The Components of Option Duration (a) The Duration of the Underlying Bond. (b) The Option Delta.**

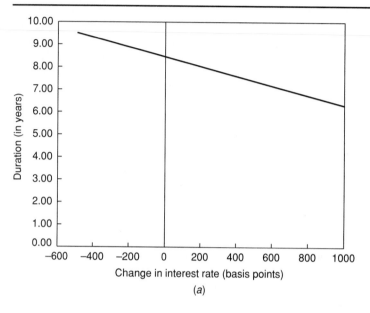

Change in interest rate (basis points)

(a)

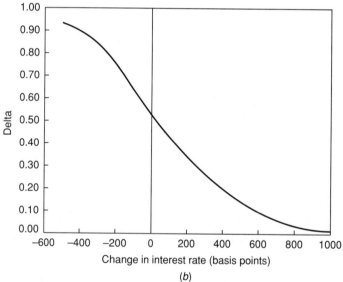

Change in interest rate (basis points)

(b)

**EXHIBIT 38–5**
**(c) Bond Price Divided by Option Price. (d) Duration of Option.**

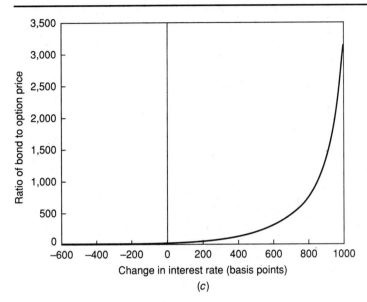

(c)

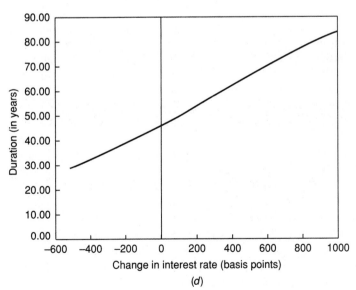

(d)

**EXHIBIT 38–6**
**Duration of a Callable Bond**

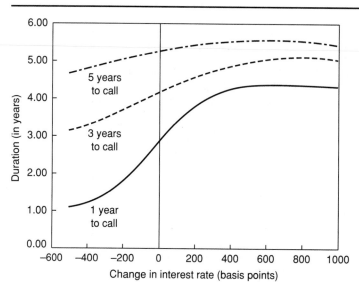

is 10 percent. An increase in interest rates of 400 basis points brings the option far enough out-of-the-money that the duration of the bond comes very close to that of the underlying bullet. A drop in interest rates pulls the duration down, with the effect being most dramatic for the case of only one year remaining to call. An interest-rate drop of over 400 basis points leads to a duration close to that of a one-year instrument.

Each of the curves is contained in an envelope of the duration of the bullet on the top and the duration of a similar coupon bond with a time to maturity equal to the time remaining to call on the bottom. The speed with which the curve shifts from one edge of the envelope to the other is a function of the time remaining to call, as well as the volatility of interest rates. The shorter the time remaining to expiration of the option is, the quicker the shift will be.

The nonlinearity or convexity of duration is increasingly manifested as the time to call approaches. For an American option, the curve will dip to zero duration for interest rates that lead to values above par, once the period of call protection is passed.[18]

---

[18] In practice, bonds are not optimally called. The bond may continue in force for a period of time after call should, theoretically, be made, and the actual duration effect will not be this dramatic.

**EXHIBIT 38–7**
**Duration of a Put Bond with Option Position**

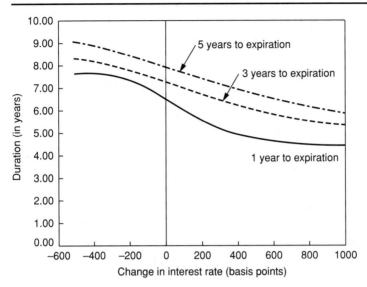

*Example 2: Put Bonds.* The key difference between callable bonds and put bonds is not that one has a call attached and the other has a put attached. The key difference is that the callable bond is *short* an option, whereas the putable bond is *long* an option. Put/call parity tells us that the put and the call are different ways of looking at the same instrument. We can just as easily look at the putable bond as a bond with an attached call option.

The long versus short option is evident when we decompose the putable bond into its bullet and option parts, expressing the duration of the bond as

$$D = \alpha D_B + (1 - \alpha)D_P \qquad (38\text{–}7)$$

Applying Equation (38–4), this then becomes

$$D = [\alpha + (1 - \alpha)\lambda]D_B + (1 - \alpha)\rho \qquad (38\text{–}8)$$

This equation differs from Equation (38–6) only by $\lambda$ here being additive.

Exhibit 38–7 traces the duration of a 15-year bond with a 10-year put as a function of interest rates. The bond and option have longer time to maturity in this example than in the callable bond example, in order to give a comparison of lengthening time to maturity on the effect of the option.[19] Like the callable

---

[19] Using put/call parity, a 15-year bond with a put with 10 years to expiration is identical to a 10-year bond with a call option on a 5-year bond, where the call has 10 years to expiration.

bond example, the exercise price of the put is at par. The duration for a time to maturity of 15, 13, and 11 years is plotted by the respective curves in Exhibit 38–7.

The long option position of the putable bond leads, not unexpectedly, to duration effects that are the opposite of those of the callable bond's short option position. The envelope is the duration of a 15-year and a 10-year bond, with the top of the envelope being approached as interest rates drop, and the bottom of the envelope being approached as interest rates increase. The duration of the short side of this bond is identical to the duration of the long side of the callable bond depicted in Exhibit 38–6: a 10-year bond with a 10 percent coupon.[20]

***Example 3: Options on bonds and options on liabilities.*** The liabilities of many financial institutions can be viewed as interest-sensitive cash-flow streams. The Guaranteed Investment Contracts (GICs) and Single Premium Deferred Annuities (SPDAs) issued by insurance companies, Certificates of Deposit (CDs) issued by banks and thrifts, as well as defined benefits pension plans, can be viewed in a liability context in the same way coupon-paying bonds are in an asset context. A bullet GIC, for example, accrues all of its interest to a single maturity date, making its cash-flow analogous to a zero coupon bond. The pension benefits for the retired-lives portion of a defined benefits pension plan can be thought of as a type of coupon-paying bond.[21]

The goal of asset/liability matching is to match the interest-rate sensitivity of these liabilities to that of the assets backing them. When duration is used as the basis for measuring this sensitivity, the first objective is to construct a portfolio of assets with the same net duration as the liability cash flows. A secondary objective is to address the convexity of the asset and liability cash flows by using a set of assets whose duration will change with interest rates and with the passage of time in the same way as the liabilities. This second-order matching will lead to low net convexity, reducing the need to make

---

[20] This example is based on a European-style option, an option that can only be exercised at the time of expiration. Most put bonds issued domestically are European-style. The bonds with detachable bond warrants issued overseas are American-style options, which can be exercised at any time on or before the expiration date. The American-style option can be exercised at any time; it is more sensitive to current changes in interest rates than is a European option with time remaining to expiration. The duration of an American-style option may drop to zero for a high enough interest rate, since a sufficiently high interest rate will trigger immediate exercise. The profile of an American-style option will differ from that of Exhibit 38–7 by dropping down more quickly with a positive change in interest rates and by asymptoting the $x$-axis rather than the duration of the shorter maturity bond.

[21] Typically, the pension benefits will be declining over time rather than being constant and therefore are not analogous to a coupon-paying bond with level coupon payments. Also, many plans include cost-of-living adjustments that further complicate the analogy to bonds with payments set in nominal terms.

adjustments in the asset/liability mix and reducing the exposure from abrupt interest-rate changes.[22]

Just as there are bonds with options, so are there liabilities with options. SPDAs and GICs have a put option written to the issuer that allows the policy holder to put the policy back to the issuer at par value before maturity.[23] Bank CDs with early redemption privileges can similarly be viewed as a combination of a pure interest-rate instrument plus a put option written by the bank to the holder of the CD.

The effect of the option on the interest sensitivity and duration characteristics of these liabilities is clear. If interest rates rise, it will be in the interest of the option holder to exercise the option, put the instrument back to the issuer, and reinvest the proceeds at the higher market rate. If interest rates drop, it will be in the interest of the option holder to maintain the instrument until maturity. These instruments will therefore drop in duration as interest rates rise and will extend in duration as interest rates decline.[24]

The interest-rate sensitivity of an SPDA contract is depicted in Exhibit 38–8a. The GIC and CD will have a similar profile, approaching the duration of their option-free counterpart for low interest rates and moving gradually to zero duration as interest rates increase.

Since these liabilities reflect a short put option position for the issuer, a put bond will provide the best duration and convexity match. The long put option position of the put bond will net out with the short put position of the liability. The net result of matching an SPDA with a put bond is illustrated in Exhibit 38-8b.

Many financial institutions are in the habit of funding their putable liabilities with callable assets such as callable bonds and mortgage-backed securities with prepayment options. The net result is a short straddle, a position consisting of both a short call option and a short put option. A short straddle will lose money if interest rates move in either direction. If interest rates rise, the put option on the liability side will be exercised, forcing the liquidation of assets that have declined in price. If interest rates drop, the call options on the asset side will be exercised, requiring the reinvestment of the proceeds at lower interest rates. This straddle is illustrated in Exhibit 38–8c. Assuming that the options

---

[22] Examples of asset/liability matching strategies are presented for banks and thrifts by Toevs and Haney (1986) and, for insurance companies, by Tilley and Latainer (1986).

[23] Some policies include a penalty for early exercise, which may be a function of time remaining to maturity. Such a penalty can be viewed as a transaction cost and does not alter the essential nature of the option feature.

[24] The impact of the option is complicated by the fact that not all option holders will exercise at the theoretically optimal time. The change in the duration characteristics will therefore be somewhat less than predicted by a model that assumes optimal exercise by all option holders. We will treat the issue of nonoptimal exercise in more detail in the next section.

**EXHIBIT 38–8a**
**Interest Sensitivity of an SPDA**

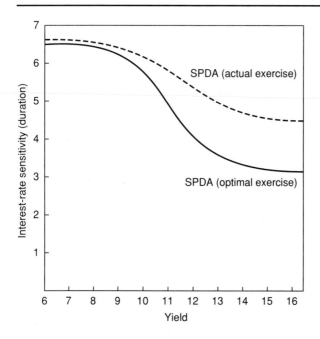

**EXHIBIT 38–8b**
**Covering an SPDA Liability with a Put Bond**

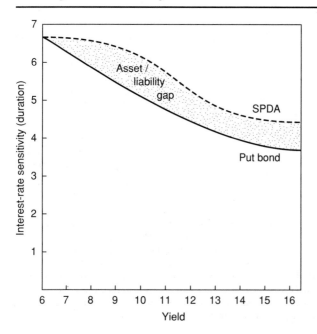

**EXHIBIT 38–8c**
**Covering an SPDA Liability with a Mortagage-Backed Security**

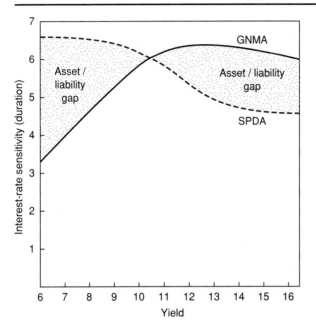

are fairly priced in the market, this risk will be compensated for by an improved yield should interest rates remain stable, but the two-sided risk to the institution remains difficult to manage.[25]

# POTENTIAL PITFALLS IN THE ANALYSIS OF BONDS
# WITH IMPLICIT OPTIONS

The principle of value additivity simplifies the pricing and exposure measurement of bonds with options. The bond and option features can each be analyzed

---

[25] The risk of the short straddle position can be managed by careful dynamic adjustment of the asset and liability position to maintain a net neutral hedge ratio. There is always a point at which the positive change in the put option will be exactly counteracted by the negative change in the call option. If the asset position is adjusted to keep the put and call effect balanced, the result will be a "delta neutral" position, with the option effect washed out. Such dynamic adjustment strategies are common among option strategists working in the listed option markets but are more difficult for fixed income securities where spreads and transactions costs are relatively high. The issues of dynamic hedging are presented in Bookstaber (1987).

separately, using the well-established tools for pricing cash flows and options. However, for those who are not well versed in option theory, a number of difficulties remain in the practical application of option tools to the interest-rate-sensitive options of the bond market. In this section we will address a few of these difficulties.

## Assessing the Performance of Bonds with Options

The increased complexity that options add to the pricing and the exposure management of fixed income securities carries over to the evaluation of the performance of fixed income securities as well. Performance evaluation is based on the relative performance of comparable bond portfolios. Portfolios with similar characteristics are ranked against one another or are compared to some other benchmark such as the Becker Universe or the Shearson-Lehman Index. This evaluation process obviously only makes sense if the portfolios being compared truly are comparable. In the absence of option-like features, it is relatively simple to test for comparability. The quality, maturity, duration, and types of bonds in the portfolios are easily observed. With options embedded in many bonds, the comparability begins to cloud.

We have already seen that options can have a dramatic effect on the interest-rate sensitivity of the bonds.[26] The duration of the bond will be far different when an option is out-of-the-money than when it moves into-the-money. Looking at the duration characteristics of the underlying bonds alone will inevitably misstate the true interest-rate sensitivity of the bonds.

The payoff distribution will also differ for bonds with different options. A bond with a short call option, such as a callable bond or a mortgage-backed security, will have truncated return potential. It will have limited opportunity for appreciation. The bondholder, as compensation for giving up the upside potential, will receive a higher yield than for a comparable noncallable bond. A bond with a long put option will be truncated on downside returns. The holder of a put bond has insurance against long-term declines in the bond price. As payment for this insurance protection, the holder of a put bond will receive a lower yield than for a comparable nonputable bond.

It is difficult to rank two portfolios strictly on the basis of yield, since the higher yield of the one may have been achieved by selling off the upside potential, whereas the lower yield of the second may be moderated by protection against loss. These option features will not be apparent when the bonds are compared in a static environment. Even a comparison of returns over time will not give a complete indication of these features, since any such comparison

---

[26] The effect of option positions on portfolio returns is discussed in Bookstaber and Clarke (1981, 1984, and 1985).

is constrained to one particular interest-rate path. A portfolio heavily weighted toward put bonds will come out the winner if interest rates move substantially up or down, but will appear to be inferior if interest rates remain unchanged.[27] A portfolio weighted toward callable bonds will perform best if interest rates remain unchanged, since the bondholder receives the premium for the call option in the form of a higher coupon. However, if interest rates move up, the call feature will prove a detriment. The callable bondholders and putable bondholders inherently are facing different risks and are holding bonds with substantially different sensitivities to the interest-rate environment. It is difficult to lump the bonds together in terms of duration, convexity, and the distribution of payoff.

The payoff distribution of bonds with default risk, specifically corporate debentures, will be affected by option features in a way that may result in apparently superior performance for bonds with a higher risk of default. Bonds with default risk are hybrid instruments, part fixed income instrument, part equity of the firm. If the firm is successful in meeting its obligations to the bondholders, the bond remains a fixed income instrument, collecting the promised cash-flow payments. However, if the firm defaults on these payments, then the bondholder has recourse to the assets of the firm. The ownership of the firm reverts to the bondholders, who in effect become the equity holders of the firm.

Corporate debentures can be thought of as a pure interest-rate vehicle, such as a Treasury bond, combined with a short put option position on the equity of the firm. The put option gives the issuer of the bond, the current equity holders, the right to put the equity of the firm to the bondholder at an exercise price equal to the payments promised the bondholders. If the value of the firm drops below this exercise price, it will be in the interest of the equity holders to exercise the put option and give the equity of the firm to the bondholders rather than give them the promised payment. If the value of the firm is above the exercise price, the equity holders will leave the option unexercised, since greater value will be found in making the promised payment and retaining the ownership of the firm.[28]

The short put option position is undesirable from the standpoint of the bondholder because in the event of default the bondholder faces a possible loss equal to the difference between the promised payment and the value of the assets of the firm. The bondholder is compensated for this through an option premium for the put option he has written. This premium is expressed in the spread between the yield of the corporate bond and the yield of a Treasury bond

---

[27] As we have seen in the previous section, the holder of a put bond has a straddle on interest rates. If rates rise, the put can be exercised, putting the investor into a bond with higher yield. If interest rates drop, the holder can let the option expire unexercised and enjoy the appreciation in the longer term bond.

[28] A description of high-yield bonds as bullet bonds with short put option positions is presented in Bookstaber and Jacob (1986).

of comparable terms. The closer the option is to being in-the-money, the greater the option premium will be, and the higher the yield differential will be.

High-yield bonds, lower quality bonds with a higher risk of default, enjoy their yield advantage as a result of this option. The put option of high-yield bonds is closer to the money than is the option of higher quality corporate issues; it therefore has a higher premium. The implicit short put option of the high-yield bonds will lead to a return distribution that is more heavily weighted on the downside and is truncated on the upside relative to other bonds without as strong a default component.[29]

The high-yield bondholder receives the value of the firm only when it is undesirable to receive it. This is obviously less desirable than a distribution that is symmetrically weighted toward receiving either higher or lower return as a result of changes in equity value. The short put option on the high-yield bond leads to all variance being "bad" variance: All the variability is on the downside. As a result, the expected return is greater than for a bond with equal variance of return but with that variance being symmetric about the mean. Symmetric variance allows an equal chance for a favorable shock and for an unfavorable shock.

Virtually all studies of the performance of high-yield bonds have failed to note the need to consider not only the mean and variance of return but also the source of variance. The result of most studies on high-yield bonds—that these bonds outperform higher quality bonds on a mean-variance basis—is not surprising when the source of that variance is considered. In a fair market, bonds with short put options should dominate unoptioned bonds in a mean-variance context.[30] The inefficiency may not rest with the bond market. Rather, it may rest with the application of the mean-variance criterion to bonds with options. Options can truncate and skew the distribution in ways that require a consideration of more than just variance to assess risk. The higher moments of the distribution must also be considered.

## Pitfalls in Option Model Design

Pricing and exposure measurement require an option model. There are a number of option pricing models in the literature for options on interest-rate-sensitive instruments. It is beyond the scope of this chapter to consider these in depth or to sketch out any particular model for applying the pricing and exposure concepts presented in the previous sections. However, here we will present some

---

[29] This distribution is similar to that of callable bonds, except that here the distribution is truncated in terms of equity rather than interest rates.

[30] The effect of option positions on the performance of securities measured in mean-variance space is discussed in Bookstaber and Clarke (1985).

of the important considerations in using option models for interest-rate-sensitive instruments.

Developing a bond option pricing model requires overcoming a number of difficulties that are not present in models for a nonstochastic interest-rate environment. The most obvious difficulty is in depicting the relationship between the yield curve and the price of the interest-rate-sensitive instrument. A model requires both the interest rate for financing the arbitrage and the interest rate for pricing the underlying asset as stochastic, and these rates must bear a relationship that preserves reasonable yield-curve structure. A second difficulty is the distributional assumptions for the interest rates and the underlying asset. The lognormal distribution conventionally used in option pricing models is inappropriate for modeling an interest-rate process because interest rates tend to vary within a fairly narrow band.[31] Since bonds bear a complex relationship to interest rates and furthermore are restricted to be priced at par at maturity, the usual assumption that bond prices are distributed lognormally is clearly inappropriate, even if interest rates are hypothesized to be lognormally distributed. These difficulties have been addressed in a number of models for interest-rate-sensitive assets.[32]

---

[31] Cox, Ingersoll, and Ross (1978) have used a mean-reverting process to model interest rates. There is reason to think interest rates are mean-reverting, since abnormally high rates will lead to a shift in monetary policy to reduce rates, while unusually low rates will lead to a less restrained policy, which will lead rates to increase. By contrast, since in a lognormal process the variance grows linearly with time, a 20 percent standard deviation for rates over one year will imply a standard deviation of rates of over 60 percent in 10 years.

[32] The effect of stochastic interest rates and term structure has been the central topic of the models of Brennan and Schwartz (1982a, 1982b) and Courtadon (1982). Courtadon, relying on earlier work on the valuation of default-free bonds by Vasicek (1977), Cox, Ingersoll, and Ross (1978), and Dothan (1978), has developed models for the valuation of American calls and puts on bonds. Brennan and Schwartz follow a methodology similar to Courtadon but use two bonds, a short-term bond and a long-term bond, to give a better picture of the term structure. As the authors of these papers note, their models are not preference free, greatly limiting their practical and theoretical appeal. Other models such as Ho and Lee (1986), have adapted the binomial framework of Cox, Ross, and Rubinstein (1979) to bond pricing.

The distributional implications for pricing debt options has been treated by Ball and Torous (1983), who attempt to overcome the restriction of bond prices approaching par at maturity by positing a Brownian bridge process as underlying bond price movements, and by Bookstaber and McDonald (1985), who develop a model based on a generalized return distribution for estimating the distributional characteristics of bond returns.

Although these models each meet some of the requirements of an option model for interest-rate-sensitive assets, inadequacies remain. The models of Courtadon and of Brennan and Schwartz, for example, are preference-dependent. Furthermore, these models do not adequately model the distributional properties of bonds. The models of Ball and Torous and Bookstaber and McDonald, while addressing these problems, are European models of limited value in assessing the options embedded in bonds—options that are often American.

The most widely used approaches to modeling interest-rate-sensitive options are based on adaptations of the binomial option pricing model.[33] These approaches have been used to price bond options by those in academics, in the insurance industry, and in the investment banking community.[34] The binomial model is also similar in its computational procedure to other bond option pricing models that use numerical integration methods.

Because of the popularity of the binomial model, we will use it as an illustration of the difficulties inherent in developing consistent option pricing models for interest-rate-sensitive instruments. We will do this by illustrating one particularly perverse failure of such models: the failure to preserve put/call parity.

In the binomial approach, interest rates are assumed to follow a binomial process each period, and the value of the underlying bond is then computed as a function of the interest rate at each point on the binomial lattice. The option values at period $T$, the time of option expiration, are determined by the option contract specifications as a function of the underlying bond's prices at period $T$. The option prices for the periods before expiration are then found recursively. The option price in any period is found by solving the three equation system describing the no-net-investment and no-net-return conditions that are required to eliminate one-period arbitrage opportunities:

No net investment: $\quad \Delta_1 B_1^o + \Delta_s B_s^o - C^o = 0$

No net return: $\quad \Delta_1 B_1^u + \Delta_s B_s^u - C^u = 0$

$$\Delta_1 B_1^d + \Delta_s B_s^d = C^d = 0$$

where $B_1$, $B_s$, and $C$ are the one-period bond prices, underlying bond prices, and option values for the current period (superscript O), the next period if interest rates follow the upward path (superscript $u$), and next period if interest rates follow the downward path (superscript $d$), respectively. The proportions of the one-period and underlying bond currently held are given by $\Delta_1$ and $\Delta_s$, respectively. This equation system involves three equations in three unknowns: $C^o$, $\Delta_1$, and $\Delta_s$. The solution will give the current option value and the required holdings of the two assets for effecting the no-net-investment/no-net-return hedge.

Exhibit 38–9 illustrates this pricing model in a two-period setting. The first lattice represents the possible price paths for interest rates and resulting bond prices. A flat yield curve is assumed so that the one-period and two-period interest rates, as well as the interest rate of the underlying bond, are equal to

---

[33] The binomial model, first suggested by Sharpe (1978), is developed by Cox, Ross, and Rubinstein (1979) and by Rendleman and Bartter(1979).

[34] See Rendleman and Bartter (1980) and Ho and Lee (1986).

this interest rate. The first point on the lattice shows that the initial interest rate is 10 percent. The rates follow an up movement of 1.2 and a down movement of .833, leading to the succession of interest rates for later periods. The prices for the underlying bond based on these interest rates are shown below the interest rate at each point on the lattice. The underlying bond is assumed to be a zero coupon bond with $100 principal amount and initially has 10 periods to maturity, leading to an initial price of $38.55.[35]

Based on these prices, the value of a two-period call option and a two-period put option, both with an exercise price of $40, are computed in the

**EXHIBIT 38–9**

Periods to expiration:    2                    1            0
Periods to bond maturity: 10                   9            8

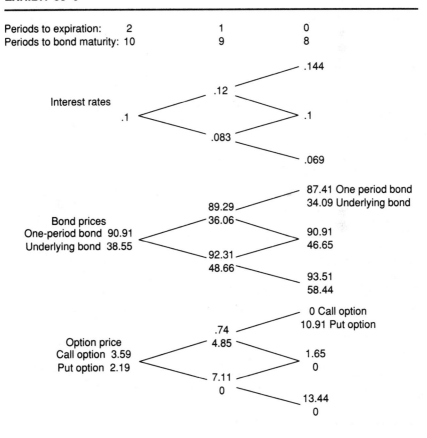

Interest rates

| | | |
| --- | --- | --- |
| | | .144 |
| | .12 | |
| .1 | | .1 |
| | .083 | |
| | | .069 |

Bond prices
One-period bond 90.91
Underlying bond 38.55

| | | |
| --- | --- | --- |
| | | 87.41 One period bond |
| | 89.29 | 34.09 Underlying bond |
| | 36.06 | |
| | | 90.91 |
| | | 46.65 |
| | 92.31 | |
| | 48.66 | |
| | | 93.51 |
| | | 58.44 |

Option price
Call option 3.59
Put option 2.19

| | | |
| --- | --- | --- |
| | | 0 Call option |
| | .74 | 10.91 Put option |
| | 4.85 | |
| | | 1.65 |
| | | 0 |
| | 7.11 | |
| | 0 | |
| | | 13.44 |
| | | 0 |

[35] The bond price is computed using simple interest: $B = 100[1/(1 + r)^T]$

second lattice. The resulting option values are $3.59 for the call and $2.19 for the put.

An inherent inconsistency with this approach to bond option pricing becomes apparent when the option values are checked against the put/call parity relationship. For zero coupon bonds, put/call parity requires

$$C - P = B^o - E[1/(1 + r)^2]$$

A violation of this condition implies arbitrage opportunities between the call, the put, the underlying security, and the two-period risk-free discount bond. Given our assumption of a flat yield curve, we can compare the option values given by the binomial model with this relationship:

Model values: $C - P = \$1.40$
Put/call parity relationship: $B^o - E[1/(1 + r)^2] = \$1.36$

It is clear that while one-period arbitrage holds in this model, put/call parity does not. The model is therefore inconsistent. The reason for the inconsistency is evident from an examination of the instruments used within the model. Since the two-period bond on which put/call parity relies is not used in the model, the resulting option price cannot be expected to maintain put/call parity. We could have alternatively developed the model in a way that would have maintained the put/call parity relationship—by using the two-period bond in place of the one-period bond in the option pricing equation—but only at the cost of not eliminating one-period arbitrage opportunities. In general, in the binomial model there will be no solution value for the put and the call that will eliminate the possibility for both put/call arbitrage and one-period arbitrage for arbitrary yield-curve assumptions. As the model is extended beyond two periods to $T$ periods, the problem expands. Besides the one-period arbitrage and the $T$-period arbitrage represented by the put/call parity relationship, there are possible arbitrage opportunities using the bonds with maturities of $2, 3, \ldots, T\text{-}1$ periods that must be addressed as well.

The failure of put/call parity is more than a curiosity. Put/call parity is a fundamental relationship that must exist between a put and call option because this relationship can be exploited to reap arbitrage profits, if it is violated. Furthermore, important strategies, such as conversions and reverse conversions, are related to the put/call parity relationship. A model that generates prices that violate put/call parity has generated prices that could not reasonably be expected to exist in the market place.[36]

---

[36] This issue is discussed further in Bookstaber, Jacob, and Langsam (1986).

## The Problem of Nonoptimal Exercise

The theory of option pricing assumes that all American options are exercised optimally, that is, they are exercised in such a way as to maximize the value of the option for the option buyer. Optimal exercise will occur when the option is worth more dead than alive—when the intrinsic value of the option is greater than the value unexercised.[37] The assumption of optional exercise is not always a good one, however. When compared with the timing of theoretically determined optimal exercise, convertible bonds, callable bonds, and mortgage-backed securities all have their own characteristics of nonoptimal exercise. Convertible bonds are often issued as a backdoor approach to the issue of equity. A firm, feeling that the equity is undervalued by the market or that it is not strong enough to attract investors for their equity, may issue convertible bonds in the hope that the bonds will later be converted and in the end give the desired result of an equity issue.[38]

The objective of enhancing the equity position outweighs the objective of minimizing the cost of the firm's short option position. As a result, calling convertible bonds to force exercise of the equity option may not be done at what appears to be the optimal time. Other callable corporate bonds may remain unexercised after the optimal call date because the refinancing of other issues is more pressing.

Mortgage-backed securities suffer more from the problems of nonoptimal exercise than any other type of security. Early exercise, which can occur either because of early prepayment or because of default, is the rule with mortgage-backed securities. The mortgage holder may prepay because of demographic concerns—a change in family size, a divorce, or a change in income level— or because the interest-rate environment makes the early exercise and refinancing

---

[37] Put options may be exercised early in order to capture the time value of the intrinsic value. For example, if a put option is far in-the-money, a greater return may be obtained by placing the proceeds of the exercise in the risk-free asset than can be obtained from further deterioration in the underlying security. For call options on bonds, early exercise may be desirable either because of favorable reinvestment rates on the proceeds of exercise relative to the return from continuing to hold the underlying security or because of the effect of pull to maturity. As the bond approaches maturity, the potential for further large price increases diminishes. The volatility of the bond drops, and therefore the time value of the option drops as well.

[38] A casebook example of this is Novo Industry. Recognizing that its domestic market, the Danish market, was too small to support its financing needs, Novo went out into the international market for capital. However, rather than issuing equity, which was not traded abroad and therfore would not be received strongly by the market, Novo issued a number of convertible bond issues. After these issues converted, a large international holding of the equity was established, making it easier to get the equity listed. Novo is now listed on the New York Stock Exchange and has options listed on the Chicago Board Option Exchange as well.

attractive financially. The demographic component is relatively easy to predict, since it is largely independent of the interest-rate level and is closely related to the age of the mortgage. The economic exercise component is also, in theory, predictable because, as with any American option, the time of optimal exercise can be determined as a function of the time remaining to the option expiration and the current price of the underlying security. However, in practice mortgage holders do not appear to exercise optimally. The prepayment increases with a drop in interest rates, but the rate of prepayment remains distributionally related to the interest-rate level, leading to uncertainty of cash flows to the investors of mortgage-backed securities.

The uncertainty of prepayment leads to a second level of complexity in exposure management. Not only is the convexity of the bond affected by the prepayment option, the prepayment option itself behaves in an unpredictable way.

## CONCLUSION

The key feature options bring to the universe of fixed income instruments is flexibility of payoffs. Options provide the means to mold return distributions to meet investment objectives.

With long options, the investor can sell off undesirable return characteristics. Investors in put bonds truncate potential downside loss in the event of interest-rate rises. Convertible bonds allow the investor to profit from equity while maintaining a known floor return (assuming that the bond does not default).

Short option positions allow the investor to generate higher yield by selling off the desirable return characteristics. Callable bond holders sell the potential for appreciation in a lower interest-rate environment. Holders of debentures agree to absorb the difference between the promised payment and the value of the firm if the assets of the issuer drop to the point where the scheduled payments of principal and interest are not made.

Just as options allow the investor to alter returns to better meet investment objectives, options can also be used to tailor interest-rate sensitivity to meet liability needs. We have illustrated how long option positions can help a bond position to better match the liability exposure from redeemable CDs, GICs, and other products with redemption features.

The increased flexibility that options bring comes at the price of greater complexity. The pricing of bonds now depends on option theory as well as the traditional methods of discounted cash-flow analysis. Options exacerbate the measurement of interest-rate exposure and magnify the convexity problems that arise in using duration for exposure management. For the investor who does not understand the role options play in bond pricing, the added complexity only leads to greater uncertainty and risk. For the investor who can use the option features intelligently, they open up an added dimension for the control of interest-rate risk and for extracting profits from the market.

## REFERENCES

Ball, C., and W. Torous. "Bond Price Dynamics and Options." *Journal of Financial and Quantitative Analysis*, 18, December 1983, pp. 517–31.

Bierwag, G.O., G.G. Kaufman, and A.L. Toevs. "Duration: Its Development and Use in Bond Portfolio Management." *Financial Analysts Journal*, July/August 1983.

Bookstaber, R. "The Use of Options in Performance Structuring." *Journal of Portfolio Management*, 11, Summer 1985, pp. 36–50.

_____. *Option Pricing and Investment Strategies*. Chicago, IL: Probus Publishers, 1987.

Bookstaber, R., and R. Clarke. "Problems in Evaluating the Performance of Portfolios with Options." *Financial Analysts Journal*, January/February 1985, pp. 48–62.

_____. "Option Portfolio Strategies: Measurement and Evaluation." *Journal of Business*, 57, October 1984, pp. 469–92.

_____. "Using Option Strategies to Alter Option Portfolio Distributions." *Journal of Portfolio Management*, Summer 1981, pp. 63–70.

Bookstaber, R., and D. Jacob. "Controlling the Credit Risk of High-Yield Bonds." *Financial Analysts Journal*, March/April 1986, pp. 25–36.

Bookstaber, R., D. Jacob, and J. Langsam. "The Arbitrage-Free Pricing of Options on Interest Sensitive Instruments." *Advances in Futures and Options Research*. JAI Press, 1986.

Bookstaber, R., and J. McDonald. "A Generalized Option Valuation Model for the Pricing of Bond Options." *Review of Research in Future Markets*, 4, 1985, pp. 60–73.

Brennan, M., and E. Schwartz. "Alternative Methods for Valuing Debt Options." Working paper 888. University of British Columbia. Vancouver, B.C., 1982a.

_____. "An Equilibrium Model of Bond Pricing and a Test of Market and Efficiency." *Journal of Financial and Quantitative Analysis*, 17 September 1982b, pp. 301–29.

Courtadon, G. "The Pricing of Options on Default-Free Bonds." *Journal of Financial and Quantitative Analysis*, 17, March 1982a, pp. 75–100.

_____. "A More Accurate Finite Difference Approximation for the Valuation of Options." *Journal of Financial and Quantitative Analysis*, 17(5), December 1982b.

Cox, J., J. Ingersoll, and S. Ross. "A Theory of the Term Structure of Interest Rates." Research paper no. 468, Stanford University, Graduate School of Business, August 1978.

Cox, J., S. Ross, and M. Rubinstein. "Options Pricing: A Simplified Approach." *Journal of Financial Economics*, 7, 1979, pp. 229–63.

Cox, J., and J. Rubinstein. *Option Markets*. Englewood Cliffs, NJ: Prentice-Hall, 1985.

Dothan, U. "On the Term Structure of Interest Rates." *Journal of Financial Economics*, January 1978.

Galai, D., and R. Masulis. "The Option Pricing Model and the Risk Factor of Stock." *Journal of Financial Economics*, 3, 1976, pp. 53–81.

Goodman, L. "Put-Call Parity with Coupon Instruments." *Journal of Portfolio Management*, 11, Winter 1985, pp. 59–60.

Ho, T.S. and S. Lee. "Term Structure Movements and Pricing Interest Rate Contingent Claims," *Journal of Finance* 41(5), 1011-1028, 1986.

Merton, R.C. "On the Pricing of Corporate Debt: The Risk Structures of Interest Rates." *Journal of Finance*, 29, May 1974, pp. 449–70.

Platt, R., ed. *Controlling Interest Rate Risk*. New York: Wiley, 1986.

———. "The Pricing of Options on Debt Securities." *Journal of Financial and Quantitative Analysis*, 9(4), December 1980.

Sharpe, W. *Investments*. Englewood Cliffs, NJ: Prentice-Hall, 1978.

Tilley, J., and G. Latainer. "Risk Control Technique for Life Insurance Companies." In *Controlling Interest Rate Risk*, ed. R. Platt. New York: Wiley, 1986.

Toevs, A., and W. Haney. "Measuring and Managing Interest Rate Risk, A Guide To Asset/Liability Models Used in Banks and Thrifts." In *Controlling Interest Rate Risk*, ed. R. Platt. New York: Wiley, 1986.

Vasicek, O. "An Equilibrium Characterization of the Term Structure." *Journal of Financial Economics*, November 1977, pp. 177–88.

# PART 7

# FIXED INCOME PORTFOLIO MANAGEMENT

# CHAPTER 39

# BOND MANAGEMENT:
# PAST, CURRENT, AND FUTURE

*H. Gifford Fong*
*President*
*Gifford Fong Associates*

Fixed income management has undergone a remarkable evolution. The range of portfolio strategies has expanded as the technology of portfolio analysis has developed over time. This broadened capability is permitting greater efficiency and effectiveness as well as the introduction of innovative strategies. Perhaps more remarkable is the prospect of a new dimension of fixed income portfolio strategy that dramatically goes beyond the traditional notions of management.

What follows is an overview of the changes that have occurred in fixed income portfolio strategy over the last 20 years. This historical survey will trace the emergence of various quantitative tools that have helped shape the world of modern fixed income portfolio management. After this review, a description of a representative strategy harnessing this technology will be presented.

## TRADITIONAL FIXED INCOME
## PORTFOLIO STRATEGY[1]

The primary functional areas of modern fixed income management are shown in Exhibit 39–1, which is a triangle with three intersections representing the

---

[1] For a more comprehensive discussion of traditional fixed income strategy, see H. Gifford Fong and Frank J. Fabozzi, *Fixed Income Portfolio Management* (Homewood, IL: Dow Jones-Irwin, 1985).

major strategies. At the bottom left can be found *active management,* made up of rate anticipation and/or sector management. Key to this area are expectations of interest-rate change and/or sector spread (yield difference from Treasury securities). To the lower right can be found *passive management,* where either a buy-and-hold strategy or indexing to a representative market bogey is typical.

Active and passive management can be differentiated on the basis of the kinds of input necessary. For example, traditional active management is "expectationally driven"; that is, the most important set of inputs will be expectations of interest-rate and spread relationship changes. Passive management, on the other hand, is based on nonexpectational inputs; in other words, the key inputs are known at the time of the analysis. In the case of indexing, these inputs are the basic characteristics of the market index chosen.

This difference in inputs corresponds to variations in the risk-return characteristics of the alternatives. The greater the expectational inputs are, all other things equal the greater the return potential and the associated variability (risk) of the strategy will be. Thus, active management will have the highest expected return but the highest associated risk, and passive management will have the lowest expected return and risk on average. The emphasis in this traditional setting is to seek higher returns by managing the expectations, which in turn increase the expected returns.

In contrast to the expectational nature of active management and nonexpectational nature of passive management, the top of the triangle, *immunization,* represents a hybrid strategy. Under some circumstances, an expectational, high expected risk-return approach may be chosen, or a nonexpectational, minimum risk posture may be assumed.

**EXHIBIT 39–1**
**Fixed Income Management**

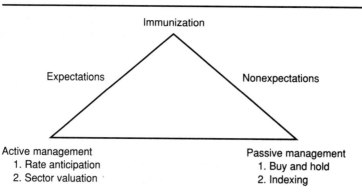

## HISTORICAL PERSPECTIVE

From a historical perspective, the early quantitative tools (*circa* 1970s) were first used to support active management. Sensitivity analysis, in which the implications of the expectations on portfolio returns could be evaluated, became a fundamental tool in active strategies. Expected scenarios of interest-rate change could be applied to the current portfolio, and prospective returns could be calculated. This analysis was extended to include insights from evaluating the implications of the expected returns.[2]

This early application represents the quantification of a traditional task that was formerly done informally by the portfolio manager. With this tool, the portfolio manager could pursue a more systematic and structured approach to portfolio decision making. It was not the case that a foreign step was introduced but rather an alternative path freeing the time of the portfolio manager. In effect, a computational task became automated so more time could be devoted to tasks that could not be automated. Given the usual demands on the available time of the portfolio manager, this quantitative assistance leveraged the ability of the manager to focus on the expectational inputs that are central to the active management process.

With the approach of the 1980s, a number of factors developed that encouraged the use of an old concept in a new form—immunization. Originally conceived in the 1930s, the immunization strategy awaited a series of theoretical and empirical developments before it could be put to practical use. So when relatively high interest rates (in relation to the typical actuarial assumption), the desire to minimize pension contributions, and the growth of new theoretical understanding[3] emerged at the same time, the basis for the use of immunization had been laid. Moreover, the tarnished reputation of traditional active management because of the performance of many portfolio managers in the 1970s further influenced the need for applying a new strategy.

In the 1980s, the further evolution of strategy took the direction of duration-controlled approaches. Given the aversion to unexpected exposure to changes in interest rates, reliance on interest-rate risk control by monitoring the duration of the portfolio became widespread. Out of this trend emerged indexing, which

---

[2] See, for example, John L. Maginn and Donald L. Tuttle, eds., *Managing Investment Portfolios: A Dynamic Process* (Charlottesville, VA.: The Institute of Chartered Financial Analysts, 1983), Chapter 9.

[3] Important advances in the nature of immunized portfolios were made in Lawrence Fisher and Roman Weil, "Coping with Risk of Interest Rate Fluctuations: Return to Bondholders from Naive and Optimal Strategies," *Journal of Business,* October 1971; and H. Gifford Fong and Oldrich A. Vasicek, "A Risk Minimizing Strategy for Portfolio Immunization," *The Journal of Finance,* December 1984, provided explicit risk measures for immunized portfolios.

targeted the portfolio duration. This is an extreme case of quantification that minimizes the need for expectational input.

More recently, other targeted-duration strategies have emerged. These, in general, have a duration target different from the popularly followed bond indexes but serve a similar function: limiting or controlling the exposure to interest-rate changes by "targeting" the duration.

This brief history traces the changes in strategy over about the last 20 years. Concurrently, the role of quantitative methods has altered. What started out as a useful means of measuring and monitoring has developed over time as an important source of portfolio strategy.

Early applications were mere alternatives to traditional practice, which allowed the automation of basic tasks. As concern for unconstrained use of expectations increased, quantitative methods provided the means of monitoring and controlling risk exposure, especially the risk of interest-rate change different from a desired duration level. These applications involved the use of quantitative techniques first to free up the time of the portfolio manager and then to help shape the appropriate policy of the portfolio management process. For example, a targeted-duration portfolio removes interest-rate forecasting from the manager's judgment yet still allows expectations to be applied in sector and individual bond selection. However, as the use of quantitative methods has increased, the potential for return has decreased. The question now becomes how to expand the horizons of return in the face of quantitative control.

## QUANTITATIVE INNOVATION

Exhibit 39–2 lists representative fixed income applications. Historically, the cornerstone of quantitative analysis has been the measurement of relevant factors providing analytical insight. And historically, the time demands of the traditional process of management could have been better served. More recent developments, such as indexing and immunization, suggest that quantitative innovation supplemented by traditional activities such as investment objective setting and trading, can be the principal expedient of portfolio management.

When one considers the important sources of management contribution to the return of a fixed-income portfolio, duration management has had the greatest impact followed by sector selection and then individual bond selection.[4] The potential for superior performance from management contribution is therefore severely handicapped if the most important potential source is taken away.

---

[4] This can be intuitively understood by considering the relative contribution to the variability of portfolio returns from these three sources.

**EXHIBIT 39–2**
**Quantitative Applications**

___

*Active Management*
    Return simulation

Predicts bond and portfolio behavior given alternative interest-rate scenario projections.

*Immunization*
    Immunization model

Creates and maintains a portfolio that will have an ensured return over a specified horizon, irrespective of interest-rate change.

*Passive Management*
    Indexing system

Creates and maintains a portfolio that will track the performance of a given bond index with a manageable set of securities.

*Individual Security Analysis*
    Swap systems

Allows for comparison of individual securities, with the objective of identifying historical price (or basis point spread) relationships.

    Term-structure analysis

Evaluates the current level of yields by producing spot, discount, and forward-rate structures. Also values Treasury securities.

    Bond valuation model

Develops a normative value for corporate and mortgage-backed securities, based on the evaluation of those characteristics of the security that contribute to overall price.

    Contingent claims model

Evaluates the embedded option in a security without forecasting interest rates.

*Other*
    Performance attribution system

Calculates the total return for a bond portfolio and attributes the return to its components.

    Risk analysis report

Calculates option-adjusted average duration, convexity, and yield for a portfolio.

___

    Active duration management may not be appropriate for all investors, but the consequences and merits of the choice should be understood.

    For example, targeted-duration strategies are designed to preclude large return departures from the chosen duration level. The choice of the level may be due to a number of considerations (including, importantly, the duration of the liabilities to be funded); however, whatever the level, if there is a consistent and reliable means of adding value through active duration management around the target, the potential for substantial incremental returns is achieved.

    Granted, the aversion to unconstrained expectational duration management may still exist. However, if a means of active duration management could operate in a controlled, nonexpectational framework, an interesting alternative would be achieved.

Drawn from modern option valuation theory, an asset allocation analysis can provide a form of active duration management.[5] The objective is to create a synthetic call option on the best performing of the two extremes of the selected duration range. What would result would be a systematic shift within this range based on an active asset allocation between the longest and shortest duration assets.

An option valuation model used for this purpose determines the appropriate proportions of the two duration extremes. The model can systematically shift the portfolio to the highest returning asset from the lowest returning asset. A synthetic option is thereby created from this active asset allocation—an option that will achieve the returns of the best performing of the two assets. The final portfolio return will be the return of the best performing asset less the synthetic option cost. This cost, which may be determined at the beginning of the analysis, arises from the return slippage due to the portfolio not using the best performing asset all of the time. Because there is a gradual shift, there is a "cost" or return differential as compared to the return of the best performing asset.

In general, the cost will vary with the number of assets, the length of the investment horizon, and the estimated risk of the assets considered (standard deviation of returns and correlation between assets). While the cost of the strategy can vary depending on the actual outcome of the risk estimates, the strategy will still achieve the desired property of a synthetic call on the best performing asset class.

Consider the management of an intermediate fixed income portfolio made up of high-grade government and corporate securities. Conventional indexing would target the duration of the index as the duration of the portfolio to be held. Value enhancement would take the form of sector selection and/or individual security selection. Return differences from the most important management activity, that of active duration management, would be eliminated.

Introducing active duration management using option valuation technology can retain the most important source of management return, without the need for interest-rate forecasting. The portfolio returns would be further enhanced by using a term-structure model to value Treasury securities and a bond valuation model for the balance of the portfolio.

---

[5] A discussion of a specific fixed income application can be found in John L. Maginn and Donald L. Tuttle, eds., *Managing Investment Portfolios,* 2nd ed. (Charlottesville, VA: The Institute of Chartered Financial Analysts), Chapter 8 (forthcoming); the discussion here is based on the theory discussed in H. Gifford Fong, and Oldrich A. Vasicek, "Forecast Free International Asset Allocation," *The Financial Analyst Journal* (forthcoming).

By harnessing the quantitative innovation of option valuation technology, a new dimension of portfolio decision making emerges. Active duration management without the need for interest-rate forecasting is made possible.

Another nonexpectational form of active duration management is tactical asset allocation. This strategy varies the duration of the portfolio based on fair value for the bond market. When the market is considered undervalued, the duration of the portfolio will be lengthened to what is considered normal; and, conversely, when the market is considered overvalued, the portfolio duration is shortened. The key is the determination of what is "fair value"; and, here tactical asset allocation differs from an option valuation approach. Expectations are required in the determination of fair value for tactical asset allocation, whereas the option valuation approach does not rely upon asset valuation expectation.

What has been described is a strategy applying quantitative innovation in the management of an active intermediate portfolio. Without the additional return potential of this technology, the return prospect would be that of a conservative duration portfolio. With the technology, the return range can be extended to much longer duration portfolios with the downside cushion of a short-duration portfolio.

## SUMMARY

A review of the main functional areas of fixed income management reveal a range of risk-return potential. Over time, the popularity of strategy has shifted in recognition of the difficulty of valid and reliable interest-rate forecasts. Recent developments in option valuation technology reintroduces the return of more active strategies, without the need for interest-rate forecasting.

# CHAPTER 40

## THE ACTIVE DECISIONS IN THE SELECTION OF PASSIVE MANAGEMENT AND PERFORMANCE BOGEYS*

*Chris P. Dialynas*
*Managing Director*
*Pacific Investment Management Company*

---

The asset allocation decision is perhaps a plan sponsor's most important decision. Within the scope of that decision, the selection of investment managers and performance bogeys are critical. Traditional asset allocation methods are based on studies of relative returns and risk over long periods of time. Performance periods, however, both for the plan itself and the investment manager entrusted with the funds, are based upon relatively short time spans. As such, there is an inherent inconsistency in the investment process.

In this chapter, the active bond management process will be explored and contrasted with the "passive management" option. We will also examine the differences in index composition. Performance inferences will be made based exclusively on the index composition and the future economic environment. We will see that successful bond management, whether active or passive, depends on good long-term economic forecasting and a thorough understanding of the mathematical dynamics of fixed income obligations. Likewise, selection of a performance bogey depends on similar considerations as well as the liability structure of the plan itself.

---

*The author expresses his gratitude to the research department at Shearson Lehman Hutton/American Express for their effort in providing data.

## ACTIVE BOND MANAGEMENT

Active management of bond portfolios capitalizes on changing relations among bonds to enhance performance. Volatility in interest rates and changes in the amount of volatility induce divergences in the relative prices between bonds. Since volatility, by definition, allows for opportunity, the fact that during the first half of 1986 active bond managers as a class underperformed the passive indexes in one of the most volatile bond markets in the past fifty years seems counter-intuitive. What went wrong then? What should we expect in the future?

Active bond managers each employ their own methods for relative value analysis. Common elements among most managers are historical relations, liquidity considerations, and market segmentation. Market segmentation allegedly creates opportunities, and historical analysis provides the timing cue. The timing of strategic moves is important because there is generally an opportunity cost associated with every strategy. Unfortunately, since the world is in perpetual motion and constant evolution, neither market segmentation nor historical analysis is able to withstand the greater forces of change. Both methods, either separately or jointly, are impotent. The dramatic increase in volatility experienced in recent years implies the world is turning and evolving more quickly. Paradoxically, many active managers are using methods voided by volatility to try to capitalize on volatility.

The mistakes of active bond managers have been costly. As a result, a significant move from active to passive (or indexed) management is in progress. Does this move make sense? To understand relative performance differentials between passive and active managers, we need to dissect the active and passive portfolios and reconstruct the macroeconomic circumstances. We will see that the composition of the indexes and the circumstances produced a dynamic combination that was most difficult to beat in 1986.

## MARKET INDEXES

While a variety of bond market indexes are popular today, only two have been notable throughout the present business cycle. The Shearson Lehman Government Corporate (SLGC) bond index was the most popular and the Salomon High Grade Long Term Bond Index was the traditional measure. Since the high-grade index sees little use today, our focus will be primarily on the SLGC index and the "new" Shearson Lehman Aggregate Index (SLAG), which includes mortgages. We will conclude with a comparison of the different indexes and their respective performance expectations given various interest-rate movements, as well as a review of historical performance comparisons.

## The SLGC Index

The SLGC is primarily composed of government and agency securities. The composition of the index is detailed in Exhibit 40–1.

The SLGC is constructed such that its composition is representative of the relative distribution of securities in the market exclusive of the mortgage market. Because the government issues the vast majority of debt, it is not surprising that the index holds such a high and increasing proportion of government securities. The index must, by definition, "buy" the debt. With the exception of some of the 30-year government bonds issued during this period, virtually all of the government and agency debt held in the index is noncallable. Because of this, between 1980 and 1989 the index has become increasingly call-protected. We will see that the callable/noncallable distribution is an important distinguishing feature between the index and active managers.

## The SLAG Index

The primary difference between the SLGC and the SLAG is the inclusion of mortgages in the SLAG. Mortgages provide the most uncertain distribution of cash flows among fixed income securities and exhibit substantial negative convexity. The degree of convexity differential between the SLGC and the SLAG is largely determined by the concentration of mortgages below par. The greater the percentage of mortgages below par is, the greater the relative convexity of the SLAG will be. Relative index performance expectations along the yield curve spectrum are sensitive to the relative coupon distribution of mortgages in the market at any point in time. That distribution, reported in Exhibit 40–2, will

**EXHIBIT 40–1**
**SLGC Distribution and Reported Characteristics***

| | Period Beginning | | | | |
|---|---|---|---|---|---|
| | 6/1980 | 6/1984 | 6/1986 | 6/1988 | 6/1989 |
| U.S. govt. | 40.77 | 57.33 | 60.35 | 61.90 | 62.41 |
| Agency | 18.20 | 14.96 | 11.14 | 10.50 | 10.87 |
| Corporates | 35.74 | 23.85 | 25.10 | 24.52 | 23.39 |
| Yankee | 5.29 | 3.87 | 3.40 | 3.07 | 3.33 |
| Duration | 5.04 | 4.02 | 5.10 | 4.03 | 5.21 |
| Yield | 10.25 | 13.59 | 8.49 | 9.07 | 9.10 |

* As reported by Shearson Lehman Hutton/American Express.

**EXHIBIT 40–2**
**SLAG Distribution and Reported Characteristics**

|  | Period Beginning | | | | |
|---|---|---|---|---|---|
|  | 6/1980 | 6/1984 | 6/1986 | 6/1988 | 6/1989 |
| U.S. govt. | 38.82 | 48.06 | 48.61 | 45.57 | 45.86 |
| Agency | 15.99 | 12.54 | 8.97 | 7.73 | 7.99 |
| Corporates | 31.40 | 19.99 | 20.22 | 18.06 | 17.19 |
| Mortgages | 10.14 | 16.18 | 19.46 | 26.35 | 26.52 |
| Yankee | 4.64 | 3.25 | 2.74 | 2.26 | 2.44 |
| Duration | 5.26 | 4.24 | 4.90 | 5.03 | 5.29 |
| Yield | 10.34 | 13.78 | 8.68 | 9.32 | 9.30 |

largely influence subsequent duration differences between the indexes and, therefore, subsequent performance differences as well.

### The Salomon Brothers High Grade Index

The Salomon Brothers high-grade, long-term bond index was a popular bond market bogey during the 1970s and early 1980s. The index is comprised primarily of high-quality (AA and AAA), long-term (10 years and longer) corporate bonds. Its reported duration approximated 8.5 years. The performance of the index was very poor during this period of increasing rates and increasing volatility in interest rates. The rate increases were so great that call options were driven well out of the money, reducing the localized cushioning effect normally associated with rate increases. The increase in volatility was tremendous and directly reduced the value of corporate bonds. Naturally, the high-grade index became perceived as too risky and not representative of the market's distribution of bonds. The SLGC was adopted as the market index. Its shorter duration allowed it to better weather the bear market. The SLAG index is most representative of the market and gained popularity during the latter half of the 1980s.

## PERFORMANCE CHARACTERISTICS
## OF CALLABLE AND NONCALLABLE BONDS

Exhibit 40–3 characterizes the expected performance characteristics of callable and noncallable bonds under different market environments. The market environments are described by two parameters: the direction of interest rates and the volatility of rates.

**EXHIBIT 40–3**

**Expected Performance Characteristics of Callable and Noncallable Bonds Under Different Market Environments**

Direction of Interest Rates

|  |  | Increase in rates | No change | Decrease in rates |
|---|---|---|---|---|
| Increase | NC | + | + | (+) |
|  | C | Amb+ | – | (–) |
| No change | NC | *i* | *i* | (+) |
|  | C | + | *i* | (–) |
| Decrease | NC | – | –*i* | +Amb |
|  | C | (+) | + | –Amb |

Volatility Changes

Performance Expectations
Relative to Comparable Duration
Govt. Securities Portfolios

| *i* | Income advantage | (+) | Big winner |
|---|---|---|---|
| (–) | Big loser | – | Loser |
| Amb | Ambiguous | NC | Non-callable portfolio |
| + | Winner | C | Callable portfolio |

Callable bonds do well in rising rate environments and decreasing volatility environments. Decreases in volatility have the profound direct effect of reducing the value of the call option imbedded within the callable bond. Since the bondholder has effectively sold the option, as its value is reduced by the lower volatility, the total value of the bond increases independent of any interest-rate movement.

Callable bonds do better than noncallable bonds in increasing rate environments because the higher rates cause the option to go out of the money. As the option goes out of the money, its value diminishes and the bond's value increases. The option value decline cushions the bond price decline induced by higher rates, thereby reducing the *effective duration*[1] of the bond. The effective duration of the bond decreases as rates increase, and the callable bond outperforms the noncallable bond, whose duration is relatively inelastic.

---

[1] Effective duration refers to the call-option-adjusted duration and, as used here, is independent in durational changes induced by liquidity or credit considerations.

Noncallable bonds perform better than callable bonds in decreasing rate and increasing volatility environments. Their effective duration[2] increases in decreasing rate environments because, exclusive of credit-risk considerations, the noncallable bonds are more *convex*[3]; that is, their *rate* of price increase outpaces that of the comparable duration callable bonds. As the volatility of interest rates increases, noncallable bonds will command a premium and, because the noncallable bonds are more convex, they will appreciate exclusively because of their relative convexity advantage.

The call features of the bond universe are summarized in Exhibit 40–4.

**EXHIBIT 40–4**
**Call Features of the Bond Universe**

| Issue Type | Refunding Protection | Call Protection | Refunding Price | Current Call Price |
|---|---|---|---|---|
| Treasury | Maturity* | Maturity | NA | NA |
| Traditional agency | Maturity | Maturity | NA | NA |
| Traditional industrial | 10 years | None | Premium | Premium |
| Traditional utility | 5 years | None | Premium | Premium |
| Traditional finance | 10 years† | None | Premium | Premium |
| GNMA pass-through | None | None | 100 | 100 |
| FNMA pass-through | None | None | 100 | 100 |
| FHLMC PC | None | None | 100 | 100 |
| CMO | None | None | 100 | 100 |
| Title XI | None‡ | None‡ | 100‡ | 100‡ |
| PAC CMO | Within prepayment range | None outside range | 100 | 100 |
| TAC CMO | Within prepayment range§ | None outside range | 100 | 100 |

* Some 30-year government bonds were issued with 25 years of call protection.
† A decline in receivables may permit an immediate par call.
‡ Default negates any refunding or call protection.
§ Call protected within a prespecified range of prepayment rates on the collateral.

[2] In this instance, effective duration refers to the expected percentage price change in the market. It is not used here in a volatility adjusted duration context.

[3] Convexity is the measure of how a bond's price change as yields change differs relative to the price change expected from its duration. Convexity is a measure of duration elasticity.

**EXHIBIT 40-5**
**6-Month Volatility from 48-Month Mean**
**30-Year Treasury Total Return: Jan 1976 through June 1989**

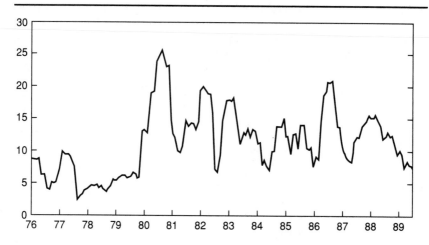

## A LOOK AT MARKET VOLATILITY

It is helpful to examine the volatility of the bond market to make inferences about performance attributes. Exhibit 40–5 displays the volatility of the bond market as described by the 6-month moving average of the 12-month standard deviation of total return on 30-year U.S. Treasury bonds.

Unprecedented, high volatility has been experienced in the bond market during the past decade. Not only has volatility been high, but the degree of variation in volatility has been high as well. It is *volatility change* that influences the value of options, which, in turn, cause relative performance differences between callable and noncallable portfolios.

## A LOOK AT INTEREST RATES

The most important piece of the puzzle is the direction of interest rates. Exhibit 40–6 depicts the movement of rates for the period January 1, 1976 to June 1989. We observe dramatic changes in the absolute level of rates. As such changes occur, the relative values of callable and noncallable bonds change. Lower rates work to the advantage of noncallable bonds, and higher rates to the advantage of callable bonds. With extreme increases in rates, ironically, U.S. Government non-callable bonds perform best. This is generally because of the importance of liquidity and credit non-callable bonds considerations to corporate bonds.

**EXHIBIT 40–6**
**Yield on 30-Year Treasuries: Jan 1976 to June 1989**

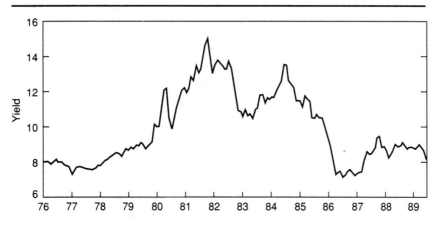

## A Look at Recent History

The volatility of the bond market increased from about 4 percent in 1976 to about 20 percent in 1982. In the period from 1976 to 1982, volatility ranged between 2 percent and 20 percent. In the period from 1982 to 1986, volatility was never less than 7 percent. Over the complete period from 1976 to 1986, average volatility tripled. This information alone would favor bond portfolios containing the *fewest* callable securities. However, all else equal, we would prefer noncallable portfolios during the period from 1976 to 1982 and callable ones during the 1982–1986 period.

Yields on long-term government bonds increased from 8 percent in 1976 to 14.5 percent in 1982. In the 1982–1986 period, rates dropped from 14.5 percent to 7.25 percent. The 1986–1989 period was one within which rates increased from 7.25 percent to 8.625 percent. The range in rates from 1976 to 1982 was 8 percent to 14.5 percent. The range for the middle period was 7.25 percent to 14.5 percent. Rates ranged from 7.25 percent to 10.00 percent during the latter period. We would naively expect portfolios containing callable securities to do best during the first period, portfolios containing noncallable bonds to do best during the middle period, and portfolios containing callable bonds to excel during the latter period. Of course, these inferences assume constant conditions in credit, volatility, and yield-curve shape.

The performance differences between callable and noncallable bonds for these periods are summarized in Exhibit 40–7.

**EXHIBIT 40–7**
**Performance Differences Between Callable and Noncallable Bonds During Prior Periods**

| | 1976–1982 | 1982–1986 | 1976–1986 | 1986–1989 |
|---|---|---|---|---|
| Portfolio composition | Interest rates increased/ Volatility increased | Interest rates declined/Volatility unchanged | Interest rates declined slightly/ Volatility increased | Interest rates increased/ Volatility declined |
| Callable | − | ⊖ | − | + |
| Non-callable | − | (+ +) | + | − |

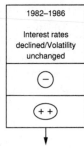
The step decline in interest rates and the virtually unchanged level of high volatility favored noncallable over callable portfolios by a wide margin. The options became in-the-money and shortened the duration of the callable portfolio, revealing the dramatic effects of negative convexity!

Interest-rate change from 8% to14.5% moved the call features out of the money. This effect swamped the increase in volatility. Thus, callable portfolios outperformed.

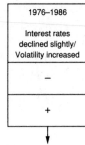
While interest rates declined only modestly, the tremendous increase in volatility served to make the option more valuable. A countervailing effect of callable issues' income advantage did not offset their decrease in principal value created by the option over short investment horizons.

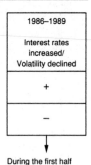
During the first half of this period, the increase in interest rates swamped the increase in volatility. Callable bonds outperformed noncallables during this subperiod. During the second half of the period rates declined and volatility declined. The drop in rates dominated and callables performed best. There were ambiguous results for the full period. Rates increased modestly and volatility was largely unchanged.

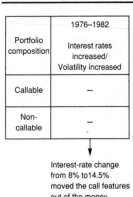

# THE IMPLICIT FORECASTS OF VOLATILITY AND INTEREST RATES

Most active bond managers are sector managers, or sector rotators. They hold portfolios composed of a high proportion of nongovernment securities. These portfolios are short the call options or, viewed alternatively, long portfolios of callable bonds. Combining this observation with the preceding historical analysis, it is obvious that, adjusting for durational differences the first six months of 1986, few people seem to have anticipated the magnitude of the change in interest rates and the profound increase in realized volatility. Both of these forecast errors were important detractors from performance. Even those managers who correctly forecasted the change in interest rates terribly underestimated the combined impact of increased volatility and declining rates on the value of the option. Thus, their selection of bonds was inconsistent with their forecast.

Bond management necessarily requires an interest-rate forecast, a volatility forecast, and a set of analytical models that calculate the future value of individual securities and portfolios of securities based upon those forecasts. It is the confluence of volatility movement and interest-rate movement that largely affects bond values.

Similarly, the decision to move from active to passive management, or from passive to active, is necessarily predicated upon an implicit forecast of interest rates, volatility, and perceived investment manager consciousness. Moreover, the choice of index as a bogey for active managers or as a source of investment value contains within it an implicit forecast of both rates and volatility.

The choice of indexes today (long government rates at 8.625%) is a choice of buying or selling convexity and duration. Convex portfolios, such as the SLGC, hold a high percentage of noncallable bonds. Portfolios with little convexity, such as the Shearson Lehman Aggregate Index (SLAG) hold many callable bonds. Thus, the durations of convex portfolios change inversely with market rates, whereas the durations of nonconvex portfolios may, perversely, change in the same direction as rates.

Simply stated, in today's world, the SLGC is a convex portfolio and the SLAG is not very convex.[4] As such, the SLGC yields less than the SLAG and is much more sensitive to changes in interest rates and changes in volatility. However, if rates decline from here, the SLAG index will underperform the SLGC by a significant margin because its duration will not increase and may actually decrease. Exhibit 40–8 compares the expected performance characteristics of the SLGC and SLAG.

The expected differences in portfolio performance are largely the result of the one-dimensional nature of duration as a descriptive risk variable. Portfolios with a high proportion of bonds containing imbedded call options that are at- or near-the-money perversely influence duration when interest rates change. Rate increases initially cause an *increase* in portfolio durations, and rate decreases cause a *decrease* in portfolio durations. The aggregate indexes, today, represent portfolios with this unconventional durational attribute because they contain a high proportion of callable bonds at- or near-the-money. Portfolios described in terms of both duration and convexity have greater explanatory power since their risk parameters are more fully defined. Implicit within a move to passive management is both a volatility and an interest-rate forecast. The move to passive management reinforces Say's Law, which holds that

---

[4] The importance of coupon concentration in the relative performance of these two indexes is explained in the next section.

**EXHIBIT 40–8**
**Comparison of the Expected Performance of the SLGC and SLAG**

| Interest rates | UNCH | Rise | Fall | UNCH | UNCH | Rise | Rise | Fall | Fall |
|---|---|---|---|---|---|---|---|---|---|
| Volatility | UNCH | UNCH | UNCH | Rises | Falls | Rises | Falls | Rises | Falls |
| Index that performs best | SLAG | SLAG | SLGC | SLGC | SLAG | Ambiguous (SLAG)* | SLAG | SLGC | Ambiguous (SLGC)* |

* Interest-rate movements are usually the prevailing force. The index in parentheses would therefore dominate unless the interest-rate movement was very small and the volatility movement great.

supply creates its own demand. Passive investment portfolios have done well in spite of their main investment criterion: Buy that which is produced independent of price or value considerations. Passive management relies upon the market forces to ensure that asset values are appropriate. Passive, narrow indexes, such as the SLGC, have even done well recently because of the circumstances— radically lower rates and increased volatility, both of which have benefitted call-protected portfolios. The past is prologue; today's investment choice will be judged by tomorrow's circumstances.

The compositional and structural differences between the narrow and aggregate indexes are, today, very pronounced. Previously, while compositionally distinct, their structural similarities caused highly correlated performance results. (See Exhibits 40–9 and 40–10.) The performance characteristics of the two indexes will now differ to a greater degree than has been previously experienced. In fact, the aggregate index will experience a gradual, unpredicatable lengthening in duration as the high percentage of low-duration premium mortgages are prepaid and refinanced with current coupon longer duration mortgages. This lengthening will occur quite independently of any changes in interest rates and as long as rates do not drop considerably. A big drop in rates will most likely cause the SLAG duration to decrease, and its performance would lag behind the performance of the SLGC substantially. The differential would probably exceed most market participants' expectations.

Those who are required to select a performance bogey for their fund have a difficult choice. The bogey performs the role of directing the risk of the assets. The choice involves a trade-off between a bogey that (1) replicates the proportional distribution of bonds in the market, (2) has risk characteristics complementary to the liability structure of the assets, and (3) has a relatively neutral market bias associated with it. Unfortunately, no bogey satisfies all of these requirements, and the trade-offs can be costly.

The choices are difficult. Ultimately, correct macroeconomic forecasts will dominate the active/passive choice. Will volatility increase or diminish and when? Will rates go up or down and when? What influences volatility? How do interest rates and volatility changes trade off? When does the volatility/interest-rate forecast favor one index over the other? These are the tough questions you should be asking your active manager or your passive index.

## THE IMPORTANCE OF COUPON CONCENTRATION IN RELATIVE SLGC/SLAG PERFORMANCE

The SLAG and SLGC have exhibited a high historical correlation. The high correlation was violated during the first half of 1986. It is important to understand why the high correlation existed and why it diverges to better understand tomorrow's expected correlation.

**EXHIBIT 40–9**
**Index Performance (%)** (Six-Month Periods)

| End Date | SLGC | SLAG | AG-GC Difference | Ratio GC to AG % | Sal High Grade |
|---|---|---|---|---|---|
| 12/78 | .99 | 1.26 | .27 | 78.57 | 1.00 |
| 06/79 | 6.62 | 6.50 | −.12 | 101.85 | 6.16 |
| 12/79 | −4.05 | −4.29 | −4.29 | 94.41 | 6.16 |
| 06/80 | 8.22 | 8.44 | .22 | 97.39 | −9.75 |
| 12/80 | −4.77 | −5.29 | −5.29 | 90.17 | 7.81 |
| 06/81 | .70 | .15 | −.55 | 466.67 | −9.80 |
| 12/81 | 6.51 | 6.09 | −.42 | 106.90 | −2.92 |
| 06/82 | 6.41 | 6.84 | .43 | 93.71 | 1.74 |
| 12/82 | 23.20 | 24.13 | .93 | 96.15 | 5.91 |
| 06/83 | 4.82 | 4.91 | .09 | 98.17 | 34.61 |
| 12/83 | 3.03 | 3.29 | .26 | 92.10 | 5.70 |
| 06/84 | −1.02 | −1.68 | −.48 | 71.43 | .53 |
| 12/84 | 16.42 | 17.11 | .69 | 95.97 | −5.03 |
| 06/85 | 10.56 | 10.95 | .39 | 96.44 | 23.05 |
| 12/85 | 9.72 | 10.05 | .33 | 96.72 | 13.65 |
| 06/86 | 9.96 | 9.05 | −.91 | 110.06 | 14.47 |
| 12/86 | 5.14 | 5.70 | .56 | 90.18 | 11.52 |
| 06/87 | −.44 | −.17 | .27 | 258.82 | 7.47 |
| 12/87 | 2.74 | 2.93 | .19 | 93.52 | −2.27 |
| 06/88 | 4.60 | 4.98 | .38 | 93.37 | 2.04 |
| 12/88 | 2.85 | 2.77 | −.08 | 102.89 | 6.35 |
| 06/89 | 9.23 | 9.20 | −.03 | 100.33 | 4.09 |

It was previously noted that the major distinction between the SLGC and the SLAG is the inclusion of mortgages in the SLAG. As such, we must determine whether these securities' options were at the money, in the money, or out of the money to establish their effect on portfolio convexity. The simplest framework we can utilize to evaluate the effect on convexity is a pricing framework. Mortgages selling at a discount exhibit positive convexity and higher durations, whereas other mortgages exhibit low or negative convexity and lower durations.

Exhibit 40–11 shows the percentage of outstanding GNMAs priced at or below par for selected time periods. We observe that in 1982 all mortgages were at par or a discount. In 1984, most mortgages were at a discount. The situation differed in June 1986 in that very few mortgages were priced at a discount. This means that the SLAG exhibited a noncallable character through 1984 and most of 1985 but reversed late in 1985. The aggregate index increased its noncallable character in 1988 and declined subsequently. At that point it took on negative convexity and a callable character. At the end of 1989, it had that callable character and therefore a shorter effective duration. In fact, under this

**EXHIBIT 40–10**
**Index Returns (%)** (Two-Year Periods)

| End Date | SLGC | SLAG | AG-GC Difference | Ratio GC to AG (%) | Sal High Grade |
|---|---|---|---|---|---|
| 06/80 | 11.81 | 11.92 | .11 | 99.08 | |
| 12/80 | 5.43 | 4.69 | −.74 | 115.78 | −6.83 |
| 06/81 | −.42 | −1.55 | −1.03 | 27.10 | −14.80 |
| 12/81 | 10.55 | 9.12 | −1.43 | 115.68 | −3.95 |
| 06/82 | 8.70 | 7.51 | −1.19 | 115.85 | −5.66 |
| 12/82 | 40.62 | 40.91 | .29 | 99.29 | 40.80 |
| 06/83 | 46.37 | 47.61 | 1.24 | 97.40 | 53.31 |
| 12/83 | 41.58 | 43.71 | 2.13 | 95.13 | 51.48 |
| 06/84 | 31.45 | 32.25 | .80 | 97.52 | 35.84 |
| 12/84 | 24.22 | 24.77 | .55 | 97.78 | 24.17 |
| 06/85 | 31.02 | 31.96 | .94 | 97.06 | 33.51 |
| 12/85 | 39.53 | 40.60 | 1.27 | 97.36 | 52.02 |
| 06/86 | 55.29 | 55.94 | .65 | 98.84 | 78.51 |
| 12/86 | 40.25 | 40.74 | .49 | 98.80 | 55.91 |
| 06/87 | 26.30 | 26.64 | .34 | 98.72 | 34.07 |
| 12/87 | 18.27 | 18.44 | .27 | 99.08 | 19.53 |
| 06/88 | 12.50 | 14.02 | 1.52 | 89.16 | 13.99 |
| 12/88 | 10.05 | 10.86 | .81 | 92.54 | 10.41 |
| 06/89 | 20.73 | 21.25 | −.48 | 97.55 | 26.16 |

condition, in contrast to noncallable indexes, its duration will decrease as rates *decline* and increase as rates increase. A similar condition existed at the end of 1989.

Exhibit 40–12 provides combined coupon distribution data of GNMA, FHLMC, and FNMA mortgage pass-throughs and the author's opinion about convexity characteristics.

The data in Exhibit 40–12 reveal that only 28 percent of the mortgages contained within the SLAG exhibit positive convexity. In a modest bull market, the SLAG index duration will decline and it will increase in a bear market. A

**EXHIBIT 40–11**
**Percentage of Outstanding GNMAs Priced at or below Par**

| June/1978 | 79 | June/1980 | 81 | June/1982 | 83 | June/1984 | 85 |
|---|---|---|---|---|---|---|---|
| 96.8% | 100 | 97.4% | 100 | 97.1% | 71.6 | 95.7% | 48.0 |

| June/1986 | | June/1987 | | June/1988 | | June/1989 | |
|---|---|---|---|---|---|---|---|
| 34.9% | | 77% | | 83% | | 77% | |

**EXHIBIT 40–12**
**Mortgage Coupon Characteristics** (May 31, 1989)

| Coupon (%) | Percentage | Price Range | Convexity |
|---|---|---|---|
| 6–7 | .78 | 85 – 88 | (+) |
| 7–8 | 3.83 | $86\frac{1}{2} - 89\frac{1}{2}$ | (+) |
| 8–9 | 22.88 | $89\frac{3}{4} - 93\frac{1}{2}$ | (+) |
| 9–10 | 42.14 | $95 - 97\frac{1}{2}$ | (−) |
| 10–11 | 19.01 | $98 - 100\frac{3}{4}$ | (−) |
| 11–12 | 7.21 | $102\frac{1}{2} - 104$ | (−) |
| 12–13 | 3.21 | $104\frac{1}{4} - 107$ | (−) |
| 13–14 | .69 | $106\frac{5}{8} - 109\frac{5}{8}$ | (−) |
| 14–15 | .07 | $107\frac{1}{4} - 112$ | (−) |
| 15–16 | .14 | $114 - 115\frac{1}{2}$ | (−) |

radical bull or bear market in interest rates will magnify these phenomenon. The opposite response will occur with the SLGC index. As such, at prevailing yield levels, the relative performance differentials between the indexes will be meaningful given some meaningful level of volatility.

Lower yields will increase performance differentials as index character diverges; higher yields will mitigate expected performance differentials because index character will merge.

## THE IMPORTANCE OF CHANGES IN THE SHAPE OF YIELD CURVE

Changing yield-curve shapes represent the other important first-order determinant of relative performance differentials. The indices are represented by various distributional holdings along the yield curve. Distributional differences between the SLGC, the SLAG,[5] and bond managers' portfolios will be important when yield-curve shapes are frequently variable and/or when changes in shape are of substantial magnitude. Yield-curve shape changes also change expected returns relative to those expected a priori because of the effects upon duration, call and put option values, prepayment behavior, and other more subtle effects.

The yield-curve effect is not included in this analysis. The difficulty in bond investment analysis is extremely complex when yield-curve shape changes

---

[5] Changes in the shape of the yield curve directly affect mortgage values. Coupon distribution relative to prevailing interest rates will influence the SLAG asset distribution along the yield curve.

are included. These complexities, including the potential correlation between interest rates and volatility, are beyond the scope of this chapter. Professional bond portfolio managers must understand these linkages if they hope to succeed.

## INDEX CONSCIOUSNESS

The extraordinary volatility of interest rates during the 70s and 80s has resulted in considerable volatility in returns. Durational differences between portfolios result in substantially different returns when interest rates are volatile. The historical return difference between the SLGC and the Salomon High Grade Index illustrate this point. Many market participants were apparently surprised by the amount of price volatility that their bond portfolios experienced in the 1960s and 1970s. In an effort to control portfolio return variability relative to the "market," some bond managers have adopted portfolio constraints wherein the durational risk relative to the market index is bound. The movement to this new investment strategy should help control variability but will nullify the relative advantages achievable through expert macroeconomic analysis and interest-rate forecasting. The movement to this policy is an admission of a flawed investment theory, risk aversion, and/or an uncertain conviction in forecasting of quantitative capability. This chapter has emphasized the importance of the contribution of good interest-rate and volatility forecasts with consistent period-dependent asset selection.

# CHAPTER 41

---

# INDEXING FIXED INCOME ASSETS*

---

*Sharmin Mossavar-Rahmani, CFA*
Senior Vice President
Fidelity Management Trust Company

---

Fixed income index funds have grown dramatically to over $75 billion since first introduced in 1979. Indeed, some of the nation's largest public, corporate, and multiple-employer pension plan sponsors, foundations, and insurance companies have indexed a significant portion, if not all, of their fixed income assets. Among the public funds, the New York City Retirement System has indexed its entire $22.3 billion of fixed income assets. In the corporate sector, AT&T has indexed as much as $4.1 billion. Other large institutions that have similarly committed a portion of their fixed income assets include California State Teachers' Retirement System, Exxon Corporation, UMWA Health and Retirement Funds, and The Rockefeller Foundation.

## ADVANTAGES AND DISADVANTAGES

The most important factor driving the interest in indexing is the poor and inconsistent performance of active investment advisors. Historically, the returns of most active investment advisors have lagged behind those of market indexes. In addition, active investment advisors who have matched or outperformed market indexes have done so inconsistently when measured over 10-year periods.

---

*This chapter has been adapted from Sharmin Mossavar-Rahmani *Bond Index Funds* (Probus Publishing Company: Chicago, 1991).

Investors therefore have turned to index funds to obtain both higher long-term returns as well as more consistent and reliable short-term performance.

Exhibit 41–1 compares the annualized returns of active investment advisors with those of a widely used market index for 1-, 3-, 5-, and 10-year periods ending December 1989. (1-, 3-, 5-, and 10-year periods are commonly used to evaluate the performance of investment advisors.) In all four periods, the overall market returns—represented by the Salomon Brothers Broad Investment-Grade Bond Index—were higher than those of the median-active investment advisor. In the 10-year period ending December 1989, market index returns ranked as high as the 19th percentile level of active investment advisors; in other words, a staggering 81 percent of active investment advisors underperformed the market index. The performance of active investment advisors during these years has not only been poor but inconsistent as well; even those active investment advisors who have outperformed the market index have done so inconsistently.

Another key attraction of indexing is the lower advisory fee schedule for index-fund management relative to that charged for active investment management. Advisory fees for index funds range between 30 and 75 percent of

**EXHIBIT 41–1**

**Annualized Total Return for Fixed Income Funds (For Periods Ending December 31, 1989)**

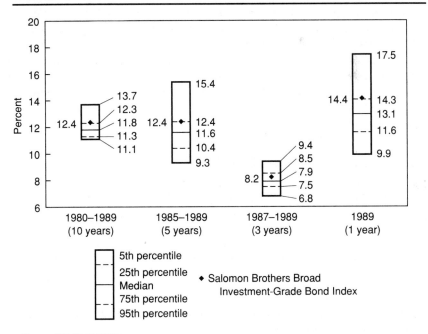

Source: SEI Corporation

advisory fees for actively managed portfolios. Fees for a $50 million index fund typically range between 5 and 17 basis points. The highest fees, about 20 basis points, are charged for enhanced or customized index funds, and significantly lower fees—a mere one or two basis points—are charged for very large index funds (say, in excess of $1 billion). The savings in advisory fees from indexing, therefore, can be substantial, particularly in the case of large funds.

Indexing also lowers costs (other than advisory fees) that are incurred in investing assets, including, for example, custodian and master trustee costs. Custodian costs vary in part as a function of transaction activity in a portfolio. Since index funds have lower turnover of assets and hence fewer transactions, the associated custodian costs also are lower.

Master trustee costs, too, vary, in part as a function of the number of portfolios that are in trusteeship. Because the size of assets given to any single advisor of an index fund is generally much larger than the size of assets given to any single advisor for active management, indexing often results in a consolidation of advisors responsible for managing a pool of assets, reducing the associated master trustee costs.

Another major advantage of indexing is the degree of control afforded the investor. When an investor hires an active investment advisor, the investor is largely at the mercy of the advisor. While an advisor is constrained by his or her investment discipline, there is, nevertheless, tremendous latitude afforded within that discipline. As such, the investor has minimal control over the advisor's investment decisions at any point in time.

Indexing, on the other hand, allows the investor to specify both the benchmark as well as the degree of latitude allowed the index-fund advisor for deviation from the benchmark characteristics. For example, an active investment advisor may have the mandate to construct a portfolio with any average duration that he or she deems appropriate based on an interest-rate forecast, whereas an index-fund advisor may be limited to, say, a 10 percent deviation from the average duration of the index.

Finally, another advantage of indexing is the ease and precision with which the value added by the investment advisor can be measured. The performance of investment advisors is reviewed by investors and consultants on a quarterly basis. The review report includes the total return of the portfolio as well as the total return of a benchmark. To date, broad market indexes have been the most widely used benchmarks. The review process for active investment advisors, in contrast, has two shortcomings: The selected benchmarks often are not the appropriate performance benchmarks for the investment advisor; and the portfolio deviations from the benchmark characteristics, which explain relative performance, are not thoroughly examined. Indexing overcomes both shortcomings. First, establishing an index fund begins with an extensive search for the appropriate index and, hence, the appropriate performance benchmark. Second, index-fund investors focus more closely on the quarterly differences in return between the portfolio and the benchmark and require investment advisors to attribute differences in return to specific deviations from the benchmark characteristics.

The rapid growth in its popularity—and its attraction—notwithstanding, indexing does pose some disadvantages. In periods of rising interest rates, which characterize bear bond market cycles, index funds tracking broad market benchmarks register relatively poor or, at best, mediocre performance. Such poor performance has occurred over all recent bear market cycles. The relatively poor performance in periods of rising interest rates, however, has been offset by the relatively high total return of the benchmark in periods of falling interest rates (which characterizes a bull bond market cycle). Over complete market cycles, therefore, index funds tracking broad market benchmarks have, at best, outperformed and, at worst, matched the median active investment advisor.

Although indexing may be more attractive than traditional active management based on interest rate anticipation, it entails a high opportunity cost, where opportunity cost is defined as the incremental returns forgone by not investing in market sectors with the highest performance. These market sectors include different maturity sectors as well as different types of securities such as Treasuries, agencies, corporates, Yankees, and mortgage-backed securities.

A few strategies have been developed over the past few years that have resulted in higher total returns than those of broad market benchmarks over a complete market cycle. Most of these strategies respond to, rather than forecast, changes in interest-rates and changes in yield spreads between short-term securities and long-term securities. Examples of such strategies include (1) momentum-based strategies that use different short-term and long-term moving averages of bond prices to determine whether to invest in bonds or in short-term instruments, (2) options-based strategies that use options theory to create, synthetically, a call option on the best performing maturity sector, (3) constant-duration strategies that assume the mean-reversion of interest rates and maintain a fixed duration over a complete market cycle of interest rates, and (4) duration-averaging strategies that also assume the mean-reversion of interest-rates and extend duration as interest rates rise and shorten duration as interest rates fall.

Some of these strategies have outperformed broad market benchmarks over bull, bear, and therefore the complete interest-rate cycles. Some of the same strategies, however, have underperformed broad market benchmarks during short periods characterized by volatile interest rates and by small overall changes in interest rate from the beginning to the end of the period. Other strategies have outperformed broad market benchmarks over complete interest cycles as well as during volatile interest-rate environments. The future long-term performance of these new strategies relative to indexing will depend on the market environment for interest rates and the actual implementation of the strategies with real assets over a market cycle.

Index funds are sometimes criticized for their rigid requirements. "True" (also called "straight," "vanilla," or "pure") index funds do not invest in instruments outside the benchmark universe, thereby forgoing the opportunities and the incremental return afforded by these instruments.

The broad market benchmarks exclude many sectors of the fixed income market including zero coupon Treasuries, nonfederal agency conventional mortgage pass-throughs, collateralized mortgage obligations, interest-only and principal-only strips, most asset-backed securities such as CARDS and CARS, medium-term notes, and bank deposit notes and derivative instruments.

Although true index funds are constrained by the holdings of their benchmarks, this constraint can be overcome readily by enhanced index funds. Enhanced index funds have the flexibility to invest in securities outside their index universe, benefitting from the incremental return from such securities and circumventing the rigid requirements posed by true index funds.

## ENHANCED INDEX FUNDS

Enhanced index funds, or "index-plus" funds, are managed with the objective of outperforming a particular index while matching the latter's major risk characteristics. Unlike pure index funds, which are passively-managed portfolios, enhanced index funds are actively managed ones where trades are intended to rebalance the portfolio *and* to capture any available investment opportunities. The magnitude of outperformance depends on several factors, including the type of index fund, the strategies employed by an index-fund advisor, the latitude given to an index-fund advisor to deviate from a selected index, and the level of volatility of interest rates and market-sector spreads.

Broad market index funds, for example, permit greater enhancement of total returns than do specialized market sector index funds. A specialized market sector index fund is restricted to one sector and, therefore, to investment opportunities in that sector only. A broad market index fund, on the other hand, can add value by allocating assets among different market sectors and by taking advantage of specific investment opportunities in each of those market sectors.

Similarly, the potential for enhancing total return is greatest if an index-fund advisor takes advantage of multiple investment strategies, including sector selection, yield-curve strategies, coupon selection, issuer selection, and use of derivative and synthetic securities. Specialization in one type of strategy limits the degree of enhancement, particularly when the prevailing market environment does not favor that strategy. It should be noted that such investment strategies are implemented while maintaining the same effective duration as that of the benchmark. These strategies are sometimes called duration-neutral strategies.

The greater the latitude to deviate from certain risk and return characteristics of the benchmark is, the greater is the potential to enhance the returns of the index fund. Of course, greater latitude to deviate means greater risk of underperforming the benchmark.

The amount of potential enhancement also depends on the level of volatility of interest rates and market-sector spreads. When volatility is low, mispricings of sectors and individual securities—and hence investment opportunities to enhance returns—are reduced. Conversely, when volatility of both interest rates and of market-sector spreads is high, an index-fund advisor can enhance returns by taking advantage of inefficiencies in the relative value of securities, changes in the shape of the yield curve, and fluctuations in yield spreads.

Notwithstanding the type of index fund, the strategies employed, the latitude given, and the level of volatility, an enhanced index fund is expected to provide at least 15 basis points of incremental value per year. Fifty basis points annually represents the maximum incremental return that typically is offered by enhanced index-fund advisors. Occasionally, an enhanced index-fund advisor may quote a multiyear target enhancement of as much as 100 basis points per year. To put this claim in perspective, it should be cautioned that such a return would require a level of performance leading to top quartile ranking among all active fixed income advisors.

Given the potential for enhancing the total return of index funds by 15—and sometimes as much as 50—basis points, the question arises as to why an index fund investor would choose pure index funds. Two factors account for the choice. First, while enhanced index funds are expected to outperform their benchmarks over a complete market cycle, such funds may underperform during some phase of the cycle. Investment strategies may require extended periods to succeed, and sometimes, they do not succeed at all. Many index fund investors are not willing to accept the risk of interim underperformance.

Second, the fees for enhanced indexing are higher than those for pure indexing. Fees alone, however, should not deter index-fund investors from selecting enhanced indexing. The additional cost is usually less than 10 basis points. And even in cases where 10 basis points appears too high, incentive (performance-based) fees can be used such that the full additional cost is only paid when the index fund has outperformed the benchmark by a certain predetermined amount.

## INDEXING METHODOLOGIES

Unlike equity index funds, bond index funds cannot purchase all securities contained in the selected index in the same proportion as that of the index itself. Most fixed income indexes contain thousands of securities; investing in all those securities in the appropriate proportion would result in an index fund whose holdings of each security are too small for portfolio rebalancing and future trading. Portfolio rebalancing is necessary as income generated by the index fund is reinvested and as securities with less than one year remaining to maturity drop out of the index. Additional trading is necessary as well because new Treasury, corporate, and mortgage-backed securities are continuously issued and added to the index. Furthermore, a significant portion of all securities contained in bond indexes are illiquid (i.e., they cannot be purchased readily in the secondary market).

The more practical approach to setting up an index fund is to select a basket of securities whose profile characteristics (such as yield, duration, and convexity) and expected total return match those of the index. Three methodologies are available for selecting and maintaining the appropriate basket: the stratified sampling approach, the optimization approach using linear programming, and the optimization approach using quadratic programming. All three methodologies are widely used.

## Stratified Sampling Method

The stratified sampling method, also known as the "cellular" approach, is the most simple and flexible of the three approaches. In stratified sampling, an index is divided into subsectors; in other words, the index is stratified into cells. The division into subsectors is made on the basis of such parameters as sector, coupon, term-to-maturity, duration, and quality. For example, two parameters can be used to divide the index: sector and term-to-maturity (or weighted average life for mortgage-backed securities). The division by sector stratifies the market index into government, mortgage-backed, corporate, and Yankee securities. The division by term-to-maturity stratifies the market index into securities with terms-to-maturity of, say, 1 to 5 years, 5 to 10 years, and greater than 10 years.

Alternatively, a market index can be divided into detailed subsectors. Using the same parameters as before, notably sector and term-to-maturity, the division by sector could stratify the market index into Treasuries and agencies instead of government securities; Ginnie Maes, Fannie Maes, Freddie Macs, and their 15-year original issue counterparts (Midgets, Dwarfs, Gnomes, and non-Gnome 15-year FHLMCs), and project loans instead of mortgage-backed securities; industrial, utility, telephone, finance, and transportation securities instead of corporate securities; and Canadian, World Bank, sovereign, and supranational securities instead of Yankee securities. The division by term-to-maturity could stratify the market index into, say, two-year intervals where the first interval includes all securities with terms-to-maturity of between one and three years. A commonly used division by term-to-maturity stratifies the market index into two- or three-year intervals for the first 10 years (1 to 3 years, 3 to 5 years, 5 to 7 years, and 7 to 10 years), and 5-year intervals thereafter (10 to 15 years, 15 to 20 years, 20 to 25 years, and greater than 25 years).

The stratification of the index is followed by the selection of securities to represent each cell. Securities are chosen such that the profile characteristics and the expected total return of each "sample" of securities representing a particular cell match the average characteristics and expected total return of all securities in that cell. Each cell may be treated differently. In some cases, the average characteristics of the cell are matched; in other cases, cells that account for a large percentage of the index may themselves be stratified further into "subcells." And still in other cases, cells that represent a nominal percentage of the index may be omitted from the index fund altogether. Of the factors that determine the number of cells and subcategories in an index fund, the size of the fund is the most critical. A large asset size enables the index-fund advisor to divide the benchmark into a greater number of cells and to select securities to represent most of the cells in the index.

The process of setting up an index fund is complete when all cells in the index have been replicated (directly through matching average characteristics or indirectly after further stratification) or eliminated from the index fund (because they represent only a nominal percentage of the index).

As noted earlier, one of the key advantages of the stratified-sampling approach is its simplicity. Stratifying an index into cells and selecting securities to represent each cell does not require sophisticated index-related analytical systems, extensive databases on security prices and dealer inventory, or even strong quantitative expertise. And unlike the linear programming and quadratic programming approaches, stratified sampling relies on portfolio management expertise to appropriately stratify the index, to eliminate unnecessary cells, to substitute one cell for another, and to select a basket of securities that will closely track the index.

Another important advantage of stratified sampling is its flexibility. This methodology is equally effective with all types of indexes. Thus, stratified sampling is as effective with a mortgage-backed securities index fund as it is with a Treasury securities index fund.

Similarly, stratified sampling is equally useful for managing a passive "vanilla" index fund as well as for an actively managed enhanced index fund. For example, securities in an actively managed enhanced index fund are often traded on a continuous basis. In stratified sampling, securities in a cell can be easily swapped without affecting the structure of the index fund.

Finally, stratified sampling lends itself to the use of securities that are not included in the index. Securities with complex structures such as derivative mortgage-backed securities can be substituted for generic mortgage-backed securities in an enhanced index fund.

Its simplicity and flexibility notwithstanding, stratified sampling does have certain shortcomings. Stratified sampling is labor intensive. An index-fund advisor must determine the ideal cellular structure for an index based on the size of portfolio and type of benchmark. The advisor must then evaluate the trade-offs between eliminating some cells and including others, and then the advisor must select securities for each cell while controlling the overall characteristics of the index fund. Such investment decisions require both time and experience in managing index funds.

Stratified sampling also may not result in an optimal portfolio. A portfolio is optimal when it achieves the highest yield and greatest convexity for a given portfolio structure with respect to parameters such as maturity, coupon, quality, sector, and call exposure. An index fund that has a higher yield and equal convexity (or equal yield and greater convexity) will outperform its benchmark over time given the same portfolio structure. But it is difficult, if not impossible, for an index-fund advisor using only stratified sampling to implement the optimal trade-offs between the yield and convexity of all securities held in the index fund (or of all those offered in the market) while maintaining the target portfolio structure.

## Optimization Approach Using Linear Programming

The key shortcomings of stratified sampling can be overcome through a more systematic and mechanistic approach. The optimization approach to indexing based on linear programming is one such comprehensive technique. This optimization approach is, in fact, a more disciplined and quantitative extension of stratified sampling.

In this approach, the goal is to maximize the likelihood that an index fund will closely track an index by allocating a finite amount of dollars among the thousands of fixed income securities available in the fixed income market. The linear programming problem is formulated by specifying three components: an objective function that, when maximized, increases the likelihood that an index fund will closely track its benchmark; a set of constraints that incorporate the target cellular structure of an index fund; and a universe of securities from which a basket of securities can be selected.

The parameter represented by the objective function can vary among different optimization problems. Objective functions based on yield measures are the most widely used. In some problems, either the par or the market-value-weighted yield-to-maturity is maximized. Some optimizations may maximize the par or the market-value-weighted effective yield to account for the call/put exposure of corporate securities and prepayment exposure of mortgage-backed securities. And still in other instances, a par or alternatively a market value-weighted adjusted yield may be maximized; the yield adjustments are designed to account for the factors specific to each security including the amount outstanding of each security, sinking-fund or special redemption features, coupon levels, and liquidity premiums. Objective functions may also be based on the expected return of the portfolio, given a probability weighting of different interest-rate scenarios, or on the par or the market-value-weighted convexity of the portfolio. These parameters typically are used when the index-fund advisor anticipates a particular change in the level or in the volatility of interest rates.

The second component that must be specified is a set of constraints. The majority of constraints in the optimization problem define the cellular structure of the index fund. Say, for example, 17.14 percent of the index is represented by one cell containing all Treasury securities with maturities of less than three years. This percentage share is matched in the index fund by using a constraint specifying that the market-value weighting in the index fund of all Treasury securities with maturities of less than three years must equal 17.14 percent.

Since constraints with exact percentages are too restrictive, most optimization problems specify a range for the market-value weight of each cell. In the above example, two constraints can be used to specify an upper and lower bound for the range—say, 18.8 percent and 15.4 percent, respectively—such that the market value of the cell is greater than or equal to 15.4 percent and less than or equal to 18.8 percent.

Additional constraints are used to match certain portfolio parameters with those of the index. The effective duration of the portfolio is the key parameter that is constrained within a very narrow range of the effective duration of the index. Other parameters include average coupon, maturity, and quality.

Some constraints are used to implement an index-fund advisor's concerns about diversification or about extensive exposure to certain sectors of the market. For example, holdings in corporate securities from one issuer can be constrained to a certain percentage of the portfolio to minimize the index fund's exposure to any single issuer.

The third component to be specified is the universe of securities from which the optimization model can select issues. This universe is critical to the worthiness of the portfolio selected by the optimization model; if the securities selected by the optimization model are not valued correctly or cannot be found at or near prices indicated in the portfolio, the value of the results of the optimization model is significantly reduced.

Pricing and availability difficulties may be partially addressed by reducing the number of securities in the universe. For example, securities below a certain issue size or those issued before a given issue date may be eliminated from the universe. Similarly, securities that are particularly illiquid, based on recent trading volume observed by broker/dealers, also may be dropped.

The optimization approach based on linear programming offers three major advantages. First, this optimization approach is systematic and comprehensive. The optimization model can be run easily on a regular basis, using the same objective function and set of constraints. The model can ensure that all appropriate cells are filled and their characteristics matched. Second, the optimization approach searches through an entire universe of securities to select the optimal combination that will provide the highest yield and convexity for a given portfolio structure. Third, the optimization approach enables an investment advisor with little or no index-fund management expertise and resources to readily acquire some index-fund management capabilities through access to such a model.

Still, while a skillful formulation of the optimization problem overcomes some of the shortcomings of stratified sampling, the optimization approach based on linear programming has its disadvantages.

One major disadvantage of the optimization approach is the broad impact of the objective function. If an objective function is specified so as to maximize effective yield, the model will seek to maximize the effective yield of every cell, irrespective of an index-fund advisor's preference to implement a yield tilt only for particular cells.

A second disadvantage of the optimization approach is the high correlation between the quality of the portfolio selected by the model and the quality of the database specified as the universe. As mentioned earlier, most publicly available fixed income databases have neither accurate data on call, put, and sinking-fund features of particular securities nor reliable prices. Furthermore, when the prices are reliable, the availability of many of the securities in the secondary market at these prices is not at all certain. Of course, one recourse would be to use as substitutes other available securities with similar characteristics; however, as an index-fund advisor starts to substitute securities and adjust prices to reflect market valuation of securities, the advisor is, in effect, moving away from a true optimization approach and toward stratified sampling.

Another recourse would be to work with dealers who offer smaller databases (containing only their own inventories or securities they believe are available in the secondary market) in order to circumvent this pricing and availability problem. The key disadvantage of such databases is the requisite reliance on one dealer who offers only house inventory or securities that can be located and re-sold at a profit. Securities available through another dealer at lower prices are therefore excluded from the portfolio.

Finally, optimization does not lend itself to partial rebalancing of an index fund or to security swaps as readily as stratified sampling. In a true optimization, an index-fund advisor cannot rebalance a particular sector of the index fund and ignore other sectors. If the mortgage-backed securities held in an index fund experience high prepayments, the additional cash generated by the mortgage-backed sector can only be reinvested by re-optimizing and rebalancing the entire portfolio. If such re-optimization is not performed, the index fund advisor again is moving towards stratified sampling.

## Optimization Approach Using Quadratic Programming

A third approach to indexing is the optimization approach using quadratic programming. This approach, also known as variance minimization, is the most complex of the three methodologies. In variance minimization, the objective is to select a basket of securities that will maximize expected return of the portfolio while minimizing the difference between the expected total return of the portfolio and that of its benchmark.

The variance minimization problem consists of three components: an objective function, a set of constraints, and a universe of securities. However, unlike linear programming, the objective function plays a far more significant role than the constraints in determining the structure of the portfolio. Also, the objective function is of quadratic rather than linear form. In variance minimization, the objective function maximizes utility where utility is defined as the difference between the expected return of an index fund and the risk of the index fund, where risk is a function of the difference between the expected return of the index fund and the expected return of the index.

In this approach, an index-fund advisor determines the optimal trade-off between higher expected return and lower risk by specifying a risk-aversion factor. A low risk-aversion factor reduces the importance of tracking the returns of a benchmark for the benefit of higher expected return, whereas a high risk-aversion factor trades off portfolio return for greater tracking of the returns of the benchmark.

The linchpin of the variance minimization approach is a risk-factor model that determines both the expected return of the index portfolio as well as the variance of expected excess return.[1]  Risk-factor models consist of, among other things, a valuation model for pricing each bond in the opportunity set. Every bond is valued based on its exposure to two types of factors: (1) interest-rates and interest-rate-related factors described as term-structure factors and (2) characteristic factors such as market sector, credit quality, coupon level, issue size, and call exposure.

The most important advantage of variance minimization relative to the linear programming and stratified sampling approaches to indexing is the use of the variance-covariance matrix. Discount factors and characteristic factors are correlated, and variance minimization is the only approach that exploits this correlation in selecting a basket of securities. If two securities are highly correlated yet fall into different cells in the stratified sampling approach and satisfy different constraints in the linear programming approach, the linear programming and stratified sampling methodologies may select both securities. Variance minimization, on the other hand, is less likely to select two highly correlated securities; it is more likely to choose a second security that will diversify issue-specific risk in the index fund.

Another advantage of variance minimization is the ability to measure the contribution to tracking error of each selected security. An index fund advisor can examine and evaluate the role each security is expected to play in minimizing tracking error and trade off the low contribution to tracking error of some selected securities for attractive features in other available securities. Of course, while securities can be substituted, it is important to note that the integrity of the initial optimal portfolio is violated; in fact, as more securities are substituted, the index fund advisor moves increasingly away from variance minimization.

---

[1] Much of the early development of fixed income risk-factor models was undertaken by BARRA, a fixed income and equity-consulting and software firm in California.

Variance minimization does have its shortcomings. One important shortcoming is the dependence of the risk factor model on historical data. The variance-covariance matrix and the variance of the discount and characteristic factors are based on historical estimates for those factors. Often, more recent data is assigned a greater weighting than older data. Nevertheless, given the volatility and dynamic structure of the fixed income market, historical estimates are not always good indicators of the future behavior of discount and characteristic factors.

A second problem associated with variance minimization is the accuracy of the bond-valuation model when data for particular characteristic factors is limited. When the market's valuation of a characteristic factor has been derived from a handful of securities, the estimate for the market's valuation may not be reliable.

Finally, while the complexities of variance minimization and its bond valuation and risk factor model can be explained, the rationale for the selection of individual securities by the optimization model in a specific index fund is somewhat obscure. In stratified sampling, securities are selected because they fall into a particular cell and are cheaper (or have certain attributes that make them more attractive) than alternative securities that also fall into the same cell. Similarly, in the linear-programming approach, if the objective function maximizes yield, securities are selected because they meet all the constraints while having the highest yield. In variance minimization, however, an intricate pattern of variances and covariances determine which security is selected. While the value of the variances and covariances for each selected security can be examined, the selection of one security over another is a function of many relationships that an index fund advisor cannot readily identify and isolate. Given such complexity, the ability of an index fund advisor to measure the full implications of swapping securities in the index fund is limited to evaluating each security's contribution to tracking error.

## IMPLICATIONS FOR THE FIXED INCOME MARKET

Increased use of bond indexing has had and will continue to have a far-reaching impact on the fixed income market. Already, the number of investment advisors providing index-fund management services has grown tenfold between 1980 and 1990; Wall Street broker/dealers have introduced dozens of bond indexes including broad market benchmarks and subsector benchmarks; and the number of firms providing analytical systems for indexing has increased.

As indexing continues to grow, profit margins throughout the investment community will be squeezed. Investment advisors increasingly will be forced to accept lower management fees; financial consultants will be retained less frequently to conduct searches for new investment advisors; and the broker/dealer community will face the tightening of bid-ask price spreads. At the same time, short-term market volatility and trading volume will decline with lower portfolio turnover and the absence of "market timing" trades in index funds. Ultimately, increased indexing will lead to a significant shake-out among investment advisors. The beneficiaries of such a shake-out will be firms with large assets as well as established specialty boutiques, and the casualties will be smaller organizations without extensive resources or particular niches.

# CHAPTER 42

## BOND IMMUNIZATION: AN ASSET LIABILITY OPTIMIZATION STRATEGY

*Peter E. Christensen*
Managing Director and Manager
Mortgage & Fixed Income Research Departments
PaineWebber, Incorporated

*Frank J. Fabozzi, Ph.D., CFA*
Visiting Professor of Finance
Sloan School of Management
Massachusetts Institute of Technology
and
Editor, The Journal of Portfolio Management

*Anthony LoFaso, Ph.D.*
First Vice President and Manager
Portfolio Strategies Group
Fixed Income Research
PaineWebber, Incorporated

The purpose of this chapter is to review the mechanics and applications of the bond immunization strategy. In the first section, we define immunization as a duration-matching strategy, then compare it to maturity-matching as an alternative approach to locking in rates. To hedge the reinvestment risk present in maturity-matching, we then explain the single-period immunization strategy and the rebalancing procedures that accompany it. Following single-period immunization, we discuss multiperiod immunization and its applications for the pension, insurance, and thrift markets. Lastly, we review the recent variations on the strategy, including combination matching, contingent immunization, immunization with futures, and immunization with options.

## WHAT IS AN IMMUNIZED PORTFOLIO?

Single-period immunization is usually defined as locking in a fixed rate of return over a prespecified horizon, such as locking in a 10 percent return for a five-year period. It can also be defined as generating a minimum future value at the end of a specified horizon, such as generating $100 million from a $50 million investment five years earlier. With multiperiod immunization, the horizon over which rates are locked in is extended to include multiple periods (such as a schedule of monthly payouts to retirees of a pension plan). Multiperiod immunization is a duration-matching strategy that permits funding of a fixed schedule of multiple future payouts at a minimum cost (such as funding a $500 million schedule of payouts at a cost of $200 million).

The actuary generally credited with pioneering the immunization strategy, F.M. Reddington, defined immunization in 1952 as "the investment of the assets in such a way that the existing business is immune to a general change in the rate of interest." [1] He also specified a condition for immunization: The average duration of assets must be set equal to the average duration of the liabilities. He thought that by matching the durations of assets and liabilities he would then immunize a portfolio from the effects of small changes in interest rates. By matching durations on both sides of the balance sheet, he felt that assets and liabilities would be equally price sensitive to changes in the general level of interest rates. For any change in yield, both sides of the ledger should be equally affected; therefore, the relative values of assets and liabilities would not be changed.

Much later, Lawrence Fisher and Roman Weil defined an immunized portfolio as follows: [2]

> A portfolio of investments is immunized for a holding period if its value at the end of the holding period, regardless of the course of rates during the holding period, must be at least as large as it would have been had the interest rate function been constant throughout the holding period.

---

[1] F.M. Reddington, "Review of the Principle of Life-Office Valuations," *Journal of the Institute of Actuaries*, vol. 78, 1952, pp. 286–340.

[2] Lawrence Fisher and Roman Weil, "Coping with the Risk of Interest-Rate Fluctuations: Returns to Bondholders from Naive and Optimal Strategies," *Journal of Business*, October 1971, pp. 408–431.

If the realized return on an investment in bonds is sure to be at least as large as the appropriately computed yield to the horizon, then that investment is immunized.

Fisher and Weil demonstrated that to achieve the immunized result, the average duration of the bond portfolio must be set equal to the remaining time in the planning horizon, and the market value of assets must be greater than or equal to the present value of the liabilities discounted at the internal rate of return of the portfolio.

Before reviewing the logic of this portfolio strategy, let's look at maturity-matching as an early approach to locking in a current level of interest rates.

## MATURITY-MATCHING: THE REINVESTMENT PROBLEM

Suppose that an investor wishes to lock in prevailing interest rates for a 10-year period. Should he or she buy 10-year bonds?

By purchasing 10-year bonds and holding them to maturity, an investor can be certain of receiving all coupon payments over the 10-year period as well as the principal repayment at redemption (assuming that no default occurs). These two sources of income are fixed in dollar amounts. The third and final source of income is the interest earned on the semiannual coupon payments. "Interest on coupon" is not fixed in dollar amounts; rather it depends on the many interest-rate environments at the various times of payment.

A reinvestment problem occurs when the reinvestment of coupon income occurs at rates below the yield-to-maturity of the bond at the time of purchase. Note from Exhibit 42–1 that as interest rates shift instantaneously and remain at the new levels for a 10-year period, the total "holding period" return on a 9 percent par bond due in 10 years will vary considerably. The initial effect will appear in the value of the asset. The immediate result will be a capital gain if rates fall (or loss, if rates rise).

As the holding period increases after a change in rates, the interest-on-coupon component of total return begins to exert a stronger influence. At 10 years, we note that interest on coupon (reinvestment income) exerts a dominance over capital gain (or loss) in determining holding period returns.

Intuitively, we know that these relationships make sense. Capital gains appear instantly, whereas changes in reinvestment rates take time to exert their effect on the total holding period return on a bond.

If rates were to jump immediately from 9 to 15 percent and a capital loss were to appear today, at what point will that capital loss be made up because

**EXHIBIT 42-1**
**Total Return on a 9 Percent Noncallable $1,000 Bond Due in 10 Years and Held Through Various Holding Periods**

| Income Source | Interest Rate at Time of Reinvestment | Holding Period in Years | | | | | |
|---|---|---|---|---|---|---|---|
| | | 1 | 3 | 5 | 6.79* | 9 | 10 |
| Coupon income | 5% | $ 90 | $ 270 | $ 450 | $ 611 | $ 810 | $ 900 |
| Capital gain or loss | | 287 | 234 | 175 | 100 | 39 | 0 |
| Interest-on-interest | | 1 | 17 | 54 | 105 | 191 | 241 |
| Total return | | $ 378 | $ 521 | $ 679 | $ 816 | $1,040 | $1,141 |
| (and yield) | | (37.0%) | (15.0%) | (11.0%) | (9.0%) | (8.5%) | (8.2%) |
| Coupon income | 7 | $ 90 | $ 270 | $ 450 | $ 611 | $ 810 | $ 900 |
| Capital gain or loss | | 132 | 109 | 83 | 56 | 19 | 0 |
| Interest-on-interest | | 2 | 25 | 78 | 149 | 279 | 355 |
| Total return | | $ 224 | $ 404 | $ 611 | $ 816 | $1,108 | $1,255 |
| (and yield) | | (22.0%) | (12.0%) | (10.0%) | (9.0%) | (8.6%) | (8.5%) |
| Coupon income | 9 | $ 90 | $ 270 | $ 450 | $ 611 | $ 810 | $ 900 |
| Capital gain or loss | | 0 | 0 | 0 | 0 | 0 | 0 |
| Interest-on-interest | | 2 | 32 | 103 | 205 | 387 | 495 |
| Total return | | $ 92 | $ 302 | $ 553 | $ 816 | $1,197 | $1,395 |
| (and yield) | | (9.0%) | (9.0%) | (9.0%) | (9.0%) | (9.0%) | (9.0%) |
| Coupon income | 10 | $ 90 | $ 270 | $ 450 | $ 611 | $ 810 | $ 900 |
| Capital gain or loss | | - 112 | - 95 | - 75 | - 56 | - 18 | 0 |
| Interest-on-interest | | 2 | 40 | 129 | 261 | 502 | 647 |
| Total return | | $ 20 | $ 215 | $ 504 | $ 816 | $1,294 | $1,547 |
| (and yield) | | (2.0%) | (6.7%) | (8.5%) | (9.0%) | (9.7%) | (9.8%) |

* Duration of a 9 percent bond bought at par and due in 10 years.

**EXHIBIT 42–2**
**"Offsetting Forces" Principle (9 Percent Coupon, 30-Year Maturity Bond, Rates Rise Instantly from 9 Percent to 15 Percent, Reinvestment Rate is 15 Percent).**

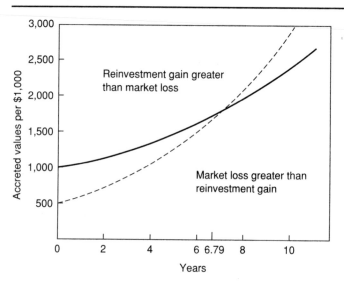

the reinvestment of coupon payments is occurring at a higher (15 percent) rate? As illustrated in Exhibit 42–2, the two "offsetting forces" of market value and reinvestment return equally offset at 6.79 years. This is the duration of the 10-year, 9 percent bond. To earn the original 9 percent target return (the yield-to-maturity at the time of purchase), it is necessary to hold that bond for the period of its duration—6.79 years in our example. If we wish to lock in a market rate of 9 percent for a 10-year period, we would select a bond with a duration of 10 years (not a maturity of 10 years). The maturity for such a par bond in a 9 percent yield environment is roughly 23 years.

From Exhibit 42–1, we note that regardless of the immediate, one-time interest-rate shift, we are still able to earn a 9 percent total return if our holding period is 6.79 years—the duration of the bond. By targeting the duration of a portfolio rather than specific maturities to the prescribed investment horizon of 6.79 years, we see the equal offsets of capital gain with lower reinvestment return occurring in the portfolio. This principle of duration-matching together with rebalancing procedures that are used over time allow us to lock in rates and minimize the reinvestment risk that is associated with the maturity-matching strategy.

# SINGLE-PERIOD IMMUNIZATION

The most straightforward approach to funding a single-period liability five years from today is to purchase a five-year, zero coupon bond maturing on the liability payment date. Regardless of future fluctuations in interest rates, the bond, or portfolio of bonds, will be price insensitive (or immune) to changes in rates as the zero coupon securities mature at par on the payment date. Because zero coupons have durations equal to their maturities, the five-year, zero coupon bonds both cash-match and duration-match the single-period liability payment.

If zero coupon bonds have insufficient yield, a portfolio of *coupon-bearing* Treasury, agency, and corporate bonds can be immunized to fund the same single-period payment only if three conditions are met: (1) the duration of the portfolio of coupon bonds must be set equal to the five-year horizon; (2) the market value of assets must be greater than the present value of liabilities; and (3) the dispersion of the assets must be slightly greater than the dispersion of the liabilities. That is,

1. $\text{Duration}_{Assets}$ $=$ $\text{Duration}_{Liabilities}$
2. $\text{PV}_{Assets}$ $>$ $\text{PV}_{Liabilities}$
3. $\text{Dispersion}_{Assets}$ $>$ $\text{Dispersion}_{Liabilities}$

## The Three Conditions for Immunization

Immunization requires that the average durations of assets and liabilities are set equal at all times. Unfortunately, simple matching of durations is not a sufficient condition.

Consider both a $200,000 par value zero coupon, five-year bond in a 9 percent rate environment and a $1 million five-year single-period liability. Obviously the durations of both the assets and liabilities are matched because they are both zero coupon, five-year obligations. However, a $200,000 par value zero coupon, five-year bond (with a market value of $128,787) cannot realistically compound to $1 million in five years. The required annual rate to compound to $1 million in five years is almost 67 percent. In a 9 percent rate environment, $643,937 is required in market value of assets to compound to $1 million in five years.

Therefore, a second condition for immunization is necessary; the market value of assets must be greater than or equal to the present value of liabilities, using the internal rate of return (IRR) of the assets as the discount factor in present-valuing the liabilities. The assets, when compounded at the "locked-in" immunized rate of 9 percent, will grow to equal or exceed the future value immunized target of $1 million in this example.

To understand the reasons for the third condition for immunization (that the dispersion of assets be greater than or equal to the dispersion of liabilities), it is important to understand the assumptions underlying the Macaulay measure of duration.[3] Since duration is defined as the present value weighted average time to payment on a bond, duration must assume a discount rate (or a series of discount rates) when calculating present value weighted time.

The discount rate assumed in the Macaulay measure of duration is the yield or internal rate of return on the bond or portfolio. By assuming only one discount rate, the Macaulay measure assumes that a flat yield curve prevails at all times, as illustrated in Exhibit 42–3. If rates shift up, say 100 basis points, the Macaulay duration calculation assumes a parallel shift to another flat yield curve 100 basis points higher.

To meet a target duration of 6.79 years as illustrated in Exhibit 42–4a, a portfolio could be constructed as either (1) a barbell of roughly equal amounts of zero- and 13-year duration securities, (2) an even ladder of equal amounts of zero- through 13-year duration securities, or (3) a bullet of only 6.79 year durations. Since the Macaulay duration calculation assumes that a flat yield curve connects every maturity point, the barbell structure incorporates the greatest amount of yield-curve risk by concentrating cash flows on both ends of the curve. If the yield curve is positive or inverted, the barbell structure will violate the assumption of a flat curve more than the even ladder or bullet structure. On the other hand, the bullet structure, by concentrating cash flows at a single maturity point, incorporates a flat slope over the relevant range on the yield curve as shown in Exhibit 42–4b.

For single-period immunization, a bullet maturity structure with tight cash flows around the liability date is generally preferred to an even ladder or barbelled portfolio because of the reduced risk exposure to the yield curve becoming steeper or twisting. In fact, to eliminate the risk of pathological shifts in yields, the investor could tighten the cash flows still further and purchase a zero coupon bond to cash-flow-match the single-period liability. Short of that, a bullet structure is the least risky and the barbell the most risky.

Therefore, for immunization the third condition of controlling the degree of barbelling must be incorporated into the process of structuring a portfolio. The measure used to control the barbelling is dispersion—a measure of the variance of cash flows around the duration date, (D), of a bond. The mathematical formula for dispersion is as follows:[4]

---

[3] See Chapter 7 for an explanation of duration and its properties.

[4] This measure, commonly referred to as $M^2$, was first developed in H. Gifford Fong and Oldrich Vasicek, "A Risk Minimizing Strategy for Multiple Liability Immunization," *Journal of Finance*, December 1984, pp. 1541–1546.

**EXHIBIT 42–3**
**Present Value of Cashflows for Macaulay Duration**

Single Discount rate for all cash flows

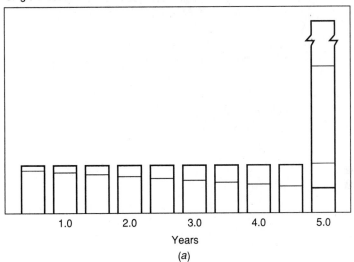

Years

(a)

Yield Curve Assumptions in Macaulay Duration (9 percent, 10-year par bond)

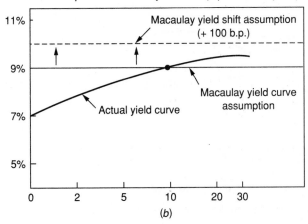

(b)

$$\text{Dispersion} = \frac{\sum (t_i - D)^2 \text{PV(CF}_i)}{\sum \text{PV(CF}_i)}$$

The dispersion of a zero coupon bond therefore is zero, while the dispersion of a 30-year current coupon U.S. Treasury bond can be 80 to 100 years squared, as illustrated in Exhibit 42–5.

**EXHIBIT 42–4**
**Maturity Structures for Portfolios—Target Duration of 6.79 Years**

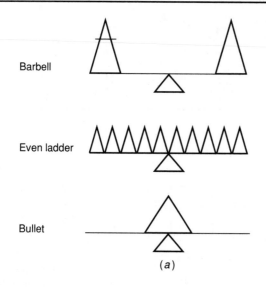

Barbell

Even ladder

Bullet

(a)

U.S. Treasury Zero-Coupon Curve (barbell versus bullet maturity structure)

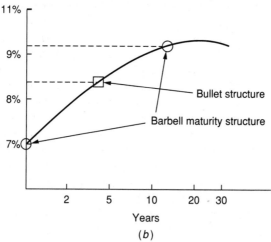

(b)

**EXHIBIT 42–5**
**Dispersions of Selected Issues** (as of May 10, 1989)

| Issuer | Coupon | Maturity | Yield | Duration | Dispersion |
|--------|--------|----------|-------|----------|------------|
| U.S. Treasury Strip | 0 | 05/15/94 | 9.310 | 5.011 | 0.000 |
| U.S. Treasury | 9.500 | 05/15/94 | 9.186 | 4.047 | 2.330 |
| U.S. Treasury | 9.375 | 05/15/96 | 9.199 | 5.226 | 5.130 |
| U.S. Treasury | 9.125 | 05/15/99 | 9.154 | 6.761 | 11.990 |
| U.S. Treasury | 8.875 | 02/15/19 | 9.115 | 10.480 | 78.720 |

## Rebalancing Procedures

As time passes, the single-period immunized portfolio must be rebalanced so that the duration of the portfolio is always reset to the remaining life in the planning period to ensure the offsetting effects of capital gains with reinvestment return. This rebalancing procedure requires that the coupon income, reinvestment income, matured principal, and proceeds from possible liquidation of longer bonds be reinvested into securities that maintain the duration equal to the remaining life in the planning period. Because of the multiple rebalancings required throughout the planning period, the bond portfolio is continually maintained in a duration-matched state and therefore should achieve its target return in spite of periodic shifts in rates.

An immunized bond portfolio, therefore, can be constructed once a time horizon is established. Since duration is inversely related to both the prevailing yields and the coupon rate, it may not be possible to immunize a portfolio beyond a certain number of years using only coupon-bearing securities. For example, when bond market yields reached their historic highs in 1981, it was not possible to immunize a bullet liability beyond seven years in the taxable markets with current coupon securities. In 1989, in an 8 percent rate environment, the maximum lock-up period was closer to 12 years. However, the use of zero coupon securities with long maturities and durations can allow the investor the opportunity to lengthen the planning period over which he or she can lock in rates.

The actual targeted return on an immunized portfolio will depend on the level of interest rates at the time the program is initiated. Though bond values may, for example, decline as interest rates rise, the future value of the portfolio (or security) based on the new higher reinvestment rate and lower principal value should still correspond to the original targeted yield. As we demonstrate later in an actual simulation of an immunized portfolio, duration is the key to controlling the equal offset of reinvestment income with asset value as interest rates fluctuate.

The important point to remember is this: *The standard deviation of return on an immunized portfolio will be much lower over a given horizon than that on a nonimmunized portfolio—whether measured around a sample mean or promised yield.* With interest-rate risk minimized (when held over an assumed time horizon), the performance of the immunized portfolio is virtually assured, regardless of reinvestment rates.

## A SIMULATION OF A SINGLE-PERIOD IMMUNIZED PORTFOLIO[5]

In this section, we will illustrate the mechanics of the immunization rebalancing procedures. The parameters for the analysis are as follows:

1. $50 million is available for investment on May 10, 1989.
2. The investment horizon is five years.
3. Only Treasury notes and bonds are eligible securities for this simulation.
4. The immunized portfolio is rebalanced annually.
5. The yield-curve assumptions used in the simulation are presented in Exhibit 42–6. These yield curves do not represent interest-rate projections. They are used only to subject the immunized portfolio to a wide variety of interest-rate fluctuations over the five-year horizon.
6. A bid-ask spread of 1/8th of a point is assumed on all transactions (1/8th of a point on bond sales, no transaction cost on bond purchases).

The target yield established on May 10, 1989 was 9.285 percent. Exhibit 42–7 presents the following information for the portfolio at the beginning of each year: (1) the individual issues in the portfolio, including par amount, coupon, maturity, price and yield, (2) the duration of each security and of the portfolio, (3) the dispersion of each security and of the portfolio, and (4) the market values plus accrued interest. *Notice that the duration of the portfolio is reset each year in order to match the remaining time in the planning horizon.* Exhibits 42–8 through 42–12 summarize the actual portfolio transactions each year.

The important conclusion to draw from the above simulation is that the target return for the immunized portfolio was achieved, even in the volatile yield environment envisioned in this scenario. We note that from Exhibit 42–8 that the target yield of 9.285 percent and target future value of $78,795,148 were exceeded by 5 basis points and $179,763, respectively.[6]   We demonstrated in this

---

[5] The authors are grateful for the assistance of Susan Fox in the preparation of this analysis and for her constructive comments on the text.

[6] Since the initial investment is $50,051,651 and the target yield is 9.285 percent, the target future value is $(1 + \frac{.09285}{2})^{10} \times \$50,051,651 = \$78,795,148$

**EXHIBIT 42–6**
**Yield-Curve Assumptions**

|  | 05/10/89 | 05/10/90 | 05/10/91 | 05/10/92 | 05/10/93 | 05/10/94 |
|---|---|---|---|---|---|---|
| 1989 | 9.12 | — | — | — | — | — |
| 1990 | 9.21 | 8.00 | — | — | — | — |
| 1991 | 9.28 | 8.00 | 8.94 | — | — | — |
| 1992 | 9.23 | 8.00 | 8.96 | 8.75 | — | — |
| 1993 | 9.23 | 8.00 | 9.00 | 8.77 | 10.50 | — |
| 1994 | 9.22 | 8.00 | 8.98 | 8.85 | 10.42 | 8.00 |
| 1995 | 9.22 | 8.00 | 8.94 | 8.86 | 10.24 | 8.10 |
| 1996 | 9.21 | 8.00 | 8.87 | 8.88 | 9.85 | 8.20 |
| 1997 | 9.18 | 8.00 | 8.75 | 8.90 | 9.70 | 8.30 |
| 1998 | 9.15 | 8.00 | 8.62 | 8.93 | 9.60 | 8.40 |
| 1999 | 9.13 | 8.00 | 8.45 | 8.97 | 9.58 | 8.50 |
| 2000 | 9.13 | 8.00 | | | | |
| 2001 | 9.14 | 8.00 | | | | |
| 2002 | 9.14 | 8.00 | | | | |
| 2003 | 9.15 | 8.00 | | | | |
| 2004 | 9.15 | 8.00 | | | | |
| 2005 | 9.16 | 8.00 | | | | |
| 2006 | 9.16 | 8.00 | | | | |
| 2007 | 9.17 | 8.00 | | | | |

*Short-term reinvestment rate*

| | 8.55% | 8.50% | 8.90% | 9.65% | 9.25% | |

example that targeted rates may be obtained over a predetermined immunization term, in spite of dramatic fluctuations in market yields.


## MULTIPERIOD IMMUNIZATION

In the discussions so far, we have documented how the three conditions are required to create a single-period immunized portfolio. These conditions can be extended to create an immunized portfolio that will satisfy the funding requirements of multiple-period liabilities, such as the monthly payouts to the retired-lives portion of a pension plan.

If a liability schedule were composed of 30 annual payments, it would be possible to create 30 single-period immunized portfolios to fund that schedule. If we then analyzed the overall duration of the 30 asset portfolios, it would equal the duration of the liabilities. As long as the dispersions of assets and liabilities are closely matched and the asset value is greater than the present value

**EXHIBIT 42–7**

**Immunization: Proposed Portfolio of Treasury Securities on May 10, 1989***

| Par Value | Coupon | Maturity | Market Price | Yield | Dispersion | Duration | % of Market | Market Value |
|---|---|---|---|---|---|---|---|---|
| $5,000,000 | 12.625 | 8/15/1994 | 113.46875 | 9.321 | 3.01 | 3.986 | 11.63 | $5,821,659.19 |
| $5,000,000 | 11.250 | 2/15/1995 | 108.43750 | 9.318 | 3.65 | 4.353 | 11.10 | $5,553,953.73 |
| $8,000,000 | 8.875 | 7/15/1995 | 98.06250 | 9.289 | 4.19 | 4.737 | 16.13 | $8,072,513.81 |
| $8,000,000 | 8.625 | 10/15/1995 | 96.84375 | 9.285 | 4.16 | 5.011 | 15.58 | $7,796,516.39 |
| $9,000,000 | 7.375 | 5/15/1996 | 90.37500 | 9.272 | 5.77 | 5.301 | 16.90 | $8,458,290.75 |
| $9,000,000 | 7.250 | 11/15/1996 | 89.21875 | 9.274 | 6.79 | 5.593 | 16.68 | $8,348,727.56 |
| $6,000,000 | 8.500 | 5/15/1997 | 95.84375 | 9.245 | 8.14 | 5.674 | 11.99 | $5,999,989.64 |
| $50,000,000 | 8.840 | 1/03/1996 | 97.20375 | 9.285 | 5.16 | 4.998 | 100.00 | $50,051,651.06 |

* Settlement date is 5/11/89.

**EXHIBIT 42–7—Continued on May 10, 1990\***

| Par Value | Coupon | Maturity | Market Price | Yield | Dispersion | Duration | % of Market | Market Value |
|---|---|---|---|---|---|---|---|---|
| $8,000,000 | 13.125 | 5/15/1994 | 117.29042 | 8.000 | 1.78 | 3.139 | 17.19 | $9,896,631.39 |
| $5,100,000 | 9.500 | 5/15/1994 | 105.05940 | 8.000 | 1.56 | 3.299 | 9.72 | $5,594,925.81 |
| $5,000,000 | 12.625† | 8/15/1994 | 116.40832 | 8.000 | 1.75 | 3.410 | 10.36 | $5,968,637.69 |
| $5,000,000 | 11.250† | 2/15/1995 | 112.64256 | 8.000 | 2.23 | 3.794 | 10.01 | $5,764,206.73 |
| $8,000,000 | 8.875† | 7/15/1995 | 103.63180 | 8.000 | 2.63 | 4.169 | 14.79 | $8,518,057.81 |
| $8,000,000 | 8.625† | 10/15/1995 | 102.69903 | 8.000 | 2.60 | 4.438 | 14.35 | $8,264,938.79 |
| $9,000,000 | 7.375† | 5/15/1996 | 97.06136 | 8.000 | 3.84 | 4.768 | 15.73 | $9,060,063.15 |
| $4,100,000 | 7.250† | 11/15/1996 | 96.24896 | 8.000 | 4.65 | 5.092 | 7.11 | $4,091,547.83 |
| $400,000 | 8.500† | 5/15/1997 | 102.64210 | 8.000 | 5.82 | 5.236 | 0.74 | $427,192.71 |
| $52,600,000 | 9.740† | 5/12/1995 | 106.06953 | 8.003 | 2.60 | 3.996 | 100.00 | $57,586,201.90 |

† Existing issue.
\* Settlement date is 5/11/90.

**EXHIBIT 42-7—Continued on May 10, 1991***

| Par Value | Coupon | Maturity | Market | | | Dispersion | Duration | % of Market | Market Value |
| | | | Price | Yield | | | | | |
|---|---|---|---|---|---|---|---|---|---|
| $8,000,000 | 13.125† | 5/15/1994 | 110.72441 | 8.980 | | 0.91 | 2.465 | 15.46 | $9,371,350.59 |
| $10,000,000 | 13.125 | 5/15/1994 | 110.72441 | 8.980 | | 0.91 | 2.465 | 19.33 | $11,714,188.24 |
| $5,100,000 | 9.500† | 5/15/1994 | 101.34353 | 8.980 | | 0.78 | 2.574 | 8.92 | $5,405,416.44 |
| $1,800,000 | 9.500 | 5/15/1994 | 101.34353 | 8.980 | | 0.78 | 2.574 | 3.15 | $1,907,794.04 |
| $5,000,000 | 12.625† | 8/15/1994 | 110.11641 | 8.970 | | 0.90 | 2.731 | 9.33 | $5,654,042.19 |
| $5,000,000 | 11.250 | 2/15/1995 | 107.25195 | 8.930 | | 1.24 | 3.123 | 9.07 | $5,494,676.23 |
| $8,000,000 | 8.875† | 7/15/1995 | 99.79609 | 8.928 | | 1.54 | 3.485 | 13.55 | $8,211,201.01 |
| $8,000,000 | 8.625† | 10/15/1995 | 98.91768 | 8.923 | | 1.52 | 3.749 | 13.14 | $7,962,430.79 |
| $5,000,000 | 7.375† | 5/15/1996 | 95.05409 | 8.870 | | 2.48 | 4.097 | 8.06 | $4,883,004.92 |
| $55,900,000 | 10.699 | 12/19/1994 | 104.45675 | 8.948 | | 1.22 | 2.998 | 100.00 | $60,604,104.44 |

† Existing issue.
* Settlement date is 5/11/91.

**EXHIBIT 42-7—Continued on May 10, 1992***

| Par Value | Coupon | Maturity | Market Price | Yield | Dispersion | Duration | % of Market | Market Value |
|---|---|---|---|---|---|---|---|---|
| $18,000,000 | 13.125† | 5/15/1994 | 107.71738 | 8.850 | 0.34 | 1.735 | 30.99 | $20,544,416.86 |
| $12,300,000 | 13.125 | 5/15/1994 | 107.71738 | 8.850 | 0.34 | 1.735 | 21.18 | $14,038,684.86 |
| $6,900,000 | 9.500† | 5/15/1994 | 101.17164 | 8.850 | 0.28 | 1.795 | 11.01 | $7,301,389.86 |
| $2,900,000 | 9.500 | 5/15/1994 | 101.17164 | 8.850 | 0.28 | 1.795 | 4.63 | $3,068,700.09 |
| $5,000,000 | 12.625† | 8/15/1994 | 107.55296 | 8.853 | 0.33 | 1.995 | 8.34 | $5,526,789.48 |
| $5,000,000 | 11.250† | 2/15/1995 | 105.72184 | 8.858 | 0.54 | 2.405 | 8.17 | $5,418,990.35 |
| $8,000,000 | 8.875† | 7/15/1995 | 100.01049 | 8.863 | 0.75 | 2.761 | 12.41 | $8,229,053.49 |
| $2,200,000 | 7.375† | 5/15/1996 | 95.01125 | 8.880 | 1.41 | 3.401 | 3.27 | $2,169,589.53 |
| $60,300,000 | 11.565† | 8/30/1994 | 104.98841 | 8.857 | 0.43 | 2.003 | 100.00 | $66,297,614.52 |

† Existing issue.
* Settlement date is 5/11/1992.

**EXHIBIT 42–7—Continued on May 10, 1993***

| Par Value | Coupon | Maturity | Market | | | | Duration | % of Market | Market Value |
|---|---|---|---|---|---|---|---|---|---|
| | | | Price | Yield | Dispersion | | | | |
| $30,300,000 | 13.125† | 5/15/1994 | 102.53007 | 10.420 | 0.07 | | 0.922 | 46.37 | $33,011,105.34 |
| $10,200,000 | 13.125 | 5/15/1994 | 102.53007 | 10.420 | 0.07 | | 0.922 | 15.61 | $11,112,649.32 |
| $9,800,000 | 9.500† | 5/15/1994 | 99.13563 | 10.420 | 0.05 | | 0.943 | 14.28 | $10,170,504.45 |
| $5,800,000 | 9.500 | 5/15/1994 | 99.13563 | 10.420 | 0.05 | | 0.943 | 8.45 | $6,019,278.14 |
| $5,000,000 | 12.625† | 8/15/1994 | 102.56533 | 10.375 | 0.06 | | 1.177 | 7.41 | $5,276,488.19 |
| $5,000,000 | 11.250† | 2/15/1995 | 101.48722 | 10.285 | 0.16 | | 1.613 | 7.31 | $5,206,439.73 |
| $400,000 | 8.875† | 7/15/1995 | 97.48937 | 10.175 | 0.27 | | 1.970 | 0.56 | $401,333.17 |
| $66,500,000 | 12.070 | 6/13/1994 | 101.62770 | 10.403 | 0.07 | | 1.002 | 100.00 | $71,197,798.34 |

† Existing issue.
* Settlement date is 5/11/93.

**EXHIBIT 42-7—Concluded on May 15, 1994***

| Par Value | Coupon | Maturity‡ | Market | | Dispersion | Duration | % of | Market Value |
| | | | Price | Yield | | | Market | |
|---|---|---|---|---|---|---|---|---|
| $40,500,000 | 13.125† | 5/15/1994 | 100.05091 | 8.000 | 0.00 | 0.011 | 72.54 | $43,119,694.86 |
| $15,600,000 | 9.500† | 5/15/1994 | 100.01246 | 8.000 | 0.00 | 0.011 | 27.46 | $16,326,568.07 |
| $56,100,000 | 12.117 | 5/14/1994 | 100.04022 | 8.113 | 0.00 | 0.011 | 100.00 | $59,446,262.93 |

† Existing issue.
‡ Note that on May 15, 1994 both securities mature.
* Settlement date is 5/11/94.

**EXHIBIT 42–8**
**Bond Immunization Year-End Transactions (May 10, 1990)**

| 1. Cash Received During Year: | Coupon Income | | Interest on Coupon | | Matured Principal | |
|---|---|---|---|---|---|---|
| | $4,420,000 | + | 221,145 | + | 0 | |
| | | | | | Total Cash Received | |
| **Plus** | Cash Carryover | | Interest on Cash Carryover | | | |
| | 0 | + | 0 | + | = | $4,641,145 |

| 2. Sell: | Par (000) | Coupon | Maturity | Yield | Price | Market Value |
|---|---|---|---|---|---|---|
| | 4,900 | 7,250 | 11/15/96 | 8.000 | 96.24896 | $4,889,898 |
| | 5,600 | 8,500 | 5/15/97 | 8.000 | 102.64210 | 5,980,698 |

Less transaction costs − 13,125

$10,857,472

| 3. Available to Reinvest: | $15,498,617 |
|---|---|

| 4. Buy: | Par (000) | Coupon | Maturity | Yield | Price | Market Value |
|---|---|---|---|---|---|---|
| | 8,500 | 13.125 | 5/15/94 | 8.00 | 117.29042 | $9,896,631 |
| | 5,100 | 9.500 | 5/15/94 | 8.00 | 105.05940 | 5,594,926 |

Cash carryover = ($15,498,617 − 15,491,557) = $7,060

**EXHIBIT 42–9**
**Bond Immunization Year-End Transactions (May 10, 1991)**

| 1. Cash Received During Year: | Coupon Income | | Interest on Coupon | | Matured Principal | |
|---|---|---|---|---|---|---|
| | $5,123,250 | + | 264,615 | + | 0 | |
| | Cash Carryover | | Interest on Cash Carryover | | Total Cash Received | |
| **Plus** | 7,060 | + | 611 | = | $5,395,536 | |

| 2. Sell: | Par (000) | Coupon | Maturity | Yield | Price | Market Value |
|---|---|---|---|---|---|---|
| | 4,000 | 7,375 | 5/15/96 | 8.870 | 94.05409 | $3,906,404 |
| | 4,100 | 7,250 | 11/15/96 | 8.810 | 93.30149 | 3,970,701 |
| | 400 | 8,500 | 5/15/96 | 8.750 | 98.84839 | 412,018 |
| | | | | **Less transaction costs** | – | 10,625 |
| | | | | | | $8,278,498 |

| 3. Available to Reinvest: | $13,674,034 |
|---|---|

| 4. Buy: | Par (000) | Coupon | Maturity | Yield | Price | Market Value |
|---|---|---|---|---|---|---|
| | 10,000 | 13.125 | 5/15/94 | 8.980 | 110.72441 | $11,714,188 |
| | 1,800 | 9.500 | 5/15/94 | 8.980 | 101.34353 | 1,907,794 |

Cash carryover = ($13,674,034 – 13,621,982) = $52,052

**EXHIBIT 42-10**
**Bond Immunization Year-End Transactions (May 10, 1992)**

**1. Cash Received During Year:**

| Coupon Income | | Interest on Coupon | | Matured Principal |
|---|---|---|---|---|
| $5,980,500 | + | 334,386 | + | 0 |

**Plus**

| Cash Carryover | | Interest on Cash Carryover | | Total Cash Received |
|---|---|---|---|---|
| 52,052 | + | 4,722 | = | $6,371,660 |

**2. Sell:**

| Par (000) | Coupon | Maturity | Yield | Price | Market Value |
|---|---|---|---|---|---|
| 8,000 | 8.625 | 10/15/95 | 8.868 | 99.28347 | $7,991,694 |
| 2,800 | 7.375 | 5/15/96 | 8.880 | 95.01125 | 2,761,296 |
| | | | | **Less transaction costs** | − 13,500 |
| | | | | | $10,739,490 |

**3. Available to Reinvest:** $17,111,150

**4. Buy:**

| Par (000) | Coupon | Maturity | Yield | Price | Market Value |
|---|---|---|---|---|---|
| 12,300 | 13.125 | 5/15/94 | 8.850 | 107.71738 | $14,038,685 |
| 2,900 | 9.500 | 5/15/94 | 8.850 | 101.17164 | 3,068,700 |

**Cash carryover** = ($17,111,150 − 17,107,385) = $3,765

## EXHIBIT 42–11
## Bond Immunization Year-End Transactions (May 10, 1993)

| 1. Cash Received During Year: | Coupon Income | | Interest on Coupon | | Matured Principal | |
|---|---|---|---|---|---|---|
| | $6,973,875 | + | 463,340 | + | 0 | |
| **Plus** | Cash Carryover | | Interest on Cash Carryover | | Total Cash Received | |
| | 3,765 | + | 371 | = | $7,441,351 | |

| 2. Sell: | Par (000) | Coupon | Maturity | Yield | Price | Market Value |
|---|---|---|---|---|---|---|
| | 7,600 | 8.875 | 7/15/95 | 10.175 | 97.48937 | $7,625,330 |
| | 2,200 | 7.375 | 5/15/96 | 9.850 | 93.68181 | 2,140,331 |
| | | | | | Less transaction costs – | 12,250 |
| | | | | | | $9,753,412 |

| 3. Available to Reinvest: | | | | | | |
|---|---|---|---|---|---|---|

| 4. Buy: | Par (000) | Coupon | Maturity | Yield | Price | Market Value |
|---|---|---|---|---|---|---|
| | 10,200 | 13.125 | 5/15/94 | 10.420 | 102.53007 | $11,112,649 |
| | 5,800 | 9.500 | 5/15/94 | 10.420 | 99.13563 | 6,019,278 |
| | Cash carryover = | ($17,194,763 – 17,131,927) = | | | | $62,836 |

**EXHIBIT 42–12**

**Bond Immunization Year-End Transactions** (May 15, 1994)

| 1. Cash Received Through 5/10/94: | Coupon Income | | Interest on Coupon | | Matured Principal |
|---|---|---|---|---|---|
| | $8,026,875 | + | 527,719 | + | 0 |
| **Plus** | Cash Carryover | | Interest on Cash Carryover | | Total Cash Received |
| | 62,836 | + | 5,929 | = | $8,623,359 |
| 2. Income from 5/10/94 – 5/15/94 | Coupon Income | | Interest on Coupon | | Matured Principal |
| | $3,398,812 | + | 0 | + | $56,100,000 |
| | | Total cash received (1 + 2) | | = | $68,122,171 |

| 3. Sell: | Par (000) | Coupon | Maturity | Yield | Price | Market Value |
|---|---|---|---|---|---|---|
| | 5,000 | 12.625 | 8/15/94 | 8.025 | 101.13270 | $5,204,857 |
| | 5,000 | 11.250 | 2/15/95 | 8.075 | 102.28331 | 5,246,244 |
| | 400 | 8.875 | 7/15/95 | 8.117 | 100.81621 | 414,640 |
| | | | | **Less transaction costs** | − | 13,000 |
| | | | | | | $10,852,741 |

| 4. Mature: 5/15/94 | Par (000) | Coupon | Maturity value & coupon |
|---|---|---|---|
| | 40,500 | 13.125 | $43,119,695 |
| | 15,600 | 9.500 | 16,326,568 |
| | | | $59,446,263 |

| 5. Final Value: | $78,974,912 |
|---|---|

of liabilities, then the liability schedule should be fully funded and the portfolio immunized.

For example, the same retired-lives payout schedule for a pension fund that will be used in the next chapter on the dedicated bond portfolio is also presented in Exhibit 42–13. The set payouts are summarized in annual amounts, but in practice they are generally converted into monthly numbers (by dividing the annual payouts into 12 equal payments).

Calculating the duration of multiperiod liabilities is not as straightforward as calculating the duration of a single-period liability, where the remaining time in the planning horizon is the liability duration. With multiple payout periods, the liability duration is derived by using, as the discount factor, the internal rate of return (IRR) on the assets. Of course, the IRR of the assets is not determinable unless we know the precise portfolio, its duration and dispersion.

As a result of this simultaneity problem, the construction of an immunized portfolio is an iterative process whereby an IRR guess for the portfolio is ad-

**EXHIBIT 42–13**
**Retired-Lives Payout Schedule for a Pension**
**Fund: Multiperiod Immunization**
**Illustration**

| Period Ending | Liability Payments |
|---|---|
| 12/31/89 (partial year @ $15MM) | $ 8,750,000 |
| 12/31/90 | 14,916,015 |
| 12/31/91 | 14,427,473 |
| 12/31/92 | 13,445,985 |
| 12/31/93 | 12,435,248 |
| 12/31/94 | 11,754,199 |
| 12/31/95 | 11,384,959 |
| 12/31/96 | 11,028,026 |
| 12/31/97 | 10,654,684 |
| 12/31/98 | 10,408,523 |
| 12/31/99 | 10,355,190 |
| 12/31/00 | 10,236,214 |
| 12/31/01 | 9,953,126 |
| 12/31/02 | 9,670,039 |
| 12/31/03 | 9,302,164 |
| 12/31/04 | 8,748,308 |
| 12/31/05 | 8,621,160 |
| 12/31/06 | 8,209,594 |
| 12/31/07 | 7,893,578 |
| 12/31/08 | 7,435,436 |
| 12/31/09 | 6,993,713 |
| 12/31/10 | 6,579,349 |
| 12/31/11 | 6,145,834 |
| 12/31/12 | 5,732,824 |
| 12/31/13 | 5,322,551 |
| 12/31/14 | 4,983,398 |
| 12/31/15 | 4,615,526 |
| 12/31/16 | 4,257,221 |
| 12/31/17 | 3,892,088 |
| 12/31/18 | 3,537,881 |
| 12/31/19 | 3,216,510 |
| 12/31/20 | 2,934,788 |
| 12/31/21 | 2,659,900 |
| 12/31/22 | 2,385,026 |
| 12/31/23 | 2,123,504 |
| 12/31/24 | 1,447,297 |
| Total | $ 276,457,331 |

**EXHIBIT 42–14**
**Multiperiod Immunization Proposed Portfolio** (May 10, 1989)

| Issue Name | Par Value | Credit | | Coupon | Maturity | Market Price | Yield |
|---|---|---|---|---|---|---|---|
| ARKLA, INC. | $2,500,000 | A3 | /BBB+ | 8.900 | 12/15/2006 | 92.24200 | 9.83 |
| BANKAMERICA | $1,000,000 | A3 | /BBB | 8.750 | 5/01/2001 | 89.15800 | 10.35 |
| BANKAMERICA | $1,000,000 | A3 | /BBB | 8.350 | 5/15/2007 | 84.17400 | 10.30 |
| BANQ NAT PARIS | $4,600,000 | AA1 | /AA | 9.875 | 5/25/1998 | 99.50200 | 9.96 |
| BENEFICIAL CORP | $2,400,000 | A3 | /A | 7.500 | 5/15/1998 | 84.98400 | 10.08 |
| BENEFICIAL CORP | $2,500,000 | A3 | /A | 8.400 | 12/01/2007 | 86.36600 | 10.03 |
| CHASE MANHATTAN | $5,000,000 | BAA2/A− | | 10.000 | 6/15/1999 | 99.27900 | 10.11 |
| CITICORP | $2,000,000 | A1 | /AA | 8.450 | 3/15/2007 | 87.19700 | 10.00 |
| CITICORP | $2,000,000 | A1 | /AA | 8.125 | 7/01/2007 | 84.42800 | 10.00 |
| FED HOME LOAN | $6,500,000 | AGY | /AGY | 8.100 | 3/25/1996 | 92.09375 | 9.70 |
| FHLMC | $2,400,000 | AGY | /AGY | 8.125 | 9/30/1996 | 91.84375 | 9.69 |
| FLORIDA POWER | $2,000,000 | AA3 | /A+ | 8.000 | 12/01/2003 | 86.09400 | 9.81 |
| GMAC | $2,700,000 | AA3 | /AA− | 8.125 | 10/15/1996 | 89.85200 | 10.10 |
| GMAC | $9,900,000 | AA3 | /AA− | 8.250 | 4/01/2016 | 85.09400 | 9.83 |
| HOUSEHOLD FIN. | $2,500,000 | A1 | /AA− | 7.500 | 10/01/1997 | 85.89200 | 10.03 |
| HOUSEHOLD FIN. | $1,100,000 | A1 | /AA− | 7.750 | 10/01/1999 | 86.06900 | 9.93 |
| HOUSEHOLD FIN. | $4,800,000 | A1 | /AA− | 8.200 | 9/15/2007 | 85.85400 | 9.88 |
| HOUSTON L&P | $3,000,000 | A3 | /BBB+ | 8.125 | 2/01/2004 | 84.92000 | 10.11 |
| HOUSTON L&P | $5,000,000 | A3 | /BBB+ | 8.375 | 10/01/2007 | 85.21400 | 10.17 |
| JERSEY BELL | $2,400,000 | AAA | /AAA | 8.000 | 9/15/2016 | 84.43100 | 9.62 |
| NIPPON TEL. | $1,000,000 | AAA | /AAA | 9.500 | 7/27/1998 | 97.82900 | 9.86 |
| OKLAHOMA G&E | $2,000,000 | AA2 | /AA | 8.250 | 8/15/2016 | 85.57700 | 9.77 |
| PACIFIC GAS | $5,000,000 | A1 | /A | 7.500 | 6/01/2004 | 81.99600 | 9.81 |
| PENN. P&L | $5,000,000 | BAA3/A− | | 8.250 | 12/01/2006 | 87.00400 | 9.82 |
| PUB SVCE E&G | $5,000,000 | A1 | /AA | 8.250 | 6/01/2007 | 86.86300 | 9.82 |
| SALLIE MAE | $1,000,000 | AGY | /AGY | 7.750 | 12/29/1996 | 89.50000 | 9.73 |
| SALLIE MAE | $25,000,000 | AGY | /AGY | 0.000 | 5/15/2014 | 9.43750 | 9.67 |
| SOC GEN | $5,000,000 | AA1 | /AA | 9.875 | 7/15/2003 | 99.73500 | 9.91 |
| SOUTHWEST BELL | $5,000,000 | AA3 | /AA− | 8.250 | 3/01/2014 | 85.88600 | 9.77 |
| TSY | $22,100,000 | TSY | /TSY | 8.500 | 9/30/1990 | 98.81250 | 9.42 |
| | $141,400,000 | AA1 | /AA+ | 6.952 | 8/05/2002 | 76.29411 | 9.86 |

\* YTC calculation for currently callable bonds assumes call on next coupon date.
† Yield to call exceeds 100 percent.

vanced; the durations and dispersion of the liabilities are then calculated based on the IRR guess; an optimal immunized portfolio is simulated to match the duration and dispersion estimates; the portfolio IRR is then compared with the estimated IRR, and, if they differ, a new IRR estimate is advanced and the procedure repeated.

Using the same portfolio constraints assumed in the dedicated portfolio,[7] a final multiperiod immunized portfolio is represented in Exhibit 42–14. Note that

---

[7] See Chapter 43 for an explanation of the portfolio constraints used in the dedicated portfolio simulation.

| | | Call Information | | | | | |
|---|---|---|---|---|---|---|---|
| Current Yield | Duration | Date | Price | YTC* | % of Market | Settlement Date | Market Value |
| 9.28 | 8.5 | | | | 2.18 | 5/17/89 | $2,399,994.44 |
| 9.78 | 7.3 | 5/01/89 | 102.710 | 42.99 | 0.81 | 5/17/89 | $895,468.89 |
| 9.92 | 8.9 | 5/15/89 | 104.340 | 58.340 | 0.76 | 5/17/89 | $842,203.89 |
| 9.48 | 5.9 | | | | 4.35 | 5/17/89 | $4,794,122.56 |
| 8.83 | 6.5 | 5/15/89 | 100.900 | 46.68 | 1.85 | 5/17/89 | $2,040,616.00 |
| 9.32 | 8.7 | 12/01/88 | 101.850 | † | 2.05 | 5/17/89 | $2,255,983.33 |
| 9.67 | 6.3 | | | | 4.69 | 5/17/89 | $5,175,061.11 |
| 9.54 | 8.8 | 3/15/89 | 104.220 | 68.11 | 1.61 | 5/17/89 | $1,773,045.56 |
| 9.29 | 8.8 | 7/01/89 | 103.710 | † | 1.59 | 5/17/89 | $1,749,948.89 |
| 8.70 | 5.3 | | | | 5.49 | 5/11/89 | $6,053,368.75 |
| 8.76 | 5.6 | | | | 2.02 | 5/11/89 | $2,226,458.33 |
| 8.92 | 8.0 | 12/01/88 | 104.420 | † | 1.63 | 5/17/89 | $1,795,657.78 |
| 8.98 | 5.6 | 10/15/89 | 101.500 | 40.25 | 2.22 | 5/17/89 | $2,445,504.00 |
| 9.58 | 10.0 | 4/01/96 | 103.600 | 11.83 | 7.73 | 5/17/89 | $8.528,668.50 |
| 8.64 | 6.1 | 10/01/89 | 100.600 | 54.13 | 1.97 | 5/17/89 | $2,171,258.33 |
| 8.91 | 7.0 | 10/01/89 | 100.800 | 54.36 | 0.87 | 5/17/89 | $957,652.06 |
| 9.40 | 9.0 | 9/15/89 | 101.690 | 64.76 | 3.80 | 5/17/89 | $4,188,788.67 |
| 9.31 | 8.1 | 2/01/89 | 104.780 | † | 2.38 | 5/17/89 | $2,619,370.83 |
| 9.71 | 8.9 | 10/01/89 | 105.400 | 72.56 | 3.91 | 5/17/89 | $4,314,206.94 |
| 9.33 | 10.2 | 9/15/89 | 105.030 | 82.56 | 1.87 | 5/17/89 | $2,059,410.67 |
| 9.44 | 6.1 | | | | 0.91 | 5/17/89 | $1,007,317.78 |
| 9.42 | 9.9 | 8/15/91 | 101.310 | 16.70 | 1.59 | 5/17/89 | $1,753,706.67 |
| 8.78 | 8.3 | 6/01/89 | 193.390 | † | 3.87 | 5/17/89 | $4,272,716.67 |
| 9.09 | 8.6 | 12/01/88 | 104.840 | † | 4.12 | 5/17/89 | $4,540,408.33 |
| 9.11 | 8.7 | 6/01/89 | 104.990 | † | 4.11 | 5/17/89 | $4,533,358.33 |
| 8.39 | 5.6 | 12/29/91 | 100.000 | 12.54 | 0.84 | 5/11/89 | $923,416.67 |
| 0.00 | 25.0 | 5/15/09 | 100.000 | 12.16 | 2.14 | 5/17/89 | $2,359,375.00 |
| 9.59 | 7.7 | | | | 4.67 | 5/17/89 | $5,154,076.39 |
| 9.42 | 9.8 | 3/01/89 | 104.380 | 82.47 | 3.97 | 5/17/89 | $4,381,383.33 |
| 8.52 | 1.3 | | | | 21.01 | 5/11/89 | $22,047,995.56 |
| 8.92 | 7.0 | 3/18/91 | 102.522 | † | 100.00 | | $110,260,534.26 |

the 6.97-year duration of assets is equal to the 6.97-year duration of the liabilities at the portfolio IRR of 9.86 percent. Furthermore, the $110,260,534 market value of assets is greater than the $110,172,000 present value of liabilities; and the 41.42 units of asset dispersion are greater than the 40.72 units of dispersion of the liabilities.

One should also note that the market value of the immunized portfolio at $110,260,534 is considerably cheaper in funding the same schedule of retired-lives payouts with the same portfolio constraints than the market value of the dedicated portfolio discussed in the next chapter. The reason is that the onerous constraint of matching every monthly liability cash flow in a dedicated portfolio strategy is not present in the immunization strategy, allowing the duration-matched solution to be more than 1 percent cheaper in price.

However, in the absence of strict cash matching it is anticipated that some liabilities will be met through a combination of asset cash flows *and* asset sales. In this regard, immunization introduces an element of market risk into the asset/liability equation that is only minimally present under a dedicated strategy.

The degree to which market risk can be limited and the cost savings of immunization thereby justified on a risk-adjusted basis depends in large part on one's ability to characterize correctly the price response of the bonds in the portfolio to changes in interest rates. This issue is especially critical when bonds containing embedded options—such as mortgages and callable corporates—are part of the asset mix and is best resolved by appealing to option-adjusted bond analytics for the relevant bond durations.[8] The immunization simulation above, which assumed that all bond cash flows were fixed, is justified in part by the degree of call protection on the callable corporates selected; but the inclusion of bonds with more call risk would require a more finely tuned analysis.

### Rebalancing Procedures for Multiperiod Portfolios

Just as with a single-period immunized portfolio, a multiperiod portfolio must be rebalanced whenever one of the three conditions is violated. If, for example, the asset and liability durations were to wander apart over time, then the portfolio must be rebalanced to return it to a duration-matched state.

In a multiperiod portfolio, the durations will tend to wander whenever a liability payment comes due. An extreme example might be a $10 million bullet liability due in one month (almost zero duration) and a $10 million bullet liability due in 10 years. The average duration of the two liabilities will be about five years.

One month from now, the one-month liability will be extinguished and the remaining liability will be 9 years and 11 months. As the asset portfolio has a duration of roughly 5 years to match what was a 5-year average duration liability, the sudden shift in liability duration from 5 years to approximately 10 years will cause a major duration mismatch and need for rebalancing.

## APPLICATIONS OF THE IMMUNIZATION STRATEGY

The major applications of the immunization strategy have been in the pension, insurance, banking, and thrift industries.

---

[8] See Chapters 36 and 37.

As illustrated in Exhibit 42–15, the pension market has made widespread use of both single-period and multiperiod immunization. Single-period immunization is generally employed as an alternative to the purchase of a guaranteed investment contract (GIC) from an insurance company. Both vehicles seek to lock in today's prevailing rates over a finite planning horizon. Immunization has the advantage of liquidity, as the portfolio is composed of marketable securities. GICs are privately written contracts between plan sponsor and insurance company and are not generally traded in the secondary market.

The additional benefit of an immunized portfolio is that the portfolio manager can take advantage of market opportunities in structuring and rebalancing these portfolios by including securities in the portfolio that are attractive on a relative value basis. Investors can actively position portfolios in sectors and credits they perceive to be cheap or upgrade candidates. By actively positioning the immunized portfolio, investors can add incremental value to the portfolios and potentially outperform the illiquid GIC over a fixed planning horizon.

The pension market has also made widespread use of multiperiod immunization. Multiperiod immunization is generally employed to fund a schedule of expected benefit payouts to the retired-lives portion of a defined benefit plan. As explained in greater detail in the next chapter on cash-flow matching, by matching the duration of an immunized portfolio with corresponding liabilities, the plan sponsor can lock in prevailing rates, raise its actuarial interest-rate assumption, and reduce cash contributions to the pension fund. Tens of billions of dollars in pension monies went into immunization and dedication strategies in the early and mid-1980s because of the strong incentive of cash-flow savings and the reduced funding risk for the retired segment of the plan.

The insurance market has also made widespread use of the multiperiod immunization strategy for their fixed-liability insurance products such as GICs and

**EXHIBIT 42–15**
**Applications for Immunization**

|  | Market | | |
| --- | --- | --- | --- |
|  | *Pension* | *Insurance* | *Banking & Thrift* |
| *Single Period* | Asset strategy (GIC alternative) | | |
| *Multiperiod* | Funding retired live payouts | Funding GIC and structured settlements | GAP management Matched growth |
|  | Single premium buy-outs | Portfolio insurance | Portfolio insurance |
|  | Portfolio insurance | | |

structured settlements. Since GIC, structured settlement, and single-premium buy-out assets and liabilities are generally segmented from general account assets and liabilities, the entire line of business can be immunized to minimize the interest-rate risk and lock in a spread. Again these portfolios can be actively positioned to take advantage of market opportunities.

Lastly, banks and thrifts have made extensive use of the multiperiod immunization strategy to assist in the management of their asset/liability gap and to ensure future duration-matched growth of assets and liabilities. *Technical Bulletin 13* (TB-13) has recently mandated for the thrift industry that the interest sensitivity of a company's assets be similar to the interest sensitivity of its liabilities. For those thrifts whose durations are not closely matched, their capital requirements will be increased.

## VARIATIONS TO IMMUNIZATION

There are several variations or enhancements to the immunization strategy, including combination-matching; contingent immunization; immunization with futures, options, mortgages, or swaps; and stochastic duration-matching.

The most popular variation of the immunization strategy is *combination-matching*, also called *horizon-matching*. A combination-matched portfolio is one that is duration-matched with the added constraint that it be cash-matched in the first few years, usually five years. The advantages of combination-matching over immunization are that liquidity needs are provided for in the initial cash flow-matched period. Also, most of the positive slope or inversion of a yield curve tends to take place in the first few years. By cash-flow matching the initial portion, we have reduced the risk associated with nonparallel shifts of a sloped yield curve.

The disadvantages of combination-matching over immunization are that the cost is slightly greater and the swapping discretion is constrained. The freedom to swap a combination-matched portfolio is partially hampered not only because the asset durations must be replaced in a swap but also because the cash flows in the initial five-year period must be replaced as well.

A variant strategy to immunization is *contingent immunization*. The contingent immunization strategy is a blend of active management with immunization such that a portfolio is actively managed with a lower floor return ensured over the horizon.[9]

The floor return, or safety net, is a rate set below the immunized rate, allowing managers discretion to actively position their portfolios. If managers

---

[9] See Martin L. Leibowitz and Alfred Weinberger, "The Uses of Contingent Immunization," *Journal of Portfolio Management,* Fall 1981, pp. 51–55.

incorrectly position their portfolios and the market moves against them, the portfolios can still be actively managed. If the market continues to move against the portfolios and the floor return is violated, then managers must commit to immunized portfolios to ensure the floor return over the remainder of the horizon.

Contingent immunization requires an abrupt change in management strategy at the moment the floor return is violated. With dynamic asset allocation (portfolio insurance), the change in strategy is gradual. In this instance, managers gradually shift out of risky assets into riskless assets to avoid violating minimum return requirements. An actively managed bond portfolio or equity portfolio is the risky asset. An immunized portfolio, with duration matched to the holding period, can serve as the riskless asset. Overall, the performance of the portfolio of risky and riskless assets replicates the performance that would be obtained were a put option added to the risky portfolio. This synthetic put gives the portfolio maximum upside potential consistent with a prespecified level of protection on the downside.

Immunized portfolios can also be created with the use of futures contracts to replicate the interest sensitivity of an immunized duration. In this form, a desired portfolio can be selected without regard to a target duration, and futures contracts can then be used to replicate the price sensitivity of an immunized portfolio at the desired duration.

Options can also be used with immunized portfolios to enhance returns over a specified horizon. Through the use of covered call writing or long put or call positions, managers can enhance returns over a specified horizon.

Finally, PAC bonds and Super-PACs are sometimes used in immunized portfolios to enhance returns.[10] Though they are mortgage derivatives, their cash flows are certain across a wide band of interest-rate scenarios (prepayment speeds). As such, they can enhance performance as long as their use is actively monitored.

## CONCLUSION

Bond immunization is an important risk-control strategy that is used extensively by the pension fund, insurance, banking, and thrift industries. In today's volatile markets, it is imperative that all asset/liability gaps be intentional. Immunization provides the tools to measure the interest-rate risk position an institution or a fund is taking with respect to its liabilities; it also provides the tools to minimize that risk when a minimum gap is desired.

---

[10] PAC bonds are discussed in Chapter 29.

# CHAPTER 43

## DEDICATED BOND PORTFOLIOS*

Peter E. Christensen
*Managing Director and Manager*
*Mortgage & Fixed Income Research Departments*
*Paine Webber Incorporated*

*Frank J. Fabozzi, Ph.D., CFA*
*Visiting Professor*
*Sloan School of Management*
*Massachusetts Institute of Technology*
*and*
*Editor, The Journal of Portfolio Management*

*Anthony LoFaso,Ph.D.*
*First Vice President and Manager*
*Fixed Income Research*
*Portfolio Strategies Group*
*Paine Webber Incorporated*

Dedication is a popular and important portfolio strategy in asset/liability management. The dedicated bond portfolio, as it is frequently called, is a cash-flow matching bond strategy that matches monthly cash flows from a portfolio of bonds to a prespecified set of monthly cash requirements or liabilities. By cash matching or prefunding these liabilities, interest-rate risk is eliminated and the liability defeased.

Applications for the dedicated strategy include pension benefit funding, defeasement of debt service, municipal funding of construction "take-down"

*The authors are grateful for the assistance of Chip Montgomery, Andy Stenwall and Susan Fox in the preparation of this analysis and for their constructive comments on the text.

schedules, structured settlement funding, GIC matching and funding of other insurance products.

## THE NEED FOR A BROADER ASSET/LIABILITY FOCUS

For financial intermediaries such as banks and insurance companies, there is a well-recognized need for a complete funding perspective. This need is best illustrated by the significant interest-rate risk assumed by many insurance carriers in the early years of their Guaranteed Investment Contract (GIC) products. A large volume of compound interest (zero coupon) and simple interest (annual pay) GICs were issued in three- through seven-year maturities in the positively sloped yield-curve environment of the mid-1970s. Proceeds from hundreds of the GIC issues were reinvested at higher rates in the longer 10- to 30-year private placement, commercial mortgage, and public bond instruments. At the time, industry expectations were that the GIC product would be very profitable because of the large positive spread between the higher "earned" rate on the longer assets and the lower "credited" rate on the GIC contracts.

By pricing GICs on a spread basis and investing the proceeds on a mismatched basis, companies gave little consideration to the rollover risk they were assuming in volatile markets. As rates rose dramatically in the late 1970s and early 1980s, carriers were exposed to extreme disintermediation as GIC liabilities matured and the corresponding assets had 20 years remaining to maturity and were valued at only a fraction of their original cost.

As a result of this enormous risk exposure, insurance carriers were induced to adopt a broader asset/liability focus in order to control the interest-rate risk associated with writing a fixed-liability product. Dedication and immunization (described in Chapter 42) have become popular matching strategies to control this market risk.

Similarly, in funding pension liabilities, there is also a need for a broad asset/liability focus. Since the future investment performance of a pension fund is unpredictable, actuaries generally incorporate conservative investment return assumptions in the calculation of annual funding requirements. This conservative approach requires current contributions much greater than the amounts needed under more realistic investment return assumptions. Such oversized contributions diminish both corporate cash flow and profits for the sponsoring entity.

Through use of the dedication strategy to fund the relatively well-defined, retired-lives portion of the pension liability, some of this conservative margin can be eliminated. In the process, the plan sponsor may elect to reduce its current contributions to the pension fund, or offer more generous benefits to plan participants, without increasing the current level of funding.

## CASH-FLOW MATCHING FOR PENSION FUNDS

The most popular application of the dedicated strategy has been to fund the payout obligations of the retired-lives portion of a pension plan. In the following simulation we illustrate, in detail, the mechanics of this strategy as it applies to pension funds.

### Determining the Liabilities

The first step in establishing a dedicated bond portfolio is to determine the schedule to be funded. For pension funds, usually it is the expected benefit payouts to a closed block of current retirees. Since the benefit payouts to *future* retirees cannot be projected with great accuracy, they are generally not included in the analysis. Since future retirees are not included in the closed block, the schedule of benefit payments declines over time due to mortality experience. Exhibit 43–1 illustrates the annual schedule of benefit payouts that are expected to be paid to current retirees.

The forecasted payouts are based on the known benefit payouts at retirement for each employee and a number of variables including expected mortality, spouse benefit assumptions, and expected cost-of-living increases. As shown in Exhibit 43–1, the total payouts in dollars over the 35-year time horizon for the retired employees are $276,457,340.

In addition to funding the retired-lives payouts, the dedicated strategy is frequently applied to a somewhat broader universe of participants that includes retirees plus terminated vested participants. Terminated vested participants are former employees who are vested in the pension plan and are entitled to benefit payouts commencing sometime in the future. Since these benefit amounts are relatively fixed, they can be readily match funded.

Several pension plans have extended the dedication strategy to include the funding of "anticipated retiree" pension obligations as well. That is, in addition to funding the retired and terminated vested liabilities, the cash-flow-matched design is used to offset liabilities associated with "active" employees aged 50 and greater. Since these benefit payments are not fixed until the employee actually retires, the various mortality, termination, and benefit assumptions must be reviewed periodically to insure that actual experience tracks the forecast.

Instead of a downward-sloping liability schedule, the profile of expected benefit payouts for this broad population of plan participants would increase dramatically in the first 10 to 15 years, level off for a brief period, then begin a downward slope. The benefit schedule peaks because the active participants who will be joining the retired population over the next 10 to 15 years are generally greater in number and have higher salaries (due to inflation) than the shrink-age in population of retirees due to mortality. The percentage reduction in actual

**EXHIBIT 43–1**
**Schedule of**
**Expected Pension**
**Payouts**

| Year | Dollar Payout |
|------|---------------|
| 1989* | $    8,750,000 |
| 1990 | 14,916,015 |
| 1991 | 14,427,473 |
| 1992 | 13,445,985 |
| 1993 | 12,435,248 |
| 1994 | 11,754,199 |
| 1995 | 11,384,959 |
| 1996 | 11,028,026 |
| 1997 | 10,654,684 |
| 1998 | 10,408,523 |
| 1999 | 10,355,190 |
| 2000 | 10,236,214 |
| 2001 | 9,953,126 |
| 2002 | 9,670,039 |
| 2003 | 9,302,164 |
| 2004 | 8,748,308 |
| 2005 | 8,621,160 |
| 2006 | 8,209,594 |
| 2007 | 7,893,578 |
| 2008 | 7,435,436 |
| 2009 | 6,993,713 |
| 2010 | 6,579,349 |
| 2011 | 6,145,834 |
| 2012 | 5,732,824 |
| 2013 | 5,322,551 |
| 2014 | 4,983,398 |
| 2015 | 4,615,526 |
| 2016 | 4,257,221 |
| 2017 | 3,892,088 |
| 2018 | 3,537,881 |
| 2019 | 3,216,510 |
| 2020 | 2,934,788 |
| 2021 | 2,659,900 |
| 2022 | 2,385,026 |
| 2023 | 2,123,504 |
| 2024 | 1,337,297 |
| Total | $ 276,457,340 |

* Partial year @ $15 million

liability and, hence, in contribution requirements associated with the anticipated retirees, is frequently larger than that for the currently retired population.

Similarly, when applying the dedication strategy to insurance company funding, a liability schedule will represent monthly projections of fixed payouts for products like GICs, single premium buyouts, or structured settlements. Once that schedule is derived, the procedures for match funding an insurance product line are similar to creating a dedicated portfolio for a pension fund.

## Setting Portfolio Constraints

With the liability schedule determined, the next step in instituting a dedicated portfolio is to specify portfolio constraints on sector, quality, issue, and lot sizes. To identify the cheapest portfolio possible that funds the fixed schedule of liabilities, the portfolio manager may wish to constrain the optimal or least-cost solution to a universe of government and corporate securities rated single A or better by one rating agency, as illustrated in Exhibit 43–2. In the simulation that follows, a minimum of 20 percent of the portfolio is constrained to be in Treasury securities and a 30 percent maximum is set for the bank and finance, utility and telephone sectors; a 25 percent maximum is established collectively for Yankee, Canadian and World Bank issues; and no industrial, Euro, PAC or Super PAC mortgages (CMOs) are allowed in this example.

Note from Exhibit 43–2 that constraints on lot size are emphasized. Round lot solutions (in lots of $1 million or more) are strongly preferred since the actual execution of the portfolio may be accomplished more efficiently without the added costs of odd lot differentials. Also, as the dedicated portfolio is swapped or reoptimized over time, additional odd lot premiums on the sale of such assets are avoided.

## The Reinvestment Rate

Since the timing of cash receipts does not always exactly match the timing of cash disbursements, surplus funds must be reinvested at an assumed reinvestment rate until the next liability payout date. This reinvestment or rollover rate is vital because it is often preferable to prefund future benefit payments with higher yielding securities rather than to purchase lower yielding issues that mature closer to the liability payment dates. The more conservative the reinvestment rate, the greater the penalty for prefunding future benefit payouts and, therefore, the tighter the cash-flow match. The more aggressive the reinvestment rate, the greater the prefunding in optimal portfolios, but the greater the risk of not earning that minimum short term reinvestment in a future period and experiencing a shortfall of cash. Frequently the actuarial investment rate assumption is used. Currently these rates are in the 5 to 6 percent range, and for the simulation that follows, we have assumed a reinvestment rate of 5 percent.

**EXHIBIT 43–2**
**Portfolio Constraints**

|  | Minimum | Maximum |
|---|---|---|
| Quality* | | |
| Treasury | 20% | 100% |
| Agency | | 100 |
| AAA | 0 | 100 |
| AA | 0 | 100 |
| A | 0 | 50 |
| BBB | 0 | 0 |
| Sector | | |
| Treasury | 20% | 100% |
| Agency | | 100 |
| Industrial | 0 | 0 |
| Utility | 0 | 30 |
| Telephone | 0 | 30 |
| Bank & Finance | 0 | 30 |
| Canadian | | |
| Yankee | 0 | 30 |
| World Bank | | |
| Euros | 0 | 0 |
| Super PACs (Mortgages) | 0 | 0 |
| Concentration | | |
| Maximum in one issue | | 10% |
| Maximum in one issuer | | 10 |
| Call Constraints on Corporate Securities | | |
| Spread between coupon and YTM | | 150 b. p. |
| Lot Size | | |
| Conditional minimum | | $1,000,000 (par) |
| Increment | | $100,000 (par) |
| Maximum | | Unlimited |

* Single-A split rated securities allowed.

## Selecting the Optimal Portfolio

Once the liability schedule, the portfolio constraints, and the reinvestment rate(s) are specified, an optimal (least cost) portfolio can be structured to defease the expected benefit payouts. The optimal portfolio is illustrated in Exhibit 43–3.

Assembling a dedicated portfolio that has a high probability of attaining its funding objective over time requires restricting the universe of available issues. The fund manager must avoid questionable credits and, most importantly, avoid those issues that may be called prior to maturity, have large sinking-fund call risk, or have significant prepayment risk. Retirement of issues prior to their

**EXHIBIT 43-3**
**Proposed Optimal Dedicated Portfolio**

| Par Value | Credit | | Issue Name | Coupon | Maturity | Market Price | Yield |
|---|---|---|---|---|---|---|---|
| $1,000,000 | AAA | /AAA | AETNA | 8.000 | 1/15/2017 | 83.72900 | 9.70 |
| 1,000,000 | AA1 | /AA+ | ALBERTA PROV | 9.250 | 11/23/1994 | 98.60700 | 9.58 |
| 1,200,000 | A3 | /BBB+ | ARKLA, INC. | 8.900 | 12/15/2006 | 92.24200 | 9.83 |
| 1,000,000 | A3 | /BBB | BANKAMERICA | 8.750 | 5/01/2001 | 89.15800 | 10.35 |
| 1,000,000 | A3 | /BBB | BANKAMERICA | 8.350 | 5/15/2007 | 84.17400 | 10.30 |
| 1,000,000 | AA1 | /AA | BANQ NAT PARIS | 9.875 | 5/25/1998 | 99.50200 | 9.96 |
| 2,500,000 | A3 | /A | BENEFICAL CORP | 8.400 | 12/01/2007 | 86.36600 | 10.03 |
| 2,900,000 | A1 | /A+ | BK OF MONTREAL | 10.000 | 9/01/1998 | 100.68900 | 9.88 |
| 1,000,000 | A2 | /A | CAROLINA P&L | 7.750 | 5/01/2003 | 85.15900 | 9.71 |
| 1,100,000 | BAA1/A | | CHASE MANHATTAN | 8.500 | 3/01/1996 | 93.01900 | 9.93 |
| 2,400,000 | BAA1/A | | CHASE MANHATTAN | 7.875 | 1/15/1997 | 88.83800 | 9.99 |
| 5,000,000 | BAA2/A− | | CHASE MANHATTAN | 10.000 | 6/15/1999 | 99.27900 | 10.11 |
| 1,700,000 | A1 | /AA | CITICORP | 8.450 | 3/15/2007 | 87.19700 | 10.00 |
| 2,000,000 | A1 | /AA | CITICORP | 8.125 | 7/01/2007 | 84.42800 | 10.00 |
| 1,500,000 | TSY | /TSY | COUPON STRIPS | 0.00 | 8/15/1991 | 81.28500 | 9.36 |
| 1,300,000 | TSY | /TSY | COUPON STRIPS | 0.00 | 11/15/1991 | 79.47700 | 9.36 |
| 1,300,000 | TSY | /TSY | COUPON STRIPS | 0.00 | 2/15/1992 | 77.67100 | 9.35 |
| 1,200,000 | TSY | /TSY | COUPON STRIPS | 0.00 | 5/15/1992 | 75.94600 | 9.35 |
| 1,300,000 | TSY | /TSY | COUPON STRIPS | 0.00 | 8/15/1992 | 74.22600 | 9.34 |
| 1,500,000 | TSY | /TSY | COUPON STRIPS | 0.00 | 11/15/1992 | 72.57800 | 9.34 |
| 1,100,000 | TSY | /TSY | COUPON STRIPS | 0.00 | 8/15/1994 | 61.93300 | 9.31 |
| 1,000,000 | AGY | /AGY | FED HOME LOAN | 9.000 | 7/26/1993 | 97.78125 | 9.65 |
| 1,000,000 | AGY | /AGY | FED HOME LOAN | 8.800 | 10/25/1993 | 97.21875 | 9.58 |
| 1,000,000 | AGY | /AGY | FED HOME LOAN | 8.500 | 4/25/1994 | 95.78125 | 9.59 |
| 1,000,000 | AGY | /AGY | FED HOME LOAN | 10.300 | 7/25/1995 | 103.09375 | 9.62 |
| 1,000,000 | AGY | /AGY | FED HOME LOAN | 8.00 | 7/25/1996 | 91.43750 | 9.67 |
| 1,000,000 | AGY | /AGY | FNMA | 10.600 | 11/10/1995 | 104.90625 | 9.57 |
| 1,000,000 | AAA | /AAA | GENERAL ELEC | 5.500 | 11/01/2001 | 70.48800 | 9.61 |
| 1,400,000 | AA3 | /AA− | GMAC | 7.250 | 3/01/1995 | 87.71200 | 10.10 |
| 1,000,000 | AA3 | /AA− | GMAC | 8.125 | 10/15/1996 | 89.85200 | 10.10 |
| 1,000,000 | AA3 | /AA− | GMAC | 5.500 | 12/15/2001 | 69.68100 | 9.73 |
| 2,600,000 | AA3 | /AA− | GMAC | 6.000 | 4/01/2011 | 66.54200 | 9.72 |
| 7,500,000 | AA3 | /AA− | GMAC | 8.250 | 4/01/2016 | 85.09400 | 9.83 |
| 2,200,000 | A1 | /AA− | HOUSEHOLD FIN | 7.500 | 10/01/1997 | 85.89200 | 10.03 |
| 1,700,000 | A1 | /AA− | HOUSEHOLD FIN | 7.750 | 10/01/1999 | 86.06900 | 9.93 |
| 3,000,000 | A3 | /BBB+ | HOUSTON L&P | 8.125 | 2/01/2004 | 84.92000 | 10.11 |
| 5,000,000 | A3 | /BBB+ | HOUSTON L&P | 8.375 | 10/01/2007 | 85.21400 | 10.17 |
| 1,000,000 | AAA | /AAA | ILLINOIS BELL | 7.625 | 4/01/2006 | 83.52300 | 9.62 |
| 2,500,000 | AA3 | /AA | MOUNTAIN TEL | 7.750 | 6/01/2013 | 82.20000 | 9.67 |
| 4,800,000 | AA3 | /AA | MOUNTAIN TEL | 8.000 | 9/15/2017 | 83.90200 | 9.67 |
| 4,400,000 | AA2 | /AA | NEW YORK TEL | 7.375 | 12/15/2011 | 79.46800 | 9.62 |

stated maturity, whether through default or call, jeopardizes the funding of the liability schedule. As a result, most current coupon callable bonds and non-Super PAC mortgage securities are not appropriate for matched portfolios.

The logic used to select the optimal or least-cost portfolio varies among purveyors of the cash-flow-matching service. There are three methods being used to identify an "optimal" portfolio. In order of sophistication, they are stepwise solutions, linear programming, and integer programming. Of the three, integer

| Current Yield | Duration | Call Information | | | % of Market | Settlement Date | Market Value |
| --- | --- | --- | --- | --- | --- | --- | --- |
| | | Date | Price | YTC* | | | |
| 9.26 | 10.0 | 1/15/97 | 104.000 | 11.60 | 0.77 | 5/17/89 | $ 864,401.11 |
| 8.98 | 4.2 | | | | 0.92 | 5/17/89 | 1,030,778.33 |
| 9.28 | 8.5 | | | | 1.03 | 5/17/89 | 1,151,997.33 |
| 9.78 | 7.3 | 5/01/89 | 102.710 | 42.99 | 0.80 | 5/17/89 | 895,468.89 |
| 9.92 | 8.9 | 5/15/89 | 104.340 | 58.34 | 0.75 | 5/17/89 | 842,203.89 |
| 9.48 | 5.9 | | | | 0.93 | 5/17/89 | 1,042,200.56 |
| 9.32 | 8.7 | 12/01/88 | 101.850 | ‡ | 2.02 | 5/17/89 | 2,255,983.33 |
| 9.74 | 6.1 | | | | 2.67 | 5/17/89 | 2,981,203.22 |
| 9.07 | 8.3 | 5/01/89 | 103.640 | 56.51 | 0.77 | 5/17/89 | 855,034.44 |
| 8.97 | 5.1 | | | | 0.93 | 5/17/89 | 1,042,947.89 |
| 8.61 | 5.6 | | | | 1.97 | 5/17/89 | 2,196,162.00 |
| 9.67 | 6.3 | | | | 4.63 | 5/17/89 | 5,175,061.11 |
| 9.54 | 8.8 | 3/15/89 | 104.220 | 68.11 | 1.35 | 5/17/89 | 1,507,088.72 |
| 9.29 | 8.8 | 7/01/89 | 103.710 | ‡ | 1.57 | 5/17/89 | 1,749,948.89 |
| 0.00 | 2.3 | | | | 1.09 | 5/11/89 | 1,219,275.00 |
| 0.00 | 2.5 | | | | 0.93 | 5/11/89 | 1,033,201.00 |
| 0.00 | 2.8 | | | | 0.90 | 5/11/89 | 1,009,723.00 |
| 0.00 | 3.0 | | | | 0.82 | 5/11/89 | 911,352.00 |
| 0.00 | 3.3 | | | | 0.86 | 5/11/89 | 964,938.00 |
| 0.00 | 3.5 | | | | 0.97 | 5/11/89 | 1,088,670.00 |
| 0.00 | 5.3 | | | | 0.61 | 5/11/89 | 681,263.00 |
| 8.96 | 3.5 | | | | 0.90 | 5/11/89 | 1,004,062.50 |
| 9.02 | 3.8 | | | | 0.87 | 5/11/89 | 976,098.61 |
| 8.84 | 4.1 | | | | 0.86 | 5/11/89 | 961,590.28 |
| 9.71 | 4.6 | | | | 0.95 | 5/11/89 | 1,061,265.28 |
| 8.53 | 5.4 | | | | 0.84 | 5/11/89 | 937,930.56 |
| 10.10 | 4.9 | | | | 0.94 | 5/11/89 | 1,049,356.94 |
| 7.78 | 8.4 | 11/01/89 | 100.000 | 99.36 | 0.63 | 5/17/89 | 707,324.44 |
| 8.13 | 4.7 | 3/01/89 | 100.700 | 58.50 | 1.12 | 5/17/89 | 1,249,395.78 |
| 8.98 | 5.6 | 10/15/89 | 101.500 | 40.25 | 0.81 | 5/17/89 | 905,742.22 |
| 7.64 | 8.2 | 12/15/88 | 100.000 | ‡ | 0.64 | 5/17/89 | 720,032.22 |
| 8.92 | 10.2 | 4/01/89 | 100.000 | ‡ | 1.57 | 5/17/89 | 1,750,025.33 |
| 9.58 | 10.0 | 4/01/96 | 103.600 | 11.83 | 5.78 | 5/17/89 | 6,461,112.50 |
| 8.64 | 6.1 | 10/01/89 | 100.600 | 54.13 | 1.71 | 5/17/89 | 1,910,707.33 |
| 8.91 | 7.0 | 10/01/89 | 100.800 | 54.36 | 1.32 | 5/17/89 | 1,480,007.72 |
| 9.31 | 8.1 | 2/01/89 | 104.780 | ‡ | 2.34 | 5/17/89 | 2,619,370.83 |
| 9.71 | 8.9 | 10/01/89 | 105.400 | 72.56 | 3.86 | 5/17/89 | 4,314,206.94 |
| 9.03 | 9.0 | 4/01/89 | 103.170 | 71.49 | 0.76 | 5/17/89 | 844,973.06 |
| 9.04 | 9.7 | 6/01/89 | 104.210 | ‡ | 1.92 | 5/17/89 | 2,144,340.28 |
| 9.39 | 10.2 | 9/15/89 | 104.870 | 84.39 | 3.66 | 5/17/89 | 4,093,429.33 |
| 8.94 | 9.7 | 12/15/88 | 104.430 | ‡ | 3.25 | 5/17/89 | 3,633,603.11 |

programming is the most technically advanced and is able to identify the lowest cost round lot solution.

## The Cash-Flow Match

Exhibit 43–4 summarizes the cash-flow match inherent in the dedicated portfolio in our example. Note that in every year, the cash flow from the maturing prin-

**EXHIBIT 43–3—Continued**

| Par Value | Credit | | Issue Name | Coupon | Maturity | Market | |
|---|---|---|---|---|---|---|---|
| | | | | | | Price | Yield |
| $ 4,900,000 | AA3 | /AA | NEW YORK TEL | 7.875 | 6/15/2017 | 82.73900 | 9.67 |
| 2,000,000 | AA2 | /AA | OKLAHOMA G&E | 8.250 | 8/15/2016 | 85.57700 | 9.77 |
| 5,000,000 | A1 | /A | PACIFIC GAS | 7.500 | 6/01/2004 | 81.99600 | 9.81 |
| 3,000,000 | AA3 | /A+ | PACIFIC TEL | 7.625 | 6/01/2009 | 82.05300 | 9.67 |
| 4,000,000 | A1 | /A | PUB SVCE E&G | 7.500 | 4/01/2002 | 84.24900 | 9.66 |
| 1,000,000 | AGY | /AGY | SALLIE MAE | 0.000 | 5/15/2014 | 9.43750 | 9.67 |
| 3,000,000 | AA1 | /AA | SOC GEN | 9.875 | 7/15/2003 | 99.73500 | 9.91 |
| 5,000,000 | AA3 | /AA− | SOUTHWEST BELL | 8.250 | 3/01/2014 | 85.88600 | 9.77 |
| 1,700,000 | A1 | /A+ | SOVRAN FIN CORP | 9.250 | 6/15/2006 | 95.20000 | 9.83 |
| 1,600,000 | TSY | /TSY | U.S. TREASURY | 7.875 | 10/31/1989 | 99.40625 | 9.17 |
| 1,300,000 | TSY | /TSY | U.S. TREASURY | 7.375 | 1/31/1990 | 98.65625 | 9.31 |
| 1,600,000 | TSY | /TSY | U.S. TREASURY | 7.625 | 4/30/1990 | 98.43750 | 9.34 |
| 1,300,000 | TSY | /TSY | U.S. TREASURY | 8.375 | 7/31/1990 | 98.84375 | 9.38 |
| 1,400,000 | TSY | /TSY | U.S. TREASURY | 8.250 | 10/31/1990 | 98.46875 | 9.39 |
| 1,500,000 | TSY | /TSY | U.S. TREASURY | 9.125 | 12/31/1990 | 99.68750 | 9.32 |
| 1,400,000 | TSY | /TSY | U.S. TREASURY | 9.250 | 4/30/1991 | 99.96875 | 9.27 |
| 1,000,000 | TSY | /TSY | U.S. TREASURY | 7.875 | 6/30/1991 | 97.37500 | 9.25 |
| 1,100,000 | TSY | /TSY | U.S. TREASURY | 7.375 | 4/15/1993 | 93.84375 | 9.28 |
| 1,300,000 | TSY | /TSY | U.S. TREASURY | 7.000 | 1/15/1994 | 91.43750 | 9.29 |
| 1,000,000 | TSY | /TSY | U.S. TSY BILL | 0.000 | 5/25/1989 | 99.68500 | 8.13 |
| 1,300,000 | TSY | /TSY | U.S. TSY BILL | 0.000 | 7/27/1989 | 98.17981 | 8.67 |
| 1,500,000 | A1 | /A+ | VIRGINIA ELEC | 7.375 | 3/01/2001 | 84.09900 | 9.66 |
| $126,000,000 | AA1 | /AA | | 7.372 | 5/06/2003 | 86.77596 | 9.80 |

Pricing date = 5/10/1989
* YTC calculation for currently callable bonds assume call on next coupon date
† Existing issue
‡ Yield-to-call exceeds 100%
§ Trades on YTC

cipal when added to the coupon income from all securities in the portfolio and the reinvestment income will almost precisely equal the liability requirements specified by the actuary in Exhibit 43–1. Since almost all cash flow is being paid out each month to fund the liability payment, the portfolio has very little cash to reinvest each period, and hence, assumes very little reinvestment risk. The plan can, therefore, lock in a rate of over 9.75 percent—the rate prevailing at the time of this writing—regardless of the future course of rates.

In this simulation the computer model has controlled reinvestment risk by structuring relatively small surplus positions in most years. However, the model sometimes prefunds distant payouts by reinvesting the proceeds of high-yielding, shorter maturing issues at the low reinvestment rate. This is frequently preferable to purchasing bonds with longer maturities and better matching characteristics, but with lower yields to maturity. Note from Exhibit 43–4 that the large amount of prefunding in the years 2017, 2018 and 2019 due to the lack of high-yielding call-protected issues in subsequent year.

| Current Yield | Duration | Call Information | | | % of Market | Settlement Date | Market Value |
|---|---|---|---|---|---|---|---|
| | | Date | Price | YTC* | | | |
| 9.16 | 10.0 | 6/15/89 | 105.180 | ‡ | 3.77 | 5/17/89 | $4,217,136.00 |
| 9.42 | 9.9 | 8/15/91 | 101.310 | 16.70 | 1.57 | 5/17/89 | 1,753,706.67 |
| 8.78 | 8.3 | 6/01/89 | 103.390 | ‡ | 3.82 | 5/17/89 | 4,272,716.67 |
| 8.92 | 9.2 | 6/01/89 | 103.690 | ‡ | 2.30 | 5/17/89 | 2,567,069.17 |
| 8.81 | 8.0 | 4/01/89 | 103.110 | 68.27 | 3.05 | 5/17/89 | 3,408,293.33 |
| 0.00 | 25.0 | 5/15/09 | 100.000 | 12.16 | 0.08 | 5/17/89 | 94,375.00 |
| 9.59 | 7.7 | | | | 2.77 | 5/17/89 | 3,092,445.83 |
| 9.42 | 9.8 | 3/01/89 | 104.380 | 82.47 | 3.92 | 5/17/89 | 4,381,383.33 |
| 9.34 | 8.4 | | | | 1.51 | 5/17/89 | 1,684,794.44 |
| 7.90 | 0.5 | | | | 1.43 | 5/11/89 | 1,594,266.30 |
| 7.32 | 0.7 | | | | 1.17 | 5/11/89 | 1,309,016.06 |
| 7.73 | 1.0 | | | | .141 | 5/11/89 | 1,578,646.74 |
| 8.28 | 1.2 | | | | 1.18 | 5/11/89 | 1,315,044.72 |
| 8.36 | 1.4 | | | | 1.24 | 5/11/89 | 1,382,014.95 |
| 8.87 | 1.5 | | | | 1.38 | 5/11/89 | 1,543,710.29 |
| 9.23 | 1.8 | | | | 1.26 | 5/11/89 | 1,403,081.52 |
| 7.86 | 2.0 | | | | 0.90 | 5/11/89 | 1,002,247.93 |
| 7.82 | 3.4 | | | | 0.93 | 5/11/89 | 1,038,044.23 |
| 7.47 | 3.9 | | | | 1.09 | 5/11/89 | 1,217,847.72 |
| 0.00 | 0.0 | | | | 0.89 | 5/11/89 | 996,850.00 |
| 0.00 | 0.2 | | | | 1.14 | 5/11/89 | 1,276,337.53 |
| 8.62 | 7.6 | 3/01/89 | 102.500 | 82.97 | 1.15 | 5/17/89 | 1,284,839.17 |
| 8.32 | 6.9 | 4/05/1990 | 103.409 | ‡ | 100.00 | | $111,737,344.59 |

## Pricing the Bonds

Notice in Exhibit 43–4 that neither prices nor yields appear in the analysis. A dedicated portfolio is concerned only with cash flows. As long as all coupon payments are made in a timely fashion and every bond matures on schedule, the liabilities specified by the actuary will be funded. Though credit ratings on some bonds in a portfolio may deteriorate over time and their market prices drop markedly, the integrity of the dedicated design is still preserved as long as all cash-flow payments are complete and punctual.

Prices and yields enter the analysis only in determining the initial cost of the optimal portfolio as seen in Exhibit 43–3. In this simulation, all bonds were priced as of May 10, 1989.

It is worth noting that the market value of the bonds in the portfolio as of

**EXHIBIT 43–4**

**Proposed Dedicated Portfolio — Yearly Cashflow Summary**

| Year | Beginning Balance | Maturing (+) Principal | Coupon (+) Income | Reinvestment (+) Cash | Liability (−) Cashflows | Ending (=) Balance |
|---|---|---|---|---|---|---|
| 1989 | $ 408,087 | $ 3,900,000 | $ 5,242,489 | $ 15,598 | $ 8,750,000 | $ 408,087 |
| 1990 | 176,956 | 5,600,000 | 9,054,263 | 30,622 | 14,916,015 | 176,956 |
| 1991 | 1,083,769 | 6,700,000 | 8,587,763 | 46,524 | 14,427,473 | 1,083,769 |
| 1992 | 1,371,381 | 5,300,000 | 8,375,825 | 57,772 | 13,445,985 | 1,371,381 |
| 1993 | 416,540 | 3,100,000 | 8,335,263 | 45,144 | 12,435,248 | 416,540 |
| 1994 | 1,144,915 | 4,400,000 | 8,028,700 | 53,875 | 11,754,199 | 1,144,915 |
| 1995 | 1,019,731 | 3,400,000 | 7,797,450 | 62,325 | 11,384,959 | 1,019,731 |
| 1996 | 631,740 | 3,100,000 | 7,490,950 | 49,085 | 11,028,026 | 631,740 |
| 1997 | 1,855,279 | 4,600,000 | 7,188,450 | 89,773 | 10,654,684 | 1,855,279 |
| 1998 | 2,313,396 | 3,900,000 | 6,879,575 | 87,066 | 10,408,523 | 2,313,396 |
| 1999 | 5,368,689 | 6,700,000 | 6,540,200 | 170,283 | 10,355,190 | 5,368,689 |
| 2000 | 1,218,741 | | 5,908,450 | 177,816 | 10,236,214 | 1,218,741 |
| 2001 | 638,321 | 3,500,000 | 5,809,388 | 63,318 | 9,953,126 | 638,321 |
| 2002 | 1,572,939 | 5,000,000 | 5,477,825 | 126,832 | 9,670,039 | 1,572,939 |
| 2003 | 1,611,667 | 4,000,000 | 5,261,575 | 79,317 | 9,302,164 | 1,611,667 |
| 2004 | 5,727,382 | 8,000,000 | 4,617,200 | 246,824 | 8,748,308 | 5,727,382 |
| 2005 | 1,611,306 | | 4,307,825 | 197,259 | 8,621,160 | 1,611,306 |
| 2006 | 442,072 | 2,700,000 | 4,269,700 | 70,660 | 8,209,594 | 442,072 |
| 2007 | 10,022,218 | 13,400,000 | 3,907,350 | 166,373 | 7,893,578 | 10,022,218 |
| 2008 | | | 2,949,125 | 409,537 | 7,435,436 | 5,945,444 |

**EXHIBIT 43-4—Continued**

| Year | Beginning Balance | Maturing (+) Principal | Coupon (+) Income | Reinvestment (+) Cash | Liability (−) Cashflows | Ending (=) Balance |
|------|-------------------|------------------------|-------------------|-----------------------|-------------------------|--------------------|
| 2009 | $ 5,945,444 | $ 3,000,000 | $ 2,834,750 | 288,309 | $ 6,993,713 | $ 5,074,790 |
| 2010 | 5,074,790 | | 2,720,375 | 175,901 | 6,579,349 | 1,391,717 |
| 2011 | 1,391,717 | 2,600,000 | 2,642,375 | 85,796 | 6,145,834 | 574,054 |
| 2012 | 574,054 | 4,400,000 | 2,402,125 | 174,406 | 5,732,824 | 1,817,761 |
| 2013 | 1,817,761 | 2,500,000 | 2,143,000 | 87,536 | 5,322,551 | 1,225,747 |
| 2014 | 1,225,747 | 6,000,000 | 1,839,875 | 213,800 | 4,983,398 | 4,296,024 |
| 2015 | 4,296,024 | | 1,633,625 | 153,991 | 4,615,526 | 1,468,114 |
| 2016 | 1,468,114 | 9,500,000 | 1,324,250 | 296,841 | 4,257,221 | 8,331,984 |
| 2017 | 8,331,984 | 10,700,000 | 809,875 | 564,244 | 3,892,088 | 16,514,015 |
| 2018 | 16,514,015 | | | 754,664 | 3,537,881 | 13,730,798 |
| 2019 | 13,730,798 | | | 621,154 | 3,216,510 | 11,135,442 |
| 2020 | 11,135,442 | | | 496,243 | 2,934,788 | 8,696,896 |
| 2021 | 8,696,896 | | | 379,112 | 2,659,909 | 6,416,100 |
| 2022 | 6,416,100 | | | 269,968 | 2,385,026 | 4,301,042 |
| 2023 | 4,301,042 | | | 168,908 | 2,123,504 | 2,346,445 |
| 2024 | 2,346,445 | | | 85,506 | 1,447,297 | 984,655 |
| | | $126,000,000 | $144,379,614 | $7,062,382 | $276,457,340 | |

Reinvestment Rate: 5.00 percent

May 11th was $111,737,345, and the internal rate of return was 9.80 percent, reflecting the market yields available at the time of this writing.

If none of the bonds in the dedicated portfolio default and if the payout projections are accurate, only $111,737,345 in assets will be required to fully fund the total retired payouts of $276,457,340 that we see illustrated in Exhibit 43–1.

## The Savings to the Pension System

As illustrated in Exhibit 43–5, using the current actuarial investment rate assumption of 5 percent, the plan must have on hand $160,756,160 in order to fully fund the $276,457,340 of payouts to retired lives. On the basis of the May 10, 1989 pricing, the portfolio can, with a yield of 9.80 percent, fully fund the same $276,457,340 in liability payouts with an initial investment of only $111,737,345. Purchase of this portfolio would generally give the actuary the comfort level necessary to increase the assumed actuarial investment rate on the retired-lives portion of the fund. In most cases, this increase may go all the way to the funding rate of 9.80 percent.

By raising the assumed rate from 5 percent to 9.80 percent on the retired portion of the plan, the plan sponsor has reduced the present value of the accumulated plan benefits by $49,018,815. This actuarial gain or potential savings of $49 million represents a 30 percent reduction from the higher present value required under a 5 percent actuarial assumption.

Increasing the assumed rate on the retired-lives portion of the pension fund decreases the present value of the funds promised as future payouts, thus reducing the actuarial liability. Reductions in actuarial liability usually translate into reductions in the current contribution requirements. The reduction in current contribution due to the dedicated strategy can be substantial.

In our example, the reduction in actuarial liability is $49,018,815. This amount cannot be realized in the form of a reduced contribution all in the first year. Pensions and tax legislation require that the gain be spread over 10 to

**EXHIBIT 43–5**
**Reduced Funding Requirements**

|  | Percent | Dollar Amount |
| --- | --- | --- |
| Total liabilities | — | $276,457,340 |
| Present value of total liabilities at | 5.00 | 160,756,160 |
| Portfolio cost (market value) at | 9.80 | 111,737,345 |
| Potential savings (2–3) | — | 49,018,815 |
| Percent savings (4/2) | 30.49 | — |
| Percent savings (4/3) | 43.87 | — |

30 years. With all other factors remaining constant, the reduction in pension contribution might amount to as much as a few million dollars per year for each of the next 10 years. However, since every pension plan is different, and different actuarial cost methods treat gains differently, the actual savings to a plan may be of a different magnitude than represented by this example.

## Reoptimizing a Dedicated Bond Portfolio

It was originally thought that once a dedicated portfolio was structured, it should be passively managed—that is, left untouched as assets roll off in tandem with liabilities. Active management techniques can, however, be applied to dedicated portfolios. In addition to bond-for-bond swapping and active sector positioning of the portfolio, a cash-matched solution can be entirely reoptimized on a periodic basis.

For example, a portfolio that was "optimized" last year, in last year's rate environment, is not an optimum portfolio in today's rate environment with a new yield curve, new yield spreads, and new available issues. As seen in Exhibit 43–6, a new least-cost portfolio can be created one year later to fund the same liability schedule with the same portfolio constraints. Since the new optimum portfolio will be less expensive than the old, a cash take-out can be generated by selling off a portion of the original portfolio and replacing the cash insufficiencies with a new combination of securities. When the take-out is significant such trades are usually executed.

The take-out generated by the computer solution can be guaranteed if the reoptimization is executed through a dealer firm. Frequently money managers and third party software vendors work in conjunction with dealer firms to obtain a trader-priced database and guaranteed take-outs. On the other hand, if a reoptimization is simulated on a database of matrix (computer-derived) prices, the take-out may disappear when market prices are obtained in the actual execution.

**EXHIBIT 43–6**
**Take-Out from Reoptimizations**

| | Market Value (000) | Average Rating | Take-Out (000) |
|---|---|---|---|
| Original dedicated portfolio | $100,000 | Aaa/AA+ | — |
| Reoptimized dedicated portfolio (marked to market 1 year later) | 99,400 | Aaa/AA+ | $600 |

Note that the new optimum portfolio will always be cheaper than the original portfolio. If the computer is not able to find a portfolio that is cheaper than the original, it will select the original portfolio again, establishing that it is still the optimum.

### Active Management of Dedicated Portfolios

In addition to adding value through comprehensive reoptimizations, bond swaps can be undertaken to pick up yield or to swap out of an undesirable credit. To preserve the integrity of the dedicated portfolio, however, the cash flows associated with the bond being sold must be replaced with those from the bond (or bonds) being purchased. As a result, bonds with identical coupons and maturities can be swapped, or bonds with higher coupons and similar maturities. Bonds with similar coupons and slightly earlier maturities can also be swapped provided an additional cash pay-up is not required.

In addition to swapping, an active manager might add significant value by actively positioning a new dedicated portfolio in cheap sectors of the market. As spreads change, the optimized portfolio will automatically overweight the newly cheapened sectors of the market and underweight the rich ones.

For example, suppose that an existing $100 million dedicated portfolio could be reoptimized, using the same set of constraints, into a $99.4 million portfolio with a $600,000 takeout. Suppose further that the portfolio manager believes that corporate spreads will widen over the next few months. The manager might desire to temporarily upgrade his portfolio from the current average rating of double-A, await the anticipated spread changes, then reverse the trade at a later date.

In this situation, the optimal strategy is to spend the $600,000 take-out to buy a higher quality portfolio. Rather than minimize cost, the portfolio can be optimized to maximize the quality rating, subject to the constraint of spending the full $100 million and cash-flow-matching every liability payment. As shown in Exhibit 43–7, the average rating of the portfolio was increased by two rating categories from double-A to agency.

Similarly, if rates were expected to rise, the portfolio could be positioned as short as possible by minimizing duration. In Exhibit 43–8, the duration of the portfolio was shortened by almost six months while still maintaining a cash-flow match. Alternatively, if rates were expected to fall, the $600,000 surplus in the portfolio could be used to maximize duration.

## ROLE OF MONEY MANAGER AND DEALER FIRM

Both money managers and dealer firms have played important roles in managing and executing cash-flow-matched portfolios. There are relative advantages to selecting a money manager over a dealer firm (and vice versa) in implementing

**EXHIBIT 43–7**
**Maximize Quality**

|  | Market Value (000) | Average Rating | Take-Out (000) |
|---|---|---|---|
| Original dedicated portfolio | $100,000 | Aaa/AA+ | — |
| Reoptimized dedicated portfolio (minimum cost) | 99,400 | Aaa/AA+ | $600 |
| Reoptimized dedicated portfolio (maximum quality) | 100,000 | Treasury/Agency | — |

the dedicated strategy. For example, all portfolio optimizations require a database of bonds that is both priced and sized by traders. Most money managers have access only to matrix pricing (computer derived pricing) that is generally reliable for corporate securities within a range of plus or minus 30 basis points. When an optimizer is applied to a matrix priced database of bonds, the optimizer will find the least-cost solution by identifying bonds that are cheap (due to mis-pricing) and select them in large blocks for the optimal solution. Since the computer-derived solution is not executable at the cheap levels specified in the database, the "least-cost" solution is not optimal when executed at market rates.

Dealer firms and software vendors with dealer connections are best positioned to simulate, structure, and execute an optimum portfolio due to the accurate pricing and sizing in their databases. However, because dealer firms are not fiduciaries, money managers direct the analysis and make the active management decisions about sector positioning, call protection, credit decisions, and spread forecasts. Money managers also oversee the execution of reoptimizations.

In short, both dealers and money managers can add value to the structuring and reoptimization of dedicated portfolios.

**EXHIBIT 43–8**
**Minimize Duration**

|  | Market Value (000) | Duration (Years) | Percent Decrease |
|---|---|---|---|
| Original dedicated portfolio | $100,000 | 5.4 | — |
| Reoptimized dedicated portfolio (minimum cost) | 99,400 | 5.4 | — |
| Reoptimized dedicated portfolio (minimum duration) | 100,000 | 4.9 | 8.3% |

## CONCLUSION

Dedication is an important portfolio investment strategy for controlling interest-rate risk and for locking in prevailing market rates. For insurance companies with fixed liability products such as GICs or structured settlements, cash flow matching has been a popular approach to lock in a spread (or profit) on the entire line of business.

For pension funds, the motivation is to control market risk by fully funding or defeasing the more quantifiable retired liabilities of a plan and locking in a market rate that is well in excess of the actuarial investment return assumption. By raising the actuarial rate to today's market levels on the dedicated portion of the plan, the plan sponsor is able to reduce pension contributions (pension expense), and thereby increase corporate cash flow and reported earnings.

The plan sponsor is also able to eliminate most funding risk (market risk) from a significant part of a plan's liability and eliminate market value fluctuations when reporting surplus asset (or unfunded liability) positions associated with that liability.

# CHAPTER 44

## EXTENSIONS OF DEDICATED BOND PORTFOLIO TECHNIQUES

*T. Dessa Fabozzi, Ph.D.*
*Vice President*
*Financial Strategies Group*
*Merrill Lynch Capital Markets*

*Tom Tong*
*Vice President*
*Financial Strategies Group*
*Merrill Lynch Capital Markets*

*Yu Zhu, Ph.D.*
*Vice President*
*Financial Strategies Group*
*Merrill Lynch Capital Markets*

As was explained in the previous chapter, cash matching has become an important portfolio strategy that has been widely applied in asset/liability management. The purpose of this chapter is to present two extensions of cash matching, which we call symmetric cash matching and reverse cash matching.

### SYMMETRIC CASH MATCHING

Cash matching uses only cash flows occurring on or before a liability date to meet the liability. An extended cash-matching strategy, which we will call "symmetric cash matching," uses cash flows occurring both before and after the liability date to meet a particular liability. We have chosen the name because the cash flows used to meet the liability stream can lie symmetrically around the liability date, although in actuality the cash flow timing and amount that result from the employment of this technique are rarely symmetric.

Symmetric cash matching requires that the firm incur short-term borrowing when using the cash flows beyond the liability date to satisfy the liability. The short-term borrowed funds are repaid immediately upon the receipt of cash flows from the investment portfolio. Thus, the loan term may range from overnight until the next liability date. Liability needs are still met with the portfolio cash flow, but the cash flow structure is less rigid than under a straight cash-matching strategy. Security selection with symmetric cash matching becomes easier and the cost may be lower.[1] Also, because the short-term debt is backed by the portfolio's cash inflow, risk is minimized.

To explain the benefits of symmetric cash matching we will compare it to a cash-matching portfolio strategy. In both cases, linear programming will be employed to find the optimal portfolio required to fund the liability stream.

## An Illustration of Symmetric Cash Matching

Suppose XYZ company must meet a liability stream totaling $105,262,000 over the period from February 1988 to February 1994. The company wishes to construct a bond portfolio to fund this liability stream. In the analysis, the firm specifies a borrowing rate of 8 percent for short-term loans (less than six months, the time period between liability dates) and a reinvestment rate for mismatched funds of 6 percent. The firm also limits the universe of bonds for the constructed portfolio to noncallable Treasury securities, thus avoiding default, call, and event risks. The liability stream the company must fund is shown in Exhibit 44–1.

**EXHIBIT 44–1**
**Liability Stream for XYZ Co.**

| Date | Liability | Date | Liability |
|---|---|---|---|
| 2/01/88 | $3,912,500 | 2/01/91 | $ 8,112,000 |
| 8/01/88 | 5,913,500 | 8/01/91 | 13,112,500 |
| 2/01/89 | 3,650,000 | 2/01/92 | 12,368,750 |
| 8/01/89 | 3,650,000 | 8/01/92 | 11,637,500 |
| 2/01/90 | 3,650,000 | 2/01/93 | 11,275,000 |
| 8/01/90 | 6,650,000 | 8/01/93 | 10,881,250 |
| | | 2/01/94 | 10,450,000 |

---

[1] A symmetric cash-matching strategy may not present a lower cost solution than a straight cash-matching approach in all cases. It will be most beneficial when the liability dates are between cash flow dates for the bonds in the portfolio.

A straight cash-matched solution will result in the purchase of 13 Treasury securities at a total dollar cost of $78,759,000. The cash flows from this portfolio and the liability stream are illustrated in Exhibit 44–2. As can be seen from this exhibit, the cash flows from the bond portfolio are more than sufficient to cover the current liabilities, resulting in a positive ending cash balance in each period. These funds will be reinvested at an annual reinvestment rate of 6 percent. At the end of the investment horizon, the firm is left with no ending surplus.

We reoptimized the problem using a symmetric cash-matching technique for two cases. In the first case, we allowed the firm to borrow 100 percent of the liability due each period. In the second case, we allowed the firm to borrow only 50 percent of the liability due each period. In both cases, the amount borrowed was repaid immediately from subsequent bond portfolio cash flows.

In the first case, the solution resulted in the purchase of 13 Treasury securities (although a basket of securities different from the one suggested under the dedication strategy) at a total dollar cost of $78,183,000. The cash flows from this portfolio and liability stream are illustrated in Exhibit 44–3. As can be seen from the "borrowing inflows," the firm borrows funds in each period to meet its current liability. The resulting cash surplus at the end of the investment horizon is $1,015. When the firm is allowed to borrow only 50 percent of the liability

**EXHIBIT 44–2**
**Cash-Matching Strategy (Reinvestment Rate = 6%).**

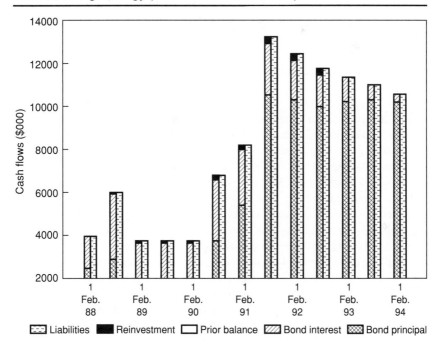

**EXHIBIT 44–3**
**Symmetric Cash-Matching Strategy (Borrowing Maximum: 100%; Rates: Reinvestment 6%; Borrow 8%).**

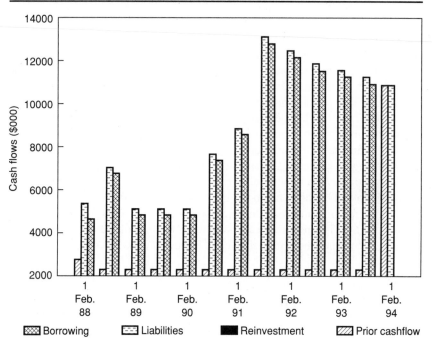

in each period, the cost of the portfolio will be $78,460,000 and the solution requires the purchase of 20 bonds. The cash balance at the end of the horizon is $1,497. The cash flows from this solution are shown in Exhibit 44–4. This exhibit clearly shows why we call this strategy symmetric cash matching.

We see that the firm can save $576,000 on the initial cost of constructing the bond portfolio by using symmetric cash matching when the firm is permitted to borrow 100 percent of the liability. When the firm may borrow only 50 percent of its liability in each period, it still can save close to $300,000 on the portfolio construction cost. Both cases offer a substantial savings to the firm compared to a straight cash-matching strategy, however, the firm is afforded greater savings when allowed to borrow more of the liability flow because of the greater flexibility allowed in constructing the portfolio.

Although the borrowing rate is 200 basis points above the reinvestment rate, using symmetric cash matching allows a better match of the timing of liability payments to cash flow receipts. The larger income received from investing in the higher yielding bond portfolio for a longer time period under this strategy outweighs the borrowing costs. In many periods, funds used to meet the liability

**EXHIBIT 44–4**
**Symmetric Cash-Matching Strategy (Borrowing Maximum: 50%; Rates: Reinvestment 6%; Borrow 8%).**

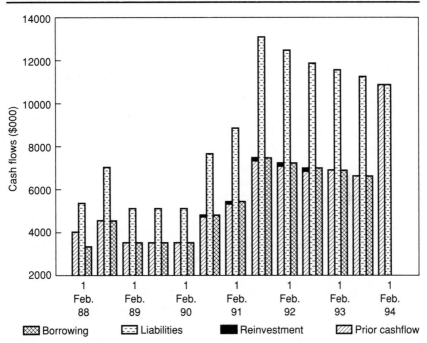

stream are borrowed for only a few days, because the cash flows received after the liability dates are used immediately to repay the debt. Because following this strategy allows a firm to better match cash flows from investment to its liabilities, it avoids having large amounts of mismatched funds reinvested at a relatively low rate.

## Risks Incurred with Symmetric Cash Matching

*Rate Risk.* The biggest concern of a portfolio manager employing a symmetric cash-matching technique is uncertainty with respect to future interest rates. Although it is unrealistic to assume a 200 basis point spread between borrowing and lending rates, we chose this very conservative assumption to illustrate that symmetric cash matching may be of benefit to the fund manager in a case where a relatively high borrowing cost is assumed.

We performed simple scenario analyses to determine the impact on the cash flows in both the straight cash-matched case and the two symmetric cash-matched cases of borrowing and reinvestment rates changes that occur just after the bond portfolio is constructed. We have summarized the results in Exhibit 44–5.

First, we analyzed what would happen to the solution if rates increased right after the creation of the bond portfolio. We shifted both interest rates up by 100 basis points. Thus the new borrowing rate is 9 percent and the new reinvestment rate is 7 percent. For this scenario, the ending balance in the 50 percent symmetric cash-matched portfolio is approximately $132,000. A negative balance of close to $35,000 occurred in the 100 percent case. The cash-matched portfolio reported a gain of over $309,000. This example demonstrates the impact of reinvestment income on the portfolios. In the 50 percent case, the gain in reinvestment income outweighs the higher borrowing cost because, in most cases, the borrowing occurs only for a short time after the liability date.[2] The 100 percent case reported a small negative ending balance. Because this case relies more heavily on short-term borrowing, the borrowing costs outweigh the benefits of additional reinvestment income. As can be seen in this example, the variance in cash flows resulting from symmetric cash matching are lower than those from the straight cash-matching strategy. This is because the impact of a change in the borrowing rate partly offsets the effect of a change in the reinvestment rate on portfolio cash flows.

When we shifted both interest rates down by 100 basis points (with a borrowing rate equal to 7 percent and a reinvestment rate of 5 percent), the cash-matched portfolio resulted in a negative ending cash balance of over $309,000, again demonstrating its strong reliance on reinvestment income. The symmet-

**EXHIBIT 44–5**
**Scenario Analysis Results**

| Scenario | Ending Cash Balance on 2/01/94 | | |
|---|---|---|---|
| | | Symmetric Cash Matching | |
| Reinvestment/ Borrowing | Cash Matching | 50% | 100% |
| 6% / 8% | $        0 | $    1,497 | $    1,015 |
| 7% / 9% | 309,047 | 132,930 | −34,758 |
| 5% / 7% | −309,045 | −126,048 | 33,487 |

---

[2] Because we chose a large spread between the borrowing rate and the reinvestment rate, the optimal solution will utilize borrowed funds only for short time periods.

ric cash-matched portfolio for the 50 percent case resulted in a loss of over $126,000 and the 100 percent case reported a small gain of approximately $33,500. The shortfall in the 50 percent borrowing case resulted from the lost reinvestment income outweighing the fall in short-term borrowing costs. In the 100 percent case, the gain from a reduction in borrowing cost outweighed the loss in reinvestment income from interim cash flows.

In the scenario analysis results presented above, we can see that there is a trade-off between a lower initial cost of constructing the portfolio with the possible risk of a rise in borrowing costs and the benefit to be derived from a cash-matched portfolio if reinvestment rates rise above those assumed in the portfolio construction. However, if reinvestment rates fall during the period, the portfolio manager could lose a substantial amount of income that he or she was relying on in the cash-matched portfolio. Given that future interest rates are uncertain and portfolio managers of structured investment funds are not in the business of predicting interest rates, this interest-rate play should not be considered when constructing a portfolio to fund a liability steam.

In addition, in a symmetric cash-matched portfolio, given that the impact of a change in the reinvestment rate to some extent offsets the impact of the change in the borrowing rate (assuming that both rates move in the same direction), the risk of an adverse change in reinvestment rates is lower than in a cash-matched fund. This is because a straight cash-matched portfolio relies heavily on the assumed reinvestment rate when the portfolio is constructed.

*Default risk.*    The difference in bond default risk of a cash-matched versus a symmetric-matched fund is insignificant if both strategies choose bonds of the same quality rating to construct the funding portfolio. All borrowing is backed by the expected cash inflows and is of very short duration, because loans are repaid as cash flows are received. Thus, the higher cost of borrowing is more than outweighed by the better matching of cash flows, allowing a higher yield portfolio to be purchased.

## REVERSED CASH MATCHING

In many cases, a firm faces a situation where it expects to receive a set of cash inflows with a large degree of predictability.[3] A relevant question to ask is: How can the firm benefit from these cash flows in the current period? One possible answer is that the firm can issue debt supported by the cash inflows, freeing current funds while immediately defeasing the issued debt. This constitutes a

---

[3] Leasing and other account receivables are examples of these cash flows.

low-risk financing strategy for the firm. We call this strategy "reversed cash matching."[4]

In a cash-matching strategy, a portfolio manager expects to fund some liability stream with an optimal combination of assets, such that the cash flows from the assets in each period are sufficient to cover the liability requirements. With optimal debt issuance the situation is reversed. The firm expects to receive measurable future cash flows and desires to issue debt in the current time period to be backed by these expected cash flows. Optimization techniques are employed to find an optimal combination of debt issues (i.e., liabilities) that are fully supported by the expected inflows.

In the following sections we use a simple example to demonstrate how reversed cash matching may be employed by a firm to find the optimal basket of debt to issue, thus maximizing the current dollar takeout to the firm. Because the debt will be fully supported by the expected cash inflows, risk is minimized. We will apply reversed cash matching to a leasing company that desires to issue the optimal amount of debt, maximizing the current dollar takeout while fully funding the liability stream with expected leasing receivables.

The reversed cash-matching strategy may be applied when designing structures of some asset-backed securities. Here, the optimal pool of bonds to be issued is determined by constructing liability cash flows that are matched by the expected cash inflows on the underlying collateral pool of assets. Although our example focuses on the issuance of lease-backed bonds, other applications can include such securities as receivable-backed bonds, mortgage-backed securities, hospital revenue bonds, and student loan securities.

### An Application of Reversed Cash Matching

*The Problem.* In January 1988, A Leasing Company projects that it will receive $1,577,118 in leasing revenues each quarter for the next nine years. The firm has decided that it wants to issue commercial paper and/or medium-term notes to be fully backed by the expected lease receivables. The borrowing rates expected for the debt issues are determined by using the current rates on Treasury bills and notes with similar maturities and adding the appropriate spreads for the credit risk associated with the debt of A Leasing Company. At the time of the analysis the rates shown in Exhibit 44–6 were available.

Based on this information, a universe is set up consisting of 18 possible debt issues whose maturities span from six months to nine years, the desired maturity range specified by A Leasing Company. The borrowing rates on debt issues for

---

[4] This strategy can also be called optimal debt issuance. However, the strategy optimizes only a local set of bond issues, not the global structure of the firm's debt.

**EXHIBIT 44–6**
**Borrowing Rates for a Leasing Company**

| Maturity | Treasury Rate (Percent) | Spread (Basis Points) | Rate for Debt (Percent) |
|----------|------------------------|----------------------|------------------------|
| 6-month  | 6.60%  | 60 b. p. | 7.20%  |
| 9-month  | 6.96   | 60       | 7.56   |
| 12-month | 7.08   | 65       | 7.73   |
| 2-year   | 7.77   | 75       | 8.52   |
| 3-year   | 8.05   | 85       | 8.90   |
| 4-year   | 8.22   | 95       | 9.17   |
| 5-year   | 8.37   | 105      | 9.42   |
| 7-year   | 8.61   | 120      | 9.81   |
| 10-year  | 8.83   | 130      | 10.13  |

maturities between those specified above, such as eight-year securities, were interpolated from the information given. It is assumed that the debt is issued at par. Initially, for simplicity, we shall omit reinvestment income.

A mixed integer programming model[5] will be employed to determine the optimal debt issuance for this firm. The objective is to maximize the total dollar value of bonds to be issued, subject to the following constraints:

1. The receivables are sufficient to cover all interest and principal payments due each period on the issued debt.
2. A minimum and a maximum dollar size are specified for each issue.
3. A limit is specified on the allowable number of separate bond issues.

Additional constraints could be included in the optimization program based on the requirements of the firm.

We included constraint (3) because a firm will usually place a limit on the number of separate new issues it will float at any one time for practical and administrative reasons. In our example, the number of separate bond issues is limited to eight.

*The Solution.* The optimal solution to the problem concludes that A Leasing Company should issue eight bonds with total proceeds of $37,310,000 and maturities ranging from 1988 to 1996. The debt portfolio, shown in Exhibit 44–7, has an average maturity of 5.77 years and an average duration of 4.36 years.

---

[5] The model represents a mixture of both linear and integer programming, where integer variables are included in the analysis.

**EXHIBIT 44–7**
**Reversed Cash Matching — Bond Issuance** (Settlement Date: 1/04/1988)

| Bond | Coupon | Maturity | Par Amount | Price | Flat Price | Accrued | Full Price |
|------|--------|----------|-----------|--------|-----------------|---------|-----------------|
| 1 | 7.200 | 06/15/1988 | 2,990 | 100.00 | 2,990,000.00 | 0.00 | 2,990,000.00 |
| 2 | 7.730 | 12/15/1988 | 1,680 | 100.00 | 1,680,000.00 | 0.00 | 1,680,000.00 |
| 3 | 8.130 | 06/15/1989 | 1,590 | 100.00 | 1,590,000.00 | 0.00 | 1,590,000.00 |
| 4 | 8.520 | 12/15/1989 | 1,660 | 100.00 | 1,660,000.00 | 0.00 | 1,660,000.00 |
| 5 | 8.900 | 12/15/1990 | 3,460 | 100.00 | 3,460,000.00 | 0.00 | 3,460,000.00 |
| 6 | 9.170 | 12/15/1991 | 3,780 | 100.00 | 3,780,000.00 | 0.00 | 3,780,000.00 |
| 7 | 9.420 | 12/15/1992 | 4,120 | 100.00 | 4,120,000.00 | 0.00 | 4,120,000.00 |
| 8 | 10.000 | 12/15/1996 | 18,030 | 100.00 | 18,030,000.00 | 0.00 | 18,030,000.00 |
| | | | | | 37,310,000.00 | | 37,310,000.00 |

The cash flow results considering both the leasing income and debt payments are shown graphically in Exhibit 44–8. The leasing cash flow is sufficient to fully service the debt requirements, with a surplus balance resulting in each period.

This solution demonstrates that with optimal debt issuance the firm can take advantage of expected future cash inflows in the current time period by issuing debt that is fully backed by the expected cash inflows. This strategy benefits the firm by minimizing the risk associated with the debt issued (because the firm is, in effect, predefeasing debt) while freeing up capital in the current time period. In this case, A Leasing Company was able to use expected receivables to back current optimal debt issuance for an initial dollar takeout of over $37 million.

***Comparison Solutions—Relaxing the Constraints.*** The constraints employed in the optimization can be tailored to meet the particular needs of the firm requesting the issuance. In the example above, we employed some assumptions that may be unrealistic for a firm using this strategy. Several of the constraints used for the initial solution will be relaxed here to determine their impact on the dollar takeout for the firm.

**EXHIBIT 44–8**
**Reversed Cash Matching** (Reinvestment Rate = 0%).

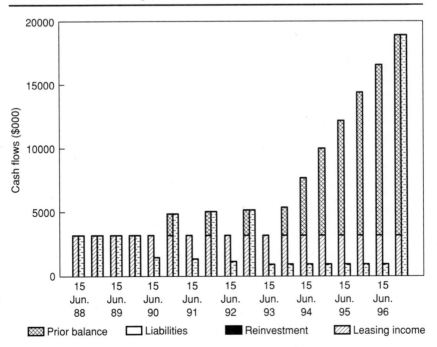

1. *Allowing for the reinvestment of mismatched funds.* Assuming a reinvestment rate of zero for mismatched funds is very conservative and often unrealistic. In most cases the firm will not keep funds idle, but will reinvest them in income-producing vehicles. We reoptimized the problem, assuming various reinvestment rates, and will present only summary results here. Exhibit 44–9 shows the results for the initial problem as well as the results obtained from allowing for the reinvestment of mismatched funds at rates of 2%, 4%, 6%, and 8%. As can be seen from the table, the higher the reinvestment rate, the larger the dollar takeout to the firm.[6] These rates were chosen for comparison purposes only. The actual reinvestment rate for the firm will probably be a rate between those given. Thus it seems reasonable to estimate that the firm's initial takeout can exceed $39 million.

2. *Relaxing the constraint on the allowable number of debt issues.* In most cases, the firm may wish to set a limit on the number of separate debt issues to be brought to the market at any one time. If this constraint is removed from the analysis, the optimal solution suggests the issuance of 11 securities. As a result, the dollar takeout to the firm is increased by $1,410,000. If a more restrictive limit on the number of bonds to be issued was imposed, say, restricting the debt to a maximum of six issues, the optimal solution would consist of six issues for a total dollar takeout of $35,420,000, which is $1,890,000 less than the solution involving a maximum of eight issues and $3,300,000 less than when no limit was placed on the number of issues. Thus, this constraint has an important impact on the profitability of the strategy.

**EXHIBIT 44–9**
**Reversed Cash Matching —**
**Comparison Solutions**

| Reinvestment Rate | Dollar Takeout |
| --- | --- |
| 0% | $37,310,000 |
| 2 | 38,730,000 |
| 4 | 39,010,000 |
| 6 | 39,290,000 |
| 8 | 39,570,000 |

[6] The relatively large discrepancy between the dollar takeout in the 0 percent and the 2 percent reinvestment cases is due mainly to the different debt structures suggested in the solution to these cases. The case with 0 percent reinvestment of mismatched funds suggests the issuance of very short term bonds along with one large issue due in December 1996. The 2 percent reinvestment case allows a more level debt structure, resulting in a lower cost of funds. In addition, allowing higher reinvestment rates suggests structures similar to the 2 percent case. Although higher reinvestment rates improve the dollar takeout, their incremental effects on the final solution become gradual.

## SUMMARY

This chapter detailed two new strategies built on the cash-matching strategy. By allowing short-term borrowing, symmetric cash matching provides a flexible and cost-effective approach to finance a firm's liabilities. This strategy allows a firm to better match cash flows from a portfolio to liability needs. By allowing the firm to meet liability cash flows both from cash inflows occurring before the liability date and from borrowing cash inflows expected just beyond the liability date, the firm may be able to realize substantial savings on the cost of constructing the portfolio. The more flexibility the manager is afforded in terms of borrowing interim cash flows, the better the firm is able to match cash outflows to actual and expected cash inflows from the bond portfolio. Even if a restriction is placed on the amount of the liability that can be borrowed each period, the cost savings may be substantial over a straight cash-matched strategy.

A reverse cash-matching strategy may be used to construct the optimal structure of debt (or asset-backed securities) for a firm. Our example shows that reversed cash matching may enable a firm to benefit from expected future cash flows, freeing capital in the current period with minimal risk. The application of the strategy can be extended to structuring other asset-backed securities.

In sum, the strategies presented here show that the cash-matching strategy can be more versatile and less costly than originally expected. Skillful application of this well-known strategy can solve a wide scope of investment problems.

# CHAPTER 45

## HIGH-YIELD
## BOND PORTFOLIOS

*Howard S. Marks, CFA*
*Managing Director*
*Trust Company of the West*

In a so-called efficient market, all potential investments are analyzed objectively with equal thoroughness and skill, and the *a priori* returns at which they sell are established proportionate to the risks entailed. This is a vast simplification of the relevant theory, but it makes sense and certainly serves adequately as a backdrop to the search for disequilibria and exceptions from which above-average risk-adjusted gains might be earned. The principal fallout from this formulation of the theory is the suggestion that on viewing any investment that appears to offer returns greater than are commensurate with the risks, the potential investor should ask, "Why should this be the case? Why am I being offered this chance?"

It appears that such an opportunity may be offered in the high-yield sector of the fixed income universe: The yields at which these bonds are available are very high, incorporating large risk premiums, but the actual historical risks have been shown to be modest. It is the purpose of this chapter to describe and define the high-yield sector, to attempt to quantify the risks and returns, and to try to explain why this opportunity may exist.

### High-Yield Bonds Defined

First of all, what are high-yield bonds? They are simply lower rated bonds. "High-yield" is a euphemism for bonds popularly perceived to entail a substantial probability that the interest payments and principal repayment will not occur as promised. Another, less kind, nickname is "junk bonds." Those in the business regret this nickname, but it does exemplify the attitude that can make unusual profit opportunities available.

Most high-yield bonds are corporate bonds. U.S. government bonds and agency obligations have not yet had their creditworthiness impugned. Most municipals have been considered worry-free—at least until New York City's difficulties shook investor confidence and the Washington Public Power Supply System became the first major default in the tax-free area.

Utilities have generally been considered unlikely to default because the essential nature of their product makes it incumbent on the regulators to establish rates that ensure their viability. But recently, uncertainties involved in building and operating nuclear generating facilities have endangered some utility debt, weakening the bonds of Long Island Lighting and causing the bankruptcy of Public Service of New Hampshire. The historical article of faith that no utility can be permitted to default has thus far been shown to be less than an absolute, but these two situations have healed and no new problems have arisen in years.

The greatest number of popularly perceived problem credits, constituting the vast bulk of the high-yield bond sector, are found in the industrial and financial areas. By and large, they are bonds that are rated Ba and below by Moody's Investor Services or BB and below by Standard & Poor's, or bonds that are unrated but considered to be equivalent in quality to those rating categories.

What do those ratings mean? In Moody's words, "bonds which are rated Ba are judged to have speculative elements; their future cannot be considered as well assured." It says further that "bonds which are rated B generally lack characteristics of the desirable investment." [1] Standard & Poor's says all bonds rated BB and below are "predominantly speculative with respect to capacity to pay interest and repay principal. . . ." [2] These statements strike fear in the hearts of would-be buyers and tend to discourage investment. Is this appropriate?

One's first reaction might be to question the propriety of assessing the desirability of an investment, as Moody's does, on the basis of the risk alone and without reference to the prospective return. After all, in the efficient market described at the outset, return is logically arrayed opposite risk. Should an investment be condemned solely because it entails high risk or uncertainty? Are venture capital investments that offer success ratios of one-in-twenty or worse necessarily bad investments? The attitude displayed by calling these junk bonds implies that an uncertain investment is an undesirable investment. But who among us does not wish that he or she had made an uncertain investment in Apple Computer or in Genentech?

Yet, many bond investors say, "I would never buy a B-rated bond." The implicit statement that a bond of low quality cannot be a good investment, regardless of price or implied return, at once shows why it is reasonable to

---

[1] *Moody's Bond Record,* Moody's Investors Service, January, 1984. p. 1
[2] *Standard & Poor's Bond Guide,* Standard & Poor's Corporation, July, 1985. p. 10.

believe that bargains can be found in low-rated bonds: *prejudice keeps investors from looking at these investment vehicles in the objective, dispassionate way required for a market to be truly efficient.*

## TRENDS IN FIXED INCOME INVESTMENTS AND OPPORTUNITIES WITH HIGH-YIELD BONDS

Historically, bonds have been a preferred investment of fiduciaries, purchased to provide secure bedrock for a portfolio. Traditionally, fiduciaries were driven by a doctrine that stressed the avoidance of risk in the absolute and emphasized the preservation of capital. "Prudent man" laws applied penalties if any risky investments were undertaken and were unsuccessful. Further, if a number of risky but potentially lucrative investments were made and one failed, the fiduciary could be sued and "surcharged" for the one that failed without being able to offset losses against the profits from the ones that succeeded. Clearly, such a climate provided great incentive to strive to avoid risk. Among the modern concepts that had yet to be invented were risk management, the portfolio approach to investing, real return, opportunity cost, and competitive performance.

In an excellent, related article in the *Financial Analysts Journal,* Dean LeBaron of Batterymarch sought to explain why, despite all of the arguments for market efficiency, departures from efficiency exist and persist. The reason he discussed first and longest is what he calls his "theory of agents." Basically, the problem is that the people who manage money are not the people whose money it is, and that they therefore have different incentives. Risk taking probably will not lead to great rewards for professional money managers if done successfully, but it can certainly produce problems—like termination—if done poorly. "The guiding principle in this environment seems to be that it is better to make a little money conventionally than to run even the smallest risk of losing a lot unconventionally."[3]

Hired money managers, especially in the fixed income world, have traditionally paid dearly for the safety (both financial and personal) they feel accompanies high ratings and have tried to avoid risk by shunning low-rated bonds despite their high yields and the historical evidence that default is a rare phenomenon.

An excellent example of extreme bias against high-yield bonds is seen in the recent enactment of a law requiring savings and loans to divest themselves of all high-yield bond investments within five years. This law was passed despite

---

[3] Dean LeBaron, "Reflections on Market Inefficiency," *Financial Analysts Journal,* May-June 1983, p. 16.

a total lack of empirical justification. As said in a *The New York Times* article titled "The $12 Billion Misunderstanding,"

> The economic case for prohibiting investment in junk bonds is far weaker than the political case. High-risk bonds have proved to be a prudent investment for savings institutions. . . . Estimates made by Wharton Economic Forecasting Associates in 1988 and confirmed [in 1989] by the General Accounting Office show that widely diversified portfolios of junk bonds have consistently outperformed Treasury bonds, investment-grade bonds and home mortgages.[4]

As time has passed, a number of trends have affected the investment world in ways that have led to alteration of this traditional approach toward risk and some increased willingness to consider high-yield investing:

- Volatile interest rates have made all fixed income investing more "risky."
- Rate volatility has led investors to attempt to anticipate interest-rate movements, but success has proved elusive.
- High ratings have not guaranteed an absence of credit losses.
- Professional investors in general have accepted the task of managing risk rather than attempting to avoid it—although traditional fixed income investors have been slow to adopt this approach.
- A public market for low-rated new issues and secondary trades has developed.
- Most important, history has consistently shown that lower rated fixed income portfolios have generated higher returns.

No doubt the preceding has demonstrated that prejudice is present in a way that can be reasonably believed to have kept high-yield bonds underpriced, and that the underpricing that is present makes a review of the sector worthwhile.

## HISTORICAL DEVELOPMENT

Prior to about 1977, companies that did not qualify for high ratings were unable to issue debt in the public market (due in large part to the prejudices against below-investment-grade debt described above). Their choices, for the most part, were limited to taking on bank debt, with its short-term nature, or selling private placement debt to insurance companies, which usually meant accepting severely restrictive covenants.

This is not to say there were no low-rated bonds in the public market. There were many, but they had not been issued as such. They were issued with investment-grade ratings (BBB/Baa or higher) and then were downgraded as

---

[4] Peter Passel, "The $12 Billion Misunderstanding," *The New York Times,* July 19, 1989.

their issuers encountered operating difficulties. Above and beyond the previously issued debt of these "fallen angels," exchanges designed to modify the financial structure of troubled companies in a way that would reduce debt service or delay maturities created additional low-rated, publicly traded bonds.

Beginning in the mid-1970s, pioneering work done primarily at the investment banking firm of Drexel Burnham Lambert led to the conclusion that historical default experience did not justify the traditional aversion to low-rated debt, and that new issues of such securities should be salable. The initial buyers consisted largely of individuals and high-yield mutual funds, which were subsequently joined by pension funds, insurance companies, banks, and savings and loans.

Through this process, new groups of issues have come to share with the fallen angels the label "high-yield bonds." These bonds receive noninvestment-grade ratings on issuance rather than as a result of being downgraded.

- The first group, often called "emerging credits," led the post-1977 parade of original issue low-rated bonds. On average, these issuers are smaller and younger than the fallen angels, and thus they receive their low ratings more because of lack of experience and critical mass than because of miscues.
- Another group came to prominence in the mid-1980s: leveraged buyouts. These bonds are issued to finance changes in ownership in which debt capital is used principally to pay off the former equity owners. Although the subject companies are generally much larger and better established than the emerging credits, the buyouts produce debt/equity ratios and interest coverage ratios that fall much higher on the risk scale.
- In quick succession, two additional groups of bonds arose as a direct consequence of the flurry of LBO activity. "Recapitalizations" are transactions through which, as in the case of LBOs, debt is substituted for equity. In these defensive transactions, cash is borrowed and paid out to shareholders in order to placate them and thus avert LBOs. The difference is that there is no change of control.
- The last group is the "divisional divestments," which emerge from bust-up type LBOs. These are the business units that are sold off to simplify structure and reduce debt. When the purchases are financed primarily with debt, issuance of high-yield bonds results.

Exhibits 45–1 and 45–2, which document the growth and size of the high-yield market, show that whereas an average $145.7 billion face value of low-rated bonds was outstanding during 1988, $139.8 billion came as new issues between 1978 and 1988. Although these figures are not directly comparable (because of the departure of some issues from the category due to redemption, bankruptcy, or upgrading), they certainly suggest the importance of the post-1977 new issues in creating the high-yield bond market of today.

**EXHIBIT 45–1**
**Public Straight Debt Outstanding 1977–1988** (Millions of Dollars)

|  | Average Par Value Public Straight Debt | Low-Rated Debt | | High-Rated Debt |
|---|---|---|---|---|
|  |  | Straight Public Debt | Percent of Public Straight Debt |  |
| 1988 | $687,590 | $145,748 | 21.2% | $541,842 |
| 1987 | 622,309 | 119,910 | 19.3 | 502,399 |
| 1986 | 505,150 | 92,985 | 18.4 | 412,165 |
| 1985 | 419,600 | 59,178 | 14.1 | 360,422 |
| 1984 | 358,100 | 41,700 | 11.6 | 316,400 |
| 1983 | 319,400 | 28,223 | 8.8 | 291,177 |
| 1982 | 285,600 | 18,536 | 6.5 | 267,064 |
| 1981 | 255,300 | 17,362 | 6.8 | 337,938 |
| 1980 | 265,100 | 15,125 | 5.7 | 249,975 |
| 1979 | 269,900 | 10,675 | 4.0 | 259,225 |
| 1978 | 252,200 | 9,401 | 3.7 | 242,799 |
| 1977 | 237,800 | 8,479 | 3.5 | 229,321 |
| Average compound growth rate | 10.1% | 29.5% | — | 8.1% |

Source: Martin Fridson, Steven B. Jones, and Fritz Wahl, *The Anatomy of the High Yield Debt Market: 1988 Update* (New York: Morgan Stanley & Co., Inc., 1989), p. 11.

Clearly there have been major changes during the time period covered by these two exhibits. Low-rated debt has risen from 3.5 percent of the public straight debt outstanding to 21.2 percent, while the rate of growth of outstandings has been three times that of high-rated bonds. In 1988, high-yield bonds accounted for almost 22 percent of new public straight debt issues, up from 7 percent in 1978. And the size of the average new issue has grown from $28 million in 1978 to $196 million in 1988.

In recent years, increasing attention on the equity side of the investment management industry has been devoted both to "indexing" portfolios so that they will mirror the broad universe and to comparing portfolio diversification against the makeup of popular indexes such as Standard & Poor's 500. In that light, it seems irrational for investors to ignore 21 percent of the public, corporate straight debt market. After all, high-yield bonds are as big a part of the bond market as all of the basic industries' stocks (chemicals, forest products, metals, oil and gas, and transportation) are of the S&P 500. Rather than dismiss a sector as significant as high-yield bonds as "too risky" because the rating agencies say it is, it makes sense to try to ascertain the actual riskiness of these bonds by reviewing the historical experience.

**EXHIBIT 45–2**
**New Straight Domestic Debt Issues: 1978–1988\*** (Millions of Dollars)

| Year | Total Par Value New Public Straight Debt Issues | | Total Par Value New High-Yield Debt Issues | | High-Yield as % New Issue Dollars |
|------|--------|------|--------|------|---------|
|      | Amount | No.  | Amount | No.  | Percent |
| 1988 | $108,598 | 655 | $30,044 | 153 | 21.67% |
| 1987 | 90,273 | 694 | 30,989 | 189 | 25.56 |
| 1986 | 121,367 | 872 | 33,433 | 229 | 21.60 |
| 1985 | 65,361 | 503 | 14,410 | 187 | 18.06 |
| 1984 | 68,379 | 351 | 14,952 | 124 | 17.94 |
| 1983 | 32,761 | 332 | 7,317 | 85 | 18.26 |
| 1982 | 44,516 | 436 | 2,760 | 46 | 5.84 |
| 1981 | 39,572 | 320 | 1,648 | 32 | 4.00 |
| 1980 | 35,328 | 347 | 1,442 | 43 | 3.92 |
| 1979 | 23,130 | 217 | 1,307 | 45 | 5.35 |
| 1978 | 19,944 | 224 | 1,493 | 52 | 6.96 |
| Total | 649,230 | 4,951 | 139,796 | 1,185 | 17.72 |

\* Not including exchange offers, secondary offerings, tax-exempts, convertibles, government agencies, mortgage- or asset-backed issues.

Source: Martin Fridson, Steven B. Jones, and Fritz Wahl, *The Anatomy of the High Yield Debt Market: 1988 Update* (New York: Morgan Stanley & Co., Inc., 1989), p. 15.

## Default Experience

When new high-yield issues began to appear in the late 1970s, widespread analysis began. The critical questions, of course, concerned the magnitude of the risk. Because there was little data on the downgraded bonds and virtually no experience with low-rated new issues, the initial recourse was to default data on the overall bond market. Although the relevance of these historical data to the new high-yield bonds was uncertain, it was quite easy to demonstrate the simple proposition that default has historically been a very rare occurrence. The results of a number of studies are combined in Exhibit 45–3, which details the percentage of all outstanding public debt going into default each year by period.

Clearly, default has occurred infrequently, and this has been especially true since 1940. In the 39 years since 1950, the default rate for all bonds has averaged .15 percent per year.

**EXHIBIT 45-3**
**Total Corporate Bond**
**Default Rates, 1900-**
**1988**

| Year | Default Rate |
|------|-------------|
| 1978-1988 | 0.30% |
| 1968-1977 | 0.20 |
| 1960-1967 | 0.03 |
| 1950-1959 | 0.04 |
| 1940-1949 | 0.40 |
| 1930-1939 | 3.20 |
| 1920-1929 | 1.00 |
| 1910-1919 | 2.00 |
| 1900-1909 | 0.90 |

Source: *Financing America's
Future* (Beverly Hills, CA: Drexel
Burnham Lambert, March 1989),
p. 13.

For years, until additional data were developed, the typical response was, "But what about defaults on low-rated bonds? Don't those bonds default more than the overall universe?" In apparent response to such questions, an article in the *Wall Street Journal* on March 6, 1985, was headlined "Study Finds Much Higher Default Rate for 'Junk Bonds' Than for All Issues." It went on to state that the default rate for bonds rated BB or lower has been 20 times higher than on all corporate bonds[5] The balance of the article and the actual study, however, detailed that the default rate between 1974 and 1984 had been only 1.5 percent of outstanding low-rated straight debt per year. Not only is this default rate modest in absolute terms, but there are reasons why it should be viewed as a conservative (i.e., high) indicator of actual losses. As Altman and Nammacher point out,

> At least 14 of these [54] defaulting firms did not actually file for bankruptcy. In several cases, interest was paid in arrears at a later date either by the firm or by a firm purchasing the defaulted entity. In others, agreements were reached with creditors to restructure the debt.[6]

---

[5] Linda Sandler, "Study Finds Much Higher Default Rate for 'Junk Bonds' Than for All Issued," *The Wall Street Journal,* March 6, 1985.

[6] Edward I. Altman and Scott A. Nammacher, "The Default Rate Experience on High Yield Corporate Debt," *Financial Analysts Journal,* July-August 1985, pp. 25–41.

Additionally, the authors point out that by selling the bonds immediately after bankruptcy, an average of 41 percent of the par value could be recouped and the loss ratio (as opposed to the default ratio) reduced to 1 percent per year. Although the exercise is not performed, adjusting for the defaults that were cured should result in a loss ratio that is even lower.

In the years since the publication of this first study, there has been a great deal of additional work done on the subject of high-yield bond default rates. In line with the increasing size, prominence, and controversiality of the high-yield market, the publication of studies on the subject has exploded. At first, the average default rates cited remained within the range of 1.5 percent to 2.0 percent, and the central estimate increased as annual default rates increased in 1986, 1987 (if one includes Texaco), and 1988.

An apparent blockbuster struck in mid-1989, however, when newspaper articles reported on a Harvard study[7] that concluded that high-yield bonds have defaulted at a 34 percent rate. It was hard to believe that both 2 percent and 34 percent could possibly be reasonable answers to the same question—and it turns out that they cannot. What the Harvard study states is that from the time of issuance through November 1988, 34 percent of the bonds issued in 1977-78 had defaulted. This "lifetime default rate" is clearly not comparable to the annual default rates discussed earlier. Instead, it should be annualized (to roughly 3.5 percent per year) and viewed as the result for a limited sample that was adversely affected because of its heavy representation of energy and steel company bonds.

Default studies have continued to proliferate, as have the conclusions. Most of their default rates have continued to fall from roughly 2.1 percent (Morgan Stanley[8]) to 3.5 percent (Harvard). Most recently, a study by employees of First Boston was published in the *Financial Analysts Journal*. It concluded that between 1977 and 1988, default (defined liberally to include "distressed exchange offers" made to avert same) affected 3.56 percent of all outstanding high-yield bonds (about 2.75 percent without exchange offers). Again, the figures fall within the general range.

The authors then continued to the next step (and an important one omitted by many researchers). They found that in the defaults, 42.7 percent of the amount invested in principal was lost; this produced, with the associated loss of interest, an overall loss rate of 1.63 percent per year. This loss rate appears to be reasonably derived, and I feel it or something like it is the figure for "actual

---

[7] Paul Asquith, David W. Mullins, Jr., and Eric D. Wolff, "Original Issue High Yield Bonds: Aging Analyses of Defaults, Exchanges, and Calls," *The Journal of Finance,* September 1989, p. 923.

[8] Fridson, op. cit., p. 15.

risk" that should be compared against high-yield bonds' promised compensation for risk bearing.[9]

Although the various figures claimed to be the actual default rate do differ materially, they are not so far apart as to preclude reasonable analysis of the opportunities offered by high-yield bonds or action based on that analysis. My own personal experience has provided the following results:

Over the last 10 years, during my employment with Citicorp and Trust Company of the West, in portfolios aggregating hundreds of millions of dollars, a total of $37.8 million was invested in bonds that went into bankruptcy or uncured default. The amount affected by default each year averaged only 0.9 percent of portfolio investments. Further, only $24.9 million was lost on these holdings. Thus, the element of recovery has been substantial, and our principal loss ratio has been only 0.6 percent per year.

I believe these last, personal statistics should be viewed in the following light:

- This experience covers a period including a double-dip recession that was the most severe contraction since the Depression. Yet the overall loss percentage was low in absolute terms.
- Most of the bankruptcies occurred in the oil industry, which was particularly hard hit by an exogenous factor: the volatile behavior of OPEC.
- The corresponding observation is that despite the harsh economic climate, there were no bankruptcies during the recession among our holdings in the manufacturing, finance, or utility sectors, which numbered in the hundreds of issues.
- Because the oil industry was "defrocked" when prices weakened starting in 1981, portfolios assembled since that time have in many cases been oil-free and, consequently, very low in defaults.

There will always be come sector like the oils that is particularly hard hit for systematic reasons (as were the REITs in the 1970s). But it is cheering that there was no random rash of bankruptcies among the balance of our portfolio holdings caused solely by the factors that prompted their low ratings.

When all of the evidence cited above—academic studies, work in the industry, and personal experience—is taken into account, the original conclusion is unchanged; in fact, it is bolstered. On the basis of history, default and bankruptcy occur infrequently, even among the issuers of high-yield bonds.

The loss rate *is* higher than on high-rated bonds, however, so we must examine the adequacy of the yields that are offered as an inducement to bear the risk.

---

[9] George T. Hradsky, and Robert Long, "High Yield Default Losses and the Return Performance of Bankrupt Debt," *Financial Analysts Journal,* July-August 1989, p. 40.

## PROMISED YIELDS ON HIGH-YIELD BONDS

The argument posed earlier was that high-yield bonds, like every other investment, should be considered in terms of the risk and the return they entail. It was already shown that credit losses in these bonds appear more frequently than they do in higher rated bonds. And it might be argued that as the history is limited and as the character of the universe has changed, the data presented could understate the eventual losses. Thus, it is reasonable to require higher *a priori* returns when purchasing these bonds.

On this topic, there is little disagreement. There consistently has been a substantial, positive spread between the yields-to-maturity at which high-yield bonds are available and the yields on higher rated debt securities.

Exhibit 45–4 details the average spread between two brokerage firms' high-yield bond indexes and U.S. Treasury bonds of comparable maturity.

Clearly, the history of the yield spread between high-yield bonds and high-grade bonds (as exemplified by risk-free Treasuries) shows the persistent presence of what has typically been a 350-450 basis point inducement to take the extra risk. The average spread has been below 300 basis points at the end of only 5 of the 117 months for which Salomon Brothers has calculated its index, and the lowest of those observations was at 287 basis points.

By all accounts, the promised yield spread on high-yield bonds has been far more than enough to compensate for the credit losses that have been experienced to date. It seems reasonable to recognize three specific aspects of the spread.

1. The spread implies higher compound returns over full cycles. This is unaffected by changes in interest rates and interim changes in the spread.

**EXHIBIT 45–4**
**Excess Return over Treasury Bonds**

| Year | DBL Composite Index | Salomon Bros. "All" High-Yield Bonds |
|------|---------------------|--------------------------------------|
| 1982 | 504 b. p.           | 526 b. p.                            |
| 1983 | 332                 | 339                                  |
| 1984 | 321                 | 348                                  |
| 1985 | 362                 | 376                                  |
| 1986 | 493                 | 483                                  |
| 1987 | 451                 | 429                                  |
| 1988 | 428                 | 422                                  |

Source: For the DBL Composite Index: *Financing America's Future* (Beverly Hills, CA: Drexel Burnham Lambert, March 1989), p. 112. For Salomon Bros.: *"All" High Yield Bonds: Monthly Letters,* Salomon Brothers, Inc., to author, January 1982 to date.

If the spread is at the same level at the corresponding point in two cycles, the yield spread will be earned—net of credit losses—for each of the intervening years. Thanks to the power of compound interest, returns grow faster than do rates: $10 million invested at 11 percent for 15 years will grow by $37.8 million; increase the rate by 28 percent to 14 percent, and the return grows by 62 percent, to $61.4 million.

2. The increased promised yield comes in the form of incremental interest. It is not a hoped-for capital gain that is "on the come." The regular receipt of higher current interest goes a long way to build a solid base for the total return and to render unfavorable relative performance unlikely. As noted investor John Neff has been described as saying, "of the two components of . . . total return— . . . yield and . . . growth—yield is worth far more because it's 'assured today.'" [10]

3. The increased yield is present as a premium for bearing risk, and it serves that purpose more than admirably. Today's 600 point average spread, for example, means that even if as much as 6 percent of the portfolio's principal value is lost to credit problems each year, the overall return on a high-yield bond portfolio will still match that on a portfolio of Treasury bonds. However, as mentioned earlier, it has been found that a substantial portion of one's investment is recovered when bonds encounter credit difficulty. Thus, if only 60 percent is lost, for example, 10 percent of the portfolio's holdings would have to experience default or bankruptcy each year in order to provide credit losses equal to 6 percent. When that figure is compared to loss estimates concentrated in the range of 2–3 percent (and my own .6 percent) the risk premium can be seen to anticipate much more risk than historically has been present.

What has been described is a risk premium that appears to more than compensate for the actual risk. The result of that combination should be disproportionately high realized returns. Next, we will review what the actual return experience has been.

## REALIZED RETURNS

With an *a priori* risk premium vastly in excess of the risks that actually materialized, superior realized returns should have come from high-yield bonds. And that is exactly what has been witnessed. In fact, the evidence on the subject of returns on low-rated bonds is extensive and appears unanimous.

---

[10] Diane Hal Gropper, "How John Neff Does It," *Institutional Investor,* May 1985, p. 88

**EXHIBIT 45–5**

**Default Experience and Yields: 1900–1943 Statistics**

|  | Life Span Default Rate | Promised Yield | Realized Yield |
|---|---|---|---|
| AAA | 5.9% | 4.5% | 5.1% |
| BBB | 19.1 | 4.9 | 5.0 |
| BB-B-C | 42.4 | 9.5 | 8.6 |

Source: John D. Fitzpatrick and Jacobus T. Severiens, "Hickman Revisited: The Case for Junk Bonds," *The Journal of Portfolio Management*, Summer 1978, p. 53.

The classic study in this field was conducted by Braddock Hickman. The Hickman study covered bond experience between 1900 and 1943. Despite the enormous default rates in the Depression, which in 1936 and 1940 reached 15 percent for all bonds[11] and which pushed 42 percent of all BB-, B-, and C-rated bonds outstanding in the 43-year period into default during their life, low-rated bonds had a superior return.

Exhibit 45–5, which is drawn from Hickman's study, shows the ability of high yields to more than offset high default experience.

In a subsequent study, John Fitzpatrick and Jacobus Severiens reviewed the period 1965–1975.[12] Their findings were similar to Hickman's. Despite the harsh implicit assumption that default results in total loss, systematically higher returns were realized as rating dropped. Exhibit 45–6 shows the unweighted average yields-to-maturity for the 11 years reduced by the default rates for B and BB bonds.

**EXHIBIT 45–6**

**Net Realized Annual Yields to Maturity**

|  | B | BB | BBB | A |
|---|---|---|---|---|
| Average of 11-year results | 9.4% | 8.4% | 8.1% | 7.1% |

Source: Fitzpatrick and Severiens, pp. 53–57.

---

[11] W.B. Hickman, *Corporate Bond Quality and Investor Experience,* (Princeton, New Jersey: Princeton University Press, 1958); and Harold G. Fraine and Robert H. Mills, "Effects of Defaults and Credit Deterioration on Yields of Corporate Bonds," *The Journal of Finance,* September 1961, p. 425.

[12] John D. Fitzpatrick and Jacobus T. Severiens, "Hickman Revisited: The Case for Junk Bonds," *The Journal of Portfolio Management,* Summer 1978, pp. 53–57.

**EXHIBIT 45–7**
**Compounded Annual Rates of Return**

|  | Low-Rated* | A | AAA |
| --- | --- | --- | --- |
| 1/82 through 5/84 | 20.3% | 16.6% | 15.0% |

* Average of DBL 100 and Salomon Brothers indexes.

A more recent academic study by Marshall Blume and Donald Keim covered the 29 months of January 1982 through May 1984.[13] Their conclusions regarding returns are summarized in Exhibit 45–7.

Finally, a tabulation of actual published results for a number of high-yield bond indexes and my investment results is shown in Exhibit 45–8 and is contrasted to the returns on a single Treasury bond and other high-grade bond indexes.

The results for the high-yield indicators are remarkably consistent and consistently superior. Further, they show an interesting pattern: They were superior when high-grade bonds did poorly and inferior when they did well. Thus, the pattern of returns is worthy of review as well.

## VOLATILITY OF RETURNS

The evidence on the volatility of returns runs uniformly in favor of high-yield bonds. At the lowest level, this can be seen on inspection. The defensive nature of the returns previously shown implies lower volatility.

Viewed statistically, the results are the same. The standard deviation of the annual returns on my high-yield bond portfolios, for example, was well below that on Shearson Lehman Huttons's Government/Corporate high-grade index over the last 9½ years.

|  | Standard Deviation of Annual Returns* (1/1/80-6/30/88) |
| --- | --- |
| Author's high-yield portfolio | 7.4% |
| SLH Gov't/Corp bonds (high-rated) | 8.2% |

* Annualized standard deviation based on monthly data.

---

[13] Marshall E. Blume and Donald B. Keim, "Risk and Return Characteristics of Lower Grade Bonds," Rodney L. White Center for Financial Research, University of Pennsylvania, 1985, pp. 3–4.

**EXHIBIT 45-8**
**Total Returns**

| Index or Portfolio | 1988 | 1987 | 1986 | 1985 | 1984 | 1983 | 1982 | 1981 | 1980 | C.A.G.R. |
|---|---|---|---|---|---|---|---|---|---|---|
| *High-Yield Bond Indicators:* | | | | | | | | | | |
| Salomon "All" High Yield Bonds | 15.20% | 4.60% | 16.50% | 23.60% | 8.60% | 21.90% | 30.80% | 3.40% | 0.40% | 13.47% |
| DBL Composite Index | 14.50 | 6.40 | 19.30 | 22.50 | 8.50 | 19.70 | 32.50 | 2.70 | 0.90 | 13.70 |
| Author's Portfolios | 15.90 | 5.02 | 21.40 | 23.40 | 5.09 | 17.70 | 27.50 | 7.80 | 4.90 | 14.00 |
| *High-Grade Bond Indicators:* | | | | | | | | | | |
| Shearson Govt/Corp | 7.58 | 2.29 | 15.62 | 21.30 | 15.02 | 8.00 | 31.09 | 7.26 | 3.06 | 12.02 |
| Shearson T-Bond Indexes | 6.99 | 2.00 | 15.61 | 20.91 | 14.47 | 7.05 | 27.84 | 9.24 | 5.61 | 11.93 |
| Shearson Corp Bond Index | 9.22 | 2.56 | 16.53 | 24.06 | 16.62 | 9.27 | 39.21 | 2.95 | −0.29 | 12.77 |

Source: Monthly Letters, Salomon Brothers to author; *Financing America's Future* (Beverly Hills, CA: Drexel Burnham Lambert, March 1989), p. 112.

Lastly, these conclusions were borne out by Blume and Keim.[14]

|  | Standard Deviation of Monthly Returns | |
|---|---|---|
|  | 1/82–5/84 | 1/80–6/84 |
| Lower rated bonds | 2.7% | 4.1% |
| A corporate bonds | 3.5 | NA |
| AAA corporate bonds | 3.5 | 4.7 |

A number of factors contribute to this reduced volatility:

- The simple receipt of higher current interest builds a foundation that restricts the downward fluctuation of returns.
- More elegantly put, the higher the coupon and stronger the sinking fund of a bond, *ceteris paribus,* the shorter its duration.
- The cycles in general bond prices, which are forced downward by higher interest rates when the economy strengthens, tend to run counter to the cycles in creditworthiness, which rises in prosperity and vice versa.
- Bond investors' fluctuating attitudes toward economic events are most often implemented via Treasury bonds.
- The discretionary nature of high-yield bond issuance takes some of the pressure off of the outstanding issues when the interest-rate environment is at its worst.

Whatever the reason, high-yield bond performance, at least during the 1980s, has been more consistent than has the performance of high-grade bonds.

## CONCLUSION

All of the evidence concerning high-yield bonds is positive. This conclusion is a strong one, and there appear to be no exceptions to the following statements:

- Default rates among high-yield bonds, while above average, have been limited to a few percent per year.
- The yield spread has been and is wide.
- The result of combining the two, realized return, has been consistently high.
- Return has been earned with above-average consistency.

The above facts argue strongly for investment in high-yield bonds.

---

[14] Blume and Keim, "Risk and Return Characteristics of Lower Grade Bonds," Tables 1 and 3.

What could be the catch? What could make investing in high-yield bonds a mistake? Put simply, past data would have to be an inaccurate indication of the future.

- There would have to be imperfections in the statistics: survey periods too short or samples too small, for example. But the conclusions are too unanimous for us to suspect previous studies' methodologies.
- The world would have to change for the worse. Perhaps one would argue that the business climate will be more treacherous, or that the character of future recessions will be different.
- The universe of bonds may change. Could the bonds of today have different risk characteristics from the historical high-yield universe in general?
- The sector may become more efficiently priced. "Junk bond" has become a household word, and the rate of issuance is up sharply. But the yield spread remains high. Unless the default rate rises greatly, therefore, today's returns will continue to more than compensate for the risk.

Perhaps Fitzpatrick and Severiens wrapped it up best:

> It is the ability to take advantage of . . . market inefficiency that results in the investment merit of junk bonds. Little reason exists to suppose that this market structure will change. Because of regulation, policy, and custom, most institutional investors shun junk bonds.[15]

---

[15] Fitzpatrick and Severiens, "Hickman Revisited," p. 57.

# CHAPTER 46

## IMPROVING
## INSURANCE COMPANY
## PORTFOLIO RETURNS

*Kevin E. Grant, CFA**
*Investment Director*
*Aetna Investment Management/Aetna Life and Casualty*

The investment utility function for a corporation is quite different than that of a pension fund or other purely investment-oriented entity. The principal difference lies in the breadth of business activities. A corporation's performance is consolidated with all business lines, creating a much more complex investment decision-making process. Pension funds adjust their portfolios in the best economic interests of the beneficiaries alone; their decisions are focused on economic factors related to only assets and liabilities.

Insurance companies and other diversified corporations operate in a highly interrelated and regulated environment; results are consolidated with business lines and are reported on a GAAP/statutory basis. This complicates the pure asset/liability economic decision-making process, requiring that corporate-wide financial performance be considered. A strategic asset move may enhance investment returns but severely limit flexibility to write new insurance business. Reactions by regulators and rating agencies further complicate the process. The insurance company portfolio manager has to consider the reaction of these overseers: The proper economic decision in a pure asset/liability framework may create a temporary distortion in financial ratios and a downgrade by the rating agencies that could impair the insurance company's ability to write new business.

* The author wishes to acknowledge the considerable contributions of Charles Melchreit, CFA, and David Canuel for their assistance in preparing the exhibits and sharing their insights.

Thus, an insurance company portfolio manager seeking to improve portfolio investment performance has to solve a very complex problem with many conflicting objectives. At first blush, the manager's objective may appear to be to maximize total return; however, it could just as easily be to minimize risk. More realistically though, an insurance company portfolio manager's objectives involve a complex risk-return function that includes not only asset/liability management but also statutory regulations, accounting treatment, rating agencies, claims-paying abilities, new business potential, and ultimately, the corporation's value to its shareholders.

## SPECIAL CONSIDERATIONS FOR INSURANCE COMPANY PORTFOLIOS

The insurance company portfolio management process is not one of academic purity, with no transaction costs or taxes, continuous prices, and arbitrage-free markets. The capital gain/loss decision, for example, involves more than just the judgment that the asset to be purchased is better than the one to be sold. There may be insurance underwriting losses that could reduce the company's ability to take losses on the portfolio. Executing a bond swap that takes a capital loss or gain has tax and statutory implications that must be viewed in light of both the corporation's overall financial position and the portfolio's assets and liabilities. Rules requiring some bonds to be carried at market rather than book value create another set of distortions and incentives, particularly when the liabilities are carried at book and the assets at market. The key to managing around the distortions is to reduce unexpected transactions: In highly active bond management strategies, many transactions result from volatility. Active strategies require transactions, and the extent of those transactions is a positive function of volatility rather than the corporation's objectives.

The most effective approach for insurance company portfolio managers is to take a long-term view of value. This doesn't mean buy and hold, which some people interpret as buy and ignore. Rather, it means buy and incubate: Construct a portfolio that you expect will provide superior returns in many economic scenarios and seek opportunities to improve the portfolio with asset swaps. The key is to develop the analytical tools that will identify long-term value and measure risk. The approach is not active management; rather, it's attentive management.

## DON'T BUY AND HOLD, BUY AND INCUBATE

The recommended approach is to look at the assets and liabilities in a wide variety of long-run economic scenarios. The cheap bonds enhance the risk-return characteristics of the portfolio in all scenarios, whereas the rich bonds enhance the risk-return characteristics in only a few. The cheap ones should be held until they become rich. This happens much more slowly than price volatility may suggest. This realization gives the portfolio manager a tremendous advantage over the market. He can wait, the players showing bids and offers cannot. If you take a long-term view, you are never forced to transact.

## EXISTING APPROACHES TO ASSET/LIABILITY MANAGEMENT

Fixed income portfolio management techniques have improved dramatically in the past few years. These include asset/liability techniques, which attempt to construct portfolios and control risk, and immunization, which attempts to continuously match the present value of assets to liabilities as interest rates change. The belief is that if their present values (prices) are always matched, as time passes assets can be sold at their present values to fund the liabilities.

Immunization uses differential calculus to parameterize the elasticity of price to interest-rate changes. The first derivative, the modified duration, is simply the percentage change in present value (price) relative to a basis point change in interest rates. Thus, if the modified durations of the assets and liabilities are equal, as rates change their present values will change by equal proportions. This assumes that the interest-rate change on all the assets and liabilities are identical; that is, the yield curve shifts in parallel.

In general, immunization models use linear programming optimization programs to find the least-cost solution (maximize the dollar-duration-weighted internal rate of return) of the assets while matching the assets' and liabilities' modified durations. As time passes and rates change, the portfolio will become mismatched and rebalancing will become necessary. Rebalancing is most frequent when volatility is high.

Several refinements have improved immunization technology over the past few years, including the development of convexity. This is simply the second derivative of the price-yield equation; that is, it is the rate of change in modified duration due to a change in yield. Incorporating convexity into simple immunization reduces the amount of rebalancing. A convenient accidental feature of the computation is that it's a summary of the dispersion of cash flows. Matching the convexities of assets and liabilities reduces the mismatch of cash flows. Other researchers have approached cash flow dispersion mismatches more directly with other measures that have the same results as matching convexity.

Matching D3 (the sensitivity of convexity to rate changes), D4, and so on, gradually will reduce risk and rebalancing in matched portfolios. However, they have diminishing importance. When more derivatives are matched than there are cash flows, only one feasible solution exists, a dedicated portfolio having no interest-rate risk. Until this point, however, yield-curve risk remains and rebalancing is required.

Exhibit 46–1 lists several bonds and an assumed five-year bullet liability. The asset weightings were derived with the immunization model previously described. In this case, only the duration was matched. Only two bonds were required to match the liability within reasonable tolerances (± 0.5%): the U. S. Treasury 6.50 percent and the Thailand 8.70 percent.

Exhibit 46–2 shows the relative present value movement of the optimal portfolio versus the liability. Under parallel yield-curve shifts, the portfolio is matched fairly well and actually becomes modestly overfunded. When the yield curve steepens, the account is underfunded. It's overfunded when the curve flattens. Exhibit 46–2 examines only instantaneous rate changes. Exhibit 46–3 examines the effects of time and rate changes on the portfolio. The reason mismatches are more dramatic in six months is that the assets' and liability's durations decay at different rates. The portfolio becomes mismatched simply because time passes. Transactions to rebalance the portfolio are necessary to maintain the match. Immunization requires frequent rebalancing due to the passage of time, without regard to value.

Immunization provides an easy way of controlling overall interest-rate risk. However, it falters because it is a static approach to dynamic yield-curve risks. Immunization exhibits several weaknesses:

1. It requires transactions. Those transactions are a result of the mathematics, not of value or opportunities in the market.
2. It overwhelmingly focuses on matching instantaneous price changes, whereas it should be concerned with the future value of the liability.
3. Transactions are a function of volatility and time, not value. This creates unpredictable capital gains and losses, which may not be appropriate for the corporation as a whole.

**EXHIBIT 46–1**
**First-Pass Immunization Noncall Assets Only***

| Security | Coupon | Maturity | PV or Price | Yield | Duration | Dollar Allocation |
|---|---|---|---|---|---|---|
| Liability | | 8/15/1994 | 65.772 | 8.50% | 4.83 | ($100.00) |
| U.S. Treasury | 6.500 | 2/15/1990 | 99.250 | 7.96 | 0.50 | $ 27.51 |
| Thailand | 8.700 | 8/1/1999 | 100.000 | 8.70 | 6.51 | 72.49 |
| U.S. Treasury | 14.250 | 11/15/1991 | 114.688 | 7.15 | 1.93 | 0.00 |
| U.S. Treasury | 8.625 | 1/15/1995 | 104.031 | 7.70 | 4.30 | 0.00 |
| U.S. Treasury | 9.125 | 5/15/2018 | 113.688 | 7.91 | 10.87 | 0.00 |
| Ford Motor Credit | 8.000 | 8/1/1994 | 100.000 | 8.00 | 4.00 | 0.00 |
| Bowater | 9.000 | 8/1/2009 | 100.000 | 9.00 | 9.12 | 0.00 |
| GMAC | 8.250 | 8/1/1996 | 100.000 | 8.25 | 5.17 | 0.00 |
| Total Assets | | | | 8.50% | 4.85 | $100.00 |

*Duration matched within 0.5 percent tolerance; convexity is not matched; all figures as of 8/3/89.

**EXHIBIT 46–2**

**Effects of Yield-Curve Shifts on Immunized Portfolio** (as of 8/3/89)

| | | Present Values | | |
|---|---|---|---|---|
| Yield Curve | Liability | Treasury 6.5% of '90 | Thailand 8.7% of '99 | Overfunded (Underfunded) |
| Unchanged* | ($100.00) | $27.51 | $72.49 | $0.00 |
| +100 b. p. | (95.26) | 27.37 | 67.92 | 0.04 |
| −100 b. p. | (105.00) | 27.65 | 77.52 | 0.17 |
| Steeper 50 b. p.† | (99.80) | 27.54 | 71.73 | (0.53) |
| Flatter 50 b. p.‡ | (100.20) | 27.48 | 73.30 | 0.59 |

\* Treasury yield curve:   2-year 7.53%
3-year 7.58
4-year 7.54
5-year 7.56
7-year 7.64
10-year 7.74
30-year 7.83
† Steeper curve pivots counterclockwise around the 5-year. The 3-month rate falls 25 basis points and the 30-year rate rises 25 basis points.
‡ Flatter curve pivots in the opposite direction.

**EXHIBIT 46–3**

**Effects of Yield-Curve Shifts and Time on Immunized Portfolio** (as of 2/3/90)

| | | Present Values | | | |
|---|---|---|---|---|---|
| Yield Curve | Liability | Treasury 6.5% of '90 | Thailand 8.7% of '99 | Cash | Overfunded (Underfunded) |
| Unchanged* | ($104.39) | $27.70 | $72.49 | $4.06 | (0.14) |
| +100 b. p. | (99.95) | 27.69 | 68.04 | 4.06 | (0.16) |
| −100 b. p. | (109.04) | 27.71 | 77.33 | 4.06 | 0.06 |
| Steeper 50 b. p.† | (104.31) | 27.70 | 71.74 | 4.06 | (0.80) |
| Flatter 50 b. p.‡ | (104.46) | 27.70 | 73.24 | 4.06 | 0.53 |

\* Position becomes underfunded in unchanged rate scenario because liability rolls down the yield curve faster than the assets. Starting Treasury curve:   2-year 7.53%
3-year 7.58
4-year 7.54
5-year 7.56
7-year 7.64
10-year 7.74
30-year 7.83
† Steeper curve pivots counterclockwise around the 5-year. The 3-month rate falls 25 basis points and the 30-year rate rises 25 basis points.
‡ Flatter curve pivots in the opposite direction.

4. The computations assume parallel yield-curve shifts. This has been a rarity, as Exhibit 46–4 illustrates.
5. Only simply structured bonds may be used in an immunized portfolio. Bonds with variable cash flows (e.g., callables, putables, mortgage-backed securities) don't fit the model and can't be used, regardless of their value.
6. Immunization assumes reinvestment into the same security. This may not be appropriate.

**EXHIBIT 46–4**
**Yield Curves.**

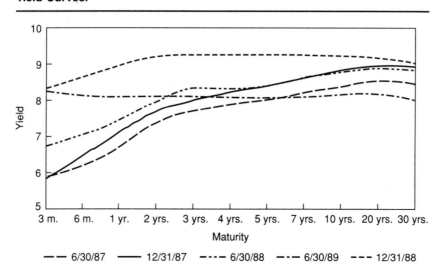

|  | 6/30/87 | 12/31/87 | 6/30/88 | 12/31/88 | 6/30/89 |
|---|---|---|---|---|---|
| 3-Month | 5.87 | 5.85 | 6.75 | 8.36 | 8.26 |
| 6-Month | 6.13 | 6.47 | 7.02 | 8.66 | 8.14 |
| 1-Year | 6.65 | 7.10 | 7.42 | 9.00 | 8.09 |
| 2-Year | 7.47 | 7.78 | 7.99 | 9.27 | 8.14 |
| 3-Year | 7.72 | 8.01 | 8.15 | 9.27 | 8.11 |
| 4-Year | 7.91 | 8.26 | 8.31 | 9.28 | 8.12 |
| 5-Year | 8.01 | 8.40 | 8.41 | 9.26 | 8.07 |
| 7-Year | 8.24 | 8.68 | 8.65 | 9.30 | 8.14 |
| 10-Year | 8.37 | 8.86 | 8.80 | 9.24 | 8.16 |
| 20-Year | 8.68 | 9.06 | 8.99 | 9.28 | 8.29 |
| 30-Year | 8.49 | 8.98 | 8.88 | 9.08 | 8.05 |

Several ad hoc approaches are available to reduce transactions and yield-curve risk. Specifically, option technology attempts to broaden the universe of assets.

## Option Valuation and Immunization

Improvements in option valuation models have helped expand the asset classes that may be included in immunized portfolios. Option-adjusted, effective, or implied durations are often substituted for modified durations. These sensitivity measures are unstable, however, and inclusion of option-related assets in an immunized portfolio may introduce risks with which the immunization model is not equipped to deal. Maximizing an option-adjusted yield while matching effective duration may seem like a reasonable approach—until risk is closely examined. Exhibit 46–5 incorporates callable corporate bonds and pass-throughs into the immunization problem. Exhibit 46–6 shows the performance of the optimal portfolio in several scenarios. Over the six-month period, the portfolio became heavily underfunded in all but one scenario. The degree of underfunding was worse than a portfolio of noncall securities. It's clear that the immunization model obscured risks inherent in the new securities.

Incorporating option technology into immunization technology has all the weaknesses of pure immunization and adds risks that neither approach is capable of evaluating fully. In fact, because effective durations are unstable, incorporating option technology into immunization may exacerbate the need for rebalancing and unexpected transactions. The term "immunization" is a misnomer; there are always bets in immunized portfolios, known and unknown. The immunization model has the capacity to neither identify nor quantify those risks.

## THE WISH-LIST FOR PORTFOLIO MANAGEMENT

The ideal portfolio construction methodology would allow the portfolio manager to

1. explicitly specify his risk-return preferences and build them into the portfolio;
2. never transact unless he wishes to (he should transact only when there is an opportunity to improve the risk-return profile of his portfolio and when it is in the corporation's overall best interest; transacting should be the portfolio manager's option, not the market's or the model's);
3. always fund his liabilities in any economic scenario (at the very least, he should be able to specify precisely what risks of underfunding liabilities he wishes to assume); and
4. most importantly, achieve his long-run return objectives within his risk and transaction tolerances.

**EXHIBIT 46–5**
**First-Pass Immunization Including Callable and Putable Assets ‡**

| Security | Coupon | Maturity | Call/Put Date | Call/Put Price | PV or Price | Yield | Effective Duration | Dollars |
|---|---|---|---|---|---|---|---|---|
| Liability | | 8/15/1994 | — | — | 64.453 | 8.92% | 4.82 | ($100.00) |
| UST | 6.500 | 2/15/1990 | — | — | 99.250 | 7.96% | 0.50 | $ 21.36 |
| Thailand | 8.700 | 8/1/1999 | — | — | 100.000 | 8.70 | 6.51 | 0.00 |
| UST | 14.250 | 11/15/1991 | — | — | 114.688 | 7.15 | 1.93 | 0.00 |
| UST | 8.625 | 1/15/1995 | — | — | 104.031 | 7.70 | 4.30 | 0.00 |
| UST | 9.125 | 5/15/2018 | — | — | 113.688 | 7.91 | 10.87 | 0.00 |
| Ford Motor Credit | 8.000 | 8/1/1994 | — | — | 100.000 | 8.00 | 4.00 | 0.00 |
| Bowater | 9.000 | 8/1/2009 | — | — | 100.000 | 9.00 | 9.12 | 41.57 |
| GMAC | 8.250 | 8/1/1996 | — | — | 100.000 | 8.25 | 5.17 | 0.00 |
| GNMA | 8.000 | 1/31/2018 | — | — | 94.813 | 8.95 | 5.94 | 0.00 |
| GNMA | 9.500 | 1/31/2019 | — | — | 100.906 | 9.43 | 4.98 | 0.00 |
| GNMA | 10.500 | 7/31/2018 | — | — | 104.219 | 9.38 | 2.55 | 37.07 |
| Xerox* | 9.200 | 7/15/1999 | 7/15/1996 | 100.00 | 99.551 | 9.36 | 5.97 | 0.00 |
| Household Finance* | 8.875 | 7/5/1999 | 7/5/1996 | 100.00 | 98.934 | 9.03 | 5.73 | 0.00 |
| ITT† | 8.250 | 8/1/2001 | 8/1/1996 | 100.00 | 100.000 | 8.25 | 5.47 | 0.00 |
| American General† | 8.125 | 8/15/2009 | 8/15/1996 | 100.00 | 99.150 | 8.29 | 7.13 | 0.00 |
| Total Assets | | | | | | 8.92% | 4.84 | $100.00 |

* Callable.
† Putable.
‡ All figures as of 8/3/89; duration matched within 0.5 percent tolerance; convexity is not matched but is constrained to exceed 0.

**EXHIBIT 46–6**
**Effects of Yield-Curve Shifts and Time on Immunized Portfolio** (as of 2/3/90)

| | Liability | UST 6.5% of '90 | Bowater 9.0% of '09 | GNMA 10.5% | Cash | Overfunded (Underfunded) |
|---|---|---|---|---|---|---|
| Unchanged* | ($104.60) | $21.50 | $41.59 | $34.97 | $6.13 | ($0.42) |
| +100 b. p. | (100.15) | 21.50 | 38.04 | 34.28 | 5.77 | (0.57) |
| −100 b. p. | (109.24) | 21.51 | 45.67 | 34.98 | 6.58 | (0.50) |
| Steeper 50 b. p. | (104.51) | 21.51 | 40.82 | 35.01 | 6.07 | (1.11) |
| Flatter 50 b. p. | (104.67) | 21.50 | 42.37 | 34.91 | 6.18 | 0.30 |

* Position becomes underfunded in unchanged rate scenario because liability rolls down the yield curve faster then the assets. Starting Treasury curve:  2-year 7.53%
3-year 7.58
4-year 7.54
5-year 7.56
7-year 7.64
10-year 7.74
30-year 7.83

† Steeper curve pivots counterclockwise around the 5-year. The 3-month rate falls 25 basis points and the 30-year rate rises 25 basis points.
‡ Flatter curve pivots in the opposite direction.

Immunization and most other common asset/liability approaches have none of these characteristics. The total return approach, however, begins to satisfy many of these needs.

# TOTAL RETURN IN THE ASSET/LIABILITY/REGULATORY/ GAAP/TAX WORLD

By examining the total returns of securities in various scenarios, many real-world constraints may be considered explicitly. Reinvestment assumptions, tax effects, regulatory restrictions, and GAAP treatment may be included in the analysis.

The total return approach involves a lot of modeling and specification by the portfolio manager. It forces the manager to think explicitly about risk. Total return approaches examine the behavior of securities in different interest-rate environments, allowing the portfolio manager to specify tolerance for loss versus liability in each scenario and then construct a portfolio that provides superior performance over the investment horizon. The portfolio manager must specify

1. an objective (he or she can maximize his expected total return, maximize it in only one scenario, or minimize risk at some minimum total return level);

2. likely and unlikely economic scenarios (the manager must specify the level of key economic variables, for example, the yield curve and credit spreads);
3. tolerances for losses in each scenario; and
4. various portfolio parameters, such as diversification.

Models must be developed for the assets to be included:

1. For corporate bonds, all the characteristics of call and put options, sinking funds, and credit risk must be modeled.

**EXHIBIT 46–7**
**Yield Curves.**

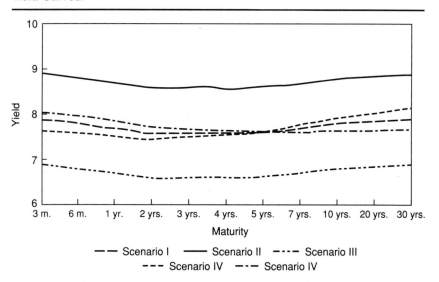

| Scenario | Horizon Interest Rates | | | Loss Tolerance | |
|---|---|---|---|---|---|
| | 3-Month | 2-Year | 10-Year | Probability | vs. Liability |
| I | 7.89 | 7.53 | 7.74 | 20% | 0.00% |
| II | 8.89 | 8.53 | 8.74 | 15 | −0.10 |
| III | 6.89 | 6.53 | 6.74 | 10 | 0.00 |
| IV | 7.64 | 7.41 | 7.90 | 30 | 0.00 |
| V | 8.04 | 7.65 | 7.58 | 25 | −0.10 |

2. For mortgage-backed securities and their various derivatives, cash flow and prepayment models must be developed. A good prepayment model may involve an econometric model with coefficients for economic refinancing, prepayment burnout, seasoning effects, and the lags in these variables.
3. Any other securities that the manager wishes to include must be modeled, for example, floating-rate notes, futures and options, swaps, and dynamic strategies.

Exhibit 46–7 shows several interest-rate scenarios specified by a portfolio manager, the assigned subjective probability, and the manager's tolerance for loss versus his liability. Exhibit 46–8 lists several assets and their modeled total return in each scenario specified by the portfolio manager. The data in Exhibits 46–7 and 46–8 are then optimized and the results reported in Exhibit 46–9. The results suggest how the manager should structure the portfolio to satisfy the risk-return objectives. As long as the specified scenarios sufficiently incorporate the actual yield-curve movement, the portfolio should not require rebalancing. However, if the manager perceives a change in value in the market, he or she has the option of taking advantage of it. The manager can also tilt the portfolio by adjusting the probabilities assigned to each scenario.

The main weakness of the total return approach is its complexity. The investment organization must commit people, computers, and research to develop the models and educating its users.

## Long-Term Arbitrage

Market makers and traders are by definition short-term-oriented. Their risk is reduced and return increased by keeping their inventory turnover high. This creates opportunities that often persist. Total return models are useful tools in identifying these opportunities.

Exhibit 46–10 shows an application of total return approaches to arbitrage. The axes of the matrix list several bonds: Each column represents a bond that may be purchased; each row represents one that may be sold. The contents of the matrix are swap suggestions where the purchased combination of bonds will outperform the one sold in each scenario.

## PROBABILITY DISTRIBUTIONS — THE NEXT FRONTIER

A particularly burdensome task involved in total return modeling is the specification of scenarios. Generally, only a small number of scenarios are specified, and it's easy to miss some important ones. This creates a potential for incomplete analysis.

**EXHIBIT 46–8**
**Pro Forma Total Returns for Specified Assets***

| Security | Coupon | Maturity | Scenario Total Return | | | | |
|---|---|---|---|---|---|---|---|
| | | | I | II | III | IV | V |
| Liability | — | 8/15/1994 | 8.77% | -0.10% | 18.08% | 8.61% | 8.93% |
| UST | 6.500 | 2/15/1990 | 7.95% | 7.89% | 8.02% | 7.97% | 7.94% |
| Thailand | 8.700 | 8/1/1999 | 8.87 | -3.41 | 22.23 | 8.31 | 9.46 |
| UST | 14.250 | 11/15/1991 | 7.24 | 4.26 | 10.27 | 7.56 | 6.92 |
| UST | 8.625 | 1/15/1995 | 7.89 | 0.13 | 16.03 | 7.71 | 8.06 |
| UST | 9.125 | 5/15/2018 | 7.93 | -11.92 | 31.76 | 2.64 | 13.42 |
| Ford Motor Credit | 8.000 | 8/1/1994 | 8.07 | 0.81 | 15.67 | 8.23 | 7.91 |
| Bowater | 9.000 | 8/1/2009 | 9.01 | -8.04 | 28.64 | 6.52 | 11.54 |
| GMAC | 8.250 | 8/1/1996 | 9.42 | -1.21 | 18.65 | 8.27 | 8.64 |
| GNMA | 8.000 | 1/31/2018 | 8.95 | -3.19 | 21.08 | 7.13 | 10.74 |
| GNMA | 9.500 | 1/31/2019 | 8.42 | -1.27 | 16.04 | 8.22 | 10.43 |
| GNMA | 10.500 | 7/31/2018 | 9.35 | 3.69 | 11.86 | 9.25 | 9.35 |
| Xerox | 9.200 | 7/15/1999 | 9.24 | -1.83 | 20.69 | 8.88 | 9.63 |
| Household Finance | 8.875 | 7/15/1999 | 9.10 | -2.15 | 20.73 | 8.71 | 9.51 |
| ITT | 8.250 | 8/1/2001 | 8.43 | -0.47 | 19.33 | 8.28 | 8.67 |
| American General | 8.125 | 8/15/2009 | 8.61 | -3.44 | 23.36 | 7.59 | 9.83 |

* Liability return assumes an initial discount rate of 8.50 percent; one-year horizon.

## EXHIBIT 46-9
### Suggested Portfolio for Specified Assets and Risk/Return Objectives*

| Security | Coupon | Maturity | Weight | Scenario Total Return | | | | |
|---|---|---|---|---|---|---|---|---|
| | | | | I | II | III | IV | V |
| Liability | — | 8/15/1994 | -100% | 8.77% | -0.10% | 18.08% | 8.61% | 8.93% |
| UST | 6.500 | 2/15/1990 | 0.0 | 7.95% | 7.89% | 8.02% | 7.97% | 7.94% |
| Thailand | 8.700 | 8/1/1999 | 0.0 | 8.87 | -3.41 | 22.23 | 8.31 | 9.46 |
| UST | 14.250 | 11/15/1991 | 0.0 | 7.24 | 4.26 | 10.27 | 7.56 | 6.92 |
| UST | 8.625 | 1/15/1995 | 0.0 | 7.89 | 0.13 | 16.03 | 7.71 | 8.06 |
| UST | 9.125 | 5/15/2018 | 0.0 | 7.93 | -11.92 | 31.76 | 2.64 | 13.42 |
| Ford | 8.000 | 8/1/1994 | 0.0 | 8.07 | 0.81 | 15.67 | 8.23 | 7.91 |
| Bowater | 9.000 | 8/1/2009 | 0.0 | 9.01 | -8.04 | 28.64 | 6.52 | 11.54 |
| GMAC | 8.250 | 8/1/1996 | 0.0 | 8.42 | -1.21 | 18.65 | 8.27 | 8.64 |
| GNMA | 8.000 | 1/31/2018 | 0.0 | 8.95 | -3.19 | 21.08 | 7.13 | 10.74 |
| GNMA | 9.500 | 1/31/2019 | 0.0 | 9.42 | -1.27 | 16.04 | 8.22 | 10.43 |
| GNMA | 10.500 | 7/31/2018 | 29.6 | 9.35 | 3.69 | 11.86 | 9.25 | 9.35 |
| Xerox | 9.200 | 7/15/1999 | 70.4 | 9.24 | -1.83 | 20.69 | 8.88 | 9.63 |
| Household Finance | 8.875 | 7/15/1999 | 0.0 | 9.10 | -2.15 | 20.73 | 8.71 | 9.51 |
| ITT | 8.250 | 8/1/2001 | 0.0 | 8.43 | -0.47 | 19.33 | 8.28 | 8.67 |
| AGC | 8.125 | 8/15/2009 | -0.0 | 8.61 | -3.44 | 23.36 | 7.59 | 9.83 |
| Total Asset Return | | | 100.0% | 9.27% | -0.19% | 18.08% | 8.99% | 9.55% |
| Assets–Liabilities Return Spread | | | | 0.50% | -0.09% | -0.00% | 0.38% | 0.62% |
| Maximum Permitted Loss | | | | 0.00% | -0.10% | 0.00% | 0.00% | -0.10% |
| Scenario Probability | | | | 20% | 15% | 10% | 30% | 25% |
| Expected Gain | | | 0.36% | | | | | |

* Selected portfolio maximizes expected total return in five probability-weighted scenarios, subject to the loss constraints enumerated in exhibit VII. The investment horizon is one year.

## EXHIBIT 46–10
## Total Return Arbitrage Matrix*

| Return Advantage | | | GN30N 7.50 | GN30N 8.00 | GN30N 8.50 | GN30N 9.00 | GN30N 9.50 | GN30N 10.00 | GN30N 10.50 | FN30N 8.00 | FN30N 8.50 | FN30N 9.00 | FN30N 9.50 | FN30N 10.00 | FH30N 8.50 |
|---|---|---|---|---|---|---|---|---|---|---|---|---|---|---|---|
| 0 BP | GN30N | 7.50 | 100.0 | .0 | .0 | .0 | .0 | .0 | .0 | .0 | .0 | .0 | .0 | .0 | .0 |
| 0 BP | GN30N | 8.00 | .0 | 100.0 | .0 | .0 | .0 | .0 | .0 | .0 | .0 | .0 | .0 | .0 | .0 |
| 0 BP | GN30N | 8.50 | .0 | .0 | 100.0 | .0 | .0 | .0 | .0 | .0 | .0 | .0 | .0 | .0 | .0 |
| 0 BP | GN30N | 9.00 | .0 | .0 | .0 | 100.0 | .0 | .0 | .0 | .0 | .0 | .0 | .0 | .0 | .0 |
| 0 BP | GN30N | 9.50 | .0 | .0 | .0 | .0 | 100.0 | .0 | .0 | .0 | .0 | .0 | .0 | .0 | .0 |
| 0 BP | GN30N | 10.00 | .0 | .0 | .0 | .0 | .0 | 100.0 | .0 | .0 | .0 | .0 | .0 | .0 | .0 |
| 23 BP | GN30N | 10.50 | .0 | .0 | .0 | .0 | .0 | .0 | .0 | .0 | .0 | 24.4 | .0 | .0 | .0 |
| 0 BP | FN30N | 8.00 | .0 | .0 | .0 | .0 | .0 | .0 | .0 | 100.0 | .0 | .0 | .0 | .0 | .0 |
| 0 BP | FN30N | 8.50 | .0 | .0 | .0 | .0 | .0 | .0 | .0 | .0 | 100.0 | .0 | .0 | .0 | .0 |
| 0 BP | FN30N | 9.00 | .0 | .0 | .0 | .0 | .0 | .0 | .0 | .0 | .0 | 100.0 | .0 | .0 | .0 |
| 0 BP | FN30N | 9.50 | .0 | .0 | .0 | .0 | .0 | .0 | .0 | .0 | .0 | .0 | 100.0 | .0 | .0 |
| 0 BP | FN30N | 10.00 | .0 | .0 | .0 | .0 | .0 | .0 | .0 | .0 | .0 | .0 | .0 | 100.0 | .0 |
| 0 BP | FH30N | 8.50 | .0 | .0 | .0 | .0 | .0 | .0 | .0 | .0 | .0 | .0 | .0 | .0 | 100.0 |
| 0 BP | FH30N | 9.00 | .0 | .0 | .0 | .0 | .0 | .0 | .0 | .0 | .0 | .0 | .0 | .0 | 100.0 |
| 0 BP | FH30N | 9.50 | .0 | .0 | .0 | .0 | .0 | .0 | .0 | .0 | .0 | .0 | .0 | .0 | 100.0 |
| 9 BP | FH30N | 10.00 | .0 | .0 | .0 | .0 | .0 | .0 | .0 | .0 | .0 | .0 | .0 | 66.4 | .0 |
| 0 BP | FH30N | 10.50 | .0 | .0 | .0 | .0 | .0 | .0 | .0 | .0 | .0 | .0 | .0 | .0 | .0 |
| 15 BP | GN30S | 8.00 | .0 | .0 | .0 | .0 | .0 | .0 | .0 | 12.7 | 63.1 | .0 | .0 | .0 | .0 |
| 13 BP | GN30S | 8.50 | .0 | .0 | .0 | .0 | .0 | .0 | .0 | .0 | 63.5 | .0 | .0 | .0 | .0 |
| 13 BP | GN30S | 9.00 | .0 | .0 | .0 | .0 | .0 | .0 | .0 | .0 | 17.7 | 29.7 | .0 | .0 | .0 |
| 0 BP | GN15N | 8.00 | .0 | .0 | .0 | .0 | .0 | .0 | .0 | .0 | .0 | .0 | .0 | .0 | .0 |
| 6 BP | GN15N | 8.50 | .0 | .0 | .0 | .0 | .0 | .0 | .0 | 9.8 | 7.4 | .0 | .0 | .0 | .0 |
| 23 BP | GN15N | 9.00 | .0 | .0 | .0 | .0 | .0 | .0 | .0 | .0 | 23.1 | .0 | .0 | .0 | .0 |
| 0 BP | FH15N | 8.00 | .0 | .0 | .0 | .0 | .0 | .0 | .0 | .0 | .0 | .0 | .0 | .0 | .0 |
| 0 BP | FH15S | 8.50 | .0 | .0 | .0 | .0 | .0 | .0 | .0 | .0 | .0 | .0 | .0 | .0 | .0 |
| 0 BP | FH15S | 8.00 | .0 | .0 | .0 | .0 | .0 | .0 | .0 | .0 | .0 | .0 | .0 | .0 | .0 |
| 0 BP | UST | 7.88 | .0 | .0 | .0 | .0 | .0 | .0 | .0 | .0 | .0 | .0 | .0 | .0 | .0 |
| 95 BP | UST | 8.25 | .0 | .0 | .0 | .0 | .0 | .0 | .0 | 10.7 | .0 | .0 | .0 | .0 | .0 |
| 101 BP | UST | 9.88 | .0 | .0 | .0 | .0 | .0 | .0 | .0 | 16.4 | 77.8 | .0 | .0 | .0 | .0 |
| 0 BP | UST | 8.00 | .0 | .0 | .0 | .0 | .0 | .0 | .0 | .0 | .0 | .0 | .0 | .0 | .0 |

Number of simulations evaluated = 13
Maximum allowable underperformance = 0BP
One-year horizon scenarios:
± 200
± 150
± 100
± 50
No change
Steeper 50, 100
Flatter 50, 100

* The column headed "Return Advantage" indicates the expected return pickup over the one-
return if we sell the new GNMA 30-year 10.5% and buy a portfolio composed of 24.4% FNMA

The arbitage is evaluated over 13 scenarios encompassing a sufficient range of curve shifts and
that does not underperform the target security in any scenario.

| FH30N 9.00 | FH30N 9.50 | FH30N 10.00 | FH30N 10.50 | GN30S 8.00 | GN30S 8.50 | GN30S 9.00 | GN15N 8.00 | GN15N 8.50 | GN15N 9.00 | FH15N 8.00 | FH15S 8.50 | FH15S 9.00 | UST 7.88 | UST 8.25 | UST 8.88 | UST 8.00 |
|---|---|---|---|---|---|---|---|---|---|---|---|---|---|---|---|---|
| .0 | .0 | .0 | .0 | .0 | .0 | .0 | .0 | .0 | .0 | .0 | .0 | .0 | .0 | .0 | .0 | .0 |
| .0 | .0 | .0 | .0 | .0 | .0 | .0 | .0 | .0 | .0 | .0 | .0 | .0 | .0 | .0 | .0 | .0 |
| .0 | .0 | .0 | .0 | .0 | .0 | .0 | .0 | .0 | .0 | .0 | .0 | .0 | .0 | .0 | .0 | .0 |
| .0 | .0 | .0 | .0 | .0 | .0 | .0 | .0 | .0 | .0 | .0 | .0 | .0 | .0 | .0 | .0 | .0 |
| .0 | .0 | .0 | .0 | .0 | .0 | .0 | .0 | .0 | .0 | .0 | .0 | .0 | .0 | .0 | .0 | .0 |
| .0 | .0 | .0 | .0 | .0 | .0 | .0 | .0 | .0 | .0 | .0 | .0 | .0 | .0 | .0 | .0 | .0 |
| .0 | .0 | .0 | 72.6 | .0 | .0 | .0 | .0 | .0 | .0 | .0 | 2.9 | .0 | .0 | .0 | .0 | .0 |
| .0 | .0 | .0 | .0 | .0 | .0 | .0 | .0 | .0 | .0 | .0 | .0 | .0 | .0 | .0 | .0 | .0 |
| .0 | .0 | .0 | .0 | .0 | .0 | .0 | .0 | .0 | .0 | .0 | .0 | .0 | .0 | .0 | .0 | .0 |
| .0 | .0 | .0 | .0 | .0 | .0 | .0 | .0 | .0 | .0 | .0 | .0 | .0 | .0 | .0 | .0 | .0 |
| .0 | .0 | .0 | .0 | .0 | .0 | .0 | .0 | .0 | .0 | .0 | .0 | .0 | .0 | .0 | .0 | .0 |
| .0 | .0 | .0 | .0 | .0 | .0 | .0 | .0 | .0 | .0 | .0 | .0 | .0 | .0 | .0 | .0 | .0 |
| .0 | .0 | .0 | .0 | .0 | .0 | .0 | .0 | .0 | .0 | .0 | .0 | .0 | .0 | .0 | .0 | .0 |
| 100.0 | .0 | .0 | .0 | .0 | .0 | .0 | .0 | .0 | .0 | .0 | .0 | .0 | .0 | .0 | .0 | .0 |
| .0 | 22.1 | .0 | .0 | .0 | .0 | .0 | .0 | .0 | .0 | .0 | .0 | .0 | .0 | .0 | .0 | .0 |
| .0 | 100.0 | .0 | 11.5 | .0 | .0 | .0 | .0 | .0 | .0 | .0 | .0 | .0 | .0 | .0 | .0 | .0 |
| .0 | .0 | .0 | 100.0 | .0 | .0 | .0 | .0 | .0 | .0 | 24.2 | .0 | .0 | .0 | .0 | .0 | .0 |
| .0 | .0 | .0 | .0 | .0 | .0 | .0 | .0 | .0 | .0 | .0 | 36.5 | .0 | .0 | .0 | .0 | .0 |
| .0 | .0 | .0 | .0 | .0 | .0 | .0 | .0 | .0 | .0 | .0 | 52.6 | .0 | .0 | .0 | .0 | .0 |
| .0 | .0 | .0 | .0 | .0 | .0 | 100.0 | .0 | .0 | .0 | .0 | .0 | .0 | .0 | .0 | .0 | .0 |
| .0 | .0 | .0 | .0 | .0 | .0 | .0 | .0 | .0 | .0 | 82.8 | .0 | .0 | .0 | .0 | .0 | .0 |
| .0 | .0 | .0 | .0 | .0 | .0 | .0 | .0 | .0 | .0 | .0 | 76.9 | .0 | .0 | .0 | .0 | .0 |
| .0 | .0 | .0 | .0 | .0 | .0 | .0 | .0 | .0 | .0 | 100.0 | .0 | .0 | .0 | .0 | .0 | .0 |
| .0 | .0 | .0 | .0 | .0 | .0 | .0 | .0 | .0 | .0 | .0 | 100.0 | .0 | .0 | .0 | .0 | .0 |
| .0 | .0 | .0 | .0 | .0 | .0 | .0 | .0 | .0 | .0 | .0 | .0 | 100.0 | .0 | .0 | .0 | .0 |
| .0 | .0 | .0 | .0 | .0 | .0 | .0 | .0 | .0 | .0 | .0 | .0 | 100.0 | .0 | .0 | .0 | .0 |
| .0 | .0 | .0 | .0 | .0 | .0 | 27.9 | .0 | .0 | .0 | 61.4 | .0 | .0 | .0 | .0 | .0 | .0 |
| .0 | .0 | .0 | .0 | .0 | .0 | .0 | .0 | .0 | .0 | 5.7 | .0 | .0 | .0 | .0 | .0 | .0 |
| .0 | .0 | .0 | .0 | .0 | .0 | .0 | .0 | .0 | .0 | .0 | .0 | .0 | .0 | .0 | .0 | 100.0 |

year horizon. The row headed GN30N 10.50 shows that we can expect to pick up 23 b. p. of total 30-year 9.0s, 72.6% new FHLMC 30-year 10.5s, and 2.9% Gnome 8.5s.

twists. The optimization finds the portfolio that shows the highest expected return advantage but

**EXHIBIT 46–11**
**Total Return Distributions—GNMA'S and 5-Year Treasury.**

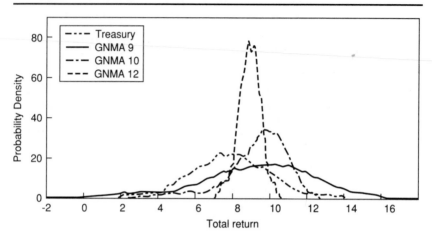

One solution is to use mathematical simulations to create many scenarios. The ideal simulation is a stochastic process that simulates movement of the entire yield curve, both its position and shape. With a large number of simulated total returns, return distributions may be examined.

Exhibit 46–11 shows total return distributions for several securities in many scenarios. They have clearly very different risk-return characteristics. Total return distributions help us to delineate clearly the risk-return characteristics of securities.

## CONCLUSION

Total return models are effective approaches to portfolio management for complex organizations. They allow their users to explicitly incorporate the realities of their businesses.

# CHAPTER 47

---

# ASSET-LIABILITY MANAGEMENT FOR PROPERTY-CASUALTY INSURERS

*Frank D. Campbell*
*Portfolio Management Division, Securities Department*
*The Travelers Companies*

---

## PROPERTY-CASUALTY INSURERS

Property-casualty (P/C) insurance includes a broad range of coverages: property, liability, workers' compensation, marine, surety, and health. P/C companies collect revenues, called premiums, in exchange for promises to indemnify the insured party for specified types of losses that may occur during the period of coverage. Some losses that occur during a policy period may not become evident until years later. In many cases, it can take years to determine the extent of loss and the liability of various parties involved. Even in lines where losses are reported quickly with no question of coverage, repair or recovery may be protracted. In the interim, inflation and judicial trends can add to the uncertainty of the ultimate costs to the insurer.

During a year, an insurer will price and write policies and collect premiums on those policies. The insurer must keep track of claims for losses that are incurred and reported during the year, and it must estimate claims for losses that were incurred during the year but which will be reported in later years. By law and regulation, the insurer must set up reserves sufficient to pay the actuarially estimated cost of those claims and any costs associated with settling those claims, usually on an undiscounted basis. In any given year, if costs of claims incurred in prior years are running above previous estimates, the insurer must add to the reserves for those prior year claims; if costs are running below earlier estimates, reserves may be reduced. The insurer invests the funds representing claim reserves as well as the surplus of the company. Current revenue (premiums and investment income) must cover marketing and administrative expenses, funds to set up the reserves for new claims, any funds needed to strengthen reserves for prior year claims, taxes, and any payments to owners. To the extent that current revenue flows are insufficient for these needs, policyholder (statutory) surplus will be drawn down; if revenue exceeds these needs, surplus is augmented. Reserves established to pay claims may be inadequate if the insurer underestimated costs of prior claims, catastrophes caused current claims to exceed levels assumed in pricing, or the insurer suffered investment losses. Surplus provides a margin to assure that policyholders are paid for all claims. Over time, surplus growth is needed to support growth in premium volume.

Historically, insurers have attempted to price insurance products so that annual premiums would cover marketing and administrative expenses, and claim and claim adjustment expenses, perhaps even leaving a margin called an underwriting profit. Insurers typically report expense ratios (marketing and administrative expenses as a percent of premium), loss ratios (claim and claim adjustment expenses as a precent of premium), and combined ratios (the sum of expense and loss ratios). Combined ratios less than 100 (%) indicate premium revenue exceeds general and claim expenses; that is, the company enjoys an underwriting profit. Combined ratios above 100 indicate an underwriting loss.

Prior to the mid-1970s, most P/C companies did manage to price for combined ratios close to 100, as shown in Exhibit 47–1. Over the 24 years from 1950 to 1973, overall industry combined ratios were above 100 in only nine years; and over the entire period, annual combined ratios averaged 98.8. Since 1974, overall industry combined ratios have been below 100 for only two years; in 1984, combined ratios reached a peak of over 120. During both periods, results varied widely among companies and among lines of insurance.

Prior to the 1980s, there was a tendency among P/C insurers to view insurance operations as separate from investment operations. Insurance pricing was aimed at achieving underwriting profits, or at least avoiding losses. Investment policy was aimed at providing steady growth in dividends and surplus. Often this meant buying long-term bonds to lock in a predictable flow of investment income, supplemented with common stock investments to raise long-run returns. Investment managers needed to anticipate movements in underwriting profits and losses to adjust the tax status of the investment portfolio, but generally there was little interaction between liability (claims) management and asset management.

In the 1980s, a number of factors caused P/C insurers to focus more on coordinating management of liabilities and assets. In the high interest-rate environment of the early 1980s, investment income began to be factored more directly into insurance pricing. In a growing number of states, insurance regulators require explicit consideration of the effect of investment income on rates of return

**EXHIBIT 47–1**
**Property-Casualty Combined Ratios**

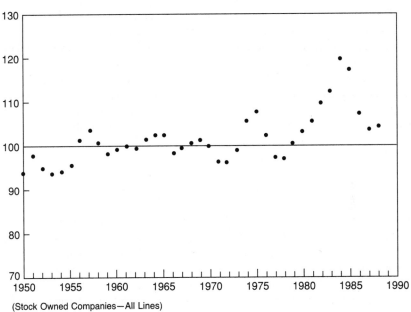

(Stock Owned Companies—All Lines)

Source: Best's Aggregates & Averages

in setting insurance prices. But competitive factors also forced pricing to reflect investment income. In the early 1980s, the industry experienced what came to be called cash-flow underwriting, whereby companies would intentionally price at an underwriting loss in order to attract premium revenues which could be invested at existing high yields. Increasingly, noninsurance corporations found it attractive to self insure, in order to keep the high investment income, rather than paying premiums to insurers and giving them the investment opportunity.

In the high interest-rate environment of the early 1980s, many insurance companies found themselves with large investment portfolios in old, low-coupon long-term bonds. The bonds could not be sold without reducing reported surplus, because market values had fallen well below book. (Accounting conventions regarding statutory surplus and bonds will be discussed later.) These companies, therefore, had to attract premium revenue to meet expenses and claim payments, to avoid selling bonds. This aggravated pressure to retain a share of market, even if it meant selling insurance products at unprofitable prices. Companies with low-coupon, long-term assets, were at a disadvantage to companies unencumbered by old long-term bonds that could price low and invest premiums at existing high interest rates. This situation lead to increased efforts by P/C companies to manage interest-rate risk which, in turn, called for management of asset/liability durations.

There remains considerable diversity in the investment objectives among P/C companies and in the methods they use to achieve those objectives. Similarly, there are wide differences in the extent to which companies coordinate the management of liabilities and assets. The remainder of this chapter will be structured around the approach to asset/liability management taken at The Travelers Companies. We view our approach to investment management as an evolving process, and there is constant, lively, internal debate with respect to many aspects of our operating methodology. This discussion really reflects one participant's views of that process.

## OVERVIEW OF THE INVESTMENT PROCESS

Within the Investment Group at Travelers, a portfolio manager is assigned to manage the portfolio representing the reserves for each business unit in the P/C companies. The portfolio manager is responsible for managing the overall characteristics of the portfolio, including interest-rate risk (duration), asset mix, liquidity, and diversification. This requires a statement of portfolio policy which establishes a normative portfolio, responsive to the characteristics of the liabilities and the needs and risk tolerance of the insurance business unit and the corporation.

The policy statement defines normal duration of assets, asset mix (for major asset classes), and cash or liquidity requirements. Policy also establishes parameters within which the portfolio manager can diverge from normal characteristics in order to take advantage of investment opportunities. A typical asset policy asset mix for a P/C portfolio might be as follows:

| Asset Class | Normal | Range |
|---|---|---|
| Cash | 5% | 3–10% |
| Bonds (Taxable & Tax-Exempt) | 70 | 60–80 |
| Mortgages | 10 | 5–15 |
| Equities | 15 | 5–20 |

The portfolio manager's performance is measured by the total return of the portfolio versus a market benchmark. The benchmark is a weighted average of market indexes, where the indexes and their weights are chosen to reflect the portfolio's normative asset allocation and liquidity and duration targets.

In developing portfolio characteristics, the portfolio manager works closely with actuaries and other contacts from the insurance business unit, the client. The insurance unit will provide information on the nature of the liabilities. The insurance unit will work with the portfolio manager to develop investment strategies that meet its needs and risk tolerances.

Since Travelers is a company consisting of several business units, overall corporate investment considerations must also influence investment strategies of individual portfolios. The Investment Committee of the Board of Directors, senior management, the Corporate Finance Department, and Investment Group management all share responsibility for addressing overall corporate investment considerations.

The portfolio manager is responsible for asset allocation decisions. Much of the responsibility for management of assets within asset classes falls to specialized groups within and outside the Investment Group. Within Travelers Investment Group are specialized Private Placement, Public Bond, and Cash Management units. Travelers Real Estate Investment Company is used as a source of mortgage loans and real estate investments.

With cooperation from the insurance business unit, the portfolio manager will develop an annual investment strategy statement. The strategy statements are reviewed by senior management to assure that portfolio strategies in aggregate are consistent with overall corporate goals and constraints. The statement will provide operating guidelines for the following investment parameters:

1. Investment goals
2. Risk tolerances
3. Asset class allocations
4. Asset diversification and characteristics
5. Performance measurement.
6. Reporting

The strategy statement is reviewed each year; it is revised if changes in company operations, insurance markets, financial markets, tax environment, or statutory constraints warrant changes in investment strategy. Revisions may be made within the year if conditions change significantly.

The remainder of this chapter will discuss the first four items listed above, particularly with respect to considerations specific to the P/C industry.

## INVESTMENT GOALS

In general terms, the overall goal of the portfolio is to support the ongoing operations of the insurance business unit. At Travelers, the philosophy of the Investment Group is to actively manage assets to maximize total return over a multiple year time horizon, subject to appropriate levels of risk. The portfolio manager's performance is measured on this total return basis. However, the insurance business units have additional requirements with respect to liquidity, current income, and contribution to surplus. These represent constraints on the portfolio manager and limit freedom to manage the portfolio on a total return basis.

A distinctive feature of the P/C industry is the cyclicality of pricing and profitability, usually referred to as the underwriting cycles. The cycles are not particularly regular, nor are they the same across all lines of business, in magnitude or in timing. The causes of the cycles are not well understood, but the cyclical nature of the P/C business is an important factor in companies' investment policies. The insurance unit's needs for current income, surplus, and liquidity and its tax status may be affected by the stage of the underwriting cycle.

The cyclical nature of P/C results is evident in the combined ratios in Exhibit 47–1. Similarly, Exhibit 47–2 shows that growth in premium revenues swings widely through the cycle. When premium growth slows for the industry as a whole, premium revenue declines for many individual companies. The

**EXHIBIT 47–2**
**Percent Growth in Written Premium**

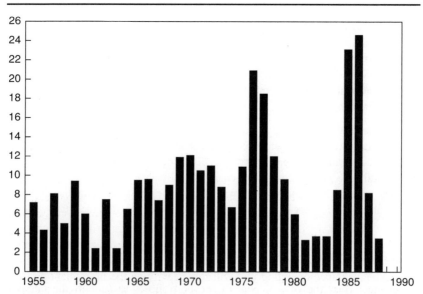

(Stock-Owned P/C Insurance Companies)

Source: Best's Aggregates & Averages

**EXHIBIT 47–3**
**Underwriting Profit or Loss**

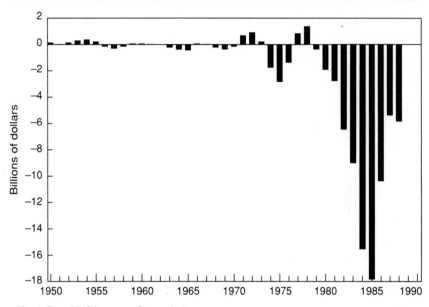

(Stock-Owned P/C Insurance Companies)

Source: Best's Aggregates & Averages

swings in premium growth result in dramatic shifts in the absolute level of underwriting profits/losses for the industry, as shown in Exhibit 47–3.

Combined ratios above 100 (underwriting losses) indicate that insurance underwriting operations are making a negative contribution to policyholder surplus. In P/C insurance, the ratio of premiums to surplus is viewed as an important measure of surplus adequacy. If surplus falls or does not grow fast enough, the insurer may be constrained in writing new business. This constraint may come from regulators or, more likely, from efforts to avoid a downgrade from rating agencies. Surplus constraints are most likely to be felt in the recovery stage of an underwriting cycle: Surplus has been growing slowly or even declining because of the negative contribution from underwriting; with prices firming, premium volume is rising fast. This is precisely the time the company wants to write business, because prices are firming. Near the bottom of an underwriting cycle, the insurance operating unit will rely heavily on the investment portfolio to generate current income and add to surplus so that it can expand insurance writings as the cycle turns. When underwriting results have been strong, there will be relatively less pressure on investments to boost surplus. Therefore, the insurance business unit's expectations for income and contribution to surplus will vary depending on the strength of insurance markets.

The insurance unit's need for liquidity in the investment portfolio will also vary with conditions in insurance markets. At any time, catastrophes have the potential to cause claim and expense payments to exceed cash flow from premiums and investment income. However, negative cash flow is more likely to occur near the bottom of an underwriting cycle, when claims have been rising faster than premiums for a period of time. At such times, when insurance pricing is very competitive, the insurance unit does not want to find itself in a position in which it has to support cash flow by writing unprofitable business.

When a company's surplus position is strong, adequate liquidity may mean just having assets that are marketable. However, near the bottom of an underwriting cycle, adequate liquidity may involve having assets that can be liquidated without negatively impacting surplus. Bonds are carried at amortized cost on P/C balance sheets. If the market value of a bond drops, surplus is not impacted until the bond is sold and the loss is realized. In the early 1980s, the market value of bonds in P/C portfolios was well below book values because interest rates had risen far above the levels of the previous decade. The inability to liquidate portfolios without impairing surplus probably caused many companies to continue writing business when pricing was clearly unprofitable.

## RISK TOLERANCE

### Marked-to-Market Exposure

Levels of risk tolerance may be developed against a number of criteria. Statutory or policyholders' surplus can affect the volume of business an insurer can write and the insurance markets that are available to that insurer. Policyholders' surplus is the difference between the statutory value of assets and liabilities; it is a margin of protection available to policyholders to assure all claims are paid. If surplus is too low relative to premium volume, state regulators may put pressure on the company to reduce its writings. More likely, an insurer with low surplus will restrict its premium volume to keep from incurring a downgrade on its financial ratings. Many corporate and institutional clients will only buy insurance coverage from an insurer whose A.M. Best financial rating is A+, A, or A−. Among many other factors, A.M. Best reviews financial leverage, including premiums to surplus and current liabilities to surplus.

As discussed in the previous section, growth in policyholders' surplus is depressed during periods of underwriting losses; in turn, capacity to write new business can be strained when pricing subsequently strengthens. Policyholders' surplus is also decreased by losses that are recognized on investments. For statutory and GAAP accounting, common and preferred stock are carried at market value; most bonds are carried at amortized cost. Changes in market values of stock are reflected on the balance sheet and in policyholders' surplus; changes in market value of bonds are not reflected in policyholders' surplus until the bonds are sold and the gain or loss is realized.

As shown in Exhibit 47–4, net investment income has risen through time, providing a steadily increasing contribution to earnings and to policyholders' surplus. Net investment income is defined as interest, dividends, fees, and rent received, net of investment expenses. When recognized gains and losses are added in, investment profit shows much more erratic growth. In 1957, 1969, and 1974, recognized losses on investments created overall investment losses at the same time the industry was incurring underwriting losses. The combined effect was large declines in surplus. Policyholder surplus is shown in Exhibit 47–5.

The willingness of a P/C insurer to recognize investment losses will vary over time, in part depending on current levels of policyholders' surplus and current and projected underwriting results. The company's risk tolerance is likely

**EXHIBIT 47–4**
**Net Investment Income and Profit**

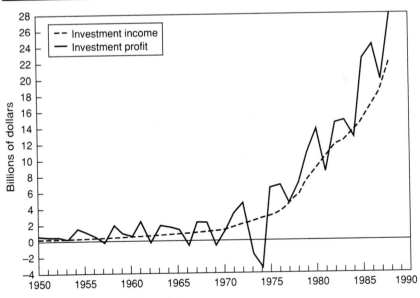

(Stock-Owned P/C Insurance Companies)

Source: Best's Aggregates & Averages

**EXHIBIT 47–5**
**Policyholders' Surplus**

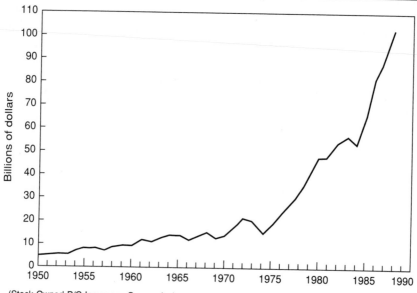

(Stock-Owned P/C Insurance Companies)

Source: Best's Aggregates & Averages

to be stated in terms of a maximum acceptable aggregate recognized capital loss at year-end, or perhaps a minimum acceptable investment contribution to surplus (net investment plus recognized gains or losses). The risk tolerance for recognizing investment losses will influence the portfolio manager's allocation between assets that are marked-to-market on the balance sheet and assets that are carried at other than market value.

## Interest-Rate Risk

The P/C industry's emphasis on policyholders' surplus has sometimes diverted attention from management of owners' equity. Due to numerous aspects of industry accounting, these concepts are not equal and are not impacted symmetrically by various types of risk. In calculating policyholders' surplus, liabilities for claim and claim adjustment expense are carried at estimated ultimate cost; most bonds are carried at amortized cost on the asset side of the calculation. Therefore, the balance sheet carrying values of major items in the calculation of policyholders' surplus are unaffected by changes in interest rates. In calculating the economic value of owners' equity, liabilities are converted to present value, and all assets are valued at market; therefore, both the liability and the asset sides of the owners' equity calculation are affected by changes in interest rates.

Over the past decade, most financial institutions have paid increasing attention to interest-rate risk and management of asset/liability duration mismatch. The P/C industry has been somewhat slow to accept the importance of asset-liability duration management. At least in part, this is due to the emphasis on policyholders' surplus and statutory accounting. Many P/C managers have doubted that investors rewarded them for managing interest-rate risk. It was never clear that investors had sufficient information to evaluate the relative interest-rate risk exposure among P/C insurers. P/C insurers publish enough data to allow calculation of reasonable estimates of market values of assets, present values of liabilities, and durations for both; however, the estimation process is cumbersome.

Duration as used here will refer to modified duration. Modified duration gives the approximate percentage change in the market or economic value of an asset or liability for a 100 basis point movement in interest rates.

Using economic values (market or present values) for assets ($A$), liabilities ($L$), and owners' equity ($S$):

$$S = A - L$$

Since surplus is the difference between asset and liability portfolios with predominantly fixed income characteristics, surplus too may have predominantly fixed income characteristics.[1] Because duration is linear in the weights of component assets or liabilities, it follows that duration of surplus ($Ds$) can be defined as follows:

$$S \times Ds = (A \times Da) - (L \times D1) \qquad (47\text{--}1)$$
$$Ds = D1 + (A/S) \times (Da - D1) \qquad (47\text{--}2)$$
$$Ds = D1 + (\text{Leverage}) \times (\text{Mismatch})$$

The duration of surplus equals the duration of the liabilities plus a term that is the product of asset leverage times the asset/liability duration mismatch. For the period 1984 to 1988, the ratio of P/C industry assets to policyholders' surplus averaged 4.1. This tends to overstate asset leverage to the extent that statutory liabilities are undiscounted (reducing surplus). Discounting loss and loss adjustment expenses, based on past payout patterns and using approximate portfolio yields as discount factors, indicates that asset leverage based on economic values was closer to 2.6.

---

[1] The discussion of surplus duration is taken from Thomas Messmore, "The Duration of Surplus," *The Journal of Portfolio Management*, Winter 1990.

Equation (47–2) can be manipulated to show that a P/C company that wishes to minimize the interest-rate risk of its economic surplus should invest for an asset duration $(Da)$ that is less than the liability duration $(D1)$. Setting duration of surplus equal to zero in equation (47–2):

$$0 = D1 + (A/S) \times (Da - D1)$$
$$Da = D1 \times [1 - (S/A)] = D1 \times (L/A) \qquad (47–3)$$

For a typical P/C company, with an asset-to-surplus ratio of 2.6, minimizing interest-rate risk of economic surplus (duration of surplus close to zero) would require an asset duration less than two thirds of the liability duration — a significant short mismatch.

## Estimating Interest-Rate Risk

The major components of P/C company liabilities are "loss and loss adjustment reserves" (more accurately described as claim and claim adjustment reserves) and "unearned premium reserves." To some extent, these liabilities may be thought of as fixed income obligations. The loss and loss adjustment reserves have been set up for claims that have already occurred; the ultimate amount of the claim cost is uncertain, but insurers estimate these amounts in establishing the reserve. In addition, based on past payout patterns, insurers can estimate the timing of payouts for existing claim obligations.

Using appropriate discount rates (based on market or company-specific yields), present values can be calculated for expected payouts of claims and adjustment expenses. This would be the amount that needs to be invested to meet the expected amount and timing of claim obligations. For sensitivity analysis, the calculations could be repeated for more or less conservative assumptions of ultimate claim amounts and payout patterns. Similarly, estimates of duration of the liabilities can be calculated, based on expected claim amounts and payout patterns. These type of calculations can be carried out by the actuarial staff and provided to the portfolio manager.

Insurers report historical payout patterns for loss and loss adjustment expenses in statutory statements that must be filed annually with state insurance commissions. Schedule O shows the payout of incurred losses by calendar year for property coverages; Schedule P does the same for liability and related coverages. This data can be used to make useful estimates of present values of liabilities for other insurers and for the industry as a whole.

Schedule P liabilities tend to have the longest average lives and account for about 85 percent of P/C loss and loss adjustment liabilities. For industry Schedule P losses incurred in 1982-83, about one third were paid within the same year the loss was incurred; 86 percent were paid within five years of the year in which the losses were incurred. Of course, these percentages are estimates since it is not certain what the ultimate loss payments for these years will be until the last claim is paid.

Assuming that industrywide loss payout patterns from earlier years continue, Schedule P losses incurred in a given calendar year have an average life (to payment) of about 2.8 years. Schedule P loss and loss adjustment expenses on P/C balance sheets at the end of 1988 had an estimated average life of 3.4 years (payouts slow after the first one to two years) and a duration of about 2.5. These estimates would vary among individual companies depending on the mix of business. For instance, auto liability claims have a shorter average life than workers' compensation claims, which in turn have a shorter average life than medical malpractice claims.

Schedule O liabilities have a shorter duration than Schedule P liabilities. Roughly two thirds of Schedule O losses are paid in the year in which they are incurred; the average life of these losses is between one and two years.

Unearned premium reserves are set up to allow for premiums that have been booked but for which the period of coverage has not been completed. Unearned premium represents obligations for claims that will be incurred in the remainder of the policy period. The liabilities represented by these future claims have a duration near 2.0, depending on the mix of premium between Schedule O and P lines. The loss and loss adjustment expense and "unearned premiums" account for 85–90 percent of P/C liabilities. Most other liabilities on P/C balance sheets are short-term in nature. Estimates prepared at Travelers indicate that for the industry as a whole P/C liabilities had durations of about 2.0–2.2 over the period 1984–1987.

The duration of P/C assets appears to be much longer than the duration of liabilities. Bonds comprise almost 60 percent of P/C admitted assets. P/C companies report the distribution of bond holdings across maturity class in Schedule D of the annual filings to state insurance commissions. At the end of 1988, those bonds had an average reported maturity of over 10 years, slightly shorter than at the end of 1987. Estimates made by Travelers indicate that for the industry as a whole P/C asset durations averaged close to 5.0–5.5 over the period 1984–1987. (These estimates assumed common stock had a duration of 4.0 and preferred stock a duration of 10.) Since the estimation process did not adjust for bond call features, these estimates should be viewed only as a rough indication of the duration of P/C assets. However, it clearly appears that P/C asset durations exceed liability durations.

Putting estimates of liability duration (2.0–2.2), asset duration (5.0–5.5), and asset-to-surplus ratio (2.6) into equation (47–2), the duration of owners' equity for the P/C industry as a whole is estimated to be close to 10. At year-end 1987, the duration of 30-year U.S. Treasury bonds was also about 10. This suggests substantial interest-rate risk for owners' equity. In general, if all interest rates were to rise one percentage point, economic surplus of P/C insurers would drop by roughly 10 percent.

Although these estimates should be viewed as illustrative only, they are consistent with work carried out by David Babbel and Kim Staking and described in a Goldman Sachs research report.[2] Babbel and Staking estimated the duration of surplus for 25 P/C writers over the period 1981–1987 and they reported the average surplus duration to be 9.7 years.

## Why So Much Interest-Rate Risk?

Being invested long allows P/C companies to take advantage of the positive slope of yield curves that exists much of the time. It is not clear, however, how large this payoff is. Managing the interest-rate exposure of owners' equity does not necessarily mean buying bills instead of bonds; it may mean buying more 5–10 year bonds and fewer 20 year bonds. During the 1980s, the Treasury yield curve had an average slope from 1 year to 30 years of 84 basis points; however the average slope from 5 years to 30 years was only 15 basis points. P/C companies have traditionally owned large holdings of tax-exempt bonds; in that market the reward for going long appears larger. During the 1980s, the municipal debt yield curve from 1 year to 30 years averaged 300 basis points, with 197 basis points of that slope between 5 years and 30 years.[3]

Moreover, P/C companies may not view interest-rate risk symmetrically because of book accounting and concern for statutory surplus. For both statutory and GAAP purposes most bonds are carried at amortized cost. If interest rates are unchanged, investing long usually offers the highest yield. If interest rates go down, P/C companies can sell bonds and realize gains and higher surplus or just keep the higher-than-market book yields. If interest rates go up, statutory bond valuations do not change, and reported surplus is not affected, unless the insurer is forced to sell the bonds.

Companies may not even view the duration of liabilities on their balance sheet at any one time as reflecting their liabilities as an ongoing concern. In general, a P/C company is constantly renewing a share of its old business and writing new business. At any time, a company can expect to write business in the future that will generate a stream of claim liabilities further into the future. Rather than considering duration of existing liabilities, P/C companies manage to a liability stream that assumes some continuing level of future insurance writings. These companies may invest long to lock in an investment yield on future business. As claims are settled, they are largely paid out of current premium and investment income flows. To adopt this view, a company should be relatively

---

[2] David F. Babbel and Kim B. Staking, *The Market Reward for Insurers That Practice Asset/Liability Management*, Goldman, Sachs & Co., November 1989.

[3] Based on weekly averages of quotes for high grade municipal bonds and notes. The source of the yield data is Bank of America.

sure that it can maintain new business at adequate volumes and prices. Locking into long-term bonds may put insurers at a pricing disadvantage if interest rates subsequently rise.

Management of stock-owned P/C companies must balance regulators' concern for statutory surplus with the need to maximize shareholder wealth. Management has often questioned whether investors pay attention to interest-rate risk of P/C insurers. Investors seem to recognize that the P/C industry is subject to interest-rate risk, but investors may be unable to distinguish relative interest-rate exposure of individual companies.

At Travelers, we attempted to study this issue. We estimated duration of owners' equity for a group of 10 P/C companies. We then compared the interest sensitivity of the stock returns of these companies with the estimates of duration of the economic value of owners' equity. For the group as a whole, the interest sensitivity of stock returns was very close to the estimate of duration of owners' equity. However, looking among individual companies there was little correlation between estimated interest sensitivity of stock returns and the estimated duration of owners' equity. There could be several explanations: estimates of duration of owners' equity are subject to error; the sample was too small; other factors influenced specific stock returns. On the other hand, it may be that investors have enough information to recognize that the P/C industry is exposed to interest-rate risk, but not enough to distinguish relative exposure among companies. This would suggest that a manager who is concerned with performance of his company's stock may not see much advantage to managing interest-rate exposure. His company will just be categorized with the rest of the industry.

The recent study by David Babbel and Kim Staking cited earlier, however, indicates that investors do recognize differences in interest-rate risk between P/C companies. Further, their work indicates that investors attach higher value to firms that control interest-rate risk. Their study of 25 P/C companies showed that market valuation of owners' equity (called liquidation value in their study) tended to be highest for firms with surplus duration near 0.0.

Travelers adopted asset-liability management techniques in the early 1980s. Today, tolerance for interest-rate risk is measured in terms of duration of owner's equity or economic surplus. Duration of liabilities is estimated two ways: looking only at liabilities currently on the balance sheet or arising from current year business; and assuming the level of new business shown in the 3-year business plan. Duration of surplus assuming no new business gives an extreme view of the interest-rate exposure of the company if it cannot write business at prices deemed profitable. On a normal basis, the risk strategy calls for minimizing the interest-rate risk of economic surplus (i.e. duration near 0.0). However, risk tolerance allows for some interest-rate risk, depending on the interest-rate forecast, the slope of yield curves, and conditions in insurance markets.

## ASSET CLASS ALLOCATION

At the end of 1988, bonds comprised 70 percent of the investment portfolios of P/C companies. Common stock accounted for 15 percent of investments, while cash and short-term assets made up an additional 8 percent. Small shares of the portfolios were devoted to preferred stock, mortgages, real estate, and other assets. The industry's asset mix is shown in Exhibit 47–6. Most types of bonds are utilized by P/C companies, including, Treasuries, agencies, municipals, corporates, mortgage-backed, and foreign issues.

In making asset allocation decisions, the portfolio manager will take into account the investment goals and risk tolerance of the insurance business unit and the overall corporation. The portfolio manager will consider expected returns, risks or volatility, and covariances among asset classes. In addition, the portfolio manager's decisions will be influenced by regulatory and tax considerations that are specific to the P/C industry. Finally, it must be realized that P/C liabilities are not certain. The number and size of claims and the timing of their payouts may be affected by such factors as the state of the economy, inflation, and interest

**EXHIBIT 47–6**
**Cash and Invested Assets: Year-end 1988**

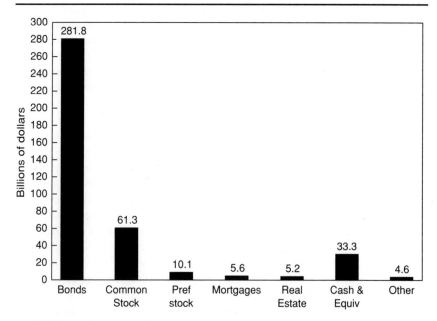

(All P,C Companies—Statutory Values)

Source: Best's Aggregates & Averages

rates; these same factors can affect the returns and risks of investment assets. This suggests the need to take into account the cross correlations among P/C liabilities and various classes of investment assets in making asset allocation decisions.

The portfolio manager must also take into account the current portfolio allocations in setting target allocations. Selling assets that are held with unrecognized losses may be in conflict with the company's needs for statutory surplus. Cash flow may limit how rapidly some asset classes can be built up if other asset classes cannot be sold off.

## Regulatory Influence on Asset Allocation

State regulations address investment policy by setting minimum standards for quality and diversification. These regulations generally are intended to prevent speculative investment activity. These standards vary among states, and some companies that operate in a number of states comply by adopting the tightest limitation (among all the states in which they operate) for each type of standard. Some of the major limitations on P/C investments include the following:

- New York requires that unsecured debt of U.S. corporations, joint stock associations and business trusts must meet certain fixed charge coverage tests, generally 1.5 times fixed charges. Secured debt of U.S. corporations must be of investment grade and meet fixed charge coverage tests.
- Illinois limits the percentage of an insurer's admitted assets that may be held in various types of obligations of states, political subdivisions, or public instrumentalities in aggregate. For example, not more than 2 percent of admitted assets may be held in the direct, general obligations of any one political subdivision of a state.
- The lesser of surplus or 10 percent of admitted assets may be held in common stock of U.S. corporations. Common stock of U.S. corporations traded over the counter is not to exceed 15 percent of surplus or 1.5 percent of admitted assets. Common stock must be traded on a national securities exchange or over the counter with a nationwide automated quotations system and the issues must meet specific net income, total asset, and minimum number of shareholder tests (New York standards).
- Not more than 50 percent of admitted assets may be held in obligations secured by first or second mortgages on U.S. real estate (New York standard).
- Not more than 12.5 percent of admitted assets may be held in U.S. real property (New York standard).
- Not more than 10 percent of admitted assets may be held in investments issued by a Canadian entity and not more than 1 percent of admitted assets may be held in other foreign investments (New York standard).

To provide more flexibility, P/C companies are allowed to put some percent of admitted assets into investments which do not meet regulatory standards (or which exceed regulatory limits); this percent is an aggregate over all investment restrictions. These exception percentages are commonly referred to as "basket" limitations. In practice, regulatory limits probably have had their greatest impact on junk bond allocations. Most noninvestment-grade bonds will not meet the coverage tests set out by many state regulators; therefore, most noninvestment grade bonds would be counted in the basket limitation. This has effectively limited P/C purchases of noninvestment grade bonds. At the end of 1988, only 1–2 percent of the bonds in P/C portfolios were below investment-grade (as designated by NAIC classifications).

A feature of regulation that probably has been more important in shaping P/C asset allocations is differential valuation methods among asset classes under statutory accounting. For purposes of measuring statutory surplus, bonds generally are carried at amortized cost, and mortgages are carried at the principal amount. In contrast, common and preferred stock are carried at market values, as determined by the Securities Valuation Office (SVO) of the National Association of Insurance Commissioners (NAIC). Preferred stock in good standing and subject to a 100 percent mandatory sinking fund is carried at cost.

A drop in the market value of a stock holding reduces statutory surplus through an unrealized loss. A decline in the market value of bonds, due to a change in the general level of interest rates or to other market conditions, does not affect statutory surplus. For P/C insurers, stocks expose statutory surplus to market risk to a greater extent than bonds. This different treatment of market value risk has tended to bias P/C investments toward bonds.

Over time, regulation that shifts portfolio investment towards bonds from stock can adversely affect the performance of P/C investments. Numerous historical studies show that stocks outperform bonds over long periods of time. Statutory accounting and surplus concerns force many insurers to pay added attention to the short-term volatility of stock.

### Taxes and Asset Allocation

For institutions engaged in spread lending, tax preferenced investment assets are of limited usefulness in their asset portfolios; for these companies, the bulk of investment income has an offsetting interest expense. For P/C insurers, since a larger share of investment income flows to net income, the tax status of investment income has greater impact on P/C companies' bottom line. For stock-owned P/C companies, investment profit (net income plus realized gains or losses) totalled $159 billion over the years 1980–1988; this was partially offset by a cumulative underwriting loss of $77 billion. This indicates that over half of investment income was exposed to income tax. This calculation understates the percentage of investment income that is potentially exposed to corporate income tax; P/C investment income in the 1980s had an implied tax payment built in, from large holdings of tax-exempt bonds. Prior to the 1980s, virtually all of investment income was exposed to corporate income tax, because on average the industry ran underwriting profits.

Not only is P/C investment income highly exposed to corporate income tax, but the exposure varies widely with the underwriting cycle. In the 1980s, on a calendar year basis, underwriting losses varied from as much as 122 percent (1984) of investment profit to as little as 14 percent (1980). This cyclicality can be smoothed for tax purposes by tax rules that allow profit and loss to be matched across time. Still, the cyclicality increases the value of tax planning in investment decisions.

Traditionally, the tax exposure of investment income has caused P/C companies to hold a large share of their portfolios in tax-exempt bonds. Tax preferences (lower capital gains tax rates and the corporate dividend exclusion) also increased the relative attraction of stock. P/C companies would shift investments toward tax-preferenced assets when underwriting losses declined, and away from tax-preferenced assets when underwriting losses were rising. According to Federal Reserve Flow of Funds data, tax-exempt bonds accounted for an average of 59 percent of all bonds in P/C portfolios over the period 1964 to 1988. (See Exhibit 47–7.) The percentage varied from 47 percent to 68 percent, and the dollar holdings of tax-exempt bond holdings actually fell in 1983 and 1984, when underwriting losses were very large. For individual companies, shifts in and out of tax-exempt bonds were much larger. Shifts in the tax value of preferenced assets adds to the need to maintain liquidity in the portfolio. As underwriting losses rise, P/C companies want to be able to move out of tax-exempt securities into taxable bonds with higher nominal yields, but at that stage of the underwriting cycle, they may have the least appetite for recognizing losses that drain statutory surplus.

The Tax Reform Act of 1986 increased the effective tax rates of P/C insurers, even though it cut the highest marginal tax rate from 46 percent to 34 percent. The Tax Reform Act accelerated the timing for recognizing taxable income by requiring adjustments for unearned premium reserves and discounting of claim reserves. It also reduced the tax benefit of tax-exempt interest and stock dividends; a new Alternative Minimum Tax further reduced the tax benefit of preferenced investment income.

Tax changes related to tax-preferenced assets are very important for asset allocation decisions. For corporations, the Tax Reform Act (and a follow-up bill in 1987) reduced the dividends-received deduction to 70 percent from 85 percent. For securities acquired after August 7, 1986, it also reduced P/C insurers' deductions for losses by 15 percent of the sum of tax-exempt interest

**EXHIBIT 47–7**
**Use of Tax-exempt Bonds**

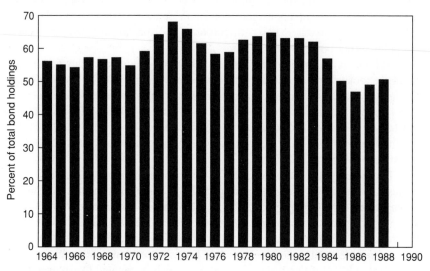

(Portfolios of Non-life Insurers)

Source: Federal Reserve, Flow of Funds

and dividends-received deduction; the decrease in deduction is called proration. In general, 15 percent of interest on tax-exempt bonds purchased after August 7, 1986 is included in taxable income; this implies a tax rate of 5.1 percent (34% × 15%). The effective tax rate on tax-exempt bonds bought before that date remains 0 percent. For stock acquired after August 7, 1986, the percent of dividends included in taxable income is 40.5 percent (30% + (15% × 70%)); and the effective tax rate is 13.77 percent (34% × 40.5%). These rates involve some simplification, but they are approximately valid when the insurer is not in an Alternative Minimum Tax (AMT) situation.

Corporations pay the larger of their regular corporate tax or AMT. AMT is 20 percent of Alternative Minimum Taxable Income (AMTI); AMTI equals regular taxable income plus certain preference items and adjustments. As preference items become larger, AMTI and AMT become larger, and the likelihood of being in an AMT-paying situation increases.

For purposes of portfolio allocation decisions, the most important preference items relate to the dividends-received deduction, 100 percent of interest on municipal bonds purchased prior to August 7, 1986, and 85 percent of interest on nongrandfathered municipal bonds. As of 1990, 75 percent of this "tax-exempt" income is included as a preference item. If a bond is a private activity bond issued after August 7, 1986 (referred to as an AMT bond), 100 percent of its tax-exempt income is included as a preference item.

Exhibit 47–8 compares effective tax rates for income (interest and dividends) from various types of securities under regular tax and under AMT.

After-tax returns on each asset class will depend on whether or not the company finds itself in an AMT position. To optimize asset allocation decisions, it is important to know what the insurer's tax situation will be. This, in turn, requires coordinated planning among the corporate finance unit, the insurance business unit, and the investment unit.

The larger preference items are relative to regular taxable income, the more likely the company will be required to pay AMT. For any given mix of investment assets, a P/C insurer's regular taxable income will decline (rise) as underwriting losses expand (shrink). Therefore, the likelihood of being in an AMT situation will depend on the stage of the underwriting cycle and on the number and severity of large catastrophe losses during the year. The income effects of underwriting cycles and large catastrophes tend to be widespread across the P/C industry. Therefore, many insurers are likely to find themselves moving toward (or away from) an AMT situation and trying to move out of (into) tax-preferenced investment assets at the same time. On the margin, this may affect spreads between tax-preferenced and fully taxable investment assets.

**EXHIBIT 47–8**
**Comparison of Tax Rates**

| | Tax Mode | |
|---|---|---|
| Security | Regular Tax | AMT |
| Taxable Bonds | 34.00% | 20.00% |
| Municipal Bonds | | |
| Purchased before 8/7/86 | 0.00 | 15.00* |
| Purchased after 8/7/86 | 5.10 | 15.75† |
| Private Activity Bonds | | |
| Purchased before 8/7/86 | 0.00 | 20.00 |
| Purchased after 8/7/86 | 5.10 | 20.00 |
| Stocks | | |
| Purchased before 8/7/86 | 10.20‡ | 16.50§ |
| Purchased after 8/7/86 | 13.77 | 17.025‖ |

* (20% × 75%)
† (20% × 15%) + (20% × 85% × 75%)
‡ (34% × 30%)
§ (20% × 30%) + (20% × 70% × 75%)
‖ (20% × 30%) + (20% × 70% × 75%) + (20% × 70% × 75% × 85%)

An asset manager who is able to anticipate shifts in insurance underwriting results may be able to make portfolio adjustments ahead of competitors. Large catastrophes are not predictable, but the insurance business unit can give useful input on the direction of underwriting cycles.

In general, if a P/C insurer expects to pay AMT, it can increase after-tax income by buying more taxable bonds. If the insurer expects to pay regular tax, buying more tax-preferenced bonds can increase after-tax income. The asset mix that maximizes after-tax income will depend on relative yields among tax-preferenced and fully taxable assets, underwriting results, and availability of tax carryovers. To maximize after-tax income over a multiple-year horizon, it is necessary to forecast all these factors.

## Liability/Asset Correlations

At any time, P/C insurers have estimates of the number of claims that have been incurred, costs of settling those claims, and the timing of payouts to settle those claims. The present value of those estimated claim payouts varies inversely with investment yields, due to the discounting effect. However even on an undiscounted basis, the timing and amount of the liabilities remain uncertain until they are finally settled. The size of the ultimate claim payment may be affected by the level of inflation between occurrence and settlement. A plaintiff in a personal injury claim may be willing to settle more quickly if interest rates are high (and settlement amounts can be invested at high yields) than if interest rates are low. Looking at current business, auto claims may increase in number during periods of strong economic activity when both personal and commercial vehicles are driven more.

It seems very reasonable to assume that the P/C liabilities are a function of general economic activity, inflation, interest rates, and numerous other factors. These factors can also affect returns and risks of investment assets. Asset/liability management in P/C companies should take into account the variability of P/C liabilities and their correlations with major classes of investment assets.

A great deal of work has been done in tracking historical returns, volatility, and cross correlations among major classes of investment assets. Various analyses have also attempted to relate asset performance and risk to various concepts such as economic activity, inflation, and interest rates. Less progress has been made in understanding the variability of P/C liabilities, the factors causing that variability, and the relationship with investment asset performance. This work will go forward as the payoffs to improved asset-liability management are recognized.

Research is underway to develop models that will provide a framework to optimize investment asset allocation taking into account many of the considerations discussed here. Such models may be based on maximizing total return on the investment assets, but constraints could be applied for current income, surplus adequacy, risk tolerance, and asset diversification. The models would include tax effects and underwriting results. The models would allow the user to include factors such as economic activity, inflation, and interest rates that affect both assets and liabilities, and therefore, the correlations among asset classes and liabilities. Travelers is participating in research along these lines. At present, work is proceeding to improve the inputs to models, especially behavior and interrelationships of asset classes and liabilities. It is hoped that this type of tool will eventually allow improved business performance, by more closely coordinating the management of assets and liabilities.

## ASSET DIVERSIFICATION

The previous section discussed factors affecting the allocation of portfolios among asset classes. The issue of what defines an asset class was intentionally avoided. Taxable bonds may be considered a separate asset class from tax-exempts, but taxable bonds may be further divided among government, corporate, and mortgage-backed bonds. Bonds may be divided by investment and noninvestment grade, or broken down even finer by quality rating. The appropriate definition of asset classes really depends on how many classes the portfolio manager wants to consider in making gross allocations and how correlated the manager perceives asset performance to be within and among asset groupings.

Regardless of how asset classes are defined there may remain a need to look beyond the asset class allocations to insure that the portfolio is adequately diversified against all identifiable sources of risk. Managing asset-liability duration mismatch may minimize interest-rate risk, but protecting against credit risk and spread risk requires making sure the portfolio is diversified over sectors, industries, and credit qualities.

For P/C insurers, assets and liabilities are often exposed to the same types of diversification risks. Therefore, there is a need to manage the diversification of assets and liabilities in a coordinated process.

Natural catastrophes can generate huge and sudden losses for P/C companies. In 1989, Hurricane Hugo, an earthquake in the Oakland-San Francisco area, and a chemical plant explosion in Texas caused billions of dollars of insured losses all within a month's time. An insurer can minimize the expected impact from any catastrophe by spreading its writings across many geographic areas, limiting the business it writes in hazard prone areas, and by reinsuring. Investments should be reviewed on a similar basis to be sure that they are not concentrated in geographic areas prone to natural catastrophes. A company's exposure to a geographic region may not look excessively large when looking separately at assets and liabilities, however, the combined asset and liability exposure may be excessive.

Economic conditions can also vary on a regional basis. In a region where unemployment is rising, insurers are likely to see a rise in theft and arson claims, and workers' compensation claims may also rise, as workers file claims for treatment they postponed when work was plentiful. This same economic weakness is likely to hurt mortgage and real estate investments, as well as performance of municipal bonds. The value of debt and stock of companies located in the region will also be affected. Liabilities and assets need to be diversified geographically, even for regions not identified with natural catastrophes. This may be difficult for regional insurance companies. Their insurance exposure will be concentrated geographically, and they may face regulatory and political pressure to keep investment funds in the region.

The liabilities of commercial insurers can be very vulnerable to the fortunes of individual industries. Asbestos manufacturers comprised a relatively small industrial group that generated billions of dollars of claims for P/C insurers. A prudent diversification program would require that the mix of insurance liabilities associated with particular industries (or the distribution of premium volume by industry) be compared with the distribution of bond and stock holdings across industries, to assure that the insurer is not inadvertently doubling its bets.

Some insurers have started to look at whether assets can be found that are inversely correlated with various types of claim liabilities. It has been suggested that investments in contracting companies and building supply firms might perform well following natural catastrophes. With large exposure to toxic waste cleanup, some insurers have looked at investments in companies that clean up toxic waste sites. Health care insurers may look for investments which either help control health care costs or benefit directly from rising health care costs. This type of diversification effort may grow as insurers get a better understanding of the factors affecting their liabilities, and more closely coordinate the management of assets and liabilities.

## SUMMARY

Traditionally, P/C companies held a bond portfolio to fund insurance reserves, while investing surplus largely in common stock. P/C insurers have accepted a great deal of interest-rate risk, because insurance pricing was viewed as insensitive to investment results. Statutory accounting methods often provided disincentives to economically efficient investment decisions. With the high interest rates of the 1980s, there has been an increased recognition of the need for asset-liability management. Asset/liability management in the P/C industry involves more than just managing interest-rate risk. P/C liabilities are affected by many of the same factors that affect asset performance: economic activity, inflation, and interest rates, as well as regional and industry factors. Management of assets and liabilities should be coordinated to improve asset allocation and assure diversification across all identifiable sources of risk.

# CHAPTER 48

## FIXED INCOME PORTFOLIO PERFORMANCE: ANALYZING SOURCES OF RETURN

*Gifford Fong*
President
*Gifford Fong Associates*

*Charles Pearson*
Director of Research
*Gifford Fong Associates*

*Oldrich Vasicek, Ph.D.*
Senior Research Associate
*Gifford Fong Associates*

*Theresa Conroy*
Applications Group
*Gifford Fong Associates*

The analysis of fixed income portfolio performance continues to evolve. From its early beginnings, in which the total return calculation was emphasized, to the first attempts at the attribution of returns, the methodology of performance analysis has changed in order to understand the process responsible for the return achieved. As the complexity of fixed income strategy as well as security type has grown, so has the need for refining the performance measurement and analysis activity.

This chapter will address recent developments in the attribution of the returns of a fixed income portfolio. We will start with a review of the basic attribution process and follow with a description of a further evolution that can accommodate the complexity of strategy and security developments.

## THE BACKGROUND

A previous approach to fixed income portfolio performance attribution revealed two main components of return:[1]

$$R = I + C \qquad (48\text{–}1)$$

where

$I$ = the effect of the external interest-rate environment beyond the control of the manager

$C$ = the contribution of the management process

The rationale was to decompose the total return into two components: the level of interest rates and the management of the portfolio.

Further decomposition of the interest-rate effect ($I$) includes:

$$I = E + U \qquad (48\text{–}2)$$

where

$E$ = expected return on default-free securities under the assumption of no change in forward rates, and

$U$ = unexpected return attributable to the actual change in forward rates

For the interest-rate environment, the expected return ($E$) is estimated from a term-structure analysis of a universe of Treasury securities.[2] From the estimated forward rates, the return implied from assuming no change in forward rates can be determined. The unexpected return ($U$) is merely the total return of all outstanding Treasury securities, weighted by capitalization, minus the expected return ($E$).

Further decomposition of the management contribution ($C$) includes:

$$C = M + S + B \qquad (48\text{–}3)$$

where

$M$ = return from maturity management

$S$ = return from spread-quality management and

$B$ = return attributable to the selection of specific securities

The management contribution ($C$) is calculated by a series of repricings. Each security in the portfolio, taking into account all transactions, is priced as if it were a default-free Treasury lying on the term structure. The return of the entire

---

[1] See Gifford Fong, Charles Pearson, and Oldrich Vasicek, "Bond Performance: Analyzing Sources of Return," *The Journal Portfolio of Management*, Spring 1983, pp. 46–50.

[2] Vasicek, Oldrich A., and H. Gifford Fong, "Term Structure Modeling," *Journal of Finance*, Vol. 37, May 1982, pp. 339–348.

Treasury universe is then subtracted from the aggregate return of these repriced securities to estimate the maturity management component ($M$). The spread-quality management component ($S$) is estimated by repricing each security in the portfolio as if it had the average yield premia of securities in that respective category. The default-free yield of each security is added to the sector premium to determine the implied price. This price is then used to calculate the gross return between evaluation dates. The interest-rate effect ($I$) and the maturity management component ($M$) are subtracted from this gross return. Finally, the return attributable to the selection of specific securities ($B$) is the total return of the portfolio minus the previously determined components.

This basic approach to fixed income performance measurement provides a framework to identify the major sources of return. It further associates the return with activities commonly linked with fixed income portfolio management.

As portfolio strategies have evolved, so has the need for a further refinement of the basic framework. In the next section, a further level of detail is used to provide an even more comprehensive attribution capability.

## ENHANCEMENTS TO THE BASIC APPROACH

The maturity management component seeks to measure the effect of overall changes in interest rates relative to the bogey chosen (all-Treasury Index). The net difference in maturity between the portfolio and the index is evaluated to determine the impact of this difference on return. For those managers who are only concerned with the direction of interest rates, this is an appropriate analysis; however, if the overall shift in the term structure is of concern, then a more refined measurement procedure is called for.[3]

Duration measures the effects of a parallel shift in the yield curve. If the yield-curve change is not parallel, the magnitude of the yield-curve shift will vary depending upon where the measurement is made. Consistent with the concept of using the Treasury index to measure the unmanaged interest-rate effect, we use the duration of the Treasury index as the point for measuring the amount of the parallel yield shift.

The duration return component of interest-rate management can then be expressed as:

$$R_{Dp} = -(D_p - D_i)S_{Di} \qquad (48\text{--}4)$$

where

$R_{Dp}$ = duration return component of interest-rate management effect for the portfolio

---

[3] Gifford Fong Associates, "Interest Rate Management," Internal Memorandum, August 1, 1989.

$S_{Di}$ = shift in Treasury yield at Treasury index duration

$D_p$ = beginning of month average adjusted portfolio duration

$D_i$ = beginning of month average adjusted Treasury index duration

As part of the maturity management analysis, a regression of the changes of the spot rate yield curve is computed. The shift in rates for the Treasury index is then:

$$S_{Di} = a + bD_i \qquad (48\text{--}5)$$

where

$S_{Di}$ = shift in Treasury yield at Treasury index duration

$a$ = intercept of the regression of the changes of the spot rate yield curve

$b$ = slope of the regression line of the changes of the spot rate yield curve

$D_i$ = beginning of month average adjusted Treasury index duration

The convexity management return component of interest-rate management actually results from two effects. The first effect is from the change in the level of interest rates. Duration can be thought of as measuring the effect of minute (or local) changes in rates on price (a first-order effect), while convexity can be thought of as measuring the change in duration as rates shift (a second-order measure). This second-order yield shift effect is calculated as

$$R_{CSp} = \frac{1}{2}(C_p - C_i)a^2 \qquad (48\text{--}6)$$

where

$R_{CSp}$ = convexity return component from the shift in the level of interest of rates

$C_p$ = adjusted convexity of the porfolio at the beginning of the month

$C_i$ = adjusted convexity of the Treasury index at the beginning of the month

$a$ = intercept of the regression of the changes of the spot rate yield curves

The other effect measured by convexity can be thought of as a "twist" effect (i.e. the effect of rotation in the yield curve). This twist effect is calculated as:

$$\begin{aligned} R_{CTp} = &-(C_p - C_i)b \\ &+(D_p - D_i)D_i b \end{aligned} \qquad (48\text{--}7)$$

where

$R_{CTp}$ = convexity return component from the twist in interest-rate change

$C_p$ = adjusted convexity of the portfolio at the beginning of the month

$C_i$ = adjusted convexity of the Treasury index at the beginning of the month

$b$ = slope of the regression line of the changes of the spot rate yield curve

$D_p$ = beginning of month average adjusted portfolio duration

$D_i$ = beginning of month average adjusted Treasury index duration

The sum of the above two effects is the convexity effect.

The parameters of duration and convexity do not measure effects resulting from changes in the shape of the yield curve (i.e., a downward sloping curve changing to a "humped" curve). We classify such effects as a "yield-curve shape change" as opposed to duration and convexity effects. Yield-curve shape change ends up being the residual component of the maturity management component after the duration and convexity effects are eliminated.

Exhibit 48–1 illustrates spot rate yield curves from October 31, 1988 and November 30, 1988. Exhibit 48–2 plots the difference between these two curves and shows the resulting linear regression line derived from this difference.

The 10-year zero (priced to the spot rate curve) not only displays duration and convexity effects but also shows yield-curve shape change interest effects as well. Using the 10-year zero, the following effects were calculated.

$$D_p = 9.585$$
$$C_p = 0.965$$

**EXHIBIT 48–1**

**U.S. Treasury Spot Rate Yield Curve**

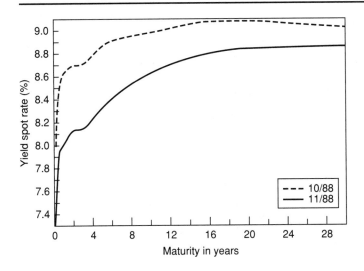

**EXHIBIT 48–2**
**Change in Spot Yield Curves**

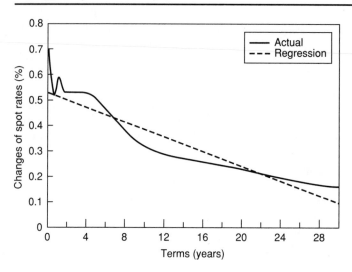

$$a = 0.005277$$
$$b = -0.0001446$$
$$D_i = 4.525$$
$$C_i = 0.4408$$

We therefore have

$$a = 0.5277\% = 0.005277$$
$$b = 0.01446\% = -0.0001446$$

$$
\begin{aligned}
\text{Duration effect} &= [-(D_p - D_i)] \times [a + (b \times D_i)] \\
&= [-(9.585 - 4.525)] \times [0.005277 + (-0.0001446 \times 4.525)] \\
&= -0.0233908 = -2.34\%
\end{aligned}
$$

Convexity effects are as follows:

$$
\begin{aligned}
\text{Yield-curve shift} &= [100 \times (C_p - C_i)] \times (0.5 \times a^2) \\
&= [100 \times (0.965 - 0.4408)] \times [(0.5 \times (0.005277)^2] \\
&= 0.000729 \\
\text{Twist} &= [-100 \times (C_p - C_i) \times b] + [(D_p - D_i) \times b \times D_i]
\end{aligned}
$$

$$= [-100 \times (0.965 - 0.4408) \times (-0.0001446)] + [(9.585 - 4.525) \times (-0.0001446) \times 4.525]$$

$$= 0.0075799 - 0.0033108$$

$$= 0.004269$$

Total convexity $= $ (Duration shift) $+$ (Twist)

$$= 0.000729 + .004269$$

$$= 0.004998 = 0.50\%$$

Yield-curve shape change effect $= $ Interest-rate management effect $-$

(Duration effect $+$ Convexity effect)

$$= -1.09 - (-2.34 + 0.50)$$

$$= 0.76\%$$

The surprising realization is that yield-curve shape change can be a very significant factor in total return. This is true not only for isolated examples as above but for actual portfolios as well.

## SUMMARY

To refine the return attribution of a fixed income portfolio, a further breakdown of the maturity management component may be accomplished. Term structure changes involve duration, convexity, and term structure shape return. The return from duration results from the effect of parallel rate changes. Convexity includes return from duration changes plus twists or rotation of the term structure. Term structure shape return results from changes in the overall shape of the term structure. This detailed decomposition of the maturity management return further highlights the sources of management skill in the portfolio management process.

For fixed income strategies that rely upon the use of these specialized approaches, this framework can be a useful monitoring tool.

# CHAPTER 49

## HEDGING WITH FUTURES
## AND OPTIONS

*Mark Pitts, Ph.D.*
*Senior Vice President*
*Lehman Brothers*

*Frank J. Fabozzi, Ph.D., CFA*
*Visiting Professor of Finance*
*Sloan School of Management*
*Massachusetts Institute of Technology*
*and*
*Editor, The Journal of Portfolio Management*

This chapter addresses a primary concern of many portfolio managers: how the futures and options markets can be used to hedge fixed-income portfolios.

In this chapter we start by discussing the prerequisites for creating an effective hedge. We then show how to derive the hedge ratio and the target rate, or price, for a hedge. For each case that we cover, examples demonstrate the performance of hedging strategies under various scenarios.

## HEDGING WITH FUTURES

### The Preliminaries

Before a hedge is ever initiated, there are several steps that the prudent manager should take in order to be completely comfortable with the hedging process. By taking these steps before the hedge is set, the potential hedger gains an understanding of what a hedge can and cannot accomplish and ensures that, if the hedge is set, it is set in the proper manner. Briefly, the preliminary steps are as follows:

1. Determine which futures contract is the most appropriate hedging vehicle.
2. Determine the target for the hedge, that is, the effective rate or price most likely to result from the hedge.
3. Estimate the effectiveness of the hedge, that is, the risk of a hedged position relative to an unhedged position.
4. Estimate the absolute (as opposed to relative) risk of the hedged position.
5. Determine the proper hedge ratio, that is, the number of futures contracts needed to hedge the underlying risk.

A primary factor in determining which futures contract will provide the best hedge is the degree of correlation between the rate on the futures contract and the interest rate that creates an unwanted underlying risk. For example, it is preferable to hedge a long-term corporate bond portfolio with Treasury bond (T-bond) futures than with Treasury bill (T-bill) futures, because long-term corporate bond rates are more highly correlated with T-bond rates than with T-bill rates. Similarly, an anticipated sale of short-term liabilities tied to the T-bill rate would generally be more effectively hedged using T-bill futures than Eurodollar time deposit futures. Using the right delivery month is also important. A manager trying to lock in a rate or price for June should use June futures contracts, because June contracts would give the highest degree of correlation. Correlation is not, however, the only consideration if the hedging program is of significant size. If, for example, a manager wanted to hedge $500 million of short-term liabilities in a distant delivery month, liquidity in the futures market would be an important consideration. In such as case, it might be necessary to spread the hedge across two or more different contracts. Consequently, a hedger of liabilities tied to the T-bill rate might hedge by selling some T-bill futures and some Eurodollar time deposit futures, eventually rolling the position entirely into T-bill futures.

Having determined the right contract and the right delivery months, the risk manager should then determine what is expected of the hedge. Obviously, if this *target rate* is too high (if hedging a sale) or too low (if hedging a purchase), hedging is perhaps not the right strategy for dealing with unwanted risk. Determining what to expect (i.e., calculating the target rate for a hedge) is not always simple. This chapter explains how the risk manager should approach this problem for both simple and complex hedges.

*Hedge effectiveness* tells the risk manager what percentage of risk is eliminated by hedging. Thus, if the hedge is determined to be 90 percent effective, over the long run a hedged position will have only 10 percent of the risk (that is, standard deviation) of an unhedged position. However, for any particular hedge, the hedged position can have more variation than the unhedged position.

The *residual hedging risk*—the absolute level of risk in the hedged position—tells us how much risk remains after hedging. While it may be comforting to know, for example, that 90 percent of the risk is eliminated by hedging, without additional statistics the hedger still does not know how much risk remains. The residual risk in a hedged position is expressed most conveniently as a standard deviation. For example, it might be determined that the hedged position has a standard deviation of 15 basis points. Assuming a normal distribution of hedging errors, the hedger will then obtain the target rate plus or minus 15 basis points two times out of three. The probability of obtaining the target rate plus or minus 30 basis points is 95 percent, and the probability of obtaining the target rate plus or minus 45 basis points is greater than 99 percent.

The target rate, the hedge effectiveness, and the residual hedging risk determine the basic trade-off between risk and expected return. Consequently, these statistics give the risk manager facts essential to making a decision with regard to hedging. Using these figures, he or she can construct confidence intervals for hedged and unhedged positions. Comparing these confidence intervals, he or she can then determine whether hedging is the best alternative. Furthermore, if hedging is the right decision, the level of confidence in the hedge is defined in advance.

The risk manager should also be aware that the effectiveness of a hedge and the residual hedging risk are not necessarily constant from one hedge to the next. Hedges for dates near a futures delivery date will tend to be more effective and have less residual risk than those lifted on other dates. The life of the hedge, that is, the amount of time between when the hedge is set and when it is lifted, also generally has a significant impact on hedge effectiveness and residual hedging risk. For example, a hedge held for six months might be 90 percent effective, whereas a hedge held for one month might be only 25 percent effective. This is because the security to be hedged and the hedging instrument might be highly correlated over the long run, but only weakly correlated over the short run. On the other hand, residual hedging risk usually increases as the life of the hedge increases. The residual risk on a six-month hedge may be 85 basis points while the residual risk for a one-month hedge may be only 35 basis points. It may seem surprising that it is possible for the longer hedges to have more risk and also be more effective. However, hedge effectiveness is a measure of *relative* risk, and because longer time periods exhibit greater swings in interest rates, the greater percentage reduction in risk for longer hedges does not mean that there is less remaining risk.

The target rate, the residual risk, and the effectiveness of a hedge are relatively simple concepts. However, because these statistics are usually estimated using historical data, the hedger should be sure that these figures are estimated with care. Statistics can be a tricky business. Well-intentioned amateurs and not-so-well-intentioned professionals have been known to produce statistics that lead to overly optimistic estimates of what a hedge can do. Consequently, the hedger should not necessarily judge the skill of a broker by how much the broker promises to accomplish with a hedge.

The final factor that must be determined before the hedge is set is the *hedge ratio*, or the number of futures contracts needed for the hedge. Usually the hedge ratio is expressed in terms of relative face amounts. Accordingly, a hedge ratio of 1.20 means that for every $1 million face value of securities to be hedged, one needs $1.2 million face value of futures contracts to offset the risk. As the following pages demonstrate, hedge ratio calculations run the gamut from trivial to esoteric.

## The Hedging Principle

Hedging is one of the primary ways that managers use interest rate futures contracts. While it is difficult to state concisely the general principle that underlies futures hedging, a one-line attempt might be as follows: do in the futures market today what you anticipate needing (or wanting) to do on a future date. For instance, if a portfolio manager owns a long bond that he anticipates selling in six months, he hedges today by selling bond futures for delivery six months hence. If the same manager does not anticipate an actual sale but wants to hedge the value of the bond six months forward, then he would, in a sense, like to sell the bond (as evidenced by the fact that he no longer wants the volatility of a long bond position), but is constrained from doing so. His course of action should be the same; he sells bond futures to hedge his position.

Similarly, an asset manager can use futures to hedge the rate at which anticipated cash flows will be invested. A manager expecting a cash inflow in one year might plan to buy long bonds when the cash is available, but she would like to hedge the rate at which that investment will be made. Anticipating a future purchase of bonds, the manager could hedge by buying bonds in the futures market today. If, on the other hand, the manager planned to invest the cash in short-term securities, she would hedge by buying short-term debt futures instead of bond futures.

Liability managers can apply the same hedging principle. The liability manager who funds operations by continually rolling over short-term debt faces substantial interest rate risk arising from the uncertainty of future rate levels. Because the manager anticipates having to sell new short-term debt in the future, a proper hedge would be to sell futures on short-term debt.[1]

The liability manager who plans to sell long-term debt to fund operations faces the risk that long-term rates will rise before the anticipated bond issuance.

---

[1] A manager who funds with floating-rate debt does not actually roll over short-term debt, but his or her interest-rate expense is determined by future short-term rates. Consequently, the best hedge will also be to sell short-term debt futures.

To hedge, the liability manager will enter into a trade in the futures market to mirror the trade anticipated for a future date. The manager thus sells futures on long-term debt to hedge the subsequent sale of long-term debt.

Some managers are responsible for both the asset and liability side of the balance sheet. Frequently, one side of the balance sheet is more sensitive to interest rate fluctuations than the other and managers find themselves managing an interest rate gap. Usually, this occurs because the assets are of much longer maturities than the liabilities. Consequently, as interest rates rise, interest expense increases while interest income stays constant. To make matters worse, as rates rise long-term assets fall below their purchase price. Because a sale of assets would then result in realized losses, managers often have few choices for correcting the imbalance.

Asset and liability managers can, however, control this exposure by combining the techniques used by asset managers and the techniques used by liability managers. Instead of reducing the interest rate sensitivity of their assets by trading into shorter maturity securities (and booking a loss), the managers can sell intermediate- or long-term debt futures and accomplish the same end. Alternatively (or concurrently), the managers can increase the interest rate sensitivity of their liabilities by lengthening their effective maturity. This is accomplished by selling short-term debt futures.

In each of the foregoing examples, the risk managers follow essentially the same rule. Whatever action they expect or want to take but are constrained from taking in the cash market, they take instead in the futures market. At the risk of oversimplification, this rule can be followed by most, if not all, asset and liability managers.

## Risk and Expected Return in a Hedge

When one enters into a hedge, the objective is to "lock in" a rate for the sale or purchase of a security. However, there is much disagreement about what rate or price a hedger should expect to lock in when futures are used to hedge. One view is that the hedger should, on average, lock in the current spot rate for the security. The opposing view is that the hedger should, on average, lock in the rate at which the futures contracts are bought or sold. As it turns out, the right answer usually lies somewhere in between these two positions. However, as the following examples illustrate, each view is entirely correct in certain situations.

*The Target for Hedges Held to Delivery:* Risk minimizing hedges that are held until the futures delivery date provide examples of hedges that lock in the futures rate of interest. A hedge with T-bill futures contracts is the most straightforward illustration of this. Suppose an investor buys a $1 million six-month T-bill at 8.5 percent and expects to sell it three months hence, at which time the bill will have three months of remaining life. To hedge this sale, the investor sells one $1 million 3-month T-bill contract for delivery in three months. Suppose further that when the hedge is set, spot 3-month bills are at 8.18 percent and three-month T-bill futures are at 9 percent. What rate does the hedger lock in for the sale of the T-bill three months hence (i.e., on the futures delivery date)?

The process of *convergence* guarantees that the hedger locks in 9 percent (the futures rate) for his sale, while the spot rates of 8.18 percent and 8.5 percent are all but irrelevant. Convergence refers to the fact that at delivery there can be no discrepancy between the spot and futures price for a given security (or commodity).[2]   If the futures price were higher than the spot price, an investor could buy in the cash market, immediately sell in the futures market, and take out money at no risk. If the futures price were lower than the spot price, an investor could buy in the futures market and immediately sell in the cash market, again taking out cash at no risk. Thus, arbitrage between the cash and futures market forces the cash and futures prices to converge on the delivery date.

To see how convergence guarantees the hedger a price equal to the futures price on the day the hedge is set, consider the cash flows associated with a T-bill contract sold at 9 percent (quoted as 91.00). For each basis point increase in the futures rate above 9 percent (or .01 decrease in the quoted futures price below 91.00), the investor receives a margin inflow of $25. Now, if the investor targets 9 percent as the expected sale rate for the T-bill (which will then have three months to maturity), every basis point above 9 percent at which the investor sells the T-bill will cost him exactly $25 (from $1,000,000 × .0001 × 90/360). Thus, ignoring transaction costs, any shortfall relative to the targeted rate is exactly offset by gains on the futures contract. Conversely, if the hedger is able to sell the T-bill at a price higher (or yield lower) than the target, losses on the futures contract offset any windfall the hedger experiences in the cash market. This guarantees that the investor does no worse and no better than the target.[3]

The Eurodollar time deposit futures work in much the same fashion as the T-bill contracts. Using the Eurodollar contract, the hedger can lock in a rate or price for an anticipated purchase or sale. If the hedge is held until delivery, the only rate that the hedger can lock in with certainty is the rate prevailing in the futures market. As the previous example shows, the rate on the securities in the cash market does not determine the rate that can be locked in.

The same principles hold true in the market for intermediate- and long-term debt, except that the hedge is a little more complicated because the hedger does not know for sure when delivery will take place or which bond will be

---

[2] In the case of more than one deliverable, this is true only for the one cheapest to deliver.

[3] For this to be exactly true, one must ignore the fact that net margin inflows from the futures contract can be invested over the life of the hedge, and net margin outflows must be borrowed (or paid out at an opportunity loss) over the life of the hedge.

delivered. However, for the sake of simplicity, consider the T-bond contract and assume that the hedger knows which bond will be delivered and that delivery will take place on the last day of the delivery month (which is frequently the most advantageous day to make delivery). Consider the $7\frac{5}{8}$ T-bonds maturing on February 15, 2007. For delivery on the June 1985 contract, the conversion factor for these bonds was .9660, implying that the investor who delivers the $7\frac{5}{8}$s would receive from the buyer .9660 times the futures settlement price, plus accrued interest. Consequently, at delivery, the (flat) spot price and the futures price times the conversion factor must converge. Otherwise, arbitrageurs would buy at the lower price and sell at the higher price and earn riskfree profits. Accordingly, a hedger could lock in a June sale price for the $7\frac{5}{8}$s by selling T-bond futures contracts equal to .9660 times the face value of the bonds. For example, $100 million face value of $7\frac{5}{8}$s would be hedged by selling $96.6 million face value of bond futures (966 contracts).

The sale price that the hedger locks in would be .9660 times the futures price. Thus, if the futures price is 70 when the hedge is set, the hedger locks in a sale price of 67.62 for June delivery, regardless of where rates are in June. Exhibit 49–1 shows the cash flows for a number of final prices for the $7\frac{5}{8}$s and illustrates how cash flows on the futures contracts offset gains or losses relative to the target price of 67.62. In each case, the effective sale price is very close to the target price (and, in fact, would be exact if the calculations were carried through to the required decimal places). However, the target price is determined by the futures price, so the target price may be higher or lower than the cash market price when the hedge is set.

When we admit the possibility that bonds other than the $7\frac{5}{8}$s of 2007 can be delivered, and that it might be advantageous to deliver other bonds, the situation becomes somewhat more involved. In this more realistic case, the hedger may decide not to deliver the $7\frac{5}{8}$s, but if she does decide to deliver them, the hedger is still assured of receiving an effective sale price of approximately 67.62. If the hedger chooses not to deliver the $7\frac{5}{8}$s, it would be because another bond could be delivered more cheaply, and thus the hedger would be able to do better than the targeted price.

In summary, if an investor sets a *risk minimizing* futures hedge *that is held until delivery*, he or she can be assured of receiving an effective price dictated by the *futures* rate (*not* the spot rate) on the day the hedge is set.

### The Target for Hedges with Short Holding Periods:   Now let us return to our original example of purchasing a $1 million, 6-month T-bill at 8.5 percent. What if the investor has no intention of holding the T-bill for three months, as in the original example, but intends to sell it in the very next term, say within a day? The investor still faces the risk that rates will rise and the sale price of the T-bill will fall. To hedge this risk the investor would sell two of the nearby T-bill futures contracts, currently trading at 9 percent and calling for delivery in three months. (Two three-month T-bill contracts are required because at the time

**EXHIBIT 49–1**
**T-Bond Hedge Held to Delivery**

*Instrument to be hedged: 7 5/8% T-bonds of 2/15/07*
*Conversion factor for June 1985 delivery = .9660*
*Price of futures contracts when sold = 70*
*Target price = .9660 × 70 = 67.62*

| Actual Sale Price for 7 5/8% T-Bonds | Final Futures Price* | Gain (Loss) on 966 Contracts ($10/.01/Contract)† | Effective Sale Price‡ |
|---|---|---|---|
| 62-0 | 64.182 | $5,620,188 | $67,620,118 |
| 63-0 | 65.217 | 4,620,378 | 67,620,378 |
| 64-0 | 66.253 | 3,619,602 | 67,619,602 |
| 65-0 | 67.288 | 2,619,792 | 67,619,792 |
| 66-0 | 68.323 | 1,619,982 | 67,619,982 |
| 67-0 | 69.358 | 620,172 | 67,620,172 |
| 68-0 | 70.393 | (379,638) | 67,620,362 |
| 69-0 | 71.429 | (1,380,414) | 67,619,586 |
| 70-0 | 72.464 | (2,380,224) | 67,619,776 |
| 71-0 | 73.499 | (3,380,034) | 67,619,966 |
| 72-0 | 74.534 | (4,379,844) | 67,620,156 |
| 73-0 | 75.569 | (5,379,654) | 67,620,346 |
| 74-0 | 76.605 | (6,380,430) | 67,619,570 |
| 75-0 | 77.640 | (7,380,240) | 67,619,760 |

\* By convergence, must equal bond price divided by the conversion factor.
† Bond futures trade in even increments of 1/32. Accordingly, the futures prices and margin flows are only approximate.
‡ Transaction costs and the financing of margin flows are ignored.

of sale the T-bill will be approximately twice as volatile as a three-month T-bill.) What rate should the hedger expect to lock in—the futures rate of 9 percent or the spot rate of 8.5 percent?

Because the hedge is lifted before delivery, the hedger can no longer be assured of locking in any particular rate, spot or future. However, the effective rate that one obtains in this example is much more likely to approximate the current spot rate of 8.5 percent interest than the futures rate of 9 percent.

The critical difference between this hedge and the example in the last section is that the hedge is not held until delivery and, therefore, convergence will generally not take place by the termination date of the hedge. In fact, because the futures delivery date is three months from the day the hedge is set and the hedge will be lifted in one day, it is much more realistic to assume that the difference between the rates on the spot six-month T-bill and the three-month T-bill future will not change over the life of the hedge, much less converge.

·

This example is not unique to T-bills. Whether the hedger is hedging with one of the other short-term contracts or hedging longer-term instruments with the intermediate- and long-term contracts, he should expect the hedge to lock in the spot rate rather than the futures rate for very short-lived hedges. To illustrate, returning to the simplified example in which the $7\frac{5}{8}$ percent of 2007 were the only deliverable bonds on the T-bond futures contract, suppose that the hedge is set three months before delivery date and the hedger plans to lift the hedge after one day. It is much more likely that the spot price of the bond will move parallel to the converted futures price (that is, the futures price times the conversion factor), than that the spot price and the converted futures price to converge by the time the hedge is lifted.

A one-day hedge is, admittedly, an extreme example. Other than underwriters, dealers, and traders who reallocate assets very frequently, few hedgers are interested in such a short horizon. The very short-term hedge does, however, illustrate a very important point: The hedger should *not* expect to lock in the futures rate (or price) just because he is hedging with futures contracts. The futures rate is locked in *only if the hedge is held until delivery*, at which point convergence must take place. If the hedge is held for only one day, the hedger should expect to lock in the one-day forward rate, which will very nearly equal the spot rate. Generally hedges are held for more than one day, but not necessarily to delivery. The proper target for these cases is examined in the next two sections.

***The Basis:***   The basis is a concept used throughout the futures markets. The *basis* is simply the difference between the spot (cash) price of a security (or commodity) and its futures price, that is:

$$\text{Basis} = \text{Spot price} - \text{Futures price}$$

In the fixed-income markets, two problems can arise when one tries to make practical use of the concept of the basis. First, the quoted futures price does not equal the price that one receives at delivery. For intermediate- and short-term contracts, the actual futures price equals the quoted futures price times the appropriate conversion factor. In the case of the short-term contracts, the quoted futures price is actually 100 minus the annualized futures interest rate. The actual invoice price must be derived using the applicable yield-to-price conventions for the instrument in question. Consequently, to be useful the basis in the fixed-income markets should be defined using actual futures delivery prices rather than quoted futures prices. Thus, the price basis for fixed income securities should be redefined as:

$$\text{Price basis} = \text{Spot price} - \text{Futures delivery price}$$

Unfortunately, problems still arise due to the fact that fixed income securities (unlike most other securities and commodities) age over time. Thus, it is not exactly clear what is meant by the "spot price." Does spot price mean the current price of the actual instrument that can be held and delivered in satisfaction of a short position, or does it mean the current price of an instrument that currently has the characteristics called for in the futures contract? For example, when the basis is defined for a three-month T-bill contract maturing in three months, should spot price refer to the current price of a six-month T-bill, which is the instrument that will actually be deliverable on the contract (because in three months it will be a three-month T-bill), or should spot price refer to the price of the current three-month T-bill? In most cases the former definition of the spot price makes the most sense.

For hedging purposes it is also frequently useful to define the basis in terms of interest rates rather than prices. The *rate basis* is defined as

$$\text{Rate basis} = \text{Spot rate} - \text{Futures rate}$$

where spot rate refers to the current rate on the instrument that can be held and delivered on the contract, and the futures rate is the interest rate corresponding to the futures delivery price of the deliverable instrument.

The rate basis is particularly useful for analyzing hedges of short-term instruments because it nets out all effects due solely to the aging process. For instance, if spot one-year T-bills and three-month T-bill futures for delivery in nine months are both trading at 12 percent, the rate basis is zero, because cash (that is, the 1-year T-bill) and futures are at the same interest rate. However, a 1-year T-bill at 12 percent has a price of 88, while a three-month T-bill at 12 percent has a price of 97, giving a price basis of −9. Furthermore, because the cash security ages, a change in the price basis does not necessarily imply that there has been a change in the rate basis, or vice versa. Accordingly, the relationship between the price basis and the rate basis is not always an obvious one.

*A More General Approach to the Target:*  Both rate and price bases are helpful in explaining the two kinds of hedges examined in the preceding sections. The first hedge was a hedge of six-month T-bills for a sale date three months in the future. By selling three-month T-bill futures for delivery in three months, the hedger was able to lock in a rate equal to the rate at which the contract was sold (9 percent in the example). The second hedge was a hedge of the same T-bill for a sale date only one day in the future. In this case, the hedger sells the same T-bill futures contract and expects to lock in a rate approximately equal to the current rate on the six-month T-bill (8.5 percent in the example). To illustrate why the two hedges are expected to lock in such different rates, we must consider the *target basis*. The target rate basis is defined as the expected rate basis on the day the hedge is lifted. In the first example, a hedge lifted on the delivery date is expected to have, and by convergence will have, a zero rate basis when the hedge is lifted. Thus, the target rate for the hedge should be the rate on the futures contract plus the expected rate basis of zero, or in other words, just the futures rate. In the latter case, one would not expect the basis to change very much in one day, so the target rate basis equals the futures rate plus the current difference between the spot and futures rate (i.e., the current spot rate).

The hedger can set the target rate for any hedge equal to the futures rate plus the target rate basis. That is,

Target rate for hedge = Futures rate + Target rate basis

The next section shows how this definition can be used to set a target for almost any hedge.

If projecting the basis in terms of price rather than yield is more manageable (as is often the case for intermediate- and long-term futures), we can work with the *target price basis* instead of the target rate basis. The target price basis is just the projected price basis for the day the hedge is to be lifted. For a deliverable security, the target for the hedge then becomes[4]

Target price for hedge = Futures delivery price + Target price basis

The idea of a target price or rate basis explains why a hedge held until the delivery date locks in a price with certainty, and other hedges do not. As is often said, hedging substitutes basis risk for price risk, and the examples illustrate this principle. For the hedge held to delivery, there is no uncertainty surrounding the target basis; by convergence, the basis on the day the hedge is lifted is certain to be zero. For the short-lived hedge, the basis will probably approximate the current basis when the hedge is lifted, but its actual value is not known. For hedges longer than one day but ending prior to the futures delivery date, there can be considerable risk because it is possible for the basis on the day the hedge is lifted to be anywhere within a wide range. Thus, the uncertainty surrounding the outcome of a hedge is directly related to the uncertainty surrounding the basis on the day the hedge is lifted, that is, the uncertainty surrounding the target basis.

The discussion so far has, of course, centered on two special cases, the very short-term hedge and the hedge held to delivery. Most hedges fall somewhere between these two extremes. The problem then is to define the target rate for hedges that are held for more than a few days, but are closed out prior to delivery. This is essentially a question of calculating a target basis because, as before, the target rate for the hedge should equal the futures rate plus the target basis.

---

[4] It should be noted that for the intermediate- and long-term instruments, the target price for the hedge does not exactly equal the price corresponding to the target rate for the hedge, or vice versa. This follows from the nonlinearity of price-to-yield functions. The expected price of a bond on a future date does *not* exactly equal the price associated with its expected yield.

To show how the target basis is used for these hedges, let us examine a simplified case in which we believe that the rate basis will decline linearly over time. The basis is thus expected to change by the same amount each day until, at delivery, the basis is zero. To show how this assumption affects the target rate for the hedge, assume that the hedger who bought 6-month T-bills at 8.5 percent plans to resell the T-bills in 30 days, that is, one-third of the way between the purchase date and the futures delivery date.[5] To account for the relative volatility of five-month T-bills and three-month T-bill futures, the investor should sell 1.67 contracts per $1 million invested. In these circumstances, what rate should the hedger target if the nearby T-bill contract is selling at 9.00 percent?

The rate basis at the outset of the hedge is −.50 percent. Assuming a linear decline in the basis, after 30 days the rate basis will equal −.33 percent. The target basis for the hedge is therefore −.33 percent. Using the formula for the target rate given in the last section, we have:

$$\text{Target rate for hedge} = \text{Futures rate} + \text{Target rate basis}$$
$$= 9.00\% - .33\%$$
$$= 8.67\%$$

Since the hedge is lifted closer to the day the hedge is set than to the delivery date, the target rate is closer to the spot rate of 8.5 percent than to the futures rate of 9 percent.

The actual outcome of the hedge will be determined by how closely the target rate basis approximates the actual basis on the day the hedge is lifted. However, if the projection is accurate, the target rate and price will be locked in by the hedge.

In the intermediate- and long-term markets it is somewhat easier (but not necessarily more accurate) to define the target for the hedge in terms of a price rather than an interest rate. Accordingly, in a hedge one might assume that the price basis, rather than the rate basis, will decline linearly over time. For example, suppose that 80 days before the assumed delivery date for the June 1985 T-bond futures contract a hedger wants to lock in a sale price for $100 million face value of $7\frac{5}{8}$s of 2007, for a sale date 20 days in the future. (To simplify, assume the $7\frac{5}{8}$s are the only deliverable bond.) The bonds may be selling at 67 in the cash market while the bond futures contract is at 68. Because the conversion factor for these bonds for the June 1985 contract was .9660, the price basis is calculated as

$$67 - (.9660 \times 68) = 67 - 65.688 = 1.312$$

---

[5] Five-month T-bills are not liquid instruments, but do provide a good example of the hedging technique.

If the price basis declines linearly through time, on the day the hedge is lifted the basis will equal .9840. Thus, the target basis, in terms of price rather than yield, is .9840. Using a formula similar to the earlier one, the target price for the hedge is given by:

$$\text{Target price for hedge} = \text{Futures price} \times \text{Conversion factor}$$
$$+ \text{Target price basis}$$

Or, in this example,

$$\text{Target price} = 65.688 + .984$$
$$= 66.672$$

As in the earlier example, if the actual price basis on the day the hedge is closed out equals the target price basis, and the hedger shorts the appropriate number of futures contracts (966 in this case), the effective sale price for the hedged security will, except for rounding, equal the targeted price. Exhibit 49–2 demonstrates this fact.

**EXHIBIT 49–2**
**T-Bond Hedge Held for 20 Days**

*Instrument to be hedged: 7 5/8% T-bonds of 2/15/07*
*Conversion factor = .9660*
*Price of futures contracts when sold = 68*
*Target price = (.9660 × 68) + .984 = 66.672*

| Actual Sale Price of Bonds | Futures Price When Hedge Is Closed Out* | Gain (Loss) on 966 Contracts ($10/.01/Contract)[†] | Effective Sale Price[‡] |
|---|---|---|---|
| 60-0 | 61.093 | $6,672,162 | $66,672,162 |
| 61-0 | 62.128 | 5,672,352 | 66,672,352 |
| 62-0 | 63.164 | 4,671,576 | 66,671,576 |
| 63-0 | 64.199 | 3,671,766 | 66,671,766 |
| 64-0 | 65.234 | 2,671,956 | 66,671,956 |
| 65-0 | 66.269 | 1,672,146 | 66,672,146 |
| 66-0 | 67.304 | 672,336 | 66,672,336 |
| 67-0 | 68.340 | (328,440) | 66,671,560 |
| 68-0 | 69.375 | (1,328,250) | 66,671,750 |
| 69-0 | 70.410 | (2,328,060) | 66,671,940 |
| 70-0 | 71.445 | (3,327,870) | 66,672,130 |
| 71-0 | 72.480 | (4,327,680) | 66,672,320 |
| 72-0 | 73.516 | (5,328,456) | 66,671,544 |

* By assumption, when closed out, the futures price equals (cash price − target basis) ÷ conversion factor.
[†] Bond futures trade in even 32nds. Thus, the futures prices and the gains and losses are approximate.
[‡] Transaction costs and the financing of margin flows are ignored.

***Basis Risk:***  As illustrated in the previous sections, for a given investment horizon, hedging substitutes basis risk for price risk. Thus, one trades the uncertainty of the price of the hedged security for the uncertainty of the basis. Consequently, when hedges don't produce the desired results, it is customary to place the blame on "basis risk." However, basis risk is the real culprit only if the target for the hedge is properly defined. Basis risk should refer only to the *unexpected* or *unpredictable* part of the relationship between cash and futures. The fact that this relationship changes over time does not in itself imply that there is basis risk. If, for example, the rate basis between a T-bill futures contract and the deliverable T-bill is 1 percent, we know for certain that the basis will decline to virtually 0 percent on the delivery date. Thus, with respect to delivery date, there is no basis risk. The basis will change by 1 percent, but this change is *completely predictable*, so there is no basis risk associated with the delivery date.

Basis risk, properly defined, refers only to the uncertainty associated with the target rate basis or target price basis. Accordingly, in order to correctly assess the risk and expected return in a hedge, it is imperative that the target basis be properly defined.

***Hedges That Do Not Minimize Risk:***  We have, until now, taken the risk minimizing hedge as our point of departure and assumed that it is the desired hedge. In so doing, we have ignored expected return in our desire to minimize risk. A different approach can be taken to achieve different targets (that is, different expected returns), but only at the cost of increasing risk.

An extreme example is when the hedge ratio is set equal to zero, that is, when there is no hedge. The risk is then the risk of holding an unhedged cash security, and the target is the expected price of the security on the anticipated sale date. Futures prices in this case are irrelevant.

Alternatively, it is possible to define the target, then work backwards to find the hedge ratio that gives this desired target. A typical example is that of a hedger who wants the target to be the current price of the security. This is not totally unreasonable since there is frequently some hedge ratio that on average (at least, historically) offsets changes in cash prices with changes in futures prices. However, if the hedger uses a hedge ratio that makes the current price the target price, he must generally take on more risk than if he chooses a hedge ratio that equates the target price to the implied futures price.

The important point here is that both the target and the risk level depend on the hedge ratio. If the manager uses the risk minimizing hedge ratio, the target and risk level are determined as described in earlier sections. If, on the other hand, the target is set equal to the current price, a hedge ratio can usually be found to give this result on average, but the hedge will not generally be the risk minimizing hedge. The hedger may thus obtain a more desirable target rate for the hedge, but does so only by assuming incremental risk.

In subsequent sections, we will continue to assume that risk minimization is the primary concern of the hedger and set up hedges accordingly.

## Cross Hedging

Previously, we defined a cross hedge in the futures market as a hedge in which the security to be hedged is not deliverable on the futures contract used in the hedge.[6] For example, an investor or issuer who wants to hedge the sale price of long-term corporate bonds might hedge with the T-bond futures contract, but since corporate bonds cannot be delivered in satisfaction of the contract, the hedge would be considered a cross hedge. Similarly, on the short end of the curve, a hedger might want to hedge a three-month rate that does not perfectly track the T-bill rate or the Eurodollar rate. A hedger might also want to hedge a rate that is of the same quality as the rate specified in one of the contracts, but that has a different maturity. For example, one must cross hedge to hedge a Treasury bond, note, or bill with a maturity that does not qualify for delivery on any futures contract. Thus, when the security to be hedged differs from the futures contract specification in terms of either quality or maturity, one is led to the cross hedge.

Conceptually, cross hedging is somewhat more complicated than hedging deliverable securities, because it involves two relationships. First, there is the relationship between the most deliverable security and the futures contract. This relationship was addressed in the foregoing sections. Secondly, there is the relationship between the security to be hedged and the most deliverable security. Practical considerations may at times lead us to shortcut this two-step relationship and focus directly on the relationship between the security to be hedged and the futures contract, thus ignoring the deliverable security altogether. However, in so doing, one runs the risk of miscalculating the target rate and the risk in the hedge. Furthermore, if the hedge does not perform as expected, the shortcut makes it difficult to tell why the hedge went awry.

*The Hedge Ratio:* The key to minimizing risk in a cross hedge is to choose the right hedge ratio. The hedge ratio depends on *volatility weighting*, or weighting by relative changes in value. The purpose of an asset hedge is to have gains or losses from a futures position to offset any difference between the target sale price and the actual sale price of the asset. Accordingly, the hedge ratio is chosen with the intention of matching the volatility (meaning, dollar change) of the futures contract to the volatility (i.e., dollar deviation from the target price) of the asset. The purpose of a liability hedge is to use futures gains or losses to offset any discrepancy between the target interest expense and the actual interest expense. In summary, then, the hedge ratio is determined by the

---

[6] Because there is never actual delivery on the Eurodollar time deposit contract, a cross hedge is defined as one in which the rate to be hedged does not perfectly correspond to the three-month LIBOR rate underlying the futures contract.

volatility of the instrument to be hedged relative to the volatility of the hedging instrument. Consequently, the hedge ratio is given by:

$$\text{Hedge ratio} = \frac{\text{Volatility of hedged security}}{\text{Volatility of hedging instrument}}$$

As the formula shows, if the instrument to be hedged is more volatile than the hedging instrument, more of the hedging instrument will be needed.

While it might be fairly clear why volatility is the key variable in determining the hedge ratio, "volatility" has many definitions. For hedging purposes, however, we are concerned with volatility in absolute dollar terms.[7] To calculate the dollar volatility of a fixed income security, one must know the precise point in time that volatility is to be calculated (because volatility generally declines as a security ages) and the price or yield at which to calculate volatility (because higher yields generally lower dollar volatility for a given yield change). The relevant point in the life of the security for calculating volatility is the point at which the hedge will be lifted. Volatility at any other point is essentially irrelevant because the goal is to lock in a price or rate only on that particular day. Similarly, the relevant yield at which to initially calculate volatility is the target yield. Consequently, the "volatility of the hedged security" referred to in the formula is the price value of a basis point for the security on the hedge lift date, calculated at its current implied forward rate.

An example shows why volatility weighting leads to the correct hedge ratio. Suppose that on April 19, 1985 an investor owned the Southern Bell $11\frac{3}{4}$ percent bonds of 2023 and sold June 1985 T-bond futures to hedge a future sale of the bonds. Because the telephone bonds are not deliverable, the investor must cross hedge. Suppose that (a) the Treasury $7\frac{5}{8}$s of 2007 were the most deliverable bond on the contract and that they were trading at 11.50 percent, (b) the Southern Bell bonds were at 12.40 percent, and (c) the T-bond futures were at a price of 70. To simplify, assume also that the yield spread between the two bonds remains at .90 percent and that the anticipated sale date was the last business day in June 1985.

The sale date corresponds to the final futures delivery date, so the target basis for the deliverable $7\frac{5}{8}$s is zero, by convergence. Because the conversion factor for the $7\frac{5}{8}$s for the June 1985 contract was .9660, the target price for hedging the $7\frac{5}{8}$s would be 67.62 (from 70 × .9660) and the target yield would be 11.789 percent (the yield at a price of 67.62). The yield on the telephone bonds is assumed to stay at .90 percent above the yield on the $7\frac{5}{8}$s, so the target

---

[7] Duration and volatility in terms of percentage change in value may be helpful in deriving the hedge ratio, but offsetting actual dollars is always the bottom line.

yield for the Southern Bell bonds would be 12.689 percent with a corresponding price of 92.628. At these target levels, the price values of a basis point (PVBP) for the $7\frac{5}{8}$s and telephone bonds are, respectively, .056332 and .072564. As indicated earlier, all of these calculations are made using a settlement date equal to the anticipated sale date, in this case the end of June 1985. Thus, the relative price volatilities of the hedged security and the deliverable security are easily obtained from the assumed sale date and target prices.

However, in the formula for the hedge ratio we need the volatility not of the deliverable security, but of the hedging instrument, that is, of the futures contract. Fortunately, knowing the volatility of the hedged security relative to the most deliverable security and the volatility of the most deliverable security relative to the futures contract, the relative volatilities that define the hedge ratio can be easily obtained as follows:

$$\text{Hedge ratio} = \frac{\text{Volatility of hedged security}}{\text{Volatility of futures contract}}$$

$$= \frac{\text{Volatility of hedged security}}{\text{Volatility of most deliverable}} \times \frac{\text{Volatility of most deliverable}}{\text{Volatility of futures contract}}$$

Or, more concisely, assuming a fixed yield spread between the security to be hedged and the most deliverable bond,

$$\text{Hedge ratio} = \frac{\text{PVBP of hedged security}}{\text{PVBP most deliverable}} \times \frac{\text{Conversion factor}}{\text{for most deliverable}}$$

where PVBP stands for the price value of a basis point.

The hedge ratio in the example at hand is therefore approximately 1.24 (from $(.072564/.056332) \times .9660$). Exhibit 49–3 shows that if the simplifying assumptions hold, a futures hedge using the recommended hedge ratio very nearly locks in the target price for $10 million face value of the telephone bonds. (Furthermore, most of the remaining error could be eliminated by frequent adjustments to the hedge ratio to account for the fact that the price values of a basis point change as rates move up or down.)

Although the example in Exhibit 49–3 is constructed for a hedge held to the futures delivery date, the technique is equally valid for hedges lifted prior to delivery. The primary difference is that if the hedge is lifted before delivery, the target basis for the deliverable issue will not generally be zero; thus, the target will be different.

***Changing Yield Spreads:*** Another refinement in the hedging strategy is usually necessary for hedging nondeliverable securities. This refinement concerns the assumption about the relative yield spread between the most deliverable

**EXHIBIT 49–3**

**Hedging a Nondeliverable Bond to a Delivery Date with Futures**

*Instrument to be hedged: Southern Bell 11 3/4% of 4/19/23*
*Hedge ratio = 1.24*
*Price of futures contract when sold = 70*
*Target price for Southern Bell bonds = 92.628*

| Actual Sale Price of Telephone Bonds | Yield at Sale | Yield on Treas. 7 5/8* | Price of Treas. 7 5/8 | Futures Price[†] | Gain (Loss) on 124 Contracts ($10/.01/ Contract) | Effective Sale Price[‡] |
|---|---|---|---|---|---|---|
| $7,600,000 | 15.468% | 14.568% | 54.590 | 56.511 | $1,672,636 | $9,272,636 |
| 7,800,000 | 15.072 | 14.172 | 56.167 | 58.144 | 1,470,144 | 9,270,144 |
| 8,000,000 | 14.696 | 13.796 | 57.741 | 59.773 | 1,268,148 | 9,268,148 |
| 8,200,000 | 14.338 | 13.438 | 59.313 | 61.401 | 1,066,276 | 9,266,276 |
| 8,400,000 | 13.996 | 13.096 | 60.887 | 63.030 | 864,280 | 9,264,280 |
| 8,600,000 | 13.671 | 12.771 | 62.451 | 64.649 | 663,524 | 9,263,524 |
| 8,800,000 | 13.359 | 12.459 | 64.018 | 66.271 | 462,396 | 9,262,396 |
| 9,000,000 | 13.061 | 12.161 | 65.580 | 67.888 | 261,888 | 9,261,888 |
| 9,200,000 | 12.776 | 11.876 | 67.134 | 69.497 | 62,372 | 9,262,372 |
| 9,400,000 | 12.503 | 11.603 | 68.683 | 71.100 | (136,400) | 9,263,600 |
| 9,600,000 | 12.240 | 11.340 | 70.233 | 72.705 | (335,420) | 9,264,580 |
| 9,800,000 | 11.988 | 11.088 | 71.773 | 74.299 | (533,076) | 9,266,924 |
| 10,000,000 | 11.745 | 10.845 | 73.312 | 75.892 | (730,608) | 9,269,392 |
| 10,200,000 | 11.512 | 10.612 | 74.839 | 77.473 | (926,652) | 9,273,348 |
| 10,400,000 | 11.287 | 10.387 | 76.364 | 79.052 | (1,122,448) | 9,277,552 |
| 10,600,000 | 11.070 | 10.170 | 77.884 | 80.625 | (1,317,500) | 9,282,500 |
| 10,800,000 | 10.861 | 9.961 | 79.394 | 82.188 | (1,511,312) | 9,288,688 |
| 11,000,000 | 10.659 | 9.759 | 80.899 | 83.746 | (1,704,504) | 9,295,496 |
| 11,200,000 | 10.463 | 9.563 | 82.403 | 85.303 | (1,897,572) | 9,302,428 |

* By assumption, the yield on the 7 5/8's is 90 basis points lower than the yield on the Southern Bell bond.
† By convergence, the futures price equals the price of the 7 5/8's divided by .9660 (the conversion factor).
‡ Transaction costs and the financing of margin flows are ignored.

security and the security to be hedged. In the last section, it was assumed that the yield spread was constant over time. However, yield spreads are not constant over time and vary with the maturity of the instruments in question, the level of rates, as well as with many unpredictable and nonsystematic factors.

*Regression analysis* is a simple technique that allows the hedger to capture the relationship between yield levels and yield spreads and use it to his advantage.[8]   The regression is a statistical technique that uses historical data to model the imperfect relationship between two variables. For hedging purposes, the variables are the yield on the security to be hedged and the yield on the most deliverable security. The regression equation takes the form:

$$\text{Yield on security to be hedged} = a + b \times \text{Yield on most deliverable security} + \text{error}$$

The regression procedure provides an estimate of $b$ (the *yield beta*) which is the expected relative yield change in the two securities. The "error" term accounts for the fact that the relationship between the yields is not perfect and contains a certain amount of "noise." The regression will, however, give an estimate of $a$ and $b$ so that over the sample period the error is on average zero. The example in the previous section that used constant spreads implicitly assumes that the yield beta in the regression equals 1.0 and $a$ equals .90 (since .90 was the assumed spread).

For the two issues in question, that is, the Southern Bell $11\frac{3}{4}$s and the Treasury $7\frac{5}{8}$s, the estimated yield beta over a recent period was 1.05. Thus, yields on the corporate issue are expected to move 5 percent more than yields on the Treasury issue. To calculate the relative volatility of the two issues correctly, this fact must be taken into account; thus, the hedge ratio derived in the last section is multiplied by the factor 1.05. Consequently, instead of shorting 124 T-bond futures contracts to hedge $10 million of telephone bonds, the investor would short 130 contracts.

The formula for the hedge ratio is revised as follows to incorporate the impact of the yield beta:

$$\text{Hedge ratio} = \text{Yield beta} \times \frac{\text{PVBP of the hedged security}}{\text{PVBP of the most deliverable}} \times \text{Conversion factor}$$

where beta is derived from the yield of the hedged security regressed on the yield of the most deliverable security. As before, PVBP stands for the change in price for a single basis point change in yield, calculated at the forward prices, for settlement on the day the hedge is to be lifted.

The hedging strategy can also be applied to hedges of short-term assets or liabilities. However, there are no conversion factors for short-term futures, so the hedge ratio for the short-term contracts simplifies to:

---

[8] The regression is very useful for noncallable bonds and bonds that are very unlikely to be called. However, the regression will not capture the effects of a call on yield spreads. Strategies for hedging callable instruments can be found in Mark Pitts and Frank J. Fabozzi, *Interest Rate Futures and Options* (Chicago: Probus Publishing, 1990), Chapters 11 and 12.

$$\text{Hedge ratio} = \text{Yield beta} \times \frac{\text{PVBP of the hedged security}}{\text{PVBP of the futures contract}}$$

***Deriving the Target for a Cross Hedge:*** It was shown earlier that the target rate for a hedge of a deliverable security should be defined as the sum of the futures rate and the target basis. That is:

$$\text{Target rate for hedge} = \text{Futures rate} + \text{Target rate basis}$$

The target rate basis is determined by the projected path of the basis through time. For simplicity, a linear decline in the basis was used in the examples.

When the discussion turned to cross hedging, the relationship between the security to be hedged and the deliverable security was modeled using the regression equation. That equation was:

$$\begin{matrix}\text{Yield on security} \\ \text{to be hedged}\end{matrix} = a + b \times \begin{matrix}\text{Yield on most} \\ \text{deliverable security}\end{matrix} + \text{error}$$

On average, the error term is equal to zero. Combining these two equations, the target for a cross hedge is easily derived.[9]

$$\text{Target rate} = a + b \times (\text{Futures rate} + \text{Target basis})$$

***Cross Hedging Summarized:*** A cross hedge is more complicated than a hedge of a deliverable security because the security to be hedged is not directly tied to the futures contract, even on the delivery date. However, the deliverable security and the futures contract are directly linked (at least at delivery). The cross hedger bridges the gap by estimating the relationship between the security to be hedged and the deliverable security (via the regression procedure), and estimating the relationship between the deliverable security and the futures contract (by projecting the future course of the basis). Combining these two estimates results in a forecast of the relationship between the security to be hedged and the futures contract. The combined estimates also forecast what the hedger can expect from the hedge (i.e., the target rate). Exhibit 49–4 shows these relationships schematically.

In a cross hedge it is sometimes necessary to take a short cut by focusing on the relationship between the security to be hedged and the futures contract, leaving out the deliverable security. This relationship is the convolution of the

---

[9] Because a regression of the deliverable security on itself would result in an intercept term equal to 0.0 and a yield beta equal to 1.0, this formulation includes the target rate for a deliverable security as a special case. Consequently, the original formula is derived when the cross hedge formula is applied to the deliverable security. The formula is also applicable if the hedger chooses to assume the yield spread will stay constant: setting the intercept ($a$) equal to the assumed yield spread and $b$ equal to 1.0, the formula will give the correct target rate for constant yield spreads.

**EXHIBIT 49-4**
**A Schematic of the Relationships in a Cross Hedge**

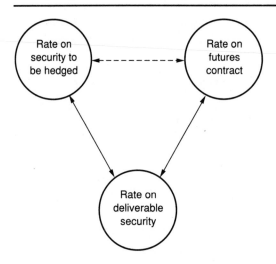

two relationships mentioned earlier—the relationship between the security to be hedged and the deliverable security, and the relationship between the deliverable security and the futures contract. The shorter route is sometimes the only practical approach, either because data is not available for the relevant regressions or because there is a need to simplify.

## HEDGING WITH OPTIONS

In this section, three of the most widely used options hedging strategies are examined. These examples show how options hedges are constructed and illustrate the basic principles of hedging with options. We also show how hedge ratios should be calculated for options hedges.

### Basic Hedging Strategies

*Protective Puts:* Consider first an investor who has a portfolio of fixed-income securities and wants to hedge against rising interest rates. The most obvious options hedging strategy is to buy puts on fixed income instruments. These *protective puts* are usually out-of-the-money puts and may be either puts on cash instruments or puts on fixed income futures. If interest rates rise, the puts will increase in value (holding other factors constant), offsetting some or all the loss on the cash instruments in the portfolio.

This strategy is a simple combination of a long put option with a long position in a spot security. The result is a payoff pattern resembling a long position in a call option alone. Such a position has limited downside risk, but large upside potential. However, if rates fall, the price appreciation on the securities in the portfolio will be diminished by the amount paid for the puts.

The protective put strategy is very often compared to purchasing insurance. Like insurance, the premium paid for the protection is nonrefundable and is paid before the coverage begins. The degree to which a portfolio is protected depends upon the strike price of the options; thus, the strike price is often compared to the deductible on an insurance policy. The lower the deductible (that is, the higher the strike on the put), the greater the level of protection and the more the protection costs. Conversely, the higher the deductible (the lower the strike on the put), the more one can lose, but the cost of the insurance is lower. No one strike price dominates any other, in the sense of performing better at all possible rate levels. Consequently, it is impossible to say that one strike price is necessarily the "best" strike price, or even that buying protective puts is necessarily better than doing nothing at all.

*Covered Call Writing:* Another options hedging strategy used by many portfolio managers is to sell calls against their fixed income portfolio; that is, to do *covered call writing*. The calls that are sold are usually out-of-the-money calls, and can be either calls on cash securities, or calls on fixed income futures. Covered call writing is just an outright long position combined with a short call position. The strategy thus results in a payoff pattern that resembles a short position in a put option alone. Obviously, this strategy entails much more downside risk than buying a put to protect the value of the portfolio. In fact, many portfolio managers do not consider covered call writing a hedge.

Regardless of how it is classified, it is important to recognize that while covered call writing has substantial downside risk, it has less downside risk than an unhedged long position alone. On the downside, the difference between the long position alone and the covered call writing strategy is the premium received for the calls that are sold. This premium acts as a cushion for downward movements in prices, reducing losses when rates rise. There is a cost associated with obtaining this cushion: the bond holder gives up some of the potential on the upside. When rates decline, the call options become greater liabilities for the covered call writer. These incremental liabilities decrease the gains the portfolio manager would otherwise have realized on the portfolio in a declining rate environment. Thus, the covered call writer gives up some (or all) of the upside potential of the portfolio in return for a cushion on the downside. The more upside potential that is forfeited (that is, the lower the strike price on the calls), the more cushion there is on the downside. Like the protective put strategy, there is no "right" strike price for the covered call writer.

*Selecting the "Best" Strategy:* Comparing the two basic strategies for hedging with options—the protective put strategy and the covered call writing strategy—it is impossible to say which is necessarily the better or more correct options hedge. An individual manager's view of the market determines the best strategy (and the best strike prices). Purchasing a put and paying the required premium is appropriate if the manager is fundamentally bearish. If, on the other hand, one is neutral to mildly bearish, it is better to take in the premium on the covered call writing strategy. If a manager has no set view on the market and prefers as little risk as possible, then the futures hedge discussed earlier in this chapter is most appropriate. If the manager is fundamentally bullish, then no hedge at all is probably the best strategy.

*Collars.* There are, of course, many options hedging strategies used by portfolio managers. For example, many managers combine the protective put strategy and the covered call writing strategy. By combining a long position in an out-of-the-money put and a short position in an out-of-the-money call, the portfolio manager creates a long position in a *collar*. The manager who uses the collar eliminates part of the portfolio's downside risk by giving up part of its upside potential. The collar has many facets. It bears a resemblance to the protective put, covered call writing, an unhedged position, and a futures or forward hedge. The collar resembles the protective put strategy in that it limits the possible losses on the portfolio if interest rates go up. It resembles the covered call writing strategy in that the portfolio's upside potential is limited. It resembles an unhedged position in that the value of the portfolio varies with interest rates, within the range defined by the strike. On the other hand, if the put strike price and the call strike price are both equal to the forward price, the collar resembles a forward hedge in that the effective sale price is not dependent upon interest rates.

## Options Hedging Preliminaries

In a manner comparable to the strategies used by the futures hedgers, there are certain preliminaries that options hedgers should consider before setting their hedges. The options hedging preliminaries include these steps:

1. Determine the options contract that is the best hedging vehicle.
2. Find the appropriate strike price. For a cross hedge, the hedger will want to convert the strike price on the options that are actually bought or sold into an equivalent strike price for the actual securities being hedged.
3. Estimate the relative and absolute risk in the hedge (not necessarily a simple matter for a cross hedge).
4. Determine the hedge ratio, that is, the number of options to buy or sell. (If not a cross hedge, the hedge ratio will usually be 1.0.)

The best options contract to use (item 1 above) depends upon several factors. These include price, liquidity, and correlation with the instrument(s) to be hedged. In imperfect markets, price is important because all options will not be priced in the same manner nor with the same volatility assumption. Consequently, some options may be overpriced and some underpriced. Obviously, other factors being equal, it is better to use the underpriced options when buying and the overpriced options when selling. Whenever there is a possibility that the option position may be closed out prior to expiration, liquidity is an important consideration. If the particular option is illiquid, closing out a position may be prohibitively expensive, and the manager loses the flexibility of closing out positions early, or rolling into other positions that may become more attractive. Correlation with the underlying instrument(s) to be hedged is another factor in selecting the right contract. The higher the correlation, the more precisely the final profit and loss can be defined as a function of the final level of rates. Poor correlation leads to more uncertainty.

Because most of the uncertainty in an options hedge usually comes from the uncertainty of interest rates themselves, but slippage between the securities to be hedged and the instruments underlying the options contracts only adds to that risk. Thus, the degree of correlation between the two underlying instruments is one of the determinants of the risk in the hedge.

The two remaining items in the list of preliminaries, determining the hedge ratio and the strike price, can best be explained with examples. Thus, the balance of this chapter is devoted to examples of options hedges. Our focus will be on hedging a long-term bond position with futures options.

## Hedging with Puts on Futures

Investors in corporate and government notes and bonds often want to hedge their positions against a possible increase in interest rates. Buying puts on futures is one of the easiest ways to purchase protection against rising rates. To illustrate the strategy of buying puts on futures in order to guard against rising interest rates, we can use the utility bond example used earlier in this chapter. (The strategy for hedging Treasury bonds is similar.) In that example, an investor held $11\frac{3}{4}\%$ bonds of 2023 and used futures to lock in a sale price for those bonds on a futures delivery date. At this point we want to show how the hedger could have used futures options instead of futures to protect against rising rates.

In the example, rates were already high; the hedged bonds were selling at a yield of 12.40 percent and the Treasury $7\frac{5}{8}\%$ of 2007 (the most deliverable bond at the time) were at 11.50 percent. For simplicity, we assumed that the yield spread would remain at 90 basis points. In terms of a yield regression, this would be equivalent to a regression in which the beta equals 1.0 and the intercept term is 0.90 percent.

From Exhibit 49–3, we can see that the current price on the bonds to be hedged is roughly equivalent to a futures price of 71–24. Thus, if the hedger wants to buy out-of-the-money puts, a futures strike price of, say, 66 might be appropriate. To see what a futures price of 66 translates into in terms of yield and price for the hedged bonds, we have to work through the most deliverable bond. Exhibit 49–5 illustrates this process schematically. We start with the 66 strike price for the options. Using the conversion factor of 0.9660 for the most deliverable bond (the $7\frac{5}{8}$% of 2007), and assuming complete convergence, a futures price of 66 implies a price of 63.756 and a yield of 12.51 percent for the Treasury $7\frac{5}{8}$ percent interest bonds.[10] Having assumed a constant yield spread of 0.90 percent between the most deliverable bond and the hedged bonds, we arrive at an equivalent yield of 13.41 percent for the bonds to be hedged. A yield of 13.41 percent for these bonds corresponds to a price of 87.668. Consequently, buying a T-bond futures option struck at 66 is roughly equivalent to buying an option struck at 87.668 on the bonds that we want to hedge.

**EXHIBIT 49–5**
**Calculating Equivalent Prices and Yields**

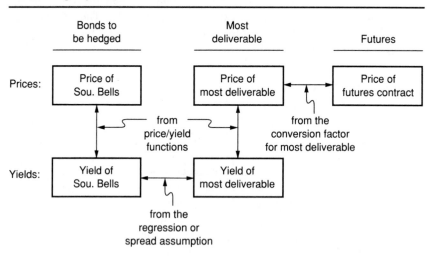

---

[10] Options on T-bond and T-note futures expire in the month preceding the futures settlement month. Thus, complete convergence is not assured. However, to keep the example simple and make the options and futures hedges directly comparable, we are treating the option as if it expired on the last day of the futures settlement month.

As explained earlier in this chapter, the futures (and futures options) hedge ratio is derived from the formula:

$$\text{Hedge ratio} = \text{Yield beta} \times \frac{\text{PVBP of the hedged security}}{\text{PVBP of the most deliverable}} \times \frac{\text{Conversion factor}}{}$$

Because we are assuming a constant yield spread between the security to be hedged and the most deliverable bond, the beta is set equal to 1.0. For increased accuracy, we calculate the price values of a basis point at the option expiration date (assumed for simplicity to be June 28, 1985) and at the yields corresponding to the futures strike price of 66 (12.51 percent for the most deliverable bond and 13.41 percent for the hedged bond). The respective price values of a basis point are 0.065214 and 0.050969. This results in a hedge ratio of 1.236 for the options hedge, or 1.24 with rounding.[11]

To create a table for the protective put hedge for $10 million in underlying bonds, we can use some of the numbers from Exhibit 49–3. Everything will be the same except the last two columns. For the put option hedge we must insert the value of the 124 futures put options in place of the 124 futures contracts in the next-to-last column. This is easy because the value of each option at expiration is just the strike price of the futures option (66) minus the futures price (or zero if that difference is negative), all times $1000. The effective sale price for the hedged bonds is then just the actual market price on the sale date, plus the value of the options at expiration, minus the cost of the options.

A reasonable price for the 66 put options would have been in the neighborhood of 24/64, or $375 per options contract. With a total of 124 options, the cost of the protection would have been $46,500 (not including financing or commissions). This cost, together with the final value of the options, is combined with the sale price for the hedged bonds to arrive at the effective sale price for the hedged bonds. These final prices are shown in the last column of Exhibit 49–6. The effective price is never less than 87.203. This equals the price of the hedged bonds equivalent to the futures strike price of 66 (i.e., 87.668), minus the cost of the puts (i.e., $0.4650 = 1.24 \times 24/64$). This minimum effective price is something that can be calculated before the hedge is ever initiated. (As prices decline, the effective sale price actually exceeds the projected effective minimum sale price of 87.203 by a small amount. This is due to rounding and the fact that the hedge ratio is left unaltered although the relative price values

---

[11] For an option on a cash market instrument, there is only one deliverable, so there is no conversion price. The hedge ratio is then

$$\text{Hedge ratio} = \text{Yield beta} \times \frac{\text{PVBP of the hedged security}}{\text{PVBP of the underlying security}}$$

**EXHIBIT 49–6**

**Hedging a Nondeliverable Bond to a Delivery Date with Puts on Futures**

*Instrument to be hedged: 11 3/4% Utility Bonds of 2023*
*Hedge ratio = 1.24*
*Strike price for puts on futures = 66*
*Target minimum price for hedged bonds = 87.203*

| Actual Sale Price of Hedged Bonds | Futures Price* | Value of 124 Put Options† | Cost of 124 Put Options | Effective Sale Price‡ |
|---|---|---|---|---|
| $7,600,000 | 56.511 | $1,176,636 | $46,500 | $8,730,136 |
| 7,800,000 | 58.144 | 974,144 | 46,500 | 8,727,644 |
| 8,000,000 | 59.773 | 772,148 | 46,500 | 8,725,648 |
| 8,200,000 | 61.401 | 570,276 | 46,500 | 8,723,776 |
| 8,400,000 | 63.030 | 368,280 | 46,500 | 8,721,780 |
| 8,600,000 | 64.649 | 167,524 | 46,500 | 8,721,024 |
| 8,800,000 | 66.271 | 0 | 46,500 | 8,753,500 |
| 9,000,000 | 67.888 | 0 | 46,500 | 8,953,500 |
| 9,200,000 | 69.497 | 0 | 46,500 | 9,153,500 |
| 9,400,000 | 71.100 | 0 | 46,500 | 9,353,500 |
| 9,600,000 | 72.705 | 0 | 46,500 | 9,553,500 |
| 9,800,000 | 74.299 | 0 | 46,500 | 9,753,500 |
| 10,000,000 | 75.892 | 0 | 46,500 | 9,953,500 |
| 10,200,000 | 77.473 | 0 | 46,500 | 10,153,500 |
| 10,400,000 | 79.052 | 0 | 46,500 | 10,353,500 |
| 10,600,000 | 80.625 | 0 | 46,500 | 10,553,500 |
| 10,800,000 | 82.188 | 0 | 46,500 | 10,753,500 |
| 11,000,000 | 83.746 | 0 | 46,500 | 10,953,500 |
| 11,200,000 | 85.303 | 0 | 46,500 | 11,153,500 |

* These numbers are approximate because futures trade in even 32nds.
† From 124 × $1000 × Max {(66 − Futures Price), 0}.
‡ Does not include transaction costs or the financing of the options position.

of a basis point that go into the hedge ratio calculation do change as yields change.) As prices increase, however, the effective sale price of the hedged bonds increases as well. Unlike the futures hedge shown in Exhibit 49–3, the options hedge protects the investor if rates rise, but allows the investor to profit if rates fall.

## Covered Call Writing with Futures Options

Covered call writing is a strategy used by many investors. Unlike the protective put strategy, covered call writing is not used for the sole purpose of protecting a portfolio against rising rates. The covered call writer, believing that the market will not trade much higher or much lower than its present level, sells out-of-the-money calls against an existing fixed income portfolio. The sale of the calls brings in premium income that provides partial protection in the event that rates increase. The premium received does not provide the kind of protection that a long put position provides, but it does provide additional income that can be used to offset declining prices. If, on the other hand, rates fall, portfolio appreciation is limited because the short call position constitutes a liability for the seller, and this liability increases as rates go down. Consequently, there is limited upside potential for the covered call writer. Of course, this is not so bad if prices are going nowhere, in which case the added income from the sale of options is obtained without sacrificing any gains.

To see how covered call writing with futures options works for the bond used in the protective put example, we construct a table much as we did before. With futures selling around 71–24 on the hedge initiation date, a sale of a 78 call option on futures might be appropriate. As in the earlier examples, it is assumed that the hedged bond will remain at a 90 basis point spread off the most deliverable bond, the US $7\frac{5}{8}\%$ of 2007. We let the price of the 78 calls be 24/64. The number of options contracts sold will be the same, namely 124 contracts for $10 million face value of underlying bonds. Exhibit 49–7 shows the results of the covered call writing strategy given these assumptions.

To calculate the effective sale price of the bonds in the covered call writing strategy, the premium received from the sale of calls is added to the actual sale price of the bonds, while the liability associated with the short call position is subtracted from the actual sale price. The liability associated with each call is the futures price minus the strike price of 78 (or zero if this difference is negative), times $1000. The middle column in the exhibit is just this value multiplied by 124, the number of options sold.

Just as the minimum effective sale price could be calculated beforehand for the protective put strategy, the maximum effective sale price can be calculated beforehand for the covered call writing strategy. The maximum effective sale price will be the price of the hedged security corresponding to the strike price of the option sold, plus the premium received. In this case, the strike price on the futures call option was 78. A futures price of 78 corresponds to a price of 75.348 for the underlying Treasury (from 78 times the conversion factor), and a corresponding yield of 10.536 percent for the most deliverable bond, the $7\frac{5}{8}\%$ of 2007. The equivalent yield for the hedged bond is 90 basis points higher, or 11.436 percent, for a corresponding price of 102.666. Adding on the premium received, 0.465 points, the final maximum effective sale price will be about 103.131.[12]  As we can see in Exhibit 49–7, if the hedged bond does trade at 90

---

[12] As in the protective put example, we assume for simplicity that the options expires on the futures expiration date and that the most deliverable bond does not change over the life of the hedge.

**EXHIBIT 49–7**
**Writing Calls on Futures against a Nondeliverable Bond**

> *Instrument to be hedged: 11 3/4% Utility Bonds of 2023*
> *Hedge ratio = 1.24*
> *Strike price for call on futures = 78*
> *Expected maximum effective price for bonds = 103.131*

| Actual Sale Price of Bonds | Futures Price* | Liability of 124 Call Options† | Premium from 124 Call Options | Effective Sale Price‡ |
|---|---|---|---|---|
| $7,600,000 | 56.511 | $   0 | $46,500 | $7,646,500 |
| 7,800,000 | 58.144 | 0 | 46,500 | 7,846,500 |
| 8,000,000 | 59.773 | 0 | 46,500 | 8,046,500 |
| 8,200,000 | 61.401 | 0 | 46,500 | 8,246,500 |
| 8,400,000 | 63.030 | 0 | 46,500 | 8,446,500 |
| 8,600,000 | 64.649 | 0 | 46,500 | 8,646,500 |
| 8,800,000 | 66.271 | 0 | 46,500 | 8,846,500 |
| 9,000,000 | 67.888 | 0 | 46,500 | 9,046,500 |
| 9,200,000 | 69.497 | 0 | 46,500 | 9,246,500 |
| 9,400,000 | 71.100 | 0 | 46,500 | 9,446,500 |
| 9,600,000 | 72.705 | 0 | 46,500 | 9,646,500 |
| 9,800,000 | 74.299 | 0 | 46,500 | 9,846,500 |
| 10,000,000 | 75.892 | 0 | 46,500 | 10,046,500 |
| 10,200,000 | 77.473 | 0 | 46,500 | 10,246,500 |
| 10,400,000 | 79.052 | 130,448 | 46,500 | 10,316,052 |
| 10,600,000 | 80.625 | 325,500 | 46,500 | 10,321,000 |
| 10,800,000 | 82,188 | 519,312 | 46,500 | 10,327,188 |
| 11,000,000 | 83.746 | 712,504 | 46,500 | 10,333,996 |
| 11,200,000 | 85.303 | 905,572 | 46,500 | 10,340,928 |

\* These numbers are approximate because futures trade in even 32nds.
† From 124 × $1000 × Max {(Futures Price − 78),0}
‡ Does not include transaction costs or the interest earned on the options premium.

basis points over the most deliverable bond as expected, the maximum effective sale price for the hedged bond is, in fact, slightly over 103. (The discrepancies shown in the exhibit are due to rounding and the fact that the position is not adjusted even though the relative price values of a basis point change as yields change.)

## The Futures Options Collar

The final strategy that we will illustrate for futures options is the long collar. As explained earlier, the collar is a combination of the examples in the previous two sections. That is, to create a long collar, the bond holder would buy protective puts and simultaneously sell covered calls. Usually, both options are out-of-the-money and the manager chooses the strike prices so that the premiums net out as nearly as possible. This strategy alters the risk-return profile of the bond portfolio, but does so without any net payment or receipt of options premiums. This strategy eliminates the portfolio's downside risk by forfeiting its upside potential.

To see how the strategy works we need only combine numbers from Exhibits 49–6 and 49–7. Exhibit 49–8 shows the actual sale price of the bond to be hedged, the value of 124 long put options on futures struck at 66, and the

**EXHIBIT 49–8**

**Hedging a Nondeliverable Bond to a Delivery Date with Futures Options Collars**

Instrument to be hedged: 11 3/4% Utility Bonds of 2023
Hedge ratio = 1.24
Strike price for puts on futures = 66
Target minimum price for hedged bonds = 87.203
Strike price for calls on futures = 78
Expected maximum price for bonds = 103.131

| Actual Sale Price of Bonds | Futures Price* | Value of 124 Put Options | Liability of 124 Call Options | Effective Sale Price† |
|---|---|---|---|---|
| $7,600,000 | 56.511 | $1,176,636 | $ 0 | $ 8,776,636 |
| 7,800,000 | 58.144 | 974,144 | 0 | 8,774,144 |
| 8,000,000 | 59.773 | 772,148 | 0 | 8,772,148 |
| 8,200,000 | 61.401 | 570,276 | 0 | 8,770,276 |
| 8,400,000 | 63.030 | 368,280 | 0 | 8,768,280 |
| 8,600,000 | 64.649 | 167,524 | 0 | 8,767,524 |
| 8,800,000 | 66.271 | 0 | 0 | 8,800,000 |
| 9,000,000 | 67.888 | 0 | 0 | 9,000,000 |
| 9,200,000 | 69.497 | 0 | 0 | 9,200,000 |
| 9,400,000 | 71.100 | 0 | 0 | 9,400,000 |
| 9,600,000 | 72.705 | 0 | 0 | 9,600,000 |
| 9,800,000 | 74.299 | 0 | 0 | 9,800,000 |
| 10,000,000 | 75.892 | 0 | 0 | 10,000,000 |
| 10,200,000 | 77.473 | 0 | 0 | 10,200,000 |
| 10,400,000 | 79.052 | 0 | 130,448 | 10,269,552 |
| 10,600,000 | 80.625 | 0 | 325,500 | 10,274,500 |
| 10,800,000 | 82.188 | 0 | 519,312 | 10,280,688 |
| 11,000,000 | 83.746 | 0 | 712,504 | 10,287,496 |
| 11,200,000 | 85.303 | 0 | 905,572 | 10,294,428 |

* Since futures trade in even 32nds, these numbers are approximate.
† Does not include transaction costs or the financing of the options positions.

**EXHIBIT 49–9**
**Alternative Strategies**

| Actual Sale Price of Bonds | Effective Sale Price with Futures Hedge | Effective Sale Price with Protective Puts | Effective Sale Price with Covered Calls | Effective Sale Price with Collar |
|---|---|---|---|---|
| $7,600,000 | $9,272,636 | $8,730,136 | $7,646,500 | $8,776,636 |
| 7,800,000 | 9,270,144 | 8,727,644 | 7,846,500 | 8,774,144 |
| 8,000,000 | 9,268,148 | 8,725,648 | 8,046,500 | 8772,148 |
| 8,200,000 | 9,266,276 | 8,723,776 | 8,246,500 | 8,770,276 |
| 8,400,000 | 9,264,280 | 8,721,780 | 8,446,500 | 8,768,280 |
| 8,600,000 | 9,263,524 | 8,721,024 | 8,646,500 | 8,767,524 |
| 8,800,000 | 9,262,396 | 8,753,500 | 8,846,500 | 8,800,000 |
| 9,000,000 | 9,261,888 | 8,953,500 | 9,046,500 | 9,000,000 |
| 9,200,000 | 9,262,372 | 9,153,500 | 9,246,500 | 9,200,000 |
| 9,400,000 | 9,263,600 | 9,353,500 | 9,446,500 | 9,400,000 |
| 9,600,000 | 9,264,580 | 9,553,500 | 9,646,500 | 9,600,000 |
| 9,800,000 | 9,266,924 | 9,753,500 | 9,846,500 | 9,800,000 |
| 10,000,000 | 9,269,392 | 9,953,500 | 10,046,500 | 10,000,000 |
| 10,200,000 | 9,273,348 | 10,153,500 | 10,246,500 | 10,200,000 |
| 10,400,000 | 9,277,552 | 10,353,500 | 10,316,052 | 10,269,552 |
| 10,600,000 | 9,282,500 | 10,553,500 | 10,321,000 | 10,274,500 |
| 10,800,000 | 9,288,688 | 10,753,500 | 10,327,188 | 10,280,688 |
| 11,000,000 | 9,295,496 | 10,953,500 | 10,333,996 | 10,287,496 |
| 11,200,000 | 9,302,428 | 11,153,500 | 10,340,928 | 10,294,428 |

liability of 124 call options on futures struck at 78. Because both the puts and the calls sold at 24/64, there is no net premium on the options positions. The effective sale price for the hedged bond is given in the last column of Exhibit 49–8.

The heart of the collar is that it allows prices to vary only within a range. Because this example was constructed using puts with strike prices roughly equivalent to a price of 87.668 on the hedged bond, and calls with strike prices equivalent to a price of about 102.666 for the hedged bond, and because there was no net options premium, the resulting collar allows prices to vary only between these ranges. As always, however, some discrepancy results from rounding and the static hedge ratio.

## SUMMARY

In this chapter, we have covered five basic strategies. For the holder of bonds, these include (1) an unhedged position, (2) a hedge with futures, (3) a hedge with out-of-the-money protective puts, (4) covered call writing with out-of-the-money calls, and (5) hedging with long collars. Similar strategies exist for those whose risks are that rates will decrease. As might be expected, there is no "best" strategy. Each strategy has its advantages and its disadvantages, and it is impossible to get something for nothing. To get anything of value, something of value must be forfeited.

In order to make a choice among strategies, it helps to lay the alternatives side by side. Using the futures and futures options examples from this chapter, Exhibit 49–9 shows the final values of the portfolio for the various alternatives. (These are the unhedged values together with the final columns from Exhibits 49–3, 49–6, 49–7, and 49–8. It is easy to see from Exhibit 49–9 that if one strategy is superior to another at one level of rates, it is inferior at some other level of rates. Consequently, we cannot conclude that any one strategy is the best strategy.

The manager who makes the strategy decision effectively makes a choice among probability distributions. Except for the perfect hedge, there is always a range of possible final values of the portfolio. Of course, exactly what that range is, and the probabilities associated with each possible outcome, is a matter of opinion. Yet, given a probability distribution of prices or rates, corresponding probability distributions for each hedging alternative can be created.[13]

---

[13] For a further discussion, see Pitts and Fabozzi, *Interest Rate Futures and Options*, pp. 379–386.

# CHAPTER 50

## ASSET ALLOCATION USING FUTURES AND OPTIONS

*Ravi E. Dattatreya, Ph.D.*
*Senior Vice President*
*Sumitomo Bank Capital Markets, Inc.*

Asset allocation refers to the task of dividing the total value of an investment portfolio among various asset classes. The asset classes can be broadly based, as in equities, fixed income, and cash. Each class can be divided more finely into industrial, high technology, and so on for equities, and short-term, long-term, investment-grade, and so on for fixed income. It has been observed that the asset allocation decision can be more important in determining the total return from an investment portfolio than any other single decision. Because of this, the allocation decision has been the focus of considerable study. In this chapter, we will review the asset allocation decision and examine ways of efficiently implementing the process using futures and options once the decision has been made.

### TYPES OF ASSET ALLOCATION

There are at least four broad types of asset allocation programs:

1. Strategic asset allocation
2. Tactical asset allocation
3. Portfolio insurance
4. Directional asset allocation

*Strategic asset allocation* (SAA) involves evaluating the needs of the investment and then determining the appropriate mix of asset classes that meets those needs. The approach largely resembles asset/liability management. The implied horizon for SAA is long term. The policy is determined more by the needs or the liabilities of the investment entity than by the state of the market. The performance of a portfolio under SAA is measured by its ability to satisfy the liability, not relative to a market index or an absolute rate of return. In the implementation and evaluation of any investment strategy, it is always best to examine both the expected (or actual) returns from the portfolio and the different types of risks associated with the strategy. Returns must be valued relative to risks taken.

A portfolio under SAA will require periodic course correction, or rebalancing, either to realign attributes that no longer match goals because of changes in the market value of the asset classes, or to realign long-term goals that have shifted as a result of changed investment strategies. In any case, the frequency of rebalancing is expected to be low.

*Tactical asset allocation* (TAA) is an active management technique that attempts to take advantage of the opportunities occurring in the market. Properly executed TAA should capture value in the market by changing the asset mix in response to changing market patterns.

*Portfolio insurance* (PI) is also a tactical allocation strategy in the sense that the asset mix is changed as the market moves. However, the goal of PI is not to enhance returns but to protect against adverse market conditions. PI has lost its popularity since the crash of October 1987.

*Directional asset allocation* (DAA) is another form of tactical allocation, where we use options to automatically modify allocation levels in response to market moves. In general, the allocation in an appreciating class is increased.

In the next section, we will review the TAA technique that has gained popularity recently and is perhaps the most important form of asset allocation. It is also the technique that can take full advantage of futures and options. DAA is discussed in detail later in this chapter.

## TACTICAL ASSET ALLOCATION

TAA is a technique that objectively estimates the returns on the asset classes under consideration, for example, stocks, bonds, and cash. As such, TAA includes a quantitative framework to measure or estimate available returns and thus to determine under- or overvalued asset classes. The technique exploits changing market patterns by shifting the asset mix in favor of the relatively attractive asset class(es).

TAA typically shifts the allocation in favor of an asset class that has experienced a sharp drop in price, thus taking a contrarian position. The implication is that after the price drop the class is undervalued relative to the other classes. The most significant property of TAA is that it provides a disciplined approach for adopting a contrarian position.

TAA depends on certain basic assumptions. First, the market provides information about the returns available from the various asset classes. Second, there is an equilibrium relationship among these implied returns. Finally, when the returns deviate from their normal behavior, the market forces will bring them back into equilibrium. It is in this return to normalcy, or equilibrium, that the asset allocator seeks to profit.

The TAA process comprises (1) a framework to recognize when the market deviates from equilibrium and where opportunities lie, (2) a procedure to evaluate whether the market can and will return to equilibrium, and (3) a way to time the allocation decision, that is, to determine whether the deviation will continue or whether the return to normalcy will occur in the short or long term.

The contrarian bent of TAA can be justified in many ways. For example, suppose that a pension fund decides to shift its assets from equities to bonds to match its liabilities more closely, perhaps by means of an immunized or a dedicated portfolio. The corresponding market impact would make those stocks available at attractive prices. Note that the price of the stocks fell not because of any negative evaluation, but because of a nonvalue-oriented preferential decision on the part of the fund. A TAA program that can distinguish between price changes due to changes in expected returns versus price changes due to nonreturn reasons can profit from such situations.

Another reason why TAA works is that investment managers tend to be segregated into fixed income users and equity users. Thus, when one asset class becomes over- (or under-) valued, there is a strong friction inhibiting free flow of capital to the undervalued asset class; any reallocation in response to market changes is done within a class rather than across classes. To the extent that a portfolio managed under TAA is to shift capital to the more attractive class, the returns from TAA should be superior.

## ASSET ALLOCATION USING FUTURES

Typically, a portfolio is restructured by selling or buying individual stocks, bonds, and money market securities or by trading blocks of these securities. The availability of futures provides a very attractive alternative to trading the individual securities. We can use the futures to alter the risk profile of the portfolio. Note that in this case, changing the risk profile gives us the *effect* of asset allocation even though capital may not flow from one market sector to another.

# USING STOCK INDEX FUTURES

In the equity market, two futures contracts are traded widely: the S&P 500 index contract and the NYSE composite index contract. The S&P index has broad acceptance, whereas the NYSE composite index contains more issues (1,700 versus 500 for the S&P), making it more representative of the broad stock market. The correlation between the two indexes is very high; therefore, either contract can be used for allocation.

To see how futures contracts can be used to modify equity exposure, suppose the S&P index is at 300. Each index point on the S&P 500 is worth $500. Therefore, the equity exposure in each S&P contract is obtained by multiplying the index value by 500. Thus, each contract is worth $150,000 (300 × 500) of exposure. To obtain $100 million of exposure, we would use 667 (100,000,000/150,000) futures contracts.

## Tracking Error

To replicate a portfolio that differs from the index, you compute a beta for the portfolio relative to the S&P index and use this factor to multiply the number of contracts. For example, if the beta of the portfolio to be mimicked or hedged were 0.90, you would use just 90 percent of the contracts computed above.

You can determine the beta of a portfolio by doing a historical regression analysis of the periodic (e.g., weekly or monthly) changes in the value of the portfolio against the periodic changes in the index. The use of a beta so obtained implicitly assumes that the relative behavior of the index and the portfolio will continue to hold. As long as the correlation coefficient is high enough, this is an acceptable situation.

There will be statistical, or tracking, error in the sense that the return obtained from the use of futures can differ from that obtained via cash market transactions. This error can be viewed as comprising two elements. The first is the random behavior of the portfolio's value relative to the index, the second is the differential movement of the futures relative to the index. However, we view the allocation process at a gross level rather than as an arbitrage. In this context, it is best to have a high tolerance for tracking error, given the various advantages of the use of futures that will be discussed later in this chapter.

# USING FIXED INCOME FUTURES

There are several futures contracts that represent the fixed income markets. They are based on Treasury obligations in the maturity sectors of 2, 5, and 10 years and on the long bond. There are also short-term futures, such as the T-bill contract and the Eurodollar contract. The CBT long bond contract is the most liquid, and we will use it in our examples. Fixed income futures are slightly more complicated than stock index futures in that a number of different bonds are deliverable against the contract. The delivery price is determined by the futures prices times a normalization factor, known as the conversion factor, for each bond. Usually, the price of the future's contract follows that of the bond that is considered most likely to be delivered, known as the cheapest deliverable bond.

In order to use bond futures to modify a portfolio's exposure to interest rates, we need a convention to measure its current and desired levels of exposure. We use the portfolio's dollar duration as a measure of interest-rate risk. Dollar duration is the dollar change in portfolio value for a 100-basis-point change in interest rates. It is also 100 times what is known as the present value of a basis point (PVBP). Duration, which is the percentage change in value for a 100-basis-point change in interest rates, is also a frequently used measure of risk. Dollar duration is the product of duration (percentage expressed as a decimal) and the market value of the portfolio. For example, if the duration of a portfolio with a market value of $50,000,00 is 5, then the dollar duration is $2,500,000 (0.05 × $50,000,000). When stated without any specific reference to a portfolio or a holding, the dollar duration of a bond is most often expressed using a notional par amount of $100.

The dollar duration of a Treasury bond (or note) contract is obtained by dividing the dollar duration (per $100 par value) of the cheapest deliverable bond by the delivery factor associated with that bond and multiplying the result by 1,000. The multiplication reflects the $100,000 par value of the futures contract. For example, the cheapest deliverable bond for the June 89 contract is the 7.25 of 2016. The dollar duration of the bond for a notional par amount of $100 is 9.146 at a price of $85 18/32 as of June 1, 1989, and the delivery factor is 0.9176. Therefore, the dollar duration of the futures contract is $9,967.31 ($1,000 × 9.146 / 0.9176).

Because the duration of the futures contract depends on the cheapest deliverable bond and because this bond can change, there is some uncertainty in determining the interest-rate risk of a futures position precisely. Some amount of error due to maturity mismatches can be mitigated by using combinations of the different available futures contracts.

## Yield Enhancement

We postulate a net pressure to sell in the financial futures markets, because the primary use of futures is to hedge assets. If this assumption is true, these futures should be cheap to buy. Therefore, a synthetic strategy using long positions in futures should show increased returns.

An argument could be made that if futures are indeed cheap, then arbitrage activity will bring them up to their fair price. However, because of the complex terms of the futures contract, for example, the choice of the deliverable bond, it is not always easy either to structure an arbitrage or to determine what the fair price should be. Thus, market inefficiency definitely exists. A corollary to this is that short positions in the bond futures could reduce the returns obtained.

In the context of yield enhancement, the advantage of futures comes with an associated cost, negative convexity, described below. The complexity of the futures contract that makes arbitrage imperfect also generates this cost.

## Convexity

The dollar duration or PVBP of a bond or a portfolio is not a constant. It changes with time as well as with market levels. If the PVBP of a portfolio increases as the market rallies, then the portfolio is said to be convex. Convexity is a desirable property because a convex portfolio gains value at an increasing rate for every successive basis point rally in the interest rates. For some portfolios, the PVBP actually decreases in rallying markets. They are said to have negative convexity. In general, the more convexity, the better.

However, convexity, being a desirable property, can be obtained only by giving up something else desirable. Even though the popular literature contains voluminous discussions of the trade-off between convexity and yield give-up, it turns out that this trade-off is not easily determined or quantified. The advantage of convexity depends on many factors, including the volatility of interest rates, and the yield is not necessarily a good measure of return. The actual rate of return obtained over a given horizon is a much better measure.

Long-maturity zero coupon bonds and options are examples of securities with high convexity. Callable bonds and mortgage-backed securities, on the other hand, have low or even negative convexity. Thus, if we wish to increase the convexity of a portfolio, we would purchase zeroes or options.

## Convexity Risk in a Futures Contract

The futures contract has associated with it certain option characteristics known as delivery options. The major ones are the rights retained by the short seller as to the timing of the delivery as well as the bond that is delivered. In effect, the buyer of the futures contract has sold these options and therefore is subject to some risk.

The market price of the bond futures contract closely follows that of the cheapest-to-deliver bond (CTDB). As its name indicates, this bond is the bond most likely to be delivered against the futures contract. As the market rallies, shorter duration bonds typically become CTDs. As the market declines, longer duration bonds become CTDs. This tendency of the shorter and longer bonds to become CTDs at low and high rate levels is dominated by the relative yield spreads among the deliverable bonds. For example, as of May 5, 1989, the 13.25s of 2014, with a dollar duration of 11.7, were almost as cheap to deliver as the 7.25s of 2016, with a dollar duration of 8.6.

Because the duration of the futures contract follows that of the CTDB, its duration tends to fall as rates fall and to rise as rates rise. As we stated earlier, this property is an undesirable property known as negative convexity. A consequence of negative convexity is that a long position in futures tends to underperform a cash portfolio of equal duration but higher convexity. Thus, the possible yield enhancement of using futures comes at a price.

It should be noted that the duration of the futures contract can change even without the CTDB changing. This change in duration is not as abrupt as a change in the CTDB indicates. We can think of it as the duration responding in anticipation of the change in the CTDB. To this extent, our formula for the computation of the duration of the futures is approximate.

The effect of the delivery option is relatively large in the case of the long bond futures. In their case, a large number of bonds are deliverable, the range of their maturities extends from 15 to 30 years, and the coupons vary from 7.25 percent to 14 percent. The dollar durations of these deliverable bonds ranged from 8.1 to 11.7 on May 5, 1989. In the case of the shorter futures on 10-, 5-, and 2-year Treasury notes, the effect is smaller. The ranges of dollar durations for these contracts on May 5, 1989 were 4.6 to 6.3, 3.4 to 4.0, and 1.6 to 1.8, respectively.

Negative convexity is undesirable because it makes the portfolio underperform another with a greater convexity. In our case, the synthetic security could underperform the cash bond. Thus, even if the futures contract appears to be cheap at the outset, it might turn out otherwise when the effect of the seller's options is included.

Fortunately, it is possible to address negative convexity. The obvious solution is to add convexity to the portfolio by purchasing appropriate quantities of highly convex instruments, such as long zero coupon bonds and options.

If options are used, out-of-the-money strangles are a reasonable choice. The long put position in the strangle protects against a rise in rates, and the long call protects against a fall in rates. The strike prices of the strangle are determined by estimating the futures prices at which changes in the cheapest-to-deliver bond are expected.

## ADVANTAGES OF USING FUTURES

The use of futures provides the asset allocator with numerous advantages:

1. minimized transaction costs
2. liquidity

3. ability to do simultaneous trades
4. isolation of asset allocation from security selection
5. stabilization of current income
6. value capture in the market
7. trading in anticipation—time shifting

## Transaction Costs

A portfolio managed under TAA will show a turnover of perhaps 100 percent per annum. Therefore, transaction costs can be a critical factor in implementation strategy selection. It has been estimated that the transaction costs can be 200 basis points for stocks and 100 basis points for bonds. Use of futures can cut this costs to 10–20 basis points. Note that transaction costs can be viewed as having two components: the stated commission or fees and market impact. The major futures contracts, such as the Treasury bond or the stock index futures contract involve negligible market impact. Thus, the added cost of active management is acceptably low.

## Liquidity

The futures markets are very deep and liquid. Large volumes can be transacted relatively quickly and efficiently. Stock index futures trade several billion dollars' worth each day. Bond futures are the most liquid market in the world, routinely trading over $25 billion daily.

## Simultaneous Trading

It is possible to execute simultaneous trades in different markets using futures. For example, a TAA fund can shift large amounts of bond exposure to cash and increase stock exposure literally in minutes. In a simultaneous transaction in the underlying securities, the different lengths of delay before settlement (e.g., five business days for stocks and one business day for Treasury bonds) is a nuisance. The use of futures avoids this complexity.

## Isolation of Asset Allocation from Security Selection

By using futures, the asset allocation decision can be made separately from the portfolio management process. Thus, the asset manager can continue to implement his or her microlevel decisions without any disruption from the macrolevel allocation process. This isolation of the two processes permits the portfolio to capture fully the value of active management within the various asset classes. Thus, asset allocation can be overlaid on traditional portfolio management.

## Stabilization of Current Income

In many cases, current income from the portfolio is important. Futures make the implementation of the allocation decision less disruptive to the income stream, because the portfolio can continue to hold the bulk of the income-producing securities. However, additional liquidity would be necessary to meet variation margin requirements. Variation margin is discussed later in this chapter.

## Value Capture in the Market

Even though we can expect that futures usually are fairly priced, there are circumstances when we can conclude that futures are cheap or rich *relative to the underlying securities*. We can incorporate this information in selecting the vehicle to trade: If futures are cheap, we buy futures; if not, we buy the underlying securities. This way, we can gain from any relative mispricing of futures.

## Trading in Anticipation—Time Shifting

One application of futures in asset allocation is to use them for time shifting, letting them stand as place holders until the completion of the transaction in the cash security. Such time shifting can be advantageous in many situations. We might wish to wait to receive funding for a purchase or to postpone the recognition of gain (or loss) due to sale. Or we might consider the market condition unsuitable for obtaining the right price for the security under consideration.

For example, suppose we wish to purchase a long Treasury bond. Assume, however, that the funding for the purchase will be available only after one month. In this case, we can hedge our decision to purchase the long bond by buying the CBT long Treasury bond contracts. If the market rallies, the price we will have to pay to purchase the bond will be greater, but a corresponding gain on the futures position will bring down the net cost of purchase. Similarly, if the market prices decline, we can buy the bond at a lower price, but there will be a loss on the futures position, bringing the net cost of purchase up. In either case, the effective purchase price of the bond will be close to the price locked in today. This price will be approximately equal to the forward purchase price for the bond.

If we are contemplating the future sale of a bond already in the portfolio, then we can hedge this action by selling bond futures. The sale price of the bond is effectively locked in by the hedge.

The time-shifting strategy using futures can also be used to implement long-term asset allocation decisions. For example, if we decide to reduce our equity exposure and increase our interest-rate exposure permanently, then we could sell stock index futures and purchase bond futures to execute our decision immediately. Then, we could select appropriate stocks and sell them as opportunities arise. We also should buy back the stock index futures at the same time as the stocks are sold to keep the equity exposure constant. A similar procedure is used on the fixed income side, until the entire allocation decision has been implemented in the underlying securities. This opportunistic buy-sell strategy using futures provides some protection from the market impact of reallocation on the relatively less liquid securities markets.

## DISADVANTAGES OF USING FUTURES

Notwithstanding the numerous advantages in using futures for asset allocation, there are also certain disadvantages. Regulatory restrictions prevent many potential investor groups from effectively using futures. Other disadvantages are

1. daily mark to market
2. need for liquidity to meet variation margin calls
3. tracking error
4. mispricing cost

### Daily Mark to Market

In order to ensure the integrity of the futures markets, the exchanges require that futures positions be marked to market daily. This results in a significant data processing burden, as well as the need to transfer funds to and from the broker. In addition, the mark-to-market process leads to immediate recognition of gains and losses. In certain circumstances, it might be more advantageous to postpone the recognition of gains and losses, an option not available with futures.

### Need for Liquidity

In order to meet the daily variation marking calls resulting from the settlement process, the investor will be required to maintain a reserve fund. As a consequence, some portion of the portfolio is forced to be in liquid assets, such as money market securities, rather than in actively managed assets. Also, large market moves might require additional assets to be liquidated to meet margin calls.

### Tracking Error

Futures are not necessarily ideal representations of the broad markets an allocator might wish to track. This is especially true in the case of interest-rate futures. For example, the CBT long bond futures tends to track a single bond, the cheapest deliverable bond, rather than an index of long bonds. In addition, the cheapest deliverable bond itself can change as a function of market conditions. Thus, there can be significant uncertainty in the behavior of the futures contract.

On the other hand, the fixed income sectors are highly correlated (relative to stock market sectors) and the tracking error is small. To the extent that any uncertainty in the behavior of the futures contract is already incorporated in the futures price, there is no cost to the investor in using futures due to this uncertainty.

Finally, it is best to view the allocation process at a gross level rather than as having a fine, arbitrage-like precision. That is, the allocator should have a good tolerance for tracking error relative to a market index.

## Mispricing Cost

The true cost of using futures is in the possibility of mispricing the futures contracts at the time they are bought and sold. Notwithstanding the very high liquidity and size of the futures markets, there is potential for favorable as well as unfavorable mispricing. The available analytical pricing models are not adequate to handle the complexities of the futures contracts, such as the largely ignored daily mark-to-market process and the numerous delivery options.

However, there is no reason to believe that the cost due to mispricing is significantly higher in futures than in the underlying securities. In fact, it is possible to take the view that the futures prices are closer to fair price than the cash market instruments because of the size and liquidity of the futures markets.

## IMPLEMENTATION EXAMPLES

Suppose we have a $1 billion pension fund that currently is 55 percent in stocks, 30 percent in bonds, and 15% in cash. The fund manager wishes to change the allocation to 45 percent stocks, 35 percent bonds, and 20 percent cash. Assume that the S&P index is at 300, the duration of the bond portfolio is 5, and the cheapest deliverable bond is the 7.25s of 2016, with a dollar duration of 9.146. The conversion factor is 0.9176, so the dollar duration of a futures contract is $9,967.31 ($1000 × 9.146/0.9176).

In a cash market transaction, the fund must sell 10 percent ($100 million) of stocks and purchase 5 percent ($50 million) of bonds. The remaining 5 percent cash is retained as cash.

As an alternative, the fund can use stock index and bond futures contracts, leaving the portfolio intact. The stock exposure can be adjusted by selling S&P index futures, and the bond exposure can be modified by buying CBT futures contracts.

To create the effect of selling $100 million of stocks, given that each contract is worth $150,000, we sell 667 (100,000,000/150,000) contracts.

To synthesize the effect of purchasing a $50 million portfolio with a duration of 5, we compute the number of futures contracts to buy as follows: Recall that the dollar duration of bonds to be purchased is obtained by the product of market value and the duration expressed as a decimal. That is, the dollar duration of the bonds to be purchased is $50 million times 0.05 (representing a duration of 5, or 5 percent), which is $2.5 million. Now, each futures contract is worth $9,967.31 in exposure. Therefore, we would purchase 251 ($2,500,000/$9,967.31) contracts.

The creation of a synthetic cash position of an additional $50 million is automatic.

## THE EFFECT OF VARIATION MARGIN

For most analytical purposes, futures contracts are approximated by forward contracts. Unlike forward contracts, futures contracts are marked to market daily. The futures contract effectively is settled every day. This results in daily cash flow to the holder of futures positions. The cash flow is positive if the position is long and the futures price goes up or if the position is short and the futures price goes down. The cash flow is negative otherwise. This daily cash flow, known as the variation margin, has two important effects on the futures contract.

The first effect is on pricing. Consider the following: Suppose that the price of the underlying security in a futures contract is positively correlated with interest rates. Then, if we are long the futures contracts, any margin flows that we receive due to an increase in the price of the security is likely reinvested at higher interest rates, resulting in higher returns. Similarly, any margin flow that results from a fall in price of the underlying security can be financed at lower interest rates, resulting in lower cost. Thus, the futures contract is attractive to buy. Therefore, its price should also be correspondingly higher.

Similarly, if the underlying security and the interest rates are negatively correlated, then the variation margin has a negative effect on the price of the futures because the margin outflows are financed at higher rates and inflows are invested at lower rates. In this case, the futures price is expected to be lower. This is perhaps the case in the fixed income markets, where the correlation between interest rates at different maturities is high. This causes a negative correlation between the short-term rate and the price of the deliverable bonds, thus forcing down the futures price. This effect partly explains why the fixed income futures prices appear cheaper compared to forward prices.

The second effect is on the hedge ratio, or the number of futures contracts needed for hedging. To illustrate this effect, suppose we wish to sell one month from now a $25 million portfolio with a duration of 5. The dollar duration of the portfolio is 5 percent of the market value, or $1.25 million ($25 million times 0.05). Assume that delivery is in one month. If the cheapest deliverable bond is the 7.25s of 2016, with a dollar duration (per $100) of 9.146 and a conversion factor of 0.9176, the dollar duration of a futures contract, using the earlier derivation, is $9,967.31 ($1000 × 9.146/0.9176). Therefore, to represent a dollar duration of $1.25 million, we need 125 futures contracts.

Suppose now that market rates immediately drop by 100 basis points and stay there for a month. The value of the portfolio will increase by $1.25 million, and we will receive approximately $26.25 million ($25 million initial value + $1.25 million increase) for our portfolio. On the futures side, because we have matched the dollar durations, the corresponding loss will also be $1.25 million. However, this cash amount has to be delivered immediately as variation margin. The cash requirement can be funded by borrowing or by liquidating interest-earning securities. In either case, the total cost to us from the futures position will be not just the $1.25 million, but the interest cost on the amount for the one month to the horizon.

Similarly, if the market rates rise by 100 basis points, we will have a loss of approximately $1.25 million, but the equal gain on the futures position is earned immediately. We can earn interest on this gain for the one month to horizon and thus more than make up the loss on the portfolio.

The implication here is that we are *overhedged* by a small amount. A little reflection will reveal that the overhedge amount depends on the interest rate at which the variation margin flows can be financed or invested and on the time to delivery. More precisely, to be properly hedged we have to multiply the hedge by a factor equal to the present value of one dollar payable at delivery, discounted at the short-term rate. For example, if the interest rate is 9 percent and the time to delivery is one month, then the factor would be 0.9926 (1/(1 + 0.09/12). Therefore, the correct number of futures contracts to use would be 124 (125 × .9926).

In other words, the futures contract has the price sensitivity (dollar duration) of a forward contract that delivers a little more than the par amount of the futures. This effective amount is obtained by multiplying the par amount by the futures value of a dollar on the delivery date, or, equivalently, by dividing by the present value of a dollar payable on the delivery date.

Clearly, given that the short-term rate (say the one-day rate) is not a constant, the futures position needs rebalancing in response to rate changes. As we approach the delivery date, the adjustment becomes smaller. For long horizons, the correction due to variation margin financing can be significant. For example, for a one-year time period, assuming a 10 percent interest rate, we would use just over 90 percent of the usual number of contracts.

# DIRECTIONAL ASSET ALLOCATION: USING OPTIONS

Just as futures represent a leveraged position in underlying securities, so do options. However, the leverage, or the participation in the market in the case of options, varies with the level of the market. For example, a call option on the S&P participates in market rallies and effectively withdraws from the market in a decline. It follows, therefore, that options can also be used for asset allocation. We call this *directional asset allocation* to draw attention to the fact that the effective allocation varies as the market moves and with the passage of time. Whether the allocation increases as the market rallies can be controlled by using short and long positions in puts and calls. All standard options strategies are available to be examined in light of tactical asset allocation. For example, writing a call on an asset class in the portfolio can be viewed in the context of asset allocation as reducing the exposure to that class. Depending on whether we buy or sell options, there would be an up-front cost or income to the portfolio.

## Factors to Consider

Options basically price market volatility. To the extent that the actual volatility differs from the volatility implied by the price of the option, the expected returns will vary. Therefore, if there is a strong opinion on the volatility, then it is relatively more straightforward to determine the appropriate options strategy. If we believe that the implied volatility is low, we would tend to use those strategies in which we buy options. Similarly, if we believe that the implied volatility is high, we would seek strategies selling options.

Options are wasting assets; their value decreases as expiration approaches. Because of this time decay, options might not be appropriate for some long-term strategies that require repeated purchase of options. The rate of time decay is not a constant. It is possible to construct strategies that make use of this fact; for example, we can purchase an option with a low time decay. This might mean buying an option with a longer time to expiration than necessary, which would minimize time decay.

Unlike futures, there is an up-front payment necessary in the case of options.

Any factor that affects the value of options will also change the effective allocation of a portfolio using the options strategy. These include volatility, time to expiration, market level, and the short-term interest rate. Of these, change in the market level is by far the most important.

## Delta Hedging

We can use two approaches to determine the amount of options to be purchased. The first, the *delta hedging* strategy, uses the duration or the price sensitivity to equate the options position to the alternative futures or cash position. For example, an at-the-money call option on the bond futures contract has a *delta* of about 0.5; that is, its value changes about half as much as that of the futures contract. Therefore we would use twice as many options as futures.

*Example.* Suppose we have a $1 billion pension fund that is 50 percent in equity and 50 percent in fixed income. Suppose also that we wish to change the ratio to 60:40. This would require us to purchase $100 million of stocks financed by the sale of $100 million of bonds. Assuming that the S&P index is at 300, the number of futures contracts necessary to increase the equity exposure to 60 percent can be computed as follows: Each index point is worth $500. Therefore, each contract is worth $150,000 ($500 × 300 S&P points). Thus, to obtain $100 million of exposure, we must purchase 667 ($100,000,000/$150,000) futures contracts. Assume now that the delta of an at-the-money option is 0.5. Then each futures contract can be represented by two options contracts. Therefore, we would need 1,334 (667 × 2) options contracts.

Note that the delta of the option changes as the market moves and with the passage of time. If the market rallies, the delta will increase and the equity exposure of the portfolio will correspondingly increase. If the market continues to rally, the delta will approach 1.0. The equity exposure added by the options position then will be $200 million, double that of the starting amount. Thus, if the option position is not adjusted, we would be overhedged in a market rally; that is, we would overperform.

Similarly, if the market declines, the delta will fall. For a severe fall in the S&P index, the delta will approach 0.0. The equity exposure added by the options position will also fall to zero.

The fixed income side of the portfolio can be similarly handled. Assuming that the cheapest deliverable bond for the June 89 contract is the 7.25s of 2016, the dollar duration of the bond is 9.146 at a price of $85\frac{18}{32}$, and the delivery factor of the bond is 0.9176, the dollar duration of the bond is $9,967.31 ($100 × 9.146/0.9176) per contract. Now, assuming that the duration of the portfolio is 5, the dollar duration for a $100 million portfolio would be $5 million (i.e., 5% of the $100 million). Therefore, the number of futures contracts required would be 502 ($5 million/$9,967.31). Alternatively, we could use 1004 contracts of an option (e.g., an at-the-money option) with a delta of 0.5.

We can maintain the allocation at desired levels by rebalancing the options position. This way we can mimic a futures position. However, the difference is that the option provides protection in the case of a sudden adverse move in the market. The cost of this protection is the premium paid for the option.

## Covered Hedging

In the second approach, the covered hedging strategy, we do not match the price sensitivity of the option to that of an alternative futures position. Rather, we simply purchase an equal par value of the option. Calls are purchased to increase participation in an asset, and puts are purchased to decrease participation. We can also construct covered hedging with short positions in options, but long positions are preferred in an asset allocation context. Covered call writing, for example, reduces participation in an asset. But the resulting downside protection is limited to the premium earned. Therefore, we would recommend using that strategy in a different context, for example, yield enhancement.

*Example.* As in the example above, suppose that the manager of a $1 billion portfolio with a current allocation of 50 percent in stocks and 50 percent in bonds wishes to change the allocation to 60:40. To reduce the proportion of bonds in the portfolio, we would have to sell $100 million worth of futures. Assuming that the cheapest deliverable bond for the June 89 contract is the 7.25s of 2016, the dollar duration of the bond is 9.146 at a price of $85\frac{18}{32}$, and the delivery factor is 0.9176, we obtain the dollar duration of the futures contract as $9,967.31 ($1,000 $\times$ 9.146/0.9176). To synthesize the effect of $100 million in bonds with an assumed duration of 5, we need a dollar duration of 0.05, or 5 percent times the $100 million—$5 million. Therefore, the number of futures contracts required is 502 ($5,000,000/$9.967.31). Alternatively, using the covered hedging strategy, we could purchase 502 put option contracts.

In this strategy, we would initially be underhedged because the price sensitivity of the option is lower than that of the bonds (or the futures). Therefore, there is still some residual bond exposure left, and the initial bond exposure will be greater than $400 million or 40 percent. As the market rallies, the size of this residue actually increases and reaches the original 50 percent. If the market falls, the delta of the put option increases and eventually reaches 1.0. At this point, the exposure will be 50 percent, as desired. A similar effect takes place as the option approaches expiration.

The stock allocation of the portfolio can be similarly handled. To increase the equity exposure by $100 million, we would need 667 futures contracts, assuming that the S&P is at 300. Alternatively, under the covered hedging strategy, we would use 667 call option contracts. Again, our initial exposure will be less than the desired amount because the delta of the option is less than 1.0. As the market moves up, the exposure will increase and eventually reach the full amount. On the other hand, if the market falls, the exposure will fall. A similar effect occurs as the option approaches expiration. The exposure will be all or none, depending on whether the option near expiration is in-the-money.

## Anticipatory Strategies

We can also use options in anticipation of buy or sell transactions. For example, if we are planning to purchase bonds, we could instead purchase call options. Then, if the market rallies, the call options would put us in bonds at a lower cost. If the bond market declines, then we would either not purchase the bonds or purchase them in the open market at the new lower price.

An alternative strategy is to sell put options. However, the net cost of the purchase can be higher than the market, and if the market rallies, we would have to purchase it at a higher price in the open market.

In both of the above applications using puts and calls, we can increase the certainty of the purchase by using options that are deep-in-the-money. The deeper the option is in-the-money, the closer the transaction would resemble a cash (or futures) transaction.

## Combinations

Using options in combination with futures can provide us with attractive return patterns. An example is disaster protection. Suppose we purchase an out-of-the-money put option on the asset class that we are buying. The put provides protection in case the asset class falls drastically in price. Similarly, we can purchase an out-of-the-money call on an asset class that we are selling to capture some returns just in case the price of that class rallies. We would use out-of-the-money options to keep the cost of the options down to acceptable levels.

## Synthesizing Options

We can also use futures to synthesize option positions dynamically. In fact, portfolio insurance is an allocation strategy that synthesizes the purchase of a put option on the market. Given that the tactical asset allocator is contrarian, it is roughly as though the portfolio insurer is purchasing the put sold by the tactical allocator. Thus, it is possible to superimpose an option-like strategy on traditional asset allocation.

## Advantages and Disadvantages of Using Options

Directional Asset Allocation using options has numerous advantages over traditional allocation strategies. It provides alternative return patterns. It can provide protection from adverse moves in the market after an allocation decision has been made and executed. In some cases, it automatically rebalances the portfolio to the intended levels. Being exchange-traded and relatively liquid instruments, options provide the most advantage of futures over cash transactions.

Option values are also sensitive to volatility. Therefore, if the perceived volatility of the market should change, the value of the options will change too. Similarly, time decay is a factor. Options have a limited life time, and they lose a part of their value every day.

The major disadvantage is cost. Options require an up-front payment of the premium. Also, available options have short expirations. Therefore, option positions must be rolled into the next expiration cycle. Unlike futures, each rollover means an additional cost.

## CONCLUSION

It has been widely recognized that the asset allocation decision is the single most important factor in determining the returns from a portfolio. In recognition of this fact, asset allocation strategies are becoming popular. Using futures in allocation strategies can provide numerous advantages. Options can also be used for directional asset allocation and as protection in case the allocation decision turns out to be incorrect.

# CHAPTER 51

## INTERNATIONAL BOND INVESTING AND PORTFOLIO MANAGEMENT

*Adam M. Greshin, CFA*
Vice President
Scudder, Stevens and Clark

*Margaret Darasz Hadzima, CFA*
Principal
Scudder, Stevens and Clark

In 1988 U.S. dollar-denominated, publicly issued bonds accounted for 46 percent of the world's total outstanding bonds.[1] Approximately 10 percent of U.S. dollar bonds were issued and traded outside the U.S. market. Taken together, these figures indicate that about 58 percent of the world's bonds are traded outside the U.S. market. New issue volume in the international bond markets regularly exceeds new issuance by U.S. corporate borrowers in the domestic market. The variety of borrowers in the international bond markets has increased dramatically in the 1980s, and financing techniques now rival the U.S. domestic market in their sophistication. While the sheer size of the U.S. economy ensures a central role for U.S. bonds in world capital markets, the growth in volume and turnover in international bonds suggests a general understanding of their characteristics is in order.

Do international bonds have a role for U.S. dollar-based investors? At the end of 1989, Lipper Analytical Services had over 40 entries listed under the

---

[1] Taken from a study published by Salomon Brothers, Inc. entitled "How Big is the World Bond Market?—1989 Update", published May 1989.

category for global and international bond mutual funds.[2] The fact that only a handful of these funds is more than two or three years old indicates how recent the phenomenon of international bond investing is among retail investors. Institutional investors in the United States have been active in the international bond markets for a much longer period, but the amount of institutional assets invested in international bonds is tiny relative to the available pool of assets. Questions remain as to the appropriateness of international bonds in U.S. dollar portfolios, particularly in light of the volatility in the foreign-exchange markets in the past two decades. Should international bonds be a core holding in U.S. portfolios? Or, should they be used on an occasional basis when foreign interest rate and currency levels appear attractive? After reviewing the characteristics of international bonds and their impact on a U.S. portfolio, this chapter will focus on the role of international bonds in an actively managed bond portfolio. The final section of the chapter will introduce currency hedged bond investing, which has become popular among international investors in the 1980s as a way of participating in the international bond markets without the attendant currency risk.

## INTERNATIONAL BONDS: U.S.-PAY VERSUS FOREIGN-PAY

The term *international bonds* is often used to describe a number of different types of bonds with a variety of characteristics relating to the issuer domicile, the nature of the underwriting syndicate, the location of the primary trading market, the domicile of the primary buyers, and/or the currency denomination. The most decisive influence on the price or yield of a bond is currency denomination. Regardless of the domicile of the issuer, the buyer, or the trading market, prices of issues denominated in U.S. dollars ("U.S.-pay") are affected principally by the direction of U.S. interest rates, whereas prices of issues denominated in other currencies ("foreign-pay") are determined primarily by movements of interest rates in the country of the currency denomination. Thus, analysis of international bond investing must be separated into two parts—U.S.-pay and foreign-pay.

## U.S.-PAY INTERNATIONAL BONDS

The U.S.-pay international bond market consists of *Eurodollar bonds*, which are issued and traded outside any one domestic market, and *Yankee bonds*, which are issued and traded primarily in the United States.

---

[2] Taken from *Mutual Fund Performance Analysis, Special Fourth Quarter 1989 Report*, published by Lipper Analytical Services, Inc., in December 1989.

## Eurodollar Bonds

Eurodollar bonds are the largest single component of the Eurobond market, which encompasses securities of all different currency denominations. Eurodollar bonds are.

*(pay 1 annually).*

1. Denominated in U.S. dollars
2. Issued and traded outside the jurisdiction of any single country
3. Underwritten by an international syndicate
4. Issued in bearer (unregistered) form

Since Eurodollar bonds are not registered with the SEC, as U.S. domestic new issues are required to be, underwriters legally are prohibited from selling new issues to the U.S. public until the issue has "come to rest" and a seasoning period has expired. An issue is usually considered seasoned 40 days after it has been fully distributed.[3] This seasoning requirement effectively locks U.S. investors out of the primary market. Even though a portion of Eurodollar outstandings end up in U.S. based portfolios after the seasoning period expires, the lack of participation of U.S. investors in new offerings ensures that the Eurodollar market will remain dominated by foreign-based investors. While no single location has been designated for Eurodollar market making, London is the de facto primary trading center for all Eurobonds.

The Eurodollar bond market has grown dramatically from its humble beginnings in the early 1960s, although the vast majority of growth has occurred only in the past decade. In 1980, total Eurodollar new issuance was a still modest $16 billion. By 1984, new-issue volume had expanded to $63 billion and in 1989, a record year for the Eurodollar bond market, over $112 billion of new issues were brought to market—almost 57 percent of total Eurobond new issuance (see Exhibit 51–1). Market turnover for Eurodollar bonds topped $2 trillion in 1989, over 40 percent of total Eurobond turnover for the year. Marketability of Eurodollar bonds has improved as the market has grown but there are still many examples of straight fixed-coupon bonds which trade infrequently, particularly among the older issues that may be only $50 million or less in individual issue size. Normal issue size today is $100 to $300 million. Despite the increase in market size, liquidity will remain somewhat constrained by the popularity of Eurodollar bonds among European retail investors who are likely to buy bonds and tuck them away until maturity. Since Eurobonds are held in bearer (unregistered) form, details about major holders of Eurodollar bonds are

---

[3] The Securities and Exchange Commission's revised Regulation S recently reduced the seasoning period from 90 to 40 days. At the time of this writing, other changes in SEC regulations, notably Regulation 144a, were proposed but not yet enacted to make the Euromarkets and the U.S. domestic bond markets more fungible.

**EXHIBIT 51–1**
**Publicized New Eurodollar Bond Issuance** (US $ Millions)

|                     | 1989    | 1988   | 1987   | 1986    | 1985   | 1984   | 1983   |
|---------------------|---------|--------|--------|---------|--------|--------|--------|
| Straights           | 46,733  | 37,414 | 22,808 | 57,335  | 41,502 | 28,352 | 19,045 |
| Floating-rate notes | 5,645   | 3,989  | 3,248  | 38,354  | 47,668 | 29,224 | 14,080 |
| Equity warrants     | 58,610  | 25,400 | 21,427 | 11,636  | 1,650  | 1,730  | 2,460  |
| Convertibles        | 1,871   | 1,986  | 8,681  | 5,104   | 3,845  | 4,038  | 1,888  |
| Total Eurodollar    | 112,859 | 68,789 | 56,164 | 112,429 | 94,665 | 63,344 | 37,473 |

Source: Data obtained from "International Bond Market Performance Indexes," copyright © by Salomon Brothers Inc. "International Bond Performance Index" is a servicemark of Salomon Brothers Inc.

often unreliable, but market participants estimate retail investors account for 40–50 percent of the market.

The structure of the Eurodollar market has also evolved from its beginnings as a forum for plain "vanilla" bonds which featured fixed, annual coupon payments and medium-term maturities. While plain vanilla bonds still account for a solid majority of Eurodollar outstandings, 1989 was the first year in which bonds with equity warrants were the largest single category of new-issue Eurodollar paper, comprising over half the new-issue market (Exhibit 51–1). This points to another important change—the increasingly prominent role played by Japanese investors in the Euromarkets. Japanese companies, drawing on the strength of their domestic equity market, have been the single largest issuers of equity-linked paper. Other financing innovations in the Eurodollar bond market have mirrored the innovations in the U.S. domestic market. These include medium-term notes, original-issue discounts, zero coupon issues, and convertibles.

Borrowers in the Eurodollar bond market may be divided into four major groups: sovereign, supranational agency, corporate, and financial. Supranational agencies, such as the World Bank and the European Investment Bank, are consistently among the top borrowers reflecting their constant need for development financing and their lack of a "home" issuance market. Sovereign and sovereign-backed borrowers are also prominent, although the growth in sovereign Eurodollar issuance has slowed in the late 1980s as governments have either cut back on their external borrowing in favor of their domestic bond market, or chosen to borrow in the non-dollar markets to diversify their currency exposure.

Financial innovations, particularly the advent of the interest-rate and currency swap markets, have greatly expanded the diversity of borrowers, notably in the corporate sector. Companies in need of floating-rate finance have been able to combine a fixed-coupon bond with an interest-rate swap to create a cheaper means of finance than a traditional floating-rate note. This is one reason for the large decline in floating-rate note issuance evident in Exhibit 51–1. Similarly, when currency swap terms are favorable, a company in need of, say, deutsche mark funds could issue a Eurodollar bond and combine it with a currency swap to create a cheaper source of deutsche mark funds than a traditional deutsche mark bond.

The future of the Eurodollar bond market is largely a function of the domestic regulatory environment in the major issuer countries. The dominating presence of Japanese companies among Eurodollar borrowers reflects the cumbersome financial regulations that often prohibit these same companies from issuing bonds in their domestic market. Japan may have accounted for as much as 50 percent of new-issue volume in the Eurodollar bond market in 1989. If and when the Japanese government loosens restrictions on domestic corporate bond issuance, many Japanese companies can be expected to use the yen domestic bond market as their primary source of funds. The course of the U.S. dollar and U.S. interest rates have the greatest short-term impact on the growth of the

Eurodollar bond market. The strength in the dollar since the end of 1987, particularly against the yen, has increased investors' appetites for dollar-denominated securities and encouraged dollar bond issuance. Similarly, the rally in the U.S. bond market in 1986 which brought interest rates down towards 7 percent, their lowest level of the decade, resulted in a horde of corporate borrowing (despite the rapidly depreciating dollar) that saw Eurodollar new issuance rise above $100 billion for the first time ever in one year.

The direction of U.S. interest rates and the value of the dollar will continue to have an impact on the size and liquidity of the Eurodollar bond market. Over the long term, however, the survivability of the market will be decided by the global trend toward financial deregulation. To the extent that national governments continue to dismantle the laws which hobble the development of domestic bond markets, the attraction of Eurodollar bonds, and all Eurobonds, to issuers and investors will diminish.

## Yankee Bonds

The other portion of the U.S.-pay international bond market, referred to as the *Yankee bond market*, encompasses those foreign-domiciled issuers who register with the SEC and borrow U.S. dollars via issues underwritten by a U.S. syndicate for delivery in the United States.[4] The principal trading market is in the United States, although foreign buyers can and do participate. Unlike Eurodollar bonds, Yankee bonds pay interest semiannually.

The Yankee market is much older than the Eurodollar market. Overseas borrowers first issued Yankee bonds in the early 1900s when the U.S. became the world's preeminent creditor nation. The repayment record of these early issues was not good—as much as one-third of the outstanding "foreign" bonds in the U.S. were in default on interest payments by the mid-1930s. The market grew slowly until 1974 when the interest equalization tax was abolished, and then expanded rapidly.[5] By the end of 1989, total outstandings were valued at approximately $65 billion, a figure rivalling other sectors of the U.S. corporate bond market in size.

Supranational agencies and Canadian provinces (including provincial utilities) are the most prominent Yankee issuers, comprising well over half the total market (see Exhibit 51–2). The World Bank is by far the largest single issuer.

---

[4] A small portion of outstanding Yankee bonds are foreign currency-denominated. These are not included in this analysis.

[5] The interest equalization tax was imposed on purchases of foreign securities by U.S. residents during the years 1963 to 1974. The intent and effect of the tax was to discourage foreign borrowing in the United States by increasing the cost of capital. To make returns after the I.E.T. competitive with rates on domestic issues, gross rates on foreign borrowings had to be higher than would otherwise have been the case.

The corporate sector, which is a major borrower in the Eurodollar bond market, is of only minor importance in the Yankee market. Exhibit 51–2 points to one important attribute of the Yankee bond market—the high credit quality of most issues. Approximately 80 percent of outstanding Yankee bonds are rated Aa/AA or better by the major credit-rating agencies. No other sector of the U.S. bond market, aside from U.S. Treasuries, can claim a comparable credit quality. This often explains the good relative performance of Yankee bonds during periods of economic instability. One additional benefit of the Yankee market is the low "event risk" assigned to most sovereign entities. While not completely free of event risk, politics being the prime example, governments are not subject to the takeover speculation that has become a major source of credit concern in the corporate sector in the late 1980s.

## The Market for Eurodollar and Yankee Bonds

Foreign investors play a major role in the Yankee market, although the market's location in the U.S. prevents foreigners from having as dominating a presence as they have in the Euromarkets. Prior to 1984, foreign investors had a preference for U.S.-pay international bonds, which include both Yankees and Eurodollar issues, because they were not subject to a 30 percent withholding tax imposed by the U.S. government on all interest paid to foreigners. When the withholding tax exception was abolished in July 1984, a major advantage of U.S.-pay international bonds over U.S. Treasuries and domestic corporate bonds was removed. The result was a cheapening of Yankees and Euros relative to the U.S.

**EXHIBIT 51–2**

**Top Ten Borrowers in the Yankee Market** (Yankee Bond Outstanding as of August 1, 1988)

| Issuer | Yankee Bonds Outstanding ($ Billions) |
| --- | --- |
| World Bank | $6.46 |
| Quebec Hydro | 4.27 |
| Province of Ontario | 4.11 |
| Inter-American Development Bank | 1.94 |
| Province of Quebec | 1.87 |
| Kingdom of Sweden | 1.81 |
| European Investment Bank | 1.67 |
| British Columbia Hydro | 1.58 |
| New Zealand | 1.55 |
| Commonwealth of Australia | 1.52 |

Source: "Credit Quality in the Yankee Bond Market—Sovereign-Backed Issuers Offer Opportunity," Salomon Brothers Inc., November 10, 1988.

domestic market but foreign investor support remained strong. U.S.-pay international bonds offer a yield advantage over U.S. government bonds, usually due to the lesser liquidity of international issues, and foreign buyers are often more familiar with Yankee and Eurodollar credits than they are with U.S. domestic credits. Finally, Yankee and Eurodollar issuers sometimes compensate for their "foreign" status in the U.S.-pay market by offering bonds with shorter maturities and greater call protection—structures that traditionally appeal to overseas investors.

For these reasons, when foreign buyers seek exposure to U.S.-pay bonds, they often buy U.S.-pay international bonds—Eurodollar or Yankee— instead of domestic issues. The degree of interest of foreign buyers in U.S.-pay securities, or lack thereof, frequently is reflected in a narrowing or widening in the spread between U.S.-pay international bond yields and U.S. domestic yields. This is particularly true of Eurodollar bonds, since foreign interest governs this market to a greater extent than the Yankee market which is more attuned to U.S. investor preferences. The fact that the Eurodollar market and the Yankee market have different investor bases occasionally leads to trading disparities between the two markets. For example, similarly structured Canadian Yankee bonds often trade at lower yields than Canadian Eurodollar bonds because U.S. investors tend to be more comfortable with Canadian credits due to the close proximity of the two countries. The opposite is true with European credits, such as The European Investment Bank or The Kingdom of Denmark, which often trade at less attractive yields in the Eurodollar market than in the U.S. market.

The globalization of the investment world has brought the Yankee and Eurodollar bond markets closer together and it is not uncommon for investors to arbitrage the two markets when yield disparities appear. One recent innovation that builds on this increased intermarket efficiency is the World Bank's pioneering "Global Bond" that came out in 1989. The $1.5 billion issue was placed in both the Yankee and the Eurodollar market, and procedures were developed to trade and settle the bond in both markets. The idea was to create an instrument that had the attributes of both a Yankee bond and a Eurodollar bond, and thereby do away with the market segmentation that inhibited liquidity and created yield disparities. The success of the issue is further evidence of the melding of the Euro and domestic markets that has accelerated as barriers to world capital movement are lowered.

## FOREIGN-PAY INTERNATIONAL BONDS

From the standpoint of the U.S. investor, foreign-pay international bonds encompass all issues denominated in currencies other than the dollar. A variety of types of issues are available to the U.S. investor, but in practically all cases the primary trading market is outside the United States.

## The Markets

Securities sold by an issuer within its own country and in that country's currency are typically termed *domestic issues*. These may include direct government issues, government agencies sometimes called semi-governments, or corporates. In most countries, the domestic bond market is dominated by government or government-backed issues. Central governments have directly issued or guaranteed approximately 57 percent of the world's outstanding bonds. Another 10 percent of outstandings is accounted for by state (provincial) or local government issues, meaning 67 percent of the publicly issued bonds outstanding are government credits.[6] The U.S. is the only country with a well-developed, actively traded corporate bond market. Other countries either have discouraged private sector bond issuance in favor of bank loans or equity financing, or companies themselves have chosen to raise funds in the Euromarkets where they have had access to a wider investor audience and fewer issuing restrictions. Recent progress in international credit-rating procedures and greater cross-border capital flows have helped to develop domestic corporate bond markets outside the U.S., but liquidity remains spotty and the number of issuers in each country is limited.

The *foreign bond market* includes issues sold primarily in one country and currency by a borrower of a different nationality. The Yankee market is the U.S.-dollar version of this market. Other examples are the Samurai market, which consists of yen-denominated bonds issued in Japan by non-Japanese borrowers, and the Bulldog market, which is comprised of United Kingdom sterling-denominated bonds issued in the U.K. by non-British entities. Relative to the size of the domestic bond markets, these foreign bond markets are quite small and liquidity can be limited. For borrowers, the major advantage of the foreign bond markets is the access they provide to investors in the country in which the bonds are issued. The Samurai market, for example, allows borrowers directly to tap the huge pools of investment capital in Japan. For investors, foreign bonds offer the convenience of domestic trading and settlement, and additional yield.

Securities issued directly into the international ("offshore") markets are called *Eurobonds*, of which Eurodollar bonds are the U.S.-pay version. These securities are typically underwritten by international syndicates and are sold in a number of national markets simultaneously. They may or may not be obligations of or guaranteed by an issuer domiciled in the country of currency denomination,

---

[6] See footnote 1. The 67 percent actually understates the government portion because some international bonds listed in the Euro or Yankee category are government or government-backed bonds that have been issued outside the domestic market (e.g. Kingdom of Sweden Eurodollar bonds).

and the issuer may be a sovereign government, a corporation, or a supranational agency. The Eurobond market encompasses any bond not issued in a domestic market, regardless of issuer nationality or currency denomination. Eurodollar bonds consistently have been the largest sector of this market, although their share of total outstandings has declined from about 65 percent in 1984 to about 50 percent in 1989, in large part due to the depreciation of the dollar from 1985 through 1987. Eurodeutsche mark bonds are the next largest sector with about a 17 percent share. As with the foreign bond markets, liquidity of Eurobonds is typically less than the liquidity of domestic government issues.

## Components of Return

To the dollar-based investor, there are only two components of return in U.S.-pay bond investing: coupon income; and capital change resulting from interest-rate movements. In foreign-pay investing, a third component of return must be considered: foreign currency movements. The U.S. investor must couple the domestic or internal price movement with income and then translate the total domestic return into dollars to assess the total return in U.S. dollars.

For the U.S. investor in foreign currency bonds, the prospects for return should not only be viewed in an absolute sense, but also be analyzed relative to returns expected in the U.S. market. The analysis can be separated into three different questions.

*What is the starting yield level relative to yield levels on U.S. bonds?* Where this spread is positive, the income advantage will, over time, provide a cushion against adverse movements of the foreign bond price relative to U.S. bonds or against deterioration in the value of the foreign currency. The longer the time horizon, the greater the cushion provided by this accumulating income advantage. If, on the other hand, the starting income level of the foreign currency issue is below that provided by U.S. bonds, this income deficiency must be offset continually by an appreciating currency or positive internal price movement relative to U.S. bonds to provide comparable returns. This may appear to be a difficult challenge, but the decade of the 1970s as a whole saw the best converted U.S. dollar total returns accruing the bond investments with the lowest income levels. The same result was achieved in the 1980s decade where Japanese yen bonds had the world's best total returns in U.S. dollar terms despite the fact that yen bonds offered the lowest interest rates of the world's major bond markets. The underlying rationale for this result is that bonds with low yields are denominated in currencies of countries with low inflation rates, which ultimately translates into currency appreciation relative to the U.S. dollar.

*What are the prospects for internal price movements relative to expectations for U.S. bond prices?* This factor can be broadly discussed in terms of changing yield spreads of foreign-pay bonds versus U.S. issues in the same way that changing yield spreads within the domestic U.S. market are discussed when describing changes in relative prices. However, several points should be considered in regard to this analogy. In the U.S. market, all bond prices generally move in the same direction, although not always to the same extent; whereas domestic price movements of foreign-pay bonds may move in a direction opposite to that of the U.S. market. Second, although yield spread relationships within the U.S. market may fluctuate broadly, in many cases there is a normal spread that has some repetitive meaning. However, changing economic, social, and political trends between the United States and other countries suggest that there are few normal relationships to serve as useful guidelines.

Finally, although both U.S. and international investors must be aware of differing price movements emanating from equal yield movements in securities of differing maturities, international bond investors must also be aware of the impact a given basis point change in yield has on the price movements of bonds with significantly different starting yield levels. For example, a 100 basis-point (1%) decline in the yield of a 10-year United Kingdom government issue starting at a 10 percent yield results in a 6.5 percent price change, whereas the same 100 basis-point move equates to a 7.8 percent price change for a 10-year Swiss franc issue with a starting yield of 6 percent. (A 10 percent discount rate shortens the duration relative to a 6 percent discount rate.) When the more commonly analyzed effects of varying maturities and differing yield changes are added to the impact of different starting yield levels, the resulting changes in relative price movements are not intuitively obvious. For example, the various combinations of starting yield, maturity, and yield change shown in Exhibit 51–3 all result in the same 10 percent capital price increases.

*What are the prospects for currency gain or loss versus the U.S. dollar?* The debate continues as to whether or not foreign currency changes can be predicted and, if so, what factors determine such changes. In many ways this debate is little different from that regarding the predictability of stock market

**EXHIBIT 51–3**

**Impact of Maturity and Starting Yield on Yield and Price Change Relationships**

| Starting Yield | Maturity (Years) | Yield Change | Price Change |
|---|---|---|---|
| 10% | 10 | −1.50% | +10% |
| 10 | 5 | −2.44 | +10 |
| 6 | 10 | −1.27 | +10 |
| 6 | 5 | −2.21 | +10 |

movements or interest rates. Like the stock and bond markets, a number of factors exert a direct influence on foreign exchange rates. The common problems faced by forecasters are whether these factors have already been fully discounted in prices—be they stock, bond, or foreign exchange—and which factor will predominate at any given time. Those factors generally regarded to affect foreign currency movements include the following:

1. The balance of payments and prospective changes in that balance.
2. Inflation and interest-rate differentials between countries.
3. The social and political environment, particularly with regard to the impact on foreign investment.
4. Relative changes in the money supply.
5. Central bank intervention in the currency markets.

A common question is whether international bond returns are almost entirely a function of currency movements. Exhibit 51–4 shows that for the 12-year period 1978 to 89, and for two of the three interim periods, the income component of return has proven to be the largest of the three components, as

**EXHIBIT 51–4**
**Average Annual Returns of International Bond Index* by Components**

| | Contribution to Return | | | |
|---|---|---|---|---|
| | Income | Domestic Capital Gain | Foreign Currency | Total Dollar-Converted Average Annual Return |
| 1978–81 | +9.5% | −4.8% | +0.3% | + 5.0% |
| 1982–85 | +9.1 | +5.0 | −1.4 | +12.7 |
| 1986–89 | +6.9 | +0.7 | +7.5 | +15.1 |
| 1978–89 | +8.5 | +0.4 | +2.0 | +10.9 |

* Market-weighted in the government bonds of Australia, Canada, France, West Germany, Japan, the Netherlands, Switzerland, and the United Kingdom. See also footnote 7.

[7] Monthly total returns in Exhibits 51–4 to 51–19 were taken from three sources: Salomon Brothers' "International Bond Market Performance Indexes," published monthly; Salomon Brothers' "World Government Bond Indexes," also published monthly; and from Scudder Stevens and Clark data. The income component of total return was imputed from monthly yield levels compiled from "World Financial Markets" published by Morgan Guaranty Trust Company of New York.

measured by an index of international bonds market-weighted in eight foreign countries.

Over a shorter time horizon, however, foreign currency or domestic capital changes can be significantly more important. Exhibit 51–5 breaks down the 1978 to 1989 period into annual returns to demonstrate the influence domestic capital changes and movements in exchange rates can have on total returns over the short term. Domestic capital changes ranged from −9.8 percent in 1979 to 9.8 percent in 1982, and currency returns varied from −11.4 percent in 1981 to +25.3 percent in 1987. (Recall that negative foreign currency returns for dollar-based investors correspond to a strengthening in the dollar versus other currencies, and vice versa.) The income component of return varied in a much narrower range throughout the period, from a low of 6.7 percent in 1987 and 1988 to a high of 11.1 percent in 1981. For individual countries, the variation in components of return was even greater. The greatest capital price changes were +36.9 percent in the United Kingdom in 1982 and −18.2 percent in Canada in 1981. Currency changes for specific countries ranged from +30.4 percent in Japan in 1987 to −20.7 percent in France in 1981. These data show

**EXHIBIT 51–5**
**Average Annual Returns of International Bond Index\* by Components**

| | | Contribution to Return | | |
|---|---|---|---|---|
| | Income | Domestic Capital Gain | Foreign Currency | Total Dollar-Converted Average Annual Return |
| 1978 | 7.6% | −1.5% | 15.1% | 21.2% |
| 1979 | 9.1 | −9.8 | −5.9 | −6.6 |
| 1980 | 10.3 | −3.3 | 5.3 | 12.3 |
| 1981 | 11.1 | −3.9 | −11.4 | −4.2 |
| 1982 | 10.2 | 9.8 | −9.4 | 10.6 |
| 1983 | 9.2 | 1.4 | −4.6 | 6.0 |
| 1984 | 9.0 | 2.1 | −10.5 | 0.6 |
| 1985 | 8.1 | 6.3 | 22.3 | 36.7 |
| 1986 | 6.9 | 6.5 | 19.3 | 32.7 |
| 1987 | 6.7 | 3.0 | 25.3 | 35.0 |
| 1988 | 6.7 | 0.2 | −4.6 | 2.3 |
| 1989 | 7.1 | −4.7 | −6.6 | −4.2 |

\* Market-weighted in the government bonds of Australia, Canada, France, West Germany, Japan, the Netherlands, Switzerland, and the United Kingdom.

clearly that all three factor of return—income, capital change, and currency movement—are important and must be considered both absolutely and relative to U.S. alternatives.

## THE RATIONALE FOR INTERNATIONAL BOND INVESTING

The rationale for foreign-pay international bond investing is two-fold. First, international bonds can from time to time enhance an investor's total rate of return relative to what is available from alternative U.S. domestic bond investments. The composition of return will vary between income, domestic price change, and foreign currency change. Second, international bonds combined with U.S. bonds can reduce the risk or the volatility of return relative to a portfolio invested solely in U.S. fixed income securities.

In analyzing the case for international bonds, there is no a priori reason why one rationale for international bond investing should receive more emphasis than the other. The relative emphasis on these rationales is properly a function of the investment objectives of the investor, and these objectives should be reflected in the composition of an international bond portfolio. To some investors with long-term time horizons, the impact of international bonds on interim volatility of returns is unimportant. For these investors, embarking on a program of international bond investing is not appropriate unless international bonds can be expected to improve the rate of return. To others, particularly investors with shorter time horizons who have been seared by the occasional roller coaster in the U.S. fixed income markets, the attraction of international bonds may be their potential for a reduction in the volatility of overall portfolio returns.

### Superior Rates of Return

One of the cornerstones of the rationale for international equity investing is that a portfolio of foreign equities should, over time, provide a higher return than a portfolio of U.S. equities, since many areas of the world are growing more rapidly than the United States and are experiencing higher rates of investment spending and productivity growth. Ultimately these superior growth characteristics should translate into more rapid increases in corporate profits and, in turn, stock prices assuming a degree of comparability in starting valuations.

No such strong fundamental arguments exist for international bonds. There have been long periods, throughout much of the late 1960s and 1970s and again from 1985 to 1987, where international bonds provided superior returns to U.S. instruments and long periods, from 1981 to 1984 and from 1988 to 1989 when the reverse was true. In the former period, foreign bonds benefited both from higher income levels than in the United States, and strengthening currencies. This, coupled with the higher unanticipated inflation rates in the United States compared with other industrialized countries, led to lackluster domestic U.S. bond returns relative to those abroad. The 1985–1987 period is most memorable for the downward spiral in the U.S. dollar which produced windfall gains for holders of foreign-pay instruments. In the 1981–1984 period, U.S. bonds benefited from income streams much higher than in other markets coupled with the improvement in the inflation outlook which resulted in generous capital gains as interest rates declined. In 1988 and 1989, renewed confidence in the U.S. dollar, and lower than expected inflation in the U.S. economy led to the superior performance of U.S. bonds relative to most foreign-pay alternatives.

These results strongly suggest that potential returns from international bonds relative to the United States must be carefully analyzed by the three components—income advantage, expected relative domestic price movements, and prospective currency changes.

The best case for ongoing observance of international bonds lies in the continual array of opportunities and risks provided by the constant shifting of international exchange rate and interest-rate relationships. The range of starting yields is continuously changing; some foreign rates provide a yield cushion against a U.S. interest-rate bogey, and others provide a disadvantage. At any time, different countries will be at different points in their economic and interest-rate cycles. Similarly, foreign currency relationships are continuously shifting, sometimes moving with interest rates and sometimes against them. Over time it should be possible to capitalize on these shifting relationships, which will, in the aggregate, supply a greater number of opportunities than can any one individual and relatively homogeneous market. This rationale is an opportunistic and selective one, which has at its heart the cyclicality of economic behavior worldwide.

In the analysis that follows, eight foreign bond markets are analyzed in relation to the U.S. market. Included are the government bond markets of Australia, Canada, France, Germany, Japan, the Netherlands, Switzerland, and the United Kingdom. The analysis focuses on the 1978–1989 period due to the availability of reliable data and a sufficient amount of time for interest-rate and currency cycles to work their way through the markets.

A comparison of eight foreign bond markets with the U.S. market shows that over the period 1978 to 1989, U.S. bonds provided a slightly inferior 9.96 percent rate of return compared to a 10.86 percent rate of return produced by a market-weighted index of foreign-pay bonds.

The superior performance of the international bond index during this period is largely a function of the time period chosen, since there is no a priori reason to expect international bond returns, over the long run, to be any better or worse than domestic returns. Furthermore, the result is largely influenced by the very strong Japanese returns which represent a large 35% of the market-weighted index. An index equally weighted in the eight foreign bond markets would have produced a return of approximately 9%, almost 1% below that of the U.S.

**EXHIBIT 51–6**
**International Bond Markets Compound Annual Rates of Return—1978–1989**

| | Components of Return | | | | |
|---|---|---|---|---|---|
| | Total Return in U. S. Dollars | Domestic Capital Change | Income | Total Domestic Return | Foreign-Exchange Change |
| Australia | 7.59% | −1.69% | 12.76% | 11.07% | −3.13% |
| Canada | 9.92 | −0.84 | 11.30 | 10.46 | −0.49 |
| France | 9.46 | −0.23 | 11.66 | 11.43 | −1.77 |
| Germany | 8.47 | −0.87 | 7.45 | 6.58 | 1.77 |
| Japan | 11.65 | 0.22 | 6.82 | 7.04 | 4.31 |
| Netherlands | 9.39 | −0.40 | 8.25 | 7.85 | 1.43 |
| Switzerland | 5.73 | −1.11 | 4.66 | 3.55 | 2.11 |
| United Kingdom | 10.06 | 0.26 | 11.45 | 11.71 | −1.48 |
| United States | 9.96 | −0.29 | 10.25 | 9.96 | — |

Exhibit 51–6 shows total returns from nine bond markets in U.S. dollar terms over the 1978–1989 period. Japan was the best performing bond market during that period due to the strong yen and marginally positive domestic capital changes. The strong performance of the United Kingdom reflects the attractive income accruals which were high enough to overcome the weakness of the British pound over the period. The United States ranked third, just ahead of Canada, which, despite its better returns in local currency terms, gave back part of its gains with currency depreciation. Switzerland lagged the other countries due to its historically low yields which more than counteracted the slight appreciation of the Swiss franc versus the U.S. dollar over the 12-year period.

The total return figures in Exhibit 51–6 mask significant disparities in annual total returns between bond markets. In Exhibit 51–7, the 1978 to 1989 period is broken down into annual return data for a better look at short run changes. Notice the large disparity between the best and worst performing bond markets in each year. The smallest difference in total returns was recorded in 1983 when the 12.55 percent return in Japan was 21 percent better than the −8.61 percent return in the Netherlands. The largest difference in returns appeared in 1985 when France had a 52.70 percent return and Australian bonds lost 12.37 percent—a 65 percent return differential. These wide disparities are far greater than the return differentials in Exhibit 51–6 which have been smoothed out with the passage of time. Exhibit 51–7 also shows that only once in the 12 year period did a country, the United Kingdom from 1979 to 1980, appear in the best or worst column in consecutive years. Seven of the nine countries, with Germany and the Netherlands the exceptions, were at least once in the best performing category, and all countries but France had at least one year in the worst category. This reinforces the idea mentioned earlier that value added from

**EXHIBIT 51–7**
**Annual Total Returns Converted to U. S. Dollars**

| | Best | | Worst | |
|---|---|---|---|---|
| | Country | Return | Country | Return |
| 1978 | Switzerland | 34.70% | Canada | −5.50% |
| 1979 | United Kingdom | 12.40 | Japan | −21.46 |
| 1980 | United Kingdom | 28.88 | Germany | −10.58 |
| 1981 | Japan | 5.50 | United Kingdom | −19.00 |
| 1982 | Canada | 35.73 | Switzerland | 1.18 |
| 1983 | Japan | 12.55 | Netherlands | −8.61 |
| 1984 | United States | 14.29 | Switzerland | −14.66 |
| 1985 | France | 52.70 | Australia | −12.37 |
| 1986 | Japan | 43.50 | United Kingdom | 15.30 |
| 1987 | United Kingdom | 47.60 | United States | −1.40 |
| 1988 | Australia | 30.30 | Switzerland | −12.50 |
| 1989 | Canada | 18.00 | Japan | −15.00 |

opportunistic international bond investing can be great, but over time, government policies and market forces tend to correct the economic disparities that lead to large gains or losses in the short run. The rates of return experienced by each of the nine countries have no necessary repetitive significance. The 1978–1989 period was unique in many respects. In the late 1970s, an acceleration in U.S. inflation and a widening gap between economic growth in the U.S. and Europe caused U.S. interest rates to rise relative to Europe and Japan. The Soviet invasion of Afghanistan and the Iran hostage crisis helped lead to a loss of confidence in the Carter administration and a weakening in the dollar. The second oil shock in 1979 was the reason for the strong performance of the United Kingdom bond markets from 1979 to 1980 and the negative returns in Japan and Germany, two oil importing countries. The 1981–1984 period was characterized by strong relative returns of U.S. and Canadian bonds due to high income levels and renewed confidence in the dollar. Japanese bonds also performed well due to Japan's success at combatting global inflation and the emergence of the yen as the world's strongest currency. The 1985-1986 period experienced one of history's great bond market rallies with interest rates retreating from the record levels reached earlier in the decade. The decline in the dollar meant foreign bond markets were once again in favor among U.S. investors. French bond returns reflected the government's retreat from state interventionism which characterized the early years of the Mitterand administration. The 1988–1989 period witnessed a return to dollar strength and declining interest rates in the U.S. relative to other countries. The political liberalization of Eastern Europe in 1989 had a negative impact on European bond markets as interest rates rose to reflect the unanticipated growth and inflation potential of a more integrated European market.

The variability of the sources of return is evident in a comparison of annual data. The components of return for 1980 are shown in Exhibit 51–8 and for 1986 are shown in Exhibit 51–9. In each case, the U.S. bond market ranked fifth or sixth out of nine markets as measured by total return in U.S. dollar terms. In 1986 the four top performers were the major hard currency countries: Japan, Germany, the Netherlands, and Switzerland. In 1980, three of these countries trailed the list, and the United Kingdom, Japan, and Australia provided the best returns. The superior performance of Japanese bonds in 1986 was due to strong yen appreciation and positive capital price movements that offset a 2.2 percent relative income disadvantage of Japanese bonds. The same is true for the other top performers in that year. Notice the high income component in Australia for 1986 was partially offset by negative returns in the currency component leading to below average total returns. In 1980, the top-ranked results for United Kingdom bonds were accounted for by all three components of return, whereas the 17.8 percent rise in the value of the yen contributed to over 70 percent of the return on Japanese bonds. The income component was the dominant positive factor in all bond markets except Japan in 1980. In contrast, currency appreciation was the leading contributor to five out of eight bond markets in 1986.

Despite some evidence of variability in the components of return, a frequent challenge to international bond investing is that favorable foreign bond returns relative to U.S. bond returns correspond to periods of dollar weakness and that the reverse is true for periods of dollar strength. Although there is considerable

**EXHIBIT 51–8**
**Variability of Components of Return** (1980)

|  | Components of Return | | |
| --- | --- | --- | --- |
|  | Total Return (Dollars) | Capital Change | Income | Foreign-Exchange Change |
| United Kingdom | 28.88% | 6.58% | 13.14% | 7.65% |
| Japan | 22.88 | −4.54 | 8.98 | 17.66 |
| Canada | 1.70 | −8.78 | 12.46 | −1.91 |
| Australia | 1.40 | −15.23 | 10.94 | 5.95 |
| United States | 0.79 | −10.61 | 11.40 | — |
| Netherlands | −5.76 | −4.66 | 10.24 | −10.74 |
| France | −8.07 | −10.06 | 13.78 | −11.37 |
| Switzerland | −9.63 | −3.94 | 4.78 | −10.38 |
| Germany | −10.58 | −6.66 | 8.51 | −12.20 |

**EXHIBIT 51–9**
**Variability of Components of Return** (1986)

| | Components of Return | | | |
|---|---|---|---|---|
| | Total Return (Dollars) | Capital Change | Income | Foreign-Exchange Change |
| Japan | 43.50% | 8.09% | 5.41% | 26.43% |
| Germany | 38.69 | 3.29 | 5.91 | 27.01 |
| Netherlands | 36.10 | 1.21 | 6.29 | 26.60 |
| Switzerland | 35.20 | 1.76 | 4.34 | 27.43 |
| France | 33.90 | 6.00 | 8.20 | 17.25 |
| United States | 21.00 | 13.41 | 7.59 | — |
| Australia | 17.60 | 7.23 | 13.37 | −2.49 |
| Canada | 17.10 | 6.45 | 9.15 | 1.30 |
| United Kingdom | 15.30 | 2.29 | 10.01 | 2.67 |

merit to this argument over short and intermediate time periods, the historical contribution of return from currency appreciation over long periods of time should not be overemphasized.

Exhibit 51–10 shows the contribution of currency movements to returns. The 1978 to 1989 period has been divided into three four-year subperiods to illustrate the impact of a longer time horizon on foreign currency returns. For each of the four-year periods, the impact of currency on return has been much higher than for the 12-year period as a whole. This is not surprising given the wide swings in foreign currency values that can occur in the short-term. Over time, as the economic imbalances that caused the currency movements have

**EXHIBIT 51–10**
**Average Annual Contribution of Foreign Currency Changes to International Bond Returns**

| | 1978-89 | 1978-81 | 1982-85 | 1986-89 |
|---|---|---|---|---|
| Australia | −3.13% | −0.30% | −12.10% | 3.71% |
| Canada | −0.49 | −2.01 | −4.04 | 4.82 |
| France | −1.77 | −4.93 | −6.49 | 6.62 |
| Germany | 1.77 | −1.80 | −2.02 | 9.56 |
| Japan | 4.31 | 2.08 | 2.44 | 8.54 |
| Netherlands | 1.43 | −2.21 | −2.58 | 9.52 |
| Switzerland | 2.11 | 2.41 | −3.22 | 7.42 |
| United Kingdom | −1.48 | −0.21 | −6.67 | 2.68 |

**EXHIBIT 51–11**
**Comparison of International Bond Returns** (1978–1989)

| | Average Annual Bond Returns Converted to U. S. Dollars | Average Annual Bond Returns in Domestic Currency |
|---|---|---|
| Australia | 7.59% | 11.07% |
| Canada | 9.92 | 10.46 |
| France | 9.46 | 11.43 |
| Germany | 8.47 | 6.58 |
| Japan | 11.65 | 7.04 |
| Netherlands | 9.39 | 7.85 |
| Switzerland | 5.73 | 3.55 |
| United Kingdom | 10.06 | 11.71 |

adjusted, currency prices have readjusted towards previous levels. Whether this trend continues will have an important impact on the place of international bonds in U.S. portfolios. Exhibit 51–11 compares local currency returns and converted dollar returns for 1978 to 1989. In half the cases currency conversion added to the results, and in half it subtracted.

A second challenge involving foreign currency exposure relates to the fact that foreign currency adds to the volatility of foreign bond returns. On a market-by-market basis, this has been true. Exhibits 51–12 and 51–13 show the standard deviation of monthly total returns in nine bond markets in both local currency and dollar-denominated terms. The data are presented for the 1978 to 1989 period and are also broken down into four-year

**EXHIBIT 51–12**
**Standard Deviation of Monthly Domestic Local Bond Market Total Returns**

| Local Currency | 1978–89 | 1978–81 | 1982–85 | 1986–89 |
|---|---|---|---|---|
| Australia | 2.41% | 1.36% | 3.22% | 2.13% |
| Canada | 3.19 | 3.92 | 3.17 | 1.91 |
| France | 1.60 | 1.82 | 1.14 | 1.59 |
| Germany | 1.61 | 2.17 | 1.19 | 1.12 |
| Japan | 1.59 | 1.95 | 1.20 | 1.50 |
| Netherlands | 1.51 | 2.03 | 1.28 | 0.91 |
| Switzerland | 1.05 | 1.42 | 0.85 | 0.70 |
| United Kingdom | 2.94 | 3.23 | 2.90 | 2.53 |
| United States | 2.96 | 3.72 | 2.77 | 1.96 |

**EXHIBIT 51–13**

**Standard Deviation of Monthly Bond Market Total Returns Converted to U. S. Dollars**

|  | 1978-89 | 1978-81 | 1982-85 | 1986-89 |
|---|---|---|---|---|
| Australia | 4.29% | 2.08% | 4.95% | 5.02% |
| Canada | 3.82 | 4.43 | 4.02 | 2.54 |
| France | 4.03 | 4.27 | 3.76 | 3.93 |
| Germany | 4.87 | 5.27 | 4.76 | 4.49 |
| Japan | 4.84 | 5.38 | 4.02 | 5.01 |
| Netherlands | 4.35 | 4.84 | 3.83 | 4.27 |
| Switzerland | 4.59 | 5.41 | 3.69 | 4.47 |
| United Kingdom | 5.21 | 5.39 | 4.99 | 5.22 |
| United States | 2.96 | 3.72 | 2.77 | 1.96 |
| International Index | 3.86 | 4.16 | 3.23 | 4.07 |

segments. For the 12-year period as a whole, the volatility of returns in the United States was greater than the volatility of local currency returns in any other market except Canada. Exhibit 51–12 also reflects the fact that volatility has decreased over the period in all countries but Australia. When foreign exchange movements are factored in, the volatility of foreign bond returns in U.S. dollar terms increased substantially. For the 1978 to 1989 period, and for each of the subperiods, the standard deviation of the U.S. return is about the lowest.

The increased volatility associated with foreign currency instruments has led to the development of *currency-hedged* investments, which neutralize the currency component of international bonds while maintaining exposure to local bond price movements. This will be discussed later in the chapter. As discussed in the next section, the increase in volatility of individual market returns due to foreign exchange movements is significantly reduced in a diversified international bond portfolio. Importantly, as Exhibit 51–13 shows, the standard deviation of the international index is lower than that of most of the individual markets. This is because the correlations of return between the individual foreign markets and currencies are less than perfect.

## Diversification

A second rationale for international bond investing is diversification. The inclusion of foreign bonds in a portfolio should reduce the risk or volatility of returns of a portfolio otherwise invested solely in U.S. fixed income securities. This is because foreign bond markets do not move with, or are not perfectly correlated with, the U.S. bond market. Intuitively this is obvious. The dynamics of the business cycle, and the role of monetary policy in dealing with the business cycle, differ by country. Institutional or structural forces, government financing practices, and tradition mean that the role of buyers and sellers varies between fixed income markets. The trend of inflation, a country's tolerance of inflation, and the sources of inflationary pressure differ among countries, as does the impact of inflation on the trend and structure of interest rates.

Finally, a host of geopolitical, foreign policy, and societal forces ensure that the movements of foreign bond prices are not perfectly correlated. Consequently, when foreign currency bonds are added to a portfolio of U.S. fixed income securities, the price movements often offset each other, and the overall volatility of returns can be reduced.

Exhibit 51–14 shows the correlation coefficients of monthly changes in total returns (bond prices plus income) in local currency terms between nine major bond markets over the 1978 to 1989 period. The highest correlation with the U.S. market is Canada—not a surprising occurrence in view of the bilateral relationships between the two economies. The correlation is lowest with Australia, which once again is reasonable in view of the lack of interdependence between the two economies. Within these two extremes lie the European markets and Japan. In most cases the correlation among the continental European markets is higher than that between those markets and the United States, reflecting the high degree of interdependence between the European economies and the existence of formal trading and currency relationships.

Exhibit 51–15 shows the correlation coefficients of monthly domestic total returns between the United States and foreign markets broken down by four-year time periods. In all cases except Australia, the degree of correlation or interdependence rose over the 12-year period. This is one more statistical manifestation of the degree to which the world is getting smaller and the increased

**EXHIBIT 51–14**

**Correlation Coefficients of Domestic Total Returns in Foreign Bond Markets — 1978-1989** (Based on Monthly Data)

|  | US | Aus | Can | Fra | Ger | Jap | Net | Swi | U.K. |
|---|---|---|---|---|---|---|---|---|---|
| United States | 1.00 | | | | | | | | |
| Australia | .18 | 1.00 | | | | | | | |
| Canada | .78 | .13 | 1.00 | | | | | | |
| France | .25 | .09 | .40 | 1.00 | | | | | |
| Germany | .52 | .18 | .57 | .45 | 1.00 | | | | |
| Japan | .39 | .14 | .37 | .35 | .61 | 1.00 | | | |
| Netherlands | .54 | .12 | .53 | .53 | .76 | .49 | 1.00 | | |
| Switzerland | .35 | .21 | .41 | .28 | .49 | .39 | .50 | 1.00 | |
| United Kingdom | .34 | .03 | .34 | .27 | .37 | .37 | .36 | .31 | 1.00 |

**EXHIBIT 51–15**

**Correlation Coefficient Between U. S. and Foreign Bond Markets Domestic Total Return** (Based on Monthly Data)

|  | 1978-89 | 1978-81 | 1982-85 | 1986-89 |
|---|---|---|---|---|
| Australia | .18 | .30 | .17 | .04 |
| Canada | .78 | .76 | .80 | .80 |
| France | .25 | .14 | .06 | .58 |
| Germany | .52 | .49 | .45 | .64 |
| Japan | .39 | .34 | .33 | .58 |
| Netherlands | .54 | .56 | .46 | .57 |
| Switzerland | .35 | .31 | .34 | .41 |
| United Kingdom | .34 | .28 | .29 | .48 |

synchronization of economic behavior resulting from freer global capital movements. Increased bond market correlation reflects the more uniform impact on the industrialized countries of a number of significant economic events during the period, notably: the second oil shock in 1979 to 1980 which led to inflation and higher interest rates in practically all industrialized countries; the global recession which ended in 1982; the economic expansion throughout the remainder of the 1980s; and the crash and quick recovery of global stock markets from 1987 to 1988. The economic policy coordination which began in the postwar era with Bretton Woods accelerated rapidly in the 1970s and 1980s. To the extent that this trend continues, increased interdependence between bond markets is to be expected. For reasons discussed above, however, international bond price trends should remain less than perfectly correlated.

Exhibit 51–16 shows the correlation coefficients of the change in monthly total returns converted to U.S. dollars for the 1978 to 1989 period overall, and again broken down into four-year segments. A comparison of Exhibits 51–15 and 51–16 shows the impact of currency movements on the correlation of returns with the United States over 12-years was negative for all countries but France, and only marginally negative for the United Kingdom. The largest impact on correlation was in the German bond market where changes in the deutsche mark/U.S. dollar exchange rate reduced the domestic bond market correlation coefficient from .52 to .32. Over shorter periods, where exchange rate movements are more marked, domestic total return and converted U.S. dollar total return correlations can diverge more substantially. For example, in the 1982 to 1985 period, the correlation coefficient of German bond market returns with U.S. returns was .45 in local currency terms and only .17 in U.S. dollar terms. Similarly, the correlation coefficient between Japanese and U.S. returns in 1986–89 was reduced from .58 to .28 when the currency factor was added.

**EXHIBIT 51–16**
**Correlation Coefficient Between United States and**
**Foreign Bond Markets Total Return Converted to U. S.**
**Dollars** (Based on Monthly Data)

|                | 1978-89 | 1978-81 | 1982-85 | 1986-89 |
|----------------|---------|---------|---------|---------|
| Australia      | .12     | .43     | .19     | .13     |
| Canada         | .72     | .72     | .75     | .64     |
| France         | .28     | .25     | .21     | .44     |
| Germany        | .32     | .41     | .17     | .37     |
| Japan          | .28     | .36     | .15     | .28     |
| Netherlands    | .37     | .45     | .28     | .33     |
| Switzerland    | .30     | .42     | .12     | .31     |
| United Kingdom | .32     | .40     | .23     | .30     |

Exhibits 51–15 and 51–16 lead to the conclusion that while local bond price movements between countries are becoming more correlated, currency volatility has continued to reduce the correlation between international bond markets when measured in U.S. dollar terms. This supports the use of international bonds for portfolio diversification.

## THE IMPACT OF INTERNATIONAL BONDS ON A U.S. BOND PORTFOLIO: THE CASE FOR INTERNATIONAL BOND INVESTING

The above analysis demonstrates that a market-weighted portfolio of foreign-pay bonds over the 12-year period from 1978 to 1989 had a U.S. dollar average annual total return of 10.86 percent, slightly higher than the 9.96 average annual return of a U.S.-pay portfolio. When broken down into shorter periods of time, however, foreign-pay bonds occasionally offered better returns, and occasionally worse. Volatility in the individual foreign markets and the aggregate markets in an international index, when measured in dollar terms, was shown always to be greater than U.S. bond volatility due to fluctuations in exchange rates. Finally, the correlation of foreign-pay bonds with U.S. bonds was shown to be relatively low, supporting the diversification benefits of international bonds in a U.S. portfolio. Given these risk-return characteristics, it is possible to examine the impact of foreign bonds on a U.S. fixed income portfolio.

Exhibit 51–17 shows a comparison of the compound rates of return of three portfolios: an international bond index market-weighted in the eight foreign markets studied above; the U.S. bond market; and a portfolio assumed to be invested 80 percent in the U.S. market average and 20 percent in the international index.

**EXHIBIT 51–17**
**Compound Annual Rates of Return**

|  | 1978-89 | 1978-81 | 1982-85 | 1986-89 |
|---|---|---|---|---|
| International Index | 10.86% | 5.04% | 12.67% | 15.11% |
| United States | 9.96 | 1.23 | 19.02 | 10.34 |
| Portfolio 1 (80 United States, 20 International Index) | 10.14 | 1.99 | 17.75 | 11.29 |

For the period as a whole, the U.S. bond market underperformed the international index by a margin of 90 basis points (.9 percent). The U.S. return was augmented by 18 basis points when a 20 percent commitment to the international bond index was added to an 80 percent commitment in U.S. bonds, as illustrated by portfolio 1. The results are more magnified if the period is divided into four-year segments. In 1978 to 1981 and again in 1986 to 1989 international bonds outperformed U.S. bonds by a large margin and a 20 percent commitment to the international bond index added 76 basis points to total return in the 1978–1981 period and 95 basis points to total return in the 1986–89 period. From 1982 to 1985, U.S. bonds had markedly better returns than the international index and the net result of a 20 percent commitment to international bonds subtracted 127 basis points from returns. Exhibit 51–17 is intuitively obvious from a total return standpoint. International bonds will add to the total returns of a U.S.-based portfolio when the foreign bond markets and/or currencies outperform the U.S. market; and they will be a drain on returns when the reverse is true.

Exhibit 51–18 shows the effect of international diversification on the standard deviation of a portfolio. Despite the substantially higher volatility of the international bond index relative to the U.S. market, a weighting in inter-

**EXHIBIT 51–18**
**Standard Deviations of Monthly Returns** (in U. S. Dollars)

|  | 1978-89 | 1978-81 | 1982-85 | 1986-89 |
|---|---|---|---|---|
| International Index | 3.86% | 4.16% | 3.23% | 4.07% |
| United States | 2.95 | 3.72 | 2.77 | 1.95 |
| Portfolio 1 (80% United States, 20% International Index) | 2.76 | 3.46 | 2.48 | 2.00 |

national bonds can lower the overall volatility of a U.S. portfolio because the correlation between U.S. bonds and international bonds is relatively low. Over the 1978 to 89 period, a 20 percent weighting in international bonds added 90 basis points to total return while lowering the standard deviation of the portfolio from 2.95 to 2.76. This supports the theory that international bonds have some diversification characteristics. However, the reduction in volatility can be relatively small. Furthermore, during only two of the three subperiods did the internationally diversified portfolio have a lower volatility than the U.S. market average. In the 1986–89 period, coinciding with strong returns in the foreign bond markets and sharp fluctuation in exchange rates, international bonds increased portfolio volatility slightly, but added 95 basis points to total return. During this period, correlations of returns to the U.S. market remained relatively low although somewhat higher than in previous periods. However, the fluctuations of the currency markets added significantly to the volatility (and return) of foreign bonds relative to U.S. bonds which were enjoying a period of relative stability. The net effect was that a combination of 20 percent international bonds and 80 percent U.S. bonds was slightly more volatile than a U.S. portfolio.

The tradeoff between low correlations of international returns with U.S. returns but higher volatility than U.S. returns also explains why most long run studies of the appropriate mix of international bonds in an overall portfolio is in the 20 to 40 percent range. This is illustrated in Exhibit 51–19 using the data from Exhibits 51–17 and 51–18. A portfolio of 100 percent U.S. bonds results in a return of 9.96 percent and a standard deviation of 2.95. As international bonds are initially added to the portfolio, volatility declines and returns increase. A portfolio of 70 percent U.S. bonds and 30 percent international bonds has the lowest overall volatility. Beyond this point, an investor can still add to total returns by increasing the portfolio weighting in international bonds, but only at the cost of higher overall portfolio volatility. At the upper end of this range the higher volatility of foreign bonds in U.S. dollar terms relative to the U.S., despite the low correlation of foreign bonds and U.S. bonds, means that the combined volatility of foreign and U.S. bonds is higher than for U.S. bonds alone.

The rationale behind foreign-pay bond investing is twofold: the opportunity for superior returns resulting from changes in relative interest rates and exchange rates; and a reduction in long-term portfolio volatility for a given return. The objectives and requirements of each different portfolio will determine which of these considerations has greater sway over the decision to invest overseas. While return enhancement and lower volatility are both important considerations in portfolio management, the evidence suggests that the potential for enhanced returns through active management should be the primary motive for international bond investing since the reduction in volatility of a combined U.S. and foreign portfolio is realtively small.

**EXHIBIT 51–19**
**Historical Risk/Return Tradeoff of International Diversification** (1978-89 Monthly Data)

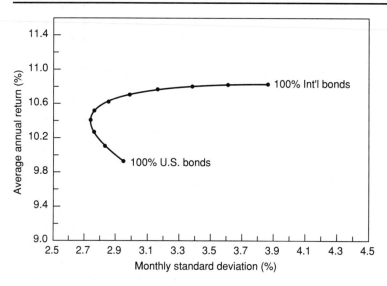

## ACTIVE INTERNATIONAL BOND MANAGEMENT

There is little question that, with the benefit of hindsight, a strategy of active international bond investing over the 12-year period from 1978 to 89 could have provided enhanced returns to a U.S.-based investor. Exhibit 51–7 showed the best and worst performing bond markets for each of the 12 years. In only one of the 12 years, 1984, was the U.S. market the best performer. In 1987, for example, a U.S. investor could have realized an almost 50 percent return enhancement by investing in United Kingdom long bonds. While choosing the best market is always difficult, *any* of the foreign bond markets in 1987 would have provided more attractive returns in dollar or local currency terms than the U.S. market. The crucial question, of course, is whether without such hindsight a portfolio manager can provide incremental return through active international investing without incurring a commensurate degree of risk. The wide disparity of returns in Exhibit 51–7 illustrates the significant opportunities in foreign-pay bonds but also points to the pitfalls of adopting an inappropriate investment strategy.

At the heart of the case for active international bond management is the ability to profit from inefficiencies in international markets. For a market to be efficient, information must be freely available, all participants must use the information similarly, and capital flows between investments must be free. In such an environment, perceived discrepancies in fiscal or monetary policies and their economic consequences in one country relative to other countries quickly would be reflected in interest rates and exchange rates so that international bond returns would be roughly equivalent over time. The more efficient the markets, the shorter the period of time required for returns to equate across markets.

While there is evidence to suggest the international bond and currency markets are becoming more efficient, they are still a long way from the relative efficiency of the U.S. market which benefits from the homogeneity of rules and regulations governing the investment community. In the international markets, the availability of information, particularly with regard to central bank policies, is much improved over earlier years but a variety of impediments prevent market information from being used in a similar fashion. Differences in tax treatment by countries, legal impediments which restrict the free flow of capital across borders, and differences in national character and institutions all create disparities in national investment postures.

A classic example of the inefficiency of international bond markets arising from differences in investment objectives is the case of Switzerland. For years the Swiss capital markets benefited from the country's reputation as a safe haven from the Cold War, and from strict secrecy laws which emphasized anonymity. The demand among private investors for Swiss franc-denominated assets and bank accounts meant Swiss interest rates were far lower than they otherwise would have been had investors been making the same analytical decisions regarding Swiss bonds as they were making regrading other international bonds. This is one reason for the unattractive total returns on Swiss bonds in the 1978–89 period. In the late 1980s, as the Cold War wound down and the secrecy laws that attracted dubious cash to Switzerland came under fire, Swiss interest rates rose to levels more in line with economic fundamentals.

The foreign exchange markets do compensate over time for the inefficiencies noticeable in various domestic bond markets, but in the short-term, currencies can actually magnify total return discrepancies. Economic theory teaches that interest-rate differentials and currency changes reflect differential inflation rates so that currency changes equal the difference in income factors. Historically high-inflation countries, such as Australia, with generous domestic bond returns due to high nominal income streams experience a loss in the value of their currency relative to moderate-inflation countries with lower domestic nominal bond returns. In this sense, currencies should smooth out international bond returns over time. Exhibit 51–6 illustrates this smoothing process for the 1978–89 period. Notice the greater discrepancy in the total domestic returns than in the returns converted into U.S. dollars.

Over shorter periods of time, however, foreign exchange movements often act counter to what theory would dictate. This is most apparent in the huge total return differentials in Exhibit 51–7. A myriad of special factors determine exchange rate movements in the short-term; inflation differentials is only one of these factors. Official foreign exchange intervention and different perceptions of political forces are among the many factors that distort fundamental exchange rate relationships. In view of these inefficiencies and the investment opportunities they present, active international bond investment can add incremental value to a U.S.-based portfolio.

## THE TOOLS OF ACTIVE MANAGEMENT

A thorough understanding of the components of total return and their interrelationships is important to any active international investor. As discussed earlier, three factors are in the return provided by international bonds—income, capital change, and currency. Of these, only income in local currency terms and the margin over the income bogey provided by U.S. alternatives are known initially, and even they are subject to change as exchange rates fluctuate. A positive yield advantage over alternative U.S. bonds will, over time, provide a cushion for deterioration in the domestic capital price or the currency relative to U.S. issues. By the same token, with time, a negative yield spread will have to be offset by relative appreciation of the domestic bond price or currency.

The shorter the investment time horizon, the less important is the yield relationship with U.S. bonds. Yield spreads are measured in annual terms so that a 2 percent yield advantage of French franc bonds over U.S. bonds means an investor in French bonds will come out ahead if, after one year, the French franc and French local bond prices do not deteriorate more than a combined 2 percent relative to the U.S. dollar and U.S. bond prices. If the investment time horizon is shortened to three months, the 2 percent annual yield cushion becomes a .5 percent quarterly cushion—a practically insignificant margin in the international bond markets in light of the potential volatility in currencies and relative interest rates that can occur over three months.

A simple, long-term strategy of investing in the highest yielding international bond markets normally is not appropriate for total return oriented investors. This is true for two reasons. First, high interest rates usually reflect domestic economic imbalances, such as inflation (real or perceived) or strong growth in the money supply, which can lead to an erosion in local bond prices. Second, high yields often are necessary to compensate investors for an expected decline in the relative value of the local currency. This is evident in Exhibit 51–6 where the four countries with the highest income streams—Australia, France, the United Kingdom, and Canada—all experienced a weakening of their currency versus the U.S. dollar. Over shorter periods of time, when foreign exchange movements and bond prices are not directly linked to domestic economic fundamentals but are a response to managed rates, a yield oriented investment strategy may be appropriate. This proved to be the case in 1988 in Australia where high yields and a strengthening currency led to generous converted U.S. dollar returns.

The factors that have a bearing on currency fluctuation, the second component of return, have been reviewed earlier. By and large, they relate to fundamental economic and political trends. From a practical viewpoint, there are two main problems in using these factors to project currency movements. One relates to the analyst's ability accurately to perceive trends not already efficiently reflected in the present currency price. The second relates to the interaction of these factors and the ability to project which factors will dominate. As pointed out earlier, the component of return provided by currency changes for an international bond index over long time periods has not been large. In Exhibit 51–4, the currency contribution to the index's total return for the 1978–89 period was shown to be two percent. Currency becomes increasingly important, however, as the time period is shortened. In Exhibit 51–5, showing annual returns of an international bond index, the range of currency contribution was shown to be from −11 percent to +25 percent. Currency changes can be even more significant for individual markets. Thus the international bond investor must be willing to make judgments on foreign exchange.

The third component of return, domestic price movements, must be analyzed both absolutely and relative to expected U.S. movements. There are substantial differences between various markets regarding the extent of government influence on the level of interest rates. However, the common key variables affecting interest-rate movements are generally viewed to be the following:

1. Monetary policy, particularly with regard to exchange rates
2. The level and direction of domestic inflation rates
3. Demand for funds, which is often related to real GNP growth
4. Supply of funds
5. Fiscal policy and budget deficits
6. Social and political developments

These variables must be analyzed to assess their likely impact on the direction of interest rates in each country. As in the United States, this analysis must distinguish between movements in short rates and long rates, which most often move in the same direction but not usually to the same extent. When the potential shape and movement of the yield curve in each country is projected, judgments on the appropriate maturity structure can be made.

Gone are the days when interest-rate projections could be made on a country-by-country basis with no regard to the impact of international economic developments on domestic bond prices. The past decade provides ample evidence of both the interrelationship between the interest rate and currency levels, and of the circular and interrelated nature of interest rates between countries with floating exchange rates. In the 1980 to 84 period, for example, domestic economic trends and apparent government desires would have suggested lower interest levels in a number of foreign economies, but record high U.S. interest rates precluded lower rates abroad without precipitating even further foreign exchange deterioration versus the U.S. dollar. In 1989, the surging Deutsche mark forced many European countries to keep short-term rates high relative to Germany to guard against currency volatility in the closely aligned European economies. Just as in the early 1980s, few projections of foreign interest-rate levels were made without reference to expectations for the United States; in 1989, analysts looked to Germany as well as the United States for a barometer of future world interest rate levels.

Clearly then, international bond portfolio management requires ongoing economic analysis and judgment to assess the prospective exchange rate and domestic price components of return. It is important to distinguish between these two components when making judgments about prospective total returns. Whereas the income component of return is predictable, exchange rates and domestic bond prices will change, and *they may not change in the same direction and with the same magnitude*. Active international investment requires separate judgments to be made about the attractiveness of the country's interest rates and its currency. There may be times when a bond market is attractive for interest rate reasons and unattractive for currency reasons. While one option in such a scenario would be to avoid foreign-pay investment until currency risk is deemed appropriate, another option would be to purchase the foreign bond and eliminate the foreign exchange risk by hedging the currency exposure in the forward currency markets. The procedure and the justification for currency-hedged bond investment are examined in the next section.

## CURRENCY-HEDGED BOND INVESTMENT

Foreign-pay bonds incorporate two kinds of risks: interest-rate risk, which is a part of all fixed income securities; and currency risk, which is unique to foreign currency-denominated securities. Once the decision is made to purchase foreign-pay bonds, the investor must decide whether the expected return from the foreign currency component of the bond is sufficient to compensate for the additional volatility inherent in a foreign currency instrument. The decision whether or not to adopt an open foreign currency position is easier to make if incremental return is the sole reason for international bond investing. However, international bonds also have important diversification benefits that result from both foreign interest rate and currency exposure. A decision to eliminate currency risk based on a pessimistic foreign currency projection will almost certainly increase the correlation of the non-dollar bond returns with the U.S. returns relative to the correlation of unhedged returns with the U.S., because foreign currency is a major factor behind the lower correlation of foreign-pay bonds with domestic bonds. This increased correlation may result in a higher overall portfolio volatility than if the position was left unhedged. This will be discussed after reviewing the mechanics of currency-hedged bond investing.

## Mechanics of Currency-Hedged Bond Investing

To purchase a foreign-pay bond, two separate transactions must be made. The bond must be purchased and then the currency in which the bond is denominated must be purchased to pay for the bond. If the decision is made to hedge the foreign currency component of the bond, a simultaneous sale of the currency purchased is transacted through the forward currency market.[8] In practice, the forward sale of a currency entails no money changing hands between the currency dealer and the investor. Instead, a sale price for the currency at some point in the future is agreed upon, and the investor commits to deliver the currency at that future point and at that price. The currency dealer commits to delivering dollars in return. In other words, the investor has locked in a sale price for the foreign currency thereby eliminating practically all exposure to currency volatility in the interim.

Currency exposure can be fully hedged using a series of forward exchange contracts matching each of the coupon payments and the final principal repayment when the foreign bond matures. Fully hedged investment is relatively unusual, mostly because investors rarely purchase a bond with the intention of holding it to maturity, but also because the liquidity of the forward currency markets beyond one or two years is fairly limited. The most common practice is to use rolling forward contracts from one month to one year in duration which may be renewed at expiration date. Rolling forward contracts are not perfect hedges because the price of the bond is difficult to predict at some point in the future, but the amount of foreign exchange exposure generally is quite small and has little impact on total return.

Hedged foreign bond investment reduces the currency volatility involved with international investing. Two components of return, income and currency gain or loss, become known quantities.[9] The only unknown is the local price change of the foreign bond. An investor can compare the foreign-pay bond yield combined with the known currency gain or loss embodied in the forward discount or premium with yields available on straight domestic bonds. This differential can then be incorporated into projections for foreign interest-rate

---

[8] Several currency-hedging alternatives are available although the forward markets are the most widely used for hedged investing. Currency swaps or options could also be used.

[9] For a more detailed analysis of forward currency contracts and the foreign exchange markets, see Roger M. Kubarych, *Foreign Exchange Markets in the United States*, Revised Edition, Federal Reserve Bank of New York, 1983.

changes relative to domestic interest-rate changes. If expected local currency returns in the foreign bond market are greater than both the yield give-up (if any) required to buy the foreign bond, and the forward currency discount (if any), then the hedged foreign bond is an attractive investment from a total return point of view. A simple example illustrates this relationship.

Assume that 10-year yields on United Kingdom (U.K.) bonds are 9.0 percent and 10-year U.S. bond yields are 8.0 percent. Further assume that the spot rate for sterling is 1.600 dollars per 1 pound sterling and the three-month forward rate is 1.595 dollars per pound—a .33 percent discount over three months.[10] The hedged U.K. bond return over a three-month period is as follows:

Income  +  Forward discount or premium  +  U.K. bond price change[11]

$$= 9/4 + (-.33) + \text{U.K. bond price change}$$
$$= 1.92\% + \text{U.K. bond price change}$$

The 1.92 percent known return from income and currency in U.K. bonds can then be compared to the 2.0 percent known income return from U.S. bonds (8 percent/4) over three months. The differential of .08 percent must be made up by price appreciation of the U.K. bond relative to the U.S. bond. If the U.K. bond appreciates by more than .08 percent on a relative basis, the currency-hedged investment earns a superior return.

---

[10] The discount or premium for the currency in the forward market is closely aligned with the yield spread on Eurodeposits of the same duration as the forward contract. In this example, three-month Eurosterling deposits are assumed to be 8.8 percent and three-month Eurodollar deposits are 7.5 percent. The discount is computed as follows:

$$\text{Spot rate} \times \left(1 + \frac{\text{Eurodollar rate} - \text{Eurosterling rate}}{4}\right)$$

$$= 1.600 \times \left(1 + \frac{.075 - .088}{4}\right)$$
$$= 1.600 \times .99675$$
$$= 1.5948.$$

Therefore, $1.5948/1.6000 = .99675$ or $-.33$

[11] These three components are not really additive since currency gain or loss should be applied to the income and local price change as well. Nonetheless, both these effects generally are quite small. More specifically, the actual formula is as follows:

Forward Discount or Premium + (Income + U.K. Bond Price Change)

$$\left(1 + \frac{\text{Forward Discount or Premium}}{100}\right)$$

Currency-hedged international bond investment reduces the decision to buy foreign-pay bonds to a projection of relative interest-rate spreads. If foreign interest rates are expected to decline relative to U.S. rates sufficiently to offset the net of the income advantage or disadvantage versus the hedge gain or cost, then hedged investment will augment total returns regardless of the course of the U.S. dollar over the holding period. The cost of the currency hedge generally is of only minor import when making total return projections, particularly over the short term.[12] In the above example, U.K. 10-year interest rates only have to decline 5 basis points relative to the U.S. to compensate for the cost of the hedge, an insignificant movement considering the lack of correlation between U.K. and U.S. local bond markets.

## Rolling Hedged Yields

When currency-hedged investment first became popular in the mid-1980s, reference occasionally was made to computing so-called rolling hedged yields on foreign bonds as a basis of comparison with U.S. bond yields. Rolling hedged yields are computed by adding the *annualized* discount or premium for the currency hedge to the yield-to-maturity of the foreign bond for an "all-in yield." In the above example using a U.K. 10-year bond, the rolling hedged yield is calculated as follows:

Yield-to-maturity of foreign bond + Annualized discount or premium

$$= 9.0 + -(.33 \times 4) = 9.0 - 1.3$$
$$= 7.7 \, percent$$

The rolling hedged yield of 7.7 percent on the U.K. bond could then be used as a measure of relative value versus the 8.0 percent yield available in the U.S.

The problem with using rolling hedged yields as yield-to-maturity equivalents is that rolling hedged yield calculations assume the cost of the hedge (i.e., the discount or premium) will not change over the life of the bond. This is almost assuredly not the case. Hedge costs vary directly with U.S. and foreign short-term interest-rate spreads. When the currency hedge is rolled out after

---

[12] Occasionally, hedge costs can be fairly high, particularly when short-term interest rates in the U.S. are low relative to foreign rates. In December 1989, three-month Eurosterling deposits were 15.2 percent and three-month Eurodollar deposits were 8.5 percent. A three-month sterling hedge back into dollars would have costed 1.7 percent. Nonetheless, this is relatively unusual and generally coincides with a time when the yield advantage of the foreign bond in question exceeds the U.S. rate by a large amount. In December 1989, 10-year U.K. government bonds yielded 10.5 percent and U.S. Treasuries yielded 7.9 percent.

each expiration date, the new hedge cost will reflect the prevailing short-term interest-rate spread, which may be very different from what it was when the hedge was last rolled. A rolling hedged yield is better used as a measure of the shape of the foreign yield curve relative to the U.S. yield curve than as a measure of prospective total returns.[13]

To restate, with currency hedged investment, the cost of the hedge and the income advantage or disadvantage of the foreign bond is known from the outset. The investor is left with the decision of whether the foreign bond market will have better local price appreciation relative to the U.S. market, and whether the expected marginal appreciation will be enough to compensate for any income or hedge costs that may accompany the foreign bond purchase.

## Hedged versus Unhedged Foreign Bonds

The ability to participate in foreign interest-rate cycles without the added volatility of currency movements is appealing from both a theoretical and a practical standpoint. Many analysts and portfolio managers have argued that currency-hedged investing is *a priori* superior to unhedged investing because of the former's more favorable risk/return characteristics over the long term. There is some theoretical justification to this argument for dollar-based investors. If forward exchange rates, which govern hedge costs, accurately reflect the expected average movement of foreign currencies versus the dollar (i.e., forward rates do not include an embedded risk premium or discount), then hedged foreign bond returns will be equivalent to unhedged returns over time. Research tends to support this theory, although, as was mentioned earlier, total return comparisons between foreign and domestic bonds, hedged or unhedged, are somewhat beholden to the time period chosen.[14]

The theoretical debate over the superiority of hedged or unhedged investment has little practical significance. In fact, the historical attractiveness of one

---

[13] This is true because hedge costs are a function of relative short rates and the yield spread between two 10-year bonds is a function of relative long rates. High rolling hedged yields reflect more positively shaped foreign yield curves which, taken alone, say little about prospective total returns.

[14] According to Salomon Brothers' "Nonbase Currency Government Bond Indexes," hedged non-dollar bonds had an 8.97 percent average annual total return in U.S. dollar terms for the 1985 to 89 period. Unhedged foreign bonds had an 18.83 percent average annual total return in dollar terms for the same period.

A Merrill Lynch study, using the January 1978–June 1988 time period, resulted in a 11.04 percent average annual return for hedged non-dollar bonds, versus 10.92 percent for unhedged non-dollar bonds. (See "How Strong is the Case for Currency Hedged Foreign Bond Funds?", *The Merrill Lynch Guide to International Fixed Income Investing*, Merrill Lynch, Pierce, Fenner & Smith Incorporated, February, 1989.)

form of investment over the other varies considerably with the base currency of the investor and the time period studied.[15] From a practical standpoint, the choice between currency-hedged and unhedged foreign bonds depends on the priorities of the international bond investor. For total return investors, whether or not to hedge is a function of the outlook for the currency in which the foreign bond is denominated. For passive long-term investors interested in lowering the overall volatility of a U.S. dollar portfolio, unhedged foreign bonds are the better choice. This is true because the currency component of unhedged bonds, which is eliminated in hedged bonds, means unhedged bonds have a lower correlation with dollar-denominated instruments. When added to a predominantly U.S. dollar bond portfolio, unhedged bonds are somewhat more effective diversifiers. For investors unable or unwilling to take currency risk but still interested in diversification, hedged bonds are an appropriate substitute.

## CONCLUSION

International bonds, both U.S.-pay and foreign-pay, represent a significant portion of the world's fixed income markets, and an understanding of their characteristics is important for all bond investors.

U.S.-pay international bonds comprise roughly 10 percent of the U.S. dollar bond market. Issuance and liquidity in these instruments has increased dramatically in the past decade, although continued growth in the Eurodollar and Yankee bond markets is subject to regulatory policies in the domestic markets, as well as the vagaries of the dollar and U.S. interest rates. Since U.S.-pay international bonds have particular appeal to non-U.S. buyers, knowledge of the reasons for this preference and an ongoing familiarity with the investment posture of non-U.S. buyers toward U.S.-pay bonds is necessary to participate effectively in this market.

Investors in foreign-pay bonds must consider income levels and prospective price movements both in absolute terms and relative to U.S.-pay alternatives. The outlook for foreign currency changes must also be evaluated. The evidence indicates that over the 1978 to 89 period, converted U.S. dollar returns for foreign-pay bonds were somewhat better than returns in the U.S. bond market, although during shorter time periods within that 12-year interval foreign-pay bonds sometimes provided inferior returns. The evidence also indicates that foreign-pay bonds converted to U.S. dollars combined with U.S. bonds gen-

---

[15] Hedged foreign bonds have been attractive from a risk/return standpoint for U.S.-based investors due to high volatility of the U.S. bond market. For investors based in Switzerland or Japan, however, hedged investing has been considerably less attractive because of the historically low volatility of Swiss and Japanese bonds. See the Merrill Lynch study cited in footnote 14.

erally would have reduced the overall volatility of a portfolio invested solely in U.S. issues and occasionally increased the returns. Although these facts by themselves have little repetitive significance, many of the factors leading to the low correlation in returns between the U.S. and foreign-pay markets continue.

Currency-hedged international bond investment has become increasingly popular in recent years as a way to participate in foreign interest-rate cycles without taking currency risk. Hedged investment is appropriate when the prospects for foreign bond markets are attractive relative to the prospects for U.S. bonds, irrespective of potential currency movements. While hedged international bonds have a greater correlation with U.S. bonds due to the lack of currency fluctuation, evidence suggests hedged bonds can reduce the volatility of a U.S.-based portfolio and occasionally augment portfolio returns.

There is no a priori reason to expect international bonds, hedged or unhedged, to provide superior long-term returns relative to U.S. bonds. To the extent that governments continue to remove the remaining constraints to world capital flows, fixed income returns and interest-rate volatility in the major markets can be expected to converge. In the meantime, the variance of monetary, fiscal, and political trends and policies between countries suggest there will be from time to time particular markets that offer better investment value than the U.S. market.

# CHAPTER 52

## INTERNATIONAL FIXED INCOME INVESTING: THEORY AND PRACTICE

*Michael R. Rosenberg, Ph.D.*
*First Vice President and Manager*
*International Fixed Income Research*
*Merrill Lynch Capital Markets*

In a recent Greenwich Associates study of institutional bond buying in the United States, two emerging trends appeared significant to the future direction of the fixed income investment business. According to the study, the primary trend emerging among U.S. bond buyers is the increasing globalization of bond portfolios. The secondary trend, which is directly related to the primary trend, is the greatly increased use of risk management instruments to deal with the risk and volatility of U.S. portfolio managers' increasingly diversified international bond portfolios.

These trends toward globalization and the more sophisticated use of risk management tools are growing at an increasingly rapid pace among European and Japanese investors as well and have caused a need for more detailed information on the theory and practice of global bond portfolio management. The purpose of this chapter is to address that need by critically analyzing the case for international fixed income diversification from a risk-return and active management standpoint, and by providing internationally minded investors with the basic tools to actively manage their global bond portfolios.

The chapter is divided into five sections. The first section examines the contribution that international bonds can make to the risk-return profile of a broadly diversified portfolio. Contrary to the generally accepted notion that substantial risk reduction opportunities are available, the evidence suggests that only a modest reduction in portfolio risk can be achieved through international diversification on an unhedged basis. The second section analyzes whether a stronger case can be made for international diversification on a hedged basis. Once again, contrary to the growing belief that hedged diversification guarantees investors less risk without sacrificing portfolio return, we demonstrate that if transaction costs and other fees associated with hedging are taken into consideration, international diversification on a currency-hedged basis may prove to be more expensive than not hedging at all.

The third section attempts to salvage the case for international fixed income investment by directing the focus away from risk reduction considerations and toward total return enhancement considerations. Sizable differences in total return exist among the domestic and overseas markets that, if exploited, can substantially enhance the total return prospects of an otherwise purely domestic bond portfolio. Thus, domestic investors will profit by viewing foreign bonds not as a *separate* asset class for *all* seasons, but as a *tactical* asset for *selected* seasons.

The fourth section provides internationally minded investors with general guidelines for setting up and constructing a global bond portfolio. The fifth and final section provides both a general framework for designing an active global bond portfolio strategy and a disciplined approach to assess the key decision criteria—the currency, market, and bond selection decisions—that global bond investors must address.

## THE CASE FOR INTERNATIONAL FIXED INCOME DIVERSIFICATION

Proponents of international fixed income diversification quite often point to reams of charts and tables that purport to show significant risk reduction possibilities from combining U.S. and foreign bonds in a passively managed diversified portfolio. Unfortunately, our research does not corroborate that evidence. Although portfolio risk reduction is possible through international diversification, our research indicates that the extent of risk reduction from passive management is fairly modest.

Exhibit 52–1 plots the cumulative total returns on U.S. and foreign dollar-denominated bonds from March 1973 (the beginning of floating exchange rates) to December 1988. U.S. bonds are represented by the Merrill Lynch Domestic Master Index, which includes government and corporate debt and, since 1975, mortgage securities. The foreign bond market performance index is InterSec Research's Non-North American Bond Index, a composite index, that measures the weighted average cumulative total returns of the German, French, Swiss, Dutch, Japanese, and British bond markets in U.S. dollar terms. Note that in Exhibit 52–1 the performance of the U.S. and overseas markets differed widely over interim periods: The foreign markets were stronger in the late 1970s, the

**EXHIBIT 52–1**
**U.S. and Foreign Bond Total Return Indexes (in U.S. Dollar Terms).**

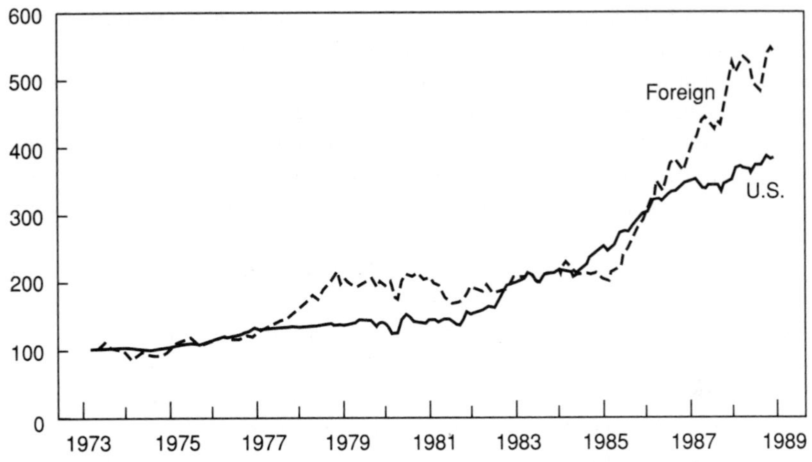

U.S. market was stronger in the early 1980s, and the foreign markets regained superiority during 1985–88. Over the entire period, the evidence shows that the average annualized return in U.S. dollar terms was 11.3 percent on foreign bonds and 9.0 percent p.a. on U.S. domestic bonds. We attribute that disparity to sampling error in the time period chosen for study. In the long run, there is no a priori reason why the expected return on foreign bonds in U.S. dollar terms should be higher or lower than the expected return on U.S. domestic bonds. Indeed, as Exhibit 52–1 shows, as recently as 1986 the cumulative returns were identical.

However, the evidence shows that the volatility of foreign bond market returns in U.S. dollar terms has been considerably greater than the volatility of U.S. domestic bond market returns. Between March 1973 and December 1988, the standard deviation of monthly returns was 12.4 percent on dollar-denominated foreign bonds whereas it was 7.1 percent on U.S. domestic bonds. The roughly 75 percent difference in volatility entirely was due to the impact of the dollar's volatility; in fact, foreign bond market returns in local currency terms were, on average, only half as volatile as U.S. bond market returns.

Although foreign bonds in U.S. dollar terms were more volatile than U.S. domestic bonds, it was still possible to combine foreign bonds with U.S. domestic bonds in a diversified bond portfolio to reduce overall portfolio risk, because the returns on U.S. and foreign bonds did not show a high positive correlation. The evidence shows that the average correlation of monthly U.S. and foreign bond returns for the 1973–88 period was only 0.34.

Exhibit 52–2 shows how much portfolio risk could have been reduced through passive international diversification on an unhedged basis. This graph demonstrates how an investor could have varied the allocation of an internationally diversified bond portfolio between dollar and nondollar bonds from March 1973 to December 1988 to achieve a certain level of return for a given level of risk. For example, if a U.S. investor had committed 100 percent of his or her funds to the U.S. domestic bond market, the average annual return would have been 9.0 percent and the annualized standard deviation of monthly returns would have been 7.1 percent. Allocating 10 percent of his or her funds to foreign bonds and leaving the balance in U.S. domestic bonds would have yielded a slightly higher annual return of 9.3 percent, with a portfolio standard deviation of 6.9 percent. That constitutes a 0.2 percent reduction in portfolio volatility from the 100 percent U.S. allocation case. At an 80 percent U.S. domestic, 20 percent nondollar mix, the average annual return would have been 9.6 percent, with the annualized portfolio standard deviation remaining at 6.9 percent. At that allocation, overall portfolio risk would have been minimized. Any commitment to foreign bonds beyond 20 percent would have increased portfolio risk.

The extent of risk reduction from passive international fixed income diversification appears quite modest, so much so that it hardly seems worthwhile. In fact, one major U.S. pension consultant, after examining the historical evidence,

**EXHIBIT 52–2**

**Passive Portfolio of U.S. and Foreign Bonds: Risk-Return Trade-off (1973–1988).**

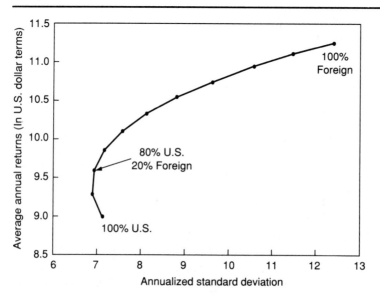

concluded that "nondollar bond investment is a diversification opportunity that U.S. investors can afford to pass up, especially those with smaller funds and limited resources for the conduct of their investment program."

## THE CASE FOR CURRENCY HEDGED FOREIGN BONDS

In order to salvage the case for nondollar bonds, a number of analysts have argued for hedged rather than unhedged foreign bonds in U.S. portfolios. Those analysts contend that because currency volatility adds to the volatility of a foreign bond portfolio, hedging away currency risk in the forward exchange market should render hedged foreign bonds less volatile than unhedged foreign bonds. At the same time, currency hedging should not involve any loss of long-term expected return, assuming no risk premium is embedded in forward exchange rates. Taken together, a policy of purchasing hedged foreign bonds should offer greater risk reduction with no loss of expected return compared to traditional unhedged international diversification. That assessment has led a number of observers to conclude that hedged foreign bonds offer U.S. investors a free lunch.

Had U.S. investors bought the idea of currency-hedged foreign bonds during the past ten years, they would have received a free lunch, as the historical evidence clearly shows (see Exhibit 52–3a). The return on hedged nondollar bonds (11.0% p.a.) over the 1978–88 period closely matched the return on unhedged nondollar bonds (10.9% p.a.), but the monthly annualized standard deviation of return on hedged foreign bonds was significantly lower than the comparable volatility of unhedged foreign bonds (5.92% vs. 13.6%). As Exhibit 52-3a shows, had U.S. investors diversified into nondollar bonds, they could have reduced portfolio risk by purchasing either hedged or unhedged nondollar bonds, but the extent of available risk reduction was much more dramatic for diversification into hedged nondollar bonds. In the case of unhedged nondollar bond diversification, the modestly lower overall portfolio risk was due to the low average monthly correlation between U.S. and unhedged foreign bonds (0.42). In contrast, in the case of hedged nondollar bond diversification, the dramatically lower overall portfolio risk was due largely to the low volatility of hedged foreign bonds (5.9%) compared to U.S. bond market volatility (10.6%).

Although the historical evidence indicates that a free lunch existed in the past, there is little reason to believe this free lunch will persist indefinitely. After all, one of the first basic principles we learn in introductory economics courses is that there is no such thing as a free lunch. We have always questioned the validity of the free-lunch hypothesis, largely because it cannot hold for all investors. Exhibit 52–3b looks at the risk-return trade-off that would have faced Japanese fund managers had they invested in hedged nonyen bonds. The evidence clearly

**EXHIBIT 52–3**
**(a) Historical Risk-Return Trade-off: U.S. Domestic Bonds versus Hedged and Unhedged Nondollar Bonds (Annualized Monthly Returns and Standard Deviations). (b) Historical Risk-Return Trade-off: Yen Bonds versus Hedged and Unhedged NonYen Bonds (Annualized Monthly Returns and Standard Deviations).**

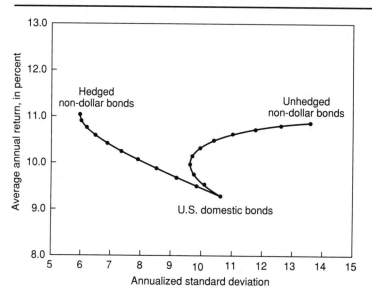

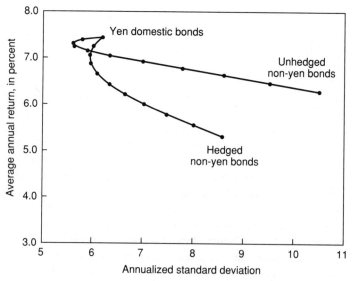

shows that hedged nonyen bonds fared poorly compared to yen domestic bonds in terms of both risk and return, which is opposite to the case for U.S. investors. The reason is fairly straightforward—U.S. domestic bonds were more volatile than their foreign counterparts in the past ten years, whereas Japanese domestic bonds were less volatile than their foreign counterparts. However, there is no reason why either of those trends must persist.

In fact, we attribute this lower average volatility of hedged foreign bonds relative to U.S. bonds to two factors that are unlikely to recur: (1) institutional rigidities, such as capital flow restrictions and heavily regulated capital markets, in a number of key overseas financial centers, which may have limited their volatility, at least artificially, and (2) monetary policies in the late 1970s and early 1980s in the U.S. that were more unstable than in Germany or Japan which accentuated the U.S. bond market's volatility.

However, we see changes on both counts that should lead to a worldwide convergence in bond market volatilities. Regarding the first point, we are presently witnessing a major liberalization and deregulation of many of the overseas markets. Regarding the second point, we see growing evidence of a convergence of world inflation rates and macroeconomic policies. Even if economic policies were to diverge again in the future, without perfect foresight it is not certain which country or countries will be pursuing more unstable policies in the future. In fact, the evidence shows that, on average, since 1985, Japanese bonds have been more volatile than U.S. bonds, and in 1990 German bonds have become more volatile than U.S. bonds.

It is more reasonable to assume not only that long-term expected returns should be the same across markets, but that their expected risks should be the same as well. If we make the assumption that both the expected returns and expected volatilities will be the same on U.S. and hedged foreign bonds, it can be shown that it makes no difference in terms of long-term risk reduction whether or not a foreign bond portfolio is hedged.

Consider the assumptions outlined in Exhibit 52–4. We assume that the expected return on passive portfolios of U.S. bonds and hedged and unhedged foreign bonds will be at 9.3 percent p.a., which was the U.S. average annualized historical return over the 1978–88 period. We also assume that the historical volatilities of U.S. and unhedged foreign bonds (10.6% and 13.6%, respectively) continue to prevail. In addition, we make the assumption that the expected future volatility of hedged foreign bonds will be 10.62 percent, which matches the U.S. historical average volatility but far exceeds that market's own historical average volatility of 5.9 percent. It is really not important to this exercise which level of expected future volatility is assumed as long as the expected volatilities of U.S. and hedged foreign bonds are assumed to be the same. Finally, we also assume that the average historical correlations between U.S. bonds and hedged and unhedged foreign bonds will continue to prevail. Note that the monthly correlation of U.S. bond returns with unhedged foreign bond returns was 0.42, which was significantly lower than the 0.54 correlation

**EXHIBIT 52–4**
**Theoretical Long-Run Expected Returns, Standard Deviations, and Correlations for U.S. Domestic, Hedged Nondollar and Unhedged Nondollar Bonds**

| | Expected Return | Expected Standard Deviation | Correlation with U.S. Bonds |
|---|---|---|---|
| U.S. Domestic Bonds | 9.3* | 10.62* | 1.00* |
| Hedged Nondollar Bonds | 9.3 | 10.62 | 0.54* |
| Unhedged Nondollar Bonds | 9.3 | 13.57* | 0.42* |

\* Historic Average

of U.S. bond returns with hedged foreign bond returns. This is because currency fluctuations reduce the degree to which the U.S. and foreign markets covary. This suggests that although unhedged foreign bonds will tend to be more volatile than their hedged counterparts, because of currency volatility, unhedged foreign bonds have the upper hand over hedged foreign bonds because they are more efficient diversifiers when a combined U.S.–foreign bond portfolio is created.

If these assumptions are plausible, then the diversification benefits derived from portfolio combinations of U.S. and hedged foreign bonds can be shown to be the same as those derived from portfolio combinations of U.S. and unhedged foreign bonds. This is demonstrated in Exhibit 52–5—whichever diversification route is taken, the same minimum risk portfolio results. Hedged foreign bonds have an advantage over their unhedged counterparts in that they are less volatile, but unhedged foreign bonds have an advantage over their hedged counterparts in that they are more efficient diversifiers. When combined with U.S. bonds, both advantages cancel each other out, such that hedged and unhedged foreign bonds offer the same long-term risk reduction benefits.

That analysis leads to what I humbly term *Rosenberg Proposition I*.

*Rosenberg Proposition I*
*In a world free of transaction costs, the amount of risk reduction available from international bond diversification in the long run is independent of whether or not currency risk is hedged.*

Followers of finance theory will recognize this to be a paraphrase of the famous Modigliani-Miller proposition that the value of the firm is independent of its

**EXHIBIT 52–5**

**Alternative Paths to Achieve the Minimum Risk Portfolio Through Diversified Combinations of U.S. and Hedged/Unhedged Foreign Bonds.**

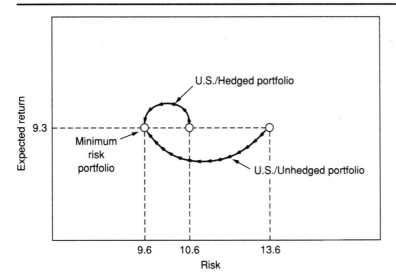

capital structure (debt/equity mix). The conclusion from Rosenberg Proposition I is that hedged international fixed income diversification offers no advantage over unhedged international fixed income diversification. Unfortunately, the story does not end there because there are transaction costs and other fees associated with continuously hedging a foreign bond portfolio. Exhibit 52–6 lists the extra costs and fees associated with always hedging an otherwise passively managed foreign bond portfolio. Those include (1) the execution costs of buying and selling forward exchange (in terms of bid-ask spreads); (2) additional set-

**EXHIBIT 52–6**

**Additional Costs Associated with Managing a Continuously Hedged Foreign Bond Portfolio**

|  | Cost in Basis Points |
|---|---|
| Execution Costs | 12–25 |
| Settlement Costs | 5–25 |
| Management Fees | 10 |
| Total | 27–60 |

Source: Ennis, Knupp & Assoc.

tlement costs in the form of custodial fees; and (3) additional management fees, because a continuously hedged foreign bond portfolio, unlike a passively managed unhedged foreign bond portfolio, requires constant rollover of short-term hedges. Ennis, Knupp and Associates, a U.S. pension consultant, estimates the additional costs to be 30–60 basis points. First Chicago Investment Advisors estimates the additional costs to be 40–50 basis points if the forward hedges are rolled over on a monthly basis. Those additional costs and fees must then be subtracted from the expected return on hedged foreign bonds, and the resulting net return can then be compared to U.S. and unhedged foreign bond market returns. If we factor that lower expected return into the theoretical diversification exercise described in Exhibit 52–5, it becomes evident that the unhedged foreign bond diversification route will yield a higher expected return for the same level of risk than the hedged foreign bond diversification route.

That leads to what I have termed **Rosenberg Proposition II**.

### Rosenberg Proposition II
*In a world where transaction costs and management fees are not insignificant, hedged foreign bonds will be a more expensive means than unhedged foreign bonds to achieve risk reduction.*

Thus, our findings suggest that from a long-term perspective, instead of offering a free lunch, currency hedging may prove to be a more expensive lunch than if one never hedged at all. This does not mean that we do not favor hedging at all. What it does mean is that we favor hedging only on a selective basis when conditions warrant it. Pursuing an alternative policy of continuously hedging will prove to be a costly means to achieve guaranteed long-term risk reduction.

## THE CASE FOR ACTIVE MANAGEMENT

If a strong case cannot be made for currency-hedged foreign bonds, can the case for international fixed income diversification be salvaged? The answer to that question is an emphatic "yes." If we are to build a case for nondollar bonds, we must admit that, in terms of reducing portfolio risk, the benefits of passive international fixed income diversification are limited, whether or not the underlying foreign currency exposure is hedged. Instead, the case for international fixed income diversification needs to be directed away from risk-reduction considerations and toward total return enhancement considerations. Foreign bonds offer U.S. investors a unique opportunity to enhance the return on their U.S. fixed income portfolios, but that return enhancement opportunity is available only through successful active management. It is widely recognized that the differences in total return performance among the competing subsectors of the U.S. domestic bond market are relatively small when compared to the sizable differences in performance that exist between the U.S. and overseas markets. If U.S. fund managers can exploit such differences by correctly shifting their portfolios from U.S. to foreign bonds and then back when conditions warrant, then there will be great interest in the use of foreign bonds, not as a separate asset class for all seasons, but as a tactical asset for selected reasons.

One way of measuring the total return opportunity set available to international investors is to examine the total return spread between the best- and worst-performing markets over time. The difference between the best and worst performers gives some indication of the return that could have been earned if an investor had correctly underweighted the weak markets and overweighted the strong markets. Another way of measuring the total return opportunity set is to examine the total return spread between the strongest market and the investor's homebase market.

Exhibit 52–7 shows the total return spread between the best- and worst-performing markets over the 1973–88 period, as well as the U.S. domestic bond market's total return over the same period. On average, there has been a 35–40 percent per annum difference (that is, 3500–4000 basis points) in total return performance between the strongest- and weakest-performing markets during that period. That suggests that there have been substantial opportunities to increase total return by correctly overweighting the strong markets and underweighting the weak. The U.S. domestic bond market was the best-performing market only twice, in 1982 and 1984. On three occasions — 1977, 1978, and 1987 — it was at or near the bottom of the international bond total return performance list. On average, the spread between the best-performing market and the U.S. market has been about 15–20 percent per annum. Thus, U.S. investors who

**EXHIBIT 52–7**
**Total Return Performances of the Best, Worst, and U.S. Bond Markets (Total Returns in U.S. Dollar Terms), 1973–1988.**

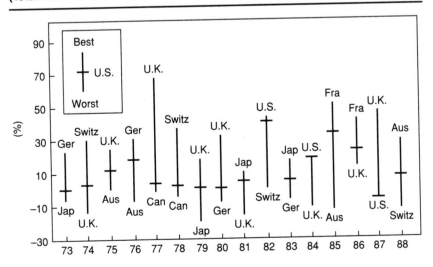

could correctly forecast market performance could have significantly enhanced their total return performance had they taken a global perspective in their bond investment decisions.

If U.S. bond investors accept the notion that the tactical use of foreign bonds can help boost the performance of their domestic portfolios, then we should expect to see a growing number of U.S. fund managers selectively adding foreign bonds in an aggressive manner to help them outperform their domestic benchmark, such as the Merrill Lynch Domestic Master Index or the Shearson Lehman Government Corporate Bond Index. In fact, we believe that the way the international fixed income investment game is played in the U.S. will change radically in the coming years, from a dedicated international bond management strategy that treats foreign bonds as a *separate* asset class to one that treats foreign bonds as a tactical asset to help domestic-oriented investors outperform their domestic benchmark and competition. To get an idea of how U.S. fund managers may use foreign bonds on a tactical basis, let's consider the following exercise.

Consider a hypothetical U.S. domestic bond fund that establishes internal investment policy guidelines in the following manner: The fund will allocate 20 percent of its portfolio to foreign bonds and the remainder to U.S. domestic and corporate bonds when it is believed that the dollar is trending lower. When the dollar is trending higher, the fund will allocate 100 percent to U.S. domestic bonds (see Exhibit 52–8). To determine whether the dollar's trend is up or down, a simple trading rule is followed. If the dollar's trade-weighted value on a monthly average basis lies below its twelve-month moving average, the dollar's trend is considered to be down, and vice versa. Hence, the crossover of the one- and twelve-month moving averages in the dollar's value is used as the criterion to adjust the domestic/foreign mix. Exhibit 52–9 shows that the dollar has had several major cycles in the past sixteen years. The one- and twelve-month moving average trading rule defines those broad cycles fairly clearly, although several moving average crossovers have proved to be false signals.

**EXHIBIT 52–8**

**Investment Policy Guidelines — Hypothetical U.S. Domestic Bond Portfolio**

*Recommended Allocation to Domestic and Foreign Bonds*

|  | Bearish on the Dollar | Bullish on the Dollar |
|---|---|---|
| U.S. Domestic Bonds | 80% | 100% |
| Foreign Bonds | 20 | 0 |

**EXHIBIT 52–9**
**Trade-Weighted Dollar—One- and Twelve-Month Moving Averages.**

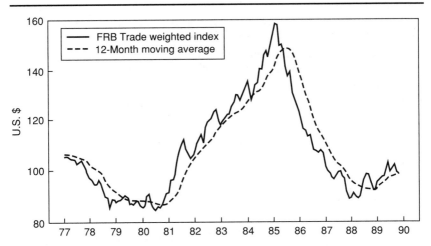

We have simulated the total return outcome (excluding transaction costs) that could have been achieved had a U.S. bond manager followed our trading rule over the 1973–88 period. Exhibit 52–10 shows the cumulative differences in total return performance between the Merrill Lynch Domestic Master Index and the active domestic/foreign bond strategy. It is assumed that a U.S. bond manager starts out owning 100 percent of the Merrill Lynch Domestic Master Index; then, when the trading signal indicates the dollar is heading lower, the manager cuts that position to 80 percent, with the remaining 20 percent allocated to the InterSec Non-North American Bond Index. When the trading signal indicates the dollar is headed higher, the foreign bond position is liquidated, returning the portfolio to the original 100 percent domestic bond allocation. Implementing that active domestic/foreign bond strategy on an ongoing basis for the period 1973–1988 yielded a total return of 10.85 percent p.a., which amounts to a 185 basis point p.a. total return pickup over the 9.0 percent p.a. return on the Merrill Lynch Domestic Master Index for the same period. The 10.85 percent p.a. return also compares favorably to the 9.6 percent average annual return that could have been earned on an 80 percent U.S./20 percent foreign *passively* managed global bond portfolio (see the first section of the chapter).

The preceding analysis highlights the importance of taking an active management approach to international fixed income investment and shows why total return enhancement issues should dominate risk reduction considerations in decisions about involvement in the overseas bond markets. The next two sections provide internationally minded investors with general guidelines for setting up and constructing a global bond portfolio and a comprehensive framework for designing an active global bond portfolio strategy.

**EXHIBIT 52–10**

**Total Return Performance on U.S. Domestic Bonds vs. an Actively Managed U.S./Foreign Portfolio.**

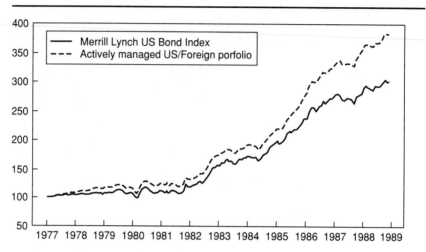

## GENERAL GUIDELINES FOR CONSTRUCTING A GLOBAL BOND PORTFOLIO

Managing a global bond portfolio is more complex than managing a domestic bond fund. Variations in government regulations, market practices, settlement procedures, yield conventions, and secondary market liquidity mean that the international investment manager must be thoroughly knowledgeable about numerous institutional details. Moreover, transaction costs in the form of commissions, taxes, bid-ask spreads, custody fees, and settlement charges differ widely among markets, so the international investment manager must have a thorough understanding of trading, regulatory and accounting practices as well. Finally, and perhaps most important, the international fixed income strategy process requires that the investment manager evaluate the complex interaction of currency movements, interest-rate changes, inter- and intramarket yield spread developments, and yield curve shifts in all of the major markets.

The investor's first step in setting up an international bond portfolio is to determine financial objectives. Some managers seek to maximize total return, whereas others seek to maximize income. Time horizons also differ widely among investment managers; some global bond investors may select a short-term time horizon to capture short-run swings in exchange rates or interest rates, whereas others may adopt a longer term to capture broad trends in currency and bond market movements. Management styles also differ regarding the level of portfolio turnover and the use of derivative products. Finally, investors with different base currencies may face different constraints on the investments they can make in other currencies.

The U.S. institutional investor market for nondollar bonds can be broken down into eleven investor types: (1) dedicated international bond mutual funds; (2) internationally dedicated accounts of U.S. pension funds; (3) active managers of U.S. domestic bond portfolios; (4) high-yield (junk) domestic bond funds; (5) the treasury departments of U.S. banks; (6) the treasury/cash management departments of U.S. corporations; (7) international property and casualty insurance companies; (8) global equity funds; (9) individuals; (10) municipalities; and (11) general investment managers. Exhibit 52–11 summarizes the broad investment objectives of those eleven investor types.

In the initial stages of setting up an international bond portfolio, the investment manager should draw up a delegation of authority list that indicates which foreign markets and credits will be approved for purchase. Based on an assessment of country and credit risk, as well as an assessment of tax and liquidity considerations, an approved list of issuers should be drawn up. Names can be added and dropped as conditions warrant.

For example, a risk-averse fund manager may choose to invest only in government and government-guaranteed issues. Another manager may approve the purchase only of AAA and AA corporate issues, and so forth. The delegation of authority list should also detail what percentage of the fund's assets can be assigned to any single credit.

Once it is clear which markets and credits will be approved for purchase, the international investor should select a global custody service (usually a large international bank with an extensive overseas branch and correspondent banking network) to arrange for the delivery and settlement of traded securities and foreign exchange, the collection of coupon income, the reclamation of any coupon tax due the investor because of double-taxation treaties, the maintenance of cash balances in various markets on deposit, the receipt of comprehensive and timely reports on portfolio activities, and the valuation of total assets under management. It would be wise for the investment manager to set up an internal bond operations unit to review all trade details (e.g. price, settlement date, and accrued interest), specify delivery instructions, and contact the global custody service to arrange for settlement and safe custody.

Once those housekeeping duties are fulfilled, the international investment manager should attend to the establishment of portfolio management guidelines for the distribution of the global bond fund's assets. Those self-imposed asset allocation guidelines should assign minimum, normal, and maximum positions that can be held in any single currency block or market. The purpose of the guidelines is to underscore the desire for diversification yet provide ample latitude for active management. For example, Exhibit 52–12 highlights the asset distribution guidelines for a hypothetical global bond fund. The guidelines define the proportion

**EXHIBIT 52–11**
**Types of U.S. Investors and Nondollar Investment Objectives**

| Investor | High Total Investment Return | High Current Income | Asset-Liability Matching | Exploit Positive Carry | Exploit Trading/ Arbitrage Opportunity | Manage Non-US$ Cash Flow |
|---|---|---|---|---|---|---|
| Individuals | • | • | | | | |
| Pension Funds | • | | | | • | • |
| Corporations | • | | | | | |
| Investment Managers | • | | | | • | |
| Municipalities | • | | | | | |
| Banks/Thrifts | • | | | • | | |
| Insurance Companies | | | • | | | |
| Global/Intl. Fixed Income Mutual Funds | • | | | | • | • |
| Domestic Fixed Income Mutual Funds | • | • | | | | |
| Domestic High-Yield Mutual Funds | | • | | | | |
| Global/Intl. Equity Mutual Funds | • | | | | | • |

**EXHIBIT 52–12**
**Asset Allocation Guidelines for Structuring
a Global Bond Portfolio** (Percent Breakdown)

| Currency Block | Minimum Position | Normal Position | Maximum Position |
|---|---|---|---|
| U.S.$ | 23.5 | 47.0 | 73.5 |
| Yen | 11.5 | 23.0 | 46.0 |
| DM, Dfl, SFr | 6.5 | 13.0 | 33.0 |
| Sterling | 3.5 | 7.0 | 25.0 |
| FFr, ECU | 2.0 | 4.0 | 20.0 |
| C$ | 2.0 | 4.0 | 20.0 |
| A$, NZ$ | 1.0 | 2.0 | 10.0 |

of the portfolio's funds that can be assigned to the major currency blocks: U.S. dollar, Canadian dollar, German mark, French franc, Japanese yen, British pound, and Australian/New Zealand dollars.

The weights chosen as "normal" should reflect the approximate relative current market value of each of the major markets in the total world bond market, or perhaps even better, the relative liquidity and tradeability of each market. If investors use a widely followed external benchmark for performance evaluation, such as the Merrill Lynch Global or Salomon Brothers World Bond Index, they might want to use the benchmark's fixed weights as the normal weights. The normal weights shown in Exhibit 52–12 are the market capitalization weights of all the key markets in the Merrill Lynch Global Government/Eurobond Index as of April 1989 (see Exhibit 52–13).

By assigning minimum and maximum guidelines in the manner shown in Exhibit 52–12, the investment manager places certain operational constraints on the asset allocation decisions. Within the limits defined by these guidelines, the investment manager is free to allocate funds among currencies and markets. Those markets and/or currencies expected to perform relatively favorably should be assigned portfolio weights in the normal-maximum range, whereas those markets and/or currencies expected to perform relatively poorly should be assigned weights in the minimum-normal range. The stronger an investor's conviction about currency and interest-rate trends, the more the assigned weight may lean toward the extreme end of the min-norm or norm-max range. Because the risk of being wrong must be factored into each investment decision, in times of uncertainty there is likely to be a tendency for the recommended portfolio weights to move closer to the market norm. That is consistent with the risk-averse behavior of most individual investors and portfolio managers.

**EXHIBIT 52–13**

**International Fixed Income Strategy Table—Recommended Asset Mix (Percent Breakdown)**

| Currency Block | Currency Decision | | Market Decision | | | Bond Selection Decision | | | | | | | Portfolio Duration | Portfolio Risk | |
|---|---|---|---|---|---|---|---|---|---|---|---|---|---|---|---|
| | | | | | | Maturity Structure | | | | | Sector Breakdown | | | | |
| | Net Currency Position | Currency Hedge | Gross Currency Position | Cash Equiv-alent | Bonds | 1–3 Years | 3–5 Years | 5–7 Years | 7–10 Years | Long | Govern-ment | Euro/ Foreign | Portfolio Duration | Currency Risk | Interest-Rate Risk |
| US$ | 49 *47* | 0 | 49 *47* | 24 | 25 *47* | 0 *17* | 0 *9* | 0 *5* | 21 *5* | 4 *11* | 25 *41* | 0 *6* | 3.3 *4.5* | 1.04 | 0.76 |
| C$ | 6 *4* | 0 | 6 *4* | 2 | 4 *4* | 2 *1* | 0 *1* | 0 *1* | 2 *0* | 0 *1* | 4 *3* | 0 *1* | 2.3 *4.5* | 1.50 | 0.77 |
| A$/NZ$ | 8 *2* | 0 | 8 *2* | 0 | 8 *2* | 4 *1* | 0 *1* | 0 *0* | 4 *0* | 0 *0* | 8 *1* | 0 *1* | 3.8 *3.0* | 4.00 | 5.07 |
| Yen | 20 *23* | 0 | 20 *23* | 8 | 12 *23* | 0 *5* | 0 *5* | 0 *5* | 12 *7* | 0 *1* | 12 *20* | 0 *3* | 4.5 *4.9* | 0.87 | 0.80 |
| European STG | 7 *7* | 0 | 7 *7* | 4 | 3 *7* | 0 *1* | 0 *1* | 0 *1* | 0 *2* | 3 *2* | 3 *6* | 0 *1* | 4.1 *5.6* | 1.00 | 0.73 |
| DM, DFl and SF | 8 *13* | 0 | 8 *13* | 0 | 8 *13* | 4 *2* | 0 *4* | 0 *3* | 3 *3* | 1 *1* | 8 *8* | 0 *5* | 5.7 *4.4* | 0.62 | 0.80 |
| FFr, ECU | 2 *4* | 0 | 2 *4* | 0 | 2 *4* | 0 *1* | 0 *1* | 0 *1* | 1 *1* | 1 *0* | 2 *3* | 0 *1* | 8.8 *4.4* | 0.50 | 1.00 |
| Total | 100 | 0 | 100 | 28 | 62 *100* | 10 *38* | 0 *22* | 0 *16* | 43 *18* | 9 *16* | 62 *82* | 0 *18* | 3.9 *4.6* | | 0.84 |

*Note:* Recommended portfolio weights are shown in standard type and the weights of the Merrill Lynch Global Government/Eurobond Index are shown in italics.

## A FRAMEWORK FOR FORMULATING INTERNATIONAL FIXED INCOME STRATEGY

This section describes a unique framework to assist investors in their formulation of a global bond portfolio strategy. The framework revolves around a strategy table, depicted in Exhibit 52–13, which highlights the key decision criteria that global bond investors must address. The strategy table breaks down the global fixed income investment process into three key decision criteria—currency, market, and bond selection. Each of those decision criteria can and should be treated separately in a forecasting context, but they need to be integrated in a portfolio construction context. In the analysis that follows, we show how to accomplish this integration process.

The strategy table shows how an investor's desired exposure to the individual currencies, markets, maturity categories, sectors, and market durations compares with the broad market capitalization and individual maturity category, sector, and duration weights of the Merrill Lynch Global Government/Eurobond Index. The recommended portfolio weights are in standard type and the weights of the Merrill Lynch Global Bond Index are shown in italics. How far investment managers will allow their portfolio stances to deviate from market capitalization weights will depend not only on their confidence about the general direction that currencies and interest rates may take, but on their outlook for yield-curve slope and sector-spread changes as well. We begin our analysis by focusing on the factors that determine an investor's optimal net currency position. We then focus on those factors that determine the level of exposure to interest-rate risk that an investor will desire across a wide range of markets. We conclude by showing how to combine currency and bond investment decisions in the portfolio construction process.

### Currency Decision

In a global bond portfolio context, currency and interest-rate decisions should be treated separately. In the strategy table, the currency and market decisions are clearly separated, with currency hedging driving a wedge between the two key decision criteria. By means of the currency hedge, an investor can simultaneously overweight (underweight) a market and underweight (overweight) the underlying currency.

The purpose of the currency decision section of the strategy table is to draw an investment manager's attention to his or her portfolio's net currency position or exposure. A portfolio's net currency exposure in a particular market equals the actual gross allocation to that market, adjusted for any currency hedges. From the strategy table, this is shown simply as

Net currency position = Gross currency position − currency hedge.

The net currency position of a global bond portfolio will be tilted in favor of one currency depending on the portfolio manager's opinion about the trend in exchange rates. To get a quick reading of how far each currency bet deviates from market norms, we introduce a summary risk measure called *currency risk*, which we define as the ratio of the portfolio's (recommended) net currency position to the benchmark index's market capitalization weight (see Exhibit 52–14). A reading above 1.0 for the currency risk measure indicates a willingness to bear more currency risk than that to which a global bond market performance index would be exposed.

By undertaking currency exposure that exceeds or falls short of market norms, investors are making relative value judgments, namely, whether one currency will do better or worse than another. In the aggregate, the composite currency risk of a global bond portfolio must equal 1.0, with those currencies enjoying a currency risk objective greater than 1.0 offset by those currencies with a currency risk objective less than 1.0.

The decision to set a currency risk objective at any particular level for any single currency depends on your outlook and conviction regarding the future path of exchange rates. There are essentially three inputs that investors need to determine their own optimal net currency exposures: (1) the projected change in currency values, (2) the projected local returns in each bond market, and (3) the levels of short-term forward premiums, which are known at the outset. To help explain how an investor can set optimal net currency exposures, let's assume a two-bond-market world consisting of the U.S. and German markets, where each makes up 50 percent of the global bond market. We will wish to have a 25 percent minimum exposure to each currency and a 75 percent maximum exposure. With two markets and the use of forward currency hedges, an investor can create four asset categories. (In an $N$ market world, an investor can create $N^2$ asset categories.) Those asset categories are listed in Exhibit 52–15, along with their projected total returns for a given investment horizon expressed in U.S. dollar terms.

## EXHIBIT 52–14

| Currency Decision | Portfolio Risk |
|---|---|
| Net Currency Position | Currency Risk |
| 49 47 | 1.04 |

$$\text{Currency Risk} = \frac{\text{Net Currency Position}}{\text{Market Capitalization Weight}}$$

**EXHIBIT 52–15**
**Asset Choices in a Two-Market World**

| Asset Choices | Projected Total Return in U.S. Dollar Terms |
|---|---|
| U.S. Dollar Bonds | $R_{US}$ |
| German Bonds | $R_G + DM$ |
| German Bonds Hedged into US$ | $R_G + FP_{DM}$ |
| U.S. Dollar Bonds Hedged into DM | $R_{US} - FP_{DM} + DM$ |

$R_{US}$ = U.S. local bond market return
$R_G$ = German local bond market return
$FP_{DM}$ = Short-term forward premium on Deutschemarks
$DM$ = Appreciation/depreciation of DM versus U.S. dollar

Given the four asset categories shown in Exhibit 52–15, there are two asset categories that allow an investor to have a net exposure to dollars: U.S. dollar bonds and German bonds hedged into dollars. Likewise, there are two categories that allow an investor to have a net exposure to Deutsche marks: German bonds and U.S. dollar bonds hedged into deutsche marks. If an investor wanted to make a currency bet in favor of the dollar (i.e. have a dollar currency risk objective greater than 1.0), two conditions would have to be met:

(1) The projected return on U.S. bonds must exceed the projected return on German bonds (unhedged) in U.S. dollar terms, that is,

$$R_{US} > R_G + DM$$

(2) The projected return on German bonds hedged into U.S. dollars on a rolling basis must exceed the projected return on German bonds (unhedged) in U.S. dollar terms, that is,

$$R_G + FP_{DM} > R_G + DM$$

If either of those conditions is not met, an investor would do better by making a currency bet in favor of the deutsche mark, either by buying DM bonds outright or by buying U.S. bonds hedged into deutsche marks. Let's assume that both conditions are met, and thus, in terms of setting strategy, we adopt a U.S. dollar currency risk objective equal to 1.5 and a deutsche mark currency risk objective equal to 0.5. Because an overweight net U.S. dollar position can be detained by being long U.S. dollar bonds or by being long German bonds hedged into U.S. dollars, it becomes evident that a variety of gross currency position/hedging schemes can satisfy those single currency risk objectives. This is demonstrated in Exhibit 52–16.

A net U.S. dollar currency position of 75 percent (i.e., a currency risk objective equal to 75%/50% = 1.5) can be arrived at by having a gross cur-

**EXHIBIT 52–16**

**How a Variety of Gross Allocation/Hedging Schemes Can Satisfy a Single Currency Risk Objective**

| Market | Currency Decision | | Market Decision | Portfolio Risk |
|---|---|---|---|---|
| | Net Currency Position (%) | Currency Hedge (%) | Gross Currency Position (%) | Currency Risk |
| U.S. | 75.0 | +50.0 | 25.0 | 1.5 |
| | 75.0 | +37.5 | 37.5 | 1.5 |
| | 75.0 | +25.0 | 50.0 | 1.5 |
| | 75.0 | +12.5 | 62.5 | 1.5 |
| | 75.0 | 0.0 | 75.0 | 1.5 |
| Germany | 25.0 | −50.0 | 75.0 | 0.5 |
| | 25.0 | −37.5 | 62.5 | 0.5 |
| | 25.0 | −25.0 | 50.0 | 0.5 |
| | 25.0 | −12.5 | 37.5 | 0.5 |
| | 25.0 | 0.0 | 25.0 | 0.5 |
| Total | 100.0 | 0.0 | 100.0 | 1.0 |

Assumption: U.S. and Germany make up 50 percent of the world bond market.

rency position or allocation in U.S. bonds of 75 percent; by having a 50 percent allocation to U.S. bonds and a 25 percent allocation to German bonds hedged into U.S. dollars; by having a 25 percent allocation to U.S. bonds and a 50 percent allocation to hedged German bonds, and so forth. Is there a difference in terms of total return outcome between choosing one particular gross allocation/hedging scheme over another, when the net currency exposure is the same? The answer is "sometimes." Remember that the decision to have an overweight U.S. dollar position depends upon the following:

$$R_U S > R_G + DM \qquad \text{Acquire U.S. dollar bonds}$$
$$\text{and}$$
$$R_G + FP_D M > R_G + DM \qquad \text{Acquire hedged German bonds}$$

If both conditions are satisfied, the appropriate method to obtain an overweight dollar position will depend on the relationship between $R_{US}$ and $(R_G + FP_{DM})$. If the projected return on U.S. dollar bonds exceeds the projected return on hedged German bonds, that is, if

$$R_{US} > R_G + FP_{DM}$$

then the optimal allocation will be a 75 percent exposure (our maximum required exposure) in U.S. bonds with nothing hedged. If the projected return on hedged German bonds exceeds the projected return on U.S. dollar bonds, that is, if

$$R_{US} < R_G + FP_{DM}$$

then the optimal allocation will be a 25 percent exposure in U.S. dollar bonds (our minimum required exposure) and a 50 percent exposure in German bonds hedged into U.S. dollars. If the projected return on U.S. dollar bonds equals the projected return on hedged German bonds, that is, if

$$R_{US} = R_G + FP_{DM},$$

then all gross allocation/hedging schemes will yield the same expected return, and thus, everything else being equal, investors who seek a certain currency risk objective will be indifferent as to allocation schemes.

In the final analysis, either the allocation/hedging scheme is irrelevant, or the optimal allocation scheme is actually a corner solution, where nothing or everything is hedged.

## Market Decision

The purpose of the market decision section of the strategy table is to draw an investment manager's attention to his or her gross currency position, or to the total allocation to each market and how that allocation is divided between cash and bonds. To get a more complete reading of a global bond portfolio's price sensitivity to changes in interest rates, we introduce a summary risk measure we call *interest-rate risk*. We define interest-rate risk in a given market as the ratio of the recommended gross currency position to the market capitalization weight multiplied by the ratio of the recommended portfolio duration to the market's average duration (see Exhibit 52–17).

By defining interest-rate risk in this manner, we highlight the fact that a global bond portfolio can achieve greater exposure to an anticipated interest-rate decline in a particular market in two ways, by increasing the size of either the gross currency position or allocation relative to market norms, leaving the portfolio's duration unchanged, or by raising the portfolio's duration relative to the market's average duration, leaving the gross allocation unchanged. Likewise, a global bond portfolio can achieve a reduced exposure to an anticipated interest-rate rise in a particular market both by cutting back the size of either the gross currency position or allocation relative to the market norm, and by lowering the duration of the existing holdings relative to the market's average duration. For an entire portfolio, the composite interest-rate risk is a weighted average of the interest-rate risks of the individual markets.

The decision to set an interest-rate-risk objective at any particular level for an individual market or for an entire multimarket portfolio depends on opinions

**EXHIBIT 52–17**

| Currency Block | Market Decision | | Portfolio Risk |
| | Gross Currency Decision | Portfolio Duration | Interest-Rate Risk |
| --- | --- | --- | --- |
| U.S.$ | 49 | 3.3 | 0.76 |
| | 47 | 4.5 | |
| C$ | 6 | 2.3 | 0.77 |
| | 4 | 4.5 | |
| A$/NZ$ | 8 | 3.8 | 5.07 |
| | 2 | 3.0 | |
| Yen | 20 | 4.5 | 0.80 |
| | 23 | 4.9 | |
| STG | 7 | 4.1 | 0.73 |
| | 7 | 5.6 | |
| DM | 8 | 5.7 | 0.80 |
| | 13 | 4.4 | |
| FFr | 2 | 8.8 | 1.00 |
| | 4 | 4.4 | |

$$\text{Interest Rate Risk} = \frac{\text{Gross Currency Position}}{\text{Market Capitalization Weight}} \times \frac{\text{Portfolio Duration}}{\text{Market Duration}}$$

regarding the future trend in interest rates. A reading above 1.0 for interest-rate risk indicates a willingness to bear more interest-rate risk than that to which a global benchmark index would be exposed.

An investor can obtain a desired interest-rate risk through a variety of gross allocation/duration schemes simply by altering the gross currency position and the portfolio's average duration in an inverse manner. To see that more clearly, assume that an investor wishes to have an overweight exposure to a projected decline in U.S. bond yields equal to 1.5 times the U.S. market's average exposure to yield changes, that is, the investor desires a U.S. bond interest-rate risk equal to 1.5. Assume that the U.S. bond market makes up 50 percent of the world bond market and that the average duration of the U.S. bond market is four years.

As illustrated in Exhibit 52–18, a variety of gross allocation/duration schemes can satisfy the 1.5 interest-rate risk for the U.S. bond market. For example, a 75 percent allocation to U.S. bonds, with the average duration of the U.S. bond holdings equal to four years (75%/50% × 4.0/4.0 = 1.5)

**EXHIBIT 52–18**
**How a Variety of Gross Allocation/**
**Duration Schemes Can Satisfy a**
**Single Interest-Rate Risk Objective**

| Market | Gross Currency Position | Portfolio Duration | Interest-Rate Risk |
|---|---|---|---|
| U.S. | 25.0 | 12.0 | 1.5 |
|  | 37.5 | 8.0 | 1.5 |
|  | 50.0 | 6.0 | 1.5 |
|  | 62.5 | 4.8 | 1.5 |
|  | 75.0 | 4.0 | 1.5 |

Assumptions: (1) U.S. makes up 50 percent of
the world bond market; (2) U.S. bond market average duration = 4 years.

satisfies the 1.5 interest-rate risk objective, or a gross allocation of 50 percent
to U.S. bonds, with the average duration of the U.S. bond holdings equal to six
years (50%/50% × 6.0/4.0 = 1.5) achieves this objective, and so forth.

If a variety of gross allocation/duration schemes generate the same interest-
rate risk, is there a difference in terms of total return outcome between one
particular allocation scheme and another? As was true in the case of currency
risk, the answer is "sometimes." The interest-rate risk as we defined it relies
on duration being a reliable proxy measure of the price sensitivity of a bond
portfolio to a given change in yield. Duration is widely viewed as a reliable
measure of interest-rate risk if it is assumed that the yield curve is flat and that
any yield changes that do occur are small and uniform across the entire yield
curve, that is, parallel. If those conditions are met, then it does not matter which
gross allocation/duration scheme is adopted, because the total return outcome
from the competing allocation schemes will be the same. If the yield curve
is assumed to be flat (with yields unchanged) the same standstill yield will be
earned along the entire maturity/duration spectrum. Thus, a small allocation/long
duration scheme will yield the same return as a large allocation/short duration
scheme.

However, if the assumption of a flat yield curve is relaxed, the standstill
yield on various gross allocation/duration schemes will differ. Consider an unchanging, upward sloping yield curve where the standstill yield on long-duration
bonds exceeds the standstill yield on short-duration notes. In that instance, the
standstill yield on a small allocation/long-duration scheme will exceed the standstill yield on a large allocation/short-duration scheme, even though both allocation schemes generate the same interest-rate risk. Thus, investors who expect
an upward sloping yield curve to exhibit little change, should use small allo-

cation/long duration schemes to meet interest-rate risk objectives. The opposite would be the case for a downward sloping yield curve environment.

Now consider the implications of a large parallel shift of a flat or upward sloping yield curve. As was true in the case of an unchanging upward sloping yield curve, the return on small allocation/long-duration schemes will once again exceed the return on large allocation/short-duration schemes, because small allocation/long-duration schemes offer greater positive convexity than do large allocation/short-duration schemes. Thus, assuming yield changes are large and yields move in a parallel fashion, the greater positive convexity of small allocation/long-duration schemes will lead to greater upside performance in a declining yield environment and less downside risk in a rising yield environment.

Let's now consider the possibility of nonparallel shifts. If the yield curve flattens because short-term interest rates rise relative to long-term interest rates or steepens because short-term interest rates decline relative to long-term interest rates, then the relative performance of competing gross allocation/duration schemes may differ considerably, even though they may generate the same interest-rate risk. In the case of a flattening yield curve, small allocation/long-duration schemes should outperform large allocation/short-duration schemes, whereas in the case of a steepening yield curve the opposite should be true.

## The Bond Selection Decision

When nonparallel shifts of the yield curve are anticipated, neither duration nor our summary measure of interest-rate risk may be adequate indicators of a bond portfolio's price sensitivity to changes in interest rates. In such cases, it may be more important to manage the maturity structure of the portfolio correctly than to get the portfolio's duration or interest-rate risk right. Therefore, in any bond investment decision, the summary measure of interest-rate risk—which considers only the gross allocation and the portfolio's relative duration—must be supplemented by comparing the portfolio's recommended maturity structure to the maturity mix of the benchmark index. That is why the strategy table breaks down the bond selection decision into component sources of bond investment risk. The bond selection section of the strategy table draws an investment manager's attention not only to his or her portfolio's average duration and how that compares to market norms, but also to the portfolio's maturity structure and how that compares with the maturity mix of the benchmark index and to the portfolio's sector breakdown (governments versus Euros) and how that compares to market norms.

## Tying the Pieces Together

In the preceding sections, we described the steps that investors should take in formulating their currency, market, and bond selection decisions. The strategy table helps investors formulate a global investment decision process by allowing them to assess just how far their currency, market, and bond selection decisions deviate from market norms. In this section, we show how those individual decision criteria can be integrated into the construction of a global bond portfolio.

An investor begins the process of assigning portfolio weights by setting out desired currency and interest-rate risk objectives for each market, with allowances made for any maturity or sector adjustments if changes are expected in yield curve slope or intramarket spread. How far the bets on currency and interest-rate risk will be allowed to deviate from market norms will depend on the investor's outlook and conviction regarding the future direction of exchange rates and interest rates.

The precise assignment of portfolio weights across currencies and markets must satisfy both the currency risk and the interest-rate risk objectives. The problem for portfolio managers is that a variety of portfolio weighting schemes can jointly satisfy any set of currency and interest-rate risk objectives. That is shown in Exhibit 52–19, which plots a range of currency risk and interest-rate risk measures between 0 and 1.5 for the U.S. dollar and the U.S. bond market on the horizontal axes and various gross currency positions or allocations consistent with those risk objectives on the vertical axis. Given a U.S. dollar currency risk objective of 1.5, for example, it is evident that a variety of gross allocation/hedging schemes can satisfy that objective—for example, a 75 percent allocation to U.S. dollar bonds with nothing hedged satisfies it, as does a 50 percent allocation to U.S. dollar bonds with an additional 25 percent coming from hedged foreign bonds, and so forth. Likewise, a variety of gross allocation/duration schemes can satisfy an interest-rate risk objective of 1.5—for example, a 75 percent U.S. allocation, with the portfolio's duration equal to the market's average duration, or a 50 percent U.S. allocation, with the portfolio's duration equal to 1.5 times the market's average duration, and so forth. As the shaded area in the graph indicates, a variety of allocations to the U.S. dollar bond market, coupled with selective currency hedges and adjustments to portfolio duration, can jointly satisfy both the 1.5 currency risk objective and 1.5 interest-rate risk objectives. Which gross allocation/hedging/duration scheme should be selected in constructing a global bond portfolio? The answer is fairly straightforward: The optimal allocation scheme is the one that maximizes portfolio return while satisfying the investor's currency and interest-rate risk objectives.

There are two important steps in deriving the optimal allocation scheme— the gross allocation/hedging decision and the gross allocation/duration decision. As we previously discussed, under certain assumptions it makes no difference which gross allocation hedging/duration scheme is selected to satisfy a desired set of currency- and interest-rate risk objectives, because they all should yield the same return. However, once those assumptions are relaxed, certain allocation schemes may yield higher expected returns than others, even though they may satisfy the same currency and interest-rate risk objectives.

**EXHIBIT 52–19**
**Integrating Currency and Market Decisions.**

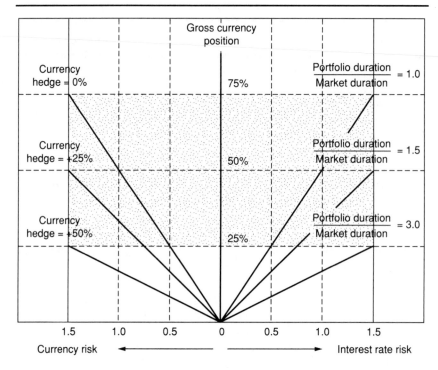

The best way to describe how an optimal portfolio allocation can be selected from a range of competing risk allocation schemes is through a simple illustration. As before, let's assume a universe consisting of the U.S. and German bond markets, where each makes up 50 percent of the global bond market. We wish to have a 25 percent minimum exposure to each currency and market and a 75 percent maximum exposure. Let's assume that, given our assessment and conviction of likely currency changes and local market return outcomes, we adopt a U.S. dollar currency-risk objective equal to 1.5 and a deutsche mark currency risk objective of 0.5. Let's assume further that interest-rate risk objectives of 1.0 are sought for both the U.S. and German bond markets. The projected local market returns for the U.S. ($R_{US}$) and German ($R_G$) bond markets are shown in Exhibit 52–20a along with the known 6 percent short-term forward premium on deutsche marks ($FP_{DM}$).

It is expected that the returns earned on U.S. and German bonds in local currency terms will amount to 10 percent and 5 percent, respectively. For now, let's assume that those returns will be invariant to the particular gross allocation/duration scheme selected; that is, we assume flat total return curves for both markets.

**EXHIBIT 52–20***a*
**Projected Total Returns on U.S. and Hedged German Bonds under Hypothetical Alternative Allocation Schemes**

| Asset Allocations | | Projected Total Return when U.S. and German Total Return Curves Are Flat | | | | Projected Total Return when German Total Return Curve is Upward-Sloping | |
|---|---|---|---|---|---|---|---|
| U.S. | Germany | $R_{US}$ | $R_G$ | $FP_{DM}$ | $R_G + FP_{DM}$ | $R'_G$ | $R'_G + FP_{DM}$ |
| 25.0% | 75.0% | 10% | 5% | 6% | 11% | 5% | 11% |
| 37.5 | 62.5 | 10 | 5 | 6 | 11 | 6 | 12 |
| 50.0 | 50.0 | 10 | 5 | 6 | 11 | 7 | 13 |
| 62.5 | 37.5 | 10 | 5 | 6 | 11 | 8 | 14 |
| 75.0 | 25.0 | 10 | 5 | 6 | 11 | 9 | 15 |

Given the 6 percent short-term forward premium on deutsche marks, the projected return on German bonds hedged into U.S. dollar terms is 11 percent (5% + 6% = 11%). Assuming that the dollar is projected to rise by 5 percent against the deutsche mark over the investment horizon, the projected return on unhedged German bonds in U.S. dollar terms will be equal to zero (5% − 5% = 0%). As shown in the total return analysis section of Exhibit 52–20*b*, assuming flat U.S. and German total return curves and a minimum 25 percent exposure to both the U.S. market and the German bond market on an unhedged basis, the desired currency risk and interest-rate risk objectives are satisfied, and total return is maximized by having a 25 percent allocation to U.S. bonds and a 50 percent exposure to German bonds hedged into U.S. dollars. That follows from the analysis described earlier when we noted that hedged German bonds would be preferred over U.S. dollar bonds outright if

$$R_G + FP_{DM} > R_{US},$$

while U.S. dollar bonds outright would be preferred over hedged German bonds if

$$R_{US} > R_G + FP_{DM}.$$

Given that the projected return on hedged German bonds equals

$$R_G + FP_{DM} = 0.05 + 0.06 = 0.11,$$

whereas the projected return on U.S. dollar bonds outright equals

$$R_{US} = 0.1,$$

it is clear that

$$R_G + FP_{DM} > R_{US}.$$

**EXHIBIT 52–20b**
**Asset Weighted Total Return Analysis**

| Assumptions | Total Return from U.S. Assets | | + | Return from Unhedged German Assets | | + | Return from Hedged German Assets | | = | Total Return |
|---|---|---|---|---|---|---|---|---|---|---|
| | Asset Weight | Total Return (%) | | Asset Weight | Total Return (%) | | Asset Weight | Total Return (%) | | (%) |
| U.S. and Germany Have Flat Total Return Curves | .250 | (10) | | .25 | (5-5) | | .500 | (11) | | 8.00 |
| | .375 | (10) | | .25 | (5-5) | | .375 | (11) | | 7.88 |
| | .500 | (10) | | .25 | (5-5) | | .250 | (11) | | 7.75 |
| | .625 | (10) | | .25 | (5-5) | | .125 | (11) | | 7.63 |
| | .750 | (10) | | .25 | (5-5) | | 0 | (11) | | 7.50 |
| Germany Has an Up-ward-Sloping Total Return Curve | .250 | (10) | | .25 | (5-5) | | .500 | (11) | | 8.00 |
| | .375 | (10) | | .25 | (6-5) | | .375 | (12) | | 8.50 |
| | .500 | (10) | | .25 | (7-5) | | .250 | (13) | | 8.75 |
| | .625 | (10) | | .25 | (8-5) | | .125 | (14) | | 8.75 |
| | .750 | (10) | | .25 | (9-5) | | 0 | (15) | | 8.50 |

Thus, the optimal allocation should be a corner solution in favor of hedged German bonds.

In this example, the specific allocation scheme that maximized total return was determined by focusing only on the optimal gross allocation/hedging scheme, because all the competing gross allocation/duration schemes must yield the same return if flat total return curves are assumed. However, if we relax the assumption that the projected local returns on U.S. and German bonds are invariant to the particular gross allocation/duration scheme selected, a different total return ranking among the competing allocation schemes will arise. Consider the case where, as before, the U.S. local bond market return (10%) is invariant to the gross allocation/duration scheme selected, but the German total return curve is positively sloped, that is, the projected return on small allocation/long duration schemes will yield a higher projected return than large allocation/short-duration schemes, even though the same interest-rate risk objective is satisfied. In Exhibit 52–20a, the projected local return on German bonds ($R'_G$) is shown to vary from 5 percent for large allocation (75%)/short-duration schemes to 9 percent for small allocation (25%)/long-duration schemes. As shown in the total return analysis section of Exhibit 52–20b, the desired currency risk and interest-rate risk objectives are satisfied and total return is maximized by having a U.S. dollar bond allocation equal to 50–62.5 percent and a hedged German bond allocation 12.5–25.0 percent. This more balanced allocation contrasts to the corner solution allocation (a 25% U.S. dollar bond allocation and a 50% allocation to hedged German bonds) in the previous example, because even though hedged German bonds have a higher expected return than U.S. dollar bonds under all allocation schemes, that is,

$$R'_G + FP_{DM} > R_{US},$$

smaller hedged German bond allocations (with larger portfolio durations) have a comparative advantage over larger hedged German bond allocations (with smaller portfolio durations) in an upward sloping total return curve environment. Thus, investors would do better to exploit the higher projected returns on such schemes. Although the projected 10 percent return on U.S. dollar bonds is lower than the projected returns on hedged German bonds (11–15%) for all allocations shown, the portfolio weight assigned to U.S. dollar bonds (50.0%–62.5%) turns out to be larger than the 25 percent U.S. dollar bond allocation when flat U.S. and German bond total return curves were assumed. The allocation to U.S. dollar bonds is larger because the currency risk and interest-rate risk objectives can both be satisfied with a higher expected return if a small rather than a large hedged German bond allocation is chosen.

## CONCLUSION

A global bond portfolio's currency and interest-rate exposure will be dictated by the investment manager's currency risk and interest-rate risk objectives. Although various portfolio weighting schemes simultaneously can satisfy both risk objectives, they may yield quite different returns. The analysis presented here reveals how a portfolio manager can find the particular weighting scheme that both maximizes total return and satisfies the investor's currency risk and interest-rate risk objectives.

# PART 8

# INTEREST RATE SWAPS, CAPS, FLOORS AND COMPOUND OPTIONS

# CHAPTER 53

## CUSTOMIZED INTEREST-RATE RISK AGREEMENTS AND THEIR APPLICATIONS*

*Anand K. Bhattacharya, Ph.D.*
Vice President
*Prudential-Bache Capital Funding*

*John Breit, Ph.D.*
Director
*Merrill Lynch Capital Markets*

In recent years, significant increases in interest rates and their volatility have resulted in a substantially higher exposure to interest-rate risk for manufacturing companies as well as financial institutions. This risk is especially severe for institutions that show a mismatch between the average duration of their assets and liabilities. In such cases, because the interest-rate sensitivity of assets and liabilities is not synchronized, any changes in market interest rates will have a disproportionate effect on the net worth of the institution. Given that direct restructuring of the asset and liability mix, which essentially involves changes in the contractual characteristics of such instruments, may not be always possible, institutions increasingly have to rely on synthetically managing the

*The views reflected in this chapter are those of the authors and do not necessarily reflect the policies or opinions of either Prudential Bache Capital Funding or Merrill Lynch Capital Markets. The authors would like to express their appreciation to Mark Jordan for assistance with the graphs in the chapter.

interest-rate exposure of the firm. In this chapter, we discuss the role of capital market innovations such as interest-rate swaps, interest-rate caps and floors (and derivatives such as interest-rate collars and corridors), and compound options in asset/liability management.

## INTEREST-RATE SWAPS

Interest-rate swaps constitute a contractual agreement between two parties to exchange cash flows at periodic intervals based on a notional amount. There is no exchange of principal; the swap transaction involves the exchange only of cash flows based on a notional principal amount. Besides determining the amount of cash flows to be exchanged, the notional amount also provides important documentation for corporate financial statements and helps determine the contingent liability of swap market makers. In the event that the market maker is a regulated financial institution, such as a bank, the notional amount of swaps is also relevant for determining capital requirements.

### Converting Floating-Rate Debt to Fixed-Rate Debt Using "Plain Vanilla" Swaps

The most common type of interest-rate swap involves the payment of fixed-rate cash flows, determined as a spread over the relevant maturity Treasury rate, and receipt of floating-rate cash flows, indexed off a floating-rate indicator, such as London Interbank Offered Rate (LIBOR), Treasury bills, Commercial Paper Composite, prime rate, Certificate of Deposit Composite, Federal funds rate, J. J. Kenney, or the 11th District cost of funds. Although the fixed rate at which the cash flows are determined is fixed over the life of the swap, the floating-rate cash flows vary based on the periodic valuation of the index at the swap reset date. Swaps may be structured so that the floating rate resets on a daily, weekly, monthly, quarterly, or semiannual basis for either monthly, quarterly, semiannual, or annual settlement. The settlement date refers to the actual date on which cash flows are exchanged.

Such swaps (fixed-rate payor–floating-rate receiver) can be used to convert floating-rate liabilities synthetically to fixed-rate liabilities, because the floating cost of liabilities is "counterbalanced" by floating-rate receipts associated with the swap. Any increase or decrease in liability costs is matched by a similar change in the floating-rate inflows, as long as the notional amount of the swap is equal to the principal amount of the liability. The net effect of this strategy is to lock-in the liability cost at a fixed rate.

As an example, consider the case of a financial institution issuing floating-rate liabilities that are priced at a spread of 10 basis points over three-month

LIBOR at a rate of 9.10 percent. The preponderance of the institution's assets, however, are fixed-rate instruments. As long as interest rates either remain stable or fall, the institution will be able to earn a spread over its floating-rate funding costs. However, if interest rates increase, the institution's spread will decrease. In order to synthetically convert the floating liability cost to fixed debt expense, the institution enters into an interest-rate swap for five years with another entity paying fixed and receiving floating cash flows. Suppose that the fixed-rate side of the swap is priced at a spread of 80 basis points over the five-year Treasury rate at a rate of 9.40 percent and that the floating side of the swap is three-month LIBOR at 9.00 percent. The funding cost to the institution in various interest-rate scenarios is illustrated in Exhibit 53–1.

In this example, if the institution had not swapped the floating-rate debt cost for fixed-rate cash flows, the liability rate would have repriced in every interest-rate scenario at a spread of 10 basis points over three-month LIBOR, assuming parallel shifts in the yield curve. By entering into the interest-rate swap, the floating outflow of the liability is partially cancelled by the floating inflow from the swap in all interest-rate scenarios. The net funding cost is determined as

floating-rate liability cost + fixed-rate of swap − floating-rate of swap.

The effectiveness of this strategy will depend on the extent of basis risk between the liability rate and the swap floating-rate index (usually LIBOR). In the previous example, because the liability rate and the floating side of the swap are both based on three-month LIBOR, there is no basis risk. However, in other instances, where the liability rate is keyed off another indicator, such as the Treasury bill index or the prime rate, the existence of basis risk may mitigate the swap's effectiveness. For instance, if the liability rate increases by

**EXHIBIT 53–1**
**Converting Floating-Rate Debt to Fixed-Rate Debt Using Interest-Rate Swaps**

| Interest Rate Scenario | Liability Cost | Swap Cash Flows | | Net Funding Cost |
|---|---|---|---|---|
| | | Fixed Outflow | Floating Inflow (LIBOR) | |
| +300 b. p. | 12.10% | 9.40% | 12.00% | 9.50% |
| +200 | 11.10 | 9.40 | 11.00 | 9.50 |
| +100 | 10.10 | 9.40 | 10.00 | 9.50 |
| Stable | 9.10 | 9.40 | 9.00 | 9.50 |
| −100 | 8.10 | 9.40 | 8.00 | 9.50 |
| −200 | 7.10 | 9.40 | 7.00 | 9.50 |
| −300 | 6.10 | 9.40 | 6.00 | 9.50 |

1 percent and LIBOR increases by only 0.85 percent, the synthetic fixed rate will be 0.15 percent higher than it would have been in the absence of such imperfect correlation. Conversely, if the liability rate increases by 0.85 percent and LIBOR by 1 percent, the synthetic liability rate will be 0.15 percent lower than the swap fixed rate. The synthetic funding rate will also be affected by any discrepancies in the repricing frequency of the liability and the reset period of the swap. Ideally, close synchronization between these dates will minimize the deviation of the synthetic liability cost from the swap fixed rate that occurs due to reset date mismatch.

## Converting Fixed-Rate Debt to Floating-Rate Debt Using Reverse Swaps

A similar strategy using reverse swaps, where the financial institution receives fixed-rate cash flows and pays floating-rate cash flows is used to convert the fixed cost of liabilities to a synthetic floating rate. In this case, the fixed-rate interest cost of the liability is offset by the fixed-rate inflow of the swap. If the liability rate is higher (lower) than the swap fixed rate, then the synthetic floating rate will be higher (lower) than the swap floating rate. A financial institution that has fixed-rate debt and a preponderance of floating-rate assets, such as adjustable-rate mortgages, collateralized mortgage obligation (CMO) floater bonds, or floating-rate notes may adopt this strategy to better match the average duration of their assets and liabilities.

As an example, consider the case of an institution that has three-year fixed-rate debt at a coupon rate of 8.85 percent. In order to convert this fixed-rate debt into floating-rate liabilities, the institution enters into a reverse swap (floating-rate payor–fixed-rate receiver) for three years. The terms of the swap involve paying three-month LIBOR and receiving fixed-rate cash flows at a spread of 65 basis points over the three-year Treasury yield at a rate of 8.70 percent. An illustration of this example is presented in Exhibit 53–2. An analysis of this illustration reveals that the effective funding cost is determined as

fixed-rate liability cost + fixed-rate of swap − floating-rate of swap.

The institution has converted fixed-rate debt to LIBOR-based debt at a spread of 15 basis points over LIBOR. A schematic of the cash flows involved in synthetically converting floating- (fixed-) rate liability costs to fixed- (floating-) rate funding is presented in Exhibit 53–3. Although the dynamics of the cash flow are essentially reversed, most dealers will charge a higher spread (offer side) for fixed-rate-paying swaps than fixed-rate-receiving swaps (bid side). This bid-ask differential, which is a function of variables such as hedging costs, dealer inventory, relative supply of fixed- and floating-rate payors in the market, conditions in the Treasury market, and quality spreads in the domestic and

**EXHIBIT 53–2**

**Converting Fixed-Rate Debt to Floating-Rate Debt Using Interest-Rate Swaps**

| Interest Rate Scenario | Liability Cost | Swap Cash Flows | | Net Funding Cost |
|---|---|---|---|---|
| | | Fixed Inflow | Floating Outflow (LIBOR) | |
| +300 b. p. | 8.85% | 8.70% | 12.00% | 12.15% |
| +200 | 8.85 | 8.70 | 11.00 | 11.15 |
| +100 | 8.85 | 8.70 | 10.00 | 10.15 |
| Stable | 8.85 | 8.70 | 9.00 | 9.15 |
| −100 | 8.85 | 8.70 | 8.00 | 8.15 |
| −200 | 8.85 | 8.70 | 7.00 | 7.15 |
| −300 | 8.85 | 8.70 | 6.00 | 6.15 |

international bond markets, is used to compensate the dealers for the market-making function.

In the foregoing discussion, it has been tacitly assumed that the payment frequencies and the payment basis of the fixed and floating legs of the swap and the liability being swapped are identical. Any differences in the frequencies or basis will change the net spread calculations. This observation also applies to asset swaps (discussed later). For example, in swapping a fixed liability to

**EXHIBIT 53–3**

**Synthetic Conversion of Interest-Rate Liability.**

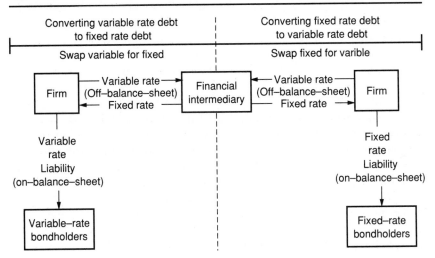

a floating-rate obligation, the net spread over LIBOR usually will be slightly different from the spread between the liability coupon and the coupon of the swap. This difference arises because swaps usually pay fixed on an $\text{actual}/_{365}$ or $^{30}/_{360}$ basis and floating on an $\text{actual}/_{360}$ basis. Hence, the net spread over LIBOR will be $^{360}/_{365}$ of the nominal spread between coupons.[1]

## INNOVATIONS IN SWAP MARKETS

In addition to allowing a firm to issue debt for which it has a comparative relative advantage and then swapping the cash flows to fine tune the asset/liability gap, interest-rate swaps also serve other useful purposes, especially due to the off-balance-sheet treatment accorded them. It often has been argued that swaps are preferable to refunding because the latter often is constrained by restrictive covenants. Periodically, firms may want to make adjustments in the capital structure with respect to the composition of debt by refinancing longer term debt with short-term debt at lower interest costs. In certain instances, this may not be easy to accomplish, especially if the debt is noncallable. Swaps provide an effective means to alter the covenants of a debt issue to accomplish asset/liability objectives without incurring the administrative, legal, and underwriting costs of issuing additional debt. In this case, the firm may swap the higher coupon debt to a cheaper floating-rate liability based on a variety of indexes, such as the Treasury-bill index, prime rate, and LIBOR.

In order to address such specific investor needs, several innovations, such as basis swaps, forward swaps, amortizing swaps, asset swaps, and swaptions have been developed over the last several years to further expand the degree of flexibility provided by generic swaps. A discussion of the salient features of these capital market innovations is presented in this section.

### Basis Swaps

Basis swaps are designed to manage the basis risk inherent in a balance sheet where the asset returns and liability costs are based on different indexes. For instance, a financial institution that invests in a CMO floater[2] with a return of 60 basis points over one-month LIBOR funded by six-month certificates of deposit at an interest cost of prime less 200 basis points is subject to basis risk, despite the minimal duration mismatch. This risk arises because the asset resets monthly off LIBOR, whereas the liability resets every six months based on movements in the prime rate. To alleviate this risk, the institution could enter

---

[1] A detailed treatment of swap mathematics is presented in the next chapter.
[2] Collateralized mortgage obligations (CMOs) are discussed in Chapter 29.

into a floating-to-floating basis swap, where the institution receives cash flows that are reset every six months at a rate of prime less 150 basis points and pays swap cash flows on a monthly basis indexed off one-month LIBOR. The basis risk will be controlled for the "tenor," or time period, of the swap.

As an illustration, assume one-month LIBOR is 9 percent and the prime rate is 10 percent. Without the basis swap, the spread earned by the institution is defined as the difference between the asset return and the liability cost, 1.60 percent (9.60% − 8.00%) in our illustration. For the sake of simplicity, it is assumed that the asset returns are not constrained by caps inherent in CMO floaters.[3] Assuming that the correlation between the prime rate and one-month LIBOR is imperfect, in that a 1 percent change in the prime results in less or more than a 1 percent change in one-month LIBOR, the spread will not be maintained in all interest-rate scenarios. As previously indicated, the institution enters into a basis swap to lock in the spread over funding costs without incurring the basis risk between the prime rate and LIBOR. Although basis swaps are used most often to refine the interest-rate sensitivity of assets and liabilities, these swaps can also be used to arbitrage spreads between various funding sources. The dynamics of the basis swap are illustrated in Exhibit 53–4.

## Forward Swaps

A forward swap allows the firm to initiate a swap with a specified delayed start. Such swaps can be used to hedge debt refinancings or anticipated debt issuance

**EXHIBIT 53–4**
**Locking in a Floating Spread over Funding Costs Using Basis Swaps**

| | | | | Swap Cash Flows | | |
| | | | | --- | --- | |
| LIBOR | Asset Return[a] | Prime | Liability Costs[b] | Floating Inflows[c] | Floating Outflows[d] | Net Spread[e] |
| --- | --- | --- | --- | --- | --- | --- |
| 7.0% | 7.60% | 9.5% | 7.5% | 8.00% | 7.00% | 1.10% |
| 9.0 | 9.60 | 10.0 | 8.0 | 8.50 | 9.00 | 1.10 |
| 11.0 | 11.60 | 12.0 | 10.0 | 10.50 | 11.00 | 1.10 |

[a] Asset return = LIBOR + 60 basis points
[b] Liability costs = prime − 200 basis points
[c] Swap floating inflows = prime − 150 basis points
[d] Swap floating outflows = LIBOR
[e] Net spread = asset return + swap inflows − liability costs − swap outflows

---

[3] The discussion of synthetically "stripping" these caps is explained later in this chapter in the section on *Interest-Rate Caps.*

in conjunction with expenditures expected in the future. For instance, suppose a firm has $200 million of noncallable fixed-rate debt maturing in three years. In order to lock in anticipated funding requirements three years hence for a period of five years at current rates, the firm could enter into a forward swap to pay fixed and receive floating cash flows starting three years from now. If rates have increased at the time of issuance, the firm would issue floating-rate debt and effectively convert the floating-rate funding to a fixed-rate liability, because the firm would be a floating-rate receiver.

From the dealer's point of view, there is a contingent liability to pay cash flows at an unknown floating rate. Assume that the three-year swap rate is 9 percent and the seven-year swap rate is 10 percent. A swap dealer enters into a forward swap to receive fixed in years 4 through 7 and pay LIBOR. The forward liability of the dealer is hedged by entering into swap transactions to pay fixed for seven years (receive LIBOR) and receive fixed for three years (pay LIBOR). This is illustrated in Exhibit 53–5.

In the first three years, the dealer receives LIBOR from the seven-year swap and pays LIBOR in the three-year swap. On the fixed side, the dealer receives 9 percent fixed in the three-year swap and pays 10 percent fixed in the seven-year swap. The net effect of these transactions is that the dealer makes a net payment of 1 percent a year for the first three years. In years 4 through 7, the dealer receives LIBOR from the seven-year swap and pays LIBOR in the forward swap. On the fixed side, the dealer receives the fixed coupon of the forward swap and pays 10 percent in the seven-year swap. The net effect of these cash flows is that the dealer earns a spread between the forward swap and 10 percent.

The forward swap fixed-rate coupon, F, is adjusted such that the present value of the 1 percent payments in the first three years is equal to the present value of earning (F% − 10%) in years 4 through 7. Although various dealers

**EXHIBIT 53–5**
**Pricing of a Forward Swap.**

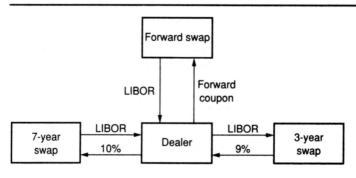

differ in the way these cash flows are discounted (some use zero coupon rates, whereas others use yield-to-maturity), the pricing of forward swaps always takes into account the cost-of-carry in the initial period. For this reason, forward swap rates are higher (lower) than conventional swap rates in an upward sloping (inverted) yield curve.

## Amorting and Accreting Swaps

In the preceding discussion, it was implicitly assumed that the notional amount does not change over the life of the swap. However, with respect to amortizing assets such as mortgage loans and other mortgage-backed instruments such as CMO bonds and automobile receivables, the spread over funding costs will not be maintained, because of the asset principal balance declining over time. This declining spread is especially critical for assets whose average life and duration may exhibit dramatic changes due to the possibility of prepayments. In such instances, if bullet swaps with the same notional amount are used, there is the risk of being either underhedged or overhedged with respect to liability costs. If interest rates decrease and prepayments increase substantially, the average life of the asset will shorten. In such instances, the asset may not generate funds sufficient to earn a positive spread. On the other hand, if interest rates rise and prepayments slow down, resulting in an extension of the average life of the asset, the swap may have to be extended or additional swap coverage obtained (at higher cost, due to bearish interest rate conditions) to maintain a positive spread.

In such instances, the institution may enter into an amortizing swap, which permits the notional amount of the swap, and hence the exchange of the cash flows, to change in accordance with the amortization rate of the asset. Note that the amortization rate of the notional amount cannot usually be changed over the life of the swap. Because the amortizing swap can be replicated by using a strip of swaps, the swap rate is determined as a blended rate of individual bullet swap rates. This feature of amortizing swaps also provides the firm with the choice of entering into a series of swaps to match the amortization rate of assets or entering into an amortizing swap at an annual blended rate.

Although amortizing swaps improve the match between the asset and hedged liability cash flows, such swaps do not completely alleviate the risk of being overhedged with respect to liability costs. A major portion of this risk is mitigated for assets such as Planned Amortization Class (PAC) CMO bonds, which provide for a specified amortization rate within a wide band of prepayment scenarios. For assets that exhibit a higher degree of prepayment volatility, if falling interest rates lead to an increase in prepayments and an attendant shortening of average life, the firm may have to continue exchanging swap cash flows for a period longer than the average life of the asset, unless the swap can be terminated.

In instances where the liability schedule is expected to increase, an interest-rate-swap with an accreting balance may be used to fix the interest cost of the liabilities. Perhaps the most common example of this type of swap application is found in the construction industry, where accreting swaps may be used to fix the rate on a project funded with a floating-rate drawdown facility.

## Swaptions

Swaptions are representative of the new class of second generation derivative products that have developed around the swaps, caps, and floor markets. Swaptions can take many forms, but typically they are options to pay or receive a predetermined fixed rate in exchange for LIBOR at some time in the future. As the market develops, it is likely that additional variable-rate indexes will be used to determine floating-rate cash flows. Alternatively, swaptions can contain an option to cancel an existing swap. The second structure is essentially the same as the first, because a swap can be canceled by entering into a new swap in the opposite direction.

In view of this overlap between options to enter swaps and options to cancel swaps, the usual shorthand terminology of puts and calls is rarely used for swaptions. Rather, the option characteristic is spelled out in more detail, for instance, an option to receive fixed at 9 percent for three years, starting two years hence. Swaption exercise can be European (exercisable on only one date in the future) or American (exercisable on any date up to and including the expiration date), with the bulk of the interbank market for European exercise. A typical American swaption structure would be to enter, say a seven-year swap paying fixed at 9 percent at any time before maturity. As an example, if the option is exercised after one year, the option holder will pay 9 percent and receive LIBOR for six years.

In terms of flexibility and costs, swaptions lie between swaps and customized interest-rate protection instruments, such as caps and floors. If LIBOR increases, the fixed payor of a swap, the holder of an option to pay fixed, and the cap buyer all benefit equally. If LIBOR decreases, the fixed payor of a swap incurs an opportunity loss and the holder of the swaption or cap loses only the up-front premium. The premium for a cap is greater than that for a swaption because the buyer of the cap essentially has purchased a strip of options, whereas the holder of a swaption owns only one option. If rates increase and the swaption is exercised, the owner of the swaption is exposed to the risk of a fall in interest rates. However, the holder of the cap can still take advantage of the beneficial movement in rates. In view of this observation, swaptions can be viewed as instruments that provide some of the protection and flexibility afforded by caps and floors.

The pricing of swaptions is still somewhat of an art. The development of models for pricing and hedging swaptions is on the cutting edge of options theory. Dealers differ greatly in the models they use to price such options, and the analytical tools range from modified Black-Scholes models to binomial lattice versions to systems based upon Monte Carlo simulations.[4] As a result, bid-ask spreads are wide, and it pays to shop around, particularly for more complicated structures that cannot be backed off in the interbank markets.

Swaptions provide the sophisticated firm with an additional, flexible tool for asset/liability management. On the liability side, the primary uses of swaptions have been in hedging uncertain funding requirements and issuing synthetically callable debt. With respect to fixing liability costs, a corporation can lock in coupon rates for future funding by paying fixed in a forward swap. However, the firm may desire to preserve the opportunity to save on these funding costs in the event that rates decline in the future by purchasing a swaption, despite the attractiveness of the current interest-rate structure. In the event that funding requirements are uncertain, the flexibility of these instruments really comes into play as swaptions can lock in current rates without committing the firm to future borrowing.

Much of the current activity in swaptions has been fueled by an arbitrage between the swaption and callable bond markets. Historically, investors have not demanded full compensation for call options embedded in corporate bonds. Hence, corporations can issue callable debt and then effectively strip off the embedded call option by writing a swaption, thereby lowering the all-in cost of the debt. On the asset side (see the discussion of asset swaps below), the primary use of swaptions has been in hedging prepayable swapped assets, such as mortgage-backed instruments. An investor may purchase fixed-rate mortgage-backed securities, swap the fixed-rate to floating, and earn an attractive spread over LIBOR. However, this spread is subject to erosion if the asset balance declines due to high prepayments. By giving up some of this spread and purchasing swaptions, the investor can reduce prepayment risk exposure.

## Asset Swaps

The foregoing discussion has focused exclusively on the use of interest-rate swaps and associated issues in swap-based liability hedging. Asset-based swaps, which use principles involved in liability hedging, are becoming increasingly popular to customize asset coupons and maturities, thereby expanding the asset universe available to portfolio managers. Asset swaps serve several useful functions, such as facilitating yield enhancement, creating assets that are not available in the marketplace, and changing the interest-rate sensitivity of the portfolio, without actually trading the securities.

---

[4] Fixed income option pricing models are reviewed in Chapter 34.

Similar to the use of swaps in converting fixed- (floating-) rate debt to floating- (fixed-) rate debt, interest-rate swaps also can be used to accomplish the same objective with fixed- and floating-rate assets. For instance, floating-rate notes (FRNs) can be converted synthetically to fixed-rate assets using a receive fixed-rate and pay floating-rate swap. Similarly, fixed-rate assets such as mortgage-backed securities, especially certain types of CMO bonds like PAC classes and receivable-backed securities, such as manufactured housing, credit card, and automobile loan collateralized bonds, can be converted to floating-rate instruments by using a receive floating-rate and pay fixed-interest-rate swap. Asset-based swaps can also be used to alter the duration characteristics and, hence, the interest-rate sensitivity of an asset portfolio. For instance, a financial institution that has a predominance of long-term fixed-rate assets can reduce the duration of its portfolio, thereby increasing the interest-rate sensitivity of the assets by creating synthetic floating-rate assets. Characteristics of interest-rate swaps, such as amortizing features and option covenants, can be used to customize and reasonably ensure a particular yield level.

The flexibility afforded by swaps in the design of such synthetic assets becomes apparent when it is realized that investors seeking a particular type of asset, say, a floating-rate asset, can evaluate traditional floating-rate instruments, such as FRNs and CMO floaters as well as fixed-rate assets, by using interest-rate swaps to synthetically convert them to floating-rate assets. Asset-based swaps can also tailor the maturity (tenor) of the swap without having to depend on conditions in the debt markets. The latter feature is especially important for institutions that have "underwater" assets. With recent developments in the asset securitization market, which portend increased securitization of a gamut of assets, firms can always use a collateralized financing structure to raise funds and then reinvest the proceeds in assets of desired maturity and coupon. However, this option, besides being time-consuming, also involves administrative, legal, and investment banking costs. Also, assets of particular maturity and coupon may not always be traded in the markets. Asset-based swaps fulfill this particular need in the market mainly due to ease of execution, customization features, and flexibility of swap termination.

## TERMINATION OF INTEREST-RATE SWAPS

The simplest way to terminate an interest-rate swap is to enter into an offsetting position. For illustrative purposes, assume that a firm entered into a 5-year swap, paying fixed at a rate of 9.40 percent and receiving three-month LIBOR. After two years, the firm decides to terminate the swap by entering into a reverse swap, paying floating rate and receiving fixed rate. By matching the reset and settlement periods of the reverse swap to those of the original swap, the floating-rate payment of the reverse swap is counterbalanced by the floating-rate inflow from the original swap. In bullish (bearish) interest-rate scenarios, the new fixed rate on the reverse swap is likely to be lower (higher) than the fixed rate on the original swap. In such cases, there will be profit (loss) associated with the transaction if the fixed rate of the reverse swap is higher (lower) than the fixed rate on the original swap. This point is illustrated in the following example (see Exhibit 53–6). In the first case, where there is a profit in the transaction, the firm has effectively created an annuity of 1 percent of the notional amount for the remaining period of the swap. Conversely, in the second case, where there is a loss associated with the transaction, the firm has created a reverse annuity of 1 percent per annum for three years.

In either case, because the closing transaction involves receiving the fixed side of a swap, the spread over Treasury is based on the bid side of the market, whereas the original swap involves payment of the swap at the offer spread.

The outcomes are summarized below. In the Exhibit 53–5 and throughout this chapter, a bearish interest-rate scenario means one in which rates are *rising* and market prices are falling (a bearish market). In a bullish interest-rate scenario, rates are falling and market prices are rising.

Instead of managing the cash flows of two swaps and the credit risk of two counterparties, the firm may sell the swap for either a profit or loss in the secondary market. In the event that current market swaps with a maturity equal to the remaining maturity of the swap to be terminated are being offered at a higher fixed rate, the swap could be sold for a fee. On the other hand, if current market swaps with a maturity similar to the swap to be liquidated are being originated at lower rates, then an exit fee may have to be paid for terminating the swap. Formally, the termination value of a swap is determined as the present value of an annuity discounted for the remaining term-to-maturity at the cur-

**EXHIBIT 53–6**

**Termination of Interest Rate Swaps**

| | Termination Interest-Rate Scenario | |
| --- | --- | --- |
| | Bearish | Bullish |
| *Swap* | | |
| Pay fixed (5-year original maturity/ | | |
| 3-year remaining maturity) | 9.40% | 9.40% |
| Receive 3-month LIBOR | LIBOR | LIBOR |
| *Reverse Swap* | | |
| Receive fixed (3-year remaining | | |
| maturity) | 10.40% | 8.40% |
| Pay 3-month LIBOR | LIBOR | LIBOR |
| *Profit (Loss)* | 1.00% | (1.00%) |

rent swap rate. The periodic value of the annuity payments is determined as the difference between the old fixed swap rate and the new fixed swap rate times the remaining notional amount of the original swap. Formally, this is stated as

$$\text{Termination value of swap} = \text{PV of Annuity at } r_s t$$

where

Annuity payments $= (r_s - r_m) \times$ notional amount;

$r_s$ = original swap fixed rate;

$r_m$ = current swap fixed rate;

$t$ = time remaining to maturity of swap.


## INTEREST-RATE CAPS AND FLOORS

Interest-rate caps and floors provide asymmetric interest-rate risk management capabilities similar to those provided by options, except that protection can be customized to a much greater degree. As indicated by the nomenclature, interest-rate caps, also referred to as interest-rate ceilings, allow the purchaser to "cap" the contractual rate associated with a liability. Alternatively, interest-rate floors allow the purchaser to protect the total rate of return of an asset. The seller of the cap pays the purchaser any amount above the periodic capped rate on the settlement date. Conversely, the purchaser of the floor receives from the seller any amount below the periodic protected rate on the relevant date. The protection provided by caps and floors is asymmetric, in that the purchaser is protected from adverse moves in the market but maintains the advantage of beneficial moves in market rates. In this respect, caps and floors differ from interest-rate swaps. Recall that interest-rate swaps seek to insulate the user from the economic effects of interest-rate volatility, regardless of the direction of interest rates.

Interest-rate protection obtained by purchasing caps and floors can be customized by selecting various contractual features. The following decision variables are commonly used in determining the parameters of either interest-rate caps or floors.

The *underlying index* from which the contractual payments will be determined can be chosen from a set of indexes based on LIBOR, commercial paper, prime rate, Treasury bills or certificates of deposit. Because these instruments are originated along several maturities, an additional variable associated with the index concerns the maturity of the index.

The *strike rate* is the rate at which the cash flows will be exchanged between the purchaser and seller of the customized interest-rate protection instrument. Caps with a higher strike rate have lower up-front premiums, although the trade-off between the premium and the strike rate is not directly proportional. Similarly, floors with a lower strike rate have a lower up-front premium. Increasing (decreasing) the strike rate does not result in a proportionate decrease in the up-front fee for interest-rate caps (floors).

The *term* of the protection may range from several months to about 30 years.

The *settlement frequency* refers to the frequency with which the strike rate will be compared to the underlying index to determine the periodic contractual rate for the interest-rate protection agreement. The most common frequencies are monthly, quarterly, and semiannually. At settlement, the cash flows exchanged could be determined on either the average daily rate prevalent during the repricing interval or the spot rate on the settlement date.

The *notional amount* of the agreement on which the cash flows are exchanged is usually fixed, unless the terms of the agreement call for the amortization of the notional amount. For instance, in "spread enhancement" strategies, which involve the purchase of an amortizing asset, such as a fixed-rate mortgage-backed security funded by floating-rate capped liabilities, amortization of the cap notional amount may be necessary in order to maintain the spread. Unless the amortization feature is included in the design of the cap, the spread between the asset cash flows and the liability costs will be eroded.

The *up-front premium* is the fee paid by the purchaser to the seller of the interest-rate agreement at the inception of the contract. This fee is similar to the premium paid to purchase options and is determined by factors such as the strike rate, volatility of the underlying index, the length of the agreement, the notional amount, and any special features, such as amortization of the notional principal.

The pricing of both caps and floors draws heavily on option pricing theory; for instance, an increase in market volatility results in a higher premium for both the cap and the floor. The strike rate for a cap is inversely related to the premium paid for the cap, because rates have to advance before the cap is in-the-money or the payoff is positive. On the other hand, the strike rate for interest-rate floors is directly related to the up-front premium. A higher strike indicates that the likelihood of the index falling below this rate is greater, which indicates a higher likelihood of positive payoff from the floor. The longer the term-to-maturity, the greater the premium, because optional protection is available for a longer period of time. Hence, there is a higher probability that the payoff associated with these instruments will be positive. With respect to the payment frequency, the agreement with a shorter payment frequency will command a higher premium, because there is a greater likelihood of payoff and the payments are determined only on the settlement date. This may be an important determinant of cash flows, especially in highly volatile markets. Any advantageous changes in market volatility for interest-rate agreements with longer settlement frequencies may not result in a payoff for the purchaser of the agreement because the option-like characteristics of caps and floors are European rather than American in design.

There also may be *additional contractual features*, such as variable premiums, cost of termination options prior to stated maturity, conversion privileges from one program to another, and purchase of a combination of programs, such as *interest rate collars* and *corridors*.

## Interest-Rate Caps

As noted above, an interest-rate cap can be used to create an upper limit on the cost of floating-rate liabilities. The purchaser of the cap pays an up-front fee to establish a ceiling on a particular funding rate. If the market rate exceeds the strike rate of the cap on the settlement date, the seller of the cap pays the difference. As an illustration, consider the following example, where an institution purchases an interest-rate cap to hedge the coupon rate of LIBOR-indexed liabilities, which reprice every 3 months.

| | |
|---|---|
| Notional amount: | $10,000,000 |
| Underlying index: | 3-month LIBOR |
| Maturity: | 3 years |
| Cap strike level: | 10% |
| Premium: | 145 basis points or 1.45% of |
| | $10,000,000 = $145,000 |
| Settlement frequency: | Quarterly |
| Day count: | Actual/360 |

The up-front premium can be converted to an annual basis point equivalent by treating $145,000 as the present value of a stream of equal quarterly payments with a future value of zero at the maturity of the cap. Ideally, this should be computed at the rate at which the up-front premium can be funded for three years. Assuming that this premium can be funded at a rate of 9 percent and the cap has 12 reset periods, the annual basis point equivalent of the up-front premium is 56 basis points.[5]

In this example, the payments to the purchaser of the cap by the seller can be determined as the quarterly difference between the three-month LIBOR index and the cap strike rate of 10% times the notional amount of the agreement. Specifically, the cap payments are computed as follows:

(index rate − strike rate) × (days in settlement period/360) × (notional amount).

For instance, where three-month LIBOR is 11 percent, the payments made by the cap seller, assuming 90-days in the settlement period, would be determined as follows:

---

[5] This represents the annuity over three years which, when discounted quarterly at an annual rate of 9 percent equals the up-front premium of 145 basis points.

$$(11\% - 10\%) \times (90/360) \times (10,000,000) = \$25,000$$

The purchaser does not receive any payments when the reference rate, as indicated by the value of three-month LIBOR, is below the strike rate of 10 percent. The payoff profile of this capped liability is illustrated in Exhibit 53–7. Because the annual amortized premium of the cap is 56 basis points, the maximum rate associated with the capped liability at a strike of 10 percent is 10.56 percent. In interest-rate scenarios where the value of three-month LIBOR is below 10 percent, the interest expense of the capped liability is higher than the unhedged interest expense by the amount of the amortization of the up-front premium. Given that the maximum risk exposure associated with the purchase of the cap is limited to the up-front premium, the dynamics of caps are similar to those of debt options. On a more specific basis, because the purchaser of the cap benefits in rising rate scenarios, the conceptual options analog is a strip of put options. However, caps can be purchased for maturities longer than those associated with a strip of puts. By increasing the strike rate of the cap, say, from 10% to 10.5%, the up-front premium (and hence the annual amortized premium) can be reduced. However, as illustrated in Exhibit 53–8, the maximum interest expense of the capped liability increases with a higher cap strike rate.

There are several advantages associated with the use of the cap in protecting the interest expense of a floating-rate liability. The purchaser of the cap can obtain protection against higher rates and also fund the liabilities at a floating

**EXHIBIT 53–7**
**Effective Interest Expense of a Capped Liability.**

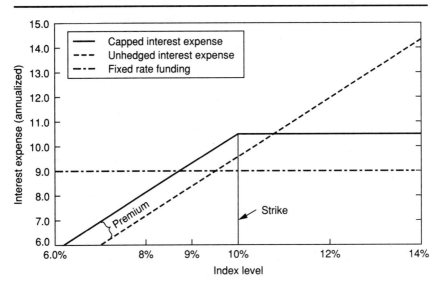

**EXHIBIT 53–8**
**Effective Interest Cost under Two Cap Levels.**

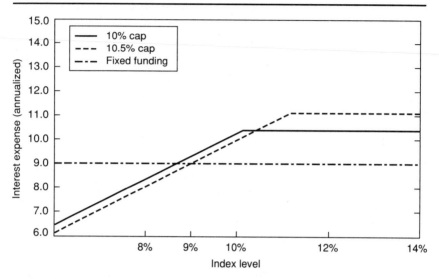

rate to take advantage of lower interest rates. In this respect, the capped liability strategy can result in a lower cost of funds than certain fixed-rate alternatives.

    In addition to capping the cost of liabilities, interest-rate caps can also be
used to synthetically strip embedded caps in floating-rate instruments such as
CMO floaters and adjustable rate mortgages. For instance, consider the case
of an institution owning a CMO floater bond that reprices monthly at a spread
of 60 basis points over LIBOR, with a cap of 600 basis points over the initial
coupon rate. Assuming that the initial coupon rate is 9.60 percent, the coupon
is capped at 15.60 percent. Because the only sources of cash flow available to
CMO bonds are the principal, interest, and prepayment streams of the underlying
mortgages, CMO floaters are by definition capped. In this respect, CMO floaters
are different from other LIBOR-indexed bonds, such as floating-rate notes. The
institution could strip off the embedded cap in the CMO floater by buying a cap
at a strike rate of 15 percent or 16 percent. With a strike rate about 600 to 700
basis points out-of-the-money, the cap could be purchased quite inexpensively.
As interest rates increase, the loss in coupon by the embedded cap feature
of the CMO bonds would be compensated by the cash inflows from the cap.
The same strategy could be applied to strip caps inherent in adjustable-rate
mortgages. However, the exercise of stripping caps associated with adjustable-
rate mortgages is somewhat more difficult due to the existence of periodic and
lifetime caps.

## Participating Caps

It is difficult to pinpoint the exact nature of financial instruments labeled as "participating" caps. A common theme in the definition of such instruments is the absence of an up-front fee used to purchase the cap. The confusion in definition arises from the variations of the term "participating." One type of participating cap involves the purchase of cap protection where the buyer obtains full protection in the event that interest rates rise. However, in order to compensate the seller of the cap for this bearish protection, the buyer shares a percentage (the participation) of the difference between the capped rate and the level of the floating-rate index in the event that interest rates fall.

For illustrative purposes, assume that a firm purchases a LIBOR-participating cap at a strike rate of 10 percent with a participation rate of 60%. If LIBOR increases to levels greater than 10 percent, the firm will receive cash flows analogous to a non-participating cap. However, if LIBOR is below the capped rate, say 8 percent, then the firm gives up 60 percent of the difference between LIBOR and the capped rate, that is, $(10\% - 8\%) \times 0.6 = 1.2$ percent. In this case the effective interest expense would be 9.20% (8.00% + 1.20%), instead of LIBOR plus the annual amortized premium, as in a non-participating cap. In bullish interest-rate scenarios, the effective interest expense using a participating cap would be higher than a non-participating cap due to the participation feature. However, in bearish interest-rate scenarios, the effective interest cost of the floating-rate liability would be higher for a non-participating cap due to the annualized cost of the up-front premium. An illustration of the effective interest costs using both hedging alternatives is presented in Exhibit 53–9.

Other participating caps, also known as participating swaps, combine the analytical elements of interest-rate swaps and caps to create a hedge for floating-rate liability costs. In a participating cap structure, the firm uses interest-rate swaps to convert the floating liability rate to a fixed rate and uses caps to create a maximum upper limit on the remainder of the interest expense of the floating-rate liability. However, what distinguishes this structure is that the caps are purchased without paying an up-front fee. The purchase is funded by executing the swap (fixed-rate payor–floating-rate receiver) at an off-market rate involving a higher spread than the current market rate for equivalent maturity swaps. Such participations can be structured in one of the following ways.

- The buyer decides the maximum rate on the floating-rate liability, which leads to the problem of determining the mixture of notional amounts of caps and swaps.
- The buyer decides on the relative mix of swaps and caps, which leads to the problem of determining the maximum rate level that can be attained with this combination.

Regardless of the choice by the buyer, the following relationship should hold in this type of participating structure:

**EXHIBIT 53–9**
**Effective Interest Expense for Participating Cap.**

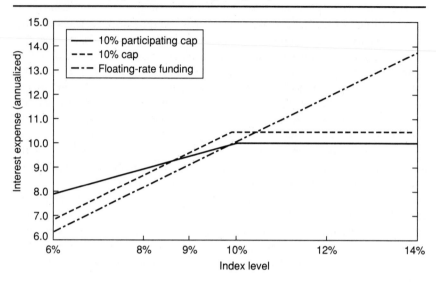

(present value of annuity at $r_0 - r_m$, $t$) $\times$ (% of swap)
$$= \text{cap premium} \times (\% \text{ of cap})$$

or

(present value of annuity at $r_0 - r_m$, $t$) $\times$ (% of swap)
$$= \text{cap premium} \times (1 - \% \text{ of swap})$$

or

$$\% \text{ of swap} = \frac{\text{present value of annuity at } r_0 - r_m, t}{\text{cap premium} + \text{present value of annuity at } r_0 - r_m, t},$$

where

$r_m$ = current market swap fixed rate for $t$ periods; and

$r_0$ = off-market swap fixed rate for $t$ periods.

As an example, consider the case of an institution desiring to cap a floating-rate liability expense that floats at a spread of 10 basis points over three-month LIBOR at a maximum rate of around 10 percent for a period of five years using this type of participating cap structure. The current market rate on a five-year pay fixed and receive floating (three-month LIBOR) swap is 80 basis points over the five-year Treasury yield at a rate of 9.40 percent. The current level of LIBOR is 9 percent and off-market five-year swaps are priced at a fixed rate of 10 percent. The cap premium for a five-year cap, indexed off three-month LIBOR at a strike rate of 10 percent is 200 basis points, or 2 percent of notional amount.

The value of the annuity for five years is the difference between the off-market and the current market swap rate, that is, $(10\% - 9.40\% = 0.60\%)$. The present value of this annuity for five years at a discount rate of 9.4 percent (current swap rate) is 2.37185 percent. Therefore, using the above equation for participating structures, the amount of the swaps is defined as $(2.37185/(2.37185 + 2.0000) = 54$ percent. Hence, the amount of the caps is $(1 - 0.54) = 0.46$, or 46 percent. Using this structure, the effective liability expense in various interest-rate scenarios is presented in Exhibit 53–10. In this example, the synthetic fixed rate using swaps is based on the higher off-market rate, whereas the blended rate is determined as a weighted average of the cap and the swap fixed rate.

In bullish interest-rate scenarios, the blended rate is higher than the unhedged expense due to the existence of the swap. The full benefit of the fall in rates is attained only partially by the portion of the liability mix that is capped. As interest rates increase, the blended rate is also higher than current market swaps due to the existence of the higher priced off-market swap that is used to fund the cap premium.

## Interest-Rate Floors

Interest-rate floors are used to protect the overall rate of return associated with a floating-rate asset. As an example, consider the case of a financial institution that owns adjustable-rate mortgages in its portfolio. In the event that interest rates decrease, the coupon payments on floating-rate assets will be lower, because the repricing of variable coupon assets is based on a floating-rate index. In order to protect the asset rate of return in bullish interest-rate scenarios, the firm could purchase an interest-rate floor. Analogous to caps, the protective features of a floor can be customized by choosing various attributes of interest-rate protection.

**EXHIBIT 53–10**
**Effective Interest Expense Using Participating Cap Structure**

| LIBOR | Unhedged | Synthetic Fixed Rate 54% Swaps | Capped Rate 46% Caps | Blended Rate |
|-------|----------|-------------------------------|---------------------|--------------|
| 11.0% | 11.10%   | 10.10%                        | 10.00%              | 10.046%      |
| 9.0   | 9.10     | 10.10                         | 9.00                | 9.506        |
| 7.0   | 7.10     | 10.10                         | 7.00                | 8.426        |

As an illustration, consider the following interest-rate floor purchased by an institution to protect the return on Treasury bill–indexed floating-rate assets:

| | |
|---|---|
| Notional amount: | $10,000,000 |
| Underlying index: | three-month Treasury bill |
| Maturity: | three years |
| Cap strike level: | 8% |
| Premium: | 85 basis points or 0.85% of $10,000,000 = $85,000 |
| Settlement frequency: | Quarterly |
| Day count: | Actual/360 |

The cash flow dynamics of interest-rate floors are opposite to those of interest rate caps, as illustrated in Exhibit 53–11. As can be seen in this illustration, a floor is beneficial in bullish interest-rate scenarios. Hence, purchasing a floor is analogous to buying a strip of call options. In bearish interest-rate scenarios, the floating-rate asset earns returns constrained only by the contractual features of such instruments (if any), such as embedded caps. However, the asset return is reduced marginally by the amortization of the floor premium. In bullish interest-rate scenarios, where the asset returns are subject to erosion, the seller of the floor pays the buyer the difference between the strike rate of the floor and the value of the underlying index, adjusted for the days in the settlement period to compensate for the loss in asset coupon.

**EXHIBIT 53–11**
**Effective Return of a Floored Asset.**

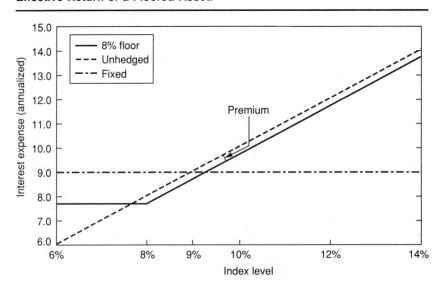

## Interest-Rate Collars

Interest-rate collars involve the purchase of a cap to hedge a floating-rate liability at a higher strike rate and the sale of a floor at a lower strike rate to offset the cost of purchasing the cap. If the underlying index rate exceeds the capped rate on the reference date, the seller of the cap pays the firm the amount above the capped rate; if the market rate is less than the floor strike rate, the firm pays the buyer the difference between the floor rate and the index level. If the market rate is between the strike rate of the cap and the strike rate of the floor, the effective interest costs of the firm are normal floating-rate funding costs plus the amortized cap premium (outflow) less the amortized floor premium (inflow). The net effect of this strategy is to limit the coupon rate of the floating-rate liability between the floor strike rate and the cap strike rate. The coupon liability rate is adjusted by the net amount of the amortized cap premium paid and the amortized floor premium received to determine the effective interest cost.

As an illustration, assume that a firm has floating-rate liabilities that are indexed at three-month LIBOR. In order to cap this floating-rate liability for 1 year, the firm purchases an interest-rate cap at a strike rate of 11 percent for a premium of 85 basis points. In order to offset this cost, the firm sells a cap at a strike rate of 8 percent for a premium of 60 basis points. The profit and loss profile of this strategy is presented in Exhibit 53–12. As interest rates rise above the cap strike

**EXHIBIT 53–12**
**Interest-Rate Collar.**

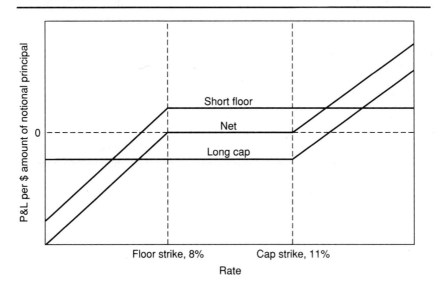

Short floor

Net

Long cap

Floor strike, 8%          Cap strike, 11%

P&L per $ amount of notional principal

Rate

rate, the firm receives cash flows from the seller of the cap offsetting the higher outflow on the floating-rate liability. As interest rates fall below the floor strike rate, the falling interest expenses associated with the floating-rate liability are offset by the cash outflows to the buyer of the floor. In interest rate scenarios between the floor and cap strike rate, there are no cash outflows or inflows associated with the hedges. This results in interest expenses associated with the floating-rate liability equal to normal borrowing costs. However, effective interest costs will be slightly higher to account for the net cap less floor premium, unless the collar is structured with a zero premium.

The main benefit obtained from an interest rate collar is that the firm obtains protection from interest rate increases at a considerably lower cost than with the purchase of cap. However, in return for the benefit of lower cost interest rate protection, the firm gives up the benefit from market rallies below the floor strike rate. Because the interest rate protection is obtained without fixing rates, interest-rate collars are sometimes also described as "swapping into a bond." However, this is an inefficient form of creating a collar because of the bid-ask volatility spread[6] associated with the structure. Given that the strategy involves buying a cap and selling a floor, the premium paid for the cap is based on a higher offer volatility, whereas the premium received for the floor is based on a lower bid volatility.

## Interest-Rate Corridors

An alternative strategy to reduce the cost of the cap premium is to buy a cap at a particular strike rate and sell a cap at a higher strike rate, reducing the cost of the lower strike cap and hedging the interest expense of a floating-rate liability. In contrast to an interest rate collar, the firm maintains all the benefit of falling interest rates, because there is no sale of a floor. As long as rates are below the strike rate of the lower strike cap, the effective interest expense of the firm is limited to normal borrowing cost plus the amortized net cap premium. As interest rates increase above the lower strike rate, the interest cost to the firm is capped until market rates are above the higher strike cap. As interest rates rise above the strike rate of the second cap, interest costs increase by the amount of the outflow of the cap.

As an illustration, consider the case of a firm that purchases a cap at a strike rate of 11 percent and sells a cap at a strike rate of 15 percent to offset the cost of the first cap. The profit and loss profile of this strategy is presented in Exhibit 53–13. At market rates below 11 percent, the caps are out-of-the-money, and the firm's effective interest cost floats at normal borrowing costs plus the

---

[6] See section on *Termination of Caps and Floors*.

**EXHIBIT 53–13**
**Interest-Rate Corridor.**

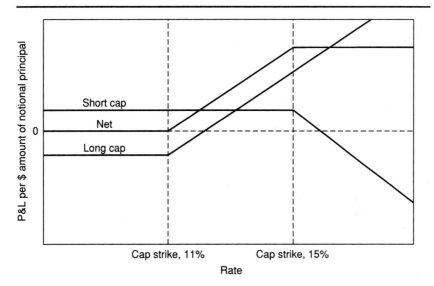

net amortized cap premium. As interest rates increase above 11 percent, the first cap is in-the-money and starts paying cash flows to the firm to offset the higher coupon associated with the floating-rate liability. This allows the firm to cap the effective interest expense at a rate 11 percent plus the net amortized cap premium. However, at rates higher than 15 percent, the second cap becomes in-the-money and the firm has to start paying cash flows to the cap buyer. The net effect of this development is to increase the liability costs by the amount of the cash outflows associated with the second cap.

Although interest rate collars allow the firm to offset the cost of capping floating-rate liabilities, a word of caution is in order, especially if the caps are struck under the auspices of a zero premium strategy. Cap premiums are determined by principles of option pricing theory; consequently, the premium received for a 15 percent cap will be less than the premium paid for the 11% cap due to the higher strike rate and bid-offer volatility spreads. Therefore, in a zero premium strategy, to equate the premium received for the higher strike cap to that paid for the lower strike cap, the notional amount of caps sold must be larger than the notional amount of caps purchased. Although this allows the firm to cap the liability rate at zero cost up to the strike rate of 15 percent, the firm is exposed to tremendous risk in a high interest-rate, or "doomsday," scenario. As market interest rates increase to over 15 percent, the cash outflows paid to the buyer of the higher strike cap may negate any cash flows received from the lower strike cap and result in much higher interest costs than the lower strike cap rate. The extent of this offsetting effect will be an inverse function of the ratio of the notional amount of higher strike to lower strike caps—the greater this ratio, the smaller the effect of the cash inflows of the lower strike cap and the higher will be effective interest cost.

## Cap/Floor Swap Parity

Similar to put-call parity for options, which essentially specifies the relationship between these types of options and the price of the underlying security, caps and floors are related to interest rate swaps. As an example, consider a strategy that involves buying a cap at 9.50 percent and selling a floor at 9.50 percent, both based off the same index, for example, LIBOR. This is equivalent to entering into an interest-rate swap, paying fixed at 9.5 percent, and receiving floating payments based on LIBOR. If interest rates increase to above the cap level, say 11 percent, the cap will pay 1.5 percent. At the same level, the holder of the swap will receive LIBOR at 11 percent. This translates into a positive cash flow of the difference between LIBOR and the fixed rate of the swap, that is, $11\% - 9.5\% = 1.5\%$. If interest rates decrease to below the floor level, say 7.5 percent, the holder of the floor pays the difference between the index and the floor strike rate, that is, $9.5\% - 7.5\% = 2\%$. At the same level, the swap holder loses the difference between the swap fixed rate and LIBOR, that is, 2%. Therefore, the cap/floor swap parity may be stated as

$$\text{long cap} + \text{short floor} = \text{fixed swap}$$

However, for cap/floor swap parity to hold, the fixed rate of the swap should be paid on the same basis ($^{\text{actual}}/_{360}$ days, $^{30}/_{360}$ days, or $^{\text{actual}}/_{365}$ days) as the floating rate, not a varying basis on the two rates. A graphical illustration of cap/floor swap parity is presented in Exhibit 53–14.

The cost of a market swap is zero because no premium cash flows are exchanged at inception. Therefore, using cap/floor swap parity, the cost of a cap should be the same as the cost of a floor struck at the same rate on an identical index. This relationship should hold irrespective of the pricing model used to value the caps and floors. Unless this relationship is true at every point, an arbitrage exists in these markets that could be used to emulate the characteristics of the overpriced instrument. For instance, if caps are overpriced, a synthetic cap could be created by buying a floor and entering into an interest-rate swap, paying fixed at the floor strike rate and receiving floating using the same underlying index as the floor. Such arbitrage possibilities due to deviation from cap/floor swap parity also ensure efficient pricing in these markets.

**EXHIBIT 53–14**
**Synthetic Swap Cap/Floor Swap Parity.**

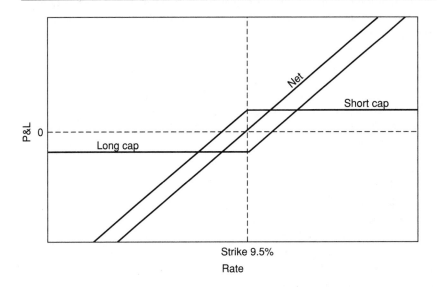

## Termination of Caps and Floors

As is apparent from the discussion on the characteristics of caps (floors), these instruments are essentially a strip of put (call) options on forward interest rates. Hence, caps and floors are priced using the same theoretical and analytical concepts involved in pricing options. The termination value of caps and floors can be determined using concepts similar to those involved in determining the market value of options (premium) prior to expiration. In contrast to interest-rate swaps, where the termination of swaps is based on the bid-ask spread to the Treasury yield, the bid-ask spread for caps and floors is stated in terms of volatility. On a practical basis, this is a much "cleaner" method of determining bid-ask spreads in the cap and floor market than deriving forward curves using bid and ask yield spreads. In order to compensate the financial intermediary for the market-making function, the offer volatility is higher than the bid volatility. Because option premiums are directly related to volatility, the difference between the offer premium and bid premium for either a cap or floor prior to maturity will be directly related to the magnitude of the spread between bid and offer volatility.

## COMPOUND OPTIONS

Interest-rate protection provided by conventional options, such as puts and calls, and derivative option-like instruments, such as caps and floors, extends over a specified period of time. During this time period, the option may be either "exercised," terminated prior to maturity, or allowed to expire worthless. The exercise (or lack thereof) is triggered by movements either in the price of the underlying security (as in the case of debt options) or in the underlying index (as in the case of caps and floors). However, any termination of the optional contract prior to maturity is incurred at the expense of the bid-offer spread. Given that swaps, caps, and floors are usually longer in maturity than conventional put and call options, termination costs are likely to be higher for such instruments. Additionally, the interest-rate protection provided by swaps, caps, and floors falls more in the category of passive hedging because, with the exception of the exchange of cash flows, there is no ongoing active management of the hedge.

For a shorter time horizon where the holding (outstanding) period of the asset (liability) is subject to change, firms can use interest-rate debt options. (A detailed discussion of the role of conventional options in asset/liability management is the subject of Chapter 49.) Such options can be used to manage asset/liability spreads or offset short-term opportunity losses associated with long-term interest-rate protection instruments. For instance, in rising interest-rate scenarios, where liability costs rise more quickly than the return on assets or the return on assets is fixed, put options can be used to offset the erosion in spread. The benefit of falling rates is still maintained as the loss on puts is limited to the up-front premium. Entities paying fixed in an interest-rate swap would be able to offset the opportunity loss in falling rate scenarios by purchasing calls on Treasuries. In recent years, an important innovation known as *compound options* or *split fee options* has allowed investors to limit losses of such short-term option strategies by permitting them to assess market conditions before purchasing additional optional coverage.

Compound options, which are essentially "options on options," allow the firm to purchase a window on the market by paying a premium that is less than the premium on a conventional option on the same underlying instrument. The optional coverage can be extended at expiration of the window period by paying another premium. In essence, compound options provide an additional element of risk management by providing the opportunity to further limit downside losses associated with asymmetric coverage without sacrificing the essential ingredients of optional coverage.

Compound options allow the investor to purchase an option to exercise another option by paying a fee known as the up-front premium for a specified period of time. At the end of this period, known as the window date, the investor may exercise the option on the option by paying another fee known as the back-end fee. Therefore, the label "split-fee" stems from the dichotomous nature of the fees paid for the combined option. Split-fee options also have been labeled "up and on" options; this terminology refers to the *up*-front fee and the back-end fee paid *on* the window date.

## Comparison with Conventional Option Strategies

Compound options offer several advantages over conventional options, such as additional leverage and greater risk management capabilities. This point is illustrated by contrasting the coverage provided by compound puts and calls with conventional options. The graphical representation of the profit profile of a long put versus a compound put is illustrated in Exhibit 53–15. As indicated in the graph, the net profit profile of a long put is the standard textbook representation. As interest rates decline, causing increases in the value of the underlying security, the losses associated with the purchase of an at-the-money conventional put are limited to the up-front premium (CE). As interest rates increase, resulting in a fall in the price of the underlying security, the option can be exercised and the underlying security sold at the higher strike price. The net profit from exercising the option is the difference between the strike price and the value of the underlying security less the cost of the option. The net profit profile of the conventional put option in bullish and bearish interest-rate scenarios is denoted by HEA.

**EXHIBIT 53–15**
**Long Put vs. Split-Fee Option.**

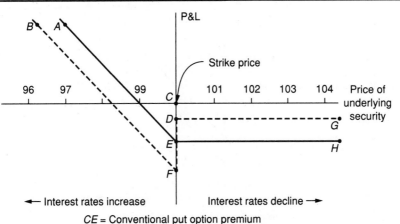

CE = Conventional put option premium
CD = Front-end fee for compound put option
DF = Back-end fee for compound put option

However, with the compound put option, the same degree of protection afforded by the conventional put is available in bullish interest-rate scenarios at a much lower cost, as indicated by the up-front premium of CD in Exhibit 53–15. In the event that interest rates continue to decline, the compound option can be allowed to expire unexercised. On the other hand, if interest rates are expected to increase, the optional coverage can be extended by exercising the second leg of the compound option. The total profit from the exercise of the compound option may be less than that obtained from exercising the conventional put if the sum of the up-front fee and the back-end fee is greater than the up-front put premium. In the event that the compound option is not exercised at the window date, the profit profile of the split-fee option strategy will be discontinuous, as indicated by GD in the graph. If the back-end fee is paid and the option exercised on the window date, the profit profile of the compound put is HEFB.

Portfolio managers frequently will purchase call options to profit from impending bullish changes in the market. The rationale underlying this strategy is based on the expectation that if interest rates decline, leading to an increase in the price of the underlying security, the portfolio manager will be able to purchase the asset at the lower strike price. The profit profile of this conventional call option is compared to that of a compound call in Exhibit 53–16. As indicated in the illustration, if interest rates remain unchanged or increase, the losses of a conventional call strategy are limited to the up-front call premium. The profit profile of the call is labeled QNJ in the graph; the call strategy is

**EXHIBIT 53–16**
**Long Call vs. Split-Fee Option.**

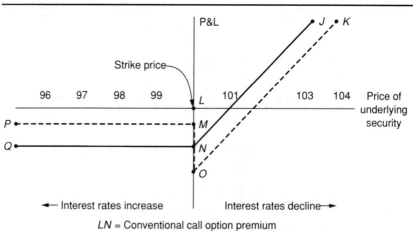

LN = Conventional call option premium
LM = Front-end fee for compound call option
MO = Back-end fee for compound call option

profitable in bullish interest-rate scenarios. In bearish interest-rate scenarios, the use of split-fee options results in losses lower than those associated with the conventional call strategy due to the lower up-front premium. However, if at the window date interest rates are lower, resulting in the exercise of the compound option, the profit profile of the compound call is denoted by PMOK. If the compound call is not exercised, the profit profile of the split-fee option will be denoted by PM.

## Uses of Compound Options

Compound options have been used mainly to hedge mortgage pipeline risk, especially the risk of applicants seeking alternative sources of financing or canceling the loan. Usually, this risk, known as "fallout" risk, is hedged by purchasing put options. The ramifications of fallout risk are especially severe if the expected mortgage production has already been sold forward. If interest rates fall and mortgage loans fall out of the pipeline, the mortgage lender can let the option expire unexercised. On the other hand, if rates increase, the lender can participate in the upside movement of the market by selling originated loans at the higher put strike price. With a compound put option, the mortgage lender can obtain the same optional protection at a much lower cost and retain the flexibility of extending the protection after assessing market conditions. If at the window date there is no need for put protection, the loss is lower than that of the premium of a conventional put. On the other hand, if additional protection is required, it can be purchased by either extending the compound option or by purchasing a conventional put option. For instance, it is possible that if forward market prices are higher (lower) on the window date, the purchase of a put (call) may be cheaper than exercising the option on the option.

Portfolios using active call-buying programs as yield enhancement vehicles may purchase compound calls when there is uncertainty regarding an impending fall in interest rates. Instead of purchasing a higher premium conventional call, the compound call allows the portfolio manager to purchase a window on the market for a lower cost. At the window date, if there is a greater degree of certainty regarding bullish market conditions, the compound options can be extended. However, if the degree of uncertainty increases, the loss is limited to the lower up-front premium.

Compound options, such as calls, can also be used in conjunction with longer term instruments, such as fixed interest-rate swaps, to offset short-term opportunity losses occurring due to a fall in interest rates. However, perhaps the largest potential use of compound option technology lies in the application of these concepts to the cap and floor market in designing long-term options on options. Recall that caps (floors) are essentially a package of European puts (calls) on forward interest rates. Although the market for options on caps and floors, which allow the buyer to either cancel or initiate customized interest-rate protection, is still fairly undeveloped, the potential uses of such instruments are enormous. As with any optional coverage, the development of such options on a series of options will add another element of flexibility provided by customized risk management instruments.

## CONCLUDING COMMENTS

In the management of interest-rate volatility and associated asset/liability structural decisions, customized risk management instruments, such as swaps, caps and floors, and split-fee options provide a high degree of coverage flexibility and customization. Interest-rate swaps can be used to either synthetically extend or shorten the duration characteristics of any asset or liability. The benefit of swaps is that direct changes in the contractual characteristics of either assets or liabilities are associated with administrative, legal, and investment banking costs. Additional swaps covenants, such as amortizing and accreting features and option riders, can be included in the contractual agreement to either better match the funding of an asset or lock in the return of a synthetic asset.

Whereas interest-rate swaps are intended to insulate the user from changes in interest-rate volatility, other customized interest-rate agreements, such as caps and floors, are designed to provide asymmetric coverage in capping liability costs and protecting the rate of return on assets. In either case, the user retains the right to participate in upside movements of the market. In order to reduce the up-front cost of purchasing caps and floors, the user can either enter into participating agreements that involve giving up a proportional share of beneficial market moves or enter into agreements, such as collars and corridors, that are analogous to option spread strategies.

Because the termination of such agreements involves exit costs, these instruments may prove beneficial for passive hedging where interest-rate protection is desired for longer periods of time. By the same token, these agreements also should not be used if the holding period of either the asset or liability is flexible or subject to change. For shorter periods of time, the user may decide to use split-fee options, which provide greater leverage and risk management capabilities similar to conventional options, although contemporary use of split-fee options has been mainly in mortgage pipeline hedging. However, compound option technology can be applied readily to develop options on caps and floors, thereby adding an additional element of flexibility for these instruments in designing customized interest-rate protection.

# CHAPTER 54

## THE INTEREST-RATE SWAP MARKET: YIELD MATHEMATICS, TERMINOLOGY, AND CONVENTIONS*

*Robert W. Kopprasch, Ph.D., CFA*
Managing Director
Hyperion Capital Management, Inc.

*John Macfarlane*
Managing Director
Salomon Brothers, Inc.
and
Treasurer
Salomon, Inc.

*Janet Showers, Ph.D.*
Director
Hedge Group
Salomon Brothers, Inc.

*Daniel Ross*
Director
Dumas West and Co.

*The authors would like to thank Daniel L. Schwartz for his contribution to the Appendix and to the development of the theories herein. Although the information in this report has been obtained from sources that Salomon Brothers Inc believes to be reliable, we do not guarantee its accuracy, and such information may be incomplete or condensed. All opinions and estimates included in this report constitute our judgment as of this date and are subject to change without notice. This report is for information purposes only and is not intended as an offer or solicitation with respect to the purchase or sale of any security. Copyright by Salomon Brothers Inc.

Since its inception in the late 1970s, the interest-rate swap[1] has developed from a negotiated device used primarily by international banks and their corporate counterparties, into a broadly based market instrument used by virtually every type of institution. The rapid growth of the over-the-counter swap market largely reflects the flexibility that it affords its participants in closing maturity, funding, and index mismatches on their balance sheets. In addition, market makers' willingness to structure swaps that meet individual counterparty needs has further stimulated the market's growth.

The expansion of the market, however, has not come without costs. Throughout this period, the market has failed to develop a consistently used yield mathematics for swaps. This lack of consistency, along with the wide variety of swap structures, has caused specific transactions to be misunderstood and mispriced.

This chapter will remove the uncertainty and imprecision that has surrounded this market and explain the mathematics fundamental to its understanding. The approach that we will use follows:

- First, we will present the terminology that is most frequently used when discussing swaps.
- Second, we will describe the *generic swap,* which can serve as the basis for structuring swaps and as the cornerstone of a valuation procedure for swaps.
- Third, we will discuss complexities of swap cash flows that initially appear to make the application of traditional bond analysis difficult.
- Fourth, we will suggest a valuation methodology for analyzing a generic interest-rate swap within the general bond math framework that is familiar to most market participants.
- Fifth, we will adapt our methodology for use in valuing nongeneric swaps.
- Finally, we will explore the typical nongeneric features actually found in the market and, using our methodology, describe their effect on a swap's "cost" or "value."

Because the mathematical techniques used in this chapter employ only traditional bond mathematics, we hope that institutions that are presented with a swap will use this approach as a framework to analyze the swap's particular features and to assess its value.

---

[1] An interest-rate swap is an agreement between two institutions in which each commits to make periodic interest payments to the other based on an agreed-upon notional principal amount, maturity, and either a predetermined fixed rate of interest or an agreed-upon floating money market index. No principal amounts change hands. This chapter will discuss only fixed-for-floating U.S. dollar interest-rate swaps, although many of the principles outlined apply to other swaps as well.

## A PRIMER ON MARKET TERMINOLOGY

Mathematics has not been the sole source of confusion for swap market participants. The lack of consistently used terminology and the fact that some terminology initially appears to be counterintuitive have left institutions unsure of how to approach the market. Thus, before we discuss mathematics, we will briefly review the following market terminology:

- The terms used when discussing the anatomy of a particular swap;
- The terms associated with positioning or making markets in swaps; and
- The interpretation of market quotations for swaps.

An interest-rate swap is a contract between two participants or *counterparties,* in which interest payments are made based on the *notional principal amount,* which itself is never paid or received. The fixed-rate payment in the swap (often called the fixed-rate coupon) is made by the *fixed-rate payer* to the *floating-rate payer.* Similarly, the floating-rate payment in the swap is made by the floating-rate payer (or variable-rate payer) to the fixed-rate payer. Both fixed and floating interest start accruing on the swap's *effective date* and cease accruing on the swap's *maturity date.* The *trade date* is the date on which the counterparties commit to the swap. On this date, the transaction is priced for value as of the *settlement date.*[2]

There are various money market indexes on which the floating-rate payment could be based. (These are presented in Exhibit 54–6 later in this chapter). The floating-rate payment stream will sometimes be calculated based on the index plus or minus an agreed-upon number of basis points, known as the floating *spread.* The overall value or cost of a swap is expressed as the *all-in-cost* (AIC), which will be discussed later. Although particular counterparties may supply credit enhancement devices (e.g., letter of credit, bank intermediaries, collateral, or insurance), the cost of such devices is not included in the AIC.

While the language relating to the structure of an individual swap is straightforward, the terminology associated with positioning or market making initially can appear to be somewhat confusing. Historically, a market maker's bias has been to "buy" or "go long" swaps by being a fixed-rate payer.[3] A market maker

---

[2] The settlement date is also the date on which any net cash payment—including any net accrued interest—changes hands. Such a cash payment could occur, for example, in secondary market or seasoned transactions as discussed in the section on nonpar swaps. In the case of entering into a swap, the settlement date is normally the same as the effective date whether or not any cash payment occurs.

[3] Given time, the market maker would "sell" his position to appropriate counterparties to offset these long positions. This trading strategy evolved because initially, floating-rate payers were limited in number and relatively inflexible in accommodating various swap structures.

who is long the swap market makes fixed-rate payments and, therefore, can be considered short the bond market (as if he had issued fixed-rate debt). This market anomaly has resulted in the widely accepted terminology shown in Exhibit 54–1.

The market convention for quoting swap levels is to quote the all-in-cost (or the internal rate of return) of the fixed side of the swap versus the opposite flow of the floating index flat.[4] The swap's all-in-cost can be expressed either as an absolute level on a semiannual basis or as a basis-point spread to the semiannual bond equivalent of the U.S. Treasury yield curve. For an example of the latter type of quote, a seven-year London Interbank Offered Rate (LIBOR) swap might be quoted to a fixed-rate payer as "the Treasury yield curve plus 60 basis points versus three-month LIBOR flat." This means that the fixed-rate payer could enter into a swap in which he receives three-month LIBOR flat and makes fixed payments, the internal rate of return of which equates to 60 basis points over the semiannual bond equivalent yield of the Treasury yield curve on the trade date.[5]

**EXHIBIT 54–1**
**Terminology of the Swap Market**

*A Fixed-Rate Payer*

Pays fixed in the swap
Receives floating in the swap
Has bought a swap
Is long a swap
Is short the bond market
Has established the price sensitivities of a longer term
  liability and a floating-rate asset

*A Floating-Rate Payer*

Pays floating in the swap
Receives fixed in the swap
Has sold a swap
Is short a swap
Is long the bond market
Has established the price sensitivities of a longer term
  asset and a floating-rate liability

---

[4] The floating index *flat* means that the floating payments equal the index itself with no spread over or under the index.

[5] The cash flows for this internal rate of return calculation include, for analytical purposes, the price of the hypothetical fixed-rate bond and redemption of principal at maturity (see the section on valuation methodology).

Market participants use several methods to define the Treasury yield curve. The most predominant methods determine at the time of execution the yield of a principal amount of Treasury securities based upon the swap's notional principal amount.[6] One method defines the curve as the semiannual yield-to-maturity of the specific note or bond with maturity closest to that of the swap. This method unfortunately often results in anomalous levels because of thin trading in the particular security or because of the presence of a discount or premium in the particular security.

We believe that a better method involves using only current coupon "on-the-run" securities. If the swap's maturity is reasonably close to the maturity of such a security, then that security's yield defines the curve. If the swap's maturity lies between that of two on-the-run securities, then the curve would be defined by interpolation of the yields.[7]

## THE GENERIC SWAP

Throughout the evolution of the market, we have observed one fundamental structure emerging as the point of reference against which all interest-rate swaps are compared. This generic (or "plain vanilla") swap may not be the final structure of most swaps completed, but it remains the single theme on which all of the countless swap variations are based. The generic swap, therefore, is a starting point for analysis.

The generic interest-rate swap combines the characteristics of a traditional fixed-income security on the fixed-rate side with the characteristics of a traditional floating-rate note on the floating side. These characteristics are outlined in Exhibit 54–2.

## COMPLEXITIES OF SWAP ANALYSIS

Several factors complicate the analysis of cost or return of an interest-rate swap within the confines of traditional bond math. Two such complications affect even the generic swap, which is the most straightforward in terms of valuation:

---

[6] The price of the Treasury securities is negotiated at the time that the parties enter the swap. Market makers have historically wanted to use the bid side to determine the curve for fixed-rate payers and the offered side to determine the curve for floating-rate payers. This convention developed because a market maker selling a swap to a fixed-rate payer traditionally sold its hedge and, hence, used the bid side. Similarly, the market maker traditionally bought a hedge when buying a swap from a floating-rate payer and, thus, used the offered side.

[7] Interpolation is straight-line based on the actual number of days between the maturity of the swap and the two securities.

**EXHIBIT 54–2**
**Terms of the Generic Swap**

| Terms | Definition |
|---|---|
| Maturity | One to fifteen years |
| Effective date | Five business days from trade date (corporate settlement). The effective date is such that the first fixed- and first floating-payment periods are full coupon periods (i.e., no long or short first coupons). |
| Settlement date | Effective date |
| Fixed payment | |
|   Fixed coupon | Current market rate |
|   Payment frequency | Either semiannually or annually |
|   Day count | 30/360 |
|   Pricing date | Trade date |
| Floating payment* | |
|   Floating index | Certain money market indexes |
|   Spread | None |
|   Determination source | Some publicly quoted source; for example, the *Reuter Monitor Money Rates Service* or the *Federal Reserve Statistical Release H.15 (519)* |
|   Payment frequency | The term of the floating-index itself |
|   Day count | Actual/360 for private sector floating-rate indexes and Actual/Actual for Treasury bills |
|   Reset frequency | The term of the floating index itself, except for Treasury bills, for which the index is reset weekly regardless of term |
|   First coupon | Current market rate for the index |
|   Premium or discount | None[†] |
| All-in-cost | Semiannual equivalent of the internal rate of return of the fixed flows versus the floating index flat[‡] |

[*] For details on floating-rate generic standards, see Exhibit 54–6.
[†] This means that no cash payment is made by either party on the effective date (see the section on nonpar swaps).
[‡] See Footnote 5.

(1) An interest-rate swap involves neither an investment at settlement date nor a repayment of principal at maturity; and (2) a swap's future floating-rate payment stream is unknown. These two factors must be addressed first in setting forth a valuation technique for swaps.

## Swapping Interest Payments or Swapping Securities?

The first obstacle to analyzing an interest-rate swap using bond math is overcome by viewing the swap as a simultaneous exchange of two separate hypothetical securities of equal maturity. This notion holds that the fixed-rate payer has sold a hypothetical fixed-rate security to the floating-rate payer and that the floating-rate payer has sold a hypothetical floating-rate note to the fixed-rate payer. Because the par amount of both "securities" is the notional principal amount of the swap, a netting of the two purchase prices upon settlement and of the two principal repayments at a maturity results in no net cash flow based upon principal dollars.[8]

This artificial construct allows us to look at the two "securities" separately for valuation purposes. Whether one thinks of a swap as an exchange of interest payments or an exchange of securities, the net cash flows of the swap are the same.

## The Uncertainty of the Floating-Rate Payments

The uncertainty of the floating-rate payment stream presents a slightly more difficult problem to overcome. The fundamental question is how can one determine the market value of a swap without knowing the precise floating-rate payments. Specifically, would a technique like Simple Margin, Total Margin, Adjusted Total Margin, or Discount Margin be required?[9]

The structure of an interest-rate swap, however, suggests a simple answer to this fundamental question. Unlike a true floating-rate note, a swap has two-way cash flows: fixed versus floating. This feature allows the swap market to value the relative attractiveness of a swap's floating index by bidding the accompanying fixed rate up or down. Consequently, the floating-rate note valuation techniques mentioned are not required. The value of the floating-rate security is incorporated into the fixed cost quoted versus the floating payments. Therefore, valuation questions for swaps focus on the hypothetical fixed security.

## THE VALUATION METHODOLOGY
## FOR GENERIC SWAPS

The basic valuation method for *generic* swaps is to find the internal rate of return of the hypothetical fixed-security flows. For analytical purposes these flows, from the perspective of the fixed-rate payer, are the "proceeds" received from the "sale" of the hypothetical fixed-rate security versus an outflow of the

---

[8] In a generic swap the prices of the exchanged "securities" are equal and, thus, no net cash payment is exchanged upon settlement. In nongeneric swaps, the prices may not be equal. In such a case, the net of the two purchase prices would determine the cash payment upon settlement (see the section on nonpar swaps).

[9] These tools attempt to measure a floater's return by quantifying an implicit change in the floating rate whenever the note deviates from par.

fixed-rate payments plus the notional principal amount at maturity.[10] The internal rate of return (expressed as a semiannual bond equivalent) of the hypothetical fixed security is quoted as the all-in-cost versus the floating flows that constitute the index flat.

## THE VALUATION METHODOLOGY FOR NON-GENERIC SWAPS: THE GENERIC EQUIVALENT CASH-FLOW APPROACH (GECA)

The structuring of swaps to meet individual counterparty needs often results in nongeneric swaps. When a swap's floating side is not generic,[11] merely determining the internal rate of return of the fixed side would not produce a meaningful number. If the floating side could be adjusted to be generic, however, both generic and nongeneric swaps could be compared on an equivalent basis. To this end, we use the *Generic Equivalent Cash-Flow Approach* (GECA) to value nongeneric swaps.

Under GECA we use the following procedure in analyzing a swap:

- First, we construct the cash flows of the two "securities" as specified in the swap contract.
- Second, we determine whether the floating payments are generic. If they are not, we artificially adjust the floating cash flows to correspond to a stream of payments satisfying the generic standard.[12] If the floating payments must be altered, we must alter the fixed cash flows by these same dollar amounts (the *adjustment flows*) so that the swap's net cash flows remain unchanged. We will refer to these adjusted cash flows as the *analytical flows* to distinguish them from the *contractual flows*.
- The final step in the GECA process is to determine the internal rate of return (on a semiannual-equivalent basis) of the analytical fixed flows. Because the floating cash flows were adjusted to be the generic standard, this internal rate of return is the swap's all-in-cost.

---

[10] The proceeds are not cash but instead are the value of the hypothetical floating-rate note received in exchange. In a generic swap the value of the floating-rate note is par. For nongeneric swaps the proceeds are the net of the value of the floater and any cash payment on the settlement date (see the section on nonpar swaps).

[11] The floating payments are generic if they fulfill the conditions set forth in the generic swap, namely: The payments equal the index flat; the payment frequency equals the index maturity; the reset frequency equals the index maturity (with the exception of Treasury bills, which are reset weekly); and the day-count convention is consistent with the basis on which the index is quoted (see Exhibit 54–6).

[12] For some nongeneric swaps, it is not possible to adjust the floating cash flows to the generic standard in a precise manner without knowing the level of the floating index. (For example, see the section on mismatches.)

## VARIATIONS ON THE GENERIC THEME

This section will discuss nongeneric swap features that often occur in the market. Where possible for each such feature, we will use our GECA methodology to describe the feature's effect on the swap's all-in-cost. Because GECA requires that the floating payments be adjusted to the generic standard, our discussion will begin with nongeneric floating-payment structures. We will then consider nongeneric fixed-payment structures.

For ease of discussion, we will use a particular generic swap as an example. Then, by varying the swap's terms, we will create nongeneric swaps and discuss how these nongeneric terms affect the all-in-cost.

The swap described in Exhibit 54–3 is clean analytically:

- The floating payment is the index flat;
- The floating rate is based on *Reuters;*
- The payment and reset frequencies of the floating payment are equal to the term of the index;

**EXHIBIT 54–3**
**The Generic Swap — A Base Case Example**

| | |
|---|---|
| Notional principal amount | $10,000,000 |
| Maturity | May 15, 1992 |
| Trade date | May 8,1985 |
| Effective date | May 15,1985 |
| Settlement date | Effective date |

*Fixed Payment*

| | |
|---|---|
| Fixed coupon | 12.50 percent |
| Payment frequency | Semiannual |
| Day count | 30/360 |
| Pricing date | Trade date |

*Floating Payment*

| | |
|---|---|
| Floating index | Six-month LIBOR |
| Spread | None |
| Determination source | *Reuter Monitor Money Rates Service* |
| Payment frequency | Semiannual |
| Day count | Actual/360 |
| Reset frequency | Semiannual |
| First coupon | Six-month LIBOR quoted for value as of the settlement date |
| Premium or discount | None |
| All-in-cost | 12.50 percent (semiannual) versus six-month LIBOR flat |

- There are no day-count discrepancies between payments and their standards;
- The initial floating coupon is a current rate;
- There is no premium or discount;
- The swap settles "corporate";
- There are no short or long first coupon payments; and
- The swap is priced on the trade date.

## Floating-Rate Variations

***Spreads above or below the floating-rate index.*** Many swaps are structured with floating-rate payments based on the floating-rate index plus or minus an agreed-upon spread. For example, a swap might be structured with a fixed-rate payment of 12.50 percent semiannual and floating-rate payment of six-month LIBOR less 25 basis points. To express this swap's AIC according to market convention against the index flat, one is tempted simply to add 25 basis points to both sides and call it 12.75 percent semiannual versus six-month LIBOR flat. Unless the fixed rate and the floating rate are calculated on the same day-count basis and paid on the same frequency, however, this procedure would be inaccurate. Analyses of two different cases of this type of swap follow.

In swaps of the first case, fixed and floating payments have the same frequency. Consider our base case example described in Exhibit 54–3, with a spread under the floating index set at 25 basis points. To find the all-in-cost, we use GECA. First, the floating payments are artificially altered to become LIBOR flat, and then the fixed flows are altered by the same dollar amounts.

The first floating payment covers the period from May 15, 1985, until November 15, 1985 — or 184 days. An increase in the LIBOR rate by 25 basis points changes the payment by

$$0.0025 \times 10,000,000 \times 184/360 = 12,777.78$$

In terms of the fixed-note, this corresponds to 25.56 basis points higher on the first coupon. On the second coupon, the increase is 25.14 basis points because the next period covers only 181 days. Each fixed-rate payment must be adjusted in this way to determine the precise analytical cash flows and yield of the fixed-rate note. This procedure, when completed, shows the all-in-cost of this swap to be 12.7537 percent versus six-month LIBOR flat. Exhibit 54–4 depicts the contractual and analytical cash flows.

In swaps of the second case, fixed and floating payments have different frequencies. For this example, consider the generic base case swap with the floating rate changed to three-month LIBOR less 25 basis points reset and paid quarterly. As in the last example, the fixed-rate payer receives 25 basis points less on the floating payment. However, here this "loss" occurs quarterly instead

**EXHIBIT 54–4**
**The Effect of a Floating Spread with the Same Payment Frequencies**

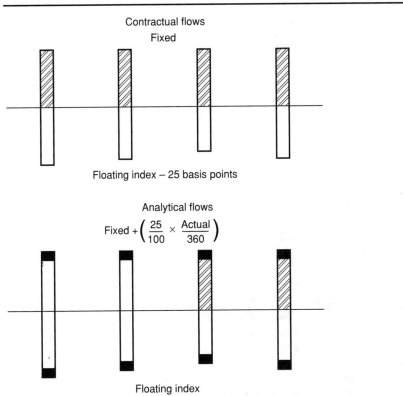

Contractual flows
Fixed

Floating index – 25 basis points

Analytical flows

$$\text{Fixed} + \left( \frac{25}{100} \times \frac{\text{Actual}}{360} \right)$$

Floating index

of semiannually, which adds a compounding effect to the day-count effect of the last example. To analyze this swap structure, we must analytically add the dollar value of the 25 basis points onto the quarterly floating-rate payments to create three-month LIBOR flat and then adjust the fixed cash flow stream by the same amounts. This procedure results in the analytical fixed-payment stream shown in Exhibit 54–5.

Exhibit 54–5 illustrates the Generic Equivalent Cash-Flow Approach: The fixed-rate payer essentially makes small quarterly payments to the floating-rate payer, while the floating-rate payer analytically pays three-month LIBOR flat. This extra quarterly analytical payment increases the all-in-cost of the fixed-rate payer to 12.7577 percent versus three-month LIBOR flat. The compounding effect is 0.4 basis point in addition to the 0.37-basis-point day-count effect seen in the previous example. Although both effects are small, it would be an error to ignore either one.

**EXHIBIT 54–5**
**The Effect of a Floating Spread with Different Payment Frequencies**

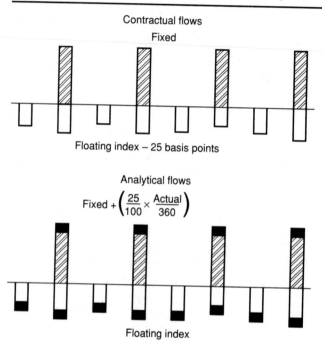

*Mismatches.*   The characteristics of the floating-rate side of a generic swap are based on the cash market in the short-term instrument on which the index is based. Specifically, the swap's reset frequency and payment frequency equal the maturity of the underlying cash instrument, and the swap's floating rate accrues on a day count consistent with its form of quotation. For example, the floating rate in a generic three-month LIBOR swap resets quarterly, pays quarterly, and accrues on an Actual/360 day count. The exception to this rule is a generic Treasury bill swap, which resets weekly.[13]

The flexibility of the interest-rate swap market, however, often creates transactions that have floating sides that deviate structurally from the underlying cash market. Any such deviation is called a *mismatch*. We will now discuss mismatches in payment frequency, day count, and reset frequency.[14]

---

[13] While inconsistent with the cash market in bills themselves, this convention appears consistent with the structure of most bill-based floating-rate notes.

[14] One swap can possess more than one mismatch. For example, consider a swap in which three-month LIBOR is reset semiannually and paid semiannually.

*Payment-frequency mismatch.* A payment-frequency mismatch occurs when the floating-rate payment frequency does not agree with the maturity of the floating-rate index. For example, a swap in which the fixed-rate payer receives interest based upon the three-month commercial paper index reset quarterly but paid semiannually is a payment-frequency mismatch swap.[15]

In this example, the fixed-rate payer loses the compounding of interest on interest that he would have received had he invested in the underlying cash instrument. Unfortunately, the precise cost of losing this "opportunity to compound" is difficult to calculate. An institution presented with a payment-frequency mismatch swap must make a largely qualitative assessment of both the amount of interest available to reinvest and the rate at which it should be compounded. Because both are impossible to determine completely in advance, no methodology can quantify precisely the effect of a payment-frequency mismatch on AIC.

Although this problem is difficult to assess, it does appear to have a reasonable solution. If the accrued floating-rate interest is compounded at the next floating rate until payment of the floating interest occurs, the fixed-rate payer should be satisfied.[16] If, however, the counterparties cannot agree on this or on some other compounding arrangement, they will be forced to make a qualitative judgment about the value of the payment-frequency mismatch.

*Day-count mismatch.* The generic interest-rate swap offers a day count consistent with the basis on which the floating-rate index is quoted. For example, if the certificate of deposit (CD) equivalent rate of one-month commercial paper is the basis for quoting the floating rate, then the floating-rate payment should accrue according to an Actual/360 day-count basis. Exhibit 54–6 outlines the most frequently used conventions.

Any inconsistencies between the swap conversion basis and the swap day count would alter the economics of the swap. Because the economic effect of a day-count mismatch varies with the absolute level of interest rates, no methodology can precisely quantify this nongeneric day-count effect. However, a counterparty can use GECA to estimate the magnitude of the day-count mismatch effect by making assumptions about the levels of the floating rate over the life of the swap.

---

[15] The receipt of a three-month index semiannually probably recurs because, for both credit and operational reasons, swap counterparties often prefer net transactions, i.e., where payment of both fixed and floating interest occurs on the same day.

[16] If there are more than two reset periods in each payment period (for example, one-month commercial paper, which is reset monthly and paid semiannually), then the total accrued before a given reset period should be compounded forward through that period at that period's rate. This compounding should occur for all resets (after the first set).

**EXHIBIT 54–6**
**Floating-Rate Generic Standards**

| Floating Index | Cash Market Quotation Basis | Swap Conversion Basis* | Swap Day Count | Payment Frequency | Reset Frequency |
|---|---|---|---|---|---|
| Treasury bills | Discount | BE | Actual/Actual | Term of index | Weekly |
| Commercial paper | Discount | CDE | Actual/360 | Term of index | Term of index |
| Bankers' acceptances | Discount | CDE | Actual/360 | Term of index | Term of index |
| LIBOR | CDE | CDE | Actual/360 | Term of index | Term of index |
| Prime | CDE | CDE | Actual/360 | Quarterly | Daily |
| Certificates of deposit | CDE | CDE | Actual/360 | Term of index | Term of index |
| Federal funds | CDE | CDE | Actual/360 | Compounded daily to mutually agreeable frequency | Daily |

* In the case of indexes quoted on a discount basis, the actual number of days in a floating-rate period—and not a predetermined notion as to the maturity of the discount instrument—should be used when converting to a bond equivalent (BE) or CD equivalent (CDE) basis. (See the *Code of Standard Wording, Assumptions and Provisions for Swaps, 1985 Edition*.) For indexes with maturities of 182 days or fewer, the following formulas can be used to convert between a rate quoted on a discount basis (d), a bond equivalent basis (b) and a CD equivalent basis (c):

$$b = \frac{365 \times d}{360 - d \times t} \qquad c = b \times \frac{360}{365}$$

where t is the actual number of days in the floating-rate period.

*Reset-frequency mismatch.* A reset-frequency mismatch occurs when the reset frequency does not agree with the maturity of the floating-rate index.[17] An illustration of this nongeneric variation would be our base case example changed to require monthly resets of the six-month LIBOR index. In this revised swap, the interval between resets is shorter than the maturity of the index.

This nongeneric feature clearly changes the value of the swap. Resetting an index more frequently than its stated term ignores the fact that, by choosing a particular maturity, cash investors choose to forfeit more frequent repricing opportunities. Because the cash investor's repricing expectations are theoretically incorporated in the index, it is inappropriate to alter the reset frequency of the index without considering its impact on value.

The value of such a structure, however, depends on the investor's expectations and portfolio considerations. For example, a fixed-rate payer who wishes to match existing short-term liabilities that are reset weekly with a three- or six-month private-sector swap index might be willing to pay more for a swap with more frequent nongeneric resets than for a swap with a generic structure. Little can be done, however, to quantify the effect of this market anomaly on the pricing of interest-rate swaps. Such nongeneric reset features, however, certainly deserve qualitative consideration when they appear.

*Short or long first floating-rate period.* A swap may trade with a first floating-rate payment period that is either shorter or longer than those in the remainder of the swap.[18] In our base case generic example, this would occur if the effective date were July 15, 1985.[19] In this case, the appropriate floating-rate index for the first floating-rate period is at issue.

We believe that the correct index in this example would be four-month LIBOR flat. In general, if a private-sector swap has a short or long first floating-rate period and the structure of the floating side is otherwise generic, then the index for the first period should have a maturity equal to the time from the effective date until the first reset date.[20] This structure is consistent with the cash market. Furthermore, if there is a spread over or under the regular index, then the same spread should apply to the first-period index.

---

[17] Therefore, the generic Treasury bill swap, in which the floating rate resets weekly, is a reset-frequency mismatch. The structure nevertheless is considered to be generic because it is consistent with the underlying market in bill-based floating-rate notes.

[18] This would most likely occur in the case of a secondary market trade or the sale of a seasoned swap. A *seasoned swap* is a swap held in a position by a market maker awaiting primary distribution.

[19] The trade date would be changed to July 8, 1985, to maintain corporate settlement. All other terms would remain the same.

[20] Because of the anomalies of the short Treasury bill market, Treasury bill swaps generally pay the stated index regardless of the term of the initial variable-rate period.

The presence of a payment-frequency or reset-frequency mismatch creates problems for determining the correct index for a long or short first coupon. For example, what would be the proper short first coupon for a five-week first floating-payment period on a swap with a regular floating-rate index of three-month LIBOR reset weekly and paid quarterly? Definitive market convention has not yet been established in this area. However, the rule proposed above for use with otherwise generic swaps could be a starting point for negotiating the appropriate short or long first coupon.

## Fixed-Rate Variations

*Payment frequencies.* By definition generic swaps have semiannual or annual fixed-rate coupons. Although rare, other fixed-rate payment frequencies do exist. The rule for computing the all-in-cost is the same whether the fixed coupons are semiannual or nonsemiannual: The AIC equals the internal rate of return (expressed on a semiannual bond-equivalent basis) of the analytical fixed flows.

For a generic (par) swap with a semiannual fixed coupon, therefore, the AIC equals the fixed-coupon rate. For an otherwise generic swap with a nonsemiannual fixed coupon, the AIC equals the semiannual equivalent of the fixed-coupon rate.

For example, if the base case example is changed to pay a 12.50 percent coupon annually, the annual yield of the hypothetical fixed-rate note becomes 12.50 percent, but the swap would be quoted at the semiannual all-in-cost of 12.132 percent. If one were to structure a generic swap with a 12.50 percent semiannual all-in-cost but with an annual fixed-rate coupon, the annual coupon would be 12.891 percent. (See the Appendix for conversion formulas.)

*Short and long first fixed-rate period.* Except when closing out an existing swap, swaps settle flat (i.e., with no accrued interest).[21] Consequently, when valuing a swap that settles on any date other than a fixed-coupon payment date, the present value calculation must incorporate a "long" or "short" first coupon period. The mathematics of this discounting is such that, on an otherwise generic swap, the all-in-cost will not equal the coupon rate if the first coupon is short or long. The Appendix contains formulas for the discounting process.

*Day counts.* Although the market convention is to structure swaps with fixed-rate payments accruing on a 30/360 day-count basis, other day-count meth-

---

[21] Closeouts are the termination of an existing swap between counterparties through a mutually agreeable cash payment. See Patrick J. Dunlavy and Thomas W. Jasper, "Secondary Trading: The Key to Further Development of the Interest Rate Swap Market," *Quarterly Statement,* November 1984.

ods are used. The Actual/360 day count, the Actual/365, and Actual/Actual all appear. To determine the price or equivalent generic all-in-cost for such a nongeneric swap, the GECA method is applied to the actual fixed-coupon cash flows to construct the analytical fixed flows, which then are discounted on a 30/360 basis.

## Effective Date

The generic swap provides for five business days to elapse between the trade date and the effective date. (For simplicity in this discussion, assume that the effective date is the settlement date.) Any variation of this "settlement period" alters the economics of the swap and, therefore, requires analysis.

The impact of an accelerated or delayed effective date is the opportunity costs afforded each counterparty by entering into the swap with an irregular settlement period. One measure of this impact is the difference between the fixed and floating interest that otherwise might have accrued. Typically, the two counterparties agree either to pay this adjustment on the settlement date or to amortize it over the life of the swap.

## Nonpar Swaps

Thus far we have examined swaps with no net cash payment at settlement and with both hypothetical securities valued at par. At this point we will generalize the GECA methodology to incorporate cash payments and situations in which the hypothetical securities are not at par. This methodology can then be applied to analyze any swap (except those with the features mentioned above that render precise analysis impossible). Exhibit 54–7 summarizes the sequence of steps in the analysis.

It may be useful to place the previously described GECA analysis into the framework of Exhibit 54–7. Steps 1, 2, and 3 are performed in the analysis of all swaps. Thus far, in our all-in-cost determination the floating-rate note has been assumed to be at par (step 4), and there were no cash payments. Therefore, the proceeds in step 7 have been par, and step 8 could be completed with 100 as the proceeds.

*Even swaps.* A swap with no cash payment at the settlement date occurs when, at pricing, the value of the hypothetical fixed-rate note equals the value of the hypothetical floating-rate note received in exchange. The two securities can be equal in two situations—when they both are at par or when they both are at the same nonpar price. We call the swap situation in which both hypothetical securities are at par a *par swap*. The second situation, in which the securities have equal but nonpar prices, is called an *even swap* (see Exhibit 54–8). Note that because the hypothetical securities in a generic swap have current, regular coupons, they are at par. Therefore, generic swaps are par swaps.

**EXHIBIT 54–7**
**Summary of Generic Equivalent Cash-Flow Approach (GECA)**

1. Determine fixed and floating contractual flows.
2. Determine adjustment flows needed to alter floating payments to generic index flat.
3. Determine fixed and floating analytical flows equal to the sum of contractual and adjustment flows plus par at maturity.
4. Find present value of next analytical floating coupon plus par discounted at current market index rate for appropriate period.

To find premium/discount, given all-in-cost:

5. Find present value of analytical fixed flows discounted at all-in-cost.
6. Calculate premium/discount equal to difference between two present values computed in Steps 4 and 5.

To find all-in-cost, given premium/discount:

7. Determine proceeds received by fixed rate payer equal to value of floating rate note received (from Step 4) plus any discount received or minus any premium paid.
8. Find semiannual equivalent internal rate of return of combination of proceeds determined in Step 7 and analytical fixed flows from Step 3.

**EXHIBIT 54–8**
**Classification of Swaps by Pricing**

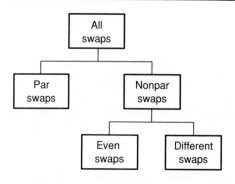

***Differential swaps: Premiums and discounts.*** A swap involving a cash payment at settlement occurs when the values of the two hypothetical securities are not equal at pricing. Because the payment compensates for the difference in value of the two securities, we call this swap a *differential* swap. By swap market convention, if a counterparty makes a payment at the settlement date of a swap, then that payment is referred to as a *premium*. If a counterparty receives a payment at the settlement date, then that payment is known as a *discount*.

Although this terminology has been borrowed from the bond market, its meaning in the swap market is distinct. In the bond market, these terms refer to the difference between the price of a security and its own par value. In the swap market, these terms refer to the difference in price between the two hypothetical securities involved in a swap. In a differential swap, the cash payment is both a premium (to the party that makes the payment) and a discount (to the party that receives the payment).

***The valuation of even and differential swaps with GECA.*** The major procedural change that must be made when analyzing nonpar swaps is that we must determine the "proceeds" of the fixed-rate note sale. This step is not necessary in analyzing a par swap for which the proceeds are always par. In a nonpar swap, the proceeds of the sale of the hypothetical fixed-rate security are the value of the hypothetical floating-rate note received in exchange less any premium paid or plus any discount received. When solving for all-in-cost, the premium or discount is known, and the hypothetical floater must be valued to determine the fixed-rate payer's proceeds. Conversely, when determining the appropriate premium or discount, one must determine the value of both hypothetical securities.

***Valuing the hypothetical floating-rate note.*** In interest-rate swap analysis, the hypothetical floating-rate note paying the index flat is considered to be at par on any of its payment dates. If at some point the index flat is not deemed to be an appropriate return in the market, the swap market will revalue the fixed security to reflect new conditions. Thus, the benchmark index-flat floater will remain at par on coupon dates.

Once a coupon rate is set, however, market variations of the appropriate maturity index can cause the hypothetical security to trade above or below par.[22] For example, in a generic swap, if three-month LIBOR is 9 percent at the reset but, one month later, two-month LIBOR is at 10 percent, the flat price of the floater will be worth less than par. To determine the full price of the floating-rate note between coupon payments, determine the present value of the next coupon, which has been previously set, plus par, which is the value of

---

[22] The appropriate maturity is the period from the settlement date to the next floating-rate reset date.

the floater on the next payment date. The discount rate used is the current market rate for the appropriate maturity of the index. In the example, the appropriate discount rate is 10 percent.

*Determining all-in-cost of a nonpar swap.* To determine the all-in-cost of a swap with a cash payment at settlement or with a nonpar floating-rate note, first the analytical fixed-bond flows paid versus the receipt of the generic index-flat note must be constructed using GECA (steps 1, 2, and 3 of Exhibit 54–7). The proceeds of this hypothetical fixed-rate note are the value of the hypothetical floating-rate note plus any discount received or minus any premium paid by the fixed-rate payer. This is step 7 of Exhibit 54–7. Then in step 8, the all-in-cost is calculated by computing the internal rate of return of the fixed-bond flows.

For example, let us alter the base case example to include a payment of 0.6 percent of the notional principal amount to the floating-rate payer on the settlement date, and let us assume that the floating-rate note has a price of 99.6; all other terms of the base case remain the same. The analytical fixed-rate security (versus six-month LIBOR flat) is a seven-year bond paying 12.50 percent semiannually with a price of 99. The semiannual all-in-cost of this swap (equal to the yield on this hypothetical bond) is 12.72 percent.

*Pricing secondary market or seasoned swaps with GECA.* In secondary market or in seasoned-swap transactions, the terms of the fixed and floating payments have previously been negotiated. Current market levels determine the all-in-cost. The premium or discount is the unknown. The process of determining this payment is known as *pricing* a swap.

The procedure for pricing a swap is similar to that described for determining a swap's all-in-cost. Referring to Exhibit 54–7, steps 1, 2, and 3 are performed as before to construct the analytical flows for the two hypothetical securities. At this point each of the two component securities is priced (steps 4 and 5). The method for pricing the floating-rate note has been described. The fixed-rate note is priced using a conventional bond math approach discounting the analytical cash flows at the all-in-cost.

The difference between the prices of the hypothetical fixed-rate and floating-rate notes is the market price of the swap. If the floating security is worth more than the fixed security, then the fixed-rate payer would make a cash payment to the floating-rate payer when entering into the swap. In the same market situation, the fixed-rate payer would receive a cash payment if closing out the swap. Conversely, if the fixed security is worth more than the floating security, the floating-rate payer would make a cash payment to the fixed-rate payer when entering into the swap, or he would receive cash payment if closing out the swap. In addition to the cash payment, net accrued is also paid.

For example, suppose that the floating-rate note is worth 99 and the fixed-rate security is worth 95. The fixed-rate payer would receive a payment of four points (plus or minus the net accrued) if closing out the swap. In essence, the fixed-rate payer is repurchasing his fixed-rate security worth 95 with the floating-rate note that he holds that is worth 99. The excess of four points is returned.


## CONCLUSION

As long as the interest-rate swap market operates as a negotiated over-the-counter market, swap structures will vary as widely as the counterparties themselves. In our approach to interest-rate swap mathematics and pricing, we do not intend to suggest that one structure is superior to another. Instead, we simply wish to establish a standard—the generic swap—against which the myriad varieties of swaps can be measured. We hope that the introduction of this standard, coupled with a fair and consistent framework for analysis of nongeneric swaps, will eliminate the uncertainty about interest rate swap mathematics. Ultimately, our goal is to increase understanding and encourage wider use of this valuable asset and liability management tool.


## APPENDIX

This Appendix provides a technical description of how to price generic and nongeneric interest-rate swaps using standard bond pricing methodology.[1] These procedures are based upon the notion that an interest-rate swap can be considered an exchange of an hypothetical fixed-income security for a hypothetical floating-rate note (see Exhibit 54–7 in the text). The Appendix will first discuss the pricing of the fixed side of the swap (including any adjustment flows required) and then describe the pricing of the floating side (which has been adjusted to the index flat). Each formula will be demonstrated through an example based upon the base case generic swap set forth in Exhibit 54–3. For simplicity, the Appendix assumes that the floating rate is based on a generic LIBOR index, with a spread introduced in the appropriate examples.

*Discounting Methods.* The pricing of the fixed and floating sides of a swap involves present value calculations. The discounting methods used are consistent with the pricing methods used in the corporate fixed-rate bond and

---

[1] The Appendix discusses only the pricing methodology for swaps and not the computation of a swap's all-in-cost. All-in-cost is determined through an internal rate of return calculation. This calculation is usually an iterative procedure that prices the swap using trial values of all-in-cost until one results in the actual price.

floating-rate note markets, respectively. This means that the flows of a fixed-rate side of the swap, including any adjustment flows due to a spread under or over the floating index, are discounted scientifically on a 30/360 day-count basis. In contrast, the flows of the floating side, adjusted to have no spread, are discounted in a straight-line manner using the Actual/360 day-count basis in the case of private-sector indexes. Because the benchmark for quoting all-in-cost is the index flat, spreads under the index can be thought of as payments from the fixed-rate payer to the floating-rate payer. As such, these payments (the adjustment flows) should be discounted at the fixed-rate payer's all-in-cost. Only by using this convention can two swaps with the same all-in-cost (one with no spread and one with a spread under the index and a correspondingly lower fixed-rate coupon) truly be called equivalent in terms of yield.

*Pricing the Hypothetical Fixed-Rate Security.* The price of the fixed-rate side of a swap can be viewed as the sum of two components: (1) the present value or full price of a fixed-rate bond (the Fixed Bond) based on the fixed-rate payer's contractual payments and (2) the present value of those flows necessary to adjust the floating side to the generic standard if possible (the Adjustment Flows). The discount rate for both present values is the swap's all-in-cost, and discounting is done using methods consistent with corporate fixed-rate bond pricing.

We begin by discussing the pricing of the Fixed Bond in a swap with semi-annual fixed payments. For such a swap, the formula for the present value of the contractual fixed-rate swap payments plus the hypothetical principal repayment at maturity is

$$\sum_{i=1}^{n} \frac{\dfrac{C}{2}}{\left(1 + \dfrac{\text{AIC}}{200}\right)^{P_i}} + \frac{100}{\left(1 + \dfrac{\text{AIC}}{200}\right)^{P_n}} \tag{54-1}$$

where

$n$ = the number of fixed coupon payments from the settlement date to maturity,

$C$ = the fixed coupon rate (expressed as a percentage),

$\text{AIC}$ = the all-in-cost (expressed as a percentage), and

$P_i$ = the number of whole and fractional fixed coupon periods from the settlement date to the ith fixed coupon payment date.

Using this formula to price the Fixed Bond in the example for May 15, 1985 settlement, at an all-in-cost of 12.50 percent, we make the following calculations:

Present value of the Fixed Bond =

$$\frac{\frac{12.50}{2}}{(1 + \frac{12.50}{200})^1} + \frac{\frac{12.50}{2}}{(1 + \frac{12.50}{200})^2} + \frac{\frac{12.50}{2}}{(1 + \frac{12.50}{200})^3}$$

$$+ \ldots + \frac{\frac{12.50}{2}}{(1 + \frac{12.50}{200})^{14}} + \frac{100}{(1 + \frac{12.50}{200})^{14}} = 100$$

Equation 54–1 applies only to swaps that have no short or long first coupons. If the first fixed coupon is short or long and the remaining fixed payments are semiannual, the following formula is appropriate:

Present value of the Fixed Bond =

$$\frac{\frac{C}{2} \times P_1}{\left(1 + \frac{\text{AIC}}{200}\right)^{P_1}} + \sum_{i=2}^{n} \frac{\frac{C}{2}}{\left(1 + \frac{\text{AIC}}{200}\right)^{P_i}} \qquad (54\text{–}2)$$

$$+ \frac{100}{\left(1 + \frac{\text{AIC}}{200}\right)^{P_n}}$$

If the base case swap had an effective date of April 1, 1985, with a short first coupon payment on May 15, 1985, the price of the Fixed Bond for settlement on April 1, 1985, at an all-in-cost of 12.50 percent would be found as follows:

Present value of the Fixed Bond =

$$\frac{\frac{12.50}{2} \times \frac{44}{180}}{\left(1 + \frac{12.50}{200}\right)^{\frac{44}{180}}} + \frac{\frac{12.50}{2}}{\left(1 + \frac{12.50}{200}\right)^{1 + \frac{44}{180}}}$$

$$+ \frac{\frac{12.50}{2}}{\left(1 + \frac{12.50}{200}\right)^{2 + \frac{44}{180}}} + \ldots + \frac{\frac{12.50}{2}}{\left(1 + \frac{12.50}{200}\right)^{14 + \frac{44}{180}}}$$

$$+ \frac{100}{\left(1 + \frac{12.50}{200}\right)^{14 + \frac{44}{180}}} = 100.034$$

For swaps in which the payment frequency is not semiannual, the following generalization of Equation 54–2 is used to price the Fixed Bond:

$$\frac{\frac{C}{\text{freq}} \times P_1}{\left(1 + \frac{\text{AIC}_c}{(100 \times \text{freq})}\right)^{P_1}} + \sum_{i=2}^{n} \frac{\frac{C}{\text{freq}}}{\left(1 + \frac{\text{AIC}_c}{(100 \times \text{freq})}\right)^{P_i}} \qquad (54\text{–}3)$$

$$+ \frac{100}{\left(1 + \frac{\text{AIC}_c}{(100 \times \text{freq})}\right)^{P_n}}$$

where

$freq$ = the number of fixed-rate payments per year, and

$AIC_c$ = the all-in-cost converted to the same compounding frequency as the number of fixed-rate payments per year (expressed as a percentage)

Under market convention, the all-in-cost is always quoted as a semiannual rate. To convert the all-in-cost to a rate with a compounding frequency consistent with the number of fixed coupon payments per year (as required in Equation 54–3), use the following formula:

$$AIC_c = \left[ \left( 1 + \frac{AIC}{200} \right)^{\frac{2}{freq}} - 1 \right] \times 100 \times freq \qquad (54\text{–}4)$$

For the base case swap changed to have a coupon of 12.75 percent paid annually, the two steps in computing the price of the fixed bond for settlement on May 15, 1985, at an all-in-cost of 12.50 Percent semiannual are the following: First, the semiannual all-in-cost is converted to its annual equivalent using Equation 54–4:

$$AIC_c = \left[ \left( 1 + \frac{12.50}{200} \right)^{\frac{2}{1}} - 1 \right] \times 100 \times 1 = 12.890625$$

Then the price of the fixed bond is computed using Equation 54–3 as follows: Present value of the fixed bond =

$$\frac{\frac{12.75}{1}}{\left( 1 + \frac{12.890625}{(100 \times 1)} \right)^{1}} + \frac{\frac{12.75}{1}}{\left( 1 + \frac{12.890625}{(100 \times 1)} \right)^{2}}$$

$$+ \ldots + \frac{\frac{12.75}{1}}{\left( 1 + \frac{12.890625}{(100 \times 1)} \right)^{7}}$$

$$+ \frac{100}{\left( 1 + \frac{12.890625}{(100 \times 1)} \right)^{7}} = 99.376$$

If the swap has a spread under or over the index, we must determine the present value of the Adjustment Flows needed to alter the floating side to the index flat. These flows correspond to the spread that accrues during each floating payment period. Since the spread accrues on the same basis as the LIBOR index (Actual/360), the actual number of days in the payment period determines the size of each Adjustment Flow. Since the adjustment for the spread is considered part of the hypothetical fixed security, the discount rate for the Adjustment Flows is the swap's all-in-cost. These ideas are reflected in the following formula for computing the present value of the Adjustment Flows:

Present value of the adjustment flows =

$$\sum_{i=1}^{n} \frac{S \times \frac{D_i}{360}}{\left(1 + \frac{AIC_c}{(100 \times freq)}\right)^{P_i}} \tag{54-5}$$

where

$n$ = the number of floating coupon payments from the settlement date to maturity,

$S$ = the spread under the index (expressed as a percentage),

$D_i$ = the actual number of days of interest accrual for the ith floating payments,

freq = the number of floating-rate payments per year,

$AIC_c$ = the all-in-cost converted to the same compounding frequency as the number of floating-rate payments per year (expressed as a percentage), and

$P_i$ = the number of whole and fractional floating coupon periods from the settlement date to the ith floating coupon payment date.

If the base base swap had a spread of 25 basis points under the six-month LIBOR index and was priced for settlement on May 15, 1985, at an all-in-cost of 12.50 percent, the formulas for calculating the present value of the Adjustment Flows (to convert the floating side to six-month LIBOR flat) would be applied as follows:

Present value of the adjustment flows =

$$\frac{0.25 \times \frac{184}{360}}{\left(1 + \frac{12.50}{(100 \times 2)}\right)^1} + \frac{0.25 \times \frac{181}{360}}{\left(1 + \frac{12.50}{(100 \times 2)}\right)^2}$$

$$+ \frac{0.25 \times \frac{184}{360}}{\left(1 + \frac{12.50}{(100 \times 2)}\right)^3} + \ldots + \frac{0.25 \times \frac{182}{360}}{\left(1 + \frac{12.50}{(100 \times 2)}\right)^{14}} = 1.161$$

Because the cash flows of the hypothetical fixed-income security are the combination of the cash flows of the Fixed Bond and the Adjustment Flows, the full price of the fixed side is simply calculated as follows:

Full price of the fixed side =

Present value of the fixed bond +

Present value of the adjustment flows

When computing the price of a swap being closed out in the secondary market, the settlement date of the transaction will often not be the beginning of a fixed or floating coupon period. The transaction, therefore, will involve accrued interest. A calculation of the accrued interest on the fixed side must include accrued interest on the Adjustment Flows to be consistent with our methodology. To compute the portion of the full price that is accrued interest, the following formulas are used:

$$\text{Accrued interest on the fixed bond} = \frac{D_F}{360} \times C \qquad (54\text{--}6)$$

$$\text{Accrued interest on the adjustment flows} = \frac{D_A}{360} \times S \qquad (54\text{--}7)$$

where

$D_F$ = The number of days (computed on a 30/360 basis) from the previous fixed payment[2] to the settlement date of the secondary market transaction,

$D_A$ = The number of days (computed on an Actual/360 basis) from the previous floating payment date to the settlement date of the secondary market transaction.

$C$ = The fixed coupon rate (expressed as a percentage),

$S$ = The spread under the index (expressed as a percentage).

If the base case swap with a spread of 25 basis points under the index were priced for a closeout in the secondary market with a settlement date of June 1, 1985, at an all-in-cost of 12.75 percent, the full price and accrued interest for the fixed side would be found by applying Equations 54–3, 54–5, 54–6, and 54–7 as follows:

Present value of the fixed bond =

$$\frac{\frac{12.50}{2}}{\left(1 + \frac{12.75}{200}\right)^{\frac{164}{180}}} + \frac{\frac{12.50}{2}}{\left(1 + \frac{12.75}{200}\right)^{1 + \frac{164}{180}}}$$

$$+ \frac{\frac{12.50}{2}}{\left(1 + \frac{12.75}{200}\right)^{2 + \frac{164}{180}}} + \ldots +$$

$$\frac{\frac{12.50}{2}}{\left(1 + \frac{12.75}{200}\right)^{13 + \frac{164}{180}}} + \frac{100}{\left(1 + \frac{12.75}{200}\right)^{13 + \frac{164}{180}}} = 99.409$$

---

[2] In this case (as well as in all cases that follow), if no payment has yet occurred, the number of days is counted from the swap's original effective date to the settlement date of this secondary market transaction.

Present value of the adjustment flows =

$$\frac{0.25 \times \frac{184}{360}}{\left(1 + \frac{12.75}{(100 \times 2)}\right)^{\frac{164}{180}}} + \frac{0.25 \times \frac{181}{360}}{\left(1 + \frac{12.75}{(100 \times 2)}\right)^{1 + \frac{164}{180}}}$$

$$+ \frac{0.25 \times \frac{184}{360}}{\left(1 + \frac{12.75}{(100 \times 2)}\right)^{2 + \frac{164}{180}}} + \ldots +$$

$$\frac{0.25 \times \frac{182}{360}}{\left(1 + \frac{12.75}{(100 \times 2)}\right)^{13 + \frac{164}{180}}} = 1.159$$

Full price of the fixed side = $99.409 + 1.159 = 100.568$

Accrued interest of the fixed bond = $\frac{16}{360} \times 12.50 = 0.566$

Accrued interest of the adjustment flows = $\frac{17}{360} \times 0.25 = 0.012$

Total accrued interest of the fixed side = $0.556 + 0.012 = 0.568$

***Pricing the Hypothetical Floating-Rate Note.*** To price the floating-rate side of a swap, we use the discounting conventions for floating-rate notes. Since the floating-rate note is assumed to have a value of par at the next payment date, the price of the floating-rate side is the present value of the next payment plus par. The discount rate used to calculate the present value should be the current market rate of the appropriate maturity index for the period from the settlement date to the next floating payment date. For example, consider a swap with a floating side that resets and pays quarterly and floats off three-month LIBOR. When priced with two months to the next floating payment, the discount rate should be the current two-month LIBOR rate. The formula for the full price of the floating-rate side, adjusted to be the index flat, is:

$$\text{Present value of the floating side} = \frac{100 + ER \times \frac{D_{PN}}{360}}{1 + \frac{CR}{100} \times \frac{D_{SN}}{360}} \qquad (54\text{–}8)$$

where

$ER$ = The current rate in effect for the next floating coupon payment (expressed as a percentage),

$D_{PN}$ = The actual number of days from the previous floating payment date to the next floating payment date,

$CR$ = The current market rate of the index for the period from the settlement date to the next floating payment date (expressed as a percentage),

$D_{SN}$ = The actual number of days from the settlement date to the next floating payment date.

The accrued interest portion of the full price of the floating side can be calculated using the following formula:

Accrued interest on the floating side =

$$\frac{ER \times (D_{PN} - D_{SN})}{360} \tag{54–9}$$

To price the floating-rate side of the base case swap with a settlement date of June 1, 1985, assuming the current floating rate in effect was set at 8.9375 percent on May 15, 1985, and that the current market rate for five and one-half month LIBOR is 9.00 percent, the aforementioned formulas would be applied as follows:

Full price of the floating side =

$$\frac{100 + (8.9375 \times \frac{184}{360})}{1 + (\frac{9.00}{100} \times \frac{167}{360})} = 100.377$$

Accrued interest on floating side =

$$8.9375 \times \frac{(184 - 167)}{360} = 0.422$$

***Pricing the Swap.*** After calculating the present values of the fixed and floating sides, we can calculate the current market price of the entire swap. Recall that we have described a swap as an exchange of two securities: a hypothetical fixed-rate note (including analytical adjustment flows) and a hypothetical floating-rate note (adjusted to the index flat). Under this notion, on closing out a swap, each party will buy back the security originally sold and sell back the other party's security originally purchased. The price of the swap will be the difference in the prices of these two securities.

Expressed as a formula, the swap's full price paid by the fixed-rate payer on closing out the swap is:

Full price paid by the fixed-rate payer =
Full price of the fixed side − Full price of the floating side

If this full price is negative, the cash payment is made by the floating-rate payer. The portion of the full price that is accounted for as accrued interest is given by the formula:

Net accrued interest paid by the fixed-rate payer =
Accrued interest on the fixed side −
Accrued interest on the floating side

If this net accrued interest is negative, the floating-rate payer has accrued a larger interest liability than the fixed-rate payer.

Consider again the base case swap with a spread of 25 basis points under six-month LIBOR and an original floating rate set at 8.9375 percent. To close out this swap on June 1, 1985, at an all-in-cost of 12.50 percent and a current market five and one-half month LIBOR rate of 9.00 percent, these equations show that the fixed-rate payer would pay the floating-rate payer 0.191 percent of the notional principal amount, of which 0.146 is net accrued interest. The calculations would be as follows:

Full price paid by the fixed-rate payer $= 100.568 - 100.377$
$$= 0.191$$
Net accrued interest paid by the fixed-rate payer $= 0.568 - 0.422$
$$= 0.146$$

# CHAPTER 55

## EURODOLLAR FUTURES/
## INTEREST-RATE
## SWAP ARBITRAGE*

*Daniel Nadler*
Shearson Lehman Hutton

It is no secret that shorter maturity interest-rate swaps are closely linked to the Eurodollar futures market. In fact, there is even a market for "IMM swaps," that is, rate swaps whose interest accrual periods coincide with the settlement dates of a sequence, or strip, of Eurodollar futures contracts. Because the markets are linked so closely, we believe it would be appropriate to define rate swap mathematics in terms of Eurodollar futures mathematics rather than in terms of the traditionally used bond analysis. The purpose of this chapter is to show how the Eurodollar futures market can be used to hedge and create shorter maturity interest rate swaps.[1]

We will begin with a description of the Eurodollar contract and an introduction to Eurodollar futures mathematics. We emphasize the mechanics of hedge ratio and target rate calculations in order to acquaint the reader with the basics of Eurodollar futures hedging. We then give an example of Eurodollar futures hedging alternatives available to a floating-rate note issuer. By looking at the problem in great detail and by carefully constructing the exposition of its solution, we lay the groundwork for analyzing shorter maturity interest-rate swaps in terms of Eurodollar futures mathematics.

The swap problem itself is then tackled. A brief overview of the market for interest-rate swaps is provided, followed by an indepth look at pricing and

*The author would like to thank the following for their contributions: Carol Bassok, Georges Courtadon, Stan Jonas, Mark Pitts and Michael Rulle.

[1] For an overview of hedging interest-rate volatility, see Chapter 49.

hedge ratio calculations for the straightforward case of a LIBOR-for-fixed IMM swap. The ability to arbitrage the interest-rate swap market or equivalently, to create swaps synthetically, follows almost immediately. Finally, we look at zero coupon and amortizing swaps which are also easily created through the use of Eurodollar futures.

## THE FUNDAMENTALS

### The Eurodollar Futures Contract

Eurodollars are deposits of U.S. dollars in institutions outside the United States. Because short-term Eurodollar lending and borrowing is so common, the International Monetary Market introduced the Eurodollar Time Deposit futures contract in 1981. Created to provide a means for managing the risks inherent in lending and borrowing Eurodollars, the futures contract is tied to the London Interbank Offered Rate (LIBOR), the rate at which Eurodollars are offered among top-tier international banks. Basically, the contract is designed to protect future interest expense (income) on $1 million for 90 days from fluctuations in three-month LIBOR. Highlights of contract specifications are presented in Exhibit 55–1.

Eurodollar futures trade in 12 contract months on a March-June-September-December cycle out for three years. The futures contract is quoted and traded in terms of a price which is equal to 100 minus the annualized futures interest rate. For example, a Eurodollar price of 92.00 is simply another way of saying that the

**EXHIBIT 55–1**
**Contract Highlights**

| | |
|---|---|
| Exchange: | International Monetary Market (IMM) of the Chicago Mercantile Exchange |
| Months traded: | March, June, September, December |
| Contract size: | $1 million |
| Price quotation: | 100 minus annualized futures yield (simple, or add-on, interest) |
| Minimum fluctuation in price: | .01% (1 basis point) @ $25/basis point |
| Daily trading limit: | None |
| Settlement: | Cash, based upon the rate at which three-month Eurodollar Time Deposits are being offered by the London market (LIBOR) |
| Last day of trading: | 2nd London business day prior to 3rd Wednesday of contract month |
| Settlement date: | Last day of trading |
| Hours of trading: | 7:20 a.m. – 2:00 p.m. (Chicago) |
| | 7:20 a.m. – 9:30 a.m. (last day of trading) |

futures LIBOR rate is 8.00% . The $25 price value of a one basis point change in the futures price follows from the fact that simple interest on $1 million for 90 days is equal to

$$\$1,000,000 \times (\text{rate} \times 90/360)$$

and that a one basis point (.01% ) change in rate corresponds to a $25 change in interest expense (income).

The final settlement price for the contract is set equal to 100 minus three-month LIBOR. Three-month LIBOR, in turn, will be determined by the rate at which three-month Eurodollar Time Deposit funds are being offered, at the time of settlement, to major banks by the London market. Since Eurodollar futures do not have an underlying cash security and consequently do not call for actual delivery, settlement is made in cash. In other words, unlike other open futures contracts which call for delivery of the underlying commodity after the last day of trading, open Eurodollar contracts are automatically offset at the final settlement price.

## Eurodollar Futures Pricing

In order to fully understand the Eurodollar futures contract, a basic knowledge of Eurodollar futures pricing is warranted. Not unlike more traditional commodities, a "carry" argument is used to establish a fair price. When market prices deviate significantly from theoretical prices, arbitrage (riskless profit) opportunities arise. Arbitrageurs, in turn, force market prices back in line with theoretical prices, thereby ensuring market efficiency. In order to illustrate this point, consider the following spot yield curve:

| Maturity (in months) | LIBOR |
|---|---|
| 1 | 7.000% |
| 2 | 7.125 |
| 3 | 7.250 |
| 5 | 7.500 |
| 6 | 7.500 |

Suppose we are trying to price the Eurodollar futures contract which stops trading exactly 60 days from today. Furthermore, consider a five-month (150-day) LIBOR borrower. The borrower is simply concerned with his dollar expense over the five-month period and should be indifferent as to whether the money is borrowed for five-months term, at the rate $r_5$, or whether it is borrowed for two months at the rate $r_2$ and then refinanced for the remaining three months at today's futures interest rate two months forward $f_{3,2}$. Consequently

$$1 + r_5 \times \frac{150}{360} = (1 + r_2 \times 60/360) \times (1 + f_{3,2} \times 90/360)$$

Using the rates in our spot yield curve and solving for $f_{3,2}$, we find that $f_{3,2} = 7.66$ percent. In other words, the fair price for the Eurodollar futures contract which stops trading in 60 days (two months forward) is equal to $100 - 7.66 = 92.34$.[2]

In order to see what would happen in the event that the Eurodollar futures price differed from 92.34, suppose the price was 92.20 which corresponds to a forward rate of 7.80 percent. Our five-month borrower would clearly prefer borrowing at 7.50 percent for five months to borrowing at 7.125 percent for two months and refinancing at 7.80 percent. On the other hand, lenders (investors) would prefer the "synthetic" strategy. At this point, the arbitrageur steps in and borrows for five months at 7.50 percent. Simultaneously, he invests the borrowed money for two months at 7.125 percent and buys futures, consequently driving its price higher, in order to lock in the 7.80 percent reinvestment for the three month period two months forward. At the end of the 5 months, the arbitrageur repays the borrowed money (with interest) and finds that interest income from the synthetic five-month investment exceeds his interest expense. Arbitrageurs will continue to exploit the inefficiency until the futures price reaches 92.34.[3] The opposite argument can be made for futures which are overpriced. Finally, futures prices for longer maturities can be derived analogously.

## The Eurodollar Strip Rate

Recall that Eurodollar futures trade in 12 contract months on a March-June-September-December cycle out for three years. As a result, the sequence of 12 contracts can be used collectively to protect interest expense (income) against changes in three-month LIBOR for a full three years (or any portion thereof). A hedger who locks in his variable LIBOR rate for three years is, in effect, creating a three-year LIBOR rate. The Eurodollar strip rate is this so-called term LIBOR rate.

One should be careful not to confuse a Eurodollar strip with the strip rate. Whereas the strip generally refers to the execution of a series of Eurodollar futures contracts, in sequence, in more than one contract month, the strip rate is the rate of return (expressed in money-market terms) which can be realized

---

[2] Transaction costs, fees, taxes, and bid-asked spreads are ignored.

[3] The return to equilibrium may occur due to changes in spot yields rather than futures prices. In either case, a sophisticated marketplace should insure fair pricing.

by earning spot LIBOR of appropriate maturity until settlement of the nearby Eurodollar contract and then compounding the earnings, each quarter, at the rates implied by the sequence of futures prices. For example, using the data presented above, we calculate the five-month strip rate $s_5$ as follows:

$$1 + s_5 \times \frac{150}{360} = (1 + r_2 \times \frac{60}{360}) \times (1 + f_{3,2} \times \frac{90}{360})$$

where $r_2$ is two-month LIBOR spot (7.125%) and $f_{3,2}$ is three-month LIBOR two months forward (7.66%, the rate implied by the price of the Eurodollar contract which stops trading in 60 days). Solving for $s_5$ we find that $s_5 = 7.50\%$, which should not surprise anyone.

Because the two-year Eurodollar strip rate will be important to us later, another example is presented. The necessary data is given below and will be used throughout the remainder of this chapter.

| Contract Month | Futures Price | Implied Rate | Days to Next Contract |
|---|---|---|---|
| Sep 87 | 92.34 | 7.66% | 91 |
| Dec 87 | 92.00 | 8.00 | 91 |
| Mar 88 | 91.80 | 8.20 | 91 |
| Jun 88 | 91.61 | 8.39 | 98 |
| Sep 88 | 91.41 | 8.59 | 91 |
| Dec 88 | 91.20 | 8.80 | 84 |
| Mar 89 | 90.99 | 9.01 | 98 |
| Jun 89 | 90.80 | 9.20 | 91 |

Suppose that the Sep 87 contract stops trading exactly 33 days from now (no longer 60 days as in the previous examples) and that 1-month LIBOR spot equals 7.00 percent. The 2-year strip rate $s_{2y}$ is calculated as follows:

$$[1 + s_{2y} \times \frac{365}{360}]^2 = [1 + .07 \times \frac{33}{360}] \times [1 + .0766 \times \frac{91}{360}] \times [1 + .08 \times \frac{91}{360}] \times$$

$$[1 + .082 \times \frac{91}{360}] \times [1 + .0839 \times \frac{98}{360}] \times \ldots \times [1 + .0901 \times \frac{98}{360}] \times [1 + .092 \times \frac{53}{360}]$$

Solving for $s_{2y}$ we find that the 2-year strip rate is equal to 8.65%.[4]

---

[4]Note the 53-day interest period associated with the Jun 89 futures contract. This is so that the period of time covered by the strip corresponds to the 730-day "2-year" period.

## Hedge Ratios and Target Rates

As we just explained, a sequence of Eurodollar futures contracts can be used to protect future interest expense (income) for up to three years against fluctuations in three-month LIBOR. Because this is the basis for our analysis, we now turn to hedge ratios and target rates, possibly the two most important elements of any hedging program. In fact, the remainder of this section is devoted to explaining, through a series of examples, the mechanics of target rate and, in particular, hedge ratio calculations. As explained in Chapter 49, the hedge ratio determines how many futures contracts are needed to minimize risk and the target rate provides a way to measure whether or not the hedge is successful.

Consider a financial institution that will be borrowing $100 million for 90 days beginning on the last trading day (hereafter, IMM date) of the Sep 87 Eurodollar contract, 33 days from "today." Furthermore, suppose that the borrowing rate will be set equal to three-month LIBOR on that date and that today's Sep 87 futures price is 92.34. Before detailing any of the calculations, three issues merit consideration. First, because Eurodollar futures contracts are tied to three-month LIBOR, the futures rate will converge to three-month LIBOR spot on the last trading day (see Exhibit 55–2). In other words, three-month LIBOR zero days forward is equal to spot. Second, short-term borrowers fearing rising interest-rates should sell Eurodollar futures whereas investors fearing a

**EXHIBIT 55–2**
**Convergence—Spot LIBOR vs. Euro Futures**

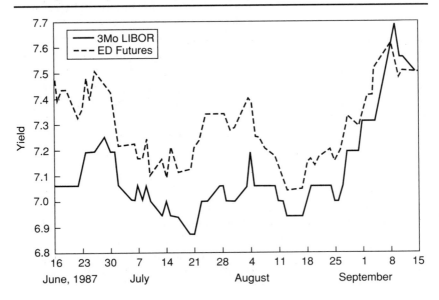

decline in rates should buy futures. Finally, the hedge lift date will be the date on which the borrowing rate is determined. When the rate is established, the uncertainty disappears and the hedge should be unwound.

Returning to our example, since the financial institution will be borrowing dollars and consequently fears an increase in three-month LIBOR over the next 33 days, it should sell contracts. As far as the hedge ratio is concerned, the basic idea is to equate the interest rate sensitivity of the futures position to that of the "cash security" being hedged. In other words,

$$\text{Hedge ratio} = \frac{\text{Dollar volatility of hedged "security"}}{\text{Dollar volatility of futures contract}}$$

Since actual interest expense will equal $100,000,000 × [3-month LIBOR × 90/360], the incremental expense caused by each basis point increase in 3-month LIBOR is $2,500. Recall that the price value of a one basis point (PVBP) change in the Eurodollar contract is $25. Consequently, the hedge is to sell $2,500/25 = 100$ Sep 87 Eurodollar contracts.

Concerning the target rate, it is the interest-rate implied by futures prices that we attempt to lock in through hedging and *not* current spot rates. In our example, since the borrower's rate is set on an IMM date, convergence to the futures rate is assumed. Therefore, the target for the hedge is set equal to the rate at which the borrower can sell 100 Sep 87 futures contracts. If the sale is transacted at 92.34, the target rate for the hedge would be equal to 7.66 percent. In other words, the targeted interest expense is $1,915,000 = $100,000,000 × [.0766 × 90/360].

In order to illustrate how the hedge performs, consider the following scenario. Suppose that by the time the $100 million is borrowed 33 days later, 3-month LIBOR has risen to 10.00 percent (futures settle at 90.00). The actual interest expense, in turn, would be $2.5 million. However, having sold 100 contracts at 92.34, the futures (hedging) gain would be 234 basis points × $25/basis point × 100 contracts = $585,000. Consequently, the borrower's interest expense net of futures gains, or effective interest expense, equals $1,915,000, the target for the hedge. A moment's reflection reveals that the actual borrowing rate (which equals the settlement futures rate) minus (plus) futures gains (losses) equals the contracted futures rate, that is, the target rate for the hedge.

## Day Count

Using the previous example, suppose that the $100 million is to be borrowed for 92 days rather than 90 days. Actual interest expense, in turn, will equal $100,000,000 × 3-month LIBOR × 92/360, and the PVBP will be $2,555.56. Since the PVBP of the Eurodollar contract is always $25, the new hedge ratio will be $\frac{2,555.56}{25} = 102.22$ contracts, or $100 × (\frac{92}{90})$. Concerning the target rate, since the borrowing rate is three-month LIBOR and the determination date (hereafter, reset date) also has not changed, the target rate will, in fact, remain the same. The targeted interest expense will, on the other hand, equal $1,957,555.56 reflecting two additional days of borrowing.

## Variation Margin Financing

Recall that the hedge ratio is designed to equate the interest-rate sensitivity of a futures position to that of the "security" being hedged. Hedging the financing of variation margin, or "tailing" the hedge, may be regarded as fine tuning and is designed to equate these interest-rate sensitivities on a present value basis.

To illustrate, let us return to our base example of a hedge created to lock in an upcoming three-month LIBOR reset on $100 million for a 90-day interest period. Recall that on the day the hedge is initiated, Sep 87 Eurodollars are trading for 92.34 and that the borrower's expected (targeted) interest expense is $1,915,000, to be paid at the end of the interest period exactly 90 days after the rate reset.

Our base example demonstrated how shorting 100 Sep 87 contracts would lock in the target rate. However, the story does not end here. To insure that participants in the futures markets fulfill their contractual obligations, and in turn insure the integrity of the futures contracts themselves, the futures exchanges have devised a system whereby all gains and losses are marked to market on a daily basis. That is, all gains and losses are recognized as they occur and are not deferred until futures delivery. Returning to our example, suppose that the change in the Eurodollar futures price from 92.34 to 90.00 occurred on the first day (just after the hedge was initiated) and that futures prices remained constant from then until the reset date. According to exchange rules and regulations, the gain on 100 futures contracts of $585,000 will be credited to the hedger's (borrower's) account by the following day. The realized gain will then be available to the hedger for short-term interest bearing investment. Consequently, the hedger's gain on the futures position with interest to the payment date will exceed the difference between targeted and actual interest expense. Conversely, had futures prices moved in the other direction, the difference (gain) between actual and targeted interest expense would not be enough to compensate the borrower for hedging losses including financing costs. In order to equate the two, the hedger

**EXHIBIT 55–3**

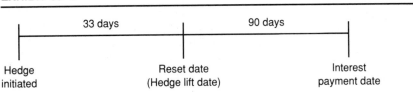

must tail his futures position so that gains or losses on the hedge will be equal, but opposite to, losses or gains on the cash side on a present value basis.

To illustrate this technique, recall that the hedge was initiated exactly 33 days prior to the reset date and suppose that the borrower's rate for lending and borrowing variation margin cash flow is 6.50 percent. Note that there are 123 days between the day on which the hedge is initiated and the day on which the actual interest payment will be made (33 days to the reset date plus 90 days from then until the payment date, as shown in Exhibit 55–3). Had the borrower sold 97.8 futures contracts

$$\frac{100}{1 + .065 \times (123/360)}$$

gains or losses on the futures position on that day, with interest to the payment date 123 days later, would equal (with only rounding errors) the loss or gain on the cash side: $97.8 \times 234$ basis points $\times$ \$25/basis point $\times [1 + .065 \times (123/360)] = \$584,836$. This is known as tailing the hedge and is designed to compensate for the effects of financing futures gains or losses to the hedging horizon.[5]

Clearly, the futures position will need to be adjusted through time as the number of days to the reset date declines toward zero. This is because the tail does not depend upon the date on which the hedge was established, but rather upon the number of days remaining until the offsetting transaction occurs (in this case, the payment date). It should also be noted that even on the reset date, the number of contracts will still be somewhat less than 100 due to the fact that interest is being paid on an add-on basis. In other words, futures gains (or losses) as of the reset date will be invested (or financed) for the remaining 90 days to the interest payment date. Since the adjustments for both marking to market (in this case 33 days) and add-on interest (90 days) are similar in nature, we have lumped the two together.

Finally, the borrowing/lending rate, which also affects the tail, will not remain constant but should move in the same direction as rates implied by futures prices. In other words, the funds rate should increase when futures prices decline and vice-versa. This too will necessitate adjustments to the futures position. Closer inspection reveals a slight advantage for the short hedger: The hedger who is shorting futures contracts will be able to invest futures gains at a higher than expected (tailed) rate and will finance futures losses at lower than expected rates. (We will take a closer look at the "drift" in a later section.)

---

[5] For the sake of clarity, simple interest was chosen. The actual tail should depend upon the hedger's margin financing arrangements and will most likely need to reflect interest compounding.

# HEDGING FLOATING-RATE NOTES

The purpose of this section is to solidify our understanding of Eurodollar futures hedging and to orient ourselves so that the transition to interest-rate swap analysis is easily made. We begin with an example in which we outline Eurodollar futures hedging techniques available to a floating-rate note issuer. Then, by concentrating on the problems of cash flow financing (distinct from variation margin financing) and the protection of "total" cost, we establish the foundation for swap analysis.

## An Example

Suppose that today is August 12, 1987 and consider an issuer who, on September 14, 1987 (the Sep 87 IMM date), plans to sell $100 million worth of floating-rate notes maturing two years hence. Suppose that the rate floats off three-month LIBOR and that interest accrual periods coincide with Eurodollar future delivery dates. In other words, resets occur on IMM dates and interest accruals go from one IMM date to the next.

Fearing a rise in short-term rates, the issuer examines two Eurodollar futures alternatives for "fixing" his floating-rate liability. The first (the "basic hedge") is designed to hedge interest-rate risk of the first order, namely interest on principal, and is computed in accordance with the calculations detailed previously. The second (the so-called "zero hedge") is designed to protect the issuer's "total" cost from fluctuations in short-term interest rates. Exhibit 55–4 summarizes hedging recommendations for both the basic and the zero hedge. The necessary data was provided earlier in this chapter, most of which is restated here.

**EXHIBIT 55–4**

| Date: | August 12, 1987 | | | |
|---|---|---|---|---|
| Financing Rate: (Variation Margin) | 6.50% | | | |

| Futures: | Contract Month | Price | Basic Hedge | Zero Hedge |
|---|---|---|---|---|
| | Sep 87 | 92.34 | − 98.97 | − 98.97 |
| | Dec 87 | 92.00 | − 97.43 | − 99.32 |
| | Mar 88 | 91.80 | − 95.91 | − 99.75 |
| | Jun 88 | 91.61 | −101.56 | −107.81 |
| | Sep 88 | 91.41 | − 92.84 | −100.80 |
| | Dec 88 | 91.20 | − 84.47 | − 93.70 |
| | Mar 89 | 90.99 | − 96.89 | −109.70 |
| | Jun 89 | 90.80 | − 88.57 | −102.73 |

The basic hedge is essentially eight distinct hedges, each protecting against increases in three-month LIBOR on $100 million for 91, 84 (Dec 88), or 98 (Jun 88, Mar 89) days. Remembering the adjustment for variation margin financing, the number of contracts in the $i^{th}$ contract month is equal to

$$\left(100 \times \frac{d_i}{90}\right) \div 1.065^{dpi/365.25}$$

where $d_i$ is the number of days of interest accrual and $dp_i$ is the number of days between "today" (August 12) and the interest payment date (end of interest accrual period).[6] The zero hedge, on the other hand, introduces a new "twist" and requires further explanation. In fact, because the issues surrounding the zero hedge are central to swap pricing and swap hedging, we will examine the problem in detail in the following subsections.

### Cash-Flow Financing—Reinvestment Risk

Consider a zero-coupon bond and an ordinary bond with semi-annual coupon payments. As we all know, the "total" return on the zero-coupon bond is known with certainty whereas the return for the coupon-bearing security is dependent upon the rate(s) at which the periodic coupons can be reinvested. Stated another way, the coupon-bearing security is subject to reinvestment risk in spite of the fact that its coupons are fixed. Analogously, the basic hedge, which "fixes" the interest payments of the floating-rate note, leaves the issuer subject to "reinvestment risk" or more accurately, the uncertainty of cash-flow financing costs. The zero hedge is designed to eliminate this second order risk and is presented as an alternative.

Exhibit 55–5 illustrates the cash-flow financing problem as well as the risk and the zero hedging solution follows immediately. We assume that the issuer is a fully leveraged LIBOR borrower (investor) and that each cash flow is (re)financed on IMM dates at three-month LIBOR.

The columns of Exhibit 55–5 represent Eurodollar futures contract months and by design, the interest accrual periods of the floating-rate note. The first row, labeled "settlement date", is self-explanatory and indicates the sequence of delivery dates of the Eurodollar contracts (IMM dates). The second row, labeled "actual days", supplies the number of days in each interest accrual period or equivalently, the number of days to the IMM date next following. For example, there are 98 days between 6/13/88 and 9/19/88 and consequently 98 days of interest accrual associated with the Jun 88 floating-rate reset. With regard to the third row, a Eurodollar futures contract, by design, converges to

---

[6] Unlike the subsection which introduced variation margin financing adjustments to the hedge ratio and which assumed simple interest financing, this calculation as well as subsequent calculations reflect interest compounding.

**EXHIBIT 55-5**

| | Sep 87 | Dec 87 | Mar 88 | Jun 88 | Sep 88 | Dec 88 | Mar 89 | Jun 89 | Sep 89 |
|---|---|---|---|---|---|---|---|---|---|
| (1) Settlement date | 9/14/87 | 12/14/87 | 3/14/88 | 6/13/88 | 9/19/88 | 12/19/88 | 3/13/89 | 6/19/89 | 9/18/89 |
| (2) Actual days | 91 | 91 | 91 | 98 | 91 | 84 | 98 | 91 | |
| (3) Target rate | 7.66% | 8.00% | 8.20% | 8.39% | 8.59% | 8.80% | 9.01% | 9.20% | |
| (4) Interest expense | $1,936,278 | 2,022,222 | 2,072,778 | 2,283,944 | 2,171,361 | 2,053,333 | 2,452,722 | 2,325,556 | |
| (5) With LIBOR cash-flow financing (+100 bp) | | | | | | | | | |
|   Dec 87 | 1,936,278 | | | | | | | | |
|   Mar 88 | | 1,975,434 (1,980,328) | | | | | | | |
|   Jun 88 | | | 3,997,656 (4,002,550) | | | | | | |
|   Sep 88 | | | | 6,153,297 (6,168,410) | | | | | |
|   Dec 88 | | | | | 8,577,779 (8,610,029) | | | | |
|   Mar 89 | | | | | | 10,935,395 (10,990,109) | | | |
|   Jun 89 | | | | | | | 13,213,268 (13,294,750) | | |
|   Sep 89 | | | | | | | | 15,990,074 (16,109,746) | 18,687,488 (18,850,665) ( 163,177) |
| (6) Days forward | | 124 | 215 | 306 | 404 | 495 | 579 | 677 | 768 |
| (7) Basic hedge | 98.97 | 97.43 | 95.91 | 101.56 | 92.84 | 84.47 | 96.89 | 88.57 | |
| (8) Zero hedge | 98.97 | 99.32 | 99.75 | 107.81 | 100.80 | 93.70 | 109.70 | 102.73 | |

three-month LIBOR on its IMM date (discussed earlier). In addition, recall that the security in question resets equal to three-month LIBOR and that said resets occur on IMM dates. As a result, the rate of interest targeted for each interest accrual period is set equal to 100 minus the corresponding Eurodollar futures price shown in Exhibit 55–4. Finally, the fourth row, labeled "interest expense," provides the coupon targeted for payment at the end of each interest accrual period. For instance, the Jun 88 futures price is 91.61 (futures interest rate equal to 8.39%) and there are 98 days of interest accrual for the Jun 88–Sept 88 interest period. Consequently, the targeted interest expense for the period, payable in Sep 88, is $2,283,944 [$100 million × .0839 × (98/360)]. If the issuer implements the basic hedge and makes the necessary adjustments through time, actual coupon payments minus (plus) hedging gains (losses) will equal those payments indicated by the target vector in row 4.

The cash-flow financing issue itself is presented in "row" 5. On 12/14/87 the first interest payment will be made which, net of hedging gains or losses, should result in an out-of-pocket expense of $1,936,278. The issuer, who is fully leveraged, must borrow this money in order to satisfy the note obligation and, by assumption, will finance the expense at 3-month LIBOR (with IMM refinancing) through the note's maturity in September 1989. Obviously, the rates at which the issuer will ultimately borrow funds to finance coupon payments depends upon then current LIBOR rates. For instance, if on 12/14/87 three-month LIBOR is 8.00 percent, the issuer will borrow $1,936,278 at 8.00 percent until refinancing 91 days later. On the other hand, if 3-month LIBOR is 9.00 percent on 12/14/87, the issuer will, of course, pay 9.00 percent for the $1,936,278. In either case, the issuer will owe

$$\$1,936,278 \times (1 + \text{rate} \times \frac{91}{360})$$

on the Mar 88 IMM date 91 days later, at which point the entire amount ($1,975,434 or $1,980,328) must be refinanced along with the additional $2,022,222 "fixed" coupon.

The diagonal in "row" 5 illustrates the financing problem through the note's maturity by comparing the issuer's "total" cost of funds with cash-flow financing at rates provided in row 3 to the issuer's cost with cash-flow financing at rates 100 basis points higher. At rates provided in row 3, the "fixed" coupon payable on 12/14/87 ($1,936,278) is financed for 91 days at 8.00 percent ($1,975,434) and added to the "fixed" coupon payable on 3/14/88 ($2,022,222) to determine the total cost as of 3/14/88 ($3,997,656). Similarly, $3,997,656 is financed at 8.20 percent for 91 days and added to the coupon payable on 6/13/88 ($2,072,778) to determine the total cost as of 6/13/88 ($6,153,297). On the other hand (at rates 100 basis points higher), $1,936,278 financed for 91 days at 9.00 percent ($1,980,328) plus the "fixed" coupon ($2,022,222) equals $4,002,550, and $4,002,550 financed for 91 days at 9.20 percent added to $2,072,778 equals

$6,168,410. As the process is carried out to the note's maturity the uncertainty surrounding total cost ($18,687,488 versus $18,850,665) becomes increasingly apparent and, all this in spite of the fact that the coupons themselves have been fixed by the basic hedge.

## The Zero Hedge

Recall our assumption that the issuer is a fully leveraged LIBOR borrower and that each cash flow is (re)financed on IMM dates at three-month LIBOR. Equivalently, and as previously illustrated, the uncertainty surrounding the financing of "fixed" coupons is directly linked to the uncertainty surrounding the path of short-term interest rates and specifically three-month LIBOR. In other words, the issuer's total cost of funds is dependent upon the level of three-month LIBOR as of the IMM financing dates in much the same way that the coupon payments themselves are dependent upon the level of three-month LIBOR as of the reset dates. And, just as the basic hedge fixes the variable coupon, a zero hedge can be constructed which protects the issuer's total cost from fluctuations in three-month LIBOR.

Recognizing that zero hedging is simply a matter of protecting interest on interest (cash-flow financing) as well as interest on principal (coupon payments), hedge ratio and target rate calculations are fairly straightforward. Because the interest accrual periods are identical, the rates of interest targeted for cash-flow financing are exactly the same as those targeted for coupon payments. For example, the target rate of 8.39 percent (row 3) for the Jun 88–Sep 88 interest accrual period, and corresponding $2,283,944 Sep 88 coupon payment, is also the target for cash-flow financing over the same period. Because total cost as of the Jun 88 IMM date equals $6,153,297, the issuer's targeted cost of funds through 9/19/88 is equal to $8,577,779\{$6,153,297 \times [1+.0839 \times (98/360)] + $2,283,944\}$.

As far as hedge ratios are concerned, consider the same 98-day Jun 88–Sep 88 interest accrual period. The issuer's coupon expense, payable in Sep 88 404 days from "today" (row 6, labeled "days forward"), is dependent upon three-month LIBOR as of 6/13/88. We have established that three-month LIBOR as of 6/13/88 also governs the issuer's cost of financing his total cost to date ($6,153,297 if hedged correctly) through the Sep 88 refinancing. As a result, in order to protect total cost through Sep 88 from fluctuations in three-month LIBOR, the issuer must hedge increases in three-month LIBOR on $100 million to "fix" the Sep 88 coupon payment *and* increases in three-month LIBOR on an additional $6,153,297 to "fix" cash-flow financing costs. It follows immediately that the zero hedge (row 8) requires the sale of 107.81

$$= \left[ (100 + 6.153297) \times \frac{98}{90} \right] \div 1.065^{404/365.25}$$

Jun 88 contracts, whereas the basic hedge (row 7) calls for only 101.56 contracts. Hedge ratios for the zero hedge in other contract months are computed similarly and, if maintained and monitored correctly, would result in a total cost to the issuer (through maturity) equal to $18,687,488.[7]

## INTEREST-RATE SWAPS

Having completed our explanation of cash-flow financing and the protection of "total" cost, an understanding of the market for LIBOR-based interest-rate swaps should come fairly easily. The purpose of this section is to detail, through an example, pricing and hedge ratio calculations for the straightforward case of a LIBOR-for-fixed IMM swap or equivalently, to analyze the swap-to-futures arbitrage. We begin with a brief overview of the market for interest-rate swaps and quickly move on to the example which, for the sake of familiarity, is governed by the same market environment as that for the floating-rate note discussed in the previous section.

### Swap Market Primer

An interest-rate swap is a contractual agreement between two parties calling for the exchange of interest payments which, in turn, accrue on different bases. The notional amount and interest accrual periods are, of course, specified in the contract along with the interest-rate index (or indices in the case of floating-for-floating) being swapped. An interest-rate swap is *not* an exchange of underlying assets or liabilities but rather, an exchange of interest payments only.

Generally used as an asset/liability management tool, the most popular swap structure is floating-for-fixed. For example, consider an interest-rate swap in which one party pays (to the other) three-month LIBOR reset quarterly and receives a fixed coupon quarterly, semi annually or even annually. As a hedge, the swap's merit is obvious: Suppose our floating-rate note issuer enters into a two-year $100 million IMM swap (resets occur on IMM dates and interest accruals go from one IMM date to the next) as fixed-rate payer and receiver of three-month LIBOR. Regardless of the path of three-month LIBOR, receipts from the swap can be used to satisfy the note obligation. The issuer, in turn, is left with fixed-rate payments to the swap counterparty and has, in effect, fixed his floating-rate liability at the swap-rate (fixed-rate side of the swap). Because the Eurodollar futures hedge developed in the previous section also serves to "fix" the issuer's floating-rate liability, we would expect swap and futures hedges

---

[7] Transaction costs, fees, taxes, and bid-asked spreads are ignored.

to produce similar results. In other words, swap pricing (the swap-rate) should be closely linked to Eurodollar futures hedging. In particular, though the swap-rate and the Eurodollar strip rate are distinct, a definitive relationship between them exists. To the degree that this relationship is violated, arbitrage would be possible.

Before moving on to detail swap pricing and the swap-to-futures arbitrage, it is important to make the following remarks about swap market conventions. The swap rate is generally quoted on a semi-annual yield basis or as a basis point spread over the Treasury yield of comparable maturity. Day count adjustments are 30/360 for fixed coupons and conventional on the floating side (actual/360 for LIBOR). In addition, although three-month LIBOR is the most popular and certainly the most interesting index from our point of view, interest-rate swaps based upon other floating-rate indices (such as six-month LIBOR, prime, commercial paper, or T-bill) are not uncommon. Finally, it is important to keep in mind that interest-rate swaps can be structured to satisfy a variety of corporate requirements and, as a result, need not necessarily conform to market convention.[8]

## Break-Even Swap Pricing

Returning to our hypothesis that shorter maturity interest-rate swaps are closely related to Eurodollar futures hedges, consider a two-year $100 million IMM swap, starting on 9/14/87 and maturing on 9/18/89, which pays a fixed coupon in exchange for three-month LIBOR. Suppose that "today" is August 12, 1987 and consider our floating-rate note issuer. As outlined in the previous subsection, said swap (with a forward start date) can be used as a hedge to "fix" the issuer's floating-rate liability. Alternatively, we have demonstrated that a zero hedge can be constructed in the Eurodollar futures market which fixes the issuer's total cost at $18,687,488. Since the two hedges accomplish the same objective, the break-even rate for the swap should be that rate which also fixes the issuer's cost at $18,687,488.

Although the break-even swap rate is comparable to the Eurodollar strip rate, it should be noted that the two rates are not identical. In the first place, the Eurodollar strip rate is generally quoted in money-market terms and, as a result, must be converted to the semiannual yield basis adopted by the swap market. More interesting is the fact that the break-even swap rate resembles the rate on a coupon-bearing security whereas the Eurodollar strip rate is, in essence, a zero-coupon rate. Consequently, the break-even swap rate is dependent upon the shape of the futures yield curve whereas the Eurodollar strip rate (day count

---

[8] For more information regarding swap market conventions, see Chapter 54.

adjustments aside) is not. In other words, given a Eurodollar strip rate there are many possibilities for the break-even swap rate which is, in turn, determined by the yield curve.

Maintaining our assumption that the issuer is a fully leveraged LIBOR borrower/lender (i.e., cash flows are financed/invested at LIBOR), consider again the two-year $100 million IMM swap, starting on 9/14/87 and maturing on 9/18/89, which pays a fixed coupon in exchange for three-month LIBOR. Supposing that fixed coupons are paid on an annual basis (on 9/19/88 and 9/18/89), the following equations can be used to calculate the break-even swap-rate $r_{be}$. Let $c$ represent the fixed dollar coupon and let $n$ be the number of fixed coupons per year (in this case, one). We use the same data as before and account for the fact that there are 365 30/360-days from 9/14/87 to 9/19/88 and 359 30/360-days from 9/19/88 to 9/18/89.

$$c \times \left[ \frac{365}{360} \times \left(1 + .0859 \times \frac{91}{360}\right) \times \left(1 + .0880 \times \frac{84}{360}\right) \right.$$

$$\times \left(1 + .0901 \times \frac{98}{360}\right) \times \left(1 + .0920 \times \frac{91}{360}\right)$$

$$\left. + \frac{359}{360} \right] = \$18,687,488$$

and

$$r_{be} = [(1 + c/100,000,000)^{n/2} - 1] \times 200$$

Noting that the equation for the fixed coupon reflects a day-count adjusted payment on 9/19/88, along with IMM (re)financing through 9/18/89, and a day-count adjusted payment on 9/18/89, we find that $c$ is equal to $8,875,497. As for the semiannual equivalent break-even swap rate, the computation is straightforward once $c$ has been determined. In our example, $r_{be}$ is equal to 8.69 percent.[9]

Of course, the formulas for both $c$ and $r_{be}$ can be rewritten to solve for the break-even swap-rate given any three-month LIBOR-for-fixed IMM swap. The generalized equations are as follows:

$$c = \frac{P \times (\prod_{i=1}^{k}[1 + f_i \times d_i/360] - 1)}{(df_k \times n/360) + \sum_{j=1}^{k-1}[(df_j \times n/360) \times \prod_{m=j+1}^{k}\{1 + f_m \times d_m/360\}]}$$

---

[9] The 735-day Eurodollar strip rate 33 days forward is 8.76 percent.

and

$$r_{be} = [(1 + \frac{c}{P})^{n/2} - 1] \times 200$$

where $k$ is the number of quarter-years, $n$ is the number of fixed coupons per year (1, 2, or 4), $P$ is the notional amount of the swap, $d_i(i = 1, k)$ is the number of days of interest accrual associated with $f_i$, the Eurodollar futures interest rate for the $i^{th}$ quarter, and $df_j$ is the number of 30/360-days associated with the fixed coupon payable at the end of the $j^{th}$ quarter. (When there is no fixed payment, $df_j$ is equal to zero.)

Returning once again to our suggestion that the break-even swap rate is not identical to the Eurodollar strip rate, consider the first equation and note the need for particular subsets of the Eurodollar strip in the denominator ($\ldots \prod[1 + f_m \times d_m/360]$). The need to incorporate the financing of fixed coupons through the swap's maturity into break-even swap pricing dictates the dependence of the break-even swap rate on the shape of the yield curve. Aside from differences attributable to the conversion from money-market to semiannual yields, the break-even swap rate will be somewhat lower than the Eurodollar strip rate in a positively sloped yield-curve environment whereas, in an inverted yield-curve environment the opposite will be true.

Finally, it should come as no surprise that the break-even swap-rate $r_{be}$ is independent of the notional amount $P$ of the swap. As a result, $P$ can be eliminated from both equations (replace $P$ with the number one) in the event that we are interested only in $r_{be}$ and not in the coupon $c$ as well.

## Swap-to-Futures Arbitrage

Exhibit 55–6 illustrates the swap-to-futures arbitrage which should, among other things, clear up any uneasiness about the meaning of break-even swap pricing. Intuitively, one would expect arbitrage to be possible when the market rate for a swap differs from the break-even rate. Aside from a subtle drift element this is true. Furthermore, because Eurodollar futures can be sold (bought) to "fix" the floating-rate payments (receipts) of a LIBOR-based swap transaction, the arbitrage itself is not very different from the zero hedging of a floating-rate note (with hedge ratio adjustments for the investment/financing of fixed coupons). Consider our two-year $100 million IMM swap maturing 9/18/89 and suppose that our frame of reference is that of market-maker rather than hedger. We note that the interest accrual periods of our swap are identical to those of our floating-rate note and investigate the break-even transaction.

Because the arbitrage is essentially a Eurodollar futures hedging problem along with cash inflows *and* outflows, Exhibit 55–6 is formatted in very much the same way as Exhibit 55–5. In fact, we pick up our de-

## EXHIBIT 55-6

|  | Sep 87 | Dec 87 | Mar 88 | Jun 88 | Sep 88 | Dec 88 | Mar 89 | Jun 89 | Sep 89 |
|---|---|---|---|---|---|---|---|---|---|
| (1) Settlement date | 9/14/87 | 12/14/87 | 3/14/88 | 6/13/88 | 9/19/88 | 12/19/88 | 3/13/89 | 6/19/89 | 9/18/89 |
| (2) Actual days | 91 | 91 | 91 | 98 | 91 | 84 | 98 | 91 | |
| (3) Target rate | 7.66% | 8.00% | 8.20% | 8.39% | 8.59% | 8.80% | 9.01% | 9.20% | |
| (4) Floating | | $1,936,278 | 2,022,222 | 2,072,778 | 2,283,944 | 2,171,361 | 2,053,333 | 2,452,722 | 2,325,556 |
| (5) Fixed ~8.69% | | | | | (8,998,768) | | | | (8,850,843) |
| (6) With LIBOR cash-flow financing | | | | | | | | | |
| Dec 87 | | 1,936,278 | | | | | | | |
| Mar 88 | | | 3,997,656 | | | | | | |
| Jun 88 | | | | 6,153,297 | | | | | |
| Sep 88 | | | | | (420,989) | | | | |
| Dec 88 | | | | | | 1,741,231 | | | |
| Mar 89 | | | | | | | 3,830,317 | | |
| Jun 89 | | | | | | | | 6,376,986 | |
| Sep 89 | | | | | | | | | 0 |
| (7) Hedge | 98.97 | 99.32 | 99.75 | 107.81 | 92.45 | 85.94 | 100.60 | 94.22 | |

scription of Exhibit 55–6 in the fourth row, labeled "floating", which supplies the coupons targeted for payment on the floating-rate side of our swap transaction. A moment's reflection reveals that these will be identical to those targeted for the floating-rate note discussed previously. As for the fixed side of our transaction, recall that the break-even coupon is equal to $8,875,497 and that said coupon, adjusted for 30/360-days, is paid annually. Row 5, labeled "fixed", provides the fixed coupons payable on our swap contract ($8, 998, 768 = $8, 875, 497 \times 365/360$; $8, 850, 843 = $8, 875, 497 \times 359/360$). Finally, "row" 6 is included to illustrate the ongoing cash balance of our swap arbitrage. Note, for example, the cash balance on 6/13/88 ($6,153,297) and consider the arbitrage from the floating-rate payer's perspective. As of 6/13/88 three floating-rate payments have been made. More importantly, it is still three months until the first fixed coupon will be received. Consequently, and not surprisingly, the debit balance (negative number signifies a credit) is equal to our floating-rate note issuer's total cost to date (Exhibit 55–5). The cash balance three months later, on the other hand, reflects coupon income ($8,998,768) as well as an additional floating-rate payment ($2,283,944 net of hedging gains/losses). The result is a credit balance on 9/19/88 equal to $420,989 ($6,153,297 \times [1 + .0839 \times (98/360)] + $2,283,944 - $8,998,768$). As the process is carried out to the swap's maturity we see that the final cash balance is equal to zero, which is indicative of a break-even transaction.

## Hedge Ratio Calculations

Concerning the structure of a swap arbitrage, recognize that the arbitrageur's risks are very similar to those of our floating-rate note issuer. The arbitrageur, like the issuer, must "fix" interest on interest along with interest on principal. In fact, the only difference is that "interest on interest", for the arbitrageur, reflects interest on the "ongoing cash balance" rather than interest on "total cost." Remember, the arbitrageur has cash coming in as well as cash going out.

With this in mind, we suggest that hedge ratio calculations for our swap arbitrage will be comparable to those for our zero hedge. We examine row 7 of Exhibit 55–6 and isolate the Sep 88–Dec 88 interest accrual period. Noting that our swap arbitrage (pay floating/receive fixed, and short Eurodollar futures) shows a credit balance on 9/19/88 equal to $420,989, the following equation can be used to verify that 92.45 Sep 88 Eurodollar contracts are required (a credit balance necessitates the purchase of Eurodollar futures or, equivalently, reduces the number that needs to be sold):

$$[(100 - .420989) \times (91/90)] \div 1.065^{495/365.25}$$

Hedge ratios for the arbitrage in other contract months are computed similarly.

## The Drift

Before moving on to apply our understanding of swap-to-futures arbitrage to other types of shorter maturity swap transactions, consider the following. Exhibit 55–6 demonstrates that arbitrage is possible when the market rate for a swap differs from the break-even rate. For instance, if the market rate is 8.59 percent, an arbitrageur can pay fixed/receive floating and buy Eurodollar futures to wind up with a credit balance at maturity. However, there is an option-like, or convexity, characteristic to Eurodollar futures hedging that does not appear in Exhibit 55–6. Our break-even calculation, in turn, will be modified slightly.

Basically, there is an asymmetry in hedging with Eurodollar futures: Hedge ratios are computed based upon an assumption about the rate at which futures gains (losses) can be invested (financed). Provided that said borrowing/lending rate remains constant, futures will perform like forwards and generate near-perfect hedges. However, the hedger's borrowing/lending rate does not remain constant. In fact, it tends to fluctuate in the same direction as rates implied by futures prices. And, as the borrowing/lending rate changes, so too will hedge ratios. As a result, and as mentioned earlier, a slight advantage belonging to the short hedger is revealed. When rates rise (prices fall), the short will buy back a portion of his futures hedge and recognize a profit. On the other hand, the long will unwind some of his position at a loss. Similarly, when rates fall and prices rise, the short will sell additional (but more expensive) contracts whereas the long will be forced to buy said contracts. Noting that the short is always rehedging by buying low and selling high, it can be said that there is a long option position embedded in a short Eurodollar futures hedge. The hedger who is buying Eurodollar futures is, of course, short the option portfolio.

Returning to the break-even calculation detailed previously, consider the floating-rate payer/fixed-rate receiver. The floating-rate payer sells Eurodollar futures and "locks in" his interest expense. In the event that the fixed-rate side of the swap transaction provides for coupon income at what we abusively labeled the "break-even swap rate," the arbitrageur is, in essence, long the option portfolio at no cost. In other words, the break-even swap rate is *not* equal to that rate described earlier but should, in fact, be somewhat lower to reflect option premium (i.e., the option premium is paid in the form of reduced fixed coupon income).

As for determining exactly how much lower, we begin by pointing out that the actual existence of an embedded option portfolio is predicated on the assumption that futures interest rates and a hedger's borrowing/lending rate are both highly and positively correlated. For example, if the rates were negatively correlated (i.e., one rate moves higher as the other moves lower), the buyer of Eurodollar futures would be long the option portfolio. And, if the degree of correlation itself were low, we would be unjustified in systematically including the option premium in break-even swap pricing. Because we believe it is reasonable to assume high positive correlation between rates, we move forward in our discussion and consider the valuation of the option portfolio.

Clearly, as with other option contracts, the value of the embedded option portfolio is an increasing function of both volatility and time to expiration. Though we have not made any effort to value the option portfolio explicitly, we do propose the following as a guideline for break-even pricing modification. The results are based upon a simulation of swap hedges for the period June 1985 through June 1988. (The variation margin financing rate is one-month LIBOR.)

| Swap Maturity | Option Premium |
| --- | --- |
| 1-year | 0 – 1 b. p. |
| 2-year | 1 – 3 b. p. |
| 3-year | 3 – 6 b. p. |

In order to avoid being misled by our guidelines for pricing modification, it is important to point out that our simulation turned out option values for three-year hedges significantly higher than six basis points. When interest rate volatility is high, particularly during the early stages of a swap hedge, the value of the embedded option portfolio can be quite large. We suggest straddles or delta hedged option positions as techniques for managing this volatility risk.

## Hedging Alternatives

Having explained how Eurodollar futures can be used to hedge/arbitrage interest-rate swaps, it is important to make the following remark regarding alternative techniques for hedging swaps. To begin with, recognize that our method is one of cash flow dedication and, as a result, requires little in the way of assumptions. It is our contention that other techniques have a much greater tendency to rely on one premise or another. Duration hedges, for instance, implicitly make flat, or parallel shift, yield-curve assumptions. Treasury hedges, which are very popular, also make a number of assumptions: A Treasury hedge assumes that the swap spread (relative to Treasury) remains constant and that the term-LIBOR/term-Repo spread remains constant. Consider the ramifications of a short Treasury hedge when the shorted Treasury goes "special." In addition, because hedgers tend to use the overnight rather than term repo market, there is a residual risk that is tied to the path of overnight-repo. (Strategies such as swapping "overnight-for-term" and hedging with Eurodollar futures do exist for managing this risk.) Although these and other hedging techniques are viable alternatives to the dedicated Eurodollar futures portfolio, we maintain that our method is the most directed.

## ODD STRUCTURES

The previous section demonstrated how an arbitrageur can create a LIBOR-for-fixed IMM swap. Because the technique used a dedicated Eurodollar futures portfolio, it will not be difficult to apply the same technique to other types of swap transactions. In other words, the method is flexible enough to accommodate a variety of swap structures. The purpose of this section is to show how Eurodollar futures can be used to create/arbitrage zero coupon as well as amortizing swaps. We use the same data as before and rely primarily on our exhibits to explain each of the transactions. We leave it as an exercise for the reader to verify the computations.

### Zero Coupon Swap

Exhibit 55–7 illustrates the swap-to-futures arbitrage for a two-year $100 million zero coupon swap (with IMM resets). A moment's reflection reveals that this is essentially our floating-rate note along with a single fixed cash flow at maturity. Quite simply, because our issuer was able to sell Eurodollar futures to "fix" his total cost at $18,687,488, the zero coupon swap arbitrageur should be able to sell (buy) the same Eurodollar strip and receive (pay) $18,687,488 at maturity to "break even."

### Amortizing Swap

Exhibit 55–8 illustrates the swap-to-futures arbitrage for a one-year $100 million IMM swap which amortizes principal at the rate of $25 million per quarter. Note, in particular, the effect that amortization has on floating-rate payments as well as the effect that it has on hedge ratios. The Mar 88 payment, for example, is equal to $1,516,667 ($75 million × .0800 × (91/360)). And, the Mar 88 hedge ratio (51.31) is computed as follows:

$$[(50 + 3.492101) \times \frac{91}{90}] \div 1.065^{306/365.25}$$

## SUMMARY

This chapter was designed to acquaint the reader with the relationship that exists between the Eurodollar futures market and the market for shorter maturity

**EXHIBIT 55-7**

|  | Sep 87 | Dec 87 | Mar 88 | Jun 88 | Sep 88 | Dec 88 | Mar 89 | Jun 89 | Sep 89 |
|---|---|---|---|---|---|---|---|---|---|
| (1) Settlement date | 9/14/87 | 12/14/87 | 3/14/88 | 6/13/88 | 9/19/88 | 12/19/88 | 3/13/89 | 6/19/89 | 9/18/89 |
| (2) Actual days | 91 | 91 | 91 | 98 | 91 | 84 | 98 | 91 | |
| (3) Target rate | 7.66% | 8.00% | 8.20% | 8.39% | 8.59% | 8.80% | 9.01% | 9.20% | |
| (4) Floating | $1,936,278 | 2,022,222 | 2,072,778 | 2,283,944 | 2,171,361 | 2,053,333 | 2,452,722 | 2,325,556 | |
| (5) Fixed | | | | | | | | | (18,687,488) |
| (6) With LIBOR cash-flow financing | | | | | | | | | |
|    Dec 87 | | 1,936,278 | | | | | | | |
|    Mar 88 | | | 3,997,656 | | | | | | |
|    Jun 88 | | | | 6,153,297 | | | | | |
|    Sep 88 | | | | | 8,577,779 | | | | |
|    Dec 88 | | | | | | 10,935,395 | | | |
|    Mar 89 | | | | | | | 13,213,268 | | |
|    Jun 89 | | | | | | | | 15,990,074 | |
|    Sep 89 | | | | | | | | | 0 |
| (7) Hedge | 98.97 | 99.32 | 99.75 | 107.81 | 100.80 | 93.70 | 109.70 | 102.73 | |

**EXHIBIT 55-8**

|  | Sep 87 | Dec 87 | Mar 88 | Jun 88 | Sep 88 |
|---|---|---|---|---|---|
| (1) Settlement date | 9/14/87 | 12/14/87 | 3/14/88 | 6/13/88 | 9/19/88 |
| (2) Actual days | 91 | 91 | 91 | 98 | |
| (3) Target rate | 7.66% | 8.00% | 8.20% | 8.39% | |
| (4) Outstanding principal | 100M | 75M | 50M | 25M | |
| (5) Floating | | $1,936,278 | 1,516,667 | 1,036,389 | 570,986 |
| (6) Fixed | | | | | (5,276,941) |
| (7) With LIBOR cash-flow financing | | | | | |
| Dec 87 | | 1,936,278 | | | |
| Mar 88 | | | 3,492,101 | | |
| Jun 88 | | | | 4,600,873 | |
| Sep 88 | | | | | 0 |
| (8) Hedge | 98.97 | 74.96 | 51.31 | 30.06 | |

interest-rate swaps. An effort was made to build an intuitive argument first by examining a floating-rate note hedge and then through the use of the straightforward LIBOR-for-fixed IMM swap. We demonstrated how a dedicated Eurodollar futures portfolio can be used to create interest-rate swap transactions. Finally, we included a brief discussion of zero coupon and amortizing swaps in order to illustrate the flexibility of our approach.

# PART 9

# MODELING AND FORECASTING

# CHAPTER 56

# THE TERM STRUCTURE OF INTEREST RATES

*Richard W. McEnally, Ph.D., CFA*
*Meade Willis Professor of Investment Banking*
*University of North Carolina*

*James V. Jordan, Ph.D.*
*Associate Professor of Finance*
*Virginia Polytechnic Institute and State University*

## INTRODUCTION

Term-structure analysis deals with the pure price of time. Exhibit 56–1 contains a three-dimensional representation of yields on coupon-bearing U.S. Treasury securities with different terms to maturity for each calendar month since 1950. Even the most casual observer of this plot cannot help but notice that in most months these yields vary with maturity and that this yield-maturity relationship itself varies from month to month. Such relationships are generally referred to as the term structure of yields. When plots of the yield-maturity relationship are examined for a single point in time, as in Exhibit 56–2, such a representation is frequently called the yield curve. When the yields to maturity are those of zero coupon bonds, as Exhibit 56–3 attempts to portray, the result is the term structure of interest rates.

Regardless of how it is examined or what it is called, awareness and appreciation of the yield-maturity relationship is absolutely essential in fixed income investment analysis and management.

Some of the uses of the term structure include the following:

1. *Analyzing the returns for asset commitments of different terms.* Fixed income investment managers vary their portfolios along many dimensions,

**EXHIBIT 56–1a**
**Term Structure of Interest Rates (January 1950–March 1963)**

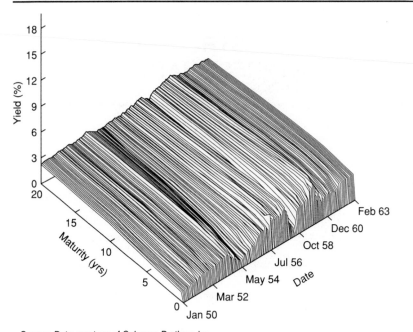

Source: Data courtesy of Salomon Brothers Inc

including quality, coupon level, and type of issuer. But no dimension is more important than the maturity dimension; it has the greatest influence on whether the portfolio will gain or lose in volatile interest-rate environments. The term structure shows the rewards that can be expected for commitments of different lengths. Properly interpreted, it can also be used to make judgments about the short-term rewards of different maturity strategies as interest rates change.

2. *Assessing consensus expectations of future interest rates.* In fixed income investment, the manager who can make better predictions of future interest rates than the consensus forecast—or even the manager who can correctly identify the direction of error in the consensus forecast—can profit immensely. But a strategy based on this principle requires a knowledge of what the consensus expectation of future interest rates is. Analysis of the term structure may help provide this information.

3. *Pricing bonds and other fixed-payment contracts.* The term structure shows the pure price of time, a price that changes from hour to hour and day to day. In pricing financial obligations, it is essential that consideration be given to the yields available on alternative investments with

**EXHIBIT 56–1b**

**Term Structure of Interest Rates (April 1963–May 1976)**

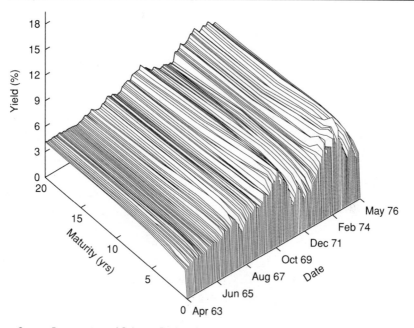

Source: Data courtesy of Salomon Brothers Inc

a similar length of commitment. The yield curve gives an idea of what these alternative yields are for coupon-bearing issues. It is common to price bonds and other contracts "off the yield curve"—that is, to set their yield equal to the yield at the same maturity point on the yield curve with some adjustment for credit quality or other considerations.

The pricing implications of term-structure analysis have become much more critical with the advent of zero coupon bonds, principal-only securities, and a host of other financial instruments with nontra-ditional cash-flow patterns. Because such securities tend to concentrate cash flows, they magnify the error from small misreadings of the price of time. Errors of this sort have allegedly accounted for large losses experienced by some investment banking firms in the past decade. An important dimension of the new "financial engineering" is the separate pricing of cash flows of different term rather than the application of average prices to them with traditional yield-to-maturity.

4. *Pricing contingent claims on fixed income securities.* Many conventional securities contain implicit options such as call or prepayment features, and of course a large market has developed in options on fixed income

**EXHIBIT 56–1c**
**Term Structure of Interest Rates (June 1976–July 1989)**

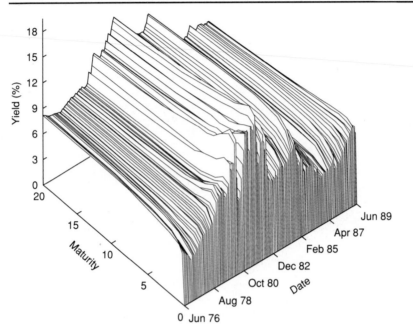

Source: Data courtesy of Salomon Brothers Inc

securities. The pricing of such contingent claims requires that the evolution of the term structure over time be modeled.

5. *Arbitraging between bonds of different maturities.* As explained in Chapter 6, swaps between somewhat similar bonds whose prices appear to be out of line is a standard fixed income portfolio management technique. Appraising the effects of term is no problem if the maturities or durations are virtually identical. When they are not, term-structure analysis can be used to make the yields more directly comparable and thereby facilitate the analysis.

In this chapter, we deal principally with two questions about the term structure: What causes it to be the way it is? And how can we measure, analyze, and interpret it? However, we should acknowledge at the outset that, despite the attention that has been given to the term structure (the term structure is a prime candidate for "most studied topic in financial economics"), there are no firm answers to these questions. Nowhere is the well-known disagreement among economists more pronounced than in the term-structure area. Thus, about the best we can hope for is more insight and understanding.

**EXHIBIT 56–2**
**Yields of Treasury Securities, June 30, 1989**

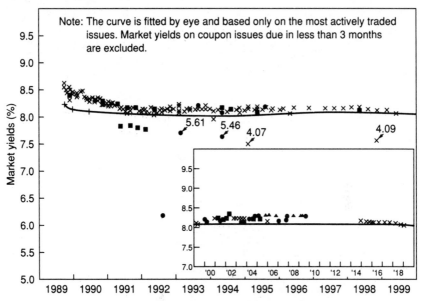

Note: The curve is fitted by eye and based only on the most actively traded issues. Market yields on coupon issues due in less than 3 months are excluded.

× Fixed maturity coupon issues under 12%.
■ Fixed maturity coupon issues of 12% or more.
+ Bills. Coupon equivalent yield of the latest 13–week, 26–week, and 52–week bills.

● Callable coupon issues under 12%.
▲ Callable coupon issues of 12% or more.
Note: Callable issues are plotted to the earliest call date when prices are above par and to maturity when prices are at par or below.

Source: *Federal Reserve Bulletin*, Summer Issue, September 1989.

## A REVIEW OF SOME BASICS

Chapter 6 deals with some basic aspects of bond prices and yield. At this point, it may be useful to review several of the concepts in that chapter.

Suppose that the available return on money committed for one year is 6 percent, and for two years it is 7 percent. These rates are *spot rates,* the annualized discount rates for money to be received at the end of years one and two. They would be the appropriate rates to be applied to zero-coupon bonds maturing at the end of these years.

Suppose also that we have two-period coupon bonds: Bond A with a 10 percent coupon and Bond B with a 5 percent coupon. Assuming annual compounding, the proper prices of these bonds are

$$P_A = \frac{10}{(1.06)} + \frac{110}{(1.07)^2} = 105.512$$

**EXHIBIT 56–3**
**Zero-Coupon Treasury Yields (April 9, 1990)\***

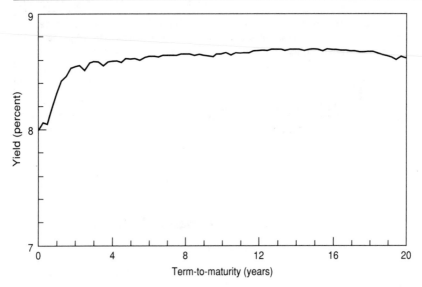

*Stripped Interest Treasuries only

Source: *Wall Street Journal*

$$P_B = \frac{5}{(1.06)} + \frac{105}{(1.07)^2} = 96.428$$

At these prices, the bonds will each provide the one- and two-period returns the market requires. However, the *yield-to-maturity* on these bonds—the single discount rate that equates the present value of the future flows to the price—is 6.953 percent for A and 6.975 percent for B.

$$P_A = \frac{10}{(1.06953)} + \frac{110}{(1.06953)^2} = 105.512$$

$$P_B = \frac{5}{(1.06975)} + \frac{105}{(1.06975)^2} = 96.428$$

The difference in the two bond yields arises because the yields to maturity are a complex average of the spot rates applied to one- and two-year money. Bond B has a somewhat greater fraction of its value tied up in more expensive year-two money, $105/(1.07)^2 = 91.711$, or 95.1 percent of its price, versus $110/(1.07)^2 = 96.078$ or 91.1 percent of the price for A, so it has the higher yield-to-maturity.

This general phenomenon, in which the yields that bonds of the same maturity offer depend on the patterns of their cash flows, is often referred to as the *coupon effect*. Notice that the yield-to-maturity on a pure discount or zero coupon bond is the same as the spot rate for money committed for the term of such a bond, provided that other factors, such as taxes, are neutral. There are no coupon effects with zeros.

In the analysis of maturity-time relationships it is usually preferable to work with spot rates rather than yields-to-maturity because such spot rates are not contaminated by coupon effects. Formally, the *term structure* deals with the relationship between spot rates and term, whereas the *yield curve* deals with yield-to-maturity and term. As this example suggests, in many instances the difference is not major, for both two-year yields are close to each other and close to the two-year spot rate. But it could be important when the length of the commitment is long or the pattern of cash flows is unusual.

One other rate deserves mention at this point. It is the *forward rate,* the spot rate at some future point that is implicit in the existing structure of spot rates. As we will establish in the next section, spot rates of 6 percent for one-year money and 7 percent for two-year money suggest that the price of one-year money at the end of one year, or the one-year forward rate in one year, is approximately 8 percent.

# THEORETICAL DETERMINANTS OF THE SHAPE OF THE TERM STRUCTURE

If buyers or issuers of fixed income securities were indifferent among securities of differing maturity, there would be no meaningful term structure; all yields would be equal. Therefore, the fact that yield curves are not perfectly horizontal suggests that some maturity preferences must exist. Reasons that have been advanced for the shape of the term structure are in effect theories or hypotheses about maturity preferences among investors. Five such theories are prominent: the market segmentation hypothesis, the expectations hypothesis, the liquidity premium hypothesis, the preferred habitat hypothesis, and the stochastic process no-arbitrage approach.[1] Let us examine each of these in turn.

## The Market Segmentation Hypothesis[2]

Suppose that buyers of fixed income securities fall roughly into two groups, one with a strong preference for short-term securities and the other with a strong

---

[1] There has also been some effort to analyze the term structure within a mean-variance framework; see Richard Roll, "Investment Diversification and Bond Maturity," *Journal of Finance,* (March 1971), pp. 51–66.

[2] The market segmentation hypothesis is frequently associated with John M. Culbertson. See his essay "The Term Structure of Interest Rates," *Quarterly Journal of Economics,* (November 1957), pp. 485–517.

preference for long-term securities. If there is little overlap in the range of maturities each group considers acceptable for portfolio investment, then the market for fixed income securities will actually be separated or segmented into two submarkets. And if one group of investors gains on the other in terms of funds available for investment, then, in the absence of an offsetting response by borrowers, this group will bid up prices and thus force down security yields in its preferred submarket. The same result might occur from a relative increase in the quantity of bonds issued by borrowers in one of the maturity ranges.[3]

This, in a nutshell, is the *market segmentation, institutional,* or *hedging pressure* theory of the term structure. It appears to be particularly popular among practicing investments professionals. Commercial banks are usually identified as the primary source of demand for short-term securities, and the demand for long-term securities is associated with life insurance companies. Advocates of this hypothesis acknowledge that these two types of institutions do not confine their investment exclusively to one end of the maturity spectrum. Moreover, they recognize the presence of other investors, including some who are comfortable operating in either maturity range. But they also believe that banks and life insurers are so dominant and their maturity preferences are so pronounced that short- and long-term yields behave as if the markets were segmented along these lines.

It is usually asserted that life insurance company demand for long-term bonds is stable over time. On the other hand, according to the market segmentation story, bank demand for short-term securities is more volatile. Banks prefer to lend directly to businesses and individuals when possible, only putting funds that are left over into securities. But demand for short-term loans by businesses and individuals is also quite volatile. In periods of strong economic activity, these borrowers demand funds for business expansion and consumption, banks sell securities to accommodate their demands, and short-term yields rise compared with long-term yields. In slack periods, these borrowers pay down their loans, and banks have excess funds for which they seek an outlet in short-term securities, driving short yields downward in comparison with long-term yields.

Opposition to the market segmentation hypothesis is based primarily on a belief that some other hypothesis provides a better explanation for the behavior of the term structure. Advocates of other hypotheses also believe that the segmentation hypothesis understates the willingness of banks, insurance com-

---

[3] Borrowers might also act to offset changes in the relative position of investors in the two submarkets by shifting their borrowing to the favored, lower interest-rate market, thereby restoring equality of interest rates. In the absence of strong maturity preferences on their part, this shifting is what we would expect rational borrowers to do, and there is evidence that some large borrowers, such as the U.S. Treasury, tend to behave in just this way. However, typical formulations of the market segmentation hypothesis assume that borrower behavior is largely unaffected by interest rates or, as it is said, is "exogenously determined."

panies, and many other investors to gravitate to the segment of the maturity structure that appears to offer the highest return, thereby eliminating temporary yield differentials.

## The "Pure" Or "Unbiased" Expectations Hypothesis[4]

*The General Idea.* The expectations hypothesis is the most widely received explanation for the shape of the term structure. This hypothesis stands in sharp contrast to the market segmentation hypothesis, for it is based on the assumption that fixed income investors, and possibly borrowers, collectively act to eliminate any comparative attraction of securities of a particular maturity. In effect, it acknowledges that maturity preferences may initially exist because of expectations about the future level of interest rates, but it asserts that market participants will respond in reasonable and rational ways to profit from these expectations. In the process they neutralize maturity preferences, but they also create systematic yield differentials among securities of different maturities.

A simple example will help us understand the expectations hypothesis. Suppose that the yield curve or term structure is flat, yields are 6 percent per annum on both one-year money and two-year money, and investors are generally in agreement that these yields will increase to 8 percent in one year. Under these conditions, the term structure would not remain flat but would become upward sloping. Plausible equilibrium or indifference yields are 6 percent on one-year (or short-term) securities and 7 percent on two-year (or long-term) securities—the same values as the spot rates in the example of the preceding section.

To see why this is so, let us first consider an investor with a long-term, or two-year, horizon. His objective is to earn the highest possible rate of return on his money over these two years and, yield aside, he is indifferent between initially buying a two-year security and holding it for two years, or purchasing a one-year security, holding it one year, and then rolling over into another one-year security for the second year. Before yields adjust, the first alternative gives him 6 percent on his money in each year. Under the second alternative, he knows he can earn 6 percent on his money for the first year and expects that he can earn 8 percent on his money in the second year, for an average yield of approximately 7 percent per annum over the two years. Thus, he will prefer the second alternative and will buy one-year securities at 6 percent rather than two-year securities at 6 percent. As he and other like-minded investors behave in this manner, prices on two-year securities will be driven down, and their yields

---

[4] The expectations hypothesis has a long history. It is frequently associated with the work of Irving Fisher, as in his "Appreciation and Interest," *Publications of the American Economic Association* (August 1896), pp. 23–29 and 88–92, and F. A. Lutz in "The Structure of Interest Rates," *Quarterly Journal of Economics*, (November 1940), pp. 36–63.

will be driven up. Only when two-year security yields reach 7 percent will the investors consider their purchases as attractive as the series of two one-year security investments.[5]

We can get to the same result by considering an investor who is seeking the largest total return (coupon yield plus price change) over the next year. She has a short-term horizon. Under our initial yield scenario, she knows that her total return on the one-year security will be 6 percent, for it will pay off at par in one year. On the other hand, her expected total return on the two-year security over the next year is initially only 4 percent.

To see this, assume that the two-year security has a 6 percent coupon. At the end of one year, it will be a one-year security—that is, it will have one year of life remaining. If the security is then to offer the expected yield-to-maturity of 8 percent, it must then sell for approximately 98. At this price, a purchaser will in the second year get a coupon of 6 and a capital gain of 2, for a total return of $(6 + 2)/98 \cong 8$ percent. But if the two-year security sells at 98 at the end of a year, its total return over the first year is only 4 percent because of the loss of value of 2; that is, $(6 - 2)/100 \cong 4$ percent. Under these circumstances, the two-year security will be unattractive to her. Thus, she will also prefer the one-year 6 percent security and avoid the two-year 6 percent security until the price of the latter drops to 98 and its yield-to-maturity rises to 7 percent. At this point she is indifferent, as the information in the table helps to establish.

|  | Maturity | |
|---|---|---|
|  | 1 Year | 2 Years |
| Coupon | 6% | 6% |
| Initial yield-to-maturity | 6% | 7% |
| Initial price | 100 | 98 |
| Capital gain, year 1 | 0 | 0 |
| Capital gain, year 2 | — | 2 |
| Return over life | 6/100 = 6% | $(6 + 6 + 2)/98 \cong 14\%$ $\cong 7\%$ per annum |
| Price at end of year 1 at 8% | — | 98 |
| Return, year 1 | 6/100 = 6% | $6/98 \cong 6\%$ |
| Return, year 2 | — | $(6 + 2)/98 \cong 8\%$ |

---

[5] In this example we are requiring that equilibrium be restored by movement in the yield of the long-term security. This is purely for expository convenience. Restoration of equilibrium might well involve both a decline in one-year yields and an increase in two-year yields.

At an initial price of 98, the two-year security offers an average yield-to-maturity of 7 percent per annum, based on its 6 percent coupon each year plus a capital gain of 2 in the second year on an initial investment of 98. However, if the price at the end of the first year remains at 98, consistent with a yield-to-maturity of 8 percent in the second year, then its total return in the first year is only 6 percent ($\cong 6/98$); there is no capital gain or loss. Thus, its total rate of return in the first year is exactly equal to the total rate of return on the one-year security, even though the yields to maturity are different. And the investor doesn't care which one she buys.

This example illustrates several significant implications of the pure expectations hypothesis. First, in each period, total rates of return—coupon plus capital gain or loss—are expected to be the same on all securities regardless of their term-to-maturity. Second, the consensus expectation of future yields or forward rates can be inferred from the presently observable term structure; for example, observing a 6 percent yield-to-maturity on one-year securities and a 7 percent yield-to-maturity on two-year securities, we know that the consensus forecast of the one-year forward rate in one year must be 8 percent. Third, yields on long-term securities are equal to an average of the present yield on short-term securities plus the expected future yield or yields on short-term securities; for instance, the 7 percent price of two-year money is approximately equal to the average of the current yield on one-year money of 6 percent and the expected future yield of 8 percent.

This last implication is believed to account for the observable tendency of short-term yields to fluctuate more than long-term yields. This tendency is readily evident in Exhibit 56–1; it is also shown directly in Exhibit 56–4, which plots the mean absolute deviation (average deviation with sign ignored) of the same yields from month to month. Yields on short-term securities fluctuate considerably. Presumably market participants regard these short rates as sometimes "high" and sometimes "low," and expect these fluctuations to more or less average out to a "normal" level over long investment horizons. This phenomenon leads to a common analogy of the yield curve with a person's waving arm: the arm is anchored to the shoulder (the long-maturity end), and the hand (short-term securities) moves up and down most as the arm is waved.

***An Algebraic Formulation.*** It is useful to formulate the pure expectations hypothesis algebraically, and over the years a somewhat standard notation has evolved for doing this. Let $_tR_n$ be the actual, observable spot rate, with the prescript denoting the time at which it is observed and the postscript indicating term. In our example, we have for the one-year spot rate $_0R_1 = 6$ percent, and for the two-year spot rate after equilibrium is reached, $_0R_2 = 7$ percent, where 0 means "now." We also need something to represent the unobservable forward rates; $_tr_{n,t}$ is used for this purpose, with the prescript representing the time at

**EXHIBIT 56–4**

**Mean Absolute Deviation of Monthly Changes in U.S. Government Security Yields and Prices (January 1950–July 1989)\***

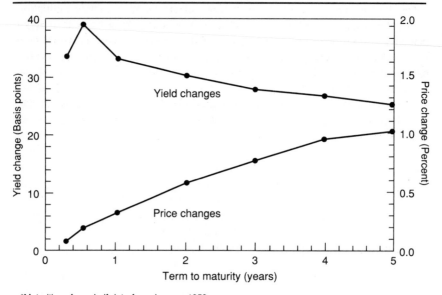

Term to maturity (years)

\*Maturities of one-half date from January 1959

Source: Data courtesy of Salomon Brothers Inc

which the rate goes into effect, the first postscript indicating the term to which it applies, and the second postscript denoting the time at which the forecast it made. In our example, rather than saying that "the presently expected price of one-year money in one year is 8 percent," we say $_1r_{1,0} = 8$ percent.

Given this notation, and acknowledging the fact that interest compounding is ignored in our example, the proposition that long rates are an average of observable and unobservable short rates can be stated as

$$(1 +_t R_n) = [(1 +_t R_1)(1 +_{t+1} r_{1,t})(1 +_{t+2} r_{1,t})\ldots(1 +_{t+n-1} r_{1,t})]^{1/n}$$
$$(56\text{–}1)$$

where there are $n$ periods.

In terms of our example values

$$(1 +_0 R_2) = [(1 +_0 R_1)(1 +_1 r_{1,0})]^{1/2}$$
$$(56\text{–}1a)$$

or

$$(1.07) \cong [(1.06)(1.08)]^{1/2}$$
$$(56\text{–}1b)$$

Notice that the average on the right side of this equation is a *geometric average,* in which we take the $n$th root of the product of $n$ values, as opposed to an arithmetic average, in which we divide the sum of $n$ values by $n$. A geometric average is necessary because, with compounding, returns combine multiplicatively rather than additively. The product of 1.06 and 1.08 is 1.1448, implying that \$1 invested for one year at 6 percent and the next at 8 percent would grow in value by 14.48 percent. Because of compounding, a yield slightly less than 7 percent earned in each of the two years would give the same appreciation. The geometric mean of 1.06 and 1.08 (i.e., the square root of 1.1448) is 1.06995, and this is the value that actually belongs on the left side of Equation 56–1b.

We can use the same notation to derive the forward rate implicit in two observed spot rates. In general form,

$$(1 +_{t+m} r_{n-m,t})^{n-m} = (1 +_t R_n)^n / (1 +_t R_m)^m \tag{56-2}$$

Thus, if we know any two points on the term structure, we can infer the yield that connects them. We can deduce the rate that is expected to prevail at the end of the shorter term-to-maturity ($m$) for the time interval that will be remaining ($n - m$) until the end of the longer term-to-maturity ($n$).

In terms of our example,

$$(1 +_1 r_{1,0})^{2-1} = (1 +_0 R_2)^2 / (1 +_0 R_1)^1 \tag{56 - 2a}$$

or

$$(1.08) \cong (1.07)^2 / 1.06 \tag{56 - 2b}$$

Use of this relationship is not limited to one-period-ahead rates. For instance, if we know the rate on four-year obligations and five-year obligations, we can readily determine the implied rate on one-year obligations that is expected to prevail in four years; if we know the rate on one-year obligations and five-year obligations, we can obtain the rate expected on four-year securities in one year.

*Alternative Statements of the Expectations Hypothesis.* The pure expectations hypothesis can be stated in at least five different ways. It is useful to spell these alternatives out, both because they are often encountered and because they have different levels of validity.[6]

---

[6] These alternatives, which have many antecedents in the financial economics literature, are all summarized in John Cox, Jonathan Ingersoll, Jr., and Stephen Ross, "A Re-examination of Traditional Hypothesis about the Term Structure of Interest Notes," *Journal of Finance,* (September 1981), pp. 769–99. The labels for each alternative come from Cox, Ingersoll, and Ross, except for the first, which is supplied by the authors of this chapter.

The *globally equal expected holding period return* alternative states that expected total returns from securities of all maturities for holding periods of all lengths are equal.

The *local expectations* version says that the expected total returns from long-term bonds over a short-term investment horizon equals today's interest rate over this horizon. Thus, the local expectations form is less comprehensive than the global version; it refers only to total returns over a horizon beginning at the *present*. It corresponds to the one-period investment horizon example discussed in the beginning of this section.

The *unbiased expectations* hypothesis states that forward rates are equal to the corresponding spot rates the market expects in the future. This is another way of saying that long-term interest rates are an average of expected future short-term rates. Both examples at the beginning of this section are consistent with this version.

The *return-to-maturity* expectations hypothesis says that the certain total return from holding a bond to maturity (a zero coupon bond with no reinvestment risk) is equal to the expected total return from rolling over a series of short-term bonds over the same horizon.

The *yield-to-maturity* version states that the periodic rate of return, or holding period yield, from holding a bond (a zero coupon bond) to maturity (a zero coupon bond with no reinvestment risk) is equal to the expected holding period yield from rolling over a series of short-term bonds over the same horizon. Thus, this version deals with periodic returns, such as annualized returns, whereas the return-to-maturity version is concerned with total or cumulative returns over the investment horizon. This version corresponds directly to the two-period example discussed at the beginning of this section.

In a journal article published in 1981 that created quite a stir in financial economics circles, Cox, Ingersoll, and Ross showed that the globally equal holding period return variant cannot be literally valid provided there is uncertainty about future interest rates. Moreover, they also proved that the remaining four versions are *not* exact equivalents or even consistent with each other with uncertain interest rates.[7] According to their analysis only the local expectations

---

[7] See Cox, Ingersoll, and Ross, pages 774–77. The reason for these conclusions has to do with what is known as Jensen's inequality, which states that the expected value of the reciprocal of a variable is not the same as the reciprocal of the expected value of the variable. Because of Jensen's inequality, if expected returns on all bonds are equal for any one holding period, the expected returns on all bonds cannot also be equal for any other holding period.

To see Jensen's inequality in an application, and to also see why the globally equal expected return variant cannot be literally valid, consider a situation in which a one-year, zero coupon bond sells for 90 while a two-year zero sells for 80, and where one year from now the two-year zero will sell for either 86.889 or 90.889 with equal probability. Thus, the total return (yield plus return of principal)

version is consistent with equilibrium; if any of the others are valid, then there are investment strategies that will earn excess returns. Others have subsequently argued that the differences in the local expectations and unbiased expectations versions, the most popular of the five, are of second-order importance.[8] Still, in light of Cox, Ingersoll, and Ross it is probably wise to stress the local expectations version and hence the equality of total returns over short investment horizons beginning immediately.

## The Liquidity Premium or Interest-Rate Risk Hypothesis

In the expectations hypothesis, investors are assumed to act only on the basis of expected returns on bonds of different maturities; they take no notice of the possibility that actual returns (and future interest rates) may deviate from their expectations. The liquidity premium, or interest-rate risk, hypothesis considers this possibility.

Let us return to our simple situation in which there is a one-year bond and a two-year bond, each of which carries a 6 percent coupon in a 6 percent interest-rate environment. Now, let us suppose that all interest rates instantaneously go to 7 percent: What happens to the prices of these two securities?

As we have already seen, the two-year security will drop to 98 in price. At this price, it offers a capital gain of 2 spread over two years, or 1 per year, and a coupon of 6 each year. If the rate of interest remains at 7 percent, then the price at the end of the first year is 99; the return in the first year is $(6 + 1)/98 \cong 7$ percent and in the second year $(6 + 1)/99 \cong 7$ percent.

---

on the two-year bond in the first year will be either $86.889/80 = 1.08611$ or $90.889/80 = 1.13611$, and the total return available on one-year bonds for the second year will be either $100/86.889 = 1.15089$ or $100/90.889 = 1.10024$. These prices have been chosen so that the expected return for one year on the two-year bond equals the certain return for one year on the one-year bond. The one-year zero will provide a total return of $100/90 = 1.11111$ with certainty, while the expected return on the two-year zero is the same, $(0.5)(86.889/80) + (0.5)(90.889/80) = (0.5)(1.13611) + (0.5)(1.08611) = 1.11111$. It cannot then also be true that the certain return for two years on the two-year bond equals the expected return for two years from rolling over the one-year bond. The two-year bond guarantees a total return of $100/80 = 1.25000$ over this time span. If one goes the route of investing in the one-year bond for one year, earning a total return of $100/90 = 1.11111$ and then rolling over into one-year bonds for the second year, the expected total return is higher, $1.11111 \times [(0.5)(100/86.889) + (0.5)(100/90.889)] = 1.11111 \times [(0.5)(1.15089) + (0.5)(1.10024)] = 1.11111 \times 1.12556 = 1.25062$. Thus, there is not equality of expected returns over all bonds for all investment horizons.

Cox, Ingersoll, and Ross do show that in continuous time, akin to continuous compounding, the yield-to-maturity and unbiased expectations versions of the expectations hypothesis are equivalent.

[8] See John Y. Campbell, "A Defense of Traditional Hypothesis about the Term Structure of Interest Rates," *Journal of Finance*, (March 1986), pp. 183–193; and Miles Livingston, *Money and Capital Markets* (Englewood Cliffs, NJ: Prentice-Hall, 1990), pp. 254–56, "Appendix: Local Versus Unbiased Expectations Hypotheses."

What about the one-year security? We would expect its price to drop immediately to 99. At this price it is like the two-year security after one year has elapsed; over the year it offers a capital gain of 1, which when added to the coupon of 6 represents a total return ≅ 7 percent on the initial investment of 99.

These price declines in response to a one percentage point increase in yields are 1 percent and 2 percent of the initial prices of the one- and two-year securities, respectively. For securities of even longer term, the price decline would be even larger. In reality the price decline would not increase *quite* proportionately with the term-to-maturity. The intuition for this nonproportionality is that the more the price drops, the smaller the initial investment is, and thus the smaller the additional price decline required to raise the yield a given amount.[9]

Exhibit 56–5 plots the actual prices at which a 12 percent coupon security must sell to yield 14 percent to maturity when it has a term-to-maturity of 1 to 25 years. The necessary price decline does increase with maturity, but at a

**EXHIBIT 56–5**

**Price of a 12 Percent Coupon Bond of Various Maturities at Yields of 10 Percent and 14 Percent**

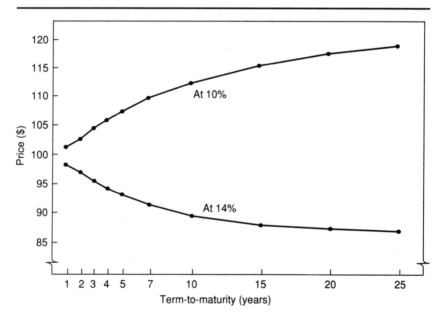

---

[9] For example, (6 + 1)/99 is actually equal to 7.07 percent, and (6 − 6− 2)/98 is actually equal to 14.28 percent; a price decline to 99.07 and to 98.25 are all that are necessary to give total returns of 7 percent and 14 percent, respectively.

decreasing rate. Exhibit 56–5 also shows the prices needed for such securities to yield only 10 percent; compared with par, these prices represent decreases or increases in price that get larger with maturity but only a decreasing rate.

This price change/yield change relationship is purely mechanical in nature; it follows from the mathematics of bond price calculations and is frequently captured via the duration of a bond. Therefore, if all yields fluctuated by the same amount, then long bonds should fluctuate more in price than short bonds. But we have already established that short-term yields fluctuate more than long-term yields; this was the message of Exhibit 56–4. Which of these influences is more important in terms of price fluctuation? That is, do short-term bonds actually vary more or less in price than long-term bonds? The answer, which can only be obtained by observation, turns out to be that longer-term bonds have greater price volatility. Exhibit 56–4 also shows mean absolute deviations of monthly bond price changes derived from yield changes for 1950 through July of 1989. Here it is evident that bond price volatility increases with maturity, first at a very rapid rate but then at a much lower rate as bond maturity lengthens.

This observation suggests a third reason investors might not be indifferent among bonds of different maturities. If most investors are adverse to fluctuations in the value of their portfolios, they will have some preference for short-term securities simply because their values are more stable. Therefore, in order to induce them to hold progressively longer-term bonds, they must expect to receive higher returns.[10] Such a return increment is usually referred to as a *liquidity premium,* on the basis that shorter term securities are more money-like and this is a premium for bearing illiquidity. It might better be described as an interest-risk premium. But regardless of what it is called, the implication is the same: Other considerations aside, longer term bonds should offer higher yields. Or to put it another way, longer term bonds should on average provide higher realized total returns.

Because actual bond price fluctuations increase with maturity but at a decreasing rate, interest-rate risk premia should also increase with maturity but at a decreasing rate. Therefore, according to the liquidity premium hypothesis, yields that would otherwise be equal regardless of term should increase but at a decreasing rate as maturity lengthens.[11]

---

[10] This justification for the existence of liquidity premia is the traditional one. In recent years the case for such premia has been made in a much more rigorous manner; for a review of such efforts see Robert J. Shiller and J. Houston McCulloch, "The Term Structure of Interest Rates," Working Paper No. 2341, National Bureau of Economic Research, August 1987, to appear in the *Handbook of Monetary Economics.*

[11] The liquidity premium hypothesis is usually attributed to J. R. Hicks. See his *Value and Capital* (Oxford: Oxford University Press, 1946). In a related vein, Reuben Kessel has argued that short yields are especially low because short securities are close substitutes for holding cash. This "money substitute" hypothesis is proposed in his essay "The Cyclical Behavior of the Term Structure of Interest Rates," *in Essays in Applied Price Theory,* (Chicago: University of Chicago Press, 1965).

A formal statement of the liquidity premium, or interest-rate risk premium, hypothesis is that the market adds premia $L_t$ to yields for term-to-maturity $t$ that would otherwise exist, with

$$0 = L_1 < L_2 < L_3 \ldots L_n$$

implying that these liquidity premia are positive and rise with longer maturities. Moreover,

$$(L_2 - L_1) > (L_3 > L_2) > \ldots (L_n - L_{n-1})$$

That is, the incremental liquidity premia decrease with lengthening maturities. If the yield curve would be flat otherwise, it should rise with maturity, at first steeply but then at a rate that decreases continuously.

### The Preferred Habitat Hypothesis

The liquidity premium hypothesis considers only price risk. Reinvestment risk may also be important. For example, a one-year bond may offer less price risk than a two-year bond to an investor with a two-year horizon, but it also exposes the investor to an uncertain reinvestment rate for the second year. The consideration of the investment horizon of investors (and borrowers) and its effect on their maturity preferences leads to the preferred habitat hypothesis.[12]

According to this theory, investors have preferred maturities that are not necessarily for the shortest term securities available. Those preferences may affect the maturity pattern of yields. Pension funds, for instance, have long-term liabilities and appear to prefer long-term investments because of the reduced risk of being forced to reinvest a large portion of their portfolios when yields are low. They might depart from their preferred maturity range, but only for a price. With a preponderance of such investors and no offsetting actions by bond issuers, risk premia might actually *decrease* with maturity. The more general point of the preferred habitat hypothesis is that market participants' maturity preferences can have a substantial but not readily predictable impact on the term structure of interest rates.

### An Eclectic Yield-Curve Hypothesis

The market segmentation, unbiased expectations, interest-rate risk premium, and preferred habitat hypotheses are not mutually exclusive ways of thinking about interest rates. It is probably fair to say the majority of those who watch the money and credit markets believe that at least two and possibly all four

---

[12] Franco Modigliani and Richard Sutch, "Innovations in Interest Rate Policy," *American Economic Review*, (May 1966), pp. 178–197.

of these influences are present in the term structure from time to time. For example, one might be of the opinion that relative yields are usually determined by supply/demand conditions in the short- and long-term securities markets, with some tendency toward lower rates in the short end, yet still believe that at some particular time the expectation of sharply lower rates is also influencing the term structure.

One composite hypothesis, the *biased expectations hypothesis,* is particularly prominent. According to this theory, the yield curve reflects future interest-rate expectations of the moment and also persistent (but not necessarily stable) liquidity premia. Formally,

$$(1 +_t R_n) = [(1 +_t R_1)(1 +_{t+1} r_{1,t} + (L_2 - L_1))(1 +_{t+2} r_{1,t} + (L_3 - L_2) \ldots$$

$$(1 +_{t+n-1} r_{1,t} + L_n - L_{n-1}))]^{1/n} \qquad (56-3)$$

where the $L_t - L_{t-1}$ are incremental liquidity premia for extending maturity an additional period.

This hypothesis appeals to many because, in addition to incorporating two elements they find intuitively appealing, it is readily able to account for "humped" yield curves, which can be observed in Exhibit 56–1 — situations in which rates initially rise with lengthening maturity but then reach a peak and decline at the longer maturities. (Of course, rising and then declining rate expectations could also account for humped yield curves.) This pattern can be rationalized in the following way. Interest rates are expected to decline moderately, and according to the unbiased expectation hypothesis this alone should produce a yield curve that declines over its entire length. However, liquidity premia, which have their largest marginal effects at short maturities, overpower this tendency toward a downward-sloping yield curve at the short end. Toward the middle of the yield curve and at its long end, the expectations component is dominant. Exhibit 56–6 summarizes these effects.

## The Stochastic-Process No-Arbitrage Approach

In the last decade, a new way of dealing with the term structure has evolved; we shall refer to it as *stochastic-process equilibrium or no-arbitrage* modeling of the term structure. This approach has three notable characteristics or underlying assumptions.[13] First, the term structure and bond prices are related to certain stochastic factors. ("Stochastic" basically means random or uncertain.) Second, these underlying factors are assumed to evolve over time according to a particular hypothesized stochastic process. Third, the interest rates and bond prices that

---

[13] See Terence C. Langetieg, "A Multivarient Model of the Term Structure," *Journal of Finance* (March 1980), p. 75.

**EXHIBIT 56–6**
**Expectations and Liquidity Effects in the Yield Curve**

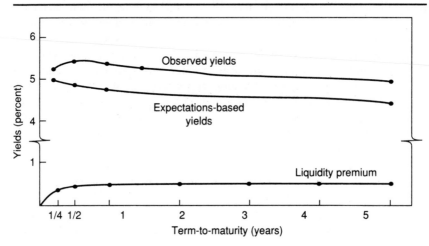

result must satisfy "no-arbitrage" or "no easy money" conditions.[14] The concept of an equilibrium term structure under uncertainty was introduced by Robert Merton in 1973.[15] Since then, a number of researchers have made significant contributions to this approach.[16]

A number of aspects of the stochastic-process equilibrium approach are worthy of comment before we examine an illustration. Possibly the most significant is that this approach is rooted in the modeling of *uncertainty;* it explicitly acknowledges that market rates are only predictable up to a point, and thus observed interest rates (or bond prices) will contain an element of surprise. With the traditional theories, this uncertainty is implicit at best, as the emphasis tends to be on expected (in a statistical sense) values.

---

[14] The actual form of the no-arbitrage condition depends on the specific model under consideration, but the bottom line is that there should be no investment strategy that can earn in excess of the risk-free rate of return on a riskless investment. For example, suppose that one-, two-, and three-year duration bonds are available. It might be possible, for example, to construct a portfolio of the one- and three-year bonds with a duration of two years and go short the two-year bond, leaving a net portfolio duration of zero. In a simple Macaulay world, such a portfolio has no interest-rate risk. Equilibrium requires that the yields on these bonds be such that the return on the net investment is equal to the riskless rate of interest.

[15] Robert C. Merton, "The Rational Theory of Options Pricing," *Bell Journal of Economics and Management Science,* (1973), pp. 141–183.

[16] For a useful overview of this approach and the related literature, see John Hull, *Options, Futures, and Other Derivative Securities* (Englewood Cliffs, NJ: Prentice-Hall 1989), especially Chapter 10, "Interest Rate Derivative Securities."

The stochastic-process equilibrium approach is described here as an *approach* or *model* rather than as a hypothesis because the critical hypotheses involve the stochastic process or processes assumed to drive the term structure. It is at this level that the individuality and opportunity for superiority of certain models arises.

The stochastic-process equilibrium approach is not inconsistent with the more traditional approaches to the term structure. For example, the pure expectations hypothesis, liquidity premium hypothesis, and biased expectations hypotheses can all be viewed as special cases generated by certain sets of assumptions about the stochastic process underlying the term structure. This approach is better viewed as an alternative way of examining the term structure rather than as a competitor to traditional theories.

Finally, the relationship of the stochastic-process, no-arbitrage approach to contingent claims should be noted. The underlying idea of a stochastic process generating the prices of fixed income securities has a parallel in the assumed process for generating stock prices that underlies many options pricing models, such as the Black-Scholes model. Moreover, the valuation of options on fixed income securities, call provisions, prepayment features, and other contingent claims all require some assumption about the term-structure generating process. Much of the research in the term-structure area has been stimulated by the desire to value such contingent claims.

Let's look at a representative model. In an effort to analyze the yield-curve notes recently issued by several financial institutions, Joseph Ogden uses a model in which only one stochastic factor drives bond prices and the term structure, the instantaneous, default-free rate of interest.[17] The process he uses to represent the evolution of this rate is a popular one:

$$dr = \beta\,(\mu - r)\,dt + \sigma r\ dz$$

where

$dr$ = the instantaneous change in this rate

$\beta$ = a speed-of-adjustment component

$(\mu - r)$ = the extent by which the current interest rate exceeds $(r > \mu)$ or falls short $(r < \mu)$ of some steady-state mean level $\mu$

$dt$ = the passage of time

$dz$ = a stochastic process

$\sigma$ = the standard deviation of the process.

In words, this equation says that the change in rates has two components, one predictable and one unpredictable. The predictable component is equal to the

---

[17] Joseph P. Ogden, "An Analysis of Yield Curve Notes," *Journal of Finance* (March 1987), pp. 99–110.

extent to which the current rate differs from its long-term value, multiplied by a coefficient that measures its rate of adjustment back toward its long-term value. Thus, this component incorporates the common observation that the interest rate tends toward some normal rate and is more likely to fall when above this normal level ($\mu - r$ is negative) and rise when below ($\mu - r$ is positive). The form of this component also implies that the size of the move in the rate is greater the further the rate is from its normal level, as the predictable component is a constant *proportion* of the difference in the two.

The unpredictable component is equal to the product of the standard deviation of the rate, the initial level of the rate, and some stochastic process. (Think of the stochastic process as something akin to a roulette wheel; we know a lot about how it operates but not the next value it will generate.) Thus, the unpredictable component corresponds with the commonsense notion that the interest rate is more volatile, in absolute terms, when it is high than when it is low. Because of this component, even though the rate *tends* to move toward $\mu$ due to the predictable component, the rate actually observed can move even further away from $\mu$.

When Ogden estimated this model for the period from 1977 through July 1985, using monthly data on 90-day Treasury bills, annualized values were 0.6384 for $\beta$, 0.1053 for $\mu$, and 0.2881 for $\sigma$. The implication is that the observed rates should have been expected to move about 64 percent of the way toward 0.1053 over the course of a year and have a standard deviation of 303 basis points per annum when $r = \mu$ (or $0.2881 \times .1053 \times 100$).

It is also possible to model the term structure by making it dependent on two stochastic factors. A common second factor, in addition to a short rate, is a long bond rate. Michael Brennan and Eduardo Schwartz have developed such a model, which is widely utilized in fixed income contingent claim valuation.[18]

Both the single factor models such as used by Ogden and two-factor models of the Brennan-Schwartz variety are consistent with the unbiased expectations theory. These models can be thought of as providing forecasts of the future rates that will be built into the term structure. They can generate term structures that rise with maturity and term structures that fall with maturity. Most stochastic-process no-arbitrage approaches also incorporate a risk premium factor that results from risk-averse investors and the tendency for longer bond

---

[18] See Michael J. Brennan and Eduardo S. Schwartz, "An Equilibrium Model of Bond Pricing and a Test of Market Efficiency," *Journal of Financial and Quantitative Analysis* (March 1982), pp. 75–100. A reasonably straightforward presentation of the Brennan-Schwartz model accompanied by some results from using the model to price actual Treasury issues appears in Michael J. Brennan and Eduardo S. Schwartz, "Bond Pricing and Market Efficiency," *Financial Analysts Journal* (September-October 1982), pp. 49–56.

returns to be more volatile than short ones. With such a risk premium factor, the stochastic-process, no arbitrage approaches are consistent with the biased expectations hypothesis. These expanded approaches can generate humped term structures in addition to the standard ascending or descending term structures.

## CLASSICAL YIELD CURVES AND THEIR RATIONALE

Exhibit 56–7 portrays four different yield curves that might be described as "classics" in the sense that they are prototypes of the forms into which all yield curves are supposed to fall. It is important to observe the level at which these yield curves are plotted, as well as their shape, for the level of rates plays an important role in the usual stories that are told to explain the shapes.

The four forms are these:

1. *Normal.* Interest rates are at moderate levels. Yields rise continuously with increasing maturity but with a gentle and continuously decreasing slope.
2. *Rising.* Interest rates are "low" by historical or other standards. Yields rise substantially with increasing term-to-maturity, but possibly with some reduction in the rate of increase at longer maturities.
3. *Falling.* Yields are extremely high by historical standards and decline over the entire maturity range of the yield curve.
4. *Humped.* This is the same as the curve in Exhibit 56–6. Interest rates are high by historical standards. The yield curve at first rises with increasing maturity but then peaks and declines at the longer maturities.

Exhibit 56–7 also summarizes the stories that can be told under a variety of term structure theories to account for these shapes. Notice that in several cases there is no adequate single explanation for the yield-curve shape under the liquidity premium hypothesis. This is consistent with the earlier discussion of the effect that the liquidity premium hypothesis is most often regarded as an "add on" rather than a "free-standing" hypothesis.

## EMPIRICAL EVIDENCE ON THE TERM-STRUCTURE HYPOTHESES

In principle, it should be possible to look at the numerical record and establish which of the various hypotheses of the term structure is most nearly valid. But in practice such validation is extremely difficult for a variety of reasons.

# EXHIBIT 56-7

## Alternative Classical Yield Curves and their Explanations

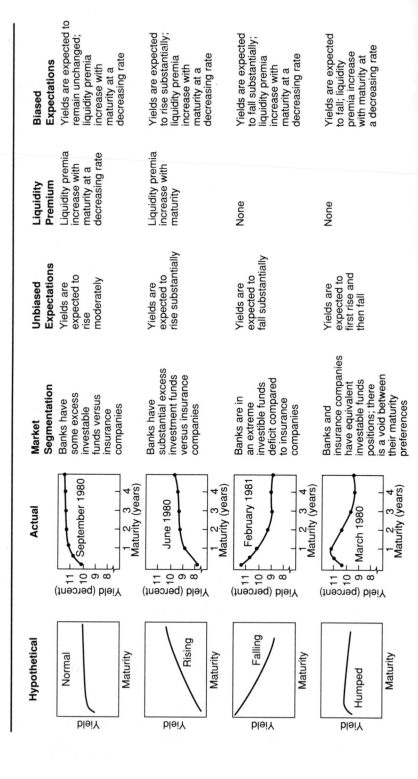

| Hypothetical | Actual | Market Segmentation | Unbiased Expectations | Liquidity Premium | Biased Expectations |
|---|---|---|---|---|---|
| Normal | September 1980 | Banks have some excess investable funds versus insurance companies | Yields are expected to rise moderately | Liquidity premia increase with maturity at a decreasing rate | Yields are expected to remain unchanged; liquidity premia increase with maturity at a decreasing rate |
| Rising | June 1980 | Banks have substantial excess investment funds versus insurance companies | Yields are expected to rise substantially | Liquidity premia increase with maturity | Yields are expected to rise substantially; liquidity premia increase with maturity at a decreasing rate |
| Falling | February 1981 | Banks are in an extreme investible funds deficit compared to insurance companies | Yields are expected to fall substantially | None | Yields are expected to fall substantially; liquidity premia increase with maturity at a decreasing rate |
| Humped | March 1980 | Banks and insurance companies have equivalent investable funds positions; there is a void between their maturity preferences | Yields are expected to first rise and then fall | None | Yields are expected to fall; liquidity premia increase with maturity at a decreasing rate |

First, market consensus expectations, which would be especially useful in verifying the expectations hypothesis, are observable only with difficulty and imperfectly. Second, interest-rate changes are characterized by surprise rather than by predictability. Thus, it is extremely difficult to conclude much about *a priori* expectations from *ex post* predictions. Third, and as we shall see, measurement of liquidity premia is extremely difficult in an uncertain world, and liquidity premia may change over time in a manner that obscure any more basic relationships.

Finally, the two theories most at odds conceptually—the segmented markets and expectation hypothesis—often are both consistent with observed yield curves. For example, when the yield curve is low by historical standards but steeply upward sloping, the implication according to the expectations hypothesis is that yields are expected to rise. But periods when interest rates are low also tend to be periods of slack economic activity and low short-term loan demand, so banks are in a surplus funds position compared with life insurance companies. These conditions should also produce upward-sloping yield curves according to the segmentation hypothesis. The two stories are readily reversed to explain downward-sloping yield curves. Unfortunately, if two theories predict similar yield patterns, then it is difficult to differentiate between them.

Nevertheless, it is useful to look at some of the evidence that has been brought forth on the various hypotheses.[19] This evidence does permit some very general, tentative conclusions. And in a number of instances the form of the evidence should be of interest to fixed income investors in its own right.

## Interest-Rate Risk or Liquidity Premia

This is the hypothesis on which the evidence is the most unequivocal, and it tends to add up to a strong case for the presence of interest-rate risk or liquidity premia.

Possibly the most obvious evidence is the behavior of yields over long periods of time. For example, analysis of the term-structure numbers underlying Exhibit 56–1 reveals that yields on securities of the shortest term have tended

---

[19] A standard term-structure reference source that reviews evidence bearing on the alternative theories in much more detail is James C. Van Horne's *Financial Market Rates and Flows* (Englewood Cliffs, NJ: Prentice-Hall, 1978), especially Chapters 4 and 5.

to be below those on longer term securities the majority of the time over the past three decades, as shown by the following tabulation:

| | Number (Proportion) of Times | |
|---|---|---|
| | Short Rate ≤ Long Rate | Short Rate > Long Rate |
| 3-month Treasury bills versus 6-month Treasury bills* | 256 (.959) | 11 (.041) |
| 3-month Treasury bills versus 1-year bonds | 349 (.931) | 26 (.069) |
| 6-month Treasury bills versus 1-year bonds* | 223 (.835) | 44 (.165) |

* Six-month Treasury bill series commenced January 1959.

It is also useful to look at long-run total returns, which consider changes in value as well as coupon income on longer-term securities. The well-known Ibbotson-Sinquefield total return series, which looks at monthly rates of return from the beginning of 1926 through the end of 1987, reveals an average annual rate of return on short-term bills (maturities of just over one month) of 3.5 percent per annum versus 4.3 percent per annum on long-term government bonds (maturities of 20 years).[20] This result occurs despite the general upward trend of interest rates over many of these years, which tended to produce capital losses on average in the long-term bond series.

While the evidence on the existence of liquidity premia is substantial, there is not consensus on their behavior over time. Some researchers find that liquidity premia are constant over time or at least that they do not vary with time, while others report time-varying liquidity premia. In the latter camp, some researchers have had limited success in relating liquidity premia to considerations such as the level of business confidence. Others have reported that liquidity premia vary directly with the level of interest rates, suggesting some sort of a proportional relationship or inverse relationship with the level of interest rates—which is consistent with the notion that interest rates are regarded as more likely to fall if they are "high" and more likely to rise if they are "low."[21]

---

[20] *Stocks, Bonds, Bills, and Inflation: 1988 Yearbook* (Chicago, IL: Ibbotson Associates, 1988), Exhibit 8, p. 25.

[21] See Van Horne, *Financial Market Rate and Flows,* pp. 124–125, for a review of some of the studies in this area.

## The Expectations Hypothesis

It is evident that if the liquidity premium hypothesis is valid, then the pure or unbiased expectations hypothesis cannot be. What about the biased expectations hypothesis, in which the term structure reflects expected future interest rates as well as liquidity premia?

There have been many tests of this hypothesis, and we will review some of them. However, it may be useful to go ahead and get the bottom line in the record: The evidence in support of the expectations hypothesis is extraordinarily weak, to say the least. As one researcher in this area has observed, "If the attractiveness of an economic hypothesis is measured by the number of papers which statistically reject it, the expectations hypothesis is a knockout."[22]

Tests of the expectations hypothesis generally take three forms. One test is to look at the equality of realized returns on securities of different maturity through time. The examination of the Ibbotson-Sinquefield results in the previous section is representative of this type of test.

In one of the classic papers on the term structure, J. M. Culbertson examined holding weekly period returns on Treasury bills (the longest outstanding) and Treasury bonds (Culbertson used a bond of approximately 19 years' maturity) for all of 1953. Culbertson detected little evidence of parallel movements in holding period returns; as a result, he indicated, "The conclusion to which we seem forced to turn is that speculative activity (i.e., activity that should equate holding period returns), dominant though it can be in very short-run movements, does not determine the broad course of interest rates or of interest-rate relationships."[23]

In contrast, Jacob Michaelson looked at weekly holding period returns on U.S. government securities with maturities ranging from one week to 10+ years over the 1951–1962 period.[24] He first observed a tendency for average realized total returns to increase with terms to maturity of from 1 to 13 weeks over this overall period and in a number of subperiods typified by cyclical upturns or downturns in interest rates. These results are consistent with what one would expect in a market dominated by the biased expectations theory in which realized returns on short-term securities conform closely to anticipations. He then looked at the correlation between total returns on the 13-week and the longer maturity series. The correlations obtained in this way were uniformly

---

[22] Kenneth Froot, "New Hope for the Expectation Hypothesis of the Term Structure of Interest Rates," *Journal of Finance*, (June 1989), p. 283.

[23] J. M. Culbertson, "The Term Structure of Interest Rates," *Quarterly Journal of Economics* (November 1957), pp. 485–517. This particular statement appears on pages 508 and 509.

[24] Jacob B. Michaelson, "The Term Structure of Interest Rates and Holding Period Yields in Government Securities," *Journal of Finance*, (September 1965), pp. 444–63.

positive. On this basis, he concluded that the biased expectations hypothesis was supported.

Another popular test of the biased expectations hypothesis examines the pattern of revisions in yield curves with the passage of time. Such tests accept the validity of the so-called error-learning model of the formation of economic expectations. According to this model, expectations of the more distant future will be revised when expectations of the more immediate future are found to be in error, and they will be revised in the same direction. As an example of this in the present context, suppose that the market routinely forecasts some rate both three months into the future and six months into the future. If after three months have elapsed the actual rate is below the forecast made three months previously, then the market might be expected to revise downward its forecast that was formerly for six months into the future but is now only three months out. That is, the revision of the rate forecast implied by the term structure should be related directly to errors that are discovered in prior implicit forecasts. If this actually seems to happen, the conclusion is that (1) the error-learning model captures the way in which forecasts are made, and (2) expectations of future rates are embedded in present rates.

This test was devised by David Meiselman, and his work on the subject is a standard reference.[25] However, for our purposes, it may be more useful to look at a more recent study utilizing a variant of this technique by Richard Worley and Stanley Diller.[26]

Their results are summarized in Exhibit 56–8. The upper panel of this figure shows the errors in forecasts of three-month rates made three months earlier; that is, the actual three-month rate is subtracted from the three-month rate that was implied by the term structure three months earlier (or $_t r_{3,t-3} - _t R_3$). Notice that an inverted scale is used, so large underestimates of actual rates are near the top of the plot and large overestimates are near the bottom. The lower panel shows the coincident changes in forecasted future rates—the difference in three-month rates expected in three months and the same three-month rate that was implied by the term structure three months previously (or $_{t+3} r_{3,t} - _{t+3} r_{3,t-3}$). These values are plotted in the usual way so, for example, a positive number means that the forecast for rates three months out has been raised. The plotted values are based on monthly observations for 1966 through most of 1976.

It is evident from the figure that there is a close correlation between forecast errors and revisions in the forecasts. Underestimates in prior forecasts are associated with increases in forecasts of the future, and conversely for overesti-

---

[25] David Meiselman, *The Term Structure of Interest Rates* (Englewood Cliffs, NJ: Prentice-Hall, 1962).

[26] Richard B. Worley and Stanley Diller, "Interpreting the Yield Curve," *Financial Analysts Journal* (November–December 1976), pp. 37–45.

**EXHIBIT 56–8**
**Worley-Diller Analysis of the Influence of Forecast Errors on Forecast Changes**

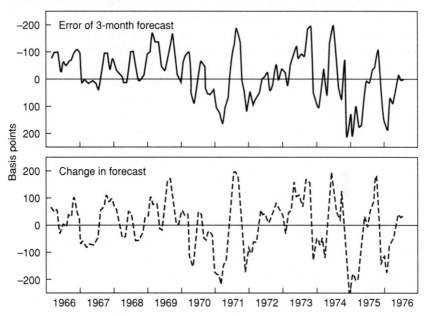

Source: R.B. Worley and S. Diller, "Interpreting the Yield Curves," *Financial Analysts Journal,* Nov.–Dec. 1976, p. 43

mates. Although such association does not prove that the term structure is based on expectations of future interest rates,[27] it is consistent with the expectations hypothesis.

A third approach to testing the expectations hypothesis is based on its implication that forecasts of future interest rates are imbedded in the present term structure of interest rates. If the expectations considered tend to dominate the slope of the yield curve *and* if the market in the aggregate possesses adequate forecasting ability, then we should find that the term structure actually does forecast future interest rates with some degree of accuracy. This is the approach that has dominated the term-structure literature and that should be of greatest interest to persons who must actually make fixed income investment decisions. Unfortunately, the evidence in this respect is also equivocal at best.

[27] As Livingston points out in *Money and Capital Markets,* such evidence simply shows that forward rates are correlated. The expectations hypothesis maintains much more than this.

If forecasts of future interest rates are embedded in the term structure, then long-term yields should lead short-term yields in time. For example, suppose that market participants raise their estimates of short-term interest rates. This change should have no impact on current short rates, but according to the expectations hypothesis it should raise current long rates. If these forecasts are correct then in the future the actual short rate should also rise. This relationship was utilized by Frederick R. Macaulay in a test reported in his landmark volume *Some Theoretical Problems Suggested by the Movement of Interest Rates, Bond Yields, and Stock Prices in the United States Since 1856.*[28] Macaulay examined the relationship for the 1890–1913 period between yields on call money and on 90-day loans and found some evidence of the latter yield series leading the former. However, he also discovered a perverse relationship at the long end of the term structure: When the yield curve was upward-sloping, long-term rates seemed to more often fall than rise. This latter relationship continues to be found by a number of researchers looking at somewhat more recent data.

The decade of the eighties saw renewed interest in forecasting tests of the term structure. Many of these tests have been unfavorable to the expectations hypothesis. In one illustrative study, Robert Shiller, John Campbell, and Kermit Schoenholtz compare actual changes in interest rates with the forecasts of these changes derived from the term structure (after adjustments for constant liquidity premia).[29] They also find that rates tend to move in the opposite direction from the theoretical predictions. Exhibit 56–9 portrays graphically the results of their analysis of the quarterly change in three-month Treasury bill rates beginning in 1959 and running through the middle of 1982; Exhibit 56–10 shows the results of an equivalent analysis of 30-year Treasury bond yields using semiannual data for the same period. These graphs, which are striking, speak for themselves. Further analysis of these data leads these researchers to conclude that their rejection of the expectations hypothesis might be due to variations in liquidity or risk premia through time—variations that, in their opinion, are so large as to destroy any information in the term structure about future rates.

On a more positive note, Eugene Fama looked at essentially the same time period but with monthly Treasury bill data.[30] He estimated two relationships. For the first, he began with the proposition that observed spot rate should be equal to the associated forward rate previously embedded in the term structure. He then subtracted the one-period spot rate from both sides of the relationship and estimated, for one-month horizons and investment periods,

---

[28] New York: National Bureau of Economic Research, 1938.

[29] Robert Shiller, John Campbell, and Kermit Schoenholtz, "Forward Rates and Future Policy: Interpreting the Term Structure of Interest Rates," *Brooking Papers on Economic Activity,* 1983, pp. 173–217.

[30] Eugene Fama, "The Information in the Term Structure," *Journal of Financial Economics* (December 1984), pp. 509–528.

**EXHIBIT 56–9**
**Actual vs. Predicted Change in Short-Term Rate, 1959:1–1982:3***

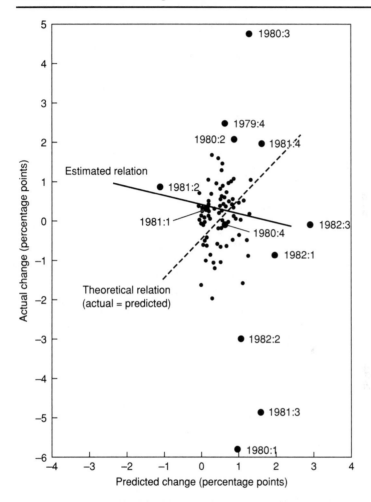

*Quarterly data, ninety-five observations, from the first day of March, June, September, and December. The short-term rate is the three-month Treasury bill rate: the predicted change from the term structure is the three-month ahead, three-month forward rate minus the current three-month rate. The forward rate is computed from the current three- and six-month rates. The predicted change is computed without allowing for a constant risk premium and thus is, by our model, the true predicted change plus a constant. The estimated relation is reported in table 3, row 1.

Source: See footnote 29.

**EXHIBIT 56–10**
**Actual vs. Predicted Change in Long-Term Rate, 1959–82\***

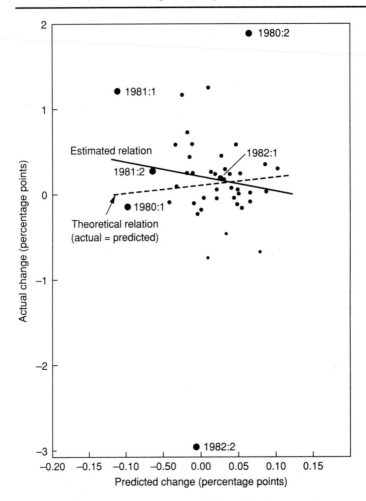

\*Semiannual data, 1959–82, forty-eight observations from the first day of January and July. The long-term rate is the thirty-year Treasury bond rate; the predicted change from the term structure is the six-month ahead, thirty-year linearized forward rate minus the current thirty-year rate. The forward rate is computed from the current six-month and thirty-year rates. Predicted change is computed without allowing for a constant risk premium and thus is, by our model, athe true predicted change plus a constant. The estimated relation is reported in table 3, row 6.

Source: See footnote 29.

$$_1R_1 -_0 R_1 = a + b_a \left(_1r_{1,0} -_0 R_1\right) \qquad (56\text{--}4a)$$

where time is measured in months. This says that the change in one-month spot rates from one month to the next is equal to a constant plus a coefficient $b_a$ times amount by which the forward rate for the second month exceeded the first month's spot rate. According to the unbiased expectation hypothesis, $b_a$ should be equal to 1.0.

Fama also related the excess of the one-month holding period return on two-month Treasury bills over the one-month rate to the right-hand side of Equation 56–4a:

$$\text{HPR}_{2,1} -_0 R_1 = a + b_b \left(_1r_{1,0} -_0 R_1\right) \qquad (56\text{--}4b)$$

where $\text{HPR}_{2,1}$ is the total return on two-month bills over the first month. The basis for this equation is that any excess return on two-month bills held for one month over the one-month risk-free return, the left-hand side, represents a realized liquidity premium for investing in two-month bills rather than in the risk-free asset. The equation relates this possible realized liquidity premium to the difference in the forward rate and the spot rate. If this latter difference is solely due to liquidity premia and if these liquidity premia actually show up in realized returns, then $b_b$ should be equal to 1.0. But $b_b$ should be equal to 0.0 if differences in forward and spot rates are solely due to interest-rate expectations embedded in the term structure. Thus, these two models gave Fama both the means to assess the forecasting ability of the term structure and an opportunity to gain insight into what was causing the term structure to vary in shape—either changing interest rate expectations or changing liquidity premia.

When the two equations were estimated with monthly interest rates and investment horizons (he also extended the analysis out to six months), $b_a$ was 0.46 with an equation $R^2$ of 0.13, while $b_b$ was 0.55 with an equation $R^2$ of 0.17. Both $b_a$ and $b_b$, while positive, were significally less than 1.0. Fama interpreted those results as providing support for the forecasting ability of the term structure and also support for the proposition that variations in the term structure show up in both realized liquidity premia and changes in spot rates. Together these two propositions lend support to the biased expectation hypothesis. Finally, Fama interpreted the fact that $b_a$ was less than 1.0 as providing evidence that the liquidity premia varied over time.

A review of one other study in this area will help us further our sense of the status of the expectations hypothesis. In a recent paper whose title is suggestive, "New Hope for the Expectations Hypothesis of the Term Structure of Interest Rates," Kenneth Froot uses collected expectation data from quarterly surveys of financial market participants collected by the *Goldsmith-Nagan Bond and Money Market Letter* for a period from the middle of 1969 through 1986.[31] With this

---

[31] Froot, "New Hope," pp. 283–305.

data, Froot was able to investigate two alternative propositions that may account for the poor showing of the expectation hypothesis: that changes in the term structure reflect something other than changing expectation about future interest rates, such as changing liquidity premia, or that expected future interest rates are simply poor forecasts of actual future rates.

Froot concludes that at the short end of the term structure (one year or less) the expectation hypothesis simply is not valid; little change in the shape of the term structure is actually due to changed expectations about future rates. Changes in observed yield spreads are predominantly attributable to time variations in term premia, and thus changes in the slope of the yield curve reflect changing perceptions of risk. At the long end of the term structure, the expectations hypothesis seems to be valid in the sense that changes in expected future interest rates on average show up one for one in the term structure. Although there are large swings in liquidity premia, they are not the primary problem. Rather, the difficulty is that interest-rate forecasting errors dominate the association between the term structure's forecasts and subsequent actual rates. Froot goes on to suggest that the primary problem with the forecasts embedded in the term structure is that the expected future rates *underreact* to changes in observed short rates.

It is disappointing that all of this research does not yield more uniform conclusions. However, it still has a number of implications that should be significant to practicing fixed income investment managers.

1. The evidence in favor of positive liquidity premia is reasonably strong. Therefore, the unbiased expectations hypothesis cannot be correct. An obvious implication is that fixed income investors should expect to earn higher returns, on average, from extending maturities. This positive reward for bearing more price risk appears to be especially pronounced at the short end of the term structure.
2. Another clear implication is that these liquidity premia cannot be assumed to be constant. This is unfortunate because it suggests that a change in the shape of the yield curve does not necessarily reveal a change in expected future interest rates. Yield curves might be decreasing in slope, for example, just when future rate expectations are increasing because of a more than offsetting decline in risk premia.[32]
3. On the other hand, changing expectations do appear to exert some impact on the term structure. For this reason it is not safe to attribute all change on the yield curve solely to changing liquidity premia either.

---

[32]Because of large time-varying risk premia, at least one group of observers has dismissed the biased expectation theory as "almost vacuous" even if it is technically correct; indeed, they regard such liquidity premia as little more than a "deus ex machina" to rescue the theory. See Gregory Mankiw and Lawrence Summers, "Do Long-Term Interest Rates Overreact to Short-Term Interest Rates?" *Brooking Paper on Economic Activity,* 1984, p. 239.

4. Finally, the forecasting accuracy of such expectations of future rates that are embedded in the term structure appears to be very poor. Therefore, even if one has deduced that a change on the shape of the yield curve is due to changing interest-rate expectations, it would be very unwise to base investment decisions on those expectations.

In sum, then, the expectations hypothesis as it is usually presented appears to be almost a caricature of reality, both as a description of how the term structure is formed and what future interest rates will be.

In light of this state of affairs, a reasonable course of action would be the same course that a person who had never been exposed to the expectations theory might follow: borrow long when long rates are below short ones, and borrow short when short rates are below long ones, or invest long when the yield curve is upward sloping and invest short when it is downward sloping. Indeed, this is just what the familiar yield-curve-riding operation attempts to do. However, in longer maturities, such a strategy might be quite risky; rejection of the expectation hypothesis does not imply that easy money can be made by betting against it.[33]

## The Market Segmentation Hypotheses

Empirical evidence on these hypotheses is limited. One of the more relevant studies, by Michael Echols and Jan Walter Elliott,[34] was part of a larger study of term-structure influences. These authors worked with monthly data from the beginning of 1964 through the end of 1971. They first made estimates of forward rates from a model that considers macroeconomic variables, changes in the money supply, the net budgetary position, net export deficit or surplus, and the like. These estimates were refined to include the measured effects of a liquidity premium. An effort was then made to explain differences in these estimated forward rates and forward rates that were actually observed by use of a supply and a demand variable. The supply measure was the ratio of the quantity of government bonds outstanding with 5 or fewer years to maturity to the quantity of bonds with 10+ years to maturity. The demand measure was the ratio of the stock of bank funds invested in U.S. govern-

---

[33] For example, Mankiw and Summers use their empirical results from the 1963–1983 period to analyze the strategy of going short in three-month Treasury bills in order to purchase 20-year Treasury bonds when the yields are 13 percent and 10 percent, respectively. This strategy would have generated an expected profit, before transactions cost, of $12 per $1,000 over a three-month period. But, at rate change levels observed in the 1979–1983 period, the standard deviation around this $12 profit would be $165, and the probability of a loss in any single period would be above 45 percent.

[34] Michael E. Echols and Jan Walter Elliott, "Rational Expectations in a Disequilibrium Model of the Term Structure," *American Economic Review*, (March 1976), pp. 28–74.

ment securities to the stock of insurance company funds invested in this way. Echols and Elliott found that an increase in bank holdings relative to insurance company holdings did tend to push down forward rates, especially at shorter maturities. This result is as predicted by the segmentation hypothesis.

The same variables were also used in an effort to explain actual yield spreads, the excess of 12-year bond yields over the three-month Treasury bill rate. In this investigation, the spread was negatively related to relative institutional participation—more bank funds in government securities compared with insurance company funds meant *smaller* spreads. Moreover, here they found that an increase in the relative quantity of short-term bonds outstanding actually tended to *raise* the spread. Both these results are not consistent with the segmented market hypothesis as it is usually conceived.

## The Stochastic-Process No-Arbitrage Approach

Most applications of the stochastic-process no-arbitrage approach to modeling the term structure have been directed toward valuing either specific options embedded in bonds or bonds with a significant options component, such as mortgage passthrough securities; while the valuations obtained in these applications have generally been reasonable and close to observed prices, the length of the time commitment has not been the critical issue.

An interesting investigation that does address term-structure applications more directly appears in a recent paper by Michael Ehrhardt, David Johnson, and Joseph Odgen.[35] These authors compared the efficiency of several bond pricing approaches by applying them to a sample of 139 Treasury bonds spread across the maturity spectrum as of July 31, 1985. Maturities ranged up to 30 years, while coupons varied from 11.465 to 16.125 and prices ranged from 88.98 to 139.42. On this date, the yield curve was upward sloping. When the stochastic-process no-arbitrage approach was used to value these bonds using historical estimates of the model inputs with no liquidity premium, the root mean squared error (RMSE, or square root of the average squared deviation of an individual bond's price from the model prediction) was 4.125 dollars per hundred dollars of par value. The introduction of a historical liquidity premium reduced the RMSE to 2.933. These values compare to an RMSE of 0.855 obtained by pricing the bonds with optimal inputs—optimal in the sense that they were chosen to fit the prices as closely as possible.

---

[35] Michael C. Ehrhardt, David Johnson, and Joseph Odgen, "An Examination of Alternative Bond Pricing Models," Working Paper, The University of Tennessee, 1988. See also Michael J. Brennan and Eduardo S. Schwartz, "Bond Pricing and Market Efficiency," pp. 49–56, for results from applying a two-factor stochastic-process model to price Treasury issues.

The errors from this approach were of the same order of magnitude as those obtained from direct statistical term-structure estimation, a standard approach to term-structure estimation described in a subsequent section of this chapter.

Ehrhardt, Johnson, and Odgen then stepped ahead to August 31, 1985 and repriced the same bonds. Using the inputs that were optimal at the end of the preceding month, the RMSE was 1.125, which compares favorably with the error obtained with the then-optimal values of 0.916.

These results, and those of other studies, are quite encouraging regarding the value of stochastic-process no-arbitrage modeling of the term structure. But much remains to be done in terms of refining and testing this approach.

## ANALYZING THE TERM STRUCTURE

For many investors, an occasional rundown on yield curves as published daily by *The Wall Street Journal* and other periodicals will be sufficient to keep an eye on the term structure. Others will want to be more formal in their analysis. In this section, we review some of the ways for monitoring the term structure.

### Published Yield Curves

Possibly the most familiar representatives of the term structure are the yield curves published each month in the *U.S. Treasury Bulletin;* the yield curve in Exhibit 56–2 comes from this source. These curves are visually fitted to month-end yields to maturity on U.S. government securities by Treasury analysts; that is, there are drawn free-hand or by eye without resorting to statistical curve-fitting techniques. As with most yield curves, the objective is to capture the yield-maturity relationship of securities that differ only by term. Thus, Treasury issues, with no default risk and only limited call options, are especially appropriate for this purpose. In fitting these curves, only the yields on approximately current coupon bonds with no special features (e.g., flower bonds) are considered. An effort is obviously made to draw the curves smoothly so that the transition from one maturity point to another is gradual.

Yield curves are also published by a number of private sources. Among the most accessible of these appear daily in *The Wall Street Journal*. Yield curves for the preceding day, one week prior, and four weeks prior are superimposed on a single graph; see Exhibit 56–11 for an example. As the exhibit indicates, the plotted yields reflect yields at the close of the trading day. While details of the fitting process are unavailable, it is obvious from the abrupt discontinuities that no effort is made to smooth the data. These yield-curve plots are particularly useful for getting a snapshot view of how the term structure is evolving.

**EXHIBIT 56–11**
**Treasury Yield (Yields as of 4:30 p.m. Eastern Time)**

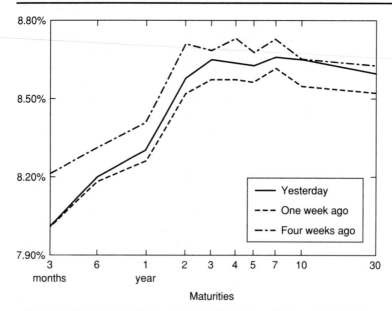

Maturities

Source: *Wall Street Journal,* Friday, April 13, 1990 (Based on Yields on April 12, 1990).

For more detailed analytical purposes, these published yield curves are not entirely satisfactory for two reasons. In the final analysis, they are judgmentally derived, and there is always uncertainty about judgmental numbers—it is unlikely, for example, that any two analysts would usually fit the same yield curve. Another problem arises when numerical yield values are needed for specific maturities. Such numbers must be read off the yield curve, and this is an activity of uncertain precision. It is unlikely that these are serious problems, and in fact they are present to a greater or lesser degree in almost all yield-curve analysis. But it has become more common to work with constructed or synthetic yield-maturity data series and to statistically fit yield curves in analyzing the term structure.

## Sources of Yield Maturity Series

A standard source of yields on U.S. government securities by maturity is a series published by Salomon Brothers, Inc. The Salomon Brothers yields have been employed to construct many of the exhibits in this chapter. This series currently shows yields at 11 maturity points ranging from three months to 30 years in numerical form. It is published weekly in Salomon Brothers' *Bond*

*Market Roundup,* and historical first-of-month (midmonth prior to 1959) yields are reported in Salomon Brothers' *An Analytical Record of Yields and Yield Spreads.* The Salomon Brothers data is prepared in much the same way as the *Treasury Bulletin* yield curves; that is, yield curves are fitted to actual bond yield data, following the yields of higher coupon bonds when a choice exists, and then the yields are read off at each maturity point. Thus the primary advantages of the Salomon Brothers series are its timeliness and that fact that the curve reading has already been done for the analyst.

In recent years, the *Federal Reserve Bulletin* (*FRB*) has contained a constant maturity yield series for U.S. government bonds and notes ranging from 1 to 30 years to maturity. This series is described as "yields on the more actively traded issues adjusted to constant maturities by the U.S. Treasury, based on daily closing bid prices." The yields are reported by calendar weeks ending on Wednesdays, by months, and by years; the weekly data represent averages of the undisclosed daily values, monthly data are averages of the weeks, and so on. Therefore, the *FRB* numbers are not directly comparable with the Salomon Brothers data. Exhibit 56–12 contains the Salomon Brothers data for January 2, 1981 and the *FRB* data for the week ending January 2, 1981. Although the two series are not identical, they are quite similar, especially in the yield-curve patterns they display.

## EXHIBIT 56–12
## A Comparison of Salomon Brothers and Federal Reserve Bulletin Yield Data

| Term-to-Maturity | Yields, Salomon Brothers, January 2, 1981 | Yields, Federal Reserve Bulletin Week Ending January 2, 1981 |
|---|---|---|
| 3 months | 15.02% | 15.05% * |
| 6 months | 14.96 | 14.96 |
| 1 year | 13.97 | 13.86 |
| 2 years | 13.01 | 13.00 |
| 3 years | 12.65 | 12.81 |
| 4 years | 12.68 | — |
| 5 years | 12.57 | 12.54 |
| 7 years | 12.47 | 12.43 |
| 10 years | 12.43 | 12.36 |
| 20 years | 11.96 | 12.05 |
| 30 years | 11.94 | 11.96 |

* Treasury bill discounts converted to coupon-equivalent yields.

Source: Data courtesy of Salomon Brothers, Inc., and from the *Federal Reserve Bulletin,* February 1981.

## Fitting Yield Curves

These two yield series are probably more useful for investment decision making than published curves because they have been reduced to numerical terms by someone who is experienced in doing this. The numbers themselves can be examined for yield patterns, or they can be plotted to obtain yield curves such as those in Exhibit 56–1, which are of the "connect the dots" variety.

Such curves are described as discontinuous. This means that they change shape at each measurement point and can do so abruptly. However, one would expect yield transitions from one maturity to another to be fairly smooth—that is, to be characterized by a continuous curve. In addition, one is often interested in maturities that are not at measurement points. Such intermediate yields could be estimated by linear interpolation, but this is clumsy and at odds with the notion of yield curves that change shape continuously. For those reasons, it is frequently desirable to fit mathematical curves to the yield points.

A number of models have been proposed for fitting such curves. Most use the method of least squares to actually fit the curve. The models differ in the form of the equation that is fitted and its number of terms. With too few terms, the estimated yield curve is excessively smooth; for example, with one term it would simply be a straight line. Too many terms will "overfit" the line; with as many terms as maturity points, the line will go precisely through each point.

One model that has proved to be particularly effective for such applications is that of Stephen Bradley and Dwight Crane.[36] The Bradley-Crane model has the form

$$ln\,(1 + R_M) = a + b_1(M) + b_2 ln(M) + e \qquad (56\text{–}5)$$

That is, values equal to the natural logarithm of one plus the observed yields for term-to-maturity of length $M$ are regressed on two variables, the term-to-maturity and the natural log of the term-to-maturity. The last term represents the unexplained yield variation. Once the estimated values of $a$, $b_1$, and $b_2$ are obtained, specific maturities of interest can be substituted to obtain estimated yields at these maturity points. Exhibit 56–13 shows the Salomon Brothers yield series as of January 2, 1981, along with a yield curve fitted by this method. It can be observed that the fit is not particularly good in the shorter maturities.

Occasionally one wishes to fit yield curves directly to yield data for individual bonds rather than to the homogenized yield series. This might be desirable as a means of avoiding possible distortions created in the process of arriving at the synthetic yield series. It might also be motivated by a particular interest in individual bonds, for example, when looking for arbitrage opportunities between

---

[36] Stephen P. Bradley and Dwight B. Crane, "Management of Commercial Bank Government Security Portfolios: An Optimization Approach Under Uncertainty," *Journal of Bank Research* (Spring 1973), pp. 18–30.

**EXHIBIT 56–13**
**Bradley-Crane Yield Curve Fitted to Salomon Brothers Yield Data for**
**January 2, 1981**

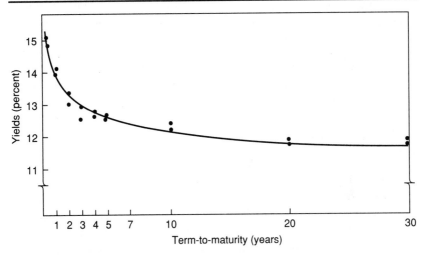

Source: Salomon Brothers Inc. Line estimated by authors.

underpriced or overpriced bonds by examining their yields in comparison with a fitted yield curve. A model for fitting such yield curves has been proposed by Elliot and Echols.[37]

The Elliot-Echols model has the form

$$ln\,(1 + R_i) = a + b_1\,(1/M_i) + b_2\,(M_i) + b_3\,(C_i) + e_i \qquad (56\text{--}6)$$

where $R_i$, $M_i$, and $C_i$ are the yield-to-maturity, term-to-maturity, and coupon rate of the $i^{th}$ bond.

Notice that yield and maturity are related in somewhat different ways than in the Bradley-Crane model. This representation also differs by the inclusion of the individual bond's coupon level. Low-coupon bonds tend to have yields that are subnormal for their term-to-maturity, presumably because of the postponable nature of the tax of their built-in capital gain. The coupon term is intended to adjust for this effect.

Elliot and Echols suggested that in obtaining yield curves from this model the coupon term should be set equal to zero so as to avoid confounding coupon effects and maturity effects. This approach is claimed to give the yield at which

---

[37] Michael E. Echols and Jan Walter Elliott, "A Quantitative Yield Curve Model for Estimating the Term Structure of Interest Rates," *Journal of Financial and Quantitative Analysis,* (March 1976), pp. 87–114.

a zero coupon bond would sell, if one existed. An alternative (if more cumbersome) procedure is to search for the coupon rate at which the coupon rate and the yield-to-maturity of a hypothetical bond of a given term-to-maturity would be the same. The resulting point on the yield curve is the estimated yield at which a current coupon bond would sell if one existed. Exhibit 56–14 shows such a yield curve fitted to individual bond and note data for this method, as of the end of March 1977. Note that because of this coupon effect there is no reason for the individual bonds to be scattered evenly around the line. Of course, a bond's actual coupon should be used in estimating its appropriate yield if the objective is to determine whether it is underpriced or overpriced.

## Measuring the Term Structure Directly

Recall the distinction between the yield curve and the term structure made at the beginning of this essay; the yield curve relates yields to maturity on coupon-bearing bonds to the term-to-maturity, whereas the term structure relates discount rates on single future payments to the term of the payment. For some purposes, yield curves adequately portray the price of time, but for others—such as pricing out single-payment securities or those with unusual patterns of cash flow or extracting implied forward rates—the term structure is preferred because it abstracts from coupon effects. Until recently it was impossible to observe the term structure directly, beyond the maturity range of Treasury bills,

**EXHIBIT 56–14**
**Elliot-Echols Yield Curve Fitted to Individual U.S. Government Bond and Note Yields, March 31, 1977**

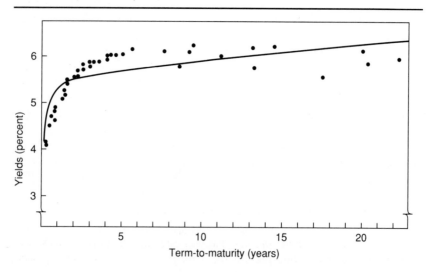

initially because there were no zero coupon securities outstanding and later because those that were outstanding were not free from some element of default risk. However, with the advent of the STRIPS (Separate Trading of Registered Interest and Principal Securities) in 1985 via the Federal Reserve's book entry accounting system, prices and yields to maturity in a wide range of zero coupon securities free from default risk have become available. Since 1989, such prices and yields at quarterly intervals for terms out to 30 years have been published in *The Wall Street Journal* on a daily basis. Such data were used to graph the term-structure relationship in Exhibit 56–3.

These discount rates change with term in a reasonably regular manner, but there are occasional jumps and dips. The usual explanation for these variations is supply-and-demand or liquidity considerations in the market for stripped securities. An analyst who wishes to smooth out these variations might find it useful to fit a curve to this data and then work with values read off the curve.

The simplicity and apparent precision of measuring the term structure with these stripped security yields is attractive. However, it may be somewhat misleading if the objective is to price future flows adjusting for their term only. The major potential problem is taxation. Stripped securities are treated as original-issue discount securities for tax purposes, and thus taxes must be paid on interest accrued under the constant or scientific yield method. (See Chapter 4 for a discussion of the tax treatment of bonds.) If STRIPS were held only by tax-exempt investors, then their yields would be true before-tax spot rates. However, this is not so if STRIPS are not held exclusively by tax-exempt investors and the valuations of such investors affect stripped bond prices. A taxed investor would have to make intermediate tax payments on the accrued discount—payments that would be akin to negative coupon receipts. In valuing these stripped bonds, the taxed investor would discount each cash flow to obtain the present value of the security and might apply different spot rates to each flow. The observed yields on the STRIPS would then be yields for instruments with intermediate cash flows.

Possible tax effects associated with coupon bonds also create a problem for term-structure estimation and, indeed, for any use of the yield curve involving such bonds. The yield curve that we observe consists of rates that have not been explicitly adjusted for taxes. The after-tax rate for a taxed investor is not simply the observed rate times 1 minus the tax rate. It depends on the timing of the tax due to the split of dollar returns between coupon income and capital gains. Furthermore, tax rates may vary among investors in this market, and the estimation of a term structure is hampered by our not knowing which bonds are held by which investors.

## Another Approach to Estimating the Term Structure

A method of term-structure analysis that was originally designed to cope with coupon effects also has some promise for dealing with tax biases. This approach, in common with much of the contemporary analytical methodology in the fixed income area, works with discount factors rather than yields.[38] Discount factors are values equal to $1/(1 + {_0}R_t)^t$; they are the entries found in the familiar present value tables.

The essence of the approach is to estimate the $d$ coefficients in the multiple regression

$$P_{i,0} = d_1 X_{i1} + d_2 X_{i2} + \ldots + d_t X_{it} + e_i \tag{56-7}$$

where

$P_{i,0}$ = the price of the $i^{\text{th}}$ bond at time zero

$X_{it}(t = 1, \ldots, T)$ = the cash flows from the bond in period $t$

In other words, prices of a number of bonds at a specific instant in time are related to their future coupons and maturity payments in a cross-sectional analysis. The estimated values of $d$ are discount factors, and from them yields that are free of coupon bias can be computed. For example, $d_1$ is an estimate of $1/(1 + R_1)$, $d_2$ is an estimate of $1/(1 + R_2)^2$, and so on, so it is easy to solve for the various values of $R$.

If a tax adjustment is to be made, the procedure is as follows. For the entire bond sample, each coupon is stated on an after-tax basis by multiplying by 1 minus the tax rate. For a discount bond, the capital gains tax is applied to the difference between the principal and the price, and the principal repayment is reduced by this amount. For a stripped bond, the income tax on imputed interest each period is treated as a negative cash flow. For a premium bond, it is assumed that the loss will be amortized linearly over the life of the bond. After the cash flows in the bond sample are adjusted in this manner, a similar regression is run with the tax-adjusted cash flows. The discount function estimated is then an after-tax discount function. The after-tax discount factors, $d_t^*$, have the form

$$d_t^* = 1/[1 + {_0}R_t(1 - \text{tr})]^t$$

where

$tr$ = the tax rate

${_0}R_t$ = the effective before-tax spot rate

All this begs the question of which tax rate to use. In several studies, different tax rates were tried until one was found to minimize the standard error

---

[38] Development and use of this methodology is reported in J. Houston McCulloch, "Measuring the Term Structure of Interest Rates," *Journal of Business,* (January 1971), pp. 19–31; Stephen M. Schaefer, "On Measuring the Term Structure of Interest Rates," paper presented to the International Workshop on Recent Research in Capital Markets, Berlin, September 1973; and Willard T. Carleton and Ian A. Cooper, "Estimation and Uses of the Term Structure of Interest Rates," *Journal of Finance* (September 1976), pp. 1067–83. The liquidity premia estimates appearing in Exhibit 56–16 were estimated by McCulloch utilizing this method.

of the regression.[39] This rate has been called the "representative investor" tax rate. This rate appears to do a good job of pricing most bonds in the sample, and in one study it was found to correspond to the tax rate of the major investors in several countries.[40]

Practical implementation of the discount factor approach involves dealing with some issues that are beyond the scope of this chapter, including data selection, constraints on the behavior of the $d_t$, and the exact form of the regression equation. These issues have been dealt with and largely resolved in the academic literature, and thus this method is worthy of consideration by persons contemplating serious term-structure analysis.

## Estimating Implicit Forward Rates

*Without liquidity premium adjustment.* Many uses of term structure do not require the estimation of forward rates. However, there will be occasions in which it is desirable to actually extract implicit forward rates from the yield curve or other data in order to get some idea of interest rates the market consensus is forecasting.

If suitably spaced yields on either synthetic or actual securities are available, then forward rates can be estimated directly by the use of Equation (56–2) without the necessity for fitting yield curves. Recall that Equation (56–2) stated

$$\left(1 +_{t+m} r^b_{n-m,t}\right)^{n-m} = (1 +_t R_n)^n / (1 +_t R_m)^m \qquad (56\text{--}2)$$

except that a $^{"b"}$ has been added to $r$, for reasons that will be discussed shortly. Use of this formula is extremely straightforward once the data are in proper form. The equation is written on the assumption that all yields are expressed in the same units of time, per annum yields being most common. For many purposes, it will be useful to measure $m$ and $n$ in units that have the effect of making $n - m = 1$.

A simple example may help illustrate the process and clarify this last point. On January 2, 1981, three-month and six-month coupon equivalent Treasury

---

[39] This method of dealing with tax effects was developed by J. Houston McCulloch, "The Tax-Adjusted Yield Curve," *Journal of Finance* (June 1975), pp. 811–30; and further studied by Robert H. Litzenberger and J. Rolfo in "An International Study of Tax Effects on Government Bonds," *Journal of Finance* (March 1984), pp. 1–22; and by James V. Jordan in "Tax Effects in Term Structure Estimation," *Journal of Finance* (July 1984), pp. 393–406. A set of monthly term-structure estimates using McCulloch's method for the period 12/46–2/87 is published in Shiller and McCulloch, "The Term Structure of Interest Rates."

[40] However, potential users should also be aware that the use of a single tax rate in term-structure estimation may not fully account for tax effects because specific tax clienteles may concentrate their holdings in certain types of bonds. For discussion of this point see, for example, Michael C. Ehrhardt, James V. Jordan, and Eliezer Z. Prisman, "Tests for Tax-Clientele and Tax-Option Effects in U.S. Treasury Bonds: Theory and Evidence," Working Paper, University of Tennessee, 1989.

bill yields as reported in *The Wall Street Journal* were 15.31 percent and 15.00 percent per annum, respectively. If we use Equation 56–2 with $m$ and $n$ expressed in years to estimate the three-month rate anticipated in three months, $n = 6$ months $= \frac{1}{2}$ year, $m = 3$ months $= \frac{1}{4}$ year, and

$$\left(1 + \tfrac{1}{4}\, r^b_{\frac{1}{4},0}\right)^{\frac{1}{4}} = \frac{(1.1500)^{\frac{1}{2}}}{(1.1531)^{\frac{1}{4}}} = \frac{1.0724}{1.0363} = 1.0349$$

This last value is for a quarter of a year because it is one plus an annual rate raised to the $\frac{1}{4}$ power. In order to make it apply to a whole year, we must raise it to the fourth power, or

$$\left[\left(1 + \tfrac{1}{4}\, r^b_{\frac{1}{4},0}\right)^{\frac{1}{4}}\right]^4 = \left(1 + \tfrac{1}{4}\, r^b_{\frac{1}{4},0}\right)$$

When we do, we get

$$(1.0349)^4 = 1.1469, \text{ or } 14.69\%$$

Alternatively, we might simply express $m$ and $n$ in three-month periods, since we are interested in a three-month forward rate. Then $n = 6$ months $= 2$ and $m = 3$ months $= 1$, and

$$\left(1 + _1 r^b_{1,0}\right)^1 = \frac{(1.1500)^2}{(1.1531)^1} = \frac{1.3225}{1.1531} = 1.1469$$

or 14.69 percent again.

Exhibit 56–15 continues the estimation of three-month forward rates as of January 2, 1981. The first rate in each series is unadjusted; the second has been adjusted for liquidity premia, as will be discussed subsequently. The exhibit also shows forward rates estimated using a simplified method proposed by Worley and Diller,[41,42] in which

$$_{t+m}r^b_{n-m,t} \cong \frac{({}_tR_n \cdot n) - ({}_tR_m \cdot m)}{n - m} \tag{56–8}$$

The values $n$ and $m$ can be expressed in days, fractions of a year, or other convenient intervals. This equation, which does not require the use of exponents or assume compounding, is quite satisfactory provided the interval $n - m$ is not large. In terms of the preceding example,

---

[41] Worley and Diller, "Interpreting the Yield Curve," p. 45.
[42] The values in the first four columns of Exhibit 56–15 are computed by reference to the actual number of days in each period because the periods are not of equal length—principally because no Treasury bill traded on January 2 matured on October 2, making it necessary to use the bill maturing October 8.

**EXHIBIT 56–15**
**Alternative Estimates of Three-Month Forward Rates** (January 2, 1981)

| Forward Rates for Three Months, Beginning | Actual Yields, Equation (56–2) | | Actual Yields, Equation (56–8) | | Fitted Yields, Equation (56–2) | |
|---|---|---|---|---|---|---|
| | Unadjusted | Adjusted | Unadjusted | Adjusted | Unadjusted | Adjusted |
| April 2, 1981 | 14.69% | 14.11% | 14.69% | 14.11% | 13.88% | 13.71% |
| July 2, 1981 | 13.02 | 12.76 | 13.01 | 12.77 | 13.40 | 13.19 |
| October 8, 1981* | 12.88 | 12.66 | 12.87 | 12.65 | 13.10 | 12.88 |
| January 2, 1982 | | | | | 12.88 | 12.66 |
| April 2, 1982 | | | | | 12.71 | 12.49 |
| July 2, 1982 | | | | | 12.58 | 12.36 |
| October 2, 1982 | | | | | 12.46 | 12.24 |
| January 2, 1983 | | | | | 12.37 | 12.15 |
| April 2, 1983 | | | | | 12.29 | 12.07 |
| July 2, 1983 | | | | | 12.21 | 11.99 |
| October 2, 1983 | | | | | 12.15 | 11.93 |

* October 2, 1982 for estimates based on fitted yields.

$$1r_{1,0}^b \cong \frac{(.1500 \cdot 2) - (.1531 \cdot 1)}{1}$$

$$\cong .1469$$

Suppose that suitably spaced yields are not available. Suppose, for example, that we want to estimate forward rates for three-month intervals beyond a year in the future. This is where curves fitted to yields or spot rates become useful. After estimating the appropriate coefficients, we can simply substitute in the appropriate values of $m$ and $n$ and use Equation (56–2) or (56–8) to obtain the forward rate. For example, the Bradley-Crane model equation for January 2, 1981 (Exhibit 56–13), is

$$ln(1 + R_M) = 0.129700 + 0.000425(M) - 0.008497\,ln(M)$$

If we are interested in the three-month rate one year into the future as of the beginning of January 1982, we substitute 1.0 and 1.25 ($m$ and $n$ equal to 1 year and $1\frac{1}{4}$ years) in the equation, obtaining 13.8970 percent for $R_1$ and 13.6933 percent for $R_{1.25}$. Equation 56–2 gives

$$\left(_1r_{.25,0}^b\right)^{.25} = \frac{(1.136933)^{1.25}}{(1.138970)^1} = 1.030756$$

or 12.88 percent per annum.

Exhibit 56–15 contains forward rates for each three-month interval beginning three months through three years into the future estimated via the fitted curve approach in addition to the forward rates for the first three-month intervals obtained earlier. The differences in the forward rates obtained by this approach and the forward rates computed with the actual Treasury bill yields are initially large but converge rapidly. (Recall that the Bradley-Crane model didn't fit the short maturities very well.) All these sets of numbers illustrate in striking fashion the decline in interest rates that was apparently expected as 1981 began.

***With liquidity premium adjustment.*** The formulas presented in the preceding discussion all had a superscript $b$ attached to the $r$'s representing forward rates. This superscript is intended as a reminder that these are "biased" forward rates; that is, to the extent that there are liquidity premia imbedded in the term structure, then forward rates are upward-biased estimates of yields the market consensus expects in the future. For many purposes, these biased forward rates are acceptable or even desirable. For example, if our interest is in monitoring the pattern of changes in expected forward rates from month to month and we are willing to ignore possible changes in liquidity premia, these biased forward rates tell us what we need to know. If we are attempting to price out a bond using forward rates, we might actually *prefer* rates with imbedded liquidity premia.

This is fortunate because satisfactory liquidity premia estimates are impossible to obtain. Ideally, we could estimate liquidity premia in any of the following ways:

- Compute differences in yields along a long-run average yield curve or term structure.
- Compute long-run differences in average total returns on bonds of different maturities.
- Compute long-run differences in implied forward rates and actual outcomes.

Conceptually, these three approaches are not the same, and in practice none is satisfying. Other problems are those we considered when reviewing empirical evidence on the expectations hypothesis: likely time variations in liquidity premia and actual interest rates that do not conform to expectations. In addition, the first approach assumes that yields are expected to remain unchanged.

The first approach was employed by Haim Levy in a paper that appeared in the *Financial Analysis Journal* in 1982.[43] Levy was attempting to assess the inflation expectation built into the yield curve at different times. In order to obtain a base-time yield curve, he studied the years 1961 through 1964, years he regarded as typifying low expected inflation and stable interest rates. The average real inflation-adjusted yields in these years, and the corresponding incremental liquidity premia for extending maturity an additional period, were as follows:

| Years to Maturity | Average Real Yield | Incremental Liquidity Premia |
|---|---|---|
| 1 | 0.80% | — |
| 2 | 1.32 | .52% |
| 3 | 1.47 | .15 |
| 4 | 1.65 | .18 |
| 5 | 1.60 | −.05 |

Using the third approach, Worley and Diller estimated incremental liquidity premia for the 1966–1976 period as follows:

| $m$ | $n-m$ | $L$ |
|---|---|---|
| 3 months | 3 months | 58 basis points |
| 6 | 3 | 26 |
| 9 | 3 | 22 |
| 6 | 6 | 24 |

$m$ = time in future when rate is effective
$n-m$ = maturity of security to which rate applies
$L$ = liquidity premium

---

[43] Haim Levy, "The Yield Curve and Expected Inflation," *Financial Analysts Journal* (November-December 1982), pp. 37–42.

**EXHIBIT 56-16**
**McCullough Liquidity Premium Estimates, March 1951–March 1966**

| m | 0 | One Month | Two Months | Three Months | Six Months | Nine Months | 1 Year | 2 Years | 3 Years | 5 Years | 10 Years | 20 Years | 30 Years |
|---|---|---|---|---|---|---|---|---|---|---|---|---|---|
| One month | 0.17 | 0.13 | 0.11 | 0.09 | 0.05 | 0.04 | 0.03 | 0.01 | 0.01 | 0.01 | 0.00 | 0.00 | 0.00 |
| Two months | 0.28 | 0.22 | 0.17 | 0.14 | 0.09 | 0.06 | 0.05 | 0.02 | 0.02 | 0.01 | 0.00 | 0.00 | 0.00 |
| Three months | 0.34 | 0.27 | 0.21 | 0.17 | 0.11 | 0.07 | 0.06 | 0.03 | 0.02 | 0.01 | 0.01 | 0.00 | 0.00 |
| Six months | 0.41 | 0.32 | 0.26 | 0.21 | 0.13 | 0.09 | 0.07 | 0.03 | 0.02 | 0.01 | 0.01 | 0.00 | 0.00 |
| Nine months | 0.32 | 0.34 | 0.27 | 0.22 | 0.13 | 0.09 | 0.07 | 0.04 | 0.02 | 0.01 | 0.01 | 0.00 | 0.00 |
| 1 year | 0.43 | 0.34 | 0.27 | 0.22 | 0.14 | 0.09 | 0.07 | 0.04 | 0.02 | 0.01 | 0.01 | 0.00 | 0.00 |
| 2 years | 0.43 | 0.34 | 0.27 | 0.22 | 0.14 | 0.09 | 0.07 | 0.04 | 0.02 | 0.01 | 0.01 | 0.00 | 0.00 |
| 3 years | 0.43 | 0.34 | 0.27 | 0.22 | 0.14 | 0.09 | 0.07 | 0.04 | 0.02 | 0.01 | 0.01 | 0.00 | 0.00 |
| 5 years | 0.43 | 0.34 | 0.27 | 0.22 | 0.14 | 0.09 | 0.07 | 0.04 | 0.02 | 0.01 | 0.01 | 0.00 | 0.00 |
| 10 years | 0.43 | 0.34 | 0.27 | 0.22 | 0.14 | 0.09 | 0.07 | 0.04 | 0.02 | 0.01 | 0.01 | 0.00 | 0.00 |
| 20 years | 0.43 | 0.34 | 0.27 | 0.22 | 0.14 | 0.09 | 0.07 | 0.04 | 0.02 | 0.01 | 0.01 | 0.00 | 0.00 |
| 30 years | 0.43 | 0.34 | 0.27 | 0.22 | 0.14 | 0.09 | 0.07 | 0.04 | 0.02 | 0.01 | 0.01 | 0.00 | 0.00 |

($n - m$ across the top)

Source: Adapted from J. Houston McCullough, "An Estimate of the Liquidity Premium," *Journal of Political Economy*, February 1975, p. 113. ©1975 The University of Chicago, publisher. All rights reserved.

J. Houston McCulloch has employed a variant of this approach to make liquidity premium estimates for the largely nonoverlapping March 1951–March 1966 period contained in Exhibit 56–16.[44] Direct comparisons of McCulloch's results with those of Levy and the Worley-Diller estimates are possible. Values derived from the Levy study are well above those from McCulloch. For example, Levy's date implies that the one-year forward rate overstates the expected interest rate in one year by 52 basis points; the McCulloch results suggest that this premium is only 7 basis points. Results from the Worley-Diller and McCulloch studies are closer. For the three-month rate in three months, the estimates are dramatically different—58 basis points for Worley-Diller versus 17 basis points for McCulloch. However, premia for three-month maturities further into the future are similar—for example, 26 and 21 basis points for rates to be effective in six months, and 22 basis points for both for rates effective in nine months. Time variation may well account for these differences.

It is interesting that the incremental liquidity premia is for practical purposes zero for yields beyond about six months into the future in both the Worley-Diller and McCullough studies. In the Levy study, leveling only occurs after four years out. If this property persists over time, forward rates estimated from the longer maturity portion of term structures should be unbiased.

Once one has formed some conclusions about incremental liquidity premia, adjustment of biased forward rates to unbiased market expectations of future spot rates simply involves subtracting the premia from the biased forward rates. Exhibit 56–15 uses the Worley-Diller and McCulloch liquidity premia to adjust the forward rates for January 2, 1981, obtained previously.

---

[44] J. Houston McCulloch, "An Estimate of the Liquidity Premium," *Journal of Political Economy* (February 1975), pp. 95–119.

# CHAPTER 57

## INTRODUCTION TO BOND PORTFOLIO RISK MODELING

*Kurt Winkelmann, Ph.D.*
*Manager, Fixed Income*
*Vestek Systems, Inc.*

A prudent investment manager makes investment decisions that balance the return on a portfolio against that portfolio's risk. Such a balancing act requires accurate and insightful measures of both risk and return. Recently, however, concern has arisen regarding the measurement of bond portfolio risk. This issue has been motivated in part by advances in both term-structure modeling and option valuation and in part by a recognition that the tried and true methods of risk measurement (duration and convexity) have shortcomings. In this chapter, the implications of these developments for bond portfolio risk measurement are discussed.

The chapter is organized around three central questions. First, what is a bond portfolio risk model and why is it necessary? Second, what issues need to be confronted in the construction of a risk model? Finally, where and how might a bond risk model be applied.

## RISK MODEL MOTIVATION

This section discusses the motivation for a bond risk model. After bond portfolio risk is defined, measurement of the factors affecting risk is considered. Discussion of the shortcomings of traditional measures of risk (duration and convexity) is used to motivate a more meaningful measure of portfolio risk.

An appropriate place to begin is with measurement. It is axiomatic to say that portfolio managers are concerned with the holding period return on a portfolio. This suggests in turn that the risk on a portfolio can be regarded as the volatility of return. Hence, a model of bond portfolio risk is really an answer to the question, what factors affect return volatility.

As explained in Chapter 58, while many factors have an impact on bond portfolio performance, by far the most dominant is movements in interest rates. As a result, the best place to begin discussion of bond portfolio risk is with the impact of interest-rate movements on portfolio returns.

Exhibit 57–1 provides an illustration of the volatility of bond returns to movements in interest rates. The table shows the standard deviation of returns to each of 12 points on the term structure over the period January 1, 1984 through September 1, 1989. Return series were constructed for the .25, .5, 1, 2, 3, 4, 5, 7, 10, 15, and 20 points on the term structure, assuming a three-month holding period. In other words, it was assumed that a zero coupon bond was purchased at each of the 11 points and sold three months later.

Exhibit 57–1 illustrates two important considerations. First, interest-rate movements constitute a considerable source of risk to a bond portfolio. Second, the volatility of return increases as the maturity of the instrument increases (all else being equal). Both of these dimensions should be reflected in any measure of portfolio risk.

As is well known, a first approximation to interest-rate risk measurement comes from two tools: duration and convexity. These tools serve two purposes. First, they provide a measure of the sensitivity of a portfolio to changes in interest rates. Second, and probably more importantly, they provide useful decision rules.

**EXHIBIT 57–1**
**Term Structure and**
**Return Volatility**

| Term Structure Point | Standard Deviation |
|---|---|
| .25 | .003 |
| .50 | .004 |
| 1.00 | .008 |
| 2.00 | .017 |
| 3.00 | .025 |
| 4.00 | .033 |
| 5.00 | .040 |
| 7.00 | .056 |
| 10.00 | .076 |
| 15.00 | .114 |
| 20.00 | .171 |

For example, suppose that a manager felt that interest rates were going to rise. In this case, if the manager wanted to outperform the bond market, the portfolio duration would be shortened relative to the market. Since long-duration bonds are more price sensitive to interest-rate movements than short-duration bonds (all else being equal), the price decline on long-duration bonds would exceed that of short-duration bonds, implying that a short-duration portfolio would outperform a long-duration portfolio. A further implication of this analysis is that long-duration portfolios have more volatile returns than do short-duration portfolios. Finally, this approach to risk measurement implies that the volatility of a portfolio is merely the duration of the portfolio times the volatility of a short portfolio.

However, duration as a measure of interest-rate risk is not without its drawbacks. Three concerns immediately suggest themselves. First, the calculation of duration and convexity are contingent upon the assumption that the only types of term-structure movements possible are parallel shifts. Second, an implication of duration as a model of portfolio risk is that the return volatility of a bond is merely its duration squared times a constant, where the constant is the volatility of the interest-rate movement. Finally, the duration model predicts that the correlation matrix of returns to the term structure is unity; that is, the correlation between the returns on zero coupon bonds of differing maturities is equal to one.

The first issue is best examined in the context of an example. Exhibit 57–2 shows term structures for three different dates: October 2, 1987, October 3, 1988, and October 2, 1989. As the graph indicates, the range of term-structure movements is not limited to parallel shifts. Indeed, it would appear that possible sources of risk to portfolio returns are the twists in the term structure.

This casual test suggests that one of the key assumptions made in the calculation of duration and convexity is not valid. However, it may still be the case that duration and convexity provide useful measures of portfolio risk. In this event, two portfolios with identical values for duration and convexity should perform identically, irrespective of the type of term-structure movement.

The following examples consider three such cases. The impact on two portfolios of U.S. government bonds with equal yields, durations, and convexities of three term-structure movements are examined. Three types of term-structure movements from a base are considered: a parallel shift in their term structure, a twist in the term structure (i.e., the long end moves down and the short end moves up), and a butterfly movement (i.e., both the long and short ends move down and the intermediate section moves up).

Exhibit 57–3 shows the characteristics of the two portfolios. Note that duration, convexity, and yield are the same in both portfolios. Thus, if these attributes are sufficient to characterize the risk due to interest-rate movements, one would expect the holding period returns to be identical, regardless of the type of term-structure movement.

**EXHIBIT 57–2**
**Treasury Term Structure**

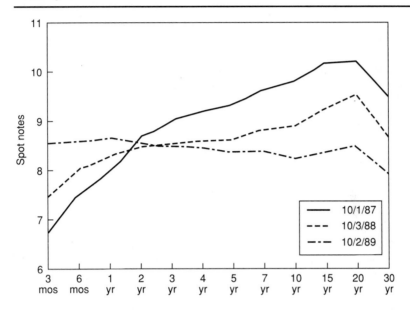

Exhibit 57–4 illustrates the three term-structure movements from a base term structure. The impact of each of these scenarios on total return over a two-month holding period is shown in Exhibit 57–5. Note that the returns are identical in the case of a parallel shift, but different in the cases of a twist or a butterfly. Hence, one might ask, what important elements affecting return volatility are omitted in the calculation of duration and convexity?

The cash-flow distributions shown in Exhibit 57–6 go a long way toward explaining the differences in total return. The graph shows the percentage of each portfolio's cash flows (in terms of present value) occurring at each point on the term structure. Note that portfolio 1 has a larger fraction of the cash flows

**EXHIBIT 57–3**
**Portfolio Characteristics**

| Characteristic | Portfolio 1 | Portfolio 2 |
|---|---|---|
| Duration | 4.60 | 4.60 |
| Convexity | .45 | .45 |
| Yield-to-maturity | 8.45 | 8.45 |

**EXHIBIT 57–4**
**Spot Rates 12/11/89**

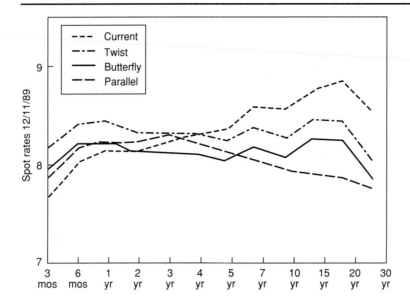

on the short end of the term structure than does portfolio 2. Given the differential cash-flow distribution, one would expect to see different performance, since total return is just the weighted average of the return to each point on the term structure. Duration (and convexity) cannot capture the affect of differential cash-flow distribution, since no unique weighting scheme is available for any fixed value of portfolio deviation.

The second drawback of the duration model relates to the first of its predictions: The volatility of a long maturity zero coupon bond number is the product

**EXHIBIT 57–5**
**Portfolio Returns** (Measured in Basis Points)

| Scenario | Portfolio 1 | Portfolio 2 |
|----------|-------------|-------------|
| Parallel | .45 | .45 |
| Twist | .03 | .05 |
| Butterfly | 2.09 | 2.04 |

**EXHIBIT 57–6**
**Cash-Flow Distribution 10/12/89**

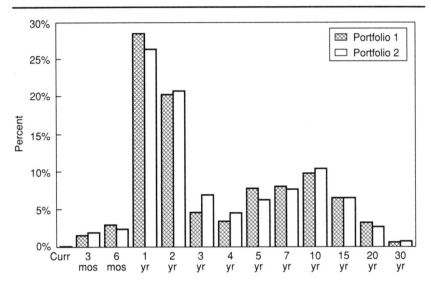

of the bond's duration and a constant. Returning to Exhibit 57–1, we easily see that no constant exists that is consistent with the proposition that volatility is duration times a constant. For example, the volatility at the one-year point is .008. However, volatility at the 20-year point is not equal to 20 times .008.

Finally, we can see that the correlation matrix of returns does not equal unity as predicted by the duration model of risk. Exhibit 57–7 shows the correlation matrix for the return series used to generate Exhibit 57–1. Notice that the correlations do not equal one. In fact, it appears as though the correlation between returns to different points on the term structure declines as the difference in maturities increases.

For example, the correlation between the return to the 90-day point and the 180-day point is .87, while the correlation between the 90-day point and the 20-year point is .39.

The examples suggest a way to proceed in the development of a bond risk model. As stated above, any such model should imply that volatility, or risk, increases as maturity increases. The examples indicate two other dimensions that should be accounted for. First, cash-flow distribution apparently makes a difference for the calculation of portfolio volatility. Second, the correlation matrix of returns is not unity. The next section addresses these issues in a discussion of the estimation of a bond risk model.

## EXHIBIT 57-7
## Correlation Matrix of Returns

*Term-Structure Point (Years)*

|       | .25  | .50  | 1.0  | 2.0  | 3.0  | 4.0  | 5.0  | 7.0  | 10.0 | 15.0 |
|-------|------|------|------|------|------|------|------|------|------|------|
| .25   | 1.00 |      |      |      |      |      |      |      |      |      |
| .50   | .87  | 1.00 |      |      |      |      |      |      |      |      |
| 1.00  | .68  | .92  | 1.00 |      |      |      |      |      |      |      |
| 2.00  | .56  | .85  | .97  | 1.00 |      |      |      |      |      |      |
| 3.00  | .52  | .81  | .93  | .99  | 1.00 |      |      |      |      |      |
| 4.00  | .49  | .78  | .90  | .98  | .99  | 1.00 |      |      |      |      |
| 5.00  | .48  | .77  | .88  | .96  | .98  | .98  | 1.00 |      |      |      |
| 7.00  | .47  | .73  | .82  | .91  | .94  | .97  | .98  | 1.00 |      |      |
| 10.00 | .46  | .71  | .78  | .88  | .90  | .94  | .96  | .98  | 1.00 |      |
| 15.00 | .40  | .58  | .61  | .72  | .75  | .81  | .85  | .92  | .95  | 1.00 |
| 20.00 | .39  | .57  | .61  | .71  | .74  | .80  | .83  | .90  | .94  | .97  |

## ISSUES IN MODEL BUILDING

Several issues arise in the construction and implementation of a bond portfolio risk model that accounts for the features discussed in the preceding section. First, the model should give rise to easily interpretable calculations that can be used for meaningful investment decision making. Second, the model should be consistent with an underlying term-structure theory, particularly if that theory is used for an option valuation model. Finally, the model should be stable over time.

The first issue that must be considered in developing a risk model is whether or not the calculations from the model can be easily interpreted and used in decision making. Put differently, the risk model should permit the user to make investment decisions.

Two useful policy calculations that arise from a risk model are *beta* and *tracking error*. Beta shows the volatility in returns on a portfolio relative to a benchmark, while tracking error shows the standard deviation of the excess return on a portfolio. Excess return is simply the difference between the return on the portfolio and the return on a benchmark.

Letting Rp be the return on a portfolio and Rb the return on a benchmark, these two calculations are given by

$$\text{Beta} \; = \; \text{cov(Rp, Rb)/var(Rb)} \tag{57-1}$$

and

$$\text{Tracking error} \; = \; \sqrt{\text{Var(Rp} - \text{Rb)}} \tag{57-2}$$

Tracking error can be rewritten in terms of beta as

$$\text{Tracking error} \; = \; (1 - \text{beta})^2 \text{var(Rb)} - \left[ \text{Var(Rp)} - \text{Beta}^2 \text{var(Rb)} \right] \tag{57-3}$$

Now, how are these calculations interpreted? Beta can be viewed as a measure of the relative volatilities of the portfolio and the benchmark. For instance, a beta of 1.2 states that the return on the portfolio can be expected to be 20 percent more variable than the return on the benchmark, all else being equal. Similarly, the return on a portfolio with a beta of .8 can be expected to be 20 percent less volatile than the return on the benchmark, again holding all else constant.

Tracking error gives a measure of expected performance. Simply put, tracking error represents the expected range (in terms of basis points) of the difference between the return on the portfolio and the return on the benchmark. If, for example, tracking error is .20, then the return on the portfolio will be within 20 basis points (plus or minus) of the return on the benchmark 66 percent of the time, and within 40 basis points (plus or minus) 97 percent of the time.

Equation (57–3) is useful in examining the interaction between beta and tracking error. Notice that Equation (57–4) breaks tracking error into two pieces. The first of these, [(1-beta$^2$) var(Rb)], reflects an investment strategy decision, while the second [var(Rp) − beta$^2$ var(Rb)], reflects an issue selection decision. For example, if a portfolio with a beta equal to one is selected (i.e., a passive strategy), then the sole source of tracking error is the selection of particular bonds. As beta varies away from one, the proportion of return differences due to the selection of a particular strategy increases. This makes sense, since a beta of one implies that the expected return on the portfolio should mimic that of the benchmark, all else being equal. Hence, the passive investment decision implies that the only source of variation between the return on the portfolio and the return on the market is in the selection of issues.

Now, how is the computation of beta related to the correlation matrix of returns? Equivalently, does a convenient method exist for computing the volatility of a portfolio's return?

These questions can be addressed by recalling that any bond or portfolio of bonds can be considered as a portfolio of zero coupon bonds. Hence, a reasonable place to start is to reallocate the cash flows of the portfolio to the points on the term structure. For example, Exhibit 57–7 considers 10 term-structure points. Thus, any portfolio can be rewritten as a portfolio of zero coupon bonds corresponding to the 10 term-structure points. As a result, the volatility of any portfolio's return is merely a weighted average of the volatility to the returns to each of the points on the term structure.

More precisely, if $x(i)$ is the proportion of the portfolio's cash flow at the $i$th point on the term structure, and cov($i,j$) is the covariance between the return on the $i$th term-structure point and the $j$th term-structure point, the variance of the return on the portfolio, var(Rp), can be written as

$$\text{var(Rp)} = \sum_i \sum_j x(i)\,\text{cov}(i, j)x(j) \qquad (57\text{–}4)$$

Notice that in this expression, the variance of the return at the $i$th term-structure point is cov($i,i$). Now, if the benchmark has holdings $y(i)$ at the term-structure points, then the covariance between the returns on the portfolio and the return on the benchmark can be written as

$$\text{cov(Rp, Rb)} = \sum_i \sum_j x(i)\text{cov}(i, j)y(j) \qquad (57\text{–}5)$$

The approach outlined in Equations (57–1) through (57–5) can be used to determine a beta for the two portfolios discussed in the previous section. In this case, the covariance matrix is represented by the correlation matrix shown in Exhibit 57–7. Using these data together with the cash-flow distributions of Exhibit 57–6 yields a beta of portfolio 1 with respect to portfolio 2 of 1.01.

Hence, one would expect the return on portfolio 1 to be 1 percent more volatile than the return on portfolio 2.

Of course, a necessary ingredient to the process is a properly specified covariance matrix. Two related issues are important in the specification of a covariance matrix. First, is the covariance matrix consistent with an underlying term-structure theory? Second, if the covariance matrix is estimated on historical data, does it pass tests for structural stability?

The concern for a covariance matrix that is consistent with an underlying term-structure theory is driven in part by recent advances in option valuation modeling. In turn, option valuation models are driven by an underlying term-structure model—that is, a model that explains the pricing of risk-free bonds that differ only in maturity. Such term-structure models in turn impose a structure upon the covariances of the excess returns to bonds of different maturities. Hence, it would be appropriate that a bond portfolio risk model made use of the theoretical restrictions implied by the term-structure model underlying option valuation model.

The final attribute that a bond portfolio risk model should possess is structural stability. Bond portfolio risk models allow the user to make predictions about the future performance of a portfolio relative to the performance of a benchmark. Estimation of a risk model implies that the user extrapolates the future behavior of bond return covariances from the past. Hence, predictions from a bond risk model can be of value only if the user believes that the factors driving the model will behave in the future as they did in the past. As a result, a risk model should pass tests for structural stability. While such tests are based upon the historical record, they can give some assurance that the covariance matrix will perform in the future as it did in the past.

The relationship between structural stability and an underlying term structure can best be seen with the following example. Suppose that over a five-year period, the term structure moved only with parallel shifts. Furthermore, suppose that these parallel shifts were consistent with an underlying model of the term structure. In this case, any covariance matrix of returns to the term structure estimated over the five-year period would obscure the potential for twists or butterfly movements. However, a covariance matrix that made use of an underlying term-structure model would fully account for the possibility of nonparallel shifts in the term structure.

## RISK MODEL APPLICATIONS

An examination of Equations (57–2) and (57–4) suggests that applications of bond risk models are defined by two characteristics. The first of these is the choice of benchmark, while the second is the choice of beta. In this context, three natural applications suggest themselves. These are indexed fund management, active management, and financial institution asset/liability management. Each of these lend themselves to policy formulation in terms of tracking error and beta.

For example, suppose that a manager wishes to track a bond index, say the Shearson/Lehman/Hutton Government Corporate bond index. The benchmark, then, is the Shearson/Lehman/Hutton index, and the goal of the manager is to minimize tracking error, or, have a beta of one. Note from Equation (57–4) that tracking error is minimized when beta is equal to one. Thus, purchases of bonds with values of beta greater than one should be balanced with purchases of bonds with betas less than one.

Consider now an active manager. In this case, the manager is rewarded for beating an index. One would expect a tracking error that is larger than that of the indexed manager. Similarly, one would expect a beta that is greater than or less than one relative to the manager's bets upon interest rates, and so on.

Finally, consider the asset/liability management problem confronting financial institutions. In this case, the benchmark is the liability side of the balance sheet, while the portfolio is the asset side. Tracking error can be shown to be the standard deviation of the return on equity (at market values) for this example. Hence, minimizing the variance of the return on equity turns out to be equivalent to setting the beta of the balance sheet equal to one. In fact, one would expect that for an institution that is borrowing short and lending long, the beta of the assets (relative to the liabilities) would be greater than one, thus implying higher volatility in return on equity.

## CONCLUSION

This chapter has discussed the motivation, construction, and implementation of bond portfolio risk models. Alternatives to standard duration/convexity models exist that take into account a broader array of the risks confronting a portfolio manager. These alternative approaches to bond portfolio risk have in turn a wide variety of applications.

# CHAPTER 58

# FIXED INCOME RISK MODELING

*Ronald N. Kahn, Ph.D.*
*Manager, Special Projects*
*BARRA*

Many years ago, bonds were boring. Returns were small and steady. Fixed income risk monitoring consisted of watching duration and avoiding low qualities. But as interest-rate volatility has increased and the variety of fixed income instruments has grown, both opportunities and dangers have flourished. Accurate fixed income risk measurement has become both more important and more difficult. The sources of fixed income risk have proliferated and intensified. Exposures to these risks are subtle and complex to estimate. Today's fixed income environment requires advanced multifactor techniques to adequately model the many sources of risk influencing the market and powerful tools to compute exposures to those risks.

Duration is the traditional fixed income risk factor and measures exposure to the risk of parallel term-structure movements. But term structures not only shift in parallel, they also twist and bend; and these movements tend to increase in magnitude as interest rates rise. In addition to interest-rate volatility, most issues are exposed to various sources of default risk, assessed by marketwide sector and quality spreads. These spreads can depend on maturity and move unpredictably over time. Beyond marketwide sources of default risk, individual issues face specific sources of default risk.

Nominal cash flows and quality ratings no longer suffice to measure risk exposures. Call and put options and sinking-fund provisions can significantly alter an instrument's risk exposures in intricate ways. Mortgage-backed securities are subject to uncertain prepayments, which influence the risk exposures of those instruments. When packaged as IOs, POs, or CMOs, the risk exposure accounting becomes even more difficult.

There is no question that building a fixed income risk model is complicated business: Forecasting risk factor covariance and analyzing the Byzantine provisions of today's fixed income instruments require sophisticated methods.

Using a fixed income risk model, however, should be intuitive and straightforward. Bond investors should find the risk factors sensible. Risk analysis results should be precise, but still conform to investor instincts. A good risk model should actually simplify the investment process, quantify risks, and increase investor insight.

Fixed income risk modeling plays a critical role in bond portfolio management, underlying benchmark tracking, immunization, active strategy implementation, and performance measurement and analysis. Benchmark tracking involves comparing the risk exposures of an investment portfolio and a benchmark. Matching those exposures should lead to investment returns that accurately track benchmark returns. Immunization involves comparing the risk exposures of a portfolio and a liability stream. Matching those exposures should immunize the portfolio's liability coverage against market changes. Active strategies involve deliberate risk exposures relative to a benchmark, aimed at exceeding benchmark returns. Performance measurement and analysis involves identifying active bets and studying their past performance so as to measure bond manager skill.

This chapter describes a multifactor approach to risk modeling. This approach consists of two basic components. First, a valuation model identifies and values the many risk factors in the market. The valuation model requires the machinery to estimate exposures to these risk factors, including an option simulation to handle the wide variety of optionable fixed income securities. Second, a risk model examines the historical behavior of these risk factors to estimate their variances and covariances. While the presentation here will be general, this chapter will conclude with evidence of the performance of multifactor risk models based on their specific application to the U.S. bond market.[1]

## THE VALUATION MODEL

The following multifactor valuation model is designed to identify and value risk factors in the market. This model estimates bond prices as

---

[1] For a more detailed description of this application to the U.S. bond market, see Ronald N. Kahn, "Risk and Return in the U.S. Bond Market: A Multifactor Approach," in Frank J. Fabozzi (ed.) *Advances and Innovations in the Bond and Mortgage Markets* (Chicago: Probus Publishing, 1989).

$$PM_n(t) = \sum_T \frac{cf_n(T) \cdot PDB(t, T)}{\exp[\kappa_n(t) \cdot T]} + \xi_n(t) \qquad (58\text{--}1)$$

$$= PF_n(t) + \xi_n(t) \qquad (58\text{--}2)$$

with

$$\kappa_n(t) = \sum_j x_{n,j} \cdot s_j(t) \qquad (58\text{--}3)$$

where

$PM_n$ = bond $n$ market price at time $t$

$PF_n$ = bond $n$ fitted price at time $t$

$cf_n(T)$ = bond $n$ option adjusted cash flow at time $T$

$PDB(t, T)$ = price at $t$ of default-free pure discount bond maturing at $T$

$x_{n,j}$ = bond $n$ exposure to factor $j$

$s_j(t)$ = yield spread due to factor $j$ at time $t$

$\xi_n(t)$ = bond $n$ price error at time $t$

$\kappa_n(t)$ = bond $n$ total yield spread at time $t$

The characteristics of the market as a whole are the term structure, represented here by the default-free pure discount bond prices $PDB(t,T)$, and the marketwide factor yield spreads $s_j(t)$. The bond-specific exposures include the option adjusted cash flows $cf_n(T)$ and the exposures $x_{n,j}$. These depend upon any call or put options or sinking-fund provisions embedded in bond $n$. The final bond specific component of this model is the price error $\xi_n(t)$. This model clearly enumerates how a bond's total exposure to the various factors determines its price. The estimated values $[PDB(t,T), s_j(t), \xi_n(t)]$ result from fitting this model to actual trading prices at time $t$.[2] All these values change unpredictably over time.

The yield-spread factors $s_j$ correspond to the nonterm-structure sources of risk and return identified by the model. Most of these are sources of default risk. For example, each corporate bond sector might have its own yield spread, measuring the default risk common to all AAA-rated members of the sector. Each quality rating would also have its own yield spread, measuring the additional default risk common to issues rated lower than AAA.

---

[2] For more details, see Ronald N. Kahn, "Estimating the U.S. Treasury Term Structure of Interest Rates," in Frank J. Fabozzi, (ed.) *The Handbook of U.S. Treasury and Government Agency Securities: Instruments, Strategies and Analysis, Revised Edition* (Chicago: Probus Publishing, 1990).

Beyond the factors that measure default risk, there exist other factors that capture risk and return in bond markets. Benchmark factors measure the uncertain liquidity premiums afforded heavily traded issues. A current-yield factor measures the market's assessment at time $t$ of the advantage of receiving return in the form of capital gains instead of interest, providing a possible tax advantage. A perpetual factor, appearing in markets containing perpetual bonds, measures the market's assessment at time $t$ of the advantage or disadvantage of owning perpetual bonds.

Observed corporate bond yield spreads tend to increase with maturity, quantifying the market's perception of the increase in default risk over time. For investors, any change in the dependence of spreads upon maturity constitutes a source of return risk. Since these spreads appear to increase linearly with duration, a duration spread can measure the extent of this increase with duration at any given time. A risk model can then measure how this dependence changes over time.

So far this analysis had concentrated on the estimated marketwide factors of value. Estimates of these factors rely on option-adjusted cash flows, however. Hence, the next section will describe the option adjustment procedure in more detail.

## Option Adjustments

Estimating the values $[PDB(t, T), s_j(t), \xi_n(t)]$ requires both market prices and cash flows and yield-spread factor exposures. However, since embedded options alter the nominal cash flows, the final step in the valuation model involves adjusting the nominal bond cash flows accordingly.

Bonds can include call and put options and sinking-fund provisions. Mortgage-backed securities include prepayment options. These securities are portfolios containing a nonoptionable security and an option. For callable and sinkable bonds and mortgages, the issuer retains the option, and so the portfolio is long a nonoptionable security and short the option:

$$\text{Optionable bond} = \text{Nonoptionable bond} - \text{Option} \qquad (58\text{--}4)$$

and

$$PF_n(t) = PFN_n(t) - PFO_n(t) \qquad (58\text{--}5)$$

where

$PFN_n$ = bond $n$ nominal fitted price
$PFO_n$ = bond $n$ option fitted price

For putable bonds, the purchaser owns the put option, so the portfolio is long both the nonoptionable security and the option.

Viewed in this portfolio framework, the key aspect of option adjustment involves modeling the embedded option. A detailed description of option modeling is beyond the scope of this chapter,[3] but basically it is three-step procedure.

First, choose a model that describes the stochastic evolution of future interest rates. This model will describe the drift and, more importantly, the interest-rate volatility, of either the short interest rate or the entire term structure. It will describe a set of possible future interest rate paths.

Second, impose a no-arbitrage condition to fairly price bonds of different maturities. This step will determine the probability weight, for valuation purposes, of each possible future interest-rate path and generate a current set of bond prices. A properly tuned model will generate prices consistent with observed bond prices.

Third, impose relevant option decision rules to apply the model to the particular option of interest. These decision rules will depend on both the specific option covenants as well as the behavioral model governing the corporation or the individual mortgage holder. Imposing these rules will lead to estimated cash flows and a price for the option. The portfolio property described in Equation (58–4) then dictates how the option cash flows adjust the optionable bond cash flows.

## Option Adjustment Example[4]

To see this work in practice, consider a simple example of a callable zero coupon bond. The bond nominally pays $V$ dollars at maturity $M$:

$$\text{PFN}_n(t) = V \cdot \text{PDB}(t, M) \tag{58–6}$$

But the traded security includes an embedded option for the issuer to call the bond at strike price $K$ and time $T$, with $t < T < M$. The option model estimates the call option value as

$$\text{PFO}_n(t) = -K \cdot Y \cdot \text{PDB}(t, T) + V \cdot X \cdot \text{PDB}(t, M) \tag{58–7}$$

where $X$ and $Y$ are cumulative distribution functions.[5] Equation (58–7) resembles the Black-Scholes stock option formula,[6] though $X$ and $Y$ are not necessarily

---

[3] See, for example, Frank J. Fabozzi and Ravi E. Dattatreya, "A Simplified Model for Valuing Debt Options," *Journal of Portfolio Management,* Spring 1989, pp. 64–72.

[4] This section covers more details of the option adjustment process for the benefit of mathematically inclined readers.

[5] These cumulative distribution functions correspond to the valuation probability — the martingale probability associated with the stochastic interest-rate model.

[6] Fischer Black and Myron Scholes, "The Pricing of Options and Corporate Liabilities," *Journal of Political Economy,* May–June 1973.

cumulative normal distributions. They do, however, act as probabilities and range between zero and one.

Now consider the interpretation of Equation (58–7): The option involves paying the amount $KY$ at time $T$, to receive $VX$ at the later time $M$. With this interpretation, and with the portfolio property (Equation 58–4), the adjusted price and cash flows for the callable security are

$$PF_n(t) = V \cdot PDB(t, M) - [-K \cdot Y \cdot PDB(t, T) + V \cdot X \cdot PDB(t, M)]$$

$$= K \cdot Y \cdot PDB(t, T) + V \cdot (1 - X) \cdot PDB(t, M) \tag{58–8}$$

$$cf_n(T) = K \cdot Y \tag{58–9}$$

$$cf_n(M) = V \cdot [1 - X] \tag{58–10}$$

As Equations (58–9) and (58–10) show, the probabilities $X$ and $Y$ adjust the nominal cash flows. An out-of-the-money option has $X$, $Y$, and PFO all equal to zero, and the option-adjusted cash flows reduce to the nominal cash flows. For this callable bond example, as $X$ and $Y$ increase, the option will shorten the nominal cash flows. More complicated options involve more cash flows (a set of $T_1, \ldots, T_N$), more probabilities, and perhaps even more complicated numerical procedures to estimate the probabilities; but, in principle, the adjustment procedure is the same.

Remember that the true option-adjusted cash flows are still not certain. The option model chooses certain cash flows $-KY$ and $VX$ to replicate both the value and duration of the modeled security. Unfortunately, it is impossible to choose these cash flows to also replicate the convexity of the modeled security. The discrepancy between the convexity of the modeled security and the convexity of the replicating cash flow—the "excess convexity" of the option—is greatest when the option is at-the-money and approaches zero elsewhere. Fortunately, this discrepancy at worst affects risk modeling only in second order—it affects only convexity, not duration. And, an additional yield-spread factor—an additional $s_j$—can account for the discrepancy.

Given a procedure for estimating these option-adjusted cash flows at time $t$, a set of market prices at time $t$ will lead to estimates of $PDB(t, T)$ and $s_j(t)$, according to a procedure designed to minimize overall pricing error. The historical behavior of these market variables will then lead to the risk model itself.

## THE RISK MODEL

Bond prices change over time in response to three general phenomena: shortening bond maturities, shifting term structures, and changing yield spreads. Bonds are risky because the last two phenomena are uncertain. The core of a bond risk model is, therefore, an estimate of the variances and covariances of the term structure and the yield-spread factor excess returns. The next two sections describe how to estimate these marketwide factor excess returns, and a third section describes how to estimate bond specific risk.

## Term-Structure Factor Returns

Building the risk model requires a history of the behavior of all relevant market factors, which the valuation model provides. How exactly does this work? Consider first the term-structure risk factors: the default-free pure discount bond prices. The price $PDB(t,T)$ represents the price at time $t$ of a certain $1.00 paid at time $T$. The return to this factor between $t - \Delta t$ and $t$ is the return to the following strategy:

> Invest $1.00 at time $t - \Delta t$ in the default-free pure discount bond $PDB(t - \Delta t, T)$. This bond has a maturity of $T - (t - \Delta t)$. Hold for a period $\Delta t$. Then sell the bond, now with a maturity $T - t$, for price $PDB(t, T)$.

The excess return to this factor follows by subtracting the risk-free rate of return. This risk-free rate is the return to the strategy:

> Invest $1.00 at time $t - \Delta t$ in the default-free pure discount bond $PDB(t - \Delta t, t)$ maturing at time $t$. This bond has a maturity of $\Delta t$. Hold for a period $\Delta t$. Then redeem the bond, which has now matured.

The fixed holding period $\Delta t$ is a defining constant of the risk model.

## Yield-Spread Factor Returns

Now consider the returns associated with the yield-spread factors. The excess return to factor $j$ at time $t$ is the return to the following artificial strategy:

> Invest $1.00 at time $t - \Delta t$ in a portfolio exposed only to factor $j$ and to term-structure risk. The portfolio duration is set to the average market duration over the risk model history. Hold for a period $\Delta t$, *and roll down the term structure over this period*. Sell the portfolio at time $t$.

This strategy is artificial because it assumes a fixed term structure. The excess return to this strategy is the change in yield spread $s_j$ over the holding period, multiplied by the average bond market duration, plus the yield spread multiplied by the holding period $\Delta t$. Duration, the fractional change in price accompanying a change in yield, enters into this formula to convert a change in yield spread into a price return.

## Specific Return

Beyond the general, marketwide sources of risk discussed, individual issues also face specific risk. Factors that influence only one particular issue, or only the bonds of a particular company, generate specific risk and return. For example,

LBO event risk constitutes a specific risk of current interest.[7] In the context of the risk model, specific returns arise because the bond pricing error $\xi_n(t)$ can change randomly over time.

The specific return to bond $n$ at time $t$ is the return to the following strategy:

> Invest \$1.00 at time $t - \Delta t$ in a portfolio long bond $n$, but with all marketwide sources of risk hedged. Hold for a period $\Delta t$, and then sell. The difference in pricing error will generate the specific return $\frac{\xi_n(t) - \xi_n(t - \Delta t)}{PM_n(t - \Delta t)}$.

The distinction between marketwide sources of risk and specific risk is important because investors can hedge marketwide sources of risk through other instruments exposed to those same risk sources. By assumption, specific risk is uncorrelated with marketwide risk.[8]

## Integration

A multifactor risk model identifies the risk factors operating in a given market and then estimates their risk. Each factor generates excess returns over the model's estimation period. The risk model analyzes those return histories to forecast their variances and covariances.

Several difficult questions arise during the course of this analysis. What historical estimation period works best for covariance forecasting? Is covariance stable over time, or does it cycle or trend? These basic questions remain the subject of continual debate.

One particular question about forecasting bond market covariance concerns whether or not covariance depends on the level of rates. Does bond market risk increase as rates increase? Is volatility higher when rates are 16 percent than when rates are 8 percent? Academics have speculated that the answer is yes, and historical investigation confirms it, for the U.S. bond market.

John Cox, Jonathan Ingersoll, and Stephen Ross[9] have developed a widely accepted model of the term structure, which prices bonds and bond options based on equilibrium arguments. Their model posits the stochastic evolution of the term structure, with interest-rate standard deviation and bond return standard deviation both proportional to the square root of the level of rates. When rates double from 8 percent to 16 percent, volatility rises by a factor of 1.4: the square root of 2.0.

---

[7] Ronald N. Kahn, "LBO Event Risk," in Frank J. Fabozzi, (ed.) *Managing Institutional Assets* (New York: Ballinger, 1990).

[8] The specific risk of two different issues may be correlated, for example, if one company issued them both.

[9] John C. Cox, Jonathan E. Ingersoll, Jr., and Stephen A. Ross, "A Theory of the Term Structure of Interest Rates," *Econometrica*, vol. 36, no. 2 (March 1985).

Historical investigation can probe the dependence of bond market risk on the level of rates. Exhibit 58–1 illustrates the results of a test comparing the standard deviation of monthly pure discount bond excess returns observed each year from 1948 to 1988, to the mean five-year spot rate observed each year. This test determined the exponent $c$ of the relationship

$$\text{volatility} \alpha (\text{rate})^c$$

If $c = 1$, then volatility is directly proportional to rates; when rates double, volatility doubles. The Cox, Ingersoll, Ross model assumes that $c = 1/2$. The empirical results illustrated in Exhibit 58–1 demonstrate that $c = 1.08 \pm 0.14$. Within the standard errors shown in Exhibit 58–1, volatility is directly proportional to rate level. Moreover, as the $R^2$ statistic reveals, the level of rates explains 61 percent of the observed difference in risk from year to year. The effect is more pronounced in high-rate periods than in low-rate periods. Further study examined the dependence of yield-spread factor risk on the level of the five-year spot rate. Results were mixed, though generally consistent with direct proportionality.

Given the broad empirical and theoretical evidence supporting the dependence of covariance upon rates, forecasts of covariance based on historical data should take account of this effect.

With all this sophisticated risk model machinery now in place and integrated, how well does the resulting risk model perform?

**EXHIBIT 58–1**
**Risk versus Level of Rates**

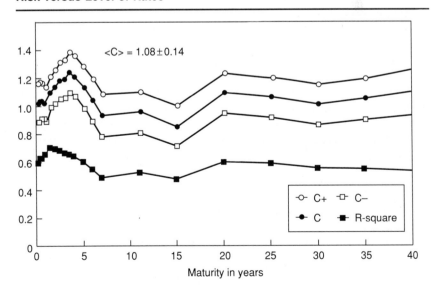

## PERFORMANCE

Multifactor risk modeling involves significant effort. Is this effort justified? Does it significantly differ from the duration approach? How well does the multifactor approach to fixed income risk modeling actually work?

To see how the multifactor approach differs from the duration and convexity approach, consider the performance of a multifactor model in the U.S. bond market. Remember that duration and convexity are both parallel yield shift concepts. They measure the risk of parallel yield shifts. But the term structure does not move in parallel.

The risk model views the term structure as a set of pure discount bonds of different maturities, each allowed to move independently. The covariance matrix then describes the extent to which they actually do move together. Exhibits 58–2 and 58–3 illustrate the two predominant, coherent movements of the term structure, as forecast in September 1989 based on the observed term-structure history throughout the 1980s. These *principal components* are the independent, uncorrelated collective movements of the term structure. Exhibit 58–2 illustrates the primary term-structure movement: a nonparallel shift, with short rates more volatile than long rates. A duration-based risk model would assume that a parallel shift completely specified term-structure risk. This nonparallel shift accounts for 95.4 percent of modeled term-structure risk. Exhibit 58–3 illustrates the secondary term-structure movement: a twist, with short and long rates moving in opposite directions. This twist accounts for an additional 4.1 percent of modeled term-structure risk.

**EXHIBIT 58–2**
**First Principal Component**

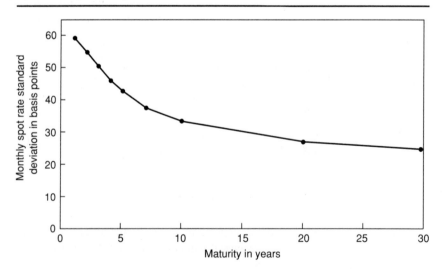

**EXHIBIT 58–3**
**Second Principal Component**

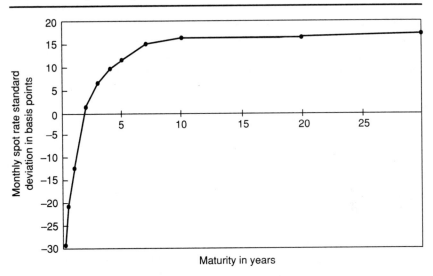

To further examine how well multifactor risk modeling performs, the following test compared a simple duration model and a duration plus convexity model with a 10-factor model (pure discount bonds with maturities of 0.25, 0.5, 1, 2, 3, 4, 5, 6, 7, 10, 30 years) in modeling noncallable U.S. Treasury security returns between January 1980 and October 1986. The noncallable U.S. Treasury market should be the simplest market to model because it requires no factors to account for default risk and no option simulation model. For demonstrating the significant enhancement resulting from the multifactor approach, this is the most difficult test. The results are as follows:

| Model | Number of Factors | Percent of Explained Variance |
|---|---|---|
| Duration | 1 | 75.8 |
| Duration + convexity | 2 | 81.1 |
| First principal component | 1 | 82.4 |
| First two principal components | 2 | 87.0 |
| Full multifactor model | 10 | 88.0 |

The full multifactor model explains significantly more of the observed variance than the simple duration model or even the duration and convexity model. The first two principal components are the optimized first two risk factors. The first principal component model employs just one factor, a nonparallel shift, and outperforms the two-factor duration and convexity model. Of course, one must construct the full multifactor risk model to identify this optimal one-factor model.

This chapter so far has described the construction of a risk model and a test of its overall performance measuring fixed income risk. How, though, does the risk model apply to a particular investment portfolio?

## PORTFOLIO RISK CHARACTERIZATION

Historical analysis captures the inherent riskiness of the factors of value present in the bond market. The riskiness of a particular bond portfolio depends upon its exposure to these sources of risk.

The fraction of a portfolio's present value at each vertex measures the portfolio's exposure to term-structure risk. Two portfolios with identical distributions of present value along the vertices face identical term-structure risk. Of course, these two portfolios have identical durations. However, two portfolios can have identical durations without having identical distributions across the entire set of vertices. Such portfolios will not face identical term-structure risk.

What about yield-spread factor risk? Consider for example the risk associated with the sector yield spread. The fraction of the portfolio in each sector, multiplied by the duration of the bonds in that sector compared to bond market average duration, measures the portfolio's sector risk exposure. Risk exposures for quality factors and other factors follow analogously.

Beyond the marketwide factors of value the model identifies, there also exist risk factors associated solely with individual issues. By definition, the specific risk for each issue is uncorrelated with all marketwide factor risk. It may be correlated, though, with the specific risk of other bonds of the same issuer. We can estimate this specific issue risk historically as the realized excess return risk of each specific issue not explained by the model.

Total risk follows from combining the risk exposures that characterize a given portfolio with the variances and covariances of the underlying risk factors that characterize the market, and adding in specific issue risk. This number is the predicted total variance of the portfolio excess return.

Portfolio risk analysis usually involves comparing the portfolio against a benchmark (or liability stream). Comparing risk exposures will quantify the manager's bets in relation to the benchmark. The risk model can then predict how well the portfolio will track the benchmark. For active managers, an optimizer can implement common factor and specific issue bets, while still controlling risk. An active manager's utility will usually increase with expected excess return and decrease with expected tracking error. An optimizer can maximize this utility.

## SUMMARY

Today's fixed income markets are characterized by complex instruments and increased volatility. In this environment, bond portfolio management must increasingly rely on sophisticated models to accurately gauge fixed income risk. Building these models requires considerable sophistication. Using them, however, should be straightforward. A good model should simplify the investment process and increase investor insight.

# CHAPTER 59

## VALUATION AND RISK ANALYSIS
## OF INTERNATIONAL BONDS

Brian K. Newton
*Senior Vice President*
*BARRA International*

Paul B. Chau
*Senior Consultant*
*BARRA*

The world of international fixed income can well be described as one composed of widely differing market structures governing an even more diverse set of assets. When addressing the problems of managing a portfolio of international fixed income securities, one must consider not only the specific nature of the bonds held but also the institutions that govern the trading of the assets in and across the various markets. Further, one must be aware of the trading patterns extant in the markets themselves. So, for example, the investor considering the purchase of Japanese government bonds (JGBs) must understand the rules for withholding on coupon payments as well as the market norms for liquidity in this highly illiquid market.

Taken together, these issues present a substantial challenge for the international investor. These problems, however, are further complicated by the imprecise linkage between markets in the form of the freely floating[1] exchange

---

[1] There are tight linkages among the European markets imposed by the EMS. The Dutch and German markets provide an interesting example where policy has long been targeted to the maintenance of a preset exchange rate with monetary policy adjusted to keep currencies in line. By extension, with EC 1992 fast approaching, there may indeed be a single exchange rate linking European with non-European markets. Of course, the structure of what is now a set of, say, five fixed income markets may be radically different at that time.

rate system. Perhaps of greatest importance over much of the 80s has been the effect of currency movements on the returns earned by international investors. It is not enough to bet on those markets that exhibit the highest (local) return over one's investment horizon—one must also get the currency right. The answers to the questions of when and to what degree to hedge currency exposure are often the most critical determinants of the decision of an international investment strategy.

Before beginning the task of devising a global investment strategy, one must understand the elements of each market that plays a significant role in defining the value of assets traded in each market. One cannot merely apply knowledge gained from investing in one's own domestic market. Simple extensions of the strategies that work well in one market may lead to extremely poor results in another.

Returning to the example of the JGB market, at the time of this writing the short end of the yield curve is extremely illiquid. This stems from the fact that the coupons associated with the JGBs issued eight or nine years ago are very high relative to more recently issued JGBs.[2] Coupons of over 7 percent are found on these very seasoned issues, while more recently issued bonds have coupons of around 5 percent.[3] For a host of reasons, investors are not willing to trade out of their positions in these high-coupon securities. Thus investors attempting to establish dedicated or immunized portfolios may find it nearly impossible to do so if they wish to stick with JGB issues.

Valuation analysis, therefore, has a decidedly market-specific component that, to be properly accounted for, requires substantial knowledge about each market individually. This knowledge includes not only a taxonomy of the types of assets traded in the market but also a full understanding of the institutions that regulate the market and the trading habits of the important classes of investors active in the market.

Turning to risk analysis, we find a similar set of issues. The traditional measures of risk in the context of a single market—duration and, more recently, convexity in both their standard and option-adjusted forms—lose all meaning in the context of an international portfolio. These statistics, of course, can be computed by applying the usual well-known formulae. However, the meaning of a 4.5-year duration for a portfolio of U.S. Treasuries, U.K. Gilts, and JGBs is unclear. In addition to the weaknesses of these measures of risk in a single—

---

[2] The bulk of large capitalization JGB coupon issues are 10-year issues. There are two-, three-, and four-year coupon bonds along with five-year discount issues in the JGB market; however, there is virtually no secondary market. For this reason, the major indexes exclude these issues from their constituent lists. There are also a few issues with 20-year maturities. These generally are included in indexes representing the JGB market.

[3] The current benchmark bond, the #111, has a coupon of 4.6 percent while other more recent issues have coupons in the range of 4.6 to 5.1 percent.

market context,[4] there is the added problem that markets do not move precisely in step with one another. Before a duration number can be sensibly interpreted for a global portfolio, the markets represented in that portfolio would all have to undergo identical interest-rate changes *simultaneously*. This assumption is not valid for nearly all markets over any recent period, and evidence to this effect is provided below.

The purpose of this chapter is to describe, in the context of today's marketplace, approaches for addressing these difficulties. In the next section, we offer an approach for devising single market valuation models to assist the investor in making trading decisions, marking portfolios to market, and so on. The approach described has been applied, with uniformly excellent results, to markets as diverse as the U.K. Gilt, U.S. investment-grade, Japanese investment-grade, and Eurocurrency bond markets. Having developed a framework for accurate valuation of fixed income securities, we then turn to the issue of forecasting the risk of a portfolio of these securities. Again we first consider local market risk—those factors of risk relevant to an individual market—and then add the new dimension inherent in global portfolios, namely currency risk. Finally, we provide a brief discussion of an approach for addressing currency risk, which separates this risk from local market risk. This approach facilitates not only risk analysis but also the analysis of alternative investment strategies.

## VALUATION ANALYSIS

Clearly, the most important element in the value of a fixed income security is the prevailing level of interest rates, because any fixed income security may be thought of as a promised stream of future cash flows. These cash flows are then discounted owing to the time value of money and the relative riskiness of the promise. Adjustments made for the relative riskiness of any individual cash-flow stream are in general much smaller than the effects of the interest rate or term structure.[5]

Adopting this point of view, the first and most important task of valuation analysis is to accurately characterize the term structure. In Chapters 9, 56, and 58, the determinants of the term structure for a given market are discussed. Briefly stated, these amount to the relative supply and demand for government securities, the market's view of the future prospects of the national economy, and the relative riskiness of those prospects. The term structure, therefore, is embodied in the prices of government securities, assuming that the sovereign borrower is the borrower of lowest risk in any fixed income market.

---

[4] An insightful discussion of this can be found in Chapter 58.

[5] The exception to this is the very risky class of bonds known as high-yield, or junk, bonds. Spreads over the term structure are normally a substantial proportion of the underlying Treasury rate and can approach the level of the term structure during periods of heightened economic uncertainty.

We can estimate the term structure at any point in time from the prices of government bonds. A very simple approach would assume that all government securities are of equal interest to investors and that the only differentiating feature is the maturity of a given issue. Making this assumption, one can derive the term structure from a cross section of prices spanning the maturity spectrum of the government market.[6] We can now apply this set of interest rates to compute fair prices of other bonds not used in the estimation. This approach provides a reasonably good approximation of the value of any bond issued in the market so long as the issue is not "too different" from the government bonds used in estimating the term structure. But, what does "too different" mean?

A precise answer to this question depends crucially on the state of the market when the question is posed. We can generally improve the approximation provided by the term structure by identifying and valuing those asset features that distinguish one bond from another in the minds of investors. Obviously the level of credit risk, most often associated with the rating of an issue, is important for an investor's valuation of a bond. For corporate debt, the economic sector in which the firm operates provides information as to the relative riskiness of the firm's prospects. Option features, whether for exercise by the issuer or the purchaser, affect the relative valuation of otherwise similar instruments. In general, any asset feature or market condition (such as relative liquidity, tax treatment, market volatility in the case of options, etc.) that substantially changes investors' willingness to pay for an issue should be considered.

Identifying the differentiating features for a particular market is the key step in refining the valuation analysis that begins with the term structure. For the U.S. market, items of relevance to investors would include those mentioned above — rating, sector, liquidity, option features — as well as relative coupon, degree of subordination, and the existence of a sinking fund, among others. The final step in valuation analysis is to take the term structure as determined from the prices of government bonds and estimate the value of exposure to the differentiating features. Having done this, one can compute the fair value for any issue in the market and compare that figure with market prices for rich/cheap trading opportunities, marking a portfolio of untraded assets to market or assessing a bid/offer on an asset not recently traded.

To formalize our arguments, we offer the following valuation model specification.[7]

$$PM_n(t) = \sum_T \frac{cf_n(T) \cdot PDB(t, T)}{\exp[\kappa_n(t) \cdot T]} + \epsilon_n(t) \qquad (59\text{–}1)$$

$$= PF_n(t) + \epsilon_n(t) \qquad (59\text{–}2)$$

---

[6] Again, technical details related to this estimation are discussed elsewhere in this volume as well as in numerous academic articles.

[7] This specification conforms to that in Chapter 58. See footnote 4.

with

$$\kappa_n(t) = \sum_j x_{n,j} \cdot s_j(t) \tag{59-3}$$

where

$PM_n(t)$ = bond $n$ market price at time $t$

$PF_n(t)$ = bond $n$ fitted price at time $t$

$cf_n(T)$ = expected cash flow at time $T$

$PDB(t, T)$ = discount for horizon date $T$

$x_{n,j}$ = bond $n$ exposure to factor $j$

$s_j(t)$ = market's assessment of factor $j$

$\epsilon_n(t)$ = bond $n$ price error at time $t$

$\kappa_n(t)$ = bond $n$ total yield spread at time $t$

The price of each bond is given by the discounted stream of promised future cash flows. The total discount function for any particular bond consists of two components; the base line term structure given by $PDB(t,T)$ and the bond-specific yield adjustment given by Equation (59–3). The term structure $PDB(t,T)$ is estimated from the prices of government bonds. This discount function represents the borrowing cost of the least risky borrower in the market—by assumption, the central government. The bond-specific component of the discount function describes how the cash flows of any individual issue are differentially discounted owing to the specific features of the asset. Hence the valuation of any security is a function of the market-wide properties of the term structure [$PDB(t,T)$] and the values of the various distinguishing asset attributes ($s_j$), together with an asset's promised stream of cash flows [$cf_n(T)$] and its exposures ($x_{n,j}$) to these distinguishing attributes.

Before turning to a discussion of the differences among the world's bond markets, recall our assumption that the government issues on which the term structure is based are identical up to maturity in the eyes of investors. In the real world, however, this can be far from the truth, depending on the market. In the U.S. Treasury market, issues have coupons ranging from 5 percent to over 15 percent, bills are issued as discounts; certain issues are subject to differential tax treatment (e.g., flower bonds); others can be stripped; and some recently issued securities are considered "on-the-run," a term connoting their very high liquidity. Therefore, a more careful analysis of the U.S. term structure should account for these differences among government issues in order to better define the true term structure of interest rates in the economy.

Similar considerations apply in most other government bond markets. Perhaps the most extreme example is again the Japanese market. The benchmark bond, currently the # 111 JGB issue, accounts for a huge share of daily trading volume. In fact, when the # 89 held benchmark status, it occasionally accounted for over 90 percent of daily volume! This pattern has relaxed recently, but it does highlight the extreme nature of some of the world's bond markets. Exhibit 59–1 below provides a comparison of the relative liquidity observed in the five largest government bond markets by capitalization for midyear 1989.

Aside from the differences in liquidity among government issues, specific attributes of each bond can lead to significant differences in prices. For example, the relative coupon of an issue may cause the bond to be priced relatively rich compared to what would be predicted from the estimated term structure. Borrowing again from the Japanese experience, JGBs with coupons in the 7 to 8 percent range are rarely traded because investors covet the cash flow and cannot replace it with recently issued bonds carrying 5 percent coupons. Many instruments have option features—calls, extensions, conversions—which effect asset values. Others have sinking funds (some with options) or have no maturity such as the War Loans of the U.K. Gilt market. Each of these attributes alters the value of the issue for the investor.

In terms of the model specified above, this implies that a set of attributes to which the market imputes value are associated with government bonds. For proper estimation of the term structure [$PDB(t,T)$], one must simultaneously estimate the values ($s_j$) of these distinguishing features ($x_{n,j}$). Only then will the true base line interest rates be revealed.

Our research has shown that the above specification is robust, both across markets and through time. In analyzing data from 10 government bond markets,[8] we found that by carefully specifying the set of attributes important in

**EXHIBIT 59–1**
**Relative Liquidity of Government Bond Markets**

| Market | Number Traded | Actively Traded | Benchmark |
|---|---|---|---|
| U.S. | 142 | 21 | 7 |
| Japan | 44 | 10 | 1 |
| Germany | 63 | 25 | 1 |
| U.K. | 25 | 25 | 8 |
| France | 32 | 17 | 3 |

Source: J.P. Morgan Securities, Inc.

---

[8] The data for this research was provided by Salomon Brothers Inc. The result of the research effort is an analytical system for assessing the risk of portfolios of government bonds from the represented markets—the BARRA Global Bond System.

each market, bond prices can be accurately predicted. Exhibit 59–2 provides representative statistics showing the accuracy of the model in several markets at two different points in time.

Given this framework for valuing individual assets, one can apply the models to such tasks as evaluating trading opportunities, marking a portfolio to market, or any other valuation-dependent analysis. Of course, there are caveats that apply in properly interpreting the results. The parameters estimated for each market are only as good as the data used in estimating them. Ideally, all prices used would reflect transactions occurring at nearly the same time. This is rarely, if ever, the case with bond price data because the source of the price is often a trader asked to quote a fair market value rather than a report of an actual transaction price. In light of the aforementioned variations in liquidity within each market, it may well be the case that only a very small fraction of the prices are "real" in this sense. One may then view portfolio valuation analyses as reasonable since the errors will tend to cancel each other when the underlying models are correct on average.

With valuation of fixed income securities now well defined, we turn to the assessment of risk in fixed income markets. The next section explores the issues involved in modeling risk for single-market portfolios as well as multi-market portfolios, which face the additional dimension of risk in their currency exposures.

**EXHIBIT 59–2**
**Root Mean Square of Pricing Errors (RMS)**

| Market | June 1989 | | September 1989 | |
|---|---|---|---|---|
| | No. of Issues | RMS | No. of Issues | RMS |
| Canada | 108 | 0.68 | 105 | 0.63 |
| U.S. | 169 | 0.56 | 167 | 0.41 |
| Japan | 101 | 0.41 | 103 | 0.34 |
| Germany | 171 | 0.34 | 168 | 0.26 |
| U.K. | 83 | 0.75 | 81 | 0.72 |
| Netherlands | 84 | 0.77 | 86 | 0.27 |
| Switzerland | 38 | 0.40 | 38 | 0.56 |
| France | 66 | 0.54 | 65 | 0.42 |
| Australia | 70 | 0.26 | 69 | 0.35 |
| Denmark | 28 | 0.36 | 26 | 0.35 |

Source: BARRA

# RISK ANALYSIS

In the preceding section, we argued that interest rates are by far the most important determinant of asset value in fixed income markets. Following directly from this, we argue that *interest-rate risk* is the most important element of risk. Our research shows that interest-rate risk is roughly 90 percent of the story in most markets. We can improve on this; that is, we can explain even more of market risk, by understanding the risk in the other factors of asset value that we identified in developing our valuation models. By modeling the linkages among the interest-rate and value factors, our risk characterization is further refined.

The remainder of this section explains our approach to modeling risk in a single fixed income market. Having devised risk models for the separate markets in a similar fashion, we then describe a model that accounts for the linkages existing across markets—essentially the covariance structure of market returns. This model considers the covariation of local market returns. The currency issue is addressed briefly in the next section.

## Local Market Risk

The variation in the term structure of interest rates accounts for the greatest amount of risk in a fixed income market. In fact, in the case of the U.S. bond market, interest-rate fluctuations account for roughly 90 percent of the risk. The remaining 10 percent is attributable to the risks inherent in asset features such as call or put options, sector membership, relative coupon, and rating. Exhibit 59–3 shows the decomposition of return variance for a universe consisting of all government and corporate bonds with a minimum maturity of one year.

**EXHIBIT 59–3**
**Decomposition of Return Variance**

|  | Variance $\%^2$ |
| --- | --- |
| Interest-rate effects | 100.95 |
| Interest-sensitive factors | 0.00 |
| Covariance of interest-rate effects and interest-sensitive factors | 0.14 |
| Quality and sector factors | 1.12 |
| Covariance of quality and sector factors and interest-rate effects | 11.67 |
| Specific issues | 0.00 |
| Total | 113.89 |

Source: BARRA

The exhibit provides evidence in support of the claim that interest rates are the dominant element of risk. The fact that interest rates are the dominant risk factor explains the usefulness of duration as a good first approximation to bond risk. Duration measures risk relative to *small* (parallel) shifts in interest rates.

But, interest rates do not always shift in parallel,[9] and the shifts are not necessarily small over time periods even as short as a week. Also, the extent to which the other valuation factors shift in unison with or in opposition to the term structure can markedly effect the risk of individual securities. Portfolios more highly exposed to these factors than the market as a whole can exhibit substantially different returns than a market index portfolio.

How then does one improve upon the duration approximation of fixed income risk? One methodology, which has proved quite useful over the past decade, is to use as a base the valuation models described above. From this model, the valuation factor returns are computed over the investment horizon of interest, say one month. The result from this exercise is a set of factor returns series embodying the returns experienced in the market over the history used in the analysis. The final step is the construction of a covariance matrix of factor returns that reveals how the various factors move with respect to one another.

The preceding paragraph contains the "recipe," if you will, for a full multiple factor risk model for a fixed income market. The key element in the risk model is the specification of the valuation model described in the previous section. The extent to which this underlying valuation model captures the important factors for explaining value in the market will set the limits on the risk model's ability to explain variation in returns.

Recalling our general valuation model, the factors explaining value in a market are the term structure (equivalently, the prices of pure discount bonds at various maturities) and the features of assets that differentiate otherwise equivalent bonds. The valuation model produces a price for each of these distinguishing features along with the pure discount bond prices.

The number of factors in any particular model will depend on the variety of assets found in the market being modeled. Taking the U.S. Treasury market as an example, the interest-rate structure can be defined very accurately by fewer than 10 interest rates. The special features in this market contributing to differential asset prices number two or three.[10] Therefore, our risk model has roughly a dozen factor returns series from which the covariance matrix is estimated.

So far this example has focused on the U.S. fixed income market—in fact, only the Treasury market. However, through suitable generalization of the under-

---

[9] Quite the contrary. A study performed by BARRA showed that for weekly intervals from 1979 through 1986 the term structure as estimated by BARRA never once shifted in a perfectly parallel fashion and often moved in a rotating, or butterfly-like, fashion.

[10] These would include coupon differential, on-the-run status, and tax treatment.

lying valuation model, this approach can be applied to any fixed income market. To date, the valuation methodology has been applied to the U.S. and Japanese investment-grade markets, the U.K. Gilt market, the Australian government and semigovernment market, and the Eurocurrency markets—all with very strong performance.

In addition, the risk modeling approach has been applied to all of these save the Eurocurrency markets,[11] as well as the 10 government markets covered by the Salomon Brothers World Government Bond Indexes. For each of these 10 markets, the risk models using between 9 and 14 parameters have performed remarkably well, explaining between 85 and 95 percent of risk.

## Global Portfolio Risk

We began this chapter with the purpose of describing methods for valuing and assessing the riskiness of international bonds and portfolios. So far we have described techniques for valuing and assessing risk of issues in a single-market context. Here we address the complication of risk analysis for portfolios composed of bonds from several markets. Again, we postpone the assessment of the currency factor until the next section.

To this point, we have devised individual market models. Each of these models, both valuation and risk, is based on roughly 10 valuation parameters. Before proceeding with the development of a multimarket risk analysis framework, we offer in Exhibit 59–4 evidence of the inappropriateness of duration as a measure of risk for a multimarket portfolio.

The exhibit shows the correlation of returns across markets over a period of roughly five years. For duration to make sense in the context of portfolios of bonds from several markets, the correlations would have to be identical, barring differences in duration across markets. In other words, if we control for the differences in duration between individual markets, then the return correlations would be unity. While individual market durations are different and vary somewhat through the sample period of December 1984 through June 1989, this does not explain the range of correlations. These are shown to range from a low of $-0.101$ to a high of $0.861$. Clearly then, duration is a poor approximation for risk in the context of multicurrency fixed income portfolios.

We can produce a more general risk analysis framework by using the risk models for the component markets. However, to move to such a multimarket framework, we must overcome one important difficulty. In the case of each single-market model, we suggested computing a covariance matrix from roughly 10 parameters. This means estimating the approximately 55 elements of the covariance matrices, one for each market. However, simply combining the returns

---

[11] The limitation here is the lack of a reasonable history of reliable pricing information.

**EXHIBIT 59–4**
**Correlation of Fixed Income Returns** (December 1984–June 1989)

| | Australia | Canada | France | Germany | Japan | Netherlands | Switzerland | U.K. | U.S. |
|---|---|---|---|---|---|---|---|---|---|
| Australia | 7.81 | −0.101 | 0.023 | 0.127 | 0.039 | 0.131 | 0.118 | 0.099 | 0.040 |
| Canada | | 8.971 | 0.523 | 0.523 | 0.447 | 0.543 | 0.270 | 0.335 | 0.861 |
| France | | | 6.150 | 0.525 | 0.462 | 0.611 | 0.300 | 0.407 | 0.596 |
| Germany | | | | 4.208 | 0.708 | 0.858 | 0.548 | 0.501 | 0.534 |
| Japan | | | | | 6.697 | 0.623 | 0.376 | 0.533 | 0.470 |
| Netherlands | | | | | | 3.758 | 0.672 | 0.361 | 0.552 |
| Switzerland | | | | | | | 2.639 | 0.198 | 0.369 |
| U.K. | | | | | | | | 8.482 | 0.335 |
| U.S. | | | | | | | | | 9.842 |

Note: Diagonal elements represent annualized standard deviation of returns.

Source: BARRA

series and attempting to estimate the resulting multimarket covariance matrix would require enough data to reliably estimate roughly 5000 parameters! Some alternative approach must be used.

Solving the problem of forming a risk model spanning 10 markets can be accomplished by using techniques that effectively reduce the dimensionality of the problem. A detailed discussion of these techniques is beyond the scope of this chapter, but the basic idea is quite straightforward. What we are after is a set of parameters that capture most of the explanatory power of the full set of parameters used in the single-market models. To construct these parameters, we appeal to the technique of principal component analysis.

Principal components is a technique that transforms the parameters of a model into a new set of *independent* parameters explaining the greatest amount of variation, the next greatest amount, and so on. As noted, these *hybrid* parameters are independent of one another within each of the individual market risk models. Where our dozen parameter models explain, say, 95 percent of the risk in a fixed income market, nearly all of this explanatory power can be embodied in two or at most three independent parameters. The results of our research in this area are presented in Exhibit 59–5.

From the exhibit, we see that for each market the first principal component captures between 89 and 98 percent of the variation explained by the full model. What this means is that a suitably defined *one-parameter* model could explain nearly all risk in these markets! An analysis of the structure of the first principal component shows that it is very much like a duration parameter in that weights on the various pure discount bond returns grow with maturity. However, this principal component is *not* identical to duration, and it accounts for a more general shift in the term structure.

**EXHIBIT 59–5**
**Risk Explained by Principal Components**

| Market | First | Second | Third |
|---|---|---|---|
| Canada | 93.3% | 98.5% | 99.4% |
| U.S. | 95.6 | 98.5 | 99.7 |
| Japan | 92.4 | 98.0 | 99.6 |
| Germany | 91.1 | 98.2 | 99.6 |
| U.K. | 89.4 | 99.2 | 99.8 |
| Netherlands | 97.8 | 99.9 | 100 |
| Switzerland | 91.8 | 97.2 | 98.4 |
| France | 94.6 | 99.1 | 99.7 |
| Australia | 96.8 | 99.4 | 99.8 |
| Denmark | 95.3 | 99.2 | 99.8 |

Source: BARRA

The second principal component exhibits weights on short interest rates of opposite sign to those on the longer rates. Roughly, this can be interpreted as a twisting of the term structure. Finally, the third principal component, which, as the exhibit shows, contributes very little to the model's total explanatory power, weights the noninterest-rate factors.

Thus, our analysis of the covariance matrix shows at most three independent risk factors in each of the single-market models. These 30 principal components (3 per market, 10 markets) can now be used to construct a risk model allowing for the analysis of portfolios with assets from any market. Of course, the currency issue remains and we now turn to this aspect of the analysis of international portfolios.


## CURRENCY RISK

A full analysis of the currency aspect of international investment is a topic for a book in itself. However, we can say a few things regarding currency in the context of the multimarket risk model we have developed in this discussion. Thus far we have a risk model that captures the "within market" variation of returns as well as the relationships of the principal component factors across markets. Further, the analysis shows that the use of principal components sacrifices nothing in terms of the power of the model to account for risk. Now, if exchange rates were perfectly determined by interest rates, the story would be basically finished. However, other factors enter into the equation of exchange rate determination, so currencies must be added explicitly.

The final step in constructing our risk model for multicurrency portfolios is adding currency returns to the covariance matrix. It is important to realize that we must carefully define the currency returns to ensure that the separation between local market returns and currency returns is valid.

In deriving the separation property of currencies versus securities, we require a few definitions:

rx ≡ return due to exchange rate changes

rc ≡ exchange return plus short-term interest

rfl ≡ local risk-free interest rate

From these definitions, we have the following relationship:

$$1 + rc = (1 + rx) \times (1 + rfl) \tag{59-4}$$

This says that an investment in a currency earns not only the return from changes in the exchange rate with the base or numeraire currency but also the risk-free rate in the foreign market. For example, a U.K. investor buying dollars would earn the return for changes in the £/$ rate plus the interest on the short-term instrument, in this case a Treasury bill.

Now we turn to the returns to assets or bonds in the fixed income case. Again we require a few definitions:

rl ≡ total return on an asset for the *local* investor

rfn ≡ risk-free return in the numeraire market

r ≡ asset return from the numeraire perspective

Thus, we have

$$(1 + r) = (1 + rx) \times (1 + rl) \qquad (59–5)$$

Finally we translate this numeraire total return figure to numeraire *excess* return:

$$\text{Numeraire excess return} \equiv (1 + r) - (1 + rfn) = r - rfn \qquad (59–6)$$

From these definitions, we can use a simple algebraic manipulation to derive the separation property we are seeking:

$$r - rfn \approx (rx + rfl - rfn) + (rl - rfl) \qquad (59–7)$$

Interpreting Equation (59–7) we see that from the numeraire perspective, that is the investor's domicile, excess return to an asset is approximately[12] equal to the sum of the numeraire excess currency return and the local excess return of the asset. We now have the desired separation of currency and local market returns.

This exercise is required to complete the risk model for multicurrency fixed income portfolios. By defining returns in the manner described above, the full risk model is complete and one can analyze the risk of any portfolio of bonds and currencies.

## SUMMARY

This chapter has presented approaches first for constructing valuation models for fixed income securities and second for assessing the risk in portfolios of these assets. The linkages across markets in the form of currencies have also been addressed in a manner that facilitates the analysis of risk by separating the local market aspects from those purely attributable to currency fluctuations.

---

[12] For this approximation, we are ignoring the cross product term $rx \cdot rl$, which, for all practical purposes is very close to zero over one-month horizons. Note, however, that we do not ignore the correlation of rx and rl, which is important for risk analysis.

The valuation models proposed are based on the estimation of the interest rate or term structure in each market along with the market-specific factors that distinguish the assets. Interest rates are found to be of greatest importance in valuing securities. However, by identifying features of assets in addition to interest rates that investors view as important, we are able to refine further the valuation models.

Having developed for each market a valuation model based on about 10 or 12 parameters, we have shown that the risk in these markets can be explained by only 2 or 3 parameters. Using the technique of principal components analysis, we derived a set of *hybrid* parameters that were independent within each market. We showed that the first three components captured essentially all of the explanatory power of the original dozen or so parameters. Hence we were able to reduce the dimensionality of the overall model to a manageable number.

Finally, we showed that by suitably defining returns, we could separate local market returns from currency returns. This facilitated the analysis by making local market return independent of the investor's domicile.

# CHAPTER 60

## FORECASTING INTEREST RATES

W. David Woolford, CFA
*Managing Director*
*Prudential Insurance Company of America*

## INTRODUCTION

There is no shortage of interest-rate forecasts, although only a small segment of the population dares to make this the sole basis for a career. Each day individuals buy and sell money for various time periods, both for their own account and as agents or investment advisors. Whether the analyses leading to their decisions are shallow or deep, rigorous or emotional, the outcome of these myriad decisions—in the cash markets, financial futures markets, with and without the assistance of financial intermediaries—is a series of interest rates for various maturities and types of securities. This series, in turn, can be decomposed—though imperfectly—into a consensus forecast for interest rates. That consensus provides a benchmark for successful forecasting. Improve on this consensus consistently (net of transaction and opportunity costs), and the forecast has been profitable. However, not everyone can succeed, for the consensus, by definition, has been established by an equal weighting of dollars on both sides.

For many market professionals, the difficulty in consistently correctly predicting shifts in the consensus has led to a refocus of their analyses toward topics outlined elsewhere in this volume. That new focus entails a goal not so much to outguess the consensus as to exploit even momentary adjustment lags, to arbitrage cash and futures markets, and to construct portfolios that offer significant upside potential but have already built-in limits to downside risk. These adjustments in focus are not free, however, and returns from such activity will not exceed the market average unless the professional can somehow combine this activity with better information, transaction or scale economies, or a cheaper access to financing.

This chapter, however, is intended to lay the groundwork for those daring (or foolish) enough to attempt to improve on the consensus. For those so determined, a large body of literature stands ready to prepare (and perhaps dissuade) the uninitiated. With few exceptions, methods can be catalogued in two groups.

At one extreme are multisector models, simplifications of the economy that seek to explain interest-rate behavior from the interactions of a wide range of hypothetical economic actors in a hypothetical economy containing various degrees of realism. Among the large multisector models providing users with excellent equation/sector descriptions and analyses are Wharton, Data Resources, and The WEBA Group. Such models need not be composed of several hundred interacting equations. They may also be grossly oversimplified—a restatement of the demand for money to forecast interest rates, for example—but they share a common element; that is, the forecast for interest rates is based on a pattern of causality from one or more economic variables that is expected to be reproduced, on average, in the future.

At the other extreme are projections that lack any causal specification but rather are based on an analysis of technical factors. Again, such technical activity may be limited to charting relationships or may be very sophisticated time series analyses. These models lack the structural specification that, say, conditions A, B, and C will be associated with result X in strength Y within time T. However, they share one commonality with structural models. Both seek to explain the future on the basis of the past. Furthermore, only a biased sample of past data can be used. When combined with the range of innovation in financial markets over the past century, and particularly in the past 25 years, this selection bias helps to explain why identical models in the hands of different forecasters can produce sharply varying results.

Just how different can be seen from a survey of interest-rate forecasts. At the end of 1980, for example, a small group of forecasters, presumably with access to identical information and to each other, saw fit to disagree on the outlook for interest rates one year later to such an extent that the range of forecasts for the interest rate on Federal funds spanned 900 basis points. For most cyclical experiences over the past two centuries, that range exceeds the actual trough-to-peak and peak-to-trough movements in interest rates. Of course, the final months of 1980 were exceptionally difficult times in which to forecast the level of interest rates, and forecasters generally agreed on their future direction (down). Recent forecasts, such as those made at the end of 1988 for year-end, 1989, are much more in agreement as to the level of interest rates one year later.

Consensus forecasts display considerably less variation, as might be expected from an average. An estimate of the consensus forecast, prepared roughly at the same time as the forecasts above, is shown in Exhibit 60–1. In retrospect, it proved to be a tough standard for 1981.

Estimates of the market consensus cannot be prepared directly from interest rates quoted in cash or futures markets, except in the case of pure discount

**EXHIBIT 60–1**

**Forecasts for the Federal Funds Rate Prepared One Year Earlier** (Actual Data Rounded)

| Forecast for Year-end | 1981 | 1985 | 1989 |
|---|---|---|---|
| Estimate for market consensus | 12.8% | 10.0% | 8.5% |
| Forecast 1 | 8.0 | 12.0 | 9.6 |
| Forecast 2 | 11.0 | 6.0 | 8.1 |
| Forecast 3 | 14.0 | 8.0 | 6.7 |
| Forecast 4 | 16.0 | 11.3 | 10.4 |
| Forecast 5 | 17.0 | 9.3 | 5.3 |
| Actual rate at year-end (weekly average) | 12.9 | 9.6 | NA |
| Actual funds rate at time of forecast (monthly average) | 18.9 | 8.4 | 8.8 |

Note: Identities of forecasters are not constant over time. The consensus has been extrapolated from forward rates implicit in the Treasury yield curve and assumes that funds carried a 100-basis point premium to Treasury instruments in 1981, and 50 basis points in 1985 and in 1989.

instruments. The usual specification of interest rates in bond markets, however, is the conventional yield-to-maturity, an internal rate of return calculation that assumes that all coupon payments can be reinvested at this internal rate of return until maturity. Furthermore, the bond markets contain a vast heterogeneity of instruments bearing differing call, default risk, liquidity premia, and other features.

The first difficulty with the conventional yield-to-maturity specification is largely computational. A complete description of the term structure can be created by estimating a well-defined concept, the *spot rate*. The spot rate is the rate that, compounded over the period, gives the return that the market would demand for a pure discount instrument for that period, say $T$. (With pure discount instruments, reinvestment risk is eliminated.) As $T$ is varied, the sequence of spot rates traces out the term structure. Equivalently, this also describes a series of forward rates—the incremental return in varying $T$. Hence the spot rate, $R_T$, is equivalent to the geometric average of all forward rates, $r_i$.

$$1 + R_T = (1 + r_1)(1 + r_2)\ldots(1 + r_R)\ldots(1 + r_T)$$

Any member of this series of forward rates, in turn, can be decomposed into an anticipated interest rate, $F$, and a liquidity premium, $L$.

$$1 + r_k = (1 + F_k)(1 + L_k) \qquad k = 1, 2, \ldots T$$

Until recently, spot rates had to be estimated from a sample of securities. (In practice, the yield curve was estimated using Treasury securities to minimize default risk and bias introduced by call features.) However, major Wall Street investment bankers have introduced a series of spot rate products—bearing various trademarks—and the U.S. Treasury has recently seen fit to recognize the success of these products by agreeing that new Treasury issues can be disaggregated (stripped) into their spot rate components and also reconstituted. The Treasury's decision makes the product more generic and easily transferable and should spawn a number of new academic studies and portfolio techniques.

This market will remove some of the errors in estimating spot rates but will not end the debate over the shape and magnitude of term premiums until more complete markets are available in forwards than the current futures markets contain. The advent of organized futures markets had been expected to provide an important laboratory for the study of financial markets and the market consensus. Results of initial experiments, however, were greeted with consternation when it became apparent that forward cash market and futures rates were not equal, despite their apparent theoretical equivalence. However, that apparent inconsistency has been resolved by noting, first, differences in tax treatments in cash and futures transactions and (a more fundamental difference) the cost of guaranteeing futures contracts in an organized market (Kane [45]).[1] Despite the reserves carried by the organized exchanges, residual risk does exist—a futures contract on a default-free security does not make the contract default free. The price to be paid for bearing the residual risk is sufficient to generate differences in prices for cash market and futures claims.

Interest will continue to focus on the stability of liquidity, or term, premiums. There is some empirical support for the following argument: Although the postwar average liquidity (term) premium has ranged from perhaps 15 to 20 basis points in very short bill maturities, to 50 to 75 basis points for three-month rates six months forward, to perhaps 200 basis points or more at longer forwards, these liquidity premia will vary procyclically over the business cycle.[2]

For the interest-rate forecaster, however, each of these considerations might pale in comparison with the more difficult task of preparing an alternative to the consensus. Empirical research, particularly work by Roll [65] and Pesando [61], has shown that the consensus sets a high standard by which to be judged. Fame and fortune have accrued to those fortunate enough to top the consensus, but forecasts by those less fortunate lie in unmarked graves. Thus, an understanding

---

[1] For clarity, numbers in brackets are used to footnote references. Corresponding numbered references are contained in the bibliography at the end of this chapter.

[2] The origin of the liquidity premium is itself a source of debate. It may reflect moneyness, perceived default risk (including credit or interest-rate controls), or changes in the volatility of interest rates. For example, Throop [75] found that the standard deviation of rates is significantly related to a measure of the liquidity premium for Treasury bill rates in some specifications. In general, however, there is no hard agreement as yet on either the underlying cause(s) or the empirical size of liquidity premiums.

of the consensus is important as a benchmark. The consensus is also useful as a neutral position when other methods offer no clear strategy, which occurs more frequently than most fixed income managers care to admit.

## STRUCTURAL MODELS

The heart of all structural models used in interest-rate forecasting is a description of the supply of funds to the credit markets and the demand for these funds. This equilibrium has been summarized (and embellished in numerous ways) in the so-called Hicksian Cross, or IS-LM framework.[3]   Exhibit 60–2 shows the determinations of interest rates and economic activity under this framework. This IS curve traces the locus of points along which savings (often assumed to be simply proportional to economic activity, although clearly responsive to interest rates as they reflect the reward for postponing expenditures, and not just anticipated inflation) are equal to investment (whose level is a function of some kind of hurdle rate derived from the marginal efficiency of capital). Clearly, both can be made conditional on various monetary and fiscal policies. This curve is downward sloping because lower interest rates would be found as higher levels of economic activity increased the flow of savings and because increased investment reduces the marginal return on investment. (However, the slope is reversed in comparing interest rates and inflation. The anticipation of accelerated inflation rates reduces savings, forcing higher interest rates.) Similarly, LM measures the locus of points along which money supply and money demand are equal and is an upward-sloping function, reflecting a higher demand for money as economic activity increases.[4]

The intersection of the proximate determinants of increments to the flow of funds, as expressed by the IS curve, and monetary factors determines the equilibrium interest rate. Forecasting interest rates would appear to be merely a matter of forecasting determinants of IS and LM. In fact, this is the route taken by early structural models and continued up to this day (though with a significant upgrading in sophistication) by many econometric model builders.

Structural models, of which IS-LM is the major form, offer the only means currently available to evaluate structural changes in the economy, including changes in operating procedures for monetary and fiscal policies. Their failure to produce above-average forecasts, however (see Pesando [61] and McNees

---

[3] This is also sometimes mistakenly called the Keynesian cross. Keynes himself may have felt that a somewhat different interpretation of the interest rate was in order. See Meltzer [51].

[4] This sidesteps both the precise definition of *moneyness*, used in forecasting interest rates, and the interest elasticity of the demand for money function. Despite the wealth of empirical tests of this elasticity, its value remains a matter of dispute. Recent discussions of the "stability" of the demand for money implicitly argue that with interest-rate volatility, estimation errors have increased.

**EXHIBIT 60–2**
**IS-LM Relationships**

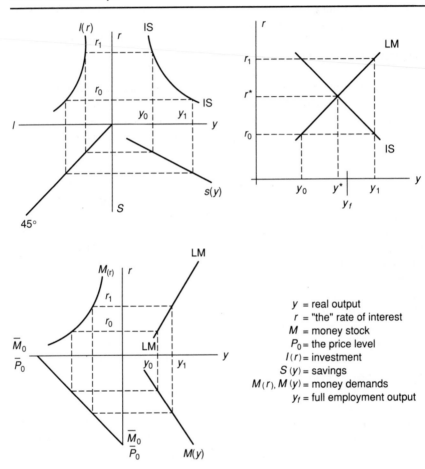

$y$ = real output
$r$ = "the" rate of interest
$M$ = money stock
$P_0$ = the price level
$I(r)$ = investment
$S(y)$ = savings
$M(r), M(y)$ = money demands
$y_f$ = full employment output

[53]), has produced a healthy skepticism directed at econometric models. Users of these models should be aware of a number of shortcomings. The following is only a partial catalogue.

## Stability

Large econometric models include a substantial number and variety of feedback relations. Changes in farm prices, for example, alter trade balances and affect farm machinery sales, industrial orders and employment, personal income, food consumption, and farm prices. Lower interest rates (e.g., from an unexpectedly expansionary monetary policy) initially increase investment and economic activity, increase prices of assets (including common stocks), and spur additional borrowing, thereby forcing interest rates to reverse their initial decline. Not infrequently, specification of individual feedback relationships produces simultaneity in which model specification must be altered (*add-factored* is the professional euphemism) to produce convergence. Usual practice is for model-building entrepreneurs to permit users to interact with the ultimate system, but such a "simulation" leaves the model's response framework unchanged; reestimation to explore alternative specifications is not particularly user-friendly. Some modelers do report dynamic Monte Carlo simulations that provide more accurate error bounds on forecasts, but again these projections of forecast errors are conditional on the future appropriateness of the underlying model structure.

Several chapters in this book deal with the portfolio and specific problems introduced by optionable securities, especially mortgage instruments. Researchers in these securities are particularly sensitive to the dangers of assuming that an underlying model structure will persist into the future. As one analyst aptly put it, "The fact that a pool has recently experienced faster-than-expected prepayment may merely indicate that the pool's fast payers are now in someone else's pools."

## Identification

The proverbial introductory economics examination question: "We observe a decline in interest rates. Investment demand must have fallen." In terms of Exhibit 60–2, a fall in investment demand (a shift to the right of $I(r)$) is consistent with a decline in interest rates, but this decline is also consistent with a host of other phenomena, including a shifting savings behavior. Identification of the large model equivalents of IS and LM relationships usually involves simplifying assumptions on the determinants and specification of interest-sensitive relationships in order to distinguish demand and supply.

## Specification Error

Pressures for convergence and identification will lead to specification bias. Forecasts of an upturn in interest rates may be conditional on a prior upturn in inflation, for example, when there is considerable evidence that the reverse is true. Wage gains may *lead* rather than (correctly) *lag* inflation. Wealth effects may operate with unacceptably long or short lags to be consistent with other equilibrium conditions. Long-run, own-price elasticities may be estimated to be no larger than short-run responses. Consequently, volatility will be damped. This is a necessary concomitant of regression procedures but one that can have the unfortunate side effect of increasing the apparent explanatory power of one-factor models while failing to capture the unique characteristics that can distinguish a correct forecast from the consensus.

A full description of various models and their specific features cannot be attempted in this chapter. However, model builders and buyers should ask for some minimum requirements if the model is to be useful in answering hypotheses on the impact of structural changes on levels of interest rates:

1. Over long periods of time, inflation is essentially a monetary phenomenon. Over that same time frame, the primary determinant of the level of interest rates is inflation. Short-run relationships of money stock, inflation, and interest rates, however, are highly variable. Nevertheless, models that seek to forecast interest rates should have steady state characteristics consistent with the long-run rate of inflation having a consistent relationship with long-run growth in the money stock. One test of a model is to double the growth rate of the quantity of money and maintain the new growth for a sustained period of time. Since no change has been made to the productivity function for money, long-run steady state should see the rate of inflation roughly double because there is no reason in this context to expect a permanent increase in the underlying demand for money balances. Does the model show the predicted response?

2. Concerning the government budget constraint, how does the model close the identity that Treasury outlays must match receipts from taxes and debt issue, including debt sales through the intermediary of the central bank? What mechanism, if any, is there for the central bank's response to the deficit? Earlier mechanisms specified this response as one in which the central bank's willingness to absorb the deficit via open-market debt purchases was a positive function of the level of interest rates.[5] These mechanisms are perhaps appropriate so long as the central bank follows an interest-rate target, but their applicability was sharply reduced by recent changes in operating procedures. Specification of the central bank's reaction function is not an easy task. Moreover, heightened recognition of the central bank's importance in the inflationary process has increased the focus on this reaction function. For example, the fear that deficits will ultimately be monetized because of pressures from political or economic events can lead to substantial term premiums.

3. Under an interest-rate target, what mechanism exists to model the central bank's reaction function when the target is incompatible with price

---

[5] Focus on this factor assumes that there is not a high interest elasticity of demand for money. If there is—Keynes' so-called liquidity trap—interest rates are insensitive to changes in money supply, and it is immaterial how the deficit is financed. Empirically, however, a liquidity trap has not characterized the postwar period.

stability? Many models contain no such bridge, pretending that an infinitely elastic reserve supply procedure can nevertheless co-exist with a determinant price level. The fault generally lies in a failure to specify a clearing mechanism for *aggregate* demand, replacing this with $n - 1$ clearing markets in a way that confuses relative prices with the aggregate price level. Such a model cannot capture interest-rate movements.

4. Is there a monetary explanation of the exchange rate (and, if applicable, central bank intervention)? External/internal balance is particularly important because of the potential to only partly specify credit demand if the Euromarket is ignored.[6] Hartman [39] found support for the hypothesis that a significant part of variation in short-term U.S. interest rates in the 1975–78 period was attributable to foreign influences. His work predates, but anticipates, the recent debate on the impact of record U.S. trade deficits on domestic capital markets.

5. How is credit market equilibrium specified? Although money supply growth is the primary determinant of the long-term level of inflation, inflation is the rate of change of the purchasing power of money. Interest rates specify the price of credit—the rate for exchanging future claims on consumption for present claims. Clearly, their most important determinant will be the time path of anticipated price changes for these consumption claims over the period, and this explains the attention paid to projecting expectations of inflation rates and actual inflation rates in interest-rate-forecasting models. In the short run, however, other factors can combine to generate sharply different interest-rate conditions than would be projected on the basis of inflation expectations. Adjustment lags, institutional conditions (disintermediation, for example), central bank and Treasury financing activity, inventory adjustments, and other factors can all produce interest-rate environments that differ, short term, from what expectations of inflation might suggest.

Ultimately such temporary conditions will be arbitraged. Many models of credit market conditions provide such arbitrage. The user should be careful to analyze the following:

1. Analyze whether or not such arbitrage exists. Can interest rates permanently fail to reflect expected inflation? If so, the model is useful only for very short-term timing activities and is inconsistent with equilibrium.

---

[6] In principle, Walras' Law ensures that if $n - 1$ markets can be shown to clear, the $n$th market must also be in equilibrium. Domestic asset markets, however, cannot be fully specified, so Walras' law cannot be used to justify omitting consideration of foreign influences on the domestic interest-rate environment. Indeed, for small countries with open capital markets, foreign influences are the most important determinant of interest rates.

2. Analyze whether or not the credit market specification closes the asset and liability sides of the relationship. For example, some flow-of-funds models contain no constraint on loan growth from funding—implicitly assuming an infinitely elastic supply of bank reserves by the central bank. In such an environment, however, no meaningful specification of the level or movement in interest rates is possible, and the entire model should be discarded. (In terms of the IS–LM framework, such a model presumes a horizontal LM function.)

## Rational Expectations

Even if these checks produce a satisfactory report, model users face a potentially insurmountable obstacle to improving on the consensus forecast in the form of rational expectations.[7] Early models of expectations merely specified some mechanically extrapolative formation of expectations—distributed lags, for example. No attempt was made to see if this was consistent with competitive equilibrium in, say, the capital markets. When such tests of equilibrium were performed, however, it became clear that mechanical formulations of expectations (whether adaptive, regressive, inertial, extrapolative, or some combination) would only be accurate if markets offered unexploited profits.[8] Market participants could consequently improve on mechanical extrapolations, and would if markets were efficient. In an efficient market, interest-rate forecasting would be defined as the solution to the following exercise:

1. Assume that the change in interest rates, $dr$, is linear in the information set, $S$, needed to forecast changes in interest rates. Then to a first-order approximation, the change in interest rates, $dr$, can be described by

$$dr = f(S, V) \qquad (60\text{--}1)$$

where $V$ is a serially uncorrelated error term independent of $S$.
2. By definition, $S$ is not known to all or even a significant number of capital market participants, or interest rates would already reflect this information. This is equivalent to saying that data on interest-rate de-

---

[7] There is a tendency to confuse rational expectations with market efficiency because tests for these phenomena are joint tests. Market efficiency implies that prices already efficiently use available information. Forecasters cannot expect to improve on the market consensus unless they have access to new information at above-average efficiency or (what amounts to the same thing) have additional information. Efficiency can be produced with all market participants behaving irrationally—that is, in ways other than consistently in their own best interests.

[8] Adaptive expectations adjust the new forecast by a proportion of the error between forecast and actual values; regressive expectations project that the actual return will adjust to its previous level (equilibrium) over a period of time. (See, for example, Dobson, Sutch, and Vanderford [17].)

terminants, $K$, can be decomposed into two components, information already available $(K_{-1})$ and $S$:

$$K = f(K_{-1} S) \qquad (60\text{-}2)$$

3. Statistically, an estimate for $S$ can be derived from errors in Equation (60-2). Efficient market theory would argue that estimates of $S$ in Equation (60-2) will be serially independent. Otherwise lagged values of $S$ could be used to improve estimates in this equation. These estimates of $S$ can then be used in Equation (60-1) to solve for $dr$. If the efficient markets hypothesis holds, lagged values of $S$ will have no significance for $dr$ in Equation (60-1). Furthermore, at the margin, the cost of collecting $S$ and estimating its impact should roughly equal its value in estimating $dr$.[9]

Note that this does not preclude improving on the market consensus in forecasting short-term rates, because there is no arbitrage opportunity in serial dependence to exploit—a one-period bond matures in the same period as information is available. References elsewhere in this chapter supporting apparent improvements in the market forecast, in fact, are uniformly limited to short-term rates. Furthermore, the longer the forecast horizon, the weaker is the evidence for market efficiency, in part because term premiums will display (cyclical) variability.[10]

The difficulty that rational expectations presents to model builders is that it hypothesizes that market participants will *alter* their behavior to reduce unexploited profit opportunities—in terms of the above framework that participants consistently reduce the expected value of information needed to forecast changes in interest rates, $E(S/S_{-1})$—to zero. Profitable arbitrages cannot persist. This means that the response coefficients estimated from a structural model, which has been of necessity based on past reactions, will change depending on the actual outcome.

The reader interested in pursuing this problem with respect to the term structure should always be aware that since rationality is specified in the sense that expectations must be consistent with predictions deriving from economic and statistical theory and since the term structure is also estimated from the same data set, the test will be a joint test of rational expectations formations and the hypothetical term structure.[11]

---

[9] For a further discussion and some estimates, see Evans [20] and Pesando [61]. Evans' estimates, however, should be carefully reviewed because of statistical problems created by overlapping sample intervals reducing degrees of freedom.

[10] For a similar but more restrictive view on the potential for successful forecasting, see Pesando [61].

[11] See, for example, Modigliani and Shiller [56].

The question of rationality also has been addressed with regard to the Fisher equation. Irving Fisher postulated that the nominal rate of interest would equal the rate of return from holding real assets together with the expected rate of inflation on these assets. The Fisher equation is easily understood in theory. Its use in practical forecasting is largely limited to longer term asset equilibrium. The equation is

$$(1 + i_t) = (1 + r_t)(1 + p_t)(1 + g_t) \qquad (60\text{–}3)$$

where
$\quad i_t$ = the nominal interest rate
$\quad r_t$ = the default–free real return
$\quad p_t$ = the anticipated rate of inflation
$\quad g_t$ = the "risk premium"

At this level of generality, $g_t$ can be linked to many sources: default risk, term or other issuer options, the volatility of inflation, or taxes, to name a few. Clearly, $g_t$ can be positive or negative. Although there is no agreement on either the size or stability of $r_t$, Friedman and Schwartz [29], in an encyclopedic study of monetary developments in the United States and United Kingdom, argue that over the past century roughly a 3 percent figure would have been appropriate. Accepting this figure, a portfolio manager would choose a rate of inflation that he or she expected to persist at the end of a given period, set $r_t$ equal to 300 basis points, and add any additional premiums to solve for $i_t$ in Equation (60–3). That solution could then be compared with forward rates available given the current term-structure vector consistent with Equation (60–1). The excess (deficient) available return, on a risk-adjusted basis, can then be used as an input in asset allocation. The real rate cannot be simulated from averaging *ex post* data. For example, Ibbotson and Sinquefield [44] found that the average real return to an investment in long-term Treasury securities was 0.7 percent between 1926 and 1987. This is an estimate of the real rate if, over the period, average errors in estimating $p$ were zero and the average value of $g$ was zero. Realized real returns are heavily impacted by unanticipated inflation. (From 1926 to 1950, realized real returns were 2.7 percent—much closer to the 3 percent figure of Friedman and Schwartz.)

The tenuous short-term connection between inflation and interest rates limits the practical use of this relation to longer term asset equilibrium. The Fisher equation holds so long as real assets and bonds are arbitraged by investors— in other words, an efficient market. Tests by Fama [21] supported the joint test of rationality and a constant real rate, but this result has been the subject of significant criticisms, particularly Fama's use of the Consumer Price Index as an index of real asset prices. However, for those determined to forecast interest rates through forecasts of inflation, Fama's tests are disturbing because they appear to support the argument that current interest rates already contain *all* relevant information about inflation (in other words, interest rates may operate as the best predictor of inflation), but the reverse does not hold.

Such a finding would deal a harsh blow to forecasts based on projections of inflation, although it would still leave open the question of whether or not it is possible to develop projections of the real rate (whether or not the real rate should properly be treated as a constant, either in analytical or forecasting applications, remains an open question). Recent evidence questioning the cyclical constancy of the natural rate of unemployment, for example, indirectly supports the hypothesis that the real rate of interest also varies. Evidence along this same vein is now available from Great Britain, where the first large-scale use of index-linked bonds in a moderate inflation environment (so that a long-term capital market exists) appears to show that most of the movement in nominal interest rates reflects changes in expected inflation, but real interest rates are sensitive to expectations of the strength of economic activity [82].

A different question is addressed by the preferred habitat thesis, which argues that interest rates on different instruments will reflect demand and supply by major participants in these sectors. For example, this thesis would forecast that a major determinant of changes in negotiable certificate of deposit rates will be the future path of bank loan demand or that prices for corporate bonds will reflect demand for these securities by such typical institutional purchasers as insurance and pension fund portfolios. Such a hypothesis is often implicitly used by flow-of-funds forecasts in projecting various kinds of new issue indigestion because traditional purchasers will be unable to absorb forthcoming supply. The Fisher equation, as noted, relies for its validity on arbitrage between real goods and bonds. As an aid to short-term run forecasts, preferred habitat rests on an even more fragile reed—the lack of arbitrage, except at substantial premiums, between various sectors of the debt markets. As initially proposed by Modigliani and Sutch [57], preferred habitat reflects differences in investor time period preferences for consumption. Cox, Ross, and Ingersoll's extension [15] to differing risk preferences does not alter the fundamental difficulty that forecasting interest rates on the basis of preferred habitat requires an institutional or other rationale for the absence of arbitrageurs. It is thus a disequilibrium situation, observable at times but extremely difficult to forecast on a systematic basis. In fact, Singleton [71, p. 612] found no evidence that maturity-specific disturbances could explain a significant part of yield movements for Treasury securities. Except for the one-year bill, he said, "the specific processes appeared to be generated by serially uncorrelated processes and, thus, [were] of no value for forecasting future interest rates." Singleton was led to conclude that "if institutional variables have an effect, then it will be through their influence on liquidity premiums and expectations."

Projecting interest-rate movements by ascribing future twists in the yield curve to preferred habitat remains a popular, if questionable, practice. The following are some examples:

1. Bank portfolios tend to purchase Treasury securities in 2- to 7- (occasionally 10-) year maturities to speculate on interest-rate movements (by mismatching asset and liability durations). This speculation has historically been associated with weakening loan demand and downward pressure on bank earnings; this correlation has weakened as banks have come to view their portfolios less as sources of liquidity for loan demand and more as separate profit centers. If the hypothesis is valid, one would expect to find, other things equal, upward pressure on these maturities when loan demand is very strong.

2. Insurance companies and pension fund managers are traditional buyers of longer term fixed income securities. Their asset allocation and available funding, then, should twist the yield curve up or down for these instruments relative to other maturities. (The author knows of no valid evidence for this statement.)

3. Many analysts view short-term interest rates as purely demand determined, arguing that the aggregate supply of short-term credit will be insensitive to interest rates because of a lack of liquid investment alternatives. The statement has been used to justify forecasts of short-term rates well below inflation rates. Though perhaps valid for some investors, it neglects the ability of other investors to alter their asset/liability structure. For example, inordinately high short-term interest rates will encourage borrowing long to lend short; the reverse will be true at levels of short-term rates viewed as excessively low.

4. The Euromarkets are typically viewed as financial markets for overnight to 15-year maturities, although the market's growth has brought a full spectrum of maturities. The view that strong foreign demand for dollars will reduce domestic interest rates is true, other things equal, but there is no reason to expect that temporary discrepancies with domestic markets in particular maturities will not be arbitraged by changes in *issuer* maturity selection. This arbitrage accounts for tightened links between domestic and Eurodollar markets. For example, in 1985, issuer interest in seven-year securities partly, and perhaps largely, reflected opportunities offered by the swap market. The swap involves exchange of fixed-rate cash flows for floating-rate cash flows over a five- or seven-year period. The Euromarket's ability to offer strong domestic credits access to the seven-year maturity spectrum at a yield competitive with Treasuries on an all-in swap basis facilitated closer links to the domestic markets. The evidence that new Eurodollar instruments will offer more fleeting above-average returns coincides with increased interest by institutions in this country and elsewhere in international dollar and nondollar floating income vehicles.

## Recap

This brief review of structural models may appear to have been a uniformly negative one. In fact, the scale of criticism that can be brought to bear is testimony to the wealth of knowledge that has been accumulated in this area. Future work directed at liquidity premia and rational expectations can pay further dividends in expanding knowledge, although it is clear that profitable forecasts are dependent on use of unprocessed or normally unavailable information or as a side benefit to necessary participation in risk-bearing. There are several directions that this may take:

1. Processing of information has improved. Time-series analysis has produced, in some instances, forecasts that improve on implicit forward rates. One recent states/space improvement on ARIMA is the contribution by Fildes and Fitzgerald [25]. Improved time-series models have become increasingly available to serious portfolio managers. Their appeal should be particularly strong to forecasters interested in constructing benchmark forecasts independent of their personal interpretation of history. There remains the hurdle of quantifying changing response patterns to new information. This is a fertile and productive field for Bayesian analysis.

2. There has now been sufficient empirical evidence to question the applicability of the simple one-factor capital asset pricing model in equity markets. Bond price variability has increased to reflect the increased variability of inflation. (This was predictable. With the acceleration of inflation, either yields could remain low and price variability low, giving bonds the character of a nominal option with a suboptimal return, or returns and risks could both rise.) Despite the more univariate character of bonds, this has spurred interest in an application of the arbitrage pricing theory [66] in which compensation for bearing risk is composed of several premia. Elsewhere in this volume, work reported on the respective values for call options, sinking funds, warrants, and other extendable/retractable features permits the price of a bond to be expressed as the sum of various risk premia. In turn, the term structure can be viewed as a piecewise continuous set of risk premia for capital and reinvestment risks.

3. Quantitative research into business cycles has improved. A review of current methodology in the following pages makes the gaps in this area readily apparent. However, the need to estimate rational expectations models incorporating predictable response coefficients stands as a major stumbling block to useful forecasting improvements to this area.[12]

---

[12]This point has been made in another context by Al Wojnilower [84, p. 278]: "Because of the major structural changes in finance between most successive cycles, the behavior of financial data, including monetary aggregates, also is likely to have different implications from cycle to cycle."

## BUSINESS-CYCLE MODELS

A charitable view of less-than-perfect performance of large-scale forecasting models would be that their useful features are already incorporated in the term structure, as market efficiency would suggest. Of course, this has also had the impact of maintaining interest in other forecasting procedures with various levels of naivete.

Any examination of the term structure over the business cycle should begin with Phillip Cagan's three intensive studies of cyclical movements in interest rates (in [36] and [37]) augmented by his exhaustive examination of trends and cycles in the quantity of money [11]. There has been a clear tendency for interest-rate cycles to better anticipate business cycles in more recent times. This undoubtedly reflects the improved frequency and quality of economic information. Just as noticeable is a tendency for the lag in cyclical swings in long- to short-term rates to tighten. Long-term rates now exhibit peaks and troughs coincident with or even in advance of swings in short-term rates. Growth in the sophistication and activity of financial markets may be one explanation for this observation; another is the increased attention given to monetary policy and attempts by portfolio managers to anticipate shifts in policy intent. To the extent these consensus expectations prove to be correct and shifts in policy intent are consistent with the economy's cyclical character, long-term rates can lead short-term rates. To the extent they are incorrect, rate movements will display a jagged trend, and each successive error in the direction of long-term rates will lead the market to extract greater risk premiums varying with the duration (interest sensitivity) of the security and to produce a steeper (or for initially inverted cases, a flatter) yield curve. Forecasting interest-rate cycles in this formulation is thus a joint forecast of (1) the economy's underlying strength and (2) the reaction function of policymakers. This is the lesson of the 1983–88 experience. The sharp drop in interest rates that accompanied the 1982 recession produced a yield curve that, in an environment of weak short-term credit demand, carried a term premium of roughly 225 basis points between three-month and 25-year maturities. Over the next two years, short-term credit demands surged while inflation rates remained low—and the term premium reached nearly 300 basis points before declining as a cycle toward tighter monetary policies produced an expectation of temporary increases in interest rates. Studies of the term structure over the business cycle have noted some general similarities, of which the following is a sampling.

1. Since business cycles incorporate an adjustment of actual inventory to desired inventory positions that typically involves some inventory liquidation (or at least a sharp reduction in accumulation), the cessation of the liquidation stage at or near the cycle trough typically produces a relatively sharp rebound in production activity and temporary sharp upward pressure on interest rates as working capital needs expand. This

pressure relaxes for two reasons: The translation of raw materials into finished products reduces the pressure on cash flow, and initial inflation expectations generated by the contemporaneous rebound in raw material and intermediate product prices (as these inventories contract to and below target levels) are softened by the evidence of more moderate price increases at the finished goods level. With the gain in productivity as capacity utilization begins to climb, expanded profit margins are possible, further contributing to moderating pressures to raise prices while improving cash flow.

2. This upward pressure on interest rates around and following the trough typically lasts at most 6 to 12 months. It is then followed by a sharp rally that will carry bond prices back to near (or through) previous highs and yields to near (or below) their previous cyclical lows (mid-86, for example). At this point, the postwar history has been one of rising demand for funds producing a fundamental inconsistency between the interest-rate targets sought by the central bank and economic reality. Since this result is perceived only with a lag, the result is a succession of policy adjustments until policy ultimately succeeds in either pricing sufficient participants out of the market or engages in direct allocation (via disintermediation, for example) to achieve this goal.

   So long as the Federal Reserve persisted on pursuing an interest-rate target that permitted credit demands to continue to be met at prices generally below inflationary expectations, projections of interest-rate turning points at peaks were equivalent to finding evidence of the onset of disintermediation. In this respect, it is important to remember that financial institutions make forward commitments and, until recently, had no organized markets in which to offset this risk.[13]

   The composite index of leading indicators is frequently followed as an indicator of the future pattern of credit demands. However, the index, despite its relatively good track record in tracing cyclical patterns, cannot be said to provide more than a rough gauge to interest-rate movements. Interest-rate turning points are more closely linked with the reference cycle, as reflected by the composite index of coincident indicators, particularly when adjusted for a lagging recognition that the economy had entered recession. Credit demands themselves, other expert opinion notwithstanding, do not give useful signals as to the peak in interest rates, save possibly over very short-run intervals. In part, this reflects the elasticity of balance sheets of financial intermediaries together with

---

[13]Commitments are an option to the borrower that he may choose not to exercise. At this writing, markets for state-contingent claims of this sort, including the interest-rate options markets, are still relatively immature.

the fact that data to estimate supply and demand for funds are available on only a piecemeal basis for the financial system.

3. Interest rates themselves typically attempt to anticipate the peak in economic activity, resulting in a flattening and, in recent cycles, inversion in the yield curve. Inversion in prewar periods was generally linked to a liquidity crunch in the midst of monetary panic. More recently, the credit markets have exhibited sustained periods of substantial inversion. An inverted yield curve is a disequilibrium phenomenon that cannot persist in the absence of new information to alter expectations, since it projects future declines in rates. Persistent inversion requires that short-term rates continue to rise, and, furthermore, is generally accompanied by more-than-proportional increases in long-term rates that will ultimately destroy the inversion. This process reflects the adjustments to:

Disappointed expectations that rates will fall and produce capital appreciation (roughly) proportional to the duration of fixed income instruments.

Larger risk premiums, since levels of interest rates have deviated more than expected and (generally) created a stretched financial fabric.

Potential or actual political pressure for more (read: inflationary) expansionary monetary policies to relieve upward pressures on interest rates.

4. Postwar peak-to-trough declines in short-term interest rates have, on a percentage basis, been so similar as to enter the rule-of-thumb mythology. A similar stability in terms of percentage peak-to-trough declines in long-term interest rates during the postwar period can be

**EXHIBIT 60–3**
**Percent Decline in Interest Rates from Peak to Trough**

|  | (1)<br>Federal<br>Funds | (2)<br>Aaa Corporate<br>Bonds | (3)<br>Increases in<br>Inflation Rate<br>(CPI) in Prior<br>Upturn | (4)<br>(3)<br>Divided by<br>Trough Rate |
|---|---|---|---|---|
| 1957–58 | −82 | −25 | + 5.7 | 1.57 |
| 1959–61 | −71 | −19 | + 2.6 | 0.59 |
| 1966–67 | −34 | −13 | + 4.1 | 0.77 |
| 1970–71 | −59 | −22 | + 5.4 | 0.71 |
| 1974–75 | −64 | −24 | + 9.9 | 1.25 |
| 1980 | −49* | −21 | +11.9 | 1.07 |
| 1981–83 | −58 | −29 | — | — |

* Decline approximated 60 percent using weekly data.

Source: *Business Conditions Digest*, U.S. Department of Commerce.

**EXHIBIT 60–4**
**Relative Behavior of Call Money and Long-Term Treasury Yields at Troughs**

| (1)<br>Reference<br>Cycle | (2)<br>Federal<br>Funds | (3)<br>Long Treasury<br>Bonds | (4)<br>(3) − (2) |
|---|---|---|---|
| April 1958 | 0.63%<br>(May 1958) | 3.12%<br>(April 1958) | 2.49% |
| February 1961 | 1.16<br>(July 1961) | 3.73<br>(May 1961) | 2.57 |
| November 1970 | 3.71<br>(March 1971) | 5.71<br>(March 1971) | 2.00 |
| March 1975 | 5.22<br>(May 1975) | 6.66<br>(February 1975) | 1.44 |
| July 1980 | 9.03<br>(July 1980) | 9.40<br>(June 1980) | 0.37 |
| November 1982 | 8.51<br>(February 1983) | 10.19<br>(April 1983) | 1.68 |

Note: Dates in parentheses are trough months on a month-average basis.

Source: *Business Conditions Digest,* U.S. Department of Commerce.

seen in Exhibit 60–3. At the same time, however, the differential in call money and long-term Treasury yields at the trough has tended to shrink, as shown in Exhibit 60–4. This may have reflected an implicit judgment on the part of the credit market at the trough that inflation would continue to decline—a judgment largely in error thus far in the postwar period. Another of the rules-of-thumb of the postwar period is that the cyclical decline in corporate bonds will typically retrace over half the preceding trough-to-peak basis-point rise (see Exhibit 60–5).

5. Until recently, the Federal Reserve has tended to follow a policy of targeting interest rates. Use of an interest-rate target, however, demands an accurate projection of the economic climate that will be produced by that target in conjunction with other factors. Exhibit 60–6 (from Poole, [59]) illustrates how an interest-rate target produces excessive shifts in monetary policy (as described by the LM function) in response to real shocks in economic activity (a shift from $IS_0$ to $IS_1$ is produced by a cyclical upswing). The interest-rate target, however, cushions shocks produced by instability in money demand (shifts in LM). Since the Federal Reserve has no special claim to prescience, its interest-rate targets were frequently inappropriate for economic conditions. One test of the appropriateness of the Federal Reserve's various targets was the tar-

**EXHIBIT 60–5**
**High-Grade Corporate Bond Yields**

| | (1) Trough | (2) Succeeding Peak | (3) Basis Points Rise | (4) Basis Points Decline | (5) (4)/(3) |
|---|---|---|---|---|---|
| 1953–54 | 2.74 (54:3) | 4.81 (57:6) | 207 | 120 | 58% |
| 1957–58 | 3.61 (58:6) | 5.37 (59:10) | 176 | 100 | 57 |
| 1960–61 | 4.37 (61:3) | 6.14 (66:9) | 177 | 79 | 45 |
| 1966–67 | 5.35 (62:2) | 9.70 (70:6) | 435 | 216 | 50 |
| 1970–71 | 7.54* (71:2) | 10.44 (74:9) | 290 | 254 | 88 |
| 1974–75 | 7.90 (76:12) | 14.08 (80:3) | 618 | 296 | 48 |
| 1980–81 | 11.12 (80:6) | 16.97 (81:9) | 585 | 568 | 97 |
| 7-cycle average | | | | | 63% |

Note: Dates in parentheses are dates of cyclical peaks and troughs in monthly average interest rates.
* Trough in 1972 was disregarded due to price controls.

Source: *Business Conditions Digest,* U.S. Department of Commerce.

get's relationship to inflation expectations. (See Exhibit 60–7.) Recall the Fisher equation (above). An attempt to maintain an interest-rate target below inflation expectations (here proxied by the average survey response to the Michigan Survey Research Center) implies an opportunity to arbitrage goods against borrowing and pressures for accelerating monetary growth, *ultimately* forcing higher interest rates. The question of just when is "ultimately" is not an easy one for which to find empirical regularities. The Federal Reserve has chosen to alter its interest-rate targets more frequently in recent years, and target adjustments now tend to be tied to actual money supply growth relative to interim targets chosen by the Federal Reserve. Since these interim operating targets for money supply growth are not released until after the end of the interim period, however, they must be deduced by careful analysis of the operating factors within which monetary policy is conducted. These

**EXHIBIT 60–6**
**Impact on Output of Real and Monetary Shocks under Alternative Monetary Policies**

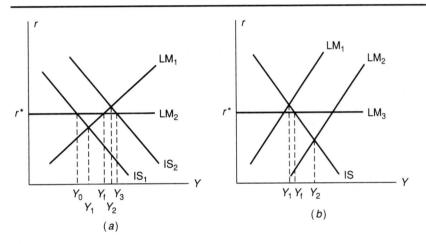

(a)

(b)

**EXHIBIT 60–7**
**Federal Funds Rate and Inflationary Expectations\* (quarterly averages)**

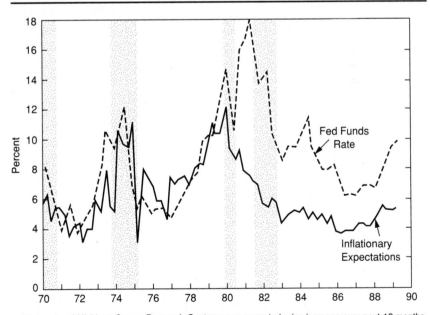

\*University of Michigan Survey Research Center; mean expected price increase over next 12 months.
Shaded areas indicate periods of contraction in business cycle activity.

Source: Federal Reserve Board; Survey Research Center, the University of Michigan.

factors are particularly important for clues to the near-term (short-run) pressures on interest rates. They do not have good predictive power for longer term trends in interest rates.

6. Cagan [37] found a "weak but significant association" between the lag in the upswing in interest rates and the duration of the following business expansion. A similar correlation was apparent for the depth of recession. The short recessions of 1960, 1970 and 1980 may reflect the nearly contemporaneous timing of reference-cycle and interest-rate peaks. However, given the increased attention to anticipating business cycles by credit market participants, it is improbable that this will be true for future business cycles.

Major interest-rate turning points have tended to complement business-cycle turning points and, increasingly, to anticipate these reference-cycle turning points. What analytical tools are available for this purpose?

The most visible and easily available is the composite index of leading economic indicators. The index is composed of indicators that tend to lead business activity and, moreover, were selected partly based on their ability to provide consistent leads with a minimum of false signals. Three consecutive one-month declines in the index do not necessarily signal impending recession; four are, however, rarely a false signal. The actual decline in the indicators prior to the peak in economic activity is not an indicator of the ultimate severity of the recession, but the author has found a good relationship between the peak-to-trough decline in the index and the depth of recession that has the intuitive appeal of rough correspondence to the cyclical component of overall economic activity.

Leading indicators have had a highly variable lead time (see Exhibit 60–8) and, during the ensuing period till recession, a substantial part of the cyclical upswing in interest rates is usually found, as credit demands become increasingly less easily postponed while credit supply is under pressure.

Interestingly, however, once the economy passes its peak, interest rates are generally already moving lower in an irregular fashion or have little upward momentum remaining. Exceptions to this statement in the 1970s tended to coincide with the clash of rising inflation and still highly regulated credit markets; with deregulation, that phase may well have passed.

An important reason for this variation lies not in the variation in cyclical experience so much as in the discrepancy between cycle and chronological time. The stages identified by Arthur Burns and Wesley Mitchell [10] in pioneering work at the National Bureau are always found in each business cycle, but as circumstances vary, the *time* necessary to complete each stage can show wide variations. Consequently, the student of business cycles seeks evidence to support an argument that the economy has passed from one stage to the next, using these points as roadposts to the potential for major sustainable turning points

**EXHIBIT 60–8**
**Leading Indicators and Cyclical Increases in Interest Rates**

| (1) Cyclical Peak | (2) Lead in Months by Composite Index of Leading Economic Indicators | Proportion of Total Cyclical Upswing Following Peak in Composite Index of Leading Economic Indicators | | Proportion of Total Cyclical Upswing Following Peak in Business Cycle | |
|---|---|---|---|---|---|
| | | (3) Yield on New Issues on Long-Term, High-Grade Corporate Bonds | (4) Three-Month Treasury Bills | (5) Yield on New Issues on Long-Term, High-Grade Corporate Bonds | (6) Three-Month Treasury Bills |
| August 1957 | 23 | 74 | 67 | — | 7 |
| April 1960 | 11 | 26 | 32 | — | — |
| September 1966* | 6 | 42 | 25 | — | 1 |
| December 1969 | 8 | 50 | 24 | 11 | 5 |
| November 1973 | 8 | 87 | 47 | 81 | 11 |
| January 1980 | 10 | 72 | 56 | 39 | 33 |
| July 1981 | 3 | 34 | 24 | 11 | 11 |
| Average, seven cycles | 10 | 55 | 39 | 20 | 10 |

* Not an official business cycle peak.

Source: U.S. Department of Commerce, *Handbook of Business Cycle Indicators.*

in interest rates, including the flattening of the yield curve and sharp run-up in interest rates that typically accompanies the final stages of the economic expansion. That evidence has become easier to gather with the widening range of easily available information. However, inflation, by increasing the dispersion and volatility of relative prices, has offset this advantage by making it more difficult to measure reference-cycle phases.

As laid out by Burns and Mitchell, the analytical study of business cycles encompasses nine stages: trough, peak, and subsequent trough, three intermediate periods of expansion, and three of contraction. For statistical purposes, their approach was to measure peaks and troughs on a centered three-month average, then divide expansions and contractions into three stages of (arbitrarily) equal length.

Most of these studies predated large-scale computers. Computers permit easy computation of inflection points, producing nine stages as before but with the initial, intermediate (inflexion), and terminal stages of unequal length. The final, more judgmental process is then to correlate various indicators as an aid to deciding the economy's current position in the cycle.

At times, cyclical indicators frequently used as indicators of interest-rate movements may have only a casual correlation to rates. Even business-cycle phases lack a perfect correlation: From 1910 to 1948 there were six cycle phases (expansions and contractions) in which there were no identifiable corresponding swings in interest rates.[14] An additional dramatic example has been provided by the behavior of spot commodity prices and long-term Treasury bond yields in 1979–81. (See Exhibit 60–9.) Casual empiricism would suggest that the weakening in commodity prices heralds an impending decline in interest rates, since either demand is weakening (lowering inflationary expectations) or supply is unexpectedly high (again with presumably beneficial effects on inflation). In 1979 and 1980 major shifts in commodity prices were nearly contemporaneous with interest-rate movements, but no such pattern was evident in 1981. The negative correlation observed in 1981 can be rationalized; high interest rates, by increasing the cost of carry, must either reduce cash prices or be matched by a rise in prices for forward (future) delivery, or both.[15] The example illustrates the undesirability of using either forward or spot prices independently in analyzing interest rates. The relationship between spot and forward prices reflects the following:

- Carrying costs including storage
- Normal backwardation (a risk premium offered cash holders)

---

[14] Phillip Cagan, "The Influence of Interest Rates on the Duration of Business Cycles," Tables 1–2, p. 15 in [37].

[15] Foreign-exchange interest parity relationships spring from the same root.

**EXHIBIT 60–9**
**Long-Term Treasury Bonds and Spot Commodity Prices**

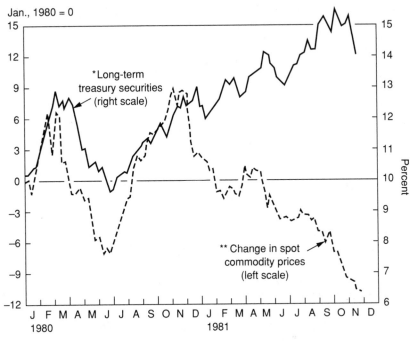

Jan., 1980 = 0

*Long-term treasury securities (right scale)

** Change in spot commodity prices (left scale)

* 20 year constant maturity.

** *Journal of Commerce*, 1947–49 = 100, change since 1/1/80. Index includes grains, foodstuffs, textiles, and metals, but does not directly measure petroleum or precious metals.

- The risk premium for noncompliance with the forward contract specifications
- The expected price change for the specific commodity

Therefore, the spot-futures arbitrage relationship will contain no new information about the *future* direction of interest rates. This also implies that analyses of the statistical relationships of spot and futures prices to forecast interest rates through inflation premia in commodity markets contain no new information. The residual information being offered by these markets as forecasts of interest rates is essentially "white noise"—a random walk that offers only the potential for arbitrage profits between markets.

Gauging a cyclical peak in economic activity has produced a relatively wide error bound on the basis of cyclical indices. Troughs can usually be gauged much more closely—largely because postwar recessions have tended to be of relatively

| Signal of Recovery | Average Lead Time (Months) |
|---|---|
| 1. Upturn in composite index of leading indicators | 3+ months |
| 2. Downturn in composite index of lagging indicators | 8 months |
| 3. Slowdown in repayments of consumer installment credit | 8+ months |
| 4. Consumer savings rate reverses the initial recession decline | 5 months |
| 5. Employment declines | 4 months |
| 6. Treasury bill rates decline | 8 months |
| 7. Long-term corporate bond yields decline | 7 months |
| 8. Net borrowed (free) reserves rise | 7+ months |
| 9. Deceleration in production decline (three-month average) | 3 months |
| 10. Housing starts rise (year-to-year) | 7+ months |
| 11. Crude material prices ease (year-to-year) | 11 months |
| 12. Adjusted-for-inflation M2 declines | 2 months |

short duration. The above compendium, by Roy Moor and Evelina Tainer of The First National Bank of Chicago, notes 12 signals of economic recovery found in the six postwar recessions to 1979.

## Spread Relationships

On the basis of published indices, business-cycle turning points are rarely identical for all types of fixed income instruments. Some frequently heard shibboleths follow:

*Municipal markets lag taxable securities.* This is a special case of the preferred habitat thesis. Banks, casualty companies, and individuals are the primary buyers of tax-exempt issues. For this statement to be correct, spreads between taxable and tax-exempt securities can tighten at and after interest-rate peaks, to the extent that buyers have a reduced need for tax-exempt income. Similarly, spreads could widen prior to the peak as demands for tax-exempt income mount, reflecting the heated pace of business activity and bracket creep. The key to arbitraging these relationships is estimating the extent to which bracket creep and tax losses will exist in upturns and downturns, respectively, and estimating the extent to which alternative vehicles, such as leasing credits, will be used to defer and manage taxes.

*Current-coupon corporate bonds will lag Treasury securities with comparable maturities in declining interest-rate environments.* Potential price appreciation in a declining rate environment will be smaller for current-coupon corporate issues than for Treasury issues because of differences in call features. Whenever interest rates are viewed to be high relative to their sustainable long-run level, the lesser call protection offered by corporate issues will cause spreads to current-coupon Treasuries to widen. To be true in a declining-rate environment for noncallable securities, however, credit quality concerns must force risk premiums to rise. This frequently happens in the initial stages of recession and then reverses as rates drop, leverage ratios improve, and balance sheets are restructured. Call option values also play a role here. At lower rate (more normal) levels, projections of volatility decline, coupon call options have less value, and spreads can tighten, even though quality premiums remain high.

*Seasonal factors tend to lead to interest-rate peaks near midyear and interest-rate troughs at the first of the new year.* In relatively efficient markets, predictable seasonal fluctuations will be anticipated. What remains will be either so variable or so damped that there is little or no profitable information from estimating the seasonal. Diller's analysis of seasonals (in [36], Chapter 2) for the early postwar period (1948–1965) found repetitive seasonality in the 1955–60 period, but seasonal movements were either damped or irregular in earlier and later periods. In the 1955–60 period, seasonals tended to peak near year-end, trough in June, and peak again in September. The evidence was consistent with seasonal characteristics in the money demand function. Lawler's [49] recent study found that the spread between negotiable certificate of deposit and bill yields displayed a seasonal peak in February, with a June trough. Though Lawler did not draw this conclusion, the seasonality again appears related as much to Federal Reserve activity as to private sector activity, reflected in management of commercial bank balance sheets.

## Longer Run Influences: Kondratieff and Kuznets Waves

War, natural calamities, sweeping technological advances, and other shocks can result in cycles overlaid on the more seasonal and cyclical swings in interest rates. The theme of very long cycles in prices and economic activity is identified with Nicolai Kondratieff, who postulated that economies followed regular cycles of roughly 50 years' duration (Phelps Brown and Hopkins [9] presented evidence of 50-year cycles for prices in the United Kingdom over the past eight centuries). According to Kondratieff (see Exhibit 60–10) the first part of the 50-year cycle is typically composed of an upcycle lasting 20 years. In this up phase, inflation gradually accelerates as entrepreneurial confidence increases, economic policies are expansive, and capacity utilization—initially very low—increases, first to levels that encourage productivity improvements and new investment but then to unsustainable levels. Economic volatility increases sharply, and the up phase usually terminates in heightened social tensions and even war. The termination of the up phase is generally followed by a 7- to 10-year interval of relative price stability, although bond prices remain close to their lows reached in the high inflation ending the up phase. The transition from recent excesses is typically accompanied by a swing to libertarian, laissez-faire philosophies and sustained

**EXHIBIT 60–10**

**U.S. Wholesale Prices and the Idealized Kondratieff Wave**

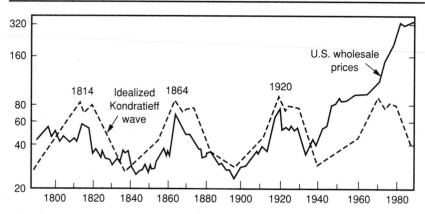

Source: Historical Statistics of the United States, Bureau of Labor Statistics. A version of this chart appeared in *Forbes* Magazine, November 9, 1981.

attempts to cut government spending and deficits. The deflationary impact of these policies, on a financial system already strained by the prior inflation, sets off a self-feeding deflationary cycle that encompasses several business cycles with steep, lengthy counteractions, short recoveries, and sharply higher levels of bankruptcy.

To be sustainable, Kondratieff cycles must somehow involve systematic underprediction of inflation in the early up phase, and equally systematic errors in the deflation period. The improvement in the measurement and frequency of economic data and the safeguards built into the financial system in recent years have reduced the likelihood that we might enter the plateau phase of a Kondratieff-like cycle.

Kuznets swings or "waves" occupy an intermediate position. In examining data over longer periods of time, Kuznets (for example, [45]) found "long swings" in growth rates of real output and population spanning roughly 20 years. More recently, the same 20-year regularity has been observed in property-casualty underwriter pricing. In the case of population, these swings have been linked to migration (which, given the selective character of international migration, has its own implications for growth rates) and technological change. Like Kondratieff cycles, moreover, Kuznets waves are associated with changes in capacity utilization. Immigration will lead to an accelerated demand for capital stock, rising real interest rates, and pressures for expansionary fiscal and monetary policies; outmigration can have the reverse effect. So long as international capital markets clear relatively efficiently, this need not have any long-term significance for interest rates, since international capital flows will shift capital from surplus to deficit countries (or asset prices will adjust). Neither labor nor capital market efficiency is perfect, however, and over/under building will produce cycles—long swings—that tend to produce unexpected pressures on credit markets over sustained periods of time.

Although an emphasis on long swing may seem at odds with the goal of predicting interest-rate movements over relatively short intervals, recall the discussion of market efficiency above. Success in forecasting the set of really *valuable* information (S) usually implies using information not generally variable or not generally used, or making use of new techniques to better understand existing information. To the extent that long waves have validity and are currently not being incorporated in existing models, they offer a relatively "cheap" source of new information, particularly since we might expect to find with efficient markets that *ex ante* changes in long-term rates increase with the forecast horizon.

## FLOW-OF-FUNDS ANALYSIS

In contrast to those who forecast future interest rates on the basis of inflation and/or monetary policies, the flow-of-funds school projects supply and demand for credit by various participants.

Flow-of-funds methods do not forecast interest rates in a reduced-form relation. The goal instead is a more modest one—to anticipate directions in movements in interest rates as a result of an examination of the *sectoral* consistency of national income projections with the implication for financing. Underlying this approach is the implicit assumption that economic plans are being based on these national income projections and will be reflected in credit demands and supplies. Also implicit, however, is the assumption that sectoral financial flows change predictably and are only moderately sensitive to interest rates in other markets (preferred habitat). Otherwise, flow-of-funds models reverse the causality above, determining sector flows from wealth, NIA components, and interest rates, subject to aggregate constraints. Dependent and independent variables are reversed.

Emphasis on the various sources of and demands for loanable funds is in no way inconsistent with the emphasis on monetary variables by monetarists. Nobel laureate Sir John Hicks [42, p. 135], writing in 1938, made perhaps the most direct statement on this point:

> Is the rate of interest determined by the supply and demand for loanable funds (that is to say, by borrowing and lending); or is it determined by the supply and demand for money itself? This last view is put forward by Mr. Keynes in his *General Theory*. I shall hope to show that it makes no difference whether we follow his way of putting it, or whether we follow those writers who adopt what

appears at present to be a rival view. Properly followed up, the two approaches lead to exactly the same results.

Hick's reconciliation noted that equilibrium was inconsistent with more than one set of spot rates.[16] Walras' Law could then be invoked to show that in an economy with $n$ commodities ($n - 1$ relative prices), a loan or credit market, and money and, with equilibrium in the $n - 1$ relative prices, if the loan/credit market were in equilibrium, then the supply of money must equal the demand for money. Put another way, the $n$ commodity markets and the supply and demand for money will determine the $n - 1$ relative prices and the price level that are consistent with only one interest rate; and that is the interest rate that clears the loan market, since only one spot rate can exist for a given maturity.

The differences between those who would forecast interest rates on the basis of the supply of and demand for money and those who would use the supply of and demand for credit are only superficial at this level of analysis. The *real* argument relates to how best to determine the interest rate that is also consistent with simultaneously clearing the $n$ goods markets. Monetarists implicitly view expectations of inflation as the primary determinant of the level and direction of interest rates and focus on this component of the Fisher equation. This view carries over to policy recommendations, which emphasize that commodity (real or goods) markets will clear quickly and efficiently in the absence of government intervention. By implication, the real rate of interest, or marginal efficiency of capital, is relatively stable. Analysts preferring flow of funds do so because they view money demand as unstable (or money supply as undefinable, or both) and see the real rate of interest as both unstable and capable of being heavily influenced by activities in certain key markets.

Viewed objectively, these differences are often a matter of the time frame of analysis. In the short term, there is a limited correlation of interest rates with inflation and at least the appearance of instability in money demand relationships. Flow of funds, as a forecasting tool, has the apparent advantage of focusing on markets closely connected with credit demands and supply, and on particular regulatory barriers. In the longer run, money demand appears stable, and inflation expectations become the proximate determinant of interest rates. One is tempted to say that the choice of forecasting procedure depends primarily on the time reference.

However, it is important not to overemphasize this distinction. Monetarists refer to the impact of money on interest rates as having three stages: liquidity,

---

[16] If, in our $n$-commodity system, demands for $n - 1$ products equal the supplies of $n - 1$ products, then the $n$th demand must equal its supply. The proof uses the fact that only $n - 1$ relative prices need to be determined and that income to be spent on the products, at any point in time, is given.

income, and price expectations effects that partition the time path into short-term and long-run influences.[17]

Beyond the forecasting horizon, it is often difficult to categorize flow-of-funds approaches to interest rates because different forecasters identify different pressure points at different points in the business cycle as the predominant determinant of the direction and level of interest rates.

The comments, below, are generally offered as a guide:

1. Flow-of-funds data are prepared by staff of the Board of Governors of the Federal Reserve from data produced by a large number of different sources. Data frequently must be massaged in one way or another to produce comparability.[18] The Board's personnel do an excellent job with this difficult task. Nevertheless, estimates are subject to wider error bounds than many financial data. For this reason, flow-of-funds forecast tends to focus on Treasury financing, bank, bond, and mortgage borrowing, and consumer credit. One way to assess the potential for error is to study the statistical discrepancy between assets and liability statistics in the various sectors (see Exhibit 60–11). Even after several revisions, unresolved statistical discrepancies remain a large part of the estimated net increase in liabilities.

2. The concept of "crowding out" plays an important role in many flow-of-funds analyses. In Exhibit 60–12, higher Treasury borrowing raises interest rates from $i_o$ to $i_1$, reducing business external borrowing for (e.g.) fixed investment by $B_0 - B_1$ and lowering consumer borrowing

---

[17] Studies of money demand generally support the contention that the demand for money is a stable function of a small number of variables—specifically, wealth or permanent income and an opportunity cost given by the real rate of return on alternative assets. A shift to a more expansionary monetary policy generates an initial drop in interest rates as economic actors attempt to shed excess balances through the purchase of other assets. These purchases bid up the price of other assets (bid down the opportunity cost of money) to enable the initial increase to be held. However, it also encourages increased production of these assets (the income effect), which bids up the demand for money and lowers prices of the competing assets whose production has been increased (raising the real interest rate). Finally, by increasing capacity utilization and raising asset prices, this process produces an upward adjustment in price expectations and money interest rates. Empirical studies find the liquidity effect of an unanticipated monetary expansion to be at most six months and the income effect to be somewhat longer and more variable. For an anticipated expansion, however, liquidity and income effects have already been largely if not totally discounted. For an elaboration, see, for example, Friedman [28], Gibson and Kaufman [32], Barro [2], and Miskin [55]. However, the variability of liquidity and income effects (depending on the validity of expectations, initial economic conditions, etc.) and the evidence of market efficiency referred to earlier in this chapter are used to justify the monetarist focus on price expectations for interest-rate forecasts and a longer run perspective.

[18] For example, bond issuance volume in the public and private new-issue markets must be gathered; retired and maturing issues must then be netted from this gross total.

**EXHIBIT 60-11**
**Statistical Discrepancy for Selected Sectors** (Three-Year Averages)

| | Average Discrepancy | | | (Percent of Sector Net Increase in Liabilities) | | |
|---|---|---|---|---|---|---|
| | ($ Billions) | | | | | |
| Sector | 1979–81 | 1982–84 | 1985–87 | 1979–81 | 1982–84 | 1985–87 |
| Household, personal trusts, and nonprofit organizations | −59 | −31 | −29 | 39% | 19% | 10% |
| Nonfinancial corporate business (excluding farms) | 35 | 14 | 44 | 23 | 10 | 26 |
| U.S. government | 4 | 2 | 9 | 6 | 5 | 4 |
| Commercial banking | −10 | −9 | −12 | 8 | 7 | 6 |

Source: Board of Governors of the Federal Reserve System, *Flow of Funds Accounts*, 1981, 1985, and 1988.

**EXHIBIT 60–12**
**Crowding Out**

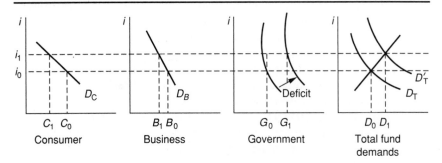

by $C_0 - C_1$. This neglects the cause of the initial deficit, which might have been due to lower tax receipts because reduced activity cut underlying consumer and business activity to levels consistent with $C_1$ and $B_1$, respectively. Furthermore, the analysis neglects the impact of a deficit created by expansionary fiscal policy on private output through operating on perceived wealth and asset values for underlying (more utilized) capital stock. The impact, for example, *might* be to produce additional internal funds, short term, to fund the deficit. Longer run, of course, expansionary policies will increase external cash needs to increment capacity. It also helps to assume only a limited elasticity of supply of savings—an assumption that has considerable support empirically. Otherwise, "crowding out" must be relatively minor, and interest-rate forecasts based on flow of funds would show little variation.[19]  On balance, Exhibit 60–12 contains a dangerous simplicity; the actual support for crowding out, short term, must be empirical.

3. Structural or regulatory constraints that prevent markets from arbitraging play a key role in many flow-of-funds forecasts. Regulation Q, which limited the monetary interest rates that banks and savings associations could pay on certain types of deposits, was an effective throttle on home mortgage lending whenever market interest rates rose above these ceilings. This effectively increased credit supplies to other participants and subsidized their cost of credit in high interest-rate environments. In recent years several deposit forms not subject to Regulation Q have developed, and the regulation itself is scheduled to be totally phased out in stages to 1986. Another less documented "structural" constraint some-

---

[19] As a general rule, this is the typical result for model-based forecasts because of the need to damp the large statistical noise in the data.

times seen in flow-of-funds analyses conforms with preferred habitat by arguing that significant new Treasury debt can only be sold at a sharp concession to current debt holdings—in other words, a very inelastic demand function exists for additions to current holdings.

4. Within the flow-of-funds school are at least two disparate groups. One group emphasizes aggregate financial ratios. Current or prospective financial conditions, in this view, will result in financial ratios that are so extreme as to lead to extremely inelastic credit supplies, thereby widening quality differentials and increasing the probability of a credit crunch as these stretched ratios strain the normal intermediary function. We might call this the "intermediary" school. The second group also uses ratios but emphasizes ratios dealing with wealth, maturity mismatch, and debt-service capacity—the "real balance" school. This second group emphasizes (explicitly or implicitly) that interest rates are the "terms of trade" between consuming in the present and postponing current consumption. The major difference between the groups, then, is that the intermediary school focuses on the potential for a given supply of savings to be channeled to various borrowers and the potential for key borrowers or intermediaries to be shut out of the credit market as a result of an actual or perceived deterioration in their risk-bearing ability. By contrast, the "real balance" group's focus is on how elastic this initial supply of savings will be to changes in economic conditions (both income and price effects), implicitly assuming the efficiency of the intermediation process. [20]

5. In some ways, the term *flow of funds* is a misnomer that tends to concentrate attention on sources of new funds and incremental demands at the expense of changes in asset allocation among existing assets. Such shifts have the potential to dwarf incremental flows. For example, at mid-year 1986, money market funds totaled more than $300 billion; there were $500 billion in money market deposit accounts (MMDA's) and over $1 trillion in bank and thrift time certificates. A 10 percent shift out of these funds was on the scale of 75 percent of personal savings flows. Furthermore, recent work on asset models has stressed that markets often clear by changes in price with modest flows. Arbitrage of international and domestic short-term money markets is a frequent example; so are the equity markets, in which net flows of funds are a miniscule part of outstanding market values.

---

[20] For a surprisingly modern exposition, see Wicksell [81]. Wicksell's legacy claims a number of distinguished economists, including Hicks [42], Keran [46] and Mundell [58], and his work is enjoying a renaissance as a basis for cyclical forecasts.

## PRODUCING A FORECAST

What might seem like the most difficult is actually the easiest part of this exercise, which is why it has been delayed until the end. Following are five ways of producing a forecast.

1. Forecasts can be read directly from the forward rate structure. In the absence of additional information or confidence in one's expertise, this is the rational choice. Exhibit 60–13 is an example of forward rates calculated by one analytical service near mid-year 1985. To these forward rates must be added any liquidity or term premiums. Furthermore, the geometric mean of a series of forward rates is the spot rate, and coupon premium, default, and call options must be added to produce a forecast of a particular interest rate. The latter are generally estimated from historical data of actual rates regressed on spot rates and proxy variables—sector and rating dummies for default risk and coupon scales, the theoretical value of the call option, and so on. (One approach to measuring the call option is found in Yawitz and Marshall [85].) For short-term rates, however, evidence to date supports using one or more of the techniques below or a survey of forecasters.

2. Use a large-scale econometric model. The evidence to date is ambiguous on this point. If experts have provided their judgmental review, there may

**EXHIBIT 60–13**
**Estimated U.S. Treasury Term Structure** (July 6, 1989)

| Maturity | Spot Rates | Current Yield on Par Bond | Discount Function | Forward |
|---|---|---|---|---|
| 1 month | 7.90% | 8.05% | .994 | 7.90% |
| 2 months | 7.91 | 8.06 | .987 | 7.91 |
| 3 months | 7.91 | 8.07 | .981 | 7.92 |
| 6 months | 7.94 | 8.10 | .962 | 7.99 |
| 12 months | 7.97 | 8.12 | .925 | 7.90 |
| 2 years | 7.73 | 7.90 | .859 | 7.43 |
| 3 years | 7.80 | 7.95 | .795 | 7.96 |
| 5 years | 7.87 | 8.01 | .680 | 7.93 |
| 7 years | 7.90 | 8.04 | .581 | 7.99 |
| 10 years | 7.95 | 8.09 | .458 | 8.09 |
| 15 years | 8.03 | 8.14 | .307 | 8.16 |
| 20 years | 8.13 | 8.19 | .203 | 8.39 |
| 30 years | 7.62 | 8.11 | .106 | 7.25 |

Source: Gifford Fong & Associates

be some gain in using this as a tool for forecasting short-term rates (e.g., Throop [75] and Pesando [61]).

3. Produce a "monetarist" forecast. These come in several variants. Perhaps the simplest solves for the interest-rate path consistent with a projected growth of the money stock, given the assumption of a stable money demand function. This involves projection of the price and income components for the money demand function and finding interest rates consistent with these projections. A variant on this method would assume some portion of the differential between money supply and money demand is made up each period that money supply growth is different than "expectations" (based either on publicly announced targets or distributed lags; for example, see Barro [2]). Naturally, the success of this procedure is dependent on the ability to correctly predict income, price, and adjustment components—a further reason monetarists tend to focus their horizon for interest-rate forecasts on the two- to five-year period where price expectations become the most important determinant. For these longer run forecasts, longer run growth of the money stock and its first and second derivatives become the prime components of a forecast.[21]

A simple example of a short-term, monetarist forecast is given below. There is general agreement that a good specification of the demand for money in terms of a small number of variables, is

$$\frac{M}{NP} = a + b + \left(\frac{Y}{PN}\right) + c(R_0) + d(R_B) + e\left(\frac{M_{-1}}{P_{-1}N_{-1}}\right) \qquad (60\text{--}4)$$

where all variables are expressed in logarithmic form, and are defined as follows:

$M$ = any variant of $M_1$ or $M_2$, depending on one's preference.

$Y$ = real (preferably permanent) income (often proxied by real GNP).

$N$ = population.

$P$ = a broad-based price index, usually proxied by the GNP deflator because of the absence of a broad-based price index for assets.

$R_0$ = an interest-rate proxying for the opportunity cost of money. Both short-term and long-term rates have been used without real discrimination, though a "transactions" view of money demand would favor the short-term rate.

---

[21] The fact that the second derivative of monetary growth is damped about zero has not, apparently, prevented its being an important part of the judgment on the direction of interest rates two to three years out!

$R_B$ = the "own" rate—passbook savings or (more recently), NOW accounts, preferably adjusted upward for nonpecuniary returns.

The subscript "−1" indicates a one-period lag to allow for partial adjustment in observed data.

Assuming that one determined a desired specification from Equation (60–4), it could be estimated over some prior period using $R_0$ as an independent variable and incorporate any desired shift variables (for price controls, changing commitment pricing terms on bank lines, etc.). The use of a lagged term to capture serial correlation is a serious statistical weakness from a forecasting standpoint. Forecasts would use these estimated coefficients to solve for $R_0$:

$$R_0 = \frac{1}{c}\frac{M}{NP} - \frac{b}{c}\left(\frac{Y}{PN}\right) - \frac{d}{c}(R_B) + \frac{e}{c}\left(\frac{M_{-1}}{P_{-1}N_{-1}}\right) - \frac{a}{c} \qquad (60\text{–}5)$$

using forecasts of $M/NP$ and $Y/PN$; $R_B$ is (generally) slowly changing or predictable on the basis of legislation, and $M_{-1}/(P_{-1}N_{-1})$ is known. $M$ can be forecast using Federal Reserve targets, if desired. $N$ is predictable; forecasts of $Y$ and $P$ can be naive (last period's growth rate), sourced from consensus forecasts or even based on recent and projected money stock growth. (A close correlation exists between nominal income growth over six-month spans and money supply growth over prior six-month spans.) There is less agreement on the stability of this relationship.[22] More important, unless consistent forecasts of $M$, $Y$, and $P$ have been created, the solution for $R_0$ lacks validity, since the coefficients were calculated based on a certain consistency. (This is a variant of the previous descriptions of rational expectations.)

4. Forecasts using business-cycle turning points, of course, rely on an ability to outperform the composite index of leading economic indicators or one of its variants (such as the ratio of composite coincident to composite lagging indicators). There have been a number of books on business cycles, but the Mitchell/Burns anthology and its offspring remain required reading for serious students. Also recommended is the critique of recent research by Lucas [50].

5. Different emphases, as noted, make it more difficult to precisely describe the creation of a forecast using flow of funds. Instead, major areas are detailed below.[23]

---

[22]Two solutions for the above equation are given in Hafer and Hein [37, pp. 13–14] and [26].
[23]This discussion relies heavily on von Furstenberg [31].

a. The basic flow-of-funds forecast typically contains key trigger points:

(1) The differential, *ex ante*, between investment demand and the flow of savings. To close this differential, prices and quantities must adjust (markets clear) and ensure *ex post* equality.

(2) The size and timing of the federal government's financing needs, as a key component of *ex ante* savings flows.

(3) The outlook for inventories and corporate cash flows as a guide to external cash needs.

(4) In recent years, sources of funds from abroad.

(5) Asset allocation by banks and insurance companies (preferred habitat).

b. Start with national income (NIA) projections as a guide to flow of funds and as a check on the internal consistency of the national income projections. (Refer to Exhibit 60–14 for NIA components to gross savings and investment.)

Sources of savings include:

(1) Household and personal savings. To personal savings from income from current production (NIA), add

- The surplus of railroad retirement and state and local retirement funds because these funds are also available for investment.
- Capital gains distributions of investment companies.
- Consumer durables (NIA, and thus gross of depreciation).
- Depreciation on other household assets.

(2) Nonfinancial business savings. To undistributed corporate profits, add capital consumption allowances, but subtract a minor item, capital gains dividends of investment companies, and the undistributed profits of the financial sector (including retained earnings of government entities.)

(3) Foreign sector saving. This is the negative of net foreign investment.

(1), (2), and (3) constitute private sources; to this, to determine gross savings, (4) must be added.

(4) Government savings—both the federal government's overall cash surplus or deficit and the surplus or deficit of state and local governments.

Since gross savings must equal gross investment, the forecast of the sum of (1)−(4) is compared with uses for these funds:

- Residential construction.
- Nonresidential outlays for structures and equipment.

**EXHIBIT 60-14**
**NIA Gross Savings and Investment**

|  | 1980 ($ Billions) |
|---|---|
| Gross savings: |  |
| Personal savings | $101.3 |
| Undistributed corporate profits | 107.2 |
| Corporate inventory valuation adjustment | −45.7 |
| Capital consumption adjustment | −17.2 |
| Corporate capital consumption allowance | 175.4 |
| Noncorporate corporate capital consumption allowance | 111.9 |
| Total gross private savings NIA | 432.9 |
| Plus: |  |
| Federal government surplus | −61.2 |
| State and local surplus | 29.1 |
| Consumer durables | 211.9 |
| Equals: Gross savings, flow of funds | 612.7 |
| Gross investment: |  |
| Consumer durables | 211.9 |
| Residential | 105.3 |
| Plant and equipment | 296.0 |
| Inventory change | −5.9 |
| Oil leases/mineral rights (U.S. government sales) | 6.5 |
| Total gross investment | 613.8 |
| Statistical discrepancy | 1.1 |

Source: Federal Reserve, November 1981, *Flow of Funds Accounts.*

- Inventories.
- Consumer durables.

To this point, the forecast is basically equivalent to describing the IS relationship. This means that it is consistent with *any* level of interest rates, although a particular interest rate would be specified were a level of economic activity known. In fact, the IS relationship specifies jointly attainable combinations of output, $y$, and interest rates, $r$. Since $y$ and $r$, are jointly determined, however, it is not sufficient to form an interest-rate forecast. Even at this level of generality, however, two features might be noted:

- Personal savings are only a part of the economy's gross savings pool. International comparisons of savings that focus only on this subcomponent may seriously distort the overall relationship. Japan's substantially higher savings rate, for example, partly reflects measurement differences and a more leveraged business sector but may also be, in part, a reaction to the destruction of capital stock during the second World War. See, for example, Christiano [13].

- At this level of aggregation, savings and investment "appear" to be independent of financial markets. The role of financial markets is to channel or gather an excess of deficiency of funds from various sectors to ration across various sectors requiring net financial investment. Their success determines the ultimate combination of output and interest rates $(y_0, r_0)$.

Exhibit 60–15 shows the derivation for 1980 of net financial investment. (Statistical discrepancies have been subsumed in net financial investment for each sector.)

Net financial investment, in turn, equals net acquisition of financial assets less debt issuance for each sector. In terms of Exhibit 60–17, this obviously places the onus on the household and financial sectors to finance business and government activities under most economic environments.

    *c.* From this point, the flow-of-funds forecast, whether econometric or intuitive, is successively disaggregative. That is partly because there is only a *weak* relationship between actual credit/GNP in aggregate and the trend in interest rates. (See Exhibit 60–16.)

Forecasts for NIA components, by sector, determine net financial investment for each sector (Exhibit 60–17).

Also shown in Exhibit 60–15 are gross flows underlying net activity. These should also be carefully examined. Too small a proportion of gross to net flows *suggests* an unexpectedly greater degree of monetary stringency with consequent upward pressure on interest rates.

Once a sector-by-sector description of net financial investment has been created using NIA data, it is necessary to determine what funds will be available to or demanded from the credit markets. This involves projecting reasonable values for items in lines 11 through 17 of Exhibit 60–15 and comparing these items with net financial investment to arrive at net investment in credit markets and related instruments (line 19). Several of the line items in line 11 to 17 are linked to other forecasts. Demand deposit and currency growth, for example, must be consistent with one's view of the policy measures followed by the Federal Reserve. Insurance and pension reserves tend to follow a relatively predictable trend. The relatively unpredictable items are the distribution of household assets between money market funds and time deposits and business demands for time deposits, particularly since distinguishing these demands from security repurchase agreements and other liquid assets is a very artificial one.

Line 19 of Exhibit 60–15 is the penultimate goal in creating a forecast. This is the forecast, by sector, of funds that will be provided to the credit markets

**EXHIBIT 60–15**
**Derivation of Net Financial Investment, 1980 ($ Billions)**

| Line Number | Transactions Category | Sector | | | | | | | | | |
|---|---|---|---|---|---|---|---|---|---|---|---|
| | | Households | | Business | | Net Foreign Sector | | State and Local Governments | | U.S. Government | |
| | | u | s | u | s | u | s | u | s | u | s |
| 1 | Gross saving | | 402.9 | | 257.6 | | 0.0 | | 2.7 | | −70.0 |
| 2 | Capital consumption | | 302.8 | | 225.0 | | | | — | | — |
| 3 | Net savings (1 − 2) | | 172.0 | | 32.6 | | | | 2.7 | | −70.0 |
| 4 | Gross investment (5 + 10) | 402.9 | | 257.7 | | 0.0 | | 2.7 | | −70.0 | |
| 5 | Private capital expenditures (6 to 9) | 313.1 | | 285.4 | | | | 0.0 | | — | |
| 6 | Consumer durables | 211.9 | | — | | | | | | | |
| 7 | Residential construction | 93.8 | | 11.4 | | | | | | | |
| 8 | Plant and Equipment | 7.4 | | 273.6 | | | | | | | |
| 9 | Inventory Change/ mineral rights | — | | 0.6 | | | | | | | |
| 10 | Net financial investment (1 − 5) = (18 − 19) | 89.8 | | −27.8 | | 0.0 | | 2.7 | | −70.0 | |
| 11 | Demand deposits and currency | 10.9 | | 2.4 | | 0.7 | | −1.1 | | −3.6 | |

**EXHIBIT 60–15—Continued**

| | | | | | | | |
|---|---|---|---|---|---|---|---|
| 12 | Time/savings deposits | 131.2 | 1.7 | 1.2 | -1.7 | | -0.2 |
| 13 | Money funds | 29.2 | — | | | | |
| 14 | Gold/foreign exchange/SDRs | | | 5.5 | | | 4.3 |
| 15 | Life insurance reserves | 11.5 | — | | | | |
| 16 | Pension fund reserves | 77.5 | — | | | | |
| 17 | Interbank items | — | | -24.5 | * | 26.5 | * | 8.8 |
| 18 | Net investment in liquidor insurance claims (11 to 17) | 260.3 | 4.1 | -28.1 | -29.3 | | -8.3 |
| 19 | Net investment in credit markets and related investments (10 − 18) | -170.5 | -31.9 | 28.1 | 32.1 | | -61.7 |
| 20 | Statistical discrepancy | -79.6 | 44.5 | 28.5 | 9.8 | | -0.8 |
| 21 | incl. in (10) = 19 − 20 | 90.0 | -76.4 | -0.4 | 22.3 | | -60.5 |

**EXHIBIT 60–15—Continued**

| Line Number | Transactions Category | Federally Sponsored Credit Agencies | | Monetary Authority | | Commercial Banking | | Private Nonbank Finance | | Total, All Sectors | |
|---|---|---|---|---|---|---|---|---|---|---|---|
| | | u | s | u | s | u | s | u | s | u | s |
| 1 | Gross saving | | 0.9 | | 0.4 | | 8.2 | | | | 612.7 |
| 2 | Capital consumption | | | | | | 5.0 | | | | 465.4 |
| 3 | Net savings (1 − 2) | | ‾0.9 | | ‾0.4 | | 3.2 | | | | 147.3 |
| 4 | Gross investment (5 + 10) | 0.9 | | 0.4 | | 8.2 | | | | 612.7 | |
| 5 | Private capital expenditures (6 to 9) | 0.0 | | 0.0 | | 11.3 | | | | 612.7 | |
| 6 | Consumer durables | | | | | | | | | 211.9 | |
| 7 | Residential construction | | | | | | | | | 105.3 | |
| 8 | Plant and Equipment | | | | | 11.3 | | 2.9 | | 295.0 | |
| 9 | Inventory Change/ mineral rights | | | | | | | | | 0.6 | |
| 10 | Net financial investment (1 − 5) = (18 − 19) | 0.9 | | 0.4 | | −3.2 | | 7.1 | | — | |
| 11 | Demand deposits and currency | 0.1 | | 2.3 | 9.0 | 0.7 | 4.9 | 3.7 | 2.1 | 16.0 | 16.0 |
| 12 | Time/savings deposits | | | | | 91.7 | 128 | 53.4 | 145.1 | 145.1 | |

**EXHIBIT 60-15—Continued**

| | | | | | | | | | | |
|---|---|---|---|---|---|---|---|---|---|---|
| | — | — | — | — | — | — | — | — | — | — |
| 13 Money funds | | | | | | | 29.2 | 29.2 | 29.2 |
| 14 Gold/foreign exchange/SDRs | | 3.9 | 2.6 | | | | | | |
| 15 Life insurance reserves | | | | | | | 11.5 | 8.1 | 8.1 |
| 16 Pension fund reserves | | | | | | | 42.3 | 11.5 | 11.5 |
| | | | | | | | | 77.5 | 77.5 |
| 17 Interbank items | | −1.9 | −1.0 | −4.5 | −29.8 | — | — | −30.8 | −30.8 |
| 18 Net investment in liquidor insurance claims (11 to 17) | 0.1 | −6.3 | | −70.6 | | −122.0 | | 0 | |
| 19 Net investment in credit markets and related investments (10 − 18) | 0.8 | +6.3 | | 67.4 | | 129.1 | | 0 | |
| 20 Statistical discrepancy | 0.6 | — | −10.6 | 56.8 | −0.9 | 128.2 | −8.6 | 8.6 | |
| 21 incl. in (10) = 19 − 20 | −1.5 | −6.3 | | | | | | | |

Note: u = use; s = source. Details may not add to totals due to rounding.
* Included in household sector.

Source: November, 1981 *Flow of Funds Accounts*, Board of Governors of the Federal Reserve System.

**EXHIBIT 60–16**
**Credit Demand and Long-Term Interest Rates**

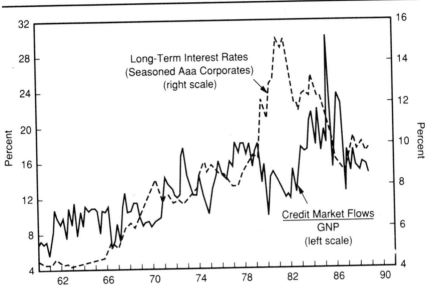

*Includes all debt obligations of business, household, and government sectors.

Source: Federal Reserve Flow of Funds. Seasonally adjusted and annualized data.

and related instruments. Note the implication, for example, of a relatively large figure for the household sector in line 10 coupled with a decline in line 18. The implication is that much more of the household's credit acquisition will be direct or through nontraditional intermediaries.

Data in Exhibit 60–17 show that in 1980 household borrowing for consumer credit and home mortgage debt accounted for 46 percent of household net investment in credit markets and related instruments, a comparatively small proportion because of the negligible rise in consumer credit. Similarly, a growing projection of funds by commercial banks relative to nonbank finance (comparing 1980 to prior years, not shown here) would tend to suggest business would be "forced" to use more bank financing or to go directly to investors, bypassing intermediaries. To go from this statement to the implication that long-term interest rates would be under upward pressure, however, requires an additional assumption. This is that businesses will pay a premium to have the somewhat longer maturity offered by public debt markets or that banks will refuse to offer longer term fixed-rate claims, or some combination of these factors. (One reason often given in recent years to expect such a premium has been the deterioration in business balance sheet flexibility.) That hypothesis may be correct, but any analysis must include the *increased* flexibility offered by new financing

**EXHIBIT 60–17**

**Net Financial Sector Investments, 1980 ($ Billions)**

Sector

| Line Number | Transactions Category | Households | | Business | | Net Foreign Sector | | State and Local Governments | | U.S. Government | |
|---|---|---|---|---|---|---|---|---|---|---|---|
| | | u | s | u | s | u | s | u | s | u | s |
| 17 | Net investment in credit market and related investments (from table 8) | | -17.5 | | -31.9 | | 28.1 | | 32.1 | | -61.7 |
| 22 | Credit market investments (lines 22 to 31) | 27.6 | 101.7 | 3.7 | 123.7 | 15.6 | 27.1 | 44.5 | 25.3 | 23.7 | 79.2 |
| 23 | U.S. government securities | 20.5 | | -2.1 | | 10.5 | | 23.6 | 24.4 | | 79.3 |
| 24 | State and local obligation | 3.0 | | -0.2 | .25 | | | 0.3 | | | |
| 25 | Corporate/foreign bonds | 3.6 | | | 30.4 | 5.1 | 0.8 | 9.7 | | | |
| 26 | Home mortgages | 6.3 | 83.4 | | -1.6 | | | 8.0 | | | |
| 27 | Other mortgages | 1.8 | 1.5 | | 38.9 | | | 2.8 | | 2.7 | |
| 28 | Consumer credit | | 2.3 | | | | | | | 4.8 | -0.1 |
| 29 | Bank loans, not elsewhere classified | | | 2.1 | | | | | | | |
| 30 | Other loans† | | 5.6 | | 31.7 | | 11.5 | | | 16.2 | |
| 31 | Commercial paper/banker's acceptances | | 8.9 | | 15.2 | | 4.7 | | 0.9 | | |
| 32 | Related instruments (lines 33 to 37) | -3.6 | — | 3.9 | 6.6 | | 10.1 | 2.8 | — | -2.5 | 3.7 |
| 33 | Corporate equity issuance (net) | -1.9 | 7.1 | 98.9 | 10.4 | 42.6 | 3.0 | 5.3 | | | |
| 34 | Security credit | 4.1 | 5.0 | | 12.9 | 5.4 | 2.1 | | | | |
| 35 | Taxes payable | | | | -6.7 | | | -1.1 | | -2.8 | |
| 36 | Trade credit (net) | 2.2 | 2.1 | 32.8 | 33.2 | 1.8 | 1.0 | 1.8 | | 1.4 | 3.7 |
| 37 | Equity in clinicorp enterprises | -18.3 | | | -18.3 | | | | | | |
| 38 | Other | -75.3 | | 66.1 | -10.3 | 35.4 | | 6.8 | | -1.1 | |
| 20 | Statistical discrepancy incl. in lines 22,32 | -79.6 | | 44.5 | | 28.5 | | 9.8 | | -0.8 | |

**EXHIBIT 60–17—Continued**

| | | \multicolumn{10}{c}{Sector} | | | | | | | | | |
| Line Number | Transactions Category | Federally Sponsored Credit Agencies u | s | Monetary Authority u | s | Commercial Banking u | s | Private Nonbank Finance u | s | Total, All Sectors u | s |
|---|---|---|---|---|---|---|---|---|---|---|---|
| 17 | Net investment in credit market and related investments (from table 8) | | 0.8 | | 6.3 | | 67.4 | | 129.1 | | 0.0 |
| 22 | Credit market investments (lines 22 to 31) | 42.1 | 43.0 / 43.0‡, § | 4.5 | 4.5 | 99.7 | 7.1 | 155.6 | 10.4 | 412.4 | 412.4 |
| 23 | U.S. government securities | | | | | 25.6 | | 39.7 | | 122.3 | 122.3 |
| 24 | State and local obligation | | | | | 13.6 | | 10.1 | | 26.9 | 26.9 |
| 25 | Corporate/foreign bonds | | | | | 0.6 | 1.5 | 20.1 | 5.6 | 38.4 | 38.4 |
| 26 | Home mortgages | 25.6‡ | | | | 11.3 | | 27.1 | −0.8 | 81.0 | 81.0 |
| 27 | Other mortgages | 7.1§ | | | | 8.1 | | 15.5 | −0.1 | 40.1 | 40.1 |
| 28 | Consumer credit | | | | | −9.7 | | 9.9 | | 2.3 | 2.3 |
| 29 | Bank loans, not elsewhere classified | 10.4 | | | | 48.4 | | −0.5 | 7.1 | 48.4 | 36.6 |
| 30 | Other loans† | | | | | | | 10.0 | | | |
| 31 | Commercial paper/ banker's acceptances | | | 0.1 | | 1.8 | 5.6 | 23.2 | −0.9 | 21.4 | 21.4 |
| 32 | Related instruments (lines 33 to 37) | 0.8 | 0.0 | 0.5 | −1.3 | −4.3 | 20.8 | 7.6 | 23.7 | 67.0 | 67.0 |

**EXHIBIT 60–17—Concluded**

| | | | | | | | Sector | | | | | |
|---|---|---|---|---|---|---|---|---|---|---|---|---|
| Line Number | Transactions Category | Federally Sponsored Credit Agencies | | Monetary Authority | | Commercial Banking | | Private Nonbank Finance | | Total, All Sectors | |
| | | u | s | u | s | u | s | u | s | u | s |
| 33 | Corporate equity issuance (net) | | | | | | | | | 21.1 | 21.1 |
| 34 | Security credit | | | | | 0.8 | 0.4 | 12.3 | 5.7 | 10.0 | 10.0 |
| 35 | Taxes payable | | | | | | 0.5 | 5.1 | 4.9 | -3.9 | -3.9 |
| 36 | Trade credit (net) | | | | | | | | 3.1 | 40.0 | 40.0 |
| 37 | Equity in clinicorp enterprises | | | | | | | | | -18.3 | -18.3 |
| 38 | Other | 0.8 | | 0.5 | -1.3 | -5.2 | 20.0 | -9.9 | 10.0 | 18.1 | 18.1 |
| 20 | Statistical discrepancy incl. in lines 22,32 | 0.6 | | | | -10.6 | | -0.9 | | -8.6 | |

Note: u = use; s = source. Details may not add to totals due to rounding.
* Line 19 also equals the negative of net sources in lines 21 and 32.
† Includes Finance company loans to business, U.S. government loans, sponsored credit agency loans, and policy loans.
‡ Includes $18.0 billion of mortgage pools.
§ Includes $16.0 billion of mortgage pools.
" Includes $7.1 billion of advances from FHLB.

Source: November 1981 *Flow of Funds Accounts*, Board of Governors of the Federal Reserve System.

vehicles—interest-rate swaps, medium-term notes, payment-in-kind securities, a wide variety of forward contracts including extendibles and retractibles, and other structures that alter or channel interest-rate exposure.

Comparing entries in Exhibit 60–17 over time also helps to pinpoint how Treasury and off-budget financing might be met. Again, some forecasters choose to draw implications, based strongly or weakly on preferred habitat, of the pressure on interest rates necessary to permit the Treasury to fund a greater-than-normal (let alone greater-than-expected) deficit, particularly if the distribution of funds for the credit markets deviates from normal and/or large inelastic entries can already be identified. (An example of the latter would be heavy business trade credit needs.)

Typical practice is to complete as many items of the array in Exhibit 60–17 from trend extrapolation or compatible figures to NIA extrapolations. Upward pressures on interest rates—and revisions to NIA estimates—are indicated by a failure of expected financial demands, whether from Treasury or private users, to meet sources. Usually, a first pass is made using only private sector uses cued to NIA projections. (For example, projections for housing sales and starts cue mortgage activity; consumer durables and employment gains can be related to consumer credit; and inventory activity will be reflected in business short-term credit needs.) These demands then leave remaining sources to meet the Treasury's deficit (or can be incremented by a surplus). This gap indicates whether pressures on interest rates, given the NIA projections, would be significant (and in some circumstances, the potential for declines in rates). A judgment on what sectors will prove most interest-elastic to meet Treasury funding requirements is then made, and NIA activity recalculated to arrive at new sources and uses. Computer simulation permits a simultaneous solution.

The problems that face all large models, described earlier, face modeling flow of funds. Also noted previously the size of the statistical discrepancy means that the standard errors attaching to projections of microelements of individual accounts must be considered to be very large. Successful flow-of-funds forecasters generally weld experience, subjective beliefs, and a substantial element of luck to detailed economic analysis.

Although this may appear to be more art than science and, as described, is a process of successive iteration, with each new entry requiring a cross-check of other projections, it must be emphasized again that flow-of-funds methods do not forecast interest rates in a reduced-form-equation fashion. The goal is a more modest one—to anticipate directions in the movement of interest rates as a result of the examination of the *sectoral* consistency of NIA projections with the implications, given institutional limitations, for financing sectoral demands. Underlying this approach is the implicit assumption that economic plans are being based on these NIA projections and will be reflected in credit demands and supplies. This need not be true. For example, Wojnilower's summation of his techniques [84, p. 232] explicitly recognized that professional projections may dovetail poorly with results:

The most interesting case of schizoid expectations comes from the financial community, although here my evidence is unfortunately entirely anecdotal. That financial managers in their professional capacities have had a more optimistic outlook than the public on security prices is surely attested by the fact that institutions have continued to acquire massive amounts of bonds in the face of virtually continual declines in real and all too often also nominal values. Meanwhile the public has clearly shifted its investment mix toward increasing its borrowings and its real estate assets, producing palpably superior investment performance.

Flow-of-funds models have a further advantage that also helps to account for their popularity. Like the "stories" that color perceptions of individual equity issues (despite the weight of evidence that on average these stories are fully discounted by current stock prices), flow of funds can be used to emphasize a particular component that the analyst views as the *current* crucial factor in interest-rate movements. The fallacy of composition, that what is true of the individual need not be true of the whole, is equally applicable for flow-of-funds analysis (personal versus gross savings, for example), but flow of funds can add the emperor's new clothes to what is otherwise the naked and relatively efficient operation of Adam Smith's "invisible hand." By giving color to a view of the operation of the economy, flow-of-funds analysis can provide a service that is as much a marketing technique as an analytical underpinning. It is a technique that many special-interest groups have honed to near perfection in interaction with the government to justify federal guarantees or other subsidies that ballooned total funding in recent years.

## CONCLUSIONS

Serious studies generally indicate that short-term forecasts of long-term interest rates contain little or no value added. Forecasts of short-term interest rates, however, have been made successfully, by comparison with naive extrapolations, both because there is no theoretical necessity for short-term rates, short term, to follow a random walk and because the Federal Reserve has frequently chosen to act in a predictable fashion.

The evidence that short-term, long-term interest rates follow a random walk has been used to

1. Support option strategies directed toward fixed income investments, such as immunization, that shift the forecast horizon to a longer term perspective (but may offset this advantage by concentrating reinvestment risk).
2. Relate interest rates and inflation over longer periods of time. Deregulation, in this writer's opinion, has only temporarily disturbed this relationship, and presumably shifted it to a different plateau.

3. Justify an approach that views flow of funds as primarily a consistency check and marketing guide rather than an efficient tool for forecasting rates.

As in all other markets, however, the maxim in forecasts is *caveat emptor*.

# REFERENCES

1. Barro, Robert J. "Rational Expectations and the Role of Monetary Policy." *The Journal of Monetary Economics*, January, 1976, pp. 1–32.
2. — —. "Unanticipated Money, Output, and the Price Level in the United States." *The Journal of Political Economy*, August 1978, pp. 549–80.
3. Black, Fischer. "The ABC's of Business Cycles." *Financial Analysts Journal*, November/December 1981, pp. 75–80.
4. Blanchard, Oliver J., and Lawrence H. Sumers. "Perspectives on High World Real Interest Rates." *Brookings Papers on Economic Activity*, 2, 1984, pp. 273–334.
5. Bodie, Zvi, Alex Kane, and Robert L. MacDonald. "Why Haven't Nominal Rates Declined?" NBER Reprint Series, #498, 1984.
6. Bodie, Zvi, and John B. Shoven. *Financial Aspects of the U.S. Pension System.* Chicago: National Bureau of Economic Research, University of Chicago Press, 1982.
7. Blinder, Alan, and Stanley Fischer. "Inventories, Rational Expectations and the Business Cycle." National Bureau of Economic Research Working Paper, No. 381, August 1979.
8. Bomberger, William A., and W. J. Frazer. "Interest Rates, Uncertainty, and the Livingston Data." *The Journal of Finance*, June 1981, pp. 661–75.
9. Brown, Earnest Phelps, and Shiela Hopkins. "Seven Centuries of the Price of Consumables, Compared with Builders' Wage Rates." *Economica*, November 1956, pp. 296–314.
10. Burns, Arthur C., and Wesley C. Mitchell. *Measuring Business Cycles.* New York: National Bureau of Economic Research, 1947.
11. Cagan, Phillip. *Determinants and Effects of Changes in the Stock of Money 1875–1960.* New York: National Bureau of Economic Research, Columbia University Press, 1965.
12. Chow, G. C. "Multiplier, Accelerator, and Liquidity Preference." *Review of Economics and Statistics*, January 1967, pp. 1–15.
13. Christiano, Lawrence J. "Understanding Japan's Savings Rate: The Reconstruction Hypothesis," Federal Reserve Bank of Minneapolis, *Quarterly Review*, Spring 1989, pp. 10–26.
14. Cox, John C., Jonathan E. Ingersoll, Jr., and Steven A. Ross. "Duration and the Measurement of Basis Risk." *The Journal of Business*, January 1979, pp. 51–61.
15. — —." A Reexamination of Traditional Hypotheses about the Term Structure of Interest Rates." *Journal of Finance*, September 1981, pp. 769–93.
16. Culbertson, John M. *Macroeconomic Theory and Stabilization Policy.* New York: McGraw-Hill, 1968.
17. Dobson, Steven W., Robert C. Sutch, and David E. Vanderford. "An Evaluation of Alternative Empirical Models of the Term Structure of Interest Rates." *Journal of Finance*, September 1976, pp. 1035–65.

18. Dwyer, Gerald P. "Are Expectations of Inflation Rational?" *Journal of Monetary Economics*, February 1981, pp. 59–84.
19. Echols, Michael E., and Jan W. Elliot. "Rational Expectations in a Disequilibrium Model of the Term Structure." *American Economic Review*, March 1976, pp. 28–44.
20. Evans, Paul. "Why Have Interest Rates Been So Volatile?" Federal Reserve Bank of San Francisco, *Economic Review*, Summer 1981, pp. 7–20.
21. Fama, Eugene. "Short-Term Interest Rates as Predictors of Inflation." *American Economic Review*, June 1975, pp. 427–48.
22. Fama, Eugene, and G. William Schwert. "Inflation, Interest and Relative Prices." *Journal of Business*, April 1979, pp. 183–210.
23. Feldstein, Martin. "Inflation, Income Taxes and the Rate of Interest: A Theoretical Analysis." *American Economic Review*, December 1976, pp. 809–20.
24. Feldstein, Martin, and Otto Eckstein. "The Fundamental Determinants of the Interest Rate." *Review of Economics and Statistics*, August 1970, pp. 363–75.
25. Fildes, Robert A., and M. D. Fitzgerald. "Efficiency and Premiums in the Short-Term Money Market." *Journal of Money, Credit and Banking*, November 1980, Part I, pp. 615–29.
26. Fisher, Irving. *The Theory of Interest*. New York: MacMillan, 1930.
27. Friedman, Benjamin, and William G. Dewald. *Financial Market Behavior Capital Formation and Economic Performance*. Conference papers published by the *Journal of Money, Credit and Banking*, Vol. 12, Part 2 (May 1980).
28. Friedman, Milton. *The Optimum Quantity of Money and Other Essays*. New York: Aldine Publishers, 1969. (See especially essays 5, 6, 10.)
29. Friedman, Milton, and Anna J. Schwartz. *Monetary Trends in the United States and the United Kingdom*. Chicago: National Bureau of Economic Research, University of Chicago Press, forthcoming, 1982.
30. Froot, Kenneth A. "New Hope for the Expectations Hypothesis of the Term Structure of Interest Rates." *The Journal of Finance*, June 1989, pp. 283–305.
31. von Furstenberg, George M. "Flow of Funds Analysis and the Economic Outlook." *Annals of Economic and Social Measurement*, February 1977, pp. 1–25.
32. Gibson, William E., and George Kaufman. "The Sensitivity of Interest Rates to Changes in Money and Income." *The Journal of Political Economy*, May/June 1968, pp. 427–78.
33. Gordon, R. A., and L. Klein, eds. *Readings in Business Cycles*. Homewood, Ill.: Richard D. Irwin, 1965.
34. Gordon, Robert J. "Large-Scale Econometric Models." Mimeographed. Washington, D.C.: U.S. Department of the Treasury, 1970.
35. Grossman, Jacob. "The Rationality of Money Supply Expectations and the Short-Run Response of Interest Rates to Monetary Surprises." *Journal of Money, Credit and Banking*, November 1981, pp. 409–24.
36. Guttentag, Jack M., ed. *Essays on Interest Rates*. Vol. 2. New York: National Bureau of Economic Research, Columbia University Press, 1971. (See especially essays 1 and 2.)
37. Guttentag, Jack M., and Phillip Cagan, eds. *Essays on Interest Rates*. Vol. 1. New York: National Bureau of Economic Research, Columbia University Press, 1969.
38. Hafer, R. W., and Scott Hein. "The Dynamics and Estimation of Short-Run Money Demand." Federal Reserve Bank of St. Louis *Review*, March 1980, pp. 26–35.

**39.** Hartman, David G. "The International Financial Market and U.S. Interest Rates." Working Paper No. 598, National Bureau of Economic Research, New York, 1981.

**40.** Hein, Scott. "Dynamic Forecasting and the Demand for Money." Federal Reserve Bank of St. Louis *Review*, June–July 1980, pp. 13–23.

**41.** Hicks, Sir John R. "Mr. Keynes and the Classics." *Econometrica*, April 1937, pp. 147–59.

**42.** — — . *Value and Capital*. 2d ed. London: Oxford at the Clarendon Press, 1946.

**43.** Houglet, Michel X. *Estimating the Term Structure of Interest Rates for Nonhomogeneous Bonds*. Ph.D. dissertation, University of California, Berkeley, 1980.

**44.** Ibbotson, Roger G., and Rex, A. Sinquefield. *Stocks, Bonds, Bills, and Inflation: Historical Returns (1926–1978)*. 2d ed. Charlottesville, Va.: The Financial Analysts Research Foundation, 1979.

**45.** Kane, E. J. "Arbitrage Pressure and Divergences between Forward and Futures Interest Rates." Working Paper No. CSFM–21 Center for The Study of Futures Markets, Columbia Business School, New York, May 1980.

**46.** Keran, Michael W. "How to Think About Foreign Capital." The Prudential *Economic Review*, October 1988.

**47.** Kessel, Reuben A. *The Cyclical Behavior of the Term Structure of Interest Rates*. New York: National Bureau of Economic Research, Columbia University Press, 1965.

**48.** Kuznets, Simon. *Economic Growth of Nations*. Cambridge, Mass.: Harvard University Press, 1971.

**49.** Lawler, T. A. "Seasonal Movements in Short-Term Yield Spreads." Federal Reserve Bank of Richmond *Economic Review*, July/August 1978.

**50.** Lucas, Robert. "Methods and Problems of Business Cycle Theory." *The Journal of Money, Credit and Banking*, November 1980, Part II, pp. 696–715.

**51.** Lutz, F. A. *The Theory of Interest*. 2d ed. New York: Aldine Publishers, 1967.

**52.** McCulloch, J. Huston. "The Tax-Adjusted Yield Curve." *Journal of Finance*, June 1975, pp. 811–30.

**53.** McNees, Stephen K. "The Recent Record of Thirteen Forecasters." *New England Economic Review*, Federal Reserve Bank of Boston, September/October 1981.

**54.** Meltzer, Allan H. "Keynes' General Theory: A Different Perspective." *Journal of Economic Literature*, March 1981, pp. 34–64.

**55.** Miskin, Frederic. "Monetary Policy and Long-Term Interest Rates." *Journal of Monetary Economics*, February 1981, pp. 29–55.

**56.** Modigliani, Franco, and R. J. Shiller. "Inflation, Rational Expectations and the Term Structure of Interest Rates." *Economica*, February 1973, pp. 12–43.

**57.** Modigliani, Franco, and Richard Sutch, "Innovations in Interest Rate Policy." *American Economic Review, Papers and Proceedings*, May 1966, pp. 178–97.

**58.** Mundell, R. A. *Monetary Theory*. Pacific Palisades, Calif.: Goodyear Publishing, 1971.

**59.** Nelson, Charles R. *The Term Structure of Interest Rates*. New York: Basic Books, 1972.

**60.** Nelson, Charles R., and G. William Schwert. "Short-Term Interest Rates as Predictors of Inflation: On Testing the Hypothesis that the Real Rate Is Constant." *American Economic Review*, June 1977, pp. 478–86.

61. Pesando, James E. "On Forecasting Long-Term Interest Rates: Is the Success of the No-Change Prediction Surprising?" *Journal of Finance*, September 1980, pp. 1045–47.

62. Poole, William R. "Optimal Choice of Monetary Policy Instruments in a Simple Stochastic Macro Model." *Quarterly Journal in Economics*, May 1970, pp. 197–216.

63. — —. The Relationship of Monetary Decelerations to Business Cycle Peaks: Another Look at the Evidence." *Journal of Finance*, June 1975, pp. 697–712.

64. Reinganum, Marc. "The Arbitrage Pricing Theory: Some Empirical Results." *Journal of Finance*, May 1981, pp. 313–21.

65. Roll, Richard. *The Behavior of Interest Rates*. Amsterdam: North Holland, 1970.

66. Ross, Stephen A. "The Arbitrage Theory of Capital Asset Pricing." *Journal of Economic Theory*, December 1976, pp. 341–60.

67. Salomon Brothers, *Prospects for Financial Markets*. Annual. New York: Salomon Brothers Bond Market Research.

68. Santoni, G. J., and Courtenay C. Stone. "What Really Happened to Interest Rates: A Longer-Run Analysis." Federal Reserve Bank of St. Louis *Review*, November 1981, pp. 3–14.

69. Shiller, Robert J., John Y. Campbell, and Kermit Schoenholtz. "Forward Rates and Future Policy: Interpreting the Term Structure of Interest Rates." *Brookings Papers on Economic Activity*, No. 1, 1983, pp. 173–224.

70. Simon, David P. "The Rationality of Federal Funds Rate Expectations Evidence from a Survey." *Journal of Money Credit and Banking*, August 1989, pp. 388–93.

71. Singleton, Kenneth J. "Maturity-Specific Disturbances and the Term Structure of Interest Rates." *Journal of Money, Credit and Banking*, November 1980, Part 1, pp. 603–14.

72. Stambaugh, Robert F. "The Information in Forward Rates: Implications for Models of the Term Structure." *Journal of Financial Economics*, May 1988, pp. 41–70.

73. Stokes, Houston H., and H. Neuberger. "The Effect of Monetary Changes on Interest Rates: A Box-Jenkins Approach." *Review of Economics and Statistics*, November 1979, pp. 534–48.

74. Telser, Lester G. "A Critique of Some Recent Empirical Research on the Explanation of the Term Structure of Interest Rates." *Journal of Political Economy*, August 1967, pp. 546–61.

75. Throop, Adrian W. "Interest-Rate Forecasts and Market Efficiency." Federal Reserve Bank of San Francisco, *Economic Review*, Spring 1981, pp. 29–43.

76. Tobin, James, and William Brainard. "Pitfalls in Financial Model Building." *American Economic Review, Papers and Proceedings*, May 1968, pp. 99–122.

77. Turnbull, Stuart M. "Measurement of the Real Rate of Interest and Related Problems in a World of Uncertainty." *Journal of Money, Credit and Banking*, May 1981, pp. 177–91.

78. Wecker, William. "Predicting the Turning Points of a Time Series." *The Journal of Business*, January 1979, pp. 35–50.

79. Wendel, Helmut F. "Interest-Rate Expectations." Washington, D.C.: Board of Governors of the Federal Reserve System, 1968.

80. Wenninger, John, Lawrence Radecki, and Elizabeth Hammond. "Recent Instability in the Demand for Money." Federal Reserve Bank of New York, *Quarterly Review*, Summer 1981, pp. 1–9.

**81.** Wicksell, Knut. *Interest and Prices*. London: MacMillan and Co., 1936.
**82.** Wilcox, James A. "Short-Term Movements of Long-Term Interest Rates: Evidence from the U.K. Indexed Bond Market." *National Bureau of Economic Research*, unpublished working paper, 1985.
**83.** — —. "Private Credit Demand, Supply, and Crunches: How Different Are the 1980s?" *American Economic Review, Papers and Proceedings*, May 1985, pp. 351–6.
**84.** Wojnilower, Albert R. "The Central Role of Credit Crunches in Recent Financial History." *Brookings Papers on Economic Activity*, Vol. 2 (1980), 30th Conference, pp. 277–326.
**85.** Yawitz, Jess B., and W. J. Marshall. "Measuring the Effect of Callability on Bond Yields." *Journal of Money, Credit and Banking*, February 1981, pp. 60–71.

# INDEX